Lecture Notes in Computer Science 3298

Commenced Publication in 1973
Founding and Former Series Editors:
Gerhard Goos, Juris Hartmanis, and Jan van Leeuwen

Sheila A. McIlraith   Dimitris Plexousakis
Frank van Harmelen (Eds.)

The Semantic Web – ISWC 2004

Third International Semantic Web Conference
Hiroshima, Japan, November 7-11, 2004
Proceedings

 Springer

Volume Editors

Sheila A. McIlraith
University of Toronto
Dept. of Computer Science
6 King's College Road, Toronto, Ontario M5S 3H5, Canada
E-mail: sheila@cs.toronto.edu

Dimitris Plexousakis
University of Crete
and Foundation for Research and Technology (FORTH)
Institute of Computer Science
711 10 Heraklion, Crete, Greece
E-mail: dp@ics.forth.gr

Frank van Harmelen
Vrije Universiteit Amsterdam
Dept. of Computer Science
De Boelelaan 1081a, 1081HV Amsterdam, The Netherlands
E-mail: frank.van.harmelen@cs.vu.nl

Library of Congress Control Number: 2004114602

CR Subject Classification (1998): H.4, H.3, C.2, H.5, F.3, I.2, K.4

ISSN 0302-9743
ISBN 3-540-23798-4 Springer Berlin Heidelberg New York

Springer is a part of Springer Science+Business Media

springeronline.com

© Springer-Verlag Berlin Heidelberg 2004
Printed in Germany

Typesetting: Camera-ready by author, data conversion by PTP-Berlin, Protago-TeX-Production GmbH
Printed on acid-free paper   SPIN: 11344568   06/3142   5 4 3 2 1 0

Preface

The 3rd International Semantic Web Conference (ISWC 2004) was held November 7–11, 2004 in Hiroshima, Japan. If it is true what the proverb says: "Once by accident, twice by habit, three times by tradition," then this third ISWC did indeed firmly establish a tradition. After the overwhelming interest in last year's conference at Sanibel Island, Florida, this year's conference showed that the Semantic Web is not just a one-day wonder, but has established itself firmly on the research agenda. At a time when special interest meetings with a Semantic Web theme are springing up at major conferences in numerous areas (ACL, VLDB, ECAI, AAAI, ECML, WWW, to name but a few), the ISWC series has established itself as the primary venue for Semantic Web research.

Response to the call for papers for the conference continued to be strong. We solicited submissions to three tracks of the conference: the research track, the industrial track, and the poster track. The research track, the premier venue for basic research on the Semantic Web, received 205 submissions, of which 48 were accepted for publication. Each submission was evaluated by three program committee members whose reviews were coordinated by members of the senior program committee. Final decisions were made by the program co-chairs in consultation with the conference chair and the senior program committee. The industrial track, soliciting papers describing industrial research on the Semantic Web, received 22 submissions, of which 7 were accepted for publication. These papers were reviewed by three members of the industrial track program committee, and final decisions were made by the industrial track co-chairs. Finally, the poster track, designed for late-breaking results and work in progress, received 68 submissions, of which 47 were accepted, following two reviews of poster summaries by the conference program committee. Final decisions were made by the poster track chair. Results of the poster track are reproduced in a separate volume.

One of the Chairs' prerogatives is to make some sense out of these submission statistics. First of all, ISWC 2004 was a truly international forum, with accepted contributions from over 20 countries worldwide. It is also instructive to look at the distribution of papers across different areas. The chart on the next page shows the number of papers submitted and accepted in the different areas. (NB: most papers were classified in multiple areas.) We see that two of the more "traditional" Semantic Web topics continue to dominate the conference: languages/tools/methodologies and ontologies. Other core topics are also strongly represented: interoperability, Web services, middleware and searching/querying. Together, these six core topics already account for 60% of the accepted papers. Some topics, although central to the Semantic Web, are surprisingly small in number, for example database technologies (5%) and inference/rules (4%). Some other topics are already "hot" in smaller workshops, but apparently haven't made it to the big conference scene yet, such as peer-to-peer and trust (each at a modest 2%).

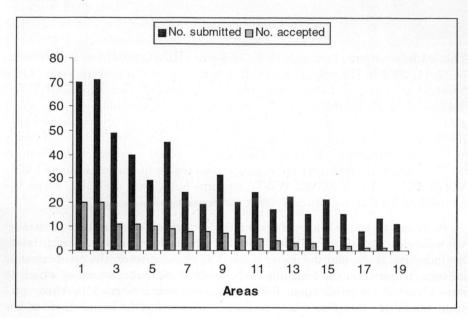

Areas:

1	Languages, tools and methodologies for Semantic Web data
2	Ontologies (creation, merging, linking and reconciliation)
3	Semantic integration and interoperability
4	Semantic Web services (description, discovery, invocation, composition)
5	Semantic Web middleware
6	Searching, querying and viewing the Semantic Web
7	User interfaces
8	Visualization and modelling
9	Data semantics
10	Database technologies for the Semantic Web
11	Semantic Web inference schemes/rules
12	Tools and methodologies for Web agents
13	Large-scale knowledge management
14	Peer-to-peer systems
15	Semantic Web mining
16	Semantic Web trust, privacy, security and intellectual property rights
17	Semantic brokering
18	Semantic Web for e-business and e-learning
19	Knowledge portals

As with any conference, the quality of the accepted papers and the integrity of the review process reflect the hard work of the program committee. We thank our senior program committee, members of both program committees, and our auxiliary reviewers for the tremendous effort they put into the task of evaluating submissions to the conference. Most importantly, we thank industrial track co-chairs Dean Allemang and Jun-Ichi Akahani, and poster track chair, Jeremy Carroll for the superb job they did, organizing and coordinating their tracks of the conference.

Invited talks constitute an integral part of the scientific program of an international conference. We were fortunate to have three excellent and diverse distinguished lectures as part of the ISWC 2004 technical program. Edward Feigenbaum, Kumagai Professor of Computer Science and Director Emeritus, Knowledge Systems Laboratory, Stanford University, communicated his views on the status and progress of Semantic Web research by speaking on "The Semantic Web Story – It's already 2004. Where are we?". Wolfgang Nejdl, Director of the Learning Lab Lower Saxony at the University of Hannover elaborated on the research issues involved in distributed search on the Semantic Web with his presentation entitled "How to Build Google2Google – An (Incomplete) Recipe –." Marie-Christine Rousset, head of the Artificial Intelligence and Inference Systems Group in the Laboratory of Computer Science at the University of Paris-Sud, renewed an old knowledge representation theme by addressing the expressiveness/tractability trade-off in her talk entitled "Small Can be Beautiful in the Semantic Web." This volume includes papers by Nejdl and Rousset that are associated with their lectures.

In addition to the paper and poster tracks, ISWC 2004 included 8 workshops, 6 tutorials, a demonstration session with 45 registered demonstrators, the Semantic Web Challenge with 18 participants, and an exhibition featuring industrial demonstrations. Large participation in these events reflects the broad interest in the Semantic Web, and how active the field is. Once again, we thank all the chairs for their dedicated efforts towards making the conference a success. The local organization of ISWC 2004 went smoothly through the extraordinary care and attention of those on the organizing committee. We are greatly indebted to Riichiro Mizoguchi, the local arrangements chair, for doing a meticulous job. His attention to detail, and the beautiful venue he selected for the conference contributed tremendously to the overall experience of the conference. John Mylopoulos and Katia Sycara, ISWC 2003 program co-chairs, also deserve our special thanks for their guidance and for sharing their experience with last year's conference.

Electronic submission of papers and reviews was driven by the Confious Conference Management system, developed at ICS FORTH by Manos Papaggelis. This was the first time Confious was used, and the system ran remarkably smoothly. We thank Manos for his around-the-clock support during the many months preceding the conference. We also owe a debt of gratitude to Akiko Inaba for her diligence and aesthetic sense in developing and supporting the ISWC 2004 Web page. Finally, we extend tremendous thanks to Jorge Baier for the fine job he did in preparing these proceedings.

We hope that the attendees found the conference both stimulating and enjoyable.

November, 2004   Sheila McIlraith and Dimitris Plexousakis
                                                                    Program Co-Chairs

                                                                    Frank van Harmelen
                                                                    Conference Chair

Organizing Committee

General Chair	Frank van Harmelen (Vrije Universiteit, The Netherlands)
Program Co-Chairs	Sheila McIlraith (University of Toronto, Canada)
	Dimitris Plexousakis (ICS FORTH and Univ. of Crete, Greece)
Local Arrangements Chair	Riichiro Mizoguchi (Osaka University, Japan)
Industrial Track Co-chairs	Dean Allemang (TopQuadrant Inc., USA)
	Jun-ichi Akahani (NTT Corporation, Japan)
Poster Track Chair	Jeremy Carroll (Hewlett-Packard Labs, UK)
Demos Chair	Stefan Decker (DERI, Ireland)
SW Challenge Co-chairs	Michel Klein (Vrije Universiteit, The Netherlands)
	Ubbo Visser (University of Bremen, Germany)
Tutorials Co-chairs	Vipul Kashyap (Partners HealthCare Systems Inc., USA)
	Takahira Yamaguchi (Keio University, Japan)
Workshops Chair	Natasha Noy (Stanford University, USA)
Exhibition Chair	Hiroshi Tsuda (Fujitsu Ltd., Japan)
Metadata Chair	Steffen Staab (University of Karlsruhe, Germany)
Publicity Chair	Akiko Inaba (Osaka University, Japan)
Sponsorship Co-chairs	Akira Maeda (Hitachi Ltd., Japan)
	Massimo Paolucci (Carnegie Mellon University, USA)
	York Sure (University of Karlsruhe, Germany)

Senior Program Committee

Hamish Cunningham (University of Sheffield, UK)
Oren Etzioni (University of Washington, USA)
Jérôme Euzenat (INRIA Rhône-Alpes, France)
Tim Finin (University of Maryland, Baltimore County, USA)
Carole Goble (University of Manchester, UK)
Benjamin Grosof (MIT, USA)
Alon Halevy (University of Washington, USA)
Ian Horrocks (University of Manchester, UK)
Toru Ishida (Kyoto University, Japan)
Boris Katz (MIT, USA)
Craig Knoblock (University of Southern California, USA)
Nicholas Kushmerick (University College Dublin, Ireland)
Deborah McGuinness (Stanford University, USA)
John Mylopoulos (University of Toronto, Canada)
Wolfgang Nejdl (L3S and University of Hannover, Germany)

Zbigniew Ras (University of North Carolina, Charlotte, USA)
Michel Scholl (CNAM, France)
Guus Schreiber (Vrije Universiteit, The Netherlands)
Rudi Studer (University of Karlsruhe, Germany)
Katia Sycara (Carnegie Mellon University, USA)
Hideaki Takeda (National Institute of Informatics, Japan)

Program Committee

Karl Aberer (EPFL, Switzerland)
Bernd Amann (CNAM, France)
Jose Luis Ambite (ISI, University of Southern California, USA)
Grigoris Antoniou (ICS FORTH, Greece)
Jean-François Baget (INRIA Alpes, France)
Sean Bechhofer (University of Manchester, UK)
Zohra Bellahsene (Université de Montpellier II, France)
Abraham Bernstein (University of Zurich, Switzerland)
Kalina Bontcheva (University of Sheffield, UK)
Paolo Bouquet (University of Trento, Italy)
Jeffrey M. Bradshaw (Institute for Human and Machine Cognition, USA)
François Bry (Institute for Informatics, University of Munich, Germany)
Mark Burstein (BBN, USA)
Diego Calvanese (Free University of Bolzano, Italy)
Jeremy Carroll (Hewlett-Packard, UK)
Pierre-Antoine Champin (Université de Lyon I, France)
Vinay Chaudhri (SRI International, USA)
Gregory Cobena (Xyleme, France)
Nigel Collier (National Institute of Informatics, Japan)
Oscar Corcho (Intelligent Software Components, Spain)
Isabel Cruz (University of Illinois, Chicago, USA)
Hasan Davulcu (Arizona State University, USA)
Mike Dean (BBN, USA)
Stefan Decker (DERI, Ireland)
Thierry Declerck (Saarland University and DFKI GmbH, Germany)
Grit Denker (SRI International, USA)
Ian Dickinson (Hewlett-Packard, UK)
Ying Ding (University of Innsbruck, Austria)
An Hai Doan (University of Illinois, Urbana-Champaign, USA)
John Domingue (Knowledge Media Institute, Open University, UK)
Andreas Eberhart (University of Karlsruhe, Germany)
Boi Faltings (EPFL, Switzerland)
Richard Fikes (Stanford University, USA)
Dana Florescu (BEA, USA)
Aldo Gangemi (CNR, Italy)
Yolanda Gil (ISI, University of Southern California, USA)

Fausto Giunchiglia (University of Trento, Italy)
Asun Gomez-Perez (Universidad Politécnica de Madrid, Spain)
Marko Grobelnik (J. Stefan Institute, Slovenia)
Michael Gruninger (NIST, USA)
Nicola Guarino (ISTC-CNR, Italy)
Ramanathan Guha (IBM Research, USA)
Mohand Said Hacid (Université de Lyon I, France)
Wendy Hall (University of Southampton, UK)
Jeff Heflin (Lehigh University, USA)
Masahiro Hori (Kansai University, Japan)
Herman ter Horst (Philips Research, The Netherlands)
Michael Huhns (University of South Carolina, USA)
Rick Hull (Bell Labs, USA)
Jane Hunter (DSTC, University of Queensland, Australia)
Zack Ives (University of Pennsylvania, USA)
Anupam Joshi (University of Maryland, Baltimore County, USA)
Subbarao Kambhampati (Arizona State University, USA)
Roger (Buzz) King (University of Colorado, USA)
David Kinny (Agentis Software, USA)
Atanas Kiryakov (Ontotext Lab, Sirma, Bulgaria)
Yasuhiko Kitamura (Kwansei Gakuin University, Japan)
Matthias Klusch (DFKI GmbH, Germany)
Manolis Koubarakis (Technical University of Crete, Greece)
Yannis Labrou (Fujitsu Labs, USA)
Georg Lausen (University of Freiburg, Germany)
Thibaud Latour (CRP Henri Tudor, Luxembourg)
Chen Li (University of California, Irvine, USA)
Robert MacGregor (ISI, University of Southern California, USA)
David Martin (SRI International, USA)
Mihhail Matskin (KTH, Sweden)
Masaki Matsudaira (OKI, Japan)
Diana Maynard (University of Sheffield, UK)
Brian McBride (Hewlett-Packard, UK)
Frank McCabe (Fujitsu Labs, USA)
Drew McDermott (Yale University, USA)
Luke McDowell (University of Washington, USA)
Sergey Melnik (Microsoft Research, USA)
Pavlos Moraitis (University of Cyprus, Cyprus)
Mark Musen (Stanford University, USA)
Tim Oates (University of Maryland, Baltimore County, USA)
Massimo Paolucci (Carnegie Mellon University, USA)
Bijan Parsia (University of Maryland, USA)
Peter Patel-Schneider (Bell Labs, USA)
Terry Payne (University of Southampton, UK)
Paulo Pinheiro da Silva (Stanford University, USA)

Alan Rector (University of Manchester, UK)
Chantal Reynaud (Université d'Orsay, France)
Mark Roantree (Dublin City University, Ireland)
Marie-Christine Rousset (Université d'Orsay, France)
Henryk Rybinski (Warsaw University of Technology, Poland)
Norman Sadeh (Carnegie Mellon University, USA)
Fereidoon Sadri (University of North Carolina, Greensboro, USA)
Ulrike Sattler (University of Manchester, UK)
Nigel Shadbolt (University of Southampton, UK)
Wolf Siberski (University of Hannover, Germany)
Michael Sintek (DFKI, Germany)
Andrzej Skowron (Warsaw University, Poland)
Steffen Staab (University of Karlsruhe, Germany)
Lynn Andrea Stein (Olin College, USA)
Heiner Stuckenschmidt (Vrije Universiteit, The Netherlands)
Gerd Stumme (University of Kassel, Germany)
Said Tabet (Nisus Inc., USA)
Val Tannen (University of Pennsylvania, USA)
Yannis Tzitzikas (University of Namur, Belgium)
Andrzej Uszok (Institute for Human and Machine Cognition, USA)
Dan Vodislav (CNAM-CEDRIC, Paris, France)
Christopher Welty (IBM Watson Research Center, USA)
Kevin Wilkinson (HP Labs, USA)
Steve Willmott (Universitat Politècnica de Catalunya, Spain)
Michael Wooldridge (University of Liverpool, UK)
Guizhen Yang (SRI International, USA)
Yiyu Yao (University of Regina, Canada)
Ning Zhong (Maebashi Institute of Technology, Japan)
Djamel Zighed (Université de Lyon, France)

Industrial Track Program Committee

Bill Andersen (Ontology Works, USA)
Jürgen Angele (Ontoprise, Germany)
Ken Baclawski (Semantx Life Sciences, Div. of Jarg Corporation, USA)
Richard Benjamins (iSOCO and UPM, Spain)
Jack Berkowitz (Network Inference, USA)
Andy Crapo (GE, USA)
John Davies (British Telecom, UK)
Michael Denny (Concurrent Technologies Corporation, USA)
Lars M. Garshol (Ontopia, Norway)
Richard Huffine (EPA, USA)
Thomas Kamps (Fraunhofer Institute, Germany)
Takahiro Kawamura (Toshiba Corporation, Japan)
Paul Keller (NASA Ames Research Center, USA)

Shoji Kurakake (NTT DoCoMo, Japan)
Jae Kyu Lee (KAIST, South Korea)
Kyu-Chul Lee (Chungnam National University, Korea)
Alain Leger (France Telecom, France)
Ryusuke Masuoka (Fujitsu Laboratories of America Inc., USA)
Alexander Morgan (General Motors Research, USA)
Holger Rath (Empolis, Germany)
Amit Sheth (Semagix, UK)
Satish Thatte (Microsoft, USA)
Mike Uschold (Boeing, USA)
Richard Watts (Lawrence Livermore National Labs, USA)
John Zimmerman (NNSA Kansas City Plant, USA)

Local Organizing Committee

Jun-ichi Akahani (NTT Communication Science Laboratories, Japan)
Kazuo Asakawa (Information Technology Media Labs., Fujitsu Labs., Japan)
Nigel Collier (National Institute of Informatics, Japan)
Kiyoshi Hara (Nihon Unisys Software, Japan)
Koiti Hasida (AIST, Japan)
Tsukasa Hirashima (Hiroshima University, Japan)
Masahiro Hori (Kansai University, Japan)
Mitsuru Ikeda (Japan Advanced Institute of Science and Technology, Japan)
Toru Ishida (Kyoto University, Japan)
Noriaki Izumi (AIST, Japan)
Akifumi Kambara (INTAP, Japan)
Yasuhiko Kitamura (Kwansei Gakuin University, Japan)
Yoshinobu Kitamura (Osaka University, Japan)
Kiyoshi Kogure (ATR Intelligent Robotics and Communication Labs., Japan)
Ken Kuriyama (Gakken, Japan)
Akira Maeda (Systems Development Laboratory, Hitachi Ltd., Japan)
Katashi Nagao (Nagoya University, Japan)
Yukio Osawa (Tsukuba University, Japan)
Nobuo Saitoh (Keio University, Japan)
Hideo Shimazu (NEC Corporation, Japan)
Kazuo Sumita (Corporate Research and Development Center, Toshiba, Japan)
Hideaki Takeda (National Institute of Informatics, Japan)
Shinichiro Tanaka (Toyota Motor Corporation (Auditor), Japan)
Hiroshi Tsuda (Information Technology Media Labs., Fujitsu Labs., Japan)
Jun-ichi Tsujii (University of Tokyo, Japan)
Takahira Yamaguchi (Keio University, Japan)
Toshio Yokoi (Tokyo Institute of Technology, Japan)
Ning Zhong (Maebashi Institute of Technology, Japan)

Additional Reviewers

Harith Alani (University of Southampton, UK)
Anupriya Ankolekar (HCI Institute, Carnegie Mellon University, USA)
Donovan Artz (ISI, University of Southern California, USA)
Ronald Ashri (University of Southampton, UK)
Roxana Belecheanu (University of Southampton, UK)
Stephan Blohdorn (University of Karlsruhe, Germany)
Alex Borgida (Rutgers University, USA)
Liliana Cabral (Knowledge Media Institute, Open University, UK)
Philippe Cudre-Mauroux (EPFL, Switzerland)
Bernardo Cuenca Grau (Universidad de Valencia, Spain)
Jose Manuel de Bruijn (DERI, Austria)
Jianchun Fan (Arizona State University, USA)
Tim Furche (Institute of Informatics, University of Munich, Germany)
Nicholas Gibbins (University of Southampton, UK)
Steve Harris (University of Southampton, UK)
Thomas Hernandez (Arizona State University, USA)
Bo Hu (University of Southampton, UK)
Liang Jin (University of California, Irvine, USA)
Yannis Kalfoglou (University of Southampton, UK)
Uwe Keller (DERI, Austria)
Francis Kwong (University of Manchester, UK)
Ruben Lara (DERI, Austria)
Holger Lausen (DERI, Austria)
Jia Li (University of California, Irvine, USA)
José Manuel López-Cobo (Intelligent Software Components, Spain)
Sameer Maggon (ISI, University of Southern California, USA)
Martin Michalowski (ISI, University of Southern California, USA)
Christopher Murphy (Olin College, USA)
Ullas Nambiar (Arizona State University, USA)
Axel Polleres (DERI, Austria)
Varun Ratnakar (ISI, University of Southern California, USA)
Roman Schmidt (EPFL, Switzerland)
Matteo Scoz (University of Trento, Italy)
Imen Sebei (CNAM-CEDRIC, Paris, France)
Marc Spraragen (ISI, University of Southern California, USA)
Naveen Srinivasan (Robotics Institute, Carnegie Mellon University, USA)
Martin Szomszor (University of Southampton, UK)
Raphael Troncy (INA, France)
Jie Wu (EPFL, Switzerland)
Baoshi Yang (ISI, University of Southern California, USA)
Weiwen Yang (University of California, Irvine, USA)
Stefano Zanobini (University of Trento, Italy)

Sponsors

Gold

TOSHIBA

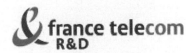

Silver

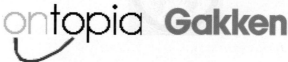

Table of Contents

Semantic Web Mining

Tools and Methodologies for Web Agents

User Interfaces and Visualization

Large Scale Knowledge Management

Semantic Web Services

Inference

Searching and Querying

Semantic Web Middleware

Integration and Interoperability

Ontologies

Industrial Track

How to Build Google2Google
– An (Incomplete) Recipe –

Wolfgang Nejdl

L3S and University of Hannover, Germany
nejdl@l3s.de

Abstract. This talk explores aspects relevant for peer-to-peer search infrastructures, which we think are better suited to semantic web search than centralized approaches. It does so in the form of an (incomplete) cookbook recipe, listing necessary ingredients for putting together a distributed search infrastructure. The reader has to be aware, though, that many of these ingredients are research questions rather than solutions, and that it needs quite a few more research papers on these aspects before we can really cook and serve the final infrastructure. We'll include appropriate references as examples for the aspects discussed (with some bias to our own work at L3S), though a complete literature overview would go well beyond cookbook recipe length limits.

1 Introduction

Why should we even think about building more powerful peer-to-peer search infrastructures? Isn't Google sufficient for every purpose we can imagine? Well, there are some areas where a centralized search engine cannot or might not want to go, for example the hidden web or community-driven search.

The hidden web requires replication of data usually stored in databases in a central search engine which seems like a bad idea, even though Froogle (http://froogle.google.com/) attempts to do this for a limited domain / purpose (shopping, of course). A central data warehouse just does not seem an appropriate infrastructure for the world wide web, even though replicating much of the surface web on the Google cluster is (still) doable.

The main characteristic of a community-driven search infrastructure is its strong search bias on specific topics / results. While the last two years have seen techniques emerging for biasing and personalizing search [1,2,3], catering for a lot of small and specific search communities in a centralized search engine neither seems easy to accomplish nor particularly useful to implement for a search engine company which has to target the average user, not specialized communities.

Besides covering these new areas, another advantage of a distributed search infrastructure is the potential for faster updates of indices, because we can exploit local knowledge about new and updated content directly at the site which provides it, without necessarily crawling all of its content again. Last, but not least, decentralized search services might also appeal to those who would rather opt for a more "democratic" and decentralized search service infrastructure instead of centralized services provided by a (beneficial) monopolist or a few oligopolists.

S.A. McIlraith et al. (Eds.): ISWC 2004, LNCS 3298, pp. 1–5, 2004.

In this talk, we will discuss some necessary ingredients for a Google2Google recipe, which have to be mixed together to provide a general decentralized search service infrastructure. Please be aware, that a well-tasting solution is still a few years away, and cooking it all together is not as simple as it might seem at the first moment.

2   Distributed Search Engine Peers

As the first ingredient, we need a large set of distributed Google2Google search peers. These are not just distributed crawlers such as the peers in the distributed search engine project Grub (http://grub.org/), but rather provide crawling, indexing, ranking and (peer-to-peer) query answering and forwarding functionalities.

Each Google2Google search peer will be responsible for a small partition of the web graph, with some overlaps to achieve redundancy, but without centralized schedulers. As the web graph is block structured, with inter-block links much sparser than links within blocks, search peers have to orient themselves on this structure [4,5].

Obviously, it will be important how we connect these peers. A super peer architecture [6,7] might be a good choice because it allows us to include task specific indexing and route optimization capabilities in these super peers. As for the exact topology, we will have a range of options, most probably building upon one of the P2P topologies derived from Cayley graphs [8] used in DHT and other P2P networks [9,10,11,12].

Typical search engine users will rely on simple text string searches, though for more sophisticated applications we certainly want to provide more sophisticated query capabilities as they are available for example in the Edutella network [13]. For certain applications we might opt for publish/subscribe infrastructures instead [14], which can re-use many of the ingredients mentioned in this talk.

3   Distributed Ranking Algorithms

One of the main reasons Google quickly replaced older search engines was its ability to rank results based on the implicit recommendations of Web page writers expressed in the link structure of the web. So we definitively have to throw in a ranking algorithm to provide Google2Google with comparable functionalities.

Unfortunately, two main ingredients of Google's ranking algorithm (TF/IDF and PageRank) rely on collection wide document properties (IDF) and central computation (PageRank). There is hope, however, that we are able to solve these problems in the future: IDF values in many cases do not change much when new documents are added [15], and distributed algorithms for computing pagerank and personalized pagerank have been proposed [16,3].

Furthermore, pagerank variants more suited to decentralized computation have recently been investigated [17,18], and promise to decrease communication costs in a Google2Google setting. These algorithms compute PageRank-like values in two separate steps, first doing local computation within a site, then computation between sites (without taking specific pages into account). Additional analysis is needed on how they compare to PageRank and how sites with a lot of non-related pages (e.g. mass hosters like Geocities) can be handled. Google2Google search peers will probably have to rely on blocks within these sites or group the pages of such sites in community-oriented clusters.

4 Top-k Retrieval and Optimization

Obviously, ranking algorithms are not enough, we also have to use them to prune Google2Google answers to the best k ones. Imagine shipping hundred thousand answers and more to the user, who only wants to look at the top ten or top twenty answers in most cases anyway.

Recent work on top-k query processing and optimization in peer-to-peer networks has addressed these issues, and has shown how (meta) data on query statistics and ranking methods can be used to retrieve only the k best resources [19,20]. Ranking in this context is used to score the results that come from distributed sources, reduce the number of answers, enable partial matches to avoid empty result sets and optimize query forwarding and answering. Briefly, these algorithms assume a super-peer network connected using for example a hypercube-derived topology [12], and implement three intertwined functionalities (more details are presented in another presentation [19]):

- Ranking: Each peer locally ranks its resources with respect to the query and returns the local top-k results to its super-peer.
- Merging: At the super-peers results from the assigned peers are ranked again and merged into one top-k list. These answers are returned through the super-peer backbone to the querying peers, with merges at all super-peers involved.
- Routing: Super-peer indices store information from which directions the top-k answers were sent for each query. When a known query arrives at a super-peer these indices are used to forward the query to the most promising (super-) peers only. A small percentage of queries - depending on the volatility of the network - has to be forwarded to other peers as well, to update the indices in a query-driven way.

5 Trust and Security

Finally, trust and security play a role even more important in our decentralized Google2Google infrastructure than in more centralized settings. Topics here range from the issue of decentralized trust establishment and policy-based access control for distributed resources [21,22] to distributed computations of trust values meant to achieve the same benefits as trust networks in social settings [16,23]. The presentations at the 1st Workshop on Trust, Security and Reputation on the Semantic Web [24] covered a large set of topics in this area and initiated a lot of fruitful discussions.

In our Google2Google setting, malicious peers could for example try to subvert information they provide, an issue especially critical for ranking information. Recent analysis of attack scenarios in a distributed PageRank setting [16,3], have been encouraging, though, and have shown that with suitable additional modifications of the distributed algorithm, PageRank computation becomes quite un-susceptible to malicious peers even in a decentralized setting. Personalized PageRank variants can be made even more resiliant if we bias them towards trusted sites / peers [25,26].

6 Conclusion

Even though a decentralized infrastructure makes seemingly simple things surprisingly difficult (for example how to implement the "Did you mean xx" functionality in Google, which relies on (global) query and answer statistics), our short search for available ingredients for a Google2Google infrastructure already turned out rather successful. It will still take quite a few more research papers (plus an appropriate business / incentive model for a distributed search engine infrastructure) until we will be able to finalize our Google2Google recipe. But once we are finished we will have most certainly realized quite a few new opportunities for searching and accessing data on the (semantic) web.

Acknowledgements. Regarding the title of the paper as well as the initial idea, let me thank my friend and colleague Karl Aberer for inventing and using the term Google2Google as a nice catch phrase for distributed web search engines, on occasion of the panel he organized at the 2nd International Workshop on Databases, Information Systems, and Peer-to-Peer Computing [27]. This workshop took place in Toronto on August 29 and 30, in the context of VLDB'04. Regarding the results and ideas described in this paper, I gratefully acknowledge all my collaborators at L3S and elsewhere for their valuable contributions on the issues discussed in this talk and mentioned in the reference list in the next section. Without their help, my cookbook recipe would not have been written.

References

1. Haveliwala, T.: Topic-sensitive pagerank. In: Proceedings of the 11th International World Wide Web Conference, Honolulu, Hawaii. (2002)
2. Jeh, G., Widom, J.: Scaling personalized web search. In: Proceedings of the 12th International World Wide Web Conference, Honolulu, Hawaii, USA (2003)
3. Chirita, P., Nejdl, W., Scurtu, O.: Knowing where to search: Personalized search strategies for peers in P2P networks. In: SIGIR Workshop on Peer-to-Peer Information Retrieval, Sheffield, UK (2004)
4. Cho, J., Garcia-Molina, H.: Parallel crawlers. In: Proceedings of the Semantic Web Workshop, 11th International World Wide Web Conference, Honolulu, Hawaii, USA (2002)
5. Kamvar, S.D., Haveliwala, T.H., Manning, C.D., Golub, G.H.: Exploiting the block structure of the web for computing pagerank. In: Proceedings of the 12th Intl. World Wide Web Conference, Budapest, Hungary (2003)
6. Yang, B., Garcia-Molina, H.: Designing a super-peer network. In: Proceedings of the 19th Internatonal Conference on Data Engineering, Bangalore, India (2003)
7. Nejdl, W., Wolpers, M., Siberski, W., Schmitz, C., Schlosser, M., Brunkhorst, I., Loser, A.: Super-peer-based routing and clustering strategies for RDF-based peer-to-peer networks. In: Proceedings of the 12th International World Wide Web Conference, Budapest, Hungary (2003)
8. Nejdl, W., Qu, C., Kriesell, M.: Cayley DHTs: A group-theoretic framework for analysing DHTs based on cayley graphs. Technical report, University of Hannover (2004) submitted for publication.
9. Ratnasamy, S., Francis, P., Handley, M., Karp, R., Shenker, S.: A scalable content addressable network. In: Proceedings of the 2001 Conference on applications, technologies, architectures, and protocols for computer communications, ACM Press New York, NY, USA (2001)

10. Stoica, I., Morris, R., Karger, D., Kaashoek, M.F., Balakrishnan, H.: Chord: A scalable peer-to-peer lookup service for internet applications. In: Proceedings of the 2001 Conference on applications, technologies, architectures, and protocols for computer communications, ACM Press New York, NY, USA (2001)
11. Aberer, K., Cudré-Mauroux, P., Hauswirth, M.: A framework for semantic gossiping. SIG-MOD Record **31** (2002) http://www.p-grid.org/Papers/SIGMOD2002.pdf.
12. Schlosser, M., Sintek, M., Decker, S., Nejdl, W.: HyperCuP—Hypercubes, Ontologies and Efficient Search on P2P Networks. In: International Workshop on Agents and Peer-to-Peer Computing, Bologna, Italy (2002)
13. Nejdl, W., Wolf, B., Qu, C., Decker, S., Sintek, M., Naeve, A., Nilsson, M., Palmér, M., Risch, T.: EDUTELLA: a P2P Networking Infrastructure based on RDF. In: Proceedings of the 11th International World Wide Web Conference, Hawaii, USA (2002) http://edutella.jxta.org/reports/edutella-whitepaper.pdf.
14. Chirita, P.A., Idreos, S., Koubarakis, M., Nejdl, W.: Publish/subscribe for RDF-based P2P networks. In: Proceedings of the 1st European Semantic Web Symposium, Heraklion, Crete (2004)
15. Viles, C., French, J.: On the update of term weights in dynamic information retrieval systems. In: Proceedings of the Fourth International Conference on Information and Knowledge Management, Baltimore, Maryland, USA (1995)
16. Kamvar, S., Schlosser, M., Garcia-Molina, H.: The eigentrust algorithm for reputation management in P2P networks. In: Proceedings of the 12th International World Wide Web Conference. (2003)
17. Wang, DeWitt: Computing pagerank in a distributed internet search system. In: Proceedings of the 30th International Conference on Very Large Databases, Toronto (2004)
18. Wu, J., Aberer, K.: Using siterank for decentralized computation of web document ranking. In: Proceedings of the 3rd Intl. Conference on Adaptive Hypermedia and Adaptive Web-Based Systems, Eindhoven, Netherlands (2004)
19. Nejdl, W., Siberski, W., Thaden, U., Balke, W.T.: Top-k query evaluation for schema-based peer-to-peer networks. In: Proceedings of the 3rd International Semantic Web Conference, Hiroshima, Japan (2004)
20. Balke, W.T., Nejdl, W., Siberski, W., Thaden, U.: Progressive distributed top-k retrieval in peer-to-peer networks. submitted for publication (2004)
21. Yu, T., Winslett, M., Seamons, K.: Supporting Structured Credentials and Sensitive Policies through Interoperable Strategies in Automated Trust Negotiation. ACM Transactions on Information and System Security **6** (2003)
22. Gavriloaie, R., Nejdl, W., Olmedilla, D., Seamons, K., Winslett, M.: No registration needed: How to use declarative policies and negotiation to access sensitive resources on the semantic web. In: Proceedings of the 1st First European Semantic Web Symposium, Heraklion, Greece (2004)
23. Ziegler, C., Lausen, G.: Spreading activation models for trust propagation. In: Proceedings of the IEEE International Conference on e-Technology, e-Commerce, and e-Service. (2004)
24. Bonatti, P., Golbeck, J., Nejdl, W., Winslett, M.: ISWC'04 workshop on trust, security, and reputation on the semantic web. http://trust.mindswap.org/trustWorkshop (2004) Hiroshima, Japan.
25. Gyöngyi, Z., Garcia-Molina, H., Pedersen, J.: Combating web spam with trustrank. In: Proceedings of the 30th International Conference on Very Large Databases, Toronto (2004)
26. Chirita, P., Nejdl, W., Schlosser, M., Scurtu, O.: Personalized reputation management in P2P networks. Technical report, University of Hannover (2004)
27. Ooi, B.C., Ouksel, A., Sartori, C.: The 2nd intl. workshop on databases, information systems and peer-to-peer computing. http://horizonless.ddns.comp.nus.edu.sg/dbisp2p04/ (2004) co-located with VLDB'04, Toronto, Canada.

Small Can Be Beautiful in the Semantic Web

Marie-Christine Rousset

LRI, CNRS – Université Paris Sud XI – INRIA Futurs,
Bâtiment 490, Université Paris Sud XI, 91405 Orsay cedex, France

Abstract. In 1984, Peter Patel-Schneider published a paper [1] entitled *Small can be Beautiful in Knowledge Representation* in which he advocated for limiting the expressive power of knowledge representation formalisms in order to guarantee good computational properties and thus make knowledge-based systems usable as part of larger systems. In this paper, I aim at showing that the same argument holds for the Semantic Web: if we want to give a chance for the Semantic Web to scale up and to be broadly used, we have to limit the expressive power of the ontologies serving as semantic marking up of resources. In addition, due to the scale of the Web and the disparity of its users, it is unavoidable to have to deal with distributed heterogeneous ontologies. In this paper, I will argue that a peer-to-peer infrastructure enriched with simple distributed ontologies (e.g., taxonomies) reconciled through mappings is appropriate and scalable for supporting the future Semantic Web.

1 Introduction

The Semantic Web [2] envisions a world-wide distributed architecture where data and computational resources will easily inter-operate based on semantic marking up of web resources using *ontologies*. Ontologies are a formalization of the semantics of application domains (e.g., tourism, biology, medecine) through the definition of classes and relations modeling the domain objects and properties that are considered as meaningful for the application. Building ontologies is a hard and time-consuming task for which there exists only some very general principles to guide the ontology designers [3,4,5] who still have to face with many modeling choices. Even for a same domain, different modeling choices can lead to very different ontologies. In particular, the choice of the basic classes and relations for modeling the basic domain vocabulary is subject to many variations depending on the ontology designers. The appropriate level of detail of the ontology descriptions is not easy to determine either and mainly depends on the purpose of the ontology construction.

Several important issues remain open concerning the building and usage of ontologies in the setting of the Semantic Web. In this talk, I will discuss some of them and I will explain my vision of the kind of infrastructure that I consider as scalable for supporting the future Semantic Web. An instance of that infrastructure is implemented in the Somewhere [6] system that I will present briefly.

S.A. McIlraith et al. (Eds.): ISWC 2004, LNCS 3298, pp. 6–16, 2004.

2   Simple Versus Complex Ontologies

A first question concerns the choice of the right expressive power for an adequate modeling of the ontologies needed in the Semantic Web. The current tendancy promoted by the knowledge representation community is to consider that formal languages with high expressive power are required because they enable a fine-grained description of domain ontologies. Such a choice is questionable for several reasons. The main argument that I would oppose against this choice is algorithmic: well-known complexity results show that exploiting ontologies modeled using expressive formal languages (e.g., OWL [7]) cannot scale up to complex or large ontologies. Another argument is that formal languages with high expressive power are difficult to handle for users having to model an application domain. In the Semantic Web setting, the purpose of ontologies is to serve as a semantic markup for web resources and as a support for querying in order to obtain more efficient and precise search engines. Therefore, they must be simple to be correctly understood and rightly exploited by humans (users or experts), and they must be expressible in a formal language for which the algorithmic complexity of reasoning is reasonable to make them really machine processable. Taxonomics of atomic classes are examples of simple ontologies that I envision as good candidates for serving as marking up resources at the Web scale. They are easy to understand for users and practitioners. They may even be automatically constructed by data or text mining. They are conform to the W3C recommandation being a subset of OWL-DL that we could call OWL-PL since they can be encoded in propositional logic. As a result, query answering becomes feasible at a large scale, which is the goal to reach eventually if we want the Semantic Web to become a reality.

3   Personalized and Distributed Versus Standardized Ontologies

Another question deals with the possibility of building consensual domain ontologies that would be broadly shared by users over the Web for marking up their data or resources. Building a universal ontology (or using an existing one, e.g., CYC [8]) that could serve as a reference set of semantic tags for labelling the data and documents of the Web is, at worst an utopia, at best an enormous enterprise which may eventually turn out to be useless in practice for the Semantic Web. The current tendency (e.g., [9,10,11]) consists in building standardized ontologies per domain. So far, it is an open question whether such an approach is likely to scale up to the Web because it cannot be taken as granted that users will appropriate those ontologies. The risk is that ontology designers spend a lot of time building an expected consensual ontology which will not be eventually broadly used because end users will prefer to use their own ontologies. In the same way as we have our own view of the nesting and the names of the different folders for structuring our personal file systems, mail files or bookmarks, it is likely that people will prefer using their own ontology to mark up the data or resources they agree to make available through the Semantic Web. There is a little chance that they will accept to use an external ontology which they are not used to for re-labelling the resources that they have already marked-up.

However, if the ontologies are simple (e.g., taxonomies of terms) users may be ready to establish mappings between their own ontology and ontologies of some users with whom they share some topics of interest.

Consider for instance a user Bob found of music who has already stored plenty of music files in three folders that he has named $Classic$, $Jazz$ and $Rock$ to distinguish pieces of classical music, jazz and rock respectively. Suppose now that by searching new music files on the web, he discovers a user Tom making available on his web page music files but marked up by the name of the composers. Establishing a mapping saying that what Tom marks as $Mozart$ (pieces of music) is a specialization of his own view of $Classic$ (pieces of music) is straighforward for Bob. This mapping will make possible for any user querying the web using Bob's ontology to get $Mozart$ files stored at the Tom's web page as an answer to his search for classical pieces of music.

In this vision of the Semantic Web introduced in [12], no user imposes to others his own ontology but logical mappings between ontologies make possible the creation of a web of people in which personalized semantic marking up of data cohabits nicely with a collaborative exchange of data. In this view, the Web is a huge Peer Data Management System based on simple distributed ontologies and mappings.

4   Peer Data Management Systems

Peer data management systems (PDMS) have been proposed recently [13,14,15,16] to generalize the centralized approach of information integration systems based on single mediators, in which heterogeneous data sources are reconciled through logical mappings between each source schema or ontology and a single mediated schema or ontology. A centralized vision of mediation is appropriate for building semantic portals dedicated to a given domain but is too rigid to scale up to the Semantic Web for which PDMSs based on distributed mediation are more adapted. In a PDMS, there is no central mediator: each peer has its own ontology and data or services, and can mediate with some other peers to ask and answer queries. The existing PDMSs vary according to (a) the expressive power of their underlying data model and (b) the way the different peers are semantically connected. Both characteristics have impact on the allowed queries and their distributed processing.

In Edutella [17], each peer stores locally data (educational resources) that are described in RDF relatively to some reference ontologies (e.g., dmoz [9]). For instance, a peer can declare that it has data corresponding to the concept of the dmoz taxonomy corresponding to the path $Computers/Programming/Languages/Java$, and that for such data it can export the $author$ and the $date$ properties. The overlay network underlying Edutella is a hypercub of super-peers to which peers are directly connected. Each super-peer is a mediator over the data of the peers connected to it. When it is asked, its first task is to check if the query matches with its schema: if that is the case, it transmits the query to the peers connected to it, which are likely to store the data answering the query ; otherwise, it routes the query to some of its neighbour super-peers according to a strategy exploiting the hypercub topology for guaranteeing a worst-case logarithmic time for reaching the relevant super-peer.

In contrast with Edutella, Piazza [13,18] does not consider that the data distributed over the different peers must be described relatively to some existing reference schemas. In Piazza, each peer has its own data and schema and can mediate with some other peers by declaring *mappings* between its schema and the schemas of those peers. The topology of the network is not fixed (as the super-peers hypercub in Edutella) but accounts for the existence of mappings between peers: two peers are logically connected if there exists a mapping between their two schemas. The underlying data model considered in the first version of Piazza [13] is relational and the mappings between relational peer schemas are inclusion or equivalence statements between conjunctive queries. Such a mapping formalism encompasses the *local-as-views* and the *global-as-views* formalisms used in information integration based on centralized single mediators for stating the mappings between the schemas of the data sources to be integrated and the mediated schema. The price to pay is that query answering is undecidable except if some restrictions are imposed on the mappings or on the topology of the network ([13]). The currently implemented version of Piazza [18] relies on a tree-based data model: the data is in XML and the mappings are equivalence and inclusion statements between XML queries. Query answering is implemented based on practical (not complete) algorithms for XML query containment and rewritings. The scalability of Piazza so far does not go up to more than about eighty peers in the published experiments and relies on a wide range of optimizations (mappings composition [19], paths pruning [20]), made possible by the centralized storage of all the schemas and mappings in a global server.

In Somewhere [6], we have made the choice of being fully distributed: there are neither super-peers (as in Edutella) nor a central server having the global view of the overlay network as in Piazza. In addition, we aim at scaling up to thousands of peers. For making it possible, we have chosen a simple class-based data model in which the data is a set of resource identifiers (URIs or URLs), the schemas are (simple) definitions of classes possibly constrained by inclusion, disjunction or equivalence statements, and mappings are inclusion, disjunction or equivalence statements between classes of different peer schemas. That data model is in accordance with the W3C recommandations since it is captured by the propositional fragment of the OWL ontology language.

5   Overview of the Somewhere PDMS

This section reports a joint work [6] with Philippe Adjiman, Philippe Chatalic, Francois Goasdoué and Laurent Simon.

5.1   Data Model

In Somewhere a new peer joins the network through some peers that it knows (its acquaintances) by declaring mappings between its own ontology and the ontologies of its acquaintances. Queries are posed to a given peer using its local ontology. The answers that are expected are not only instances of local classes but possibly instances of classes of peers distant from the queried peer if it can be infered from the peer ontologies and the mappings that they satisfy the query. Local ontologies, storage descriptions and mappings are defined using a fragment of OWL DL which is the description logics fragment of the Ontology Web Language recommended by W3C. We call OWL-PL the fragment of OWL-DL that we consider in Somewhere, where PL stands for propositional logic. OWL PL is the fragment of OWL DL reduced to the union ($\sqcup$), intersection ($\sqcap$) and complement ($\neg$) constructors for building class descriptions.

Peer ontologies: Each peer ontology is made of a set of axioms of class (partial or complete) definitions that associate class identifiers with class descriptions, and disjointness, equivalence or inclusion statements between class descriptions. Class identifiers are unique to each peer: we use the notation $P{:}CI$ for a class identifier CI of the ontology of a peer P.

Peer storage descriptions: The specification of the data that is stored locally in a peer P is done through assertional statements relating data identifiers (e.g., URLs or URIs) to class identifiers of the ontology of the peer P. The class identifiers of P involved in such statements are called the *extensional classes* of P and their extensions are the sets of data identifiers associated with them.

Mappings: Mappings are disjointness, equivalence or inclusion statements involving classes of different peers. They express the semantic correspondence that may exist between the ontologies of different peers.

Schema of a Somewhere peer-to-peer network: In a Somewhere network, the schema is not centralized but distributed through the union of the different peer ontologies and the mappings. The important point is that each peer has a partial knowledge of the schema: it just knows its own data and local ontology, and mappings with its acquaintances.

Let $\mathcal{P}$ be a Somewhere peer-to-peer network made of a collection of peers $\{P_i\}_{i \in [1..n]}$. For each peer P_i, let O_i and M_i be respectively the local ontology of P_i and the set of mappings stated at P_i between classes of O_i and classes of the ontologies of the acquaintances of P_i. The schema $\mathcal{S}$ of $\mathcal{P}$ is the union $\bigcup_{i \in [1..n]} O_i \cup M_i$ of the ontologies and of the sets of mappings of all the peers composing $\mathcal{P}$.

Semantics: The semantics is a standard logical formal semantics defined in terms of *interpretations.* An interpretation I is a pair $(\Delta^I, .^I)$ where Δ is a non-empty set, called the domain of interpretation, and $.^I$ is an interpretation function which assigns a subset of Δ^I to every class identifier and an element of Δ^I to every data identifier.

An interpretation I is a *model* of the distributed schema of a Somewhere peer-to-peer network $\mathcal{P} = \{P_i\}_{i \in [1..n]}$ iff each axiom in $\bigcup_{i \in [1..n]} O_i \cup M_i$ is satisfied by I.

Interpretations of axioms rely on interpretations of class descriptions which are inductively defined as follows:

- $(C_1 \sqcup C_2)^I = C_1^I \cup C_2^I$
- $(C_1 \sqcap C_2)^I = C_1^I \cap C_2^I$
- $(\neg C)^I = \Delta^I \backslash C^I$

Axioms are satisfied if the following holds:

- $C \sqsubseteq D$ is satisfied in I iff $C^I \subseteq D^I$
- $C \equiv D$ is satisfied in I iff $C^I = D^I$
- $C \sqcap D \equiv \bot$ is satisfied in I iff $C^I \cap D^I = \emptyset$
- $C(a)$ is satisfied in I iff $a^I \in C^I$

A Somewhere peer-to-peer network is *satisfiable* iff its (distributed) schema has a model.

Given a Somewhere peer-to-peer network $\mathcal{P} = \{P_i\}_{i \in [1..n]}$, a class description C *subsumes* a class description D iff in each model I of the schema of $\mathcal{P}$, $D^I \subseteq C^I$.

5.2   Illustrative Example of the Somewhere Data Model

Let us consider four persons Ann, Bob, Chris and Dora, each of them bookmarking URLs about restaurants they know or like. Each has his/her own taxonomy for categorizing restaurants. In addition, they have to describe their stored available data, i.e., the sets of URLs that they accept to make available to the PDMS. They do it by declaring some *extensional classes* (denoted $P{:}ViewX$) as subclasses of some classes $(P{:}X)$ of their ontology and by assigning to them the set of corresponding URLs as their instances.

Ann, who is working as a restaurant critics, organizes its restaurant URLs according to the following classes:

- the class $Ann{:}G$ of restaurants considered as offering a "good" cooking, among which she distinguishes the subclass $Ann{:}R$ of those which are rated:
  $Ann{:}R \sqsubseteq Ann{:}G$.
- the class $Ann{:}R$ is the union of three disjoint classes $Ann{:}S1$, $Ann{:}S2$, $Ann{:}S3$ corresponding respectively to the restaurants rated with $1, 2$ or 3 stars:
  $Ann{:}R \equiv Ann{:}S1 \sqcup Ann{:}S2 \sqcup Ann{:}S3$
  $Ann{:}S1 \sqcap Ann{:}S2 \equiv \bot$ $Ann{:}S1 \sqcap Ann{:}S3 \equiv \bot$ $Ann{:}S2 \sqcap Ann{:}S3 \equiv \bot$
- the classes $Ann{:}I$ and $Ann{:}O$, respectively corresponding to Indian and Oriental restaurants,
- the classes $Ann{:}C$, $Ann{:}T$ and $Ann{:}V$ which are subclasses of $Ann{:}O$ denoting Chinese, Taï and Vietnamese restaurants respectively:
  $Ann{:}C \sqsubseteq Ann{:}O$, $Ann{:}T \sqsubseteq Ann{:}O$, $Ann{:}V \sqsubseteq Ann{:}O$

Suppose that the data stored by Ann she accepts to make available are data on restaurants of various specialties, but that among the rated restaurants she stores and makes available those rated with 2 stars. The extensional classes declared by Ann are then:
$Ann{:}ViewS2 \sqsubseteq Ann{:}S2$, $Ann{:}ViewC \sqsubseteq Ann{:}C$
$Ann{:}ViewV \sqsubseteq Ann{:}V$, $Ann{:}ViewT \sqsubseteq Ann{:}T$
$Ann{:}ViewI \sqsubseteq Ann{:}I$

Bob, who is found of Asian cooking and likes high quality, organizes his restaurant URLs according to the following classes:

- the class $Bob{:}A$ of Asian restaurants,
- the class $Bob{:}Q$ of restaurants of high quality that he knows.

Suppose that he wants to make available every data that he has stored. The extensional classes that he declares are $Bob{:}ViewA$ and $Bob{:}ViewQ$ (as subclasses of $Bob{:}A$ and $Bob{:}Q$):

$Bob{:}ViewA \sqsubseteq Bob{:}A$, $Bob{:}ViewQ \sqsubseteq Bob{:}Q$

Chris is more found of fish restaurants but recently discovered some places serving a very nice cantonese cuisine. He organizes its data with respect to the following classes:

– the class $Chris{:}F$ of fish restaurants,
– the class $Chris{:}CA$ of Cantonese restaurants

Suppose that he declares the extensional classes $Chris{:}ViewF$ and $Chris{:}ViewCA$ as subclasses of $Chris{:}F$ and $Chris{:}CA$ respectively:

$Chris{:}ViewF \sqsubseteq Chris{:}F$, $Chris{:}ViewCA \sqsubseteq Chris{:}CA$

Finally, Dora organizes her restaurants URLs around the class $Dora{:}DP$ of her preferred restaurants, among which she distinguishes the subclass $Dora{:}P$ of pizzerias and the subclass $Dora{:}SF$ of seafood restaurants.

Suppose that the only URLs that she stores concerns pizzerias: the only extensional class that she has to declare is $Dora{:}ViewP$, as a subclass of $Dora{:}P$:

$Dora{:}ViewP \sqsubseteq Dora{:}P$

Ann, Bob, Chris and Dora are modelled as four peers. Each of them is able to express what he/she knows about others using mappings stating properties of class inclusion or equivalence.

Ann is very confident in Bob's taste and agrees to include Bob'selection as good restaurants by stating $Bob{:}Q \sqsubseteq Ann{:}G$. Finally, she thinks that Bob's Asian restaurants encompass her concept of Oriental restaurant : $Ann{:}O \sqsubseteq Bob{:}A$.

Bob: Bob knows that what he calls Asian cooking corresponds exactly to what Ann classifies as Oriental cooking. This may be expressed using the equivalence statement : $Bob{:}A \equiv Ann{:}O$ (note the difference of perception of Bob and Ann regarding the mappings between $Bob{:}A$ and $Ann{:}O$).

Chris: Chris considers that what he calls fish specialties is a particular case of what Dora calls seafood specialties : $Chris{:}F \sqsubseteq Dora{:}SF$

Dora: Dora counts on both Ann and Bob to obtain good Asian restaurants : $Bob{:}A \sqcap Ann{:}G \sqsubseteq Dora{:}DP$

Figure 1 describes the peer network induced by the mappings. In order to alleviate the notations, we omit the local peer name prefix except for the mappings. Edges are labeled with the class identifiers that are shared through the mappings between peers.

5.3   Query Answering

Queries and answers: Queries are combinations of classes of a given peer ontology. The corresponding answer sets are expressed in intention in terms of the combinations of extensional classes that are *rewritings* of the query. The point is that extensional classes

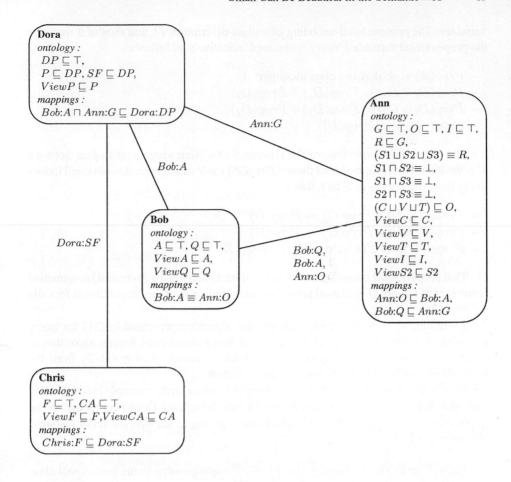

Fig. 1. The restaurants PDMS

of distant peers can participate to the rewritings and thus their instances to the answer set of a query posed to a given peer.

Given a Somewhere peer-to-peer network $\mathcal{P} = \{P_i\}_{i\in[1..n]}$, a logical combination Q_e of extensional classes is a *rewriting* of a query Q iff Q subsumes Q_e. Q_e is a *maximal rewriting* if there does not exist another rewriting Q'_e of Q subsuming it.

In the Somewhere setting, query rewriting can be equivalently reduced to distributed reasoning over logical propositional theories by a straighforward propositional encoding of the distributed ontologies and mappings composing the distributed schema of a Somewhere peer-to-peer network.

Propositional encoding: The propositional encoding concerns the schema of a Somewhere peer-to-peer network and the queries. It consists in transforming each query and schema statement into a propositional formula using class identifiers as propositional variables. The propositional encoding of a class description D, and thus of a query, is the propositional formula $Prop(D)$ obtained inductively as follows:

- $Prop(A) = A$, if A is a class identifier
- $Prop(D_1 \sqcap D_2) = Prop(D_1) \wedge Prop(D_2)$
- $Prop(D_1 \sqcup D_2) = Prop(D_1) \vee Prop(D_2)$
- $Prop(\neg D) = \neg(Prop(D))$

The propositional encoding of the schema S of a Somewhere peer-to-peer network $\mathcal{P}$ is the distributed propositional theory $Prop(S)$ made of the formulas obtained inductively from the axioms in S as follows:

- $Prop(C \sqsubseteq D) = Prop(C) \Rightarrow Prop(D)$
- $Prop(C \equiv D) = Prop(C) \Leftrightarrow Prop(D)$
- $Prop(C \sqcap D \equiv \perp) = \neg Prop(C) \vee \neg Prop(D)$

That propositional encoding transfers satisfiability and maps (maximal) conjunctive rewritings of a query Q to clausal proper (prime) implicates of the propositional formula $\neg Prop(Q)$.

Therefore, we can use the message passing algorithm presented in [21] for query rewriting in Somewhere. That algorithm is the first consequence finding algorithm in a peer-to-peer setting: it is anytime and computes consequences gradually from the solicited peer to peers that are more and more distant.

We illustrate the distributed resulting query processing on the example in Section 5.2. Consider that a user queries the restaurants PDMS through the **Dora** peer by asking the query $Dora{:}DP$, meaning that he is interested in getting as answers the set of favourite restaurants of Dora:

- He will get as a first rewriting $Dora{:}ViewP$ corresponding to the extensional class of the URLs of pizzerias stored locally by Dora.
- Then, the mapping $Chris{:}F \sqsubseteq Dora{:}SF$ leads to a new rewriting, $Chris{:}ViewF$, meaning that a way to get restaurants liked by Dora is to obtain the Fish restaurants stored by Chris.
- Finally, the mapping $Bob{:}A \sqcap Ann{:}G \sqsubseteq Dora{:}DP$ leads to the splitting of $Bob{:}A \sqcap Ann{:}G$ into the two subqueries $Bob{:}A$ and $Ann{:}G$; they are transmitted respectively to the peers Bob and Ann, which process them independently:
  - $Bob{:}ViewA$ is a local rewriting of $Bob{:}A$, which is transmitted back to the Dora peer, where it is queued for a future combination with rewritings of the other subquery $Ann{:}G$. In addition, guided by the mapping $Ann{:}O \equiv Bob{:}A$, the Bob peer transmits to the Ann peer the query $Ann{:}O$; the Ann peer processes that query locally and transmits back to the Bob peer the rewriting: $Ann{:}ViewC \sqcup Ann{:}ViewT \sqcup Ann{:}ViewV$, which in turn is transmitted back to the Dora peer as an additional rewriting for the subquery $Bob{:}A$ and queued there,
  - $Ann{:}ViewS2$ is a local rewriting of $Ann{:}G$, which is transmitted back to the Dora peer, and combined there with the two queued rewritings of $Bob{:}A$ ($Bob{:}ViewA$ and $Ann{:}ViewC \sqcup Ann{:}ViewT \sqcup Ann{:}ViewV$).

As a result, two rewrirings are sent back to the user:

- $Ann{:}ViewS2 \sqcap Bob{:}ViewA$, meaning that a way to obtain restaurants liked by Dora is to find restautants that are both stored by Ann as rated with 2 stars and by Bob as Asian restaurants,

- $Ann{:}ViewS2 \sqcap (ViewC \sqcup Ann{:}ViewT \sqcup Ann{:}ViewV)$, meaning that another way to obtain restaurants liked by Dora is to find restautants stored by Ann as restaurants rated with 2 stars and also as Chinese, Thai or Vietnamese restaurants. Note that this rewriting, which is obtained after several splitting and re-combining turns out to be composed of extensional classes of the same peer (Ann).

- Because of the mapping $Bob{:}Q \sqsubseteq Ann{:}G$, Ann transmits the query $Bob{:}Q$ to Bob, which transmits back to Ann $Bob{:}ViewQ$ as a rewriting of $Bob{:}Q$ and then of $Ann{:}G$. Ann then transmits $Bob{:}ViewQ$ back to Dora as a rewriting of $Ann{:}G$. At Dora's side, $Bob{:}ViewQ$ is now combined with the queued rewritings of $Bob{:}A$ ($Bob{:}ViewA$ and $Ann{:}ViewC \sqcup Ann{:}ViewT \sqcup Ann{:}ViewV$). As a result, two new rewrirings are sent back to the user:

  - $Bob{:}ViewQ \sqcap Bob{:}ViewA$, meaning that to obtain restaurants liked by Dora you can take the restaurants that Bob stores as high quality restaurants and also as Asian restaurants,

  - $Bob{:}ViewQ \sqcap (Ann{:}ViewC \sqcup Ann{:}ViewT \sqcup Ann{:}ViewV)$, providing a new way of getting restaurants liked by Dora (restaurants that are both considered as high quality restaurants by Bob and stored as Chinese, Thai or Vietnamese restaurants).

A peer-to-peer architecture implementing this distributed query rewriting algorithm has been developed and the first experimental results of its scalability are promising [6]. This architecture is used in a joint project with France Télécom, which aims at enriching peer-to-peer web applications with semantics in the form of taxonomies (e.g., Someone [12]).

6   Conclusion

Most of the concepts, tools and techniques deployed so far by the Semantic Web community correspond to the "big is beautiful" idea that high expressivity is needed for describing domain ontologies. As a result, when they are applied, the so-called Semantic Web technologies are mostly used for building thematic portals but do not scale up to the Web.

In this paper, I have argued in favour of a "simple-is-beautiful" vision of the Semantic Web consisting in progressing step by step from the current web towards a more semantic web. The first challenging step (which is far being reached) should be to do best than Google for searching through the whole Web. My vision of a "Semantic Google" would be to replace the use of words for annotating web documents by terms of a taxonomy. Though terms of a taxonomy are words, the (big) difference is that the taxonomy provides a kind of context of interpretation for those terms which is most of the time sufficient in practice to desambiguate their meaning. Therefore, it is important that taxonomies whose terms are used for annotating web resources are attached to those web resources. In this vision, any user is allowed to annotate freely web resources with terms of the taxonomies of his choice but he must attach those taxonomies to the web resources he has annotated. The glue of such a semantic web would be provided by mappings between taxonomies, and the infrastructure implementing it would be a peer-to-peer one.

References

1. Patel-Schneider, P.: Small can be beautiful in knowledge representation. In: IEEE Workshop on Principles of Knowledge-Based Systems. (1984)
2. Berners-Lee, T., Hendler, J., O.Lassila: The semantic web. Scientific American, 279 (2001)
3. Sure, Y., Staab, S., Studer, R.: Methodology for development and employment of ontology based knowledge management applications. SIGMOD Record **34** (2002) 8–24
4. Studer, R., Benjamins, R., Fensel, D.: Knowledge engineering: Principles and methods. Data and Knowledge Engineering **25** (1998) 161–197
5. Fernandez-Lopez, M., Gomez-Perez, A.: Overview and analysis of methodologies for building ontologies. Knowledge Engineering Review **17** (2002) 129–156
6. Adjiman, P., Chatalic, P., Goasdoué, F., Rousset, M.C., Simon, L.: Somewhere in the semantic web. Technical report, http://www.lri.fr/~goasdoue/biblio/ACGRS-TR-SW.pdf (2004)
7. W3C: Owl web ontology language semantics and abstract syntax (2004)
8. Lenat, D.: Cyc: A large-scale investment in knowledge infrastructure. Communication of the ACM **38** (1995) 32–38
9. Dmoz: The open directory project (http://dmoz.org/)
10. OTA: Open travel alliance (http://www.opentravel.org/)
11. IEEE: Ieee learning object metadata (http://ltsc.ieee.org/wg12)
12. Plu, M., Bellec, P., Agosto, L., van de Velde, W.: The web of people: A dual view on the WWW. In: Int. World Wide Web Conf. (2003)
13. Halevy, A., Ives, Z., Suciu, D., Tatarinov, I.: Schema mediation in peer data management systems. In: ICDE'03. (2003)
14. Ooi, B., Shu, Y., Tan, K.L.: Relational data sharing in peer data management systems. **23** (2003)
15. Arenas, M., Kantere, V., Kementsietsidis, A., Kiringa, I., Miller, R., Mylopoulos, J.: The hyperion project: From data integration to data coordination. (2003)
16. Bernstein, P., Giunchiglia, F., Kementsietsidis, A., Mylopoulos, J., Serafini, L., Zaihraheu, I.: Data management for peer-to-peer computing: A vision. In: WebDB Workshop. (2002)
17. Nedjl, W., Wolf, B., Qu, C., Decker, S., Sintek, M., Naeve, A., Nilsson, M., Palmer, M., Risch, T.: Edutella: a p2p networking infrastructure based on rdf. In: WWW'02. (2002)
18. Halevy, A., Ives, Z., Tatarinov, I., Mork, P.: Piazza: data management infrastructure for semantic web applications. In: WWW'03. (2003)
19. Madhavan, J., Halevy, A.: Composing mappings among data sources. In: VLDB 03. (2003)
20. Tatarinov, I., Halevy, A.: Efficient query reformulation in peer data management systems. In: SIGMOD 04. (2004)
21. Adjiman, P., Chatalic, P., Goasdoué, F., Rousset, M.C., Simon, L.: Distributed reasoning in a peer-to-peer setting. In: ECAI 04. (2004)

A Method for Converting Thesauri to RDF/OWL

Mark van Assem[1], Maarten R. Menken[1], Guus Schreiber[1], Jan Wielemaker[2], and Bob Wielinga[2]

[1] Vrije Universiteit Amsterdam, Department of Computer Science
{mark,mrmenken,schreiber}@cs.vu.nl
[2] University of Amsterdam, Social Science Informatics (SWI)
{wielemaker,wielinga}@swi.psy.uva.nl

Abstract. This paper describes a method for converting existing thesauri and related resources from their native format to RDF(S) and OWL. The method identifies four steps in the conversion process. In each step, decisions have to be taken with respect to the syntax or semantics of the resulting representation. Each step is supported through a number of guidelines. The method is illustrated through conversions of two large thesauri: McSH and WordNet.

1 Introduction

Thesauri are controlled vocabularies of terms in a particular domain with hierarchical, associative and equivalence relations between terms. Thesauri such as NLM's Medical Subject Headings (MeSH) are mainly used for indexing and retrieval of articles in large databases (in the case of MeSH the MEDLINE/PubMed database containing over 14 million citations[1]). Other resources, such as the lexical database WordNet, have been used as background knowledge in several analysis and semantic integration tasks [2]. However, their native format, often a proprietary XML, ASCII or relational schema, is not compatible with the Semantic Web's standard format, RDF(S). This paper describes a method for converting thesauri to RDF/OWL and illustrates it with conversions of MeSH and WordNet.

The main objective of converting existing resources to the RDF data model is that these can then be used in Semantic Web applications for annotations. Thesauri provide a hierarchically structured set of terms about which a community has reached consensus. This is precisely the type of background knowledge required in Semantic Web applications. One insight from the submissions to the Semantic Web challenge at ISWC'03[2] was that these applications typically used simple thesauri instead of complex ontologies.

Although conversions of thesauri have been performed, currently no accepted methodology exists to support these efforts. This paper presents a method that

---

[1] http://www.ncbi.nlm.nih.gov/entrez/
[2] http://www-agki.tzi.de/swc/swc2003submissions.html

S.A. McIlraith et al. (Eds.): ISWC 2004, LNCS 3298, pp. 17–31, 2004.

can serve as the starting point for such a methodology. The method and guidelines are based on the authors' experience in converting various thesauri. This paper is organized as follows. Section 2 provides introductory information on thesauri and their structure. In Sect. 3 we describe our method and the rationale behind its steps and guidelines. Sections 4 and 5 each discuss a case study in which the conversion method is applied to MeSH and WordNet, respectively. Additional guidelines that were developed during the case studies, or are more conveniently explained with a specific example, are introduced in these sections. Related research can be found in Sect. 6. Finally, Sect. 7 offers a discussion.

2 Structure of Thesauri

Many thesauri are historically based on the ISO 2788 and ANSI/NISO Z39.19 standards [3,1]. The main structuring concepts are terms and three relations between terms: Broader Term (BT), Narrower Term (NT) and Related Term (RT). *Preferred terms* should be used for indexing, while *non-preferred terms* are included for use in searching. Preferred terms (also known as *descriptors*) are related to non-preferred terms with Use For (UF); USE is the inverse of this relation. Only preferred terms are allowed to have BT, NT and RT relations. The Scope Note (SN) relation is used to provide a definition of a term (see Fig. 1).

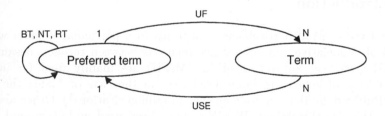

Fig. 1. The basic thesaurus relations. Scope note is not shown.

Two other constructs are *qualifiers* and *node labels*. Homonymous terms should be supplemented with a qualifier to distinguish them, for example "BEAMS (radiation)" and "BEAMS (structures)". A node label is a term that is not meant for indexing, but for structuring the hierarchy, for example "KNIVES By Form". Node labels are also used for organizing the hierarchy in either *fields* or *facets*. The former divides terms into areas of interest such as "injuries" and "diseases", the latter into more abstract categories such as "living" and "non-living" [3].

The standards advocate a *term-based* approach, in which terms are related directly to one another. In the *concept-based* approach [7], concepts are interrelated, while a term is only related to the concept for which it stands; i.e. a *lexicalization* of a concept [12]. The concept-based approach may have advantages such as improved clarity and easier maintenance [6].

3   Method Description

The method is divided into four steps: (0) a preparatory step, (1) a syntactic conversion step, (2) a semantic conversion step, and (3) a standardization step. The division of the method into four steps is an extension of previous work [15].

3.1   Step 0: Preparation

To perform this step (and therefore also the subsequent steps) correctly, it is essential to contact the original thesaurus authors when the documentation is unclear or ambiguous. An analysis of the thesaurus contains the following:

- Conceptual model (the model behind the thesaurus is used as background knowledge in creating a sanctioned conversion);
- Relation between conceptual and digital model;
- Relation to standards (aids in understanding the conceptual and digital model);
- Identification of multilinguality issues.

Although we recognize that multilinguality is an important and complicating factor in thesaurus conversion (see also [8]), it is not treated in this paper.

3.2   Step 1: Syntactic Conversion

In this step the emphasis lies on the syntactic aspects of the conversion process from the source representation to RDF(S). Typical source representations are (1) a proprietary text format, (2) a relational database and (3) an XML representation. This step can be further divided into two substeps.

Step 1a: structure-preserving translation. In Step 1a, a *structure-preserving* translation between the source format and RDF format is performed, meaning that the translation should reflect the source structure as closely as possible. The translation should be complete, meaning that all semantically relevant elements in the source are translated into RDF.

Guideline 1: USE A BASIC SET OF RDF(S) CONSTRUCTS FOR THE STRUCTURE-PRESERVING TRANSLATION.   Only use constructs for defining classes, subclasses, properties (with domains and ranges), human-readable rdfs:labels for class and property names, and XML datatypes. These are the basic building blocks for defining an RDF representation of the conceptual model. The remaining RDF(S) and OWL constructs are used in Step 2 for a semantically oriented conversion. However, one might argue that the application of some constructs (e.g. domains and ranges) also belongs to semantic conversion.

Guideline 2: USE XML SUPPORT FOR DATATYPING. Simple built-in XML Schema datatypes such as xsd:date and xsd:integer are useful to supply schemas with information on property ranges. Using user-defined XML Schema datatypes is still problematic[3]; hopefully this problem will be solved in the near future.

Guideline 3: PRESERVE ORIGINAL NAMING AS MUCH AS POSSIBLE. Preserving the original naming of entities results in more clear and traceable conversions. Prefix duplicate property names with the name of the source entity to make them unique. The meaning of a class or property can be explicated by adding an rdfs:comment, preferably containing a definition from the original documentation. If documentation is available online, rdfs:seeAlso or rdfs:isDefinedBy statements can be used to link to the original documentation and/or definition.

Guideline 4: TRANSLATE RELATIONS OF ARITY THREE OR MORE INTO STRUCTURES WITH BLANK NODES. Relations of arity three or more cannot be translated directly into RDF properties. If the relation's arguments are independent of each other, a structure can be used consisting of a property (with the same name as the original relation) linking the source entity to a blank node (representing the relation), and the relation's arguments linked to the blank node with an additional property per argument (see examples in Sect. 4).

Guideline 5: DO NOT TRANSLATE SEMANTICALLY IRRELEVANT ORDERING INFORMATION. Source representations often contain sequential information, e.g. ordering of a list of terms. These may be irrelevant from a semantic point of view, in which case they can be left out of the conversion.

Guideline 6: AVOID REDUNDANT INFORMATION. Redundant information creates representations which are less clear and harder to maintain. An example on how to avoid this: if the Unique Identifier (UI) of a resource is recorded in the rdf:ID, then do not include a property that also records the UI.

Guideline 7: AVOID INTERPRETATION. Interpretations of the meaning of information in the original source (i.e., meaning that cannot be traced back to the original source or documentation) should be approached with caution, as wrong interpretations result in inconsistent and/or inaccurate conversions. The approach of this method is to postpone interpretation (see Step 2b).

Instead of developing a new schema (i.e., thesaurus metamodel), one can also use an existing thesaurus schema, such as the SKOS (see Sect. 3.4), which already defines "Concept", "broader", etc. This may be a simpler approach than to first develop a new schema and later map this onto the SKOS. However, this

---

[3] http://www.w3.org/2001/sw/WebOnt/webont-issues.html#I4.3-Structured-Datatypes

is only a valid approach if the metamodel of the source and of SKOS match. A drawback is that the naming of the original metamodel is lost (e.g. "BT" instead of "broader"). For thesauri with a (slightly) different metamodel, it is recommended to develop a schema from scratch, so as not to lose the original semantics, and map this schema onto SKOS in Step 3.

Step 1b: explication of syntax. Step 1b concerns the *explication* of information that is implicit in the source format, but intended by the conceptual model. The same set of RDF(S) constructs is used as in Step 1a. For example, the AAT thesaurus [11] uses node labels (called "Guide Terms" in AAT), but in the AAT source data these are only distinguished from normal terms by enclosing the term name in angle brackets (e.g. <KNIVES by Form>). This information can be made explicit by creating a class `GuideTerm`, which is an `rdfs:subClassOf` the class `AATTerm`, and assigning this class to all terms with angle brackets. Other examples are described in Sects. 4 and 5.

3.3   Step 2: Semantic Conversion

In this step the class and property definitions are augmented with additional RDFS and OWL constraints. Its two substeps are aimed at explication (Step 2a) and interpretation (Step 2b). After completion of Step 2a the thesaurus is ready for publication on the Web as an "as-is" RDF/OWL representation.

Step 2a: explication of semantics. This step is similar to Step 1b, but now more expressive RDFS and OWL constructs may be used. For example, a `broaderTerm` property can be defined as an `owl:TransitiveProperty` and a `relatedTerm` property as an `owl:SymmetricProperty`.

A technique that is used in this step is to define certain properties as specializations of predefined RDFS properties, e.g. `rdfs:label` and `rdfs:comment`. For example, if a property `nameOf` is clearly intended to denote a human-readable label for a resource, it makes sense to define this property as a subproperty of `rdfs:label`. RDFS-aware tools will now be able to interpret `nameOf` in the intended way.

Step 2b: interpretations. In Step 2b specific *interpretations* are introduced that are strictly speaking not sanctioned by the original model or documentation. A common motivation is some application-specific requirement, e.g. an application wants to treat a `broaderTerm` hierarchy as a class hierarchy. This can be stated as follows: `broaderTerm rdfs:subPropertyOf rdfs:subClassOf`. Semantic Web applications using thesauri will often want to do this, even if not all hierarchical links satisfy the subclass criteria. This introduces the notion of metamodeling. It is not surprising that the schema of a thesaurus is typically a metamodel: its instances are categories for describing some domain of interest.

Guideline 8: CONSIDER TREATING THE THESAURUS SCHEMA AS A METAMODEL. The instances of a thesaurus schema are often general terms or concepts, that occur as classes in other places. RDFS allows one to treat instances as a classes:

simply add the statement that the class of those instances is a subclass of rdfs:Class. For example, an instance i is of class C; class C is declared to be an rdfs:subClassOf rdfs:Class. Because instance i is now also an instance of rdfs:Class, it can be treated as a class.

The above example of treating broader term as a subclass relation is similar in nature.

A schema which uses these constructions is outside the scope of OWL DL. Application developers will have to make their own expressivity vs. tractability trade-off here.

The output of this step should be used in applications as *a specific interpretation of the thesaurus*, not as a standard conversion.

3.4   Step 3: Standardization

Several proposals exist for a standard schema for thesauri.[4] Such a schema may enable the development of infrastructure that can interpret and interchange thesaurus data. Therefore, it may be useful to map a thesaurus onto a standard schema. This optional step can be made both after Step 2a (the result may be published on the web) and Step 2b (the result may only be used in an application-specific context). Unfortunately, a standard schema has not yet been agreed upon. As illustration, the schema of the W3C Semantic Web Advanced Development for Europe (SWAD-E) project[5] is mapped to MeSH in Sect. 4.

The so-called "SKOS" schema of SWAD-E is concept-based, with class Concept and relations narrower, broader and related between Concepts. A Concept can have a prefLabel (preferred term) and altLabels (non-preferred terms). Also provided is a TopConcept class, which can be used to arrange a hierarchy under special concepts (such as fields and facets, see Sect. 2). TopConcept is a subclass of Concept. Note that because SKOS is concept-based, it may be problematic to map term-based thesauri.

4   Case One: MeSH

This section describes how the method has been applied to MeSH (version 2004[6]). The main source consists of two XML files: one containing so-called *descriptors* (228 MB), and one containing *qualifiers* (449 Kb). Each has an associated DTD. A file describing additional information on descriptors was not converted. The conversion program (written in XSLT) plus links to the original source and output files of each step can be found at http://thesauri.cs.vu.nl/. The conversion took two persons approximately three weeks to complete.

---

[4] http://www.w3.org/2001/sw/Europe/reports/thes/thes_links.html
[5] http://www.w3.org/2001/sw/Europe/reports/thes/1.0/guide/
[6] http://www.nlm.nih.gov/mesh/filelist.html

4.1 Analysis of MeSH

The conceptual model of MeSH is centered around Descriptors, which contain Concepts [9]. In turn, Concepts consist of a set of Terms. Exactly one Concept is the preferred Concept of a Descriptor, and exactly one Term is the preferred Term of a Concept. Each Descriptor can have Qualifiers, which are used to indicate aspects of a particular Descriptor, e.g. "ABDOMEN" has the Qualifiers "pathology" and "abnormalities". Descriptors are related in a polyhierarchy, and are meant to represent broader/narrower *document retrieval sets* (i.e., not a subclass relation). Each Descriptor belongs to one (or more) of fifteen Categories, such as "Anatomy" and "Diseases" [10]. The Concepts contained within one Descriptor are also hierarchically related to each other.

This model is inconsistent with the ISO and ANSI standards, for several reasons. Firstly, the model is concept-based. Secondly, Descriptors contain a set of Concepts, while in the standards a Descriptor is simply a preferred term. Thirdly, Qualifiers are not used to disambiguate homonyms.

4.2 Converting MeSH

Step 1a: structure-preserving translation. In the XML version of MeSH, Descriptors, Concepts, Terms and Qualifiers each have a Unique Identifier (UI). Each Descriptor also has a TreeNumber (see [1]). This is used to indicate a position in a polyhierarchical structure (a Descriptor can have more than one TreeNumber), but this is implicit only. Relations between XML elements are made by referring to the UI of the relation's target (e.g. <SeeRelatedDescriptor> contains the UI of another Descriptor). In Step 1a, this is converted into instances of the property `hasRelatedDescriptor`. The explication of TreeNumbers is postponed until Step 1b.

Most decisions in Step 1a concern which XML elements should be translated into classes, and which into properties. The choice to create classes for Descriptor, Concept and Term are clear-cut: these are complex, interrelated structures. A so-called <EntryCombination> relates a Descriptor-Qualifier pair to another Descriptor-Qualifier pair. Following Guideline 4, two blank nodes are created (each representing one pair) and related to an instance of the class EntryCombination. As already mentioned, relations between elements in XML MeSH are made by referring to the UI of the target. However, each such relation also includes the *name* of the target. As this is redundant information, the name can be safely disregarded.

Guideline 9: GIVE PREFERENCE TO THE RELATION-AS-ARC APPROACH OVER THE RELATION-AS-NODE APPROACH. In the relation-as-arc approach, relations are modeled as arcs between entities (RDF uses "properties" to model arcs). In the relation-as-node approach, a node represents the relation, with one arc relating the source entity to the relation node, and one arc relating the relation node to the destination entity [7]. The relation-as-arc approach is more natural to the RDF model, and also allows for definition of property semantics (symmetry, inverseness, etc.) in OWL.

It is not always possible to follow Guideline 9, e.g. in the case of MeSH <ConceptRelation>. Although the straightforward choice is to create a property that relates two Concepts, this is not possible as each ConceptRelation has an additional attribute (see Guideline 4). Again, a blank node is used (the relation-as-node approach).

Guideline 10: CREATE PROXY CLASSES FOR REFERENCES TO EXTERNAL RESOURCES IF THEY ARE NOT AVAILABLE IN RDF. Each Concept has an associated SemanticType, which originates in the UMLS Semantic Network[7]. This external resource is not available in RDF, but might be converted in the near future. In MeSH, only the UI and name of the SemanticType is recorded. One could either use a datatype property to relate the UI to a Concept (again, the redundant name is ignored), or create SemanticType instances (empty proxies for the actual types). We have opted for the latter, as this simplifies future integration with UMLS. In this scenario, either new properties can be added to the proxies, or the existing proxies can be declared `owl:sameAs` to SemanticType instances of a converted UMLS.

Guideline 11: ONLY CREATE `rdf:ID`s BASED ON IDENTIFIERS IN THE ORIGINAL SOURCE. A practical problem in the syntactical translation is what value to assign the `rdf:ID` attribute. If the original source does not provide a unique identifier for an entity, one should translate it into blank nodes, as opposed to generating new identifiers. A related point is that if the UI is recorded using `rdf:ID`, additional properties to record an entity's UI would introduce redundancy, and therefore shouldn't be used.

Guideline 12: USE THE SIMPLEST SOLUTION THAT PRESERVES THE INTENDED SEMANTICS. In XML MeSH, only one Term linked to a Concept is the preferred term. Some terms are permutations of the term name (indicated with the attribute `isPermutedTermYN`), but unfortunately have the same UI as the Term from which they are generated. A separate instance cannot be created for this permuted term, as this would introduce a duplicate `rdf:ID`. Two obvious solutions remain: create a blank node or relate the permuted term with a datatype property `permutedTerm` to Term. In the first solution, one would also need to relate the node to its non-permuted parent, and copy all information present in the parent term to the permuted term node (thus introducing redundancy). The second solution is simpler and preserves the intended semantics.

Step 1b: explication of syntax. In Step 1b, three explications are made. Firstly, the TreeNumbers are used to create a hierarchy of Descriptors with a [Descriptor] `subTreeOf` [Descriptor] property. Secondly, the TreeNumber starts with a capital letter which stands for one of fifteen Categories. The

---

[7] http://www.nlm.nih.gov/pubs/factsheets/umlssemn.html

class Category and property [Descriptor] inCategory [Category] are introduced to relate Descriptors to their Catogories. Thirdly, the ConceptRelations are translated into three properties, brd, nrw and rel, thus converting from a relation-as-node to a relation-as-arc approach (see Guidelines 12 and 9). This requires two observations: (a) the values NRW, BRD and REL of the attribute relationName correspond to narrower, broader and related Concepts; and (b) the relationAttribute is not used in the actual XML, and can be removed. Without the removal of the relationAttribute, the arity of the relation would have prevented us from using object properties.

Some elements are not explicated, although they are clear candidates. These are XML elements which contain text, but also implicit information that can be used to link instances. For example, a Descriptor's <RelatedRegistryNumber> contains the ID of another Descriptor, but also other textual information. Splitting this information into two or more properties changes the original semantics, so we have chosen to create a datatype property for this element and copy the text as a literal value.

Step 2a: explication of semantics. In Step 2a, the following statements are added (a selection):

- The properties brd and nrw are each other's inverse, and are both transitive, while rel is symmetric;
- A Concept's scopeNote is an rdfs:subPropertyOf the property rdfs:comment;
- All properties describing a resource's name (e.g. descriptorName) are declared an rdfs:subPropertyOf the property rdfs:label;
- Each of these name properties is also an owl:InverseFunctionalProperty, as the names are unique in the XML file. Note that this may not hold for future versions of MeSH;
- All properties recording a date are an owl:FunctionalProperty;
- The XML DTD defines that some elements occur either zero or once in the data. The corresponding RDF properties can also be declared functional;
- As a Term belongs to exactly one Concept, and a Concept to exactly one Descriptor, [Concept] hasTerm [Term] as well as [Descriptor] hasConcept [Concept] is an owl:InverseFunctionalProperty;

Unfortunately, the relation represented by class EntryCombination cannot be supplied with additional semantics, e.g. that it is an owl:SymmetricProperty (see Guideline 9).

Step 2b: interpretations. In Step 2b, the following *interpretations* are made, following Guideline 8. Note that these are examples, as we have no specific application in mind.

- brd is an rdfs:subPropertyOf rdfs:subClassOf;
- Descriptor and Concept are declared rdfs:subClassOf rdfs:Class.

Step 3: standardization. In Step 3, a mapping is created between the MeSH schema and the SKOS schema. The following constructs can be mapped (using `rdfs:subPropertyOf` and `rdfs:subClassOf`):

- `mesh:subTreeOf` onto `skos:broader`;
- `mesh:Descriptor` onto `skos:Concept`;
- `mesh:hasRelatedDescriptor` onto `skos:related`;
- `mesh:descriptorName` onto `skos:prefLabel`.

There is considerable mismatch between the schemas. Descriptors are the central concepts between which hierarchical relations exist, but it is unclear how MeSH Concepts and Terms can be dealt with. SKOS defines datatype properties with which terms can be recorded as labels of Concepts, but this cannot be mapped meaningfully onto MeSH' Concept and Term classes. For example, `mesh:conceptName` cannot be mapped onto `skos:prefLabel`, as the former's domain is `mesh:Concept`, while the latter's domain is `skos:Concept` (skos:Concept is already mapped onto mesh:Descriptor). Furthermore, the `mesh:Category` cannot be mapped onto `skos:TopCategory`, because TopCategory is a subclass of `skos:Concept`, while `mesh:Category` is not a subclass of `mesh:Descriptor`.

5   Case Two: WordNet

This section describes how the method has been applied to WordNet release 2.0. The original source consists of 18 Prolog files (23 MB in total). The conversion programs (written in Prolog) plus links to the original source as well as the output files of each step can be found at `http://thesauri.cs.vu.nl/`. The conversion took two persons approximately three weeks to complete. Note that Step 3 for WordNet is not discussed here for reasons of space, but is available at the forementioned website.

5.1   Analysis of WordNet

WordNet [2] is a concept-based thesaurus for the English language. The concepts are called "synsets" which have their own identifier. Each synset is associated with a set of lexical representations, i.e. its set of synonyms. The synset concept is divided into four categories, i.e. nouns, verbs, adverbs and adjectives. Most WordNet relations are defined between synsets. Example relations are hyponymy and meronymy.

There have been a number of translations of WordNet to RDF and OWL formats. Dan Brickley[8] translated the noun/hyponym hierarchy directly into RDFS classes and subclasses. This is different from the method we propose, because it does not preserve the original source structure. Decker and Melnik[9] have created a partial RDF representation, which does preserve the original

---

[8] http://lists.w3.org/Archives/Public/www-rdf-interest/1999Dec/0002.html
[9] http://www.semanticweb.org/library/

structure. The conversion of the KID Group at the University of Neuchatel[10] constitutes an extension of representation both in scope and in description of semantics (by adding OWL axioms). We follow mainly this latter conversion and relate it to the steps in our conversion method. In the process we changed and extended the WordNet schema slightly (and thus also the resulting conversion).

5.2   Converting WordNet

Step 1a: structure-preserving translation. In this step the baseline classes and properties are created to map the source representation as precisely as possible to an RDF representation:

- Classes: `SynSet`, `Noun`, `Verb`, `Adverb`, `Adjective` (subclasses of `SynSet`), `AdjectiveSatellite` (subclass of `Adjective`);
- Properties: `wordForm`, `glossaryEntry`, `hyponymOf`, `entails`, `similarTo`, `memberMeronymOf`, `substanceMeronymOf`, `partMeronymOf`, `derivation`, `causedBy`, `verbGroup`, `attribute`, `antonymOf`, `seeAlso`, `participleOf`, `pertainsTo`.

Note that the original WordNet naming is not very informative (e.g. "s" represents synset). For readability, here we use the `rdfs:labels` that have been added in the RDF version. All properties except for the last four have a synset as their domain. The range of these properties is also a synset, except for `wordForm` and `glossaryEntry`. Some properties have a subclass of `SynSet` as their domain and/or range, e.g. `entails` holds between `Verbs`.

The main decision that needs to be taken in this step concerns the following two interrelated representational issues:

1. Each synset is associated with a set of synonym "words". For example, the synset 100002560 has two associated synonyms, namely `nonentity` and `nothing`. Decker and Melnik represent these labels by defining the (multi-valued) property `wordForm` with a literal value as its range (i.e. as an OWL datatype property). The Neuchatel approach is to define a word as a class in its own right (`WordObject`). The main disadvantage of this is that one needs to introduce an identifier for each `WordObject` as it does not exist in the source representation, and words are not unique (homonymy).
2. The last four properties in the list above (`antonymOf`, etc.) do not represent relations between synsets but instead between *particular words* in a synset. This also provides the rationale for the introduction of the class WordObject in the Neuchatel representation: antonymOf can now simply defined as a property between WordObjects.

We prefer to represents words as literal values, thus avoiding the identifier problem (see Guideline 11). For handling properties like `antonymOf` we defined a helper class `SynSetWord` with properties linking it to a synset and a word. For each subclass of SynSet, an equivalent subclass of `SynSetWord` is introduced (e.g. `SynSetVerb`). A sample representation of an antonym looks like this:

---

[10] http://taurus.unine.ch/GroupHome/knowler/wordnet.html

```
<SynSetWord>
  <inSynSet rdf:resource="#100017087"/>
  <relevantWord>natural_object</relevantWord>
  <antonymOf>
    <SynSetWord>
      <inSynSet rdf:resource="#100019244"/>
      <relevantWord>artifact</relevantWord>
    </SynSetWord>
  </antonymOf>
</SynSetWord>
```

In this example, the word `natural object` in synset 100017087 is an antonym of the word `artifact` in synset 100019244.

Step 1b: explication of syntax. The source representation of WordNet does not contain many implicit elements. The only things that need to be added here are the notions of hypernymy and holonymy (three variants). Both are only mentioned in the text and are apparently the inverse[11] of respectively the hyponym relation and the three meronym variants. Consequently, these four properties were added to the schema.

Step 2a: explication of semantics. In this step additional OWL axioms can be introduced to explicate the intended semantics of the WordNet classes and properties. A selection:

- `Noun`, `Verb`, `Adverb`, and `Adjective` together form disjoint and complete subclasses of `SynSet`;
- `hyponymOf` and `hypernymOf` are transitive properties;
- `hyponymOf` only holds between nouns or verbs;[12]
- `hyponymOf`/`hypernymOf` and the three variants of `meronymOf`/`holonymOf` are inverse properties;
- `verbGroup` and `antonymOf` are symmetric properties.

In addition, we defined the properties `wordForm` and `glossaryEntry` as subproperties of respectively `rdfs:label` and `rdfs:comment`.

From the WordNet documentation it is clear that these properties have this type of intended semantics. The alternative for defining these as subproperties would have been to use `rdfs:label` and `rdfs:comment` directly in the RDF representation, thus dropping the original names. This makes the traceability of the conversion less clear.

---

[11] The WordNet documentation uses the term "reflexive", but it is clear that inverseness is meant.

[12] In the Neuchatel representation an intermediate class `NounsAndVerbs` is introduced to express these constraints. This is not needed, as OWL supports local property restrictions which allow one, for example, to state that the value range of the `hyponymOf` property for `Noun` must be `Noun`.

Step 2b: interpretations. We have used WordNet heavily in semantic annotation of images (see e.g. [5]). In that application we used the WordNet hierarchy as an RDFS subclass tree by adding the following two metastatements:

- `wn:SynSet rdfs:subClassOf rdfs:Class;`
- `wn:hyponymOf rdfs:subPropertyOf rdfs:subClassOf`

Tools such as Triple20[13] will now be able to visualize the synset tree as a subclass tree. The repercussions of this type of metamodeling for RDF storage and retrieval are discussed in [14].

6 Related Research

Soualmia *et al.* [13] describe a migration of a specialized, French version of MeSH to an OWL DL representation. Their goal is to improve search in a database of medical resources. We mention a few of their modeling principles. Firstly, they "clean" the taxonomy by distinguishing between part-of and is-a relationships (the former type are translated into a `partOf` property, the latter into `rdfs:subClassOf`). Secondly, qualifiers are translated into properties, and their domains are restricted to the union of the descriptors on which they may be applied. The properties are hierarchically organized using `rdfs:subPropertyOf` according to the qualifier hierarchy.

Wroe *et al.* [16] describe a methodology to migrate the Gene Ontology (GO) from XML to DAML+OIL. Their goal is to "support validation, extension and multiple classification" of the GO. In each step, the converted ontology is enriched further. For example, three new part_of relations are introduced. Also, new classes are added to group part_of instances under their parent components, which enables visualization of the hierarchy. MeSH and the KEGG enzyme database are used to enrich class definitions so a new classification for Gene enzyme functions can be made by a reasoner. Additional modeling of class restrictions allowed the same reasoner to infer 17 is-a relationships that were omitted in the original source.

Goldbeck *et al.* [4] describe a conversion of the NCI (National Cancer Institute) Thesaurus from its native XML format to OWL Lite. Their goal is to "make the knowledge in the Thesaurus more useful and accessible to the public". A mapping of XML tags onto OWL classes and properties is defined, based on an analysis of the underlying conceptual model and NCI's thesaurus development process. `rdf:IDs` are created using a transformation of the original concept names (spaces removed, illegal characters substituted). This is a reasonable approach, under the assumption that names are indeed and will remain unique (see Guideline 11).

There are two main differences with our work. Firstly, the forementioned projects do not separate between "as-is" conversion and enrichment steps, as our method does. Therefore, the conversions may only be usable for the project's

---

[13] http://www.swi-prolog.org/packages/Triple20/

own goals. Secondly, we try to generalize over specific conversions and aim to define a more general conversion process.

In the SWAD-Europe project a schema is being developed to encode RDF thesauri. Additionally, work is in progress to produce a guideline document on converting multilingual thesauri [8]. The development of a standard schema influences our standardization step, and guidelines on converting multilingual thesauri may be incorporated to broaden the scope of our method.

7   Discussion

This paper has presented a method to convert existing thesauri to RDF(S) and OWL, in a manner that is sanctioned by the original documentation and format. Only in a separate step may interpretations be made for application-specific purposes.

Two additional aims of converting existing resources to the RDF model may be identified. Firstly, the quality of a thesaurus may be improved using the semantics of RDF(S), as some thesauri use relations with weak or unclear semantics, or apply them in an ambiguous way [12]. Secondly, converted thesauri can be checked using standard reasoners, identifying e.g. missing subsumption and inverse relations (e.g. BT/NT).

Recently the W3C has installed the Semantic Web Best Practices and Deployment (SWBPD) Working Group[14], which aims to provide guidelines for application developers on how to deploy Semantic Web technology. This method may serve as input for and might be extended by this Working Group.

Several issues remain as future research in developing a methodology. Firstly, translating between the source model and the RDF model is a complex task with many alternative mappings, especially for thesauri that do not conform to or define extensions of the ISO and ANSI standards. Secondly, more guidelines are required on how to convert multilingual thesauri. Thirdly, a standard thesaurus schema is required to perform step three of our method. It is clear that the current SWAD-E proposal does not completely cover complex thesauri such as MeSH. An open question is whether the proposal might be extended or that this type of thesaurus is simply outside the scope, as MeSH deviates from the ISO and ANSI standards.

Acknowledgements. This work was partly supported by the IST project IST-2002-507967 "HOPS" and the CHIME project, part of the NWO ToKeN2000 programme. The authors are grateful for the useful discussions with and feedback of their colleagues.

References

1. ANSI/NISO. Guidelines for the construction, format, and management of monolingual thesauri. Ansi/niso z39.19-2003, 2003.

---

[14] http://www.w3.org/2001/sw/BestPractices/

2. Christiane Fellbaum, editor. *WordNet: An Electronic Lexical Database*. Bradford Books, 1998.
3. International Organization for Standardization. Documentation - guidelines for the establishment and development of monolingual thesauri. Iso 2788-1986, 1986.
4. Jennifer Goldbeck, Gilberto Fragoso, Frank Hartel, James Hendler, Bijan Parsia, and Jim Oberthaler. The National Cancer Institute's Thesaurus and Ontology. *Journal of Web Semantics*, 1(1), Dec 2003. URL: http://www.mindswap.org/papers/WebSemantics-NCI.pdf.
5. L. Hollink, A. Th. Schreiber, J. Wielemaker, and B. J. Wielinga. Semantic annotation of image collections. In S. Handschuh, M. Koivunen, R. Dieng, and S. Staab, editors, *Knowledge Capture 2003 – Proceedings Knowledge Markup and Semantic Annotation Workshop*, pages 41–48, 2003.
6. Douglas Johnston, Stuart J. Nelson, Jacque-Lynne A. Schulman, Allan G. Savage, and Tammy P. Powell. Redefining a thesaurus: Term-centric no more. In *Proceedings of the 1998 AMIA Annual Symposium*, 1998.
7. Alistair Miles and Brian Matthews. Review of RDF thesaurus work. Deliverable 8.2, version 0.1, SWAD-Europe, 2004. URL: http://www.w3c.rl.ac.uk/SWAD/deliverables/8.2.html.
8. Alistair Miles, Brian Matthews, and Michael Wilson. RDF encoding of multilingual thesauri. Deliverable 8.3, version 0.1, SWAD-Europe, 2004. URL: http://www.w3c.rl.ac.uk/SWAD/deliverables/8.3.html.
9. U.S. National Library of Medicine. Introduction to MeSH in XML format, November 2001. URL: http://www.nlm.nih.gov/mesh/xmlmesh.html.
10. U.S. National Library of Medicine. MeSH tree structures, May 2004. URL: http://www.nlm.nih.gov/mesh/intro_trees.html.
11. T. Peterson. *Introduction to the Art and Architecture Thesaurus*. Oxford University Press, 1994. See also: http://www.getty.edu/research/tools/vocabulary/aat/.
12. Dagobert Soergel, Boris Lauser, Anita Liang, Frehiwot Fisseha, Johannes Keizer, and Stephen Katz. Reengineering thesauri for new applications: the AGROVOC example. *Journal of Digital Information*, 4(4), March 2004.
13. L.F. Soualmia, C. Goldbreich, and S.J. Darmoni. Representing the mesh in owl: Towards a semi-automatic migration. In *Proceedings of the First International Workshop on Formal Biomedical Knowledge Representation (KR-MED 2004)*, pages 81–87, Whistler, Canada, June 2004.
14. J. Wielemaker, A. Th. Schreiber, and B. J. Wielinga. Prolog-based infrastructure for rdf: performance and scalability. In D. Fensel, K. Sycara, and J. Mylopoulos, editors, *The Semantic Web - Proceedings ISWC'03, Sanibel Island, Florida*, volume 2870 of *LNCS*, pages 644–658, Berlin/Heidelberg, October 2003. Springer Verlag.
15. Bob Wielinga, Jan Wielemaker, Guus Schreiber, and Mark van Assem. Methods for porting resources to the semantic web. In C. Bussler, J. Davies, D. Fensel, and R. Studer, editors, *Proceedings of the First European Semantic Web Symposium (ESWS2004)*, number 3053 in LNCS, pages 299–311, Heraklion, Greece, May 2004. Springer-Verlag.
16. C.J. Wroe, R. Stevens, C.A. Goble, and M. Ashburner. A methodology to migrate the Gene ontology to a description logic environment using DAML+OIL. In *Proceedings of the 8th Pacific Symposium on Biocomputing (PSB 2003)*, pages 624–635, Lihue, Hawaii, USA, January 2003.

Contexts for the Semantic Web

Ramanathan Guha[2], Rob McCool[1], and Richard Fikes[1]

[1] Artificial Intelligence Laboratory, Stanford University, USA
[2] IBM Research, USA

Abstract. A central theme of the Semantic Web is that programs should be able to easily aggregate data from different sources. Unfortunately, even if two sites provide their data using the same data model and vocabulary, subtle differences in their use of terms and in the assumptions they make pose challenges for aggregation. Experiences with the TAP project reveal some of the phenomena that pose obstacles to a simplistic model of aggregation. Similar experiences have been reported by AI projects such as Cyc, which has led to the development and use of various context mechanisms. In this paper we report on some of the problems with aggregating independently published data and propose a context mechanism to handle some of these problems. We briefly survey the context mechanisms developed in AI and contrast them with the requirements of a context mechanism for the Semantic Web. Finally, we present a context mechanism for the Semantic Web that is adequate to handle the aggregation tasks, yet simple from both computational and model theoretic perspectives.

1 Introduction

The ease with which web sites could link to each other doubtless contributed to the rapid adoption of the World Wide Web. It is hoped that as the Semantic Web becomes more prevalent, programs will be able to similarly weave together data from diverse sites. Indeed, the data model behind RDF was significantly motivated by the fact that directed labeled graphs provided a simple, but effective model for aggregating data from different sources.

Unfortunately, while the languages of the Semantic Web (RDF, RDFS, OWL, etc) provide a method for aggregation at the data model level, higher level differences between data sources sometimes make it inappropriate to directly merge data from them. Just as with the human readable web, Semantic Web publishers make assumptions and use the same term in subtly different ways. On the human readable web, the human consumers of web pages are able to use their common sense to reconcile these differences. On the Semantic Web, we need to develop the mechanisms that allow us to explicitly represent and reason with these assumptions and differences. This will enable the programs that consume data from the Semantic Web to reconcile these differences, or at least avoid the problems that arise by applying an overly simple aggregation model to such data sources.

S.A. McIlraith et al. (Eds.): ISWC 2004, LNCS 3298, pp. 32–46, 2004.

In the past, AI researchers have encountered similar issues when aggregating structured knowledge from different people or even the same person at different times. To handle these issues, mechanisms such as contexts and micro-theories have been proposed and implemented in projects such as Cyc [17]. While the kind of phenomena encountered in those projects are substantially more intricate and unlikely to be encountered in the near future on the Semantic Web, the scale and federated nature of the Semantic Web pose a new set of challenges. We believe that a context mechanism that is similar in spirit to the earlier context mechanisms will be not only useful, but required to achieve the Semantic Web vision. However, the differences between AI systems and the Semantic Web also mean that a context mechanism for the Semantic Web will have substantial differences from the AI context mechanisms. In this paper, we discuss the motivation for some of the basic requirements and present some possibilities for a context mechanism for the Semantic Web.

We begin by recounting some of the problems in aggregating data from different sources that were encountered on the TAP [20] project. These examples provide the motivation for the capabilities required of a context mechanism for the Semantic Web. We then present a simple context mechanism for handling these problems. After that, we discuss the model theory extensions required to incorporate this mechanism into RDF. Finally, we discuss related work and Semantic Web issues and constructs related to contexts.

2   Overview of TAP

The TAP project [20], [18] has over the last three years attempted to create platforms for publishing to and consuming data from the Semantic Web. Using this platform, we have built a number of applications [19] both to validate our assumptions and to help bootstrap the Semantic Web.

Building anything more than the simplest toy applications requires a substantial amount of data. Unfortunately, the Semantic Web, in its current stage, has little to offer in this regard. On the other hand, we do have a very large body of unstructured knowledge in the human readable World Wide Web. So, both to solve our problem and to bootstrap the Semantic Web, we have created a large scale knowledge extraction and aggregation system called onTAP. onTAP includes 207 HTML page templates which are able to read and extract knowledge from 38 different high quality web sites. The HTML template system has currently read over 150,000 pages, discovering over 1.6 million entities and asserting over 6 million triples about these entities. The system that aggregates this data can run in either a dynamic mode, in response to a query from an application, or in a batch mode. In batch mode, this aggregator is used to create a classification index for keyword-based queries and for scanning of documents for referenced entities.

onTAP also includes a system to read political news articles from Yahoo! News. The articles in this news feed are matched against natural language patterns to extract entities, attributes of and relationships between these entities.

Work is currently underway to expand this system to read more news sources. This system has read 46,113 articles to discover 6,052 unique entities and 137,082 triples about them.

Most of the content of TAP is obtained via these templates that draw on HTML pages that are targeted at humans. However, we believe that observations regarding the contextual phenomena associated with this data can be extrapolated to the case where the data is directly published by the sites in a structured form. Most of the sites that TAP uses do have their content in a structured form in a database. Front end processors query the database and format the data into HTML. When a site such as Amazon makes its data available in a structured form, they publish the same data. That is, the format and markup language used are different, but the assumptions, approximations and other contextual phenomena that are in their HTML pages are also present in the structured data that they publish.

3 Contextual Phenomena

In this section we discuss some of the contextual phenomena that we observed in the process of building the TAP knowledge base that cause problems in data aggregation. The examples of contextual phenomena we observed can be classified into a small number of varieties of contexts. Here we describe each of these varieties along with some examples that we encountered. We also discuss how we would like to handle each of these cases during aggregation.

Class Differences. Different sites often use a particular class in slightly different ways. Sites may differ on the meaning of seemingly unambiguous concepts such as *Person*. For example, the site Who2 classifies C3PO (the robot in Star Wars) as a person, whereas most other sites classify it as a robot. During aggregation, we should map Who2's use of *Person* to something more general. Alternately, we can believe what Who2 has to say about some resource, unless what it says contradicts what some other site says.

Propositional Attitude. A related phenomenon is that of a site having an implicit propositional attitude. For example, many sites providing reviews of television shows specify that Josiah Bartlet (a character who plays the role of the President of the US in the television series 'West Wing') is the President of the United States. During aggregation, the propositional attitude of these statements should be made explicit.

Property Type Differences. A common source of differences between sites is that property types such as *capacity* and *price* are used differently. An example is the capacity of nuclear power plants. These plants have two different kinds of capacities: a design capacity and an actual capacity. Some sites specify the design capacity while others specify the actual capacity, but in most cases they just refer to it as the capacity. When aggregating, we need to either create a generalization of the two capacities or determine which capacity a particular site is referring to and map the *capacity* on that site to the appropriate version of capacity in the aggregate.

Point of View. More substantial differences occur when there are conflicting points of view. Is Taiwan a country of its own, or a province of China? The answer depends very strongly on which site is queried. Similarly, different sites classify Hamas as a terrorist organization, a freedom fighting organization and a humanitarian organization. This kind of subjective data is often mixed in with more objective data (like the head of Hamas or the capital of Taiwan). When aggregating data from these sites, we would like to either make the subjectivity explicit (through the use of propositional attitudes) or only selectively import those facts that are not contentious.

Implicit Time. Sites often publish a piece of data that is true at the time of publication, with the temporal qualification being left implicit. Equally often, this data does not get updated when it no longer holds. There are a number of sites that list Bill Clinton as the President of the US, that refer to Yugoslavia as a country, etc. Unfortunately, such implicitly temporally qualified data is often mixed in with data that is not temporally qualified. For example, it is still true that Bill Clinton graduated from Yale and the latitude and longitude of Sarajevo have not changed. When aggregating data from these sites, we would like to either make the time explicit or only selectively import those facts that are not likely to have changed.

A similar phenomenon is that of a site leaving the unit of measure associated with an attribute value implicit. So, instead of specifying the price as US$40, they might simply say 40. In such cases, we need to either make the unit of measure explicit or perform the appropriate conversion.

Approximations. Approximations are another source of differences between sites. For example, the CIA World Factbook provides approximate values for the population, area, etc. of all countries. More accurate numbers are typically available from the governments of each of these countries, only some of which are online. We like to be able to combine data from the CIA World Factbook and data from the governments, preferring the government data when it is available.

We recognize that these differences could be because the TAP data was obtained by extracting structured data from HTML pages that were intended for human consumption. However, these phenomena are not an artifact of the information being published in an unstructured format. Most of the information on these sites is drawn from structured databases and these phenomena manifest themselves in these databases as well. Consequently, we believe that these problems will persist even when the data is made available in a machine readable form.

These kinds of differences between sites pose problems when data from these sites is aggregated. The problem is not that some of these sites are not trustworthy or that all of their data is bad. In fact, sources of data such as the CIA Factbook and Who2 are rich and useful repositories that should be part of the Semantic Web. What we need is a mechanism to factor the kinds of differences listed above as part of the data aggregation process. Various formalizations of context mechanisms have been proposed in the AI literature to handle this process of factoring differences in representations between knowledge bases. In the next section we first briefly review some of the context-related concepts from AI, note the differences between those and our requirements for the Semantic Web and then, in the following section, propose a simplified version to solve our problem for the Semantic Web.

4   Contexts in AI

Contexts as first class objects in knowledge representation systems have been the subject of much study in AI. KR systems as early as KRL [2] incorporated a notion of contexts. The first steps towards introducing contexts as formal objects were taken by McCarthy ([14], [15]) and Guha [10] in the early 1990s. This was followed by a number of alternate formulations and improvements by Buvac [6] [4], Fikes [5], Giunchiglia [8], Nayak [16] and others. Contexts/Microtheories are an important part of many current KR systems such as Cyc [17]. Contexts remain an active area of research in AI and Philosophy.

Contexts have been used in AI to handle a wide range of phenomena, a categorization of which can be found in [9]. They have been used in natural language understanding to model indexicals and other issues that arise at the semantic and pragmatic processing layers. They have found extensive use in common-sense reasoning systems where they are used to circumscribe the scope of naive theories. These systems use nested contexts, with the system being able to *transcend* the outermost context to create a new outer context. Both common sense and natural language systems also have a class of contexts that are ephemeral, that might correspond to a particular utterance or to a particular problem solving task. The ability to easily introduce a new context and infer attributes of that context adds substantial complexity to these context mechanisms. Contexts have also been used in model based reasoning [16] to partition models at different levels of abstraction.

The scope and complexity of the AI problems that contexts have been employed for is substantially more than anything we expect to encounter on the Semantic Web. The primary role for contexts on the Semantic Web is to factor the differences (like the ones described earlier) between data sources when aggregating data from them. Consequently, we do not need nested contexts, ephemeral contexts and the ability to transcend contexts.

On the other hand, the expected scale and highly distributed nature of the Semantic Web is in contrast to AI systems, most of which are much smaller and centralized. So, while we don't need the level of functionality provided by the AI formulations of contexts, we do place stronger constraints on the computational complexity and ease of use of the context mechanism.

In the next section, we develop a context mechanism for the Semantic Web. In the following section, we discuss the model theory extensions required for this mechanism.

5   Contexts for the SW

We present our context mechanism in the following setting. We have Semantic Web content (in RDFS or one of the OWL dialects) from a number of different URLs. The content from each URL is assumed to be uniform, but there may be differences like the ones described earlier between the content from the different URLs. We would like to create an internally consistent aggregate of the data from these different sites. The aggregate should be maximal in the sense that it should incorporate as much of the data from the different URLs as possible.

Each data source (or collection of data sources) is abstracted into a context. Contexts are first class resources that are instances of the class *Context*[3]. We define a PropertyType (*contextURL*) whose domain is *Context* that specifies the location(s) of the data source(s) corresponding to the context. The contents of the data source(s) are said to be true in that context. For the sake of keeping the description simple, for the remainder of this paper, unless otherwise specified, we will assume that the context has a single data source and that the URL of the context is that of the data source. So, for example, if a chunk of RDF is available at the URL *tap.stanford.edu/People.rdf*, we can have a context corresponding to this URL and the contents of this URL are said to be true in that context. Since the context is a resource, like any other resource on the Semantic Web, other chunks of RDFS/OWL can refer to it.

We are interested in defining contexts that aggregate data from other contexts. In keeping with the spirit of the Semantic Web, we would like to do this by declaratively specifying these new *Aggregate Contexts*. The different mechanisms that may be used in specifying these aggregate contexts define our design space. We start by examining the very general mechanism used in [10], [15] which has been followed by others in the AI community. We then present a much simpler, though less expressive variant that might be adequate for the semantic web.

Guha [10] and McCarthy [15] introduced a special symbol *ist* and the notation $ist(c_i, \varphi)$ to state that a proposition φ is true in the context c_i. Further, these statements can be nested, so that statements like $ist(c_i, ist(c_j, \varphi))$ can be used to contextualize the interpretation of contexts themselves. The system is always *in* some context. The system can enter and exit contexts. At any point in time, there is an outermost context, which can be *transcended* by creating a new outer context. A symbol can denote different objects in different contexts and the domains associated with different contexts can be different. Since contexts are first class objects in the domain, one can quantify over them, have functions whose range is a context, etc. All this allows one to write very expressive formulae that **lift** axioms from one context to another. While this is very convenient, it also makes it quite difficult to provide an adequate model theory and extremely difficult to compute with.

Nayak [16], Buvac [3] and others have tried to simplify this general formulation by introducing restrictions. Nayak considers the case where no nesting is

---

[3] We will drop namespace qualifiers, etc. for the sake of readability. Terms in *this* font refer to RDF resources.

allowed, contexts may only appear as the first argument to *ist* and are not first class objects (i.e., cannot be quantified over, etc.). Under these constraints, a classical modal logic like S5 can be used to provide a model theory for contexts. Buvac considers the case where a symbol is restricted to denote the same object in all contexts. For the purposes of the Semantic Web, Nayak's restrictions seem rather severe, but Buvac's may be acceptable. Both assume the Barcan formula:

$$\forall(x)ist(c, \varphi(x)) \leftrightarrow ist(c, \forall(x)\varphi(x)) \tag{1}$$

While these restrictions allow them to define a clean model theory, they are not enough to give us computational tractability. In fact, it is easy to show that all of these logics are not even semi-decidable.

Giunchiglia [8] and other researchers at Trento have used the notion of a bridge rule to formalize contexts. Much of their work is in the propositional realm and hence not directly relevant to the Semantic Web.

A general theme behind all these approaches is the introduction of the single interpreted symbol *ist*. *ist* is the only new symbol for which the underlying logic provides an interpretation. This is in contrast with RDF, RDFS, etc. in which a number of symbols (e.g., *Class*, *PropertyType*, *subClassOf*, ...) are all interpreted by the logic. We now extend this approach to handle contexts.

An aggregate context is a context whose contents (i.e., the statements that are true in that context) are lifted from other contexts. That is, they are imported into the aggregate context from other contexts after appropriate normalization/factoring. We now introduce a number of vocabulary elements that can be used to specify this lifting. This list is not exhaustive, but is adequate to cover the most common types of contextual differences that we discussed in section 3. We give informal descriptions and axiomatic definitions of these terms here and in the next section, outline the approach for defining the model theory for these constructs. We will use *ist* as a predicate in the meta-theory for the axiomatic definitions, even though it is not part of the base language.

- **AggregateContext**: This subclass of contexts corresponds to aggregate contexts. Since the Semantic Web allows anyone to make statements about any resource, there can be complications when different sites provide different definitions for a particular aggregate context. More specifically, allowing other contexts to specify what should be imported into a context, while safe in simple languages like RDF/S, opens the doors to paradoxes in more expressive languages like OWL. Even with RDF/S, it is important that the lifting process be simple to execute. To achieve this, we constrain the URL of an aggregate context to contain the full specification of what it imports. In other words, a lifting rule for importing into a particular context is true only in that context. We will later consider a semantic constraint for enforcing this.
- **importsFrom**: This is a property type whose domain is *AggregateContext* and whose range is *Context*. If c_1 *importsFrom* c_2, then everything that is true in c_2 is also true in c_1. The defining axiom for *importsFrom* is as follows.

$$ist(c_2, p) \wedge ist(c1, importsFrom(c_1, c_2)) \rightarrow ist(c_1, p) \tag{2}$$

We do not allow cycles in the graph defined by *importsFrom*. *importsFrom* is the simplest form of lifting and corresponds to the inclusion of one context into another. The more sophisticated forms of lifting require us to create a resource for the lifting rule.

- **LiftingRule**: This class has all the lifting rules as its instances. Each *LiftingRule* must have a single *AggregateContext* as the value for *targetContext* and single *Context* for *sourceContext*. We have subclasses of *LiftingRule* for the different kinds of lifting we would like to perform. An *AggregateContext* may have any number of lifting rules that lift into it. Lifting rules generally ignore some of the triples in the source context, import some of the triples without any modification, transform and then import some other set of triples and optionally add some new set of triples into the aggregate context. The specification of a lifting rule involves specifying which triples to import or which triples to add and how to perform the necessary transformations. Some lifting rules may also specify a preference for one source over another for some class of triples. Our goal here is not to specify an exhaustive set of transformations, but to cover some of the important ones and provide a flavor for the general approach.

  An important factor that impacts the representation of these *LiftingRules* is whether the aggregation process is restricted to be monotonic. If the process is allowed to be non-monotonic, the addition of a new LiftingRule to an aggregate context may cause certain triples to no longer hold. Non-monotonic lifting rules have the ability to say that everything not explicitly specified to be ignored or modified is to be imported. Consequently, they are easier to write, but do have the disadvantages of non-monotonicity. We describe the monotonic version and then suggest how it might be made more terse by introducing a non-monotonic construct.

- **Selective Importing**: These lifting rules explicitly specify the triples that should be directly imported from the source to the destination. Each triple may be specified by the property type or the first argument or the second argument. Optionally, these importing rules can specify the constraints on the first/second argument or combinations of property type and constraints on first/second argument etc. Examples: import *capitalCity* and *area* from the CIA Factbook. Import everything for instances of *Book* and *AudioCD* from Amazon. Import *manufacturer* for instances of *ElectronicsProduct* from Amazon. The defining axiom for Selective Importing Rules is as follows:

$$ist(c_i, targetContext(lr, c_i) \land sourceContext(lr, c_j) \land sourceFilter(lr, sc) \land$$
$$targetFilter(lr, tc) \land propFilter(lr, p) \land$$
$$type(lr, SelectiveImportLiftingRule)) \land$$
$$ist(c_j, type(x, sc) \land type(y, tc) \land p(x, y)) \rightarrow$$
$$ist(c_i, p(x, y))$$

$$(3)$$

- **Preference Rules**: In many cases, a number of sources have sparse data about a set of entities i.e., each of them might be missing some of the attributes for some of the entities they refer to and we might want to mitigate this sparcity by combining the data from the different sources. However, we might have a preference for one source over another, if the preferred source has the data. A preference rule can either specify a total preference ordering on list of sources or simply that one particular source is preferred over another. As with Selective Importing lifting rules, a preference rule can be constrained to apply to only a particular category of triples. Example: Who2 has more detailed information about more celebrities than IMDB, but IMDB's data is more accurate. This class of lifting rule allows us to combine Who2 with IMDB, preferring IMDB over Who2 if both have values for a particular property type for the same individual.

A more sophisticated (but substantially more computationally complex) version of preference lifting rules is in terms of consistency, i.e., if an inconsistency is detected in the target context, then triples from the less preferred context are to be eliminated first (to try and restore consistency).

Preference Lifting rules are non-monotonic across contexts in the sense that the addition of a new triple in one of the source contexts can cause another triple in the target context to be removed. However, they do not induce non-monotonicity within a context. The defining axiom for Preference Lifting Rules is as follows:

$$
\begin{aligned}
ist(c_i, \; &targetContext(lr, c_i) \wedge sourceContext(lr, c_j) \wedge sourceContext(lr, c_k) \wedge \\
&propFilter(lr, p) \wedge sourceFilter(lr, sc) \wedge targetFilter(lr, tc) \wedge \\
&preferred(lr, c_k) \wedge type(lr, PreferenceLiftingRule)) \wedge \\
&ist(c_j, p(x, y) \wedge type(x, sc) \wedge type(y, tc)) \wedge \\
&\neg ist(c_k, (\exists(z)p(x, z) \wedge type(x, sc) \wedge type(z, tc) \wedge (z \neq x)) \rightarrow \\
ist(c_i, \; &p(x, y))
\end{aligned}
$$

$$(4)$$

– **Mapping Constants**: One of the most common transformations required is to distinguish between slightly different uses of the same term or to normalize the use of different terms for the same concept. These lifting rules specify the source term and the target term. As with selective importing lifting rules, we can constrain the application of these mappings to specific categories of triples. Example: Many different sites use the term *price*, some referring to price with tax, some to price with tax and shipping, etc. This class of lifting rules can be used to distinguish between them in the aggregate context. The earlier example of nuclear power plant capacity also falls into this category. The defining axiom of Term Mapping rules is as follows:

$$
\begin{aligned}
ist(c_i, \; &targetContext(lr, c_i) \wedge sourceContext(lr, c_j) \wedge \\
&propMapTo(lr, p_2) \wedge sourceFilter(lr, sc) \wedge targetFilter(lr, tc) \wedge \\
&propMapFrom(lr, p_1) \wedge type(lr, TermMappingLiftingRule)) \wedge \\
ist(c_j, \; &p_1(x, y) \wedge type(x, sc) \wedge type(y, tc)) \rightarrow ist(c_i, p_2(x, y))
\end{aligned}
$$

$$(5)$$

- **Mapping more complex graph patterns**: All the above lifting rules deal with cases where the target graph is isomorphic to (portions of) the source graph. Sometimes, this constraint cannot be satisfied. For example, if the source leaves time implicit and the target has an explicit model of time, the source and target graphs are not likely to be isomorphic.

  Assuming we don't use an explicit *ist* in the base language, we can introduce a special construct for each phenomenon, such as making implicit time explicit. With this approach, we would introduce a property type (*contextTemporalModel*) to specify the model of time used by a context (implicit, Situation Calculus, Histories, etc.). In the case where the context used implicit time, we use another property type (*contextImplicitTime*) to specify the implicit time. Using a reified version of the Situation Calculus to represent time, the following axiom defines these property types.

$$ist(c_i, contextTemporalModel(c_i, ImplicitStaticTime) \wedge$$
$$contextImplicitTime(c_i, t_i)) \wedge$$
$$ist(cj, targetFilter(lr, tc) \wedge contextTemporalModel(c_j, SitCatModel) \wedge$$
$$type(lr, SitCalLiftingRule) \wedge propFilter(lr, p) \wedge sourceFilter(lr, sc)) \wedge$$
$$targetContext(lr, ci) \wedge sourceContext(lr, cj) \wedge$$
$$ist(c_j, type(x, sc) \wedge type(y, tc) \wedge p(x, y)) \rightarrow$$
$$ist(c_i, (\exists z)type(z, SitProp) \wedge time(z, t_i) \wedge$$
$$sitProp(z, p) \wedge sitSource(z, x) \wedge sitTarget(z, y))$$

$$(6)$$

  A more general solution is to identify common transformation patterns (as opposed to particular phenomenon) and introduce vocabulary to handle these. For example, a common pattern involves reifying a particular triple to make something explicit. Examples of this include making time and propositional attitudes. Another common pattern involves transforming a literal into a resource. A common example of this is to make the unit of measure or language explicit.

- **Default Lifting**: The constructs described above are monotonic. In practice, it is often convenient to be able to say that all of the contents of one context should be included in the aggregate context without any modification unless one of the other lifting rules applies. To do this, we introduce a property type analogous to *importsFrom*, called *defaultImportsFrom* that specifies this.

While not exhaustive, we believe this vocabulary and associated set of lifting rules are sufficient to solve many issues that arise in data aggregation on the Semantic Web. More importantly, this functionality can be incorporated into the Semantic Web with fairly small and simple additions to the existing standards.

6   Model Theory

In the last section we discussed some potential alternatives for introducing contexts into the Semantic Web. In this section, we discuss issues related to contexts and the model theory of the Semantic Web representation languages. Of course, the particular alternative used has significant impact on the model theory. But there are some basic changes that are required, independent of the approach used. We discuss these first and then consider the impact on the model theory corresponding to the different approaches.

We restrict our attention to the model theory for RDFS. We expect it will be possible to provide a similar treatment for at least the simpler versions of OWL.

The most basic change introduced by the addition of contexts is that the denotation of a resource is not just a function of the term and the interpretation (or structure), but also of the context in which that term occurs. We will assume that the denotation of literals is not affected by the context. This context dependence can be incorporated as follows. The definitions of interpretation and satisfaction (as given in the RDF Model Theory [11]) are changed as follows.

A simple interpretation I of a vocabulary V is defined by:

1. A non-empty set IR of resources, called the domain or universe of I. C is a subset of IR corresponding contexts.
2. A set IP, called the set of properties of I.
3. A mapping IEXT from IP into the cross product of IR x IR i.e. the set of pairs $< x, y >$ with x and y in IR .
4. A non-empty set $CURI \subset (URI \cap V)$ used to denote contexts. A mapping IS from the cross product $(URI \cap V)$ x $CURI$ into $(IR \cup IP)$. $(URI \cap V)$ corresponds to the URIs used to refer to resources. The cross product $(URI \cap V)$ x $CURI$ corresponds to resource-context pairs. We impose the constraint $IS(CURI, CURI) \in C$ so that CURIs denote contexts.[4] So, under this modified definition, IS maps resources to objects in the domain *in a context*. This is the primary substantial change.
5. A mapping IL from typed literals in V into IR.
6. A distinguished subset LV of IR, called the set of literal values, which contains all the plain literals in V

The denotation of a ground graph is now with respect to the context it occurs in, which manifests itself as the second URI in the argument to IS in (4) above. We update and extend the definition of satisfaction so that instead of defining satisfaction for a graph, we define it for a set of graphs, each in a context. The updated definition of satisfaction is as follows:

1. if E is a plain literal "aaa" occurring in c in V then I(E,c) = aaa
2. if E is a plain literal "aaa"@ttt in V occurring in c then I(E,c) = $< aaa, ttt >$
3. if E is a typed literal in V occurring in c then I(E,c) = IL(E)
4. if E is a URI reference in V occurring in the context c, then I(E,c) = IS(E,c)
5. If E is a ground triple s p o in the context c then I(E,c) = true if c, s, p and o are in V, IS(p,c) is in IP and $< IS(s, c), IS(o, c) >$ is in IEXT(IS(p,c)). Otherwise I(E,c)= false.

---

[4] If we want a flat context space wherein a CURI denotes the same context irrespective of where it occurs, we impose the additional constraint that $IS(CURI_a, CURI_j) = IS(CURI_a, CURI_i)$ for all i, j.

6. if E is a ground RDF graph in the context c then I(E,c) = false if I(E',c) = false for some triple E' in E, otherwise I(E,c) =true.
7. if $< E_i, c_i >$ are a set of ground graphs occuring each occurring in the corresponding context, then I($< E_i, c_i >$) = false if I(E_i, c_i) = false for some grap E_i associated with the context c_i, otherwise I($< E_i, c_i >$) = true.

Finally, the definition of entailment is updated so that a ground graph G_1 in a context C_1 is entailed by a set of graph-context pairs $< G_i, C_i >$ if $< G_1, C_1 >$ is true under every interpretation under which ($< G_i, C_i >$) is true.

It is easy to see that the primary substantial change in the model theory is the addition of the context argument to the interpretation. The change in the definition of satisfaction is that we can no longer simply merge graphs without regard to where they occur. This is, of course, the point of this whole exercise.

Additional changes to the model theory depend on whether we have a predicate/modal like *ist* in the vocabulary, the constraints we impose on quantifying over contexts and into contexts, whether we want the Barcan formula, etc. Since this approach has been discussed quite exhaustively in the literature ([3], [16], Giunchiglia [8], [7]) and since the use of an explicit *ist* is not very appropriate for the Semantic Web, we will not go into the details of that approach here.

The less expressive approach which eschews the use of an explicit symbol like *ist* in favour of a suite of specialized interpreted symbols (such as *importsFrom*) appears to require a less substantial, though more cumbersome additions to the model theory. Following the pattern of sections 3 and 4 of [11], interpretations can be provided for the different context-specific vocabulary items introduced in the last section. For example, the interpretation for the term *importsFrom* is: *if I(c1 importsFrom c2, c1) is true and I(E,c2) is true then I(E, c1) is true.* The interpretations for the other vocabulary terms, though more verbose, are still straightforward model theoretic equivalents of the axiomatic definitions given earlier.

Finally, we need to add a semantic constraint so that a *LiftingRule* for specifying what to lift into a particular context is true only in that context. So, *if I(c1, c2) $\neq$ I(c2, c2) then I(c2 targetContext lr, c1) is false.*

It is important to note that all the theorems and lemmas of [11] continue to hold. Overall, it appears that a restricted context mechanism that does not use an explicit *ist* can be accommodated into the model theory without substantial perturbations.

7 Related Work and Discussion

The issue of contextuality and contexts as first class objects has been a topic of much discussion since the early days of RDF. In this section, we first discuss the relation between the context mechanism presented in this paper and reification (and related proposals). We then discuss the issue of non-monotonicity that is raised by contexts.

7.1   Reification

RDF provides reification as a mechanism for making statements about statements. There are significant differences between reification and contexts both in what they are intended for and in their structure. Reification is intended to enable statements about potential statements (which may or may not be true). For example, they can be useful for making statements about provenance. Since they have no coupling with the truth of the triple that has been reified, they cannot be used to relate the truth of a triple in one graph to its truth in another graph. Consequently, it is difficult to see how reification can be used to mediate aggregation.

In contrast, the primary goal of the context mechanism presented here is to enable the aggregation while factoring in the differences between the data sources being aggregated. It is only incidental that the context mechanism may be used to make other kinds of statements about graphs. Since the goal is to aggregate triples that are true in the graphs being aggregated, contexts and truth are very closely related. Contexts and reification are also very different in their structure and in where they appear in the model theory. Because of the close coupling between truth and contexts, they cannot be a posteriori introduced at the RDF Vocabulary level. They appear in the guts of the model theory, in the definition of an interpretation. This is in contrast to the reification which does not play any significant role in the model theory.

In addition to the reification mechanism in RDF, the system/language CWM/N3 supports a construct called contexts. As far as we can determine, this notion of context is not substantially different from reification.

The shortcomings of reification have lead to numerous alternative proposals, the most substantial of which are those by Klyne [13], [12]. Indeed some of the constructs presented there, drawn from earlier work by Guha [10] and McCarthy [15], are very similar in spirit to those presented here. The extension to the model theory presented here is simpler. Unlike that work we avoid the use of an *ist* construct and significantly reduce the complexity. Further, our focus in this paper is on data aggregation, not on introducing contexts as a general piece of functionality into the Semantic Web. The general problem of contextual dependence is much too complex to tackle head-on (at least for the Semantic Web). We believe that we need to be driven by concrete tasks such as data aggregation to achieve progress.

7.2   Non-monotonicity

The context mechanism discussed in this paper leads to non-monotonic aggregation in the following sense. A graph G_1 might imply φ, but because of selective lifting, preferential lifting or transformation during lifting, the aggregation of this graph with zero or more other graphs might not imply φ. It has been argued [1] that the Semantic Web should be based purely on classical monotonic logics for reasons of scalability. While monotonicity might be desirable at the local level, it is neither desirable nor feasible at the level of the Semantic Web as a whole.

Further, the computational intractability associated with non-monotonic logics in AI are not because of non-monotonicity itself, but because of the particular mechanisms used to introduce it.

What we need is the ability to say that a particular theory T_1 implies φ without the fear that additions to T_1 cause φ to no longer be true. However, T_1, when aggregated with other theories T_2, T_3, ... might lead to a superior theory which does not imply φ. The examples given in section 3, especially the example of the CIA Factbook combined with census data from particular countries is a good example of why this is desirable. The issue is not that of the CIA Factbook not being trustworthy. It has a lot of good data that we would like to be able to use. It would be undesirable if we had to choose between it and data from the census bureaus. In the past, lacking a proper context mechanism, we have been unable to associate a granularity with the monotonicity. With the context mechanism, we are able to control the points of non-monotonicity and we are able to distinguish between non-monotonicity within a context versus non-monotonicity across contexts. For example, one could remain monotonic within contexts, but can be non-monotonic across contexts.

8   Conclusions

As shown by the experience with TAP and in many other projects that aggregate independently created data, differences in assumptions, use of terms, etc. lead to problems during aggregation. In this paper, we present an adaptation of the context mechanism from AI to solve these problems. We avoid the general *ist* construct and the associated complexity but provide enough support to solve the contextual problems that typically arise in aggregation on the Semantic Web.

References

1. Tim Berners-Lee. Semantic web architecture.
   `http://www.w3.org/DesignIssues/Rules.html`.
2. Daniel G. Bobrow and Terry Winograd. On overview of krl, a knowledge representation language. *Cognitive Science*, 1:3–46, 1997.
3. Sasa Buvač. Quantificational logic of context. In Howard Shrobe and Ted Senator, editors, *AAAI 1996*, pages 600–606, Menlo Park, California, 1996. AAAI Press.
4. Saša Buvač, Vanja Buvač, and Ian Mason. Metamathematics of contexts. *Fundamenta Mathematicae*, 23(3), 1995. Available from http://www-formal.stanford.edu/buvac.
5. Saša Buvač and Richard Fikes. A declarative formalization of knowledge translation. In *Proceedings of the ACM CIKM: the Fourth International Conference in Information and Knowledge Management*, 1995. Available from http://www-formal.stanford.edu/buvac.
6. Saša Buvač and Ian Mason. Propositional logic of context. In *AAAI*, pages 412–419, 1993.
7. Valeria de Paiva. Natural deduction and context as (constructive) modality. In *CONTEXT 2003*, pages 116–129, 2003.

8. Fausto Giunchiglia and Chiara Ghidini. Local models semantics, or contextual reasoning = locality + compatibility. In Anthony G. Cohn, Lenhart Schubert, and Stuart C. Shapiro, editors, *KR'98: Principles of Knowledge Representation and Reasoning*, pages 282–289. Morgan Kaufmann, San Francisco, California, 1998.

9. R. Guha and John McCarthy. Varieties of contexts. In *CONTEXT 2003*, pages 164–177, 2003.

10. Ramanathan V. Guha. Contexts: a formalization and some applications. Technical Report STAN-CS-91-1399, Stanford CS Dept., Stanford, CA, 1991.

11. Pat Hayes. Rdf semantics. `http://www.w3.org/TR/rdf-mt/`.

12. Graham Klyne. Contexts and the semantic web. `http://public.research.mimesweeper.com/RDF/RDFContexts.html`.

13. Graham Klyne. Contexts for the semantic web. `http://www.ninebynine.org/RDFNotes/UsingContextsWithRDF.html`.

14. John McCarthy. Generality in artificial intelligence. In Vladimir Lifschitz, editor, *Formalizing Common Sense: Papers by John McCarthy*, pages 226–236. Ablex Publishing Corporation, Norwood, New Jersey, 1990.

15. John McCarthy. Notes on formalizing contexts. In Ruzena Bajcsy, editor, *Proceedings of the Thirteenth International Joint Conference on Artificial Intelligence*, pages 555–560, San Mateo, California, 1993. Morgan Kaufmann.

16. P. Pandurang Nayak. Representing multiple theories. In B. Hayes-Roth and R. Korf, editors, *AAAI-94*, pages 1154–1160, Menlo Park, CA, 1994.

17. R.Guha and D. Lenat. Context dependence of representations in cyc. In *Colloque ICO*, 1993.

18. R.Guha and R. McCool. Tap: A semantic web platform. *Computer Networks*, 42:557 – 577, 2003.

19. R.Guha, R. McCool, and E. Miller. Semantic search. In *WWW 2004, Budapest, Hungary*, 2003.

20. R.Guha and Rob McCool. Tap: Towards a web of data. `http://tap.stanford.edu/`.

Bipartite Graphs as Intermediate Model for RDF[*]

Jonathan Hayes[1,2] and Claudio Gutierrez[1]

[1] Center for Web Research, Dept. of Computer Science, Universidad de Chile
`cgutierr@dcc.uchile.cl`
[2] Dept. of Computer Science, Technische Universität Darmstadt, Germany
`jonathan.hayes@gmx.de`

Abstract. RDF Graphs are sets of assertions in the form of subject-predicate-object triples of information resources. Although for simple examples they can be understood intuitively as directed labeled graphs, this representation does not scale well for more complex cases, particularly regarding the central notion of connectivity of resources.

We argue in this paper that there is need for an intermediate representation of RDF to enable the application of well-established methods from graph theory. We introduce the concept of *RDF Bipartite Graph* and show its advantages as intermediate model between the abstract triple syntax and data structures used by applications. In the light of this model we explore the issues of transformation costs, data/schema-structure, and the notion of RDF connectivity.

Keywords: RDF Model, RDF Graph, RDF Databases, Bipartite Graph.

1 Introduction

The World Wide Web was originally built for human consumption, and although everything on it is machine-readable, the data is not machine-understandable [1]. The Resource Description Framework, RDF [2], is a language to express metadata about information resources on the Web proposed by the WWW Consortium (W3C). It is intended that this information is suitable for processing by applications and thus is the foundation of the Semantic Web [3]. RDF statements are triples consisting of a subject (the resource being described), a predicate (the property), and an object (the property value). A set of RDF triples is called an *RDF Graph*, a term formally introduced by the RDF specification [4] and motivated by the underlying graph data model.

The graph-like nature of RDF is indeed intuitively appealing, but a naive formalization of this notion presents problems. Currently, the RDF specification does not distinguish clearly among the term "RDF Graph", the mathematical

---

[*] The first author was supported by Millennium Nucleus, Center for Web Research (P01-029-F), Mideplan. The second author was supported by FONDECYT No 1030810.

S.A. McIlraith et al. (Eds.): ISWC 2004, LNCS 3298, pp. 47–61, 2004.

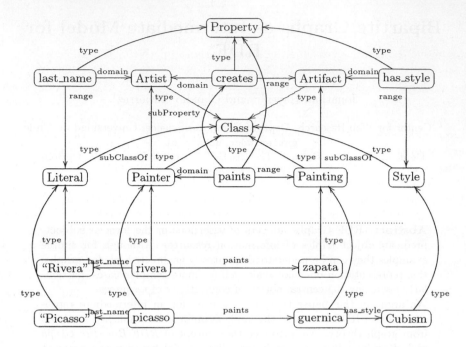

Fig. 1. The museum example. A non-standard graph where edge labels and nodes can represent the same object. For example, *paints* occurs as a node as well as arbitrarily often in the role of edge labels.

concept of graph, and the graph-like visualization of RDF data. An RDF Graph is a set of triples and therefore, by itself, not a graph in the classic sense. *RDF Concepts and Abstract Syntax* [4] presents "node and directed-arc diagrams" (or, as referred to in [1], *directed labeled graphs*) as a visualization scheme for RDF by representing a triple <a b c> by $a \xrightarrow{b} c$. However, the document leaves open how to deal with a statement property (an edge label) which occurs as the subject or object of another statement: one could either duplicate resources as nodes and as edge labels (as shown in figure 1), or allow edges to connect not only to nodes, but also to other edges.

Both approaches are inconvenient from several points of view: allowing multiple occurrences of resources as labels jeopardizes one of the most important aspects of graph visualization, which is the implicit assumption that the complete information regarding a node in a graph is obtained by its place in the drawing and its incident edges. On the other hand, the essential drawback of the second approach is the fact that the resulting construct is not a graph in the standard sense to which we could apply well-established techniques from graph theory. However, this is a principal reason for representing RDF by graphs: when reasoning formally over RDF data, e.g., as described in *RDF Semantics* [5], one has to operate with sets of triples. Although well-defined formally, a set of triples is a model that due to multiple occurrences of the same resource in the data structure leads to undesirable redundancies and does not capture the graph-like nature of RDF data, particularly regarding the connectivity of resources.

We propose to model RDF Graphs as bipartite graphs. RDF Graphs can be represented naturally by hypergraphs, and hypergraphs can be represented naturally by bipartite graphs. (Bipartite) graphs are well-known mathematical objects which, as formal representation, have several advantages over the triple or directed labeled graph representation discussed above. Among these advantages are: algorithms for the visualization of data for humans [6,7], a formal framework to prove properties and specify algorithms, the availability of libraries with generic implementations of graph algorithms, and of course, techniques and results of graph theory. Representing RDF data by (standard) graphs allows to reduce application demands to well-studied problems of graphs. A few examples at hand: Difference between RDF Graphs: When are two RDF Graphs the same? [8,9] Entailment: Determining entailment between RDF Graphs can be reduced to graph mappings: Is graph A isomorphic to a subgraph of graph B? [5]. Minimization: Finding a minimal representation of an RDF Graph is important for compact storage and update in databases [10]. Semantic relations between information resources: metrics and algorithms for semantic distance in graphs [11,12]. Clustering [13,14] and graph pattern mining algorithms [15] to reveal regularities in RDF data.

Contributions. In this paper we provide a formal graph-based intermediate model of RDF, which intends to be more concrete than the abstract RDF model to allow the exploit of results from graph theory, but still general enough to allow specific implementations. The contributions are the following: (1) We present a class of *RDF bipartite graphs* as an alternate graph representation for RDF. (2) We study properties of this class of graphs and the transformation of RDF data into it. (3) We provide an approach to stratify an RDF Graph into data and schema layers. (4) We explore the notion of *RDF connectivity* and how it is conveyed by the graph model.

Related Work. There is little work on formalization of the RDF graph model besides the guidelines given in the official documents of the W3C, particularly *RDF Concepts and Abstract Syntax* [4] and *RDF Semantics* [5]. There are works about algorithms on different problems on RDF Graphs, among them T. Berners-Lee's discussion of the *Diff* problem [8] and J. Carroll's study of the RDF graph matching problem [9]. Although not directly related to graph issues, there is work on the formalization of the RDF model itself that touches our topic: a logical approach that gives identities to statements and so incorporates them to the universe [16], a study oriented to querying that gives a formal typing to the model [17] and results on normalization of RDF Graphs [10].

In the thesis [18] there is an extended discussion of the model to be presented in this paper, containing all the proofs and further investigations on RDF maps and applications to RDF storage and querying.

2   Preliminaries

RDF. The atomic structure of the RDF language is the statement. It is a triple, consisting of a subject, a predicate and an object. These elements of a triple can be *URIs* (Uniform Resource Identifiers), representing information resources; *literals*, used to represent values of some datatype; and *blank nodes*, which represent anonymous resources. There are restrictions on the subject and predicate of a triple: the subject cannot be a literal, and the predicate must be a URI resource. Resources, blanks and literals are referred to together as *values*.

An *RDF Graph* is a set of RDF triples. Let T be an RDF Graph. Then univ(T), the set of all values occurring in all triples of T, is called the *universe* of T; and vocab(T), the *vocabulary* of T, is the set of all values of the universe that are not blank nodes. The *size* of T is the number of statements it contains and is denoted by $|T|$. With subj(T) (respectively pred(T), obj(T)) we designate all values which occur as subject (respectively predicate, object) of T.

Let V be a set of URIs and literal values. We define RDFG(V) := $\{T \mid T$ is RDF Graph and vocab(T) $\subseteq V\}$, i.e. the set of all RDF Graphs with a vocabulary included in V. There is a distinguished vocabulary, *RDF Schema* [19] that may be used to describe properties like attributes of resources (traditional attribute-value pairs), and to represent relationships between resources. It is expressive enough to defines classes and properties that may be used for describing groups of related resources and relationships between resources.

Example RDF Graph 1 The `prefix:suffix` notation abbreviates URIs. The *wor* prefix identifies a "Web of Researchers" vocabulary (*rdfs* is RDF Schema)

1: <wor:Ullman> <wor:coauthor> <wor:Aho>
2: <wor:Greibach> <wor:coauthor> <wor:Hopcroft>
3: <wor:coauthor> <rdfs:subPropertyOf> <wor:collaborates>
4: <wor:Greibach> <wor:researches> <wor:topics/formalLanguages>
5: <wor:Valiant> <wor:researches> <wor:topics/formalLanguages>
6: <wor:Erdös> <wor:researches> <wor:topics/graphTheory>
7: <wor:Aho> <wor:collaborates> <wor:Kernighan>
8: <wor:Hopcroft> <wor:coauthor> <wor:Ullman>

Graphs. A *graph* is a pair $G = (N, E)$, where N is a set whose elements are called *nodes*, and E is a set of unordered pairs $\{u, v\}$ of nodes $u, v \in N$, the *edges* of the graph. A node v and an edge e are *incident* if $v \in e$; two edges e_1 and e_2 are *adjacent* if they both are incident to a node v. Observe that the definition implies that the sets N and E are disjoint.

A graph G is a *multigraph* if multiple edges between two nodes are permitted. A graph $G = (N, E)$ is said to be *bipartite* if $N = U \cup V, U \cap V = \emptyset$ and for all $\{u, v\} \in E$ it holds that $u \in U$ and $v \in V$. A *directed graph* is a graph where the elements of E are ordered, i.e. there are functions from $: E \to N$ and to $: E \to N$ which yield the source and the target of each edge. In order to express more information, a graph can be *labeled*. A graph (N, E), together with

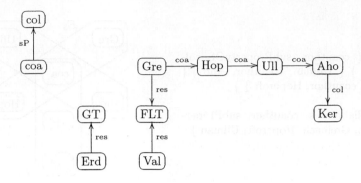

Fig. 2. Example RDF Graph 1 represented by a directed labeled graph. URI prefixes have been omitted, and labels have been abbreviated as follows: **co**llaborates, **subProperty**Of, **coa**uthor, **G**raph **T**heory, **res**earches, **Erd**ős, **Gre**ibach, **F**ormal **L**anguage **T**heory, **Val**iant, **Hop**croft, **Ull**man, **Aho**, **Ker**nighan.

a set of labels L_E and an edge labeling function $l_E : E \to L_E$ is an *edge-labeled* graph. A graph is said to be *node-labeled* when there is a node label set and a node labeling function, as above. We will write (N, E, l_N, l_E) for a node- and edge-labeled graph.

The notions of path and connectivity will be important in what follows. A *path* is a sequence of edges $e_1, \ldots, e_n$ where each edge e_i is adjacent to e_{i-1}, for $i \in [2, n]$. The *label* of the path is $l_E(e_1) \cdot l_E(e_2) \cdot \ldots \cdot l_E(e_n)$ Two nodes x, y are *connected* if there exists a path $e_1, \ldots, e_n$ with $x \in e_1$ and $y \in e_n$. The *length* of a path is the number of edges it consists of.

RDF as Directed Labeled Graphs. Now we can formalize the *directed labeled graph* representing an RDF Graph, as outlined in [4]. Let T be an RDF Graph. Then define $\delta(T) = (N, E, l_N, l_E)$ as the node- and edge-labeled multigraph with $N = \{n_x : x \in \text{subj}(T) \cup \text{obj}(T)\}$ with $l_N(n_x) = x$ and $E = \{e_{s,p,o} : (s, p, o) \in T\}$ with $\text{from}(e_{s,p,o}) = n_s$, $\text{to}(e_{s,p,o}) = n_o$, and $l_E(e_{s,p,o}) = p$.

Figures 1 and 2 presents examples of such a graph. This definition yields a standard graph, but observe that node and edge label sets might not be disjoint (in figure 2, the resource `coa` appears at the same time as edge label and as node). This leads to problems as described in the introduction.

Hypergraphs. Informally, hypergraphs are systems of sets which extend the notion of graphs allowing edges to connect any number of nodes. For background see [20]. Formally, let $V = \{v_1, \ldots, v_n\}$ be a finite set, the *nodes*. A *hypergraph* on V is a pair $\mathcal{H} = (V, \mathcal{E})$, where $\mathcal{E}$ is a family $\{E_i\}_{i \in I}$ of subsets of V. The members of $\mathcal{E}$ are called *edges*. A hypergraph is *simple* if all edges are distinct. A hypergraph is said to be *r-uniform* if all edges have the cardinality r. An r-uniform hypergraph is said to be *ordered* if the occurrence of nodes in every edge is numbered from 1 to r.

$\mathcal{E} = \{$ { coauthor, subPropertyOf, collaborates }, { Ullman, coauthor, Aho },{ Greibach, coauthor, Hopcroft } }

V= { collaborates, coauthor, subPropertyOf, Aho, Greibach, Hopcroft, Ullman }

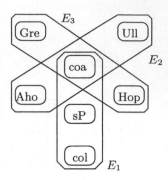

Fig. 3. Example of a simple 3-uniform hypergraph. This hypergraph represents the first three statements of the example RDF Graph 1.

Hypergraphs can be described by binary edge-node *incidence matrices*. In this matrix rows correspond to edges, columns to nodes: entry $m_{i,j}$ equals 1 or 0, depending on whether E_i contains node n_j or not. To the incidence matrix of a hypergraph $\mathcal{H} = (V, \mathcal{E})$ corresponds a *bipartite incidence graph* $B = (N_V \cup N_{\mathcal{E}}, E)$, which is defined as follows. Let N_V be the set of node names of $\mathcal{H}$ which labeled the columns of the matrix, and $N_{\mathcal{E}}$ the set of edge names labeling its rows. Then E contains an edge $\{e_i, v_j\}$ for each $e_i \in N_{\mathcal{E}}, v_j \in N_V$ where the matrix entry $m_{i,j}$ is 1. The obtained graph B can be read to have an edge $\{e, v\}$ exactly when the hypergraph node represented by v is member of the hypergraph edge represented by e. It is evident that B is bipartite. Figure 4 shows the incidence matrix of a hypergraph and the bipartite incidence graph derived from it.

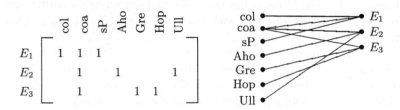

Fig. 4. Incidence matrix representing the hypergraph of Example 3 and the corresponding incidence graph. In the case of an ordered hypergraph, matrix entries will indicate the position of the occurrence of the node in the edge.

3   RDF Bipartite Graphs

Deriving Bipartite Graphs from Hypergraphs. One of the major problems encountered in trying to model RDF Graphs as classical graphs is the fact that an edge or labeled edge cannot represent the ternary relation given by an RDF triple. Therefore it is natural to turn the attention to graphs with 3-node-connecting edges instead of classical 2-node edges, that is, hypergraphs.

Proposition 1. *Any RDF Graph can be represented by a simple ordered 3-uniform hypergraph: every RDF triple corresponds to a hypergraph edge, the nodes being the subject, predicate and object in this order. The node set of the hypergraph is the union of all the edges. (Trivial)*

The converse of the proposition also holds when imposing constraints on the occurrences of blank nodes and literals: blank nodes may not be predicates and literals may not serve as subjects or predicates.

As stated in the preliminaries section, hypergraphs can be represented by incidence matrices where membership of a node in an edge is marked with a '1'. In the case of the hypergraph representing an RDF Graph, the nodes of an edge are ordered and we label them by S, P, or O to represent the role (subject, predicate, or object) of the information resource. Hence, when deriving the bipartite incidence graph of this incidence matrix, an edge will be added for every S, P, O entry of the matrix, and this edge will be labeled with the corresponding character. Thus, the only difference between the graph derived from the incidence matrix of any hypergraph and an RDF Graph hypergraph is the fact that each edge has one of three labels.

Mapping RDF to RDF Bipartite Graphs. This section presents a map of RDF Graphs to bipartite graphs. Let $\mathcal{B}$ be the set of bipartite labeled graphs

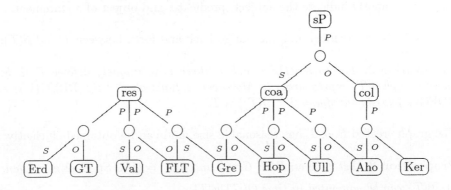

Fig. 5. The RDF bipartite graph of the example RDF Graph 1. Statement nodes are represented by circles; edge labels S, P, O indicate their subject, predicate and object.

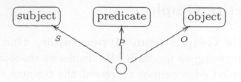

Fig. 6. A statement as RDF bipartite graph.

$G = (V \cup St, E, \text{nl}, \text{el})$, $V \cap St = \emptyset$, where each edge in E connects a node in V with a node in St, and $\text{el} : E \to \text{EL}$ and $\text{nl} : V \to \text{NL}$ are labeling functions. The elements of V are called the *value nodes* and those of St the *statement nodes*.

Definition 1 (RDF Bipartite Graph). *Let V be a vocabulary and T an RDF Graph. Then we define a map $\beta : \text{RDFG}(V) \to \mathcal{B}$ as follows: $\beta(T) = (V \cup St, E, \text{nl}, \text{el}) \in \mathcal{B}$ is the RDF bipartite graph representing T, with $V = \{v_x : x \in \text{univ}(T)\}$; $St = \{st_t : t \in T\}$; and the set of edges E is built as follows: for each triple $t = (x, y, z) \in T$ add the edges $\{st_t, v_x\}$ with label S, $\{st_t, v_y\}$ with label P, and $\{st_t, v_z\}$ with label O. The labeling of the nodes is given by:*

$$\text{nl}(v_x) := \begin{cases} (x, d_x) & \text{if } x \text{ is literal } (d_x \text{ is the datatype identifier of } x) \\ x & \text{else} \end{cases}$$

Note that $\beta(T)$ is a *3-regular* bipartite graph, because the degree of each node in St is 3. This representation incorporates explicitly the statements as nodes into the graph.

Example 1. Figure 6 illustrates how a single statement is represented as RDF bipartite graph. Figure 5 shows the RDF bipartite graph representation of the Web Of Scientists example. The drawing convention is as follows: unlabeled circles represent statement nodes, boxes with rounded corners value nodes. Edge labels S, P, and O indicate the subject, predicate, and object of a statement.

The model is well-defined and one can go back and forth between T and $\beta(T)$:

Proposition 2. *For each RDF Graph T there is a uniquely defined RDF bipartite graph $\beta(T)$ representing it. Moreover, a function $\beta^{-1} : \beta\,(\text{RDFG}(V)) \to \text{RDFG}(V)$ exists satisfying $\beta^{-1}(\beta(T)) = T$.*

The graph created from T has reasonable size, and can be obtained efficiently[1]:

Proposition 3. *Let T be an RDF Graph and $\beta(T) = (V \cup St, E, \text{nl}, \text{el})$. Then:*

1. *$\beta(T)$ can be computed in time $O(|T| \lg |T|)$.*
2. *The graph $\beta(T)$ is bounded as follows: $|St| = |T|$, $|V| = |\text{univ}(T)|$ and $|E| = 3\,|T|$.*

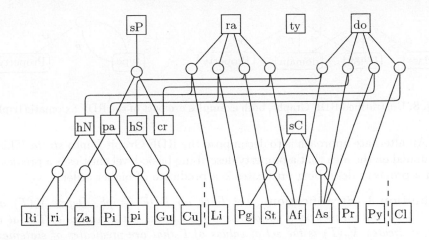

Fig. 7. RDF bipartite graph of the museum example. Edge labels have been omitted for clarity. Drawing levels indicate the order of the values nodes. At the bottom level are values which never occur as predicates: class instances like (bold letters indicate the abbreviations) the literal "**Ri**vera", **ri**vera (resource), **Za**pata, classes such as **P**ainting, **A**rtifact, **Ar**tist, **P**ainter, **P**roperty, and the meta-class **Cl**ass. Simple properties include **h**as_**N**ame and **pa**ints, and properties of properties are **s**ub**P**roperty, **do**main, **ra**nge and **ty**pe. Declarations with property "type" are shown in figure 10.

4   The Structure of RDF Graphs

RDF Graphs consist of values and statements. A first coarse-grained division of the statements is the following: those that define a schema, and those that are data structured under this schema (see figure 1—the dotted line represents this division). Although RDF does not distinguish between schema-defining and data statements, this distinction is natural when considering storage [21] and querying [17] in databases. Unfortunately, a plain discrimination between the data and schema parts of an RDF specification is not always possible. Moreover, features like extensibility of specifications and reification make this divide difficult to grasp formally. In the following we present two approaches to this issue.

Definition 2. *A* data subgraph *of an RDF Graph* T *is a maximal subgraph* T' *satisfying* $(\mathrm{subj}(T') \cup \mathrm{obj}(T')) \cap \mathrm{pred}(T') = \emptyset$. *The* schema subgraph *associated to* T' *is* $T \setminus T'$.

The terms of data and schema subgraph correspond to the *description base* and *description schema* in the wording of [22]. By the definition, note that an RDF Graph T does not have a uniquely defined data subgraph, e.g. consider $\{(a, b, c), (b, d, e)\}$ where each statement alone is a data subgraph. Moreover, an RDF Graph could have exponentially many different ones (proposition 13 in [18]).

---

[1] The proofs of all propositions can be found in [18].

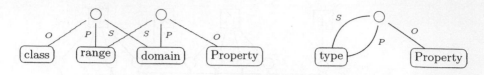

Fig. 8. Unstratified RDF Graphs, both examples are part of the RDF axiomatic triples.

An alternate approach is to decompose the RDF Graph T into *strata*. This is grounded on the idea that a property describing basic-level entities is a predicate, and a property describing predicates is a predicate of higher order.

Definition 3 (Stratification). *Let T be an RDF Graph. Define $V_i(T)$ and $St_j(T)$ by mutual recursion as follows: $V_0(T)$ is the set of values of T that are not predicates, $V_n(T)$ is the set of values of T that are predicates of statements in $St_n(T)$, and $St_{n+1}(T)$ is the set of statements of T whose subject and object are elements of $\bigcup_{j \leq n} V_j(T)$.*
The order of T is the maximum n such that V_{n-1} is not empty.

T is stratified if $\operatorname{univ}(T) = \bigcup_{j \geq 0} V_j(T)$.

Example 2 (Stratification).
- $T = \{(a, a, b)\}$ cannot be stratified: $V_0(T) = \{b\}$ and $V_j(T) = \emptyset$ for $j > 0$. (e.g., `<rdf:type rdf:type rdf:Property>` is an RDF *axiomatic triple* [5]— see figure 8.)
- The reification of a triple `<a b c>` is stratified (see figure 9).
- The museum example (figure 1) can be partitioned into 3 levels (see figure 7).

Proposition 4 (Unstratifiedness). *T is not stratified if and only if there is a cycle from a value node in $\beta(T)$ with label in $[(O|S)P]^+$.*

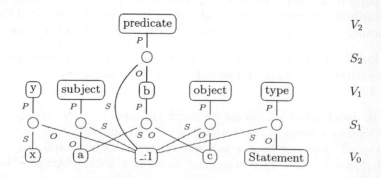

Fig. 9. Stratified drawing of a reification. A resource x makes a proposition y about the statement `<a b c>`.

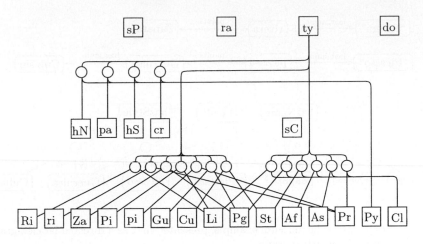

Fig. 10. Type declarations of the RDF bipartite graph in figure 7.

Although the complete axiomatic specification of RDF is not stratified (see figure 8), most RDF data currently found in practice is stratified—if RDF axiomatic triples are not considered—and has small order (no bigger than 3). Also, if T is stratified, the graph obtained by reifying each of its triples is stratified. However, the union of two stratified RDF Graphs is not necessarily stratified.

Both approaches embrace RDF's extensibility in that they do not rely on the rdfs namespace prefix. The proposition of an alternate RDF Schema *RDFS(FA)* by Pan and Horrock [23,24] is based on similar considerations and also provides a potentially unbounded stratification.

5   Connectivity of RDF Data

An RDF Graph conveys more meaning than the sum of its statements considered individually. For example, Greibach is a coauthor of Hopcroft, who is a coauthor of Ullman (figure 2). We can deduce that Greibach and Ullman are related by a "transitive co-authorship", although this is not stated explicitly by a single statement. In the museum example—consider the fragment in figure 11—Picasso and Rodin are related in that they both paint. Complex relationships between resources are called *semantic associations* in [25,11]; for storage and querying the importance of considering the *connectedness* of resources has been argued in [21,26,27,28]. Guha et al. distinguish between a *logical* and a *physical* model for querying and inferencing RDF [26]. Such a logical model would have to truly represent the graph nature of RDF in contrast to a concrete serialization syntax (the "physical model") such as RDF/XML or triple storage in databases.

This section introduces the concept of *connectivity* for RDF by means of *paths* and relates these terms to their counterparts from graph theory.

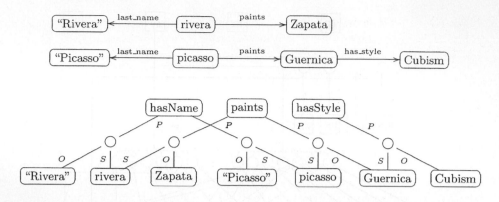

Fig. 11. Fragment of the museum example, presented first as a directed labeled graph, and below as RDF bipartite graph.

Definition 4 (Triple Path). *Let T be an RDF Graph. A path in an RDF Graph—or triple path—P is a sequence of RDF triples $(t_1, t_2, \ldots, t_n)$ with $t_k = (s_k, p_k, o_k) \in T$, for which it holds that*

$$\text{for all } i < n, \{s_i, p_i, o_i\} \cap \{s_{i+1}, p_{i+1}, o_{i+1}\} \neq \emptyset.$$

From this notion the concept of *RDF Connectedness* naturally follows: A triple path $(t_1, t_2, \ldots, t_n)$ is said to be *connecting* resources x and y if it holds that $x \in \{s_1, p_1, o_1\}$, $x \notin \{s_i, p_i, o_i : 1 < i \leq n\}$ and $y \in \{s_n, p_n, o_n\}$, $y \notin \{s_i, p_i, o_i : 1 \leq i < n\}$. The concepts "triple path" and "RDF connectedness" stress the anchoring in the RDF model and are independent of the graph representation (e.g., RDF bipartite graph or directed labeled graph) or serialization syntax.

RDF connectivity corresponds to the well-established notion of connectedness in classical graphs:

Proposition 5. *Let T be an RDF Graph. The resources x, y are connected in T if and only if there exists a path in $\beta(T)$ between the corresponding nodes v_x and v_y.*

Example 3 (Paths in RDF Bipartite Graphs). The lower part of figure 11 shows the RDF bipartite graph version of the directed labeled graph depicted above. All paths of the former also exist in the latter, but not vice versa: the resources `picasso` and `rivera` now appear connected (via the property `paints`, or `hasName`), although the directed labeled graph version does not show this. In the sense of the definition of RDF Graph connectivity given above, these resources are indeed related, and the directed labeled graph version fails to represent that.

The example shows that not all paths which exist in an RDF Graph are present in its directed labeled graph. The following definition describes those paths which are represented:

Definition 5 (Horizontal Path). *A horizontal (triple) path P in an RDF Graph T is a sequence of RDF triples $(t_1, t_2, \ldots, t_n)$, $t_k = (s_k, p_k, o_k) \in T$, for which it holds that for all $i < n$, $\{s_i, o_i\} \cap \{s_{i+1}, o_{i+1}\} \neq \emptyset$.*
A horizontal path is said to be oriented *if $o_i = s_{i+1}$ for all $i < n$.*

Proposition 6. *For every oriented horizontal path P in an RDF Graph T there exists a corresponding path $\delta(P)$ in its directed labeled graph $\delta(T)$, and vice versa.*

Note that the non-horizontal paths are sequences of triples $t_1, \ldots, t_n$ where for some j, t_j and t_{j+1} are linked via a predicate. Examples are the relation of Picasso and Rivera via `paints` presented at the beginning of the section, reifications, and statements about a predicate. If we make a parallel to relational databases, the notion of horizontal path corresponds roughly to values of tuples linked via joins; on the other hand, "vertical" paths are paths passing through the schema of the database. Vertical paths are also relevant for RDF querying when sub-class and sub-property semantics are incorporated (e.g., RQL [29]). Other examples for the use of vertical connectedness arise from the various types of "semantic associations" presented in [25]: *similar* paths are horizontal paths where the properties are sub-properties of a common ancestor property.

6   Conclusions

We introduced a representation of RDF Graphs in terms of classical bipartite graphs as an intermediate model between the abstract RDF triple syntax and concrete implementations. We presented preliminary results about the structure and lines of development of the model. We argued the advantages of the model compared to the triple representation and to the directed labeled graph representation used currently by default.

One of the main advantages of our model from a developer point of view is the possibility to directly use standard graph libraries. We are using the model to approach diverse algorithmic problems of RDF databases, particularly graph-like notions in querying and storage. Future work includes refinement of the RDF bipartite graph model and aspects of visualization.

References

1. Lassila, O., Swick, R.R.: Resource Description Framework (RDF) Model and Syntax Specification. W3C Recommendation. World Wide Web, http://www.w3.org/TR/1999/REC-rdf-syntax-19990222, (1999)
2. Miller, E., Swick, R., Brickley, D.: Resource Description Framework (RDF) / W3C Semantic Web Activity. World Wide Web, http://www.w3.org/RDF/ (2004)
3. Berners-Lee, T.: Semantic Web Road Map. World Wide Web, http://www.w3.org/DesignIssues/Semantic.html (September 1998)
4. Klyne, G., Carroll, J.J.: Resource Description Framework (RDF): Concepts and Abstract Syntax. W3C Recommendation. World Wide Web, http://www.w3.org/TR/2004/REC-rdf-concepts-20040210/ (10 February 2004)

5. Hayes, P.: RDF Semantics. W3C Recommendation. World Wide Web, http://www.w3.org/TR/2004/REC-rdf-mt-20040210/ (10 February 2004)
6. di Battista, G., Eades, P., Tamassia, R., Tollis, I.G.: Algorithms for Drawing Graphs: An Annotated Bibliography. Comput. Geom. Theory Appl. 4 (1994) 235–282 http://www.cs.brown.edu/people/rt/gd-biblio.html.
7. Mäkinen, E.: How to Draw a Hypergraph. Intern. J. Computer Math. 34 (1990) 177–185
8. Berners-Lee, T., Connolly, D.: Delta: an Ontology for the Distribution of Differences between RDF Graphs. World Wide Web, http://www.w3.org/DesignIssues/Diff (2004)
9. Carroll, J.J.: Matching RDF Graphs. Technical Report HPL-2001-293, Digital Media Systems Laboratory, HP Laboratories, Bristol, http://www.hpl.hp.com/techreports/2001/HPL-2001-293.html (2001)
10. Gutierrez, C., Hurtado, C., Mendelzon, A.O.: Foundations of Semantic Web Databases. In: Proceedings of the Twenty-third ACM SIGACT-SIGMOD-SIGART Symposium on Principles of Database Systems (PODS), June 14-16, 2004, Paris, France, ACM (2004)
11. Aleman-Meza, B., Halaschek, C., Arpinar, I.B., Sheth, A.P.: Context-Aware Semantic Association Ranking. In Cruz, I.F., Kashyap, V., Decker, S., Eckstein, R., eds.: Proceedings of SWDB'03. (2003)
12. Rodríguez, A., Egenhofer, M.: Determining Semantic Similarity Among Entity Classes from Different Ontologies. IEEE Transactions on Knowledge and Data Engineering 15(2) (2003) 442–456
13. Carrasco, J.J.M., Fain, D., Lang, K., Zhukov, L.: Clustering of Bipartite Advertiser-Keyword Graph. IEEE Computer Society (2003)
14. Zha, H., He, X., Ding, C.H.Q., Gu, M., Simon, H.D.: Bipartite Graph Partitioning and Data Clustering. In: Proceedings of the 2001 ACM CIKM, Atlanta, USA, ACM (2001) 25–32
15. Vanetik, N., Gudes, E., Shimony, S.E.: Computing Frequent Graph Patterns from Semistructured Data. In: Proceedings of ICDM 2002, Maebashi City, Japan, IEEE Computer Society (2002)
16. Yang, G., Kifer, M.: On the Semantics of Anonymous Identity and Reification. In Meersman, R., Tari, Z., eds.: On the Move to Meaningful Internet Systems, 2002 - DOA/CoopIS/ODBASE, Irvine, USA, Proceedings. Volume 2519 of Lecture Notes in Computer Science., Springer (2002)
17. Karvounarakis, G., Alexaki, S., Christophides, V., Plexousakis, D., Scholl, M.: RQL: A Declarative Query Language for RDF. In: Proceedings of 2002 WWW Conference, ACM Press (2002) 592–603
18. Hayes, J.: A Graph Model for RDF. Diploma thesis, Technische Universität Darmstadt, Department of Computer Science, Germany, http://purl.org/net/jhayes/rdfgraphmodel.html (2004)
19. Brickley, D., Guha, R.: RDF Vocabulary Description Language 1.0: RDF Schema. W3C Recommendation. World Wide Web, http://www.w3.org/TR/2004/REC-rdf-schema-20040210/ (10 February 2004)
20. Duchet, P.: Hypergraphs. In Graham, R., Grötschel, M., Lovász, L., eds.: Handbook of Combinatorics. Elsevier Science B.V., Amsterdam (1995) 381–432
21. Matono, A., Amagasa, T., Yoshikawa, M., Uemura, S.: An Indexing Scheme for RDF and RDF Schema based on Suffix Arrays. In Cruz, I.F., Kashyap, V., Decker, S., Eckstein, R., eds.: Proceedings of SWDB'03. (2003) 151–168

22. Karvounarakis, G., Magkanaraki, A., Alexaki, S., Christophides, V., Plexousakis, D., Scholl, M., Tolle, K.: RQL: A Functional Query Language for RDF. In Gray, P., Kerschberg, L., King, P., Poulovassilis, A., eds.: The Functional Approach to Data Management. Springer-Verlag (2004)

23. Pan, J., Horrocks, I.: Metamodeling Architecture of Web Ontology Languages. In Cruz, I.F., Decker, S., Euzenat, J., McGuinness, D.L., eds.: Proceedings of SWWS'01, The first Semantic Web Working Symposium, Stanford University, California, USA, July 30 - August 1, 2001. LNCS, Springer-Verlag (2001)

24. Pan, J., Horrocks, I.: RDFS(FA) and RDF MT: Two Semantics for RDFS. In Fensel, D., Sycara, K., Mylopoulos, J., eds.: Proc. of the 2003 International Semantic Web Conference (ISWC 2003). Number 2870 in Lecture Notes in Computer Science, Springer (2003) 30–46

25. Anyanwu, K., Sheth, A.: ρ-Queries: Enabling Querying for Semantic Associations on the Semantic Web. In: Proceedings of the Twelfth International World Wide Web Conference, ACM Press (2003) 690 699

26. Guha, R., Lassila, O., Miller, E., Brickley, D.: Enabling Inferencing. World Wide Web, http://www.w3.org/TandS/QL/QL98/pp/enabling.html (1998)

27. Karvounarakis, G., Christophides, V., Plexousakis, D.: Querying Semistructured (Meta)Data and Schemas on the Web: The case of RDF and RDFS. Technical Report 269, FORTH Institute of Computer Science (2000)

28. Haase, P., Broekstra, J., Eberhart, A., Volz, R.: A Comparison of RDF Query Languages. World Wide Web, http://www.aifb.uni-karlsruhe.de/WBS/pha/rdf-query/rdfquery.pdf (2004)

29. FORTH Institute of Computer Science http://139.91.183.30:9090/RDF/RQL/Manual.html: RQL v2.1 User Manual. (2003)

A Model Theoretic Semantics for Ontology Versioning

Jeff Heflin and Zhengxiang Pan

Department of Computer Science and Engineering, Lehigh University
19 Memorial Dr. West, Bethlehem, PA 18015, U.S.A.
{heflin,zhp2}@cse.lehigh.edu

Abstract. We show that the Semantic Web needs a formal semantics for the various kinds of links between ontologies and other documents. We provide a model theoretic semantics that takes into account ontology extension and ontology versioning. Since the Web is the product of a diverse community, as opposed to a single agent, this semantics accommodates different viewpoints by having different entailment relations for different ontology perspectives. We discuss how this theory can be practically applied to RDF and OWL and provide a theorem that shows how to compute perspective-based entailment using existing logical reasoners. We illustrate these concepts using examples and conclude with a discussion of future work.

1 Introduction

The Semantic Web (Berners-Lee, Hendler, and Lassila 2001)[1] has been proposed as the key to unlocking the Web's potential. The basic idea is that information is given explicit meaning, so that machines can process it more intelligently. Instead of just creating standard terms for concepts as is done in XML, the Semantic Web also allows users to provide formal definitions for the standard terms they create. Machines can then use inference algorithms to reason about the terms and to perform translations between different sets of terms. It is envisioned that the Semantic Web will enable more intelligent search, electronic personal assistants, more efficient e-commerce, and coordination of heterogeneous embedded systems.

Unfortunately, the Semantic Web currently lacks a strong underlying theory that considers its distributed aspects. To date, the semantics for semantic web languages have looked little different from the traditional semantics of knowledge representation languages. Traditional knowledge bases assume a single consistent point-of-view, but the knowledge of the Semantic Web will be the product of millions of autonomous parties and may represent many different viewpoints. We argue that the Semantic Web is not just AI knowledge representation using an XML syntax, but actually changes the way we should think about knowledge representation. Semantic web knowledge bases must deal with an additional level of abstraction, that of the document or resource that contains assertions and formulas. Furthermore, the semantics of the knowledge base must explicitly account for the different types of links that can exist between documents. Although languages such as RDF and OWL currently give a definitive account of the meaning of any single document, things become more ambiguous when you consider how documents should be combined. In this respect, semantic web systems are in a state

S.A. McIlraith et al. (Eds.): ISWC 2004, LNCS 3298, pp. 62–76, 2004.
© Springer-Verlag Berlin Heidelberg 2004

analogous to the early days of semantic nets. A quote from Brachman [3] about links between concepts in early semantic nets seems just as appropriate for "links" between semantic web documents today:

> ... the meaning of the link was often relegated to "what the code does with it" - neither an appropriate notion of semantics nor a useful guide for figuring out what the link, in fact means.

Without a better understanding of inter-document links on the Semantic Web, we will have serious interoperability problems. This paper will examine the relationship between different types of inter-document links and propose an unambiguous semantics for them. In particular we focus on links that indicate that one document is a revision of another.

2 Ontology Versioning

Ontologies have come to be seen as a critical component of the Semantic Web. An ontology provides a common vocabulary to support the sharing and reuse of knowledge. When two parties agree to use the same ontology, they agree on the meanings for all terms from that ontology and their information can be combined easily. Unfortunately, there is no widely accepted definition of an ontology. We prefer this definition from Guarino [4]: "An ontology is a logical theory accounting for the intended meaning of a formal vocabulary."

The first author [7] initially described the problems of ontology versioning in distributed environments such as the Web. The Web is a dynamic place, where anyone can instantaneously publish and update information. It is important that this ability is not lost when it is described by a Semantic Web language. People must be able to publish semantic web ontologies as easily as other documents, and they must be allowed to revise these ontologies as well. Ontologies may be changed in order to correct errors, to model new phenomenon, or simply to represent the world in a different way.

When we decide to change an ontology, then we must consider that in a distributed ontology framework such as the one needed by the Semantic Web, there will often be information resources that depend on it. Since the owner of the resource may find these changes undesirable, we should not actually update the original ontology but intstead create a new file that represents the new version.

However, this can lead to problems. Consider the example in Fig.1. The original version of the ontology incorrectly states that all Dolphins are Fish. There is another web page that states that Flipper is a Dolphin. Later, the ontology is corrected to say all Dolphins are Mammals. In RDF and OWL, there are no semantics associated with versioning, so we have to attempt to approximate them using existing language constructs. On the left of Fig.1, we could consider making each version2 class be a subclass of a corresponding version1 class. This means version2 Dolphin will not be version2 Fish, but also means that Flipper will not be a member of any version2 classes. In other words, version1 data is lost in version2. Alternatively, on the right of Fig. 1, we could consider making each version1 class be a subclass of a corresponding version2 class, this means Flipper will be a version2 Dolphin and a version2 Mammal, but will also

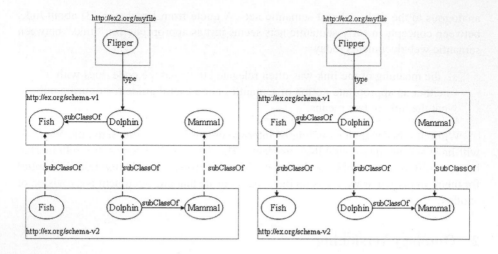

Fig. 1. Ontology revision example. On the left: version 2 classes are subclasses of version 1 classes. On the right: version 1 classes are subclasses of version 2 classes.

be a version2 Fish. If the Fish and Mammal classes are disjoint, this will lead to an inconsistent ontology.

An additional complexity deals with the intended meanings of the ontology. Consider the case that in version 1, "Dolphin" actually meant "Dolphin Fish." Perhaps because this term was confusing users, we decide to change it to mean a kind of porpoise, which is the more common usage. The resulting ontology would be indistinguishable from the one described in the preceding paragraph. Yet, the implications are very different. In the first case, we were correcting an error in our definitions and would like to retroactively apply this correction to existing information resources. In the second case, we have decided to change our concept of "Dolphin", and consequently changed our definition to correspond to the new meaning. In this case, it would be a mistake to retroactively apply the new definitions to old resources. That is no instance of version1 Dolphin should be considered instance of version2 Dolphin. Note that there is no syntactic distinction between these two cases.

The first author [6] has shown how to resolve such problems by allowing ontology authors to specify backwards-compatibility. Essentially an ontology version is backward compatible with a prior version if it contains all of the terms from the earlier ontology and the terms are supposed to mean the same thing in both ontologies.

Since backwards-compatibility depends on knowledge of the intended models of an ontology, it cannot be computed automatically, instead it must be specified by an ontology's author. This is driven by the fact that ontologies only specify a theory partially, and that the intended meaning of a term may change even though the ontology's theory remains the same. Since the ontology can only restrict unintended models, there is no way to formally describe the intended models of an ontology. Furthermore, we suggest that an ontology may not correctly describe the real world, thus it may be missing models that were intended, may include models that are undesirable.

In fact, OWL has already taken ontology versioning into account. For example, owl:backwardCompatibleWith and owl:incompatibleWith are dedicated to specifying the compatibility. However, the Web Ontology Group felt that versioning was not understood well enough to provide semantics for those features when the language was designed. Associating formal semantics to those language constructs can help OWL support ontology versioning.

This paper builds on the first author's previous work and provides a model theoretic semantics for ontology versioning, particularly the concept of backward compatibility. Meanwhile, these inter-document links on the Semantic Web are established: extension, prior Version, backward compatible version and commitment to an ontology by a resource.

3   Preliminary Definitions

We now provide formal definitions to describe our model of the Semantic Web. We need to have structured representations of the data associated with information resources, and these resources must be able to commit to ontologies which provide formal definitions of terms. We will describe this by defining ontologies and resources using a a logical language and by providing a model theoretic semantics for these structures. These definitions improve upon those given by the first author [6].

Let D be the domain of discourse, i.e., the set of objects that will be described. Let R be a subset of D that is the set of information resources, such as web pages, databases, and sensors.

There are many candidate representation languages for an ontology. In order to maintain the generality of this theory, we will use first-order logic as the representation language. Due to the expressivity of FOL, this theory will still apply to the languages commonly used for semantic web systems, such as description logics, as well as proposed Horn logic extensions. We will assume that we have a first-order language $\mathcal{L}^S$ with a set of non-logical symbols S. The predicate symbols of S are $S_P \subset S$, the variable symbols are $S_X \subset S$, and the constant symbols are $S_C \subset S$. For simplicity, we will not discuss function symbols, since an n-ary function symbol can be represented by a $n+1$-ary predicate. The well-formed formulas of $\mathcal{L}^S$ are defined in the usual recursive way. We will use $L(V)$ to refer to the infinite set of well-formed first-order logic formulas that can be constructed using only the non-logical symbols V. We define interpretation and satisfaction in the standard way.

Now, we define the concept of semantic web space, which is a collection of ontologies and information resources.

Definition 1. *A semantic web space* $\mathcal{W}$ *is two-tuple* $\langle \mathcal{O}, R \rangle$, *where* $\mathcal{O}$ *is a set of ontologies and* R *is a set of resources. We assume that* $\mathcal{W}$ *is based on a logical language* $\mathcal{L}^S$.

In the next two subsections, we formally define ontology and resource.

3.1   Ontology Definitions

We begin by formally defining an ontology that supports versioning.

Definition 2. *Given a logical language $\mathcal{L}^S$, an ontology O in $\mathcal{O}$ is a five-tuple $\langle V, A, E, P, B \rangle$, where*

1. *$V \subseteq S$ (the vocabulary V is a subset of the non-logical symbols of $\mathcal{L}^S$)*
2. *$V \supset S_X$ and $V \supset S_C$ (V contains all of the variable and constant symbols of $\mathcal{L}^S$)*
3. *$A \subseteq L(S)$ (the axioms A are a subset of the well-formed formulas of $\mathcal{L}^S$.*
4. *$E \subset \mathcal{O}$ is the set of ontologies extended by O.*
5. *$P \subset \mathcal{O}$ is the set of prior versions of the ontology, such that for all $O_i \in P$ with $O_i = \langle V_i, A_i, E_i, P_i, B_i \rangle$, $P \supset P_i$.*
6. *$B \subset P$ is the set of ontologies that O is backwards compatible with. For each $B_i \in B$, $V \supseteq V_i$.*

As a result of this definition, an ontology defines a logical language that is a subset of the language $\mathcal{L}^S$, and defines a core set of axioms for this language. Note, the second condition is for convenience in defining well-formed formulas below.

There are three basic kinds of "links" between ontologies. An ontology can extend another, which means that it adds new vocabulary and or axioms. The set E is the set of ontologies extended by O. Ontologies also have a set P of prior ontologies and set B of prior ontologies that they are backward compatible with. Note that the prior versions P of an ontology need only be a superset of the prior versions of those ontologies in P. Thus, versioning need not be a total order.

It is important to note that this definition requires that an ontology include the vocabulary of any ontology with which it is backward compatible. This is in order to guarantee that formulas that were well-formed with respect to one version are also well-formed with respect to the backward-compatible version.

Note that backwards-compatibility does not require that the revision contains a superset of the axioms specified by the original version. This allows us to remove axioms that are no longer correct or that would be better expressed in another ontology.

For convenience, we define the concept of an ancestor ontology. An ancestor of an ontology is an ontology extended either directly or indirectly by it.[1] If O_2 is an ancestor of O_1, we write $O_2 \in anc(O_1)$. The formal definition of an ancestor is:

Definition 3 (Ancestor function). *Given two ontologies $O_1 = \langle V_1, A_1, E_1, P_1, B_1 \rangle$ and $O_2 = \langle V_2, A_2, E_2, P_2, B_2 \rangle$, $O_2 \in anc(O_1)$ iff $O_2 \in E_1$ or there exists an $O_i = \langle V_i, A_i, E_i, P_i, B_i \rangle$ such that $O_i \in E_1$ and $O_2 \in anc(O_i)$.*

Since the ontology defines a language, we can talk about well-formed formulas with respect to an ontology. Essentially, a formula is well-formed with respect to an ontology if it is a well-formed formula of the logic that only uses the ontology's vocabulary. First, we must identify the vocabulary accessible to an ontology. Ancestor ontologies play a role in this. Since an ontology should have access to all symbols defined in its ancestors, a formula of that ontology should still be well-formed if it uses symbols from the ancestor ontologies.

---

[1] Extension is sometimes referred to as inclusion or importing. The semantics of our usage are clarified in Definition 7

Definition 4. *The vocabulary closure of an ontology is given by a function vclose* : $\mathcal{O} \rightarrow \mathcal{P}(S)^2$ *such that for each ontology* $O = \langle V, A, E, P, B \rangle$, $vclose(O) = V \cup \bigcup_{\{j \mid O_j \in anc(O)\}} V_j$ *(where* $O_j = \langle V_j, A_j, E_j, P_j, B_j \rangle$*).*

Using the vocabulary closure, we can define well-formedness.

Definition 5. *A formula* ϕ *is well-formed with respect to an ontology* O *iff* $\phi \in L(vclose(O))$.

We also need the definition of a well-formed ontology. We must consider two factors. First, we must consider whether or not a well-formed ontology can extend itself, either directly or indirectly. We will remain agnostic on the issue and not place any restrictions on cycles for the extension relation here. We only insist that all of an ontology's ancestor ontologies be well-formed. Second, we must ensure that no resource or ontology can commit to (or extend) two different versions of the same ontology.

Definition 6. *An ontology* $O = \langle V, A, E, P, B \rangle$ *is well-formed iff:*

1. *A is well-formed with respect to* O
2. *for each* $O_i \in anc(O)$, O_i *is well-formed*
3. *there does not exist any ontology* $O_i \in anc(O)$, *where* $O_i = \langle V_i, A_i, E_i, P_i, B_i \rangle$, *such that there is an* $O_j \in anc(O)$ *and* $O_j \in P_i$.

We will now provide meaning for ontologies by defining models of ontologies. Recall that in logic, a model of a theory is an interpretation that satisfies every formula in the theory. Thus, we must first determine the structure of our interpretations. One possibility is to use interpretations of $\mathcal{L}^V$, the language formed using only the non-logical symbols in V. However, this will limit our ability to compare interpretations of different ontologies, so we will instead use interpretations for $\mathcal{L}^S$. As such, each interpretation contains mappings for any predicate symbol in any ontology, and thus a single interpretation could be a model of two ontologies with distinct vocabularies.

For ontology extension to have its intuitive meaning, all models of an ontology should also be models of every ontology extended by it.

Definition 7. *Let* $O = \langle V, A, E, P, B \rangle$ *be an ontology and* $\mathcal{I}$ *be an interpretation of* $\mathcal{L}^S$. *Then* $\mathcal{I}$ *is a model of* O *iff* $\mathcal{I}$ *satisfies every formula in A and* $\mathcal{I}$ *is a model of every ontology in E.*

Thus an ontology attempts to describe a set of possibilities by using axioms to limit its models. Some subset of these models are those intended by the ontology, and are called the intended models of the ontology. Note that unlike a first-order logic theory, an ontology can have many intended models because it can be used to describe many different states of affairs [4]. The axioms of an ontology limit its models by restricting the relations that directly or indirectly correspond to predicates in its vocabulary, while allowing models that provide for any possibility for predicate symbols in other domains.

---

[2] We use $\mathcal{P}$ to refer to the powerset.

3.2   Resource Definitions

Definition 8 (Knowledge Function). *Let $K : R{\to}\mathcal{P}(L(S))$ be a function that maps each information resource into a set of well-formed formulas.*

We call K the *knowledge function* because it provides a set of formulas for a resource. For example, this could be the first order logic expressions that correspond to the RDF syntax of the resource.

Now we need to associate an ontology with each resource.

Definition 9 (Commitment Function). *Let R be the set of information resources and $\mathcal{O}$ be the set of ontologies. The commitment function $C : R \to \mathcal{O}$ maps resources to ontologies.*

We call this the *commitment function* because it returns the ontology that a particular resource commits to. When a resource commits to an ontology, it agrees to the meanings ascribed to the symbols by that ontology.

The vocabulary that a well-formed resource may use is limited by the ontology to which it commits.

Definition 10. *An information resource $r \in R$ is well-formed iff*

1. *there exists an $O \in \mathcal{O}$ such that $C(r) = O$*
2. *O is well-formed*
3. *$K(r)$ is well-formed with respect to O.*

We now wish to define the semantics of a resource. When a resource commits to an ontology, it has agreed to the terminology and definitions of the ontology. Thus every interpretation that is a model of resource must also be a model of the ontology for that resource.

Definition 11. *Let r be a resource where $C(r) = O$ and $\mathcal{I}$ be an interpretation of $\mathcal{L}^S$. $\mathcal{I}$ is a model of r iff $\mathcal{I}$ is a model of O and $\mathcal{I}$ satisfies every formula in $K(r)$.*

A possible limitation imposed by the commitment function is that it only allows each resource to commit to a single ontology. However, a virtual ontology can be created that represents multiple ontologies committed to by a single resource. If we assume that committing to two ontologies means that the vocabulary from the resource can come from either ontology and that its models must be models of both ontologies, then committing to two ontologies $O_1 = \langle V_1, A_1, E_1, P_1, B_1 \rangle$ and $O_2 = \langle V_2, A_2, E_2, P_2, B_2 \rangle$ is equivalent to committing to the ontology $O_{union} = \langle \emptyset, \emptyset, \{O_1, O_2\}, \emptyset, \emptyset \rangle$. The well-formed formulas of O_{union} are equivalent to well-formed formulas of the union of O_1 and O_2, and the models of O_{union} are precisely the intersection of the models of O_1 and O_2.

In section 4, we will provide a semantics for ontology extension and versioning in terms of ontology perspectives.

3.3   Relationship to RDF(S) and OWL

Since OWL is essentially a description logic, all OWL axioms can be expressed in $\mathcal{L}^S$. Unfortunately, OWL does not distinguish between resources and ontologies; instead all OWL documents are ontologies.[3] We reconcile this situation by introducing a rule:

---

[3] This decision was not endorsed by all members of the working group that created OWL

any OWL document that contains a description of a class or a property is an ontology; otherwise, the document is a resource.

After having made this distinction, some language constructs can be associated to the ontology definition (Definition 2). From an OWL DL ontology, we can construct an ontology $O = \langle V, A, E, P, B \rangle$

1. for each symbol s in rdf:ID, rdf:about and rdf:resource, $s \in V$
2. for each axiom a in class axioms and property axioms, $a \in A$
3. for each O_i in triple $\langle O$ owl : imports $O_i \rangle, O_i \in E$
4. for each O_i in triple $\langle O$ owl : priorVersion $O_i \rangle, O_i \in P$
5. for each O_i in triple $\langle O$ owl : backwardCompatibleWith $O_i \rangle, O_i \in P$ and $O_i \in$ B.

Note if the subject of owl:imports is a resource document in our definition, then $\langle r$ owl : imports $O \rangle \rightarrow C(r) = O$. In the case that a resource document imports multiple ontologies, $C(r) = O_{union}$. O_{union} is a virtual ontology where
$$O_{union} = \langle \emptyset, \emptyset, \{O_i | O_i \in \langle r \text{ owl : imports } O_i \rangle \}, \emptyset, \emptyset \rangle.$$
RDF and RDFS have a model theoretic semantics [5], but do not have any explicit support for versioning, nor do they have explicit semantics for inter-document links. One possible way to assign such a semantics is to treat each RDF schema as an ontology and each reference to a namespace as an implicit commitment or extension relationship.

4   Ontology Perspectives

Now that we have defined models of individual resources and ontologies, we need to return our attention to a set of distributed information resources, as is the case with a semantic web space. What does it mean to be a model of multiple resources? The first author [6] has suggested that there should not be a universal model of all the resources and ontologies on the Web. In fact, it is extremely unlikely that one could even exist. Instead, we must allow for different viewpoints and contexts, which are supported by different ontologies. He defines perspectives which then allow the same set of resources to be viewed from different contexts, using different assumptions and background information. However, This definition of perspectives was somewhat ad-hoc, and did not have a solid theoretical basis. Here we present a model theoretic description of perspectives.

Each perspective will be based on an ontology, hereafter called the basis ontology or base of the perspective. By providing a set of terms and a standard set of axioms, an ontology provides a shared context. Thus, resources that commit to the same ontology have implicitly agreed to share a context. When it makes sense, we also want to maximize integration by including resources that commit to different ontologies. This includes resources that commit to ancestor ontologies and resources that commit to earlier versions of ontologies that the current ontology is backward compatible with.

Given these guidelines, we can define an ontology perspective model of a set of resources that incorporates backward-compatibility. This model cannot be based solely on the models of some subset of the resources. Since one of the problems we want to be able to solve is to correct an ontology that has incorrectly specified its models, we need to be able to substitute the models for a new version of an ontology where the models of the older version sufficed before. We will start with a supporting definition that allows us to define the model of a resource assuming the ontology it commits to has been replaced with a newer, backward-compatible one.

Definition 12. *Let r be an information resource, O be an ontology such that $C(r) = O$, $O' = \langle V', A', E', P', B' \rangle$ be an ontology such that $O \in B'$. An O'-updated model of r is an interpretation $\mathcal{I}$ such that $\mathcal{I}$ is a model of O' and $\mathcal{I}$ satisfies every formula in $K(r)$.*

We can now define an ontology perspective model of a semantic web space. Any perspective model must also be an updated model of those resources that commit to ontologies with which the basis ontology is backwards-compatible, and updated models of those resources that commit to ontologies that the base's ancestor ontologies are backwards-compatible with. In essence the following definitions define the semantics of the document links we have discussed by determining the logical consequences of a semantic web space based on the extensions, backward-compatibilities and commitment relations. Note, prior versions play no role, and thus are essentially "semantic-free".

Definition 13 (Ontology Perspective Model). *An interpretation $\mathcal{I}$ is an ontology perspective model of a semantic web space $\mathcal{W} = \langle \mathcal{O}, R \rangle$ based on $O = \langle V, A, E, P, B \rangle$ (written $\mathcal{I} \models_O \mathcal{W}$) iff:*

1. *$\mathcal{I}$ is a model of O*
2. *for each $r \in R$ such that $C(r) = O$ or $C(r) \in anc(O)$ then $\mathcal{I}$ is a model of r.*
3. *for each $r \in R$ such that $C(r) \in B$ then $\mathcal{I}$ is an O-updated model of r*
4. *for each $r \in R$ such that $\exists O_i, O_i = \langle V_i, A_i, E_i, P_i, B_i \rangle \in anc(O) \wedge C(r) \in B_i$, then $\mathcal{I}$ is an O_i-updated model of r*

Note the first part of the definition is needed because there may be no resources in R that commit to O, and without this condition, O would not have any impact on the models of the perspective.

We now turn our attention to how one can reason with ontology perspectives.

Definition 14 (Ontology Perspective Entailment). *Let $\mathcal{W} = \langle \mathcal{O}, R \rangle$ be a semantic web space and O be an ontology. A formula ϕ is a logical consequence of the ontology perspective of $\mathcal{W}$ based on O (written $\mathcal{W} \models_O \phi$) iff for every interpretation $\mathcal{I}$ such that $\mathcal{I} \models_O \mathcal{W}, \mathcal{I} \models \phi$.*

It would also be useful if we can define a first order logic theory that is equivalent to the definition above.

Definition 15 (Ontology Perspective Theory). *Let $\mathcal{W} = \langle \mathcal{O}, R \rangle$ be a semantic web space where $\mathcal{O} = \{O_1, O_2, \ldots, O_n\}$ and $O_i = \langle V_i, A_i, E_i, P_i, B_i \rangle$. An ontology perspective theory for $\mathcal{W}$ based on O_i is:*

$$\Phi = A_i \cup \bigcup_{\{j | O_j \in anc(O_i)\}} A_j \cup \bigcup_{\{r \in R | C(r) \in B_i\}} K(r)$$

$$\cup \bigcup_{\{r \in R | C(r) = O_i \vee C(r) \in anc(O_i)\}} K(r)$$

$$\cup \bigcup_{\{r \in R | \exists j, O_j \in anc(O_i) \wedge C(r) \in B_j\}} K(r)$$

These theories describe a perspective based on a selected ontology. Each theory contains the axioms of its basis ontology, the axioms of its ancestors, the assertions of all resources that commit to the basis ontology or one of its ancestors, and the assertions of all resources that commit to an ontology with which the basis ontology is backward compatible, or one of its ancestors is backward compatible.

Theorem 1. *Let $\mathcal{W} = \langle \mathcal{O}, R \rangle$ be a semantic web space, $O = \langle V, A, E, P, B \rangle$ be an ontology, and Φ be a ontology perspective theory for $\mathcal{W}$ based on O. Then $\Phi \models \phi$ iff $\mathcal{W} \models_O \phi$.*

PROOF. (Sketch) We can show that the sets of models are equivalent. The models of Definition 13, part 1 are exactly the models of $A_i \cup \bigcup_{\{j \mid O_j \in anc(O_i)\}} A_j$ (from Definition 7). From Definition 11 we can conclude that the models of both part 1 and 2 are exactly the models of $A_i \cup \bigcup_{\{j \mid O_j \in anc(O_i)\}} A_j \cup \bigcup_{\{r \in R \mid C(r) = O_i \vee C(r) \in anc(O_i)\}} K(r)$

From Definition 12 we can conclude that models of part 3 are $A_i \cup \bigcup_{\{r \in R \mid C(r) \in B_i\}} K(r)$. Finally, from the same definition, we can conclude that the models of part 4 are exactly the models of $\bigcup_{\{j \mid O_j \in anc(O_i)\}} A_j \cup \bigcup_{\{r \in R \mid \exists j, O_j \in anc(O_i) \wedge C(r) \in B_j\}} K(r)$. The union of these axioms corresponds to the conjunction of the conditions, and when simplified is equivalent to the theory specified in Definition 15.

The implication of Definition 15 is that we do not need special purpose reasoners to perform ontology perspective reasoning. Since the entailments of an ontology perspective theory are equivalent to ontology perspective entailment (by Theorem 1), you can create the corresponding FOL theory and use an FOL theorem prover to reasoner about ontology perspective entailments. Furthermore, if we restrict the logic used in defining the resources and ontologies, then we should be able to use the more efficient reasoners that correspond to these restricted logics.

5 Example

We will reconsider the "Dolphin" example from Figure 1 using our definitions. In Figure 2, Ontology O_A is the original ontology which contains an incorrect axiom. Ontology O'_A is a backward compatible revision of O_A (as indicated by the fifth element in the tuple) that replaces the offending axiom with a correct one.

What are the logical consequences of r in Figure 2? That depends on what perspective we choose. The ontology perspective theory of $\mathcal{W}$ based on O_A is simply

$\Phi_{O_A} = \{Dolphin(flipper), Dolphin(x) \rightarrow Fish(x)\}$

It is clear that $\Phi_{O_A} \models Fish(flipper)$, and thus $\mathcal{W} \models_{O_A} Fish(flipper)$. On the other hand, the perspective theory of $\mathcal{W}$ based on O'_A is:

$\Phi_{O'_A} = \{Dolphin(flipper), Dolphin(x) \rightarrow Mammal(x)\}$

Consequently, $\mathcal{W} \models_{O'_A} Mammal(flipper)$.

As shown here, semantic web spaces essentially have multiple consequence relations, where each corresponds to the perspective of a particular ontology or version of an ontology. This allows users to decide whether or not they want to reason in terms of the old version of the ontology or the newer version.

$$O_A = \quad \langle \{Fish, Mammal, Dolphin\},$$
$$\{Dolphin(x) \to Fish(x)\},$$
$$\emptyset,$$
$$\emptyset,$$
$$\emptyset \rangle$$

$$O'_A = \quad \langle \{Fish, Mammal, Dolphin\},$$
$$\{Dolphin(x) \to Mammal(x)\},$$
$$\emptyset,$$
$$\{O_A\},$$
$$\{O_A\} \rangle$$

$$K(r) = \{Dolphin(flipper)\}$$
$$C(r) = O_A$$
$$W = \quad \langle \{O_A, O'_A\}, \{r\} \rangle$$

Fig. 2. Ontology revision using the formal model.

Furthermore, the effects are limited to relevant resources. Consider the example where in O_A, *Dolphin* actually means "dolphin fish", but in O'_A it is decided to give it the new meaning "a kind of porpoise." In this case, O'_A is not backward-compatible with O_A because it has different intended interpretations. This is expressed by changing the last element of the O'_A tuple to $\emptyset$. In this case, Φ_{O_A} is as above, but $\Phi_{O'_A}$ is:

$$\Phi_{O'_A} = \{Dolphin(x) \to Mammal(x)\}$$

Note, that in this case $Dolphin(flipper) \notin \Phi_{O'_A}$ because of the definition of ontology perspective models. Consequently, $\mathcal{W} \nvDash_{O'_A} Mammal(flipper)$

Now we turn to a more complex example that combines the extension and versioning (Figure 3 and 4).

The Semantic Web can be used to locate documents for people or to answer specific questions based on the content of the Web. These uses represent the document retrieval and knowledge base views of the Web. The knowledge base view uses the logical definition of queries: a query is a formula with existentially quantified variables, whose answers are a set of bindings for the variables that make the formula true with respect to the knowledge base. But what is a knowledge base in the context of the Semantic Web? In order to resolve a number of problems faced by the Semantic Web we have extensively discussed means of subdividing it. Theoretically, each of these perspectives represents a single model of the world, and could be considered a knowledge base. Thus, the answer to a semantic web query must be relative to a specific perspective.

Consider the set of ontologies and resources presented in Figure 4. There are four ontology perspective theories generated from this semantic web space: $\Phi_{O_C}, \Phi_{O'_C}, \Phi_{O_V}$ and $\Phi_{O'_V}$. Based on Definition 15, different ontologies and resources appear in each perspective theory. As shown in Fig. 5, Φ_{O_C} includes the axioms from O_C and the knowledge from r_1. Φ_{O_V} includes the axioms from O_V, and because O_C is an ancestor of O_V, those of O_C. It also includes the resources r_1 and r_3, which commit to these ontologies. On the other hand, $\Phi_{O'_C}$ includes axioms only from O'_C, and the resources r_1 and r_2. Note that $\Phi_{O'_C}$ does not include axioms in O_C, because the theory in Definition

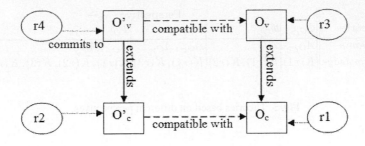

Fig. 3. Ontology extension and revision example.

$$O_C = \quad \langle \{Car, Convertible\},$$
$$\{Convertible(x) \rightarrow Car(x)\},$$
$$\emptyset,$$
$$\emptyset,$$
$$\emptyset \rangle$$

$$O'_C = \quad \langle \{Car, Convertible, SUV\},$$
$$\{Convertible(x) \rightarrow Car(x),$$
$$SUV(x) \rightarrow Car(x)\},$$
$$\emptyset,$$
$$\{O_C\},$$
$$\{O_C\} \rangle$$

$$O_V - \quad \langle \{Vehicle, Motorcycle\},$$
$$\{Motorcycle(x) \rightarrow Vehicle(x)$$
$$O_C : Car(x) \rightarrow Vehicle(x)\},$$
$$\{O_C\},$$
$$\emptyset,$$
$$\emptyset \rangle$$

$$O'_V = \quad \langle \{Vehicle, Motorcycle, Automobile\},$$
$$\{Motorcycle(x) \rightarrow Vehicle(x),$$
$$Automobile(x) \rightarrow Vehicle(x),$$
$$Automobile(x) \leftrightarrow O'_C : Car(x)\},$$
$$\{O'_C\},$$
$$\{O_V\},$$
$$\{O_V\} \rangle$$

$$C(r_1) = O_C$$
$$K(r_1) = \{Car(beetle), Convertible(mustang)\}$$
$$C(r_2) = O'_C$$
$$K(r_2) = \{Car(jetta), Convertible(z3), SUV(yukon)\}$$
$$C(r_3) = O_V$$
$$K(r_3) = \{Vehicle(humvee), Motorcycle(yamaha)\}$$
$$C(r_4) = O'_V$$
$$K(r_4) = \{Vehicle(bradley), Motorcycle(harley), Automobile(s600)\}$$

Fig. 4. Example ontologies and resources.

| | Perspective | | | |
Theories	Φ_{O_C}	$\Phi_{O'_C}$	Φ_{O_V}	$\Phi_{O'_V}$
Axioms	A_{O_C}	$A_{O'_C}$	A_{O_C}, A_{O_V}	$A_{O'_C}, A_{O'_V}$
Knowledge	$K(r1)$	$K(r1), K(r2)$	$K(r1), K(r3)$	$K(r1), K(r2), K(3), K(r4)$

Fig. 5. Theories based on different perspectives.

15 does not contain the prior version's axioms. $\Phi_{O'_V}$ includes axioms from O'_V and O'_C, and the resources r_1, r_2, r_3 and r_4.

As a result, the answer to any particular query depends on which perspective it is issued against. For example, the answers to Car(x) based on O_C's perspective will be {beetle, mustang}. The answers to same query based on O'_C's perspective will be {jetta, z3, yukon, beetle, mustang}. The answers to Vehicle(x) based on O_V's perspective will be {humvee, yamaha, beetle, mustang}, while the answers to that query based on O'_V's perspective will be {bradley, harley, s600, humvee, yamaha, jetta, z3, yukon, beetle, mustang}.

6   Related Work

Prior to the concept of the Semantic Web, there was little work related to ontology versioning. Perhaps this is because most ontology systems were centralized, and in such cases versioning is less of an issue. One exception is CONCORDIA [10], which provides a model of change with applications in medical taxonomies. However, this model is limited to simple taxonomic ontologies and does not have a formal semantics.

Klein and Fensel [8] were the first to compare ontology versioning to database schema versioning [11]. They proposed that both prospective use (viewing data from the point of view of a newer ontology) and retrospective use (viewing data from the point of view of an older ontology) of data should be considered. However, Klein and Fensel do not describe a formal semantics.

Stuckenschmidt and Klein [12] provide a formal definition for modular ontologies and consider the impact of change in it. However, their approach involves physical inclusion of extended ontologies and requires that changes be propagated through the network. This approach is unlikely to scale in large, distributed systems. Furthermore, they do not allow for resources to be reasoned with using different perspectives, as is described here.

Bouquet et al. [2] have also argued that it often does not make sense to have a global interpretation of a set of on semantic web ontologies. Their solution involves creating local interpretations and providing bridge rules between different contexts. By contrast, our paper shows that ontologies can provide the benefits of contexts too. Furthermore, Bouquet et al. do not consider the impact of versioning.

An orthogonal problem to the one described in this paper is how to determine the correspondences and differences between two different versions of an ontology. PROMPT-DIFF [9] is an example algorithm intended for that purpose.

7   Conclusion

We have discussed the problem of ontology versioning and in particular the need for a formal semantics of the links that can exist between ontologies. We mathematically described the components of the Semantic Web and provided a model theoretic semantics for these components. we also discussed how this semantics relates to RDF(S) and OWL. We then showed how Heflin's perspectives [6] could also be defined using model theoretic semantics. This provided a formal account for three kinds of links between semantic web documents: commitment to an ontology by a resource, extension of one ontology by another, and backward-compatibility of an ontology with a prior version. We described a simple approach for reasoning with perspectives and finally gave examples to illustrate their utility.

There are a number of directions for future work. First, we intend to look at other kinds of versioning. For example, we will consider a model theoretic semantic for retrospective as well as prospective use of data. The incompatible prior versions will also be considered. A possible approch would be introducing deprecation, which is similar to the retired concept in CONCORDIA [10]. Second, although our theory presents a good logical account of reasoning with distributed ontologies, it has some practical limitations. Ontology perspectives divide the information resources into subsets that were likely to have the same viewpoint, but still cannot guarantee consistency. Since perspectives could be very large, containing millions of resources, it is a shame if a single inconsistency trivialized the whole thing. An important problem is to find a theory that allows useful reasoning in the face of these inconsistencies. Third, we will look at how a model theoretic approach can be used as a basis for beginning to formalize semantic notions of trust.

Acknowledgement. This work was supported by the Defense Advanced Research Projects Agency under a subcontract from ISX Corporation and by the National Science Foundation under Grant No. IIS-0346963.

References

1. T. Berners-Lee, J. Hendler, and O. Lassila. The Semantic Web. *Scientific American*, May 2001.
2. P. Bouquet, F. Giunchiglia, F. van Harmelen, L. Serafini, and H. Stuckenschmidt. C-OWL: Contextualizing ontologies. In *Proc. of the 2003 Int'l Semantic Web Conf. (ISWC 2003)*, LNCS 2870, pages 164–179. Springer, 2003.
3. R. Brachman. What IS-A is and isn't: An analysis of taxonomic links in semantic networks. *IEEE Computer*, 16(10):30–36, October 1983.
4. N. Guarino. Formal ontology and information systems. In *Proceedings of Formal Ontology and Information Systems*, Trento, Italy, June 1998. IOS Press.
5. P. Hayes. RDF semantics. Proposed Recommendation, December 2003. http://www.w3.org/TR/2003/PR-rdf-schema-20031215/.
6. J. Heflin. *Towards the Semantic Web: Knowledge Representation in a Dynamic, Distributed Environment*. PhD thesis, University of Maryland, 2001.

7. Jeff Heflin and James Hendler. Dynamic ontologies on the Web. In *Proc. of the Seventeenth National Conference on Artificial Intelligence (AAAI-2000)*, pages 443–449, Menlo Park, CA, 2000. AAAI/MIT Press.
8. M. Klein and D. Fensel. Ontology versioning for the semantic web. In *Proc. of the 1st Int'l Semantic Web Working Symposium (SWWS)*, pages 75–91, 2001.
9. N. Noy and M. Musen. PROMPTDIFF: A fixed-point algorithm for comparing ontology versions. In *Proc. of the Eighteenth National Conference on Artificial Intelligence (AAAI-2002)*, Menlo Park, CA, 2002. AAAI/MIT Press.
10. D. E. Oliver, Y. Shahar, M. A. Musen, and E. H. Shortliffe. Representation of change in controlled medical terminologies. *Artificial Intelligence in Medicine*, 15(1):53–76, 1999.
11. J. Roddick. A survey of schema versioning issues for database systems. *Information and Software Technology*, 37(7):383–393, 1995.
12. H. Stuckenschmidt and M. Klein. Integrity and change in modular ontologies. In *Proc. IJCAI'03*, Acapulco, Mexico, 2003.

Extending the RDFS Entailment Lemma

Herman J. ter Horst

Philips Research, Eindhoven, The Netherlands
herman.ter.horst@philips.com

Abstract. We complement the RDF semantics specification of the W3C by proving decidability of RDFS entailment. Furthermore, we show completeness and decidability of entailment for RDFS extended with datatypes and a property-related subset of OWL.

The RDF semantics specification provides a complete set of entailment rules for reasoning with RDFS, but does not prove decidability of RDFS entailment: the closure graphs used in the completeness proof are infinite for finite RDF graphs. We define partial closure graphs, which can be taken to be finite for finite RDF graphs, which can be computed in polynomial time, and which are sufficient to decide RDFS entailment.

We consider the extension of RDFS with datatypes and a property-related fragment of OWL: FunctionalProperty, InverseFunctional-Property, sameAs, SymmetricProperty, TransitiveProperty, and inverseOf. In order to obtain a complete set of simple entailment rules, the semantics that we use for these extensions is in line with the 'if-semantics' of RDFS, and weaker than the 'iff-semantics' defining D-entailment and OWL (DL or Full) entailment. Classes can be used as instances, the use of FunctionalProperty and TransitiveProperty is not restricted to obtain decidability, and a partial closure that is sufficient for deciding entailment can be computed in polynomial time.

1 Introduction

The language RDF (Resource Description Framework) plays a foundational role in the W3C's Semantic Web vision. The RDF semantics specification [2] provides a model-theoretic description of the semantics of RDF and RDFS (RDF Schema). This specification also contains the RDFS entailment lemma, describing a complete set of entailment rules, used to implement RDF reasoners. The RDFS entailment lemma moreover makes clear to people, in syntactic terms, what RDFS entailment is. This paper extends the RDFS entailment lemma in three directions: decidability of entailment, reasoning with datatypes, and reasoning with property-related vocabulary such as owl:FunctionalProperty.

Decidability of RDFS entailment is a fundamental issue, which has not yet been settled. The existence of a complete set of entailment rules does not imply decidability of entailment; compare first-order logic, with Gödel's completeness theorem and Church's theorem showing undecidability. The completeness proof for RDFS [2] makes use of closure graphs which are infinite for finite graphs, in view of the container membership properties rdf:_i. The proof shows that

S.A. McIlraith et al. (Eds.): ISWC 2004, LNCS 3298, pp. 77–91, 2004.

in order to decide whether a finite graph H rdfs-entails a finite graph G, it is sufficient to check whether a finite subgraph of the closure of H simply entails G. However, since the closure of H is infinite, and therefore the number of candidate subgraphs is infinite, this is not a finite algorithm. In this paper we define partial closure graphs, which can be taken to be finite for finite graphs and which can be computed in polynomial time, and prove that these can be used to decide rdfs-entailment. Comparing the closure graphs described in [2], to decide whether a graph H rdfs-entails a graph G, it is allowed to omit the addition to H of the axiomatic triples for the URIs rdf:_i that do not appear in either H or G, as long as these axiomatic triples are added to H for at least one URI rdf:_i.

The RDF semantics specification [2] defines a notion of reasoning with data-types, called D-entailment, for which no completeness or decidability result is known. We show that a completeness and decidability result can be obtained for a somewhat weaker semantics of datatypes, by making a relatively small modification to the entailment rules: rule rdf2 is replaced by a rule rdf2-D, with the same effect not only for the datatype XMLLiteral but for all datatypes in a datatype map D. This result requires a mild assumption, that datatype maps are 'discriminating', as will be explained below.

For OWL (Web Ontology Language) [5] no complete set of entailment rules is known. OWL Full entailment is known to be undecidable. For OWL DL, restrictions were imposed on the use of the language to obtain decidability. OWL DL entailment and OWL Lite entailment are known to be in NEXPTIME and EXPTIME, respectively [3]. Several people have stated that owl:FunctionalProperty is the single most useful element of the OWL vocabulary. We consider reasoning with RDFS extended with this and other property-related vocabulary: Inverse-FunctionalProperty, sameAs, SymmetricProperty, TransitiveProperty, and inverseOf. We show that 12 simple entailment rules, in combination with the 18 entailment rules for RDFS, form a complete set. Just like for the notion of datatype reasoning that we use, the semantics considered is in line with the 'if-semantics' of RDFS, rather than the stronger 'iff-semantics' underlying D-entailment and OWL (DL or Full) entailment. In a similar way as for RDFS, we prove that entailment can be decided with a partial closure graph which can be computed in polynomial time, and that the problem to decide whether a finite graph H entails a finite graph G is in NP, and in P when G has no blank nodes. No restrictions are imposed: for example, classes can be used as instances, and FunctionalProperty and TransitiveProperty can be freely combined.

In this paper, the descriptions of the proofs are largely restricted to places where the finiteness of a partial closure or the considered semantic extensions of RDFS lead to a difference with the proof of the RDFS entailment lemma.[1]

2   RDF Graphs and Simple Entailment

This section summarizes terminology, introduces notations, and recalls the interpolation lemma which characterizes simple entailment [2] [4].

---

[1] A version of this paper with complete proofs is available on request.

2.1 URI references, blank nodes, literals. Let U denote the set of *URI references* and B the set of *blank nodes*, which is assumed to be infinite. Let L be the set of *literals*; L is the union of the set L_p of *plain literals* and the set L_t of *typed literals*. A typed literal l consists of a lexical form s and a datatype URI t: we shall write l as a pair, $l = (s, t)$. The sets U, B, L_p and L_t are pairwise disjoint. A *name* is an element of $U \cup L$, and a *vocabulary* is a subset of $U \cup L$. RDF has a special datatype URI, called `rdf:XMLLiteral`, which will also be written as X. An *XML literal* is a typed literal of the form (s, X).

2.2 RDF graphs. An *(RDF) graph* G is defined to be a subset of the set

$$U \cup B \;\times\; U \;\times\; U \cup B \cup L. \qquad (1)$$

The elements (s, p, o) of an RDF graph are called *RDF triples*, which consist of a *subject*, a *predicate* (or *property*), and an *object*, respectively. We shall write triples as $s\,p\,o$ and introduce one-letter abbreviations for several standard URI references (see Tables 1 and 4), to obtain a shortening of definitions and proofs. The notation can be viewed as an abbreviation of the N-Triples notation [1].[2]

Denoting the projection mappings on the three factor sets of the product set given in (1) by π_i, the *set of nodes* of an RDF graph G is

$$nd(G) = \pi_1(G) \cup \pi_3(G),$$

which is a subset of $U \cup B \cup L$. The set of *blank nodes* of G is denoted by

$$bl(G) = nd(G) \cap B.$$

The *vocabulary of a graph* G, which will be denoted by $V(G)$, is the set of names that occur as subject, predicate or object of a triple in G.

Two RDF graphs G and G' are *equivalent* if there is a bijection $f : nd(G) \to nd(G')$ such that $f(bl(G)) \subset bl(G')$, such that $f(v) = v$ for each $v \in nd(G) \cap (U \cup L)$, and such that $s\,p\,o \in G$ if and only if $f(s)\,p\,f(o) \in G'$.

A *subgraph* of an RDF graph is a subset of the graph.

A graph is *ground* if it has no blank nodes.

Given a partial function $h : B \rightharpoonup U \cup B \cup L$, an *instance* of a graph G is a graph obtained from G by replacing some (or all) blank nodes v in G by $h(v)$.

Given a set S of graphs, a *merge* of S is a graph that is obtained by replacing the graphs G in S by equivalent graphs G' that do not share blank nodes, and by taking the union of these graphs G'. The merge of a set of graphs S is uniquely defined up to equivalence. A merge of S will be denoted by $M(S)$.

2.3 Simple interpretations. A *simple interpretation* I of a vocabulary V is a 6-tuple $I = (R_I, P_I, E_I, S_I, L_I, LV_I)$, where R_I is a nonempty set, called the set of *resources*, P_I is the set of *properties*, LV_I is the set of *literal values*, which is a subset of R_I that contains at least all plain literals in V, and where E_I, S_I, and L_I are functions:

$$E_I : P_I \;\to\; \mathcal{P}(R_I \times R_I),$$

---

[2] As in the expression $s\,p\,o \in G$, where G is an RDF graph, the context will always make clear what the triple is.

$$S_I : V \cap U \ \to \ R_I \cup P_I,$$

$$L_I : V \cap L_t \ \to \ R_I.$$

Here $\mathcal{P}(X)$ denotes the power set of the set X, that is, the set of all subsets of X. The function E_I defines the *extension* of a property as a set of pairs of resources. The functions S_I and L_I define the interpretation of URI references and typed literals, respectively.

If I is a simple interpretation of a vocabulary V, then I also denotes a function with domain V, in the following way. For plain literals $l \in L_p \cap V$, we have $I(l) = l \in LV_I$. For typed literals $l \in L_t \cap V$, $I(l) = L_I(l)$. For URI references $a \in U \cap V$, $I(a) = S_I(a)$.

If $E = s\,p\,o$ is a ground triple, then a simple interpretation I of a vocabulary V is said to *satisfy* E if $s, p, o \in V, I(p) \in P_I$, and $(I(s), I(o)) \in E_I(I(p))$. If G is a ground RDF graph, then I satisfies G if I satisfies each triple $E \in G$.

Given a simple interpretation I and a partial function $A : B \rightharpoonup R_I$, a function I_A is defined that extends I by using A to give an interpretation of blank nodes in the domain of A. If $A(v)$ is defined for $v \in B$, then $I_A(v) = A(v)$. If G is any RDF graph, then I satisfies G if I_A satisfies G for some partial function $A : B \rightharpoonup R_I$, that is, if

$$(I_A(s), I_A(o)) \in E_I(I(p))$$

for each triple $s\,p\,o \in G$. If I is a simple interpretation and S a set of graphs, then I satisfies S if I satisfies G for each G in S; it is not difficult to see that I satisfies S if and only if I satisfies $M(S)$.

2.4 Simple entailment. A set S of graphs *simply entails* a graph G if each simple interpretation that satisfies S also satisfies G. In this case we shall write

$$S \models G.$$

2.5 Interpolation lemma. *If S is a set of RDF graphs and G is an RDF graph, then $S \models G$ if and only if a subgraph of $M(S)$ is an instance of G.*

This lemma is proved in [2]. It shows that the simple entailment relation $S \models G$ between finite sets S of finite RDF graphs and finite RDF graphs G is decidable. It also shows that this problem is in NP: guess and check an instance function h. It is clear that this problem is in P when G is assumed to be ground. According to [2], this problem (without restrictive assumptions) is NP-complete.

3   RDFS Interpretations and D* Interpretations

As preparation for the proof of decidability of entailment for RDFS, possibly extended with datatypes, this section defines D* interpretations, a generalization of RDFS interpretations extending the semantics of XMLLiteral to all datatypes in a datatype map. We first consider RDFS interpretations.

3.1 RDFS interpretations. The *RDF and RDFS vocabulary, $rdfV \cup rdfsV$,* is a set of URI references listed with one-letter abbreviations in Table 1, plus 18 other URI references [2] (which play a smaller role in the semantics).

Table 1. Abbreviated notation for standard URI references

t	rdf:type	L	rdfs:Literal
P	rdf:Property	D	rdfs:Datatype
X	rdf:XMLLiteral	C	rdfs:Class
r_i	rdf:_i	s_C	rdfs:subClassOf
d	rdfs:domain	s_P	rdfs:subPropertyOf
r	rdfs:range	m	rdfs:member
R	rdfs:Resource	γ	rdfs:ContainerMembershipProperty

Let V be a vocabulary and I a simple interpretation of $V \cup \{t, C\}$ such that $I(t) \in P_I$, so that $E_I(I(t))$ is defined. In this case, the set C_I of *classes* of I is defined to be

$$C_I = \{a \in R_I : (a, I(C)) \in E_I(I(t))\},$$

and the *class extension function* $CE_I : C_I \to \mathcal{P}(R_I)$ of I is defined by

$$CE_I(a) = \{b \in R_I : (b, a) \in E_I(I(t))\} \quad (a \in C_I).$$

An *rdfs-interpretation* of a vocabulary V is a simple interpretation I of $V \cup rdfV \cup rdfsV$ that satisfies the following conditions:

- I satisfies all triples in Table 2, plus 32 other ground triples [2]. These triples are together called the *RDF* and *RDFS axiomatic triples*.
- $a \in P_I$ if and only if $(a, I(P)) \in E_I(I(t))$
- $a \in R_I$ if and only if $(a, I(R)) \in E_I(I(t))$
- $a \in LV_I$ if and only if $(a, I(L)) \in E_I(I(t))$
- If $(a, b) \in E_I(I(d))$ and $a \in P_I$ and $b \in C_I$ and $(e, f) \in E_I(a)$, then $e \in CE_I(b)$ [3]
- If $(a, b) \in E_I(I(r))$ and $a \in P_I$ and $b \in C_I$ and $(e, f) \in E_I(a)$, then $f \in CE_I(b)$
- $E_I(I(s_P))$ is transitive and reflexive on P_I
- If $(a, b) \in E_I(I(s_P))$ then $a \in P_I$ and $b \in P_I$ and $E_I(a) \subset E_I(b)$
- If $a \in C_I$ then $(a, I(R)) \in E_I(I(s_C))$
- If $(a, b) \in E_I(I(s_C))$ then $a \in C_I$ and $b \in C_I$ and $CE_I(a) \subset CE_I(b)$
- $E_I(I(s_C))$ is transitive and reflexive on C_I
- If $a \in CE_I(I(\gamma))$ then $(a, I(m)) \in E_I(I(s_P))$
- If $a \in CE_I(I(D))$ then $(a, I(L)) \in E_I(I(s_C))$
- If $l = (s, X) \in V$ is a well-typed XML literal, then $L_I(l) = xml(l) \in LV_I$ and $(L_I(l), I(X)) \in E_I(I(t))$
- If $l = (s, X) \in V$ is an XML literal that is not well-typed, then $L_I(l) \notin LV_I$ and $(L_I(l), I(X)) \notin E_I(I(t))$

---

[3] This condition and the next condition have been slightly reformulated, to make clear that the definition uses the functions E_I and CE_I inside their domains, as required. See the explanation following the definition. Lemma 3.2 below shows that exactly the same class of rdfs-interpretations is defined as in [2].

Table 2. RDF and RDFS axiomatic triples

$t\,t\,P$	$s_P\,d\,P$	$r\,r\,C$	$X\,s_C\,L$
$r_i\,t\,P$	$s_C\,d\,C$	$s_P\,r\,P$	$D\,s_C\,C$
$t\,d\,R$	$m\,d\,R$	$s_C\,r\,C$	$r_i\,t\,\gamma$
$d\,d\,P$	$t\,r\,C$	$\gamma\,s_C\,P$	$r_i\,d\,R$
$r\,d\,P$	$d\,r\,C$	$X\,t\,D$	$r_i\,r\,R$ $(i = 1, 2, ...)$

Here the function xml assigns to each well-typed XML literal its value [4]. Note that the first axiomatic triple $t\,t\,P$ shows that for each rdfs-interpretation I, $I(t) \in P_I$, so that $E_I(I(t))$, C_I, and CE_I are defined, as is used in the statement of the remaining conditions. By using the functions E_I and CE_I, the definition assumes, implicitly, that certain values of I, such as $I(d)$ and $I(r)$, are in P_I, and that other values of I, such as $I(D)$, are in C_I. That this is allowed is demonstrated in the next lemma. This lemma also justifies some other conclusions that can be stated for each rdfs-interpretation, and that are constantly used in the manipulation of rdfs-interpretations.

3.2 Lemma. *The first condition in the definition of rdfs-interpretations ensures that each invocation of the functions E_I and CE_I in this definition is allowed. If I is an rdfs-interpretation of a vocabulary V, then*

- *$I(t)$, $I(d)$, $I(r)$, $I(s_C)$, $I(s_P)$, and $I(m)$ are in P_I and $P_I \subset R_I$*
- *$I(P)$, $I(R)$, $I(C)$, $I(L)$, $I(D)$, $I(X)$, and $I(\gamma)$ are in C_I*
- *$P_I = CE_I(I(P))$, $C_I = CE_I(I(C))$, $R_I = CE_I(I(R))$, and $LV_I = CE_I(I(L))$*
- *if (a,b) is in $E_I(I(d))$ or $E_I(I(r))$, then $a \in P_I$ and $b \in C_I$*
- *if $(a,b) \in E_I(I(t))$, then $b \in C_I$ and $a \in CE_I(b)$*
- *if $(a,b) \in E_I(I(d))$ and $(e,f) \in E_I(a)$, then $e \in CE_I(b)$*
- *if $(a,b) \in E_I(I(r))$ and $(e,f) \in E_I(a)$, then $f \in CE_I(b)$*

3.3 Datatype maps. Before defining D* interpretations, we summarize some terminology and introduce some notation related to datatype maps [4] [2]. A *datatype* d is defined by a nonempty set of strings $L(d)$, the *lexical space*, a nonempty set $V(d)$, the *value space*, and a mapping $L2V(d) : L(d) \to V(d)$, the *lexical-to-value mapping*. A *datatype map* is a partial function D from the set U of URI references to the class of datatypes. Each datatype map is required [2] to contain the pair (X, x), where X is `rdf:XMLLiteral` and x is the built-in XML literal datatype, defined by $L(x) = \{s : (s, X) \in L_X^+\}$, $V(x) = XV$, and $L2V(x)(s) = xml((s, X))$ for each $(s, X) \in L_X^+$. Here L_X^+ is the set of well-typed XML literals [4].

Suppose that a datatype map D is given. The *D-vocabulary* is the *domain* $dom(D)$ of D, i.e., the set of URI references $a \in U$ such that $(a, d) \in D$ for some datatype d. The *range* of D, i.e., the set of datatypes d such that $(a, d) \in D$ for some $a \in U$, is denoted by $ran(D)$. The set of *D-literals* is the set of typed literals $(s, a) \in L_t$ with $a \in dom(D)$. The set of all well-typed literals with type in D, i.e., the set of all *well-typed D-literals*, is denoted by L_D^+:

$$L_D^+ = \{(s, a) \in L_t : a \in dom(D), s \in L(D(a))\}.$$

The function val_D is defined to map each well-typed D-literal to its value:

$$val_D : L_D^+ \to \bigcup_{d \in ran(D)} V(d) \, ,$$

$$val_D((s, a)) = L2V(D(a))(s) \quad (a \in dom(D), s \in L(D(a))) \, .$$

Injective datatype maps whose value spaces are disjoint and whose literal-to-value mappings are injective are of special importance in this paper; such datatype maps will be called *discriminating*. The assumption that a datatype map is discriminating is satisfied, for example, when it consists only of the four datatypes rdf:XMLLiteral, xsd:string, xsd:integer, and xsd:boolean.

3.4 Definition (D* interpretations). If D is a datatype map, a D^* *interpretation* of a vocabulary V is an rdfs-interpretation I of $V \cup dom(D)$ that satisfies the following conditions for each pair $(a, d) \in D$:

- $I(a) = d$
- I satisfies the following triples: $a\,t\,D$ and $a\,s_C\,L$
- if $l = (s, a') \in L_t \cap V$ and $I(a') = d$ and $s \in L(d)$, then $L_I(l) = L2V(d)(s) \in LV_I$ and $(L_I(l), d) \in E_I(I(t))$
- if $l = (s, a') \in L_t \cap V$ and $I(a') = d$ and $s \notin L(d)$, then $L_I(l) \notin LV_I$ and $(L_I(l), d) \notin E_I(I(t))$

If D is a datatype map, the triples $a\,t\,D$ and $a\,s_C\,L$ appearing in this definition are combined for $a \subset dom(D)$ to form the *D-axiomatic triples*. It should be noted that D* interpretations generalize the XMLLiteral-related conditions on rdfs-interpretations.[4]

4 RDFS Entailment and D* Entailment

4.1 Definition (D* entailment). Given a datatype map D, a set S of graphs D^* *entails* a graph G if each D* interpretation I that satisfies S also satisfies G.

RDFS entailment coincides with D* entailment when the datatype map D is assumed to consist of only the type rdf:XMLLiteral. We shall use the notation

$$S \models_s G$$

for D* entailment (and also for the special case of RDFS entailment).

---

[4] This correspondence with the XMLLiteral-related conditions would be exact when the phrase "if $l = (s, a') \in L_t \cap V$ and $I(a') = d$" starting the last two conditions on D* interpretations would in both cases be simplified to "if $l = (s, a) \in L_t \cap V$". In fact, this change can be made without leading to a change in entailments, as can be seen by checking the proof of the D* entailment lemma described below; only minor changes to the proof are needed. With the definition chosen, D* interpretations can be related in a simple way to the D-interpretations of [2]: If I is an rdfs-interpretation of a vocabulary V, then I is a D-interpretation of V if and only if I is a D* interpretation of V that satisfies $CE_I(d) = V(d)$ for each $d \in ran(D)$.

Table 3. D* entailment rules

	If G contains		where	then add to G
lg	$v\,p\,l$		$l \in L$	$v\,p\,b_l$
gl	$v\,p\,b_l$			$v\,p\,l$
rdf1	$v\,p\,w$			$p\,t\,P$
rdf2-D	$v\,p\,l$		$l = (s,a) \in L_D^+$	$b_l\,t\,a$
rdfs1	$v\,p\,l$		$l \in L_{\mathrm{p}}$	$b_l\,t\,L$
rdfs2	$p\,d\,u$	$v\,p\,w$		$v\,t\,u$
rdfs3	$p\,r\,u$	$v\,p\,w$	$w \in U \cup B$	$w\,t\,u$
rdfs4a	$v\,p\,w$			$v\,t\,R$
rdfs4b	$v\,p\,w$		$w \in U \cup B$	$w\,t\,R$
rdfs5	$v\,sp\,w$	$w\,sp\,u$		$v\,sp\,u$
rdfs6	$v\,t\,P$			$v\,sp\,v$
rdfs7	$p\,sp\,q$	$v\,p\,w$	$q \in U$	$v\,q\,w$
rdfs8	$v\,t\,C$			$v\,sc\,R$
rdfs9	$v\,sc\,w$	$u\,t\,v$		$u\,t\,w$
rdfs10	$v\,t\,C$			$v\,sc\,v$
rdfs11	$v\,sc\,w$	$w\,sc\,u$		$v\,sc\,u$
rdfs12	$v\,t\,\gamma$			$v\,sp\,m$
rdfs13	$v\,t\,D$			$v\,sc\,L$

4.2 Definition (D* entailment rules). Given a datatype map D, the D* entailment rules are defined in Table 3. They consist of exactly the 18 rules defined in [2] for RDFS, the only difference being that rule rdf2 is replaced by the more general rule rdf2-D. In words, the first rule lg ('literal generalization') says that if G contains $v\,p\,l$, where l is a literal, then add $v\,p\,b_l$ to G, where b_l is a blank node allocated to l by this rule. Here *allocated to* means that the blank node b_l has been created by an application of rule lg on the same literal l, or if there is no such blank node, in which case it must be a new node which is not yet in the graph. In rule rdfs1, b_l is a blank node that is allocated by rule lg to the plain literal $l \in L_{\mathrm{p}}$. In rule rdf2-D, b_l is a blank node that is allocated by rule lg to the well-typed D-literal $l \in L_D^+$. Note that rule rdf2-D is a direct generalization of entailment rule rdf2 from [2], which has the same effect only for well-typed XML literals $l \in L_X^+$. If D contains only the datatype rdf:XMLLiteral, then rule rdf2-D becomes exactly rule rdf2.

The notion of XML clash from [2] is generalized in a straightforward way to any datatype map.

4.3 Definition (D-clash). Given a datatype map D, a *D-clash* is a triple $b\,t\,L$, where b is a blank node allocated by rule lg to an ill-typed D-literal.

We turn to completeness and decidability. As was also done in earlier versions of [2], we extract from the completeness proof the notions of closure and Herbrand interpretation, as well as a satisfaction lemma. In view of the finiteness of a partial closure, the closure notion is of practical interest and is no longer just an 'abstraction in the proof'. The Herbrand construction of [2] will need to be refined, to deal with the finiteness of a partial closure and with datatypes.

4.4 Definition (partial and full RDFS and D* closures). Suppose that G is an RDF graph and D a datatype map. In the definitions that follow, the axiomatic triples containing the URI references r_i (i.e., the four triples $r_i\,t\,P$, $r_i\,t\,\gamma$, $r_i\,d\,R$, and $r_i\,r\,R$) are treated in a special way. Suppose that K is a nonempty subset of the positive integers $\{1, 2, ...\}$ chosen in such a way that for each $r_i \in V(G)$ we have $i \in K$. The *partial D^* closure $G_{s,K}$* of G is defined in the following way. In the first step, all RDF and RDFS axiomatic triples and D-axiomatic triples are added to G, except for the axiomatic triples including r_i such that $i \notin K$. In the next step, rule lg is applied to each triple containing a literal. Then, rules rdf2-D and rdfs1 are applied to each triple containing a well-typed D-literal or a plain literal, respectively. Finally, the remaining D^* entailment rules are applied until the graph is unchanged. In addition to the partial D^* closure $G_{s,K}$ obtained in this way, the *full D^* closure G_s* of G is defined by taking $G_s = G_{s,K}$ where K is the full set $\{1, 2, ...\}$. When the datatype map D consists of only the datatype `rdf:XMLLiteral`, a partial and a full D^* closure of an RDF graph G are called a *partial* and a *full RDFS closure* of G, respectively. With respect to a partial (or full) D^* closure $G_{s,K}$ and a literal $l \in V(G) \cap L$, the unique blank node allocated by rule lg to l is denoted by b_l.

4.5 Lemma. *Let D be a finite datatype map. If G is a finite RDF graph, then each partial D^* closure $G_{s,K}$ of G is finite for K finite, and a partial D^* closure of G can be computed in polynomial time.*

Proof. The graph obtained from a finite graph G in the first step of the definition of partial closure is clearly finite when K is finite. Then, rule lg adds only finitely many new triples, leading to a finite graph G' containing G. In the remaining steps, no new names or blank nodes are added to G', so it follows that there exist finite sets $U_0 \subset U$, $B_0 \subset B$, and $L_0 \subset L$ such that

$$G_{s,K} \subset \; U_0 \cup B_0 \; \times \; U_0 \; \times \; U_0 \cup B_0 \cup L_0 \,. \tag{2}$$

Hence $G_{s,K}$ is a finite graph.

To prove that a partial D^* closure can be computed in polynomial time, choose a finite, nonempty set $K \subset \{1, 2, ...\}$ such that $i \in K$ for each $r_i \in V(G)$. Let $g = |G|$, $d = |D|$, and $k = |K|$. We prove that $G_{s,K}$ can be computed in time polynomial in g, d, and k. It will follow that a partial D^* closure can be computed in time polynomial in g, since k can clearly be taken to be $3g + 1$, and d can be viewed as a bounded parameter. The first step of the closure construction process adds $48 + 4k$ RDF and RDFS axiomatic triples and $2d$ D-axiomatic triples. In the next step, rule lg adds at most g triples. It follows that the graph G' resulting from these steps has at most $2g + 2d + 4k + 48$ triples, so that the sets U_0, B_0, and L_0 in (2) can be chosen to satisfy $|U_0 \cup B_0 \cup L_0| \leq 3(2g + 2d + 4k + 48)$, and $|G_{s,K}| \leq 27(2g + 2d + 4k + 48)^3$. Therefore, in the remaining steps at most $27(2g + 2d + 4k + 48)^3$ rule applications can add a new triple to the partial closure graph under construction. For each of the entailment rules used, it can be determined whether a successful rule application exists in at most linear or quadratic time as a function of the size of the partial closure graph under construction (cf. Table 3). For example, for rule rdf1 linear time is sufficient, and for rule rdfs2 quadratic time is sufficient. It follows that $G_{s,K}$ can be computed in time polynomial in g, d, and k.

4.6 Definition (D* Herbrand interpretation). Suppose that D is a discriminating datatype map. A *D* Herbrand interpretation* of a graph G is a simple interpretation $S_K(G)$ of $V(G_s)$ defined as follows. K is a nonempty subset of $\{1, 2, ...\}$ chosen such that for each $r_i \in V(G)$ we have $i \in K$. R_I is defined as the union of four pairwise disjoint sets:

$$val_D(V(G_s) \cap L_D^+)$$

$$V(G_s) \cap (L - L_D^+)$$

$$V(G_s) \cap (U \cup B - dom(D))$$

$$ran(D)$$

The remainder of the definition makes use of the function

$$sur : R_I \to nd(G_{s,K}) \cap (U \cup B)$$

('surrogate'), which replaces the elements of R_I by non-literal nodes in $G_{s,K}$. The function sur is defined as follows, using the assumption on D:

- If $l \in V(G_s) \cap L_D^+$, then $sur(val_D(l)) = b_l$.
- If $l \in V(G_s) \cap (L - L_D^+)$, then $sur(l) = b_l$.
- If $v \in V(G_s) \cap (U \cup B - (dom(D) \cup \{r_i : i \notin K\}))$, then $sur(v) = v$.
- If $i \notin K$, then $sur(r_i) = r_n$, where $n \in K$ is fixed.
- If $(a, d) \in D$, then $sur(d) = a$.

The other parts of the $S_K(G)$ are defined in the following way:

$$LV_I = \{x \in R_I : sur(x)\, t\, L \in G_{s,K}\}$$

$$P_I = \{x \in R_I : sur(x)\, t\, P \in G_{s,K}\}$$

$$S_I(v) = v \quad (v \in V(G_s) \cap U - dom(D))$$

$$S_I(a) = D(a) \quad (a \in V(G_s) \cap dom(D))$$

$$L_I(v) = v \quad (v \in V(G_s) \cap L_t - L_D^+)$$

$$L_I(l) = val_D(l) \quad (l \in V(G_s) \cap L_D^+)$$

$$E_I(p) = \{(s, o) : s \in R_I, o \in R_I, sur(s)\, sur(p)\, sur(o) \in G_{s,K}\} \quad (p \in P_I)$$

Note that for each $v \in V(G_s) \cap (U - \{r_i : i \notin K\})$, we have $sur(I(v)) = v$, and that $sur(I(r_i)) = r_n$ for $i \notin K$. Moreover, if $l \in V(G_s) \cap L$, then $sur(I(l)) = b_l$.

4.7 D* satisfaction lemma. *Let G be an RDF graph and D a discriminating datatype map. If the partial D* closure $G_{s,K}$ of G does not contain a D-clash, then $S_K(G)$ is a D* interpretation that satisfies $G_{s,K}$.*

Proof. In the proof the D* Herbrand interpretation $S_K(G)$ of G is denoted by I. Define the function $A : bl(G_{s,K}) \to R_I$ by $A(b_l) = val_D(l)$ if $l \in L_D^+$, $A(b_l) = l$ if $l \in L - L_D^+$, and by $A(b) = b$ for other blank nodes b. Rule rdf1 shows that for each triple $v\,p\,w$ in $G_{s,K}$, $G_{s,K}$ contains the triple $p\,t\,P = sur(I(p))\,t\,P$, so that $I(p) \in P_I$. In order to prove that I_A satisfies $v\,p\,w$, i.e. that $(I_A(v), I_A(w)) \in E_I(I(p))$, it is sufficient to prove that $sur(I_A(v))\,p\,sur(I_A(w)) \in G_{s,K}$, since $sur(I(p)) = p$. In order to prove that this triple is indeed in $G_{s,K}$, note first that

$$sur(I_A(v)) = v \quad (v \in nd(G_{s,K}) - L).$$

Namely, as is easy to see, this holds in each of the following cases where $v \in nd(G_{s,K}) - L$: $v \in U$, $v \in B$ allocated to a literal in L_D^+ or in $L - L_D^+$, other blank nodes v. Moreover, we have $sur(I_A(l)) = b_l$ for each $l \in nd(G_{s,K}) \cap L$, as was already noted. It follows that if $v\,p\,w \in G_{s,K}$, then $sur(I_A(v))\,p\,sur(I_A(w)) \in G_{s,K}$, as desired: the only case that needs checking is where $w \in L$. In this case rule lg shows that $v\,p\,b_w \in G_{s,K}$, as required: there is no entailment rule that can be applied with a literal in object position but that cannot be applied with a blank node in object position, so rule applications used to derive $v\,p\,w$ can be followed in parallel with other rule applications to provide a derivation of $v\,p\,b_w$.

Note that $S_K(G)$ satisfies all axiomatic triples, even though $G_{s,K}$ may not contain all of them: if $i \notin K$ then $sur(r_i) = r_n$, and the axiomatic triples including r_i are also satisfied. For example, the triple $r_i\,t\,P$ is satisfied because $sur(r_i)\,t\,P = r_n\,t\,P \in G_{s,K}$.

We turn to the assumptions on D* interpretations. Suppose that $(a, d) \in D$. If $l = (s, a') \in V(G_s) \cap L_t$ and $I(a') = d$, then the assumption on D shows that $a = a'$. Suppose therefore that $l = (s, a)$ is a well-typed D-literal in $V(G_s)$. Then $I(l) = val_D(l) = L2V(d)(s) = A(b_l)$. In order to prove that $I(l) \in LV_I$, we need to prove that $sur(I(l))\,t\,L = b_l\,t\,L \in G_{s,K}$. Rule rdf2-D shows that the triple $b_l\,t\,a$ is in $G_{s,K}$. With the axiomatic triple $a\,s_C\,L$ and rule rdfs9 it follows that $b_l\,t\,L \in G_{s,K}$. We also have $(L_I(l), d) = (I_A(b_l), I_A(a)) \subset E_I(I(t))$, since $sur(I_A(b_l))\,t\,sur(I_A(a)) = b_l\,t\,a \in G_{s,K}$.

Suppose that $(a, d) \in D$ and that $l = (s, a) \in V(G_s)$ is a D-literal that is not well-typed. Then $A(b_l) = l$. Suppose that $(L_I(l), d) \in E_I(I(t))$; then $b_l\,t\,a = sur(L_I(l))\,t\,sur(d) \in G_{s,K}$, so that with the axiomatic triple $a\,s_C\,L$ and rule rdfs9 it follows that $b_l\,t\,L \in G_{s,K}$: $G_{s,K}$ contains a D-clash. Suppose that $L_I(l) \in LV_I$; then, again, $b_l\,t\,L = sur(L_I(l))\,t\,L \in G_{s,K}$: $G_{s,K}$ contains a D-clash.

We show that $a \in R_I$ if and only if $(a, R) \in E_I(t)$. If $(a, I(R)) \in E_I(t)$, then clearly $a \in R_I$. Suppose that $a \in R_I$. It is sufficient to prove that $sur(a)\,t\,R \in G_{s,K}$. If $a = val_D(l)$, $l \in V(G_s) \cap L_D^+$, then $sur(a) = b_l$ and $G_{s,K}$ contains triples $v\,p\,l$ and $v\,p\,b_l$. Rule rdfs4b shows that $sur(a)\,t\,R = b_l\,t\,R \in G_{s,K}$. If $a = l \in V(G_s) \cap (L - L_D^+)$, then $sur(l) = b_l$ and $G_{s,K}$ contains triples $v\,p\,l$ and $v\,p\,b_l$. Again, rule rdfs4b shows that $sur(l)\,t\,R = b_l\,t\,R \in G_{s,K}$. If $a \in V(G_s) \cap (U \cup B - (dom(D) \cup \{r_i : i \notin K\}))$, then $sur(a) = a$ and $G_{s,K}$ contains, by rule rdf1, a triple of the form $a\,p\,v$ or $v\,p\,a$, so that by rule rdfs4a or rdfs4b, we have $sur(a)\,t\,R = a\,t\,R \in G_{s,K}$. If $a = r_i$ and $i \notin K$, then $sur(r_i)\,t\,R = r_n\,t\,R \in G_{s,K}$ in view of $r_n\,t\,P \in G_{s,K}$ and rule rdfs4a. If $a = d \in ran(D)$, then D contains a pair (a', d) and $G_{s,K}$ contains the axiomatic triple $a'\,t\,D$. Rule rdfs4a shows that $G_{s,K}$ contains the triple $sur(d)\,t\,R = a'\,t\,R$.

4.8 D* entailment lemma. *Let D be a discriminating datatype map, S a set of RDF graphs, and G an RDF graph. Then, $S \models_s G$ if and only if there* *is a graph H that can be derived from $M(S)$ combined with RDF and RDFS axiomatic triples and D-axiomatic triples, by application of the D* entailment rules, and that either simply entails G or contains a D-clash.*

The next statement gives a more precise version of this lemma.

4.9 D* entailment lemma (alternative statement). *Let D be a discriminating datatype map, S a set of RDF graphs, and G an RDF graph. Let H be a partial D* closure $M(S)_{s,K}$ of $M(S)$ and suppose that $i \in K$ for each $r_i \in V(G)$. Then, $S \models_s G$ if and only if either H simply entails G or H contains a D-clash.*

4.10 Corollary. *Let D be a finite discriminating datatype map. The D* entailment relation $S \models_s G$ between finite sets S of finite RDF graphs and finite RDF graphs G is decidable. This problem is in NP, and in P when G is ground.*

Proof of corollary. Take a partial D* closure $H = M(S)_{s,K}$ of $M(S)$ such that K is finite and $i \in K$ for each $r_i \in V(G)$, and check whether this graph contains a D-clash or whether this graph simply entails G. By Lemma 4.5, H can be computed in time polynomial in $|M(S)| + |G|$. The proof is concluded by using the remarks following the interpolation lemma (see 2.5).

Proof of D* entailment lemma (completeness part). Let $H = M(S)_{s,K}$ be a partial D* closure of $M(S)$ such that $i \in K$ for each $r_i \in V(G)$, and let I be the associated D* Herbrand interpretation $S_K(M(S))$. If H does not contain a D-clash, then I is a D* interpretation which satisfies H, so I satisfies S. By $S \models_s G$, I satisfies G. Choose $A : bl(G) \to R_I$ such that I_A satisfies G. It follows that for each triple $s\,p\,o \in G$, $E_I(I(p))$ contains the pair $(I_A(s), I_A(o))$. Therefore, for each triple $s\,p\,o \in G$, H contains the triple

$$sur(I_A(s))\ sur(I(p))\ sur(I_A(o)).$$

The assumption that $i \in K$ for each $r_i \in V(G)$ implies that if $v \in V(G) \cap U$, then $sur(I(v)) = v$. Moreover, if $l \in nd(G) \cap L$ then $sur(I(l)) = b_l$. Define the mapping $h : bl(G) \to nd(H)$ to be $h = sur \circ A$, and extend h to all of $nd(G)$ by $h(v) = v$ for each $v \in nd(G) - bl(G)$. It follows that

- if $s\,p\,o \in G$ and o is not in L, then $h(s)\,p\,h(o) \in H$
- if $l \in L$ and $s\,p\,l \in G$, then $h(s)\,p\,b_l \in H$.

In the second of these two cases, it also follows that $h(s)\,p\,h(l) = h(s)\,p\,l \in H$, in view of rule gl. Hence there is a subgraph of H that is an instance of G, with respect to the instance mapping h. It follows that H simply entails G.

5   pD* Interpretations and pD* Entailment

In this section, we extend the above results on RDFS entailment and D* entailment to a subset of OWL related to properties (see Table 4). We do not obtain the full power of the 'iff-semantics' of the W3C's OWL semantics specification [5]. We consider a weaker semantics, in line with the 'if-semantics' of RDFS. This leads to simple and useful entailment rules, which can be used to extend RDF reasoners. This weaker semantics, which is computationally less complex, seems to be sufficient for many applications of this subset of OWL.

Table 4. Abbreviations of property-related vocabulary

F	FunctionalProperty	S	SymmetricProperty
F'	InverseFunctionalProperty	T	TransitiveProperty
s	sameAs	i	inverseOf

Table 5. P-axiomatic triples

$F\,sc\,P$	$S\,sc\,P$	$st\,P$	$id\,P$
$F'\,sc\,P$	$T\,sc\,P$	$it\,P$	$ir\,P$

5.1 Definition (pD* interpretations). The *P-vocabulary*, denoted by *propV*, is a set of URI references listed in Table 4, together with one-letter abbreviations.

Let D be a datatype map. A *pD* interpretation* of a vocabulary V is a D* interpretation I of $V \cup propV$ that satisfies the following conditions:

- I satisfies the triples in Table 5, which are called the *P-axiomatic triples*.
- If $p \in CE_I(I(F))$ and $(a,b),(a,c) \in E_I(p)$ then $(b,c) \in E_I(I(s))$
- If $p \in CE_I(I(F'))$ and $(a,c),(b,c) \in E_I(p)$ then $(a,b) \in E_I(I(s))$
- If $p \in CE_I(I(S))$ and $(a,b) \in E_I(p)$ then $(b,a) \in E_I(p)$
- If $p \in CE_I(I(T))$ and $(a,b),(b,c) \in E_I(p)$ then $(a,c) \in E_I(p)$
- $E_I(I(s))$ is an equivalence relation on R_I
- If $(p,q) \in E_I(I(i))$ then $(a,b) \in E_I(p)$ if and only if $(b,a) \in E_I(q)$
- If $a \in C_I$ and $(a,b) \in E_I(I(s))$ then $(a,b) \in E_I(I(s_C))$
- If $p \in P_I$ and $(p,q) \in E_I(I(s))$ then $(p,q) \in E_I(I(s_P))$

5.2 Lemma. *The first condition in the definition of pD* interpretations ensures that each invocation of the functions E_I and CE_I in this definition is allowed. If I is a pD* interpretation of a vocabulary V, then $I(s)$ and $I(i)$ are in P_I, and $I(F)$, $I(F')$, $I(S)$, and $I(T)$ are in C_I.*

5.3 Definition (pD* entailment). Given a datatype map D, a set S of RDF graphs *pD* entails* an RDF graph G if each pD* interpretation I that satisfies S also satisfies G. In this case, we shall write

$$S \models_{\mathrm{p}} G.$$

It is clear that each OWL interpretation [5] is a pD* interpretation, so that if $S \models_{\mathrm{p}} G$, then S OWL Full entails G.

5.4 Definition (P-entailment rules). See Table 6.

5.5 Definition (partial and full pD* closures). Suppose that G is an RDF graph and D a datatype map. The *partial pD* closure* $G_{\mathrm{p},K}$ of G, and the *full pD* closure* G_{p} of G, are defined in a way similar to the definition of the partial and full D* closures $G_{\mathrm{s},K}$ and G_{s} of G (see 4.4). The only differences are in the first and last steps. In the first step, the 8 P-axiomatic triples are also added to G. In the last step, the P-entailment rules are used as well.

Table 6. P-entailment rules

	If G contains			where	then add to G
rdfp1	$pt\,F$	$u\,p\,v$	$u\,p\,w$	$v \in U \cup B$	$v\,s\,w$
rdfp2	$pt\,F'$	$u\,p\,w$	$v\,p\,w$		$u\,s\,v$
rdfp3	$pt\,S$	$v\,p\,w$		$w \in U \cup B$	$w\,p\,v$
rdfp4	$pt\,T$	$u\,p\,v$	$v\,p\,w$		$u\,p\,w$
rdfp5a	$v\,p\,w$				$v\,s\,v$
rdfp5b	$v\,p\,w$			$w \in U \cup B$	$w\,s\,w$
rdfp6	$v\,s\,w$			$w \in U \cup B$	$w\,s\,v$
rdfp7	$u\,s\,v$	$v\,s\,w$			$u\,s\,w$
rdfp8a	$p\,i\,q$	$v\,p\,w$		$w \in U \cup B$ and $q \in U$	$w\,q\,v$
rdfp8b	$p\,i\,q$	$v\,q\,w$		$w \in U \cup B$ and $q \in U$	$w\,p\,v$
rdfp9	$v\,t\,C$	$v\,s\,w$			$v\,s_C\,w$
rdfp10	$pt\,P$	$p\,s\,q$			$p\,s_P\,q$

5.6 Lemma. *Let D be a finite datatype map. If G is a finite RDF graph, then each partial pD^* closure $G_{p,K}$ of G is finite for K finite, and a partial pD^* closure of G can be computed in polynomial time.*

Proof. This is proved as for partial D^* closures (see 4.5). For the last part of the proof, note that for rules rdfp1, rdfp2 and rdfp4, the existence of a successful rule application can be detected in time $O(|G''|^3)$, where G'' is the partial closure graph under construction. The other P-entailment rules can be handled in linear or quadratic time, just like the D^* entailment rules.

5.7 Definition (pD^* Herbrand interpretation). Given a discriminating datatype map D and an RDF graph G, a *pD^* Herbrand interpretation* $P_K(G)$ is defined in a similar way as a D^* Herbrand interpretation $S_K(G)$ (see 4.6). The only differences are that G_s is replaced by G_p and $G_{s,K}$ by $G_{p,K}$.

5.8 pD^* satisfaction lemma. *Let G be an RDF graph and D a discriminating datatype map. If the partial pD^* closure $G_{p,K}$ of G does not contain a D-clash, then $P_K(G)$ is a pD^* interpretation that satisfies $G_{p,K}$.*

Proof. We consider here only the most complicated addition to be made to the proof of the D^* satisfaction lemma (see 4.7), which is reflexivity. To prove reflexivity of $E_I(I(s))$ on R_I, where $I = P_K(G)$, the four parts of the definition of R_I need to be considered separately. Suppose first that $l \in V(G_p) \cap L_D^+$. Then by rule rdfp5b, $G_{p,K}$ contains the triple $b_l\,s\,b_l = sur(val_D(l))\,s\,sur(val_D(l))$, so that $(val_D(l), val_D(l)) \in E_I(s)$, as desired. Suppose next that $l \in V(G_p) \cap (L - L_D^+)$. Again by rule rdfp5b, $G_{p,K}$ contains the triple $b_l\,s\,b_l = sur(l)\,s\,sur(l)$, so that $(l, l) \in E_I(I(s))$, as desired. Suppose next that $a \in V(G_p) \cap (U \cup B - (dom(D) \cup \{r_i : i \notin K\}))$. Then, $sur(a) = a$ and $G_{p,K}$ contains, by rule rdf1, a triple of the form $a\,p\,v$ or $v\,p\,a$, so that by rules rdfp5a and rdfp5b, it follows that $G_{p,K}$ contains the triple $a\,s\,a = sur(a)\,s\,sur(a)$, so that $(a, a) \in E_I(I(s))$. If $i \notin K$, then $sur(r_i) = r_n$ and $G_{p,K}$ contains the axiomatic triple $r_n\,t\,P$, so that by rule rdfp5a, $sur(r_i)\,s\,sur(r_i) = r_n\,s\,r_n \in G_{p,K}$ and $(r_i, r_i) \in E_I(I(s))$. If $d \in ran(D)$, then D contains a pair (a, d) and $G_{p,K}$ contains the axiomatic triple $a\,t\,D$. In view of rule rdfp5a, it follows that $G_{p,K}$ contains the triple $a\,s\,a = sur(d)\,s\,sur(d)$, so that $(d,d) \in E_I(I(s))$.

5.9 pD* entailment lemma. *Let D be a discriminating datatype map, S a set of RDF graphs, and G an RDF graph. Then, $S \models_p G$ if and only if there is a graph H that can be derived from $M(S)$ combined with RDF and RDFS axiomatic triples and D-axiomatic triples and P-axiomatic triples, by application of D* entailment rules and P-entailment rules, and that either simply entails G or contains a D-clash.*

5.10 pD* entailment lemma (alternative statement). *Let D be a discriminating datatype map, S a set of RDF graphs, and G an RDF graph. Let H be a partial pD* closure $M(S)_{p,K}$ of $M(S)$ and suppose that $i \in K$ for each $r_i \in V(G)$. Then, $S \models_p G$ if and only if either $H \models G$ or H contains a D-clash.*

5.11 Corollary. *Let D be a finite discriminating datatype map. The pD* entailment relation $S \models_p G$ between finite sets S of finite RDF graphs and finite RDF graphs G is decidable. This problem is in NP, and in P when G is ground.*

Proof. Most of the work to be added to the proof for D* entailment involves the validity of the P-entailment rules, and this does not present problems.

6   Conclusion

In this paper we proved that rdfs-entailment is decidable, by using partial closure graphs that are finite for finite RDF graphs. It was also proved that these partial closure graphs can be computed in polynomial time, and that the problem 'H rdfs-entails G', with H and G finite RDF graphs, is in NP, and in P when G is assumed to have no blank nodes. Results on RDFS completeness, decidability, and complexity were extended to include reasoning with datatypes and a property-related subset of OWL.

Acknowledgment. I would like to thank Warner ten Kate, Jan Korst, and the anonymous referees for comments that helped to improve the manuscript.

References

1. J. Grant, D. Beckett (Eds.), RDF Test Cases, W3C Recommendation, 10 February 2004, http://www.w3.org/TR/2004/REC-rdf-testcases-20040210/
2. P. Hayes (Ed.), RDF Semantics, W3C Recommendation, 10 February 2004, http://www.w3.org/TR/2004/REC-rdf-mt-20040210/
3. I. Horrocks, P.F. Patel-Schneider, Reducing OWL Entailment to Description Logic Satisfiability, Proceedings of the 2nd International Semantic Web Conference, Springer-Verlag LNCS 2870, 2003, pp. 17-29.
4. G. Klyne, J. Carroll (Eds.), Resource Description Framework (RDF): Concepts and Abstract Syntax, W3C Recommendation, 10 February 2004, http://www.w3.org/TR/2004/REC-rdf-concepts-20040210/
5. P.F. Patel-Schneider, P. Hayes, I. Horrocks (Eds.), OWL Web Ontology Language Semantics and Abstract Syntax, W3C Recommendation, 10 February 2004, http://www.w3.org/TR/2004/REC-owl-semantics-20040210/

Using Semantic Web Technologies for Representing E-science Provenance

Jun Zhao[1], Chris Wroe[1], Carole Goble[1], Robert Stevens[1], Dennis Quan[2], and Mark Greenwood[1]

[1] Department of Computer Science
University of Manchester
Oxford Road Manchester
United Kingdom M13 9PL
{zhaoj,carole,robert.stevens,cwroe}@cs.man.ac.uk
[2] IBM T. J. Watson Research Center
1 Rogers Street Cambridge
MA 02142 USA
dennisq@us.ibm.com

Abstract. Life science researchers increasingly rely on the web as a primary source of data, forcing them to apply the same rigor to its use as to an experiment in the laboratory. The ^{my}Grid project is developing the use of *workflows* to explicitly capture web-based procedures, and *provenance* to describe how and why results were produced. Experience within ^{my}Grid has shown that this provenance metadata is formed from a complex web of heterogenous resources that impact on the production of a result. Therefore we have explored the use of Semantic Web technologies such as RDF, and ontologies to support its representation and used existing initiatives such as Jena and LSID, to generate and store such material. The effective presentation of complex RDF graphs is challenging. Haystack has been used to provide multiple views of provenance metadata that can be further annotated. This work therefore forms a case study showing how existing Semantic Web tools can effectively support the emerging requirements of life science research.

1 Introduction

Life science researchers have made early and heavy use of Web technologies to access large datasets and applications [1]. Initiatives such as the Human Genome Project [2] have meant that rather than sequencing human genes in the laboratory, it is possible to download sequences from the Web. As well as data, tools are also available on the Web, and data are moved between tools to perform analyses [1]. The greater reliance on these resources as primary sources of data means *ad hoc* web browsing is giving way to a more systematic approach embodied by the term e-Science within the UK research community [3]. By analogy to the laboratory, web-based procedures to analyze or integrate data are called *in silico* experiments.

S.A. McIlraith et al. (Eds.): ISWC 2004, LNCS 3298, pp. 92–106, 2004.
© Springer-Verlag Berlin Heidelberg 2004

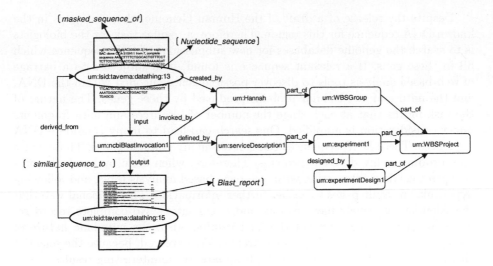

Fig. 1. An example e-Science provenance log.

The results of an *in silico* experiment are of reduced value if the materials, methods, goals, hypotheses and conclusions of an experiment are not recorded. Traditionally, in the lab, a scientist records such information in a lab-book and uses these records of where, how and why results were generated in the process of analysing, validating and publishing scientific findings. These records are the *provenance* of an experiment. Provenance data are also needed for e-Science *in silico* experiments, in order to help e-Scientists to verify results, draw conclusions and test hypotheses. In e-Science provenance logs, each piece of data used in an *in silico* experiment; the tools used to analyse those data; the results generated; and the associations and derivations of these data and tools need to be recorded. Part of such a provenance log for an e-Science experiment is shown in Fig 1. The recording, indexing, organisation and use of these provenance data are a key aspect of e-Science.

^{my}Grid [1], as a pilot e-Science project in the U.K., aims to provide middleware services not only to automate the execution of *in silico* experiments as workflows in a Grid environment, but also to manage and use results from experiments [4]. Currently this project is being developed using several molecular biological scenarios. This paper uses the collaboration with biologists and bioinformaticians at Manchester University, researching the genetic basis of Williams-Beuren Syndrome [5]. Williams-Beuren Syndrome is a congenital disorder associated with the deletion of a small region of Human Chromosome 7. There is significant interest in characterising the genes in this region, in order to gain an insight into how an apparently small number of genes can lead to a complex set of cognitive and physical phenotypes.

---

[1] http://www.mygrid.org.uk.

Despite the release of a draft of the Human Genome, there are gaps in the known DNA sequence for this region. Therefore, a regular task for the biologists is to search the genome databases for new submissions of DNA sequence which fill in these gaps. If a relevant sequence is found, it is subjected to a barrage of web-based analysis tools to discover possible genes encoded within the DNA, and the nature of any cellular proteins produced by those genes. The nature of the task means that at each stage the number of resources and data fragments under consideration is amplified. One search can lead to many candidate DNA sequences. These DNA sequences can contain many possible genes. Those genes may produce many different proteins. Therefore, when done by hand, the process can take days interacting with web page based analysis tools, and following hyperlinks in result pages to gather further information. This personal web that the scientist selectively navigates around is transitory. No complete record remains to explain the origin of the final results. Also, the mundane nature of the task often means not all possible avenues are explored, because the scientist either misses possible routes or discards apparently uninteresting results.

^{my}Grid was used to automate this process, and so each web-based analysis tool and data resource were wrapped as a web service. Workflows were designed to automatically orchestrate the access to these resources and data flow between them. Figure 2 shows a graphical representation of one workflow from this project, which uses two main bioinformatics applications RepeatMasker and NCBI BLAST, in order to discover new DNA sequences in the gap region for this disease. The previously transient relationships between resources have been captured as a web of provenance information, part of which is shown in Fig 1. Often discarded intermediate results are assigned identifiers and published locally, so that they become first class resources of this personal web of science [6]. In order to build this personal web, Life Science Identifiers (LSIDs) [7] are used to provide location-independent access to these resource data and metadata. The Resource Description Framework (RDF) is used to represent the web of relationships between resources by associating semantic information with these resources and their relationships, creating a Semantic Web of Provenance data. Haystack, a Semantic Web browser [8], is used to deliver these provenance webs to the end user.

If provenance information is to be shared, we need to overcome their heterogeneiety and agree on a common understanding (or semantics) as to what the contents of each data item and service represents and the relationships we provide between resources. Semantic Web ontology languages such as DAML+OIL and its successor OWL have been used to capture this semantic information [9].

As with previous web technologies, there is much interest in the life science community in the potential uses of the Semantic Web. Key organisations such as Affymetrix are publishing data in RDF format [10] and mailing lists such as the WWW Semantic Web Life Sciences mailing list are discussing how best to embrace the new technology[2]. By using existing Semantic Web technology and software such as RDF repositories, ontologies, Haystack and Life Science

---

[2] Archives at http://lists.w3.org/Archives/Public/public-semweb-lifesci/

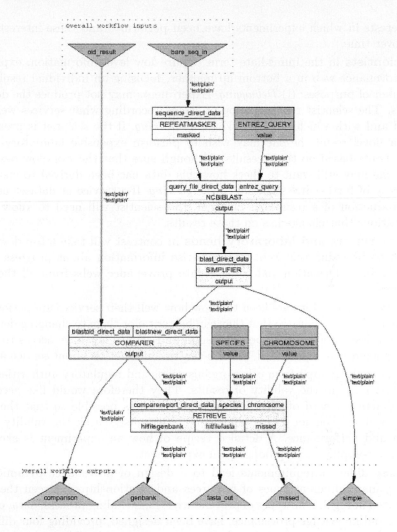

Fig. 2. An example workflow from the Williams-Beuren Syndrome scenario.

Identifiers, this work acts as a case study describing what is already possible in supporting life scientists with a Semantic Web. In this paper Sect 2 describes scientists' requirements for provenance and the implications of the information recorded. Section 3 describes why Semantic Web technologies are well suited to supporting our requirements. Section 4 describes the implementation of provenance recording and visualization.

2   Provenance Requirements and Design

Provenance has a very broad scope within e-Science. At its simplest, it describes from where something has arisen. But many different parties may have a variety of interests in which experiments have been performed and these interests will vary over time.

Scientists in the immediate term require low level information, exploring the provenance web in a bottom up manner, focusing on individual results for a number of purposes: (i) *Debugging*. Experiments may not produce the desired results. The scientist requires a log of events recording what services were accessed and with which data; (ii) *Validity checking*. If the scientist is presented with a novel result, he/she may wish to perform expensive laboratory-based experiments based on these results. Although sure that the workflow design is valid, she may still want to check how this data has been derived to ensure it is worthy of further investigation; (iii) *Updating*. If a service or dataset used in the production of a result has changed, the scientist will need to know what implications that change has on those results.

Supervisors and laboratory heads in contrast will take a top down approach to browsing this web, to summarise information about progress made in gathering information and to aggregate provenance webs from all their researchers.

Service providers are keen to know how well their services are performing and their patterns of use so that they can better tailor them to changing demand. They are less interested in specific results and should not have access to them but focus more on aggregated, process-centric information about service access.

Research groups from other organisations and regulatory authorities may have less trust in the validity of results. They therefore would like access to as complete a record of the *in silico* experiment as possible so that they can replicate it in their local environment and rigorously check the validity of its design and performance. A detailed recipe of how an experiment is executed should be supplied for reproducing an experiment.

These different requirements lead to a design of provenance pyramid embracing many different types of resources and relationships between them, as illustrated in Fig 3. Four types of provenance logs, including process, data, organisation and knowledge provenance, have been designed, providing four different views over this provenance web and supporting a personalised web of provenance data for these different user requirements.

The *process* provenance, which is similar to traditional event logs, recording the order of services called and data parameters used for these services, with all the time-stamps of service invocations and workflow executions. The *data* derivation provenance, builds a graph of data objects in a workflow run, including inputs to a workflow, data parameters for services, intermediate results from services and final results of a workflow. Data are linked to the services that used them, to other data they were generated from, to the source they came from with a version snapshot. *Contextual* information are provided for most if not all the provenance resources, to state the user of the data or service, the experiment design of this run, the project this experiment belongs to, the hypothesis this experiment or project is based on, etc. This contextual information not only provides additional materials for organising and exploring resources, but also provides another means by which we can integrate provenance logs, based on a common user, a common hypothesis, or a common design. The *organisation* provenance records who, when and where these contextual information was created and how they evolved during experiments. The fourth type of provenance presents domain specific links between experiment resources, e.g. a BLAST service input which is a nucleotide sequence is a *similar sequence* to the output of this BLAST service. As shown in Fig 3, *associations* between experiment objects are built when attaching organisation provenance to data and building knowledge linking between experiment resources. Similarly, associations are made to record *derivations* of these objects through process and data provenance. Direct data linking is the focus of data provenance, which is partly inferred from process provenance. A personalised web of provenance logs is supported by their associated organisation and annotated knowledge level information.

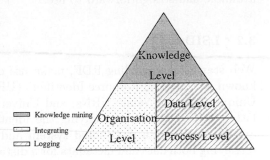

Fig. 3. Provenance design in ^{my}Grid.

Based on this core design of provenance, logs are automatically recorded during and after the workflow execution process in ^{my}Grid. Inter-related resources are identified and linked in a personal web, with an opportunity for users or third parties to annotate these logs either in free text or controlled vocabularies. Bioinformaticians, however, find it difficult to find information from a highly inter-linked provenance web. A higher level integration over this personal web is therefore required. By navigating and querying this web of provenance, scientists are able to verify results by tracing how they are produced, to test hypotheses and draw their conclusions supported by the historical record in provenance logs.

3   Semantic Web Technologies

In this section we present the Semantic Web technologies used in this project, which includes RDF, LSIDs and ontologies, in order to represent provenance logs and build a Semantic Web of these resources.

3.1   RDF

RDF was chosen as a representation model for provenance because: (i) it provides a more flexible graph based model with which to relate resources than for example the tree model of XML; (ii) it provides an explicit identification system (Universal Resource Identifiers (URIs)) for resources that allows metadata about a resource to be merged from several sources; (iii) and it provides a well-defined, but not overly constraining association with an ontology. This guides what can be said about a resource, but does not limit description to this schema. Also from a practical standpoint several mature open source RDF repositories are available and straightforward to use.

3.2   LSIDs

Web standards, including RDF, make use of a family of identifiers collectively known as Universal Resource Identifiers (URIs). Members of this family include Unique Resource Name (URNs) and Universal Resource Locators (URLs). The latter is used for both specifying the identity and location of a resource. We are implementing a distributed system and so we must have a mechanism for retrieving both data and metadata for a distant resource from its identifier. URLs are therefore an obvious candidate. However, the ^{my}Grid project has chosen to use a type of URN called LSIDs.

LSIDs promise to uniquely and consistently identify data resources in life science, and provide a resolution protocol for the retrieval of that data and any associated metadata [7]. They have been initially developed under the umbrella of the I3C[3] and are now undergoing formal standardisation by OMG[4].

Every LSID is made up of five parts: the Network Identifier (NID); the root domain name system (DNS) name of the issuing authority; the namespace chosen by the issuing authority; the object id unique in that namespace; and finally an optional revision id for storing versioning information [7]. The structure of an LSID is shown as below:

```
urn:lsid:AuthorityID:NamespaceID:ObjectId[:RevisionID]
```

The resolution process of an LSID guarantees the persistence and uniqueness of the data object identified by the LSID, independent of the location of the data source. When resolving LSIDs, two software components are necessary, an LSID server and an LSID client. An LSID *server* is operated by the authority who publishes informatics data and assigns LSIDs to the data. An LSID client communicates to the server over the network by the LSID protocol to retrieve data or metadata identified by the LSID. Given an LSID, the *AuthorityID* is first resolved to identify the location of the LSID resolution service for that Authority by querying the Internet DNS. Once the Authority is identified, its IP address or hostname and TCP/IP port number are returned and used to construct an HTTP/SOAP endpoint URL of the following form:

```
http://hostname:80/authority
```

The LSID is then used as a parameter when querying the endpoint. A Web Service Description Language (WSDL) [11] description is returned, providing the means to retrieve the data or metadata object identified by the LSID. This WSDL document details all the functionalities available for that LSID supported

---

[3] Interoperable Informatics Infrastructure Consortium http://www.i3c.org
[4] Object Management Group http://www.omg.org

by the Authority. A wide variety of protocols can be indicated using this mechanism, including HTTP, FTP, file system and SOAP methods. Though the persistence of data identified by the LSID is guaranteed in the resolution process, the metadata associated with an LSID can change over time.

The perceived benefits of LSIDs to ^{my}Grid are:

1. A clean separation of data and metadata: there is no convention to define what the client receives when it resolves a URL. A document that is obtained can represent metadata, data or more likely a combination of both. The most accepted model on the web is to incorporate some RDF metadata inline into a document. However this is not applicable in ^{my}Grid:
   a) We are dealing with raw data rather than published documents. The workflow system needs to pass raw data between services without any metadata annotations ;
   b) Data and metadata can reside in different locations;
   c) Metadata may be attached to resources for which we have no control (3rd party metadata);
2. An explicit social commitment to maintaining immutable and permanent data. Provenance becomes worthless if we can allow the data resolved by a URL to change. However provenance becomes more valuable the more metadata is attached and updated.
3. A potential to apply compatible standards: we could have implemented a convention for how to retrieve metadata and data from a URL but that would have been ^{my}Grid-specific. LSIDs provided us with a ready built protocol that is undergone a standardisation procedure. By using this standard, we ensure that this RDF-based web of provenance can be merged with other Semantic Webs of information, such as protein structure metadata in the Protein Data Bank. Trial LSID authorities currently exist for the Protein Data Bank, GenBank (a genomic database) and PubMed (a life science literature database). Again, from a practical point of view, developers at IBM have supported the LSID standard by providing client and server implementations in Java, C++ and Perl, together with a demonstration user client called LSID Launchpad that forms a plug-in to Internet Explorer[5].

3.3   Ontologies

If information is to be integrated and shared across a large community, there must be an agreement on the domain semantics of that information. This is true, even for a single user. We must be able to specify semantics at two levels: first, we need a high level schema describing the classes of resource that can be linked together such as `data_item` and `service_invocation` and the relationships that can hold between them such as `output`; second, one needs a large domain vocabulary that further classifies types of resource such as data type (e.g. BLAST report), service type (e.g. sequence alignment service), and topic of interest (Williams-Beuren Syndrome). Such a shared understanding of the domain greatly facilitates querying by increasing recall and precision.

---

[5] http://www-124.ibm.com/developerworks/oss/lsid/

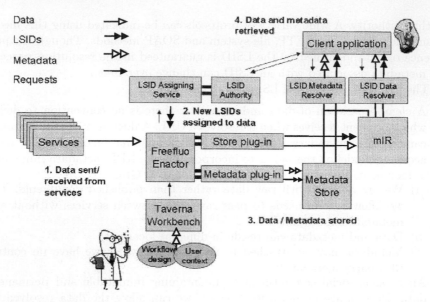

Fig. 4. Architecture for provenance generation and visualization in ^{my}Grid

4 Implementation

Having chosen RDF to describe our resources, LSIDs to identify them and ontologies to deliver a common semantic view of those data, provenance support has to be delivered within an environment for performing *in silico* experiments. Figure 4 shows the architecture of the provenance providing components in ^{my}Grid and how provenance data are drawn together. First the user starts a workflow using the Taverna workflow workbench[6]. The workbench holds organisation information such as user identity, which is passed to the workflow enactor together with input data and workflow specification. As the workflow is run, the enactor stores data (using the mySQL RDBMS), and metadata (in a Jena RDF repository[7]) corresponding to our four views of provenance. Each resource (including person, organisation, data and service) is assigned an LSID and made available via an LSID authority implemented using an open source framework[8]. Client applications can then visualize both metadata and data using the LSID protocol.

4.1 Supporting Provenance Recording with Ontologies

Section 3 described the benefits gained from committing to formally specified common semantics. Therefore, before generating any provenance, we must spec-

---

[6] Taverna and FreeFluo are both open source projects available from
http://taverna.sourceforge.net and http://freefluo.sourceforge.net

[7] Jena is an open source Semantic Web framework for Java including an RDF repository http://jena.sourceforge.net/

[8] An LSID Java server stack available for download at:
http://www-124.ibm.com/developerworks/projects/lsid

ify the schema by which it will be generated and the vocabulary of concepts used to classify, at a domain level, the resources involved. ^{my}Grid used the DAML+OIL ontology language because much of the work predated the later development and release of the OWL specification. We are currently migrating to OWL.

The schema ontology is relatively small in size (<30 classes, <20 properties) and specifies (at a domain independent level) each class of resource and the properties that can be held between them for the four views of provenance that we record.

1. To describe the *in silico* experiment execution process, we have modelled classes such as `service_invocation` describing the web service process, `invocation_event` describing specific sub-events of an often multifaceted process and `data_item` identifying the data flow in and out of the web service process. The property `created_by` relates data items to the service invocation that created them.
2. The data derivation view (at a domain independent level) is currently simple and uses a single property `derived_from` to link web service outputs with their associated inputs. Any more specific relationships are domain dependent and go to form the knowledge view of the provenance web.
3. Domain dependent relationships between data are specific to an individual service and may even be specific to the context of a particular workflow. For example, the output of a BLAST service is a `similar_sequence_to` the input. Therefore the author of the workflow is responsible for determining exactly which properties are used. He/she chooses appropriate properties that go to form a statement *template*.
4. The experimental organisation view relates the specific workflow run with the person, project and organisation for which it was run and a simple description of the scientific motivation.

The larger domain specific ontologies[9] (yet still small in biomedical informatics terms) contain ~600 classes and ~50 properties. As many concepts have multiple parents (a feature hard to maintain by hand), each concept is assigned a single parent manually together with a formal concept definition in DAML+OIL. A description logic reasoner then uses the formal concept definitions to check consistency and infer additional subsumption relationships. A detailed description of this is beyond the scope of this paper. More information can be found in [12]. To be effective, the uses of the ontology must pervade the system:

1. The schema acts as a specification for the Taverna/FreeFluo workflow enactor of how to encode the provenance information. The enactor automatically generates RDF statements relating to information it has about what services were called, with what parameters, how long the service took to process the request, any sub events that occurred and the outcome in terms

---

[9] ^{my}Grid ontology available from `http://www.mygrid.org.uk/` in the ontology component section

of either result data or failure. All properties are sourced from the ontology, and all resources are typed with ontology concepts. LSIDs are generated corresponding to the workflow run, each service invocation, and sub-events. The relevant RDF statements are then published as the metadata of these resources. The enactor also relates this process-based view to a data derivation view. It directly links data items by first assigning each data item a unique LSID, and then generating RDF statements linking items together. As above, these statements form the metadata for the data items. The Taverna workflow workbench holds organisation information about the identity of the experiment, person, project,and organisation under which this workflow is run. Each is also identified by LSID, so RDF statements linking these to the specific workflow run can be published as additional metadata of these resources. Given the example workflow in Fig 2, users can semantically trace through its provenance logs: From where the *protein sequence* output of the workflow is *derived*, which service *created* this protein output, who is the *owner* of this protein sequence, etc. When integrating provenance logs from different runs, users are able to group all the logs that generate a *protein sequence* as outputs that were, for example, either *created* by a particular user or those that contain sequences that are *similar to* this protein output. Figure 1 shows the provenance graph generated by the workflow in Fig 2. The data graph is an inversion of the workflow graph, but further extended to co-ordinate with the process provenance.

2. The domain specific ontologies are used by the workflow enactor to classify at a domain level the data items produced or used by the workflow.
3. The domain specific ontologies provide properties that the scientist can use to relate inputs and outputs of a service to provide the knowledge view described above.
4. Both schema and domain specific ontologies are used by Haystack to aid visualization as described in the next section.

4.2   Visualizing RDF Based Provenance

Having generated these provenance data, we need to enable a scientist to perform the kind of provenance-based tasks described in Sect 2. Analysis and validation will often be based upon browsing. Yet this browsing needs to be done along many axes and from many viewpoints, according to the goal of the task. This means we need a generic, flexible basis for the scientist to interact with the provenance data.

By using the LSID protocol for retrieval of both data and metadata, we have been able to cleanly separate visualization components from those generating and storing provenance information, so much so that we have been able to reuse existing externally developed software with pre-existing LSID client functionality. The first such client we have used is the LSID Launchpad that renders RDF metadata associated with an LSID in the browser. Entering an LSID into Internet Explorer results in the LSID client finding the relevant LSID authority, and retrieving the associated metadata for that resource. As is common when retrieving web documents, client applications can be registered to deal with particular MIME types so that when the data itself is retrieved it is displayed in the appropriate way.

Although a useful demonstration of LSID infrastructure, this style of RDF metadata visualization is intentionally naive. Users only see a restricted area of the graph one relationship wide. A few richer tools do exist to deliver Semantic Web technology to the user. One such Semantic Web browser, Haystack, from MIT, enables developers to provide customised views over RDF metadata [8]. To rapidly obtain a high level view of how resources interrelate, the user can view the provenance RDF as a labelled directed graph in Haystack, as with many other Semantic Web visualization tools.

Figure 5 shows an extract of such a graph, giving an example of how Haystack helps to visualize the *semantic* linking between these semantically enriched provenance resources for the experiment in Figure 2. In fact, we have found that the network of relationships is so dense that a complete rendering of the graph becomes difficult to interpret. We therefore filter out all but a small set of semantic relationships relevant to the user and task. In the case of Fig 5, only 13 RDF properties are being displayed: showing the relationship between data item (derived_from), the data flow between services (input, output), some organisation information of resources (e.g. created_by, design, group, project, etc), and some knowledge linking between data from different provenance logs (similar_sequence_to). By making use of Haystack's ability we can also separate these semantic links into four levels according to our provenance pyramid, which can be chosen from the view panel in Haystack, as shown in Fig 5.

However, we expect this graph based view of the whole provenance log will not provide a complete solution for the end user. The traditional web is itself a graph of documents related by hyperlinks, yet it is rarely rendered as such. Therefore, much more of our attention has been focused on providing a web browser metaphor for users to browse the provenance web. Haystack provides an application framework that allows the developer to render complex RDF subgraphs into user interface screens that behave like the much more familiar frames of web pages. Each class of resource can be associated with one or more of what Haystack terms "views". This is a specification, written in a novel high level programming language, Adenine, of how the metadata associated with that resource should be interpreted in order to construct a web page like interface for that resource. For more information see Quan *et al.* [13] and [8].

Our experience in using Haystack is promising. It has provided a rapid prototyping environment in which we can explore with our users the most effective way of interacting with RDF-based provenance information. By providing an application framework in which we can build up provenance views, it has enabled us to bypass the considerable effort needed to code core application and user interface components. When showing RDF-encoded provenance in Haystack to our collaborating bioinformaticians, they are satisfied that semantic relationships are made explicit when browsing these RDF logs in Haystack. By navigating and clicking, they can follow the hyperlinks between resources, directed by underlying

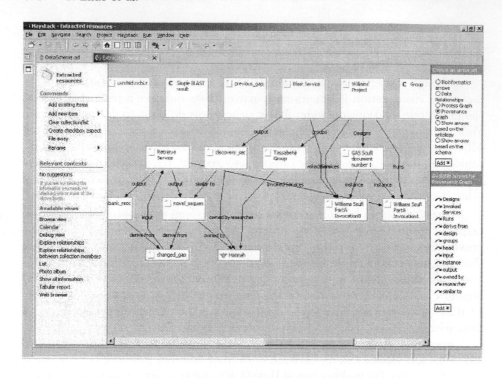

Fig. 5. Haystack screenshot of visualizing example provenance log.

semantic relationships. Also, when facing large amounts of data from provenance logs, users can choose different sets of predicates, in order to conceptually group provenance data in multiple ways according to the task at hand. For example, as introduced in Sect 2, when scientists at the stage of "debugging" experiment results, they could be interested in viewing provenance logs from a *process* aspect, to trace how experiments are executed. During the stage of "validity checking", a *data* view can be more supportive for scientists to track the data derivation path in an experiment.

Haystack's reliance on ontologies to drive the presentation of metadata fits well with the core role of ontologies in our provenance. Ontology classes associated with resources during provenance generation in the Taverna application have a direct impact on how those resources are displayed to the user in Haystack.

Haystacks LSID client functionality has also been of benefit. The user can enter an LSID of a provenance resource in Haystack and the metadata will be retrieved from the ᵐʸGrid LSID metadata resolver and displayed appropriately.

However, within ᵐʸGrid we have come across several issues with the Haystack and LSID approach. Haystack is a large desktop application requiring significant resources. This contrasts with bioinformaticians preference for light-weight web-based applications. Also using the architecture shown in Fig 4 we must rely on retrieving provenance metadata via the LSID protocol. As the protocol only allows for retrieval one resource at a time, to provide a high level expansive view covering many resources we must enter into a piecemeal repetitive retrieval process and slowly build up the complete picture in the local Haystack RDF repository.

5   Discussion

The capture of *in silico* experiments as workflows and their outputs form a natural web of data. These can be described and identified by RDF and LSIDs respectively. In the ^{my}Grid project, these provenance data are recorded along four views: process, data derivation, organisation and knowledge. The knowledge or semantic component is needed in order to offer a common view over the heterogeneous semantic types within the provenance data and allows the provenance-based tasks to be accomplished.

Our implementation automatically traces the process and data derivation provenance and attaches the necessary organisational provenance to an experiment's data. The Taverna workflow environment offers the facility to attach knowledge level provenance through its template mechanism, supported by the ^{my}Grid ontology of bioinformatics services. This machinery also automatically provides RDF descriptions linked to the data through LSIDs. These provenance data can then be browsed by a scientist through the Haystack tool.

This success has, however, revealed several issues. As suggested in Sect 4.2, there is an issue of how these provenance data are presented to users — is a graph or a familiar web form appropriate? There is also a wider issue of usability, from the micro-scale of button and link labels, keystrokes and speed, to a macro-scale of effectiveness, efficiency and satisfaction in its support for provenance-based tasks in *in silico* experiments. Our current implementation and experience has offered no clues about the scalability of our handling and presentation of provenance data. As many users run many experiments, vast quantities of highly linked and annotated data will be generated. There is an issue about whether both the presentation and computational handling of all these data are scalable.

Given our addition of a semantic description of these data, we fully expect to be able to add *machine processing* of these data to the current human emphasis of our work. By fully implementing and managing an ontology for provenance data, such semantically supported processing over these data could be enabled by reasoning over the semantics associated with data resources. This would allow semantic querying of these logs, provide trust information about data based on logs, etc.

In our description of the use of provenance, we have presented a scenario where all users can browse all provenance data and even make annotations on other people's data. Obviously there are profound *security and authorisation* issues in such a scenario. Biologists are, as are other people, very security conscious about new data and associated discoveries etc. Many levels of authorisation need to be incorporated into the RDF paradigm in order to support access to subgraphs within an experiment repository.

These points do not contradict, but build upon the success of our demonstration of a Semantic Web of provenance for *in silico* experiments. The provision of such support for provenance is vital for the performance of *in silico* experiment and offers a rich test-bed for the concepts and technology of the Semantic Web.

Acknowledgements. The ^{my}Grid project, grant number GR/R67743, is funded under the UK e-Science programme by the EPSRC. The authors would like to acknowledge the other members of the ^{my}Grid team for their contributions.

References

1. Karp, P.: A Strategy for Database Interoperation. Journal of Computational Biology **2** (1995) 573–586
2. Program, H.G.: Genomics and its impact on science and society: A 2003 primer. Technical report, U.S. Department of Energy (2003)
3. Fox, G., Walker, D.: e-Science Gap Analysis. Technical report, Indiana University and Cardiff University, UK e-Science Center (2003)
4. Stevens, R., Robinson, A., Goble, C.: myGrid: Personalised Bioinformatics on the Information Grid. In: International Conference on Intelligent Systems in Molecular Biology. (2003)
5. Preus, M.: The Williams Syndrome: Objective Definition and Diagnosis. Clinical Genetics **25** (1984) 422–428
6. Hendler, J.: Communication: Enhanced Science and the Semantic Web. Science **299** (2003) 520–521
7. Martin, S., Senger, M., Niemi, M.: Life Sciences Identifiers second revised submission. Technical report, I3C (2003)
8. Quan, D., Karger, D.R.: How to make a semantic web browser. In: Proc. of the Thirteenth International World Wide Web Conference (WWW2004), ACM (2004) 255–265
9. Horrocks, I., Patel-Schneider, P.F., van Harmelen, F.: From SHIQ and RDF to OWL: The making of a web ontology language. Journal of Web Semantics **1** (2003) 7–26
10. Cline, M., Shigeta, R., Wheeler, R., Siani-Rose, M., Kulp, D., Loraine, A.: The effects of alternative splicing on transmembrane proteins in the mouse genome. In: Pacific Symposium on Biocomputing. Volume 9. (2004) 17–28
11. Christensen, E., Curbera, F., Meredith, G., Weerawarana, S.: Web Services Description Language (WSDL) 1.1 (2001) W3C Note.
12. Wroe, C., Stevens, R., Goble, C., Roberts, A., Greenwood, M.: A Suite of DAML+OIL Ontologies to Describe Bioinformatics Web Services and Data. the International Journal of Cooperative Information Systems **12** (2003) 597–624
13. Quan, D., Huynh, D., Karger, D.R.: Haystack: A platform for authoring end user semantic web applications. In Fensel, D., Sycara, K., Mylopoulos, J., eds.: Proc. of the 2003 International Semantic Web Conference (ISWC 2003). Number 2870 in Lecture Notes in Computer Science, Springer (2003) 738–753

GridVine: Building Internet-Scale Semantic Overlay Networks[*]

Karl Aberer[1], Philippe Cudré-Mauroux[1], Manfred Hauswirth[1], and
Tim Van Pelt[2]

[1] School of Computer and Communication Sciences
Swiss Federal Institute of Technology (EPFL), Switzerland
{karl.aberer, manfred.hauswirth, philippe.cudre-mauroux}@epfl.ch
[2] Department of Computer and Information Science
Linköpings Universitet, Sweden
tim@vanpelt.com

Abstract. This paper addresses the problem of building scalable semantic overlay networks. Our approach follows the principle of data independence by separating a logical layer, the semantic overlay for managing and mapping data and metadata schemas, from a physical layer consisting of a structured peer-to-peer overlay network for efficient routing of messages. The physical layer is used to implement various functions at the logical layer, including attribute-based search, schema management and schema mapping management. The separation of a physical from a logical layer allows us to process logical operations in the semantic overlay using different physical execution strategies. In particular we identify iterative and recursive strategies for the traversal of semantic overlay networks as two important alternatives. At the logical layer we support semantic interoperability through schema inheritance and Semantic Gossiping. Thus our system provides a complete solution to the implementation of semantic overlay networks supporting both scalability and interoperability.

1 Introduction

Research on semantic overlay networks has recently received a lot of attention in the emerging area of peer-to-peer data management [10,6,15,17]. All of these approaches are based on a generalization of the concept of federated databases, where peers store data or (content) metadata according to their local schemas and freely define mappings (translations, views) from their schemas to those of

---

[*] The work presented in this paper was (partly) carried out in the framework of the EPFL Center for Global Computing and was supported by the National Competence Center in Research on Mobile Information and Communication Systems (NCCR-MICS), a center supported by the Swiss National Science Foundation under grant number 5005-67322 and in part and by the Swiss National Funding Agency OFES as part of the European project KnowlegeWeb No 507482.

S.A. McIlraith et al. (Eds.): ISWC 2004, LNCS 3298, pp. 107–121, 2004.

other peers. Thus a network is constructed where peers are logically interconnected through schema mappings and where queries can be propagated to other peers using different schemas, even over multiple hops. The main concern of these works is on the problem of consistent query answering and reconciliation of different mappings occurring in the semantic overlay network [8,22].

In parallel, structured overlay networks, e.g., Chord [21] or P-Grid [2], have been developed as new infrastructures for routing requests for resources that are distributed over large populations of peers using application-specific keys in an efficient manner. Naturally, such networks can be employed in order to efficiently respond to simple keyword-based queries. Structured overlay networks clearly also have the potential to support the efficient operation of a semantic overlay network. However, research on how to take advantage of this potential is in its infancy.

In this paper, we introduce an architecture and implementation leveraging on the potential for scalability offered by structured overlay networks in the realization of interoperable, large-scale semantic overlay networks. A key aspect of the approach we take is to apply the principle of data independence [13] by separating a logical from a physical layer. This principle is well-known from the database area and has largely contributed to the success of modern database systems. At the logical layer, we support various operations to maintain the semantic overlay network and to support semantic interoperability, including attribute-based search, schema management, schema inheritance and schema mapping. We also provide support for a specific schema reconciliation technique, i.e., Semantic Gossiping, that we have introduced earlier [3]. We provide these mechanisms within the standard syntactic framework of RDF/OWL. At the physical layer, we provide efficient realizations of the operations exploiting a structured overlay network, namely P-Grid. This requires mappings of operations and data to the physical layer. Important aspects of this mapping are:

- The mapping of data and metadata to routable keys.
- The introduction of a specific namespace for resources present in the peer space, such that the infrastructure can resolve resource requests.
- The implementation of traversals of the semantic network taking advantage of intermediate schema mappings. An interesting aspect is the possibility to use different strategies to implement such traversals at the structured overlay network layer, in ways that are substantially different from naive solutions. We analyze two types of processing strategies, iterative and recursive. As in standard database query processing, the data independence principle thus opens up the possibility of optimization using different query processing strategies.

We have developed a first implementation following the architectural principles outlined above building on the existing implementation of the P-Grid structured overlay network. We report on initial experiments showing the effect of using different query processing strategies for semantic network traversal.

The rest of this paper is structured as follows: We start with an overview of our approach in Section 2. Our architecture and implementation use P-Grid as a physical layer, which is briefly described in Section 3. Section 4 presents the mechanisms used to index metadata and schemas and to resolve queries. Section 5 describes semantic interoperability while Section 6 is dedicated to GridVine, the implementation of our approach. Finally, we discuss related work in Section 7 and conclude.

2 Overview of Our Approach

2.1 Data Independence

Following the principle of data independence enounced above, our approach revolves around a two-layer model: a physical layer based on the P-Grid access structure underpinning GridVine, a logical semantic overlay layer (see Fig. 1). P-Grid (Section 3) is an efficient, self-organizing and fully decentralized access structure based on a distributed hash table (DHT). GridVine uses two of P-Grid's basic functionalities: the *Insert(key, value)* primitive for storing data items based on a key identifier and the *Retrieve(key)* primitive for retrieving data items given their key.

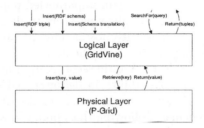

Fig. 1. The two-layer model

Taking advantage of these two rather limited primitives, we build a full-fledged semantic overlay network on top of P-Grid. The system exposes a new set of primitives (depicted on top of Fig. 1) allowing end-users to insert metadata, schemas and schema translations as well as retrieve semantic information using expressive query languages. Capitalizing on recent developments, we chose the RDF / RDFS pair as languages to encode metadata and vocabulary definitions in GridVine. These two languages represent the fundamental building blocks of the emerging Semantic Web [23] and are predestined to become *de facto* standards for encoding metadata as well as their corresponding schematic information.

The exact mechanisms we choose for inserting metadata into the P-Grid are naturally of utmost importance, since they directly influence the query capabilities of the overall system, and are extensively discussed in the following (Section 4). In order to support the processing of schema-specific information, we introduce a meta-schema specifying common characteristics for all custom schemas derived by the users. Also, we introduce new addressing spaces, i.e., URI schemes, to identify resources both in the physical (P-Grid data items) and logical (semantic information) layers.

2.2   Decentralized Semantics

Classification of resources and definition of vocabularies are essential for leveraging metadata creation and fostering semantic interoperability through reuse of conceptualizations. Legacy information sharing systems typically support static sets of centrally imposed, predefined schemas. We consider such a monolithic approach as far too rigid for adequately capturing information sources in a network of autonomous and heterogeneous parties. Not only is this not desirable from an ideological perspective, it also misses out on the power of P2P. Seeing users as experts of the information they share, they themselves are most fit to come up with a proper schema to describe their data. However desirable it may be to let users come up with their own schemas in a bottom-up manner, it also severely endangers global semantic interoperability and search capabilities: How could one ensure optimal precision and recall when searching for data items that might be referred to by a large variety of terms? Our answer to this question if twofold, including both schema inheritance and Semantic Gossiping mechanisms.

Schema inheritance provides GridVine with basic schema reusability and interoperability capabilities. As for other social networks [7], we expect the popularity of schemas in GridVine to follow scale-free preferential attachment laws, such that a small subset of schemas gain unparalleled popularity while the others remain mainly confidential. By allowing users to derive new schemas from well-known base schemas, we implicitly foster interoperability by reusing sets of conceptualizations belonging to the base schemas.

Semantic Gossiping [3,4] is a semantic reconciliation method that can be applied to foster semantic interoperability in decentralized settings. The method aims at establishing global forms of agreement starting from a graph of purely local mappings among schemas. Following this approach, we allow peers in GridVine to create, and possibly index, translation links mapping one schema onto another. These links can then be used to propagate queries in such a way that relevant data items annotated according to different schemas can also be retrieved. Query forwarding can be implemented using several approaches. In the following, we identify two radically different strategies for forwarding queries: iterative forwarding, where peers process series of translation links repeatedly, and recursive forwarding, where peers delegate the forwarding to other peers. Schema inheritance and Semantic Gossiping are further described in Section 5.

3   The P-Grid P2P System

GridVine uses our P-Grid [2] P2P system as its physical layer. P-Grid is based on the principles of distributed hash tables (DHT) [18]. As any DHT approach, P-Grid associates peers with data keys from a key space, i.e., partitions of the underlying distributed data structure. Each peer is responsible for some part of the overall key space and maintains additional (routing) information to forward queries and requests. Without constraining general applicability, we use binary keys in the following. P-Grid peers refer to a common underlying tree structure in order to organize their routing tables. In the following, we assume that the tree is binary. This is not a fundamental limitation as a generalization of P-Grid to k-ary structures has been introduced in [5], but will simplify the presentation.

Each peer $p \in P$ is associated with a leaf of the binary tree. Each leaf corresponds to a binary string $\pi \in \Pi$. Thus each peer p is associated with a path $\pi(p)$. For search, the peer stores for each prefix $\pi(p, l)$ of $\pi(p)$ of length l a set of references $\rho(p, l)$ to peers q with property $\overline{\pi(p, l)} = \pi(q, l)$, where $\overline{\pi}$ is the binary string π with the last bit inverted. This means that at each level of the tree the peer has references to some other peers that do not pertain to the peer's subtree at that level, which enables the implementation of prefix routing for efficient search. The cost for storing the references (in routing tables) and the associated maintenance cost are scalable as they are proportional to the depth of the underlying binary tree.

Each peer stores a set of data items $\delta(p)$. For $d \in \delta(p)$ the binary key $key(d)$ is calculated using an order-preserving hash function. $key(d)$ has $\pi(p)$ as prefix but we do not exclude that temporarily also other data items are stored at a peer, that is, the set $\delta(p, \pi(p))$ of data items whose key matches $\pi(p)$ can be a proper subset of $\delta(p)$. In addition, peers also maintain references $\sigma(p)$ to peers having the same path, i.e., their replicas.

P-Grid supports two basic operations: *Retrieve(key)* for searching a certain key and retrieving the associated data item and *Insert(key, value)* for storing new data items. Since P-Grid uses a binary tree, *Retrieve(key)* intuitively is efficient, i.e., $\mathcal{O}(log(|\Pi|))$, measured in terms of messages required for resolving a search request, in a balanced tree. For skewed data distributions we show in [1] that due to the probabilistic nature of the P-Grid approach, the expected search cost measured by the number of messages required to perform the search remains logarithmic, independently how the P-Grid is structured. This is important as it allows us to apply simple order-preserving hashing functions to metadata annotations, which may lead to non-uniformly distributed key distributions. As P-Grid uses an order-preserving hash function to compute keys and define their association with peers, it processes prefix and range queries of arbitrary granularity efficiently, i.e., $O(log(|\Pi|) + |\{p|\kappa \text{ } is \text{ } prefix \text{ } of \text{ } \pi(p)\}|$. Prefix queries will be an important constituent in the generic implementation of metadata queries. *Insert(key, value)* is based on P-Grid's more general update functionality [11] which provides probabilistic guarantees for consistency and is efficient even in highly unreliable, replicated environments, i.e., $\mathcal{O}(log(|\Pi|) + replication \text{ } factor)$.

4   Semantic Support

In the following, we elaborate on how GridVine handles the creation and indexing of RDF triples (Section 4.1) and schemas (Section 4.2). Section 4.3 discusses then query resolution mechanisms.

4.1   Metadata Storage

In GridVine, statements are stored as RDF triples and refer to data items shared in the P-Grid infrastructure. A structured overlay network allows to implement an application specific addressing space. In our case, we introduce a specific URI schemes *pgrid* : // for resources, and *pgrids* : //, for schema-elements. This does not exclude the use of other URI schemes in conjunction with P-Grid's specific ones, as long as the infrastructure ensures that all the identifiers can be resolved.

In the case were all resources are identified by P-Grid URIs, a typical situation would be a statement where the subject is identified by a P-Grid key, i.e., a binary string such as *11110101*, whereas the predicate and object refer to P-Grid's specific RDF schemas (or literals). This allows us to constrain the applicability of the schema constructs. An example of such a statement would be *the P-Grid resource 11110101 (subject) is entitled (predicate) Rain, Steam and Speed (object)*, which, translated into the XML syntax of RDF, would result in a file like the one transcribed in Fig. 2.

```
<?xml version="1.0"?>
<rdf:RDF xmlns:rdf="http://www.w3.org/1999/02/22-rdf-syntax-ns#">
  <rdf:Description rdf:about="pgrid://11110101">
    <Title xmlns="pgrids://01001101:bmp#">Rain, Steam and Speed</Title>
  </rdf:Description>
</rdf:RDF>
```

Fig. 2. An RDF statement encoded in XML

Since most RDF query languages [19] are based on constraint searches on the triples' *subject, predicate* or *object*, we reference each individual triple three times, generating separate keys based on their *subject, predicate* and *object* values. Thus, the insertion operation of a triple $t \in T$ is performed as follows:

$$Insert(t) \equiv Insert(t_{subject}, t), Insert(Hash(t_{predicate}), t), Insert(Hash(t_{object}), t).$$

Prefix searches, e.g., on the beginning of a string representing an object value, are inherently supported by P-Grid's routing mechanisms. Supporting substring searches imposes to index all the suffixes of a generated key as well. Thus, if we introduce l as the average length of the strings representing *subjects, objects* or *predicates*, $3l$ *Insert()* operations incur on average when indexing an RDF triple in GridVine.

4.2   Schema Definition and Storage

We encode category descriptions using RDF Schema (RDFS). RDFS is an extension of RDF providing mechanisms for describing groups of resources and their relationships. Among other capabilities, it allows to define classes of resources (*classes*) and predicates (*properties*) and to specify constraints on the subject (*domain*) or the object (*range*) of a given class of predicates.

GridVine schemas allow to declare new *categories* to describe application specific resources. The categories are all derived by subclassing from a generic RDF class called $P - GridDataItem$ representing any P-Grid addressable resource. Properties referring to this class as domain allow to declare application-specific vocabularies (i.e., metadata attributes) with arbitrary values as ranges.

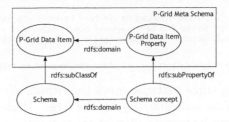

Fig. 3. Relations of a P-Grid custom schema to the P-Grid meta schema

All properties derive from a generic $P - GridDataItemProperty$ property. P-Grid meta-schema and its relation to user-defined RDF schemas are summarized in Fig. 3.

We create distinct RDFS files for every category, grouping the definition of a subclass as well as all its affiliated properties. We create a unique identifer for the category by concatenating the path $\pi(p)$ of the peer creating a category to the category itself. We then insert it into P-Grid as any other file:

$$Insert(rdf\_schema) \equiv Insert(Hash(\pi(p) : class\_name), rdf\_schema).$$

Note that due to the possibility of performing substring searches, schemas can also be searched by their category name only.

4.3 Resolving Queries in GridVine

The simplest query one may pose against the system consists in a triple pattern with only one bound variable, i.e., a query retrieving (parts of) a set of triples given the value of their *subject, predicate* or *object*. For example, the following RDQL [20] query: *SELECT ?y WHERE (<pgrid://01101000>, ?y, ?z)* returns all the predicates used to annotate data item *01101000*. In GridVine, we call such a query a *native query*. Native queries are resolved routing one message through the P-Grid infrastructure. In our case, a message containing the above query and the address of the peer p from which the query originates is routed as explained in Section 3 to the peer(s) q responsible for storing data item d with $key(d) = 01101000$. Upon reception of the query, q checks its local database and sends back to p the set of data items $\delta(q)$ matching the query, which in turn parses the answer and displays the result. The whole process still generates $\mathcal{O}(log(|\Pi|))$ messages: $\mathcal{O}(log(|\Pi|))$ messages to resolve the P-Grid entry plus one message for the answer. Native queries on literals (e.g., searches on the value of a property) are resolved exactly in the same way, but start beforehand by hashing the literal in order to get its corresponding key.

Variables can be introduced as subject, predicate or object of a triple pattern. GridVine resolves triple patterns differently depending on the number of unbound variables they contain:

Three unbound variables triple patterns would retrieve all the triples stored in the system, implying $\mathcal{O}(|\Pi|log(|\Pi|))$ messages. They are not allowed in GridVine.
Two unbound variables triple patterns are standard native queries, and may as such be resolved using the method described above.

One unbound variable triple patterns can be resolved by issuing a native query; The predicate of the query may either be the first or the second bound expression of the triple patterns. The query issued must include both predicates in order for the query destination to filter out the triples correctly.

Zero unbound variable triple patterns are constant and require no further resolution.

The cost of resolving triple patterns grows logarithmically with the number of peers, making GridVine scale gracefully in the large. Triple patterns are powerful primitives that can be used to support more expressive query languages as well. GridVine supports RDQL query resolution through simple triple pattern combinations, following strategies similar to the ones presented in [10].

5   Semantic Interoperability

As previously mentioned, we believe that semantic heterogeneity is a critical threat for large-scale semantic networks. We detail below the mechanisms we take advantage of in order to foster semantic interoperability in GridVine.

5.1   Schema Inheritance

We let users derive new categories from the existing ones. However, we impose that the new class representing the subcategory subclasses the base category class. RDFS enforces monotonic inheritance of properties through class hierarchies; In our case, the subcategory automatically inherits the properties defined in the base category through the *domain* definitions. Additionally, subcategories may introduce sets of new properties specific to the subclass. Fig. 4 below provides an example where a category for annotating JPEG files is derived from a more generic category of image files.

The process can of course be applied recursively in the sense that a subcategory may in turn serve as a super-category for a new derivation, creating complex hierarchies of categories and classes from the most popular base schemas. Since subcategories subsume their base categories, subcategories of a given category may be used indifferently as instances of the base category. In particular, searches on a property belonging to a base category automatically affect subcategory instances as well (least-derived property indexation). Thus, we create

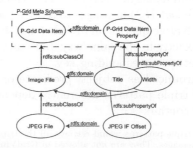

Fig. 4. A simple example of category inheritance

sets of semantically interoperable schemas through properties inherited by all descendants of a (potentially very popular) base schema.

5.2 Semantic Gossiping

In [3,4], we introduced Semantic Gossiping as a new semantic reconciliation method. Semantic gossiping aims at establishing global forms of agreement starting from a graph of purely local mappings among schemas. Peers that have annotated their data according to the same schema are said to belong to the same *semantic neighbourhood*. Each peer has the possibility to create (either manually or automatically) a mapping between two schemas, in effect creating a link between two semantic neighbourhoods. The network as such can be seen as a directed graph of translations.

This translation graph exhibits two interesting properties: First, using local translations and with the possibility to learn about other existing translations in the system, transitivity allows for the forwarding of queries to semantic domains for which there is no direct translation link (transitive closure). A second observation is that the graph has cycles. One of the fundamental assumptions that underlies the approach is that the translations between different semantic domains may be partially or totally *incorrect*. Analysis of composite cycles and returned results makes it possible to check the quality of translations and to determine the degree of semantic agreement in a community, as described in [3].

Following this approach, we allow peers in GridVine to create translation links mapping one schema onto another. Translations are used to propagate queries from one semantic domain to another (see Section 6.1). Since RDFS does not support schema mapping, we encode translations using OWL [23]. Translation links consist of series of *owl:equivalentProperty* statements which characterize the correspondences between the two categories at the property level. Fig. 5 below is an example of translation. Individual property equivalence statements are reified in order to account for partially-overlapping properties: Peers can thus refer to the various equivalence statements and qualify the individual mappings with a semantic similarity value as introduced in our Semantic Gossiping papers [3,4].

```
<?xml version="1.0"?> <?xml version="1.0" encoding="ISO-8859-1" ?>
<rdf:RDF xmlns:owl ="http://www.w3.org/2002/07/owl#"
  xmlns:rdf ="http://www.w3.org/1999/02/22-rdf-syntax-ns#">
  <Image_Description xmlns="pgrids://10000101:exif#">
    <owl:equivalentProperty rdf:ID="m1" rdf:resource="pgrids://01001101:bmp#Title"/>
  </Image_Description>
  <Exif_Image_Width xmlns="pgrids://10000101:exif#">
    <owl:equivalentProperty rdf:ID="m2" rdf:resource="pgrids://01001101:bmp#Width"/>
  </Exif_Image_Width>
</rdf:RDF>
```

Fig. 5. An example of translation

To forward queries properly, we need to retrieve all the translation links relating a given schema to other schemas. Thus, we index the translations based on their source schemas (e.g., *pgrids://10000101:exif* in Fig. 5):

$$Insert(owl\_file) \equiv Insert(Hash(\pi(p_{source}) : source\_class\_name), owl\_file).$$

Forwarding a query is then logically handled using gossiping as described in [3, 4]: Starting from a given semantic domain, the query gets transformed and iteratively traverses other semantic domains following translations links until it is considered as being too different (either from a syntactic or a semantic point of view) from the original query. A new query is issued after each translation step. In the following section, we show that different physical implementations of Semantic Gossiping can be realized using the P-Grid overlay network.

6   Implementation

6.1   Architectural Overview

GridVine was implemented by extending our existing Java-based P-Grid library which is available upon request. Fig. 6 shows the architecture of the implementation as a UML class diagram. The left side shows the P-Grid library with the Gridella GUI and the right side shows GridVine's semantic extensions. The arrows in the figure denote "uses" relationships. The *Gridella* component provides a GUI and uses the *P-Grid* component to issue queries; the *Semantics* component uses the *P-Grid* component to issue and receive queries and uses the *RDF*, *RDFS*, and *OWL* components to handle incoming requests. The *RDF* component is responsible for creating and managing RDF based metadata and provides the gossiping functionality. The *Extractors* subcomponent facilitates automatic metadata extraction to leverage the burden of manual annotation (e.g., automatic extraction of EXIF information from images). Functionalities related to schemas are provided by the *RDFS* component, while the *OWL* component handles all issues regarding translations. The *P-Grid*, *Semantics*, *RDF*, *RDFS*, and *OWL* components are implemented as *Singletons*, i.e., only a single instance of each of these classes exists at runtime and handles all requests.

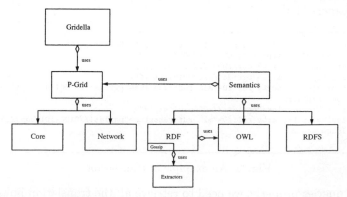

Fig. 6. The GridVine component model

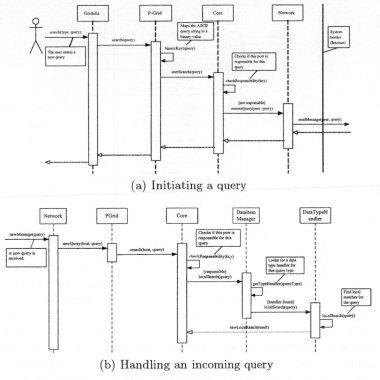

(a) Initiating a query

(b) Handling an incoming query

Fig. 7. GridVine queries

Querying. Fig. 7(a) shows the initiator's side of a query in P-Grid which Grid-Vine uses to provide its semantic search capabilities.

The user initiates a query via the Gridella GUI which hands it over to the P-Grid component to perform the actual search. The parameter type defines the type of data to search for (GUID, File, RDF, RDFS, OWL) and is implicitly assigned by the system (and encoded in the query). The query is then routed to other peers which are "closer" to the required result as described in Section 3.

If a peer receives a query, it checks whether it can answer the query, i.e., wether it is responsible for the partition of the key space the query belongs to, otherwise the query will be forwarded as shown in Fig. 7(a). If the peer can answer the query, as shown in Fig. 7(b), it checks the type of the query (GUID, File, RDF, RDFS, OWL) and hands it over to the corresponding datatype handler which processes the query according to its type. Datatype handlers are defined and registered with the P-Grid library by the users of the library, i.e., the *Gridella* and *Semantics* components.

Semantic Gossiping. The introduction of RDF type queries enables Semantic Gossiping which is explicitly activated by the issuer of a query through a special flag in the query. Fig. 8 sketches how gossiping is implemented. In the figure,

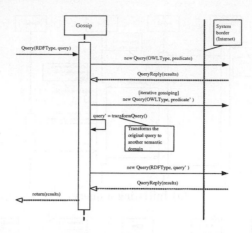

Fig. 8. Gossiping mechanism

we just show the relevant part and omit the preceding flow of control (incoming message – P-Grid – Datatype handler (Semantics)) for simplicity.

In resolving translation links we support two approaches: iterative and recursive. In iterative resolution, the peer issuing the RDF query tries to find and process all the translations links by itself; It first issues a query to retrieve the translation links capable of transforming the category used in the original query; Upon finding a translation, it translates the original query into a transformed query (Query') and issues a search for the transformed query. Furthermore, the gossiping peer issues a query for a translation of the translation (Predicate'). This continues until no more translation is available or the transformed query is considered as being too different from the original query following syntactic and semantic similarity measures [4].

In recursive resolution, the issuing peer tries to resolve the translation by delegating it rather than doing it itself: First, it looks for translations of the predicates used in the query and translates the query upon finding a translation. The transformed query is issued and results for the query are returned to the issuer of the query. The receiver of the transformed query follows the same procedure recursively.

6.2   Experimental Evaluation

We briefly discuss below an initial performance evaluation of the two Semantic Gossiping techniques GridVine implements. The tests were performed using the current implementation on a Fast Ethernet network of 60 SUN Ultra10 stations (Solaris 8). We first created 15 different semantic domains (i.e., 15 different categories C_0 to C_{15}) related to each other through 15 translation links as depicted in Fig. 9(a). We chose to organize the translations in a very regular way (i.e., a tree) in order to get a better grasp on the results obtained; Note however that our approach and implementation work equally well on more complex translation graphs (see also [3,4]).

We launched 15 peers, each on a separate computer and each locally storing a triple related to a different category. By issuing a query from the peer using C_0, we could retrieve all the 15 triples from the 15 semantic domains by forwarding the query through the translation link hierarchy. A second setting was created by replicating this first setting four times, running 60 peers using the same category setting (i.e., we had 4 peers per category each storing one triple locally).

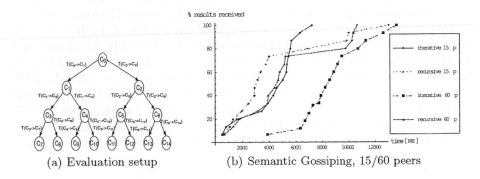

(a) Evaluation setup   (b) Semantic Gossiping, 15/60 peers

Fig. 9. Semantic gossiping evaluation, 15/60 peers, 15 translation links

The results, time elapsed versus quantity of results (up to 15/60 results) received by the peer issuing the query, for both settings and for iterative and recursive forwarding are displayed on Fig. 9(b). As expected, iterative forwarding works in a fairly linear manner. Also, note the initial delay incurred by letting one peer process and send all the queries for iterative forwarding with 60 peers. Our recursive approach proceeds more in stages, as it delegates the whole process of query forwarding to intermediary peers. This second approach proves to be particularly scalable with the number of peers: Results are rather independent of the number of peers or results returned, since the number of peers processing and forwarding the query increases with the network size.

7   Related Work

Hyperion [9] is an on-going project which proposes an architecture and outlines a set of challenges for decentralized data management in P2P systems. SWAP [12] is an approach combining P2P and Semantic Web techniques. It relies on an RDF(S) model and on structure extraction for handling queries in a P2P setting. Edutella [15] employs a super-peer topology and facilitates the clustering of data based on ontology, rule, or query. In PeerDB [17], each peer holds a set of locally available metadata (*Local Dictionary*) and a set of metadata that can be accessed by other nodes in the network (*Export Dictionary*). Metadata can be added through an SQL query facility. The system if based on BestPeer [16] which employs mobile agents to satisfy queries. No global schema is imposed but the process is not fully automated, as the user has to decide which mappings are actually meaningful. The Piazza peer data management project [22] takes an approach to semantic heterogeneity that is similar to Semantic Gossiping. Unlike our approach, Piazza does not provide any measures to judge the (in)correctness of mappings. The indexing is centralized and thus the scalability of the system is limited.

All the above approaches address semantic interoperability but offer limited scalability. Other approaches address scalability but do not deal with semantic interoperability. For example, Peer-to-Peer Information Exchange Retrieval (PIER) [14] is a database-style query engine built on top of a DHT. Its main focus is to provide database query processing facilities to widely distributed environments. One of PIER's restrictions is that it imposes global, standard schemas following the rational that some schemas will become de facto standards. RDF-Peers [10] builds on the Multi-Attribute Addressable Network (MAAN), which extends Chord, to efficiently answer multi-attribute and range queries on RDF triples. RDFPeers is a scalable RDF store, but does not provide any schematic support (e.g., to handle user-defined schemas or to address semantic interoperability issues).

8   Conclusions

To the best of our knowledge, GridVine is the first semantic overlay network based on an scalable, efficient and totally decentralized access structure supporting the creation of local schemas while fostering global semantic interoperability. Following the principle of data independence, our approach separates the logical and physical aspects such that it can be generalized to any physical infrastructure that provides functionalities similar to our P-Grid P2P system.

References

1. K. Aberer. Efficient Search in Unbalanced, Randomized Peer-To-Peer Search Trees. Technical Report IC/2002/79, Swiss Federal Institute of Technology, Lausanne (EPFL), 2002. http://www.p-grid.org/Papers/TR-IC-2002-79.pdf.
2. K. Aberer, P. Cudré-Mauroux, A. Datta, Z. Despotovic, M. Hauswirth, M. Punceva, and R. Schmidt. P-grid: A self-organizing structured p2p system. *ACM SIGMOD Record*, 32(3), 2003.
3. K. Aberer, P. Cudré-Mauroux, and M. Hauswirth. Start making sense: The Chatty Web approach for global semantic agreements. *Journal of Web Semantics*, 1(1), 2003.
4. K. Aberer, P. Cudré-Mauroux, and M. Hauswirth. The Chatty Web: Emergent Semantics Through Gossiping. In *International World Wide Web Conference (WWW)*, 2003.
5. K. Aberer and M. Punceva. Efficient Search in Structured Peer-to-Peer Systems: Binary v.s. k-ary Unbalanced Tree Structures. In *International Workshop On Databases, Information Systems and Peer-to-Peer Computing*, 2003.

6. K. Aberer (ed.). Special issue on peer to peer data management. *ACM SIGMOD Record*, 32(3), 2003.
7. R. Albert and A.-L. Barabási. Statistical mechanics of complex networks. *Reviews of Modern Physics*, 74(47), 2002.
8. A. Anaby-Tavor, A. Ga, and A. Trombetta. Evaluating matching Algorithms: the Monotonicity Principle. In *IJCAI Workshop on Information Integration on the Web*, 2003.
9. M. Arenas, V. Kantere, A. Kementsietsidis, I. Kiringa, R. J. Miller, and J. Mylopoulos. The Hyperion Project: From Data Integration to Data Coordination. *SIGMOD Record*, 32(3), 2003.
10. M. Cai and M. Frank. RDFPeers: A Scalable Distributed RDF Repository based on A Structured Peer-to-Peer Network. In *International World Wide Web Conference (WWW)*, 2004.
11. A. Datta, M. Hauswirth, and K. Aberer. Updates in Highly Unreliable, Replicated Peer-to-Peer Systems. In *International Conference on Distributed Computing Systems (ICDCS)*, 2003.
12. M. Ehrig, P. Haase, R. Siebes, S. Staab, H. Stuckenschmidt, R. Studer, and C. Tempich. The SWAP Data and Metadata Model for Semantics-Based Peer-to-Peer Systems. In *Multiagent System Technologies (MATES)*, 2003.
13. J. M. Hellerstein. Toward network data indepence. *ACM SIGMOD Record*, 32(3), 2003.
14. R. Huebsch, J. M. Hellerstein, N. Lanham, B. T. Loo, S. Shenker, and I. Stoica. Querying the Internet with PIER. In *Conference On Very Large Data Bases (VLDB)*, 2003.
15. W. Nejdl, B. Wolf, C. Qu, S. Decker, M. Sintek, A. Naeve, M. Nilsson, M. Palmér, and T. Risch. EDUTELLA: a P2P networking infrastructure based on RDF. In *International World Wide Web Conference (WWW)*, 2002.
16. W. S. Ng, B. C. Ooi, and K. L. Tan. BestPeer: A self-configurable peer-to-peer system. In *International Conference on Data Engineering (ICDE)*, 2003.
17. B. C. Ooi, Y. Shu, and K.-L. Tan. Relational Data Sharing in Peer-based Data Management Systems . *ACM SIGMOD Record*, 32(3), 2003.
18. C. G. Plaxton, R. Rajaraman, and A. W. Richa. Accessing Nearby Copies of Replicated Objects in a Distributed Environment. In *Annual ACM Symposium on Parallelism in Algorithms and Architectures (SPAA)*, 1997.
19. E. Prud'hommeaux and B. Grosof. Rdf query and rules: A framework and survey. http://www.w3.org/2001/11/13-RDF-Query-Rules/.
20. A. Seaborne. Rdql - a query language for rdf. http://www.w3.org/Submission/RDQL/.
21. I. Stoica, R. Morris, D. Karger, F. Kaashoek, and H. Balakrishnan. Chord: A Scalable Peer-To-Peer Lookup Service for Internet Applications. In *ACM SIGCOMM Conference*, 2001.
22. I. Tatarinov, Z. Ives, J. Madhavan amd A. Halevy, D. Suciu, N. Dalvi, X. Dong, Y. Kadiyaska, G. Miklau, and P. Mork. The Piazza Peer Data Management Project. *ACM SIGMOD Record*, 32(3), 2003.
23. World Wide Web Consortium. Semantic web activity at the w3c. http://www.w3.org/2001/sw/.

Bibster – A Semantics-Based Bibliographic Peer-to-Peer System

Peter Haase[1], Jeen Broekstra[3], Marc Ehrig[1], Maarten Menken[2], Peter Mika[2],
Mariusz Olko[4], Michal Plechawski[4], Pawel Pyszlak[4], Björn Schnizler[1],
Ronny Siebes[2], Steffen Staab[1], and Christoph Tempich[1]

[1] Institute AIFB, University of Karlsruhe, D-76128 Karlsruhe, Germany
{ehrig, haase, staab, tempich}@aifb.uni-karlsruhe.de, schnizler@iw.uka.de
[2] Vrije Universiteit Amsterdam, The Netherlands
{mrmenken, pmika, ronny}@cs.vu.nl
[3] Aduna, Amersfoort, The Netherlands jeen@aduna.biz
[4] Empolis, Warsaw, Poland {pap, mpl}@empolis.pl

Abstract. This paper describes the design and implementation of Bibster, a Peer-to-Peer system for exchanging bibliographic data among researchers. Bibster exploits ontologies in data storage, query formulation, query routing and answer presentation: When bibliographic entries are made available for use in Bibster, they are structured and classified according to two different ontologies. This ontological structure is then exploited to help users formulate their queries. Subsequently, the ontologies are used to improve query routing across the Peer-to-Peer network. Finally, the ontologies are used to post-process the returned answers in order to do duplicate detection. The paper describes each of these ontology-based aspects of Bibster. Bibster is a fully implemented open source solution built on top of the JXTA platform.

1 Introduction

The advantages of Peer-to-Peer architectures over centralized approaches have been well advertised, and to some extent realized in existing applications: no centralized server (thus avoiding a bottleneck for both computational performance and information update), robustness against failure of any single component, scalability both in data volumes and the number of connected parties. However, besides being the solution to many problems, the large degree of distribution of Peer-to-Peer systems is also the cause of a number of new problems: The lack of a single coherent schema for organizing information sources across the Peer-to-Peer network hampers the formulation of search queries, duplication of information across the network results in many duplicate answers to a single query, and answers to a single query often require the integration of information residing at different, independent and uncoordinated peers.Finally, query routing and network topology (which peers to connect to, and which peers to send/forward queries to) are significant problems.

S.A. McIlraith et al. (Eds.): ISWC 2004, LNCS 3298, pp. 122–136, 2004.

The research community has recently turned to the use of semantics in Peer-to-Peer networks to alleviate these problems [1], [2], [3]. The use of semantic descriptions of datasources stored by peers and indeed of semantic descriptions of peers themselves helps in formulating queries such that they can be understood by other peers, in merging the answers received from other peers, and in routing queries across the network. In particular, the use of ontologies and of Semantic Web technologies has been identified as promising for Peer-to-Peer systems.

The scenario that we have envisioned is that researchers share bibliographic metadata in a community with a Peer-to-Peer system. The data may have been obtained from local BibTeX files or from bibliography servers like the DBLP database[1] or CiteSeer[2]. As one may easily recognize, this scenario (like some others that we do not elaborate upon in this paper) exhibits two characteristics that strongly require a semantics-based Peer-to-Peer system.

First, a centralized solution does not exist and cannot exist, because of the multitude of informal workshops that researchers refer to, but that do not show up in centralized resources such as DBLP. Any such centralized resource will only cover a limited scientific community. For example, DBLP covers a lot of Artificial Intelligence, but almost no Knowledge Management, whereas a lot of work is being done in the overlap of these two fields. At the same time, many individual researchers are willing to share their resources, provided they do not have to invest work in doing so.

Second, the use of Semantic Web technology is crucial in this setting. Although a small common-core ontology of bibliographic information exists (title, author/editor, etc), much of this information is very volatile and users define arbitrary add-ons, for example to include URLs or abstracts of publications.

In this paper we will describe the design of the Bibster system and emphasize the semantic components and their use: semantic extraction of bibliographic metadata in section 4, semantic querying in section 5, peer selection using semantic topologies in section 6, and semantic duplicate detection in section 7. Furthermore, Bibster has been fully implemented and we present evaluation results from a field experiment in section 8.

2   Major Bibster Use Cases

Bibster is aimed at researchers that share bibliographic metadata. Requirements for Bibster must include capabilities that support their daily work. Researchers may want to:

1. query a single specific peer (e.g. their own computer, because it is sometimes hard to find the right entry there), a specific set of peers (e.g. all colleagues at an institute) or the entire network of peers (to obtain the maximal recall at the price of low precision).

---

[1] http://dblp.uni-trier.de/
[2] http://citeseer.org/

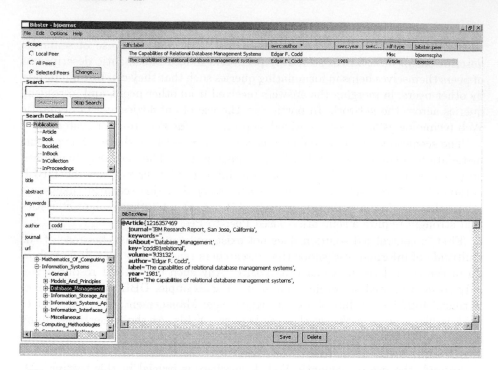

Fig. 1. Searching for publications about database management authored by Codd

2. search for bibliographic entries using simple keyword searches, but also more advanced, semantic searches, e.g. for publications of a special type, with specific attribute values, or about a certain topic.
3. integrate results of a query into a local knowledge base for future use. Such data may in turn be used to answer queries by other peers. They may also be interested in updating items that are already locally stored with additional information about these items obtained from other peers.

The screenshot in figure 1 partially indicates how these use cases are realized in Bibster. The *Scope* widget allows for defining the targeted peers, the *Search* and *Search Details* widgets allow for keyword and semantic search; *Results Table* and *BibtexView* widgets allow for browsing and re-using query results. The query results are visualized in a list grouped by duplicates. They may be integrated into the local repository or exported in formats such as BibTeX and HTML.

3   Design of Bibster

3.1   Ontologies in Bibster

Ontologies are crucial throughout the usage of Bibster, viz. for importing data, formulating queries, routing queries, and processing answers.

Firstly, the system enables users to import their own bibliographic metadata into a local repository. Bibliographic entries made available to Bibster by a user (cf. section 4) are automatically aligned to two common ontologies: The first ontology (SWRC[3]) describes different generic aspects of bibliographic metadata (and would be valid across many different research domains), the second ontology (ACM Topic Hierarchy[4]) describes specific categories of literature for the Computer Science domain.

Secondly, queries are formulated in terms of the two ontologies: Queries may concern fields like author, publication type, etc. (using terms from the SWRC ontology) or queries may concern specific Computer Science terms (using the ACM Topic Hierarchy).

Thirdly, queries are routed through the network depending on the expertise models of the peers describing which concepts from the ACM ontology a peer can answer queries on. A matching function determines how closely the semantic content of a query matches the expertise model of a peer. Routing is then done on the basis of this semantic ranking.

Finally, answers are returned for a query. Due to the distributed nature and potentially large size of the Peer-to-Peer network, this answer set might be very large, and contain many duplicate answers. Because of the semistructured nature of bibliographic metadata, such duplicates are often not exactly identical copies. Ontologies help to measure the semantic similarity between the different answers and to remove apparent duplicates as identified by the similarity function.

3.2   Bibster Architecture and Modules

The Bibster system has been implemented as an instance of the SWAP System architecture as introduced in [1]. Figure 2 shows a high-level design of the architecture of a single node in the Peer-to-Peer system. We will now briefly present the individual components as instantiated for the Bibster system.

Communication Adapter: This component is responsible for the network communication between peers. It serves as a transport layer for other parts of the system, for sending and forwarding queries. It hides and encapsulates all low-level communication details from the rest of the system. In the specific implementation of the Bibster system we use JXTA as the communication platform.

Knowledge Sources: The knowledge sources in the Bibster system are sources of bibliographic metadata, such as BibTeX files stored locally in the file system of the user.

Knowledge Source Integrator: The Knowledge Source Integrator is responsible for the extraction and integration of internal and external knowledge sources into the Local Node Repository. In section 4 we describe the process of semantic extraction from BibTeX files. In section 7 we explain how the knowledge of local and remote sources can be merged, i.e. how duplicate query results are detected.

---

[3] http://www.semanticweb.org/ontologies/swrc-onto-2001-12-11.daml
[4] http://www.acm.org/class/1998/

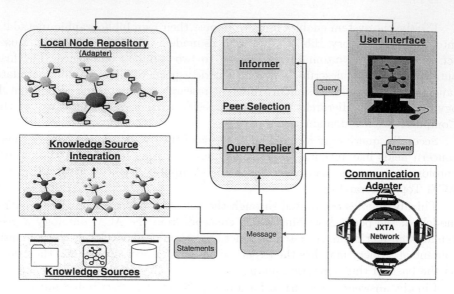

Fig. 2. SWAP System Architecture

Local Node Repository: In order to manage its information models and views as well as information acquired from the network, each peer maintains a Local Node Repository providing the following functionality: (1) Mediate between views and stored information, (2) support query formulation and processing, (3) specify the peer's interface to the network, and (4) provide the basis for peer ranking and selection. In the Bibster system, the Local Node Repository is based on the RDF-S Repository Sesame [4]. The query language SeRQL is used to formulate semantic queries against the Local Node Repository, as described in section 5.

Informer: The task of the Informer is to proactively advertise the available knowledge of a peer in the Peer-to-Peer network and to discover peers with knowledge that may be relevant for answering the user's queries. This is realized by sending advertisements about the expertise of a peer. In the Bibster system, these expertise descriptions contain a set of topics that the peer is an expert in. Peers may accept – i.e. remember – these advertisements, thus creating a semantic link to the other peer. These semantic links form a semantic topology, which is the basis for intelligent query routing (cf. section 6 for details).

Query Replier: The Query Replier is the coordinating component controlling the process of distributing queries. It receives queries from the User Interface or from other peers. Either way it tries to answer the query or distribute it further according to the content of the query. The decision to which peers a query should be sent is based on the knowledge about the expertise of other peers.

User Interface: The User Interface (Figure 1) allows the user to import, create and edit bibliographic metadata as well as to easily formulate queries.

4   Semantic Extraction of Bibliographic Metadata

Many researchers have accumulated extensive collections of BibTeX files for their bibliographic references. However, these files are semi-structured and thus single attributes may be missing or may not be interpreted correctly. For interchanging bibliographic data in a semantically based Peer-to-Peer network it has to be represented in a structured and formal way. *BibToOnto* is a component of Bibster for extracting explicit knowledge of bibliographic items. Plain BibTeX files are transformed into an ontology based knowledge representation.

The target ontology is the Semantic Web Research Community Ontology (SWRC), which models among others a research community, its researchers, topics, publications, tools, and properties between them. The SWRC ontology defines a shared and common domain theory which helps users and machines to communicate concisely and supports the exchange of semantics.

BibToOnto automatically classifies bibliographic entries according to the ACM topic hierarchy. Additionally, it is possible to reclassify the entries manually in the user interface of Bibster. The ACM topic hierarchy is a standard schema for describing and categorizing computer science literature. It covers 1287 topics of the computer science domain. In addition to the sub- and supertopic relations, it also provides information about related topics.

The following example shows a transformation of a BibTeX entry to a SWRC ontology based item. The result[5] is represented as an RDF graph in figure 3.

Example 1. @ARTICLE{codd70relational
```
            author   = "Edgar F. Codd",
            year     = "1970",
            title    = "A relational model for large shared data banks",
            journal  = "Communications of ACM",
            volume   = "13",
            number   = "6",
            pages    = "377--387"}
```

5   Semantic Querying

Each peer node in the Bibster system manages a local RDF repository with bibliographic data extracted by BibToOnto or integrated from other peers. The query language interface to the local RDF repository is SeRQL [5].

SeRQL (Sesame RDF Query Language) is an RDF/RDF-S query language that was developed in the context of the SWAP project to address practical requirements that were not sufficiently met by other query languages.

SeRQL Design Principles. Several characteristics are urgently required in the context of Bibster (but also of many other systems) for an RDF/RDF-S query language like SeRQL. In particular, it must:

---

[5] For better readability we used a concatenation of the author name and the title of the publication as a URI in this example. In the Bibster system however we calculate hash codes over all attribute values to guarantee the uniqueness of URIs.

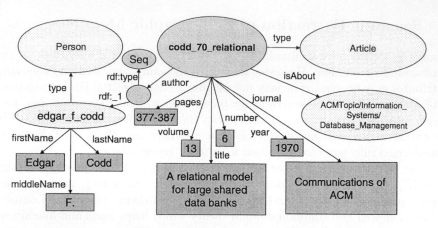

Fig. 3. SWRC Sample Metadata

1. be functional such that each query returns a RDF graph, which may be integrated into the local repository or queried again,
2. be aware of the (optional) schema,
3. let the user formulate path expressions for navigating the RDF graph, e.g. the combination of SWRC and ACM topic hierarchy,
4. be able to deal with *optional* values, e.g. a publisher field may be given or not.

Without showing all capabilities of SeRQL in full detail[6], we briefly show how SeRQL queries are composed, and how tasks in the Bibster system are performed using SeRQL.

(1) SeRQL uses a `select-from-where` or `construct-from-where` filter, where the `select` or `construct` clauses specify projections, the `from` clause specifies a graph match template (by means of path expressions), and the `where` clause allows the definition of additional boolean constraints on matched values in the path expressions.

(2) SeRQL takes the RDF schema into account by mapping from the given graph to its formal model.

(3) When navigating the RDF graph, SeRQL exploits the formal semantics of path labels. For example, `<rdfs:subClassOf>` is interpreted as a reflexive transitive relation and upward inheritance of instances is interpreted (through the `<rdf:type>` relation (cf. [5] for full details).

(4) Bibtex entries may be incomplete. SeRQL allows to distinguish between optional and required elements in the query and, hence, is flexible enough to deal with these circumstances.

A Querying Scenario. In our running example, a researcher is querying for journal articles written by the author Codd about database management. Internally, this request is formulated as a SeRQL query that looks as follows:

---

[6] See http://www.openrdf.org/doc/SeRQLmanual.html for a complete overview.

Example 2.
```
construct distinct
    {s} prop {val};
        <rdf:type> {t};
        <swrc:author> {x} <rdf:type> {<rdf:Seq>};
                          <rdfs:member> {author} prop_author {val_author}
from
    {s} <serql:directType> {t};
        <rdf:type> {<swrc:Article>};
        prop {val};
        <swrc:isAbout> {<acm:ACMTopic/Information_Systems/Database_Management>};
        <swrc:author> {x} <rdfs:member> {} <swrc:lastName> {lname},
        [{x} <rdfs:member> {author} prop_author {val_author} ]
where prop != <rdf:type> and lname like "Codd"
using namespace
    swrc = <!http://www.semanticweb.org/ontologies/swrc-onto-2001-12-11.daml#>,
    acm =  <!http://daml.umbc.edu/ontologies/classification#>
```

Compare the structure of the from-clause to the representation of the RDF graph given in figure 3. The from-clause retrieves not only the identifier for the particular journal entry ("codd_70_relational", matched by s), but also the graph structure surrounding it, which essentially gives the entry its meaning: the name of the author, the type of publication, the year it was published, the number of pages, etc. Also, if the first and middle names of an author are known, the query retrieves those (but it does not fail if these are not known).

The use of schema-awareness is evident in the use of typing information on s: s need not only be of type swrc:Article, we also retrieve its *specific* (or *direct*) type. Being functional plays a role as well: A graph transformation is used to create a query result that can be easily processed to be given back to the user through the GUI.

6   Expertise Based Peer Selection

The scalability of a Peer-to-Peer network is essentially determined by the way how queries are propagated in the network. Peer-to-Peer networks that broadcast all queries to all peers do not scale – intelligent query routing and network topologies are required to be able to route queries to a relevant subset of peers that are able to answer the queries.

Modern routing protocols like Chord [6] and CAN [7] allow for sophisticated query routing based on distributed indices. More recently, in the Semantic Web context, schema based Peer-to-Peer networks such as the one described in [8] have emerged based on complex, extensible semantic descriptions of resources. They allow for complex queries against these metadata instead of simple keyword-based queries. Another semantic-based approach is pSearch [9], a decentralized non-flooding Peer-to-Peer information retrieval system. pSearch distributes document indices through the Peer-to-Peer network based on document semantics generated by Latent Semantic Indexing (LSI). The search cost (in terms of nodes searched and data transmitted) for a given query is thereby reduced, since the indices of semantically related documents are likely to be co-located in the network. Here we give an overview of the model of expertise based peer selection as proposed in [10] and how it is used in the Bibster system. In this model, peers use a shared ontology to advertise semantic descriptions of their expertise in the Peer-to-Peer network. The knowledge about the expertise of other peers forms a semantic topology, independent of the underlying network topology. If the peer receives a query, it can decide to forward it to peers about which it knows that their expertise is similar to the subject of the query. The advantage of this approach is that queries will not be forwarded to all or a random set of known peers, but only to the ones that have a good chance of answering it.

Semantic Description of Expertise

Peers. The Peer-to-Peer network consists of a set of peers P. Every peer $p \in P$ has a Local Node Repository, which stores the bibliographic metadata.

Common Ontology. The peers share an ontology O, which is used for describing the expertise of peers and the subject of queries. In our case, O is the ACM topic hierarchy that contains a set of topics T.

Expertise. An expertise description is an abstract, semantic description of the Local Node Repository of a peer based on the shared ontology O. The expertise E of a peer is thus defined as $E \subseteq 2^T$, where each $e \in E$ denotes a set of ACM topics, for which a peer provides classified instances.

Advertisements. Advertisements $A \subseteq P \times E$ are used to promote descriptions of the expertise of peers in the network. An advertisement $a \in A$ associates a peer p with an expertise e. Peers decide autonomously, without central control, whom to promote advertisements to and which advertisements to accept. This decision is based on the semantic similarity between expertise descriptions.

Matching and Peer Selection

Queries. Queries $q \in Q$ are posed by a user and are evaluated against the local node repositories of the peers. First a peer evaluates the query against its local node repository and then decides which peers the query should be forwarded to.

Subjects. A subject is an abstraction of a given query q expressed in terms of the common ontology. The subject specifies the required expertise to answer the query. In our scenario, the subjects of queries are defined as $S \subseteq 2^T$, each s is the set of ACM topics that are referenced in the query. E.g., the extracted subject of the query in example 2 would be *Information Systems/Database Management*.

Similarity Function. The similarity function $Sim : S \times E \mapsto [0,1]$ yields the semantic similarity between a subject $s \in S$ and an expertise description $e \in E$. An increasing value indicates increasing similarity. If the value is 0, s and e are not similar at all, if the value is 1, they match exactly. Sim is used for determining to which peers a query should be forwarded. In Bibster, the similarity function Sim_{Topics} is based on the idea that topics which are close according to their positions in the topic hierarchy are more similar than topics that have a larger distance. For example, an expert on the ACM topic *Information Systems/Information Storage and Retrieval* has a higher chance of giving a correct answer on a query about *Information Systems/Database Management* than an expert on a less similar topic like *Hardware/Memory Structures*.

To be able to define the similarity of a peer's expertise and a query subject, which are both represented as a set of topics, we first define the similarity for individual topics. [11] have compared different similarity measures and have shown that for measuring the similarity between concepts in a hierarchical structured semantic network, like the ACM topic hierarchy, the following similarity measure yields the best results:

$$
sim_{Topic}(t_1, t_2) = \begin{cases} e^{-\alpha l} \cdot \frac{e^{\beta h} - e^{-\beta h}}{e^{\beta h} + e^{-\beta h}} & \text{if } t_1 \neq t_2, \\ 1 & \text{otherwise} \end{cases}
$$

Here l is the length of the shortest path between topic t_1 and t_2 in the graph spanned by the *SubTopic* relation. h is the level in the tree of the direct common subsumer from t_1 and t_2. $\alpha \geq 0$ and $\beta \geq 0$ are parameters scaling the contribution of shortest path length l and depth h, respectively. Based on their benchmark data set, the optimal values are: $\alpha = 0.2$, $\beta = 0.6$.

Peer Selection Algorithm. The peer selection algorithm returns a ranked set of peers, where the rank value is equal to the similarity value provided by the similarity function. Therefore, peers that have an expertise more similar to that of the subject of the query will have a higher rank. From this set of ranked peers one can, for example, select the best n peers, or all peers whose rank value is above a certain threshold. In the Bibster system we select the best n peers that have not yet received the query along the message path, where n can be specified. A maximum number of hops (set to 4 for the field experiment) further limits the forwarding of queries.

Semantic Topology

The knowledge of the peers about the expertise of other peers is the basis for a semantic topology. Here it is important to state that this semantic topology is independent of the underlying network topology. At this point, we do not make any assumptions about the properties of the topology on the network layer. The semantic topology can be described by the following relation:

$Knows \subseteq P \times P$, where $Knows(p_1, p_2)$ means that p_1 knows about the expertise of p_2.

The relation $Knows$ is established by the selection of which peers a peer sends its advertisements to. Furthermore peers can decide to accept an advertisement, e.g. to include it in their registries, or to discard the advertisement. The semantic topology in combination with the expertise based peer selection is the basis for intelligent query routing.

7   Semantic Duplicate Detection

When querying the Bibster network one receives a large number of results with an often high number of duplicates. This is due to the fact that we do not have a centralized but many distributed local repositories. Furthermore, the representation of the metadata is very heterogeneous and possibly even contradicting. To enable an efficient and easily usable system Bibster presents query results grouping duplicates together. Duplicates in Bibster are bibliographic entries which refer to the same publication, person, or organization in the real world, but are modelled as different resources. Bibster uses specific similarity functions to recognize two resources as being duplicates.

Similarity Function. A similarity function for RDF resources R of the local node repository is a function $sim : R \times R \rightarrow [0..1]$.

For each resource type (publication, person, organization), we have compiled a set of specific features used to assess the similarity between two of its instances. For instance, publications are assessed based on their titles, publication types, authors, years, ACM topics, etc. For each of the features we use different *individual similarity functions*, which are grouped as follows:

The *data value level* focuses on comparisons of data values, which in RDF are represented as typed literals. For example, to determine the similarity of data values of type string (e.g. to compare the last names of persons) we use the *syntactic similarity* of [12]. At the *graph structure level* we check how resources are related to each other. For example, a publication resource is linked to person resources, e.g. authors. Thus we can compare two publications on the basis of the similarity of the sets of authors. This feature alone is not deciding, but it supports the hypothesis of having duplicate entries.

Similarity measures at the *ontology level* extend the ones at the graph structure level by ontology specific characteristics. To determine the similarity of two publications based on their topics we make use of the ACM topic hierarchy. We apply the hierarchical similarity function as presented earlier in this paper [13].

Applying background *knowledge about a specific domain*, we can define more appropriate similarity functions. For example, in the SWRC domain ontology there are many subconcepts of publications: articles, books, and technical reports to just name a few. Unknown publication types are often provided as Misc. We can thus define a function that returns a value of 1 if the publication type is identical, a value of e.g. 0.75 if Misc is one of it, and 0 otherwise.

From the variety of individual similarity functions, an overall value is obtained with an aggregated similarity function, using a weighted average over the individual functions. For Bibster, the weights have been assigned based on experiments with sample data. More precisely, several duplicates were detected manually. From these training duplicates the weights were adjusted to achieve a maximal f-measure (combination of precision and recall) value.

The Duplicate Relation. As duplicates we consider those pairs of resources whose similarity is larger than a certain threshold

$$t \in [0..1] : D_t := \{(x, y) | sim(x, y) \geq t\}$$

If we assume that the duplicate relation is transitive, we can define the transitive closure as:

$$TC(D_t) := \{(x, z) | (x, y) \in D_t \wedge (y, z) \in D_t\}$$

This transitive closure essentially represents clusters of semantically similar resources.

Resource Merging. Instead of presenting all individual resources of the query result, duplicates are visualized as one, merged, resource. The merged resources comprise the union of statements of the individuals identified as duplicates. In the case of conflicting property values, we apply heuristics for the merging of resources (e.g. for booktitles to select the most detailed value with the least abbreviations).

8   Results

The Bibster system that implements the methods presented in this paper has been evaluated by means of a public field experiment. The user actions and system events are continuously logged and analyzed to evaluate the user behavior and system performance. We have analyzed the results for a period of two months (June and July 2004) and have obtained the following interesting results: A total of 146 peers from various organizations spread mainly over Europe and North America used the Bibster system. The users shared more than 70000 bibliographic entries. While seventeen peers shared more than 1000 items each, accounting for 84% of the total content, a lot of peers provided only little content or were "free-riding".

The users performed a total of 1782 queries. The SWRC ontology was used for about half of all queries, mainly for the purpose to search for special types of publications (e.g. only for articles) or for publications of a given author. In 348 queries the users asked for topics of the ACM topic hierarchy. Thereby it is obvious that the users are accepting the ontology based searching capabilities and that there is a benefit for them in using these ontologies.

With respect to query routing, with the expertise based peer selection we were able to reduce the number of query messages by about 50 percent, while retaining the same recall of documents compared with a naive broadcasting approach. Figure 4 shows the number of forwarded query messages sent per query and the precision of the peer selection (the percentage of the reached peers that actually provided answers to a given query). Although we have shown an improvement in the performance, the results also show that with a network of the size as in the field experiment, a naive approach is also acceptable. On the other hand, with a growing number of peers, query routing and peer selection becomes critical: In simulation experiments with larger peer networks with thousands of peers, we have shown improvements in the order of one magnitude in terms of recall of documents and relevant peers [10].

Lessons Learned

This section summarizes some experiences we have gained from the development and application of Bibster.

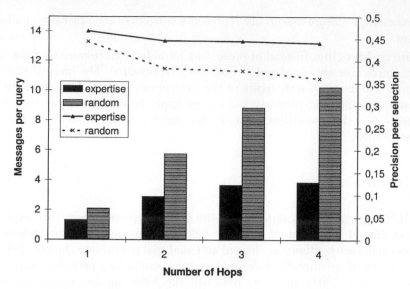

Fig. 4. Number of Messages and Precision of Peer Selection

For Bibster and similar applications the usage of Semantic Web technologies and ontologies provide an *added value* — in fact it is almost a strict requirement given its semi-structured, volatile data structures. Semantic structures serve important user concerns like high quality duplicate detection or comprehensive searching capabilities.

Unsurprisingly, in small networks with *small user groups*, intelligent query routing is not a major issue. While it is beneficial to direct queries to specific peers known to the user (a trust issue!), advanced routing algorithms may only be beneficial for a much larger number of users in a network. Based on our experience we now conjecture that content-based routing and trust issues will have to converge for such larger networks, too.

9   Related Work

In the previous sections, related work on the individual aspects of semantics-based Peer-to-Peer technology has already been discussed. Therefore in this section our study of related work focuses on complete systems. Edutella (*cf.* *eg.* [8]) is a Peer-to-Peer system based on the JXTA platform, which offers similar base functionality as the SWAP system. The Edutella network focuses on the exchange of learning material. They use super-peer based topologies, in which peers are organized in hypercubes to route queries. In contrast to their work, Bibster is embedded in the general SWAP architecture and a running application.

[14] describes the design of a Peer-to-Peer network for open archives, where data providers, i.e. research institutes, form a Peer-to-Peer network which sup-

ports distributed search over all the connected metadata repositories. This scenario which is similar to our bibliographic Peer-to-Peer scenario, however, their system has not been implemented up to this point.

P-Grid [15] is a structured, yet fully-decentralized Peer-to-Peer system based on a virtual distributed search tree. It aims at providing load-balancing and fault-tolerance, assuming that peers fail frequently and are online with low probability. P-Grid also considers updates with an update algorithm based rumor spreading.

The DFN Science-to-Science (S2S) [16] system enhances content based searching by using peer-to-peer technology to make locally generated indexes accessible in an ad hoc manner. Whereas Bibster is fully distributed, S2S uses a kind of super peers (Search Hubs) to route queries and cache information.

Various systems address the issue of heterogeneity in Peer-to-Peer systems on the schema level, such as the Piazza peer data management system [17], which allows for information sharing with different schemas relying on local mappings between schemas.

10   Conclusion

In this paper, we have described the design and implementation of Bibster, a semantics-based Peer-to-Peer system for the exchange of bibliographic metadata between researchers. For this purpose, Bibster exploits lightweight ontologies, expressed in RDF Schema in all its crucial aspects: data-organisation, query formulation, query routing and duplicate detection. To our knowledge, Bibster now constitutes the first ontology-based Peer-to-Peer systems ready for fielded deployment.

In general, there are interesting alternatives for each of the different aspects (e.g., [2] for querying or [15] for query routing) and, actually, we are still exploring multiple approaches to optimize the overall system (e.g., [18] for query routing). In practice, however, it constitutes a major challenge to integrate these different components into a coherent system like Bibster.

The next steps in the development of Bibster are, *(i)* its optimization (e.g., manual query optimization), *(ii)* its spreading to further user groups and, *(iii)* the extension of Bibster to better account for personalized semantic structures, based on the two common core ontologies, e.g. peer-local extensions of the ACM topic hierarchy.

The reader may find further reading material on Bibster, its underlying technologies and related material in the open available project deliverable documentation at `http://swap.semanticweb.org/` and `http://bibster.semanticweb.org/`.

Acknowledgments. Research reported in this paper has been partially financed by the EU in the IST projects SWAP (IST-2001-34103) and SEKT (IST-2003-506826). We would like to thank our colleagues for fruitful discussions.

References

1. Broekstra, J., Ehrig, M., Haase, P., van Harmelen, F., Kampman, A., Sabou, M., Siebes, R., Staab, S., Stuckenschmidt, H., Tempich, C.: A metadata model for semantics-based peer-to-peer systems. In: Proceedings of the WWW'03 Workshop on Semantics in Peer-to-Peer and Grid Computing. (2003)
2. Nejdl, W., Wolf, B., Qu, C., Decker, S., Sintek, M., Naeve, A., Nilsson, M., Palmér, M., Risch, T.: Edutella: A P2P networking infrastructure based on rdf. In: Proceedings to the Eleventh International World Wide Web Conference. (2002)
3. Castano, A., Ferrara, S., Montanelli, S., Pagani, E., Rossi, G.: Ontology-addressable contents in p2p networks. In: Proceedings of the WWW'03 Workshop on Semantics in Peer-to-Peer and Grid Computing. (2003)
4. Broekstra, J., Kampman, A., van Harmelen, F.: Sesame: An architecture for storing and querying rdf data and schema information (2001)
5. Broekstra, J., Kampman, A.: Serql: An rdf query and transformation language (2004) Submitted to the International Semantic Web Conference, ISWC 2004.
6. Stoica, I., Morris, R., Karger, D., Kaashoek, M.F., Balakrishnan, H.: Chord: A scalable peer-to-peer lookup service for Internet applications. In: Proceedings of the ACM SIGCOMM '01. (2001)
7. Ratnasamy, S., Francis, P., Handley, M., Karp, R., Shenker, S.: A scalable content-addressable network. In: Proc. of ACM SIGCOMM '01. (2001)
8. Nejdl, W., et al.: Super-peer-based routing and clustering strategies for rdf-based peer-to-peer networks. In: Proceedings of the Twelfth International World Wide Web Conference (WWW 2003), Budapest, Hungary (2003)
9. Tang, C., Xu, Z., Mahalingam, M.: pSearch: Information retrieval in structured overlays. In: ACM HotNets-I. (2002)
10. Haase, P., Siebes, R., van Harmelen, F.: Peer selection in peer-to-peer networks with semantic topologies. In: International Conference on Semantics of a Networked World: Semantics for Grid Databases, June 2004, Paris. (2004)
11. Li, Y., Bandar, Z.A., McLean, D.: An approach for measuring semantic similarity between words using multiple information sources. Transactions on Knowledge and Data Engineering 15 (2003) 871–882
12. Maedche, A., Staab, S.: Comparing ontologies - similarity measures and a comparison study. In: Proc. of EKAW-2002. (2002)
13. Rada, R., Mili, H., Bicknell, E., Blettner, M.: Development and application of a metric on semantic nets. In: IEEE Transactions on Systems, Man and Cybernetics. (1989) 17–30
14. Ahlborn, B., Nejdl, W., Siberski, W.: OAI-P2P: A peer-to-peer network for open archives. In: Workshop on Distributed Computing Architectures for Digital Libraries - ICPP2002. (2002)
15. Aberer, K., Mauroux, P.C., Datta, A., Despotovic, Z., Hauswirth, M., Punceva, M., Schmidt, R.: P-Grid: a self-organizing structured p2p system. ACM SIGMOD Record 32 (2003) 29–33
16. Wertlen, R.: Dfn science-to-science: Peer-to-peer scientific research. In: Proceedings of the Terena Networking Conference (TNC 2003), Zagreb, Croatia (2003)
17. Tatarinov, I., Ives, Z., Madhavan, J., Halevy, A., Suciu, D., Dalvi, N., Dong, X., Kadiyska, Y., Miklau, G., Mork, P.: The piazza peer data management project. SIGMOD Record 32 (2003)
18. Tempich, C., Staab, S., Wranik, A.: REMINDIN': Semantic query routing in peer-to-peer networks based on social metaphors. In: Proc. of the 13th Int. World Wide Web Conference, WWW 2004. (2004)

Top-k Query Evaluation
for Schema-Based Peer-to-Peer Networks

Wolfgang Nejdl[1], Wolf Siberski[1], Uwe Thaden[1], and Wolf-Tilo Balke[2]

[1] L3S and University of Hannover, Hannover
{nejdl,siberski,thaden}@l3s.de
[2] EECS, University of California, Berkeley
balke@eecs.berkeley.edu

Abstract. Increasing the number of peers in a peer-to-peer network usually increases the number of answers to a given query as well. While having more answers is nice in principle, users are not interested in arbitrarily large and unordered answer sets, but rather in a small set of "best" answers. Inspired by the success of ranking algorithms in Web search engine and top-k query evaluation algorithms in databases, we propose a decentralized top-k query evaluation algorithm for peer-to-peer networks which makes use of local rankings, rank merging and optimized routing based on peer ranks, and minimizes both answer set size and network traffic among peers. As our algorithm is based on dynamically collected query statistics only, no continuous index update processes are necessary, allowing it to scale easily to large numbers of peers.

Keywords: Top-k retrieval, peer-to-peer query processing, ranking.

1 Introduction

Meaningful querying for information, whether on the Web or in information systems and databases, often retrieves answers together with an indication of how well the results match the query. Various kinds of metadata available through the Semantic Web offer additional semantic information which may be integrated into the retrieval process. However, this generally comes at the price of large result set sizes that are often unmanageable for the individual user. Since users are usually only interested in a few *most relevant* answers to their query, the goal in top-k retrieval techniques is to return manageable result sets consisting of these most relevant answers.

This paper is concerned with querying peer-to-peer networks, which in recent years turned out to be a good basis for distributed information storage and exchange infrastructures. We will focus on *schema-based* peer-to-peer networks like Edutella [1], which is a peer-to-peer infrastructure for storing and retrieving RDF metadata in a distributed environment.

Let us consider a sample scenario, where the need for restricting the number of answers to a given query becomes apparent. Suppose that a student, John, prepares for an exam in logic programming and looks for appropriate exercises. We can assume that the educational ontology he uses allows him to specify his request for exercises, and his topic ontology ACM-CCS[1] lets him specify 'Logic Programming' as topic. As this is a

---

[1] ACM Computing Classification System, http://www.acm.org/class/1998/

S.A. McIlraith et al. (Eds.): ISWC 2004, LNCS 3298, pp. 137–151, 2004.
© Springer-Verlag Berlin Heidelberg 2004

fairly common area, we'll expect him to get a large list of matches more or less matching the query (e.g. some exercises specifically on logic programming, some exercises that contain logic programming questions among others and a number of exercises discussing just a few aspects of the topic). With current peer-to-peer infrastructures (including Edutella) there is no way for John to retrieve a list where all exercises are ordered by relevance, and only the best ones are presented in the first step, to be expanded whenever needed. John might also try to be more restrictive in subsequent queries until a sufficiently small result set is retrieved, but without knowing exactly which data are available this is a quite tedious process.

The situation gets even worse if we allow approximate keyword search. Suppose John looks specifically for Prolog programming exercises, but the corresponding entry is not part of the used topic ontology. A good solution would be to allow a combined schema-based and keyword search. John could then add the keyword 'Prolog' to his query. Again, keyword searches which return unordered lists of matching documents are not particularly useful. Similar to internet search engines, the success of any keyword search depends on its ability to identify a limited set of the most relevant documents.

Ranking scores each resource that matches a query using a certain set of criteria and then returns it as part of a ranked list. Additionally, we need to restrict the number of results, to make it easier for the user to use the results, and to minimize traffic in a peer-to-peer environment. John then gets a manageable number of results which includes those answers that are the most relevant for his query. This approach is referred to as top-k retrieval in database query processing, where only the k best matching resources are returned to the user.

In this paper we present a distributed top-k algorithm for peer-to-peer infrastructures. Our algorithm retrieves the k most relevant results in a peer-to-peer network without having to rely on any centralized or global knowledge and without need for a complete distributed index. Furthermore, our top-k algorithm does not only deliver more relevant results, it also allows us to optimize query distribution and routing. Based on statistics gathered at super-peers, queries are distributed only to the most promising peers. Compared to current approaches like PlanetP [2], because we do not need to maintain a complete distributed index, we avoid continuous updates whenever peers join or leave the network. Instead we show how information can be gathered dynamically based on the queries posed to the network, enabling advanced routing and top-k answers based on previous query statistics.

2   Peer-to-Peer Infrastructures and Ranking for Top-k Routing

2.1   Schema-Based Peer-to-Peer Networks

Schema based querying.   Let us first start with the necessary background on peer-to-peer infrastructures for our algorithm. In previous papers, we have described the RDF-based peer-to-peer infrastructure Edutella [1,3] which is an example of a more advanced approach to peer-to-peer networks called schema-based peer-to-peer networks. Schema-based peer-to-peer networks have a number of advantages compared to simpler peer-to-peer networks such as Napster or Gnutella. Instead of prescribing one global schema to describe content, they support arbitrary metadata schemas and ontologies, which is crucial for the Semantic Web, and thus have been investigated heavily during the last years [4,5,6,7]. These systems allow complex and extensible descriptions of resources, and provide more complex query capabilities than simple keyword-based search. Edutella uses RDF and RDFS for resource and schema description. The distributed nature of RDF is a perfect match to the distributed nature of peer-to-peer networks, and the flexibility and extensibility of RDFS allows us to combine arbitrary schema elements for resource description as well as for query formulation.

Semantic Routing. If we have additional semantic information about the data available in the network, we can use this information to optimize query routing. [8] uses this approach for an unstructured peer-to-peer network and evaluates different kinds of routing indices used to forward requests in the right direction. Other peer-to-peer approaches which support routing based on semantic characteristics are P-Grid [9,4] and Piazza [5].

Edutella uses a super-peer topology, where super-peers form the network backbone and take care of routing queries through the network [3]. Only a small percentage of nodes are super-peers, but these are assumed to be highly available nodes with high computing capacity. In the Edutella network they are arranged in the HyperCuP topology [10]. The HyperCuP algorithm is capable of organizing peers into a recursive graph structure from the family of Cayley graphs, out of which the hypercube is the most well-known topology. This topology allows for $\log_2 N$ path length and $\log_2 N$ number of neighbors, where N is the total number of nodes in the network (i.e. the number of super-peers in our case). The algorithm works as follows: All edges are tagged with their dimension in the hypercube. A node invoking a request sends the message to all its neighbors, tagging it with the edge label on which the message was sent. Nodes receiving the message forward it only via edges tagged with higher edge labels (see [10] for details).

The super-peers employ routing indices which explicitly take schema information into account. Queries are analyzed regarding the schema elements used, and only peers which actively use these are considered when distributing the query.

2.2 Ranking Results

The second ingredient for our algorithm is ranking. Ranking allows us to reduce the overall number of answers in the result set and also to return close matches to avoid empty result sets in case no exact matches are found. Answers returned are ordered using a score value computed for each resource. We will use this score to limit the number of answers and return only the k best matching results. Let us describe two particularly useful ranking-methods, which we will then use in our algorithm presented in 3.2.

Topic-distances in Taxonomies. In the context of the Semantic Web, the use of ontologies and taxonomies to classify resources is very common. Given such a taxonomy, resources are associated with topics/concepts in the hierarchy using appropriate metadata annotations, and we can use methods as discussed in [11] to measure how similar and thus how relevant a resource is with respect to a query.

TFxIDF. TFxIDF stands for Term Frequency and Inverse Document Frequency and is a content-based ranking method. It calculates the relevance of a document, based on how often a search term appears in a document (term frequency TF), and how often the term exists in the whole document collection (inverse document frequency IDF). The more search terms are found in a document, the more important the document is, taking into account how often the search term is found in the collection, i.e. weighting rare terms in documents higher. A detailed introduction can be found in [12]. For a term t_i from a set of keywords and a document d_j from a document collection T_r TFxIDF is defined as

$$TFxIDF(t_i, d_j) = \underbrace{n(t_i, d_j)}_{TF} \cdot \underbrace{\log \frac{|T_r|}{n(t_i)}}_{IDF} \tag{1}$$

where $n(t_i, d_j)$ denotes the number of occurrences of the term t_i in the document d_j and $n(t_i)$ is the number of documents that contain the term t_i.

3 Top-k Query Answering and Routing

3.1 Challenges

Top-k ranking in peer-to-peer networks has to address four challenges:

Mismatch in scoring techniques and input data used by the different peers can have a strong impact on getting the correct overall top-scored objects. Since we want to minimize network traffic, but nevertheless integrate the top-scored objects from all different peers (and super-peers) within each super-peer, each super-peer has to decide how to score answers to a given query. In this paper we will assume that every peer throughout the network uses the same methods to score documents with respect to a query, though input data to compute these scores may be different.

Using only distributed knowledge and thus different input data to score answers complicates top-k retrieval, because many scoring measures that take global characteristics into account simply cannot be evaluated correctly with limited local knowledge. For our TFxIDF measure we can calculate term frequency locally for each document, but inverted document frequency depends on all documents in the peer network and thus can only be determined globally. Joining and leaving peers influences the calculation further. When we calculate IDF based on the local knowledge of each peer only, monotonicity of local rankings will not be preserved at the super-peer (who has more complete input to calculate IDF) and thus the overall top score list at the super-peer may miss relevant results. In the following we therefore will distinguish between two different kinds of measures: those that can be evaluated locally, i.e. that rely on the characteristics/content of the resources in a peer's local collection only (possibly in connection with some network-wide constants), and those that incorporate collection wide information, that depends on the resources in the (global) collection of all peers.

Minimizing network data transfer means that we should strive to only exchange the minimal amount of information necessary between peers and super-peers. A good example for limiting network data transfer is semantic-based routing. Queries and results are only routed through those (super-)peers that are associated with resources relevant to the query. This is also relevant for merging result sets in super-peers, where we want to minimize incoming data yet still produce a complete top-k answer list.

No continuous index updates. In peer-to-peer networks peers join and leave the network at unpredictable intervals. Top-k retrieval and routing has to take this into account without requiring continuous index updates limiting scalability of the algorithm. As a tradeoff we are willing to accept a certain degree of non-optimality in our top-k results as long as changes in the network are reflected "fast enough" in our results. Obviously, volatility of the peers cannot be arbitrarily high, as no kind of statistics would be meaningful then.

Taking this considerations into account, we will describe a top-k answering and routing algorithm, which is based on local rankings at each peer, aggregated during routing of answers for a given query at the super-peers involved in the query answering process. Each peer computes local rankings for a given query, results are merged and ranked again at the super-peers and routed back to the query originator. On this way back, each involved super-peer again merges results from local peers and from neighboring super-peers and forwards only the best results, until the aggregated top k results reach the peer that issued the corresponding query. While results are routed through the super-peers, we maintain statistics which peers / super-peers returned the best results. This information is subsequently used to directly route queries that were answered before mainly to those peers able to provide top answers. Additionally, a small percentage of queries will additionally be forwarded randomly to enable lazy update of these indices to adapt to changes in the peer-to-peer network. The more volatile the network is, the higher the percentage routed to random peers has to be in order to adapt to changing data allocations.

The following sections describe the different parts of the algorithm, starting with local ranking, then covering the merging of the results at the super-peers, and then finally showing how we can improve routing based on query / answer statistics.

3.2 Ranking at Single Peers

When a super-peer receives a query, it asks its peers to rank their resources locally. The results are top-k ranked variable bindings from each peer, which are sent back to the super-peer, along with score information for merging at the super-peer. To simplify the presentation we describe the algorithm taking the view of a user who wants to retrieve URIs of the best matching RDF-resources. Thus, we will only refer to the resource instead of complete variable bindings.

In the context of this paper, we restrict ourselves to queries which allow conjunctive triple matching with constraints. Current Semantic Web query languages like RDQL [13] allow only 'hard' constraints, i.e. only resources for which all constraints are fulfilled match the query. On the other hand, for SQL additional language constructs for specification of 'weak' constraints, weighting of constraints and specification of the max number of results have already been defined in previous work [14].

Here we do not propose a language extension, but use a formal notation for our queries instead. A query Q is a tuple $Q = (Atoms_Q, \ k)$ where $Atoms_Q = \{(q, w_q)\}$ define the constraints of the query together with a weight w_q which is used to specify how important the different atoms are for the query-result-rankings. Constraints have the form $q = (prop_q, op_q, c_q)$ where prop is an RDF property , op is an operator and c is a constant RDF literal or resource.

Using this notation our scenario query from section 1 (find all 'lom-edu:Exercise's with a subject-classification in the ACM CCS most similar to 'acm-ccs:LogicProgramming' and where the content of the property 'dc:description' is most relevant with respect to the keyword 'prolog') looks as follows:

$Q = (\{(q_1, \ 0), \ (q_2, \ 0.7), \ (q_3, \ 0.3)\}, \ 12)$ with

$q_1 = (rdf : type, \ =, \ lomedu\text{:}Exercise)$

$q_2 = (dc : subject, \ \approx, \ acmccs\text{:}LogicProgramming)$

$q_3 = (dc : description, \ \sqsupseteq, \ 'prolog')$.

The operators that can be used in queries are distinguished into 'hard' and 'soft' operators: $OP_{hard} = \{=, \ <, \ >\}$ and $OP_{soft} = \{\approx, \ \sqsupseteq\}$: $OP = OP_{hard} \cup OP_{weak}$. In our example the hard operator $=$ specifies that the results must be of the type lom-edu:Exercise. Our soft operators are a similarity operator ('$\approx$') and a keyword search operator('$\sqsupseteq$') ('$\approx$' measures similarities between topics in a taxonomy and '$\sqsupseteq$' triggers a measurement based on keyword search in text).

In general our approach can build upon any kind of similarity measures. In this paper we focus on two methods as examples: a measurement for distances in taxonomies and TFxIDF for plain text searches. In contrast to the taxonomy distance calculation, TFxIDF also needs non-local information.

Li et al. have developed and compared several measures for topic similarity in tax-onomies [11]. We chose the following measure which yielded the best results in their study. The similarity of two topics in a taxonomy is defined as

$$\text{sim}_p(r, \ prop, \ c) = \begin{cases} e^{-\alpha l} \cdot \frac{e^{\beta h} - e^{-\beta h}}{e^{\beta h} + e^{-\beta h}} & : \ \text{if value}(r, \ prop) \neq \ c \\ 1 & : \ \text{otherwise} \end{cases} \qquad (2)$$

where l is the shortest path between the topics in the taxonomy tree and h is the depth level of the direct common subsumer. α and β are parameters to optimize the similarity measurement (best setting is usually $\alpha = 0.2$ and $\beta = 0.6$). We might sometimes get different results on different peers due to different property values for the same resource. This can be caused either by annotation errors or if the property value is user-dependent, e.g. user ratings.

Centralized IR system use a global index containing term and inverse document frequencies. In a distributed context this approach is not feasible. PlanetP solves this problem by maintaining a replicated network-wide index which is updated using gos-siping within the network [2]. In contrast, our approach does not build a complete index in advance at all, but rather retrieves the necessary non-local information as soon as it is needed for the evaluation of a query. For TFxIDF, this is the inverse document fre-quency, and idf denotes the non-local value. In section 3.3 we describe how this value is calculated and distributed to the peers. Corresponding to equation 1 we define tfidf for a peer p and a resource r as

$$\mathrm{tfidf}_p(r,\ prop,\ c) = \mathrm{tf}_p(r,\ prop,\ c) \cdot \mathrm{idf}(prop,\ c) \tag{3}$$

where $\mathrm{tf}_p(r,\ prop,\ c)$ is the term frequency (= number of occurrences) of constant c in property $prop$ of resource r and $\mathrm{idf}(prop, c)$ is the network-wide inverse occurrence frequency of c in property $prop$.

We use the index '$_p$' to specify that a function or set is related to the context of peer p. In this section we restrict ourselves to simple peers; in 3.3 we will also take super-peers into account.

Depending on the type of property and constant used in the atom the appropriate measure is selected.

$$\mathrm{score}_p(q,\ r) = \begin{cases} \mathrm{tfidf}_p(r,\ prop_q,\ c_q) &:\ op_q =\sqsupseteq \\ \mathrm{sim}_p(r,\ prop_q,\ c_q) &:\ op_q =\approx \wedge (c_q \text{ is a topic}) \end{cases} \tag{4}$$

Using the weights from the atoms we can calculate the overall score of a resource with respect to a complex query.

$$\mathrm{score}_p(Q,\ r) = \begin{cases} 0 &:\exists q\ \mathrm{score}(q,\ r) = 0 \wedge op_q \in OP_{hard} \\ \sum\limits_{q \in Atoms_Q} w_q \cdot \mathrm{score}_p(q,\ r) &:\text{otherwise} \end{cases}$$

$$\tag{5}$$

3.3   Query Distribution and Result Merging

In order to use the peer scores from single peers to determine the top k resources within the network, peers do not only return the scores, but will need to provide some additional information that will be used at the super-peer to do a ranking over the top k results from the peers.

Let us first extend the single-peer measures discussed in the last section to take super-peers into account. P denotes the set of all peers and SP the set of all super-peers. For the set of all peers connected to a super-peer p we use the notation P_p and the notation $SP_p(Q)$ for the set of super-peers a query has to be forwarded to from super-peer p[2].

Score aggregation. Aggregation of taxonomy scores is straightforward, because this measure is independent of the originating peer's context. We use the maximum score of a resource as consolidated score[3]:

$$\mathrm{sim}_p(r,\ prop,\ c) = \begin{cases} \mathrm{Max}_{o \in P_p \cup SP_p(Q)}(\mathrm{sim}_o(r,\ prop,\ c)) : p \in SP \\ \text{same as for simple peer} \qquad\qquad : p \in P \end{cases} \tag{6}$$

---

[2] We could introduce this set formally as well, but give only an informal sketch here, because the HyperCuP topology is not our main focus in this paper. In HyperCuP, each super-peer can be represented as a vector with binary entries, which describe the location regarding the dimension in the graph. A super-peer will only forward queries to other super-peers that are one dimension higher. To know which super-peers will send results for a query to the current super-peer we use a difference-function on the vectors. This gives us a list of vectors representing the super-peers that will return results.

[3] In this and all following equations o and p always represent peers, r and s resources.

Aggregating the TFxIDFs from the peers means we have to compute an overall TFx-IDF measurement for all results delivered from the peers. We calculate the aggregation of the occurrences of a constant in a text property (=TF) together with the number of all resources at the peers related to the number of all matching resources at the peers (=IDF). To cope with different TF values for one resource in different peers we will always use the maximum value. The extended TFxIDF functions are defined as

$$
\begin{aligned}
\mathrm{df}(prop,\ c) &= \sum_{o \in P} \mathrm{df}_o(prop,\ c) \\
R(prop) &= R_p(prop) = \bigcup_{o \in P} R_o(prop) \\
\mathrm{idf}(prop,\ c) &= \log \frac{|R(prop)|}{\mathrm{df}(prop,\ c)}
\end{aligned}
\tag{7}
$$

where $R_o(prop)$ is the set of all resources of peer o having the property $prop$ and $\mathrm{df}_o(prop,\ c) = |\{r\ |\ r \in R_o \wedge \mathrm{tf}_o(r,\ prop,\ c) > 0\}|$ which is the same weighting as used in equation 1.

As mentioned in the previous section, we do not build an index over idf values in advance, but calculate the necessary values on demand. Already calculated values are cached in an index, so repeated evaluations of the same query can reuse them. If a query is not yet in this index, we have to distribute it twice. In the first round the peers deliver only their local document count and document frequency. This information is merged according to equation 7, and added to the super-peer index. In the second round, the necessary idf values are added to the query message, so that the aggregated information becomes available to all peers and super-peers. The other super-peers also add these values to their indices. The peers can calculate resource scores now, and return them as well as their current local document count and document frequency. That way an idf value is updated during each evaluation of a query which contains the corresponding query atom. No additional messages are necessary to maintain the index.

Investigating distributed information retrieval techniques over document collections in the Web, Viles and French [15] propose to use statistical averages that are updated only once in a while. They show that the effectiveness of retrieval is usually only slightly affected by this simplification, because changes in the collections usually tend to compensate each other on average and major changes generally need some time to develop. Thus relying on slightly outdated information based on a previous query evaluation will only lead to deterioration in extremely volatile P2P networks[4].

Query driven update of indices is possible because queries are not posed randomly but usually follow a Zipf distribution, where few queries make up the majority of requests. Zipf distributions are ubiquitous in content networks, the Internet and other collections. The distribution was first discovered by the Harvard linguistic professor G. K. Zipf, and has become one of the most empirically validated laws in the domain of linguistic quantities. If we count the number of times each word appears in a text (called frequency) and assign each word a rank based on its frequency (i. e. rank=1 is the word that appears the most), we can see that the product frequency · rank for each word is roughly equal to a constant. In a more general context, this corresponds to the observation that the frequency of occurrence of an event as a function of the rank is a power-law function.

---

[4] To improve the precision further, we can re-evaluate the query if the difference of an idf value stored in the index and the value updated from the responses exceeds a certain threshold.

Recent research has discovered this distribution as a typical distribution of information on the Internet [16,17,18,19]. In P2P networks typical consumers are interested in only subsets of all available content and content categories [20]. Documents are also distributed following Zipf's law, i.e. many consumers are interested in resources which are held by a few providers.

This makes it safe to assume that also the occurrence frequency of query atoms rsp. of the property/constant pairs they contain will also follow a Zipf distribution., and therefore, for most queries posed to the network, the necessary idf values will already be in the index, and we only seldom have to distribute a query twice.

$$\text{tf}_p(r,\ prop,\ c) = \begin{cases} \text{Max}_{o \in P_p \cup SP_p(Q)}(\text{tf}_o(r,\ prop,\ c)) : p \in SP \\ \text{same as for simple peer} \qquad : p \in P \end{cases} \tag{8}$$

These definitions as well as the following are recursive; the calculation terminates at the super-peers which do not need to forward the query to other super-peers.

Merging. Having defined the scores for peers and super-peers we can now use equations 4 and 5 to calculate an aggregated query score for each resource at the super-peer.

Simply collecting all top k resources from each peer and merging these sets would cause more network traffic than necessary. A simple top-2 examples illustrates this: In order to get the overall top scored resource in the super-peer we only need the maximum-scored resource of all its local peers and super-peers along the spanning tree starting at the query originator. Having chosen the maximum resource from any of the peers, we can select the top-2 of this set and exclude all peers which didn't get their top-1 resource placed in the selection. All the other peers still offer their top-scored resources. So for determining the overall second best resource for our merged top 2 result set, we only additionally need to ask the two best peers that already delivered our top-scored resources. For higher numbers of query results this process can be repeated inductively until all top k resources are delivered, as we show below.

Since the best objects are determined one by one, the merging super-peer can immediately deliver each result resource to the super-peer directly up the super-peer backbone, enabling it in turn to also return its merged results at the earliest point in time. This successive query result delivery behavior not only optimizes bandwidth use, but also helps to improve the psychologically felt response time for the user by offering correct result objects for consideration already at an early stage.

To formalize this approach let us first define some sets in each peer for bookkeeping:

For a resource $r \in M$ the set $BetterThan(Q, r, M)$ contains all resources $s \in M$ with a better score than r with respect to query Q:

$$BetterThan_p(Q, r, M) = \{s \in M \mid score_p(Q, s) > score_p(Q, r)\} \tag{9}$$

$Top_p(i, Q, M)$ is the subset of the i best scoring resources in a set M:

$$Top_p(i, Q, M) = \{r \in M \mid \quad |BetterThan_p(Q, r, M)| < i\} \tag{10}$$

For a peer p we define the resource(s)[5] with the i-th most score as

$$\begin{aligned} ResAt_p(1, Q) &= Top_p(1, Q, R_p) \\ ResAt_p(i, Q) &= Top_p(i, Q, R_p) \setminus Top_p(i-1, Q, R_p) \end{aligned} \tag{11}$$

---

[5] This can be more than one resource, if there are several resources with the same score.

where R_p is the set of all resources at peer p. For super-peers, we define $ResAt$ at the end of this section (16).

We define the following sets for a super-peer sp doing the merge: $ConsideredPeers_{sp}(Q, i)$ is the set of all peers, which have to be asked (are considered) for resources in the i-th iteration to guarantee a correct result set. $TopResCandidates_{sp}(Q, i)$ is an intermediate set of resources which could be in the top k set for the i-th iteration, i.e. the current best scored resources from all contributing peers, where peers that already contributed to the merged result delivered their respective next best resources. $TopRes_{sp}(Q, i)$ is a set of cardinality k of top resources after i iterations. Since we always get a guaranteed overall i-th best resource by choosing the maximum resource from $TopResCandidates_{sp}(Q, i)$ we can also guarantee that the top i resources of $TopRes_{sp}(Q, i)$ are already correct, while our current $(i + 1)...k$-th resources may still be replaced with better ones (as shown at the end of this section).

In the first iteration we have to consider all connected peers. In the i-th iteration we can consider only those peers from which at least one resource made it into $TopRes$ during the $i - 1$-th iteration, because all other peers still offer their current best resources:

$$ConsideredPeers_{sp}(Q, 1) = P_{sp} \cup SP_{sp}(Q)$$
$$ConsideredPeers_{sp}(Q, i) = \{p \mid TopRes_{sp}(Q, i - 1) \cap ResAt_p(i - 1, Q) \neq \emptyset\}$$
(12)

For a super-peer $AllResAt$ is the union of all $ResAt$-sets of connected peers

$$AllResAt_{sp}(i, Q) = \bigcup_{o \in ConsideredPeers(Q, i)} ResAt_o(i, Q)$$
(13)

To determine the $TopRes(Q, i)$, we first merge $TopRes(Q, i - 1)$ with the new resources delivered from the considered peers $(AllResAt_{sp}(i, Q))$, and then select the top i resources from this union.

$$TopResCandidates_{sp}(Q, 1) = AllResAt_{sp}(1, Q)$$
$$TopResCandidates_{sp}(Q, i) = AllResAt_{sp}(i, Q) \cup TopRes_{sp}(Q, i - 1)$$
(14)

$$TopRes_{sp}(Q, i) = Top_{sp}(k, Q, TopResCandidates_{sp}(Q, i))$$
(15)

Example. The following top-4 example shows how our algorithm works. We assume that super-peer sp is connected to peers p_1, p_2 and p_3. We denote resources with numbers and assume that the resource number is equal to its score for query Q.

$R_{p_1} = \{r_{11}, r_{12}, r_{13}\}$ with $score(Q, r_{11}) = 0.9$, $score(Q, r_{12}) = 0.8$, $score(Q, r_{13}) = 0.1$
$R_{p_2} = \{r_{21}, r_{22}, r_{23}\}$ with $score(Q, r_{21}) = 0.7$, $score(Q, r_{22}) = 0.3$, $score(Q, r_{23}) = 0.1$
$R_{p_3} = \{r_{31}, r_{22}, r_{33}\}$ with $score(Q, r_{31}) = 0.6$, $score(Q, r_{32}) = 0.5$, $score(Q, r_{33}) = 0.4$

Then we get:
$ConsideredPeers_{sp}(Q, 1) = \{p_1, p_2, p_3\}$, $AllResAt_{sp}(Q, 1) = \{r_{11}, r_{21}, r_{31}\}$,
   $TopRes_{sp}(Q, 1) = \{r_{11}, r_{21}, r_{31}\}$
$ConsideredPeers_{sp}(Q, 2) = \{p_1, p_2, p_3\}$, $AllResAt_{sp}(Q, 2) = \{r_{12}, r_{22}, r_{32}\}$,
   $TopRes_{sp}(Q, 2) = \{r_{11}, r_{12}, r_{21}, r_{31}\}$
$ConsideredPeers_{sp}(Q, 3) = \{p_1\}$, $AllResAt_{sp}(Q, 3) = \{r_{13}\}$,

$TopRes_{sp}(Q,3) = \{r_{11}, r_{12}, r_{21}, r_{31}\}$
$ConsideredPeers_{sp}(Q,4) = \emptyset$

We can stop here, because no more resources have to be considered.

Our final result is $TopRes_{sp}(Q,k)$, but in step i we can already identify (and forward) the i-th most scored resource (set). The $ResAt$ definition extended for the super-peer case is:

$$ResAt_{sp}(1,Q) = \qquad\qquad TopRes_{sp}(Q,1)$$
$$ResAt_{sp}(i,Q) = TopRes_{sp}(Q,i) \setminus TopRes_{sp}(Q,i-1) \qquad\qquad (16)$$

We can stop the iteration as soon as $ConsideredPeers_{sp}(Q,i) = \emptyset$, because in this case $TopRes_{sp}(Q,i) = TopRes_{sp}(Q,i-1))$:

$TopRes_{sp}(Q,i)$
$\quad = Top_{sp}(k,Q,TopResCandidates_{sp}(Q,i))$
$\quad = Top_{sp}(k,Q,AllResAt_{sp}(i,Q) \cup TopRes_{sp}(Q,i-1))$
$\quad = Top_{sp}(k,Q,\displaystyle\bigcup_{o \in ConsideredPeers(Q,i)} ResAt_o(i,Q) \cup TopRes_{sp}(Q,i-1))$
$\quad = Top_{sp}(k,Q,\displaystyle\bigcup_{o \in \emptyset} ResAt_o(i,Q) \cup TopRes_{sp}(Q,i-1))$
$\quad = Top_{sp}(k,Q,\emptyset \cup TopRes_{sp}(Q,i-1))$
$\quad = Top_{sp}(k,Q,TopRes_{sp}(Q,i-1))$
$\quad = TopRes_{sp}(Q,i-1))$

Now we only have to show that $TopRes_{sp}(Q,i)$ contains the i resources with the highest score. We do this by induction. Be r_i the resource with network-wide rank i, $r_{p,i}$ the resource with rank i at peer p. For case 1 the assertion is obviously correct: $\exists p\ r_1 = r_{p,1} \Rightarrow r_1 \in AllresAt_{sp}(1,Q) \Rightarrow r_1 \in TopRes_{sp}(Q,1)$.

Assume that $r_{i-1} \in TopRes(Q,i-1)$. If $r_i \in TopRes_{sp}(Q,i-1)$, then obviously $r_i \in TopRes_{sp}(Q,i)$. In the case $r_{i-1} \notin TopRes_{sp}(Q,i-1)$ we have to show that $r_i \in AllResAt_{sp}(i,Q)$ which we can do by showing that $\exists p\ r_i = r_{p,i}$. We know $\exists p,j\ r_i = r_{p,j}$. Both $i > j$ and $i < j$ can't be true: If $\exists j\ j > i \wedge r_i = r_{p,j}$ $\Rightarrow score_p(r_{p,i}) > score_p(r_i) \Rightarrow |BetterThan_p(Q,r_i,R_p)| \geq i$ which contradicts our assumption that r_i is at rank i.

On the other hand, if $\exists j\ j < i \wedge r_i = r_{p,j} \Rightarrow \exists j\ j > i \wedge r_i \in AllResAt_{sp}(j,Q)$. Also, $\quad \forall l: 1 \leq l \leq j-1\ r_{p,l} \in TopRes(Q,l) \quad \Rightarrow \quad \forall l: 1 \leq l \leq j-1$ $p \in ConsideredPeers_{sp}(Q,l) \Rightarrow r_i \in TopRes_{sp}(Q,j) \Rightarrow r_i \in TopRes_{sp}(Q,i-1)$ which contradicts our initial assumption. Therefore, $r_i = r_{p,i} \Rightarrow r_i \in ResAt_p(Q,i)$ $\Rightarrow r_i \in AllResAt_{sp}(Q,i) \Rightarrow r_i \in TopRes_{sp}(Q,i)$. $\square$

So the iteration terminates after at most k steps, delivering the top k resources.

3.4 Routing Optimization

We can use the query answering information collected at the super-peers to optimize routing. Let us define the set of peers at super-peer p, which have contributed to the top k resources, as

$$TopPeer_p(Q) = \{o \in P_p \cup SP_p \mid \exists r \in R_o \wedge r \in TopRes_p(Q)\} \qquad (17)$$

Routing can be optimized significantly if each super-peer sends a query Q to the (super-)peers in $TopPeer_p(Q)$ only. To achieve this goal, the super-peer has to store this set for each query it evaluates. The routing index created in this way is a map of $(Q, TopPeer_p(Q))$ pairs.

Every time a super-peer receives a query, it checks whether the query is already in its index or if it is a new query. If the query matches a previous query then the super-peer will use the associated $TopPeer(Q)$ set to determine the direction in which the query should be forwarded to retrieve the top k. To find the matching index entry for a new query, we use the query containment algorithm introduced in [21]. Note that for the application in top k retrieval the number k of objects that have to be returned is an integral part of the query. It is easy to see that if a local routing index contains a query Q, every query Q' also matches Q, if Q' contains exactly the same predicates as Q, but the value k' of requested results in Q' is smaller than the value k in Q.

As we already remarked before, in a peer-to-peer network peers may join and leave at any time and the content at peers may change. Since we do not have (and do not want to have) any kind of notification of those changes, the routing of the queries must adapt to such changes automatically. To achieve this, super-peers send the query to other arbitrary (super-)peers as well, with a specific probability, depending on the volatility of the network, to capture the network dynamics. This also updates the idf values stored in the indices for these queries.

For a peer-to-peer network there are three typical distributions that we consider. Under an *arbitrary distribution* resources at one peer are not related. For this case, our hypothesis is that the more arbitrarily the resources are distributed among peers, the less optimization will be achieved by our routing indices. In contrast we have a *clustered distribution* when the resources provided by each peer are highly related. In this case our index/routing algorithm will result in much reduced message forwarding.

4   Related Work

In the context of peer-to-peer networks, only very few authors have explored retrieval algorithms taking rankings into account. The idea of PeerSearch [22] is comparable to our approach, since they are also creating an aggregation of the top k results from the peers. In contrast to our ranking-algorithm they do not use any broadcast-topology, but use CAN [23] in combination with the vector space model (VSM) and latent semantic indexing (LSI) to create an index which is stored in CAN using the vector representations as coordinates.

PlanetP [2] concentrates on peer-to-peer communities in unstructured peer-to-peer networks with sizes up to ten thousand peers. They introduce two data structures for searching and ranking which create a replicated global index, using gossiping. Each peer maintains an inverted index of its document and spreads the term-to-peer index. Based on this replicated index a TFxIDF-ranking algorithm is implemented.

Aberer and Wu provide a good theoretical background in [24] where they present a ranking algebra as a formal framework for ranking computation. They show that not only one global ranking should be taken into account, but several rankings must be seen in different contexts. Their ranking algebra allows aggregating the local rankings into global rankings.

[25] discusses the combination of distributed information retrieval and unstructured peer-to-peer networks. The basic idea is to filter results while they are routed back to the query originator. Each peer maintains a list of neighbors. These lists change over time to keep the better neighbors (i.e. the ones giving better results, which is defined as the peers which can offer more results).

In the context of databases Agrawal et al. [26] propose several approaches to rank database query results, under the assumption that there is only one table, and only conjunctive queries are used. Instead of returning only complete matches, a similarity value (similarity between query and table row) is calculated. If a condition is matched by the row data, the frequency factor (analogous to inverse document frequency) is added to the similarity value. They present similarity-measures for numerical data and range conditions.

Bruno et al. [27] use a similar formalisation like we do, but discuss the characteristics of retrieval in web databases, when several web accessible databases are used to create a top-k list, where each atom maybe answered from a different database.

5 Conclusion

Large peer-to-peer networks with semantically meaningful cooperative query answering capabilities may lead to vast result sets, which makes it necessary to investigate how to rank answers and return only the best ones in such a distributed environment. Inspired by the success of ranking algorithms in Web search engines and top-k retrieval algorithms in databases, this paper provides a solution to this problem by presenting a decentralized top-k retrieval and routing algorithm for peer-to-peer networks. The algorithm makes use of local rankings, rank merging and optimized routing based on peer ranks, and does not have to maintain a central index or locally replicated copies of such an index. The algorithm guarantees a manageable result set size and at the same time minimizes network traffic among peers. While we do assume a super-peer network, no specific network topology is required. In contrast to other approaches, our top-k indices need only to be updated during query answering, and therefore do not involve further update traffic in addition to query forwarding. We also showed two examples of how to integrate different ranking methods into our algorithm.

We are currently simulating our algorithm in the Edutella/HyperCuP environment, using different assumptions about data and query distribution, to further quantify the effects and advantages of our approach for different distributions.

Acknowledgements. We especially want to thank Kevin Chang from the DAIS group at Urbana-Champaign for giving valuable input to an earlier draft of this report as well as for providing several very useful references on top-k query answering and information retrieval.

References

1. Nejdl, W., Wolf, B., Qu, C., Decker, S., Sintek, M., Naeve, A., Nilsson, M., Palmér, M., Risch, T.: EDUTELLA: a P2P networking infrastructure based on RDF. In: Proceedings of the Eleventh International World Wide Web Conference (WWW2002), Hawaii, USA (2002)
2. Cuenca-Acuna, F.M., Peery, C., Martin, R.P., Nguyen, T.D.: PlanetP: Using gossiping to build content addressable peer-to-peer information sharing communities. In: Twelfth IEEE International Symposium on High Performance Distributed Computing (HPDC-12), IEEE Press (2003)
3. Nejdl, W., Wolpers, M., Siberski, W., Löser, A., Bruckhorst, I., Schlosser, M., Schmitz, C.: Super-peer-based routing and clustering strategies for RDF-based peer-to-peer networks. In: Proceedings of the Twelfth International World Wide Web Conference (WWW2003), Budapest, Hungary (2003)
4. Aberer, K., Cudré-Mauroux, P., Hauswirth, M.: The chatty web: Emergent semantics through gossiping. In: Proceedings of the Twelfth International World Wide Web Conference, New York, USA, ACM Press (2003) 197–206
5. Halevy, A.Y., Ives, Z.G., Mork, P., Tatarinov, I.: Piazza: Data management infrastructure for semantic web applications. In: Proceedings of the Twelfth International World Wide Web Conference (WWW2003), Budapest, Hungary (2003)
6. Bernstein, P.A., Giunchiglia, F., Kementsietsidis, A., Mylopoulos, J., Serafini, L., Zaihrayeu, I.: Data management for peer-to-peer computing: A vision. In: Proceedings of the Fifth International Workshop on the Web and Databases, Madison, Wisconsin (2002)
7. Nejdl, W., Siberski, W., Sintek, M.: Design issues and challenges for RDF- and schema-based peer-to-peer systems. SIGMOD Records (2003)
8. Crespo, A., Garcia-Molina, H.: Routing indices for peer-to-peer systems. In: Proceedings International Conference on Distributed Computing Systems. (2002)
9. Aberer, K.: P-Grid: A self-organizing access structure for P2P information systems. In: In Proceedings of the Sixth International Conference on Cooperative Information Systems (CoopIS), Trento, Italy (2001)
10. Schlosser, M., Sintek, M., Decker, S., Nejdl, W.: HyperCuP—Hypercubes, ontologies and efficient search on P2P networks. In: International Workshop on Agents and Peer-to-Peer Computing, Bologna, Italy (2002)
11. Li, Y., Bandar, Z.A., McLean, D.: An approach for measuring semantic similarity between words using multiple information sources. IEEE Transactions on Knwoledge and Data Engineering 15 (2003)
12. Witten, I., Moffat, A., Bell, T.: Managing Gigabytes. Morgan Kaufman, Heidelberg (1999)
13. Hewlett Packard Research Labs: RDQL - RDF data query language (2004) http://www.hpl.hp.com/semweb/rdql.html.
14. Ilyas, I.F., Aref, W.G., Elmagarmid, A.K.: Supporting top-k join queries in relational databases. In: Proceedings of the 29th International Conference on Very Large Databases, Berlin, Germany (2003) 754–765
15. Viles, C.L., French, J.C.: On the update of term weights in dynamic information retrieval systems. In: Proceedings of the International Conference on Information and Knowledge Management (CIKM '95), Baltimore, MD, USA, ACM (1995) 167–174
16. Faloutsos, M., Faloutsos, P., Faloutsos, C.: On power-law relationships of the internet topology. In: ACM SIGCOMM Computer Communication Review, Vol 29(4). (1999)
17. Chen, Q.: The origin of power laws in internet topologies revisited. In: 21st Annual Joint Conference of the IEEE Computer and Communications Societies. (2002)
18. Medina, A., Matta, I., Byers, J.: On the origin of power laws in internet topologies. ACM SIGCOMM Computer Communication Review 30(2) (2000)

19. Adamic, L.A., Huberman, B.A.: Zipf's law and the internet. Glottometrics **3** (2002)
20. Crespo, A., Molina, H.G.: Semantic overlay networks for P2P systems. Technical report, Stanford University (2003)
21. Chirita, P.A., Idreos, S., Koubarakis, M., Nejdl, W.: Publish/subscribe for RDF-based P2P networks. In: In Proceedings of the 1st European Semantic Web Symposium. (2004)
22. Tang, C., Xu, Z., Mahalingam, M.: Peersearch: Efficient information retrieval in peer-to-peer networks. Technical Report HPL-2002-198, Hewlett-Packard Labs (2002)
23. Ratnasamy, S., Francis, P., Handley, M., Karp, R., Shenker, S.: A scalable content addressable network. In: Proceedings of the 2001 Conference on applications, technologies, architectures, and protocols for computer communications. (2001)
24. Aberer, K., Wu, J.: A framework for decentralized ranking in web information retrieval. In: Proceedings of the fifth Asia Pacific Web Conference (APWeb2003). (2003)
25. Yu, B., Liu, J., Ong, C.S.: Scalable P2P information retrieval via hierarchical result merging. Technical report, Dep. of CS, University at Urbana-Champaign (2003)
26. Agrawal, S., Chaudhuri, S., Das, G., Gionis, A.: Automated ranking of database query results. In: Proceedings of the Second Conference on Innovative Data Systems Research. (2003)
27. Bruno, N., Gravano, L., Marian, A.: Evaluating top-k queries over web-accessible databases. In: Proceedings of the 18th International Conference on Data Engineering, San Jose, CA, USA, IEEE Computer Society (2002)

Learning Meta-descriptions of the FOAF Network

Gunnar AAstrand Grimnes, Pete Edwards, and Alun Preece

Computing Science Dept.
King's College
University of Aberdeen
AB24 3UE Scotland
{ggrimnes,pedwards,apreece}@csd.abdn.ac.uk
www.csd.abdn.ac.uk/research/agentsgroup

Abstract. We argue that in a distributed context, such as the Semantic Web, ontology engineers and data creators often cannot control (or even imagine) the possible uses their data or ontologies might have. Therefore ontologies are unlikely to identify every useful or interesting classification possible in a problem domain, for example these might be of a personalised nature and only appropriate for a certain user in a certain context, or they might be of a different granularity than the initial scope of the ontology. We argue that machine learning techniques will be essential within the Semantic Web context to allow these unspecified classifications to be identified. In this paper we explore the application of machine learning methods to FOAF, highlighting the challenges posed by the characteristics of such data. Specifically, we use clustering to identify classes of people and inductive logic programming (ILP) to learn descriptions of these groups. We argue that these descriptions constitute re-usable, first class knowledge that is neither explicitly stated nor deducible from the input data. These new descriptions can be represented as simple OWL class restrictions or more sophisticated descriptions using SWRL. These are then suitable either for incorporation into future versions of ontologies or for on-the-fly use for personalisation tasks.

1 Introduction

If a Semantic Web as set in out [1] becomes reality one might imagine that machine learning will no longer be required, as by manipulation of logical statements about semantic resources and their descriptions anything can be inferred and understood. However, we believe that no matter how wide-spread and extensive the Semantic Web becomes, every little fact is still unlikely to be explicitly stated, and in addition agents will need to know personalised facts, that although not generally true may be true in a certain context for a certain user. The fundamental organising structure of the Semantic Web is that of a set of inter-related classes; individual resources are members of one or more classes. A large part of the challenge in defining RDF Schemas [2] and OWL [3] ontologies is to identify a sufficiently rich set of classes to capture the various kinds of resources that exist. Inevitably, in any such effort, some potentially interesting and useful classes will be left unidentified. In some cases, they may be alternative ways of viewing an existing conceptualisation (for example, dividing people into subsets according to the kind of

S.A. McIlraith et al. (Eds.): ISWC 2004, LNCS 3298, pp. 152–165, 2004.
© Springer-Verlag Berlin Heidelberg 2004

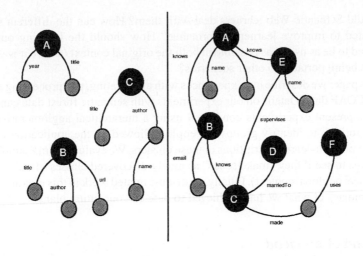

Fig. 1. Schematic Illustration of Semantic Forests and Semantic Webs.

work they do, instead of by their gender). In some cases, these may reflect conceptualisations that are true only locally, in a particular context for a specific user (for example, the class of all restaurants liked by a particular individual).

We believe that machine learning techniques have enormous potential to discover such unspecified classes. In some cases, the designers of schemas and ontologies may be prompted to add the new classes into future versions of their conceptualisations. In other cases, the discovered classes may be created on-the-fly in order to derive some inference or perform some task.

For our discussion of learning from the Semantic Web, we assume it is using the standard RDF representation based on *(subject, object, predicate)* triples [4]. We identify two types of Semantic Web data:

- "Semantic forests" - these consist of many small, disconnected, shallow resource trees. The structure of such a forest is isomorphic to that of an XML document. Real world examples of such semantic forests include meta-data using Dublin Core[1], or the use of RDF Site Summary (RSS)[2]. See Figure 1(left).
- "Semantic webs" - consist of a large graph of resources linking to each other, with no clear distinction where one resource description ends and another begins. Such data cannot easily be expressed in pure XML, and a richer representational language, like RDF, is really needed. The only significant real-world example we are aware of to date is Friend of a Friend (FOAF)[3]. See Figure 1(right).

Currently semantic forest data is pre-dominant. The number of true semantic webs should increase as the Semantic Web develops, however we do not expect semantic forests to disappear altogether. These different types of data present us with a challenge:

---

[1] http://dublincore.org
[2] http://web.resource.org/rss/1.0/
[3] http://www.foaf-project.org

How should Semantic Web learners deal with them? How can the different structures be exploited to improve learner performance? How should the learning outcome be represented to be as useful as possible in both the original context (where it was learned) as well as being portable to other scenarios?

In this paper we describe our experiences with aggregating, pre-processing and learning from FOAF data. Details on our experiments with semantic forest data can be found in [5]. We present experiments conducted using a hierarchical agglomerative clustering [6] algorithm to identify groups of people, followed by the application of the ILP system Aleph [7] to learn descriptions of these clusters. We evaluate some sample learned descriptions to see if they "make sense" as newly-discovered classes of individuals (either in a local or global context). Finally we discuss related work in this area and conclude with a summary of what we have achieved to date and our future plans.

2   Friend of a Friend

The Friend of a Friend (FOAF)[4] project aims to create a Web of machine-readable homepages describing people, the links between individuals and the things they create and do. The FOAF ontology is described using the Ontology Web Language (OWL) [3]. To join the FOAF world all one has to do is generate a FOAF profile describing oneself and publish it on the Web. The profile must adhere to the ontology and could either be generated by hand, or more often, by copy, paste and edit of other people's FOAF, or by semi-automated tools such as FOAF-a-matic[5]. Part of an example profile is shown in Figure 2 [6]. This example illustrates several important things about FOAF:

- The *foaf:knows* property points to other people known by this person, creating a networked community.
- People in the FOAF world don't need URIs, they are identified through their *foaf:mbox* (or *foaf:mbox_sha1sum*), i.e. the email address. In the FOAF ontology these are identified as *owl:inverseFunctionalProperty*, meaning they uniquely identify a person.
- *foaf:knows* properties do not take the value of the URI of other people's FOAF, instead they point to an anonymous RDF node of type *foaf:Person*, which contains the *foaf:mbox* of the other person. Whether two anonymous nodes represent the same person can then be decided based on the *foaf:mbox* values; merging these nodes is known as "smushing"[7].
- *foaf:mbox_sha1sum* is used to disguise email-addresses for privacy reasons. The use of a checksum rather than just omitting the value allows people to confirm that the address actually does belong to a person.
- Other FOAF files are linked through *rdfs:seeAlso*, allowing Semantic Web bots to crawl through FOAF space.

---

[4] http://www.foaf-project.org/
[5] http://www.ldodds.com/foaf/foaf-a-matic.html
[6] The full example can be found at: http://www.csd.abdn.ac.uk/~ggrimnes/foaf.rdf
[7] http://rdfweb.org/topic/Smushing

```
<foaf:Person>

  <foaf:mbox rdf:resource="mailto:ggrimnes@csd.abdn.ac.uk" />
  <foaf:name>Gunnar AAstrand Grimnes</foaf:name>
  <foaf:homepage rdf:resource="http://www.csd.abdn.ac.uk/~ggrimnes" />
  <foaf:workplaceHomepage rdf:resource="http://www.csd.abdn.ac.uk"/>
  <foaf:projectHomepage rdf:resource="http://www.csd.abdn.ac.uk/research/agentcities"/>
  <foaf:groupHomepage rdf:resource="http://www.csd.abdn.ac.uk/research/agentsgroup" />
  <foaf:phone rdf:resource="tel:+441224272835" />

  <foaf:depiction rdf:resource="http://www.csd.abdn.ac.uk/~ggrimnes/gfx/me.jpg" />

  <foaf:interest rdf:resource="http://www.w3.org/2001/sw/" />
  <foaf:interest rdf:resource="http://www.agentcities.net" />

  <foaf:made rdf:resource="http://www.csd.abdn.ac.uk/research/AgentCities/GraniteNights" />

  <contact:nearestAirport>
   <airport:Airport rdf:about='http://www.daml.org/cgi-bin/airport?ABZ' />
  </contact:nearestAirport>

  <foaf:knows><foaf:Person>
     <foaf:mbox rdf:resource="mailto:maym@foobar.lu" />
     <rdfs:seeAlso rdf:resource="http://martinmay.net/foaf.rdf"/>
  </foaf:Person></foaf:knows>
  <foaf:knows><foaf:Person>
     <foaf:mbox rdf:resource="mailto:apreece@csd.abdn.ac.uk" />
  </foaf:Person></foaf:knows>
  <foaf:knows><foaf:Person>
     <foaf:mbox rdf:resource="mailto:pedwards@csd.abdn.ac.uk" />
  </foaf:Person></foaf:knows>
  <foaf:knows>
   <foaf:Person foaf:name="Sonja A Schramm">
     <foaf:mbox_sha1sum>
     83276f91273f2900cf0b6657b3708b736276ef81
     </foaf:mbox_sha1sum></foaf:Person>
  </foaf:knows>

  <rdfs:seeAlso rdf:resource="http://www.csd.abdn.ac.uk/~ggrimnes/codepict.rdf" />
  <rdfs:seeAlso rdf:resource="http://www.csd.abdn.ac.uk/research/agentsgroup/foaf.rdf" />

</foaf:Person>

<rdf:Description rdf:about="">
 <wot:assurance rdf:resource="foaf.rdf.asc" />
</rdf:Description>
```

Fig. 2. Parts of Example FOAF File.

- The *wot:assurance* property at the bottom of the file points to a signature of this file, signed with the person's PGP key, providing a secure way to know who made these statements. This provides a basis for the trust layer of the Semantic Web architecture.

2.1 Topology

The FOAF project began around 1999, but only gained significant momentum in the past two years, due to the increased awareness of the Semantic Web and the existence of FOAF visualisation tools such as Foafnaut[8] and the FOAF co-depiction project[9]. The

---

[8] http://jibbering.com/foaf/foafnaut.svg
[9] http://swordfish.rdfweb.org/discovery/2001/08/codepict/

Agents@Aberdeen   Foaf Universe

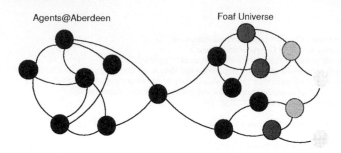

Fig. 3. FOAF Group with Narrow Connection to FOAF World.

co-depiction project allows searches to be made for pictures depicting multiple people, effectively proving their *foaf:knows* relationship, in addition is allows one to visually document the link from oneself to famous people, for example Bill Clinton or Frank Sinatra, increasing the fun-factor and "instant-gratification" of creating a FOAF profile.

For our experiments we used a FOAF crawl from September 2003[10], which contains 9097 nodes of type person. When smushed, this is equivalent to 8908 people, of which 1980 people know at least one other person, i.e. they are not leaf-nodes of the FOAF knows-graph. The data consists of 147527 triples, using 201 different namespaces, and 1066 distinct properties (compared to 49 in the FOAF ontology). Many of these properties are not widely used, only 116 are used more than 100 times.

Within the FOAF graph one can typically identify groups of people that are very "close" in real-life. For example, the people within a single research group. In such a group there are many interconnecting *foaf:knows* links, and the level of detail about each person is similar since their profiles are often generated by copy and pasting one person's FOAF, or because they are all generated by the same person or from a database. A group often has only a very narrow connection to the rest of the FOAF graph, or in certain cases no connection at all. In the Aberdeen Computing Science FOAF graph for example most people know each other, but as shown in Figure 3, the only link to the rest of the FOAF network is through a single person node.

2.2 Problems

While the heterogeneity and distributed nature of FOAF is clearly a good thing and makes a data-set based on FOAF very realistic, it does introduce a number of problems when one attempts to reason with or learn from the data. These are summarised below:

– Human errors. The majority of FOAF content is manually generated using a text editor, causing several types of human error:
  • Simple typing mistakes, i.e. *foaf:knosw.*
  • Using properties with the wrong namespace, e.g. *rdf:seeAlso* vs. *rdfs:seeAlso.*
  • Misunderstanding or misinterpretation of the FOAF ontology, e.g. using *foaf:mbox* with the email address as a literal string as opposed to an *rdf:resource* with a *mailto:* link.

---

[10] http://jibbering.com/foaf/dumps/

- Weaknesses and/or inconsistencies of the FOAF ontology:
  - *foaf:mbox* vs *foaf:mbox_sha1sum*. Both properties are declared as *owl:inverseFunctionalProperty* as detailed above. However, nowhere is it formally declared that *foaf:mbox_sha1sum* is the Secure Hash Algorithm[11] checksum of the *foaf:mbox* property. The intention is of course that a node with a *foaf:mbox_sha1sum* matching the checksum of another's *foaf:mbox* should be smushed together. At the moment this must be hard-coded in an application specific manner.
  - No standard way of expressing interest. *foaf:interest* has range *foaf:Document*, and most commonly points to the URL of a page about the concept. Again, the use of literals vs. *rdf:resource* is inconsistent, but the main problem is that people use different URLs for the same concept. For example: http://www.w3.org/RDF/, http://rdfweb.org, http://rdfweb.org/, http://www.rdfweb.org/.
- Level of detail varies greatly. Our initial experiments with learning from FOAF returned several rules based simply on the presence of an attribute, such as *foaf:groupHomepage*, rather than the value of the attribute.

2.3   Enriching FOAF

The Advanced Knowledge Technologies (AKT) project[12] aims to tackle a number of challenges of knowledge management, and as a show-case has created an ontology for representing academic researchers and their organisations. An RDF dataset conforming to this ontology has been created by "screen-scraping" the Web pages of UK based research institutions. The lack of detail in the FOAF data could be addressed by enriching it using the information available in the AKT RDF repository. However, this would involve further complicating the learning task by including yet another ontology. We therefore decided to map the instances from the AKT ontology to FOAF, as the ontologies have very similar domains; the majority of the mappings were straightforward, such as :

[*akt:has-email-address* ⇒ *foaf:mbox*]

Others were more complicated, for instance:

[*rdf:type akt:Professor-In-Academia* ⇒
(*rdf:type foaf:Person* & *foaf:title 'Professor'*)].

For the sake of re-usability these mappings were represented in OWL using *owl:equivalentProperty* for the trivial mappings and our own RDF mapping of RuleML[13] (this work predates the SWRL effort) for the more sophisticated rules, like the rule shown in Figure 4.

---

[11] http://www.w3.org/PICS/DSig/SHA1_1_0.html

[12] http://www.aktors.org

[13] http://www.csd.abdn.ac.uk/~qhuo/program/generaltool_sources/ruleml.rdfs

rdf__type(A, *'akt__Professor-In-Academia'*):-
  rdf__type(A,*'foaf__Person'*),
  foaf__title(A, *'Dr'*).

Fig. 4. Ontology Mapping Excerpts.

rdf__type(*'genid:002'*, *'foaf__type'*).
foaf__name(*'genid:002'*, *'Gunnar AAstrand Grimnes'*).
foaf__mbox(*'genid:002'*, *'ggrimnes@csd.abdn.ac.uk'*).
foaf__knows(*'genid:002'*, *'genid:003'*).
foaf__mbox(*'genid:003'*, *'apreece@csd.abdn.ac.uk'*).
. . .

Fig. 5. FOAF Fragment Converted to Prolog.

3   RDF and ILP

Encouraged by our earlier experiences with learning from semantic forests using ILP [5], the next step was to explore the application of these techniques to FOAF data. The mapping of RDF to Prolog is straightforward. Figure 5 illustrates a fragment of the FOAF profile in Figure 2 converted to Prolog. Some things to note about the representation are:

– Namespace handling. Namespaces of properties were converted to prefixes in Prolog, with *namespace* predicates giving the mapping from prefixes to actual namespaces. For example *foaf:mbox* becomes:
  foaf__mbox(A, *'mailto:ggrimnescsd.abdn.ac.uk'*).
  namespace(*'foaf'*, *'http://xmlns.com/foaf/0.1/'*).
– RDF types. For each class in the ontology Prolog rules are created to determine if a resource is a member of the specific class, or any sub-class thereof. This allows RDF types to be mapped to ILP internal types, used for limiting which predicates may be applied to a given resource, reducing the search-space dramatically. Figure 6 contains an example.
– Normalisation and inference over interests. In our initial experiments with the FOAF data we attempted to fix the inconsistent *foaf:interest* problem by "smushing" nodes that represented the same concept, for example *http://rdfweb.org/foaf/* and *http://www.foaf-project.org/*. In addition super/sub-concept links were created between concepts such as *http://www.debian.org/* and *http://www.linux.org/*, and some general nodes that did not appear in the original data, e.g. *#ProgrammingLanguages* were added. Our preliminary experiments demonstrated that the ILP learner did not use these generalisations, probably due to the low number of *foaf:interest* links actually appearing in the data. As a result, these extra rules were not included in our full experiments.

An additional advantage of using ILP with RDF is that converting the learned results back into RDF is trivial, given some way of representing Horn clause rules in RDF, e.g. the Semantic Web Rule Language (SWRL) [8].

```
foaf__Person(A):-
   instanceOf(A,'http://xmlns.com/foaf/0.1/Person').
foaf__Document(A):-
   instanceOf(A,'http://xmlns.com/foaf/0.1/Document').

instanceOf(A,B):-rdf__type(A,B).
instanceOf(A,B):-rdf__subClassOf(B,C),instanceOf(A,C).
instanceOf(A,unknown):-nonvar(A).

castAsfoaf__Person(A,A):-foaf__Person(A).

:-modeb(*,foaf__interest(+foaf__Person, -foaf__Document)).
:-modeb(1,castAsfoaf__Person(+resource,-foaf__Person)).
:-modeb(1,castAsResource(+foaf__Person,-resource)).
```

Fig. 6. RDF Type Inference in Prolog.

4   Learning from FOAF

For our experiments with FOAF data we used Aleph [7]. Before attempting to learn from the FOAF data it was pre-processed by first smushing it, and then removing any duplicate properties resulting from this merger. Aleph was initially configured to use any of the predicates appearing in the input data when constructing a hypothesis, only restricted by the RDF typing as detailed above. However, as there were 1066 predicates in the full dataset, this was too much for Aleph to deal with and we moved to only using a subset based on the most frequent occurring predicates. The 15 most frequently predicates are shown in Figure 7, and the preliminary experiments were done with these, excluding *rdf:type* as it is applied to every person node. However, this did not give very good results and we moved instead to using the 100 most frequent predicates; for space reasons that list is not re-produced here.

Initial exploratory experiments with Aleph highlighted problems with the scale of the FOAF dataset. Even with a very small subset of the full data (less than 10% of the people in the full crawl), the search-space was still far too large, and Aleph was unable to make any generalisations over the data. To reduce the size of the search space the problem was broken into sub-problems by first applying a clustering algorithm and then feeding each

Frequency	Property
1244	http://www.w3.org/1999/02/22-rdf-syntax-ns#type
1120	http://jibbering.com/foaf/jim.rdf#isKnownBy
1119	http://xmlns.com/foaf/0.1/knows
908	http://xmlns.com/foaf/0.1/mbox_sha1sum
906	http://xmlns.com/foaf/0.1/name
846	http://www.w3.org/2000/01/rdf-schema#seeAlso
419	http://xmlns.com/foaf/0.1/depiction
392	http://xmlns.com/foaf/0.1/surname
344	http://xmlns.com/foaf/0.1/firstName
327	http://purl.org/dc/elements/1.1/title
273	http://xmlns.com/foaf/0.1/codepiction
266	http://xmlns.com/foaf/0.1/mbox
246	http://xmlns.com/foaf/0.1/nick
236	http://xmlns.com/foaf/0.1/homepage
230	http://purl.org/dc/elements/1.1/description

Fig. 7. 15 Most Frequent Predicates in FOAF.

cluster to Aleph separately. Such an operation does make sense in the context of FOAF, as there are often clusters of people, reflecting real-life groups, e.g. research groupings, where the group membership may not be explicitly stated. To perform the clustering step a hierarchical agglomerative clustering algorithm (HAC) [6] has been employed. HAC is a greedy bottom-up clusterer which works by initially creating one cluster for each individual, then repeatedly merging the two closest clusters until there is only one left or some threshold for similarity is reached. Our version of HAC computes the distance between two clusters as the average distance between each of the individuals in the two clusters.

Initially, a modified version of Hamming distance [9] is used as similarity metric; modifications were as follows: each RDF property appears as an attribute of the instance, as does each (property, value) pair. All properties and values are treated as nominal, including anonymous nodes. Although there could have been some scope for treating datatyped properties as ordinal, few of the properties used in FOAF are typed, so dealing with extra complexity was unlikely to pay off. The intention behind this similarity metric is that two people that both have a certain property, say *foaf:interest*, are more similar than two people who do not share any attributes, but less similar than two people who have the same value for *foaf:interest*. Initial clustering experiments with this similarity metric were unsuccessful, manual inspection of the clusters showed that they did not in any way re-produce groups of people a human might have identified. It was clear that considering only direct attributes of the Person node was flawed. A similarity metric is needed that can take into account the FOAF graph immediately around a person, and her position in the bigger graph, not just the immediate attributes. We are not aware of any work to date on the subject of similarity metrics for RDF data. However, in [10] a similarity metric for conceptual graphs is presented. Conceptual graphs are a data-structure commonly used for natural language processing. They consist of a network of concept nodes, representing entities, attributes, or events and relation nodes between them. A simple conceptual graph representing *John loves Mary* is as follows:

$$[\text{John}] \Leftarrow (\text{subj}) \Leftarrow [\text{love}] \Rightarrow (\text{obj}) \Rightarrow [\text{Mary}]$$

The similarity metric developed is based on the idea of the Dice coefficient [11], but incorporating a combination of two complementary sources of similarity: the *conceptual similarity* and the *relational similarity*, i.e. the overlap of nodes and the overlap of edges within the two graphs. Full details of the similarity metric can be found in [10].

Conceptual graphs and RDF instances are sufficiently similar that the same similarity metric should be appropriate in both cases. The similarity metric is designed to work on separate graphs, and in order to apply it to RDF we had to modify the algorithm to extract a sub-graph around each person. The RDF graph is traversed in either direction from the person node, i.e. triples were considered where the node in question is either the subject or the object. To limit the size of the sub-graph the number of triples traversed is limited. Trial and error showed that the optimal sub-graphs for clustering were obtained if traversal was allowed two triples forwards and one backwards. Note that these traversals may **not** be in any order, and backward-traversals are only permitted from the initial node. Consider for instance Figure 8, the subgraph for the person "Gunnar Grimnes" would include one backwards traversal, i.e. the "Comp. Sci. Dept" node, but not the

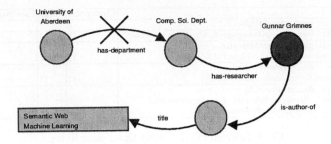

Fig. 8. Example of Extracting Person Subgraph.

"University of Aberdeen" node. It would also include two forward traversals, to both the anonymous node and the literal title node.

Clustering with this similarity metric gave acceptable results. For example the algorithm was able to discover clusters of people from different research-groups at Aberdeen. Aleph was then applied to the generated clusters (as detailed above), to learn a concise description of each cluster.

5 Results

The descriptions presented here were learned using the method detailed above on a subset of 869 of the total FOAF people.

Initially experiments were conducted using the 100 most frequent predicates for both clustering and rule learning; these included *fouf:knows* and its generated inverse predicate. With these settings 219 clusters had rules generated by Aleph, out of the total 825 clusters generated. Most of the learned rules were of the type:

> **member**(A) :-
> **jibbering__isKnownBy**(A, *'http://norman.walsh.name/knows/who#norman-walsh'*). (This rule covered all the 216 people in the cluster it described.)

Specifically, out of the 219 rulesets 177 used either *foaf:knows* or its inverse. It was apparent that the *foaf:knows* relation was so predominant in the FOAF data that it overshadowed everything else. Rules using *foaf:knows* are not very re-usable, and do not really express general classifications of the data. Therefore, the next experiments were conducted using the same 100 predicates, but removing *foaf:knows* and its inverse. The results for these experiments were much more interesting, as the lack of *foaf:knows* forced Aleph to generate rules using the other predicates. In addition, clustering and learning from the FOAF data excluding *foaf:knows* was much more efficient, the clustering step alone took only a third of the time when done without *foaf:knows*.

For space reasons we will not present all the learned descriptions here, but only discuss a selection of rules describing interesting clusters. Figure 9 shows for each rule the following: the size of the cluster; a recall measure (the number of instances covered by the rule); the false negatives (the members of the cluster not covered by this rule); and the false positives (people covered by this rule who are not a member of the cluster).

#	Rule	Cluster Size	Recall	False Neg.	False Pos.
1	member(A) :- trust__trustsHighly(B,A).	8	8	0	0
2	member(A) :- foaf__groupHomepage(A, *'http://www.aktors.org'*).	13	13	0	0
3	member(A) :- pim__nearestAirport(A, *'http://www.daml.org/cgi-bin/airport?ABZ'*).	12	12	0	2
4	member(A) :- dc__creator(B,A), dc__format(B, *'application/postscript'*).	17	15	2	0
5	member(A) :- dc__creator(B,A), dc__title(B, *'Managing Reference: Ensuring Referential Integrity of Ontologies for the Semantic Web'*).	8	8	0	0

Fig. 9. Selected FOAF Cluster Description Rules.

Rule 1 appears interesting as it characterises people who are highly trusted by someone. The *trust:trustedHighly* predicate comes from the namespace *http://www.mindswap.org/~golbeck/web/trust.daml#*, and is part of an effort to extend the FOAF network with the concept of trust; one application being email filtering [12]. Although the rule at first sight looks meaningful it becomes apparent that there are very few people in (our subset of) the FOAF world that use this particular predicate. The rule has no false positives, so the 8 people in this cluster represent all the uses of this predicate in our data, and in fact 7 of them are trusted by the primary author of the paper cited above. If the use of FOAF for enabling a Web of trust becomes more popular in the future such a rule would indeed be interesting. However, the question that must be raised is whether such a rule is too general to be useful, or if it is sufficient to know that a person is highly trusted by someone. In a local context this might be significant, but in a global context such knowledge is unlikely to have any great utility.

Rule 2 describes the Advanced Knowledge Technologies group at Aberdeen; these people were originally described using the AKT ontology, but the descriptions were converted to FOAF as described earlier. Based on the subset of data used for our experiments this rule perfectly describes the AKT group of people. However, in the real world there are other AKT groups at other institutions, and although this rule describes a meaningful group of people, namely the group of all members of the AKT project, it is not specific to the local Aberdeen group.

Rule 3 describes the Aberdeen Agents research group (Agents@Aberdeen), the airport referenced in the rule being Aberdeen airport, Dyce (ABZ). Although the people in the AKT research group are also situated in Aberdeen, the AKT ontology has no information regarding location, and so the FOAF description is lacking this information. A better description of the agent group might have been :

member(A) :- **foaf__groupHomepage**(A, *'http://www.csd.abdn.ac.uk/research/agentsgroup/'*).

However, as there is one person who is a member of both the AKT and the Agents research group, and in this experiment was inserted into the AKT cluster, this rule would have had an additional false positive, and rule 3 was chosen in its place.

Rule 4 describes a cluster of people who have all created a postscript document. There are 4 postscript documents in our dataset, and the 15 people covered by this rule are the authors of these documents; all the people and documents are from the same UK institution. This is a good example of the bizarre clusters and rules that sometimes occur within the FOAF space. Although a human might perhaps identify this rule as less significant than for instance one using *foaf:groupHomepage*, Aleph has no way of making the distinction. This rule also illustrates how RDF created by copy and paste or from a database can produce artificial clusters, based on the use of certain schemas or predicates particular to that cluster.

Rule 5 describes a cluster made up of 8 people who co-authored a paper. This is clearly a meaningful cluster, although quite small and the scope for using it for classification is limited. This rule is also interesting because the actual publication (Variable B) is sometimes given a URI, and sometimes just referred to as an anonymous node. Aleph must therefore use another clause to identify it. This is analogous to the FOAF use of *foaf:mbox* to identify people. However, in the FOAF case we can pre-process the data and smush the nodes because *foaf:mbox* is declared to be inverse functional in the ontology; this illustrates how background knowledge in an ontology can facilitate learning.

6   Related Work

Improving learning performance by taking advantage of the structure that is inherit in data that is marked up using XML is discussed in [13]. XML documents are represented as ordered and labeled trees and the authors present an algorithm called XMiner to extract the most frequent sub-trees for a given class; these are then converted into rules for classifying new instances. The authors demonstrate that their classifier out-performs information retrieval or association rule classifiers when learning from XML data.

Exploiting structure and semantics for learning is also discussed in [14], where ontologies are used to enrich plain text and do feature selection and aggregation. The aim being to improve clustering results. The authors also use semantic meta-data about Web pages to perform web-mining; a user's navigational path through a site becomes a path through semantic concepts, which might be more comprehensible than the raw access-log. The paper also includes a brief discussion of applying ILP to Semantic Web data, highlighting the challenge of solving the scalability problems of ILP to make it usable on the Semantic Web.

Alani et al [15] uses ontologies to detect Communities of Practice (COP) that are only implicitly expressed. For instance, two people might not have a direct relation, but they might have written a paper together. The detection is based on analysis of the graph of people and properties and allows weights to be attached to possible relations. For example, it is more significant that two people have written a paper together, than the fact that they subscribe to the same journal. Experiments are performed using the same AKT ontology used for the work described in this paper. In [16], the COP detection mechanism is combined with ontologies to generate an initial user-profile for a hybrid-recommender system called Quickstep. Analysis of a user's publications taken from her homepage are used to determine interest weights for concepts in the ontology, the user is then matched with similar users in the COP and their combined profiles are in turn matched with the concept weights of research papers to recommend papers of interest, even to new users of the system. Middleton et al also present experiments comparing ontology supported recommendations to those made without ontological inference. This work is continued further in [17], where a new system called Foxtrot which includes profile visualisation, email notification and user feedback.

The European Elena project[14] aims to demonstrate the feasibility of smart spaces for education, and is using Semantic Web technology to achieve this. In [18] RDF meta-data for educational resources is combined with an RDF profile to provide a personalised and adaptive view of a hypermedia learning-space.

7   Conclusion

In this paper we have shown how clustering and inductive logic programming can be used to learn descriptions of groups of people from FOAF data. We believe that the type of descriptions that have been shown in this paper identify interesting classifications in the data that were not initially specified in the RDF schemas or OWL ontologies. Additionally, these new classes could be integrated back into the original ontologies or instance data, for example by expressing them either as OWL descriptions (using restrictions on property values) or using the Semantic Web Rule Language [8].

Evaluating the information value of the newly-learned descriptions must ultimately be done by a human, since the semantics can never truly be understood by a machine. However, some steps can be taken to filter out the less useful descriptions. We have shown that removal of the *foaf:knows* relation eliminated the generation of very specific clusters surrounding a particular person. These clusters were less useful as it appears in general very hard to generalise a *foaf:knows* relationship any further. Moreover, rules without literal values have less information content than rules specifying a value. Although to an ILP algorithm the presence of a predicate looks significant, we must consider the open world assumption of RDF, in that other FOAF profiles outside our current dataset may also make use of the predicate, which might render classification by this rule incorrect.

We are planning to extend this work by conducting experiments in which we integrate the learned knowledge into the original data, and then re-run the clustering and learning steps, effectively creating a form of feedback learning. Our hope is that by using the additional descriptors it should be possible to learn even richer and more interesting classifications.

Any attempt to apply machine learning techniques to the Semantic Web will have the problem of scale, and even in the limited domain of FOAF we had to restrict our experimental study to a relatively small dataset to gain acceptable performance from the clustering and ILP steps. We will conduct further research into how the scalability of the learning algorithms can be improved to a level where we can at least learn from the whole FOAF crawl. However, for a global Semantic Web of interconnected information, like FOAF, the scalability challenge is huge.

---

[14] http://www.elena-project.org/

References

1. Berners-Lee, T., Hendler, J., Lassila, O.: The semantic web. Scientific American (2001) 28–37
2. Brickley, D., Guha, R.V.: Resource Description Framework (RDF) Schema Specification. W3c recommendation, World Wide Web Consortium (2000)
3. McGuinness, D.L., van Harmelen, F.: Web Ontology Language (OWL): Overview. W3c recommendation, World Wide Web Consortium (2003)
4. Lassila, O., Swick, R.R.: Resource Description Framework (RDF) Model and Syntax Specification . W3c recommendation, World Wide Web Consortium (1999)
5. Grimnes, G.A., Edwards, P., Preece, A.: Learning from Semantic Flora and Fauna. In: Semantic Web Personalization Workshop, AAAI, San Jose, USA. (2004)
6. Vorhees, E.: Implementing agglomerative hierarchical clustering algorithms for use in document retrieval. In: Information Processing & Management. Volume 22. (1986) 465–476
7. Srinivasan, A.: The Aleph Manual. (2001) http://web.comlab.ox.ac.uk/oucl/research/areas/machlearn/Aleph/.
8. Horrocks, I., Patel-Scheider, P., Boley, H., Tabet, S., Groshof, B., Dean, M.: SWRL: A Semantic Web Rule Language Combining OWL and RuleML. DARPA DAML Program. (2003)
9. Hamming, R.: Error Detecting and Error Correcting Codes. Bell System Techincal Journal **29** (1950) 147–160
10. Montes-y-Gómez, M., Gelbukh, A., López-López, A.: Comparison of Conceptual Graphs. In: Lecture Notes in Artificial Intelligence. Volume 1793. Springer Verlag (2000) 548–556
11. Rasmussen, E.: Clustering Algorithms. In Frakes, W., Baeza-Yates, R., eds.: Information Retrieval: Data structures & Algorithms, Prentice Hall (1992)
12. Golbeck, J., Parsia, B., Hendler, J.: Trust Networks on the Semantic Web. In: Proceedings of Cooperative Intelligent Agents 2003, Helsinki, Finland (2003)
13. Zaki, M.J., Aggarwal, C.C.: XRules: An Effective Structural Classifier for XML Data. In: 9th International Conference on Knowledge Discovery and Data-mining. (2003) 316–325
14. Berendt, B., Hotho, A., Stumme, G.: Towards Semantic Web Mining. In: International Semantic Web Conference. (2002) 264 – 278
15. Alani, H., Dasmahapatra, S., O'Hara, K., Shadbolt, N.: Identifying Communities of Practice through Ontology Network Analysis. In: IEEE IS. IEEE (2003) 18–25
16. Middleton, S., Alani, H., Shadbolt, N., De Roure, D.: Exploiting Synergy Between Ontologies and Recommender Systems. In: 11th International WWW Conference, Semantic Web Workshop. (2002) 41–50
17. Middleton, S., Shadbolt, N., Roure, D.D.: Ontological User Profiling in Recommender Systems. In: ACM Transactions on Information Systems. Volume 22(1). (2004) 54–88
18. Dolog, P., Henze, N., Nejdl, W., Sintek, M.: Towards the Adaptive Semantic Web. In: 1st Workshop on Principles and Practice of Semantic Web Reasoning. (2003) 51–68

From Tables to Frames

Aleksander Pivk[1,2], Philipp Cimiano[2], and York Sure[2]

[1] Josef Stefan Institute, Department of Intelligent Systems, Ljubljana, Slovenia
http://ai.ijs.si/
aleksander.pivk@ijs.si
[2] Institute AIFB, University of Karlsruhe, Karlsruhe, Germany
http://www.aifb.uni-karlsruhe.de/WBS/
{pivk,cimiano,sure}@aifb.uni-karlsruhe.de

Abstract. Turning the current Web into a Semantic Web requires automatic approaches for annotation of existing data since manual approaches will not scale in general. We here present an approach for automatic generation of F-Logic frames out of tables which subsequently supports the automatic population of ontologies from table-like structures. The approach consists of a methodology, an accompanying implementation and a thorough evaluation. It is based on a grounded cognitive table model which is stepwise instantiated by our methodology.

1 Introduction

Turning the current Web into a Semantic Web requires automatic approaches for annotation of existing data since manual annotation approaches such as presented in [6] will not scale in general. More scalable (semi-)automatic approaches known from ontology learning (cf. [11]) deal with extraction of ontologies from natural language texts. However, a large amount of data is stored in tables which require additional efforts.

We here present an approach for automatic generation of F-Logic frames [9] out of tables which subsequently supports the automatic population of ontologies from table-like structures. The approach consists of a methodology, an accompanying implementation and a thorough evaluation. It is based on a grounded cognitive table model which is stepwise instantiated by our methodology. In practice it is hard to cover every existing type of a table. We identified a couple of most relevant table types which were used in the experimental setting during the evaluation of our approach.

The paper is structured as follows. In the next Section 2 we first introduce the grounding table model which forms the base for our stepwise approach to generate frames out of tables. Subsequently we explain each step in detail and show relevant substeps. In Section 3 we present a thorough evaluation of the accompanying implementation. Before concluding and giving future directions, we present related work.

2 Methodological Approach

Linguistic models traditionally describe natural language in terms of syntax, semantics and pragmatics. There also exist models to describe tables in similar ways (cf. [7,8])

S.A. McIlraith et al. (Eds.): ISWC 2004, LNCS 3298, pp. 166–181, 2004.
© Springer-Verlag Berlin Heidelberg 2004

Table 1. Example of a possible table, found in [1]

Tour Code			DP9LAX01AB	
Valid			01.05. - 30.09.04	
Class/Extension			Economic	Extended
Adult	P	Single Room	35,450	2,510
		Double Room	32,500	1,430
	R	Extra Bed	30,550	720
Child	I	Occupation	25,800	1,430
	C	No occupation	23,850	720
	E	Extra Bed	22,900	360

where tables are analyzed along the following dimensions: (i) **Graphical** – the image level description of the pixels, lines and text or other content areas, (ii) **Physical** – the description of inter-cell relative location, (iii) **Structural** – the organization of cells as an indicator of their navigational relationship, (iv) **Functional** – the purpose of areas of the tables in terms of data access, and (v) **Semantic** – the meaning of text in the table and the relationship between the interpretation of cell content, the meaning of structure in the table and the meaning of its reading.

Our approach builds on the model described above. However, we will not consider the *graphical* dimension as no image processing will be necessary. Regarding the *physical* dimension, we process the tables encoded in HTML format in order to get a physical model of the table. In principle it can be seen as a graph describing the cells being connected together. In order to capture the *structural* dimension of the table, further processing is necessary (i) to determine the orientation of the table, i.e. top to down or left to right, and, (ii) to discover groups of cells building logical units. When talking about the function of a table, Hurst [8] distinguishes between two functional cell types *access* and *data*. Cells of type *data* are the ones we are interested when reading a table and which contain the actual information, while cells of type *access* determine the path to follow in the table in order to find the *data* cell of interest. Further, he distinguishes *local* (looking for one specific *data* cell) from *global* (comparing the value of different *data* cells) search in a table. In our approach we describe the *functional* dimension of a table in order to support *local* search. Such a functional description requires (i) finding all the *data* cells in a table as well as (ii) all the *access* cells to reach a given *data* cell of interest. In terms of database terminology, we need to find the keys for a certain field in the table. In our approach we distinguish between two *functional types* of cells: A(ttribute)-cells and I(nstance)-cells. A-cells describe the conceptual nature of the instances in a column or row. I-cells represent instances of the concepts represented by a certain A-cell. I-cells can have the two *functional roles* described by Hurst, i.e. they can play the role of *data* or *access* cells. Regarding the *semantic* description we follow a different paradigm as Hurst. Instead of adopting the relational model [2], we describe the semantics of a table in terms of F-Logic frames [9]. F-Logic combines the intuitiveness of modeling with frames with the expressive power of logic. Furthermore, existing F-Logic inference engines such as Ontobroker [4] allow later on e.g. for processing and query answering. Therefore it was our primary choice as representation language.

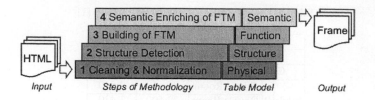

Fig. 1. Building blocks of the methodology

We briefly introduce our running example. As input we use Table 1 which is taken from the tourism domain and is (roughly speaking) about room prices. The ideal description in terms of an F-Logic frame of this table, i.e. the output after applying our approach, could look as follows:

Tour[TourCode => ALPHANUMERIC
    Validity => DATE
    EconomicPrice(PersonType,RoomType) => LARGE_NUMBER
    ExtendedPrice(PersonType,RoomType) => LARGE_NUMBER]

By resorting to F-Logic we are thus able to describe the semantics of tables in a model-theoretic way. Furthermore, as required by Hurst, the frame makes explicit (i) the meaning of cell contents (ii) the functional dimension of the table, and (iii) the meaning of the table abstracting from its particular structure. In this line, different tables with different structures but identical meaning would be described by one and the same frame. In what follows we describe how we process the table in order to yield intermediate descriptions of a table along the dimensions described above as well as how as a last step the table is translated into a F-Logic frame.

As depicted in Figure 1 our methodology consists of four main steps. For each building block of the table model there exists a corresponding methodological step to create this part of the table model. In the following subsections we will describe all steps in detail.

2.1   Cleaning and Normalization

Web documents are often very noisy in a sense that their syntactic structure is incorrect. Web browsers (i.e. Opera) are capable of dealing with such poorly structured, inconsistent, and incomplete documents. In order to remove this noise we perform the following two steps: a) syntactic correction/cleaning, and b) normalization.

First, we assume that documents are represented with the DOM[1] (Document Object Model). A DOM tree is an ordered tree, where each node is either an element or a text node. An element node includes an ordered list of zero to many child nodes, and contains a string-valued tag (such as table, h1 or title) and zero to many string-valued attributes (such as href or src). A text node normally contains a single text string and has no child nodes.

In the two substeps we construct an initial table model out of an updated DOM tree. In order to clean the code and make it syntactically correct, we employ the CyberNeko HTML

---
[1] http://www.w3.org/DOM/

Table 2. Table 1 after cleaning and normalization step

Tour Code	Tour Code	Tour Code	DP9LAX01AB	DP9LAX01AB
Valid	Valid	Valid	01.05 - 30.09.04	01.05 - 30.09.04
Class/Ext.	Class/Ext.	Class/Ext.	Economic	Extended
Adult	PRICE	Single Room	35,450	2,510
Adult	PRICE	Double Room	32,500	1,430
Adult	PRICE	Extra Bed	30,550	720
Child	PRICE	Occupation	25,800	1,430
Child	PRICE	No occupation	23,850	720
Child	PRICE	Extra Bed	22,900	360

Parser[2]. The normalization step of the rendered 'table' element node in the DOM tree is only necessary, when an explicit child node's attribute, such as rowspan or colspan, indicates multiple row or column spanning cells, where the actual total number of rows or columns is lower than the attribute value. In both steps our system updates the corresponding DOM subtrees accordingly.

Table 2 shows the final reformulation of the example in Table 1, where cleaning has been performed and copies of cells with rowspan and rowspan attributes have been properly inserted into the matrix structure.

2.2 Structure Detection

Assignment of functional types and probabilities to cells. In the initial pass over the table element node (of the DOM tree), we convert a sub-tree into a matrix structure, which is populated by cells according to its layout information. During this step the text of each cell is tokenized, and each token is assigned a *token type* according to the tree (leaves) presented in Figure 2. At the same time, we assign each cell in the rendered table a *functional type* and a probability of the type. By default, a cell is assigned no functional type (probability value equals zero), or I-cell type in case the cell includes only/mostly tokens, recognized as dates, currencies, or numerical values. Its probability is then calculated based on the distribution of cell's token types. Finally, we assume that the cell in the lower-right corner is always an I-cell, and the cell in the upper-left corner is an A-cell. Therefore we assign those two cells the types, regardless of their content, with probability one.

Detecting table orientation. One problem related to the interpretation of a table is that its logical orientation is a priori not clear. In fact, when performing a local search on a table, the data of interest can be either ordered in a top-to-down (vertical orientation) or left-to-right manner (horizontal orientation). For example, in figure 1 the relationship *"Tour Code, DP9LAX01AB"* reads left-to-right, but price values of an attribute *"Economic Class"* appear top-to-down. When trying to determine the table orientation we rely on the similarity of cells. The intuition here is that, if rows are similar to each other,

---

[2] http://www.apache.org/andyc/neko/doc/html

then orientation is vertical and on the contrary, if columns are similar, then interpretation is horizontal.

In order to calculate the differences among rows and columns of the table, we need first to define how to calculate the difference between two cells. For this we represent a cell as a vector c of *token types* of all the tokens in the cell. Henceforth, c_i will denote the i-th component of the vector c, corresponding to the token type of the i-th token in the cell. Furthermore, $|c|$ will denote the size of the vector. The token types we consider are given in Figure 2. They are ordered hierarchically thus allowing to measure the distance δ between two different types as the edges between them. This representation is flexible and can be extended to include domain specific information. For example, the numeric type is divided into categories that include range information about the number, i.e. LARGE_NUM ($\geq$ 10.000), MED_NUM ($100 \leq n <$ 10.000), SMALL_NUM ($<$ 100), and CURRENCY, which can be treated as a domain specific information.

Now when comparing the vectors of two cells, we compare the token types with same indices in case the vectors have equal length; otherwise, we calculate the distance for the left-side tokens (tokens aligned at the head) and for the right-side tokens (tokens aligned at the tail). The distance is in both cases also normalized.

$$\delta_{cells}(c_P, c_Q) := \begin{cases} \frac{v}{2*u} \left(\sum_{i=1}^{u} \delta(c_{P_i}, c_{Q_i}) + \sum_{i=w}^{v} \delta(c_{P_i}, c_{Q_i}) \right) & \text{if } u \neq v \\ \frac{1}{u} \sum_{i=1}^{u} \delta(c_{P_i}, c_{Q_i}) & \text{if } u = v \end{cases} \tag{1}$$

where $u = min(|c_P|, |c_Q|)$, $v = max(|c_P|, |c_Q|)$ and $w = v - u + 1$. Now given a table with r rows and s columns, the total distance (Δ_{cols}) between columns is calculated by summing up the distance between the last column and each of the preceding $m - 1$ columns, where $m = min(r, s)$, i.e.

$$\Delta_{cols} = \sum_{i=1}^{m-1} \delta_{cols}(col_{s-i}, col_s) \tag{2}$$

$$\delta_{cols}(col_p, col_q) = \sum_{i=m}^{s} \delta_{cells}(c_{i,p}, c_{i,q}) \tag{3}$$

where $c_{x,y}$ is the cell in row x and column y.

The total distance (Δ_{rows}) between rows is by analogy calculated by summing up the distance between the last row and each of the $m - 1$ preceding rows:

$$\Delta_{rows} = \sum_{i=1}^{m-1} \delta_{rows}(row_{r-i}, row_r) \tag{4}$$

$$\delta_{rows}(row_p, row_q) = \sum_{i=m}^{r} \delta_{cells}(c_{p,i}, c_{q,i}) \tag{5}$$

Here we only compare equal number of rows and columns, starting at the lower-right corner, thus optimizing the number of comparisons (not all the rows and columns to the top of the table need to be compared). Finally, to determine the orientation of the

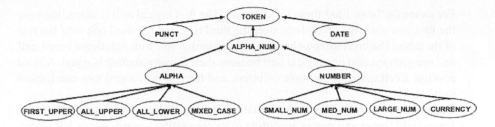

Fig. 2. Hierarchy of token types

table, we compare both results. If the distance between columns is greater than among rows ($\Delta_{cols} > \Delta_{rows}$), orientation is set to *vertical* (top-to-down). On the other hand, if the distance between columns is lower than among rows ($\Delta_{cols} < \Delta_{rows}$), then orientation is set to *horizontal* (left-to-right). In the last case, where the two results are equal, orientation is assigned the default, i.e. *vertical*.

Discovery of regions

Definition 1 (Logical unit). *A logical unit is a part of a table produced by a horizontal split in case of vertical orientation or by a vertical split in case of horizontal orientation.*

Definition 2 (Region). *A region is a rectangular area of a table consisting of cells with the same functional type. Regions cannot extend over multiple logical units and can therefore only appear within one logical unit.*

Here we will present a step-by-step algorithm for discovery of regions in tables. Pseudocode of the algorithm is given in Table 3.

1. *Initialize logical units and regions.* First, the system splits a table into *logical units*. In particular, when table orientation is column-wise (vertical), the horizontal split is done at every row containing cells spanning multiple columns, or when dealing with row-wise (horizontal) orientation, vertical split is done at every column containing cells spanning multiple rows. Consecutive logical units may then be merged if their layout structure is equal. Over-spanning cells of type I-cell also represent a sign for a split. Note that a table itself is by definition one logical unit.

Table 3. Algorithm for discovery of regions

---

1. Initialize logical units and regions
2. Learn string patterns of regions
for all logical units
  do while (logical unit is not uniform)
   3. Choose the best coherent region
   4. Normalize logical unit

For example, Table 1 has three logical units. The first logical unit is extending over the first two rows, the second one over the third row, and the third one over the rest of the table. The first two rows have an over-spanning cell with functional type I-cell and are grouped into one logical unit because their layout structure is equal. A third row has a cell spanning multiple columns, and the rest is grouped into one logical unit.

Once splitting is over, the region initialization step begins. The system starts at a lower-right corner and moves according to its orientation towards upper-left corner over all logical units, thus generating all distinct initial regions. The cell c_N is added to a region r if the following conditions apply (otherwise a new region is created):

a) the cell c_N is within the same logical unit as other cells
b) its size is equal to the size of cells already in the region, and
c) it keeps the distance among cells in r within a treshold value:

$$\delta_{cells}(c_N, c_{1(r)}) \leq 2 \tag{6}$$

where the value of 2 reflects a significant token type change according to the hierarchy in figure 2.

2. *Learn string patterns for regions.* For each region r we learn a set P_r of significant patterns, which are sequences of token types and tokens, describing the content of a significant number of cells. The patterns are of two types: the first represents the content of cells from left-to-right (forward) and the second from right-to-left (backward). The pattern 'FIRST_UPPER Room' for example covers the cells 'Single Room' and 'Double Room'. For the purpose of pattern construction we have implemented the DATAPROG algorithm, which is described in [10] together with a detailed pattern learning process. In case there are not enough examples (less than 20) to statistically choose the most significant patterns, only the most specific (having their coverage over the treshold value) are chosen.

Before entering the loop (compare table 3), the system checks the uniformity of every logical unit. In our case, a logical unit is uniform when it consists of logical sub-units and each sub-unit includes only regions of the same size and orientation. Only the units that are not uniform are further processed within the following steps of the loop.

3. *Choose the best coherent region.* If a logical unit is not uniform, the system chooses its *best region*, which is used to normalize neighboring regions and consequently the logical unit itself. The best region r_{max} is chosen according to the formula $\Phi_{r_{max}} = max_{r \, in \, l} \phi_{r,l}$, which is calculated by the following equation:

$$\phi_{r,l} := \left(\frac{|r|}{|l|} + \frac{1}{|r|} \sum_{c \, in \, r} P(c) + \frac{1}{2*|r|*|P_r|} \sum_{p \in P_r} covers(p,r) \right) \tag{7}$$

where l denotes a *logical unit*, r denotes a *region* in the unit, c denotes *cells* in the region, and P_r is the set of *significant string (forward and backward) patterns* for the region as described above. The function $covers(p,r)$ returns a number of cells covered by pattern p in region r. According to the above formula, the selected region maximizes the sum of averaged region size (1st operand of the sum), averaged cell probabilities (2nd operand) and averaged pattern coverage over a particular region (3rd operand).

4. *Normalize neighboring regions of the best region.* The intuition here is to use the best region as a propagator for other regions in their normalization process. First, the system selects (based on the orientation) all neighboring regions, i.e. those that appear in the same rows (left/right) for column-wise orientation, or in same columns (up/down) for row-wise orientation. Now, two possibilities exist: (a) neighboring regions within a common column/row (orientation dependent) do not extend over the boundaries of the best region. In this case, the solution is straightforward, because the 'new' region is extended in a way to cover all common column/row regions. (b) neighboring regions within a common column/row do extend over the boundaries of the best region. In this case, the best region is extended accordingly, and this step repeated.

The logical unit is being processed within the loop as long as the system is not able to divide it into logical sub-units, where each sub-unit includes only regions of the same size and orientation (uniformity condition). Note that string patterns, probabilities and functional types of normalized regions are also updated in every iteration. Finally, in this way all logical units are being normalized and prepared for further processing.

2.3   Building of a Functional Table Model

The key step of translating a table into a frame is building a model of the functional dimension of the table. This model is called *Functional Table Model* (FTM) and essentially arranges regions of the table in a tree, whereby the leaves of the tree are all the regions consisting exclusively of I-cells. Most importantly, in the FTM these leaves are assigned their functional role, i.e. *access* or *data*, and semantic labels as described in Section 2.4.

The construction of the FTM proceeds bottom up: we start with the lowest logical unit in the table and proceed with further logical units towards the top. For each logical unit in question we first determine its type. There are three possibilities: (a) the logical unit consists only of A-cells, in which case all its regions will be turned into inner nodes of the tree and thus connected to some other nodes in the tree, (b) it consists only of I-cells, in which case they will constitute leaves and will be connected to appropriate inner nodes, and (c) it consists of I-cells and A-cells, in which case we determine the logical separation between them by taking the uniformity condition into account.

In some cases a special *connection node* (see Figure 3) needs to be inserted into the tree. This occurs when we encounter a logical unit that reflects a split in the table, in particular when a previous logical unit contained only A-cells, but the present logical unit again contains I-cells. In such cases, we check (described later in this paragraph) if reading orientation of the present logical unit is different from the previous one and needs to be changed. If this is true, the logical unit needs to be recalculated, as described in Section 2.2. For example, the first logical unit (first two rows) in Table 1 has four regions (each 'logical' cell) and there is no logical unit on top of it. So, if the orientation was vertical (i.e. like in lower logical unit), there would be no inner node (consisting of A-cells) to connect the I-cells to. Thus orientation has to be changed from vertical to horizontal for this logical unit.

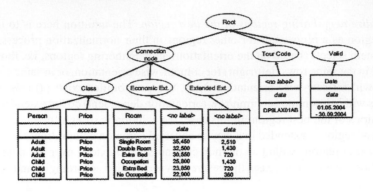

Fig. 3. A functional table model (FTM) of the running example (Table 1) with square components representing I-cells and rounded components representing A-cells.

As already mentioned above, each region in a leaf position is assigned its corresponding functional role. The role *access* is assigned to all consecutive regions (starting at the left subnodes of a subtree) together forming a unique identifier or key in the database terminology. The rest of the leaf nodes in the subtree get assigned the role *data*.

When all logical units have been processed, we connect the remaining unconnected nodes to a root node. For example, the FTM constructed out of our running example is depicted in Figure 3. After the FTM is constructed, we examine if there are any multi-level (at least two levels of inner A-cell nodes) subtrees that might be merged. The candidate subtrees for merging must have the same tree structure (same number of levels and nodes on each level) and at least one level of matching A-cells. If there are any candidates that fulfill the requirements, we perform a process called *recapitulation*, where we merge the nodes at same positions in both subtrees. As we only require one level of matching A-cells, there might be some A-cells that do not match. For every such case, the following steps are taken: (a) find a semantic label of a 'merged' A-cell node (described in Section 2.4), (b) connect the 'merged' A-cell to a new leaf node, which is populated by the A-cell contents of merged nodes, and (c) assign the functional role of the new leaf node to *access*. In this way we check and merge all possible multi-level subtrees of a FTM and finalize the construction process.

2.4 Semantic Enriching of the Functional Table Model

Discovery of semantic labels. In order to find semantic labels for each table region (node), we resort to the WordNet lexical ontology [5] to find an appropriate hypernym covering all tokens in the cells contained in the region. Furthermore, we also make use of the GoogleSets[3] service to find synonyms for certain tokens. For example, the first region in Table 2 consists of the tokens *adult* and *child*, for which WordNet suggests the hypernym *person*. However, the tokens are not always so 'pure', therefore we stepwise remove words in the cells by the following transformations and consult WordNet after each step to yield a suitable hypernym:

---

[3] http://labs.google.com/sets

1. punctuation removal
2. stopword removal
3. compute the IDF measure (where the documents are cells in our case) for each word and filter out the ones with value lower than the threshold
4. select words that appear at the end of the cells as they are more significant[4]
5. query GoogleSets with the remaining words in order to filter words which are not mutually similar

Map Functional Table Models into Frames. In order to define how to transform a FTM into a frame, we first give a formal definition of a method and a frame:

Definition 3 (Method). *A method is a tuple* $M := (name_M, range_M, P_M)$, *where (i)* $name_M$ *is the name of the method, (ii)* $range_M$ *is a string describing the range of the method and (iii)* P_M *is a set of strings describing the parameters of the method.*

The method $Price(PersonType, RoomType) \Rightarrow NUMBER$ would for example be formally represented as the tuple (Price,NUMBER,{PersonType,RoomType}). Further, a frame is defined as follows:

Definition 4 (Frame). *A Frame F is a pair* $F:=(name_F, M_F)$ *where* $name_F$ *is the name of the frame and* M_F *is a set of methods as described above.*

Now when generating a frame, we create one method m for every region with functional role *data* with all the regions of type *access* as parameters of this method. This parameters must either be located on the same level within the same subtree or on a parent path to the root node. Here it is crucial to find appropriate names for the method ($name_M$) and parameter identifiers $p \in P_M$. The semantic label for each identifier is a combination of a region label (described in procedure above) and parent A-cell node labels. For better understanding, compare the FTM tree depicted in Figure 3 and the example of the generated frame given below. Further, we also set the range $range_M$ of the method m to the syntactic token type of the region with functional role *data* for which the method was generated. Finally, the frame for the running example, generated by the system, looks as follows:

Tour [Code => ALPHANUMERIC
    DateValid => DATE
    EconomicExtension (PersonClass, RoomClass) => LARGE_NUMBER
    ExtendedExtension (PersonClass, RoomClass) => LARGE_NUMBER]

3 Evaluation

In order to evaluate our approach, we compare the automatically generated frames with frames manually created by two different subjects in terms of Precision, Recall and F-Measure. In particular, we considered 21 different tables in our experiment and asked 14

---

[4] The intuition here is that for nominal compounds the nominal head is at the end.

Trip Code	Trip Duration (in days)	Cost	Insurance
LM202	-7	520	50
LM208	9-15	725	70
LM209	16-23	949	90
LM311	23-31	1495	120
LM223	32-45	2275	195
XM001	46-60	3180	220

(a) 1D

	Departure	Arrival
City:	Dallas/Ft Worth, TX (DFW)	Honolulu, HI (HNL)
Scheduled:	Mar 16 - 11:45am	Mar 16 - 4:20pm
Actual:	Mar 16 - Not Available	Mar 16 - Not Available
Gate/Terminal:	A29	18
Baggage Claim:	-	F2

(b) 2D

Rate (%)	Regular	Float
Regular Fixed Deposit		
1 Year	5,05	5,05
2 Years	5,1	5,1
3 Years	5,1	5,1
Fixed Deposit		
3 Months	4,35	4,35
6 Months	4,6	4,6
9 Months	4,7	4,7
1 Year	5	5
2 Years	5,05	5,05
3 years	5,05	5,05

(c) Partition table

Fig. 4. Examples of Tables

subjects to manually create a frame for three different tables such that each table in our dataset was annotated by two different subjects with the appropriate frame ($14 \times 3 = 21 \times 2 = 42$). In what follows we first describe the dataset used in the experiments. Then we describe the evaluation methodology and present the actual results of the experiment. The definition of the task as well as the instructions for the annotators can be found at http://www.aifb.uni-karlsruhe.de/WBS/pci/FromTables2Frames.ps

Table Classes. We have identified three major table classes according to their layout that appear frequently on the web: *1-Dimensional* (1D), *2-Dimensional* (2D), and *Complex* tables. The first two classes are more simple and also appear more often compared to the last class. A similar classification into classes has also been introduced in [16].

1-Dimensional tables: this class of tables has at least one row of A-cells above the rows of I-cells. If there are more than one row of A-cells then we assume that they are hierarchically connected. The content of the I-cells in different columns represent instances of the A-cells above. An example of this type is given in Figure 4 (a).

2-Dimensional tables: this class has a rectangular area of I-cells appearing within columns. This class has at least one row of A-cells above the rectangular area, and at least one column of A-cells on the left side of the rectangular area. Discovering and handling of this class is hard as it is difficult for a system (without any other knowledge) to decide if the first column consists of A-cells or I-cells. Our solution here is to interpret the leading column as A-cells only if its first row cell is a non-spanning cell with an empty label or a label containing a character '/'. An example for this type of table is given in Figure 4 (b).

Complex tables: this class of tables shows a great variety in layout structure. Therefore a table might have the following features:

– **Partition data labels:** Special over-spanning data labels between the data and/or attribute labels can make several partitions of the table. Each partition shares the same attributes, such as in Figure 4 (c). In this case the relation among attribute and data value cannot be obtained directly.

– **Over-expanded labels:** some entries might expand over multiple cells. There are two options: (a) data values span over multiple rows in the same column or (b) an attribute label spans over multiple columns. An example of this class is the part of Table 1 consisting in the lower seven rows.

– **Combination:** large tables might consist of several smaller, simpler ones. For example, Table 1 consists of two structurally 'independent' tables.

In our experiment, we have gathered 21 tables, each belonging to at least one class. Since the first two classes are a bit less interesting, we used only three different tables for each class, but for each complex subclass we used five different tables. All tables were gathered from two distinctive sources: one from tourist domain and another from a source dealing with food research. Domains were quite different, and also tables were selected from different sources in a way that their distribution over classes is uniform.

Evaluation Methodology. We evaluated our approach by considering the well-known information retrieval measures Precision, Recall and F-Measure. In particular, for each table we evaluated the frame automatically generated for it by the system with respect to the two frames manually created by two different subjects along the following lines: *Syntactic Correctness, Strict Comparison, Soft Comparison, Conceptual Comparison.* In order to assess how similar two strings are, we will introduce a string comparison operator $\sigma : String \times String \rightarrow [0..1]$.

In particular, in our evaluation we use a string comparison operator based on a combination of a TFIDF weighting scheme with the Jaro-Winkler string-distance scheme. Cohen et al. [3] showed that the operator produces good results in such tasks. The *Syntactic Correctness* measures how well the frame captures the syntactic structure of the table, i.e. to what extent the number of arguments matches the number of parameters as specified by the human annotator for a given method. In what follows we define three functions *Syntactic* giving the syntactic correctness between two methods as well as a method and a frame, respectively.

$$Syntactic_{M \times M}(m_1, m_2) := \begin{cases} \frac{|P_{m_1}|}{|P_{m_2}|} & \text{if } |P_{m_2}| > 0 \\ 1 & \text{if } |P_{m_1}| = |P_{m_2}| = 0 \\ 0 & otherwise \end{cases}$$

$$Syntactic_{M \times F}(m, f) = Syntactic_{M \times M}(m, m'),$$

where m' is that method in f_M which maximizes $\sigma'(m, m') * Syntactic_{M \times M}(m, m')$. Note that the above measures are directed; they will be used in one direction to obtain the Precision and in the other direction to obtain the recall of the system.

Strict Evaluation then checks if the identifier for the method name, the range and the parameters are identical. We also define a corresponding functions *Strict* again defined on two methods and a method and a frame, respectively:

$$Strict_{M \times M}(m_1, m_2) := \begin{cases} 1 & \text{if } name_{m_1} = name_{m_2} \\ 0 & otherwise \end{cases}$$

$$Strict_{M \times F}(m, f) = max_{m' \in M_f} Strict_{M \times M}(m, m')$$

The Soft Evaluation also measures in how far the identifiers for the method name, the range and the parameters match, but makes use of the string comparison operator defined above:

$$Soft_{M \times M}(m_1, m_2) = \sigma(name_{m_1}, name_{m_2})$$

$$Soft_{M \times F}(m, f) = max_{m' \in M_f} Soft_{M \times M}(m, m')$$

Further, we have a modified string comparison σ which returns 1 if the string to compare are equivalent from a conceptual point of view and σ otherwise, i.e.

$$\sigma'(s_1, s_2) := \begin{cases} 1 & \text{if } s_1 \text{ and } s_2 \text{ are conceptually equivalent} \\ \sigma(s_1, s_2) & \text{otherwise} \end{cases}$$

The *Conceptual* measure was introduced to check in how far the system was able to learn the frame for a table from a conceptual point of view. In order to assess this, two of the authors compared the frames produced by the system and the ones given by the human subjects and determined which identifiers can be regarded as conceptually equivalent. In this line *RegionType*, *Region* and *Location* can be regarded as conceptual equivalent. Here are the formal definitions of the corresponding functions:

$$Conceptual_{M \times M}(m_1, m_2) = \sigma'(name_{m_1}, name_{m_2})$$

$$Conceptual_{M \times F}(m, f) = max_{m' \in M_f} Conceptual_{M \times M}(m, m')$$

For all the above measures we compare two frames as follows:

$$X_{F \times F}(f, f') = \frac{\sum_{m \in f_M} X_{F \times F}(m, f')}{|f_M|},$$

where X stands either for *Syntactic, Strict, Soft* or *Conceptual*.

In our evaluation study, we give results for Precision, Recall and F-Measure between the frame F_S produced by the system and the frames $F_1, ... F_n$ (in our case $n = 2$) produced by the human annotators. In particular, we will consider the above evaluation functions *Syntactic, Strict, Soft* and *Conceptual* in order to calculate the Precision, Recall and F-Measure of the system. Thus, in the following formulas, X stands either for *Syntactic, Strict, Soft* or *Conceptual*: $Prec_{Avg,X}(F_S, \{F_1, ... F_n\}) = \frac{\sum_{1 \leq i \leq n} X(F_S, F_i)}{n}$
And Recall is defined inversely, i.e. $Rec_{Avg,X}(F_S, \{F_1, ... F_n\}) = \frac{\sum_{1 \leq i \leq n} X(F_i, F_S)}{n}$.
Obviously, according to the definitions of the measures, the following equations hold:
$Prec_{Strict} \leq Prec_{Soft} \leq Prec_{Conceptual}$, $Rec_{Strict} \leq Rec_{Soft} \leq Rec_{Conceptual}$.
Furthermore, we also give the value of the precision and recall for the frame which maximizes these measures, i.e. $Prec_{max,X}(F_S, \{F_1, ... F_n\}) = max_i X(F_S, F_i)$ And Recall is defined inversely, i.e. $Rec_{max,X}(F_S, \{F_1, ... F_n\}) = max_i X(F_i, F_S)$. Obviously, here the following equations hold: $Prec_X \leq Prec_{max,X}, Rec_X \leq Rec_{max,X}$.
The reason for calculating precision and recall against the frame given by both annotators which maximizes the measures is that some frames given by the annotators were not modelled correctly according to the intuitions of the authors. Thus, by this we avoid

Table 4. Results of the different evaluation measures

	Average				Maximum			
	Syntactic	Strict	Soft	Conceptual	Syntactic	Strict	Soft	Conceptual
Precision	48.71%	36.78%	44.88%	56.01%	62.85%	48.84%	58.26%	71.02%
Recall	50.53%	38.81%	47.75%	58.50%	67.54%	51.83%	61.95%	77.65%
F-Measure	49.60%	37.77%	46.27%	57.22%	65.11%	50.29%	60.05%	74.18%

to penalize the system for an answer which is actually correct. As a byproduct of calculating $Recall_X$ and $Recall_{max,X}$ we can also indirectly judge how good the agreement between human subjects is.

Finally, as is usual we balance Recall and Precision against each other by the F-Measure given by the formula: $F_X(P_X, R_X) = \frac{2P_X R_X}{P_X + R_X}$

The system is now evaluated by calculating the above measures for each automatically generated frames and the corresponding frames given by the human annotator.

Discussion of Results. Table 4 gives the results for the Precision, Recall and F-Measure as described above. The first interesting observation is that the values for the *maximum* evaluation are quite higher than the ones of the *average* evaluation, which clearly shows that there was a considerable disagreement between annotators and thus that the task we are considering is far from being trivial.

The results of the *Syntactic* comparison are an F-Measure of $F_{avg,Syntactic} = 49.60\%$ for the *average* evaluation and $F_{max,Syntactic} = 65.11\%$. The values show that the system is interpreting the table to a satisfactory extent from a syntactic point of view, i.e. it is determining the number of parameters correctly in most of the cases. Regarding the naming of the methods, their range and their parameters, the results vary considerable depending on the measure in question. For the *average* evaluation the results are: $F_{avg,Strict} = 37.77\%$, $F_{avg,Soft} = 46.27\%$ and $F_{avg,Conceptual} = 57.22\%$. These results show that the system has indeed problems to find the appropriate name for methods, their ranges and their parameters. However, as the conceptual evaluation shows, most of the names given by the system are from a conceptual point of view equivalent to the ones given by the human annotator. For the *maximum* evaluation we have: $F_{max,Strict} = 50.29\%$, $F_{max,Soft} = 60.05\%$ and $F_{max,Conceptual} = 74.18\%$. Thus, we can conclude that from a conceptual point of view the system is getting an appropriate name in almost 75% of the cases and it is getting the totally identical name in more than 50% of the cases. Actually, our system only failed in processing two of the 21 tables, such that in general we conclude that our results are certainly very promising.

4   Related Work

A very recent systematic overview of related work on table recognition can be found in [18]. Several conclusions can be drawn from this survey. Firstly, only few table models have been described explicitly. Apart from the table model of Hurst which we have applied in our approach [7,8] the most prominent other model is from Wang [17].

However, the model of Hurst is better suited for our purpose since it is targeted towards table *recognition* whereas Wang is targeted towards table *generation*.

Secondly, it becomes clear that research so far in table recognition focused on recovering tables from encoded documents, i.e. Ng et al. [13] applied machine learning techniques to identify the location of the table (rows and columns) in the text, where McCallum et al. [12] and Pinto et al. [15] dealt also with row labeling and cell classification. Chen et al. [1] also worked on table recognition (using heuristic rules), and interpretation, but only from web documents. Table extraction methods have also been applied in the context of question answering, such as in [14,16].

In contrast, we assume that tables are already harvested. Furthermore, we provide a methodology and implementation which completely instantiates a table model and additionally closes the gap to formal semantics provided by ontologies. Our approach allows subsequently for using the full potential ontologies offer e.g. for query answering or knowledge retrieval over a set of tables.

5 Conclusion

We have shown how our methodology stepwise instantiates the underlying table model which consists of *Physical, Structural, Functional* and *Semantic* components. The core steps of the methodology are (i) Cleaning and Normalization, (ii) Structure Detection, (iii) Building of the Functional Table Model (FTM) and (iv) Semantic Enriching of the FTM. We demonstrated and evaluated the successful automatic generation of frames from HTML tables. Additionally, our experimental results show that from a conceptual point of view the system is getting appropriate names for frames in almost 75% of the cases and it is getting the totally identical name in more than 50% of the cases. These results are certainly very promising.

Acknowledgments. This work has been supported by the IST-projects Dot.Kom and SEKT, sponsored by the EC as part of the frameworks V and VI, respectively. During his stay at the AIFB, Aleksander Pivk has been supported by a Marie Curie Fellowship of the European Community program 'Host Training Sites' and by the Slovenian Ministry of Education, Science and Sport. Thanks to all our colleagues for participating in the evaluation of the system as well as to the reviewers for useful comments on the paper.

References

1. H. Chen, S. Tsai, and J. Tsai. Mining tables from large scale HTML texts. In *Proc. of the 18th Int. Conf. on Computational Linguistics (COLING)*, pages 166–172, 2000.
2. E.A. Codd. A relational model for large shared databanks. *Communications of the ACM*, 13(6):377–387, 1970.
3. W. Cohen, P. Ravikumar, and S. Fienberg. A comparison of string distance metrics for name-matching tasks. In *Proceedings of the IIWeb Workshop at the IJCAI 2003 conference*, 2003.
4. S. Decker, M. Erdmann, D. Fensel, and R. Studer. Ontobroker: Ontology Based Access to Distributed and Semi-Structured Information. In R. Meersman et al., editors, *Database Semantics: Semantic Issues in Multimedia Systems*, pages 351–369. Kluwer, 1999.

5. C. Fellbaum. *WordNet, an electronic lexical database*. MIT Press, 1998.

6. S. Handschuh and S. Staab, editors. *Annotation in the Semantic Web*. IOS Press, 2003.

7. M. Hurst. Layout and language: Beyond simple text for information interaction - modelling the table. In *Proc. of the 2nd Int. Conf. on Multimodal Interfaces, Hong Kong*, 1999.

8. M. Hurst. *The Interpretation of Tables in Texts*. PhD thesis, University of Edinburgh, 2000.

9. M. Kifer, G. Lausen, and J. Wu. Logical foundations of object-oriented and frame-based languages. *Journal of the ACM*, 42:741–843, 1995.

10. K. Lerman, S. Minton, and C. Knoblock. Wrapper maintenance: A machine learning approach. *J. of Artificial Intelligence Research*, 18:149–181, 2003.

11. A. Maedche. *Ontology Learning for the Semantic Web*. Kluwer Academic Publishers, 2002.

12. A. McCallum, D. Freitag, and F. Pereira. Maximum entropy markov models for information extraction and segmentation. In *Proceedings of the ICML 2000*, pages 591—598, 2000.

13. H. T. Ng, C. Y. Kim, and J. L. T. Koo. Learning to recognize tables in free text. In *Proceedings of the 37th Annual Meeting of the Association for Computational Linguistics*, pages 443—450, 1999.

14. D. Pinto, W. Croft, M. Branstein, R. Coleman, M. King, W. Li, and X. Wei. Quasm: A system for question answering using semi-structured data. In *Proceedings of the Joint Conference on Digital Libraries (JCDL) 2002*, pages 46–55, 2002.

15. D. Pinto, A. McCallum, X. Wei, and W.B. Croft. Table extraction using conditional random fields. In *Proceedings of the 26th annual international ACM SIGIR conference on Research and development in informaion retrieval*, pages 235–242. ACM Press, 2003.

16. H. L. Wang, S. H. Wu, I. C. Wang, C. L. Sung, W. L. Hsu, and W. K. Shih. Semantic Search on Internet Tabular Information Extraction for Answering Queries. In *Proc. of the Ninth Int. Conf. on Information and Knowledge Management, Washington DC*, pages 243–249, 2000.

17. X. Wang. *Tabular Abstraction, Editing and Formatting*. PhD thesis, U. of Waterloo, 1996.

18. R. Zanibbi, D. Blostein, and J.R. Cordy. A survey of table recognition: Models, observations, transformations, and inferences. *International Journal of Document Analysis and Recognition*, to appear.

The Specification of Agent Behavior by Ordinary People: A Case Study

Luke McDowell, Oren Etzioni, and Alon Halevy

University of Washington, Department of Computer Science and Engineering
Seattle, WA 98195 USA
{lucasm,etzioni,alon}@cs.washington.edu,
http://www.cs.washington.edu/research/semweb/email

Abstract. The development of intelligent agents is a key part of the Semantic Web vision, but how does an ordinary person tell an agent what to do? One approach to this problem is to use RDF *templates* that are authored once but then instantiated many times by ordinary users. This approach, however, raises a number of challenges. For instance, how can templates concisely represent a broad range of potential uses, yet ensure that each possible instantiation will function properly? And how does the agent explain its actions to the humans involved? This paper addresses these challenges in the context of a case study carried out on our fully-deployed system[1] for *semantic email agents*. We describe how high-level features of our template language enable the concise specification of flexible goals. In response to the first question, we show that it is possible to verify, in polynomial time, that a given template will always produce a valid instantiation. Second, we show how to automatically generate explanations for the agent's actions, and identify cases where explanations can be computed in polynomial time. These results both improve the usefulness of semantic email and suggest general issues and techniques that may be applicable in other Semantic Web systems.

1 Introduction

The vision of the Semantic Web has always encompassed not only the declarative representation of data but also the development of intelligent agents that can consume this data and act upon their owner's behalf. For instance, agents have been proposed to perform tasks like appointment scheduling [2], meeting coordination [26], and travel planning [22]. A significant difficulty with this vision, however, is the need to translate the real-world goals of untrained users into a formal specification suitable for agent execution [31,30]. In short, how can an ordinary person tell an agent what to do?

One approach to this problem is to encapsulate classes of common behaviors into reusable *templates* (cf., *program schemas* [7,10] and *generic procedures* [22]). Templates address the specification problem by allowing a domain-specific template to be *authored* once but then *instantiated* many times by untrained users. In addition, specifying such templates declaratively opens the door to automated reasoning with and composition of templates. Furthermore, the resulting declarative specifications can be much more concise than with a procedural approach (see Table 1).

---

[1] See http://www.cs.washington.edu/research/semweb/email for a publicly accessible server (no installation required); source code is also available from the authors.

S.A. McIlraith et al. (Eds.): ISWC 2004, LNCS 3298, pp. 182–197, 2004.
© Springer-Verlag Berlin Heidelberg 2004

Table 1. Comparison of the size of an E-Agent specification in our original procedural prototype [9] (using Java/HTML) vs. in the declarative format described in this paper (using RDF). Overall, the declarative approach is about 80-90% more concise.

E-Agent name	Procedural approach (number of lines)	Declarative approach (number of lines)	Size Reduction for Declarative
Balanced Potluck	1680	170	90%
First-come, First-served	536	99	82%
Meeting Coordination	743	82	89%
Request Approval	1058	109	90%
Auction	503	98	81%

However, specifying agent behavior via templates presents a number of challenges:

- **Generality:** How can a template concisely represent a broad range of potential uses?
- **Safety:** Templates are written with a certain set of assumptions — how can we ensure that any (perhaps unexpected) instantiation of that template by a naive user will function properly (e.g., do no harm [32], generate no errors)?
- **Understandability:** When executing a template, how can an agent explain its actions to the humans (or other agents) that are involved?

This paper investigates these challenges via a case study that leverages our deployed system for *semantic email agents* (E-Agents).[2] E-Agents provide a good testbed for examining the agent specification problem because they offer the potential for managing complex goals and yet are intended to be used by a wide range of untrained people. For instance, consider the process of scheduling a meeting with numerous people subject to certain timing and participation constraints. E-Agents support the common task where an *originator* wants to ask a set of *participants* some questions, collect their responses, and ensure that the results satisfy some set of *constraints*. In order to satisfy these constraints, an E-Agent may utilize a number of *interventions* such as rejecting a participant's response or suggesting an alternative response.

Our contributions are as follows. First, we identify the three key challenges for template-based agents described above. We then examine specific solutions to each challenge in the context of our fully-deployed system for semantic email. For *generality*, we describe the essential features of our template language that enable authors to easily express complex constraints without compromising important computational properties. The sufficiency of these features is demonstrated by our implementation of a small but diverse set of E-Agents. For *safety*, we show how to verify, in polynomial time, that a given template will always produce a valid instantiation. Finally, for *understandability*, we examine how to automatically generate explanations of *why* a particular response could not be accepted and *what* responses would be more acceptable. We also identify suitable restrictions where such constraint-based explanations can be generated in polynomial time. These results both greatly increase the usefulness of semantic email as well as highlight important issues for a broad range of Semantic Web systems.

---

[2] Our prior work [19] referred to *semantic email processes*; in this work we call them E-Agents to be more consistent with standard agent terminology.

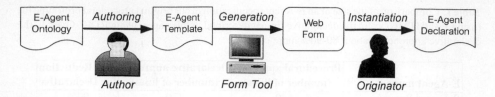

Fig. 1. The creation of a Semantic Email Agent (E-Agent). Initially, an "Author" *authors* an E-Agent template and this template is used to *generate* an associated web form. Later, this web form is used by the "Originator" to *instantiate* the template. Typically, a template is authored once and then instantiated many times.

The next section gives a brief overview of E-Agents while Section 3 discusses the salient features of our template language with an extended example. Sections 4 and 5 examine the problems of instantiation safety and explanation generation that were discussed above. Finally, Section 6 considers related work and Section 7 concludes with implications of our results for both email-based and non-email-based agents.

2   Overview of Semantic Email Agents

We illustrate E-Agents with the running example of a "balanced potluck," which operates as follows. The E-Agent originator initially creates a message announcing a "potluck-style" event — in this case, the message asks each participant whether they are bringing an `Appetizer`, `Entree`, or `Dessert` (or `Not-Coming`). The originator also expresses a set of constraints for the potluck, e.g., that the difference in the number of appetizers, entrees, or desserts should be at most two (to ensure "balance").

Figure 1 demonstrates how a template is used to create a new E-Agent. Initially, someone who is assumed to have some knowledge of RDF and semantic email authors a new template using an editor (most likely by modifying an existing template). We call this person the E-Agent *author*. The template is written in RDF based on an ontology that describes the possible questions, constraints, and notifications for an E-Agent. For instance, the potluck template defines some general balance constraints, but has place-holders for *parameters* such as the participants' addresses, the specific choices to offer, and how much imbalance to permit. Associated with each template is a simple *web form* that describes each needed parameter; Section 4 describes a tool to automatically generate such forms. An untrained originator finds an appropriate web form from a public library and fills it out with values for each parameter, causing the corresponding template to be instantiated into an E-Agent *declaration*. The semantic email server executes the declaration directly, using appropriate algorithms to direct the E-Agent outcome via message rejections and suggestions.

In our implementation, E-Agents are executed by a central server. When invoked, this server sends initial messages to the participants that contain a human-readable announcement along with a corresponding RDF component. These messages also contain a simple text form that can be handled by a human with any mail client, or by another agent based on an associated RDQL query. Participants fill out the form and reply via mail directly to the server, rather than to the originator, and the originator receives status messages from the server when appropriate.

3   Concise and Tractable Representation of Templates

Our first challenge is to ensure that a template can concisely represent many possible uses while still ensuring the tractability of E-Agent reasoning (e.g., to check the acceptability of a participant's response). This section first describes our template language via an extended example and then discusses how the language meets this challenge.

3.1   Template Example

An E-Agent *template* is a (parameterized) RDF document that specifies
- a set of **participants**,
- **questions** to ask the participants,
- **constraints** to enforce on the participants' responses, and
- **notifications** to send to the originator and/or participants at appropriate times.

We illustrate the latter three parts below with a balanced potluck template. In these declarations (shown in N3 format), variables in bold such as **$Choices$** are parameters provided by the originator; other variables such as x are computed during execution.

Questions: The set of questions to ask each participant. For instance, a potluck E-Agent might ask everyone for the food items and number of guests that they are bringing:

```
[a               :StringQuestion;
 :name           "Bring";
 :enumeration    "$Choices$"; ]

[a               :IntegerQuestion;
 :guard          "$AskForNumGuests$";
 :name           "NumGuests";
 :minInclusive   "0"; ]
```

The enumeration and minInclusive properties constrain the legal responses to these questions. In addition, the latter question is "guarded" so that it applies only if the parameter AskForNumGuests is true. Because a question defines data that may be accessed in multiple other locations in the template, it is important to be able to reason about whether its guard might evaluate to false (see Section 4). Finally, each question item also specifies a RDQL query (not shown) that defines the semantic meaning of the requested information and is used to map the participant's textual response to RDF [19].

Constraints: The originator's goals for the E-Agent's outcome. Each goal may be expressed either as a constraint that must be satisfied at every point in time (a MustConstraint) or as a constraint that should, if possible, be *ultimately satisfied* by the final outcome (a PossiblyConstraint). Section 5 defines the behavior of these constraints more precisely. Our simple example uses a quantified MustConstraint to require balance among the counts of the different choices:

```
[a               :MustConstraint;
 :forAll         ([:name    "x";    :range  "$Choices$-$OptOut$"]
```

```
                [:name    "y";        :range "$Choices$-$OptOut$"]);
   :suchThat    "$x$ != $y$";
   :enforce     "abs($Bring.{$x$}.count()$ - $Bring.{$y$}.count()$)
                   <= $MaxImbalance$";
   :message     "Sorry, we can't accept a $Bring.last()$ now."; ]
```

The constraint applies to every possible combination (x,y) from the set (Choices – OptOut); OptOut is for choices such as "Not Coming" that should be excluded from the constraints. The message property is an optional message to send to a participant in case this constraint causes their message to be rejected. This particular message is not very helpful, but specifying messages with enough detail to entice the desired cooperation from the participants can be a challenge for the E-Agent author. Section 5 discusses techniques for automatically constructing more informative messages.

Notifications: A set of email messages to send when some condition is satisfied, e.g., to notify the originator when the total number of guests reaches GuestThreshold:

```
  [a          :OnConditionSatisfied;
   :guard      "$GuestThreshold$ > 0";
   :define     [ :name   "TotalGuests";
                  :value "[SELECT SUM(NumGuests) FROM CURR_STATE]"];
   :condition  "$TotalGuests$ >= $GuestThreshold$";
   :notify     :Originator;
   :message    "Currently, $TotalGuests$ guests are expected.";]
```

3.2   Discussion

The example above illustrates two different ways for accessing the data collected by the E-Agent: via a pre-defined variable (e.g., Bring.last(),Bring.x.count()) or, less commonly, by utilizing an explicit SQL query over a virtual table constructed from the RDF (e.g., as with TotalGuests). The former method is more convenient and allows the author to easily specify decisions based on a variety of views of the underlying data. More importantly, if the constraints refer to response data only through such pre-defined variables, then they are guaranteed to be *bounded*, because they enable the agent to summarize all of the responses that have been received with a set of counters, where the number of counters is independent of the number of participants. For this type of constraints (which still enables many useful E-Agents), the optimal decision of whether to accept a message can always be computed in polynomial time [19]. Thus, the language enables more complex data access mechanisms as necessary but helps authors to write E-Agents that are computationally tractable.

This example also highlights additional key features of our language, including:

- Guards (e.g., with $AskForNumGuests$)
- Sets, membership testing, and set manipulation (e.g., $Choices$-$OptOut$)
- Universal quantification (e.g.. forAll x... enforce this constraint)
- Question types/restrictions (e.g., IntegerQuestion, minInclusive)
- Multiple constraint types (e.g., MustConstraint vs. PossiblyConstraint)
- Math. functions and comparisons (e.g., abs(x-y) <= $MaxImbalance$)
- Pre-defined queries over the supporting data set (e.g., $Bring.last()$)

Among other advantages, guards, sets, and universal quantification enable a single, concise E-Agent template to be instantiated with many different choices and configurations. Likewise, question types and restrictions reduce template complexity by ensuring that responses are well-formed. Finally, multiple constraint/notification types, mathematical functions, and pre-defined queries simplify the process of making decisions based on the responses that are received. Overall, these features make it substantially easier to author useful agents with potentially complex functionality.

Using this template language, we have authored and deployed a number of E-Agents for simple tasks such as collecting RSVPs, giving tickets away (first-come, first-served), scheduling meetings, and balancing a potluck. Our experience has demonstrated that this language is sufficient for specifying a wide range of useful E-Agents (see Table 1).

4 Template Instantiation and Verification

The second major challenge for template-based specifications is to ensure that originators can easily and safely instantiate a template into an E-Agent declaration that will accomplish their goals. This section first briefly describes how to acquire and validate instantiation parameters from the originator. We then examine in more detail the problem of ensuring that a template cannot be instantiated into an invalid declaration.

Each E-Agent template must be accompanied by a web form that enables originators to provide the parameters needed to instantiate the template into a declaration. To automate this process, our implementation provides a tool that generates such a web form from a simple RDF *parameter description*:

Definition 1. *(parameter description) A parameter description ϕ for a template τ is a set $\{R_1, ..., R_M\}$ where each R_i provides, for each parameter P_i in τ, a name, prompt, type, and any restrictions on the legal values of P_i. Types may be simple (Boolean, Integer, Double, String, Email address) or complex (i.e., a set of simple types). Possible restrictions are: (for simple types) enumeration, minimal or maximal value, and (for sets) non-empty, or a subset relationship to another set parameter.*

For instance, the following (partial) parameter description relates to asking participants about the number of guests that they will bring to the potluck:

```
[a          :TypeBoolean;
 :name      "AskForNumGuests";
 :enumeration (
  [:value :True;  :prompt "Yes, ask for the number of guests";]
  [:value :False; :prompt "No, don't ask about guests";] ) ]

[a          :TypeInteger;
 :name      "GuestThreshold";
 :prompt    "Notify me when # of guests reaches (ignored if 0):";
 :minInclusive "0"; ]
```

The form generator takes a parameter description and template as input and outputs a form for the originator to fill out and submit. If the submitted variables comply with all parameter restrictions, the template is instantiated with the corresponding values and the resulting declaration is forwarded to the server for execution. Otherwise, the tool redisplays the form with errors indicated and asks the originator to try again.

4.1   Instantiation Safety

Unfortunately, not every instantiated template is guaranteed to be executable. For instance, consider instantiating the template of Section 3 with the following parameters:

```
AskForNumGuests = False
GuestThreshold  = 50
```

In this case the notification given in Section 3 is invalid, since it refers to a question symbol NumGuests that does not exist because the parameter AskForNumGuests is false. Thus, the declaration is not executable and must be refused by the server. This particular problem could be addressed either in the template (by adding an additional guard on the notification) or in the parameter description (by adding a restriction on GuestThreshold). However, this leaves open the general problem of ensuring that *every* instantiation results in a *valid declaration*:

Definition 2. *(valid declaration) An instantiated template δ is a valid declaration if:*

1. **Basic checks:** δ *must validate without errors against the E-Agent ontology, and every expression $e \in \delta$ must evaluate to a valid numerical or set result.*
2. **Enabled symbols:** *For every expression $e \in \delta$ that is* enabled *(i.e., does not have an unsatisfied guard), every symbol in e is defined once by some enabled node.*
3. **Non-empty enumerations:** *For every enabled* enumeration *property $p \in \delta$, the object of p must evaluate to a non-empty set.*

Definition 3. *(instantiation safety) Let τ be a template and ϕ a parameter description for τ. τ is instantiation safe w.r.t. ϕ if, for all parameter sets ξ that satisfy the restrictions in ϕ, instantiating τ with ξ yields a valid declaration δ.*

Instantiation safety is of significant practical interest for two reasons. First, if errors are detected in the declaration, any error message is likely to be very confusing to the originator (who knows only of the web form, not the declaration). Thus, an automated tool is desirable to ensure that a deployed template is instantiation safe. Second, constructing instantiation-safe templates can be very onerous for authors, since it may require considering a large number of possibilities. Even when this is not too difficult, having an automated tool to ensure that a template remains instantiation safe after a modification would be very useful.

Some parts of verifying instantiation safety are easy to perform. For instance, checking that every *declaration* will validate against the E-Agent ontology can be performed by checking the *template* against the ontology, and other checks (e.g., for valid numerical results) are similar to static compiler analyses. However, other parts (e.g., ensuring that a symbol will always be enabled when it is used) are substantially more complex because of the need to consider all possible instantiations permitted by the parameter description ϕ. Consequently, in general verifying instantiation safety is difficult:

Theorem 1. *Given τ, an arbitrary E-Agent template, and ϕ, a parameter description for τ, then determining* instantiation safety *is co-NP-complete in the size of ϕ.*

This theorem is proved by a reduction from $\overline{SAT}$. Intuitively, given a specific counter-example it is easy to demonstrate that a template is *not* instantiation-safe, but proving that a template is safe potentially requires considering an exponential number of parameter combinations. In practice, ϕ may be small enough that the problem is feasible. Furthermore, in certain cases this problem is computationally tractable:

Theorem 2. *Let τ be an E-Agent template and ϕ a parameter description for τ. Determining instantiation safety is polynomial time in the size of τ and ϕ if:*
- *each* forAll *and* enumeration *statement in τ consists of at most some constant J set parameters combined with any set operator, and*
- *each* guard *consists of conjunctions and disjunctions of up to J terms (which are boolean parameters, or compare a non-set parameter with a constant/parameter).*

These restrictions are quite reasonable and still enable us to specify all of the E-Agents described in this paper (using $J \leq 4$). Note that they do not restrict the total number of parameters, but rather the number that may appear in any one of the identified statements. The restrictions ensure that only a polynomial number of cases need to be considered for each constraint/notification item, and the proof relies on a careful analysis to show that each such item can be checked independently while considering at most one question at a time.[3]

4.2 Discussion

In our implementation, we provide a tool that approximates instantiation safety testing via limited model checking. The tool operates by instantiating τ with all possible parameters in ϕ that are boolean or enumerated (these most often correspond to general configuration parameters). For each possibility, the tool chooses random values that satisfy ϕ for the remaining parameters. If any instantiation is found to be invalid, then τ is known to be not instantiation safe. Extending this approximate, non-guaranteed algorithm to perform the exact, polynomial-time (but more complex) testing of Theorem 2 is future work.

Clearly nothing in our analysis relied upon the fact that our agents are email-based. Instead, similar issues will arise whenever 1.) an author is creating a template that is designed to be used by other people (especially untrained people), and 2.) for flexibility, this template may contain a variety of configuration options. A large number of agents, such as the RCal meeting scheduler [26], Berners-Lee et al.'s appointment coordinator [2], and McIlraith et al.'s travel planner [22], have the need for such flexibility and could be profitably implemented with templates. This flexibility, however, can lead to unexpected or invalid agents, and thus produces the need to verify various safety properties such as "doing no harm" [32] or the instantiation safety discussed above. Our results highlight the need to carefully design the template language and appropriate restrictions so that such safety properties can be verified in polynomial time.

---

[3] See McDowell [18] for details on the proofs of this paper's theorems.

5 Automatic Explanation Generation

While executing, an E-Agent utilizes rejections or suggestions to influence the eventual outcome. However, the success of these interventions depends on the extent to which they are understood by the participants. For instance, the rejection "Sorry, the only dates left are May 7 and May 14" is much more likely to elicit cooperation from a participant in a seminar scheduling E-Agent than the simpler rejection "Sorry, try again." The E-Agent author can manually encode such explanations into the template, but this task can be difficult or even impossible when constraints interact or depend on considering possible future responses. Thus, below we consider techniques for simplifying the task of the E-Agent author by automatically generating explanations based on *what* responses are acceptable now and *why* the participant's original response was not acceptable.

We begin by defining more precisely a number of relevant terms. Given an E-Agent, the *supporting data set* is an RDF data store that holds responses from the participants to the questions posed by the E-Agent. The *current state* D is the state of this data set given all of the responses that have been received so far. We assume that the number of participants is known and that each will eventually respond.

A *constraint* is an arbitrary boolean expression over constants, parameters, and variables. Variables may be arbitrary expressions over constants, parameters, other variables, and queries that select or aggregate values for some question in the data set. Constraint satisfaction may be defined in two different ways. First,

Definition 4. *(MustConstraint) A* MustConstraint C *is a constraint that is satisfied in state* D *iff evaluating* C *over* D *yields* True.

If a response would lead to a state that does not satisfy a MustConstraint C, it is rejected. For example, for the potluck we would not accept a dessert response if that would lead to having 3 more desserts than entrees or appetizers. In many cases, however, such a conservative strategy will be overly restrictive. For instance, we may want to continue accepting desserts so long as it is still *possible* to achieve a balanced final outcome. Furthermore, a MustConstraint is usable only when the constraints are initially satisfied, even before any responses are received, and thus greatly limits the types of goals that can be expressed. Hence, we also define a second constraint type:

Definition 5. *(PossiblyConstraint) A* PossiblyConstraint C *is a constraint that is ultimately satisfiable in state* D *if there exists a sequence of responses from the remaining participants that leads to a state* D' *so that evaluating* C *over* D' *yields* True.

This approach permits more flexibility with the constraints and with the sequence of responses, though computing satisfaction for such constraints is more challenging.

For simplicity, we assume that the constraints C_D are either all MustConstraints or all PossiblyConstraints, though our results for PossiblyConstraints also hold when C_D contains both types. In addition, some results below mention *bounded* constraints (see Section 3.2), a restricted type that still supports a wide range of agents (including all those discussed in this paper). Recall that a sufficient condition for being bounded is for the constraints to access data only via "pre-defined" variables.

5.1   Acceptable Responses

Often the most practical information to provide to a participant whose response led to an intervention is the set of responses that would be "acceptable" (e.g., "An Appetizer or Dessert would be welcome" or "Sorry, I can only accept requests for 2 tickets or fewer now"). This section briefly considers how to calculate this *acceptable set*.

Definition 6. *(acceptable set) Let Λ be an E-Agent with current state D and constraints C_D on D. Then, the* acceptable set A *of Λ is the set of legal responses r such that D would still be satisfiable w.r.t. C_D after accepting r.*

For a `MustConstraint`, this satisfiability testing is easy to do and we can compute the acceptable set by testing a small set of representative responses. For a `PossiblyConstraint`, the situation is more complex:

Theorem 3. *Given an E-Agent Λ with N participants and current state D, if the constraints C_D are bounded, then the acceptable set A of Λ can be computed in time polynomial in N, $|A|$, and $|C_D|$. Otherwise, this problem is NP-hard in N.*

In this case we can again compute the acceptable set by testing satisfiability over a small set of values; this testing is polynomial if C_D is bounded [19]. In addition, if C_D is bounded then either $|A|$ is small or A can be concisely represented via ranges of acceptable values, in which case the total time is polynomial in only N and $|C_D|$.

5.2   Explaining Interventions

In some cases, the acceptable set alone may not be enough to construct a useful explanation. For instance, suppose an E-Agent invites 4 professors and 20 students to a meeting that at least 3 professors and a quorum of 10 persons (professors or students) must attend. When requesting a change from a professor, explaining *why* the change is needed (e.g., "We need you to reach the required 3 professors") is much more effective than simply informing them *what* response is desired (e.g., "Please change to Yes"). A clear explanation both motivates the request and rules out alternative reasons for the request (e.g., "We need your help reaching quorum") that may be less persuasive (e.g., because many students could also help reach quorum). This section discusses how to generate explanations for an intervention based on identifying the constraint(s) that led to the intervention. We do not discuss the additional problem of translating these constraints into a natural language suitable for sending to a participant, but note that even fairly simple explanations (e.g., "Too many Appetizers (10) vs. Desserts (3)") are much better than no explanation.

Conceptually, an E-Agent decides to reject a response based on constructing a *proof tree* that shows that some response r would prevent constraint satisfaction. However, this proof tree may be much too large and complex to serve as an explanation for a participant. This problem has been investigated before for expert systems [24,29], constraint programming [14], description logic reasoning [20], and more recently in the context of the Semantic Web [21]. These systems assumed proof trees of arbitrary complexity and handled a wide variety of possible deduction steps. To generate useful

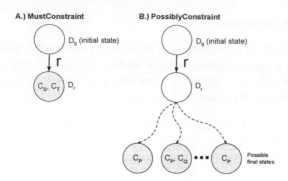

Fig. 2. Examples of proof trees for rejecting response r. Each node is a possible state of the data set, and node labels are constraints that are *not* satisfied in that state. In both cases, response r must be rejected because every leaf node (shaded above) does not satisfy some constraint.

explanations, key techniques included abstracting multiple steps into one using rewrite rules [20,21], describing how general principles were applied in specific situations [29], and customizing explanations based on previous utterances [4].

In our context, the proof trees have a much simpler structure that we can exploit. In particular, proofs are based only on constraint satisfiability (over one state or all possible future states), and each child node adds one additional response to the parent's state in a very regular way. Consequently, we will be able to summarize the proof tree with a very simple type of explanation. These proof trees are defined as follows:

Definition 7. *(proof tree) Given an E-Agent Λ, current state D, constraints C_D, and a response r, we say that P is a proof tree for rejecting r on D iff:*

- *P is a tree where the root is the initial state D.*
- *The root has exactly one child D_r, representing the state of D after adding r.*
- *If C_D is all* MustConstraints, *then D_r is the only non-root node.*
- *If C_D is all* PossiblyConstraints, *then for every node n that is D_r or one of its descendants, n has all children that can be formed by adding a single additional response to the state of n. Thus, the leaf nodes are only and all those possible final states (e.g., where every participant has responded) reachable from D_r.*
- *For every leaf node l, evaluating C_D over the state of l yields* False.

Figure 2A illustrates a proof tree for MustConstraints. Because accepting r leads to a state where some constraint (e.g., c_T) is not satisfied, r must be rejected. Likewise, Figure 2B shows a proof tree for PossiblyConstraints, where C_P and C_Q represent the professor and quorum constraints from the example described above. Since we are trying to prove that there is no way for the constraints to be ultimately satisfied (by any outcome), this tree must be fully expanded. For this tree, every leaf (final outcome) does not satisfy some constraint, so r must be rejected.

We now define a simpler explanation based upon the proof tree:

Definition 8. *(sufficient explanation) Given an E-Agent Λ, current state D, constraints C_D, and a response r such that a proof tree P exists for rejecting r on D, then we say that E is a sufficient explanation for rejecting r iff,*

- *E is a conjunction of constraints that appear in C_D, and*
- *for every leaf node n in P, evaluating E over the state of n yields* False.

Intuitively, a sufficient explanation E justifies rejecting r because E covers every leaf node in the proof tree, and thus precludes ever satisfying C_D. Note that while the proof tree for rejecting r is unique (modulo the ordering of child nodes), an explanation is not. For instance, an explanation based on Figure 2A could be C_S, C_T, or $C_S \wedge C_T$. Likewise, a valid explanation for Figure 2B is $C_P \wedge C_Q$ (e.g., no way satisfy both the professor and quorum constraints) but a more precise explanation is just C_P (e.g., no way to satisfy the professor constraint). The smaller explanation is often more compelling, as we argued for the meeting example, and thus to be preferred [6]. In general, we wish to find the explanation of minimum size (i.e., with the fewest conjuncts):

Theorem 4. *Given an* E-*Agent Λ with N participants, current state D, constraints C_D, and a response r, if C_D consists of* MustConstraints, *then finding a minimum sufficient explanation E for rejecting r is polynomial time in N and $|C_D|$. If C_D consists of* PossiblyConstraints, *then this problem is NP-hard in N and $|C_D|$.*

Thus, computing a minimum explanation is feasible for MustConstraints but likely to be intractable for PossiblyConstraints. For the latter, the difficulty arises from two sources. First, checking if any particular E is a sufficient explanation is NP-hard in N (based on a reduction from ultimate satisfiability [19]); this makes scaling E-Agents to large numbers of participants difficult. Second, finding a minimum such explanation is NP-hard in the number of constraints (by reduction from SET-COVER [12]). Note that this number can be significant because we treat each forAll quantification as a separate constraint; otherwise, the sample potluck described in Section 3 would always produce the same (complex) constraint for an explanation. Fortunately, in many common cases we can achieve a polynomial time solution:

Theorem 5. *Given an* E-*Agent Λ with N participants, current state D, constraints C_D, and a response r, if C_D is bounded and the size of a minimum explanation is no more than some constant J, then computing a minimum explanation E is polynomial time in N and $|C_D|$.*

This theorem holds because a candidate explanation E can be checked in polynomial time when the constraints are bounded, and restricting E to at most size J means that the total number of explanations that must be considered is polynomial in the number of constraints. Both of these restrictions are quite reasonable. As previously mentioned, bounded constraints arise naturally when using our template language and permit a wide range of functionality. Likewise, E-Agent explanations are most useful to the participants when they contain only a small number of constraints, and this is adequate for many E-Agents (as in the meeting example above). If no sufficient explanation of size J exists, the system could either choose the best explanation of size J (to maintain a simple explanation), approximate the minimum explanation with a greedy algorithm, or fall back on just providing the participant with the acceptable set described in the previous section.

Many different types of agents can describe their goals in terms of a set of constraints [17,23], and often need to explain their actions to users. Our results show that while generating such explanations can be intractable in general, the combination of simple explanations and modest restrictions on the constraint system can enable explanation generation in polynomial time.

6 Related Work

McDowell et al. [19] describe work related to the general notion of semantic email, including its relation to existing workflow and collaboration systems. Here we focus on research relevant to the agent specification problem.

Other projects have considered how to simplify the authoring of Semantic Web applications, e.g., with Haystack's Adenine programming language [27]. Adenine resembles our template language in that it can be compiled into RDF for portability and contains a number of high-level primitives, though Adenine incorporates many more imperative features and does not support the types of declarative reasoning that we describe. Languages such as DAML-S and OWL-S [5] enable the description of an application as a Semantic Web *service*. These languages, however, focus on providing details needed to *discover* and *invoke* a relevant service, and model every participant as another web service. Our work instead concisely specifies an E-Agent in enough detail so that it can be directly *executed* in contexts involving untrained end users.

More generally, E-Agent templates could be viewed as an instance of *program schemas* [7,10] that encapsulate a general class of behavior, e.g., for automated program synthesis [10] or software reuse [7,1]. Similarly, McIlraith et al. [22] propose the use of *generic procedures* that can be instantiated to produce different compositions of web services. Concepts similar to our definition of instantiation safety naturally arise in this setting; proposals for ensuring this safety have included manually-generated proofs [7], automatically-generated proofs [10], and language modification [1]. Our work focuses on the need for such schemas to be safely usable by ordinary people and demonstrates that the required safety properties can be verified in polynomial time.

Recent work on the *Inference Web* [21] has focused on the need to explain a Semantic Web system's *conclusions* in terms of base data and reasoning procedures. In contrast, we deal with explaining the agent's *actions* in terms of existing responses and the expected impact on the E-Agent's constraints. In this sense our work is similar to prior research that sought to explain decision-theoretic advice (cf., Horvitz et al. [11]). For instance, Klein and Shortliffe [16] describe the VIRTUS system that can present users with an explanation for why one action is provided over another. Note that this work focuses on explaining the relative impact of multiple factors on the choice of some action, whereas we seek the simplest possible reason why some action could *not* be chosen (i.e., accepted). Other relevant work includes Druzdzel [8], which addresses the problem of translating uncertain reasoning into qualitative verbal explanations.

For constraint satisfaction problems (CSPs), a *nogood* [28] is a reason that no *current* variable assignment can satisfy all constraints. In contrast, our explanation for a PossiblyConstraint is a reason that no *future* assignment can satisfy the constraints, given the set of possible future responses. Potentially, our problem could be reduced to nogood calculation, though a direct conversion would produce a problem that might take time that is exponential in N, the number of participants. However, for bounded constraints, we could create a CSP with variables based on the *aggregates* of the responses, rather than their specific values [19]. Using this simpler CSP, we could then exploit existing, efficient nogood-based solvers (e.g., [15,13]) to find candidate explanations in time polynomial in N. Note though that most applications of nogoods have focused on their use for developing improved constraint solving algorithms [28,15] or for debugging constraint programs [25], rather than on creating explanations for average users. One exception is Jussien and Ouis [14], who describe how to generate user-friendly nogood explanations, though they require that a designer explicitly model a user's perception of the problem as nodes in some constraint hierarchy.

7   Conclusions and Implications for Agents

This paper has examined how to specify agent behavior. We adopted a template-based approach that shifts most of the complexity of agent specification from untrained originators onto a much smaller set of trained authors. We then examined the three key challenges of generality, safety, and understandability that arise in this approach. For E-Agents, we discussed how high-level features of our template language enable the concise specification of complex agent behavior. We also demonstrated that it is possible to verify the instantiation-safety of a template in polynomial time, and showed how to generate explanations for the agent's actions in polynomial time. Together, these techniques both simplify the task of the E-Agent author and improve the overall execution quality for the originator and the participants of an E-Agent. In addition, our polynomial time results ensure that these features can scale to E-Agents with large numbers of participants, choices, and constraints.

While we focused on the context of semantic email, our results are relevant to many other agent systems. For instance, almost any agent needs some ability to explain its behavior, and many such agents react to the world based on constraints. We showed that generating explanations can be NP-hard in general, but that the combination of simple explanations and modest constraint restrictions may enable explanation generation in polynomial time. Likewise, an agent template should support a wide range of functionality, yet ensure the *safety* of each possible use. There are several different types of safety to consider, including that of doing no harm [32], minimizing unnecessary side-effects [32], and accurately reflecting the originator's preferences [3]. We motivated the need for instantiation safety, a type that has been previously examined to some extent [10,1], but is particularly challenging when the instantiators are non-technical users. Our results also highlight the need to carefully design template languages that balance flexibility with the ability to efficiently verify such safety properties.

Thus, many agents could benefit from a high-level, declarative template language with automatic safety testing and explanation generation. Collectively, these features would simplify the creation of an agent, broaden its applicability, enhance its interaction with the originator and other participants, and increase the likelihood of satisfying the originator's goals. Future work will consider additional ways to make agent authoring and instantiation easier with the goal of bringing the Semantic Web vision closer to practical implementation.

Acknowledgements. This research was supported in part by NSF grant DARPA contract NBCHD030010, IIS-0312988, and ONR grant N00014-02-1-0324 for Oren Etzioni; NSF CAREER grant IIS-9985114 and ITR grant IIS-0205635 for Alon Halevy; and by NSF Graduate Research and Microsoft Endowed Fellowships for Luke McDowell. Jeff Lin assisted with the implementation. Thanks to Gerome Miklau, Natasha Noy, Stani Vlasseva, and the anonymous reviewers for their helpful comments on improving this work.

References

1. E. E. Allen. *A First-Class Approach to Genericity.* PhD thesis, Rice University, Houston, TX, 2003.
2. T. Berners-Lee, J. Hendler, and O. Lassila. The Semantic Web. *Scientific American*, May 2001.
3. C. Boutilier. A POMDP formulation of preference elicitation problems. In *AAAI-02*, pages 239–246, 2002.
4. G. Carenini and J. D. Moore. Generating explanations in context. In *Intelligent User Interfaces*, pages 175–182, 1993.
5. DAML Services Coalition. DAML-S and OWL-S. http://www.daml.org/services.
6. M. G. de la Banda, P. J. Stuckey, and J. Wazny. Finding all minimal unsatisfiable subsets. In *Proceedings of the 5th ACM SIGPLAN international conference on Principles and practice of declarative programming*, pages 32–43. ACM Press, 2003.
7. N. Dershowitz. Program abstraction and instantiation. *ACM Trans. Programming. Language Systems*, 7(3):446–477, 1985.
8. M. Druzdzel. Qualitative verbal explanations in bayesian belief networks. *Artificial Intelligence and Simulation of Behaviour Quarterly*, 94:43–54, 1996.
9. O. Etzioni, A. Halevy, H. Levy, and L. McDowell. Semantic email: Adding lightweight data manipulation capabilities to the email habitat. In *WebDB*, 2003.
10. P. Flener, K.-K. Lau, M. Ornaghi, and J. Richardson. An abstract formalisation of correct schemas for program synthesis. *Journal of Symbolic Computation*, 30(1):93–127, July 2000.
11. E. J. Horvitz, J. S. Breese, and M. Henrion. Decision theory in expert systems and artificial intelligence. *International Journal of Approximate Reasoning*, 2:247–302, 1988.
12. D. S. Johnson. Approximation algorithms for combinatorial problems. *Journal of Computer and System Sciences*, 9:256–278, 1974.
13. U. Junker. QUICKXPLAIN: Conflict detection for arbitrary constraint propagation algorithms. In *IJCAI'01 Workshop on Modelling and Solving problems with constraints*, 2001.
14. N. Jussien and S. Ouis. User-friendly explanations for constraint programming. In *ICLP 11th Workshop on Logic Programming Environments*, Paphos, Cyprus, Dec. 2001.
15. G. Katsirelos and F. Bacchus. Unrestricted nogood recording in csp search. In *Principles and Practice of Constraint Programming*, October 2003.
16. D. A. Klein and E. H. Shortliffe. A framework for explaining decision-theoretic advice. *Artificial Intelligence*, 67(2):201–243, 1994.
17. A. K. Mackworth. Constraint-based agents: The ABC's of CBA's. In *Constraint Programming*, pages 1–10, 2000.
18. L. McDowell. *Meaning for the Masses: Theory and Applications for Semantic Web and Semantic Email Systems.* PhD thesis, University of Washington, Seattle, WA, 2004.
19. L. McDowell, O. Etzioni, A. Halevey, and H. Levy. Semantic email. In *Proc. of the Thirteenth Int. WWW Conference*, 2004.

20. D. L. McGuinness and A. Borgida. Explaining subsumption in description logics. In *IJCAI (1)*, pages 816–821, 1995.
21. D. L. McGuinness and P. Pinheiro da Silva. Infrastructure for web explanations. In *Second International Semantic Web Conference*, October 2003.
22. S. McIlraith, T. Son, and H. Zeng. Semantic web services. *IEEE Intelligent Systems. Special Issue on the Semantic Web*, 16(2):46–53, March/April 2001.
23. A. Nareyek. *Constraint-Based Agents*, volume 2062 of *Lecture Notes in Computer Science*. Springer, 2001.
24. R. Neches, W. R. Swartout, and J. D. Moore. Explainable (and maintainable) expert systems. In *IJCAI*, pages 382–389, 1985.
25. S. Ouis, N. Jussien, and P. Boizumault. *k*-relevant explanations for constraint programming. In *FLAIRS'03*, St. Augustine, Florida, USA, May 2003. AAAI press.
26. T. Payne, R. Singh, and K. Sycara. Calendar agents on the semantic web. *IEEE Intelligent Systems*, 17(3):84–86, 2002.
27. D. Quan, D. Huynh, and D. R. Karger. Haystack: A platform for authoring end user semantic web applications. In *Second International Semantic Web Conference*, October 2003.
28. T. Schiex and G. Verfaillie. Nogood Recording fot Static and Dynamic Constraint Satisfaction Problems. *International Journal of Artificial Intelligence Tools*, 3(2):187–207, 1994.
29. W. Swartout, C. Paris, and J. Moore. Design for explainable expert systems. *IEEE Expert*, 6(3):58–647, 1991.
30. L. G. Terveen and L. T. Murray. Helping users program their personal agents. In *CHI*, pages 355–361, 1996.
31. R. Tuchinda and C. A. Knoblock. Agent wizard: building information agents by answering questions. In *Intelligent User Interfaces*, pages 340–342, 2004.
32. D. Weld and O. Etzioni. The first law of robotics (a call to arms). In *Proc. of AAAI*, 1994.

Visual Modeling of OWL DL Ontologies Using UML

Sara Brockmans, Raphael Volz, Andreas Eberhart, and Peter Löffler

Institute AIFB, University of Karlsruhe, D-76128 Karlsruhe
{brockmans, volz, eberhart, loeffler}@aifb.uni-karlsruhe.de
http://www.aifb.uni-karlsruhe.de/WBS/

Abstract. This paper introduces a visual, UML-based notation for
OWL ontologies. We provide a standard MOF2 compliant metamodel
which captures the language primitives offered by OWL DL. Similarly,
we invent a UML profile, which allows to visually model OWL ontologies
in a notation that is close to the UML notation. This allows to develop
ontologies using UML tools. Throughout the paper, the significant differences to some earlier proposals for a visual, UML-based notation for
ontologies are discussed.

1 Introduction

An ontology defines a common set of concepts and terms that are used to describe
and represent a domain of knowledge. Recently, several standardization committees have taken up research results form the AI community and defined standard
ontology languages. For example, the Word Wide Web Consortium (W3C) has
recently finished its work on the Web Ontology Language (OWL) [5].

The utility of a visual syntax for modelling languages has been shown in
practice and visual modelling paradigms such as the Entity Relationship (ER)
model or the Unified Modelling Language (UML) are used frequently for the
purpose of conceptual modeling. Consequently the necessity of a visual syntax
for knowledge representation (KR) languages has been argued frequently in the
past [7,14]. Particular KR formalisms such as conceptual graphs [19] or Topic
Maps [1] are based on well-defined graphical notations.

Description logic based ontology languages such as OWL, however, are usually defined in terms of an abstract (text-based) syntax and most care is spent
on the formal semantics. The absence of a visual syntax[1] has lead to several
proposals. [7] proposed a particular visual notation for the CLASSIC description
logic. Newer developments have abandoned the idea of a proprietary syntax and
proposed to rely on UML class diagrams. [4] suggested to directly use UML
as an ontology language, whereas [2] proposed to predefine several stereotypes
such that a more detailed mapping from UML to the primitives offered by the
DAML+OIL description logic can be achieved. [2] further argue that the UML

---

[1] Which can be seen as a direct result of the criticisms about the semantics of early
diagrammatic semantic networks [21,3].

S.A. McIlraith et al. (Eds.): ISWC 2004, LNCS 3298, pp. 198–213, 2004.
© Springer-Verlag Berlin Heidelberg 2004

metamodel should be extended with elements such as property and restriction such that UML is more compatible with KR languages such as OWL.

A metamodel for the purpose of defining ontologies, called Ontology Definition Metamodel (ODM), has recently been requested by the OMG [18], with specific focus on the OWL DL language. In answer to this request four proposals were submitted. [12] defines stereotypes for representing the new aspects introduced by ontologies in UML. In our opinion, the proposal has several weaknesses. For example, OWL properties are visually modelled as UML classes instead of mapping them to UML associations. Similarly, the different kind of class constructors found in OWL are reflected by associations, while we believe that an appropriate specialization of UML classes is more appropriate. Obviously there are no strict metrics for intuitiveness and clarity. Consequently, in this paper we argue by showing head to head comparisons of the different representations. Ultimately, the choice is up to the reader.

[8] follows the RDF serialization of OWL documents and represents the ontology in a graph-like notation that is close to the actual RDF serialization. Also various kinds of OWL properties are modeled as a hierarchy of UML classes. Complex OWL class definitions, i.e. using union and other operators, are modeled as comments associated to a class.

[13] departs from the OMG request and introduces a metamodel for the Open Knowledge Base Connectivity (OKBC) standard. [6] suggests the OWL Full language, but neither provides a visual syntax nor introduces a metamodel.

At the moment [12,6,8,13] are merged into one proposal. While this is work in progress, a first presentation [10] suggests that the proposal will be based on OWL Full and is being extended to capture further KR languages such as Simple Common Logic (SCL). Obviously the scope of this merged proposal is quite extensive.

The benefit from this design decision is that different ontology formats such as KIF, Description Logics, or Topic Maps can be mapped into one very general and expressive metamodel. Also, a single mapping to the visual UML profile in which actual ontologies are defined suffices.

However, these advantages do not come for free. By encompassing many paradigms, the resulting ODM and the mappings become quite complex. We believe that, for the sake of readability and usability, several separate metamodels should be introduced for each KR, e.g. OWL DL. In order to map between the individual KRs the requested metamodel mapping facilities [17] can be used. While this results in a higher number of mappings, the individual mappings will be a lot more lightweight and easier to specify.

Therefore this paper defines an ODM for OWL DL. Our goals are to achieve an intuitive notation, both for users of UML and OWL DL. Naturally, the proposed metamodel has a one-to-one mapping to the abstract syntax of OWL DL and thereby to the formal semantics of OWL.

The remainder of this paper is organized as follows: Section 2 introduces the Meta Object Facility (MOF). Section 3 introduces our Ontology Definition Metamodel for OWL DL. Section 4 introduces a UML Profile for ontology modeling and explains the major design choices taken in order to make the notation readable for both users with UML and users with OWL background. We conclude by summarizing our work and listing points for future work.

2   UML-MOF

This section introduces the essential ideas of the Meta Object Facility (MOF) of UML 2.0 and shows how an Ontology Definition Metamodel (ODM) fits into the overall picture. The need for a dedicated ontology modeling language stems from the observation that an ontology cannot be sufficiently represented in UML [11]. Both representations share a set of core functionalities such as the ability to define classes, class relationships, and relationship cardinalities. Despite this overlap, there are many features which can only be expressed in an ontology language. Examples for this disjointness are transitive and symmetric properties in OWL or methods in UML.

UML methodology, tools and technology, however, seem to be a feasible approach for supporting the development and maintenance of ontologies. Consequently, the OMG issued a request for proposals for an Ontology Definition Metamodel (ODM) [9]. The following key requirements were given:

1. As shown in Figure 1, an ODM has to be grounded in the Meta Object Facility (MOF2), which is explained in the following section. This requirement is common for any other metamodel, e.g. UML.
2. A UML profile defining a visual notation for ontologies must be provided. Furthermore, partial mappings in both directions between the metamodel and this profile need to be established.
3. From the ODM, one must be able to generate an ontology representation in a language such as OWL DL. Figure 1 shows this process. In particular a mapping to OWL DL was requested.
4. An XMI serialization and exchange syntax for ODM must be provided. This XMI format allows exchanging an ODM metamodel between tools.

We target the first two requirements in this paper, since the remaining two requirements directly follow from a good ODM.

2.1   Meta Object Facility

The Meta Object Facility (MOF) is an extensible model driven integration framework for defining, manipulating and integrating metadata and data in a platform independent manner. The aim is to provide a framework that supports any kind of metadata, and that allows new kinds to be added as required. MOF plays a crucial role in OMG's four-layer metadata architecture shown in Figure 2. The bottom layer of this architecture encompasses the raw information to be described. For example, Figure 2 contains information about a person called Pete and a car with the license plate ABC-1234. The model layer contains the

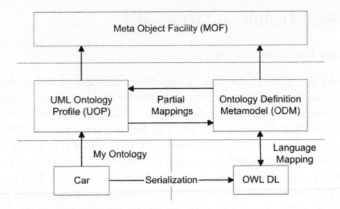

Fig. 1. A partial ontology to UML mapping allows existing tools to operate on compatible aspects of ontologies.

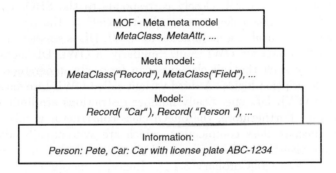

Fig. 2. OMG Four Layer Metadata Architecture.

definition of the required structures. Our domain might use records for grouping information. Consequently, the records car and person are defined. If these are combined, they describe the model for the given domain. The metamodel defines the terms in which the model is expressed. In our example, we would state that models are expressed with records and fields by instantiating the respective meta classes. Finally, the MOF lies at the top. This layer is called the meta meta model layer. Note that MOF is hard wired, while the other layers are flexible and allow to express various metamodels such as the UML metamodel.

We provide the ODM for OWL DL in the following section using the core modeling features provided by MOF. We primarily use classes, attributes and associations, the notation of which is well-known from UML. Additionally, our metamodel is augmented with OCL constraints which specify invariants that have to be fulfilled by all models that instantiate the ODM. Such models are visually encoded using the UML profile introduced in Section 4.

3   Ontology Definition Metamodel

3.1   Design Considerations

A metamodel for a language that allows the definition of ontologies naturally follows from the modelling primitives offered by the ontology language. OWL ontologies themselves are RDF documents. They instantiate the RDF data model, and use URIs to name entities. The formal semantics of OWL is derived from Description Logics (DL), an extensively researched KR formalism. Hence, most primitives offered by OWL can also be found in a Description Logic. Three species of OWL have been defined. One variant called OWL Full can represent arbitrary RDF components inside of OWL documents. This allows, for example, to combine the OWL language with arbitrary other representation languages. From a conceptual perspective a metamodel for OWL Full necessarily has to include elements for the representation of RDF.

Another variant called OWL DL states syntactic conditions on OWL documents, which ensure that only the primitives defined within the OWL language itself can be used. OWL DL closely corresponds to the SHOIN(D) description logic and all language features can be reduced[2] to the primitives of the SHOIN(D) logic. Naturally, a metamodel for OWL DL is smaller and less complex than a metamodel for OWL Full. Similarly, a OWL DL metamodel can be built in a way such that all elements can be easily understood by people familiar with description logics. A third variant called OWL Lite disallows some constructors of OWL DL, specifically number restrictions are limited to cardinalities 0 and 1. Furthermore, the oneOf class constructor is missing. Other constructors such as class complement, which are syntactically disallowed in OWL Lite, can nevertheless be represented via the combination of syntactically allowed constructors [20][Corollary 3.4.1]. Hence, a metamodel for OWL DL necessarily includes OWL Lite.

3.2   An ODM for OWL DL

The rest of this section will provide a summary of the OWL language whilst introducing our metamodel. Interested readers may refer to the specifications [16] for a full account of OWL. The metamodel is augmented with several OCL constraints. Some important constraints are given here in footnotes.

3.2.1   Ontologies. URIs are used to identify all objects in OWL. In order to provide an efficient notation, we replicate the namespace concept of XML and introduce a separate Namespace metaclass which manages the abbreviation (name) that is assigned to a certain URI (cf. Figure 3). Every element of an ontology is a NamedElement and hence a member of a Namespace. All elements of an Ontology are specializations of OntologyElement[3] which is itself derived

---

[2] Some language primitives are shortcuts for combinations of primitives in the logic.
[3] member->forAll(ocllsKindOf(OntologyElement))

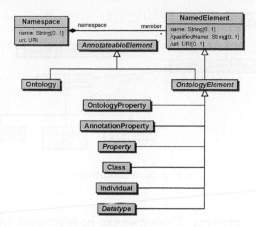

Fig. 3. Ontologies and Namespaces

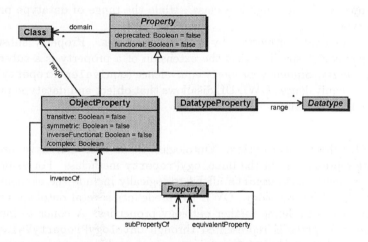

Fig. 4. Properties and property axioms

from `NamedElement`. Anonymous elements of the ontology belong to a dedicated anonymous namespace[4]. The qualifiedName attribute is the global name of an element and can be derived[5] from the local `name` attribute and the `Namespace` name.

3.2.2   Properties. Properties represent named binary associations in the modeled knowledge domain. OWL distinguishes two kinds of properties, so called object properties and datatype properties. Both are generalized by the

---

[4] `allInstances()->size(name->isEmpty())) <=1`
[5] `name->notEmpty() and namespace.name->notEmpty() implies qualifiedName = namespace.name.concat(":").concat(name).`

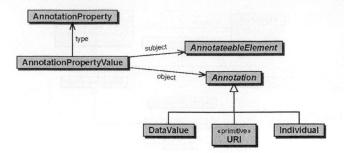

Fig. 5. Annotations

abstract metaclass `Property`. Properties can be functional, i.e. their range may contain at most one element. Their domain is always a class. Object properties may additionally be inverse functional, transitive, symmetric or inverse to another property. Their range is a class[6], while the range of datatype properties is a datatype.

Users can relate properties by using two axioms. Property subsumption (`subPropertyOf`)[7] specifies that the extension of a property is a subset of the related property. Similarly, property equivalence (`equivalentProperty`) defines extensional equivalence. OWL DL disallows that object and datatype properties are related via axioms.

3.2.3 Ontology properties. Ontologies themselves can have properties, which are represented via the `OntologyProperty` metaclass. For example, the ontology property `owl:imports` allows to logically include the elements of one ontology in another ontology. OWL DL predefines several ontology properties and allows users to define further ontology properties. A concrete instance of an ontology property is represented through `OntologyPropertyValue`, which instantiates a certain type of `OntologyProperty` and is a reference between two ontologies.

3.2.4 Annotation properties. Given elements of an OWL ontology can be annotated with metadata. Several annotation properties, e.g. `owl:versionInfo`, are predefined and users can define further annotation properties. We treat annotation properties similarly to ontology properties. However, the subject of an `AnnotationPropertyValue` is an `AnnotateableElement`

---

[6] OWL DL mandates that no complex role may be transitive:
```
complex=functional or inverseFunctional or NumberRestriction.
allInstances()->exists(onProperty=self) or inverseOf->exists(complex)
or subPropertyOf->exists(complex) and complex implies not transitive.
```
[7] This association is transitive:
```
Property.allInstances()-> forAll(r,s,t|(r.subPropertyOf->includes(s)
and s.subPropertyOf->includes(t) implies r.subPropertyOf->includes(t))).
```

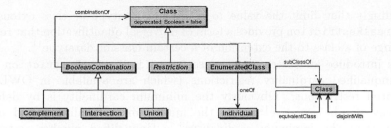

Fig. 6. Class constructors and axioms

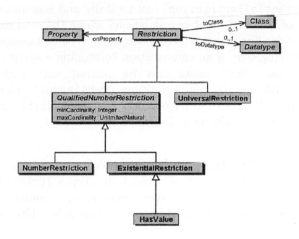

Fig. 7. OWL Restrictions

and the object is a Annotation, which can be either a `DataValue`, a `URI` or an `Individual` (cf. Figure 5).

3.2.5 Class Constructors.

In comparison to UML, OWL DL does not only allow to define simple named classes. Instead, classes can be formed with several class constructors (cf. Figure 6). One can conceptually distinguish the boolean combination of classes, restrictions and enumerated classes. `EnumeratedClass` is only available in OWL DL and is defined through a direct enumeration of named[8] individuals. Boolean combinations of classes are provided through `Complement`[9], `Intersection` and `Union`.

Restrictions are class constructors that restrict the range of a property for the context of the class (cf. Figure 7). Restrictions can be stated *on* datatype and object properties, as indicated by `toClass` and `toDatatype`.

---

[8] `oneOf->forAll(name.notEmpty())`
[9] `combinationOf->size()=1`

Accordingly they limit the value *to* a certain datatype or class extension[10]. UniversalRestriction provides a form of universal quantification that restricts the range of a class to the extension of a certain class or datatype[11].

We introduce an abstract metaclass QualifiedNumberRestriction to relate unqualified cardinality restrictions (which are available in OWL) and existential restrictions. Obviously the minimum cardinality is by default 0 and may not be negative[12] while the maximum cardinality should not be smaller than the minimum cardinality[13]. Unqualified number restrictions (NumberRestriction) are available in OWL and define how many elements the range of the given property has to have while not restricting the type of the range[14]. (ExistentialRestriction) can logically and semantically be seen as a special type of qualified number restrictions where the cardinality is fixed[15]. OWL also provides HasValue, which is a special type of existential restriction where the qualifying class is an enumeration containing a single individual[16].

Figure 6 shows that classes can be related with each other using class axioms, such as class subsumption (subClassOf), class equivalence (equivalentClass)[17] and class disjointness (disjointWith). These relations between classes are naturally modelled as associations.

3.2.6 Datatypes. The datatype system of OWL is provided by XML Schema, which provides a predefined set of named datatypes (PrimitiveType), e.g. strings xsd:string. Additionally, users may specify enumerated datatypes (EnumeratedDatatype) which consist of several data value of items (DataValue).

3.2.7 Knowledge Base. OWL does not follow the clear conceptual separation between terminology (T-Box) and knowledge base (A-box) that is present in most description logics and in MOF, which distinguishes between model and information. The knowledge base elements (cf. Figure 8) are

---

[10] 1. toClass->size()=1 xor toDatatype->size()=1

2. onProperty.ocllsKindOf(DatatypeProperty) implies toDatatype->size()=1

[11] The reader may note that this is logically not understood as a constraint but as an entailment rule.

[12] minCardinality>=0

[13] Even though OWL allows this by making the class definition become inconsistent. We disallow this situation through the constraint:
maxCardinality>=minCardinality.

[14] toClass=owl::Thing or toDatatype=rdfs::Literal

[15] minCardinality=1 and maxCardinality=*

[16] toClass.oclssTypeOf(EnumeratedClass) and
toClass.oclAsType(EnumeratedClass).oneOf->size()=1)
or (toDatatype.ocllsTypeOf(EnumeratedDatatype) and
toDatatype.oclsAsType(EnumeratedDatatype).oneOf->size()=1)

[17] Every equivalent class is trivially a superclass:
subClassOf->includesAll(equivalentClass).

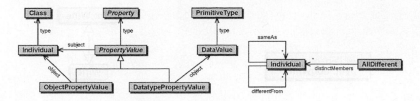

Fig. 8. Knowledge Base Items and Axioms

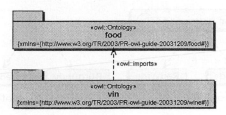

Fig. 9. owl:imports

part of an ontology. An `Individual` is an instantiation of a `Class` and is the subject of a `PropertyValue`, which instantiates a `Property`. Naturally, an `ObjectPropertyValue` relates its subject with another `Individual` whilst a `DatatypePropertyValue` relates its subject with a `DataValue`, which is an instance of a primitive datatype.

Individuals can be related via three axioms. The `sameAs` association allows users to state that two individuals (with different names) are equivalent. The `differentFrom` association specifies that two individuals are not the same[18]. `AllDifferent` is a simpler notation for the pairwise difference of several individuals.

4 A UML-Profile for Ontologies

This section describes a UML profile which supports reusing UML notation for ontology definition. Since the UML profile mechanism supports a restricted form of metamodeling, our proposal contains a set of extensions and constraints to the UML metamodel. This tailors UML such that models instantiating the ODM can be defined. We heavily rely on the custom stereotypes, which usually carry the name of the corresponding OWL language element.

4.1 Ontologies

Figure 9 shows that a `Namespace` is represented by packages, while a stereotype indicates an `Ontology`. Ontology properties correspond to appropriately stereotyped UML dependencies. The deprecation of a given element, e.g. the *deprecated class* JugWine in Figure 10, is achieved using a stereotype.

---

[18] The reader may note that OWL does not take the unique names assumption.

Fig. 10. owl:DeprecatedClass   **Fig. 11.** owl:EquivalentClass

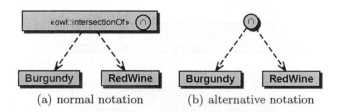

(a) normal notation   (b) alternative notation

Fig. 12. owl:intersectionOf

4.2 Classes

Atomic classes are depicted in the most trivial way, namely as UML classes. The reader may note, that we only use the first segment of the UML class notation, which contains the name of the class, stereotypes, and keyword-value pairs. The second segment specifies concrete properties, while the third segment is missing, since OWL does not contain methods. *Class inclusion* is depicted using the UML generalization symbol, which is the most natural way.

Class equivalence could be expressed by two class inclusions. As a simpler notation for two generalization arrows in the opposite direction next to each other, the bi-directional generalization arrow is introduced. An example of this notation is shown in Figure 11. Dependencies could also be used but are not intuitive. [12,10] propose to use stereotyped UML associations to state class axioms, which does not translate well to the UML object level. For this reason, *Class disjointness* is depicted as a bi-directional, stereotyped dependency.

For the representations of OWL class constructors, we use individual stereotypes and the UML class notation. Dependencies to the classes which form the complement, part of the union or part of the intersection of a class are depicted as UML dependencies. We suggest specific pictograms to be used instead of dependencies as allowed in UML. Figure 12 depicts alternative graphical notations for an intersection of classes. An `EnumeratedClass` is connected to the enumerated individuals by dependencies (cf. Figure 13). Alternatively, we allow a more compact string-based notation. The reader may note that UML associations can only be used between classes, an `EnumeratedClass` can therefore not be consistently represented with associations, if the UML notation for objects is used for individuals.

In general, a *restriction* is depicted by a class with a corresponding stereotype. If the property which participates in the restriction is an object property,

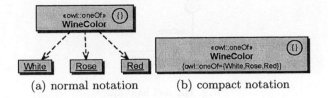

(a) normal notation   (b) compact notation

Fig. 13. owl:oneOf

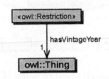

Fig. 14. owl:cardinality

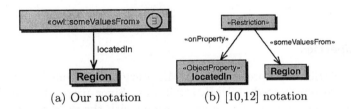

(a) Our notation   (b) [10,12] notation

Fig. 15. owl:someValuesFrom

we depict it as an association to the participating class. Otherwise, in case of a datatype property, it is depicted as an attribute. Figure 14 shows that cardinalities involved in restrictions are depicted in the standard UML notation, viz. next to the attribute's association. We mentioned that OWL has only unqualified cardinality restrictions. Thus, the class participating in a cardinality restriction is always owl:Thing and attribute types are rdfs::Literal, which means that they can have every data value.

ExistentialQuantification can and ValueRestriction has to be indicated by a DEDICATED stereotype. Figure 15 demonstrates the notation for an existentially quantified restriction. The reader can compare our notation with the notation proposed by [12,10] (cf. Figure 15). Clearly, our presentation is more compact and elegantly uses the available features of UML.

When modeling HasValue, no separate notation is introduced. If properties are represented as associations, the endpoints have to be classes. Under these circumstances, combining existence restriction and enumeration is the most compact notation conforming to the UML-metamodel. One could think to model it more directly from the class which has the restriction, but an association cannot be built between a class and an individual. Although our solution looks

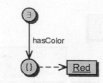

Fig. 16. owl:hasValue

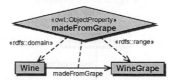

Fig. 17. An ObjectProperty with domain and range

quite complex, it keeps the consistency with restrictions. Figure 16 shows our notation.

4.3 Properties

Object properties are represented as UML n-ary associations[19], while datatype properties are represented as UML attributes. Since properties can have multiple domains and ranges, several associations with the same name are needed, therefore our proposal uses an association class which is connected to the association itself. If the domain is itself a restriction, we end up with two associations and it would be unclear which one counts for the restriction and which one for the domain of the property. In this case, we provide a extended graphical representation (cf. Figure 17).

Analogous to classes, specific properties are assigned a respective stereotype. Figure 18 demonstrates the *functionality* and *inverse functionality* stereotype. Naturally, *Deprecation*, *transitivity* and *symmetry* are represented in the same way. Figure 18 also shows how a property is connected to its inverse using a bi-directional UML dependency.

Similar to classes, *Property inclusion* is depicted with a generalization arrow, and *property equality* with a bi-directional generalization arrow.

4.4 Data Types

Data types are represented in the form of a stereotyped UML class. An EnumeratedDatatype is depicted similar to the enumeration of individuals, viz. a stereotyped UML class is connected to the enumerated data values through dependencies and we provide a text-based shorthand notation (cf. Figure 19).

---

[19] This notation of associations is in fact provided by UML although rarely seen in practice.

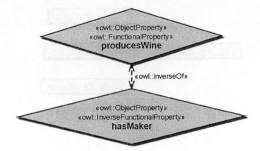

Fig. 18. Property characteristics

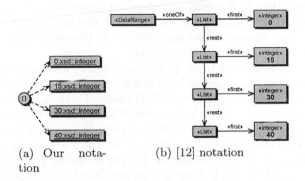

(a) Our nota- (b) [12] notation
tion

Fig. 19. Enumerated Datatypes

Figure 19 also shows the proposed notation by [12], which uses associations and additional stereotyped classes. Sticking to the RDF-notation makes the representation unnecessarily complex since there is no order in data enumerations.

4.5 Individuals

Individuals are depicted in the object notation of UML, viz. in the form 'Object : Class'. [12] proposes to use a Class Thing for individuals, but this does not clearly show the difference between the object and model level, which is pursued in UML. We represent axioms specifying the equivalence or difference of individuals through stereotyped associations between individuals. We conclude with Figure 20, which shows our notation for `AllDifferent`. Here, associations lead from an anonymous instance of owl::AllDifferent to those individuals which are defined to be different.

5 Conclusion

We have presented an Ontology Definition Metamodel for the DL variant of OWL. Unlike previous proposals, our metamodel directly corresponds to the

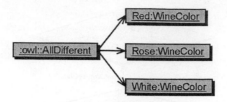

Fig. 20. owl:AllDifferent

language primitives available in OWL DL. The validity of instances of this meta-model is ensured through various OCL constraints, some of which were given here (cf. [15] for a full account). We additionally provided a UML profile, of which we believe that it is cognitively more adequate for folks familiar with UML *and* OWL. Our profile utilizes the maximal intersection of UML features and OWL features. Hence, classes are depicted as classes, properties as n-ary associations and individuals as UML objects.

We believe that leveraging UML for the development and maintenance of ontologies is a very promising approach. It is a first step to bring the W3C vision of a Semantic Web technology and the OMG vision of a Model Driven Architecture together. We can now use a large array of industrial strength tools that is available for UML and other related OMG standards for the purpose of ontology development. Besides graphical editors, other kinds of utilities offer further benefit. For example, we can utilize the Eclipse Modeling Framework (EMF) to derive a Java API for OWL directly from the ODM. Ontologies can benefit from UML based system development, but in turn ontologies can also contribute to system development. One of the prime application areas is the management of policies and the enforcement of regulatory compliance in logistics, the financial sector, or other industries. These very advantages and application areas prompted OMG's call for proposals for an ontology definition model.

Acknowledgments. Research for this paper has been partially funded by the EU in the IST projects KnowledgeWeb (IST-2004- 507482) and Sekt (IST-2003-506826), as well as by the Graduate School IME - University Karlsruhe. We would like to thank our colleagues for discussion as well as the reviewers for the ISWC conference for valuable comments on our paper.

References

1. Topic Maps: Information Technology – Document Description and Markup Languages. ISO/IEC standard 13250:2000, December 1999.
2. K. Baclawski, M. Kokar, P. Kogut, L. Hart, J. Smith, W. Holmes, J. Letkowski, and M. Aronson. Extending UML to Support Ontology Engineering for the Semantic Web. In *4th Int. Conf. on UML (UML 2001)*, Toronto, Canada, October 2001.
3. R.J. Brachman. On the Epistemological Status of Semantic Nets. In N.V. Findler, editor, *Associative Networks: Representation and Use of Knowledge by Computers*, pages 3–50, 1979.

4. S. Cranefield and M. Purvis. UML as an Ontology Modelling Language. In *Proceedings of the Workshop on Intelligent Information Integration*, volume 23 of *CEUR Workshop Proceedings*, Stockholm, Sweden, July 1999.
5. M. Dean and G. Schreiber. Web Ontology Language (OWL) Reference Version 1.0. Technical report, World Wide Web Consortium (W3C), 2003.
6. DSTC. Ontology Definition MetaModel Initial Submission. http://www.omg.org/docs/ad/03-08-01.pdf, August 2003.
7. B. R. Gaines. An Interactive Visual Language for Term Subsumption Languages. In J. Mylopoulos and R. Reiter, editors, *Proc. of 12th Int. Joint Conf. on Art. Int.*, pages 817–823, Sydney, Australia, August 1991. Morgan Kaufmann.
8. Gentleware. Ontology Definition Meta-Model. http://www.omg.org/docs/ad/03-08-09.pdf, August 2003.
9. Object Management Group. Ontology Definition Metamodel - Request For Proposal, March 2003.
10. L. Hart, P. Emery, B. Colomb, K. Raymond, D. Chang, Y. Ye, E. Kendall, and M. Dutra. Usage Scenarios and Goals For Ontology Definition Metamodel. http://www.omg.org/docs/ontology/04-01-01.pdf, January 2004.
11. L. Hart, P. Emery, B. Colomb, K. Raymond, S. Taraporewalla, D. Chang, Y. Ye, and M. Dutra E. Kendall. OWL Full and UML 2.0 Compared, March 2004.
12. IBM. Ontology Definition Metamodel (ODM) Proposal. http://www.omg.org/docs/ad/03-07-02.pdf, August 2003.
13. Sandpiper Software Inc. and Stanford University Knowledge Systems Laboratory. UML for Knowledge Representation. A Layered, Component-Based Approach to Ontology Development. http://www.omg.org/docs/ad/03-08-06.pdf, March 2003.
14. R. Kremer. Visual Languages for Knowledge Representation. In *Proc. of 11th Workshop on Knowledge Acquisition, Modeling and Management (KAW'98)*, Voyager Inn, Banff, Alberta, Canada, April 1998. Morgan Kaufmann.
15. P. Loeffler. UML zur Visuellen Modellierung von OWL DL. Master's thesis, University of Karlsruhe (TH), June 2004.
16. D. L. McGuinness and F. van Harmelen. OWL Web Ontology Language Overview. Technical report, World Wide Web Consortium (W3C), August 2003. Internet: http://www.w3.org/TR/owl-features/.
17. Object Management Group. MOF 2.0 Query / Views / Transformations - Request for Proposal. http://www.omg.org/docs/ad/02-04-10.pdf, 2002.
18. Object Management Group. Ontology Definition Metamodel - Request for Proposal. http://www.omg.org/docs/ontology/03-03-01.rtf, 2003.
19. J. F. Sowa. Conceptual Graphs Summary. In P. Eklund, T. Nagle, J. Nagle, and L. Gerholz, editors, *Conceptual Structures: Current Research and Practice*, pages 3–52, 1992.
20. R. Volz. *Web Ontology Reasoning with Logic Databases*. Phd thesis, University of Karlsruhe (TH), Karlsruhe, Germany, http://www.ubka.uni-karlsruhe.de/cgi-bin/psview?document=2004/wiwi/2, February 2004.
21. W.A. Woods. What's in a Link: Foundations for Semantic Networks. In D.G. Bobrow and A.M. Collins, editors, *Representation and Understanding: Studies in Cognitive Science*, pages 35–82, 1975.

What Would It Mean to Blog on the Semantic Web?

David R. Karger[1] and Dennis Quan[2]

[1] MIT Computer Science and Artificial Intelligence Laboratory
32 Vassar Street
Cambridge, MA 02139 USA
karger@mit.edu

[2] IBM T. J. Watson Research Laboratory
1 Rogers Street
Cambridge, MA 02142 USA
dennisq@us.ibm.com

Abstract. The phenomenon known as Web logging ("blogging") has helped realize an initial goal of the Web: to turn Web content consumers (i.e., end users) into Web content producers. As the Semantic Web unfolds, we feel there are two questions worth posing: (1) do blog entries have semantic structure that can be usefully captured and exploited? (2) is blogging a natural way to encourage growth of the Semantic Web? We explore empirical evidence for answering these questions in the affirmative and propose means to bring blogging into the mainstream of the Semantic Web, including ontologies that extend the RSS 1.0 specification and an XSL transform for handling RSS 0.9x/2.0 files. To demonstrate the validity of our approach we have constructed a semantic blogging environment based on Haystack. We argue that with tools such as Haystack, semantic blogging will be an important paradigm by which metadata authoring will occur in the future.

1 Introduction

The Web is arguably the most successful open information distribution mechanism in existence. Despite its success, a few issues were not worked out initially, such as easy publication and machine-readable metadata. Web logs ("blogs") have emerged as a potential solution to the publication problem. The idea is based on the premise that publication occurs incrementally in discrete units—blog entries—and that users manage their own content (as opposed to newsgroups). A number of different software packages have grown around this simplified abstraction. Separately, the problem of machine-readable content is being attacked by the Semantic Web. Here the idea is that Web sites would host content in a language such as RDF, mostly devoid of human-readable artifacts such as prose, instead opting for more precise machine-readable specifications [7].

On the surface, these efforts seem to have little to do with each other, besides being both based on the Web. However, we argue that they are actually bound to converge at a common destination—a metadata-rich version of today's Web. Even today, there is a lot of family resemblance between blogs and the Semantic Web model. Blogs enable the average user to talk about—i.e., annotate—resources on the Web and pub-

S.A. McIlraith et al. (Eds.): ISWC 2004, LNCS 3298, pp. 214–228, 2004.

lish these annotations for others to see. A large portion of these blogs already have machine-readable "table of contents" files encoded in an XML format called RSS. Furthermore, blog entries themselves are first class—blog entries can be searched over, replied to, and referred to in other blogs.

In this paper we wish to examine two questions. First, if blogs could take full advantage of the RDF representation, what benefits would be realized? Second, do blogs form the basis of a nascent Semantic Web? In pursuit of answers to these questions, we characterize the notion of *semantic blogging*—the publication of RDF-encoded Web logs. Furthermore, to explore the practical benefits of semantic blogging, we have constructed a prototype semantic blogging tool on top of Haystack, our Semantic Web metadata exploration, visualization, and authoring tool [1, 8].

1.1   Approach

Our approach to semantic blogging focuses on adding unobtrusive extensions to the current blog creation interface paradigm—one of the key elements of the success of blogging—while producing machine-readable content for the benefit of blog content consumers. We argue that there is no added user effort involved in creating a semantic blog versus a conventional one, because the real work is done by the software in capturing semantics that are already being provided by the user. For example, when the user clicks on the "blog this" button on the Google toolbar in the Web browser to blog about the current page [19], instead of just recording a hyperlink, the system can record the fact that the current Web page is the *topic* of the blog entry. (Furthermore, one is not bound to using Google's blogging service.) In addition to these and other semantics inherent to blogs today, we also provide a mechanism for more advanced users to embed arbitrary RDF in a blog using a forms mechanism similar to that seen in Annotea [6].

In either case, the consumers of blog content benefit from having information from multiple blogs and the rest of the Semantic Web being integrated together and displayed in a variety of ways. Instead of being restricted to viewing one blog at a time, users can view cross-blog reply graphs to track the flow of a conversation, without requiring that publication be controlled by a central authority, as with a newsgroup. When browsing Web or Semantic Web content, one can see opinions, instructions, or descriptions from blogs alongside the content itself, as is done in tools such as the Haystack Semantic Web browser and Annotea [6]. Possibilities for automation are also created from the precise recording of semantics such as movie or product ratings, interest levels, and statistics such as sports scores.

1.2   Outline of the Paper

The paper is organized as follows. First, we first explore how blogs are written and used today and compare and contrast the blog paradigm with other Web publication paradigms. Based on these observations, we propose ontologies that extend the RSS 1.0 specification [12] and enable one to capture the semantics of blog entries in RDF. Afterwards, we describe our prototype semantic blogging environment, which allows users to both read existing blogs and to maintain their own blogs. We describe an XSL transform that translates existing RSS 0.9x/2.0 feeds [13, 14] into RDF, allowing us to take advantage of both existing and new RDF-enabled blogs. Finally, we put the pieces together and outline a scenario of how semantic blogging can enable more powerful forms of information retrieval and automation across blogs and other Semantic Web content.

2   The Essence of Blogging

At its core, blogging incorporates three distinct, key concepts, and analyzing blogging with respect to these concepts helps to clarify how blogging (and by extension semantic blogging) compares with other approaches. The first concept is of enabling users to publish information in small, discrete notes, as opposed to large, carefully-organized Web sites. Blogger remarks that "blog posts are like instant messages to the web" [9]. This analogy is borne out by the observation that interfaces for popular blogging tools including Blogger, Moveable Type [29], and Radio Userland [10] resemble those used by Web-based e-mail systems such as Hotmail [28]. Looking purely from this perspective, one might also note that the same kinds of brief, subjective comments can be found in the feedback bulletin boards of Web sites such as Amazon.com, Epinions.com, and Slashdot.org. Similarly, systems such as Annotea, which allows users to attach RDF-encoded "sticky note" annotations to text on Web pages [6], accumulate content one note at a time. Of course, blogs are not restricted to being lists of comments and criticisms; a wide variety of content exists in blogs today [24].

The second key concept is decentralized, per-user publication. Blog entries very often take the form of annotations to pages or critiques of products, but blog entries are primarily kept together based on common authorship, not common subject. In other words, the content author is the one who controls publication, and the feeling of "ownership" is part of the blogging experience. Bloggers write on a variety of topics and categorize their content as they choose, in contrast to a discussion site or a newsgroup, where deviation from predefined topics is often frowned upon and can result in censorship. Additionally, bloggers have control over the structure of individual blog entries. In a discussion group or with an annotation server, users are sometimes forced to conform to preset rating schemes or other attribute sets.

Furthermore, blogs generally exist independent of a centralized server. In this sense, maintaining a blog is conceptually similar to maintaining a single-user version of Annotea that has been reformulated to publish a table of contents of recent annotations to selected Web sites. However, the lack of a central point of aggregation has its disadvantages. With the Annotea model, where annotations are stored on a centralized server, it is easy to determine what other annotations exist for a resource of interest. Similarly, with the Internet newsgroup model, it is a simple task to trace reply chains because messages are grouped by thread. Later in the paper, we discuss ways in which semantic blogging can be used to overcome these limitations.

The last key concept—exposing machine-readable listings—is a property that many blogs possess in order to allow individual blog entries to be aggregated together. A family of XML-based standards for describing the contents of a blog loosely affiliated by the acronym "RSS" plays an important role in the thesis of this paper. The Really Simple Syndication 0.92 [14] (and its related standards hereafter referred to as RSS 0.9x) and 2.0 standards originated by Dave Winer [13] are not based on RDF but are by far the most widely adopted. The RDF Site Summary 1.0 standard [12] encodes essentially the same information and is based on RDF, but relatively few sites produce RSS files to this specification. There are other specifications for XML-based blog listing formats, such as Atom [17], which contain similar information. What is agreed upon is the basic notion of producing a machine-processable listing of blog entries in an XML format, and we build upon these XML formats in this paper.

Machine-readable listings are often used by blog readers, such as SharpReader [21] and NetNewsWire [20], as well as those built into blogging tools such as Radio Userland mentioned earlier. Like newsgroup readers and e-mail clients, blog readers typically offer users the ability to view lists of blog entries sorted by date, name, and other attributes—even lists that span multiple blogs. In order to emulate the threaded message displays found in other messaging tools, blog readers such as SharpReader find embedded hyperlinks in common between different blog entries and use them as the basis for determining threading. With semantic blogging we attempt to find cleaner ways to support the already-extant notion of inter-blog threading.

3   Bringing Out the Hidden Semantics in Blogs

Superficially, the existence of machine-readable listings is the strongest link between blogging and the Semantic Web. The connection, however, runs deeper. The discrete units being published in bulletin boards, in blogs, and with Annotea often have considerable internal structure: e-mails, instant messages, annotations, and bulletin board posts have a from field, a send date, and sometimes more specific information such as the product or other object being reviewed, a rating, etc. Put another way, the process of blogging inherently emphasizes metadata creation more than traditional Web publishing methodologies (e.g., direct HTML composition). The success of blogging points to its role as a socially viable means for encouraging users to publish certain forms of metadata. In this section, we elaborate on three specific forms of metadata that are inherent to the process of blogging. We also discuss possible benefits that would be realized from more precise, machine-readable metadata records.

3.1   Blogs as Annotations

Bloggers are free to write about anything they want in their blogs, from what they ate for breakfast that morning to the traffic problems on the commute home. Despite this freedom, bloggers frequently comment on things that exist on the Web. More specifically, bloggers spend much of their time creating focused annotations of Web resources. This observation is of interest to us to the extent to which these annotations can be modeled by taxonomies and ontologies.

Blog entries that talk about Web resources can be classified into a number of different types, and different annotation types can be modeled by differing levels of structure. For example, it may be useful to model criticism annotations using a numerical rating. At the moment, blog entries that embody criticisms may contain a numerical rating but that rating is rarely recorded in a machine-readable form, although there have been proposals based on non-RDF formats such as structured blogging [25] or Review Module for RSS 2.0 [23]. Using an ontology to model such annotations would make it easier to do automated filtering and analyses, such as finding the average rating for a given resource; such analyses are already done by specialized data mining sites such as blogosphere.us [26], but they usually do not track anything more semantic than just the frequency with which specific sites are hyperlinked to. Also, because blogs are managed on a per-user basis, users have the flexibility to adopt such ontologies to mark up their annotations.

Additionally, in moving blogging to the Semantic Web, an obvious extension is allowing blogs to talk about arbitrary Semantic Web resources. This extension not only broadens the set of available topics but also allows resources that previously had to go unnamed (e.g., "teddy bear model #22321") to be identified more precisely, improving search capabilities.

3.2 Blogs as Message Chains

Emphasizing a point from Section 2, blogs act as logs of messages, usually written to a general audience but at times focused towards specific parties. This phenomenon is most evident when an event of interest occurs, such as a product release. A flood of blog posts appear coincidentally, and the debate that ensues results in blogs containing entries that comment on other blog entries [5]. This structure is reminiscent of e-mail or newsgroups: a blog entry has a sender, a set of (sometimes targeted) recipients, a subject line, and often one reply-to entry (or more, although today notating that a blog entry is in reply to another blog entry may need to be done with human-readable prose and a hyperlink, depending on the blogging system in use).

3.3 Blogs as *Ad Hoc* Tables of Contents

Many blogs are devoted to a specific topic; alternatively, many bloggers intentionally divide their content into topics. The collections of commentary presented in these blogs often end up serving as a useful introduction to some esoteric subject. In other words, blogs can act as tables of contents for some field of interest. This combination of intentionally-recorded domain knowledge and a machine-readable listing format creates a number of possibilities for enhancing information retrieval. The main problem with a blog serving as a permanent archive of introductory material is that RSS listings produced by blog servers typically only include the n most recently published blog entries. One way of overcoming this problem would be to have blog servers also produce archival "back-issue" RSS files. We discuss alternative ways of dealing with this issue throughout the paper.

4 Ontologies for Enabling Semantic Blogging

Having identified the core semantics imparted by blog entries, we proceed to use Semantic Web tools, including RDF and OWL, to find ways to capture these semantics in a standard fashion. In this section we describe various ontologies and strategies for recording blog entries in RDF. We refer to blogs that have been represented in this fashion as "semantic" blogs to highlight that important elements of blog entries that were once recorded in prose are now being described with machine-readable metadata.

4.1 Building on RSS 1.0

There are many benefits to using RDF as the basis for recording machine-readable blog listings. Most important of these is that the notion of resource identity is built into RDF: resources are always referred to by their URIs. This provision simplifies processes such as notating what resource is being annotated or what blog entry is being replied to. Also, there is a well-defined mechanism for adding custom properties or attributes to blog entries. Furthermore, there are well-defined semantics for merging multiple RDF files. As a result, one can accumulate the RSS files generated by a blog over time and keep a historical record of the blog easily.

As noted earlier, RSS 1.0 is an already-extant RDF-based mechanism for publishing machine-readable blog listings. While RSS 0.9x/2.0 is the predominant format, many blogs also provide listings in RSS 1.0 format. Furthermore, most of the concepts in RSS 0.9x/2.0 map directly onto the RSS 1.0 ontology. In Section 5.1 we discuss an XSL transform for converting RSS 0.9x/2.0 files into RDF. These observations make RSS 1.0 a natural standard to build on.

4.2 Categorization

More and more, bloggers have begun to categorize their individual blog entries. Categorization allows a single blogger to distinguish multiple trains of thought or topic areas in a single blog. The RSS 0.92 and 2.0 standards support categorization, but apart from a URI naming a taxonomy, category labels themselves are just strings. The RSS 1.0 standard does not include any explicit support for categorization.

The Haystack ontology, developed for the Semantic Web Browser project discussed later [1], defines a class called **hs:Collection**, and one of the roles of a collection is to act as a category for classification purposes. A single predicate, **hs:member**, binds a collection to its members, regardless of type. In this way, collections named by URIs are used as the basis for category labeling and can hence be shared by multiple blogs. Universal naming also avoids name collisions between blogs that have coincidentally named categories (e.g., "Jaguar" in a zoologist's blog and "Jaguar" in an operating system researcher's blog are likely to mean different things) and facilitates the construction of mappings between different categorization schemes.

4.3 Message Ontology

Blog entries, as discussed earlier, have a lot in common with other forms of electronic messages, such as e-mails and instant messages. A previous paper on modeling messages in RDF [3] proposed an ontology for messaging, and we have reused the portions of this ontology that are applicable to blogging. At the heart of this ontology is the **msg:Message** class, which is the base class for all messages. We define **rss:item** from the RSS 1.0 ontology as deriving from **msg:Message**. This allows us to reuse the **msg:inReplyTo** predicate, which declares one message to be in reply to another message. (**msg:inReplyTo** is simply a sub-property of **ann:annotation**, which is used to indicate the resource being annotated by a message.)

An argument that was presented in the earlier paper on messaging was that conversations are often spread across multiple messaging channels, such as e-mail, instant messaging, and chat. Blogging has a similar phenomenon: not only do users send e-mails to bloggers in response to their blog entries or use the comment bulletin board feature attached to many blogs, but they also respond to others' blog entries in their own blogs. E-mails, bulletin board messages, and blog entries are all acting as messages within a greater conversation, and using a general messaging ontology enables us to capture these semantics in a uniform fashion across an entire conversation. More specifically, predicates such as **msg:to** and **msg:from** are used to characterize e-mails and instant messages, and in the case of a blog posting, we use a "blog audience" resource associated with the blog for the recipient (i.e., value of the **msg:to** property).

4.4   Encoding Custom Semantics

Our messaging ontology defines a **msg:body** predicate, which is used to associate a message with textual content. However, the value of the **msg:body** property need not be human-readable. By allowing an RDF file to serve as the body of a blog, we can enable arbitrary Semantic Web content to be included. While we do not see this sort of "pure" semantic blogging taking off immediately, we feel that this provision provides space for semantic blogging to progress in the future.

Haystack supports a form-based mechanism for allowing users to input a variety of different kinds of RDF metadata. Forms for entering specific kinds of semantics are likely to be generated in accordance with specific RDF Schemas or ontologies. Haystack includes support for schema-based form generation, similar to those found in Annotea [6] and Protégé [16]. Our forms mechanism is described in previous work [15].

5   A Semantic Blog Client

To demonstrate the benefits of semantic blogging, we constructed a semantic blog client built into Haystack that incorporates publishing, aggregation, and browsing capabilities. Haystack's paradigm is similar to that of a Web browser; users navigate to resources by typing in their URIs or by clicking on hyperlinks, and the toolbar exposes the familiar back, forward, refresh, and home buttons for ease of navigation. However, unlike a Web browser, which simply renders the HTML content of a resource, Haystack contains user interface templates called *views* that are used to transform machine-readable RDF metadata relating to the current resource into a human-readable, hyperlinked, on-screen presentation. We have extended Haystack with specialized views and user interface commands called *operations* that enable blogging functionality within Haystack. The technical details of how views and operations are defined are described in previous papers on Haystack [1, 8]. In this section we characterize these views and operations and show how they contribute to the end user experience.

5.1   Subscribing to Blogs

Most blogs are published as Web sites, allowing users with a normal Web browser to view and search them. Haystack includes a Web browser view, meaning that when a user browses to a Web resource (i.e., a Web page named by an HTTP URL), Haystack's functionality reduces to that of a traditional Web browser. As a result, users can browse the HTML versions of blogs from within Haystack. In addition, most blogs also provide an RSS file that can be used to subscribe to a blog, as noted earlier. By convention, an "RSS" or an "XML" button is placed on the blog's home page to signify the availability of an RSS file, and when the user clicks on the button, the browser navigates to the RSS file. When the user browses to an RSS file, Haystack detects that it is an RSS file and allows the user to subscribe to it using the Subscribe to RSS Feed operation. After the user subscribes to the blog, Haystack will automatically download the RSS file on a regular basis. Over time, Haystack accumulates a historical record of a blog, which can be useful when a blog contains helpful reference material that may want to be looked up later.

Today, relatively few blogs are encoded in RDF, and since Haystack deals primarily with RDF-encoded metadata, RSS 0.9x/2.0 files need to be converted into RDF before they can be subscribed to. The mechanism we have elected to use in handling the various forms of RSS currently extant on the Web today is to transform RSS 0.9x/2.0 files into RDF files based on RSS 1.0 and our extension ontologies discussed earlier. Being able to convert RSS 0.9x/2.0 files into RDF enables a number of powerful Semantic Web capabilities to be used over a large, pre-existing corpus of blogs, such as search, semantic exploration, etc.

The XSL Transformations language (XSLT) is a standard means for transforming one XML format into another, and we have implemented our translation process in XSLT. The complete source for our XSLT can be found on our Web site[1]. The majority of the XSLT converter is straightforward and simply converts RSS 0.9x/2.0 syntax into well-formed RDF. The primary challenge is coming up with a URI for blogs and blog entries. Fortunately, the permalink feature of RSS 0.9x/2.0 allows a blogger to assign a permanent URL name to a blog entry, but its use is optional. When it exists, our XSLT uses it as the blog entry's URI; otherwise, it defaults to the value of the link element. Many features of semantic blogging are missing from RSS 0.9x/2.0, but it is possible to use techniques such as scraping for hyperlinks as to fill in the list of resources being annotated or replied to as an approximation.

5.2   Viewing Blogs

Once a user has subscribed to a blog, it appears on the news home page in Haystack. This screen is like the front page of a newspaper in that it shows the recent news articles from all of the subscribed feeds. By using the preview pane controls on the toolbar, the user can introspect individual articles: when the user clicks on a link on the news pane, the associated article appears in the pane on the right.

In addition, individual blogs can be viewed separately. The list of entries in a blog (sometimes known as a channel) maps onto Haystack's collection concept introduced earlier. There are a number of collection views built into Haystack, and as a result,

---

[1] http://haystack.lcs.mit.edu/rss.xslt

blogs can be visualized in many different ways, including as a list, a calendar, or a multi-column table. In addition, some specialized views, such as the Explore relationships between collection members view, are provided to aid in certain forms of information exploration. In this case, the Explore relationships between collection members view displays a labeled directed graph, drawing the members of the collection (in this case, the articles in the blog) as nodes and allowing the user to select which arcs (i.e., predicates) to show between the articles. The built-in Reply graph arc set is selected in Fig. 2 and shows the **msg:inReplyTo** relationships between the messages in the display.

5.3   Organizing Blog Content of Interest

In Section 4.2 we discussed the use of collections as a categorization mechanism for bloggers. These collections are first class resources and browseable in their own right from within Haystack. In addition, a user reading a blog can also create his or her own collections and use them to file blog entries of interest. Looking at an article, the user can invoke the File away operation on the left hand pane. This operation reveals a customizable list of collections on the right hand pane into which the article can be filed. Each collection has a checkbox next to it, making it easy to file an article into multiple collections at once [11]. Collections can also be hierarchical; adding a new collection can be accomplished by right-clicking on the parent collection and selecting Add new item/Create a collection from the context menu.

5.4   Creating a Semantic Blog

We have implemented support for allowing users to blog from within Haystack. As noted earlier, blogging tools expose forms that resemble an e-mail editor for creating new blog entries. In Haystack, we have adapted the existing mail composition and transmission functionality to be able to post messages to servers (including possibly a local server built into Haystack, as in the case described below) that speak protocols like the Blogger XML-RPC protocol [30].

To implement our enhanced semantic capabilities, we have extended the Blojsom Open Source blog server, which runs on a standard Java Servlet-compliant Web server such as Apache Tomcat. Blojsom stores blog entries in text files on the file system. (One benefit of the file system approach is that a user can work on a local copy of the blog and use CVS to synchronize it with a blog server; Haystack includes built-in support for CVS.) These files contain a header that includes a one-line title for the blog entry and a series of metadata declarations. We have introduced five metadata tags, meta-inReplyTo, meta-annotates, meta-fileInto, meta-rdfBody, and meta-uri[2] in order to support our semantics, and have written a new Haystack messaging driver that allows Haystack to serialize blog entries in this form.

---

[2] This declaration permits the file to state the URI to be assigned to the blog entry and allows, in theory, for a blog entry to be posted to multiple blogs but retain the same URI. The rss:link property, which provides the URL of the content for the blog entry, can be specific to the blog server without disrupting this scheme.

Users gain access to blogging functionality through a combination of views and operations. First, a user clicks on the Blogging link in Starting Points. Haystack then shows a list of the user's existing blogs. To connect to an existing blog server via XML-RPC or to create a new semantic blog, the user can choose either the Connect to Blog Server or Create New Semantic Blog operations from the left hand pane, respectively. After filling in the appropriate configuration parameters, the user is taken to a screen that shows the blog entries that exist for that blog. Creating a new blog entry is accomplished by selecting the New text blog entry operation from the left hand pane.

The key benefits of blogging in Haystack versus current blogging tools (or even an e-mail client) are twofold. First, Haystack can produce specialized forms that capture various levels of semantics. At one end of the spectrum are simple message editors such as those seen in today's blogging tools and Web-based e-mail products. At the other extreme are specialized forms, such as those proposed by structured blogging [25] or used by Annotea [6], which can be derived from RDF Schemas automatically by Haystack.

The other benefit is that the semantics surrounding the reason for a blog entry's creation can be captured immediately. When the user is viewing a Web page, a Semantic Web resource of interest, or even another blog entry, and wishes to blog about it, he or she can click on semantically-specialized operations such as "Blog a reply" or "Blog a complaint". In contrast, those semantics are often lost in the transition between the program the annotated resource is being viewed in (e.g., the Web browser) and the blogging tool.

6 A Scenario

To concretize the benefits of our approach, consider the following fictitious scenario. John Doe is a bioinformatician who is thinking about whether to attend the Semantic Bio 2005 conference. He goes to the conference Web site and sees an overwhelming 20 page listing of all of the papers to be presented. Like many futuristic (and fictitious) conference sites, this site also offers an RDF version of the program. Using Haystack, John downloads the program and uses Haystack to browse it.

John takes a look at the multi-day Inference Track category to see just those papers. One in particular catches his eye—one called "Using the COOL Algorithm for Protein Folding Analysis". Clicking on the article, he sees the paper's abstract and references. John, like many people, has friends who are avid bloggers and maintain blogs that review the latest findings in their particular fields. These friends have already seen this paper and blogged about it; their blog entries appear alongside the article. Refer to Fig. 1.

Glancing through the subject lines, it isn't clear which blog entry came first and which came last. John clicks Extract Relevant Discussion, selects the Explore Relationships between Collection Members view, and selects the Message Reply Graph arrow set. This allows him to see which blog entries are in response to which others.

Some of the blog entries appear emptier than others. He clicks on one of them and finds it is a blog article from the initial author. He clicks on the RSS link on the page and subscribes to the entire blog. When he goes back to the relationship diagram, the missing nodes are filled in. (This process might be automated in the future.) See Fig. 2.

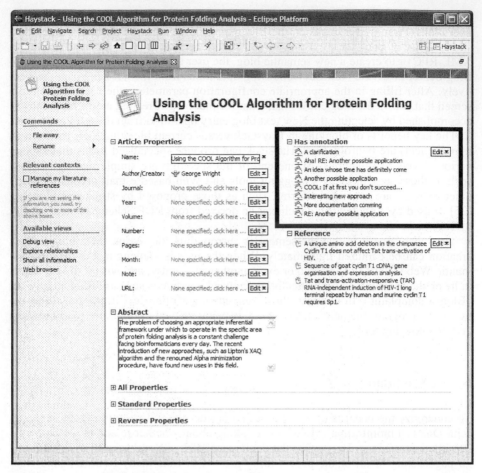

Fig. 1. Screen integrating information about a conference paper and annotations from semantic blogs (boxed area).

Furthermore, he can tell at a glance that two of the initial blog entries are commendations while the other is a criticism; however, looking down the line of conversation, he can see that the critic was eventually convinced and issued a commendation. Seeing all three of his friends in agreement is unique, and John decides to invest some time in reading through the articles. He creates a bookmark collection on the right hand docking pane and drags and drops some of the more interesting blog entries into it.

John decides to delve deeper into the approach. Scanning through the references in the paper, he finds a reference to the author's ontology. He browses to it in Haystack and clicks on one of the terms labeled "Analysis Engine". Just looking at the properties it supports does not give John a clear enough picture. However, the author has written a blog entry about it; by clicking on it, John is taken to the entire blog. A quick glance through the blog reveals that the author had been bombarded with requests for more explanation about his ontology, and he responded by blogging about

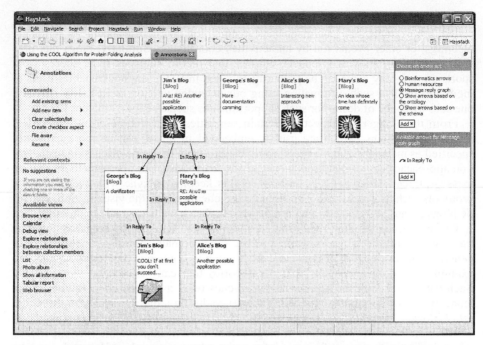

Fig. 2. Messages from multiple blogs displayed together as a reply graph.

various parts of the ontology over time, resulting in what is in essence a tutorial of how to use the ontology. John then browses through the blog, clicking on links to ontology elements embedded within the blog from time to time. In the end, John is himself convinced of the benefits of the approach and makes an entry in his own blog in concurrence, commenting on its applicability to his own research. In particular, he points out the one important argument that was critical to convincing him by dragging that blog entry from the bookmark collection he created earlier and dropping it in the In regards to field, making his blog entry an annotation for that argument.

7 Discussion

In the above scenario, we presented several examples of potential benefits for the integration of blogging and the Semantic Web. From the Semantic Web's perspective, blogging can be seen as a user-friendly metaphor for encouraging semantic annotation. Blogs already provide reviews, commentary, and human-readable instructions for many domains, and when directed towards Semantic Web resources, such blogs may be useful for documenting how to best make use of Semantic Web ontologies, schemas, and services. The contents of semantic blogs' annotations may also contain machine-readable metadata, such as numerical ratings, that could be consumed by Semantic Web agents to automatically determine aggregate ratings or other summary information.

In the future, there may be blogs that end up being completely semantically encoded. For example, one can imagine a semantic blog that notifies people of seminars, meetings, or other events run by an activities coordinator. Similarly, blogs that provide reviews (of movies, products, etc.) or that record statistics (e.g., scores from sports games) may someday be primarily encoded in RDF. Haystack enables users to input and publish such information using our extended version of RSS 1.0. Already, one sees evidence of desire for such support in sites such as Ripe Tomatoes [27].

From the blogger's perspective, certain semantics can be more cleanly recorded. The reply-to chains, which are usually embedded in prose, can be more explicitly specified as metadata, and bloggers would benefit from the same discussion visualization approaches that e-mail users have had for years. Also, our approach to displaying message threads does not rely on blog servers keeping in sync with each other via protocols such as TrackBack [18]; because the client creates the visualization, semantic blogs do not need to keep a record of what replies have been made to them.

Categories can be more easily shared not only between specific blogs, as could be the case if multiple bloggers worked in the same domain, but also among blogs in general. Simple category or type indications, such as commendation or complaint, are examples of more universally-shared categories that can be used by blog readers. Such categories could be exposed as visual cues (e.g., a thumbs up or thumbs down icon), which would improve the user experience during a quick visual scan through a set of blogs.

Also, the semantic annotation of blogs can be used to improve the user experience when dealing with various forms of information. A system such as Haystack can take advantage of these annotations in order to help users make sense of their information. For example, Haystack can help not only in bringing together the content from different blogs but also in integrating blog content with other information sources, such as conference programs. In this sense, blogs are acting as editorial "glue" that helps the reader to make sense of large bodies of information. Related scenarios can be made involving e-commerce product catalogs, online taxonomies, travel accommodation directories, etc.

Furthermore, Haystack allows blogs to be viewed in different ways, depending on the task at hand. Standard blogging tools allow users to view the articles in blogs and to group articles together in various ways. Less explored are the benefits of making use of the relationships between blogs. The example we cited earlier is Haystack's Explore relationships between collection members view, which allows the user to see the flow of a conversation even if it spans multiple blogs. One major consequence is that a group of people that wants to publish a conversation needs not do so through a single blog or a centralized mechanism, such as a newsgroup. Because URIs are used to name the blog entries, the various blogs can be aggregated by the blog reader and displayed together, while individual users are allowed to maintain the identities of and control over their own blogs—one of the key social motivational factors underlying blogging.

Acknowledgements. The authors would like to thank Kushal Dave for his helpful comments on the state of the art in blogging and Martin Wattenberg for useful pointers to relevant blogging literature.

Prefixes Used in This Paper

hs: http://haystack.lcs.mit.edu/schemata/haystack#
ann: http://haystack.lcs.mit.edu/schemata/annotation#
msg: http://haystack.lcs.mit.edu/schemata/mail#
rss: http://purl.org/rss/1.0/

References

1. Quan, D. and Karger, D. How to Make a Semantic Web Browser. Proceedings of WWW 2004.
2. Karger, D. and Quan, D. Collections: Flexible, Essential Tools for Information Management. Proceedings of CHI 2004.
3. Quan, D., Bakshi, K., and Karger, D. A Unified Abstraction for Messaging on the Semantic Web. Proceedings of WWW 2003.
4. Karger, D., Katz, B., Lin, J., and Quan, D. Sticky Notes for the Semantic Web. Proceedings of IUI 2003.
5. Kumar, R., Novak, J., Raghavan, P., and Tomkins, A. On the Bursty Evolution of Blogspace. Proceedings of WWW 2003.
6. Kahan, J. and Koivunen, M. Annotea: an open RDF infrastructure for shared web annotations. Proceedings of WWW10.
7. Berners-Lee, T., Hendler, J., and Lassila, O. The Semantic Web. *Scientific American*, May 2001.
8. Quan, D., Huynh, D., and Karger, D. Haystack: A Platform for Authoring End User Semantic Web Applications. Proceedings of ISWC 2003.
9. Blogger. http://www.blogger.com/.
10. Radio Userland. http://radio.userland.com/.
11. Quan, D., Bakshi, K., Huynh, D., and Karger, D. User Interfaces for Supporting Multiple Categorization. Proceedings of INTERACT 2003.
12. RDF Site Summary 1.0 Specification. http://web.resource.org/rss/1.0/spec.
13. RSS 2.0 Specification. http://blogs.law.harvard.edu/tech/rss.
14. RSS 0.92 Specification. http://backend.userland.com/rss092.
15. Quan, D., Karger, D., and Huynh, D. RDF Authoring Environments for End Users. Proceedings of the International Workshop on Semantic Web Foundations and Application Technologies 2003.
16. Noy, N., Sintek, M., Decker, S., Crubezy, M., Ferguson, R., and Musen, M. Creating Semantic Web Contents with Protege-2000. *IEEE Intelligent Systems* 16 (2), 2001, pp. 60-71.
17. The Atom Syndication Format 0.3. http://www.atomenabled.org/developers/syndication/atom-format-spec.php.
18. TrackBack Technical Specification. http://www.movabletype.org/docs/mttrackback.html.
19. Google Toolbar. http://toolbar.google.com/.
20. NetNewsWire. http://ranchero.com/netnewswire/.
21. SharpReader. http://www.sharpreader.net/.
22. Technorati. http://www.technorati.com/.
23. Review (RVW) Module for RSS 2.0. http://www.pmbrowser.info/rvw/0.1/.
24. Nardi, B., Schiano, D., Gumbrecht, M., and Swartz, L. "I'm Blogging This": A Closer Look at Why People Blog. Submitted to *Communications of the ACM*. http://www.ics.uci.edu/%7Ejpd/classes/ics234cw04/nardi.pdf.

25. Paquet, S. Towards Structured Blogging.
    http://radio.weblogs.com/0110772/stories/2003/03/13/towardsStructuredBlogging.html.
26. blogosphere.us. http://www.blogosphere.us/trends.php.
27. Rotten Tomatoes. http://www.rottentomatoes.com/vine/register.php.
28. Hotmail. http://www.hotmail.com/.
29. Moveable Type. http://www.movabletype.org/.
30. Blogger API. http://www.blogger.com/developers/api/.

The Protégé OWL Plugin:
An Open Development Environment
for Semantic Web Applications

Holger Knublauch, Ray W. Fergerson, Natalya F. Noy, and Mark A. Musen

Stanford Medical Informatics, Stanford School of Medicine
251 Campus Drive, Stanford, CA 94305-5479
holger@smi.stanford.edu

Abstract. We introduce the OWL Plugin, a Semantic Web extension of the Protégé ontology development platform. The OWL Plugin can be used to edit ontologies in the Web Ontology Language (OWL), to access description logic reasoners, and to acquire instances for semantic markup. In many of these features, the OWL Plugin has created and facilitated new practices for building Semantic Web contents, often driven by the needs of and feedback from our users. Furthermore, Protégé's flexible open-source platform means that it is easy to integrate custom-tailored components to build real-world applications. This document describes the architecture of the OWL Plugin, walks through its most important features, and discusses some of our design decisions.

1   Introduction

Efficient development tools are a prerequisite for the wide adoption of a new technology. For example, visual Web design tools like DreamWeaver have significantly reduced the development costs of Internet content, and have brought Web technology to the fingertips of people who are not familiar with the details of HTML. The concept of the Semantic Web [3] is often regarded as the next "big" technology leap for the Internet. Now that the Web Ontology Language (OWL) [16] has been officially standardized, it is the task of tool builders to explore and provide suitable infrastructures that help make the Semantic Web vision a reality. This document reports on our work and results in the construction of such a tool.

Our goal was to build an extensible tool with support for the most commonly needed features for the development of Semantic Web applications. *Ontologies* play a central role in the Semantic Web: They provide formal models of domain knowledge that can be exploited by intelligent agents. As a result, a development tool for Semantic Web applications should provide services to access, visualize, edit, and use ontologies. Furthermore, since ontologies may be notoriously hard to build [13], a tool should provide intelligent assistance in ontology construction and evolution. Finally, since the Semantic Web is open to so many potential application areas, a tool should be customizable and extensible.

We have developed the OWL Plugin, an extension of Protégé. Protégé [4,8] is an open platform for ontology modeling and knowledge acquisition. The OWL Plugin can

S.A. McIlraith et al. (Eds.): ISWC 2004, LNCS 3298, pp. 229–243, 2004.

be used to edit OWL ontologies, to access description logic (DL) reasoners, and to acquire instances for semantic markup. As an extension of Protégé, the OWL Plugin profits from the benefits of a large user community, a library of reusable components, and a flexible architecture. The OWL Plugin therefore has the potential to become a standard infrastructure for building ontology-based Semantic Web applications.

This document describes the main features of the Protégé OWL Plugin and illustrates how it can be used and customized to build real-world Semantic Web applications. Section 2 lists requirements and design goals that motivated the development of the OWL Plugin. Section 3 provides background on the Protégé platform and architecture. Section 4 describes how Protégé has been extended with support for OWL, and how other components can be built on top of it. Section 5 shows how the OWL Plugin can be used to edit OWL classes and properties. Section 6 describes features that help evolve, test and maintain ontologies, including intelligent reasoning based on description logics. Section 7 shows how Protégé can serve as an editor of Semantic Web contents (e.g., OWL individuals). Section 8 discusses our results and points at ongoing and future work. This paper assumes that the reader is familiar with OWL, but not necessarily with Protégé.

2   Requirements and Design Goals

The nature of the Semantic Web and its languages has implications for tool builders. A rather well-known aspect is that the cryptic and error-prone RDF syntax of OWL [16] makes it extremely hard to build valid OWL ontologies manually. Graphical ontology editing tools with a simple syntax and built-in validation mechanisms could significantly improve this situation.

A more critical aspect is that the Semantic Web is based on ontologies, and ontologies are notoriously difficult to build [13]. One reason for this difficulty is that ontologies are formal models of human domain knowledge. While human knowledge is often tacit and hard to describe in formal models, there is also no single correct mapping of knowledge into discrete structures. Although some rules of thumb exist that facilitate selected ontology-design tasks (e.g., [13,15]), there are hardly any comprehensive ontology development methods in routine use. As an alternative to systematic and comprehensive guidelines, development tools should at least support rapid turn-around times to encourage ontology evolution and iteration. User interfaces should simplify and accelerate common tasks and at the same time encourage best practices and design patterns. Furthermore, tools should expose somewhat intelligent assistance for ontology builders, and point out obvious modeling errors. Another important criteria is that ontologies can become very large, so that tools need to be scalable, and should support the coordination of efforts among multiple people.

A final issue for Semantic Web development tools is that they should be *open*. First, they should be open-source so that interested people can more easily try and understand them. Second, tools should also be open to project-specific customizations and extensions. Nobody knows where the Semantic Web will be in the future, and it may offer boundless opportunities for innovative services, methods, and applications. An open tool that allows for the integration of these future components more easily may significantly reduce development costs. For example, developers of OWL reasoners could integrate their reasoning component into an OWL editor so that they can much easier experiment with different ontologies. Also, developers of Web services could reuse the tool's infrastructure without having to write their own base platform first.

3   Protégé

Protégé is an open-source tool developed at Stanford Medical Informatics. It has a community of thousands of users. Although the development of Protégé has historically been mainly driven by biomedical applications [4], the system is domain-independent and has been successfully used for many other application areas as well.

Like most other modeling tools, the architecture of Protégé is cleanly separated into a "model" part and a "view" part. Protégé's *model* is the internal representation mechanism for ontologies and knowledge bases. Protégé's *view* components provide a user interface to display and manipulate the underlying model.

Protégé's *model* is based on a simple yet flexible metamodel [11], which is comparable to object-oriented and frame-based systems. It basically can represent ontologies consisting of classes, properties (slots), property characteristics (facets and constraints), and instances. Protégé provides an open Java API to query and manipulate models. An important strength of Protégé is that the Protégé metamodel itself is a Protégé ontology, with classes that represent classes, properties, and so on. For example, the default class in the Protégé base system is called :STANDARD-CLASS, and has properties such as :NAME and :DIRECT-SUPERCLASSES. This structure of the metamodel enables easy extension and adaption to other representations [12]. For example, we have extended this metamodel to handle UML and OWL.

Using the *views* of Protégé's user interface, ontology designers basically create classes, assign properties to the classes, and then restrict the properties' facets at certain classes. Using the resulting ontologies, Protégé is able to automatically generate user interfaces that support the creation of individuals (instances). For each class in the ontology, the system creates one *form* with editing components (*widgets*) for each property of the class. For example, for properties that can take single string values, the system would by default provide a text field widget. The generated forms can be further customized with Protégé's form editor, where users can select alternative user interface widgets for their project. In addition to the predefined library of user interface widgets, Protégé has a flexible architecture that enables programmers to develop custom-tailored widgets, which can then be plugged into the core system. Another type of plugin supports full-size user interface panels (*tabs*) that can contain arbitrary other components. In addition to the collection of standard tabs for editing classes, properties, forms and instances, a library of other tabs exists that perform queries, access data repositories, visualize ontologies graphically, and manage ontology versions.

Protégé currently can be used to load, edit and save ontologies in various formats, including CLIPS, RDF, XML, UML and relational databases. Recently, we have added support for OWL. Our decision to build our system on top of Protégé was driven by various factors. Since ontologies play such an important role in Semantic Web applications, it was straight-forward to take an existing ontology development environment as a starting point. Extensions to Protégé can benefit from the generic services provided by the core platform, such as an event mechanism, undo capabilities, and a plugin mechanism. By basing the OWL Plugin on top of Protégé, we could also reuse Protégé's client-server-based multi-user mode that allows multiple people to edit the same ontology at the same time. Protégé also provides a highly scalable database back-end, allowing users to create ontologies with hundreds of thousands of classes. Also, there is already a considerable library of plugins which can be either directly used for OWL or adapted to OWL with little effort. Furthermore, the fact that Protégé is open-source also encourages plugin development. Last but not least, Protégé is backed by a large community of active users and developers, and the feedback from this community proved to be invaluable for the development of the OWL Plugin.

Our decision to base the OWL Plugin on Protégé also had some risks. In order to be able to reuse as much of the existing Protégé features as possible, we had to create a careful mapping between the Protégé metamodel and OWL that maintains the traditional Protégé semantics where possible. Furthermore, none of the generic Protégé widgets and tabs is optimized for OWL, and not all of the editing metaphors for frame-based systems are appropriate for OWL. In particular, OWL's rich description logics features such as logical class definitions required special attention. The following sections will show how we have addressed these issues.

4   The Architecture of the OWL Plugin

The OWL Plugin is a complex Protégé extension that can be used to edit OWL files and databases. The OWL Plugin includes a collection of custom-tailored tabs and widgets for OWL, and provides access to OWL-related services such as classification, consistency checking, and ontology testing.

4.1   OWL Plugin Metamodel

As illustrated in Figure 1, the OWL Plugin extends the Protégé model and its API with classes to represent the OWL specification. The OWL Plugin supports RDF(S), OWL Lite, OWL DL (except for anonymous global class axioms, which need to be given a name by the user) and significant parts of OWL Full (including metaclasses).

In order to better understand this extension mechanism, we need to look at the differences between the Protégé metamodel and OWL. OWL is an extension of RDF(S) [7]. RDF has a very simple triple-based model that is often too verbose to be edited directly in a tool. Fortunately, RDF Schema extends RDF with metamodel classes and properties which can be mapped into the Protégé metamodel. As a result, the extensions that OWL adds to RDF(S) can be reflected by extensions of the Protégé metamodel.

Although this extension has been successfully implemented for the OWL Plugin, not all aspects of the metamodels could be mapped trivially. It was straight-forward to represent those aspects of OWL that just extend the Protégé metamodel. For example, in order to represent disjoint class relationships, it was sufficient to add a new property :OWL-DISJOINT-CLASSES to Protégé's owl:Class metaclass. It was also relatively easy to represent OWL's complex class constructors that can build class descriptions out of logical statements. For example, OWL classes can be defined as the complement

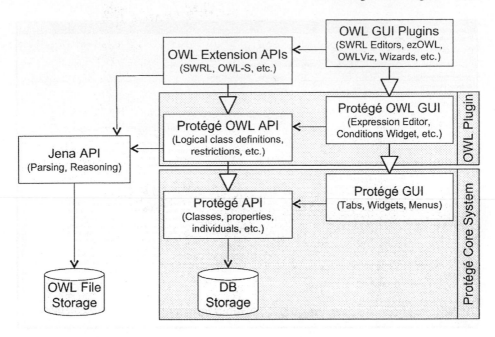

Fig. 1. The OWL Plugin is an extension of the Protégé core system.

of other classes, using the `owl:complementOf` constructor. In the OWL Plugin, complements are represented by instances of a metaclass `:OWL-COMPLEMENT-CLASS` that inherits from other Protégé system classes. As illustrated in Figure 2, the other types of OWL class constructors such as restrictions and enumerated classes, and the various kinds of properties are mapped into similar metaclasses.

Other aspects of OWL required some work to maintain a maximum of backward compatibility with traditional Protégé applications. There is a semantic difference between Protégé and OWL if multiple restrictions are defined at the same time. In particular, Protégé properties with multiple classes as their range can take as values instances of all classes (union semantics), whereas OWL properties with multiple classes in their range can only take values that are instances of all classes at the same time (intersection semantics). In order to solve this mismatch, the OWL Plugin uses an internal `owl:unionOf` class if the user has defined more than one range class. The same applies to a property's domain. Another difference is that OWL does not have the notion of facets, which in Protégé are used to store property restrictions at a class. While a maximum cardinality restriction at a class in Protégé is represented by a single quadruple (class, property, facet, value), the same is stored as an anonymous superclass in OWL. OWL even supports attaching annotation property values to such anonymous classes, and therefore it would be insufficient to map OWL restrictions into facets only. We have implemented a mechanism that automatically synchronizes facet values with restriction classes, so that the traditional semantics of Protégé are maintained while using the syntax of OWL.

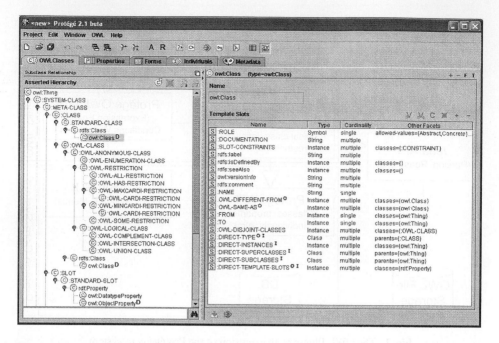

Fig. 2. The OWL metaclasses are implemented as subclasses of the Protégé system classes. As shown here, they can be browsed with Protégé as well.

4.2   OWL Plugin API

Reflecting the Protégé metamodel extensions, the OWL Plugin also provides an extended Java API to access and manipulate OWL ontologies. While the core API already provides access to ontology classes, properties, and instances, the OWL Plugin extends this API with custom-tailored Java classes for the various OWL class types. This API basically encapsulates the internal mapping and thus shields the user from error-prone low-level access. It is possible to further extend this API to define custom-tailored classes for OWL extensions like OWL-S and the Semantic Web Rule Language (SWRL) [6]. For example, individuals of the SWRL class `AtomList` could be represented by instances of a corresponding Java class such as `AtomListInstance`. Algorithms for SWRL could then operate on more convenient objects than with the generic classes, while non-SWRL-aware Protégé components would handle these objects as normal `Instances`. We are currently working such a SWRL library.

The OWL Plugin provides a comprehensive mapping between its extended API and the standard OWL parsing library Jena [1]. After an ontology has been loaded into a Jena model, the OWL Plugin generates the corresponding Protégé objects. It then keeps the Jena model in memory at all times, and synchronizes it with all changes performed by the user. Thus, if the user creates a new Protégé class, a new Jena class with the same name is created as well. The presence of a secondary representation of the ontology in

---

[1] `http://jena.sourceforge.net`

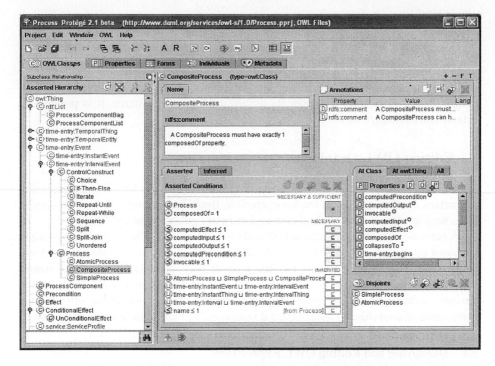

Fig. 3. A screenshot of the classes tab in the OWL Plugin (displaying the OWL-S ontology). The screenshot shows the logical definition of the selected class `CompositeProcess`, its properties, disjoints and annotations.

terms of Jena objects means that the user is able to invoke arbitrary Jena-based services such as interfaces to classifiers, query languages, or visualization tools permanently. The mapping into Jena also makes it much easier to embed existing and future Semantic Web services into the OWL Plugin. Also, when the ontology is saved, it is sufficient to call the corresponding Jena API method to serialize the Jena objects to a file. The immediate Jena mapping is not available in the OWL Plugin's database or multi-user modes, where it is replaced with a conventional, monolithic translation.

4.3   OWL Plugin User Interface

Based on the above mentioned metamodel and API extensions, the OWL Plugin provides several custom-tailored graphical user interface components for OWL. When started, the system displays the five tabs shown in Figure 3. Most ontology designers will focus on the *OWL classes* and *Properties* tabs which are described in sections 5 and 6. The *Forms* and *Individuals* tabs are mostly geared for the acquisition of Semantic Web contents (instance data, detailed in Section 7), while the *Metadata* tab allows users to specify global ontology settings such as imports and namespaces.

Note that the generic architecture of Protégé and the OWL-specific extensions make it relatively easy to add custom-tailored components. For example, optimized editors for

SWRL or OWL-S could be added to the system. Likewise, description-logic reasoners could be directly implemented on top of the Protégé OWL API or Jena. In fact, several developers from around the world have already developed extensions of the OWL Plugin, some of them even without interacting with us. In the remainder of this document, we will focus on the standard set of user interface components and features of the OWL Plugin. Since all of these components are available as open-source, it is possible to extend and customize them.

5   Editing OWL Ontologies

In this section we will walk through some of the forms and tabs for editing classes and properties. Further details on the user interface (including a comparison with similar tools such as OilEd) can be found in complementary publications [10,9].

A screenshot of the OWL classes tab is shown in Figure 3. The main class hierarchy is shown on the left, and the details of the currently selected class are shown in a form on the right. The upper section of the class form displays class metadata such as names and annotations. Annotation properties are ignored by OWL DL reasoners. Instead, they are very suitable to manage metadata about a class, such as versioning information, comments, relationships to other external resources, and labels in multiple languages.

5.1   Displaying and Editing OWL Expressions

A key question for developers of an OWL tool is how to represent and edit logical class descriptions in a way that makes them easy to read and, at the same time, efficient to enter. With OWL's RDF-based syntax [16], expressions quickly become extremely verbose and hard to read. The OWL Abstract Syntax [17] is much more user-friendly, but still quite verbose. Although Protégé also has some support for the Abstract Syntax, we chose to develop an expression syntax based on standard DL symbols [1] such as $\forall$ and $\sqcup$ as the primary display format. These symbols (Table 1) allow the system to display complex nested expressions in a single row.

This notation is used consistently throughout the user interface and is supported by a comfortable expression editor. Using this editor, users can rapidly enter OWL class expressions either with mouse or keyboard. The special characters are mapped onto keys known from languages such as Java (e.g., `owl:intersectionOf` is entered with the & key). To simplify editing, keyboard users can exploit a syntax completion mechanism known from programming environments, which semi-automatically completes partial names after the user has pressed `tab`. For very complex expressions, users can open a multi-line editor in an extra window, which displays the expression using indentation.

The OWL Plugin helps new users to get acquainted with the expression syntax. English prose text is shown as a "tool tip" when the mouse is moved over the expression. For example, "$\exists$ *hasPet* Cat" is displayed as "Any object which has a cat as its pet".

5.2   Editing Class Descriptions

Traditional Protégé users are accustomed to an object-centered view to the interface that has required some effort to adapt to OWL. In the Protégé metamodel, classes are typically

Table 1. Protégé uses traditional description logic symbols to display OWL expressions. In this table, property names such as *hasChildren* appear in italics. A common naming convention is to use uppercase names such as Parent to represent classes, while individuals like yellow should be written in lower case.

OWL element	Symbol	Key	Example expression in Protégé
owl:allValuesFrom	∀	*	∀ *hasChildren* Female
owl:someValuesFrom	∃	?	∃ *hasHabitat* University
owl:hasValue	∋	$	*hasGender* ∋ male
owl:minCardinality	≥	>	*hasChildren* ≥ 1 (at least one value)
owl:maxCardinality	≤	<	*hasDegree* ≤ 5 (at most five values)
owl:cardinality	=	=	*hasGender* = 1 (exactly one value)
owl:intersectionOf	⊓	&	Student ⊓ Parent
owl:unionOf	⊔	|	Male ⊔ Female
owl:complementOf	¬	!	¬Parent
owl:oneOf	{ ... }	{ }	{yellow green red}

only related through simple superclass/subclass relationships, and therefore a simple tree view was enough to edit classes. OWL on the other hand not only distinguishes between necessary conditions (superclasses) and necessary and sufficient conditions (equivalent classes), but furthermore allows users to relate classes with arbitrary class expressions. As shown in Figure 3, the OWL Plugin's class editor addresses this complexity by means of a list of conditions, which is organized into blocks of necessary & sufficient, necessary, and inherited conditions. Each of the necessary & sufficient blocks represents a single equivalent intersection class, and only those inherited conditions are listed that have not been further restricted higher up in the hierarchy. In addition to the list of conditions, there is also a custom-tailored widget for entering disjoint classes, which has special support for typical design patterns such as making all siblings disjoint. This rather object-centered design of the OWL classes tab makes it possible to maintain the whole class definition on a single screen.

5.3 Editing Properties

The class form provides a listing of all properties for which instances of the selected class can take values. This includes those properties which have the class in their domain, and those that don't have any domain restrictions. The details of the properties are edited by means of a separate form. Similar to the class form, the upper part of the property form displays name and annotation properties. The lower part contains widgets for the property's domain, range, and characteristics such as whether a property is transitive or symmetric.

Note that Protégé and OWL support user-defined metaclasses that extend the standard system classes. For example, ontologies can define a subclass of owl:ObjectProperty and then add other properties to it. This allows users to specify additional property characteristics such as *hasUnit*. The system automatically creates widgets for the additional properties of the metaclass.

6   Ontology Maintenance and Evolution

As mentioned in Section 2, ontology design is a highly evolutionary process. Ontology developers almost certainly will need to explore various iterations before an ontology can be considered to be complete. A development tool should assist in ontology evolution, and (where appropriate) help the user to prevent or circumnavigate common design mistakes. In the OWL Plugin, we are exploring some promising approaches for ontology maintenance, partly comparable to modern tools for programming languages. With programming tools, developers can get instant feedback using the *compile* button. Compiler errors are listed below the source code and enable the programmer to quickly navigate to the affected area. Another very efficient means of detecting programming errors is using so-called *test cases*, which have become popular in conjunction with agile development approaches such as Extreme Programming [2]. A test case is a small piece of code that simulates a certain scenario and then tests whether the program behaves as expected. It is a good programming style to maintain a library of test cases together with the source code, and to execute all test cases from time to time to verify that none of the recent changes has broken existing functionality. To a certain extent, the idea of test cases is related to the formal class definitions in description logics such as OWL DL. For example, by formally stating that a Parent is the intersection of Person and a minimum cardinality restriction on the *hasChildren* property we ensure that future statements about Parents don't contradict the original developer's intention. This is especially important in an open-world scenario such as the Semantic Web. Thus, DL reasoners can help build and maintain sharable ontologies by revealing inconsistencies, hidden dependencies, redundancies, and misclassifications [14]. How the OWL Plugin integrates such reasoners is illustrated in Section 6.1. In addition to reasoners, the OWL Plugin also adopts the notions of test cases and compile buttons with an "ontology testing" feature, which is described in Section 6.2.

6.1   Reasoning Based on Description Logics

The OWL Plugin provides direct access to DL reasoners such as Racer [5]. The current user interface supports two types of DL reasoning: Consistency checking and classification (subsumption). Support for other types of reasoning, such as instance checking, is work in progress.

Consistency checking (i.e., the test whether a class could have instances) can be invoked either for all classes with a single mouse click, or for selected classes only. Inconsistent classes are marked with a red bordered icon.

Classification (i.e., inferring a new subsumption tree from the asserted definitions) can be invoked with the classify button on a one-shot basis. When the classify button is pressed, the system determines the OWL species, because some reasoners are unable to handle OWL Full ontologies. This is done using the validation service from the Jena library. If the ontology is in OWL Full (e.g., because metaclasses are used) the system attempts to convert the ontology temporarily into OWL DL. The OWL Plugin supports editing some features of OWL Full (e.g., assigning ranges to annotation properties, and creating metaclasses). These are easily detected and can be removed before the data are sent to the classifier. Once the ontology has been converted into OWL DL, a

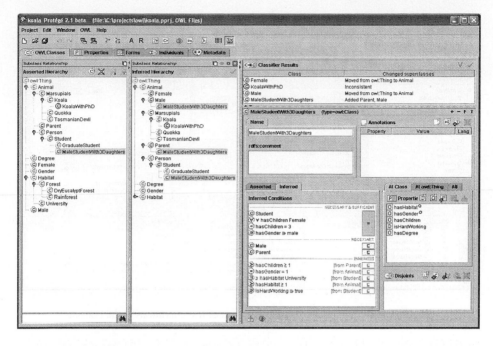

Fig. 4. The OWL Plugin can be used to invoke a classifier and to visualize classification results in support of ontology maintenance. The asserted and the inferred hierarchy are shown side by side.

full consistency check is performed, because inconsistent classes cannot be classified correctly. Finally, the classification results are stored until the next invocation of the classifier, and can be browsed separately. Classification can be invoked either for the whole ontology, or for selected subtrees only. In the latter case, the transitive closure of all accessible classes is sent to the classifier. This may return an incomplete classification because it does not take incoming edges into account, but in many cases it provides a reasonable approximation without having to process the whole ontology.

OWL files store only the subsumptions that have been asserted by the user. However, experience has shown that, in order to edit and correct their ontologies, users need to distinguish between what they have asserted and what the classifier has inferred. Many users may find it more natural to navigate the inferred hierarchy, because it displays the semantically correct position of all the classes.

The OWL Plugin addresses this need by displaying both hierarchies and making available extensive information on the inferences made during classification. As illustrated in Figure 4, after classification the OWL Plugin displays an inferred classification hierarchy beside the original asserted hierarchy. The classes that have changed their superclasses are highlighted in blue, and moving the mouse over them explains the changes. Furthermore, a complete list of all changes suggested by the classifier is shown in the upper right area, similar to a list of compiler messages. A click on an entry navigates to the affected class. Also, the conditions widget can be switched between asserted and inferred conditions. All this allows the users to analyze the changes quickly.

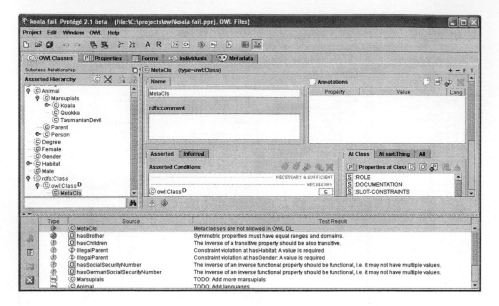

Fig. 5. The OWL Plugin displays violations of test conditions at the bottom.

6.2 Ontology Testing

The OWL Plugin provides a mechanism to execute small test cases. Users can press an ontology test button, and the system will execute a configurable list of tests. These tests are small Java programs that basically take a class, property, individual, or ontology as its input, verify arbitrary conditions on them, and in case of failure, return an error message. For example, one of the predefined tests ensures the invariant that the inverse of a transitive property should also be transitive. As illustrated in Figure 5, if a property in the ontology violates this conditions, then the system displays a warning. In some cases it even provides a "repair" button, which attempts to remove the source of the violation automatically.

The OWL Plugin provides a standard set of ontology tests for various best ontology design practices. It also contains tests against OWL DL compliance (e.g., to warn the user when OWL Full features such as metaclasses have been used). The ontology test mechanism has also been exploited to implement a simple but powerful "to-do-list" feature. For example, if a class has the value "TODO: Add German label" as its value of the *owl:versionInfo* annotation property, then the ontology test button will display a corresponding to-do item in the list of warnings. This simple mechanism helps coordinate shared ontology design efforts.

The list of standard ontology tests can be easily extended by programmers, so that the system will execute additional user-defined tests uniformly. These additional tests could for example ensure the application of project-specific design patterns, naming conventions, or other best practices.

7 Editing Semantic Web Contents

Ontologies provide Semantic Web agents with background knowledge about domain concepts and their relationships. This knowledge can be exploited in various ways, for example to drive context-sensitive search functions. Ontologies can also be instantiated to create individuals that describe Semantic Web resources or real-world entities. For example, individuals of an ontology for travel agents could represent specific holiday destinations or activities. In such a scenario, a Semantic Web repository would provide instance data about these individuals, and agents can use their ontological knowledge to match user requests with available offers.

Protégé provides out-of-the-box support for editing individuals. The OWL Plugin's *Individuals* tab can be used to instantiate classes from the ontology, and to edit the characteristics of the individuals with comfortable forms. Users could import an ontology into their project, create instances for its classes, and then store the instances into separate files. These files can then be distributed on the Web, so that intelligent agents could find them.

In another application scenario, Protégé could be used to associate existing Web resources such as images to ontological concepts. In the context of another Protégé plugin, we have implemented a convenient drag-and-drop mechanism that allows users to drag a Web link or image from their Web browser into Protégé, and thus establish a relationship between the external Web resource and the selected object in the ontology. These relationships could be exploited by arbitrary Web Services. Thus, Protégé is not only limited to being used as an ontology authoring tool, but also as a platform for arbitrary other services that *use* the ontologies.

8 Discussion

While real Semantic Web applications are still in their infancy, there is a clear demand for tools that assist in application development. The intention of the Protégé OWL Plugin is to make Semantic Web technology available to a broad group of developers and users, and to promote best practices and design patterns.

One of the major benefits of using Protégé is its open architecture. The system provides various mechanisms to hook custom-tailored extensions into it, so that external components like reasoners and Web services can be integrated easily. Since the source code is open and freely available as well, existing base components can be used as templates for customized solutions. Projects don't need to spend time developing their own base infrastructure with standard features such as loading and managing OWL ontologies. Instead, they can start with the OWL Plugin as it comes out-of-the-box and then gradually adapt or remove the features that don't completely match their requirements.

Since its first beta versions in late 2003, the OWL Plugin has been widely embraced by OWL users around the world. Although we don't have exact numbers and statistics about our users, we know that Protégé has more than 20,000 registered users. Of these, a significant portion is very interested in OWL and many use it routinely. The protege-owl@smi.stanford.edu discussion list currently has more than 650 subscribed members. The traffic on this list is very large and provides useful critiques for the developers, as well as encouraging feedback and success stories. There is already a considerable number of external plugins for the OWL Plugin, demonstrating that the open architecture of Protégé provides a suitable platform for custom extensions. Also, many existing Protégé Plugins either directly work in OWL mode, or are being optimized for OWL.

The decision to implement the OWL Plugin as an extension to Protégé did not have only advantages though. In particular, the Protégé core metamodel and API support some functionality that does not have a default mapping into OWL, such as numeric range restrictions, assigning duplicate values to a property, or stating that a class is abstract (i.e., cannot have any instances). As a result, some existing widgets could not be used in the OWL mode, and programmers should not use all low-level API functions. We have made some efforts to simulate some Protégé-specific language elements with OWL. For example, if users want to state that a class is abstract, then the system fills a pre-defined annotation property. Furthermore, invalid API calls are rejected whenever possible. We believe that the many advantages of reusing the functionality and components of the Protégé platform clearly outweigh these inconveniences.

Another point to keep in mind is that the existing collection of user interface components in the OWL Plugin should only be regarded as a core configuration. For example, many users may be put off by the symbolic notation used to edit class expressions. These users often don't require the advanced description logic features of OWL but simply want to define classes and properties similar to the conventional Protégé user interface or object-oriented tools. These users may find it helpful to simplify their user interface. This would allow them to use the advanced features later, once they are accustomed to the basics of OWL. We have recently added an alternative default mode of the OWL Classes tab (called "Properties View"), which shows properties together with their restrictions instead of the generic conditions widget. This view is closer to the view that traditional Protégé users are accustomed to, but has some limitations on the full expressivity of OWL.

The focus of our work on the OWL Plugin until now has been to provide a complete, scalable and stable editor for most of the features of OWL (Full). Ongoing and future work addresses the question of how to make ontology design more accessible to people with limited formal training in description logics. In this context, we collaborate with the University of Manchester to explore more intuitive visual editing components, wizards, and debugging aids. We will also support additional design patterns, improve reasoning capabilities, and build editors and APIs for OWL extensions such as SWRL.

Acknowledgements. This work has been funded by a contract from the US National Cancer Institute and by grant P41LM007885 from the National Library of Medicine. Additional support for this work came from the UK Joint Information Services Committee under the CO-ODE grant. Our partners from Alan Rector's team and the OilEd developers at the University of Manchester have made very valuable contributions.

References

1. F. Baader, D. Calvanese, D. McGuineness, D. Nardi, and P. Patel-Schneider, editors. *The Description Logic Handbook.* Cambridge University Press, 2003.
2. K. Beck. *Extreme Programming Explained: Embrace Change.* Addison-Wesley, 1999.
3. T. Berners-Lee, J. Hendler, and O. Lassila. The Semantic Web. *Scientific American,* 284(5):34–43, 2001.
4. J. Gennari, M. Musen, R. Fergerson, W. Grosso, M. Crubézy, H. Eriksson, N. Noy, and S. Tu. The evolution of Protégé-2000: An environment for knowledge-based systems development. *International Journal of Human-Computer Studies,* 58(1):89–123, 2003.
5. V. Haarslev and R. Moeller. Racer: A core inference engine for the Semantic Web. In *2nd International Workshop on Evaluation of Ontology-based Tools (EON-2003),* Sanibel Island, FL, 2003.
6. I. Horrocks and P. F. Patel-Schneider. A proposal for an OWL rules language. In *Proc. of the Thirteenth International World Wide Web Conference (WWW 2004),* New York City, NY.
7. I. Horrocks, P. F. Patel-Schneider, and F. van Harmelen. From SHIQ and RDF to OWL: The making of a web ontology language. *Journal of Web Semantics,* 1(1), 2003.
8. H. Knublauch. An AI tool for the real world: Knowledge modeling with Protégé. *JavaWorld,* June 20, 2003.
9. H. Knublauch, O. Dameron, and M. A. Musen. Weaving the biomedical semantic web with the Protégé OWL plugin. In *International Workshop on Formal Biomedical Knowledge Representation,* Whistler, BC, Canada, 2004.
10. H. Knublauch, M. A. Musen, and A. L. Rector. Editing description logics ontologies with the Protégé OWL plugin. In *International Workshop on Description Logics,* Whistler, BC, Canada, 2004.
11. N. Noy, R. Fergerson, and M. Musen. The knowledge model of Protégé-2000: Combining interoperability and flexibility In *2nd International Conference on Knowledge Engineering and Knowledge Management (EKAW'2000),* Juan-les-Pins, France, 2000.
12. N. Noy, M. Sintek, S. Decker, M. Crubézy, R. Fergerson, and M. Musen. Creating Semantic Web contents with Protégé-2000. *IEEE Intelligent Systems,* 2(16):60–71, 2001.
13. N. F. Noy and D. L. McGuinness. Ontology development 101: A guide to creating your first ontology. Technical Report SMI-2001-0880, Stanford Medical Informatics, 2001.
14. A. L. Rector. Description logics in medical informatics. Chapter in [1].
15. A. L. Rector. Modularisation of domain ontologies implemented in description logics and related formalisms including OWL. In *Second International Conference on Knowledge Capture (K-CAP),* Sanibel Island, FL, 2003.
16. World Wide Web Consortium. OWL Web Ontology Language Reference. W3C Recommendation 10 Feb, 2004.
17. World Wide Web Consortium. OWL Web Ontology Language Semantics and Abstract Syntax. W3C Recommendation 10 Feb, 2004.

OntoTrack: Combining Browsing and Editing with Reasoning and Explaining for OWL Lite Ontologies

Thorsten Liebig and Olaf Noppens

Dept. of Artificial Intelligence
University of Ulm
D-89069 Ulm
{liebig|noppens}@informatik.uni-ulm.de

Abstract. OntoTrack is a new browsing and editing "in-one-view" ontology authoring tool that combines a hierarchical graphical layout and instant reasoning feedback for (the most rational fraction of) OWL Lite. OntoTrack provides an animated and zoomable view with context sensitive features like click-able miniature branches or selective detail views together with drag-and-drop editing. Each editing step is instantly synchronized with an external reasoner in order to provide appropriate graphical feedback about relevant modeling consequences. The most recent feature of OntoTrack is an on demand textual explanation for subsumption and equivalence between or unsatisfiability of classes. This paper describes the key features of the current implementation and discusses future work as well as some development issues.

1 Introduction

High quality ontologies are crucial for the Semantic Web [1]. Unfortunately, the task of building and maintaining mature ontologies turned out to be difficult even for KR experts. The analysis of three different efforts of formalizing knowledge for a given domain within the Halo project [2] may serve as a prime example here. This evaluation showed, that up to 75 % of the system failures were caused by modeling problems which in most cases were concerned with the act of writing down non-conflicting axioms [3]. In order to avoid those modeling problems the authors suggest to enforce development of convenient and interactive tools for building, maintaining and evaluating ontologies.

However, many ontology authoring tools currently use functionally disjunct interfaces for either editing, browsing, or reasoning with ontologies. Editing interfaces commonly use list-based representations for selection of classes or properties together with predefined forms and pop-up windows for manipulation in an additional display area. From a usability perspective, those interfaces inherently have substantial drawbacks concerning search and navigation speed as well as user orientation and editing efficiency in our opinion [4]. First, the number of visible classes is limited by the screen height requiring scrolling even for middle

S.A. McIlraith et al. (Eds.): ISWC 2004, LNCS 3298, pp. 244–258, 2004.

sized ontologies. Second, because of the tree centered representation, multiple inheritance needs to be approximated with help of "cloned" classes appearing in the list of descendants of every superclass. Third, accessing or selecting other classes during editing temporally requires additional expand and contract style selection lists for a class hierarchy already on screen.

In order to compensate some of those deficits most editors include additional browsing interfaces based on layout techniques like nested interchangeable views [5], venn diagrams [6], spring embedding [7], or hyperbolic trees [8], [9]. However, the majority of those interfaces do not allow for substantial editing and are designed as view-only plugins in most cases. Furthermore, hyperbolic tree visualization is based on a mapping of euclidian to hyperbolic geometry typically resulting in translocation of nodes after each focus change [10]. In addition, hyperbolic trees have the disadvantage of "fisheye distortion" which makes it difficult to read off-center labels for example. Other visualization techniques like tree maps or venn diagrams heavily exploit nested graphical structurings overlapped with edges, obscuring the greater structure of ontologies in most cases. In our opinion, none of these layout techniques are well suited for typical ontology browsing tasks like comparison of different expansion paths concerning level depth or common ancestors.

ONTOTRACK implements a novel approach using one integrated view for straightforward browsing, manipulating, and understanding even large OWL Lite schemas (also called TBoxes in Description Logics). Within this view ontologies are layouted as directed root graphs according to their primary structuring relation, the subsumption relationship. ONTOTRACK provides animated expansion and de-expansion of class descendants, continuous zooming, panning and uses elaborated layout techniques like click-able miniature branches or selective detail views. At the same time ONTOTRACK allows for quite a number of editing features like mouse-over anchor buttons and graphical selections without switching into a special editing layout. In addition, every single editing step is send to an external reasoner in order to make implicit modeling consequences explicitly available for graphical feedback. ONTOTRACK is currently enhanced with an on demand component for textual explanation of subsumption and equivalence between or unsatisfiability of classes.

The remainder of this paper is organized as follows. The next section contains a detailed description of the ontology authoring tool ONTOTRACK. In section 3 we discuss some implementation issues and describe the system architecture as well as work in progress. We will end with an outlook about possible future extensions.

2   OntoTrack: A New Graphical Authoring Tool for OWL Lite⁻

ONTOTRACK is a multi-platform Java application combining authoring of ontologies with reasoning about ontologies. As a consequence, running ONTOTRACK requires to have access to an appropriate reasoning system. Currently,

ONTOTRACK is adapted to the RACER server [11] via its TCP-based client interface.

The next subsection specifies the OWL language constructs ONTOTRACK is currently able to handle. For sake of broad usability and a clear and concise graphical representation we restrict this language to a sensible fraction of OWL Lite. This is followed by a more detailed explanation of ONTOTRACKs browsing, editing, reasoning as well as explaining abilities.

2.1   OWL Lite⁻: A Sensible Fraction of OWL Lite

ONTOTRACK is designed to be an authoring tool for ontology languages with an expressivity almost comparable to that of OWL Lite. The expressivity of OWL Lite is about that of the DL language $\mathcal{SHIF}(\mathbf{D})$ [12]. OWL Lite is a fraction of OWL DL aiming to provide a useful subset of language features, that are easier to present to naive users and relatively straightforward for tool developers to support [13]. In particular, OWL Lite excludes syntax constructs for unions, complements, and individuals in descriptions or class axioms. In addition, it limits cardinalities to either 0 or 1 and nested descriptions to concept identifiers. However, these restrictions come with relatively little loss in expressive power. With help of indirection and syntactical "tricks" all of OWL DL can be captured in OWL Lite except those descriptions containing either individuals or cardinalities greater than 1 [12]. Atomic negation for example, is easily simulated via complementary cardinality restrictions (e. g. $A \equiv (\geq 1\ r)$ and $negA \equiv (\leq 0\ r)$, where r is a new property). A general concept inclusion (GCI) is expressible by introducing two new classes with one complete and one partial definition for each class (e. g. $C \sqsubseteq D$ together with two complete class descriptions for C and D). A disjunction of two (or more) classes A and B can be simulated by negating the conjunction of the negation of A and B (following the laws of deMorgan and double negation). E. g. the expression $(A \sqcup B)$ is semantically equivalent to $negD$ where $negD \equiv (\leq 0\ q)$ and $D \equiv (negA \sqcap negB) \equiv (\geq 1\ q)$.

Simulating GCIs or disjunction in OWL Lite with help of multiple definitions for a single class identifier is kind of obscure and obviously conflicts with the design goal of OWL Lite. Very likely most of the above will rarely occur in real world OWL Lite ontologies. Instead, users will presumably use OWL DL when it comes to disjunction or GCIs for a certain application domain. Beyond that, there is no intuitive and unambiguous way for rendering classes with multiple, possibly mixed partial and complete, definitions. We therefore decided to restrict the usage of OWL Lite in a way we believe it was originally intended by the language designers itself (called OWL Lite⁻ in the following). In particular, we restrict classes to be defined only once in a way that could be equally expressed by one single `owl:equivalentClass` or `rdfs:subClassOf` statement over the conjunction of the collection of superclasses and restrictions (i. e. the definition of a class A is A ⊑ D or A ≡ D where A is an atomic name and has no other definition). In terms of the normative abstract syntax and semantic of OWL Lite [14] this prohibits the use of the *EquivalentClasses* axiom. As a result, GCIs and disjunction are not expressible within OWL Lite⁻.

Within this context, it is worth mentioning that different analyses of online available ontologies (e. g. [15] or [16]) showed, that most users only exploit a very limited set of the available language constructs. More concrete, only a very small fraction of those ontologies would be outside the scope of the OWL Lite subset processable with ONTOTRACK.

2.2 Browsing

The primary structuring element of ontologies is the subsumption relationship between classes and properties. Consequently, ONTOTRACK layouts an ontology as a directed acyclic graph with either classes or properties as nodes and the subsumption relationship as directed edges either in top-down, left-right, bottom-up, or right-left orientation. The drawn hierarchy may vary from the explicitly given subclass statements of the loaded ontology source document. This is due to ONTOTRACKS most important layout principle aiming to visualize the most relevant ontological commitments only. As a consequence, ONTOTRACK will only show direct subsumption relationships while hiding all those which are redundant due to the transitivity of this relationship. Furthermore, by taking modeling consequences explicitly into account, ONTOTRACK is sensitive not only to syntactically given but also to semantically implied subsumption relationships.

Figure 1 shows the ONTOTRACK application window. It solely consists of a menu bar, a search bar, and a combined browsing and manipulation area.

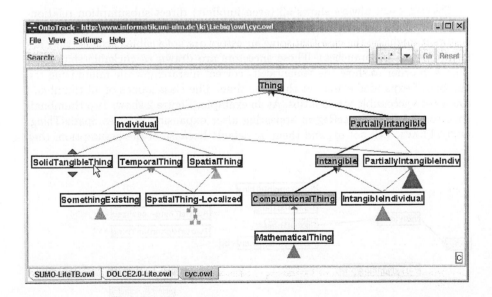

Fig. 1. Upper fraction of the OpenCyc ontology with triangle and miniature subbranches. Anchor buttons for SolidTangibleThing show up because of mouse over action.

ONTOTRACK can handle multiple ontologies in parallel, which are accessible via corresponding tabs at the bottom of the application window. The ontology displayed in Figure 1 is a fraction of the OpenCyc knowledge base (version 0.7) in top-down orientation. Note, that the subsumption path of the currently selected class (ComputationalThing) up to the OWL root class (Thing) is outlined by a darker node background and thicker edges in order to provide an optimal overview concerning depth and branching.

As an option, not expanded sub-branches of classes are rendered as triangles of varying length, width, and shading, approximating the depth, branching and number of subclasses (see class SomethingExisting in Figure 1 for an example). Depending on the number of descendants, a not expanded sub-branch will alternatively be symbolized as a miniature graph in order to give an overview about the structure of the sub-branch (see SpatialThing-Localized in Figure 1). The icons of miniature graphs are expandable on mouse click and show their class names via mouse-over tool tip. In addition, the whole ontology layout can continously be zoomed or panned simply by right button mouse-down movements.

The direct descendants of a class are expanded resp. de-expanded in an animated fashion on left mouse button click. ONTOTRACKs ontology layout is driven by the expansion direction of the user. The layout strategy aims at "clustering" the descendants of a selected class (locally simulating an ordinary tree representation). This means that an ontology with multiple inheritance may end up with a different layout for exactly the same set of expanded classes – depending on the users expansion order.

ONTOTRACK always shows all (even implicit) direct subsumption relationships between classes. However, when dealing with classes having multiple ancestors it might be the case that some ancestors are not visible (because they are in not expanded branches). Those ancestors are drawn as clickable thumbnail classes in order to show the semantically correct hierarchy while minimizing the number of expanded classes at the same time. The class names of all thumbnail classes are accessible via tool tips. As an example, Figure 2 shows two thumbnail ancestors of class SpaceRegion appearing after expansion of class SpatialThing. ONTOTRACK will not expand them by default because of the assumption, that

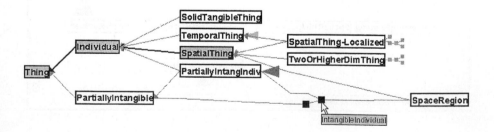

Fig. 2. Ancestor thumbnails of class SpaceRegion after expansion of class SpatialThing.

the user is much more interested in the descendants of SpatialThing (the user actually asked for) instead of their ancestors.

An auxiliary navigation feature of ONTOTRACK is the radar view, which will appear in the upper left corner of the workspace only if the ontology will exceed the available rendering area at its current scale factor. The radar view consists of a miniaturized graph of the current ontology expansion and an overlayed rectangle representing the current rendering area. The latter can be moved via mouse which will result in a corresponding relocation of the original view. Figure 9 shows a larger ontology together with a radar view.

ONTOTRACK also implements a string matching search with graphical highlighting based on the principles of the dynamic query approach [17]. Each modification of the search string directly results in an updated highlighting of matching parts of the ontology (expanded or not). Figure 3 shows the sub-string matches

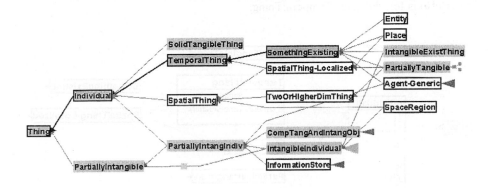

Fig. 3. Match highlighting for sub-string search for "ang" within class names.

for the search string "ang" within class identifiers. Note, that even thumbnails or triangle sub-branches are highlighted. Optionally, the user can fan out the ontology resulting in an expansion of all matching classes via one click.

2.3 Editing

Browsing and editing in ONTOTRACK is done within one single view. This allows to re-use already available navigation principles for the task of building and manipulating ontology definitions. A new sub- or superclass can easily be added by using ONTOTRACKs anchor mode for example. Here, clickable triangle buttons appear when moving with the mouse pointer over a class node (see class SolidTangibleThing in Figure 1). These anchor buttons allow for specifying an additional superclass or new subclass via mouse click and are sensible with respect to the layout orientation. An existing subclass relationship can be changed via mouse drag-and-drop or deleted by selection and "Del"-key usage as long as this relationship is not implied by other logical axioms of the ontology.

In addition, ONTOTRACK offers further editing functions while in its "detailed view" mode. The detailed view mode is activated or deactivated for each class separately using the mouse-wheel down- resp. up-wards while being over the class with the mouse pointer (alternatively PgDown/PgUp). When activated, ONTOTRACK uses an UML-style class diagram showing the list of defined property restrictions for this class in abstract DL syntax in its bottom compartment. ONTOTRACK currently supports all OWL Lite restrictions: unqualified cardinality restrictions ($\leq$, $\geq$, $=$ with cardinality 0 or 1) as well as existential and universal ($\exists$, $\forall$) quantifications. A restriction can be deleted by clicking on the round (red) button at the right hand side of the corresponding row and a new restriction will be added by clicking on the round (green) button at the bottom of the class box. At present, properties as well as classes within those restrictions are chosen with help of selection lists. In future versions, properties as well as classes may be selectable by mouse click. The example in Figure 4 shows some restrictions for the class TemporalThing.

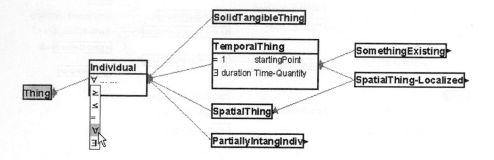

Fig. 4. Detailed view mode for classes Individual and TemporalThing with restrictions resp. specification of an universal quantification.

Semantically, a class is equivalent to (if complete) or subclass of (if partial) the conjunction of the collection of superclasses and restrictions in ONTOTRACK.

Additional editing features like class deletion or switching between complete and partial definitions are accessible via a right mouse button context menu. In order to visually distinguish between a complete and a partial class definition[1] we adopt the UML notation of *derived types* for complete class definitions. In concrete, a complete class definition is characterized by a slanted line in the upper left corner of the class box (see Figure 8 for examples).

In addition to the class hierarchy view, ONTOTRACK also provides an analogous graphical representation for properties. Here, different detailed property views allow for manipulation of global domain and range restrictions, global car-

---

[1] In OWL Lite⁻ we allow for exactly one definition per class identifier (see subsection 2.1).

dinality constraints as well as logical characteristics of the property with help of selection lists or checkboxes as exemplarily shown in Figure 5.

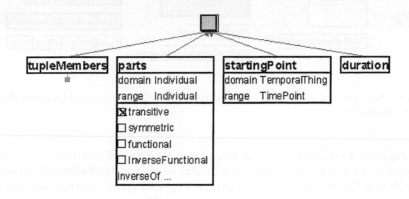

Fig. 5. Property hierarchy with examples of different detailed view modes.

As an extra feature, the property representation can be rendered as a read-only transparent layer onto the class representation and vice versa. The transparency rate of the secondary layer is freely adjustable.

2.4   Reasoning

As mentioned before, ONTOTRACK is equipped with an interface for interaction with an external OWL reasoner, namely RACER. All changes after each editing step (e.g. list selection, subclass manipulation) are immediately send to RACER. This reasoner will then make all modeling consequences explicitly available. ONTOTRACK will hand over relevant consequences to the user by providing appropriate graphical feedback. Relevant consequences currently cover subsumption and equivalence between as well as unsatisfiability of classes. For example, adding an existential restriction (minimal or exact cardinality restriction with 1 or existential quantification) on a property with a domain restriction will result in a subsumption relationship between the edited class and the property domain. Those updates are also animated in order not to confuse the user with a new hierarchy layout in one step.

As an example, in Figure 6 we have a contradiction between a restriction in class Individual and a restriction in class TemporalThing. The latter requires exactly one filler for the property duration. The restriction in class Individual however demands for exactly zero fillers. As a consequence, TemporalThing and all subclasses thereof are unsatisfiable and therefore outlined in red.

Note, that the last edited class is not necessarily the (only) one which potentially will become inconsistent. ONTOTRACK will therefore query its reasoner for conflicting or equivalent definitions in any part of the ontology after each

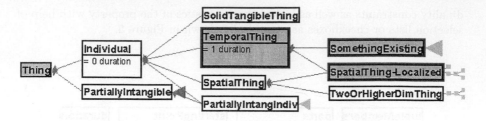

Fig. 6. Contradicting restrictions cause TemporalThing (and at least all its descendants) to be unsatisfiable.

editing step. Concerning the example shown in Figure 6 one may notice that there is at least one unsatisfiable descendant of PartiallyIntangibleIndiv (its sub-branch triangle is colored red). This user triggered query strategy also applies for implicit subsumption relationships between classes.

2.5   Explaining

Providing feedback about the logical consequences of recent user changes help users to check for imprecise, redundant or faulty modeling. Important consequences with respect to an ontology authoring tool are subsumption, equivalence and unsatisfiability. Those consequences often depend on logical interrelations of nested definitions, which itself may depend on other definitions. As a result, most consequences are not easily traceable or intuitive to non-experienced users. Current reasoning systems provide no or only limited support for explanation of logical consequences.[2] ONTOTRACKs most recent extention is a prototypical facility for an on demand explanation of subsumption, equivalence and unsatisfiability. This component is based on the work of Borgida et. al. [19] about a sequent calculus for $\mathcal{ALC}$. In [19] the authors sketch an extended DL tableaux algorithm for the generation of sequent proof steps needed for explanation. However, currently available tableaux reasoners potentially capable of handling OWL are either not avaliable as source code or based on highly optimized algorithms not easily extensible for explanation generation. We therefore implemented our own tableaux based explanation generator for ONTOTRACK.

Currently, this component is able to generate explanations within unfoldable $\mathcal{ALEN}$ ontologies, i. e. ontologies with unique acyclic definitions (negation and disjunction comes implicit due to the refutation strategy of the tableaux proofs). The actual prototype uses a naive tableaux implementation with lazy unfolding. It will generate a quasi natural language explanation compiled of text patterns which correspond to applied rules of the underlying tableaux proof. Note, that this explanation facility does not aim to replace RACER as core reasoning component and will only be activated on user request.

---

[2] The CLASSIC system is a notable exception here [18].

Explanation for A ⊑ B:

It holds that A is subsumed by B:

A ⊑ B

which is equivalent to the unfolded subsumption problem:

$(\exists r E) \sqcap (\forall r C) \sqsubseteq (\exists r D)$

In order to check that $(\exists r E)$ and $(\forall r C)$ is subsumed by $(\exists r D)$ we need to check whether the conjunction of E and C is subsumed by D:

E ⊓ C ⊑ D

which is equivalent to the unfolded subsumption problem:

$E \sqcap (\exists q E) \sqsubseteq (\geq 1 q)$

In order to check that $(\exists q E)$ is subsumed by $(\geq 1 q)$ we need to check whether E is subsumed by Thing:

E ⊑ Thing

By definition everything is subsumed by Thing.

Fig. 7. Explanation of a subsumption relationship of an example ontology shown in Figure 8.

Figure 7 displays a textual explanation of the subsumption relationship between the two classes A and B which would appear in a separate window.

Figure 8 shows the relevant definitions and their graphical representation in ONTOTRACK of the appertaining ontology within this small explanation example of Figure 7 (which has been adapted from an example in [19]).

```
ObjectProperty(r)
ObjectProperty(q)
Class(E partial)
Class(A complete
        restriction(r someValuesFrom(E))
        restriction(r allValuesFrom(C)))
Class(C complete
        restriction(q someValuesFrom(E)))
Class(B complete
        restriction(r someValuesFrom(D)))
Class(D complete
        restriction(q minCardinality(1)))
```

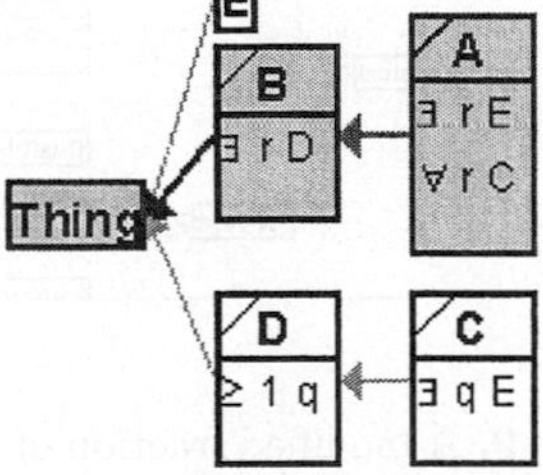

Fig. 8. Example ontology for subsumption explanation in OWL abstract syntax as well as in ONTOTRACK (relevant definitions are shown in detailed view mode).

3   Implementation Issues and Current Work

A recent analysis of online available ontologies [15] showed, that most ontologies contain more than hundred classes. Upcoming ontologies very likely will consist of several hundreds of classes presumably referencing dozen of other ontologies. Obviously, performance and scalability of ontology authoring tools are key for user acceptance and wide adoption of Semantic Web techniques. We therefore have chosen Piccolo [20] as our graphical library for ONTOTRACK, which has proven to be sufficiently fast and reliable even for large numbers of graphical objects. Piccolo is a Java2D interface toolkit supporting animation, zooming, multiple cameras, layers, etc. Our implementation of ONTOTRACKs visualization components also adopts the linked tree diagram approach of SpaceTree [10] which itself uses the Piccolo toolkit. SpaceTree makes use of elaborated layout techniques to dynamically zoom and layout tree branches in an animated fashion. Figure 9 shows, that ONTOTRACKs layout technique is even suitable to depict the greater structure of ontologies with more than 60 classes.

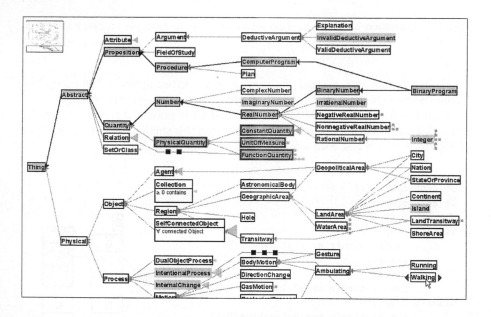

Fig. 9. A modified fraction of the IEEE SUMO ontology [21] with more than 60 classes expanded and radar view in the upper left corner.

For importing and exporting of ontologies we use the Jena 2.1 [22] RDF API and parser functionality. ONTOTRACKs core ontology model is also based on Jena which we enriched with a high-level event notification mechanism needed for propagating changes from the core model to their corresponding graphical or external reasoner representations resp. vice versa.

The RACER server is used to provide reasoning feedback about logical implied consequences. However, implementing this feedback functionality turned out to become difficult for some reasons. For example, in order to become aware of a new subsumption relationship due to a just added property restriction, ONTOTRACK needs to query the reasoner about direct superclasses for almost all classes of the ontology in turn.[3] Instead of querying for all possible changes with respect to a specific consequence for each editing step we would like to have an event-triggered publish-subscribe mechanism on reasoner side [23]. Another problem is concerned with incremental reasoning and retraction of definitions. Because of lack of algorithms for appropriately handling incremental additions to a knowledge base [24] complete reclassification after each user interaction is necessary.

A current extension is concerned with the handling of direct and follow-up consequences of user changes. E. g. a user manipulation may result in one unsatisfiable class (not necessarily the one which has been changed) or even many unsatisfiable classes in worst case. Depending on this outcome the editor should inform or even warn the user about the impact of his action in order to identify faulty modeling as early as possible.

ONTOTRACKs prototypical explanation facility is currently implemented in CommonLisp as an external component in parallel to RACER. In order to avoid redundant computation, it is desired to combine reasoning and explaining within one system component in the future. Beyond that, we plan to enhance the explanation presentation with additional mouse-enabled features and different levels of detail information.

Current work also focuses on further editing features. Comments, labels as well as ontology header information are imported as well as exported correctly but are not editable in ONTOTRACK at the moment. We also work on the integration of further editing and searching functionality like undo operations or regular expression search. Because of user demand we also plan to add a view-only mode for OWL DL ontologies with a detail view showing OWL abstract syntax. Actual graphical extensions cover the optional visualization of entailed disjointness between classes.

4   Summary and Outlook

The broad adoption of Semantic Web technology strongly depends on the availability of convenient and flexible tools for browsing, editing, and evaluation of ontologies. A clear presentation, intuitive editing abilities, and subsidiary reasoning services are key properties of ontology editors suitable even for users

---

[3] One could of course narrow this set to those classes that also have an explicit or inherited restriction on that particular property or a subproperty thereof. But this requires to have explicit knowledge about inherited restrictions or subproperties, which in turn may result in additional queries.

without much logical background. Traditional expand and contract style interfaces, template based editing forms, or tree-centered visualizations inherently have substantial drawbacks in this respect. To our knowledge, there is currently no appropriate tool for displaying the greater structure of more than 60 directly editable classes together with additional information about unsatisfiable classes, selective detail information and search results, as it is shown in Figure 9.

Our new ontology authoring tool ONTOTRACK combines navigation and direct manipulation in one single hierarchical view together with instant reasoning feedback and rudiments of an explanation component. We see ONTOTRACK as a first step towards an easy-to-use interactive ontology editor even for non experienced users and large ontologies.

Future work will be concerned with the visualization and manipulation of individuals in ONTOTRACK, either with help of an additional visualization component optimized for this purpose (e. g. like in [25]) or embedded within our current hierarchy-based layout.

Support for cross ontology references between different definitions is also a point of further investigations and are still under discussion within the Web Ontology Working Group [26]. In a first naive approach our plan was to draw a superclass from a different ontology as a thumbnail ancestor using a dashed subsumption link (in order to distinguish between local and external ancestors). In case of selecting such an ancestor the corresponding ontology should be loaded and expanded up to the referred class in a new tab of ONTOTRACK. Unfortunately, this functionality bears some problems regarding import statements and referencing mechanisms of OWL/RDF. E. g. OWL allows to distribute a class specification across multiple definitions at various RDF documents. It is even possible to define a class bearing a virtual URI not related to any of the defining documents. Now, when referring to this class from elsewhere its corresponding definition cannot be found at the URI implied by the class ID. In other words, we can't infer the location of a definition from its URI reference. Beyond that, the meaning of the referenced description can only be taken into account when importing those documents which contain RDF triples about the description. Furthermore, the notion of an ontology is an additional but optional structuring concept within OWL. In fact, the relationship between class/property descriptions and an ontology definition is unclear. More complex, even it is optional or may appear more than once in a document, an ontology header is the only way to import other documents. This means that a serious OWL authoring tool needs to carefully distinguish between documents, ontologies and references.

Another serious issue of general future research is concerned with debugging of ontologies not developed from scratch within ONTOTRACK. Here standard inference services provide only little help to resolve inconsistencies in logical incoherent ontologies. In [27] a new reasoning service for pinpointing logical contradictions within $\mathcal{ALC}$ ontologies has been introduced. A likewise methodology would obviously be helpful within ONTOTRACK.

Other novel inference services intended to support building an ontology have been developed (see sec. 6.3 in [28] for a summary). One interesting service consists of matching of class patterns against class descriptions in order to find already defined classes with a similar structure. Another approach tries to create class definitions by generalizing one or more user given ABox assertions. Other non-standard inference services like least common subsumer (e. g. like in [29]) or most specific concept are also relevant during authoring of ontologies.

We also see ONTOTRACK as a platform for further tasks like cooperative ontology construction, ontology merging and alignment, or ontology evaluation.

This contribution tries to inspire the Semantic Web community in two ways. Concerning research we hope to stimulate the development of non-standard inference services and incremental reasoning systems. On user side we aim to motivate even non experienced domain experts to build, understand and use ontologies more widely in order to push the Semantic Web from academia to industry.

References

1. Baader, F., Horrocks, I., Sattler, U.: Description Logics as Ontology Languages for the Semantic Web. In Hutter, D., Stephan, W., eds.: Festschrift in honor of Jörg Siekmann. Lecture Notes in Artificial Intelligence, Springer (2003) To appear.
2. Project-Website: Project Halo. http://www.projecthalo.com/ (2004)
3. Fiedland, N.S., Allen, P.G., Witbrock, M., Matthews, G., Salay, N., Miraglia, P., Angele, J., Stab, S., Israel, D., Chaudhri, V., Porter, B., Barker, K., Clark, P.: Towards a Quantitative, Plattform-Independent Analysis of Knowledge Systems. In: Proc. of the Ninth International Conference on Principles of Knowledge Representation and Reasoning, Whistler, BC, Canada, AAAI Press (2004) 507–514
4. Liebig, T., Noppens, O.: OntoTrack: Fast Browsing and Easy Editing of Large Ontologies. In: Proc. of the 2nd International Workshop on Evaluation of Ontology-based Tools (EON2003), Sanibel Island, USA (2003)
5. Storey, M.A., Musen, M., Silvia, J., Best, C., Ernst, N., Fergerson, Noy, N.: Jambalaya: Interactive visualization to enhance ontology authoring and knowledge acquisition in Protégé. In: Proc. of the Workshop on Interactive Tools for Knowledge Capture (K-CAP 2001), Victoria B.C., Canada (2001)
6. Kalyanpur, A.: Venn diagram approach for visualizing OWL in SVG. University of Maryland, http://www.mindswap.org/~aditkal/svg_owl.shtml (2003)
7. Mutton, P., Golbeck, J.: Visualization of Semantic Metadata and Ontologies. In: Proc. of Information Visualization 2003 (IV03), London, UK (2003)
8. Eklund, P., Green, S., Roberts, N.: OntoRama: Browsing RDF Ontologies Using a Hyperbolic Browser. In: Proc. of the 1st International Symposium on Cyber Worlds (CW2002), Tokyo, Japan (2001)
9. Hu, B., Shadbolt, N.: Visualising a DL Knowledge Base with DeLogViz. In: Proc. of the International Workshop on Description Logics (DL2003), Rome, Italy (2003)
10. Plaisant, C., Grosjean, J., Bederson, B.B.: SpaceTree: Supporting Exploration in Large Node Link Tree, Design Evolution and Empirical Evaluation. In: Proc. of the IEEE Symposium on Information Visualization (INFOVIS 2002), Boston, USA (2002) 57 – 64
11. Haarslev, V., Möller, R.: RACER System Description. In: Proc. of the International Joint Conference on Automated Reasoning (IJCAR'2001), Siena, Italy, Springer Verlag (2001) 701–705

12. Horrocks, I., Patel-Schneider, P.F., van Harmelen, F.: From SHIQ and RDF to OWL: The making of a web ontology language. Journal of Web Semantics **1** (2003) 7–26
13. Bechhofer, S., van Harmelen, F., Hendler, J., Horrocks, I., McGuinness, D.L., Patel-Schneider, P., Stein, L.A.: OWL Web Ontology Language Reference. W3C Recommendation (2004)
14. Patel-Schneider, P., Hayes, P., Horrocks, I.: OWL Web Ontology Language Semantics and Abstract Syntax. W3C Recommendation (2004)
15. Tempich, C., Volz, R.: Towards a benchmark for Semantic Web reasoners – an analysis of the DAML ontology library. In: Proc. of the 2nd International Workshop on Evaluation of Ontology-based Tools (EON2003), Sanibel Island, USA (2003)
16. van Harmelen, F.: The Complexity of the Web Ontology Language. IEEE Intelligent Systems **17** (2002) 71 – 72
17. Shneiderman, B.: Dynamic queries for visual information seeking. IEEE Software **11** (1994) 70–77
18. McGuinness, D.L., Borgida, A.: Explaining Subsumption in Description Logics. Technical Report LCSR-TR-228, Dept. of Computer Sciences, Rutgers University (1994)
19. Borgida, A., Franconi, E., Horrocks, I., McGuinness, D., Patel-Schneider, P.F.: Explaining $\mathcal{ALC}$ subsumption. In: Proc. of the International Workshop on Description Logics (DL1999). (1999) 37–40
20. Bederson, B., Grosjean, J., Meyer, J.: Toolkit Design for Interactive Structured Graphics. Technical Report CS-TR-4432, University of Maryland (2002)
21. Niles, I., Pease, A.: Towards a Standard Upper Ontology. In: Proc. of the 2nd International Conference on Formal Ontology in Information Systems (FOIS-2001), Ogunquit, Maine (2001)
22. Carroll, J.J., Dickinson, I., Dollin, C., Reynolds, D., Seaborne, A., Wilkinson, K.: Jena: Implementing the Semantic Web Recommendations. In: Proc. of the 13th International World Wide Web Conference (WWW2004), New York, NY, USA (2004) 74–83
23. Liebig, T., Pfeifer, H., von Henke, F.: Reasoning Services for an OWL Authoring Tool: An Experience Report. In: Proc. of the 2004 International Workshop on Description Logics (DL2004), Whistler, BC, Canada (2004) 79–82
24. Möller, R., Haarslev, V.: Description Logics Systems. In: The Description Logic Handbook. Cambridge University Press (2003)
25. Fluit, C., Sabou, M., van Harmelen, F.: Supporting User Tasks through Visualisation of Light-weight Ontologies. In: Handbook on Ontologies in Information Systems. Springer Verlag (2004) 414–432
26. Mail-Archives: Web Ontology Working Group. http://lists.w3.org/Archives/Public/www-webont-wg/ (2004)
27. Schlobach, S., Cornet, R.: Non-Standard Reasoning Services for the Debugging of Description Logic Terminologies. In: Proc. of the Belgian-Dutch Conference on AI (BNAI03), Nijmegen, The Netherlands (2003)
28. Baader, F., Küsters, R., Wolter, F.: Extensions to Description Logics. In: The Description Logic Handbook. Cambridge University Press (2003)
29. Baader, F., Sertkaya, B., Turhan, A.Y.: Computing the Least Common Subsumer w.r.t. a Background Terminology. In: Proc. of the 2004 International Workshop on Description Logics (DL2004), Whistler, BC, Canada (2004) 11–20

Tracking Changes During Ontology Evolution

Natalya F. Noy[1], Sandhya Kunnatur[1], Michel Klein[2], and Mark A. Musen[1]

[1] Stanford Medical Informatics, Stanford University,
251 Campus Drive, x-215, Stanford, CA 94305, USA
{noy, kunnatur, musen}@smi.stanford.edu
[2] Vrije University Amsterdam
De Boelelaan 1081a, 1081 HV Amsterdam, The Netherlands
Michel.Klein@cs.vu.nl

Abstract. As ontology development becomes a collaborative process, developers face the problem of maintaining versions of ontologies akin to maintaining versions of software code or versions of documents in large projects. Traditional versioning systems enable users to compare versions, examine changes, and accept or reject changes. However, while versioning systems usually treat software code and text documents as text files, a versioning system for ontologies must compare and present *structural* changes rather than changes in text representation of ontologies. In this paper, we present the PROMPTDIFF ontology-versioning environment, which address these challenges. PROMPTDIFF includes an efficient version-comparison algorithm that produces a structural diff between ontologies. The results are presented to the users through an intuitive user interface for analyzing the changes that enables users to view concepts and groups of concepts that were added, deleted, and moved, distinguished by their appearance and with direct access to additional information characterizing the change. The users can then act on the changes, accepting or rejecting them. We present results of a pilot user study that demonstrate the effectiveness of the tool for change management. We discuss design principles for an end-to-end ontology-versioning environment and position ontology versioning as a component in a general ontology-management framework.

1 Need for Ontology Versioning

Ontologies constitute an integral and important part of the Semantic Web. For the Semantic Web to succeed, it will require the development and integration of numerous ontologies, from general top-level ontologies, to domain-specific and task-specific ontologies. For this development to happen on the scale that the Semantic Web success requires, ontology development will have to move from the purview of knowledge engineers with artificial intelligence training to the purview of web developers and domain experts. The WYSIWYG HTML editors are in large part responsible for the pervasiveness of today's web, enabling people without formal hypertext training to create web pages and put them on the web. In the same vein, easy-to-use graphical ontology editors that use simple visual metaphors and hide many of the syntactic and semantic complexity behind intuitive interfaces will be an essential component of the success of the Semantic Web.

S.A. McIlraith et al. (Eds.): ISWC 2004, LNCS 3298, pp. 259–273, 2004.

As ontology development becomes a more ubiquitous and collaborative process, support for *ontology versioning* becomes necessary and essential. This support must enable users to compare versions of ontologies and analyze differences between them.

Furthermore, as ontologies become larger, collaborative development of ontologies becomes more and more common. Ontology designers working in parallel on the same ontology need to maintain and compare different versions, to examine the changes that others have performed, and to accept or reject the changes. In fact, this process is exactly how authors collaborate on editing software code and text documents.

Change tracking in Microsoft Word, while far from perfect, has significantly facilitated collaborative editing of Word documents. Users can easily see the changes between document versions, determine which text was added or deleted, and accept or reject the changes. Intuitive interfaces and tool support must make ontologies just as easy to maintain and evolve as Word documents. Rather than reinvent the wheel, we can build on the successes of tried and tested technologies, adapt them to the wold of ontologies and in fact improve on these technologies using the additional structural knowledge that we have in ontology definitions.

In an ontology-versioning environment, given two versions of an ontology, users must be able to: (1) examine the changes between versions visually; (2) understand the potential effects of changes on applications; and (3) accept or reject changes (when an ontology is being developed in a collaborative setting).

The fields of software evolution and collaborative document processing have faced these challenges for many years. There is one crucial difference however: In the case of software code and documents, what is usually compared—with only a few exceptions—are *text files*. For ontologies, we must compare the *structure* and *semantics* of the ontologies and not their textual serialization. Two ontologies can be exactly the same conceptually, but have very different text representations. For example, their storage syntax may be different. The order in which definitions appear in the text file may be different. A representation language may have several mechanisms for expressing the same semantic structure. Thus, text-file comparison is largely useless for ontologies.

We have developed the PROMPTDIFF ontology-versioning tool to address these issues. PROMPTDIFF automatically performs structural comparison of ontology versions, identifies both simple and complex changes (such as moving classes, or adding or deleting a tree of classes), presents the comparison results to the user in an intuitive way, and enables the user to accept or reject the changes between versions, both at the level of individual changes and groups of changes.

PROMPTDIFF is a component in the larger PROMPT ontology-management framework [13] and serves an important role in maintaining ontology views or mappings between ontologies [3]. PROMPTDIFF provides an ontology-comparison API that other applications can use to determine for example if the mapping needs to be updated when new versions of mapped ontologies appear.

In this paper, we present our general ontology-versioning architecture, describe the user interface for presenting ontology changes; the mechanism for accepting and rejecting changes and ways to custom-tailor this mechanism. We then present the results of our pilot user study aimed at evaluating the usability of our ontology-versioning tools and discuss how PROMPTDIFF is integrated in the general ontology-management framework.

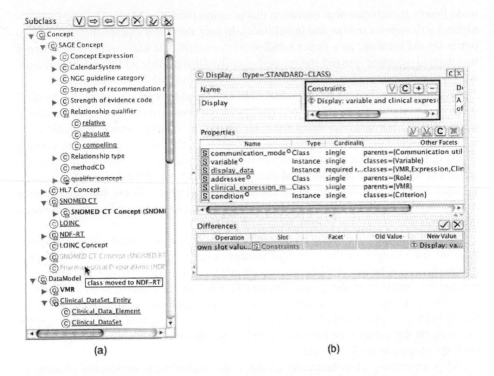

Fig. 1. Displaying changes in PROMPTDIFF. (a) Class hierarchy changes. Different styles represent different types of changes: added classes are underlined and in blue; deleted classes are crossed out and in red; moved classes are grayed out in their old positions and appear in bold in their new ones; tooltips provide additional information. (b) Individual class changes

2   Scenario: Tracking Changes in an Ontology

Consider a project where multiple authors are working on the same ontology.[1] The lead ontology editor receives a new version of the ontology from one of the authors and has the responsibility of examining the changes and accepting or rejecting them. He starts by opening the new ontology version in the Protégé ontology editor [16] and fires up the PROMPTDIFF engine to compare the new ontology version to the baseline. He then examines the results in the PROMPTDIFF interface, a snapshot of which is shown in Figure 1. This figure presents the differences between the two class hierarchies. The editor can see the classes that were added, deleted, moved, and changed.

He starts by focusing in on the subtree for the *Concept* class, which has a number of changes. The color and the font of the class names correspond to the types of the changes. He can see, for example, that $SNOMED\ CT$ is a new class (its class name is in blue and

---

[1] The ontology versions that we use in this section and in Section 6 are the actual ontology versions from a large collaborative project in our laboratory, the SAGE project (http://www.sageproject.net/). The goal of the project is to provide an infrastructure that will enable encoding and dissemination of computable medical knowledge.

underlined). Its subclass was moved to this position from another location in the class hierarchy (it appears in blue and in boldface). In fact, the editor can see the class grayed out in its old location, as a direct subclass of $Concept$. The class $qualifier\ concept$ was deleted (its name is in red and crossed-out). Tooltips provide additional information, such as a new location for the moved class $Pharmaceutical\ Preparations$.

In addition to changes to individual classes, the editor can see operation on class subtrees. The status of a subtree is conveyed by the icon that is overlaid with the traditional class icon (©). For instance, when the class $qualifier\ concept$ was deleted, all of its subclasses were deleted as well (the class icon has on overlaid delete icon ⊘). The warning icon ⚠ indicates whether or not the subtree rooted at a class has any changes in it. So, the editor knows that there are additional changes in the subtree of the NDF-RT class. At the same time, no special icons on the roots of other subtrees indicate that those subtree or individual classes in the subtrees have not changed at all and the editor does not need to look there.

Having examined the changes, the editor can now accept or reject them. He agrees with all the changes in the $Concept$ subtree, except for the addition of the class $compelling$, a subclass of $Relationship\ qualifier$. He starts by selecting the class $compelling$ and presses the "reject" button (✗). The class is removed from the new version of the ontology. He then selects the $Concept$ class and presses the "accept subtree" button (⇘) to accept the rest of the changes in the $Concept$ subtree. Once he completes the work on this subtree, he uses the "next" button to move to the next change (in this case, the change to the VMR class).

After examining class-hierarchy changes, the editor starts examining changes to specific classes. Figure 1b shows the individual changes for the class $Display$. The editor can see that two properties were added to the class, $display\_data$ and $clinical\_expression\_model$. These properties are also in blue and underlined, just like the added classes in the hierarchy. He can see changes to class-level properties, such as $constraints$ in the table at the bottom of the class definition. When he selects a line in the table, the corresponding property is highlighted. Again, the editor has the option of accepting or rejecting all changes individually or for the entire class.

In fact, if the editor received the new ontology version from the author that he trusts completely, he can simply select the root of the class hierarchy, and accept all the changes in the entire hierarchy tree with one "accept tree" button.

After the editor examines and acts upon all the changes he can save the result of his work as the new baseline version.

3   Design Principles

The scenario illustrates design principles for an ontology-versioning environment. We collected this set of requirements and design principles through our interaction with users of the Protégé ontology-development environment. These are the capabilities the users asked for in mailing lists and in private communications.

Automatic comparison of versions. Given two versions of the same ontology, we must identify what has changed from one version to the next. This identification should be performed at conceptual level, that is, it should be expressed in terms of changes to ontology concepts, such as classes, instances, their properties, and property constraints and values.

Identification of complex changes. The higher the granularity of changes presented to the user, the easier it is for the user to analyze. For example, if a class was moved to a different place in the class tree, we would like to present this change as a move rather than a sequence of an add and delete operation. Similarly, if a whole subtree of classes was deleted from the ontology, we would like to identify it as a subtree delete rather than a sequence of deletes for all classes in the subtree (and constraints and restrictions associated with them).

Contextual presentation of changes. If the user needs to understand or assess a change in an ontology (for example, a deleted class), he should be able not only to see the change itself, but also to see its context. For example, if a class was deleted, the user may want to know where in the class tree was the class located, whether it had any subclasses or instances, what were its properties, and so on.

Navigation among changes. Changes often occur in different and unrelated places in an ontology. Having examined one of the changes, the user must be able to navigate easily to the next change, even if it is in a "remote" part of the ontology.

Access to old and new values. Understanding and assessing changes is impossible without ready access to both old and new values. Just knowing that the class name has changed and its new name is "foo" is not enough: when examining the change, we would like to know what the old value was.

Mechanism for accepting and rejecting changes. There are many scenarios when users need not only to understand the change but also to make a decision on whether or not the change was correct and to be able to accept or reject the change. Collaborative ontology development is probably the best example of such use. In one use case that we considered—the development of the NCI Thesaurus [4]—managers delegate development of particular portions of the ontology to respective editors. The managers then assemble the new edits, verify them, and have the final word on whether the new edits were correct and should go in the production version.

Different levels of granularity for accepting and rejecting changes. When accepting or rejecting changes, users often do not want to go through each change and mark it for acceptance or rejection. For example, a user may want to say that all the changes in a particular subtree are correct and must be accepted or to reject one of the changes in the subtree and accept all the others.

We tried to follow these design principles in implementing the PROMPTDIFF ontology-versioning environment described in Sections 4 and 5.

4   Presenting Ontology Diff

Figure 2 shows the overall architecture of the PROMPTDIFF ontology-versioning system. Two versions of an ontology, V_1 and V_2, are inputs to the system. The heuristic-based algorithm for comparing ontology versions (the PROMPTDIFF algorithm), which we describe in detail elsewhere [11] and briefly in Section 4.2, analyzes the two versions and

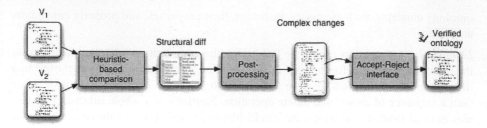

Fig. 2. The architecture of the PROMPTDIFF ontology-versioning system

automatically produces a diff between V_1 and V_2 (we call it *a structural diff* and we define it below). The post-processing module uses the diff to identify complex changes. The results are presented to the user through the intuitive interface (Section 4.3). The user then has the option of accepting or rejecting changes and these actions are reflected in the updated diff (Section 5). We implemented PROMPTDIFF as a Protégé plugin [16].

In this work, we mainly consider ontologies expressed in RDF Schema and therefore consisting of classes, their properties, constraints on properties, property values, and instances [18]. All these elements are also present in other representation formalisms such as OWL and we have used PROMPTDIFF with ontologies specified in OKBC, RDFS, and OWL.

4.1   Structural Diff

We will now introduce the definition of diff between ontology versions. Suppose that we are developing an ontology of wines. In the first version (Figure 3a), there is a class *Wine* with three subclasses, *Red wine*, *White wine*, and *Blush wine*. The class *Wine* has a property *maker* whose values are instances of *Winery*. The class *Red wine* has two subclasses, *Chianti* and *Merlot*. Figure 3b shows a later version of the same ontology fragment. Note the changes: we changed the name of the *maker* property to *produced_by* and the name of the *Blush wine* class to *Rosé wine*; we added a *tannin level* property to *Red wine*; and we discovered that *Merlot* can be white and added another superclass to the *Merlot* class. Figure 3c shows the differences between the two versions in a table produced automatically by PROMPTDIFF.[2] The columns in the table are pairs of matching frames from the two ontologies. Given two versions of an ontology O, V_1 and V_2, two frames F_1 from V_1 and F_2 from V_2 **match** if F_1 became F_2.

Similar to a diff between text files, the table in Figure 3c presents a **structural diff** between ontology versions.

Definition 1 (Structural diff). *Given two versions of an ontology* O, V_1 *and* V_2, *a* **structural diff** *between* V_1 *and* V_2, $D(V_1, V_2)$, *is a set of concept pairs* $\langle C_1, C_2 \rangle$ *where:*

---

[2] PROMPTDIFF puts additional information in the table, such as the level of changes, and specific types of changes between a frame and its image [13]

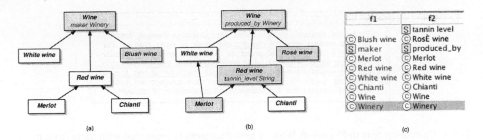

Fig. 3. Two versions of a wine ontology (a and b). Several things have changed: the property name for the *Wine* class, the name of the *Blush wine* class, a new property was added to the *Red wine* class, the *Merlot* class has another superclass. (c) The PROMPTDIFF table showing the difference between the versions

- $C_1 \in V_1$ or $C_1 = null$; $C_2 \in V_2$ or $C_2 = null$
- C_2 is an **image** of C_1 (**matches** C_1), that is, C_1 became C_2. If C_1 or C_2 is null, then we say that C_2 or C_1 respectively does not have a match.
- Each frame from V_1 and V_2 appears in at least one pair.
- For any frame C_1, if there is at least one pair containing C_1, where $C_2 \neq null$, then there is no pair containing C_1 where $C_2 = null$ (if we found at least one match for C_1, we do not have a pair that says that C_1 is unmatched). The same is true for C_2.

4.2   The PromptDiff Algorithm

The PROMPTDIFF algorithm for comparing ontology versions consists of two parts: (1) an extensible set of heuristic matchers and (2) a fixed-point algorithm to combine the results of the matchers to produce a structural diff between two versions. Each matcher employs a small number of structural properties of the ontologies to produce matches. The fixed-point step invokes the matchers repeatedly, feeding the results of one matcher into the others, until they produce no more changes in the diff.

Our approach to automating the comparison is based on two observations: (1) When we compare two versions of the same ontology, a large fraction of concepts remains unchanged (in fact, in our experiments, 97.9% of concepts remained unchanged) and (2) If two concepts have the same type (i.e., they are both classes, both properties, etc.) and have the same or very similar name, one is almost certainly an image of the other.

After identifying the concepts that have not changed, PROMPTDIFF invokes a set of heuristic matchers to match the remaining concepts. One matcher for example looks for unmatched classes where all siblings of the class have been matched. If multiple siblings are unmatched, but their sets of properties differ, another matcher will pick up this case and try to match these classes to unmatched subclasses of the parent's image. Another matcher looks for unmatched properties of a class when all other properties of that class have been matched. There are matchers that look for lexical properties such as all unmatched siblings of a class acquiring the same suffix or prefix. The architecture is easily extensible to add new matchers. With the introduction of OWL, for example, we implemented additional matchers that compared anonymous classes.

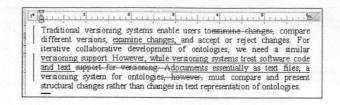

Fig. 4. Comparing text in Microsoft Word: a new document is presented with parts from the old document crossed out and new parts highlighted.

We describe all matchers that we used in detail elsewhere [13]. We have also shown that our algorithm is extremely accurate: it identifies 96% of matches in large ontologies and 93% of the matches that it identifies are correct [11].

The post-processing step enriches the structural diff with the following information: (1) complex changes, such as class moves and tree-level operations; and (2) diffs between individual matching frames

We combine the information in the structural diff with the hierarchical information to identify complex changes. To identify tree-level changes, we recursively traverse the class hierarchy to determine whether all classes in the tree have the same change operation associated with them. To identify class moves, we look for parents of the class and its image to see if they are images of each other. If they are not, then the class was moved.

Since we need this information only when the user views the corresponding part of the ontology, in practice, for efficiency reasons, the post-processing step is intertwined with the visualization step: we find the complex operations only for the trees and classes that the user has displayed on the screen.

4.3   Visualizing Structural Diff

Our user interface for tracking changes between ontology versions was inspired by the interface that Microsoft Word uses to present changes. Figure 4 shows how Microsoft Word presents the result of comparing two versions of a document. The text that was deleted is crossed out and the added text is underlined. There is also color coding for these two types of changes. Note however, that Word does not identify complex operations, such as move. For example, the phrase "examine changes" in the first sentence was moved to a new location. However, Word shows the phrase as being deleted in one place and added in another.

Visual metaphors. We have described many of the visual metaphors we use in PROMPT-DIFF in Section 2. To summarize, we visualize two types of changes in the class hierarchy: (1) class-level changes and (2) tree-level changes.

For class-level changes, the class-name appearance indicates whether the class was added, deleted, moved to a new location, moved from an old location, or its name or definition was changed. The variations in class-name appearance include color, font (bold or regular), names that are underlined or crossed-out.

We say that there is a tree-level change if all classes in a subtree have changed in the same way: they were all added or all deleted, for example. The changed icon at the subtree root indicates a tree-level operation. In addition, a warning icon ⚠ indicates that the subtree rooted at the class has undergone some changes.

We use the same visual metaphors to indicate changes in properties in individual class definitions. For changes in property values, we use a table that shows both the old and the new values for the properties (Figure 1b). When a user selects a line in the table, the corresponding property is highlighted.

Semantics of Parent–Child Relationship in the PROMPTDIFF **Tree.** Most ontology editors use the indented-tree display to present a class hierarchy to the user. In the tree, children of a tree node representing a class C are subclasses of C. The PROMPTDIFF tree shows two versions of a class hierarchy in a single tree. Consequently, the exact semantics of the parent–child relationship in a tree is different.

Let V_{old} be an old version of the ontology O and V_{new} be a new version of the ontology O. In a PROMPTDIFF tree, if a tree node N represents a class C_{new} from V_{new}, then its children in the PROMPTDIFF tree are:

1. all subclasses of C_{new} in V_{new}; and
2. all subclasses $subC_{old}$ of $source(C_{new})$ in V_{old} such that $image(subC_{old})$ is *not* a subclass of C_{new}.

As a result, the node N representing C_{new} will have children for all subclasses of C_{new} and for all subclasses of its source that were deleted or moved away from the tree.

If a tree node N represents a class C_{old} from V_{old} (this class will necessarily be a deleted or a moved class), then its children in the PROMPTDIFF are determined as follows. For each subclass $subC_{old}$ of C_{old} in V_{old}:

1. if there is an image of $subC_{old}$ in V_{new}, then $image(subC_{old})$ is a child of the node N (it will be shown as moved, i.e., in grey).
2. if there is no image of $subC_{old}$ in V_{new}, then $subC_{old}$ is a child of the node N (it will be shown as deleted).

5   Accepting and Rejecting Changes

When a user examines changes in the new version V_{new} of the ontology compared to a baseline (old) version V_{old}, he may have the need and the authority to accept or reject the changes. In rejecting a change, the user will be effectively changing V_{new}. For instance, if V_{new} contains a new class C and the user decides to reject the class addition, the rejection will have the effect of deleting C from V_{new}.

Accepting a change technically has no implication on the state of V_{new}. It does change the state of the visualization of the diff between V_{old} and V_{new}, since the accepted change should no longer show as a change. For instance, if a user decides to accept the addition of the class C in the example above, the class should no longer show as added (it will now be shown in plain font and without the underline).

As we have shown in the example in Section 2, PROMPTDIFF allows users to accept and reject changes between versions at several levels of granularity:

1. individual changes to property values and definitions
2. all changes in a definition of a class
3. all changes in class definitions and class-hierarchy positions in a subtree rooted at a particular concept

While determining the effects of accepting or rejecting individual operations is relatively straightforward, matters become more complicated as we move from individual changes in properties to class-level changes. Consider for example one of the added classes in the earlier example in Figure 1a, such as $Clinical\_DataSet$. When we accept the addition of the class, do we automatically accept the addition of all of its instances? The same problem arises for an action of rejecting a class delete (such as $qualifier\ concept$). Rejecting a class delete means putting the class back into the new version. Should its instances be reinstated as well? If we reject the addition of the $Clinical\_DataSet\_Entity$ class from Figure 1a, should we also reject the addition of its subclasses and their instances, automatically removing them from the new version?

These issues are similar to the issues discussed by Stojanovic and colleagues [17] in the context of supporting ontology evolution in KAON. When a user deletes a class for example, should its subclasses and instances be deleted as well, or should they become direct subclasses and instances of the parent of the removed class? In the KAON framework, the solution is to enable users to specify evolution strategies to define what happens in each case. However, in the setting of accepting and rejecting changes, the number of strategies to consider is much larger. The examples above show that we must consider not only the status of a single class (added, deleted, moved, etc.) but also various combinations of the class status with the statuses of its subclasses and superclasses.

Our long-term solution to the problem is to classify these strategies and allow users to custom-tailor them. In our current implementation, we implement what we consider to be the most common strategies based on our experience with the users. In our user study (Section 6), all subjects said that the result of accepting and rejecting changes fully met their expectations (all of them gave this question the highest rank of 5). However, since some users may want to custom-tailor this behavior, we are currently working on classifying and identifying the strategies to provide the users with the interface to custom-tailor them.

6   Usability Evaluation

We performed initial user studies to assess the usability of PROMPTDIFF and the ability of users to analyze and verify changes in versions of an ontology. We evaluated both the visualization itself and the mechanism for accepting and rejecting changes. We asked a group of users to compare two versions of an ontology and to accept or reject changes based on a set of rules that we provided.

6.1   Experiment Setup

For the experiment, we presented the subjects with two versions of an ontology describing clinical guidelines and asked them to examine the changes based on a set of provided rules.

Source ontology. We used the actual versions of the clinical-guideline ontology that were recorded in the course of the SAGE project.[3] The ontology contains approximately 400 classes and 300 properties. Between the two versions that we used in the experiment, 3 classes were removed, 2 classes were added, 5 new properties were added and 15 class definitions were changed. In all, there were 47 changes to 20 classes. The changes included moves in the class hierarchy, class name changes, addition of values for class properties, addition of new properties and restrictions.

Rules. We have generated a set of rules for the users to follow in accepting and reject-ing changes. The rules covered all the changes that the two ontology versions in the experiment had. Therefore, the experiment was designed to have all users come to the same final version in the end. We made an effort to provide the rules that are formulated around the state of the final version—what should and should not be included—and not in terms of what should be accepted or rejected. Here are some examples of the rules that we gave the users:

- All spelling corrections are ok
- All additions of documentation are ok
- The class *qualifier concept* should not be in the new version
- The *role* property of *Supplemental_Material* class should have the following allowed values: *source, consent_from, illustration, comment, evidence*

Users. There were 4 users in the study. All of them were experienced users of Protégé and therefore were familiar with knowledge modeling. None of them has used PROMPTDIFF before. Also, none of them was familiar with the SAGE ontology before the experiment.

Training. Prior to the experiment we asked users to follow a brief online tutorial that explained the features of PROMPTDIFF and gave several examples of its use

6.2   Results and Discussion

After we received the resulting ontologies from the users, we compared them with the benchmark ontology that we have prepared. We used PROMPTDIFF to find the changes between the ontologies that the users produced and the benchmark. Our results showed that the users correctly accepted or rejected a change in 93% of the cases. In their comments, users indicated that sometimes they were not sure they were interpreting the change rules correctly and therefore the fact that they did not do what we expected them to do in the remaining 7% of the cases could be partially attributed to that.

On the usability of the tool, the user's satisfaction level was fairly high. We asked the users to rank their answers to a number of usability questions on a scale of 1 to 5 (5 being the highest). Table 1 shows the summary of their responses. In free text comment, users indicated that the navigation through changes (using the next and previous buttons) had bugs in the implementation.

---

[3] http://www.sageproject.net/

Table 1. Results of the user study. The numbers in the second column are the average value for the users' responses. We asked the users to rank their agreement on a scale of 1 to 5, with 5 being the highest.

Was Prompt easy to use?	4
Was the presentation of changes intuitive?	4.25
Was it easy to navigate through changes	3.75
When you performed accept/reject, did the result meet your expectations	5
Was the granularity provided for accepting/rejecting changes satisfactory?	4.5

These results demonstrate that the users in general had high marks for the usability of the tool. The study has also provided us with many useful suggestions that we plan to implement in the future versions of the tool.

7   Ontology Versioning as Part of Ontology-Management Framework

We treat ontology-versioning as one of the tasks in the set of ontology-management tasks. The domain of multiple-ontology management includes not only versioning, but also creating and maintaining mappings between ontologies; merging ontologies; translating between them; creating views of ontologies; and other tasks [12].

Currently, most researchers treat these tasks as completely independent ones and the corresponding tools are independent from one another. There are tools for ontology merging (e.g., Chimaera [8]) and they have no relation to tools for ontology mapping (e.g., ONION [9]) or ontology versioning (e.g., OntoView [6]). Researchers working on developing formalisms for specifying transformation rules from one version of ontology to another, do not apply these rules to related ontologies that are not versions of each other.

However, many of the tasks in management of multiple ontologies are closely inter-related and have common elements and subtasks. Tools for supporting some of the tasks can benefit greatly from their integration with others. For example, the methods that we develop to help users find overlap between ontologies for the tasks of ontology merging can be used successfully in finding differences between ontology versions [11]. In both cases, we have two overlapping ontologies and we need to determine a mapping between their elements. When we compare ontologies from different sources, we concentrate on *similarities*, whereas in version comparison we need to highlight the *differences*, which can be a complementary process. In a previous study, we used heuristics that are similar to the ones we present in this paper to provide suggestions in interactive ontology merging [10].

Looking at the issue from another angle, PROMPTDIFF proved extremely useful in maintaining declarative ontology mappings and views. Consider for example any definition D of a mapping between two ontologies, O_1 and O_2 that explicitly refers to concepts in O_1 and O_2. Suppose we now have a new version of O_1. We must determine if our old mapping is "dirty" and requires re-definition. We say that a declarative mapping between O_1 and O_2 is "dirty" if it explicitly refers to the concepts in O_1 and

O_2 that were changed. Note however that even if the mapping is not "dirty" after a new version of an ontology is introduced, it may still be incomplete or incorrect given the new information.

We use the PROMPTDIFF API to compare the old and the new version of O_1. PROMPT-DIFF informs the user not only whether the mapping is "dirty," but also points him to the part of the mapping that refers to the changed concepts and indicates how much the concept has changed.

8 Related Work

Researchers have proposed several directions in supporting ontology versioning (although the field is still fairly nascent). One direction is based on specifying and using explicit logs of changes. For example, Oliver and colleagues [15] specified a set of changes in controlled vocabularies and described mechanisms for synchronizing different versions (with user's input) based on the change logs.

Stojanovich and colleagues [17], in the context of the KAON suite of tools for ontology management, introduce the notion of an *evolution strategy*: allowing developers to specify complex effects of changes. For example, when a class is deleted from an ontology, whether its subclasses are deleted or become subclasses of its superclass, are two different evolution strategy. KAON uses logs of changes at the granularity of single knowledge-base operations as versioning information.

Ognyanov and Kiryakov [14] propose a formal model for tracking changes in RDF repositories. RDF statements are the pieces of knowledge on which they operate. The granularity level of RDF statements is significantly lower however than the level of class and property changes that we consider here.

All of these approaches however rely on using logs or something similar to trace changes between versions. However, both in the context of de-centralized ontology development on the Semantic Web and in the context of collaborative development of ontologies, logs may not be available or do not contain the necessary change information. While many ontology development tools now provide logs of changes, there is no uniform mechanism for publishing the changes along with ontologies. But even if we do have an agreed-upon ontology of changes [7], many versions of ontologies are likely to exist without explicit change information being made public. Thus, we need tools that compare ontology versions themselves to produce the information about changes at the structural level.

The OntoView tool [6] performs a pairwise comparison of the sets of RDF statements that form the old and new version of the class- and property-definitions in an ontology. In this way, changes in syntax and specific representations of RDF are ignored. OntoView focuses on finding and representing changes between concepts in *different* versions. For example, a concept in the new version may become more general than it was in the old version. These types of changes are complementary to the ones we explore in PROMPTDIFF.

The database community has addressed similar problems in the area change-tracking in hierarchical databases and XML documents. In both of these cases researchers must compare tree-like structures, which is part of the ontology-comparison as well. However, most formulations of a tree diff problem are NP-hard [19]. Mainly, this result applies to finding a minimal edit script—the minimal set of changes to transform one tree to another. Therefore, researchers addressed variations of this problem, using heuristics and trading some of the minimality for good performance result [1,2]. The approach resonates with our PROMPTDIFF algorithm described in Section 4: while we cannot provably find the minimal set of changes between ontology versions, our heuristic approach finds the changes efficiently and our experimental results show that in practice it also finds the minimal set of changes [11]. In ontology comparison, however, we can and do also use domain knowledge (e.g., class properties, their domains and ranges) to compare hierarchical class structures—the luxury not directly available in database or XML context.

On the visualization side, visualization of changes in XML trees is the work closest to ours. IBM's XML Diff and Merge Tool [5] is a representative example of these tools. After comparing two XML trees, the tool shows the user the nodes that were added, deleted, or changed. It does not however, identify the moves, or highlight specific changes to a node (It just indicates that a node has been changed and it is up to the user to find what the changes are).

9   Conclusions and Future Work

We have presented a system for tracking changes between ontology versions. Our evaluation demonstrated that PROMPTDIFF is effective in helping users analyze and verify changes.

In order to support fully collaborative ontology development, we need to integrate systems such as PROMPTDIFF with version-control systems, such as CVS, which support other components of the versioning process—tracking versions, checking in and checking out of versions, user profiles, and so on. Other ontology-development support for versioning should include tracking changes directly during edits (rather than determining what the changes are by comparing two versions), enabling users to add design rationale during edits, and allowing users to custom-tailor effects of accepting and rejecting complex changes.

PROMPTDIFF can be downloaded at http://protege.stanford.edu/plugins/prompt/prompt.html.

Acknowledgments. This work was supported in part by a contract from the US National Cancer Institute This work was conducted using the Protégé resource, which is supported by grant LM007885 from the United States National Library of Medicine.

References

1. S. Chawathe and H. Garcia-Molina. Meaningful change detection in structured data. In *ACM SIGMOD Int Conf on Management of Data*. ACM Press, 1997.
2. G. Cobena, S. Abiteboul, and A. Marian. Detecting changes in xml documents. In *IEEE International Conference on Data Engineering, ICDE*, San Jose, CA, 2002.
3. M. Crubézy, Z. Pincus, and M. Musen. Mediating knowledge between application components. In *Workshop on Semantic Integration at ISWC-2003*, FL, 2003.

4. J. Golbeck, G. Fragoso, F. Hartel, J. Hendler, B. Parsia, and J. Oberthaler. The NCI's thesaurus and ontology. *Journal of Web Semantics*, 1(1), 2003.

5. IBM. XML diff and merge tool, 2004.

6. M. Klein, A. Kiryakov, D. Ognyanov, and D. Fensel. Ontology versioning and change detection on the web. In *13th Int Conf on Knowledge Engineering and Management (EKAW02)*, Sigüenza, Spain, 2002.

7. M. Klein and N. F. Noy. A component-based framework for ontology evolution. In *Workshop on Ontologies and Distributed Systems at IJCAI-03*, Mexico, 2003.

8. D. L. McGuinness, R. Fikes, J. Rice, and S. Wilder. An environment for merging and testing large ontologies. In *Principles of Knowledge Representation and Reasoning (KR2000)*. Morgan Kaufmann, San Francisco, CA, 2000.

9. P. Mitra, G. Wiederhold, and M. Kersten. A graph-oriented model for articulation of ontology interdependencies. In *Conf on Extending Database Technology (EDBT'2000)*, Germany, 2000.

10. N. Noy and M. Musen. PROMPT: Algorithm and tool for automated ontology merging and alignment. In *17th Nat Conf on Artificial Intelligence (AAAI-2000)*, Austin, TX, 2000.

11. N. F. Noy and M. A. Musen. PromptDiff: A fixed-point algorithm for comparing ontology versions. In *18th Nat Conf on Artificial Intelligence (AAAI-2002)*, Edmonton, Alberta, 2002.

12. N. F. Noy and M. A. Musen. The PROMPT suite: Interactive tools for ontology merging and mapping. *Int Journal of Human-Computer Studies*, 59(6), 2003.

13. N. F. Noy and M. A. Musen. Ontology versioning in an ontology-management framework. *IEEE Intelligent Systems*, page in press, 2004.

14. D. Ognyanov and A. Kiryakov. Tracking changes in RDF(S) repositories. In *13th Int Conf on Knowledge Engineering and Management, EKAW 2002*, Spain, 2002.

15. D. E. Oliver, Y. Shahar, E. H. Shortliffe, and M. A. Musen. Representation of change in controlled medical terminologies. *AI in Medicine*, 15:53–76, 1999.

16. Protege. The Protégé project, http://protege.stanford.edu, 2002.

17. L. Stojanovic, A. Maedche, B. Motik, and N. Stojanovic. User-driven ontology evolution management. In *13th International Conference on Engineering and Knowledge Management (EKAW02)*, Sigüenza, Spain, 002.

18. W3C. Resource description framework (RDF), 2000.

19. K. Zhang, J. T. L. Wang, and D. Shasha. On the editing distance between undirected acyclic graphs and related problems. In *6th Annual Symposium on Combinatorial Pattern Matching*, pages 395–407, 1995.

An Evaluation of Knowledge Base Systems for Large OWL Datasets

Yuanbo Guo, Zhengxiang Pan, and Jeff Heflin

Computer Science and Engineering Department, Lehigh University, Bethlehem, PA18015,
USA
{yug2, zhp2, Heflin}@cse.lehigh.edu

Abstract. In this paper, we present an evaluation of four knowledge base systems (KBS) with respect to use in large OWL applications. To our knowledge, no experiment has been done with the scale of data used here. The smallest dataset used consists of 15 OWL files totaling 8MB, while the largest dataset consists of 999 files totaling 583MB. We evaluated two memory-based systems (OWLJessKB and memory-based Sesame) and two systems with persistent storage (database-based Sesame and DLDB-OWL). We describe how we have performed the evaluation and what factors we have considered in it. We show the results of the experiment and discuss the performance of each system. In particular, we have concluded that existing systems need to place a greater emphasis on scalability.

1   Introduction

Various knowledge base systems (KBS) have been developed for processing Semantic Web information. They vary in a number of important ways. Many KBSs are main memory-based while others use secondary storage to provide persistence. Another key difference is the degree of reasoning provided by the KBS. Many systems are incomplete with respect to OWL [2], but still useful because they scale better or respond to queries quickly.

In this paper, we consider the issue of how to choose an appropriate KBS for a large OWL application. Here, we consider a large application to be one that requires the processing of megabytes of data. Generally, there are two basic requirements for such systems. First, the enormous amount of data means that scalability and efficiency become crucial issues. Second, the system must provide sufficient reasoning capabilities to support the semantic requirements of the application. However, increased reasoning capability usually means an increase in query response time as well. An important question is how well existing systems support these conflicting requirements. Furthermore, different applications may place emphasis on different requirements.

It is difficult to evaluate KBSs with respect to these requirements, particularly in terms of scalability. The main reason for this is that there are few Semantic Web data sets that are of large size and commit to semantically rich ontologies. The Lehigh

S.A. McIlraith et al. (Eds.): ISWC 2004, LNCS 3298, pp. 274–288, 2004.

University Benchmark [12] is our first step in order to fill this gap. In this work, we have made a further step: by making use of the benchmark, we have evaluated four KBSs for the Semantic Web from several different aspects. We have evaluated two memory-based systems (OWLJessKB and memory-based Sesame) and two systems with persistent storage (database-based Sesame and DLDB-OWL). We present our experiment, discuss the performance of each system, and show some interesting observations. Based on that, we highlight some issues with respect to the development and improvement of the same kind of systems, and suggest some potential ways in using and developing those systems. We also discuss some issues related to the evaluation of Semantic Web KBSs.

The outline of the paper is as follows: Section 2 briefly introduces the aforementioned Lehigh University Benchmark. Section 3 describes the target systems. Section 4 discusses the results. Section 5 talks about some related work. Section 6 concludes.

2 Lehigh University Benchmark for OWL

The Lehigh University Benchmark [12] was originally developed to evaluate the performance of Semantic Web repositories with respect to extensional queries over a large DAML+OIL [9] data set that commits to a single realistic ontology. For this paper, we extended the benchmark to provide support for OWL ontologies and datasets. The benchmark suite for OWL consists of the following:
- A plausible OWL ontology named univ-bench[1] for the university domain.
- Repeatable synthetic OWL data sets that can be scaled to an arbitrary size. Both the univ-bench ontology and the data are in the OWL Lite sublanguage.
- Fourteen test queries that cover a range of types in terms of properties including input size, selectivity, complexity, assumed hierarchy information, and assumed inference, etc. (Refer to the appendix for a list of them).
- A set of performance metrics including data loading time, repository size, query response time, and query answer completeness and soundness. With the exception of completeness, they are all standard database benchmarking metrics [3, 4, 8, 25]. Completeness is described in Section 3.2.
- The test module.

In addition to the language change, the major differences from the original benchmark include: one more query (Query 14); more individuals in the data sets to be classified; more RDFS vocabulary used in the ontology (e.g., *rdfs:domain*); and some domain constraint changes to allow emphasis on description logic subsumption.

Using this benchmark, we have conducted an experiment on the aforementioned systems. We describe it in next section. The benchmark suite is accessible at http://www.lehigh.edu/~yug2/Research/SemanticWeb/LUBM/LUBM.htm.

---

[1] http://www.lehigh.edu/~zhp2/2004/0401/univ-bench.owl

3   The Experiment

3.1   Target Systems

In this experiment, we wanted to evaluate the scalability and support for OWL Lite in various systems. We believe a practical KBS must be able to read OWL files, support incremental data loading, and provide programming APIs for loading data and issuing queries. As a result, we have settled on four different knowledge base systems, including two implementations of Sesame, OWLJessKB, and DLDB-OWL. We briefly describe each system below.

Sesame [6] is a repository and querying facility based on RDF and RDF Schema [27]. It features a generic architecture that separates the actual storage of RDF, functional modules offering operation on this RDF, and communication with these functional modules from outside the system. Sesame supports RDF/RDF Schema inference, but is an incomplete reasoner for OWL Lite. It can evaluate queries in SeRQL, RQL and RDQL. We evaluate two implementations of Sesame, main memory-based and database-based.

OWLJessKB [22] is a memory-based reasoning tool for description logic languages, particularly OWL. It uses the Java Expert System Shell (Jess) [19], a production system, as its underlying reasoner. Current functionality of OWLJessKB is close to OWL Lite plus some. We evaluate it as a system that supports most OWL entailments.

The fourth system, DLDB-OWL [23], is a repository for processing, storing, and querying large amounts of OWL data. Its major feature is the extension of a relational database system with description logic inference capabilities. Specifically, DLDB-OWL uses Microsoft Access® as the DBMS and FaCT [16] as the OWL reasoner. It uses the reasoner to precompute subsumption and employs relational views to answer extensional queries based on the implicit hierarchy that is inferred.

Originally, we had targeted four other systems. The first is Jena [18], a Java framework for building Semantic Web applications. Jena currently supports both RDF/RDFS and OWL. We have done some preliminary tests on Jena (v2.1) (both memory-based and database-based) with our smallest data set. Compared to Sesame, the most similar system to Jena here, Jena with RDFS reasoning was much slower in answering nearly all the queries. Some of the queries did not terminate even after being allowed to run for several hours. The situation was similar when Jena's OWL reasoning was turned on. For this reason, and also due to space constraints, we have decided not to include Jena in this paper. Those who are interested in more details are referred to [13] instead. The second is KAON [20], an ontology management infrastructure. KAON provides an API for manipulating RDF models, however, it does not directly support OWL or RDFS in its framework. We had also considered TRIPLE [24] and Racer. TRIPLE is an RDF query, inference, and transformation language and architecture. Instead of having a built-in semantics for RDF Schema, TRIPLE allows the semantics of languages on top of RDF to be defined with rules. For languages where this is not easily possible, TRIPLE also provides access to external programs like description logic classifiers. We were unable to test TRIPLE because it does not support incremental file loading and it does not provide a programming API either. Racer [15] is a description logic inference engine currently supporting RDF, DAML+OIL and OWL. Running as a server, Racer provides inference services via HTTP or TCP protocol to client applications. Racer's query interface predefines some queries and query patterns, but these are insufficient for the test queries in the benchmark. Furthermore, there is no API in Racer for importing customized queries. Thus we were unable to test Racer either.

3.2   Experiment Methodology

System Setup

The systems we test are DLDB-OWL (04-03-29 release), Sesame v1.0, and OWLJessKB (04-02-23 release). As noted, we test both the main memory-based and database-based implementations of Sesame. For brevity, we hereafter refer to them as Sesame-Memory and Sesame-DB respectively. For both of them, we use the implementation with RDFS inference capabilities. For the later, we use MySQL (v4.0.16) as the underlying DBMS since it is reported that Sesame performs best with it. The DBMS used in DLDB-OWL is MS Access® 2002. We have created a wrapper over each target system as an interface to the benchmark's test module.

Data Sets and Loading

To identify the data set, we use LUBM(N, S) in the subsequent description to denote the data set that contains N universities beginning at University0 and is generated by the benchmark tool using a seed value of S. (Readers are referred to [12] for details about synthetic data generation in the benchmark.)

We have created 5 sets of test data: LUBM(1, 0), LUBM(5, 0), LUBM(10, 0), LUBM(20, 0), and LUBM(50, 0), which contain OWL files for 1, 5, 10, 20, and 50 universities respectively, the largest one having over 6,800,000 triples in total. To our knowledge, prior to this experiment, Sesame has been tested with at most 3,000,000 statements. We have easily exceeded that by virtue of the benchmark supporting tool.

In the test data, every university contains 15 to 25 departments, each described by a separate OWL file. These files are loaded to the target system in an incremental fashion. We measure the elapsed time for loading each data set, and also the consequent database sizes for Sesame-DB and DLDB-OWL. We do not measure the occupied memory sizes for Sesame-Memory and OWLJessKB because it is difficult to accurately calculate them. However, since we evaluate all systems on a platform with a fixed memory size, the largest data set that can be handled by a system measures its memory efficiency.

Query Test

For query testing, the 14 benchmark queries are expressed in RQL [21], Jess, and a KIF[11]-like language (see the appendix) and issued to Sesame, OWLJessKB, and DLDB-OWL respectively. We do not use a common language in the test to eliminate affect of query translation to the query response time.

Query response time is collected in the way defined by the benchmark, which is based on the process used in database benchmarks [3, 4, 8, 25]. To account for caching, each of the fourteen queries is executed for ten times consecutively and the average time is computed.

We also examine query answer completeness of each system. In logic, an inference procedure is complete if it can find a proof for any sentence that is entailed by the knowledge base. With respect to queries, we say a system is complete if it generates all answers that are entailed by the knowledge base, where each answer is a binding of the query variables that results in an entailed sentence. However, on the Semantic Web, partial answers will often be acceptable. So it is important not to measure completeness with such a coarse distinction. Instead, we measure the degree of completeness of each query answer as the percentage of the entailed answers that are returned by the system. Note that we request that the result set contains unique answers.

In addition, as we will show in next section, we have realized in this evaluation that query soundness is also worthy of examination. With similar argument to the above, we in this evaluation measure the degree of soundness of each query answer as the percentage of the answers returned by the system that are actually entailed.

Test Environment

We have done the test on a desktop computer. The environment is as follows:
- 1.80GHz Pentium 4 CPU; 256MB of RAM; 80GB of hard disk
- Windows XP Professional OS; Java SDK 1.4.1; 512MB of max heap size

In order to evaluate OWLJessKB, we needed to adjust this configuration slightly. With the standard setting for max heap size in Java, the system failed to load the one-university data set due to out of memory errors. As a workaround, we increased the maximum heap size to 1GB, which requests large amount of virtual memory from operating system. This change allowed OWLJessKB to properly load the dataset.

4   Results and Discussions

4.1   Data Loading

Table 1 shows the data loading time for all systems and the on-disk repository sizes of DLDB-OWL and Sesame-DB. Fig. 1 depicts how the data loading time grows as the data set size increases and compares the repository sizes of the two database-based systems.

The test results have reinforced scalability as an important issue and challenge for Semantic Web knowledge base systems. One of the first issues is how large of a data set each system can handle. As expected, the memory-based systems did not perform as well as the persistent storage systems in this regard. OWLJessKB, could only load the 1-university data set, and took over 20 times longer than any other system to do so. On the other hand, we were surprised to see that Sesame-Memory could load up to 10 universities, and was able to do it in 5% of the time of the next fastest system. However, for 20 or more universities, Sesame-Memory also succumbed to memory limitations.

Table 1. Load Time and Repository Sizes

	Data Set	Instance Num	Load Time (hh:mm:ss)	Repository Size (KB)
DLDB-OWL			00:05:43	16,318
Sesame-DB	LUBM	103,074	00:09:02	48,333
Sesame-Memory	(1, 0)		00:00:13	-
OWLJessKB			03:16:12	-
DLDB-OWL			00:51:57	91,292
Sesame-DB	LUBM	645,649	03:00:11	283,967
Sesame-Memory	(5, 0)		00:01:53	-
OWLJessKB			-	-
DLDB-OWL			01:54:41	184,680
Sesame-DB	LUBM	1,316,322	12:27:50	574,554
Sesame-Memory	(10, 0)		00:05:40	-
OWLJessKB			-	-
DLDB-OWL			04:22:53	388,202
Sesame-DB	LUBM	2,781,322	46:35:53	1,209,827
Sesame-Memory	(20, 0)		-	-
OWLJessKB			-	-
DLDB-OWL			12:37:57	958,956
Sesame-DB	LUBM	6,888,642	-	-
Sesame-Memory	(50, 0)		-	-
OWLJessKB			-	-

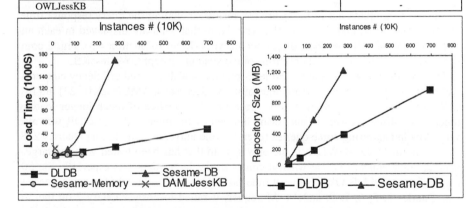

Fig. 1. Load Time and Repository Sizes. The left hand figure shows the load time. The right hand figure shows the repository sizes of the database-based systems.

Using the benchmark, we have been able to test both Sesame-Memory and Sesame-DB on larger scale data sets than what has been reported so far. The result reveals an apparent problem for Sesame-DB: it does not scale in data loading, as can be seen from Fig. 2. As an example, it took over 300 times longer to load the 20-university data set than the 1-university data set, although the former set contains only about 25 times more instances than the later. We extrapolate that it will take Sesame-DB over 3 weeks to finish up loading the 50-university data set. Therefore, we have decided not to do that unrealistic test.

In contrast, DLDB-OWL displays good scalability in data loading. We suspect the different performance of the two systems is caused by the following two reasons. First, to save space, both DLDB-OWL and Sesame map resources to unique IDs maintained in a table. When a resource is encountered during the data loading, they will look up that table to determine if it has not been seen before and need to be assigned a new ID. As mentioned in [23], querying the ID table every time is very likely to slow down the data loading as the data size grows. In its implementation, Sesame also assigns every literal an ID, while DLDB-OWL stores literals directly in the destination tables, which means Sesame has to spend even more time on ID lookup. Moreover, in order to improve performance, DLDB-OWL caches resource-ID pairs during current loading.

A second reason for the performance difference is related to the way Sesame performs inference. Sesame is a forward-chaining reasoner, and in order to support statement deletions it uses a truth maintenance system to track all deductive dependencies between statements. As [5] shows, this appears to affect the performance significantly if there are many inferred statements or the data set is fairly large. We should note that this scalability problem was not as noticeable in our previous study involving a DAML+OIL benchmark [14]. We believe this is because the prior experiment used *daml:domain* (as opposed to *rdfs:domain*) in its ontology, which does not trigger inferences in Sesame.

4.2   Query Response Time

Table 2 is a complete list of the query test results, including the query response time, number of answers, and their completeness. Note that what are displayed in each answer row are only the numbers of correct answers (Refer to Section 4.3). Fig. 2 compares by graphs the query response time of the systems except OWLJessKB.

In terms of query, the results also lead to some scalability and efficiency concerns. Although compared to the performance of its predecessor DAMLJessKB [22] in [14], OWLJessKB improves its query time greatly at the sacrifice of much longer loading time, it is still the slowest in answering thirteen of the queries. Sesame-DB was also very slow in answering some queries (even for one university), including Queries 2, 8, and 9. As for DLDB-OWL, it is the only system that has been tested with the largest data set. One concern is that when it comes to the larger data sets especially the 50-university set, DLDB-OWL's query time no longer grows linearly for some queries, i.e., Queries 2, 5, 6, 7, 9, and 14. Moreover, it failed to answer Query 2 on the 50-univeristy data set after MS Access ran out of temporary space. Compared to other systems, Sesame-Memory, is the fastest in answering all of the queries. It is also the fastest in data loading. This suggests that it might be the best choice for data of small scale if persistent storage and OWL inference is not required.

We have observed that those queries for which Sesame-DB's performance goes down dramatically are common in that they do not contain a specific URI as a subject or object in the statements. On the other hand, Sesame-DB shows a nice property in answering some other queries like Queries 3, 4, 5, 7, and 8: there was no proportional increase in the response time as the data size grows. We have also noticed a common feature of these queries, i.e., they have constant number of results over the test data sets. Whether these are the causes or coincidences is a subject for future work.

It is beyond the scope of this paper to analyze in depth the query evaluation and optimization mechanism in each system. Instead, we propose some topics for future investigation. One is to explore the potential relationship between query types and the

Table 2. Query Test Results. (* correct answers only, refer to Table 3)

Query	Metrics	LUBM(1.0)				LUBM(5.0)			LUBM(10.0)			LUBM(20.0)		LUBM(50.0)
		DLDB-OWL	Sesame-DB	Sesame-Mem	OWLJessKB	DLDB-OWL	Sesame-DB	Sesame-Mem	DLDB-OWL	Sesame-DB	Sesame-Mem	DLDB-OWL	Sesame-DB	DLDB-OWL
1	Time(ms)	59	46	15	9203	226	43	37	412	40	106	887	96	2211
	Answers	4	4	4	4	4	4	4	4	4	4	4	4	4
	Completeness	100	100	100	100	100	100	100	100	100	100	100	100	100
2	Time(ms)	181	51878	87	116297	2320	368423	495	14556	711678	1068	392392	1474664	failed
	Answers	0	0	0	0	9	9	9	28	28	28	59	59	-
	Completeness	100	100	100	100	100	100	100	100	100	100	100	100	-
3	Time(ms)	218	40	0	13990	2545	53	1	5540	59	0	11956	56	36160
	Answers	6	6	6	6	6	6	6	6	6	6	6	6	6
	Completeness	100	100	100	100	100	100	100	100	100	100	100	100	100
4	Time(ms)	506	768	6	211514	2498	823	4	5615	762	4	14856	881	10115
	Answers	34	34	34	34*	34	34	34	34	34	34	34	34	34
	Completeness	100	100	100	100	100	100	100	100	100	100	100	100	100
5	Time(ms)	617	2945	17	5929	4642	3039	17	11511	3214	17	27756	3150	135055
	Answers	719	719	719	719	719	719	719	719	719	719	719	719	719
	Completeness	100	100	100	100	100	100	100	100	100	100	100	100	100
6	Time(ms)	481	253	48	1271	4365	1517	251	11158	3539	543	28448	12717	151904
	Answers	7790	5916	5916	7790*	48582	36682	36682	99566	75547	75547	210603	160120	519842
	Completeness	100	76	76	100	100	76	76	100	76	76	100	76	100
7	Time(ms)	478	603	3	128115	2639	606	4	7028	634	4	18073	657	121673
	Answers	67	59	59	67	67	59	59	67	59	59	67	59	67
	Completeness	100	88	88	100	100	88	88	100	88	88	100	88	100
8	Time(ms)	765	105026	273	164106	3004	108384	262	5937	108851	264	13582	103779	39845
	Answers	7790	5916	5916	7790*	7790	5916	5916	7790	5916	5916	7790	5916	7790
	Completeness	100	76	76	100	100	76	76	100	76	76	100	76	100
9	Time(ms)	634	34034	89	87475	7751	256770	534	19971	460267	1123	57046	1013951	323579
	Answers	208	103	103	208	1245	600	600	2540	1233	1233	5479	2637	13639
	Completeness	100	50	50	100	100	48	48	100	49	49	100	48	100
10	Time(ms)	98	20	1	141	1051	36	0	2339	40	0	5539	50	15831
	Answers	4	0	0	4	4	0	0	4	0	0	4	0	4
	Completeness	100	0	0	100	100	0	0	100	0	0	100	0	100
11	Time(ms)	48	65	1	1592	51	73	1	61	84	3	78	82	143
	Answers	0	0	0	224	0	0	0	0	0	0	0	0	0
	Completeness	0	0	0	100	0	0	0	0	0	0	0	0	0
12	Time(ms)	62	4484	12	11266	78	4659	14	123	4703	12	310	4886	745
	Answers	0	0	0	15*	0	0	0	0	0	0	0	0	0
	Completeness	0	0	0	100	0	0	0	0	0	0	0	0	0
13	Time(ms)	200	4	1	90	2389	9	1	5173	12	1	11906	21	34854
	Answers	0	0	0	1	0	0	0	0	0	0	0	0	0
	Completeness	0	0	0	100	0	0	0	0	0	0	0	0	0
14	Time(ms)	187	218	42	811	2937	1398	257	7870	14021	515	19424	11175	106764
	Answers	5916	5916	5916	5916	36682	36682	36682	75547	75547	75547	160120	160120	393730
	Completeness	100	100	100	100	100	100	100	100	100	100	100	100	100

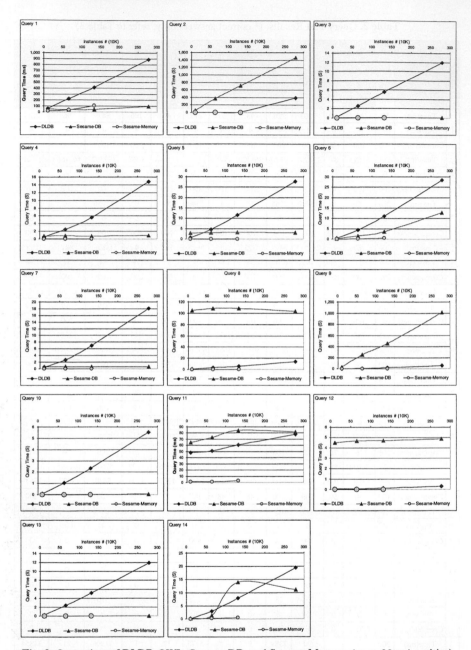

Fig. 2. Query time of DLDB-OWL, Sesame-DB, and Sesame-Memory (up to 20 universities)

performance of a certain system and its characteristics. Of course how to categorize queries is yet another issue. As another, Sesame-DB implements the main bulk of the evaluation in its RQL query engine while its query engine for another query language

SeRQL pushes a lot of the work down to the underlying DBMS. As for DLDB-OWL, it directly translates as much of the query for the database. Further work should be done to investigate how these design differences as well as the underlying DBMS used impact performance.

4.3 Query Completeness and Soundness

As described in [12], we have chosen the benchmark test queries according to several criteria. In fact, another effort we have made in defining these queries is to make them as realistic as possible. In other words, we want these queries to represent, to some extent, those in the real world. We are very interested in seeing what queries can be answered by each system.

As mentioned before, Sesame is able to address RDF/RDFS semantics while DLDB-OWL and OWLJessKB integrate extra OWL inference capability. As the results turned out, all systems could answer Queries 1 through 5 and Query 14 completely. As we expected, DLDB-OWL was able to find all the answers for Queries 6 to 10, which requires subsumption inference in order to get complete results, while Sesame could only find partial or no answers for them. It is interesting to notice that DLDB-OWL and Sesame found complete answers for Query 5 in different ways: DLDB-OWL made use of subsumption, while Sesame, although not able to figure out the subsumption, used an *rdfs:domain* restriction to determine the types of the individuals in the data set and thus achieved the same result. OWLJessKB could find all the answers for every query, and was the only system to answer Queries 11 and 13 completely, which assume *owl:TransitiveProperty* and *owl:inverseOf* inference respectively. Nevertheless, we have discovered that OWLJessKB made unsound inferences with respect to some queries. Specifically, it returned incorrect answers to Queries 4, 6, 8, and 12 because it incorrectly inferred that Lecturer is a Professor, Employee a Student, and Student a Chair. We list in Table 3 the completeness and soundness of OWLJessKB for each query.

Table 3. Query Soundness of OWLJessKB.

	1	2	3	4	5	6	7	8	9	10	11	12	13	14
Total/ Correct answers	4/4	0/0	6/6	41/34	719/719	8330/ 7790	67/67	8330/ 7790	208/208	4/4	224/224	540/15	1/1	5916/5916
Soundness	100	100	100	83	100	94	100	94	100	100	100	3	100	100

4.4 A Combined Metric

As the previous section shows, the target systems in this evaluation differ a lot in their inference capability. We feel it is insufficient to evaluate the query response time and answer completeness and soundness in isolation. We need a metric to measure them in combination so as to better appreciate the overall performance of a system and the potential tradeoff between the query response time and inference capability. At the same time, we have realized that this is a challenging issue. We introduce here our initial attempt to address this issue.

First, we use the F-Measure metric to compute the tradeoff between query completeness and soundness, since essentially they are analogous to recall and precision in Information Retrieval. In the formula below, C_q and S_q ($\in [0, 1]$) are the answer completeness and soundness for query q. b determines the weighting of C_q and S_q. We set it to 1 here, which means we equally weight completeness and soundness.

$$F_q = \frac{2b * C_q * S_q}{b^2 * C_q + S_q}$$

Then, we define a composite metric CM of query response time and answer completeness and soundness as the following, which is also inspired by F-Measure:

$$CM = \frac{1}{M} \sum_{q=1}^{M} \frac{2\alpha * P_q * F_q}{\alpha^2 * P_q + F_q}$$

In the above, M is the total number of test queries; $P_q \in [0, 1]$ is defined as

$$P_q = \max\left(1 - \frac{T_q}{N}, \varepsilon\right)$$

T_q is the response time (ms) for query q and N is the total number of instances in the data set concerned. We have used a timeout value to eliminate undue affect of those query response time that is extremely far away from others in the test results: if to a certain query q, a system's response time per instance is greater than 1- ε, where ε is a very small positive value, we will use ε for P_q instead. We use ε of 0.0001 in this evaluation. α has the same role as b in F_q and is also set to 1.

Generally speaking, the CM metric will reward those systems that can answer queries faster, more completely and more soundly. We calculate the metric value of each target system with respect to each data set. Fig. 3 shows the results. We find that these numerical results are very helpful for us to appreciate the overall performance of each system. DLDB-OWL achieves higher scores across all the data sets than the others. This helps us believe that its extra inference capability is not counterproductive. On the contrary, OWLJessKB receives the lowest value, emphasizing the need of performance improvement in it. And the higher CM values Sesame-Memory gets than Sesame-DB again suggest that it is a reasonable choice for small scale application if persistent storage is not required, particularly if completeness is not significant.

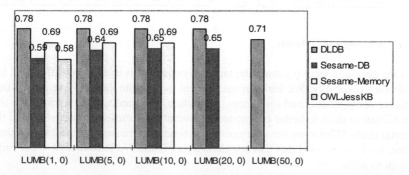

Fig. 3. CM values with weights b=1 and α=1

5   Related Work

To the best of our knowledge, the Lehigh University Benchmark we used in the evaluation is the first one for Semantic Web systems. [1] has developed some benchmark queries for RDF, however, these are mostly intensional queries, while we are concerned with extensional queries for OWL. Some attempts have been done to benchmark description logic systems [10, 17]. The emphasis of this work is to evaluate the reasoning algorithms in terms of the tradeoff between expressiveness and tractability in description logic. Our benchmark is not a description logic benchmark. We are more concerned about the issue of storing and querying large amount of data that are created for realistic Semantic Web systems. Detailed discussion on related work to the benchmark can be found in [12].

The Web Ontology Working Group provides a set of OWL test cases [7]. They are intended to provide examples for, and clarification of, the normative definition of OWL and focus on the completeness and soundness with respect to individual features. Different from our benchmark suite, they are not suitable for the evaluation of scalability.

Tempich and Volz [26] have done some preliminary work towards a benchmark for Semantic Web reasoners. They also point out that the response time as well as the correctness and completeness should be taken into account when formulating benchmark metrics. Though their benchmark is still under construction, they analyze the publicly available ontologies and report them to be clustered into three categories. According to the characteristics of each category, our univ-bench ontology happens to be a synthetic "description logic-style" ontology, which has a moderate number of classes but several restrictions and properties per class. Therefore we argue that our evaluation represents at least a considerable portion of the real word situations. The other two categories are terminological ontologies and database schema-like ontologies. We plan to extend our benchmark suite to those two categories in the future.

6   Conclusions

We presented an evaluation of four knowledge base systems (KBS) with respect to use in large OWL applications, including two memory–based systems (OWLJessKB and memory-based Sesame) and two systems with persistent storage (database-based Sesame and DLDB-OWL). The experiment was conducted in a systematic and standard way by using the Lehigh University Benchmark. We tested those systems with 5 sets of benchmark data and 14 extensional queries. To our knowledge, no experiment has been done with the scale of data used here. The smallest data size used consists of 15 OWL files totaling 8MB, while the largest data size consists of 999 files totaling 583MB.

It is clear that a number of factors must be considered when evaluating a KBS. From our analysis, of the systems tested: DLDB is the best for large data sets where an equal emphasis is placed on query response time and completeness. Sesame-Memory is the best when the size is relatively small (e.g., 1 million triples) and only RDFS inference is required; while for a larger data set (e.g., between 1 and 3 million triples), Sesame-DB may be a good alternative. OWLJessKB is the best for small datasets when OWL Lite reasoning is essential, but only after its unsoundness has been corrected.

It should be pointed out that we believe that the performance of any given system will vary depending on the structure of the ontology and data used to evaluate it. Thus the Lehigh University Benchmark does not provide the final say on what KBS to use for an application. However, we believe that is appropriate for a large class of applications. Furthermore, the basic methodology can be used to generate ontologies and datasets for other classes of applications.

Acknowledgements. Some of the material in this paper is based upon work supported by the Air Force Research Laboratory, Contract Number F30602-00-C-0188 and by the National Science Foundation (NSF) under Grant No. IIS-0346963. Any opinions, findings and conclusions or recommendations expressed in this material are those of the author(s) and do not necessarily reflect the views of the United States Air Force or NSF.

References

1. Alexaki, S. et al. On Storing Voluminous RDF Description: The case of Web Portal Catalogs. In Proc. of the 4th International Workshop on the Web and Databases. 2001.
2. M. Dean and G. Schreiber ed. OWL Web Ontology Language Reference. http://www.w3.org/TR/owl-ref/
3. Bitton, D., DeWitt, D., and Turbyfill, C. Benchmarking Database Systems, a Systematic Approach. In Proc. of the 9th International Conference on Very Large Data Bases. 1983
4. Bitton, D. and Turbyfill, C. A Retrospective on the Wisconsin Benchmark. In Readings in Database Systems, Second Edition. 1994.
5. Broekstra, J. and Kampman, A. Inferencing and Truth Maintenance in RDF Schema: exploring a naive practical approach. In Workshop on Practical and Scalable Semantic Systems (PSSS). 2003.
6. Broekstra, J. and Kampman, A. Sesame: A Generic Architecture for Storing and Querying RDF and RDF Schema. In Proc. of ISWC2002.
7. Carroll, J.J. and Roo, J.D. ed. OWL Web Ontology Test Cases. http://www.w3.org/TR/2004/REC-owl-test-20040210/
8. Cattell, R.G.G. An Engineering Database Benchmark. In Readings in Database Systems, Second Edition. 1994.
9. Connolly, D. et al. DAML+OIL (March 2001) Reference Description. http://www.w3.org/TR/daml+oil-reference
10. Elhaik, Q, Rousset, M-C, and Ycart, B. Generating Random Benchmarks for Description Logics. In Proc. of DL'98.
11. Genusereth, M. and Fikes, R. Knowledge Interchange Format. Stanford Logic Report Logic-92-1, Stanford Univ. http://logic.standford.edu/kif/kif.html
12. Guo, Y., Heflin, J., and Pan, Z. Benchmarking DAML+OIL Repositories. In Proc. of ISWC2003.

13. Guo, Y., Heflin, J., and Pan, Z. An Evaluation of Knowledge Base Systems for Large OWL Datasets. Technical report, CSE department, Lehigh University. 2004. To appear.
14. Guo, Y., Pan, Z. and Heflin, J. Choosing the Best Knowledge Base System for Large Semantic Web Applications. Poster paper at WWW2004.
15. Haarslev, V. and Moller, R. Racer: A Core Inference Engine for the Semantic Web. In Workshop on Evaluation on Ontology-based Tools, ISWC2003.
16. Horrocks, I. The FaCT System. In Automated Reasoning with Analytic Tableaux and Related Methods International Conference (Tableaux'98).
17. Horrocks, I. and Patel-Schneider, P. DL Systems Comparison. In Proc. of DL' 98.
18. Jena – A Semantic Web Framework for Java. http://jena.sourceforge.net/
19. Jess: the Rule Engine for the Java Platform. http://herzberg.ca.sandia.gov/jess
20. KAON: The KArlsruhe ONtology and Semantic Web tool suite. http://kaon.semanticweb.org/
21. Karvounarakis, G. et al. Querying Community Web Portals. http://www.ics.forth.gr/proj/isst/RDF/RQL/rql.pdf
22. Kopena, J.B. and Regli, W.C. DAMLJessKB: A Tool for Reasoning with the Semantic Web. In Proc. of ISWC2003.
23. Pan, Z. and Heflin, J. DLDB: Extending Relational Databases to Support Semantic Web Queries. In Workshop on Practical and Scalable Semantic Systems, ISWC2003.
24. Sintek, M. and Decker, S. TRIPLE – A Query, Inference, and Transformation Language for the Semantic Web. In Proc. of ISWC2002.
25. Stonebraker, M. et al. The SEQUIOA 2000 Storage Benchmark. In Readings in Database Systems, Second Edition. 1994.
26. Tempich, C. and Volz, R. Towards a benchmark for Semantic Web reasoners–an analysis of the DAML ontology library. In Workshop on Evaluation on Ontology-based Tools, ISWC2003.
27. W3C. Resource Description Framework (RDF). http://www.w3.org/RDF/

Appendix: Test Queries

We herein describe each query in a KIF like language, in which a query is written as a conjunction of atoms. Following that we describe the characteristics of the query.

Query1

(type GraduateStudent ?X)
(takesCourse ?X http://www.Department0.University0.edu/GraduateCourse0)

This query bears large input and high selectivity. It queries about just one class and one property and does not assume any hierarchy information or inference.

Query2

(type GraduateStudent ?X) (type University ?Y) (type Department ?Z)
(memberOf ?X ?Z) (subOrganizationOf ?Z ?Y) (undergraduateDegreeFrom ?X ?Y)

This query increases in complexity: 3 classes and 3 properties are involved. Additionally, there is a triangular pattern of relationships between the objects involved.

Query3

(type Publication ?X)
(publicationAuthor ?X http://www.Department0.University0.edu/AssistantProfessor0)

This query is similar to Query 1 but class Publication has a wide hierarchy.

Query4

(type Professor ?X) (worksFor ?X http://www.Department0.University0.edu)
(name ?X ?Y1) (emailAddress ?X ?Y2) (telephone ?X ?Y3)

This query has small input and high selectivity. It assumes *subClassOf* relationship between Professor and its subclasses. Class Professor has a wide hierarchy. Another feature is that it queries about multiple properties of a single class.

Query5
(type Person ?X) (memberOf ?X http://www.Department0.University0.edu)

This query assumes *subClassOf* relationship between Person and its subclasses and *subPropertyOf* relationship between memberOf and its subproperties. Moreover, class Person features a deep and wide hierarchy.

Query6
(type Student ?X)

This query queries about only one class. But it assumes both the explicit *subClassOf* relationship between UndergraduateStudent and Student and the implicit one between GraduateStudent and Student. In addition, it has large input and low selectivity.

Query7
(type Student ?X) (type Course ?Y)
(teacherOf http://www.Department0.University0.edu/AssociateProfessor0 ?Y)(takesCourse ?X ?Y)

This query is similar to Query 6 in terms of class Student but it increases in the number of classes and properties and its selectivity is high.

Query8
(type Student ?X) (type Department ?Y) (memberOf ?X ?Y)
(subOrganizationOf ?Y http://www.University0.edu) (emailAddress ?X ?Z)

This query is further more complex than Query 7 by including one more property.

Query9
(type Student ?X) (type Faculty ?Y) (type Course ?Z)
(advisor ?X ?Y) (takesCourse ?X ?Z) (teacherOf ?Y ?Z)

Besides the aforementioned features of class Student and the wide hierarchy of class Faculty, this query is characterized by the most classes and properties in the query set. Like Query 2, there is a triangular pattern of relationships.

Query10
(type Student ?X) (takesCourse ?X http://www.Department0.University0.edu/GraduateCourse0)

This query differs from Query 6, 7, 8 and 9 in that it only requires the (implicit) *subClassOf* relationship between GraduateStudent and Student, i.e., *subClassOf* relationship between UndergraduateStudent and Student does not add to the results.

Query11
(type ResearchGroup ?X) (subOrganizationOf ?X http://www.University0.edu)

Query 11, 12 and 13 are intended to verify the presence of certain OWL reasoning capabilities in the system. In this query, property subOrganizationOf is defined as transitive. Since in the benchmark data, instances of ResearchGroup are stated as a sub-organization of a Department individual and the later suborganization of a University individual, inference about the subOrgnizationOf relationship between instances of ResearchGroup and University is required to answer this query. Additionally, its input is small.

Query12
(type Chair ?X) (type Department ?Y)
(worksFor ?X ?Y) (subOrganizationOf ?Y http://www.University0.edu)

The benchmark data do not produce any instances of class Chair. Instead, each Department individual is linked to the chair professor of that department by property headOf. Hence this query requires realization, i.e., inference that that professor is an instance of class Chair because he or she is the head of a department. Input of this query is small as well.

Query13
(type Person ?X) (hasAlumnus http://www.University0.edu ?X)

Property hasAlumnus is defined in the benchmark ontology as the inverse of property degreeFrom, which has three subproperties: undergraduateDegreeFrom, mastersDegreeFrom, and doctoralDegreeFrom. The benchmark data state a person as an alumnus of a university using one of these three subproperties instead of hasAlumnus. Therefore, this query assumes *subPropertyOf* relationships between degreeFrom and its subproperties, and also requires inference about *inverseOf*.

Query14
(@everyInstance UndergraduateStudent ?X)

This query is the simplest in the test set. This query represents those with large input and low selectivity and does not assume any hierarchy information or inference.

Structure-Based Partitioning of Large Concept Hierarchies

Heiner Stuckenschmidt and Michel Klein

Vrije Universiteit Amsterdam
de Boelelaan 1081a, 1081HV Amsterdam
{heiner, mcaklein}@cs.vu.nl

Abstract. The increasing awareness of the benefits of ontologies for information processing has lead to the creation of a number of large ontologies about real-world domains. The size of these ontologies and their monolithic character cause serious problems in handling them. In other areas, e.g. software engineering, these problems are tackled by partitioning monolithic entities into sets of meaningful and mostly self-contained modules. In this paper, we suggest a similar approach for ontologies. We propose a method for automatically partitioning large ontologies into smaller modules based on the structure of the class hierarchy. We show that the structure-based method performs surprisingly well on real-world ontologies. We support this claim by experiments carried out on real-world ontologies including SUMO and the NCI cancer ontology. The results of these experiments are available online at http://swserver.cs.vu.nl/partitioning/.

1 Motivation

The increasing awareness of the benefits of ontologies for information processing in open and weakly structured environments has lead to the creation of a number of such ontologies for real-world domains. In complex domains such as medicine these ontologies can contain thousands of concepts. Examples of such large ontologies are the NCI cancer ontology [5] with about 27.500 and the Gene ontology [8] with about 22.000 concepts. Other examples can be found in the area of e-commerce where product classification such as the UNSPSC or the NAICS contain thousands of product categories. While being useful for many applications, the size and the monolithic nature of these ontologies cause new problems that affect different steps of the ontology life cycle.

Maintenance: Ontologies that contain thousands of concepts cannot be created and maintained by a single person. The broad coverage of such large ontologies normally requires a team of experts. In many cases these experts will be located in different organizations and will work on the same ontology in parallel. An example for such a situation is the gene ontology that is maintained by a consortium of experts.

Publication: Large ontologies are mostly created to provide a standard model of a domain to be used by developers of individual solutions within that domain. While existing large ontologies often try cover a complete domain, the providers of individual solutions

S.A. McIlraith et al. (Eds.): ISWC 2004, LNCS 3298, pp. 289–303, 2004.
© Springer-Verlag Berlin Heidelberg 2004

are often only interested in a specific part of the overall domain. The UNSPSC classification, for example, contains categories for all kinds of products and services while the developers of an online computer shop will only be interested in those categories related to computer hardware and software.

Validation: The nature of ontologies as reference models for a domain requires a high degree of quality of the respective model. Representing a consensus model, it is also important to have proposed models validated by different experts. In the case of large ontologies it is often difficult—if not impossible—to understand the model as a whole due to cognitive limits. What is missing is an abstracted view on the overall model and its structure as well as the possibility to focus the inspection on a specific aspect.

Processing: On a technical level, very large ontologies cause serious scalability problems. The complexity of reasoning about ontologies is well known to be critical even for smaller ontologies. In the presence of ontologies like the NCI cancer ontology, not only reasoning engines but also modelling and visualization tools reach their limits. Currently, there is no OWL-based modelling tool that can provide convenient modelling support for ontologies of the size of the NCI ontology.

All these problems are a result of the fact that the ontology as a whole is too large to handle. Most problems would disappear if the overall model consists of a set of coherent modules about a certain subtopic that can be used independently of the other modules, while still containing information about its relation to these other modules.

- In distributed development, experts could be responsible for an single module and maintain it independently of other modules thus reducing revision problems.
- Users of an ontology could use a subset of the overall ontology by selecting a set of relevant modules. While only having to deal with this relevant part, the relations to other parts of the model are still available through the global structure.
- Validation of a large ontologies could be done based on single modules that are easier to understand. Being related to a certain subtopic, it will be easier to judge the completeness and consistency of the model. Validated modules could be published early while other parts of the ontology are still under development.
- The existence of modules will enable the use of software tools that are not able to handle the complete ontology. In the case of modelling and visualization tools, the different modules could be loaded one by one and processed individually. For reasoning tasks we could make use of parallel architectures where reasoners work on single modules and exchange partial results.

Recently, some proposals concerning the representation of modules and their connections have been made [9,3,7]. These papers propose languages and discuss issues like the organization of modules and dependencies between them. A problem that has not been addressed yet concerns the creation of modules from existing ontologies. This problem which we call *partitioning* or *modularization* is discussed in the remainder of this paper.

2 Structure-Based Partitioning

The key question connected to modularization is about suitable criteria for determining the assignment of concepts to modules. This requires a good intuition about the nature of a module as well as of the purpose of the modularization. As we have seen above, there are many different use cases that come with different requirements for criteria for determining modules. Further distinctions have to be made with respect to the nature of the ontologies addressed by the method. On the semantic web, we find all kinds of ontologies starting from simple class hierarchies to complex description logic models encoded in OWL. As an attempt to develop a method that works equally well for all kinds of ontologies is likely to fail, we focus on a particular type of ontology and a certain use of the resulting partitioning.

> **Contribution:** We propose a method for partitioning large light-weight ontologies that mainly consists of a class hierarchy into disjoint and covering sets of concepts for the purpose of easier browsing and exploring the hierarchy.

Note that the method we propose can be applied to any kind of ontology that contains some kind of hierarchy. In cases where concepts are further described by their features or logical axioms, however, our method is likely to produce sub-optimal results as the information in the definitions is not taken into account. Our method is sensitive to the intended use of the resulting model, as other purposes can require partially overlapping modules or the partitioning into sets of axioms rather than concepts.

2.1 Intuition and Assumptions

Intuitively, we can say that a module should contain information about a coherent subtopic that can stand for itself. This requires that the concepts within a module are semantically connected to each other and do not have strong dependencies with information outside the module. These considerations imply the need for a notion of *dependency* between concepts that needs to be taken into account. There are many different ways in which concepts can be related explicitly or implicitly. At this point we abstract from specific kinds of dependencies and choose a general notion of dependency between concepts. The resulting model is the one of a weighted graph $O = \langle C, D, w \rangle$ where nodes C represent concepts and links D between concepts represent different kinds of dependencies that can be weighted according to the strength of the dependency. These dependencies can be reflected in the definitions of the ontology or can be implied by the intuitive understanding of concepts and background knowledge about the respective domain. Looking for an automatic partitioning method, we are only interested in such kinds of dependencies that can be derived from the ontology itself. This leads us to the central assumption underlying our approach:

> **Assumption:** Dependencies between concepts can be derived from the structure of the ontology.

Depending on the representation language, different structures can be used as indicators of dependencies. These structures can be subclass relations between classes, other relations linked to classes by the range and domain restrictions or the appearance of a class name in the definition of another class. It can be argued that a method purely based on the structure of the ontology is not able to capture important dependencies that could be found by analyzing the names of classes and the logical definitions of concepts. Our motivation for ignoring these additional aspects is of a practical nature: we want our method to scale up to large ontologies that contain hundreds of thousands of concepts. A semantical investigation of the dependencies of such ontologies would suffer from the same scalability problems we hope to solve with out partitioning method. Therefore, the question addressed in this paper is not so much about an optimal method for determining modules but about how far we can get with a rather simple and scalable method based on the structure of the ontology.

2.2   Partitioning Steps

Our method consists of two tasks that are executed in five independent steps. The first task is the creation of a weighted graph from an ontology definition. This is done in two steps: extraction of the dependency structure and determination of the weight of the dependency. The second task concerns the identification of modules from the dependency graph. The first step in this task is the detection of strongly related sets of concepts. In the following we discuss the techniques currently used in these steps.

Step 1: Create Dependency Graph: In the first step a dependency graph is extracted from an ontology source file. We implemented a PROLOG-based tool that reads OWL and RDF schema files using the SWI semantic web library [10] and outputs a graph format used by the networks analysis tool Pajek [2] that we use for detecting related sets of nodes. The tool can be configured to use different kinds of dependencies. Currently it can extract dependencies corresponding to the subclass hierarchy and dependencies created by the domain and range restrictions in property definitions.

Step 2: Determine strength of Dependencies: In the second step the strength of the dependencies between the concepts has to be determined. Following the basic assumption of our approach, we use the structure of the dependency graph to determine the weights of dependencies. In particular we use results from social network theory by computing the proportional strength network for the dependency graph. The strength of the dependency of a connection between a node c_i and c_j is determined to be the proportional strengths of the connection. The proportional strength describes the importance of a link from one node to the other based on the number of connections a node has. In general it is computed by dividing the sum of the weights of all connections between c_i and c_j by the sum of the weights of all connections c_i has to other nodes (compare [4], page 54ff):

$$w(c_i, c_j) = \frac{a_{ij} + a_{ji}}{\sum_k a_{ik} + a_{ki}}$$

Here a_{ij} is the weight preassigned to the link between c_i and c_j - in the experiments reported below this will always be one. As a consequence, the proportional strength used in the experiments is one divided by the number of nodes c_i is connected to. The intuition behind it is that individual social contacts become more important if there are only few of them. In our setting, this measure is useful because we want to prevent that classes that are only related to a low number of other classes get separated from them. This would be against the intuition that classes in a module should be related. We use node **d** in Figure 1 to illustrate the calculation

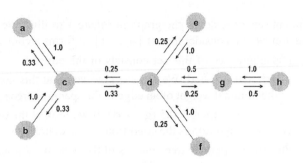

Fig. 1. An Example Graph with proportional strength dependencies

of weights using the proportional strength. The node has four direct neighbors, this means that the proportional strength of the relation to these neighbors is 0.25 (one divided by four). Different levels of dependency between **d** and its neighbors now arise from the relative dependencies of the neighbors with **d** (the proportional strength is non-symmetric). We see that **e** and **f** hoaving no other neighbors completely depend on **d**. The corresponding value of the dependency is 1. Further, the strength of the dependency between **g** and **d** is 0.5, because **g** has two neighbors and the dependency between **b** and **d** is 0.33 as **b** has 3 neighbors.

Step 3: Determine Modules: The proportional strength network provides us with a foundation for detecting sets of strongly related concepts. For this purpose, we make use of an algorithm that computes all maximal line islands of a given size in a graph [1].

Definition 1 (Line Island). *A set of vertices $I \subseteq C$ is a line island in a dependency graph $G = (C, D, w)$ if and only if*
- *I induces a connected subgraph of G*
- *There is a weighted graph $T = (V_T, E_T, w_T)$ such that:*
  - *T is embedded in G*
  - *T is an maximal spanning tree with respect to I*
  - *the following equation holds:*

$$\max_{\{(v,v')\in D|(v\in I\wedge v'\notin I)\vee(v'\in I\wedge v\notin I)\}} w(v,v') < \min_{(u,u')\in E_T} w(u,u')$$

Note that for the determination of the maximal spanning tree the direction of edges is not considered.

This criterion exactly coincides with our intuition about the nature of modules given in the introduction, because it determines sets of concepts that are stronger internally connected than to any other concept not in the set. The algorithm requires an upper and a lower bound on the size of the detected set as input and assigns an island number to each node in the dependency graph. We denote the island number assigned to a concept c as $\alpha(c)$. The assignment $\alpha(c) = 0$ means that c could not be assigned to an island.

We use different sets of nodes in the graph in Figure 1 to illustrate the concept of a line island. Let us first consider the set $\{a, ..., f\}$. It forms a connected subgraph. The maximal spanning tree of this set consists of the edges $a \xrightarrow{1.0} c$, $b \xrightarrow{1.0} c$, $c \xrightarrow{0.33} d$, $e \xrightarrow{1.0} d$, and $f \xrightarrow{1.0} d$. We can see however, that this node set is not an island, because the minimal weight of an edge in the spanning tree is 0.33 and there is an incoming edge with strength 0.5 ($g \xrightarrow{0.5} d$). If we look at the remaining set of nodes $\{g, h\}$, we see that it fulfills the conditions of an island: it forms a connected subgraph, the maximal spanning tree consists of the edge $h \xrightarrow{1.0} g$ and the maximal value of in- or outgoing links is 0.5 ($g \xrightarrow{0.5} d$). This set, however, is not what we are looking for because it is not maximal: it is included in the set $\{d, ..., h\}$. This set is a line island with the maximal spanning tree consisting of the edges $e \xrightarrow{1.0} d$, $f \xrightarrow{1.0} d$, $g \xrightarrow{0.5} d$ and $h \xrightarrow{1.0} g$ where the minimal weight (0.5) is higher than the maximal weight of any external link which is $c \xrightarrow{0.33} d$. Another reason for preferring this island is that the remaining node set $\{a, b, c\}$ also forms a line island with maximal spanning tree $a \xrightarrow{1.0} c$, $b \xrightarrow{1.0} c$ and the weaker external link $c \xrightarrow{0.33} d$.

Using these steps as a starting point we carried out a number of experiments in order to test our hypothesis that the structure of the ontology can actually be used to create a sensible partitioning of large ontologies. The most relevant of these experiments are reported in the following.

3   Experiments I: Iterative Partitioning

The different steps described above lead us to a partitioning of the input ontology into modules that satisfy the formal conditions mentioned in the previous section. We applied the steps to a number of ontologies available in OWL or RDF schema, including the SUMO [6] the NCI cancer ontology [5] as well as DICE, a large medical ontology used in one of our projects. Due to lack of space, we do not discuss the results of these initial experiments in details, but concentrate on the problems we identified. The complete results of all experiments can be found at the website that accompanies this article.[1]

One of the main problems with the approach as described above is the fact that we have to determine the size of modules that we want to be generated. The reason is that the optimal size of modules heavily depends on the size and the nature of the ontology.

---

[1] See http://swserver.cs.vu.nl/partitioning/.

In some preliminary experiments we found a module size of one to ten per percent of the size of the complete ontology works quite well for some example ontologies that had between 1000 and 2000 concepts. This heuristic, however, did not work for larger or more fragmented ontologies. In some cases a bad choice of the upper and lower bound for the size of modules also led to an extremely high number of unassigned nodes, i.e. nodes that were not part of any 'island'. In order to avoid these problems, we defined an iterative partitioning strategy that avoids some of the problems mentioned above. In the following, we present the iterative partitioning strategy and summarize the results of applying this strategy to real world ontologies.

3.1   Iterative Partitioning

The idea of the iterative assignment algorithm is to not prescribe the size of modules to be generated but to let them be determined solely by the island criterion given in the last section. A way of doing this is to set the lower bound to 1 and the upper bound to $s - 1$ where s is the size of the complete ontology. Reducing the limit by one forces the algorithm to split up the ontology in some way as the complete model exceeds the upper size limit for an island. Choosing a limit that is just one below the size of the complete ontology does not further restrict the selection of islands. This way we get the most natural grouping of concepts into strongly dependent sets. Even in this case where we do not restrict the size of island it can still happen, that nodes cannot be assigned to islands. Therefore we have to perform the expansion step afterwards in order to assign these nodes to a module.

Step 4: Assign Isolated Concepts: Our experiments showed that leftover nodes can occur at different places in the graph and are not necessarily related. Therefore we chose to assign them to existing modules. The assignment is based on the strength of the relations to nodes already assigned to a module. In particular leftover nodes are assigned to the island of the neighboring node they have the strongest relation to. In cases where all neighboring nodes are unassigned as well, these nodes are assigned first.

As a result of this strategy the islands found by the algorithm can significantly differ in size. In particular, we often get large islands that cover most of the ontology. In order to get modules of a reasonable size, we iteratively apply the algorithm to islands that are too large to be useful modules. Often this applies only for a single large island, but there are also cases especially in the case of very large ontologies where the algorithm has to be applied recursively on different parts of the ontology. Nodes in islands that are small enough get a unique number assigned and form a module of the ontology.

Algorithm 1 shows the corresponding labelling algorithm that takes a graph and labels the nodes of the graph with numbers that correspond to a partitioning assignment. The algorithm also needs the upper limit of the size of a module as input in order to determine when to stop the iterating. The counter is used in the recursive calls to make sure that modules have unique numbers. When starting the iteration, the counter has to be set to zero.

Algorithm 1 Partition

Require: limit: integer
Require: ontology: graph
Require: counter:integer
  CURRENT := ontology
  if $|current| > limit$ then
    MIN := 1
    MAX := $|current| - 1$
    CANDIDATES := islands(min,max,current)
    for all module $\in$ candidates do
      Expand(module,current)
      Partition(limit,module,counter)
    end for
  else
    COUNTER := counter + 1
    for all $c \in current$ do
      $\alpha(c)$:= counter
    end for
    return counter
  end if

3.2   Evaluation of Partitions

Looking at the result of the example application we get a first idea about the strengths
and weaknesses of the algorithm. We can see that the algorithm generates some modules
that meet our intuition about the nature of a module quite well. In some cases subtrees
that could be considered to form one module are further split even if the complete
subtree does not exceed the upper size limit. This can be explained by an unbalanced
modelling of the ontology as subtrees tend to be split up at concepts with a high number
of direct subclasses compared to its sibling classes. This phenomenon often reflect
a special importance of the respective concept in the ontology that also justifies the
decision to create a separate model for this concept. The iterative strategy frees us from
determining a lower bound for the size of modules. As a result, however, the algorithm
sometimes create rather small modules. This normally happens when the root concept
of a small subtree is linked to a concept that has many direct subclasses. For the result
of the partitioning method these subsets are often pathological because a coherent topic
is split up into a number of small modules that do not really constitute a sensible model
on their own.

When inspecting the dependencies in the relevant parts of the hierarchy, we discovered that most of the problematic modules have very strong internal dependencies.
In order to distinguish such cases, we need a measure for the strength of the internal
dependency. The measure that we use is called the 'height' of an island. It uses the
minimal spanning tree T used to identify the module: the overall strength of the internal
dependency equals the strength of the weakest link in the spanning tree.

$$height(I) = \min_{(u,u') \in E_T} w(u, u')$$

We can again illustrate the the concept of height using the example from figure 1. WE identifies two islands, namely $\{a, b, c\}$ and $\{d, ..., h\}$. As the maximal spanning tree of the first island consists of the two edges a $\xrightarrow{1.0}$ c, b $\xrightarrow{1.0}$ c, the height of this island is 1.0. In the maximal spanning tree of the second island the edge g $\xrightarrow{0.5}$ d is the weakest link that therefore sets the height of the island to 0.5.

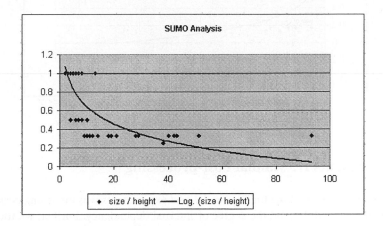

Fig. 2. Sizes and heights of partitions in the SUMO ontology

We found many cases where generated modules that do not make sense had an internal dependency of strength one. In a post-processing step this allows us to automatically detect critical modules. While for the case of an internal strength of one we almost never found the corresponding module useful in the context of the original ontology, it is not clear where to draw the line between a level of internal dependency that still defines sensible modules and a level that overrules important dependencies to concepts outside the module. In our experiments we made the experience that a threshold of 0.5 leads to good results in most cases.[2]

Figures 2 and 3 show the results of comparing the size and the height of computed islands. The plots clearly show a correlation between these properties. We also see that— except for one case—islands with a height of one are quite small.[3] The results of these experiments provided us with sufficient evidence that the height of an island is a useful criterion for judging the quality of a module. In successive experiments reported below we used this result to improve the partitions created by the iterative strategy. The results of these experiments are reported below.

---

[2] Note that due to the calculation of the dependency value, the internal strength is always of the form $\frac{1}{n}$.

[3] The exception is a part of the NCI ontology that lists all countries of the world and therefore contains 1 class with more than 200 subclasses

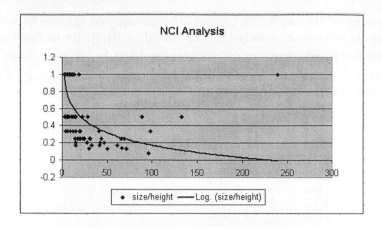

Fig. 3. Sizes and heights of partitions in the NCI ontology

4   Experiments II: Manual Post-processing

As described above, on of the findings in the first experiments was the strong correlation between size of modules and the degree of internal dependency. Further, we found out that small modules were unnatural in most cases. In a second experiment, we wanted to find out whether this result can be used to 'repair' the result of the straightforward partitioning.

Step 5: Merging: All modules with a height of 1.0 or 0.5 are merged into adjacent modules with a lower height. In many cases, there is only one adjacent module to merge with. In cases where more than one adjacent module exist, we decided for the most natural choice. In principle, the strength of the dependencies between the modules can be used to also determine a candidate for merging automatically.

The merging process was done manually using the functionality of the Pajek tool and some supporting scripts. In the following, we present and discuss the results of this experiment for the SUMO and the NCI administration ontology.

4.1   The SUMO Ontology

The partitioning of the SUMO ontology resulted into 38 partitions of which 17 had a height of lower than 0.5 (see complete results at http://swserver.cs.vu.nl/ partitioning/). These 17 partitions and their sizes after the merging process are listed in table 1. We see that the topics of the modules—which we derived from the top concept of the respective module—represent sensible subtopics of the overall ontology, which are not too close to each other. The average size of the modules is 37 concepts. Comparing this list to the modules created in the first experiment, we see that the use of the height criterion for merging enabled us to get rid of most of the problems that had occurred. An example is a high number of small modules for different kinds of measures that were created by the partitioning algorithm and that are now contained in

Table 1. Modules Generated for the SUMO Ontology

	Topic	Size			
1	Text	14	9	Real Number	14
2	Biological Attribute	12	10	Self-Connected Object	24
3	Substance	38	11	Language	23
4	Intentional Process	33	12	Proposition	11
5	Linguistic Communication	36	13	Relation	51
6	Declaration	21	14	Constant Quantity	77
7	Making	111	15	Agent	40
8	Artifact	20	16	Entity (Top-Level)	51
			17	Corpuscular Object	54

the module 'Constant Quantity'. The only problematic modules are the ones concerned with actions. The module 'making' is quite large and contains different types of actions that a human knowledge engineer would not necessarily put in the same module. Looking at the original graph we see that this part of the hierarchy is quite tangled which makes it difficult to find split points.

More striking than the pure list of concepts, however, is the module graph created in the second experiment. The graph shown in Figure 4 provides a very useful overview over the different topics covered by SUMO. We think that this representation is more useful for getting an overview of the content of SUMO than any visualization based on the individual concepts.

4.2 The NCI Cancer Ontology

In a second experiment, we took the partitioning created for the administrative part of the NCI Cancer ontology and removed partitions with a height of 1 or 0.5 by merging them with partitions of a lower height. The initial partitioning contained 108 modules many of which were quite small (compare Figure 3. Often, clearly related parts of the hierarchy had been cut up into a number of small modules. A good examples are cell lines. The initial partitioning distinguished between six different cell lines in addition to the general module about cell lines. Each of these cell line modules contained less than ten concepts. A similar situation could be observed in connection to medical occupations like different kinds of surgeons and nurses. The manual merging process based on the height of the partitions created a single cell line partition. For the case of surgeons the result is less optimal as different kinds of occupations had to be merged into a single module when using the height criterion.

Only 38 of the modules had a height of lower than 0.5. Table 2 lists these 38 modules and their respective sizes after the merging process. The average size of a module is 57 which higher than for SUMO but still a reasonable value. We have to notice, however that the variance is much higher as we find module sizes between 4 and 268. Most of

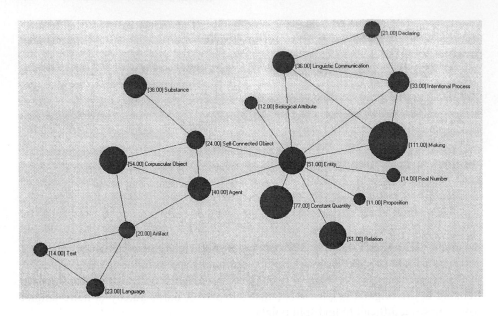

Fig. 4. Module Graph of the SUMO Ontology after Merging

the extreme cases can be explained by the special structure of the ontology. The concept conceptual entity for example has about 100 direct subconcepts that create a rather large module. The same holds for the concept country. More problematic are the modules 'clinical sciences' and occupation or discipline' that are rather large and heterogenous. In future work, we will have to analyze these modules in detail and determine a strategy for avoiding these problems by adjusting the dependency measure or the merging process.

5 Discussion

In this paper we describe a method for structure-based ontology partitioning that is practically applicable to very large ontologies. We show that a modularization based on structural properties of the ontology only already results in modules that intuitively make sense. Because modularizing an ontology essentially is a modelling activity, there is no "golden standard" to compare our results with. To come up with a more validated assessment of the quality of our modules, we need to do an experiment in which we compare the result of human modularization with our result[4].

An advantage of the method described in this paper is that there are no arbitrary choices – apart from the maximum size of a module which in many cases can be derived from the limitations of the technology used – that have to be made in advance (e.g. the number of modules required). However, there are several choices we made

---

[4] Creating a human modularization might be difficult in practice, as one of the major reasons for partitioning is that a human is not able to overlook the ontology as a whole.

Table 2. Modules Created for the NCI Administration Ontology

	Topic	Size
1	Biology	48
2	Pharmacology	20
3	Epidemiology	30
4	Clinical sciences	189
5	Medicine	85
6	Public Health	24
7	Occupation or Discipline	193
8	Social Sciences	25
9	Medical Economics	14
10	Technology	50
11	Information Science	27
12	NCI Administrative Concept	4
13	Training and Education	15
14	Board Certification	12
15	Information and Media	16
16	Database	15
17	Media / Document Type	111
18	Business Rule	61
19	Patient or Public Education	20
20	Nursing	46
21	Funding	130
22	Funding Categories	30
23	Research Career Programs	24
24	Costs	9
25	Professional Organization	56
26	Component of the NCI	75
27	NCI Boards and Groups	32
28	Population Group	71
29	Social Concept	66
30	Conceptual Entity	170
31	Sites of Care Delivery	268
32	Cancer Science	4
33	Model System	42
34	Miscellaneous Terms	23
35	Cancer Biology	17
36	Carciogenesis Mechanism	17
37	Specimen	26
38	Cell Line	101

when designing the method that need to be discussed in the light of the experiments. The first one is the choice of using the ontology structure as a basis for determining modules. We think that the experiments reported here show that we can achieve good results even with a minimal approach that uses the concept hierarchy only. It remains to be investigated whether the use of more structural information than the hierarchy and produces better results. We plan to investigate the performance of our method on graphs that include dependencies resulting from user defined relations and from the use of concepts in definitions and axioms.

Another direction for future research is the dependency measure. Currently, we use the proportional strengths, a measure adopted from social network theory that is only based on the direct connections of a node giving each connection an equal importance. It is possible that the development of dependency measures specifically for ontologies could improve our results. There are two directions in which such measures can be developed.

- **Context-aware measures:** dependency measures that do not only use the direct relations of a node but also look at relations further away and the "importance" of nodes. Measures of this type could vary in the depth in which they take other relations into account, the weight that is given to them, and the way in which the importance of nodes is calculated.
- **Semantics-based measures:** measures that use the semantics of relations for determining the dependency. Possible measures of this type are ones that give "isa"

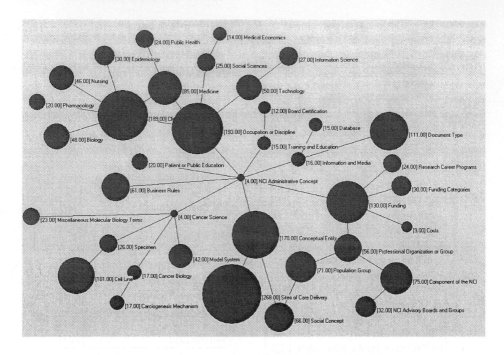

Fig. 5. Module Graph of the NCI Administration Ontology after Merging

relations a higher weight than other relations and measures that give a higher initial value to subrelations than their superrelations.

Experiments with other dependency measures should tell us whether such measures results in better modules than the ones that result from the basic measure that we used.

Another choice involves the level of abstraction at which we create the partitioning, i.e. the number of modules produced and their respective size. There are two parameters that control the abstraction level:

1. the termination point of the partitioning process, and
2. the criteria for merging modules.

In our current approach, we use the size of the module as termination criterium. This criterium can be seen as subjective; however, often the simple fact that the size of an ontology exceeds a certain threshold is the major motive to start modularizing an ontology. Using the size of the modules as termination criterium therefore is defendable. For the merging process, we currently use the coherence as criterium. For both parameters, we could experiment with the other measures than the one currently used. Further research is necessary to tell what measures perform well in which situations and what are useful threshold values for specific ontologies.

Besides experimenting with the different factors discussed above, we plan to work on automating the partitioning process as a whole. Ideally, this would result in tool that partitions an ontology and allows to adapt the abstraction level on the fly. For this to happen, we first need to do more work on the merging process and create a method that precisely describes how to perform the merging.

References

1. V. Batagelj. Analysis of large networks - islands. Presented at Dagstuhl seminar 03361: Algorithmic Aspects of Large and Complex Networks, August/September 2003.
2. V. Batagelj and A. Mrvar. Pajek - analysis and visualization of large networks. In M. Jünger and P. Mutzel, editors, *Graph Drawing Software*, pages 77–103. Springer, 2003.
3. P. Bouquet, F. Giunchiglia, F. van Harmelen, L. Serafini, and H. Stuckenschmidt. C-owl: Contextualizing ontologies. In *Proceedings of the 2nd International Semantic Web Conference ISWC'03*, Lecture Notes in Computer Science, pages 164–179, Sanibal Island, Florida, 2003. Springer Verlag.
4. R.S. Burt. *Structural Holes. The Social Structure of Competition*. Harvard University Press, 1992.
5. Jennifer Golbeck, Gilberto Fragoso, Frank Hartel, Jim Hendler, Jim Oberthaler, and Bijan Parsia. The national cancer institute's thesaurus and ontology. *Journal of Web Semantics*, 1(1), 2003.
6. I. Niles and A. Pease. Toward a standard upper ontology. In Chris Welty and Barry Smith, editors, *Proceedings of the 2nd International Conference on Formal Ontology in Information Systems (FOIS-2001)*, 2001.
7. H. Stuckenschmidt and M. Klein. Integrity and change in modular ontologies. In *Proceedings of the International Joint Conference on Artificial Intelligence - IJCAI'03*, pages 900–905, Acapulco, Mexico, 2003. Morgan Kaufmann.
8. The Gene Ontology Consortium. Gene ontology: tool for the unification of biology. *Nature Genetics*, 25:25–29, 2000.
9. R. Volz, A. Maedche, and D. Oberle. Towards a modularized semantic web. In *Proceedings of the ECAI'02 Workshop on Ontologies and Semantic Interoperability*, 2002.
10. J. Wielemaker, G. Schreiber, and B. Wielinga. Prolog-based infrastructure for RDF: performance and scalability. In D. Fensel, K. Sycara, and J. Mylopoulos, editors, *The Semantic Web - Proceedings ISWC'03, Sanibel Island, Florida*, pages 644–658, Berlin, Germany, october 2003. Springer Verlag. LNCS 2870.

Semantic Web Service Interaction Protocols: An Ontological Approach*

Ronald Ashri[1], Grit Denker[2], Darren Marvin[3], Mike Surridge[3], and Terry Payne[1]

[1] University of Southampton, Southampton, UK
{ra, trp}@ecs.soton.ac.uk
[2] SRI International, Menlo Park, California, USA
denker@csl.sri.com
[3] IT Innovation, Southampton, UK
{djm, ms}@it-innovation.soton.ac.uk

Abstract. A central requirement for achieving the vision of run-time discovery and dynamic composition of services is the provision of appropriate descriptions of the operation of a service, that is, how the service interacts with agents or other services. In this paper, we use experience gained through the development of real-life Grid applications to produce a set of requirements for such descriptions and then attempt to match those requirements against the offerings of existing work, such as OWL-S [1] and IRS-II [2]. Based on this analysis we identify which requirements are not addressed by current research and, in response, produce a model for describing the *interaction protocol* of a service in response. The main contributions of this model are the ability to describe the interactions of multiple parties with respect to a single service, distinguish between interactions initiated by the service itself and interactions that are initiated by clients or other cooperating services, and capture within the description service state changes relevant to interacting parties that are either a result of internal service events or interactions. The aim of the model is not to replace existing work, since it only focuses on the description of the interaction protocol of a service, but to inform the further development of such work.

1 Introduction

Recent years have seen a redoubling of effort, both within industry and academia, to provide appropriate solutions to the problem of run-time discovery and composition of services [3,4]. Such a capability is central to the needs of a wide range of application domains and its importance is underlined by a significant amount of industrial backing in terms of willingness to agree on underlying standards and to provide tools in support of application development. For example, within the context of e-business it is required to support

---

* Supported by the Defense Advanced Research Projects Agency through the Air Force Research Laboratory under Contract F30602-00-C-0168 to SRI. Supported by Engineering and Physical Sciences Research Council Semantic Firewall project (ref. GR./S45744/01)

S.A. McIlraith et al. (Eds.): ISWC 2004, LNCS 3298, pp. 304–319, 2004.

the dynamic provision of services selected at run-time from an ever-changing pool of competing service providers based on user preferences, or the creation of coalitions of service providers working towards a common goal [5,6]. Within the context of e-science it can enable researchers to better take advantage of Grid infrastructure to create complex solutions involving the use of computational resources and highly specialised services across institutional boundaries [7]. The majority of such efforts focus on the use of Web Services (WS) [8] as the enabling infrastructure, which provides the necessary standardization of message transportation [9], low-level service description [10], service discovery (e.g. UDDI [11]) and service composition (e.g. BPEL4WS [12]). However, WS technologies, *on their own*, are judged as insufficient to provide effective solutions to the problem of *dynamic* discovery and composition, due to the lack of appropriate semantic descriptions of the services involved and insufficient support for flexible run-time dynamic binding of services [13,3].

In response to these limitations, a number of solutions have been proposed, which either attempt to provide an overarching model, which is then linked to the underlying WS infastructure (top-down approach - e.g. OWL-S [1], IRS-II [2]), or attempt to embed appropriate solutions *within* the WS infrastructure (bottom-up approach - e.g. [13], [14]). The latter approach, although it often supports rapid progress, has the obvious limitation of being restricted in the type of solutions it produces by the WS infrastructure it attempts to integrate with. Furthermore, as the infrastructure itself is evolving the solutions will have to adapt to newer versions of standards. The former approach allows for the development of more generalised solutions that can find application outside a WS context and as the WS standards evolve. It supports a clear distinction between an abstract model of service description, which can then be used to support service discovery and composition, and the implementation of that model within the context of a specific set of enabling technologies, such as WS. Nevertheless, even these overarching models still have some way to go before they adequately address the range of issues related to service description.

In this paper we identify some of the shortcomings of current approaches as they relate to the description of the *operational process* of a service, or in other words, its *interaction protocol*, based on a set of requirements derived through an analysis of real-life Grid application scenarios implemented using the GRIA infrastructure [15]. We then propose a model for describing the interaction protocol, which furthers the state of the art through the following specific contributions.

- The ability to describe *multi-party interactions* with respect to a single service, with the different parties distinguished by the *roles* they occupy within the service operation. This is a result of the the need to be able to describe, with respect to a single service, either strict requirements or simply the capability it has to cooperate with other services and *what form that cooperation can take* during operation.
- The ability to describe interactions initiated by the described service as well as interactions that are initiated by other parties. This provides a more

flexible model than what is currently available and enables the support of more sophisticated services, which can, for example, notify clients about the state of progress or call upon other services to perform specific actions.

– The ability to describe the state changes a service goes through that are relevant to the interacting parties, caused either by events internal to the service or as a result of interactions with outside parties. This enables a client to distinguish between the results of actions it initiates, and those that depend on the service itself or other third parties. Furthermore, it enables other parties, such as security devices integrated in the underlying infrastructure [16], to monitor the progress of interaction with a service, so as to ensure that the service is not misused.

Our aim while developing this work has not been to provide yet another alternative for service description, but rather to address specific needs that arose as a result of the demands of real-life grid application that were not addressed by existing work. As such, we view our work as complementary to existing approaches and focused on the description of the interaction protocol of the service, rather than the grounding of such descriptions to WS technologies or generalised service descriptions, since existing methods can easily be used in coordination with our work.

The rest of the paper is structured as follows. Section 2 provides a motivating example that illustrates our requirements for service description. Section 3 discusses existing technologies and their limitations with respect to those requirements. Section 4 presents our service interaction protocol model, using an ontological approach, and illustrates its use with the help of the example presented in Section 3. Section 5 offers two examples of the use of the model. The first discusses how the service description can be used by a semantic web security device to regulate access to services, while the second discusses how the service description can be used to infer what dependencies a service has with respect to other services. Finally, Section 6 indicates the future directions of this work.

2   Motivating Example

Our motivating example is based on a straightforward usage scenario for Grid applications that is supported by the GRIA (Grid Resources for Industrial Applications) infrastructure [15]. It involves a *client* that submits a computation job to a *job service*, where the computation job specifies a particular application to execute, such as a renderer. Furthermore, due to the typically significant amount of data over which the computation will be run the use of a *data staging service* is also required. The data staging service manages the provision of input data to the job service and provides the results to the client once the computation is completed. Below, we discuss in more detail the specifics of the implementation of this scenario within the GRIA infrastructure.

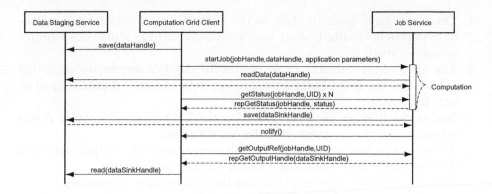

Fig. 1. An Example Grid Workflow

2.1 Grid Application Support Through GRIA

The GRIA framework is a Grid infrastructure developed using just the basic web service specifications, as part of the EC IST GRIA project [17].[1] It provides the necessary infrastructure for exposing computationally intensive applications across the Grid, with ancillary facilities for data staging and quality of service negotiation. A Grid service within GRIA can be considered as a *contextualised* web service, which exposes its functionality through a well-defined interface. It is contextualised since the interactions with the web service are based on a well-defined process, which demands that a context is maintained throughout the lifetime of the interactions. It is this interaction protocol that we aim to make explicit by providing an appropriate ontological model that will allow us to describe it.

In GRIA, a scenario as the one described above actually makes use of a number of other services and systems, both external and internal. Internal systems and services include resource schedulers, accounting systems and databases, while external services include data staging services, certificate authorities, and so forth. GRIA also provides features such as negotiation over the quality of service, long-term accounts with service providers. We do not discuss this issues in detail here, but the interested reader is referred to [15], in which a more complete description of the GRIA system is available.

Here we focus on just the interactions between the client, the job service and the data staging service, which are illustrated in Figure 1. The scenario is described below.

---

[1] A comparable system to GRIA is the Globus Toolkit 3 reference implementation of OGSI [18]. However, the OGSI model extends web service standards and explicitly introduces Grid-related concepts through those extensions. This is something that GRIA has avoided by adopting only web service standards. WSRF (Web Services Resource Framework - http://www.oasis-open.org/committees/tc_home.php?wg_abbrev=wsrf) is closer in nature to GRIA, but has only been released very recently and has no implementations available.

1. The Grid client saves its data to the data staging service supplying the `dataHandle` it obtained, along with a `jobHandle`, from a previous resource allocation stage.
2. The Grid client submits a job request to the job service including the `jobHandle`, the `dataHandle` for the source data and any additional application parameters.
3. During the lifetime of the computation the Grid client can obtain status information as to the progress of the computation.
4. At the end of the computation the job service saves the output data to a data staging service, obtaining a handle to data in response.
5. The job service notifies the client that the computation is complete.[2]
6. The Grid client retrieves a handle to the output data from the job service.
7. The Grid client reads the output data from the data staging service using the output data handle.

2.2   Job Service Description Requirements

Given this relatively straightforward example of service usage within a Grid environment we now turn our attention to identifying what are the necessary requirements for adequately describing the job service in a manner that will make clear the allowed sequence of interactions, the different parties involved and who is the initiator of which interactions. The specific requirements are discussed below.

Interaction Sequence. The most basic feature that a service description should cater for is a description of the appropriate sequence of interactions between the client and the service provider and who is the initiator of those interactions. For example, it should be clear that the client needs to request the `dataSinkHandle` from the job service, once the client has been notified that the computation is complete.

Multiple Parties and Roles. The description needs to clearly identify the various parties involved in the interactions, and who is the initiator of the interaction. Note, that while the client's main goal is to make use of a job service it cannot achieve that without also interacting with a data staging service. The use of the job service is *dependent* on the data staging service. Therefore, the description of the job service *must* make clear this dependence and describe the exact interaction the client and the job service will have with the data staging service. However, since these descriptions cannot identify specific instances of a client or a data staging service, as these are bound at runtime, it should identify the *roles* the various parties occupy. A role can be considered as identifying a well defined behaviour in terms of interaction with the service, such as *client* or *data staging service*.

Service State Changes. It is also desirable to be able to describe state changes that take place due to events that are not related to the interactions

---

[2] GRIA does not at present support notification because firewall policies at client sites are likely to deny them.

between services, but may impact on what interactions are allowed following that state change. For example, once the computation has completed the client can no longer request the status of the service.

3   Existing Technology and Current Limitations

Given the basic set of requirements identified above, we discuss in this next section the extent to which they are met by existing models for service description or related technologies.

3.1   OWL-S

The OWL-S [1] model attempts to provide a comprehensive approach to service description. The model has found considerable uptake by the Semantic Web Services community and as such has set a certain bar against which any other proposals are typically compared. It is used within the context of prototype applications (e.g. [19,20]) and extensions to the model relating to security have been suggested (e.g. [21]), as well as extensions in order to provide a more principled, theoretically grounded, view of the model [22].

Underpinning OWL-S is a separation of concerns along the lines of a *service profile* that describes what the service does, a *service process model* that describes how the services operates, and a *service grounding* that links the service model to the enabling Web Service infrastructure.

We focus on the descriptive capabilities of the OWL-S *process model*, since that is our central concern. The process model allows the specification of the operation of a service based on the combination of processes using control constructs such as sequence, split, split+join, and so forth. Necessary input, outputs, preconditions and effects can be described for each process, as well as conditional outputs and effects.

The process model, although well suited to deal with a large range of situations, does not adequately fulfill the requirements that we identified in Section 2. The main reason is that there are not constructs to indicate the *direction* of the interaction, i.e. whether the client or the service initiate it, or the fact that other parties may be involved in the interaction. As we discussed, these parties may be *necessary* as was the case in our example or may simply represent parties that could be involved to provide additional support (e.g. the use of a provenance service within the context of a grid application). Finally, there is also no representation of the state of a service.

The lack of such constructs may simply be a result of the fact that the underlying bias of the OWL-S model is to accommodate interaction with *stateless* web services with no individual thread of control, and as such any control of dataflow between processes should be handled entirely by the client.

3.2   IRS-II

The *Internet Reasoning Service-II*(IRS-II) [2] takes a broader view of the entire task of service discovery and composition, based on the UPML framework [23]. The framework distinguishes between *domain models* (describing the domain of application), *task models* (generic descriptions of the task, including inputs, outputs and preconditions), *problem solving methods* (abstract descriptions of the reasoning process), and *bridges* (mappings between different model components of an application). Individual services are described based on their inputs and outputs and the preconditions to their invocation. Services can be coupled by defining problem solving methods that describe their combinations. However, there is no support for complex interactions between services nor a flexible way to describe the operation of single services along the lines of the OWL-S process model. As such, although IRS-II makes a significant contribution towards providing a comprehensive approach to service discovery and composition based on an explicit theoretical model, it does not allow for a great deal of flexibility in describing complex individual services.

3.3   Web Services Choreography

Web Services Choreography [24] represents a relatively recent effort within the W3C, with the goal of providing a language that describes interactions between services. The underlying motivation is to provide a language that better reflects long-term, complex interactions between *stateful* services. The WS-Choreography model supports the definitions of roles, the definitions of message exchange based on either a request or a request+response protocol and the exchange of state information. The language makes use of pi-calculus as a grounding to formal, conceptual model [25].

In essence, a choreography document describes the interactions between a number of participants, with each participant occupying specific roles. The choreography is divided into work units, with work units containing activities. A number of process flow constructors enable the combination of activities. Finally, choreographies provide for progressively more specific definitions starting from an abstract definition that does not include an WSDL or SOAP constructs to portable and finally concrete implementations.

WS-Choreography addresses several of the issues that we aim to address, such as describing more complex interactions between stateful services through an abstract model that can then be grounded to specific WS technologies such as BPEL4WS. However, WS-Choreography does not address the need for describing *individual* services so as to then support the automatic composition of more complex interaction protocols, a goal that we aim to support. Furthermore, although the need for integration with Semantic Web technologies is stressed by the WS-Choreography working group it is currently not addressed. As such, our work can be seen as complementary to this effort, since we focus on descriptions of individual services and their needs in terms of interaction with a client or other supporting services. Such description could then be used to facilitate the composition of choreographies as envisaged by WS-Choreography.

3.4   BPEL4WS

Business Process Execution Language for Web Services (BPEL4WS) [12] defines a notation for specifying business processes composed of Web services. It supports the description of both executable process models (i.e. the actual behaviour of the web service) and business protocols (i.e. just the mutually visible message exchange). The language includes constructs for declaring process flow including iteration and choice as well as provides facilities for failure handling and compensation. A single process imports and exports functionality through WSDL interfaces. In this way, the process acts as a Web service itself and can invoke other Web services as part of the process. BPEL4WS also supports the declaration of partners and their roles, while state that should be public within a business process can be exposed through message correlation constructs.

   In general, BPEL4WS is a flexible language, with facilities for the addition of new constructs and attributes to the existing BPEL4WS standard without rendering existing engines incapable of utilising a BPEL document. However, BPEL4WS remains a low-level language that is heavily dependent on WSDL constructs, since it is aimed to tightly integrate within the general framework of Web Service standards. Furthermore, although semantic annotations could be added this would again be restricted to annotations of WSDL constructs, rather than more generalised notions. Our aim, as discussed in Section 1 is to take a top-down approach so that we are not restricted by low-level standards such as BPEL4WS and to provide a model that describes the interactions with respect to a single service.

   Nevertheless, we realise that in order for our model to find practical implementation within a wider setting that includes service composition dependent on description of individual services, it should be amenable to a grounding to a BPEL4WS description.

4   Service Description Through Interaction Protocols

As pointed out in Section 2, the desirable features for describing interaction protocols of services include multi-party interaction, explicit representation of who initiates the interaction, and representation of the relevant state changes of the service. Parts of these requirements can be found in some existing approaches as discussed in Section 3. For example, WS-Choreography defines roles and request and response protocols. Nevertheless, there exists no approach that captures all required features that resulted from our requirement analysis for real-world grid services. Therefore, we propose a new model for service description, basing it on an initial proposal for the definition of Interaction Protocols in DAML [26] and extending it with additional concepts such as events to reflect internal state changes of services, roles, and different types of messages to express direction of message flow (incoming vs outgoing).

   The approach we take is describing the interactions with a service as an interaction protocol, using a *service-centric* point of view. The protocol defines what are the appropriate messages that can be exchanged at any given moment from any of the parties involved in the interaction, and it is *service-centric* in the sense that we focus on just those interactions that include the service we wish to describe. For example, the service description of the job service need not include the first and the last interaction in Figure 1 between the client and the data staging service. That interaction should be described by the service description of the data staging service, which the client should have access to as well (this point is discussed further in Section 5). The reason for such a service-centric view is simply because a service can only define what interaction *it* can participate in and should avoid making assumptions about the nature of interactions that it is not party to.

4.1   Interaction Protocol Model

The proposed interaction protocol model is described in this section. The model is defined as an OWL ontology (see `www.csl.sri.com/users/denker/ sfw/wf/ip.owl`) and Figure 2 illustrates the main elements. In the figure, squares depict classes, arrows depict object properties, and the dashed boxes depict enumeration classes of individuals.

The appropriate interactions with a service are described through an *inter-action protocol*. This protocol corresponds to a set of *states*, where each state has a set of *options*. Options describe either the messages each party taking part in the interaction can perform while the interaction protocol is at that state or what events can take place at that state. Once one of the possible options in a state is taken our model describes which state follows that option, which in turn describes the next set of available options and so forth. Each option has a label to describe that option as either an *event* or a *message*.[3] In addition to labels attached to options, we further refine the model to include three types of options: *request*, *request+response*, and *internal*. A request option corresponds to the exchange of one message, whereas a request+response option includes two sequential message exchanges, the first one being the request message and the second one being the response message. Naturally, request and request+response options have messages associated with them. An internal option corresponds to an internal state change and always has an event associated with it.

Each message has a *name*, a *type*, a *role*, and *content*. The name of the message serves to identify the message within the domain of discourse. For example, if the service use an agent communication language, along the lines of the FIPA ACL [27], the name would correspond to the performative in question. If the service message exchanges correspond to lower-level WSDL messages, the name of the message would correspond to the WSDL operation.[4] The message type specifies whether the message is *incoming* (In) or *outgoing* (Out), so that we

---

[3] Restrictions like these are specified in the OWL ontology using appropriate operators.

[4] In this case some type of *grounding* between the interaction protocol and WSDL messages is required, similarly to the OWL-S approach.

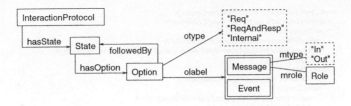

Fig. 2. Overview: (Partial) Interaction Protocol Ontology

can distinguish between messages that are initiated by the service or by other parties. The role defines the role of the party sending or receiving the message. Note that since the interaction protocol is service-centric we always know one of the parties involved in the interaction, i.e. the service under description, so the role serves to identify the other party involved. Finally, events are simply identified by a *name*.

In the case of the request option, the message may be either ingoing or outgoing. Similarly, in the request+response option, one message has to be of type ingoing message and the other of type outgoing, though there is clearly no restriction on whether the request or the response message are ingoing or outgoing. This enables the description of two directions of request+response interactions, one initiated by the service itself, the other initiated by an outside service.

With request+response we are modeling *two* subsequent states, with restrictions imposed on those states. Each state has only one option and each option has one message associated with it, to one state. In order to achieve this, in our ontology we require that a request+response option is followed by exactly one state. The successor state is in any case a state that has only one option. Thus, there are two possibilities (modeled using the union operator): (a) The message associated with the request+response option is an ingoing message, and the successor state is a state with one request option that has an outgoing message associated to it, or (b) the message associated with the request+response option is an outgoing message, and the successor state is a state with one request option that has an ingoing message associated with it (see Figure 3 for the definition).

The definition in Figure 3 guarantees the kind of request+response option that we aim for. In the future we aim to further refine the definition of the content class, including specification of multiple, typed parameters.

4.2 Applying the Model

The interaction protocol of the job service described in Section 2 is illustrated in Figure 4 and can be described using our OWL ontology for interaction protocols (see www.csl.sri.com/users/denker/sfw/wf/ip-ex.owl for OWL specification). In the figure states are numbered $S1, S2, .., S11$, while options are represented by the arrows that lead from one state to the other. Attached to options are descriptions of the events or messages concerned. Finally, request+response

```
<owl:Class rdf:about="#ReqAndRespOption">
 <owl:intersectionOf rdf:parseType="Collection">
  <owl:Restriction>
   <owl:onProperty rdf:resource="#followedBy"/>
   <owl:cardinality rdf:datatype="&xsd;nonNegativeInteger">1</owl:cardinality>
  </owl:Restriction>
  <owl:Class>
   <owl:unionOf rdf:parseType="Collection">
    <owl:Class>
     <owl:intersectionOf rdf:parseType="Collection">
      <owl:Restriction>
       <owl:onProperty rdf:resource="#olabel"/>
       <owl:allValuesFrom rdf:resource="#IngoingMessage"/>
      </owl:Restriction>
      <owl:Restriction>
       <owl:onProperty rdf:resource="#followedBy"/>
       <owl:allValuesFrom rdf:resource="#StateWithOneReqOptionWOutgoingMessage"/>
      </owl:Restriction>
     </owl:intersectionOf>
    </owl:Class>
    <owl:Class>
     <owl:intersectionOf rdf:parseType="Collection">
      <owl:Restriction>
       <owl:onProperty rdf:resource="#olabel"/>
       <owl:allValuesFrom rdf:resource="#OutgoingMessage"/>
      </owl:Restriction>
      <owl:Restriction>
       <owl:onProperty rdf:resource="#followedBy"/>
       <owl:allValuesFrom rdf:resource="#StateWithOneReqOptionWIngoingMessage"/>
      </owl:Restriction>
     </owl:intersectionOf>
    </owl:Class>
   </owl:unionOf>
  </owl:Class>
 </owl:intersectionOf>
</owl:Class>
```

Fig. 3. Request+Response Definition

options are shown with the intermediate state, as described above, within a dashed line boundary.

The information contained within the model allows us to identify the parties/roles involved, the direction of the interaction, the allowed sequence of interaction as well as relevant state changes of the service which affect the allowed interactions. As a result, when a client attempts to use this service and obtains a description of the service it will reveal that the job service requires a data staging service, and how the interaction with the data staging service takes place. Furthermore, the client can see that the service will attempt to notify it when the computation has completed, implying that the client should be able to accept such messages (we discuss this issue further in Section 5.1). Finally, the client can also identify that there is an event generated by the service after which it can no longer request the status. As an example of the use of the ontology, see Figure 5 specification of the first state transition between states $S1$ and $S2$.

5   Use of Models

In this section we discuss how the service description model can be used to enable reasoning in two crucial cases: first, within the context of providing adaptive

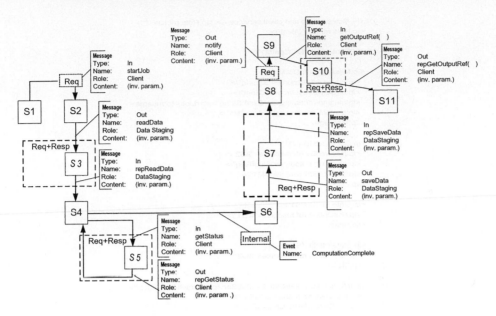

Fig. 4. Job service interaction protocol

security devices that make use of semantic descriptions; and, secondly, within the context of service composition.

5.1   Securing Services

In a previous paper we outlined the requirements for an adaptive security device (a *semantic firewall*), which makes use of semantic descriptions of services to dynamically control lower-level security devices, such as traditional firewalls, so as to enable only *appropriate interactions* [28]. Appropriate interactions are defined as those that are expected given the current context and satisfy any policy requirements associated with the interactions. In that paper, we indicate that OWL-S would be considered as a language for providing the required semantic descriptions of services. However, as discussed earlier some crucial features are missing that would enable its use.

The service description model described here addresses these limitations and enables a *semantic firewall* to establish at runtime which are the appropriate interactions at each stage of the process. Domains offering services to clients can ensure that their services are only used as the service developer defined through the interaction protocol of the service and prevent inappropriate messages from going through. Furthermore, client domains can establish exactly which interactions are initiated by the service and directed towards the client. This will solve a significant shortcoming of existing grid systems where clients are typically behind firewalls that disable any externally initiated messages. Consequently, clients are currently forced to *poll* the job service as to whether the computation has been

```
<!-- Roles for job and client services --> <ip:Role rdf:ID="J"/>
<ip:Role rdf:ID="Client"/>

<ip:Content rdf:ID="ContM1"/>

<ip:Message rdf:ID="M1">
  <ip:mtype rdf:resource="&ip;#In"/>
  <ip:mrole rdf:resource="#Client"/>
  <ip:mname rdf:datatype="&xsd;String">startJob</ip:mname>
  <ip:content rdf:resource="#ContM1"/>
</ip:Message>

<ip:Option rdf:ID="O1">
  <ip:followedBy rdf:resource="#S2"/>
  <ip:otype rdf:resource="&ip;#Req"/>
  <ip:olabel rdf:resource="#M1"/>
</ip:Option>

<ip:State rdf:ID="S1">
  <ip:hasOption rdf:resource="#O1"/>
</ip:State>

<ip:State rdf:ID="S2">
  <ip:hasOption rdf:resource="#O2"/>
</ip:State>

<ip:InteractionProtocol rdf:ID="JobServiceInteractionProtocol">
  <ip:hasState rdf:resource="#S1"/>
  <ip:hasState rdf:resource="#S2"/>

  ...
  <ip:hasState rdf:resource="#S11"/>
</ip:InteractionProtocol>
```

Fig. 5. Ontology use example for job service description

completed. By deploying semantic firewalls and making use of the interaction protocol model described to identify when and which incoming messages should be expected we can overcome this problem.

5.2   Inferring Service Dependencies

Application development using the GRIA infrastructure reveals that services are often developed with other required services in mind. For example, in our motivating scenario the required service was the data staging service. By describing such dependencies through our interaction protocol, clients, having identified a required service, can determine exactly what dependencies the service has on any other services and use that information to attempt to discover suitable services to fulfill those requirements. The use of *roles* to define such required services can aid the discovery process by indicating *classes* of services that can conform to such behaviour.

6   Conclusions and Future Work

In this paper we have present a novel model for describing how a service can interact with clients and other services. This model was developed in response to the identification of a set of requirements based on *real-life* experience with

Grid application development. Existing approaches for service description, most significantly OWL-S, do not adequately fulfill those requirements and as such this work can be seen as informing and furthering the discussion on what is an appropriate model for describing services. In particular, our model offers three specific features that are crucial for enabling the types of Grid-based scenarios we aim to support. Firstly, we are able to describe *multi-party interactions*, with respect to a single service and the different *roles* those parties occupy. Secondly, we can differentiate between interactions initiated by the service and those initiated by other parties. Finally, we can describe relevant service states that influence the subsequently allowed interactions. As discussed in Section 5 such a model can play a crucial role in enabling the development of security devices that take advantage of semantic web-based descriptions of services [28] as well as more sophisticated compositions of services. We now aim to develop appropriate reasoning engines that can be integrated within GRIA for handling such interaction protocol descriptions, with the particular aim of using them within a *semantic fireall*. In addition, we will investigate the integration of policies within the description as well as the verification of an interaction protocol against domain-wide policies. Finally, any high level description techniques adopted to describe and analyse interaction protocols must eventually be grounded in existing and emerging security specifications like WS-Security [29], WS-SecurityPolicy [30] and web service standards such as BPEL4WS [12]) in order to enable their enforcement at the message level. In consequence, further research will include investigation of techniques for mapping high level descriptions on to these Web service standards.

References

1. Ankolenkar, A., Burstein, M., Hobbs, J.R., Lassila, O., Martin, D.L., Drew McDermott, S.A.M., Narayanan, S., Paolucci, M., Payne, T.R., Sycara, K.: DAML-S: Web Service Description for the Semantic Web. In Cruz, I.F., Decker, S., Euzenat, J., McGuinness, D.L., eds.: The First Semantic Web Working Symposium, Stanford University, California (2001) 411–430
2. Motta, E., Dominique, J., Cabral, L., Gaspari, M.: IRS-II: A Framework and Infrastructure for Semantic Web Services. In Fensel, D., Sycara, K., Mylopoulos, J., eds.: The Semantic Web - ISWC03. Volume 2870 of LNAI., Springer (2003) 306–318
3. Sycara, K., Paolucci, M., Ankolenkar, A., Srinivasan, N.: Automated Discovery, Interaction and Composition of Semantic Web Services. Journal of Web Semantics 1 (2003) 27–46
4. Staab, S., van der Aalst, W.M.P., Benjamins, V.R., Sheth, A.P., Miller, J.A., Bussler, C., Maedche, A., Fensel, D., Gannon, D.: Trends and Controversies: Web Services: Been There, Done That? IEEE Intelligent Systems 18 (2003) 72–85
5. Oliveira, E., Rocha, A.P.: Agents Advanced Features for Negotiation in Electronic Commerce and Virtual Organisations Formation Processes. In Dignum, F., Sierra, C., eds.: Agent Mediated Electronic Commerce, The European AgentLink Perspective. Volume 1991. Springer (2001) 78–97

6. Anuj K. Jain, Manuel Aparico, M.P.S.: Agents for process coherence in virtual enterprises. Communications of the ACM **42** (1999) 62–69
7. de Roure, D., Jennings, N.R., Shadbolt, N.: The Semantic Grid: A future e-Science infrastructure. In Berman, F., Fox, G., Hey, A., eds.: Grid Computing: Making the Gloab Infrastructure a Reality. Wiley (2003) 437–470
8. W3C: Web Services Activity. (http://www.w3.org/2002/ws/)
9. W3C: Simple Object Access Protocol. (http://www.w3.org/TR/SOAP/)
10. Christensen, E., Curbera, F., meredith, G., Weerawarana, S.: Web Services Description Language (WSDL) 1.1. Technical report, (W3C)
11. Bellwood, T., Cl'ement, L., von Riegen, C.: UDDI Version 3.0.1- UDDI Spec Technical Committee Specification. Technical report, OASIS (2003)
12. (Ed.), S.T.: Business Process Execution Language for Web Services Version 1.1. Technical report, BEA Systems, IBM, Microsoft, SAP, Siebel Systems (2003)
13. Mandell, D.J., McIlraith, S.A.: Adapting BPEL4WS for the Semantic Web: The Bottom-Up Approach to Web Service Interoperation. In Fensel, D., Sycara, K., Mylopoulos, J., eds.: The Semantic Web - ISWC03. Volume 2870 of LNAI., Springer (2003) 227–241
14. Verma, K., Akkiraju, R., Goodwin, R., Doshi, P., Lee, J.: On Accommodating Inter Service Dependencies in Web Process Flow Composition. In Payne, T.R., Decker, K., Lassila, O., Mcilraith, S., Sycara, K., eds.: First International Semantic Web Services Symposium (2004 AAAI Spring Symposium Series), AAAI (2004)
15. Taylor, S., Surridge, M., Marvin, D.: Grid Resources for Industrial Applications. In: 2004 IEEE International Conference on Web Services (ICWS'2004). (2004)
16. Ashri, R., Payne, T., Marvin, D., Surridge, M., Taylor, S.: Towards a Semantic Web Security Infrastructure. In Payne, T.R., Decker, K., Lassila, O., Mcilraith, S., Sycara, K., eds.: First International Semantic Web Services Symposium (2004 AAAI Spring Symposium Series), AAAI (2004)
17. GRIA: Grid Resources for Industrial Applications. (http://www.gria.org)
18. Tuecke, S., Czajkowski, K., Foster, I., Frey, J., Graham, S., Kesselman, C., Maquire, T., Sandholm, T., Snelling, D., Vanderbilt, P.: Open Grid Services Infrastructure. Technical report, Global Grid Forum (GGF)
19. Richards, D., Sabou, M.: Semantic Markup for Semantic Web Tools: A DAML-S Description of an RDF-Store. In Fensel, D., Sycara, K., Mylopoulos, J., eds.: The SemanticWeb - ISWC 2003. Volume 2870., Springer (2003) 274–289
20. Paolucci, M., Ankolenkar, A., Sinivasan, N., Sycara, K.: The DAML-S Virtual Machine. In Fensel, D., Sycara, K., Mylopoulos, J., eds.: The SemanticWeb - ISWC 2003. Volume 2870., Springer (2003) 290–305
21. Denker, G., Kagal, L., Finin, T., Paolucci, M., Sycara, K.: Security for DAML Services: Annotation and Matchmaking. In Fensel, D., Sycara, K., Mylopoulos, J., eds.: The SemanticWeb - ISWC 2003. Volume 2870 of LNCS., Springer (2003) 335–350
22. Mika, P., Sabou, M., Gangemi, A., Oberle, D.: Foudations for DAML-S: Aligning DAML-S to DOLCE. In Payne, T.R., Decker, K., Lassila, O., Mcilraith, S., Sycara, K., eds.: First International Semantic Web Services Symposium (2004 AAAI Spring Symposium Series), AAAI (2004)
23. Fensel, D., Benjamins, V.R., Motta, E., Wielinga, B.J.: UPML: A Framework for Knowledge System Reuse. In Dean, T., ed.: Proceedings of the Sixteenth International Joint Conference on Artificial Intelligence, Morgan Kaufmann (1999) 16–23
24. Burdett, D., Kavantzas, N.: Ws choreography model overview. Technical report, W3C (2004)

25. Milner, R.: Communicating and Mobile Systems: The Pi Calculus. Cambridge University Press (1999)
26. Toivonen, S., Helin, H.: Representing interaction protocols in DAML. In van Elst, L., Dignum, V., Abecker, A., eds.: Agent Mediated Knowledge Management, International Symposium AMKM 2003, Stanford, CA, USA, March 24-26, 2003, Revised and Invited Papers. Volume 2926 of LNCS., Springer (2004) 310–321
27. FIPA ACL Message Structure Specification. Technical report, Foundation for Intelligent Physical Agents (2002)
28. Ashri, R., Payne, T., Marvin, D., Surridge, M., Taylor, S.: Towards a Semantic Web Security Infrastructure. In Payne, T.R., Decker, K., Lassila, O., Mcilraith, S., Sycara, K., eds.: First International Semantic Web Services Symposium (2004 AAAI Spring Symposium Series), AAAI (2004)
29. Nadalin, A., Kaler, C., Hallam-Baker, P., Monzillo, R.: Web Services Security: SOAP Message Security 1.0 (WS-Security 2004. Technical report, OASIS (2004)
30. Nadalin, A.: Web services security policy. Technical report, IBM, Microsoft, RSA Security and Verisign (2002)

ASSAM: A Tool for Semi-automatically Annotating Semantic Web Services

Andreas Heß, Eddie Johnston, and Nicholas Kushmerick

Computer Science Department, University College Dublin, Ireland
{andreas.hess, eddie.johnston, nick}@ucd.ie

Abstract. The semantic Web Services vision requires that each service be annotated with semantic metadata. Manually creating such metadata is tedious and error-prone, and many software engineers, accustomed to tools that automatically generate WSDL, might not want to invest the additional effort. We therefore propose ASSAM, a tool that assists a user in creating semantic metadata for Web Services. ASSAM is intended for service consumers who want to integrate a number of services and therefore must annotate them according to some shared ontology. ASSAM is also relevant for service producers who have deployed a Web Service and want to make it compatible with an existing ontology. ASSAM's capabilities to automatically create semantic metadata are supported by two machine learning algorithms. First, we have developed an iterative relational classification algorithm for semantically classifying Web Services, their operations, and input and output messages. Second, to aggregate the data returned by multiple semantically related Web Services, we have developed a schema mapping algorithm that is based on an ensemble of string distance metrics.

1 Introduction

The vision of semantic Web Services is to provide the means for fully automated discovery, composition and invocation of loosely coupled software components. One of the key efforts to address this "semantic gap" is the well-known OWL-S ontology [1].

However, software engineers who are developing Web Services usually do not think in terms of ontologies, but rather in terms of their programming tools. Existing tools for both the Java and .NET environments support the automatic generation of WSDL. We believe that it would boost the semantic service web if similar tools existed to (semi-) automatically generate OWL-S or a similar form of semantic metadata.

In this paper we will present a tool called ASSAM—Automated Semantic Service Annotation with Machine Learning—that addresses these needs. AS-SAM consists of two parts, a WSDL annotator application, and OATS, a data aggregation algorithm.

We describe the WSDL annotator application in Sec. 2. This component of ASSAM uses machine learning to provide the user with suggestions on how to

S.A. McIlraith et al. (Eds.): ISWC 2004, LNCS 3298, pp. 320–334, 2004.

annotate the elements in the WSDL. In Sec. 3 we describe the iterative relational classification algorithm that provides these suggestions. We evaluate our algorithms on a set of 164 Web Services.[1]

Second, in Sec. 4, we will describe OATS, a novel schema mapping algorithm specifically designed for the Web Services context, and empirically demonstrate its effectiveness on 52 invokable Web Service operations. OATS addresses the problem of aggregating the heterogenous data from several Web Services.

2   ASSAM: A Tool for Web Service Annotation

One of the central parts of ASSAM is the WSDL annotator application. The WSDL annotator is a tool that enables the user to semantically annotate a Web Service using a point-and-click interface. The key feature of the WSDL annotator is the ability to suggest which ontological class to use to annotate each element in the WSDL.

Use Cases. ASSAM is designed primarily for users who want to annotate many similar services. Typically, these will be end users wanting to integrate several similar Web Services into his or her business processes. But the annotation task might also be performed by a centralized semantic Web Service registry.

Our tool could also be useful for programmers who are only interested in annotating a single Web Service they have created.[2] In order to make his or her service compatible with existing services, a developer might want to annotate it with the same ontology that has already been used for some other Web Services. The developer could import the existing Web Services in ASSAM and use them as training data in order to obtain recommendations on how to annotate his or her own service.

Functionality. Fig. 1 shows the ASSAM application. Note that our application's key novelty—the suggested annotations created automatically by our machine learning algorithm—are shown in the small pop-up window.

The left column in the main window contains a list of all Web Services currently and the category ontology. Web Services can be associated with a category by clicking on a service in a list and then on a node in the category tree. When the user has selected a service and wants to focus on annotating it this part of the window can be hidden.

The middle of the window contains a tree view of the WSDL. Port types, operations, messages and complex XML schema types are parsed from the WSDL and shown in a tree structure. The original WSDL file is also shown as well as plain text descriptions from the occasional documentation tags within the WSDL or a plain text description of the service as a whole, such as often offered by a UDDI registry or a Web Service indexing web site.

---

[1] All our our experimental data is available in the Repository of Semantic Web Services http://smi.ucd.ie/RSWS.

[2] Thanks to Terry Payne who pointed out this use case.

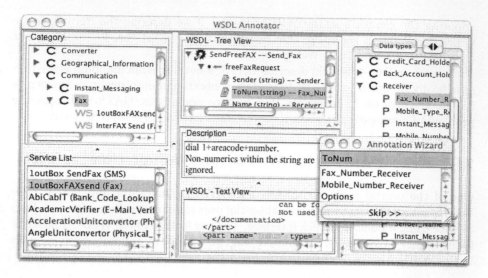

Fig. 1. ASSAM uses machine learning techniques to semi-automatically annotate Web Services with semantic metadata.

When the user clicks on an element in the WSDL tree view, the corresponding ontology is shown in the right column and the user can select an appropriate class by clicking on an element in the ontology view. Currently different ontologies for datatypes and operations are used. At present we allow annotation for operations, message parts and XML schema types and their elements. Port types or messages cannot be annotated, because there is no real semantic meaning associated with the port type or the message itself that is not covered by the annotation of the operations or the message parts.

Once the annotation is done it can be exported in OWL-S. The created OWL-S consists of a profile, a process model, a grounding and a concept file if complex types where present in the WSDL. Note that this also includes XSLT transformations as needed in the OWL-S grounding to map between the traditional XML Schema representation of the input and output data and the OWL representation.

Limitations. Because we do not handle composition and workflow in our machine learning approach, the generated process model consists only of one atomic process per operation. The generated profile is a subclass from the assigned category of the service as a whole – the category ontology services as profile hierarchy. The concept file contains a representation of the annotated XML schema types in OWL-S. Note that it is up to the ontology designer to take care that the datatype ontology makes sense and that it is consistent. No inference checks are done on the side of our tool. Finally, the a grounding is generated that also contains the XSLT mappings from XML schema to OWL and vice versa.

For the OWL export, we do not use the annotations for the operations at the moment, as there is no direct correspondence in OWL-S for the domain of an operation. Atomic processes in OWL-S are characterized only through their inputs, outputs, preconditions and effects; and for the profile our tool uses the service category.

Related Work. Paolucci et al addressed the problem of creating semantic metadata (in the form of OWL-S) from WSDL [2]. However, because WSDL contains no semantic information, this tool provides just a syntactic transformation. The key challenge is to map the XML data used by traditional Web Services to classes in an ontology.

Currently, Patil et al [3] are also working on matching XML schemas to ontologies in the Web Services domain. They use a combination of lexical and structural similarity measures. They assume that the user's intention is not to annotate similar services with one common ontology, rather they also address the problem of choosing the right domain ontology among a set of ontologies.

Sabou [4] addresses the problem of creating suitable domain ontologies in the first place. She uses shallow natural language processing techniques to assist the user in creating an ontology based on natural language documentation of software APIs.

3 Iterative Relational Classification

In this section, we will describe the machine learning algorithms behind AS-SAM's annotation wizard in greater detail. The OATS algorithm for data aggregation will be explained in the next section.

For our learning approach, we cast the problem of classifying operations and datatypes in a Web Service as a text classification problem. Our tool learns from Web Services with existing semantic annotation. Given this training data, a machine learning algorithm can generalize and predict semantic labels for previously unseen Web Services.

In a mixed-initiative setting, these predictions do not have to be perfectly accurate to be helpful. In fact, the classification task is quite hard, because the domain ontologies can be very large. But for that reason it is already very helpful for a human annotator if he or she would have to choose only between a small number of ontological concepts rather than from the full domain ontology. In previous work [5] we have shown that the category of a services can be reliably predicted, if we stipulate merely that the correct concept be one of the top few (e.g., three) suggestions.

Terminology. Before describing our approach in detail, we begin with some terminology. By introducing this terminology we do not advocate a new standard. Instead we believe that our approach is generic and independent of the actual format used for the semantic Web Service description.

We use the word *category* to denote the semantic meaning of the service as a whole, such as "E-Mail", "Weather Information" etc. The category ontology corresponds to a profile hierarchy in OWL-S.

We use the word *domain* to denote the semantic meaning of an operation, such as "Send an email" or "Query weather by ZIP code". An operation in WSDL usually maps to an atomic process in OWL-S, but there is no direct relation of the domain of an operation to OWL-S, as atomic processes are only characterized through their inputs, outputs, preconditions and effects. One could think of the *domain* as describing the semantics of the preconditions and effects, but we currently do not use the domain annotation for our OWL-S export.

We use the word *datatype* to denote the semantic type of a single variable, such as "Receiver's email address", "ZIP Code" or "temperature". This usage of the word *datatype* is consistent with how the word is used when describing a property in an ontology, but should not be confused with low-level syntactic datatypes such as "integer" or "string".

For information retrieval or classification tasks the objects that are classified or searched are usually referred to as *documents*. When we use the word *document*, we mean the Web Service as whole as represented by its WSDL. We use *document part* to denote an object within the Web Service that we want to classify: Operations, input and output messages, XML schema types etc. are *document parts*.

Iterative Classification Ensemble. The basic idea behind our approach is to exploit the fact that there are dependencies between the category of a Web Service, the domains of its operations and the datatypes of its input and output parameters. In previous work [5], we exploited these dependencies in a Bayesian setting and evaluated it on Web forms. In this paper, we present an iterative classification algorithm similar to the one introduced by Neville and Jensen in [6].

Like any classification system, our algorithm is based on a set of features of the services, operations and parameters. Following [6], we distinguish between *intrinsic* and *extrinsic* features. The intrinsic features of a document part are simply its name and other text that is associated with it (e.g., text from the occasional `documentation` tags). Extrinsic features derive from the relationship between different parts of a document. We use the semantic classes of linked document parts as extrinsic features.

Initially, when no annotations for a service exist, the extrinsic features are unknown. After the first pass, where classifications are made based on the intrinsic features, the values of the extrinsic features are set based on the previous classifications. Of course, these classifications may be partially incorrect. The classification process is repeated until a certain termination criterion (e.g. either convergence or a fixed number of iterations) is met. Fig. 2 shows an illustration of the classification phase of the algorithm.

Our iterative algorithm differs in some points from Neville's and Jensen's algorithm. In their approach, one single classifier is trained on all (intrinsic and extrinsic) features. In a variety of tasks, ensembles of several classifiers have been shown to be more effective (e.g., [7]). For this reason, we train two separate classifiers, one on the intrinsic features ("*A*") and one on the extrinsic features ("*B*"), and vote their predictions. Another advantage of combining the evidence in that way is that the classifier cannot be mislead by missing features in the beginning when the extrinsic features are yet unknown, because the classifier trained on the extrinsic features is simply not used for the first pass.

This split approach, where the A and B classifiers are combined using voting, works best, when both views would by themselves be sufficient to make a prediction. However, the fact that a Web Service belongs to a certain category (e.g. "book selling") is by itself not sufficient to classify its input parameters, but the information is still useful. We therefore introduce a second mode for incorporating the extrinsic features: We train a set of classifiers on the intrinsic features of the datatypes, but each of them is only on Web Services that belong to one category[3]. We denote this set of specialized classifiers as C. To avoid biasing the algorithm too strongly, we still combine the results of the C classifier with the A classifier in each iteration. For each level we use either B or the C classifiers, but not both. We chose the C method for the datatypes and the B method for the category and the domain.

We did not exploit every possible dynamic extrinsic feature. We used *static* extrinsic features on the domain and datatype level by incorporating text from children nodes: Text associated with messages was added to the text used by the operations classifier, and text associated with elements of complex types were added to the text used by the datatype classifier classifying the complex type itself. In Fig. 2 we denote this as "add". Note that this appears to contradict our earlier results [5], where we claimed that simply adding text from child nodes does not help. In [5], we where classifying the category level only, and the bag of words for the domain and datatype classifiers consisted of text for all operations/datatypes in that service. In our present experiment, the classifier for the operations and datatypes classify one single operation or element only, and in this case it apparently helps to add more text. The features we used and the feedback structures for the dynamic features are based on empiric preliminary tests. We used a fixed number of 5 iterations. Fig. 2 shows the setup that was eventually used.

In the evaluation section, we report results for this setup. For a more detailed discussion of the parameters of our algorithm and their effects the reader is referred to our paper [8] that describes the algorithm in greater detail from a machine learning point of view.

Evaluation. We evaluated our algorithm using a leave-one-out methodology. We compared it against a baseline classifier with the same setup for the static features, but without using the dynamic extrinsic features.

To determine the upper bound of improvement that can be achieved using the extrinsic features, we tested our algorithm with the correct class labels given as the extrinsic features. This tests the performance of predicting a class label

---

[3] To avoid an over-specialization, these classifiers are actually not trained on instances from a single category, but rather on instances from a complete top-level branch of the hierarchically organized category ontology. Note that this is the only place where we make use of the fact that the class labels are organized as an ontology, and we do not do any further inference.

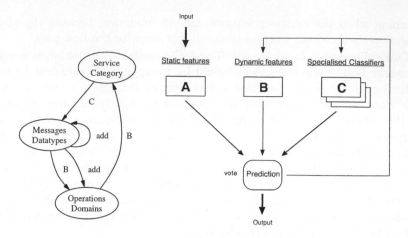

Fig. 2. Feedback structure and algorithm.

for a document part when not only the intrinsic features but also the dynamic features, the labels for all other document parts, are known.

We also compared it against a non-ensemble setup, where the extrinsic features are not added using a separate classifier but rather are just appended to the static features. Classification is then done with a single classifier. This setup closely resembles the original algorithm proposed by Neville and Jensen. Again, the same set of static features was used.

In the evaluation we ignored all classes with one or two instances, such as occurred quite frequently on the datatype level. The distributions are still quite skewed and there is a large number of classes. There are 22 classes on the category level, 136 classes on the domain level and 312 classes on the datatype level.

Fig. 3 show the accuracy for categories, domains and datatypes. As mentioned earlier, in mixed-initiative scenario such as our semi-automated ASSAM tool, it is not necessary to be be perfectly accurate. Rather, we strive only to ensure that that the correct ontology class is in the top few suggestions. We therefore show how the accuracy increases when we allow a certain tolerance. For example, if the accuracy for tolerance 9 is 0.9, then the correct prediction is within the top 10 of the ranked predictions the algorithm made 90% of the time.

We could not achieve good results with the non-ensemble setup. This setup scored worse than the baseline. For the datatypes, even the ceiling accuracy was below the baseline.

Note that on the category level incorporating the additional evidence from the extrinsic features does not help. In fact, for some tolerance values the ceiling accuracy is even worse than the baseline.

On the datatype level, our algorithm achieves 31.2% accuracy, where as the baseline scores only at 24.5%. Thus, our algorithm improves performance by almost one third. The overall performance might be considered quite low, but due to the high number of classes it is a very hard classification problem. Given that

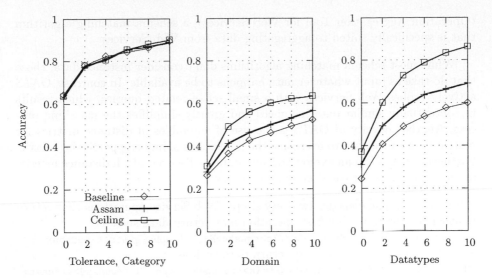

Fig. 3. Accuracy of our algorithm on the three kinds of semantic metadata as a function of prediction tolerance.

in two of three cases the user has to choose only between 10 class labels rather than between all 312 labels in the datatype ontology we are still convinced that this could save a considerable amount of workload. We evaluated the statistical significance of the performance improvement of our algorithm with a Wilcoxon Matched-Pairs Signed-Ranks Test. Our algorithm performs significantly better with a confidence value of over 99.9%. On the domain level, our approach increases the accuracy for exact matches from 26.3% to 28%. This is statistically significant with a confidence value of 96% according to a Wilcoxon Test. For both significance tests we performed a 20-fold random split.

Related work. We already mentioned the algorithm by Neville and Jensen [9], but iterative classification algorithms were also used for link-based hypertext classification by Lu and Getoor [10]. Relational learning for hypertext classification was also explored by Slattery et al., e.g. [11,12]. A difference between their problem setting and ours is that the links in our dataset are only within one Web Services, where in the hypertext domain potentially all documents can link to each other.

4   Aggregating Data from Web Services

ASSAM uses the machine learning technique just described to create semantic metadata that could assist (among other applications) a data integration system that must identify and invoke a set of Web Services operations that can answer some query. In order to automatically aggregate the resulting heterogeneous data into some coherent structure, we are currently developing OATS

(Operation Aggregation Tool for Web Services), a schema matching algorithm that is specifically suited to aggregating data from Web Services.

While most schema matching algorithms don't consider instance data, those that do take as input whatever data happens to be available. In contrast, OATS actively probes Web Services with a small set of related queries, which results in contextually similar data instances and greatly simplifies the matching process. Another novelty of OATS is the use of ensembles of distance metrics for matching instance data to overcome the limitations of any one particular metric. Furthermore, OATS can exploit training data to discover which distance metrics are more accurate for each semantic category.

As an example, consider two very simple Web Service operations that return weather information. The first operation may return data such as

`<weather><hi>87</hi><lo>56</lo><gusts>NE, 11 mph</gusts></weather>`
while the second operation may return data such as
`<fcast><tmax>87</tmax><tmin>57</tmin><wndspd>10 mph (N)</wndspd></fcast>`.
The goal of data aggregation is to consolidate this heterogeneous data into a single coherent structure. This sort of schema matching task is challenging in many ways. The schemas to be matched are usually created by different people, so there may be major differences in the structure and the vocabulary used. Related schemas may well not overlap much – the element set of one schema S may form only a small subset of the element set of another schema T. Furthermore, mappings between elements may be complex: an element of S may not match a single element, but some combination of elements in T. Finally, schema matching is computationally expensive because the number of potential matches is exponential in the size of the schemas.

In order to aggregate Web Service operation outputs, the semantically related elements among this heterogeneous XML data must be identified and grouped. Web Service aggregation can therefore be viewed as an instance of the schema matching problem. A major difference between traditional schema matching and our Web Service aggregation task is that we can exert some control over the instance data. Our OATS algorithm probes each operation with arguments that correspond to the same real-world entity. For example, to aggregate operation O_1 that maps a ZIP code to its weather forecast, and operation O_2 that maps a latitude/longitude pair to its forecast, OATS could first select a specific location (e.g., Seattle), and then query O_1 with "98125" (a Seattle ZIP code), and query O_2 with "47.45N/122.30W" (Seattle's geocode). Probing each operation with the related arguments should ensure that the instance data of related elements will closely correspond, increasing the chances of identifying matching elements.

As in ILA [13], this probe-based approach is based on the assumption that the operations overlap, i.e, there exists a set of real-world entities that are covered by all of the sources to be aggregated. For example, while two weather Web Service need not over exactly the same locations in order to be aggregated, we do assume that there exists a set of locations covered by both.

We assume that the data integration system knows how to invoke the operations being aggregated, i.e that it can map the real-world probe entities to values for the operations' input parameters.

The OATS algorithm. The input to the OATS algorithm is a set of Web Service operations $O = \{o_1, o_2, \ldots, o_n\}$, a set of probe objects $P = \{p_1, \ldots, p_m\}$, sufficient metadata about the operations so that each operation can be invoked on each probe ($V = \{v_1, \ldots, v_n\}$, where v_i is a mapping from a probe $p_k \in P$ to the input parameters that will invoke o_i on p_k)[4], and a set of string distance metrics $D = \{d_1, d_2, \ldots\}$.

When invoked, an operation $o_i \subset O$ generates data with elements $E_i = \{e_1^i, e_2^i, \ldots\}$, where $E = \cup_i E_i$ is the set of all the operations' elements. The output of the OATS algorithm is thus a partition of E. The intent is that this partition should correspond to semantically equivalent sets of elements.

One of the distinguishing features of our algorithm is the use of an ensemble of distance metrics for matching elements. For example, when comparing the gusts and wndspd instance data above, it makes sense to use a token based matcher such as TFIDF, but when comparing hi and tmax, an edit-distance based metric such as Levenshtein is more suitable. The OATS algorithm calculates similarities based on the average similarities of an ensemble of distance metrics. Later, we describe an extension to OATS which assigns weights to distance metrics according to how well they correlate with a set of training data.

The OATS algorithm proceeds as follows. Each of the n operations are invoked with the appropriate parameters for each of the m probe objects. The resulting nm XML documents are stored in a three-dimensional table T. The $T[i, \cdot, \cdot]$ entries of this table relate to operation $o_i \in O$, and the $T[\cdot, \cdot, k]$ entries relate to probe $p_k \in P$. Specifically, $T[i, j, k]$ stores the value returned for element $e_j^i \in E_i$ by operation o_i for probe p_k.

Each element is then compared with every other element. The distance between an element pair $(e_j^i, e_{j'}^{i'}) \in E \times E$ is calculated for each string distance metric $d_\ell \in D$, and these values are merged to provide an ensemble distance value for these elements. The similarity between two elements $e_j^i \in E_i$ and $e_{j'}^{i'} \in E_{i'}$ is defined as $D(e_j^i, e_{j'}^{i'}) = \frac{1}{|D|} \sum_\ell (\bar{d}_\ell(e_j^i, e_{j'}^{i'}) - \mathrm{m}(\bar{d}_\ell))/R(\bar{d}_\ell)$, where $\bar{d}_\ell(e_j^i, e_{j'}^{i'}) = \frac{1}{m} \sum_k d_\ell(T[i, j, k], T[i', j', k])$, $\mathrm{M}(\bar{d}_\ell) = \max_{(e_j^i, e_{j'}^{i'})} \bar{d}_\ell(e_j^i, e_{j'}^{i'})$, $\mathrm{m}(\bar{d}_\ell) = \min_{(e_j^i, e_{j'}^{i'})} \bar{d}_\ell(e_j^i, e_{j'}^{i'})$, and $R(\bar{d}_\ell) = \mathrm{M}(\bar{d}_\ell) - \mathrm{m}(\bar{d}_\ell)$.

By computing the average distance $\bar{d}_\ell$ over m related sets of element pairs, we are minimizing the impact of any spurious instance data. Before merging the distance metrics, they are normalized relative to the most similar and least similar pairs, as different metrics produce results in different scales.

To get the ensemble similarity $D(e_j^i, e_{j'}^{i'})$ for any pair we combine the normalized distances for each d_j. In the standard OATS algorithm, this combination is

---

[4] In our implementation, the probes are encoded as a table of attribute/value pairs, and v_i is the subset of attributes needed for operation o_i.

simply an unweighted average. We also show below how weights can be adaptively tuned for each element-metric pair.

Given the distances between each pair of elements, the final step of the OATS algorithm is to cluster the elements. This is done using the standard hierarchical agglomerative clustering (HAC) approach. Initially, each element is assigned to its own cluster. Next, the closest pair of clusters is found (using the single, complete, or average link clustering methods) and these are merged. The previous step is repeated until some termination condition is satisfied. At some point in the clustering, all of the elements which are considered similar by our ensemble of distance metrics will be merged, and further iterations would only force together unrelated clusters. It is at this point that we should stop clustering. Our implementation relies on a user-specified termination threshold.

Learning distance metric weights. Instead of giving an equal weight to each distance metric for all elements, it would make sense to treat some metrics as more important than others, depending on the characteristics of the data being compared. We now show how we can exploit training data to automatically discover which distance metrics are most informative for which elements. The key idea is that a good distance metric should have a small value between pairs of semantically related instances, while at the same time having a large value between pairs of semantically unrelated instances.

We assume access to a set of training data: a partition of some set of elements and their instance data. Based on such training data, the *goodness* of metric d_j for a non-singleton cluster C is defined as $G(d_j, C) = G'(d_j, C) / \frac{1}{c} \sum_{C'} G'(d_j, C')$, where c is the number of non-singleton clusters C' in the training data, $D_{\text{intra}}(d_j, C)$ is the average *intra*-cluster distance—i.e., the average distance between pairs of elements within C, $D_{\text{inter}}(d_j, C)$ is the average *inter*-cluster distance—i.e., the average distance between an element in C and an element outside C, and $G'(d_j, C) = D_{\text{inter}}(d_j, C) - D_{\text{intra}}(d_j, C)$. A distance metric d_j will have a score $G(d_j, C) > 1$ if it is "good" (better than average) at separating data from cluster C from data outside the cluster, while $G(d_j, C) < 1$ suggests that d_j is a bad metric for C.

Given these goodness values, we modify OATS in two ways. The first approach (which we call "binary") gives a weight of 1 to metrics with $G > 1$, and gives weight 0 to (ie, ignores) metrics with $G < 1$. The second approach ("proportional"), assigns weights that are proportional to the goodness values.

Evaluation. We evaluated our Web Service aggregation tool on three groups of semantically related Web Service operations: 31 operations providing information about geographical locations, 8 giving current weather information, and 13 giving current stock information. To enable an objective evaluation, a reference partition was first created by hand for each of the three groups. The partitions generated by OATS were compared to these reference partitions. In our evaluation, we used the definition of precision and recall proposed by [5] to measure the similarity between two partitions.

address	city	state	fullstate	zip	areacode	lat	long	icao
110 135th Avenue	New York	NY	New York	11430	718	40.38	-74.75	KJFK
101 Harborside Drive	Boston	MA	Massachusetts	02128	781	42.21	-71.00	KBOS
18740 Pacific Highway South	Seattle	WA	Washington	98188	206	47.44	-122.27	KSEA
9515 New Airport Drive	Austin	TX	Texas	78719	512	30.19	-97.67	KAUS

Fig. 4. The four probe objects for the zip and weather domains.

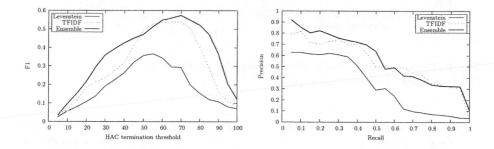

Fig. 5. Comparison of ensemble method against Levenshtein and TFIDF: F1 as a function of the HAC termination threshold (left), and precision/recall curve (right).

We ran a number of tests on each domain. We systematically vary the HAC termination threshold, from one extreme in which each element is placed in its own cluster, to the other extreme in which all elements are merged into one large cluster.

The ensemble of distance metrics was selected from Cohen's SecondString library [14]. We chose eight of the most effective metrics, consisting of a variety of character-based, token-based and hybrid metrics: TFIDF, SlimTFIDF, Jaro, CharJaccard, Levenstein, SmithWaterman, Level2Jaro and Level2JaroWinkler.

Each probe entity is represented as a set of attribute/value pairs. For example, Fig. 4 shows the four probes used for the weather and location information domains. We hand-crafted rules to match each of an operation's inputs to an attribute. To invoke an operation, the probe objects (ie, rows in Fig. 4) are searched for the required attributes. With semantically annotated Web Services, attributes could be *automatically* matched with the input fields of operations.

Results. First, we show that by using an ensemble of different string metrics, we achieve better results than using the metrics separately. Fig. 5 compares the ensemble approach to the Levenshtein and TFIDF metrics individually. We report the average performance over the three domains in two ways: F1 as a function of the HAC termination threshold, and a precision/recall curve. Note that, as expected, F1 peaks at an intermediate value of the HAC termination threshold. The average and maximum F1 is higher for the ensemble of metrics, meaning that it is much less sensitive to the tuning of the HAC termination threshold.

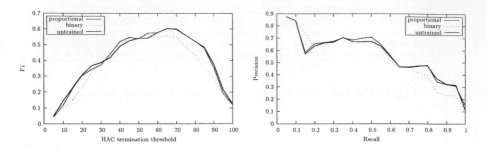

Fig. 6. Performance of OATS: F1 as a function of the HAC termination threshold (left), and precision/recall curve (right).

We now compare the performance of OATS with our two methods (binary and proportional) for using the learned string metric weights. These results are based on four probes. We used two-fold cross validation, where the set of operations was split into two equal-sized subsets, S_{train} and S_{test}. We used just two folds due to the relatively small number of operations. S_{train} was clustered according to the reference clusters, and weights for each distance metric were learned. Clustering was then performed on the entire set of elements. Note that we clustered the training data along with the test data in the learning phase, but we did not initialize the clustering process with reference clusters for the training data prior to testing. We measured the performance of the clustering by calculating precision and recall for just the elements of S_{test}. Fig. 6 shows F1 as a function of the HAC termination threshold, and the precision/recall curves for the binary and proportional learners and the original algorithm. Although neither of the learning methods increase the maximum F1, they usually increase the average F1, suggesting that learning makes OATS somewhat less sensitive to the exact setting of the HAC termination threshold.

Finally, we have found that accuracy improves with additional probe queries, but that performance is beginning to level off after just a few probes. Recall that we used up to four probe queries. We note that accuracy improved more between one and two queries, than between three and four. We anticipate that the performance increase will rapidly slow beyond a relatively small number of probes. Note that we did not carefully select the probe objects in order to maximize performance. Indeed, some of the operations returned missing elements for some probes. Our experiments show that the active invocation approach means makes OATS robust to even a "bad" choice of probes.

Related Work. The schema matching problem has been studied in various domains since the early 1980's, and many different approaches have been suggested, each exploiting various features of the instance data and/or schema. This previous work can be broadly classified according to whether it is schema vs. instance based, and whether it is structural or linguistic based. While most prior research on matching systems has focused on the schema level (e.g. [15,16,17]), the OATS algorithm demonstrates that instance-based methods are well suited to scenarios such as Web Service aggregation where instance data can be *actively requested*.

OATS has been influenced specifically by two prior research efforts: LSD [18] and ILA [13]. LSD uses similarities computed at both the schema and the instance level. LSD treats schema matching as a classification task – a number of trained learner-modules predict labels for each element and these predictions are combined with a meta learner. In contrast to OATS, a training phase is obligatory in LSD.

ILA [13] learns models of relational Web information sources, where each model consists of a number of attributes and values. ILA maps between its own and the source's relational schemas by probing the information source with values from its model, and explaining each field of the resulting string in terms of its own internal model categories. Like OATS, ILA assumes that there is some overlap between its objects and the contents of each source.

5 Discussion

In this paper, we have presented ASSAM, a tool for annotating Semantic Web Services. We have presented the WSDL annotator application, which provides an easy-to-use interface for manual annotation, as well as machine learning assistance for semi-automatic annotation. Our application is capable of exporting the annotations as OWL-S.

We have presented a new iterative relational classification algorithm that combines the idea of existing iterative algorithms with the strengths of ensemble learning. We have evaluated this algorithm on a set of real Web Services and have shown that it outperforms a simple classifier and that it is suitable for semi-automatic annotation.

We have also shown how semantically annotated Web Services could be used to enhance data aggregation systems, and how Web Service aggregation can be viewed as an instance of the schema matching problem *in which instance data is particularly important*. We have illustrated how actively probing Web Services with a small number of inputs can result in contextually related instance data which makes matching easier. Our experiments demonstrate how using an ensemble of distance metrics performs better than the application of individual metrics. We also proposed a method for adaptively combining distance metrics in relation to the characteristics of the data being compared, which although not always successful, usually increased the average F1. We plan to examine the use of more sophisticated techniques for aggregating the ensemble matchers.

One of the constraints of our aggregation system is that there must be an overlap between the sources, i.e all of the sources must "know about" the entity being queried. Ultimately, we would like our system to learn new objects from some information sources that could be used to probe other partially overlapping sources. We envisage a tool that, given a set of seed Web Services and probe queries, could find sets of related Web Services and learn new probe objects to query them with. Such visions would require the automated discovery, composition and invocation of Web Services, but this interoperability requires Services to be semantically annotated. We believe that the methods we have presented here are a reasonable first step towards the realization of these goals.

Acknowledgments. This research was supported by grants SFI/01/F.1/C015 from Science Foundation Ireland, and N00014-03-1-0274 from the US Office of Naval Research. We thank Martina Naughton, Jessica Kenny, Wendy McNulty and Andrea Rizzini for helping us manually annotating the corpus of semantic Web Services used in our evaluation. Thanks to Thomas Gottron for a helpful discussion.

References

1. The DAML Services Coalition: OWL-S 1.0. White Paper (2003)
2. Paolucci, M., Srinivasan, N., Sycara, K., Nishimura, T.: Towards a semantic choreography of web services: From WSDL to DAML-S. In: ISWC. (2003)
3. Patil, A., Oundhakar, S., Sheth, A., Verma, K.: Meteor-s web service annotation framework. In: 13th Int. WWW Conf., New York, USA (2004)
4. Sabou, M.: From software APIs to web service ontologies: a semi-automatic extraction method. In: ISWC, Hiroshima, Japan (2004)
5. Heß, A., Kushmerick, N.: Learning to attach semantic metadata to web services. In: ISWC, Sanibel Island, FL, USA (2003)
6. Neville, J., Jensen, D.: Statistical relational learning: Four claims and a survery. In: Workshop SRL, Int. Joint. Conf. on AI. (2003)
7. Dietterich, T.G.: Ensemble methods in machine learning. In: Lecture Notes in Computer Science. (Volume 1857.)
8. Heß, A., Kushmerick, N.: Iterative ensemble classification for relational data: A case study of semantic web services. In: ECML, Pisa, Italy (2004)
9. Neville, J., Jensen, D.: Iterative classification in relational data. In: AAAI Workshop SRL. (2000)
10. Lu, Q., Getoor, L.: Link-based classification. In: Int. Conf. on Machine Learning, Washington, D.C. (2003)
11. Ghani, R., Slattery, S., Yang, Y.: Hypertext categorization using hyperlink patterns and meta data. In: 18th Int. Conf. on Machine Learning. (2001)
12. Yang, Y., Slattery, S., Ghani, R.: A study of approaches to hypertext categorization. Journal of Intelligent Information Systems **18** (2002) 219–241
13. Perkowitz, M., Etzioni, O.: Category translation: Learning to understand information on the internet. In: Int. Joint Conf. on AI. (1995)
14. Cohen, W.W., Ravikumar, P., Fienberg, S.E.: A comparison of string distance metrics for name-matching tasks. In: Int. Joint Conf. on AI, Workshop on Inf. Integr. on the Web. (2003)
15. Popa, L., Velegrakis, Y., Miller, R.J., Hernandez, M.A., Fagin, R.: Translating web data. In: VLDB. (2002) 598–609
16. Do, H., Rahm, E.: Coma - a system for flexible combination of schema matching approaches. In: VLDB. (2002)
17. Madhavan, J., Bernstein, P.A., Rahm, E.: Generic Schema Matching with Cupid. In: VLDB, Rome, Italy (2001)
18. Doan, A., Domingos, P., Halevy, A.: Learning to match the schemas of data sources: A multistrategy approach. Machine Learning **50** (2003) 279–301

Information Gathering During Planning for Web Service Composition

Ugur Kuter[1], Evren Sirin[1], Dana Nau[1], Bijan Parsia[2], and James Hendler[1]

[1] Department of Computer Science,
University of Maryland, College Park, MD 20742, USA,
{ukuter,evren,nau,hendler}@cs.umd.edu
[2] MIND Lab, University of Maryland,
8400 Baltimore Ave., College Park, MD 20742, USA
bparsia@isr.umd.edu

Abstract. Hierarchical Task-Network (HTN) based planning techniques have been applied to the problem of composing Web Services, especially when described using the OWL-S service ontologies. Many of the existing Web Services are either exclusively information providing or crucially depend on information-providing services. Thus, many interesting service compositions involve collecting information either during execution or during the composition process itself. In this paper, we focus on the latter issue. In particular, we present ENQUIRER, an HTN-planning algorithm designed for planning domains in which the information about the initial state of the world may not be complete, but it is discoverable through plan-time information-gathering queries. We have shown that ENQUIRER is sound and complete, and derived several mathematical relationships among the amount of available information, the likelihood of the planner finding a plan, and the quality of the plan found. We have performed experimental tests that confirmed our theoretical results and that demonstrated how ENQUIRER can be used in Web Service composition.

1 Introduction

Web Services are Web accessible, loosely coupled chunks of functionality with an interface described in a machine readable format. Web Services are designed to be *composed*, that is, combined in workflows of varying complexity to provide functionality that none of the component services could provide alone. AI planning techniques can be used to automate Web Service composition by representing services as actions, and treating service composition as a planning problem. On this model, a service composition is a ground sequence of service invocations that accomplishes a goal or task.

OWL-S [1] provides a set of ontologies to describe Web Services in a more expressive way than allowed by the Web Service Description Language (WSDL). In OWL-S, services can be described as complex or atomic processes with preconditions and effects. This view enables us to translate the process-model constructs

S.A. McIlraith et al. (Eds.): ISWC 2004, LNCS 3298, pp. 335–349, 2004.

directly to HTN methods and operators [2]. Thus, it is possible to use HTN planners to plan for composing Web Services that are described in OWL-S.

However, using AI planning techniques for Web Services composition introduces some challenges. Traditional planning systems assume that the planner begins with complete information about the world. However, in service composition problems, most of the information (if it is available at all) must be acquired from Web Services, which may work by exposing databases, or may require prior use of such information-providing services. For example, an appointment making service might require the planner to determine an available appointment time first. In many cases, it is not feasible or practical to execute all the information-gathering services up front to form a complete initial state of the world. In such cases, it makes sense to gather information during planning.

In this paper, we describe ENQUIRER, an HTN-planning algorithm that can solve Web Service composition problems that require gathering information during the composition process. ENQUIRER is based on the SHOP2 planning system [3], and designed for planning domains in which the information about the initial world state may not be complete. In such cases, ENQUIRER issues queries to obtain the necessary information, it postpones all decisions related to that information until a response comes in, and it continues examining alternative branches of the search space. By gathering extra information at plan time, the planner is able to explore many more branches in the search space than the initial state ordinarily permits. Since external queries often dominate planning time, and, being distributed, are strongly parallelizable, ENQUIRER's non-blocking strategy is sometimes able to dramatically improve the time to find a plan.

We also provide the sufficient conditions to ensure the soundness and completeness of ENQUIRER, derive a recurrence relation for the probability of ENQUIRER finding a plan, and prove theoretical results that give mathematical relationships among the amount of information available to ENQUIRER and the probability of finding a plan. These relationships are confirmed by our experimental evaluations. We describe how the generic ENQUIRER algorithm can be used to solve the problem of composing Web Services, and test the efficiency of the algorithm on real-world problems.

2   Motivations

HTN-planning algorithms have proven promising for Web service composition. Many service-oriented objectives can be naturally described with a hierarchical structure. HTN-style domains fit in well with the loosely-coupled nature of Web services: different decompositions of a task are independent so the designer of a method does not have to have close knowledge of how the further decompositions will go. Hierarchical modeling is the core of the OWL-S [1] process model to the point where the OWL-S process model constructs can be directly mapped to HTN methods and operators. In our previous work [2], we have shown how such a translation can be done for SHOP2 [3]. In this work, we have kept the basic SHOP2-language mapping intact, and focused on extending the way SHOP2 deals with plan-time information gathering.[1] We call the extended algorithm ENQUIRER.

We have identified three key features of service-oriented planning:

- *The planner's initial information about the world is incomplete.* When the size and nature of Web is considered, we cannot assume the planner will have gathered all the information needed to find a plan. As the set of operators and methods grows very large (i.e., as we start using large repositories of heterogeneous services) it is likely that trying to complete the initial state will be wasteful at best and practically impossible in the common case.

- *The planning system should gather information during planning.* While not all the information relevant to a problem may have already been gathered, it will often be the case that it is accessible to the system. The relevance of possible information can be determined by the possible plans the planner is considering, so it makes sense to gather that information while planning.

- *Web Services may not return needed information quickly, or at all.* Executing Web Services to get the information will typically take longer time than the planner would spend to generate plans. In some cases, it will not be known a priori which Web Service gives the necessary information and it will be required to search a Web Service repository to find such capable services. It may not be possible at all to find those services. Furthermore, in some cases the found service cannot be executed because the service requires some password that the user cannot provide or the service is inaccessible due to some network failure. The system should not cease planning while waiting for answers to its queries, but keep planning to look for other plans that do not depend on answering those specific queries.

ENQUIRER is designed to address all of the issues above. In the subsequent sections, we first give a brief background on the HTN Planning and the SHOP2 planning system, and then we present the ENQUIRER planning algorithm, as well as our theoretical and experimental evaluations of it.

3   Background: HTN Planning and SHOP2

The purpose of an HTN planner is to produce a sequence of actions that perform some activity or *task*. The description of a planning domain includes a set of planning *operators* and *methods*, each of which is a prescription for how to decompose a task into its *subtasks* (smaller tasks). The description of a planning problem contains an initial state as in classical planning. Instead of a goal formula, however, there is a partially-ordered set of tasks to accomplish.

---

[1] In this paper, we focus on information gathering as plan-time execution of Web Services. Nothing in this work, however, is specific to information-providing Web Services, and could be immediately adapted to any oracular query-answering mechanism, e.g., a user could interactively supply answers to the system.

Planning proceeds by decomposing tasks recursively into smaller and smaller subtasks, until *primitive tasks*, which can be performed directly using the planning operators, are reached. For each task, the planner chooses an applicable method, instantiates it to decompose the task into subtasks, and then chooses and instantiates other methods to decompose the subtasks even further. If the constraints on the subtasks or the interactions among them prevent the plan from being feasible, the planning system will backtrack and try other methods.

SHOP2 is an HTN planner that generates actions in the order they will be executed in the world. Its backtracking search considers the methods applicable to the same task in the order they are specified in the knowledge base given to the planner. This feature of the planner allows for specifying *user preferences* among such methods, and therefore, among the solution that can be generated using those methods. For example, Figure 1(c) shows a possible user preference among the three methods for the task of delivering a box from UMD to MIT.

An example is in order. Consider a Delivery Domain, in which the task is to deliver a box from one location to another. Figure 1(a) shows two SHOP2 methods for this task: *delivering by car*, and *delivering by truck*. Delivering by car involves the subtasks of loading the box to the car, driving the car to the destination location, and unloading the box at the destination. Note that each method's preconditions are used to determine whether or not the method is applicable: thus in Figure 1(a), the *deliver by car* method is only applicable if the delivery is to be a fast one, and the *deliver by truck* method is only applicable if it is to be a slow one. Now, consider the task of delivering a box from the University of Maryland to MIT and suppose we do not care about a fast delivery. Then, the *deliver by car* method is not applicable, and we choose the *deliver by truck* method. As shown in Figure 1(b), this decomposes the task into the following subtasks: *(1)* reserve a truck from the delivery center at Laurel, Maryland to the center at Cambridge, Massachusetts, *(2)* deliver the box from the University of Maryland to Laurel, *(3)* drive the truck from Laurel to Cambridge, and *(4)* deliver the box from Cambridge to MIT. For the two delivery subtasks produced by this decomposition, we must again consider our delivery methods for further decomposing them until we do not have any other task to decompose.

During planning, the planner evaluates the preconditions of the operators and methods with respect to the world state it maintains locally. It is assumed that planner has all the required information in its local state in order to evaluate these preconditions. For example, in the delivery example, it is assumed that the planner knows all the distances between the any initial and final locations so that it can determine how long a truck will be reserved for a delivery task. Certainly, it is not realistic to assume that planner will have all this information before the planning process starts. Considering the amount of information available on the Web is huge, planner should gather the information as needed by the planning process. Since gathering information may take some considerable amount of time, it would be wise to continue planning while the queries are being processed. For example, the planner can continue planning with the *truck delivery* method until the answer to the query about train schedules has been received.

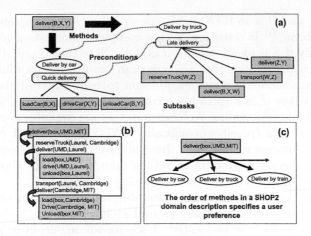

Fig. 1. Delivery planning example.

4   Definitions and Notation

We use the same definitions for logical atoms, states, task symbols, tasks, task networks, actions, operators, methods, and plans as in SHOP2. The ENQUIRER planning procedure extends SHOP2 to be able to cope with incomplete information about the initial state of the world. The following definitions establish the framework for the ENQUIRER procedure.

An *askable list* is a set of logical atoms that are eligible for the planner query during the planning process. Note that we do not require the atoms in an askable list to be ground. In many realistic application domains, the planner can only obtain certain kinds of information, regardless of whether that information is needed for planning. Intuitively, an *askable list* specifies the kinds of information that is guaranteed to be available to the planner during planning, although this information may not be given the planner at the start of the planning process.

A *query* is an expression of the form $(h\ p)$, where h is the unique label of the query and p is a logical atom. Note that we do not require p to be ground. The intent of a query is to gather information during planning about the relation p in the state of the world before planning started (i.e., in the initial state).

Let A be an askable list. We let $\delta(A)$ denote the set of all possible instantiations of the atoms in A. Then, a query $(h\ p)$ is said to be *askable with respect to A* if and only if p unifies with an atom in $\delta(A)$ – i.e., there exists a variable substitution Θ such that $\Theta(p) \in \delta(A)$. An *answer* for an already-asked query $(h\ p)$ is an expression of the form $(h\ R)$ such that $R \subseteq \delta(A)$, and for each $p' \in R$, there exists a substitution Θ such that $\Theta(p) = p'$.

A *complete-information planning problem* is a tuple $P^C = (S, T, D)$, where S is a complete initial state, T is a task network, and D is an HTN-domain description that consists of a set of planning operators O and methods M, respectively. An *incomplete-information planning problem* is a tuple $P^I = (J, A, T, D)$, where J is a set of ground atoms that are initially known, A is an askable list, T is a task network, and D is an HTN-domain description. An incomplete-information planning problem P^I is *consistent* with a complete-information planning problem P^C if only if S is identical with $J \cup \delta(A)$. Note that $J \cup \delta(A)$ denotes the total amount of information that a planner can possibly obtain while solving P^I.

We define a *service-composition problem* to be a tuple of the form $W = (J, X, C, K)$, where J is a (possibly incomplete) initial state, X is a set of all possible information-providing Web Services that are available during the planning process, C is a (possibly) composite OWL-S process, and K is a collection of OWL-S process models such that we have $C \in K$. We assume that the information-gathering services in X return information only about the initial state, and they do not have any world-altering effects.

An explanation about the set of available services X is in order. When a query $(h\ p)$ for a possibly partially ground atom p is asked, Web Service that answer this query needs to be located. A service whose output or postcondition specification matches with p is said to be a possible match.[2] For example, a query (find-airports airport(US,?x)) can be answered by a service that is specified as (:input ?c - country, :output ?x - airport, :postcondition airport(?c, ?x)). Note that, such a service description can be written in OWL-S 1.1 using the recently added Result and Expression structures.

Let $W = (J, X, C, K)$ be a service-composition problem. We let $\tau(X)$ denote the total amount of information that can possibly be gathered from the Web Services in X – i.e., $\tau(X)$ denotes the set of all possible ground atoms that are specified by the outputs or the postconditions of the services in X. Then, we say that W is *equivalent* to an incomplete-information problem $P^I = (J, A, T, D)$ if and only if $\tau(X) = \delta(A)$, where T is the SHOP2 translation for the OWL-S process C, and $D = \text{TRANSLATE}(K)$ is the HTN-domain description generated by the translation algorithm TRANSLATE of [2].

5   The ENQUIRER Algorithm

ENQUIRER starts with an incomplete initial world state, gathers relevant information during planning, and continues to explore alternative possible plans while waiting for information to come in. The algorithm is shown in Fig.2. The input is an incomplete-information planning problem (J, A, T, D) as defined above. ASKED is the set of all queries that have been issued by ENQUIRER and that have not been answered yet. ANS is the set of all queries for which answers have been received. The OPEN list is the set of triples of the form (J, T, π), where J is a (possibly) incomplete state, T is a task list, and π is a plan. Intuitively, the OPEN list holds the information on the leaf nodes of the search tree generated during the planning process. Initially, each of these lists is the empty set, except the OPEN list which is initialized to $\{(J, T, \pi)\}$.

At each iteration of the planning process, we first check if the OPEN list is empty. If so, then we report *failure* since this means that every branch in the

---

[2] In this paper, we assumed the existence of matched services. The problem of discovery and location of a matched Web Service is beyond the scope of this paper.

```
procedure ENQUIRER(J, A, T, D = (O, M))
 ASKED ← ∅; ANS ← ∅; π ← ∅; OPEN ← {(J,T,π)}
 loop
  if OPEN = ∅ then return(failure)
  OPEN ← {(J',T,π) | (J,T,π) ∈ OPEN, (h p) ∈ ASKED, an answer (h R) has
                     been received for (h p), and J' ← ProcessAnswers(J, R)}
  for each query (h p) ∈ ASKED that has been answered recently
   remove (h p) from ASKED and insert it into ANS
  select a tuple (J,T,π) from OPEN and remove it
  if T = ∅ then return(π)
  nondeterministically choose a task t ∈ T that has no predecessors
  if t is a primitive task then
   U ← {(o,Θ) | o ∈ O,  and ∃ a substitution Θ such that Θ(t) = Θ(head(o))}
   S ← {(J',Θ(T − {t}), π ∪ {Θ(o)}) | (o,Θ) ∈ X,  Θ(o) is applicable in J, and
                            J' ← ApplyOp(J, Θ(o))}
  else
   U ← {(m,Θ) | m ∈ M,  and ∃ a substitution Θ such that Θ(t) = Θ(head(m))}
   S ← {(J,T',π)|(m,Θ) ∈ X, Θ(m) is applicable in J, and
                    T' ∈ ApplyMeth(J,T,t,m,Θ)}
  OPEN ← OPEN ∪ S
  Q ← {(h p) | (u,Θ) ∈ U,  p is a precondition of u such that Θ(p) is askable w.r.t. A,
           Θ(u) is not applicable in J,  and ∄ a query (h Θ(p)) ∈ ANS}
  if Q ≠ ∅ then
   ASKED ← ASKED ∪ {(h p) | (h p) ∈ Q, and (h p) ∉ ASKED}
   OPEN ← OPEN ∪ {(J,T,π)}
```

Fig. 2. The ENQUIRER algorithm.

search space is exhausted without success. Otherwise, we start processing the answers for our previously-issued queries that have arrived at this point. Let $(h\ R)$ be such an answer for the query $(h\ p)$. Then, for every triple (J,T,π) in OPEN, we insert a ground atom $p' \in R$ into J if $p' \notin J$ and there is no action $a \in \pi$ that makes p' false in the world. Note that this condition is necessary to ensure the correctness of our algorithm since ENQUIRER's queries provide information about the initial state of the world: if we insert an atom into J that is in the delete-list of an action in π, then J becomes inconsistent. In Fig.2, the subroutine ProcessAnswers is responsible for checking this condition and updating the states in OPEN accordingly.

After processing the answered queries, the next step is to select a tuple (J,T,π) from OPEN, and remove it. We then check if the current task network T is empty or not. If so, we have π as our plan since all of the goal tasks have been accomplished successfully. Otherwise, we nondeterministically choose a task t in T that has no predecessors in T. If t is primitive then we decompose it using the operators in O. Otherwise, the methods in M must be used.

Due to the space limitations, we only describe the case in which t is primitive. The case in which t is not primitive is very similar. If t is primitive, then we first select each operator o that matches to the task t — i.e., there exists a variable substitution Θ such that $\Theta(t) = \Theta(head(o))$. The operator instance $\Theta(o)$ is applicable in J, if all of its preconditions are ground and satisfiable in J. Otherwise, it is not applicable. In the former case, we generate the next state J' and the next task network T' by applying $\Theta(o)$ in J and by removing t from T, respectively. We update the current partial plan π by adding $\Theta(o)$ to it, and update the OPEN list with the tuple $(J', T', \pi \cup \{\Theta(o)\})$.

If the operator instance $\Theta(o)$ is not applicable in J then this means that there is a precondition p of $\Theta(o)$ such that either p is not ground, or p is ground but cannot be satisfied in J. In either case, we cannot immediately come to a conclusion on whether $\Theta(o)$ is applicable in J or not. Instead, we must do the following. We first check if p is askable with respect to the askable list A; if it is not then there is no way we can obtain further information about it so we conclude that it is false. Otherwise, we check if there is a query for p in the ANS list. If so, then this means that p was queried before and an answer has been received for it. Then, since we still cannot infer any information about p from J, p must be false in the world and we cannot apply $\Theta(o)$ in J.

If there is no query related to p in ANS, then this means one of the following conditions holds: we have queried p before but no answer has come yet, or this is the first time we need to query it. To determine which case we are in, we check the ASKED list if there is a query for p in it. If so, then the former is the case and we defer our decision on the applicability of $\Theta(o)$ in J. If there is no query regarding to p in ASKED, then we create a new query for p and insert it into ASKED. In this case, we again defer our decision on $\Theta(o)$.

Note that if the precondition p is unground in $\Theta(o)$, there may be additional information related to p that cannot be inferred in J, even if p is satisfiable in that state. For example, in the delivery domain, an unground precondition may be used to get the schedule of all trains for a particular route. In the current state, there may already be some related information, e.g. results of a previous queries returned by one Web Service invocation. However, there may still be other Web Services that will return additional information that could be crucial for finding a plan. Therefore, in order to ensure completeness, ENQUIRER queries all the related Web Services about p regardless of what is inferred in J.

The ENQUIRER algorithm also uses two subroutines called ApplyOp and ApplyMeth. ApplyOp takes as input the current state J and the action to be applied in J, and outputs the successor state that arises from applying that action in J. The definition for ApplyMeth is more complicated; intuitively, it takes a method m and a non-primitive task t to be decomposed by m, and it modifies the current task network T by removing t and adding its subtasks to T (for the full definition of this subroutine, see [3]).

6   Formal Properties of ENQUIRER

Due to space limitations, we omit the proofs of our theorems here. They can be found at [4]. We first establish the soundness and completeness of our algorithm.

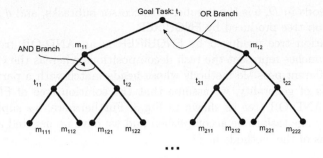

Fig. 3. The solution tree that ENQUIRER generates for an incomplete-information planning problem.

Theorem 1. *Let $W = (J, X, C, K)$ be a service-composition problem, and $P^I = (J, A, T, D)$ be an incomplete-information planning problem that is equivalent to W. If ENQUIRER returns a plan for P^I, then that plan is a solution for every complete-information planning problem that is consistent with P^I. If ENQUIRER does not return a plan, then there exists at least one planning problem P^C that is consistent with P^I, and P^C is unsolvable (i.e., no plans for P^C exist).*

The following theorem establishes the correctness of our approach.

Theorem 2. *Let $W = (J, X, C, K)$ be a service-composition problem, and $P^I = (J, A, T, D)$ be an incomplete-information planning problem that is equivalent to W. ENQUIRER returns a plan π for P^I if and only if π is a composition for W.*

Let $\chi(P^I)$ be the set of all solutions returned by any of the non-deterministic traces of ENQUIRER on an incomplete-information problem P^I. Furthermore, we let π_{P^I} be the shortest solution in $\chi(P^I)$, and let $|\pi_{P^I}|$ denote the length of that solution (i.e., plan). We now establish our first informedness theorem:

Theorem 3. *Let $P_1^I = (J_1, A_1, T, D)$ and $P_2^I = (J_2, A_2, T, D)$ be two incomplete-information planning problems. Then $\chi(P_1^I) \subseteq \chi(P_2^I)$, if $J_1 \cup \delta(A_1) \subseteq J_2 \cup \delta(A_2)$.*

A corollary immediately follows:

Corollary 1. *Let $P_1^I = (J_1, A_1, T, D)$ and $P_2^I = (J_2, A_2, T, D)$ be two incomplete-information planning problems. Then $|\pi_{P_2^I}| \leq |\pi_{P_1^I}|$, if $J_1 \cup \delta(A_1) \subseteq J_2 \cup \delta(A_2)$.*

Let $P^I = (J, A, T, D)$ be an incomplete-information planning problem. For the rest of this section, we will assume that there are constants c, p, q, m, k, b, and d such that c is the probability of a task being composite, p is the probability of a ground atom a being true, q is the probability of the truth-value of an atom a being known to ENQUIRER, m is the average number of methods that are applicable to a composite task, k is the average number of distinct preconditions for the methods in D, b is the number of successor subtasks, and d is the depth of the solution tree produced by ENQUIRER.

The solution tree produced by ENQUIRER is an AND-OR tree, in which the AND branches represent the task decompositions whereas the OR branches represent different possible methods whose heads match with a particular task. Without loss of generality, we assume that the solution tree of ENQUIRER is a complete AND-OR tree as shown in Fig.3. Furthermore, we suppose that T contains only one task to be accomplished and we have no negated atoms in the preconditions of the methods in D.

Lemma 1. *Given an incomplete-information planning problem $P^I = (J, A, T, D)$ that satisfies the assumption given above, the probability ρ of ENQUIRER finding a solution for P^I is*

$$\rho_0 = 1; \text{ and}$$
$$\rho_d = (1 - c) * (p.q)^k + c * [1 - (1 - \gamma_d)^m],$$

where $\gamma_d = (p.q)^k \times (\rho_{d-1})^b$.

The following theorem establishes our second informedness result.

Theorem 4. *Let $P_1^I = (J_1, A_1, T, D)$ and $P_2^I = (J_2, A_2, T, D)$ be two incomplete-information planning problems satisfying the assumption given earlier. Furthermore, let ρ_1 and ρ_2 be the probabilities of ENQUIRER finding solutions for P_1^I and P_2^I, respectively. Then, $\rho_1 \leq \rho_2$, if $J_1 \cup \delta(A_1) \subseteq J_2 \cup \delta(A_2)$.*

7   Experimental Evaluation

For our experiments, we wanted to investigate (1) how well ENQUIRER would perform in service-composition problems where some of the information was completely unavailable, and (2) the trade-off between the time performance and the desirability of the solutions generated by the planner by using different query-processing strategies. We built a prototype implementation of the ENQUIRER algorithm that could be run with different query strategies. We also built a simulation program that would generate random response times for the queries issued by ENQUIRER. We ran our experiments on a Sun SPARC Ultra1 machine with 192MB memory running Solaris 8.

Experimental Case 1. In this case, we have investigated how the number of solutions (i.e., plans) found by the ENQUIRER algorithm is affected by the amount of the information available during planning. In these experiments, we used a set of Web Service composition problems on the Delivery domain described in Section 3. In these problems, a delivery company is trying to arrange the shipment of a number of packages by coordinating its several local branches. The company needs to gather information from the branches about the availability of vehicles (i.e., trucks and planes) and the status of packages. Such information is provided by Web Services, and the goal is to generate a sequence of confirmation messages that tells the company that every package is delivered to its destination.

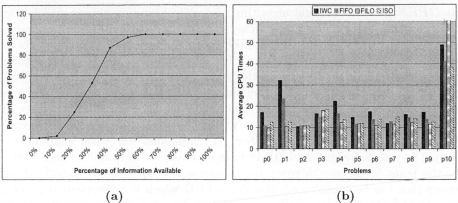

(a)   (b)

Fig. 4. Chart (a) shows the percentage of times ENQUIRER could find plans for the Delivery problems, as a function of the amount of information available during planning. Chart (b) shows the comparison of the average CPU times (in secs.) of the four query-processing strategies in ENQUIRER.

In these experiments, we have ENQUIRER run the planner on 100 randomly-generated problem instances. For each problem instance, we ran ENQUIRER several times as described below, varying the amount of information available about the initial state by varying the following quantities: $|J|$, the number of atoms of S that were given initially; and $|A|$, the amount of atoms of S that were made available in the askable list, where S is the set of all possible ground atoms in the domain.

We measured the percentage of times that ENQUIRER could find plans, as a function of the quantity $\frac{|J \cup A|}{|S|}$. The fraction $\frac{|J \cup A|}{|S|}$ is the fraction of atoms about the initial state that are available during planning. We varied $\frac{|J \cup A|}{|S|}$ from $f = 0\%$ to 100% in steps of 10% as follows: we first randomly chose a set of atoms for $|S|$ such the size of this set is equal to the fraction specified by the particular f value. Then, for each atom in this set, we randomly decided whether the atom should go in J – the incomplete initial state –, or in A – the askable list. Using this setup, we performed 100 runs of ENQUIRER for each value of $\frac{|J \cup A|}{|S|}$. The results, shown in Fig.4(a), show that the success rate for ENQUIRER increased as we increased $\frac{|J \cup A|}{|S|}$. ENQUIRER was able to solve 100% of the problem instances even when $\frac{|J \cup A|}{|S|}$ was as low as 60%.

Experimental Case 2. We also aimed to investigate the comparison between the time performance of the non-blocking nature of the search performed by the ENQUIRER algorithm and the desirability of the plans generated — i.e., how much the generated plans conforms to the user preferences encoded in the domain descriptions given to the algorithm in terms of the ordering among the methods applicable to the same task.

In this respect, we have implemented three variations of the ENQUIRER algorithm. All of these variations are based on how the planning algorithm maintains its $OPEN$ list. The original algorithm, shown in Figure 2, always searches for solutions that can be found regardless of the incompleteness of the information about the initial state: when ENQUIRER issues a query, it does not wait for an answer; instead it continues its search for solutions that can be found without issuing any queries at all. We call this strategy as the Issue-Search-Other (ISO) strategy. Similar to ISO, all the other three strategies are also based on different implementations of the OPEN list. The Issue-Wait-Continue (IWC) strategy involves blocking the search until a query, which is issued recently, gets answered. In the First-In-Last-Out (FILO) strategy, if the planner has asked many queries during its search and several of them have been answered, then it always returns to the point in the search space that corresponds to the most recently-issued query that has been answered. Finally, in FIFO which is a complete symmetric version of FILO, the planner always considers the answers corresponding to the least-recent query it has asked. Due to space limitations, we do not give the details of these strategies; for further information see [4].

In our experiments with these variations of ENQUIRER, we compared their time performances on the domain used in [2], which is partly based on the scenario described in the Scientific American article about the Semantic Web [5]. This scenario describes two people who are trying to take their mother to a physician for a series of treatments and follow-up meetings. The planning problem is to come up with a sequence of appointments that will fit in to everyone's schedules, and at the same time, to satisfy everybody's preferences.

We have created 11 random problems in this domain and we have run all strategies 10 times in each problem. We have set the maximum response time for a query asked by ENQUIRER to be 1 seconds. Fig.4(b) reports the average CPU times required by the four strategies described above.

These results provide several insights regarding the trade-off between time performance of ENQUIRER and the desirability of the solutions it generates under incomplete information. From a performance-oriented point of view, they showed that it is very important for the planner not to wait until its queries get responded, especially when it takes a very long time to get responses for those queries. In our experiments, the IWC strategy performed worst than the others in most of the problems. However, IWC was able to generate the most-desirable solutions for our problems, since it always considers the methods in ENQUIRER knowledge base in the order they were specified.

In most of the problems, the FILO strategy was able to find solutions more quickly than the other strategies; in particular, it was consistently more efficient than IWC. However, these solutions were usually less-desirable ones with respect to the user preferences encoded as orderings among the methods in ENQUIRER knowledge base, since FILO always tends to consider the answers for the most-recently issued queries, which usually correspond to less-desirable preferences because of the queries waiting for an answer.

Our experiments also suggest that the ISO strategy can be particularly useful on planning problems that have few solutions. In particular, the problem $p10$ of our experiments is one such problem, and ISO was able to find solutions for this problem more quickly than others. The reason for this behavior is that ISO performs a less organized and less structured search compared to other strategies, enabling the planner to consider different places in the search space. On the problem $p10$ which has only 48 solutions compared to the 4248 solutions of the problem $p9$, this characteristic enabled ISO to perform better than the other strategies. However, in most of the problems, the solutions generated by the planner using ISO were not the desirable ones.

8 Related Work

[6] describes an approach to building agent technology based on the notion of generic procedures and customizing user constraints. This work extends the Golog language to enable programs that are generic, customizable and usable in the context of the Web. Also, the approach augments a ConGolog interpreter that combines online execution of information-providing services with offline simulation of world-altering services. Although this approach is similar to our work, we suspect that a logic-based approach will not be as efficient as a planning approach. We intend to test this hypothesis empirically in the near future.

In the AI planning literature, there are various approaches to planning with incomplete-information, designed for gathering information during execution by inserting sensing actions in the plan during planning time and by generating conditional plans conditioned on the possible pieces of information that can be gathered by those actions. [7] presents a planning system that implements these ideas. [8] presented a planning language called UWL, which is an extension of the STRIPS language, in order to distinguish between (1) the world-altering and the observational effects of the actions, and (2) the goals of satisfaction and the goals of information. [9] describes he XII planner for planning with both complete and incomplete information, which is an extension of UCPOP [10], and is able to generate sensing actions for information gathering during execution.

ENQUIRER differs from these approaches in that it does not explicitly plan for sensing actions to obtain information at execution time. Instead, it is a planning technique for gathering the necessary information during planning time. As a result, ENQUIRER can generate simple plans since observational actions are not included in the plan, and it can interact with external information sources and clear out the "unknown"s during planning time as much as possible. In this respect, it is very suitable for the problem of composing Web Services.

[11] describes a speculative execution method for generating information-gathering plans in order to retrieve, combine, and manipulate data located in remote sources. This technique exploits certain hints received during plan execution to generate speculative information for reasoning about the dependencies between operators and queries later in the execution. ENQUIRER differs from this method in two aspects: (1) it searches different branches of the search space when one branch is blocked with a query execution, and (2) it runs the queries in planning time, whereas speculative execution was shown to be useful for executing plans. Combining speculative execution with our approach would enable

us to run queries down in a blocked branch; however, since the time spent for a query is lost when speculations about that query are not valid, it is not clear if combining the two approaches will lead to significant results.

9   Conclusions and Future Work

In our previous work [2], we have shown how a set of OWL-S service descriptions can be translated to a planning domain description that can be used by SHOP2. The corresponding planning problem for a service composition problem is to find a plan for the task that is the translation of a composite process. This approach differentiates between the information-gathering services, i.e. services that have only output but no effects, and the world-altering services, i.e. services that have effects but no outputs. The preconditions of information-gathering services include an external function to call to execute the service during planning and add the information to the current state. This can be seen as a specialized application of the ENQUIRER algorithm, when the queries are explicitly specified as special primitive tasks that correspond to atomic service executions.

ENQUIRER overcomes the following limitations in our previous work:

- The information providing services do not need to be explicitly specified in the initial description. The query mechanism can be used to select the appropriate Web Service on the fly when the information is needed. Note that matching service description does not need to be an atomic service. A composite service description matching the request could be recursively fed to the planner, or an entirely different planner could be used to plan for information gathering.
- The planning process does not need to wait for the information gathering to finish and can continue planning while the service is still executing.

In this paper, we have assumed that information-providing services cannot have world-altering effects. Otherwise, the correctness of the plans generated cannot be guaranteed since the changes done by the information-providing service may invalidate some of the steps planner already committed to. However, this restriction is not necessary when the effects of the information-gathering services do not interact with the plan being sought for. As an example, consider a service that charges a small amount of fee for the service. If we are looking for a plan that has nothing to do with money, then it would be safe to execute this service and change the state of the world. In general, this safety can be established when the original planning problem and information-gathering problem correspond to two disconnected task networks that can be accomplished without any kind of interaction. Verifying that there is no interaction between two problems is a challenging task that we will address in our future work.

ENQUIRER is designed for information gathering at plan time; however, it is important to do so in execution time as well. We hypothesize that it should possible to extend our framework for this purpose as follows. ENQUIRER's queries are about the initial state of a planning problem, to ensure that the planner is sound and complete. However, in principle, we should be able to issue queries about any state during planning. This would allow us to insert queries, similar to sensing actions, in the plan generated by the planner, leading conditional plans to be generated by the planner based on the possible answers to such queries. We are currently exploring this possibility and its ramifications on planning.

Acknowledgments. This work was supported in part by the following grants, contracts, and awards: Air Force Research Laboratory F30602-00-2-0505, Army Research Laboratory DAAL0197K0135, the Defense Advanced Research Projects Agency (DARPA), Fujitsu Laboratory of America at College Park, Lockheed Martin Advanced Technology Laboratories, the National Science Foundation (NSF), the National Institute of Standards and Technology (NIST), and NTT Corp. The opinions expressed in this paper are those of authors and do not necessarily reflect the opinions of the funders.

References

1. OWL Services Coalition: OWL-S: Semantic markup for web services (2003) OWL-S White Paper http://www.daml.org/services/owl-s/0.9/owl-s.pdf.
2. Wu, D., Parsia, B., Sirin, E., Hendler, J., Nau, D.: Automating daml-s web services composition using SHOP2. In: Proceedings of ISWC-2003, Sanibel Island, Florida (2003)
3. Nau, D., Au, T.C., Ilghami, O., Kuter, U., Murdock, W., Wu, D., Yaman, F.: SHOP2: An HTN planning system. Journal of Artificial Intelligence Research **20** (2003)
4. Kuter, U., Sirin, E., Nau, D., Parsia, B., Hendler, J.: Information gathering during planning for web service composition. Technical Report 4616-2004-58, Department of Computer Science, University of Maryland, College Park (2004)
5. Berners-Lee, T., Hendler, J., Lassila, O.: The Semantic Web. Scientific American **284** (2001) 34–43
6. McIlraith, S., Son, T.: Adapting Golog for composition of semantic web services. In: Proceedings of the Eighth International Conference on Knowledge Representation and Reasoning, Toulouse, France (2002)
7. Bertoli, P., Cimatti, A., Roveri, M., Traverso, P.: Planning in nondeterministic domains under partial observability via symbolic model checking. In: IJCAI 2001. (2001) 473–478
8. Etzioni, O., Weld, D., Draper, D., Lesh, N., Williamson, M.: An approach to planning with incomplete information. In: Proceedings of KR-92. (1992)
9. Golden, K., Etzioni, O., Weld., D.: Planning with execution and incomplete information. Technical Report TR96-01-09, Department of Computer Science, University of Washington (1996)
10. Penberthy, J.S., Weld, D.: UCPOP: A Sound, Complete, Partial Order Planner for ADL. In: Proceedings of KR-92. (1992)
11. Barish, G., Knoblock, C.A.: Planning, executing, sensing, and replanning for information gathering. In: Proceedings of AIPS-2002, Menlo Park, CA, AAAI Press (2002) 184–193

Applying Semantic Web Services to Bioinformatics: Experiences Gained, Lessons Learnt

Phillip Lord[1], Sean Bechhofer[1], Mark D. Wilkinson[2], Gary Schiltz[3], Damian Gessler[3], Duncan Hull[1], Carole Goble[1], and Lincoln Stein[4]

[1] Department of Computer Science, University of Manchester
Oxford Road, Manchester, M13 9PL, UK
[2] University of British Columbia, James Hogg iCAPTURE Centre
St. Paul's Hospital, 1081 Burrard St., Vancouver, BC, V6Z 1Y3, Canada
[3] National Center for Genome Resources
2935 Rodeo Park Drive East, Santa Fe, NM 87505, US
[4] Cold Spring Harbor Laboratory
1 Bungtown Road, Cold Spring Harbor, NY 11724, US

Abstract. We have seen an increasing amount of interest in the application of Semantic Web technologies to Web services. The aim is to support automated discovery and composition of the services allowing seamless and transparent interoperability. In this paper we discuss three projects that are applying such technologies to bioinformatics: ^{my}Grid, MOBY-Services and Semantic-MOBY. Through an examination of the differences and similarities between the solutions produced, we highlight some of the practical difficulties in developing Semantic Web services and suggest that the experiences with these projects have implications for the development of Semantic Web services as a whole.

1 Introduction

In the past 10 years, the ability to perform biological *in silico* experiments has increased massively, largely due to the advent of high-throughput technologies that have enabled the industrialisation of data gathering.

There are two principal problems facing biological scientists in their desire to perform experiments with these data. The first of these is distribution–many of the data sets have been generated by individual groups around the world, and they control their data sets in an autonomous fashion. Secondly, biology is a highly heterogeneous field. There are large numbers of data types and of tools operating on these data types. Integration of these tools is difficult but vital. [2]

Biology has coped with this in an effective and yet very *ad hoc* manner. Almost all of the databases and tools of bioinformatics have been made available on the Web; the browser becoming an essential tool of the experimental biologist. The reasons for this choice of technology are partly chance in that the growth in genomic technologies happened to occur contemporaneously with the growth

S.A. McIlraith et al. (Eds.): ISWC 2004, LNCS 3298, pp. 350–364, 2004.

of the Web. But many of the key benefits of the Web are also important for biologists. Publishing is economically cheap, technically straightforward, innately distributed, decentralised, and resilient to change. Accessing the Web is likewise simple, requiring no knowledge of specific query languages but enabling "query by navigation" [6].

While this has worked well in the past, it has obvious problems. Many bioinformatics analyses use fragile screen-scraping technologies to access data. Keeping aware of the Web sites on offer is, in itself, a full-time and highly skilled task, mostly because of the complexity of the domain. The application of Semantic Web services to bioinformatics seems a sensible idea as Web services provide a programmatic interface which avoids screen-scraping [14], while semantic descriptions could enable their discovery and composition.

In this paper we describe three architectures, ^{my}Grid, MOBY-Services and Semantic-MOBY, which have been designed to address these problems. All three are aimed mainly at bioinformatics. All three are based on Web or Web-services technologies and use an additional specification of their services to describe the semantics of their operations. All three are high-profile projects in the domain of bioinformatics and come from groups with previous track records of providing solutions for problems of interoperability[1].

The three solutions are also different from each other and from the "idealised" Semantic Web services architecture. In examining these differences, we raise a set of key questions about the applicability of Semantic Web services in practice and present our (partial) solutions for these difficulties.

2   A Day in the Life: Bioinformatics as It Is

Bioinformatics as a discipline has largely grown directly out of the molecular-biology laboratories where it was born. In general, each lab investigated a small region of biology and there are very few labs world-wide working on a single problem. Many of these labs have made their own data available for use on the Web. This data is often un- or semi-structured. Much of the data is composed of DNA or protein sequences, but this has generally been accompanied by large quantities of "annotation"–descriptions (generally in free-text form) of the sources of the sequences, literature citations and the possible function(s) of the molecules. In addition to this raw data, many different tools that operate on it have been developed, most of them with restricted functionality and targeted at performing highly specific tasks.

This situation is slowly changing, largely due to the appearance of large **service providers**, such as the genome-sequencing and -annotating centres. These centres are now increasing their scopes and often provide many different types of information. The primary **service consumer** still remains the small laboratory. Much of the information remains openly accessible.

---

[1] To our knowledge, at the time of writing these were the only substantial projects using Semantic Web Services within bioinformatics

The primary "integration layer" so far has been expert biologists and bioinformaticians. Using their expert knowledge of the domain, they will navigate through the various Web pages offering data or tool access. Information about new resources often comes by word of mouth, through Web portals or paper publications. Data transfer, between applications, is by cut and paste, often with additional data "massaging" (*e.g.*, small alterations in formatting, selections of subsets, simple local transformations such as DNA-to-protein translation). Automation of these processes is achieved largely by bespoke code, often screen-scraping the same Web pages that the manual process would use, sometimes using more programmatically amenable forms of access.

From this description we identify the following:-

– Actors

Service Providers. Generally, but not exclusively, from specialised "genome" centres.

Service Consumers. Generally from smaller laboratories, normally with smaller, non-specialist resources.

– Requirements for integration

Discovery and Description. Finding the right data or tool resources is a complex task. Service providers need to be able to describe their services, and consumers discover services by these descriptions.

Remote Programmatic Access. Current screen-scraping technologies are fragile. Organised and preferably uniform access is required.

Message Formatting. Bespoke data massaging is complex and difficult to automate.

3   Semantic Web Services in a Nutshell

The core task of this a generic semantic web architecture is to enable seamless and inter-operable communication between service providers and service consumers.

It achieves this end with five key components:

Service Interfaces. Service providers publish interfaces to their services using some form of programmatic access.

Semantic Descriptions. In addition to the interface description, semantic descriptions of services are provided. OWL-S is the most prominent framework for these descriptions.

A Domain Ontology. Terms from an ontology describing the key concepts in the domain are used within the semantic descriptions.

Registry/Matchmaker. A matchmaker service searches over the semantic descriptions made available to it. This may be combined with a registry, a service which advertises the availability of other services.

Messaging. The domain ontology is used as a *lingua franca* that enables the service consumer to treat data from different providers in a uniform fashion.

Probably the best known work on supporting such architectures is OWL-S, following on from DAML-S [18]. OWL-S is an upper ontology that describes three key aspects about a service: its *profile*, which describes what the service does; its *process*, which describes how one interacts with the service; and its *grounding*, which relates the ontological concepts to the implementation, usually via a mapping to the WSDL operations.

In this paper we compare the architectures of the three projects with that of an idealised "Semantic Web Services architecture". All three of the projects are attempting to fulfill the requirements specified in Section 2 and are building components that aim to fulfill the role of the five key components described above.

From this comparison we draw the following conclusions:

- The importance of fully automated service discovery and composition is an open question. It is unclear whether it is either possible or desirable, for all services, in this domain, and is an area of research [22].
- Requiring service providers and consumers to re-structure their data in a new formalism for external integration is also inappropriate. External formalisms that adapt to the existence of legacy structuring is sufficient for many purposes.
- The service interfaces within bioinformatics are relatively simple. An extensible or constrained interoperability framework is likely to suffice for current demands: a fully generic framework is currently not necessary.
- If service discovery is to serve the user, descriptions based on users' own models of services are needed. Furthermore, contextual, outcome or task-oriented descriptions are required.
- Semantic services require a domain ontology, but the best way to construct one is not clear. We present three potential solutions for this problem.

4   The Projects

In this section, we present a brief introduction to the three projects. We then give a description of how a traditional "Semantic Web Services" architecture might be applied and explain how this has been implemented in the three projects.

The ^{my}Grid project is part of the UK government's e-Science programme [17]. It is aimed at providing open-source, high-level middleware to support personalised *in silico* experiments in biology. Although still at a prototype stage, ^{my}Grid has been used for two case studies. These have operated as focal points for the technology based around two diseases namely Graves' Disease [12] and Williams-Beuren syndrome [15]. The core ^{my}Grid "philosophy" has been to adopt Web services standards wherever possible and build additional middleware to add value to these. The key components described in Section 3 are realised within ^{my}Grid as follows:

Service Interfaces. Services are published as Web services described with WSDL.

Semantic Descriptions. A lightweight RDF data model is used to structure a service description, with a domain ontology providing a vocabulary. Descriptions can be provided by third parties. Previously ^{my}Grid used full DAML+OIL descriptions.

Domain Ontology. The ontology is curated and stored centrally, and generated by an expert using DAML+OIL.

Registry/Matchmaker. A centralised UDDI registry built over a Jena back end, augmented to enable semantic discovery [7].

Messaging. Pre-existing domain formats are used.

The Bio-Moby project[2] has grown from the "model organism" communities–those supporting the investigation of biological problems in different organisms. These communities have evolved standards which are often specific to one community. However, biologists increasingly wish to ask questions requiring data gathered from many different organisms, thus creating a severe integration problem. The Bio-Moby project has a dual development track with different architectures. The first of these, MOBY-Services (also known as "MOBY-S"), has "simplicity and familiarity" as its core philosophy. MOBY-Services [21] exists as a prototype that is in practical use at a number of sites. The key components are realised within MOBY-Services as follows:

Service Interfaces. Services are simplified compared to WSDL, having single operations, inputs and outputs.

Semantic Descriptions. A data model is enforced by the API of registry with a domain ontology providing a vocabulary.

Domain Ontology. The ontology is user curated, stored centrally, generate by community collaboration, and structure as a Gene Ontology style DAG.

Registry/Matchmaker. A centralised bespoke registry called "MOBY-Central", which enables searching by input and output types, augmented with graph crawling.

Messaging. A thin XML envelope with embedded legacy formats is used.

The second of these, Semantic-MOBY [20] (also known as S-MOBY), has been heavily influenced by the REST architectural style [3] and makes extensive use of Semantic Web technology, in particular OWL-DL. It attempts to embrace the autonomous nature of the Web wherever possible. Also at a prototype stage, Semantic-MOBY has extensive publicly available requirements[3] and design[4] documentation. The key components are realised within Semantic-MOBY as follows:

Service Interfaces. Services are simply Web resources accessible by standard protocols such as HTTP and FTP. For example, via HTTP, a simple GET returns an RDF graph that defines the underlying service interface.

---

[2] http://www.biomoby.org
[3] http://www.biomoby.org/S-MOBY/doc/Requirements/S-MOBY_Requirements.pdf
[4] http://www.biomoby.org/S-MOBY/doc/Design/S-MOBY_Design.pdf

Semantic Descriptions. Service descriptions are expressed in OWL-DL and conform to a canonical format, or upper ontology. This upper ontology creates the context for ontological concepts, which are resolvable into OWL-DL graphs themselves by dereferencing their URIs. Service providers create service-specific subclasses of the ontology, grounding them with their own data-type requirements.

Domain Ontology. One, or several, ontologies are developed by the community, and distributed across the Web, and written in OWL-DL.

Matchmaker. One or more centralised search engines are provided. Service locations can be published, or semantic descriptions can be discovered by Web crawlers. Querying uses the same upper ontology as the semantic descriptions.

Messaging. All communication uses OWL-DL and the same upper ontology.

All three projects therefore share a strong biological focus. They are interested in easing the difficulty of connecting existing service providers to existing service consumers within this domain. This is more important than providing a generic solution.

5   Automated Service Composition

As a domain, bioinformatics has a number of characteristics of relevance to automated service composition.

Complexity. It is unlikely that any representation of the domain and background knowledge will come close to matching the knowledge of the expert bioinformatician.

Fluidity. Key concepts in the domain are open to change. Any codified representation of the domain is likely to be out of date.

Diversity. Opinions differ. Bioinformaticians wish to be involved in the selection of services to ensure that their opinions are reflected.

Automated composition is likely to be useful where transparent seamless access is the most overriding requirement, such as booking appointments [23]. Here, users will be happy to accept the results, so long as they are reasonable and they gain the advantage of not having to perform such tasks themselves. It is not likely to serve the needs of expert, knowledgeable, opinionated scientists who may invest large quantities of money and time in further experiments based on the results and who may be required to justify their methodologies under peer review. In the short term, these scientists are unlikely to trust automated service invocation and composition, probably with justification, as it is unlikely to improve on their own selections. We wish to support biologists' activities, not replace them. In this way, bioinformatics seems to be following the path of medical informatics, where early decision-making systems have given way to later decision-support systems [9].

Our requirements analyses showed one exception to this: the selection of one service from a collection of mirrors. Like most computer users, biologists are fond of asking for ways to "make it go faster". However, a set of services that are mirrors (particularly databases) must have a coordinated update strategy, probably on a daily basis. This coordination indicates that they are not truly autonomous. They are also likely to share the same user and service interfaces (and probably the same code base), so there is no heterogeneity between the mirrors either. Given this, it seems that semantic descriptions are unlikely to be useful in choosing between them. The ^{my}Grid project is also investigating other services, for which automated discovery and composition may be useful; these are described in Section 6.

6   Structured Messages and Middleware

Combined with the complexity of biology, the autonomous nature of bioinformatics has made integration of the different data resources extremely difficult. Most of the key data types, in bioinformatics, have no standard representation or many "standard representations"; there are at least 20 different formats for representing DNA sequences, most of which have no formal specification[5]. As a simple two-bit code, a DNA sequence is at its essence one of the simplest biological data types, and there are many data types which are considerably more complex.

Where standards do exist, they have often arisen as a result of many years of collaborative work. Both the service providers and service consumers have a high degree of buy-in to the formalisms that exist. The service consumers want their data in legacy formats because their tools can operate over them. While some of the data types are simple, many, however, are highly complex and internally structured[6]

Previous work has highlighted this difficulty with web services from other domains. Paolucci et al. [11], note that "the [complex] types used in a WSDL specification [for accessing amazon.com] are totally arbitrary". This problem is taken to an extreme in bioinformatics in that complex types are simply not used. To demonstrate this point, we gathered 30 bioinformatics service descriptions[7]. Of these only two defined any complex types at all and one of these was a simple list type. Bioinformaticians are just not structuring their data in XML schema, because it provides little value to them. All three projects have accepted that much of the data that they receive will not be structured in a standard way. The obvious corollary of this is that without restructuring, the information will be largely opaque to the service layer.

---

[5] http://www.hgmp.mrc.ac.uk/Software/EMBOSS/Themes/SequenceFormats.html

[6] The Swissprot database, for instance, has a 30 pages human readable specification for their format. Alternatively a regexp grammar designed to parse the database is about 300 lines long, and it does not fully parse all the implicit structure

[7] http://www.ebi.ac.uk/~tmo/mygrid/webservices/

The projects have coped with this in different ways. The simplest approach is that of ^{my}Grid. Service providers are largely autonomous and are unlikely to change their data formats unless there are compelling reasons. ^{my}Grid therefore imposes no additional structuring on the data. While there are problems stemming from the lack of a formal representation of many of the formats, bioinformatics has had a long time to solve these problems; there are many good tools and parsers that are capable of coping with this multitude of formats. Within the ^{my}Grid project, the existence of these formats is described; this then should enable us to discover services that can translate between these formats, even though these formats are opaque to the middleware. This process has been previously described as *automatic semantic translation* [8]. We describe these services as "shim services"[8]. In addition to format translation there are several other situations where users can be supported in composing services by the discovery of shims. Firstly, identifier dereferencing–bioinformatics makes extensive use of identifiers, and substituting an identifier for the data it describes is a common task [16]; and secondly, decomposition–selecting a subset of the data produced by one service, for use by another.

In these cases, it appears that services can be automatically composed in a "safe" manner, *i.e.* that is, they do not change the intended meaning of the experimental design, but enable it to work.

Both MOBY-Services and Semantic-MOBY do provide additional structuring for their messaging format. MOBY-Services uses a specialised XML schema, that defines all of its messages, which mostly acts as a thin envelope around the opaque structuring of the legacy formats. However, having accepted the existence of a wrapper, MOBY-Services now has a migration path to the increasing structuring of data. Currently it has used this facility to introduce "Cross-References"; one of the most characteristic features of the bioinformatics data has been the addition of links to other "related" data encoded mainly as hyperlinks to other databases. The cross-references provide a similar facility for programmatically accessed services.

Semantic-MOBY on the other hand uses OWL-DL RDF-XML as a messaging layer and OWL-DL for content structuring. Ontological concepts are mapped to XSD data types by providers in the description of their resource. The rich expressivity of OWL means that, over time, concept descriptions can be customized by extending domain ontologies with new properties, combining concepts across ontologies, and constraining usage with OWL-DL property restrictions.

In short, while none of the projects assume that providers will automatically restructure their data into formats defined in XML Schemas, they all provide migration paths to methodologies that can reduce the problem of syntactic heterogeneity.

---

[8] A shim is a small piece of material used to fill gaps to ensure a tight fit or level a surface

7   Service Provision and Service Interfaces

The key sociological problem that any interoperability middleware faces is attempting to gain support from the service providers. They are semi-autonomous tending to respond well to requests from service consumers. This is unlikely to happen until the system is usable, but a usable system requires the existence of many services.

The MOBY-Services project has taken a different approach. It assumes that service providers are more likely to support MOBY-Services-specific service interfaces if they are easy to generate and require minimal changes to the way the service providers already work. Within the realm of bioinformatics, most existing services look somewhat like a command-line application. Each has one input and one output. There are usually a set of parameters, *i.e.*, values which modify the way the service works, much like command-line options. We describe this style of interface in Table 1 as "Document Style". MOBY-Services therefore uses a subset of the full Web services functionality, thus limiting service interfaces to this basic data model. Each service is atomic, stateless and unrelated to other services.

The ^{my}Grid project assumes that various service providers will develop Web service interfaces for their own purposes and the middleware solutions should just be able to cope with these. Additionally, it has developed a set of services of its own with a package called "SOAPLAB" [13]. Interestingly, most of the available services conform to one of two paradigms. Most of the services have operations which conform to the simplified model of MOBY-Services: inputs, outputs, parameters. Many service providers group related, although independent, operations into a single service; MOBY-Services services only ever have a single operation. The second paradigm, described in Table 1 as "Object Style", is used by SOAPLAB[9]. The service operations define an *ad hoc* object model. This creates a problem in terms of invocation. Any client that uses these services must understand the semantics of the operations. Within the ^{my}Grid project, this has been enabled by using an extensible invocation framework within "freefluo": the workflow-enactment engine [10]. This approach falls short of a generic solution in that the framework needs to be extended for different "styles" of Web services. But within the constrained domain of bioinformatics, with its relatively few service providers, it is likely to be sufficient.

The Semantic-MOBY service interface is somewhat different. Following the REST architecture, each service has an interface based on, for example, HTTP. The underlying messages provide a richer interface defined by the Semantic-MOBY upper ontology. Like MOBY-Services, this service interface is atomic, stateless, and unrelated to other services.

Compared to general WSDL services, the simplified approach that all three projects have taken to service interfaces has some important consequences.

---

[9] It has been argued that web services are not designed to support such object style interfaces [19]. This may be true; however if ^{my}Grid aims to use services from autonomous providers it needs to cope with them.

Table 1. Two different service interfaces to BLAST, a widely used bioinformatics tool. BLAST operates over a biological sequence, has a number of parameters and returns a single complex BLAST report. The "Document Style" interface has a single method taking a complex set of parameters, while the "Object Style" interface uses object identifiers to provide an *ad hoc* object orientation.

Document Style	BlastReport performBlast(Sequence, gap, etc. . .);
Object Style	ObjectIdentifier getInstance();
	void setSequence(ObjectIdentifier, Sequence);
	void setGap(ObjectIdentifier, Gap);
	. . .
	BlastReport invoke(ObjectIdentifier);

OWL-S defines a *grounding* ontology, which describes the relationships between the ontological concepts in the underlying invocation description (*e.g.*, WSDL). This is not required for any of the projects: Semantic-MOBY because its "service interface" is defined by its upper ontology; MOBY-Services because its service interfaces are not heterogeneous; and, ^{my}Grid because the enactment engine deals with the small amount of heterogeneity.

The services are all atomic and not decomposable. As a result, nothing similar to the OWL-S *process* ontology has been used. Only ^{my}Grid uses services that require complex interaction (namely the SOAPLAB services), and this interaction is handled by the enactment engine.

8   User-Centred Service Descriptions

A Semantic Web Services architecture requires a set of semantic service descriptions, which a matchmaker service can then use to discover services.

Within these three projects, all are seeking to enable discovery of services by the user. All three projects share similar ideas about the questions that users wish to ask.

Context. The user has a specific piece of data and wishes to know which services can operate on that type of data.
Outcome. The user wishes to get a specific type of data and wishes to know which services can produce this kind of data.
Task. The user knows what kind of task, *e.g. alignment, retrieval or search.*, to perform, and wishes to known how.

The ^{my}Grid project has introduced a number of other properties of services, including one called "uses resource". Many bioinformatics tools can operate over different data sources. The underlying data has a critical impact on the use of a service, but may well not affect the interface it presents.

In a user-centred approach the users' concepts of "services" do not necessarily confirm to that of the underlying middleware. For example, within ^{my}Grid, services are generally a collection of independent, but related, operations. However, with object-style interfaces, as described in Section 7, the user wishes to find the whole service; the individual operations are essentially an implementation detail. With MOBY-Services, this abstraction is directly represented in the middleware in that each service has only one operation. A second example of this is the distinction between *inputs* and *parameters*[10]. This distinction can be understood by analogy to a command line which has a main argument and a set of options, or switches. In general, users are interested in searching for inputs, while parameters can be safely ignored until invocation time. As well as serving the users' needs, this distinction has the serendipitous effect of greatly reducing the space over which any technology must search.

The biggest limitation of service descriptions at the moment is their assumption of a single class of user. For example, the ^{my}Grid ontology is aimed at bioinformaticians, as this seemed the main user base. Previous systems, such as TAMBIS [4], have been more aimed at biologists; hence biological concepts such as "protein" are modelled and presented instead of bioinformatics concepts such as "Swissprot ID".

The three projects have somewhat differing ideas about who will provide service descriptions. Both MOBY-Services and Semantic-MOBY have systems based on service providers who describe their own services. Conversely, as with its approach to service provision, the ^{my}Grid project has concluded that service providers may or may not choose to do so, and that, at least in the short term, descriptions by third-party members (*e.g.*, those within the ^{my}Grid project!) are essential, and may be desirable even in the long term.

Service descriptions are currently manually generated by all three projects. The relatively simple and familiar formalism used by MOBY-Services (see Section 9) ensures that this process is relatively straightforward. Alternatively, Semantic-MOBY and ^{my}Grid are relying on the provision of good tool support to ease the process. The ^{my}Grid project has made perhaps the most effort in this area reusing a tool from the PEDRo project[11] which presents the user with a fill in form, and then generates services descriptions from this. Describing services is still, however, an arduous process–even though the simplified service interfaces reduce the required complexity of the service descriptions (Section 7). In addition the use of legacy formats (Section 6), means very little information can be mined from the WSDL files; tools such as WSDL2DAML-S are relatively ineffective when they have no information to work on. Most information has been gained from reading associated documentation, guesswork based on service/operation names and experimental execution of the services followed by manual inspection of the results[12].

It is clear that these approaches are not scalable. It is possible that more automated techniques [5] may become applicable in the future. Within the re-

---

[10] *primary* and *secondary* inputs in MOBY-Services parlance
[11] http://pedro.man.ac.uk/
[12] That it is so difficult to work out what services actually do, demonstrates clearly that better service descriptions are genuinely needed!

stricted domain of bioinformatics, it should be possible to partially automate experimental service execution. In the short term, however, the authoring of service descriptions will remain a major bottleneck.

9   Generating an Ontology for a Complex Domain

One fundamental difficulty of any Semantic Web Services architectures is the requirement for a domain ontology. The ontology must reflect the users' understanding of the domain and enable the description of services by service providers or helpful third parties, particularly in support of user-oriented service discovery. In a complex and changing domain such as bioinformatics this is no small undertaking.

Fortunately, within bioinformatics the community is already conversant and are generally convinced of the value of ontological descriptions. Over the last four years, the community has developed the *Gene Ontology* (GO). This is a hierarchically organised controlled vocabulary. The ontology is structurally simple; having subsumption (*is-a*) and partonomy (*part-of*) hierarchies. The ontology is widely used; it now consists of $\sim$17,000 terms and has been used to describe several million database entries. GO is the flagship ontology of a collection of biological ontologies, called OBO (Open Biological Ontologies), which describe various aspects of biology.

GO has provided much of the inspiration for the MOBY-Services approach to ontology development. One of the biggest factors in the success of GO has been the large level of community involvement in its construction[1]. The MOBY-Services central registry *MOBY-Central* therefore contains functionality for adding new terms and relationships. It has adopted the same representational formalism as GO as this is already familiar to the community; familiarity is considered more important than expressivity. Combined with reasonable editorial guidelines and an active mailing list it is hoped that those using the ontology will extend it to fulfil their requirements. Additionally, MOBY-Services has already constructed tools for viewing their ontology; it is essential that finding existing appropriate concepts is easy, in order to discourage the recreation of existing concepts. We call this the *collaborative community* style of ontology building.

^{my}Grid has learnt a different lesson from the GO, namely the importance of the role of a curator. To this end a large ontology has been already been constructed by the project. In this case, ^{my}Grid chose to use DAML+OIL as its underlying formalism because of the existence of tooling (*e.g.*, OilEd) and reasoning capabilities. Wherever possible, existing classifications from the community were used. By analysing use cases from the other two projects that were unavailable at the time the ontology was constructed, it is clear that it has reasonable, but incomplete, coverage of the domain. It is clear that, like MOBY-Services, methods to encourage feedback from the community are essential. We call this *centralised, curated* ontology building.

These two methods are not exclusive, however. MOBY-Services and ^{my}Grid are therefore making significant efforts to align their ontologies. As the largest currently available ontology of bioinformatics services, it is hoped that a view of the ^{my}Grid ontology can be constructed so that it can be used with the MOBY-Services project. The collaborative community would then be aiding knowledge capture rather than ontology building *per se*. This is perhaps closest to the Gene Ontology process. It still, however, suffers from the problem that the cost of curating the ontology must be borne centrally rather than distributed through the community.

Finally, Semantic-MOBY has sought to embrace a *distributed, autonomous* style of ontology building, reflecting the nature of bioinformatics. It seems likely that, over time, the community will build ontologies describing some or all of the domain. The independent development of the ^{my}Grid ontology seems to prove that this assumption is accurate. The Semantic-MOBY infrastructure has been designed to cope with a free market of ontology development. However, ontologies provide interoperability only so far as they are shared by members of the community. If multiple ontologies are allowed or encouraged yet mechanisms for interoperability are not embedded, there is a risk that independent "city states" will develop.

The use of a highly compositional style of ontology development, backed by a well-defined semantics and inference is critical to avoiding this development. It is hoped that core concepts can be created with community agreement and that these concepts can be extended by smaller specialist groups. This approach is also supported by the existence of the other projects. Any ontology developed by either or both projects that is reflective of community opinion will be likely to find favour within Semantic-MOBY's free market.

Of all the aspects of the three architectures, ontology building is where the three differ the most. Perhaps this stems from the fundamental difficulty of the issue.

Given these differences, it is ironic, although heartening, that ontology building is also the activity where all three projects have shown the highest degree of collaboration, engaging in active efforts to align semantics, share the knowledge already represented explicitly, and gather additional knowledge implicit within the community.

10   Discussion

Semantic Web Services technologies offer the prospect of increased interoperability and of (semi)automated service discovery and invocation. The advent of high-throughput biological techniques has made the requirement for such a technology within bioinformatics immediate and pressing.

In this paper we have described three architectures that are applying these technologies. We have also described some of the large practical problems that have presented themselves.

Clearly all three projects are aimed at supporting bioinformatics. We feel, however, that some of the experiences may be relevant to other domains. We suggest:-

- The inappropriateness of automated service invocation and composition is likely to be found in other scientific or highly technical domains.
- The difficulties in providing a domain ontology are likely to be shared by any domain with complex data types; structuring of data is likely to be difficult where significant legacy systems exist. We suspect that our solutions may be practical for use only within a restricted domain.
- Semantic Service Discovery tailored toward the users' notions of services is likely to be a useful augmentation to all domains.

At the current time, we are unsure as to the applicability of simple service interfaces to other domains, although we suspect this may remain relatively unique to bioinformatics.

Despite these difficulties it seems likely that the development of Semantic Web Services technologies should ease the difficulty of service discovery and composition within bioinformatics. Conversely, we believe that bioinformatics offers good opportunities for testing these technologies in a practical setting.

Acknowledgements. PL and DH are supported by the UK e-Science programme EPSRC grant GR/R67743 as part of the ^{my}Grid project. SB was supported by the WonderWeb project (EU grant IST-2001-33052). DG, GS and LS thank Andrew Farmer, Ardavan Kanani, Fiona Cunningham and Shuly Avraham for their contributions to Semantic-MOBY. Semantic-MOBY is funded by a National Science Foundation grant 0213512 to L.S. and D.G. The MOBY-Services project wishes to thank Dr. William Crosby, Mr. Matthew Links, Mr. Luke McCarthy, and the National Research Council Canada for their advice, intellectual, and financial contributions. The work on MOBY-Services was supported by a grant from Genome Canada/Genome Prairie to MDW.

References

1. Michael Bada, Robert Stevens, Carole Goble, Yolanda Gil, Michael Ashburner, Judith A. Blake4, J. Michael Cherry, Midori Harris, and Suzanna Lewis. A Short Study on the Success of the Gene Ontology. Accepted for publication in the Journal of Web Semantics, 2004.
2. Marina Chicurel. Bioinformatics: bringing it all together. *Nature*, 419:751–757, 2002.
3. Roy T. Fielding. *Architectural styles and the design of network-based software architectures*. PhD thesis, University of California, Irvine, 2000.
4. C.A. Goble, R. Stevens, G. Ng, S. Bechhofer, N.W. Paton, P.G. Baker, M. Peim, and A. Brass. Transparent Access to Multiple Bioinformatics Information Sources. *IBM Systems Journal Special issue on deep computing for the life sciences*, 40(2):532 – 552, 2001.
5. Andreas Heß and Nicholas Kushmerick. Learning to attach semantic metadata to web services. In *Proceedings of 2nd International Semantic Web Conference (ISWC2003)*, Sanibel Island, Florida, October 2003.
6. P. Karp. A Strategy for Database Interoperation. *Journal of Computational Biology*, 2(4):573–586, 1995.

7. Phillip Lord, Chris Wroe, Robert Stevens, Carole Goble, Simon Miles, Luc Moreau, Keith Decker, Terry Payne, and Juri Papay. Semantic and Personalised Service Discovery. In W. K. Cheung and Y. Ye, editors, *WI/IAT 2003 Workshop on Knowledge Grid and Grid Intelligence*, pages 100–107, Halifax, Canada, October 2003.

8. Daniel J. Mandell and Sheila A. McIlraith. Adapting BPEL4WS for the Semantic Web: The Bottom-Up Approach to Web Service Interoperation. In *Proceedings of 2nd International Semantic Web Conference (ISWC2003)*, Sanibel Island, Florida, October 2003.

9. R. A. Miller. Medical diagnostic decision support systems–past, present, and future: a threaded bibliography and brief commentary. *J Am Med Inform Assoc*, 1(1):8–27, Jan-Feb 1994.

10. T. Oinn, M. Addis, J. Ferris, D. Marvin, M. Greenwood, T. Carver, A. Wipat, and P. Li. Taverna: A tool for the composition and enactment of bioinformatics workflows. *Bioinformatics*, 2004. Accepted for publication.

11. Massimo Paolucci, Anupriya Ankolekar, Naveen Srinivasan, and Katia Sycara. The DAML-S Virtual Machine. In *Internaional Semantic Web Conference*, pages 290 – 305, 2003.

12. Stevens R, K. Glover, C. Greenhalgh, C. Jennings, S. Pearce, P. Li, M. Radenkovic, and A. Wipat. Performing *in silico* Experiments on the Grid: A Users' Perspective. In *Proc UK e-Science programme All Hands Conference*, 2003.

13. Martin Senger, Peter Rice, and Tom Oinn. Soaplab – a unified sesame door to analysis tools. In *Proc UK e-Science programme All Hands Conference*, 2003.

14. Lincoln Stein. Creating a bioinformatics nation. *Nature*, 417:119 – 120, 2002.

15. R. Stevens, H.J. Tipney, C. Wroe andT. Oinn, M. Senger, C.A. Goble P. Lord, A. Brass, and M. Tassabehji. Exploring Williams-Beuren Syndrome using ^{my}Grid. In *Proceedings of 12th International Conference on Intelligent Systems in Molecular Biology*, 2004. Accepted for Publication.

16. R.D. Stevens, C.A. Goble, P. Baker, and A. Brass. A Classification of Tasks in Bioinformatics. *Bioinformatics*, 17(2):180–188, 2001.

17. Robert D. Stevens, Alan J. Robinson, and Carole A. Goble. ^{my}Grid: personalised bioinformatics on the information grid. *Bioinformatics*, 19(90001):302i–304, 2003.

18. Katia Sycara, Massimo Paolucci, Anupriya Ankolekar, and Naveen Srinivasan. Automated discovery, interaction and composition of semantic web services. *Journal of Web Semantics*, 1(1):27–46, September 2003.

19. Werner Vogels. Web services are not distributed objects. *IEEE Internet Computing*, 7(6):59–66, 2003.

20. M. D. Wilkinson, D. Gessler, A. Farmer, and L. Stein. The BioMOBY Project Explores Open-Source, Simple, Extensible Protocols for Enabling Biological Database Interoperability. *Proc Virt Conf Genom and Bioinf*, 3:16–26, 2003.

21. M. D. Wilkinson and M. Links. BioMOBY: an open-source biological web services proposal. *Briefings In Bioinformatics*, 3(4):331–341, 2002.

22. C. Wroe, C. Goble, M. Greenwood, P. Lord, S. Miles, J. Papay, T. Payne, and L. Moreau. Automating experiments using semantic data on a bioinformatics grid. *IEEE Intelligent Systems*, 19(1):48–55, 2004.

23. Dan Wu, Bijan Parsia, Evren Sirin, James Hendler, and Dana Nau. Automating DAML-S web services composition using SHOP2. In *Proceedings of 2nd International Semantic Web Conference (ISWC2003)*, Sanibel Island, Florida, October 2003.

Automating Scientific Experiments on the Semantic Grid

Shalil Majithia, David W. Walker, and W. Alex Gray

Cardiff School of Computer Science, Cardiff University,
Queens Building, Newport Road, Cardiff, UK
{shalil.majithia, david.w.walker, w.a.gray}@cs.cardiff.ac.uk

Abstract. We present a framework to facilitate automated synthesis of scientific experiment workflows in Semantic Grids based on high-level goal specification. Our framework has two main features which distinguish it from other work in this area. First, we propose a dynamic and adaptive mechanism for automating the construction of experiment workflows. Second, we distinguish between different levels of abstraction of loosely coupled experiment workflows to facilitate reuse and sharing of experiments. We illustrate our framework using a real world application scenario in the physics domain involving the detection of gravitational waves from astrophysical sources.

1 Introduction

Grid computing is emerging as a key enabling infrastructure for "flexible, secure, coordinated resource sharing among dynamic collections of individuals, institutions, and resources" [38,39]. Scientific communities, including biology and physics, are embracing Grid technologies to manage and process large datasets, execute and share scientific experiments and simulations. Additionally, applications to process data intensive scientific experiments are no longer developed as monolithic code; instead autonomous services are combined together as required into a workflow to process the data [3,4]. In this context, service-oriented Grids can provide significant new capabilities to scientists by facilitating the composition and execution of experiments from a large pool of available services. Current manual composition techniques [12,13,14,15] are of limited value in dynamic and complex service-rich environments like the Grid for several reasons. First, the potential number of suitable services in Grid environments can be extremely large. It would be unrealistic to expect a user to be able to locate a suitable service. Second, the user is expected to ensure that the data being passed to services are semantically and syntactically correct. Finally, it is possible there may be no single service which can provide the functionality required. To resolve these problems and facilitate automated composition, mechanisms are needed to specify and manipulate rich descriptions of available resources. One promising approach is the Semantic Grid [40,41,42]. The Semantic Grid concept represents the use of Semantic Web technologies in Grid computing and promises the seamless interoperability of autonomous, heterogeneous, distributed applications across the

S.A. McIlraith et al. (Eds.): ISWC 2004, LNCS 3298, pp. 365–379, 2004.
© Springer-Verlag Berlin Heidelberg 2004

Grid by enabling the automation of many tasks for example discovery, selection, composition, and execution of workflows. Current automated composition techniques [4,6,17,31,7,8,9,10,11,18,33,34,35,36,37] typically make assumptions that render them of limited value in complex dynamic environments, for example they do not address issues like autonomy, adaptation, reuse, and sharing of workflows. This implies a need for an autonomic approach to workflow composition. In such an approach, the service composition process should be able to dynamically configure services in a way that can satisfy a service request. Autonomic models are suited for Grid environments where services are constantly added, modified or removed. By facilitating autonomic service composition, scientists can:

- Easily and efficiently discover a service that is more suitable to their needs.
- Focus on the conceptual basis of their experiments rather than understand the low level details of locating services.
- Easily create and share high quality complex workflows with varying levels of abstraction.

In this paper, we present a novel framework for the autonomic composition of experiment workflows in Semantic Grids. The framework presented in this paper has a number of important features. First, we distinguish between different levels of abstraction of loosely coupled workflow representations. Second, the framework uses a dynamic fault tolerant composition algorithm which adapts to the available resources. Third, the framework allows the user to specify and refine a high level objective. As a consequence, we propose that our framework:

- has a higher probability of successfully generating executable workflows compared to existing automated composition algorithms.
- allows users to share workflows with different levels of granularity.
- allows users to specify and refine high level objectives.
- is domain independent.

The remainder of this paper is structured as follows. First we review related research in the area of workflow composition in service-oriented architectures (Section 2). Second, we present an overview of the framework (Section 3). Third, we examine the main components of the framework (Sections 4 - 7). Fourth, we present an example application and evaluate our framework (Section 8). Finally, we conclude by discussing future directions.

2   Background

Workflow composition in Grids and more generally, in Service-Oriented Architectures has been the focus of much research recently, although the composition problem has been actively investigated in the database and agent communities [23-26]. Workflow composition is an active field of research and we review the major frameworks that are most closely related to our research. Workflow composition can be broadly classified into three categories: manual, semi-automated and automated composition. Manual composition frameworks [12, 13, 15, 27] expect the user to generate workflow scripts either graphically or through a text editor, which are then submitted to a workflow execution engine. Triana [12, 13] is used in astrophysics community and provides a graphical user interface, allowing the user to select the service required from a toolbox and "drag-and-drop" onto a canvas. The services are retrieved from UDDI using a simple keyword search. Additionally, Triana allows the composition of services with locally available tools. The composed graph can then be distributed over a P2P or Grid network for execution. BPWS4J [15] provides an Eclipse plug-in to allow the user to compose a graph at the XML level. This composed graph, along with a WSDL document for the composite service, is submitted to the execution engine. Self-Serve [27] allows the user to build the workflow by locating the services required by using the service builder. The service builder interacts with UDDI to retrieve service meta-data. The composed graph, an annotated state chart, is then executed using a P2P based execution model. An interesting feature of this system is the use of a service container that aggregates services offering the same functionality. At run time, the service container selects the actual service based on membership modes and a scoring service. These systems have several drawbacks. First, the discovery and selection of services is un-scalable as the number of services increases. Second, they require the user to have low-level knowledge, e.g. in the case of BPWS4J, the user is expected to set up a workflow at the XML level. Although Triana provides a graphical drag and drop interface, this is not feasible for a large workflow. Third, if the service is no longer available, the execution will fail, although in the case of Self-Serve, the service container would probably substitute another functionally-equivalent service. Also, recent research [19] has 'extended' BPWS4J to allow runtime selection and substitution of services.

Semi-automated composition techniques [4, 6, 17, 31] are a step forward in the sense that they make 'semantic suggestions' for service selection during the composition process; the user still needs to select the service required from a shortlist of the appropriate services and link them up in the order desired. The myGrid project [43] is one of the first Semantic Grid projects and aims to provide a problem-solving workbench for biologists. Specifically, myGrid allows scientists to compose, store and execute workflows. The scientist browses a registry and selects a workflow template. This template is then submitted to an enactment engine which then either asks the user to select actual instances of the workflow components or automatically selects services based on user's personal preferences. The myGrid project is also investigating other related issues like provenance. Sirin et. al. [17] propose a system that provides service choices which are semantically compatible at each stage. The generated workflow is then executed. Cardoso and Sheth [4] propose a framework which provides assistance to the user by recommending a service meeting the user's needs. This is done by matching the user-specified Service Template (ST) with the Service Object (SO). Chen et. al. [6] outline a knowledge-based framework which provides advice as the user constructs a workflow. The system allows the user to store workflows, hence facilitating reuse. Although these systems solve some of the problems of manual composition frameworks, they are still un-scalable as the user is expected to browse a registry to select the appropriate template or service. The filtering process may provide numerous matching services for the user to select from. For example in the myGrid project, the user is expected to select the actual instance of the service desired, although an automated workflow harmonization mechanism is envisaged. Additionally, there are few, if any, fault-handling mechanisms built into these systems. For example in Cardoso and Sheth, if a ST fails to match an SO, composition will fail. Similarly in Sirin et. al., Chen et. al., and myGrid project the composed workflow is sent to the enactment engine for execution. At this stage, if a service becomes unavailable, workflow execution will fail. Finally, except for Chen et al., there is no support for generating workflows of differing levels of granularity.

Automated composition techniques [7-11, 18, 33-37] automate the entire composition process by using AI planning or similar technology. McIlraith and Son [10] address the automated composition problem by proposing an agent-based Web services composition framework which uses generic procedures and semantically marked up services to guide composition. The Agent Broker acts as a gateway to Web services and is responsible for selecting and invoking the services. The framework assumes the existence of a generic procedure. In the absence of one, composition cannot proceed. Additionally, if the Agent Broker cannot match a service, execution will fail. The SWORD toolkit [11] automates service composition by using rule-based service descriptions. The user specifies the initial and final state facts. Based on this, the planner attempts to put together a chain of services that can satisfy these requirements. The user is expected to be able to specify the state facts. More importantly, there is no automated service discovery mechanism built in. As a result, composition will fail if the service required cannot be found. Also, composition is based on specific implementations of services; this makes it difficult to share workflows as the service may no longer be available. An important component of automated composition is the discovery of the services required. Research in this area has focused on the use of DAML-S to describe service capabilities. A matchmaker engine then compares the DAML-S description of the service requested with those of the services advertised [20, 21]. This work is extended by Sycara et. al. [16] to propose a preliminary discovery and execution framework based on AI planning technology, the DAML-S Matchmaker and the DAML-S Virtual Machine. The framework assumes a composition plan is available and hence concentrates on identification of suitable services and execution of the plan. Additionally, the framework does not incorporate the use of a workflow repository. Hence, a workflow has to be recomputed each time a request is received. Also, the framework does not distinguish between executable and non-executable workflows; all workflows are based on implemented services available. As a result, the workflows are not reusable or cannot be shared as there is no guarantee that any component service will be available in the future. Sheshagiri et. al. [8] propose a framework with two key features: use of DAML-S to describe service capabilities and a planner to generate simple workflow graphs using a backward chaining algorithm. A very similar framework is proposed by Wu et al., [7] that uses SHOP2, an HTN planning system, to generate workflows. The Pegasus project [9, 33-37] used to generate workflows in high energy physics applications proposes two workflow generation systems. The Concrete Workflow Generator (CWG) maps an abstract workflow onto an executable workflow. The second system (ACWG) uses AI planning technology to generate workflows in Grid environments. An interesting feature of this work is the distinction between abstract and concrete workflows. These frameworks suffer from the same drawbacks: there is no fault handling mechanism - if a service implementation is not available, execution will fail. Additionally, the frameworks proposed do not include a workflow repository which would make it possible to reuse previously constructed workflows. Further, there is no distinction between abstract and concrete workflows. This makes it difficult to share workflows. Although the Pegasus system does make this distinction, it does not provide mechanisms to expose the abstract and the concrete workflows as services. Finally, Koehler and Srivastava [29] point out several problems with current AI planning technology when applied to the service composition problem. Laukkanen and Helin [28] put forward a model which includes simple fault handling mechanisms. The model assumes that a workflow already exists in a repository and the user selects the workflow required. This workflow is then validated to ensure that all the participating services are available. If a service is not available, a matchmaker is used to retrieve similar services. Interestingly, if a single alternative cannot be found, the composer agent attempts to put together a simple chain of service which can provide the functionality. The workflow is then rewritten to include these new services and their network locations and sent to the execution engine. The drawbacks of this model are as follows: First, the model assumes a workflow is available. There is no mechanism for the user to create one. This is a severe drawback as it completely side-steps the issue of composition. Second, workflows are stored with the network locations of the services encoded within the workflow. This means that when a workflow is reused and all the participating services are available, there is no option for the user to select alternative implementations of the service based on changed optimization criteria. The IRS-II [18] framework provides an infrastructure which can be used to publish, compose and execute Semantic Web services. The system distinguishes between a task (generic description of the task to be solved) and a Problem Solving Method (an abstract, implementation-independent description of how to accomplish a task). A task may correspond to several PSMs. The user selects a task to be performed. A broker locates an appropriate PSM (which can satisfy the task) and then invokes the corresponding services. Although the system proposes an interesting distinction between a task and a PSM, this increase in the number of artifacts required merely enhances the probability that workflow composition will fail. First, a service developer has to manually associate a PSM to a service. This becomes un-scalable as the number of PSMs and services increase. Second, composition and/or execution will fail if a task, PSM or a service is not available. There appear to be no fault-handling mechanisms to tackle such a scenario.

In this section, we reviewed briefly several service composition frameworks, some of which are used to generate experiment workflows on the Grid. We identified gaps in existing systems; lack of an autonomic composition algorithm, and non-distinction between different abstract levels of workflows.

3   Framework Overview

In this section, we outline the general requirements for the framework and present the proposed architecture. In order to successfully generate scientific workflows, an automated workflow composition framework must adhere to certain basic requirements.

- High degree of fault-tolerance: The framework must be able to handle common fault scenarios. There is no guarantee in a Grid environment that a particular service will be available at some particular time. In this case, there should be intelligent mechanisms to discover and invoke another service, or compose services which provide the same functionality. Similarly, in case a rulebase is not available for a particular objective, there must be mechanisms to chain services to achieve the objective. We define fault tolerance to mean the non-availability of the service and exclude other possible faults, for e.g. a service returns an invalid response, at this time.
- Workflow granularity: The framework should support mechanisms to allow users to generate workflows of varying levels of granularity. For example, abstract and concrete workflows. Abstract workflows specify the workflow without referring to any specific service implementation. Hence all services are referred to by their logical names. A concrete workflow specifies the actual names and network locations of the services participating in the workflow. An abstract workflow allows users to share workflows without reference to any specific service implementation. This is particularly useful as there is no guarantee of the availability of any service in Grids. On the other hand, a concrete workflow could be useful for provenance purposes. Additionally, workflows of differing levels of granularity should be loosely coupled, i.e. with minimum interdependence.
- Specify and refine high-level objectives: The framework should support mechanisms to allow users to specify and dynamically refine a high-level objective which is then translated into a workflow. It should be possible to carry out "what-if" analysis in an efficient manner with only the changed sub-graphs being recomposed.
- User-specified optimization criteria: The framework should provide a mechanism which allows users to specify the workflow composition/execution optimization criteria. For example, the user may want to minimize the total runtime of the workflow or minimize the use of expensive resources.
- Scalable: The framework should be scalable to a large number of services.
- Domain independent: The framework should be as generic as possible in order to allow its use within any domain.

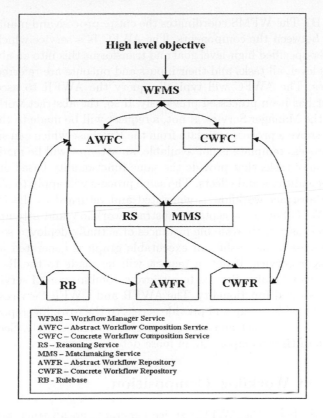

High level objective

WFMS

AWFC   CWFC

RS   MMS

RB   AWFR   CWFR

WFMS – Workflow Manager Service
AWFC – Abstract Workflow Composition Service
CWFC – Concrete Workflow Composition Service
RS – Reasoning Service
MMS – Matchmaking Service
AWFR – Abstract Workflow Repository
CWFR – Concrete Workflow Repository
RB - Rulebase

Fig. 1. The Framework Architecture.

- Other important requirements include security and ability to record and reason over provenance.

Our proposed framework provides the following:

- Support for dynamic fault-tolerant, adaptive workflow composition mechanism
- Support for generating, storing, and reusing workflows with differing levels of granularity.
- Support for specification and refinement of high-level user objectives.

The framework architecture is shown in Figure 1. Everything is a service. Services are described and invoked based on their descriptions. The key bootstrap operation is the location of the Workflow Manager Service (WFMS). The WFMS puts together the framework required based on available services and user-specified preferences. The framework consists of two core and five supporting services: Abstract Workflow Composer (AWFC), Concrete Workflow Composer (CWFC), Reasoning Service (RS), Matchmaker Service (MMS), Abstract Workflow Repository (AWFR), Concrete Workflow Repository (CWFR) and the

Rulebase (RB). The WFMS coordinates the entire process and manages the flow
of messages between the components. The AWFC is a service which accepts an
incoming user-specified high-level goal and transforms this into an abstract workflow. At this level, all tasks and their inputs and outputs are referred to by their
logical names. The AWFC will typically query the AWFR to ascertain if the
same request has been processed previously. If so, the abstract workflow will be
returned to the Manager Service. If not, a request will be made to the Reasoning
Service to retrieve a process template from the Rulebase which can satisfy the request. If a process template is not available, an attempt will be made to retrieve
a combination of tasks that provide the same functionality based on the inputs,
outputs, preconditions and effects. The same process will apply to all constituent
services. An abstract workflow is generated and returned to the Manager Service. The CWFC Service accepts an abstract workflow and attempts to match
the individual tasks with available instances of actually deployed services. If the
matching process is successful, an executable graph is generated and returned
to the Manager Service. If not, a request will be made to the Reasoning Service and the Matchmaker Service to retrieve a combination of services that can
provide the required functionality. The AWFR and CWFR Services are domain
specific services which wrap and provide access to the workflow repositories. The
repositories store abstract and concrete workflows respectively. Sections 4 to 7
describe each of these components in more detail.

4   Abstract Workflow Composition

As introduced above, the AWFC Service generates an abstract workflow from
a high-level objective. The AWFC uses a dynamic adaptable algorithm (Fig. 2)
which tries to build an abstract workflow by using at least three different sources
of information.

- AWF Repository. The AWF Repository stores semantically annotated descriptions of services and workflows. The AWFC queries the AWFR Service
  to ascertain if the same workflow has been processed previously. This is done
  by semantically matching the workflow name by referring to an ontology. If
  a match is found, the AWF is returned.
- Rulebase. If no match is found, the AWFC queries a rule base to retrieve
  a rule which can provide the template to achieve this goal. Given this rule,
  the AWFC again queries the AWFR, but this time an attempt is made to
  semantically match the inputs and outputs required to those of the abstract
  workflows in the repository. If an AWF is matched, this is returned. If the
  matching does not succeed, the AWFC analyzes and splits the rule into
  component rules. This is done recursively until an atomic rule is reached.
  The AWFC will then query the AWFR to ascertain if any AWFs match the
  rule.
- Chaining Services. The AWFC uses the Reasoning Service (see Section 6) to
  create a chain of services that when put together can fulfil the user objective.

```
AWFC(name){
    retrieveFromAWFR(name);
    if (!found) {
        retrieve rule from rulebase;
        retrieveFromAWFR(input,output);
        if (!found) {
            split rule into smallest rule;
            for (each rule) {
                get rule output;
                get rule input;
                retrieveFromAWFR(input,output);
                if (!found) {
                    chain services(input,output);
                }
                concatenate;
            }
        }
    }
    return AWF
}
```

Fig. 2. AWFC algorithm

5   Concrete Workflow Composition

The CWFC uses a dynamic adaptable algorithm to match each services in the abstract workflow with an instance of an executable service available on the network at that time. It does this in two different ways:

- Matchmaking: Each abstract service is passed to the Matchmaker Service (see Section 7) which then attempts to retrieve a semantically matching service available on the network. Depending on the degree of the match, the CWFC Service may accept the service. The degree of match may vary from exact to plug-in.
- Chaining Services: The CWFC uses the Reasoning Service (see Section 6) to chain together services which can provide the same functionality. It is possible that a service implementation may not be available. In this case, the AWFC is invoked through the WFMS, and asked to provide alternative AWFs for that particular sub-graph. This provides a high degree of fault tolerance.

Matching is done in two stages. First, a semantic match is made. If this is successful, the number and the types of the input and output messages are compared: if they are the same, the match is successful, else an attempt is made to chain services starting from the output desired.

6   Reasoning Service

The Reasoning Service provides support to the two core composer services. Specifically, this service provides a back-tracking algorithm to produce a chain of services which can provide the output required using the given input. More specifically, the following steps are performed:

- For each service available, find a service that matches the output of the service requested. Let one such service be Sn.
- Ascertain the input of Sn. Find a service that can generate the input for Sn. Let this service be Sn-1.
- This process is iterated until the input of the service Sn-x matches the input of the service requested.
- Formulate the workflow which specifies the order of execution of the components S1 to Sn.

An interesting feature of our chaining algorithm is that it uses the Matchmaking Service to match the inputs and outputs of the services. As a result, it is not essential that matching be exact; plug-in matches are acceptable. This makes our chaining algorithm more robust and with a higher rate of success than similar other algorithms.

7   Matchmaking Service

The Matchmaking Service (MMS) provides an intelligent matchmaking mechanism. Its core functionality is to match two services based on the inputs, outputs, pre-conditions and effects (IOPEs). The Matchmaking Service is used by the Reasoning Service to match inputs and outputs of the service that it is chaining. Additionally, the MMS is used by the CWFC Service to match abstract services to concrete services. Our algorithm is based on that proposed by Paolucci et. al. [20]. However, only exact and plug-in matches, as defined by Paolucci et al., are calculated as there is no guarantee that a subsumes match would be able to provide the required functionality. As a consequence, we would expect the algorithm to be more suitable and efficient for use in automated composition frameworks.

8   Implementation and Evaluation

In this section, we first describe the implementation of our framework. We then illustrate our approach by using a scenario from the physics domain and provide some preliminary results of performance evaluation experiments.

All the main components are implemented as Web services using the Axis server to expose them. We use existing Semantic Web tools, like RDF, OWLS, and reasoning mechanisms to provide the basic representation and reasoning

```
<profileHierarchy:SignalProcessing rdf:ID="FFT">
  <profile:input>
    <profile:ParameterDescription rdf:ID="FFTInput">
      <profile:restrictedTo rdf:resource="Concepts.owl#VectorType"/>
    </profile:ParameterDescription>
  </profile:input>
  <profile:output>
    <profile:ParameterDescription rdf:ID="FFTOutput">
      <profile:restrictedTo rdf:resource="Concepts.owl#ComplexSpectrum"/>
    </profile:ParameterDescription>
  </profile:output>
</profileHierarchy:SignalProcessing>
```

Fig. 3. Snippet of OWL-S Profile for FFT

technology. Services are described using OWL-S. The Reasoning and Match-making Services use DQL/JTP server to carry our subsumption reasoning. The repositories are currently implemented as flat files containing the OWL-S profiles and process models (see figure 3). The WFMS forms the core of the framework. It locates and coordinates all the other components required to form the framework. The AWFC Service generates an abstract workflow as a DAML-S Process Model. This abstract workflow is passed to the CWFC Service, which then matches all the services taking part in the workflow with available implementations. Finally, a BPEL4WS document containing the network locations and protocol details of all the tasks is generated and this can now be submitted to any BPEL4WS engine for execution. To illustrate the main features of our framework, we present the following scenario.

Compact binary stars orbiting each other in a close orbit are among the most powerful sources of gravitational waves. As the orbital radius decreases, a characteristic chirp waveform is produced whose amplitude and frequency increase with time until eventually the two bodies merge together. Laser interferometric detectors such as GEO600, LIGO, VIRGO should be able to detect the waves from the last few minutes before collision. Interferometric gravitational wave detectors are inherently broadband, sensitive to radiation coming from almost all directions in the sky, and output data at rates in excess of several megabytes per second. Consequently, searching for gravitational wave signals buried in the detector output and identifying the sources is a challenging task. To analyze this data, thousands of templates, representing the theoretical knowledge of relativistic binary systems, are correlated with the signal using fast correlation by a technique known as matched filtering. This implementation uses approximately 50 separate services connected together to form a workflow. The AWFC generates a DAML-S Process model referring to the services by their logical names, for example FFT, Conjugate, Scaler, OneSide, and Wave. These are then matched to actual implementations available on the network.

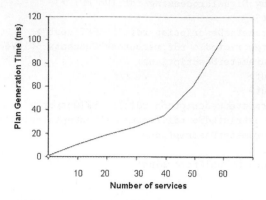

Fig. 4. Plan Generation Times.

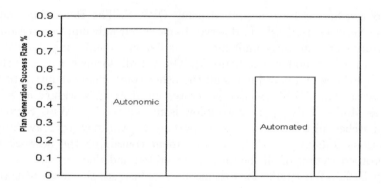

Fig. 5. Plan Generation Success Rates.

The purpose of our experiments is two-fold: to assess plan generation times and success rates. We present here preliminary results. We ran our experiments on a Windows machine with a 1.4GHz Intel processor and 512Kb RAM. We first evaluate the time for generating concrete workflows (see Figure 4). There is an exponential relationship between the number of services in a plan and the time required to match and compose an executable graph. We also looked at the workflow generation success rates(see Figure 5). We compared our framework with a simple automated back-tracking composition algorithm. We used the same process ontologies and composition requests for both of these techniques. Based on 50 requests, the results show that our framework had a success rate of 80% while the back-tracking algorithm had a success rate of about 60%. This confirms our expectation that our autonomic framework has a higher probability of successfully generating workflows. Further experiments are currently being done to ascertain the range over which this results apply.

9   Conclusion

In this paper, we propose a framework to facilitate automated composition of scientific experiment workflows in Semantic Grids made up of a Manager Service and other supporting services, including an abstract and a concrete workflow generator. We have described these components in detail and outlined their interactions. We have also described our implementation and its use within the physics domain. The important features of our approach are: an autonomic workflow generation algorithm and distinction between different levels of abstraction of the workflow in order to allow reuse and sharing. These features ensure that our framework has a higher possibility of successfully generating workflows compared to other similar algorithms. Future work involves the use our model in other application domains. We also plan to integrate user-specified optimization criteria to guide the generation of workflow. Finally, we intend to investigate the use of user specified policies to guide decisions which need to made when composing services.

References

1. Casati, F., Shan, M., and Georgakopoulos, D. 2001. E-Services - Guest editorial. The VLDB Journal. 10(1):1.
2. Tsalgatidou, A and Pilioura, T. 2002. An Overview of Standards and Related Technology in Web services. Distributed and Parallel Databases. 12(3).
3. Fensel, D., Bussler, C., Ding, Y., and Omelayenko, B. 2002. The Web Service Modeling Framework WSMF. Electronic Commerce Research and Applications.1(2).
4. Cardoso, J. and Sheth, A. 2002. Semantic e-Workflow Composition. Technical Report, LSDIS Lab, Computer Science, University of Georgia.
5. Paolucci, M., Sycara, K., and Takahiro Kawamura. 2003. Delivering Semantic Web Services. In Proc. Of the Twelfth World Wide Web Conference.
6. Chen, L, Shadbolt, N.R, Goble, C, Tao, F., Cox, S.J., Puleston, C., and Smart, P. 2003. Towards a Knowledge-based Approach to Semantic Service Composition. 2nd International Semantic Web Conference
7. Wu, D., Sirin, E., Hendler, J., Nau, D., and Parsia, B. 2003. Automatic Web Services Composition Using SHOP2. Twelfth World Wide Web Conference.
8. Sheshagiri, M., desJardins, M., and Finin, T. 2003. A Planner for Composing Service Described in DAML-S. Workshop on Planning for Web Services, International Conference on Automated Planning and Scheduling.
9. Deelman, E., J. Blythe, Y. Gil, C. Kesselman, G. Mehta, K. Vahi, K. Blackburn, A. Lazzarini, A. Arbree, Cavanaugh, R. and Koranda, S. Mapping Abstract Complex Workflows onto Grid Environments. Journal of Grid Computing. Vol. 1, 2003
10. McIlraith, S. and Son, T.C. 2002. Adapting golog for composition of semantic web services. In Proc. of the 8th International Conference on Knowledge Representation and Reasoning (KR '02), Toulouse, France.
11. Ponnekanti, S. R., and Fox, A. 2002. SWORD: A Developer Toolkit for Web Service Composition. In Proc. Of the Eleventh International World Wide Web Conference, Honolulu.
12. Taylor, I., Shields, M., Wang, I., and Philp, R: Grid Enabling Applications Using Triana, Workshop on Grid Applications and Programming Tools, June 25, 2003, Seattle. In conjunction with GGF8

13. Taylor, I., Shields, M., Wang, I., and Philp, R: Distributed P2P Computing within Triana: A Galaxy Visualization Test Case. To be published in the IPDPS 2003 Conference, April 2003
14. Mayer, A., McGough, S., Furmento, N., Lee, W., Newhouse,S., and Darlington, J: ICENI Dataflow and Workflow: Composition and Scheduling in Space and Time In UK e-Science All Hands Meeting, p. 627-634, Nottingham, UK, Sep. 2003
15. IBM Alphaworks, BPWS4J, http://www.alphaworks.ibm.com/tech/bpws4j [12.01.2004]
16. Sycara, K., Paolucci, M., Ankolekar, A., and Srinivasan, N.: Automated Discovery, Interaction and Composition of Semantic Web Services, Journal of Web Semantics, Volume 1, Issue 1, December 2003
17. Sirin, E., Hendler, J., and Parsia, B: Semi-automatic composition of web services using semantic descriptions. In Web Services: Modeling, Architecture and Infrastructure Workshop in conjunction with ICEIS 2003
18. Motta, E., Domingue, J., Cabral, L. and Gaspari, M: IRS-II: A Framework and Infrastructure for Semantic Web Services. 2nd International Semantic Web Conference (ISWC2003) 20-23 October 2003, Sundial Resort, Sanibel Island, Florida, USA
19. Mandell, D.J., and McIlraith, S.A: A Bottom-Up Approach to Automating Web Service Discovery, Customization, and Semantic Translation. In The Proceedings of the Twelfth International World Wide Web Conference Workshop on E-Services and the Semantic Web (ESSW '03). Budapest, 2003.
20. Paolucci, M., Kawamura, T., Payne, T., Sycara, K: Semantic Matching of Web Services Capabilities. Proceedings of the 1st International Semantic Web Conference (ISWC), pp. 333-347, 2002.
21. Lei Li and Ian Horrocks. A software framework for matchmaking based on semantic web technology. In Proc. of the Twelfth International World Wide Web Conference (WWW 2003), pages 331-339. ACM, 2003.
22. Berners-Lee, T., Hendler, J., Lassila, O. The Semantic Web, Scientific American, May, 2001.
23. Parent, C. and Spaccapietra, S: Issues and Approaches of Database Integration. Communications of the ACM 41(5): 166-178.
24. Kashyap, V. and A. Sheth: Semantic Heterogeneity in Global Information Systems: The Role of Metadata, Context and Ontologies, Academic Press.
25. Preece, A.D., K.Y. Hui, Gray, W.A., Marti, P., Bench-Capon, T.J.M., Jones, D.M., and Cui, Z: The KRAFT Architecture for Knowledge Fusion and Transformation. 19th SGES International Conference on Knowledge-based Systesm and Applied Artificial Intelligence (ES'99) , Springer, Berlin
26. Bayardo, R.J., W. Bohrer, R. Brice, A. Cichocki, J. Fowler, A. Helal, V. Kashyap, T. Ksiezyk, G. Martin, M. Nodine, M. Rashid, M. Rusinkiewicz, R. Shea, C. Unnikrishnan, A. Unruh and D. Woelk: InfoSleuth: Agent-Based Semantic Integration of Information in Open and Dynamic Environments. Proceedings of the ACM SIGMOD International Conference on Management of Data, ACM Press, New York. pp. 195-206.
27. Benatallah, B., Sheng, Q.Z., and Dumas, M.: The Self-Serv Environment for Web Services Composition, Jan/Feb, 2003, IEEE Internet Computing. Vol 7 No 1. pp 40-48.
28. Laukkanen, M., and Helin, H: Composing Workflows of Semantic Web Services.In AAMAS Workshop on Web Services and Agent-Based Engineering, 2003.

29. Koehler, J., and Srivastava, B: Web Service Composition: Current Solutions and Open Problems. ICAPS 2003 Workshop on Planning for Web Services, pages 28 - 35.
30. Medjahed, B., Bouguettaya, A., and Elmagarmid A: Composing Web Services on the Semantic Web. The VLDB Journal, Special Issue on the Semantic Web, Volume 12, Number 4, November 2003.
31. Stevens, R.D., Robinson, A.J., and Goble, C.A: myGrid: Personalised Bioinformatics on the Information Grid. Bioinformatics Vol. 19 Suppl. 1 2003, (Eleventh International Conference on Intelligent Systems for Molecular Biology)
32. Business Integration, http://www.bijonline.com/default.asp [12.01.2004]
33. Blythe, J., Deelman, E., Gil, Y., and Kesselman C: Transparent Grid Computing: a Knowledge-Based Approach. 15th Innovative Applications of Artificial Intelligence Conference (IAAI 2003), 2003.
34. Blythe, J., Deelman, E., Gil, Y., Kesselman, C., Agarwal, A., Mehta, G., and Vahi, K: The Role of Planning in Grid Computing, 13th International Conference on Automated Planning and Scheduling, 2003.
35. Blythe, J., Deelman, E., and Gil, Y: Planning for workflow construction and maintenance on the Grid. ICAPS 2003 Workshop on Planning for Web Services.
36. Deelman, E., Blythe, J., Gil, Y., and Kesselman, C: Pegasus: Planning for Execution in Grids., GriPhyN technical report 2002-20, 2002
37. Deelman, E., Blythe, J., Gil, Y., Kesselman C., Mehta, G., Vahi, K., Koranda, S., Lazzarini, A., Papa, M A: From Metadata to Execution on the Grid Pegasus and the Pulsar Search. , GriPhyN technical report 2003-15
38. Foster, I. and Kesselman, C. eds., The Grid: Blueprint for a New Computing Infrastructure, Morgan Kaufmann, San Francisco, 1999.
39. Foster, I. et al., "The Physiology of the Grid: An Open Grid Services Architecture for Distributed Systems Integration," tech. report, Globus Project;
40. De Roure, D., Jenning, N.R., and Shadbolt, N., Research Agenda for the Semantic Grid: A Future e-Science Infrastructure. http://www.semanticgrid.org
41. The Grid: An Application of the Semantic Web by Carole Goble and David De Roure, 2002, www.semanticgrid.org
42. Semantic Web and Grid Computing by Carole Goble and David De Roure, 2002, www.semanticgrid.org
43. Stevens,R., Robinson, A., and Goble, C.A., myGrid: Personalised Bioinformatics on the Information Grid in proceedings of 11th International Conference on Intelligent Systems in Molecular Biology, 29th June–3rd July 2003, Brisbane, Australia, published Bioinformatics Vol. 19 Suppl. 1 2003, i302-i304

Automated Composition of Semantic Web Services into Executable Processes

Paolo Traverso[1] and Marco Pistore[2]

[1] ITC-IRST, Trento, Italy
traverso@itc.it
[2] University of Trento, Italy
pistore@dit.unitn.it

Abstract. Different planning techniques have been applied to the problem of automated composition of web services. However, in realistic cases, this planning problem is far from trivial: the planner needs to deal with the nondeterministic behavior of web services, the partial observability of their internal status, and with complex goals expressing temporal conditions and preference requirements. We propose a planning technique for the automated composition of web services described in OWL-S process models, which can deal effectively with nondeterminism, partial observability, and complex goals. The technique allows for the synthesis of plans that encode compositions of web services with the usual programming constructs, like conditionals and iterations. The generated plans can thus be translated into executable processes, e.g., BPEL4WS programs. We implement our solution in a planner and do some preliminary experimental evaluations that show the potentialities of our approach, and the gain in performance of automating the composition at the semantic level w.r.t. the automated composition at the level of executable processes.

1 Introduction

One of the big challenges for the taking up of web services is the provision of automated support to the composition of service oriented distributed processes, in order to decrease efforts, time, and costs in their development, integration, and maintenance. Currently, the problem of the composition of web services is addressed by two orthogonal efforts. From the one side, most of the major industry players propose low level process modeling and execution languages, like BPEL4WS [1]. These languages allow programmers to implement complex web services as distributed processes and to compose them in a general way, e.g., by interleaving the partial execution of different services with programming control constructs, like if-then-else, while-loops, fork, choice, etc. However, the definition of new processes that interact with existing ones must be done manually by programmers, and this is a hard, time consuming, and error prone task. From the other side, research within the Semantic Web community proposes a top down unambiguous description of web services capabilities in standard languages like DAML-S [2] and OWL-S [10], thus enabling the possibility to reason about web services, and to automate tasks like discovery and composition. However, the real taking up of Semantic Web Services for practical applications needs the ability of generating automatically

S.A. McIlraith et al. (Eds.): ISWC 2004, LNCS 3298, pp. 380–394, 2004.
© Springer-Verlag Berlin Heidelberg 2004

composed services that can be directly executed, in the style of BPEL4WS programs, thus reducing effort, time and errors due to manual composition at the programming level.

Several works have proposed different automated planning techniques to address the problem of automated composition (see [17,18,21,23]). However, the planning problem is far from trivial, and can be hardly addressed by "classical planning" techniques. In realistic cases, OWL-S process models describe nondeterministic processes, whose behaviors cannot be predicted prior to of execution (e.g., a flight reservation service cannot know in advance whether a reservation will be confirmed or canceled). Moreover, the internal status of a service (e.g., whether there are still seats available in a flight) is not available to external services, and the planner can only observe services invocations and responses. Finally, composition goals need to express complex requirements that are not limited to reachability conditions (like get to a state where both the flight and the hotel are reserved). Most often, goals need to express temporal conditions (e.g., do not reserve the hotel until you have reserved the flight), and preferences among different goals (try to reserve both the flight and the hotel, but if not possible, make sure you do not reserve any of the two). As a consequence, automated composition needs to interleave (the partial executions of) available services with the typical programming language constructs such as conditionals, loops, etc., similarly to composed services that are programmed by hand, e.g., in BPEL4WS.

In this paper, we propose a technique for the automated composition of web services described in OWL-S, which allows for the automated generation of executable processes written in BPEL4WS. Given a set of available services, we translate their OWL-S process models, i.e., declarative descriptions of web service processes, into nondeterministic and partially observable state transition systems that describe the dynamic interactions with external services. Goals for the service to be automatically generated are represented in the EAGLE language [11], a language with a clear semantics which can express complex requirements. We can thus exploit the "Planning as Model Checking" approach based on symbolic model checking techniques [13,9,6,11,5], which provides a practical solution to the problem of planning with nondeterministic actions, partial observability, and complex goals, and which has been shown experimentally to scale up to large state spaces. As a result, the planning algorithm generates plans that are automata and that can be translated to BPEL4WS code.

We implement the proposed techniques in MBP [4], a planner based on the planning as model checking approach, and perform an experimental evaluation. Though the results are still preliminary, and deserve further investigation and evaluation, they provide a witness of the potentialities of our approach. Moreover, we compare the experimental results with those obtained by applying the same technique to (state transition systems generated from) BPEL4WS processes. The comparison shows that automated composition performed at the high level of OWL-S process models is orders of magnitudes more efficient than the one applied at the low level of executable processes, thus demonstrating experimentally a practical advantage of the Semantic Web approach to web services.

The paper is structured as follows. In Section 2, we give an overview of the approach and introduce an explanatory example that will be used all along the paper. In Section 3, we explain how OWL-S process models can be translated into state transition systems,

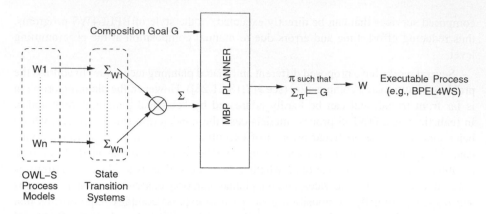

Fig. 1. OWL-S based Automated Composition.

while in Section 4 we describe the goal language. We explain how we do planning for web service composition in Section 5. We provide a preliminary experimental evaluation in Section 6, and a comparison with related work in Section 7.

2   Overview of the Approach

By automated composition we mean the task of generating automatically, given a set of available web services, a new web service that achieves a given goal by interacting with (some of) the available services. More specifically, we take as our starting point the OWL-S Process Model ontology [10], i.e., a declarative description of the program that realizes the service. Given the OWL-S process model description of n available services $(W_1, \dots, W_n)$, we encode each of them in a state transition system $(\Sigma_{W_1}, \dots, \Sigma_{W_n})$, see Fig. 1. State transition systems provide a sort of operational semantics to OWL-S process models. Each of them describes the corresponding web service as a state-based dynamic system, that can evolve, i.e., change state, and that can be partially controlled and observed by external agents. This way, it describes a protocol that defines how external agents can interact with the service.

From the point of view of the new composed service that has to be generated, say W, the state transition systems $\Sigma_{W_1}, \dots, \Sigma_{W_n}$ constitute the environment in which W has to operate, by receiving and sending service requests. They constitute what, in planning literature, is called a planning domain, i.e., the domain where the planner has to plan for a goal. In our case, the planning domain is a state transition system Σ that combines $\Sigma_{W_1}, \dots, \Sigma_{W_n}$. Formally, this combination is a parallel composition, which allows the n services to evolve independently. Σ represents therefore all the possible behaviors, evolutions of the planning domain, without any control performed by the service that will be generated, i.e., W.

The Composition Goal G (see Fig. 1) imposes some requirements on the desired behavior of the planning domain. Given Σ and G, the planner generates a plan π that controls the planning domain, i.e., interacts with the external services $W_1, \dots, W_n$ in

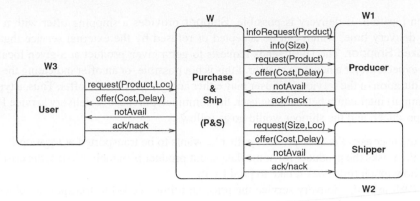

Fig. 2. A Simple Example.

a specific way such that the evolutions satisfy the goal G. The plan π encodes the new service W that has to be generated, which dynamically receives and sends invocations from/to the external services $W_1, \ldots, W_n$, observes their behaviors, and behaves depending on responses received from the external services. The plan π must therefore have the ability of encoding normal programming constructs, like tests over observations, conditionals, loops, etc. As we will see, π is encoded as an automaton that, depending on the observations and on its internal state, executes different actions. We can translate π into process executable languages, like BPEL4WS.

In the rest of the paper, we will describe step by step the automated composition task introduced above through the following example.

Example 1. Our reference example consists in providing a purchase & delivery service, say the **P&S** service, which satisfies some user request. We do so by combining two separate, independent, and existing services: a producer **Producer**, and a delivery service **Shipper**. The idea is that of combining these two services so that the user may directly ask the composed service **P&S** to purchase and deliver a given product at a given place. To do so, we exploit a description of the expected interaction between the **P&S** service and the other actors. In the case of the **Producer** and of the **Shipper** the interactions are defined in terms of the service requests that are accepted by the two actors. In the case of the **User**, we describe the interactions in terms of the requests that the user can send to the **P&S**. As a consequence, the **P&S** service should interact with three available services: **Producer**, **Shipper**, and **User** (see Fig. 2). These are the three available services W_1, W_2, and W_3, which are described as OWL-S process models and translated to state transition systems. The problem is to automatically generate the (plan corresponding to the) **P&S** service, i.e., W in Fig. 1.

In the following, we describe informally the three available services. **Producer** accepts requests for information on a given product and, if the product is available, it provides this information (e.g., the size). The **Producer** also accepts requests for buying a given product, in which case it returns an offer with a cost and production time. This offer can be accepted or refused by the external service that has invoked the **Producer**. The **Shipper** service receives requests for transporting a product of a given size to a given location. If delivery is possible, Shipper provides a shipping offer with a cost and delivery time, which can be accepted or refused by the external service that has invoked Shipper. The User sends requests to get a given product at a given location, and expects either a negative answer if this is not possible, or an offer indicating the cost and duration of the service. The user may either accept or refuse the offer. Thus, a typical (nominal) interaction between the user, the combined purchase & delivery service P&S, the producer, and the shipper would go as follows:

1. the user asks P&S for product p, that he wants to be transported at location l;
2. P&S asks the producer for some data about product p, namely its size, the cost, and how much time does it take to produce it;
3. P&S asks the delivery service the price and time needed to transport an object of such a size to l;
4. P&S provides the user an offer which takes into account the overall cost (plus an added cost for P&S) and time to achieve its goal;
5. the user sends a confirmation of the order, which is dispatched by P&S to the delivery and producer.

Of course this is only the nominal case, and other interactions should be considered, e.g., for the cases the producer and/or delivery services are not able to satisfy the request, or the user refuses the final offer. At a high level, Fig. 2 describes the data flow amongst our integrated web service, the two services composing it, and the user. This can be perceived as (an abstraction of) the WSDL description of the dataflow.   □

3   From OWL-S Process Models to State Transition Systems

OWL-S process models [10] are declarative descriptions of the properties of web service programs. Process models distinguish between *atomic processes*, i.e., non-decomposable processes that are executed by a single call and return a response, and *composite processes*, i.e., processes that are composed of other atomic or composite processes through the use of control constructs such as sequence, if-then-else, while loops, choice, fork, etc.

Example 2. The OWL-S process model of the Shipper service (see Example 1) is shown in Fig. 3 (left). The OWL-S model has been slightly simplified for readability purposes, by removing some (redundant) tags in the description of the processes. The Shipper service is a composite service consisting of the atomic processes DoShippingRequest, AcceptShippingOffer, and RefuseShippingOffer. DoShippingRequest receives in input a description of the Size and of the destination Location of the product to be delivered. The conditional output models the fact that the service returns as output an offer only if the shipping is possible, and returns a NotAvailable message otherwise. The offer includes the price (Cost) and the duration (Delay) of the transportation. If the transportation is possible (control construct IfThenElse), the shipper waits for a nondeterministic external decision (control construct Choice) that either accepts (AcceptShippingOffer) or refuses (RefuseShippingOffer) the offer.

Similarly, we can model the interactions with the producer with a composition of atomic processes AskProductInfo, DoProductRequest, AcceptProductOffer, and

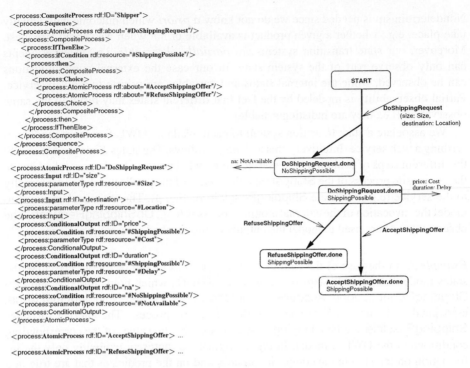

```
<process:CompositeProcess rdf:ID="Shipper">
 <process:Sequence>
  <process:AtomicProcess rdf:about="#DoShippingRequest"/>
  <process:CompositeProcess>
   <process:IfThenElse>
    <process:ifCondition rdf:resource="#ShippingPossible"/>
    <process:then>
     <process:CompositeProcess>
      <process:Choice>
       <process:AtomicProcess rdf:about="#AcceptShippingOffer"/>
       <process:AtomicProcess rdf:about="#RefuseShippingOffer"/>
      </process:Choice>
     </process:CompositeProcess>
    </process:then>
   </process:IfThenElse>
  </process:CompositeProcess>
 </process:Sequence>
</process:CompositeProcess>

<process:AtomicProcess rdf:ID="DoShippingRequest">
 <process:Input rdf:ID="size">
  <process:parameterType rdf:resource="#Size">
 </process:Input>
 <process:Input rdf:ID="destination">
  <process:parameterType rdf:resource="#Location">
 </process:Input>
 <process:ConditionalOutput rdf:ID="price">
  <process:coCondition rdf:resource="#ShippingPossible"/>
  <process:parameterType rdf:resource="#Cost">
 </process:ConditionalOutput>
 <process:ConditionalOutput rdf:ID="duration">
  <process:coCondition rdf:resource="#ShippingPossible"/>
  <process:parameterType rdf:resource="#Delay">
 </process:ConditionalOutput>
 <process:ConditionalOutput rdf:ID="na">
  <process:coCondition rdf:resource="#NoShippingPossible"/>
  <process:parameterType rdf:resource="#NotAvailable">
 </process:ConditionalOutput>
</process:AtomicProcess>

<process:AtomicProcess rdf:ID="AcceptShippingOffer> ...

<process:AtomicProcess rdf:ID="RefuseShippingOffer> ...
```

Fig. 3. The OWL-S Process Model and the State Transition System of the Shipper Service.

RefuseProductOffer; and the interaction with the user with the processes DoP&SRequest and EvaluateOffer (with the latter process the user specifies whether an P&S offer is accepted or not).   □

We encode OWL-S process models as state transition systems. These describe dynamic systems that can be in one of their possible *states* (some of which are marked as *initial states*) and can evolve to new states as a result of performing some *actions*. A *transition function* describes how (the execution of) an action leads from one state to possibly many different states. System's evolutions can be monitored through *observations* describing the visible part of the system state. An *observation function* defines the observation associated to each state of the domain.

Definition 1 (state transition system). *A* (nondeterministic, partially observable) state transition system *is a tuple* $\Sigma = \langle S, A, O, I, T, X \rangle$, *where:*

- *S is the set of* states, *A is the set of* actions, *and O is the set of* observations.
- $I \subseteq S$ *is the set of* initial states.
- $T : S \times A \to 2^S$ *is the* transition function; *it associates to each current state* $s \in S$ *and to each action* $a \in A$ *the set* $T(s, a) \subseteq S$ *of next states.*
- $X : S \to O$ *is the* observation function.

State transition systems are *nondeterministic*, i.e., an action may result in several different outcomes. This is modeled by the fact that the transition function returns sets of states.

Nondeterminism is needed since we do not know *a priori* which outcome will actually take place, e.g., whether a given product is available or not when we submit a request. Moreover, our state transition systems are *partially observable*, i.e., external agents can only observe part of the system state. In our case the external communications can be observed, while the internal status and variables are private to a given service. Partial observability is modeled by the fact that different states may result in the same observation (i.e., they are indistinguishable).

We associate a state transition system to each available OWL-S process model describing a web service. Intuitively, this is done as follows. The states S are used to codify the different steps of evolution of the service (e.g., what position has been reached inside the composite process of the Shipper) and the values of the predicates defined internally to the service (e.g., predicate ShippingPossible of Fig. 3). The actions A are used to model the invocation of the external atomic processes (e.g., DoShippingRequest). The observations O are used to model the outputs of the invoked external processes.

Example 3. In the case of the Shipper service process model (see Fig. 3 (right)), the states model the possible steps of the service: START, which holds initially, and DoShippingRequest.done, AcceptShippingOffer.done, RefuseShippingOffer.done, associated to the intermediate phases of the composite process. The internal variables ShippingPossible and NoShippingPossible describe the values of the corresponding conditions in the OWL-S model. In Fig. 3 (right), we represent explicitly only the information on the step in the composite process and on the predicates that are true in a given state. For simplicity, we do not represent the values for the the input and output parameters of the service invocation. Therefore, a single rounded box in Fig. 3 (right) corresponds to several states of the actual state transition structure.

The actions correspond to the invocation of the atomic processes DoShippingRequest, AcceptShippingOffer, and RefuseShippingOffer. The most complicated action is the first one: it has two parameters specifying the size and the destination location. Moreover, it has two possible non-deterministic outcomes. The first one, corresponding to the case the shipper is able to do the delivery, leads to the state where condition ShippingPossible is true. The second outcome, corresponding to the case the shipper is not able to do the delivery, leads to the state where condition NoShippingPossible is true.

The observations associated to each state define an assignment to the OWL-S conditional outputs. For instance, in the state corresponding to DoShippingRequest.done and ShippingPossible, values are defined for the output parameters price and duration.

□

The formal definition of the translation of an OWL-S process model into a state transition system is conceptually simple, but it is complicated by several technical details. For this reason, and for lack of space, we do not present this definition here. The interested reader may refer to [19] for a detailed discussion of a translation similar to ours. In that case, Petri nets are used as target models. The states of our state transition systems can be seen as the markings in the Petri nets of [19].

4   Composition Goals

Composition goals express requirements for the service to be automatically generated. They represent conditions on the evolution of services, and as shown by the next example, they express requirements of different strengths and at different levels of preference.

Example 4. In our example (see Fig. 2), a reasonable composition goal for the P&S service is the following:

Goal 1: The service should try to reach the ideal situation where the user has confirmed his order, and the service has confirmed the associated (sub-)orders to the producer and shipper services. In this situation, the data associated to the orders have to be mutually consistent, e.g., the time for building and delivering a product shall be the sum of the time for building it and that for delivering it.

However, this is an ideal situation that cannot be enforced by the P&S service: the product may not be available, the shipping may not be possible, the user may not accept the total cost or the total time needed for production and delivery ... We would like the P&S service to behave properly also in these cases, otherwise it is likely to loose money. More precisely, it has to reach a consistent situation, where the P&S confirms none of the two services for production and delivering:

Goal 2: The P&S service should absolutely reach a fall-back situation where every (sub-)order has been canceled. That is, there should be no chance that the service has committed to some (sub-)order if the user can cancel his order.

Some remarks are in order. First of all, there is a difference in the "strength" in which we require Goal 1 and Goal 2 to be satisfied. We know that it may be impossible to satisfy Goal 1: we would like the P&S service to *try* (do whatever is possible) to satisfy the goal, but we do not require that the service guarantees to achieve it in all situations. The case is different for Goal 2: there is always a possibility for the P&S service to cancel the orders to the producer and shipper, and to inform the user. We can require a guarantee of satisfaction of this goal, in spite of any behavior of the other services. Moreover, Goal 1 and Goal 2 are not at the same level of desire. Of course we would not like a P&S service that satisfies always Goal 2 (e.g., by refusing all requests from the user) even when it would be possible to satisfy Goal 1. We need then to express a strong preference for Goal 1 w.r.t. Goal 2. Informally, we can therefore describe the composition goal as follows:

Composition Goal: *Try* to satisfy Goal 1, *upon failure, do* satisfy Goal 2.   □

As the previous example shows, composition goals need the ability to express conditions on the whole behavior of a service, conditions of different strengths, and preferences among different subgoals. The EAGLE language [11] has been designed with the purpose to satisfy such expressiveness requirements. Let propositional formulas $p \in \mathcal{P}rop$ define conditions on the states of a state transition system. *Composition goals* $g \in \mathcal{G}$ over $\mathcal{P}rop$ are defined as follows:

$$g := p \mid g \textbf{ And } g \mid g \textbf{ Then } g \mid g \textbf{ Fail } g \mid \textbf{Repeat } g \mid$$
$$\textbf{DoReach } p \mid \textbf{TryReach } p \mid \textbf{DoMaint } p \mid \textbf{TryMaint } p$$

Goal **DoReach** p specifies that condition p has to be eventually reached in a strong way, for all possible non-deterministic evolutions of the state transition system. Similarly, goal **DoMaint** q specifies that property q should be maintained true despite non-determinism. Goals **TryReach** p and **TryMaint** q are weaker versions of these goals, where the plan is required to do "everything that is possible" to achieve condition p or maintain condition q, but failure is accepted if unavoidable. Construct g_1 **Fail** g_2 is used to model preferences among goals and recovery from failure. More precisely, goal g_1 is considered first. Only if the achievement or maintenance of this goal fails, then goal g_2 is used as a recovery or second-choice goal. Consider for instance goal **TryReach** c **Fail DoReach** d. The sub-goal **TryReach** c requires to find a plan that tries to reach condition c. During the execution of the plan, a state may be reached from which it is not possible to reach c. When such a state is reached, goal **TryReach** c fails and the recovery goal **DoReach** d is considered. Goal g_1 **Then** g_2 requires to achieve goal g_1 first, and then to move to goal g_2. Goal **Repeat** g specifies that sub-goal g should be achieved cyclically, until it fails. Finally, goal g_1 **And** g_2 requires the achievement of both subgoals g_1 and g_2. A formal semantics and a planning algorithm for EAGLE goals in fully observable nondeterministic domains can be found in [11].

Example 5. The EAGLE formalization of the goal in Example 4 is the following.

> **TryReach** /* Goal 1 */
> (AcceptProductOffer.done & AcceptShippingOffer.done &
> EvaluateOffer.done & EvaluateOffer.accepted &
> DoP&SRequest.price = DoShippingRequest.price + DoProductRequest.price &
> DoP&SRequest.duration = DoShippingRequest.duration + DoProductRequest.duration)
> **Fail**
> **DoReach** /* Goal 2 */
> (RefuseProductOffer.done & RefuseShippingOffer.done &
> EvaluateOffer.done & ¬ EvaluateOffer.accepted)

Propositions like AcceptProductOffer.done are used to describe the states of the planning domain Σ corresponding to specific states of state transition systems obtained from the OWL-S processes (process Producer in our case). Propositions like DoShippingRequest.price or EvaluateOffer.accepted refer to the values of the input/output messages in service invocation.   □

5   Automated Composition

The planner has two inputs (see Fig. 1): the composition goal and the planning domain Σ which represents all the ways in which the existing services can evolve. Formally, this combination is defined as the parallel composition $\Sigma = \Sigma_{W_1} \times \ldots \times \Sigma_{W_n}$ of the state transition systems of the existing services. The automated composition task consists in finding a plan that satisfies the composition goal G over a domain Σ. We are interested in complex plans, that may encode sequential, conditional and iterative behaviors, and are thus expressive enough for representing the flow of interactions of the synthesized composed service with the other services as well as the required observations over the other services. We therefore model a plan as an automaton.

Definition 2 (plan). *A plan for planning domain* $\Sigma = \langle S, A, \mathcal{O}, \mathcal{I}, \mathcal{T}, \mathcal{X} \rangle$ *is a tuple* $\pi = \langle C, c_0, \alpha, \epsilon \rangle$, *where:*

- C *is the set of* plan contexts.
- $c_0 \in C$ *is the* initial context.
- $\alpha : C \times \mathcal{O} \rightharpoonup A$ *is the* action function; *it associates to a plan context c and an observation o an action* $a = \alpha(c, o)$ *to be executed.*
- $\epsilon : C \times \mathcal{O} \rightharpoonup C$ *is the* context evolutions function; *it associates to a plan context c and an observation o a new plan context* $c' = \epsilon(c, o)$.

The contexts are the internal states of the plan; they permit to take into account, e.g., the knowledge gathered during the previous execution steps. Actions to be executed, defined by function α, depend on the observation and on the context. Once an action is executed, function ϵ updates the plan context. Functions α and ϵ are deterministic (we do not consider nondeterministic plans), and can be partial, since a plan may be undefined on the context-observation pairs that are never reached during plan execution.

The execution of a plan over a domain can be described in terms of transitions between configurations, where each configuration (s, c) describes the current state s of the domain and the current context c of the plan (see [7] for a formal definition). Due to the nondeterminism in the domain, we may have an infinite number of different executions of a plan. However, they can be presented in a compact way as an *execution structure*, i.e, a state transition system defined by the configurations of the plan and by the transition among these configurations. In the following, we denote by Σ_π the execution structure that represents the evolutions of the domain Σ controlled by the plan π. In a planning problem, the execution structure Σ_π that must satisfy the composition goal G (see Fig. 1). If $\Sigma_\pi \models G$, we say that π *is a valid plan for G on* Σ. A formal definition of $\Sigma_\pi \models G$ can be found in [11].

However, notice that when executing a plan, the plan executor cannot in general get to know exactly what is the current state of the domain: the limited available access to the internal state of each external service inhibits removing the uncertainty present at the initial execution step, or introduced by executing nondeterministic actions. For instance, in the case of the Shipper service describe in Fig. 3, the executor has no access to the values of predicates ShippingPossible and NoShippingPossible, even if it can infer these values from the observable outcomes of action DoShippingRequest (namely, an offer or a NoAvailable message).

In presence of partial observability, at each plan execution step, the plan executor has to consider a set of domain states, each equally plausible given the initial knowledge and the observed behavior of the domain so far. Such a set of states is called a *belief state* (or simply *belief*) [8,6]. Executing an action a evolves a belief B into another belief B' which contains all of the possible states that can be reached through a from some state of B. The available sensing is exploited initially, and after each action execution: if observation o holds after executing action a, the resulting belief shall rule out states not compatible with o. Thus in general, given a belief B, performing an action a (executable in all the states of B) and taking into account the obtained observation o gets to a new belief $Evolve(B, a, o)$:

$$Evolve(B, a, o) = \{s' : \exists s \in B.s' \in \mathcal{T}(s, a) \wedge \mathcal{X}(s') = o\}.$$

Planning in this framework consists in searching through the possible evolutions of initial beliefs, to retrieve a conditional course of actions that leads to beliefs that satisfy the goal. The search space for a partially observable domain is what is called a *belief space*; its nodes are beliefs, connected by edges that describe the above *Evolve* function. The search in a partially observable domain can be described as search inside a fully observable "belief-level" domain Σ_K whose states are the beliefs of Σ, and whose nondeterministic transition function mimics *Evolve*.

Algorithms for planning under partial observability can be obtained by suitably recasting the algorithms for full observability on the associated knowledge-level domain. Actually, the following result holds [7]:

Fact 3. *Let Σ be a ground-level domain and g be a knowledge-level goal for Σ (i.e., a goal expressing conditions on the beliefs reached during plan execution). Let also Σ_K be the knowledge level domain for Σ. Then π is a valid plan for g on Σ if, and only if, π is a valid plan for g on Σ_K.*

Thus, given a composition goal and a planning domain, solving the problem implies using dedicated algorithms for planning under partial observability with EAGLE goals, or, alternatively, planning for the fully observable associated knowledge level domain. We pursue this latter approach, so that we can reuse existing EAGLE planning algorithms under full observability [11]. We generate the knowledge level domain by combining the state transition systems defined previously. Similarly to what happens for the ground level domains, this computation consists of a parallel composition. Finally, we plan on this domain with respect to an EAGLE goal. Fact 3 guarantees that the approach outlined above for planning under partial observability with EAGLE goals is correct and complete. A potential problem of this approach is that, in most of the cases, knowledge-level domains are exponentially larger than ground domains. In [6], efficient heuristic techniques are defined to avoid generating the whole (knowledge-level) planning domain. These techniques can be extended to planning with EAGLE goals.

We have therefore the algorithms for generating a valid plan π that satisfies the composition goal. Since π is an automaton, it can be easily translated to executable process languages, like BPEL4WS. The generated code is not human-readable, however, it reflects the contexts defined in the plan (see Definition 2), which in turn reflect the structure of the goal. This makes it possible to monitor the execution of the BPEL4WS code and detect, for instance, when the primary goal of a composition (e.g., Goal 1 in Example 4) fails and a subsidiary goal (e.g., Goal 2) becomes active.

6   Experimental Evaluation

In order to test the effectiveness and the performance of the approach proposed in this paper, we have conducted some experiments using the MBP planner.

We have run MBP on six variants of the purchase and ship case study, of different degrees of complexity. In the easiest case, CASE 1, we considered a reduced domain with only the user and the shipper, and with only one possible value for each type of objects in the domain (product, location, delay, cost, size). In CASE 2 we have considered all three protocols, but again only one possible value for each type of object. In CASE 3 we

		With refuse		Without refuse	
	Building K	Planning	Result	Planning	Result
CASE 1	0.2 sec.	0.1 sec.	YES	0.1 sec.	NO
CASE 2	0.3 sec.	0.3 sec.	YES	0.3 sec.	NO
CASE 3	1.5 sec.	5.1 sec.	YES	3.4 sec.	NO
CASE 4	3.8 sec.	19.5 sec.	YES	17.9 sec.	NO
CASE 5	4.1 sec.	65.9 sec.	YES	71.5 sec.	NO
CASE 6	12.3 sec.	2899 sec.	YES	3885 sec.	NO

Fig. 4. Results of the Experiments.

have considered the three protocols, with two objects for each type, but removing the parts of the shipper and producer protocols concerning the size of the product. CASE 4 is the complete example discussed in Section 2. In CASE 5, one more web service is added to the domain, which provides support for the installation the product, once it has been delivered. CASE 6, finally, extends CASE 5 by allowing three values for each type of object. We remark that CASE 1 and CASE 2 are used to test our algorithms, even if they are admittedly unrealistic, since the process knows, already before the interaction starts, the product that the user will ask and the cost that will be charged to the user. In the other cases, a real composition of services is necessary to satisfy the goal. In all six cases we have experimented also with a variant of the shipper service, which does not allow for refusing an offer. This variant makes the composition goal unsatisfiable, since we cannot unroll the contract with the shipper and satisfy the recovery goal (see Example 5) in case of failure of the primary goal.

The experiments have been executed on an Intel Pentium 4, 1.8 GHz, 512 MB memory, running Linux 2.4.18. The results, in Fig. 4, report the following information:

- Building K: the time necessary to build the three knowledge-level domains.
- Planning: the time required to find a plan (or to check that no plan exists) starting from the knowledge-level domains.
- Result: whether a plan is found or not.

The last two results are reported both in the original domains and in the domains without the possibility of refusing a shipping offer. The experiments show that the planning algorithm returns the expected results. The performance is satisfactory: also in CASE 5, where the composition involves four external services, the composition is built in about one minute. The time required to obtain the composition grows considerably if we increase the number of available values for each object (CASE 6). Indeed, the different values are encoded into the domain states and have a strong impact on the size of the search space. A different, more advanced management of data types and variables, not requiring a direct encoding into the states, would mitigate this effect.

We perform a further set of experiments where we apply the same approach to the composition of web services at the level of BPEL4WS code. We translate the BPEL4WS code implementing the three existing services into state transition systems. The translation is technically different from (but conceptually similar to) the one described for OWL-S models, and is described in [20]. We perform this translation for the same cases

	Building K	With refuse		Without refuse	
		Planning	Result	Planning	Result
CASE 1	2 sec.	6 sec.	YES	5 sec.	NO
CASE 2	5 sec.	30 sec.	YES	13 sec.	NO
CASE 3	289 sec.	2008 sec.	YES	1642 sec.	NO
CASE 4	1058 sec.	16536 sec.	YES	13327 sec.	NO

Fig. 5. Results of the Experiments with BPEL4WS Domains.

considered in the previous experiment. Then we run the same MBP planning algorithm on the resulting planning domains. The results are reported in Fig. 5 (in CASE 5 and 6 we have stopped the planner after more than 5 hours of execution time). The comparison shows that automated composition performed at the level of OWL-S process models is much more efficient than composition applied at the level of executable processes. For instance, in CASE 4, both the time needed to generate the planning domain and the time for planning are three orders of magnitude higher for BPEL4WS domains. The reason is that OWL-S process models are at a higher level of abstraction w.r.t. BPEL4WS process models. Planning with BPEL4WS domains is done at the level of single messages between processes, while planning with OWL-S models is at the level of atomic web services. These results are a demonstration of the fact that OWL-S process models shift the representation at the right level of abstraction for composing web services, and show a practical advantage of the Semantic Web approach to web services composition.

7   Conclusions, Related and Future Work

In this paper, we have shown how OWL-S process models can be used to generate automatically new composed services that can be deployed and executed on engines for modern process modeling and execution languages, like BPEL4WS. This is achieved by translating OWL-S process models to nondeterministic and partially observable state transition systems and by generating automatically a plan that can express conditional and iterative behaviors of the composition. Our preliminary experimental evaluation shows the potentialities of the approach, and the practical advantage of automated composition at the semantic level w.r.t. the one at the level of executable processes.

Different planning techniques have been applied to the composition of web services, however, to the best of our knowledge, only the approach proposed in this paper is able to generate BPEL4WS processes that are directly executable. Existing approaches apply different planning approaches, ranging from HTNs [23] to regression planning based on extensions of PDDL [12], to STRIPS-like planning for composing services described in DAML-S [21], but how to deal with nondeterminism, partial observability, and how to generate conditional and iterative behaviors (in the style of BPEL4WS) in these frameworks is still an open issue. In [17], web service composition is achieved with user defined re-usable, customizable, high level procedures expressed in Golog. The approach is orthogonal to ours: Golog programs can express control constructs for the generic composition of web service, while we generate automatically plans that encode web service composition through control constructs. In [16], Golog programs are used to encode complex actions that can represent DAML-S process models. However, the planning problem is reduced to classical planning and sequential plans are generated for reachability goals. In [19], the authors propose an approach to the simulation, verification, and automated composition of web services based on a translation of DAML-S to situation calculus and Petri Nets, so that it is possible to reason about, analyze, prove properties of, and automatically compose web services. However, the automated composition is again limited to sequential composition of atomic services for reachability goals, and does not consider the general case of possible interleavings among processes and of extended business goals.

Other techniques have been applied to related but somehow orthogonal problems in the field of web services. The interactive composition of information gathering services has been tackled in [22] by using CSP techniques. In [14], given a specific query of the user, an interleaving of planning and execution is used to search for a solution and to re-plan when the plan turns out to violate some user constraints at run time. In [3] automated reasoning techniques, based on Description Logic, are used to generate a composite web service. In that paper, however, the composition is seen as the problem of coordinating the executions of a given set of available services, and not as the problem of generating a new web service interacting with them.

The work in [15] is close in spirit to our general objective to bridge the gap between the semantic web framework and the process modeling and execution languages proposed by industrial coalitions. However, [15] focuses on a different problem, i.e., that of extending BPEL4WS with semantic web technology to facilitate web service interoperation, while the problem of automated composition is not addressed.

In the future, we aim at a solution that avoids the computationally complex power-set construction of the knowledge level domain, by providing algorithms for natively planning with extended goals under partial observability. Some preliminary results in this directions for a different goal language are presented in [7]. Moreover, we plan to integrate the automated composition task with reasoning techniques for discovery and selection at the level of OWL-S service profiles. Finally, we intend to test our approach over realistic case studies in projects for private companies and for the public administration we are currently involved in.

Acknowledgements. Special thanks to Piergiorgio Bertoli, Loris Penserini and Mark Carman for the interesting discussions on automated composition of web services. This work has been partially funded by the FIRB-MIUR project RBNE0195K5, "Knowledge Level Automated Software Engineering".

References

1. T. Andrews, F. Curbera, H. Dolakia, J. Goland, J. Klein, F. Leymann, K. Liu, D. Roller, D. Smith, S. Thatte, I. Trickovic, and S. Weeravarana. Business Process Execution Language for Web Services Version 1.1, 2003.
2. A. Ankolekar. DAML-S: Web Service Description for the Semantic Web. In *Proc. 1st Int. Semantic Web Conference (ISWC'02)*, 2002.

3. D. Berardi, D. Calvanese, G. De Giacomo, M. Lenzerini, and M. Mecella. Automatic Composition of E-services That Export Their Behavior. In *Proc. 1st Int. Conf. on Service-Oriented Computing (ICSOC'03)*, 2003.

4. P. Bertoli, A. Cimatti, M. Pistore, M. Roveri, and P. Traverso. MBP: a Model Based Planner. In *Proc. IJCAI'01 Workshop on Planning under Uncertainty and Incomplete Information*, 2001.

5. P. Bertoli, A. Cimatti, M. Pistore, and P. Traverso. A Framework for Planning with Extended Goals under Partial Observability. In *Proc. 13th Int. Conf. on Automated Planning and Scheduling (ICAPS'03)*, 2003.

6. P. Bertoli, A. Cimatti, M. Roveri, and P. Traverso. Planning in Nondeterministic Domains under Partial Observability via Symbolic Model Checking. In *Proc. 17th Int. Joint Conference on Artificial Intelligence (IJCAI'01)*, 2001.

7. P. Bertoli and M. Pistore. Planning with Extended Goals and Partial Observability. In *Proc. 14th Int. Conf. on Automated Planning and Scheduling (ICAPS'04)*, 2004.

8. B. Bonet and H. Geffner. Planning with Incomplete Information as Heuristic Search in Belief Space. In *Proc. 5th Int. Conf. on Artificial Intelligence Planning and Scheduling (AIPS 2000)*, 2000.

9. A. Cimatti, M. Pistore, M. Roveri, and P. Traverso. Weak, Strong, and Strong Cyclic Planning via Symbolic Model Checking. *Artificial Intelligence*, 147(1-2):35–84, 2003.

10. The OWL Services Coalition. OWL-S: Semantic Markup for Web Services — Technical White paper (OWL-S version 1.0), 2003.

11. U. Dal Lago, M. Pistore, and P. Traverso. Planning with a Language for Extended Goals. In *Proc. 18tn National Conference on Artificial Intelligence (AAAI'02)*, 2002.

12. D. Mc Dermott. The Planning Domain Definition Language Manual. Technical Report 1165, Yale Computer Science University, 1998. CVC Report 98-003.

13. F. Giunchiglia and P. Traverso. Planning as Model Checking. In *Proc. 5th European Conf. on Planning (ECP'99)*, 1999.

14. A. Lazovik, M. Aiello, and Papazoglou M. Planning and Monitoring the Execution of Web Service Requests. In *Proc. 1st Int. Conf. on Service-Oriented Computing (ICSOC'03)*, 2003.

15. D. Mandell and S. McIlraith. Adapting BPEL4WS for the Semantic Web: The Bottom-Up Approach to Web Service Interoperation. In *Proc. 2nd Int. Semantic Web Conference (ISWC'03)*, 2003.

16. S. McIlraith and R. Fadel. Planning with Complex Actions. In *Proc. 9th Int. Workshop on Non-Monotonic Reasoning (NMR'02)*, 2002.

17. S. McIlraith and S. Son. Adapting Golog for composition of semantic web Services. In *Proc. 8th Int. Conf. on Principles of Knowledge Representation and Reasoning (KR'02)*, 2002.

18. S. McIlraith, S. Son, and H. Zeng. Semantic Web Services. *IEEE Intelligent Systems*, 16(2):46–53, 2001.

19. S. Narayanan and S. McIlraith. Simulation, Verification and Automated Composition of Web Services. In *Proc. 11th Int. World Wide Web Conference (WWW'02)*, 2002.

20. M. Pistore, P. Bertoli, F. Barbon, D. Shaparau, and P. Traverso. Planning and Monitoring Web Service Composition. In *Proc. 11th Int. Conf. on Artificial Intelligence: Methodology, Systems, Applications — Semantic Web Challenges (AIMSA'04)*, 2004.

21. M. Sheshagiri, M. desJardins, and T. Finin. A Planner for Composing Services Described in DAML-S. In *Proc. AAMAS'03 Workshop on Web Services and Agent-based Engineering*, 2003.

22. S. Thakkar, C. Knoblock, and J.L. Ambite. A View Integration Approach to Dynamic Composition of Web Services. In *Proc. ICAPS'03 Workshop on Planning for Web Services*, 2003.

23. D. Wu, B. Parsia, E. Sirin, J. Hendler, and D. Nau. Automating DAML-S Web Services Composition using SHOP2. In *Proc. 2nd Int. Semantic Web Conference (ISWC'03)*, 2003.

A Conceptual Architecture for Semantic Web Services

Chris Preist[1]

HP Labs, Filton Rd, Stoke Gifford, Bristol BS32 8QZ, UK
chris.preist@hp.com

Abstract. In this paper, we present an abstract conceptual architecture for semantic web services. We define requirements on the architecture by analyzing a set of case studies developed as part of the EU Semantic Web-enabled Web Services project. The architecture is developed as a refinement and extension of the W3C Web Services Architecture. We assess our architecture against the requirements, and provide an analysis of OWL-S.

1   Motivation

In this paper, we present an abstract conceptual architecture for semantic web services. The motivation behind this is (i) To provide a conceptual model to aid in the principled design and implementation of semantic web service applications; (ii) To allow the principled application of existing semantic web service ontologies such as OWL-S and WSMO; (iii) To contribute to the evolution of such languages, or the design of new ones, through the identification of appropriate features such a language needs; (iv) To motivate the development of appropriate infrastructure to support a variety of semantic web service applications. The main impetus behind this work has been provided by the European Union Semantic Web–enabled Web Services project (SWWS). This project aims to develop appropriate Semantic Web Services infrastructure to support four case-studies, inspired by the design principles proposed in the Web Services Modeling Framework [2]. Although these four case studies provide the primary source of requirements on our architecture, to encourage generality, we also consider a variety of other applications of SWS described in the literature.

We take the W3C Web Services Architecture (WSA) [14] as an important input. This provides a conceptual model for understanding web service technology and its relationship with other components. In particular, it adopts the view that the semantics of a service is provided by a contract (agreeing what the service does) between the service provider and service requestor. Such a contract can be explicit or implicit, and can be agreed in a variety of ways.

The potential role of contracts in supporting web service interactions is becoming increasingly recognised. The use of contracts in supporting interactions between agents in open systems has long been recognised by the agent community (e.g. [5]).

---

[1] The following people have contributed to this work through discussion and/or feedback: The HP Semantic Web Services team; the EU Semantic Web-enabled Web Services team, Dieter Fensel, Mark Burstein, Ian Dickinson, Terry Payne, Bijan Parsia and the ISWC reviewers.

S.A. McIlraith et al. (Eds.): ISWC 2004, LNCS 3298, pp. 395–409, 2004.
© Springer-Verlag Berlin Heidelberg 2004

Proposals have been made to use contracts in semantic web services [3]. The adoption of contracts as representing semantics in the WSA is further evidence of this trend.

Though the WSA adopts the contractual view, the implications of this are not explored as fully as is required if the semantics are to be made explicit. Specifically, it does not make a clear separation between the semantics of a service provider agent and the semantics of a particular performance of a service. Furthermore, it does not provide a model to show the activities involved in agreeing the 'semantics' of a particular service interaction (though it does informally discuss this process.) The conceptual architecture we present builds on the WSA to provide appropriate separation of concepts and additional constructs.

The WSA presents four different views on the architecture, focused around different core concepts; message, service, resource and policy. Our focus is primarily on the service-oriented view. In particular, we do not consider policy, security or reliability issues and how these are affected by the addition of explicit semantics. To do so requires additional analysis beyond the scope of this paper.

The paper is structured as follows. Firstly, we discuss the semantics of the word 'service', and consider the different ways it can be used. Next, we briefly describe the SWWS case studies, and refer to additional applications discussed in the literature. We then present a set of requirements on a semantic web services architecture, derived from analysis of this set of applications. Next, we briefly summarise the service oriented model of the WSA, and present our conceptual architecture as an extension of this. We assess the architecture against our requirements, present an analysis of OWL-S and conclude.

2   What Is a 'Service'?

The word 'service' can be used in several different ways. If a clear conceptual architecture is to be developed for semantic web services, we believe that it is necessary to make these different uses explicit.

1. 'Service' as Provision of Value in Some Domain

In the economy nowadays, a great variety of different services are traded; provision of stock quotes, shipment of crates, translation of documents, provision of a broadband connection etc. In each case, the customer receives something of value to them in return for a payment to the supplier. The service received can be described in terms of the domain of application. Such a description does not need to refer to the way in which the supplier and customer interact. This is what an economist or businessperson would refer to as a service.

On the internet, services can be provided which involve a payment, and so correspond closely to the above perspective. We can broaden this view of service without losing what is essential. A service can be provided without any payment, and the value the service provides need only be 'in the eyes of the requestor', not necessarily something with monetary value in the commercial world. For example, the provision of a specific piece of information from a database or the provision of a plan to achieve some goal. Hence, a service is *the provision of something of value, in the context of some domain of application, by one party to another.*

We also need to distinguish between a particular provision of value from the general capability to provide. We refer to the former as a *concrete service*, and the latter as an abstract service. Hence an *abstract service* is defined as *the capacity to perform something of value, in the context of some domain of application.*

2. 'Service' as a Software Entity Able to Provide Something of Value

This usage is common in the computer science and IT community. Papers often speak of sending messages to services, receiving results from services, executing services etc. While this is clearly appropriate in the context of web services and service oriented architectures, it can cause some confusion when mixing usage of this definition with the definitions above. For that reason, we believe that it is more accurate to speak of such an entity as being (part of) a service provider agent (SPA). We also use the term 'web service' to refer to a specific application with a WSDL/SOAP interface.

3. 'Service' as a Means of Interacting Online with a Service Provider

A common example of this usage is 'negotiation service'; A negotiation service provides the means to interact (negotiate) with a given actor. This usage is clearly different from usage 1, in that negotiation in itself does not provide something of value. However, the outcome of the negotiation may do so (and hence may be a service in the first sense.) For this reason, we refer to this as the provision of a negotiation 'protocol' or 'choreography'.[2]

All three of these aspects of service provision are essential; the 'value' in some domain, the interactions involved, and the implementation of the entity able to deliver what is needed. However, we believe that for conceptual reasons it is best to make clear distinctions between them.

3   Example Scenarios

In the interests of space, we present very brief overviews of five of the example scenarios used. Fuller descriptions are available in an extended version of this paper. Of these, scenarios 2, 3 and 5 are from case studies in the SWWS project.

Example A: Currency Conversion Quotation[3]

A simple service provider, providing a currency quotation for the conversion of a given amount of one currency into another currency, at a given time.

Example B: Design of a SPA to Proactively Manage Virtual ISP Problems

A system designer develops a complex service provider agent for managing faults. This requires the coordination of several internal applications, including a workforce management system (to timetable an engineer to fix the problem) and a customer relationship management system (to inform the customer). These applications have web service interfaces. The system designer develops a complex process out of these and 'wraps' the resulting system with a service provider agent front-end.

---

[2] A 'negotiation service' can exist in the first sense; this is a service where you 'subcontract' some negotiation problem to a service provider, and they negotiate on your behalf.

[3] By Terry Payne: http://www.daml.ecs.soton.ac.uk/services/SotonCurrencyConverter.html

Example C: Discovery, Selection, and Execution of a Customer Notification Service

A service requestor, OAS, needs to send a message to one of their customers. It does to by dynamically discovering a set of notification services, interacting with them to see if they can contact the specific person, selecting one based on functionality and cost, and interacting with it to send the message and provide payment.

Example D: 'Smart' Book Buying from Several Online Book Suppliers

A purchasing agent requiring several books locates several book sale SPAs, and interacts with them all simultaneously using their 'shopping cart' conversations to get quotes for purchase and delivery. It calculates the best SPA (or possibly set of SPAs) to use and 'checks out' an appropriate set of books, confirming the purchase. It monitors progress by using an 'order progress' conversation with the SPA.

Example E: Provision of a Logistics Supply Chain [1]

A company has a 'broken link' in a logistics supply chain and must rapidly locate a new shipping service between two ports. It makes a complex service request to a discovery service, and locates possible providers. It negotiates with them about the exact terms and conditions, and selects one. As the shipment takes place, it is accompanied by a complex exchange of messages between service provider and service requestor. This scenario requires two forms of 'service composition'. Firstly, the shipment service must 'slot in' with the other services in the logistics chain (arriving at the right time, etc). Secondly, the conversations with the service provider must be coordinated with conversations with other service providers in the chain.

4   Requirements Analysis

Based on the above case studies (and others) we identify requirements on a conceptual architecture (CA) for semantic web-enabled web services[4]:

1. The architecture should define the functionality of service discovery, but should not constrain the way in which it is enacted.
2. Discovery should be possible either using an explicit description of a required capability (E) or an implicit description through 'service provider type'.
3. Discovery identifies a set of SPAs which may meet the requestor's need. (C,D)
4. It should be possible to do discovery through informal browsing by a user (B).
5. Discovery should be symmetric; the functionality should not restrict a provider to advertise and a requestor to actively discover.
6. After the discovery process, there may (D) or may not (A) be a need for a contract agreement conversation to define the exact service to be provided.
7. The initiator should know prior to contacting them whether a conversation is necessary with the discovered agents to define the service.
8. A contract agreement conversation may involve negotiation of service parameters, selection of parameters from a set of possibilities (E), or a 'constructive' process such as the 'shopping trolley' metaphor (D).
9. A CA should enable negotiation to take place, but not place any requirements on either the structure of the contract agreement conversation required or on the negotiation strategies any participant may use

---

[4] The letters in brackets give the examples in section 2 which generate the requirement.

10. At the end of a contract agreement conversation, there will be an explicit contract which is identifiable as the 'semantics' (at the application level) of the agreed service. If there is no such conversation, then the discovery process should provide something identifiable as an explicit contract.

11. A service may be delivered directly as an output of an interaction with a Service Provider Agent (A), immediately as the effect of an interaction with a SPA (C), or as a later event or sequence of events after the defining interaction (E).

12. A post-agreement conversation may be directly linked to the execution/delivery of a service (E) or may simply monitor progress without directly affecting it (D).

13. A conversation about a service may be a simple request-respond pair(A), or may be a more complex interaction(D).

14. Conversations about a service may be initiated by the requestor(A), by the provider(E), or by either party (C)

15. A conversation may involve an asynchronous exchange of messages (E)

16. The semantics of a post-agreement conversation should be conceptually different from the domain-level semantics of the agreed service itself. However, there should be a means of linking the conversation with its domain level effect (E).

17. A service provider agent may in turn act as a service requestor agent to 'outsource' parts of the functionality it needs to deliver its service (B,C,D,E).

18. Some SPAs may achieve this outsourcing by executing processes of more simple elements created statically or dynamically using an internal planner (B); other SPAs may use very different reasoning methods (D).

19. It may be necessary to 'compose' service instances either to enable them connect in some way (E) or to provide a 'service bundle' that meets some need (D).

20. It may be necessary to 'compose'/coordinate conversations about services, to allow two services to interact appropriately (E).

21. Parts of the functionality required to support a conversation may themselves be treated as component services (D).

5   The Conceptual Architecture

In this section, we present a conceptual architecture (CA) which aims to meet the requirements listed in section 4. We now give a brief overview of the WSA service-oriented model [14] upon which our CA is based. The concept of a service is core, which is defined as an abstract resource representing a capability to perform some coherent set of tasks. The performance of a given task involves some exchange of messages between the requestor and provider agents. A choreography defines a pattern of possible message exchanges (i.e. conversations). The WSA associates a choreography with a task's performance. The task may also have effects in the virtual or real world. Such effects may be publicly observable, but will often be private (such as a database update). The success or otherwise of a given task (from the perspective of one party) can be assessed by whether some goal state has been achieved. Such a goal state can be defined formally or informally.

As Sycara et al observe [10], tasks can be defined in three ways. They can be represented explicitly, using name labels with a well defined semantics in some ontology of tasks. They can be represented implicitly, using a language of preconditions and effects of a task. Or they can be defined using a combination of these two approaches. The WSA makes no commitment as to which approach is used.

A service has a description, which specifies its interface and messages in a machine-processable way. This may also include a description of the service's semantics. The semantics specifies (formally, informally or implicitly) the intended effect of using the service: specifically, the tasks that constitute it. The WSA views this semantics as 'a contract between the requestor entity and provider entity concerning the effects and requirements pertaining to the use of a service.' We adopt the majority of this model unchanged. The two changes we make are:

1. Distinction Between Abstract Service, Agreed Service, and Concrete Service

In the WSA, a service has a semantics which can be described, advertised and discovered by a service requestor. However, the service semantics is defined as the contract between the provider entity and requestor entity. This creates a problem: How can something which is defined as an agreement between the two entities be advertised prior to the two entities communicating? We believe this can be solved by making a distinction in the model between the *abstract service* a provider entity offers and the *agreed service* which appears within a contract, and assigning semantics to each. Additionally, (as outlined in section 2) we introduce the *concrete service* which is the performance of a specific service at a particular time. We give more complete definitions and examples of these concepts below. Similarly, we consider *abstract tasks*, *agreed tasks* and *concrete tasks*.

2. Distinction Between Service and Service Provider Agent

The WSA specifies that a Service Provider Agent realises a service. The word 'realises' (and the explanation in WSA) implies that the provider agent is an embodiment of the service. We believe that this confuses a service as the capability to provide something of value with the entity or software implementation which has the capability. For this reason, we say that a provider agent *provides* an abstract or agreed service, and *performs* a concrete service.

We now present our conceptual architecture(CA). Firstly, we present definitions of the concepts we introduce. Then we present and explain the architecture. For clarity, we separate it into three diagrams, representing the entities and relationships involved in discovery, service definition and service execution. We omit the entities and relationships which appear in the WSA if they remain unchanged in our model and are not relevant to the discussion of service semantics.

Firstly, we define the concept of a concrete service. This is the core 'building block' with which to define the semantics of more abstract descriptions of services.

Definition: A *Concrete Service* is an actual or possible performance of a set of tasks that represent a coherent functionality (and therefore deliver some value) within some domain of interest to its associated requestor and provider entities.

A concrete service: has a set of one or more concrete tasks; has a set of messages; has a service provider and service requestor; has one or more post-agreement choreographies associated with it; has a service provider interface and/or a service requestor interface which are used by the choreographies; may have a service description.

A concrete service is effectively a (possible or actual) specific and detailed set of tasks carried out at a given time, and the messages exchanged in association with this. The messages are exchanged between a specific provider and requestor, according to certain choreographies and using certain interfaces. A service provider, however, does not offer a specific concrete service. Rather, they are able to provide many different possible concrete services. Similarly, a requestor is rarely after a specific concrete service; they are interested in many possible services which meet their needs. For that reason, we define the concept of abstract service:

Definition: An *Abstract Service* is some set of concrete services. A concrete service is said to be a *realization* of an abstract service if it appears in this set.

Definition: An *Abstract Service Description* is some machine-processable description D which has, as its model, an abstract service C. (We write `Model(D)` = C)

An Abstract Service Description is some specification of a set of services. The format of this description is not specified as part of this architecture. There are several possibilities: (1) An extensional listing of concrete services. (2) A label representing the name of some abstract service in some ontology of services. (3) A template or formal description in some knowledge representation language.

Option one is the most conceptually straightforward, but in practice will be infeasible except in the simplest of cases. In option two, the semantics of the label is defined as the (possibly infinite) set of concrete services which correspond to that label within the ontology. This correspondence may be well-defined and explicit, with a service specification or contract template associated with the label. Often, however, the correspondence will be more informal. For example, a label 'bookselling' may have as its semantics the set containing any possible concrete services where books (and only books) are being sold. The third option specifies the set of concrete services by explicitly and formally defining an abstract service using some knowledge representation (KR) language such as OWL or F-logic. This may involve explicit descriptions of abstract tasks, possibly including parameters. The set-theoretic semantics of the KR language then defines the set of concrete services to be those which formally satisfy the concept description.

A resource representing an abstract service will have an abstract service description associated with it. In addition, it may be associated with: (i) a contract agreement choreography (ii) a service provider, and an associated service provider interface (iii) a service requestor, and an associated service requestor interface.

Whereas a concrete service is always associated with a specific requestor and provider, an abstract service may have one or both of these undefined. Similarly, an abstract task may be less completely defined than a concrete task is.

An abstract service, as we shall see below, can be used for advertising or requesting. However, it is not precise enough to define what a requestor and provider agree. For that we define the following;

Definition: An *Agreed Service* is an abstract service agreed between two parties Hence it is associated with a specific service provider and service requestor, together with their associated interfaces. It also has specific post-agreement choreographies associated with it. Its definition is such that: (i) any further decisions necessary to select a realization will occur as choices made during a post-agreement choreography. (ii) Any choice made by one party during the post-agreement choreography is such that the other party is indifferent to how that choice is made. The agreed service forms the core of the service contract between two parties, which defines the semantics of their interaction:

Definition: A *Service Contract* is an agreement between a service provider and requestor that the provider will supply an agreed service to the requestor. The contract: has a service provider; has a service requestor; has an agreed service description; has an association between the tasks involved in the agreed service description and choreographies and message interfaces which will be used to have conversations about the tasks; may have information about who is responsible and what compensation may occur in the case that a service is not delivered correctly; may have additional legal terms and conditions.

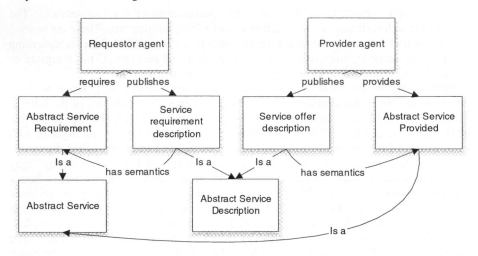

Fig. 1. Discovery Model of Conceptual Architecture

The agreed service description will be (explicitly or implicitly) in terms of the tasks to be performed. It may include tasks to be performed by the requestor (e.g. payment transfer in the case of e-commerce applications.) The task/choreography association defines how the interaction between the parties can take place during delivery of the agreed service. This may be done by including the choreographies explicitly in the contract. This is appropriate where a choreography may vary and require agreement between two parties. Alternatively, it may be done by referencing a choreography definition elsewhere. This is appropriate when the service provider agent offers a specific choreography and is not able or willing to alter it, or provides a choice between a small number of choreographies, or the parties use some standard choreography defined elsewhere.

Fig. 1 illustrates the concepts involved in discovery. A requestor agent requires one of a class of abstract service; to this end, they publish a description of their requirements. Similarly, a provider agent is able to provide services within a certain class of abstract service. It publishes a description of the services it can provide.

Ideally, in each case, the description of the abstract service will correspond exactly to the actual abstract service which is required or offered. However, in practice, this may not be possible. For this reason, we define correctness and completeness of descriptions:

Definition: A description D of an abstract service C is said to be *correct* if any element in the model of D also appears in C. i.e. $\text{Model}(D) \subseteq C$.

Definition: A description D of an abstract service C is said to be *complete* if any element of C also appears in the model of D. i.e. $C \subseteq \text{Model}(D)$.

Often, it is possible to achieve completeness but not correctness in service descriptions. For example, a bookseller can state 'I sell books' in an advert, but cannot guarantee that every title is in stock. The role of the discovery process is to determine if a given service provider may be able to meet the needs of a given service requestor, and to inform one or both parties of this. As the WSA discusses, discovery can be achieved in several different ways, including the use of a discovery service. Note that we say that both the requestor and the provider publish a service description. Such a publication may be as an entry into some discovery service, as a query to such a service, or as a local advertisement or request in a peer-to-peer system [2]. Following requirement 5, we make no commitment as to which party advertises and which party queries. In general, we would anticipate that providers would advertise and requestors would query the advertisements; however, there are exceptions such as when a requestor issues a public Request For Quotes describing the kind of service it requires.

Assuming that descriptions of service requirements and service offers are complete but not correct, then the minimal functionality required of the discovery system is to determine if the two abstract service descriptions intersect [11]. If this is the case, an agreement between the two parties may be possible. Paolucci et. al. [8] describe a more sophisticated matchmaker which uses a hierarchy of different definitions of matching to determine which matches are more likely to be fruitful.

Following discovery, two parties need to determine if they can agree on a service instance which the provider will supply to the requestor. This is done through the contract agreement phase. In some cases, this phase will be unnecessary and the results from the discovery phase will be enough. This is the case if the following criteria are satisfied; (i) The published service offer description is correct (but not necessarily complete). (ii) The offer description provides a complete and explicit service description which includes post-agreement choreographies. (iii) Any aspect of the offer description which has variability (for example, a parameter which is not defined) is such that the provider is indifferent with regard to the choice.(iv) The delivery choreography (see below) is structured such that choices within this variability (such as a parameter instantiation) can be input through it.

If all four of these criteria hold[5], then the contract agreement phase is unnecessary. The service offer description defines a set of concrete services, and the provider doesn't care which is selected. The delivery choreography allows the selection of a concrete service to be made by inputting parameter values chosen by the requestor. We call a service which has an abstract service description satisfying these criteria a **basic** service.

---

[5] This is phrased assuming the provider advertises and the requestor queries and selects. However, it is equally possible (though a lot rarer) that the requestor is indifferent, and the provider makes the selection using the requestor's delivery choreography.

If the published abstract service description does not satisfy the criteria, but the service provider agent is able to give a abstract service description which does, then the contract agreement phase becomes a straightforward 'take-it-or-leave-it' process. The contract agreement choreography simply consists of the requestor accessing the description. It then goes on to execute the delivery choreography if it chooses to use this service provider, and does nothing otherwise.

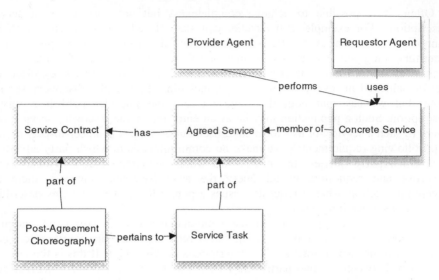

Fig. 2. Contract Agreement Model of Conceptual Architecture

In general, the contract agreement phase can be more complex than this. Fig. 2 illustrates the concepts it involves. At least one provider and at least one requestor agent participate in a choreography to agree a contract between them. The choreography involves discussing some abstract service, and may explicitly involve the manipulation of a description of it. If the choreography terminates successfully, it results in a service contract agreed between two parties; this contract contains a description of an agreed service which specifies the concrete service to be delivered. The agreed service will be a specialization of the abstract service found during discovery.

The decision making within the contract agreement phase has three aspects: *Partner selection*: Often, one or both parties can choose which partner will deliver/receive a service. *Service selection*: One party, usually the requestor, may need to select and specify certain parameters of a service instance which weren't specified during discovery. *Negotiation*: Often, when a service specification is fully defined, other contract parameters (e.g. price) will be fixed. However, in some cases, they may be open to negotiation.

Any given contract agreement phase does not necessarily involve all three of these. Furthermore, they can take place in any order, and may be interleaved.

Definition: A *contract agreement choreography* is a choreography between at least one service requestor and at least one service provider which, on successful termination, results in the agreement of a service contract between two of the parties.

Definition: A *service contract* is an agreement between a service provider and requestor that the provider will supply a specific service instance to the requestor. A service contract has (i) a service provider, (ii) a service requestor and (iii) a service instance with associated service description and resource identifier.

A contract agreement choreography may explicitly involve service selection and/or negotiation. Service selection protocols can take different forms: A service provider may offer a list of all contracts they are willing to offer, and the requestor simply selects one. A requestor may iteratively build a definition of the service they wish to receive using the 'shopping trolley' metaphor, and are given a price quote for it. A requestor may refine a service template through dialog with the provider about different options available. Example negotiation protocols include propose/counter-propose (where each party proposes a contract, and the other party either accepts it or proposes an alternative) and constraint relaxation (where parties relax constraints on a contract template until both sets are satisfiable [12]). Many other possible approaches to negotiation exist ([4], [13]).

The association of a contract agreement choreography to a given set of provider and requestor agents must take place following discovery. The simplest way to do this is for the advertising agent to associate a (pointer to) a contract agreement choreography description with their advert, or to return a contract agreement choreography when they are first queried directly.

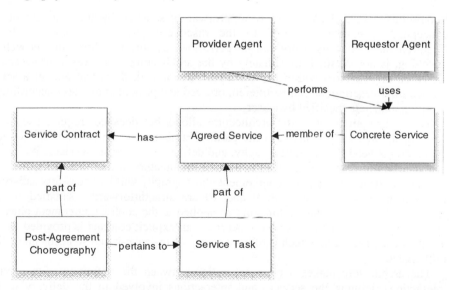

Fig. 3. Service Delivery Model of Conceptual Architecture

When a contract agreement choreography has terminated successfully, then service delivery can take place. This may commence immediately on agreement of the contract, or may be initiated later by a subsequent choreography. Fig. 3 illustrates the concepts involved in the service delivery phase. A concrete service is supplied by the provider agent to the requestor agent. This concrete service must be a member of the agreed service (which, recall, is a set of concrete services). The agreed service has an associated service contract which contains a description of the service agreed together with a mapping from the agreed tasks within the service to choreographies about these tasks. To distinguish these choreographies from the contract agreement choreographies, we refer to them as post agreement choreographies:

Definition: A post-agreement choreography is a protocol for a conversation between a service requestor and service provider about a contract which has been previously agreed, or one or more tasks within such a contract.

There are at least three different kinds of post-agreement choreography. A *delivery choreography* governs conversations which directly initiate and/or control the execution of one or more tasks in a contract. A *monitoring choreography* allows the requestor to monitor the task's progress. A *cancellation/renegotiation choreography* allows the termination or alteration of a service within a contract in certain circumstances.

This completes the Semantic Web-enabled Web Services conceptual model (CA). We now assess the architecture against the requirements of section 4.

6   Assessment of the Conceptual Architecture

Requirements 1, 2, 3 and 5 are straightforwardly satisfied by the structure of the conceptual architecture applied to the discovery phase as discussed above. Requirement 4, that discovery can be performed by informal browsing as well as matching, is not satisfied immediately by the architecture. However, a browser can easily be implemented within the conceptual framework described above; a set of service offer descriptions can be filtered, ordered and presented to a user according to certain parameters specified by a user.

To meet requirement 6, the architecture allows but does not require a contract agreement choreography between the parties. Furthermore, we characterise services which do not need such a choreography, and define them as basic services. While this characterisation is not technically part of the architecture, a discovery service could use it to determine if a contract agreement choreography will be necessary, satisfying requirement 7. Requirements 8, 9 and 10 are straightforwardly satisfied by the structure of the conceptual architecture as applied to the contract agreement phase as discussed above. In the case of basic services, an explicit contract is provided by the service offer description which is offered as take-it-or-leave-it and so needs no further refinement.

The architecture makes a clear separation between the definition of a service, interactions defining the service, and interactions involved in the delivery of the service. In particular, the delivery of a service can take place independently of its definition, satisfying requirement 11 and part of 16. The requirement that there be a means of linking a conversation with its effect is enabled but not satisfied by the architecture; use of a language which allows this is necessary. The other requirements on service delivery choreographies (12, 13, 14, 15) are straightforwardly satisfied by the structures defined above.

The conceptual architecture, like the WSA, allows 'outsourcing' of functionality (17) as agents can act simultaneously both as service providers and service requestors, possibly of several different services. We place no restrictions on the internal reasoning used to determine how this is done. One option is to use a planner to determine which service requests to make (18).

By separating out the definition of an agreed service from the choreographies to define and deliver the service, the architecture allows different kinds of 'composition' to take place. In particular, it enables parties to reason over possible service definitions at the domain level during the contract agreement phase to ensure coordination between the different services agreed(19). It also enables parties to reason about, and coordinate, choreographies associated with the agreement and deployment of different services (20). However, both of these are merely enabled by the architecture; reasoning strategies to do these must be embodied within specific requestor/provider agents.

A third form of what could loosely be called 'composition' is the application of some service to enable a choreography between provider and requestor of some other service (21). For example, a 'shopping trolley' choreography to define a book purchase may be enabled by component services, with functionality such as 'book search' or 'put in trolley'. The domain of application of these component services is 'shopping trolley choreography' as opposed to 'book delivery', the domain of the 'higher level' service being defined. However, within their domain, they can be considered as services with associated contractual definitions, and can be located and reasoned over by an agent which brings about the choreography between requestor and provider of the book delivery service. Such an arrangement, as opposed to fixed choreography definitions, would enable more flexible interactions between the two parties. It is conceivable to imagine a hierarchy of services nested in this way; though in the end it would bottom-out to fixed choreographies or basic services.

7   Analysis of OWL-S with Respect to the Conceptual Architecture

OWL-S ([7],[9]) (formerly DAML-S [6]) is an ontology for use in providing semantic markup for web services, developed by a coalition of researchers as part of the DARPA Agent Markup Language program. In this section, we compare the conceptual model implicit in OWL-S with our conceptual architecture.

The OWL-S ontology defines a service in terms of three top-level classes; the profile, the service model and the grounding. The profile characterises what a service requires and provides, and is used primarily in the discovery phase. The service model describes how a service works, primarily in terms of a process model. This defines a service's functionality as the execution of a (potentially complex) process of component web services. The grounding defines how a component web service can be interacted with, primarily through WSDL/SOAP. These three classes roughly correspond to our requirement for a service definition at the domain level, a description of how to interact with a service provider, and an implementation of that interaction. However, there are some differences which mean that OWL-S would need to be adapted and augmented if it were applied within our architecture.

In OWL-S, the profile is used almost exclusively as an advertisement/request. Hence it focuses on the description and categorization of an abstract service, but does not consider what is necessary to refine it to define an agreed service and to use this as a specification of what interactions accomplish. To do this, the service model (either within or outside the profile) would need to be augmented to provide complex structured descriptions of abstract services, and the ability to constrain and instantiate service parameters. The profile does not make a clear distinction between what a service does and the way in which one interacts with a service provider to receive the service. In particular, it is not clear that inputs/outputs should appear in the domain-level description of an agreed service. (For example, the domain level agreed service description may state that 'provider pays £10 by credit card'; the associated choreography will require a credit card number as its input. Hence the domain level definition and the choreography to deliver it are kept separate.)

The process model in OWL-S appears to serve two separate functions. Firstly, it can be used to define the exchange of messages with a service provider about a service; secondly, it can be used to define how a service provider implements the functionality of a service as a process of component web services. Both of these are valid uses, but the conceptual architecture requires that they be separated out.

The required exchange of messages about a service is defined by one or more post agreement choreographies in our conceptual architecture. The process model could be used to represent this. Note that the architecture can have several choreographies associated with a service, each performing different functions. Hence a given service may need several process models, and links between the process models and the domain-level service description to define what each does.

The definition of a service's functionality in terms of a process over component web services is a particular method of delivering a service. The CA requires that such a method should not be proscribed and that a provider using such a method should not be required to make public their method. For this reason, using the process model in this way would not be compliant. A separate structure defining the internal process should be used, and the publication of it would be optional. (Such a separation is being adopted in the nascent WSMO [15])

8   Conclusions and Future Work

We have presented a conceptual architecture developed out of a requirements analysis of a set of case studies in the SWWS project and example applications from the literature. The architecture makes a clear separation between the domain-level definition of a service to be provided, the message exchanges which bring about the service, and the internal logic which provides the appropriate functionality. Inevitably, the architecture is at an abstract level; however, it does shed light on the required characteristics of service ontologies and infrastructure services to realise it. We are currently working on an extension of the CA to include sub-communities of service agents which share a problem-solving method (in particular, planning). We also hope to expand it to cover mediation more effectively.

The conceptual architecture is being used to define, design and implement a general technical architecture for Semantic Web Services able to demonstrate the four case studies within the SWWS program. It is also being used as the underlying conceptual model in the development of WSMO-full [15] and has been submitted for consideration by the architecture subcommittee of the Semantic Web Services Initiative.

References

1. Esplugas-Cuadrado, J., Preist, C. and Williams, S.: Integration of B2B Logistics using Semantic Web Services. To appear, Proc. Artificial Intelligence: Methodology, Systems, and Applications, 11th International Conference, (2004)
2. Fensel, D. and Bussler, C.: The Web Service Modeling Framework WSMF. Electronic Commerce: Research and Applications, 1 (2002) 113-117
3. Grosof, B. and Poon, T.: SweetDeal: Representing Agent Contracts with Exceptions using Semantic Web Rules, Ontologies and Process Descriptions. To appear, International Journal of Electronic Commerce (2004)
4. He, M., Jennings, N.R. and Leung, H: On Agent Mediated Electronic Commerce. IEEE Transactions on Knowledge and Data Engineering 15(4) (2003) 985-1003
5. Jennings, N.R., Faratin, P.,Johnson,M.J., O'Brien,P. and Wiegand, M.E.: Using Intelligent Agents to Manage Business Processes. Proceedings of the First Int. Conference on the Practical Application of Intelligent Agents and Multi-Agent Technology (1996) 345-360
6. McIlraith, S. and Martin, D.: Bringing Semantics to Web Services. IEEE Intelligent Systems, 18(1) (2003) 90-93
7. OWL-S 1.0 Release. http://www.daml.org/services/owl-s/1.0/
8. Paolucci, M., Kawamura, T., Payne, T.R. and Sycara, K: Semantic Matching of Web Service Capabilities. Proc. International Semantic Web Conference (2002) 333-347
9. Paolucci, M. and Sycara, K.: Autonomous Semantic Web Services. IEEE Internet Computing, (September 2003) 34-41
10. Sycara, K., Paolucci, M., Ankolekar, A. and Srinivasan, N.: Automated Discovery, Interaction and Composition of Web Services. Journal of Web Semantics 1(1), Elsevier (2003)
11. Trastour, D., Bartolini, C. and Gonzalez-Castillo,J.: A Semantic Web Approach to Service Description for Matchmaking of Services. In Proceedings of the Semantic Web Working Symposium, Stanford, CA, USA, July 30 - August 1, 2001
12. Trastour, D., Bartolini, C. and Preist, C.: Semantic Web Support for the B2B E-commerce pre-contractual lifecycle. Computer Networks 42(5) (August 2003) 661-673
13. Vulkan, N.: The Economics of E-Commerce. Princetown University Press, Princetown, New Jersey (2003)
14. W3C. Web Services Architecture. W3C Working Group Note, 11 February 2004. http://www.w3.org/TR/ws-arch/
15. Web Services Modelling Ontology: http://www.wsmo.org/

From Software APIs to Web Service Ontologies: A Semi-automatic Extraction Method

Marta Sabou

Dept. of AI, Vrije Universiteit, Amsterdam, The Netherlands, marta@cs.vu.nl

Abstract. Successful employment of semantic web services depends on the availability of high quality ontologies to describe the domains of these services. As always, building such ontologies is difficult and costly, thus hampering web service deployment. Our hypothesis is that since the functionality offered by a web service is reflected by the underlying software, domain ontologies could be built by analyzing the documentation of that software. We verify this hypothesis in the domain of RDF ontology storage tools. We implemented and fine-tuned a semi-automatic method to extract domain ontologies from software documentation. The quality of the extracted ontologies was verified against a high quality hand-built ontology of the same domain. Despite the low linguistic quality of the corpus, our method allows extracting a considerable amount of information for a domain ontology.

1 Introduction

The promise of the emerging Semantic Web Services field is that machine understandable semantics augmenting web services will facilitate their discovery and integration. Several projects used semantic web service descriptions in very different application domains (bioinformatics grid[17], Problem Solving Methods[10]). A common characteristic of these descriptions is that they rely on a generic description language, such as OWL-S[3], to specify the main elements of the service (e.g. inputs, outputs) and on a ontology containing knowledge in the domain of the service such as the type of offered functionality (e.g. TicketBooking, CarRental) or the types of service parameters (e.g. Ticket, Car).

The quality of the domain ontologies used influences the complexity of reasoning tasks that can be performed with the semantic descriptions. For many tasks (e.g. matchmaking) it is preferable that web services are described according to the same domain ontology. This implies that the domain ontology used should be *generic* enough to be used in many web service descriptions. Domain ontologies also formally depict the complex relationships that exist between the domain concepts. Such *rich* descriptions allow performing complex reasoning tasks such as flexible matchmaking. We conclude that building quality (i.e. generic and rich) domain ontologies is at least as important as designing a generic web service description language such as OWL-S.

The acquisition of semantic web service descriptions is a time consuming and complex task whose automation is desirable, as signaled by many researchers in

S.A. McIlraith et al. (Eds.): ISWC 2004, LNCS 3298, pp. 410–424, 2004.

this field, for example [16]. Pioneer in this area is the work reported in [6] which aims to learn web service descriptions from existing WSDL[1] files using machine learning techniques. They classify these WSDL files in manually built task hierarchies. Complementary, we address the problem of building such hierarchies, i.e. domain ontologies of web service functionalities (e.g. TicketBooking). This task is a real challenge since in many domains only a few web services are available. These are not sufficient for building generic and rich ontologies.

Our approach to the problem of building quality domain ontologies is motivated by the observation that, since web services are simply exposures of existing software to web-accessibility, there is a large overlap (often one-to-one correspondence) between the functionality offered by a web service and that of the underlying implementation. Therefore we propose to build domain ontologies by analyzing application programming interfaces(APIs). We investigate two research questions:

1. *Is it possible and useful to build a domain ontology from software APIs?*
2. *Can we (semi-)automatically derive (part of) a domain ontology from APIs?*

This paper reports on work performed in the domain of RDF based ontology stores. Section 2 tackles the first question by presenting an ontology which was manually built from API documentation and reporting on using this ontology to describe existing web services. To address the second question, we present a (semi-) automatic method to derive (part of) a domain ontology in Section 3 and describe experimental results in Section 4. We use the manually built ontology as a Golden Standard for evaluating the result of the extraction process. We list related work in Section 5, then conclude and point out future work in Section 6.

2   Constructing a Golden Standard

Tools for storing ontologies are of major importance for any semantic web application. While there are many tools offering ontology storage (a major ontology tool survey [5] reported on the existence of 14 such tools), only very few are available as web services (two, according to the same survey). Therefore, in this domain it is problematic to build a good domain ontology by analyzing only the available web services. Nevertheless, a good domain ontology is clearly a must since we expect that many of these tools will become web services soon. We attempted to build a domain ontology by analyzing the APIs of three tools (Sesame [1], Jena [9], KAON RDF API[7]). We report on this ontology[2] in Section 2.1 then show that we could use it to describe web services in Section 2.2.

2.1   Manually Building the Domain Ontology

Method hierarchy. We identified overlapping functionalities offered by the APIs of these tools and modelled it in a hierarchy (see Fig. 2). The class *Method* depicts one specific functionality (similar to the OWL-S *Profile* concept).

---

[1] WSDL is the industry standard for syntactic web service descriptions.
[2] Available at http://www.cs.vu.nl/~marta/apiextraction.

According to our view, there are four main categories of methods for: adding data (*AddData*), removing data (*RemoveData*), retrieving data (*RetrieveData*) and querying (*QueryMethod*). Naturally, several specializations of these methods exist. For example, depending on the granularity of the added data, methods exist for adding a single RDF statement (*AddStatement*) or a whole ontology (*AddOntology*). Note, that this hierarchy reflects our own conceptualization and does not claim to be unique. Indeed, from another perspective, one can regard query methods to be a subtype of data retrieval methods. We have chosen however to model them as a separate class as they require inputs of type *Query*. Besides the method hierarchy, we also describe elements of the RDF Data Model (e.g. *Statement, Predicate, ReifiedStatement*) and their relationships.

During ontology building we introduced a main functionality category (a direct subclass of *Method*) if at least two APIs offered methods with such functionality (e.g. querying is only supported by Sesame and Jena). Functionalities offered just by one API were added

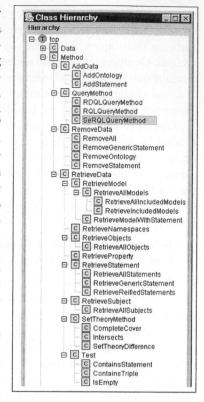

Fig. 1. The Method hierarchy.

as more specialized concepts with the goal of putting them in the context of generally offered functionality (e.g. SeRQL querying is only provided by Sesame).

Ontology richness. We enriched our ontology by identifying knowledge useful for several reasoning tasks. We enhanced the definition of methods in multiple ways such as: imposing restrictions on the type and cardinality of their parameters, describing their effects and types of special behavior (e.g. *idempotent*). We also identified methods which have the same effect, i.e *equivalent*. Knowledge about equivalent methods is important for tasks such as matchmaking. For more information on this ontology the reader is referred to [13]. We conclude that APIs are rich enough to make the building of a rich domain ontology *possible*.

2.2   Using the Domain Ontology for Web Service Description

We used the domain ontology to describe the web-interface of Sesame. The domain ontology offered all required concepts to describe the functionality of the web service and also indicated how the concepts we have used fit in a larger spectrum of possible functionalities. This is a clear advantage in comparison to the domain ontology[3] we have built in a previous project solely for the Sesame web

---

[3] Available at http://www.cs.vu.nl/~marta/apiextraction.

service [12]. While that ontology was satisfactory for the goals of that project, it was qualitatively inferior to the one we have obtained by analyzing the APIs of multiple tools.

We checked the generality of our domain ontology by using it to describe a web-interface which was not considered during ontology building. This is the recent W3C RDF Net API submission[4] which proposes a generic interface to be implemented by any service that wishes to expose RDF to client applications, therefore making the first step towards a standard RDF based web service interface. The submission distills six functionalities that any RDF engine should offer. Four of them (*query, getStatements, insertStatements, removeStatements*) are instances of the *QueryMethod, RetrieveGenericStatement, AddStatement* and *RemoveStatement* concepts respectively. The other two (*putStatements, updateStatements*) are complex operations and they correspond to sequences of concepts (*RemoveAll, AddStatement* and *RemoveStatement, AddStatement* respectively).

The manually built ontology is also an integrated part of the KAON Application Server, a middleware system which facilitates the interoperability of semantic web tools (e.g. ontology storages, reasoners). Many middleware tasks can be enhanced by reasoning with the semantic descriptions of the functionality and implementation details of registered tools [14]. Also, the middleware can expose the functionality of any registered tool as a web service and generate the semantic description of the web service from that of the underlying tool.

Summarizing Section 2, we note that by analyzing software APIs we were able to build a rich domain ontology and successfully employ it to describe (1) a web service whose API served as material for defining the ontology, (2) an emerging standard in this domain and (3) RDF storage tools registered with a semantic middleware. The manually built ontology serves as a Golden Standard for evaluating the semi-automatic extraction process presented next.

3   Semi-automatically Extracting Concepts

In this section we present our semi-automatic ontology extraction process (Section 3.1) and two possible refinements of this method (Sections 3.3 and 3.2).

3.1   The Extraction Process

The goal of the extraction process is to identify, by analyzing software API documentation, a set of concepts describing generally offered functionalities in the application domain of that software. It consists of several steps.

Step1 - Tokenise/POS tag the corpus - Automatic. This step preprocesses the corpus. After tokenisation we use the QTAG probabilistic Part Of Speech (POS) tagger[5] to determine the part of speech of each token.

Step2 - Extract Pairs - Automatic. This step extracts a set of potentially useful verb-noun pairs from the POS tagged documents. We extract all

---

[4] http://www.w3.org/Submission/2003/SUBM-rdf-netapi-20031002/
[5] http://web.bham.ac.uk/o.mason/software/tagger/index.html

pairs where the verb is in present tense, past tense or gerund form. Between the verb and the noun(phrase) we allow any number of determiners(e.g. "the", "a") and/or adjectives. The choice for such a pattern is straightforward since in javadoc style documentation verbs express the functionality offered by the methods and the following noun phrase (often their object) usually identifies the data structure involved in this functionality. We reduce the number of extracted pairs by lemmatization, so if "removes model" and "remove models" are extracted, the resulting pair is "remove model". We define the resulting pairs as *distinct*.

Step3 - Extract Significant Pairs - Manual, with some support. This step identifies all the significant pairs from the set of previously extracted distinct pairs. We define a pair to be *significant* for our task if it reflects the functionality of the method from whose description it was extracted. The ontology engineer has to decide by himself which of the extracted pairs are significant. Manually inspecting these pairs is time consuming, especially in cases when the set of extracted pairs contains many pairs of low importance for the ontology engineer. To solve this problem we adopted two strategies. First, we fine-tuned the extraction process so that the output contains a minimal number of insignificant pairs (Section 3.2). Second, we developed a set of ranking schemes to order the pairs according to their significance (Section 3.3). We present these refinement methods in different subsections due to their complexity, but we consider them closely related to the extraction process itself.

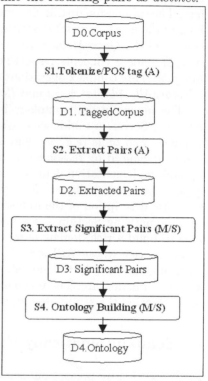

Fig. 2. The Extraction process.

Step4 - Ontology Building - Manual with support. Finally, the ontology engineer derives a concept from each significant pair. Often different pairs represent the same concept. For example, both "load graph" and "add model" correspond to the *AddOntology* concept. These concepts are the bases of the final ontology. Even if arranging them in a hierarchy is still a manual task, we support the ontology engineer with visual methods in discovering subclass relationships (Section 4.2). Further, we present the two refinement methods.

3.2   Refining the Extraction by Evaluation

Using a multi-stage evaluation method we aim to fine-tune the extraction process so that the output contains a minimum number of insignificant pairs. We present the evaluation metrics here and exemplify their use for fine-tuning in Section 4.3.

Stage 1 - evaluating pair extraction. At this stage we evaluate the quality of the first two steps of the ontology extraction process, i.e. the POS tagging and the pair extraction steps. We denote with all_{pairs} all manually identified pairs that we wish to extract and with $valid_{pairs}$ the subset of these pairs that are extracted. Extracted pairs that do not fulfill the extraction pattern are denoted by $invalid_{pairs}$. We define two metrics, adapted from the well-known information retrieval recall and precision.

$$Recall = \frac{valid_{pairs}}{all_{pairs}} \quad \text{and} \quad Precision = \frac{valid_{pairs}}{valid_{pairs} + invalid_{pairs}}$$

Quality criteria. We consider a pair extraction successful if both metrics have a high value. High recall testifies that many valid pairs were extracted from the corpus and high precision shows a low number of invalid pairs.

Stage 2 - evaluating pair significance. Evaluating the extraction process from the point of view of pair significance targets the improvement of the third ontology extraction step. For this, we count all pairs that were classified as significant during the manual inspection of the corpus (all_sign_{pairs}), all extracted significant ($sign_{pairs}$) and all extracted insignificant ($insign_{pairs}$) pairs. Similar to the previous stage, we compute recall and precision for the significant pairs as follows.

$$SRecall = \frac{sign_{pairs}}{all\_sign_{pairs}} \quad \text{and} \quad SPrecision = \frac{sign_{pairs}}{sign_{pairs} + insign_{pairs}}$$

Quality criteria. An extraction is successful if the ontology builder is presented with a high ratio of significant pairs from those existent in the corpus (high SRecall), and if there are only few insignificant pairs (high SPrecision).

Stage 3 - evaluating ontology coverage. At this stage we compare the extracted ontology with the manually built ontology. There has been little work in measuring similarity between two ontologies, one of the recent advances being the work published in [8]. We are interested to know how many of the concepts contained in the Golden Standard could be extracted, and therefore a simple lexical overlap measure, as introduced in [2], suffices. Let L_{O_1} be the set of all extracted concepts and L_{O_2} the set of concepts of the Golden Standard. The lexical overlap (LO) equals to the ratio of the number of concepts shared by both ontologies and the number of concepts we wish to extract.

$$LO(O_1, O_2) = \frac{|L_{O_1} \cap L_{O_2}|}{|L_{O_2}|} \quad \text{and} \quad OI(O_1, O_2) = \frac{|L_{O_1} \setminus L_{O_2}|}{|L_{O_2}|}$$

Human ontology building is not perfect. We encountered cases when the extraction process prompted us to introduce new concepts which were overlooked during the manual process, as illustrated in Section 4.2. We introduce an ontology improvement (OI) metric which equals to the ratio of new concepts (expressed as the set difference between extracted and desired concepts) and all concepts of the manual ontology. As a quality criteria we aim to increase the value of both metrics.

3.3   Refining the Extraction by Measuring Significance

The previous subsection addressed the problem of decreasing the effort of the ontology engineer when determining significant pairs (step 3) by evaluating and fine-tuning the extraction so that the number of extracted insignificant pairs is minimal. In this section we adopt a different strategy: we use pair ranking schemes to order the extracted pairs according to their significance. We built these schemes on pair frequency, term weight and API relevance considerations.

Pair Frequency. Our first intuition was that significant pairs are pairs that appear often and also in many different method descriptions. Denoting pf_{pair} the frequency of the pair in the corpus and df_{pair} the number of documents in the corpus in which the pair appears, we compute the rank of a pair as:

$$rank_{pair} = pf_{pair} * df_{pair}$$

Term Weight. This weighting scheme considers that the rank of a pair is directly proportional with the weight of its components. We give the same importance to the weight of the component verb and noun. Other variations in which one of these terms is considered more important could be investigated in the future.

$rank_{pair} = w_{verb} * w_{noun}$ where the weight of a term in the corpus is:

$$w_i = \sum_k wd_{i,k} = \sum_k (tf_{i,k} * df_i) = df_i * \sum_k tf_{i,k} = df_i * cf_i$$

- $wd_{i,k}$ - is the weight of term i in document k. It is defined as $wd_{i,k} = tf_{i,k} * df_i$;
- $tf_{i,k}$ - is the frequency of term i in document k;
- df_i - is the number of documents in which term i appears;
- cf_i - is the frequency of term i in the whole corpus.

API Relevance. Our final ranking scheme filters the pairs based on the number of APIs in which they appear. Intuitively, this corresponds to a different ontology building strategy than the one supported by the previous two schemes. Before we derived the "union" of all functionalities while here the focus is on their "intersection". Accordingly, pairs found in the maximum number of APIs are given the highest rank. Pairs belonging to the same number of APIs, are ordered using the Term Weight ranking scheme.

4   Experimental Results

4.1   Experimental Setup

The goal of our experiments is to test the basic extraction process and the enhancements achieved with the refinement methods. We conduct three sets of experiments. First, we apply the basic extraction process and examine the extracted concepts (4.2). Second, we use the evaluation method (1) to get an insight in the internal working of the basic extraction, (2) to suggest improvements for the extraction method and (3) to evaluate if the enhanced extraction is superior to the basic one (4.3). Finally, we perform a comparative evaluation of the pair ranking schemes on the output of the basic extraction process (4.4).

Corpora. We used two distinct corpora[6] in our experiments. The first corpus, *Corpus 1*, contains the documentation of the tools we used to build the manual ontology (Jena, KAON RDF API, Sesame) and accounts to 112 documents. The second corpus, *Corpus 2*, contains 75 documents collected from four tools: InkLing[7], the completely rewritten API of Sesame, the Stanford RDF API[8] and the W3C RDF model[9]. Each document in the corpora contains the javadoc description of one method. This description consists of a general description of the method functionality (termed "text"), followed by the description of the parameters, result type and the exceptions to be thrown (termed "parameters"). See for example the *add* method of the Jena API. We exclude the syntax of the method because it introduces irrelevant technical terms such as *java, com, org*.

```
add
     Add all the statements returned by an iterator to this model.
  Parameters:
     iter - An iterator which returns the statements to be added.
  Returns:this model
  Throws: RDFException - Generic RDF Exception
```

4.2   Extracting Concepts with the Basic Extraction Process

From Corpus 1 we extracted 180 pairs (80 distinct after lemmatization in Step 2) from which 31 distinct concepts were distilled. The first half of Table 1 lists these concepts, divided in 18 concepts already identified in the manual ontology (first column) and 13 new concepts which were ignored during the manual ontology building due to several reasons, as follows (second column). First, concepts that denote implementation related details (transactions, repositories) are tool specific functionalities and were not interesting for our task to determine RDF based functionalities. Then, concepts related to the creation of elements were ignored because only Jena offers such methods. "ModifyModel" actually denotes the effect of many methods that we ignored while modelling.

To check the applicability of our method to data sets that did not influence its design, we have applied it to Corpus 2. The extraction resulted in 79 pairs (44 distinct) synthesized in 14 concepts shown in the second half of Table 1. We conclude that our method worked on a completely new corpus allowing us to extract concepts for each four main categories identified manually.

The significant pairs identified in the third extraction step are currently only used to derive a set of concepts, however it is possible to determine their (and the

---

[6] The corpora are available on http://www.cs.vu.nl/~marta/apiextraction.
[7] http://swordfish.rdfweb.org/rdfquery/
[8] http://www-db.stanford.edu/ melnik/rdf/api.html
[9] http://dev.w3.org/cvsweb/java/classes/org/w3c/rdf/

Table 1. Extracted existing and new concepts from both experimental corpora.

Corpus 1		Corpus 2	
Concept	New Concept	Concept	New Concept
AddData	AbandonChanges	AddData(4)	CreateOntology
AddOntology (2)	BeginTransaction	AddOntology	VerifyData
AddStatement(2)	CommitTransaction	AddStatement	
ContainsStatement	CreateOntology	ContainsTriple	
ContainsTriple	CreateProperty	EvalauteQuery (3)	
QueryMethod	CreateResource	RemoveAll	
RDQLQueryMethod	CreateStatement (2)	RemoveStatement(3)	
RQLQueryMethod	GetURL	RetrieveAllStatements	
SerQLMethod	GetUsername	RetrieveData	
RemoveAll	ModifyModel	RetrieveObject	
RemoveOntology	RetrieveRepositories	RetrieveProperty	
RemoveStatement(2)	SupportSetOperations	RetrieveSubject	
RetrieveAllStatements	SupportsTransactions		
RetrieveData (2)			
RetrieveObject(2)			
RetrieveOntology(2)			
RetrieveProperty			
RetrieveResource			

corresponding concepts') hierarchical relationships. We experimented with the Cluster Map [4] visualization technique, developed by Aduna (www.adnua.biz), to highlight potential subclass relationships. The Cluster Map was developed to visualise the *instances* of a number of *classes*, organized by their classifications.

Figure 3 displays API methods (small spheres - playing the role of *instances*) grouped according to the significant pairs that were extracted from their descriptions (bigger spheres with an attached label stating the name of the pair - considered *classes* here). Balloon-shaped edges connect instances to the class(es) they belong to. We observe that all *instances* of the rql, rdql and serql query pairs (i.e. all methods from which these pairs were

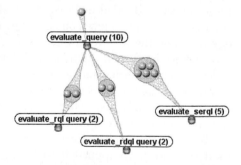

Fig. 3. Hierarchy visualisation.

extracted) are also *instances* of the query pair, hence intuitively indicating that the concepts resulting from these pairs are in a subclass relationship, where the concept derived from the "evaluate query" pair is the most generic concept.

We observe that, in both corpora, the number of distinct pairs (80, 44) is mush higher than the finally derived concepts (31, 14). To better understand this behavior of the extraction process we employ the evaluation method defined in Section 3.2, as described in the next Section.

4.3   Fine-Tuning the Extraction Process by Evaluation

In this section we describe the fine-tuning of the extraction process by using the evaluation method. Methodologically, there are three main steps in a fine tuning process. First (A), we evaluate the performance of the extraction process for the evaluation metrics defined. Second (B), according to its performance we decide on several modifications that could enhance the performance. Finally (C), we evaluate the enhanced process (on the original and a new corpus) to check if the predicted improvements took place, i.e. if the fine-tuning process was successful.

A) Evaluating the extraction process. The original extraction process was applied on Corpus 1. We observed that, in this corpus, the text section is grammatically more correct than the parameters section. Also, the predominant number of verbs were in present form, especially those that describe method functionalities. Accordingly, to verify our observations, we have evaluated the ontology extraction process in these two different parts of the method description and for the three different verb forms. A summary of the performance evaluation for the original extraction is shown in the third column of Table 2. Readers interested in the detailed evaluation data are referred to [13].

Stage 1 - evaluating pair extraction. We have counted the extracted valid and invalid pairs and computed the precision and recall of the pair extraction per verb category. The recall of pairs with present tense verbs is quite low (0.65) because, in the text area, these verbs appear in an unusual position - the first word in the sentence - a position usually being attributed to nouns. The POS tagger often fails in such cases, especially when the verbs can be mistaken for nouns (e.g. lists). In contrast, the precision of extracting present tense verbs is high. Both the recall and the precision of the extraction on the corpus as a whole are low (see Table 2) due to the existence of many present tense verbs which are often mistaken for nouns (recall) and the past tense verbs (precision).

Stage 2 - evaluating pair significance. Low significance recall (0.64 for text, 0.69 for parameters, 0.65 globally) shows that a lot of significant pairs are not extracted from the corpus. This is a direct consequence of the low extraction recall of pairs in general (e.g. many of the pairs which are not extracted are significant). The significance precision is almost double in the text (0.59) versus the parameter (0.28) section. Therefore pairs extracted from the textual part are much more likely to be significant than pairs extracted from the parameter part. This heavily affects the precision of the whole corpus (0.5).

Stage 3 - evaluating ontology coverage. The first half of Table 1 shows all distinct extracted concepts. Eighteen concepts from the manual ontology were identified yielding in a lexical overlap of $LO = 0.5$, a very good result given that a lot of significant pairs were not extracted from the corpus. Besides this, 13 new concepts were identified resulting in an ontology improvement of $OI = 0.36$. In other words, we extracted half of the concepts that we identified manually and we suggested improvements that could enlarge the ontology with 36%.

B) Conclusions for enhancements. We decided (1) to ignore the parameter section, because it heavily lowers the SPrecision of the whole corpus. Also, (2) we will only extract pairs with present tense verbs, because there are only a few verbs in other forms but they negatively influence the pair retrieval precision of the corpus. These measures serve the decrease of insignificant pairs extracted from the corpus in step 2 but do not solve the recall problem. For that we need to train the POS tagger, a task regarded as future work.

C) Quality increase of the enhanced process. The particularities of Corpus 1 influenced the fine-tuning of the process. Therefore we check the improvement of the performance on both corpora. Table 2 summarizes the evaluation results for the original and the enhanced extraction process. The enhanced process uses a modified linguistic pattern (only extracts present tense verbs) and is only applied on the textual part of the method descriptions.

Table 2. Comparison of the original and the enhanced extraction for two corpora.

Ev.Step	Ev. Matrics	Corpus 1		Corpus 2	
		Original	Enhanced	Original	Enhanced
1	Recall	0.69	0.65	-	-
	Precision	0.76	0.98	-	-
2	SRecall	0.65	0.62	-	-
	SPrecision	0.5	0.78	0.48	0.67
3	LO	0.5	0.39	0.3	0.25
	OI	0.36	0.36	0.05	0.03

For Corpus 1 the precision of the output was highly increased in both evaluation stages: 22% for the first stage and 28% for the second. This serves our goal to reduce the number of insignificant pairs extracted in step 2. Despite the heavy simplifications the ontological loss was minimal (11%). The enhanced process only missed 4 concepts because their generating pairs appeared in the parameter section (*QueryMethod*) or had verbs in past tense form (*RetrieveObject, RetrieveProperty, RetrieveResource*). For Corpus 2, we did not perform any manual inspection and therefore could only compute the SPrecision and the ontology comparison metrics. Similarlly, the pair significance increased (with 20%) resulting in a small decrease of ontology overlap (with 5%).

4.4   Refining the Extraction by Measuring Significance

Pair ranking schemes order the extracted pairs according to their significance. We evaluated which of them is the best discriminator for pair significance. To evaluate the performance of ranking schemes, we have manually determined the type of all pairs, extracted in the second step of the basic extraction process from Corpus 1, as: (1) insignificant, (2) significant leading to a new concept and (3) significant leading to an already identified concept in the manual ontology. We represented the output of each ranking scheme by plotting the rank position assigned to pairs against their significance. We drew a linear trendline (and computed its equation) to determine the behavior of the scheme. Considering the highest rank positions the most significant, in the optimal case, the trendline would have an increasing tendency, assigning high ranks to high significance. A high slope of the trendline indicates a good performance of the ranking scheme.

Pair Frequency. Fig. 4 shows the performance of the Pair Frequency ranking scheme. The slope of the linear trendline has a low value (0,0044) denoting a suboptimal behavior. Indeed, several significant pairs still appear on the lowest rank positions and then insignificant pairs predominate until the highest positions. The very top of the ranked

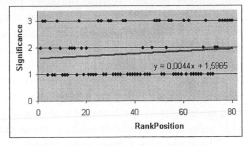

Fig. 4. Pair Frequency Scheme.

set consists indeed of significant pairs. The reason for this behavior is that often very frequent pairs do not reflect functionality while rare pairs do. Often rare pairs interrelate a significant verb (e.g. "add") with a significant noun (e.g. "model"). This prompted us to consider the weights of the constituent terms, as in the next scheme.

Term Weight. Observe in Fig. 5 that, comparatively to the previous scheme, the behavior of the Term Weight scheme is closer to the desired one: the slope of the linear trendline is higher (0,0137). Also, many insignificant pairs are identified for low rank positions and no significant pair is placed on the lowest 20 position (bottom quarter). However, there is

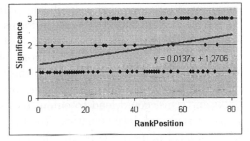

Fig. 5. Term Weight Scheme.

a mixed amount of significant and insignificant pairs for a large interval of rank positions. On top positions fewer insignificant and more significant pairs exist.

API Relevance. The API Relevance ranking performs slightly better comparatively to the Term Weight method, having a higher slope for the linear trendline (0,0151). The number of shared pairs within APIs is surprisingly low. There is a single pair shared by all three APIs ("add statement"), and three pairs shared by two of the

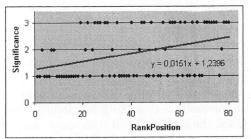

Fig. 6. API Relevance Scheme.

three APIs ("support transaction", "remove statement" , "contain statement"). Note that we only measured the intersection of lexical pairs, however, the intersection of concepts derived from the lexical pairs would yield in a much larger set (since different lexical pairs often denote the same concept).

4.5   Discussion

The basic extraction process proved very helpful: it extracted half of the concepts existent in the manually built ontology and also suggested some new additions which were ignored during ontology building. We checked the applicability of the extraction method on a different corpus than the one which served for its design and obtained concepts from all major categories of functionalities. While the extracted concepts are already a valuable help in ontology building, early experiments show that hierarchical information could be derived automatically as well. However, many of the pairs extracted in the second step were insignificant causing considerable time delays when filtering out the significant pairs. Also, we had no insight in the internal working of the process to understand its behavior. Our refinement methods address these two issues.

The evaluation refinement method allowed us to get a better understanding of the corpus and the behavior of the extraction process on this corpus. The derived observations helped us to fine-tune to extraction so that much less insignificant pairs were extracted in the second step and the loss of ontological information was minimal. The improvements were verified on the original and a new corpus as well.

Our experiments show that ranking schemes based on simple frequency measures can filter some of the significant pairs, making step 3 less time consuming. The Term Weight based scheme performs better than the Pair Ranking scheme, and the API relevance achieves the best performance. We experimented with many more possible schemes, but none of them performed significantly better. We conclude that there is a limit to the performance of simple frequency based methods, however additional background knowledge, specifically of synonymy between terms, could lead to enhanced results. For example knowing which actions (verbs) and data structures (nouns) are synonyms would help determining which lexical pairs are conceptually equivalent and allow us to work with concepts rather than lexical pairs. Our intuition is that synonymy between verbs could be determined from generic knowledge (e.g. WordNet) but more specialized domain knowledge is required for the synonymy of data structures.

5   Related Work

The problem of automating the task of web service semantics acquisition was addressed by the work of two research teams. Heß[6] employs the Naive Bayes and SVM machine learning algorithms to classify WSDL files (or web forms) in manually defined task hierarchies. Our work is complementary, since we address the acquisition of such hierarchies. Also, our method does not rely on any manually built training data as the machine learning techniques do. Patil[11] employ graph similarity techniques to determine a relevant domain for a WSDL file and to annotate the elements of the WSDL file. Currently they determine the semantics of the service parameters and plan to concentrate on functionality semantics in the future. They use existent domain ontologies and acknowledge that their work was hampered by the lack of these ontologies.

There has been several efforts in the ontology learning community to learn concept hierarchies (e.g. [2], [15]), but none of them used sources similar to API documentation. The work that is methodologically closest to our solution is the work of Cimiano[2]. They identify a set of verb-noun pairs with the intention to build a taxonomy by using the Formal Concept Analysis theory. As a result, their metrics for filtering the best pairs are different from ours. They define and evaluate three such metrics. Finally, they compare their extracted ontology to a manually built one. We adopted one of their ontology comparison metrics.

6   Conclusions and Future Work

The hypothesis of the presented work is that, given the similarity in functionality between web services and their underlying implementation, functionality focused domain ontologies could be derived from the underlying software's documentation. In this paper we answer two research questions. First, we prove that it is *possible* and *useful* to build domain ontologies from software documentation, by manually building such an ontology from API documentation and using it to describe several web services. Second, we investigate the possibility of automating the ontology extraction process and present a low-investment method for extracting concepts denoting functionality semantics. Even if these concepts represent only part of the available information in the APIs, extracting them is a considerable help for the ontology engineer. We plan to check the applicability of our method in other domains than that of RDF ontology stores.

We plan several enhancements to our extraction method. First, we wish to fine-tune the used linguistic tools (POS tagger) to the grammatical characteristics of our corpus. Second, we want to automate the conceptualization step possibly using synonymy considerations. Finally, we will investigate automatic learning of hierarchical relationships. The visualisation techniques we used suggested several good heuristics in determining such relationships and promise to become intuitive tools for non professional ontology builders.

We are aware of some limitations of our work. First, our corpora are too small for applying statistical techniques. We plan to enlarge them by adding other API documentations or including other sources such as internal code comments, user manuals etc. Also, we consider using extraction methods better suited for small corpora, for example clustering methods. Second, we ignore all existent structural information, therefore loosing a lot of semantics. We plan to build methods which leverage on the structured nature of the javadoc descriptions. For example, terms appearing in the textual description should have a higher weight than those appearing in the parameter section. Also, we wish to take into account the structure of the code (e.g. package/class hierarchies) to determine the main data structures and their relationships.

We conclude that software APIs are rich sources for ontology building and even simple statistical methods are able to extract much of the contained knowledge. The promising results published in this paper prompt us to further pursue our work towards boosting a web of semantic web services.

Acknowledgements. We thank P. Cimiano and J. Tane for their support with the TextToOnto tool and W. van Atteveldt, F. van Harmelen, P. Mika and H. Stuckenschmidt for their review and comments on earlier versions of this paper.

References

1. J. Broekstra, A. Kampman, and F. van Harmelen. Sesame: A Generic Architecture for Storing and Querying RDF and RDF Schema. In I. Horrocks and J. A. Hendler, editors, *Proceedings of the First International Semantic Web Conference*, LNCS, Sardinia, Italy, 2002.
2. P. Cimiano, S. Staab, and J. Tane. Automatic Acquisition of Taxonomies from Text: FCA meets NLP. In *Proceedings of the ECML/PKDD Workshop on Adaptive Text Extraction and Mining, Cavtat–Dubrovnik, Croatia*, 2003.
3. The OWL-S Services Coalition. OWL-S: Semantic Markup for Web Services. White Paper. http://www.daml.org/services/owl-s/1.0/owl-s.pdf, 2003.
4. C. Fluit, M. Sabou, and F. van Harmelen. *Handbook on Ontologies in Information Systems*, chapter Supporting User Tasks through Visualisation of Light-weight Ontologies. International Handbooks on Information Systems. Springer-Verlag, 2003.
5. A. Gomez Perez. A survey on ontology tools. OntoWeb Delieverable 1.3, 2002.
6. A. Heß and N. Kushmerick. Machine Learning for Annotating Semantic Web Services. In *AAAI Spring Symposium on Semantic Web Services*, March 2004.
7. A. Maedche, B. Motik, and L. Stojanovic. Managing Multiple and Distributed Ontologies in the Semantic Web. *VLDB Journal*, 12(4):286–302, 2003.
8. A. Maedche and S.Staab. Measuring similarity between ontologies. In *Proceedings of EKAW*. Springer, 2002.
9. B. McBride. Jena: A Semantic Web Toolkit. *IEEE Internet Computing*, 6(6):55–59, November/December 2002.
10. E. Motta, J. Domingue, L. Cabral, and M. Gaspari. IRS-II: A Framework and Infrastructure for Semantic Web Services. In *Proceedings of the Second International Semantic Web Conference*, LNCS. Springer-Verlag, 2003.
11. A. Patil, S. Oundhakar, A. Sheth, and K. Verma. METEOR-S Web service Annotation Framework. In *Proceeding of the World Wide Web Conference*, 2004.
12. D. Richards and M. Sabou. Semantic Markup for Semantic Web Tools: A DAML-S description of an RDF-Store. In *Proceedings of the Second International Semantic Web Conference*, LNCS, pages 274–289, Florida, USA, 2003. Springer.
13. M. Sabou. Semi-Automatic Learning of Web Service Ontologies from Software Documentation. Technical report. http://www.cs.vu.nl/ marta/papers/techreport/olws.pdf, 2004.
14. M. Sabou, D. Oberle, and D. Richards. Enhancing Application Servers with Semantics. In *Proceedings of AWESOS Workshop*, Australia, April 2004.
15. C. Sporleder. A Galois Lattice based Approach to Lexical Inheritance Hierarchy Learning. In *Proccedings of the Ontology Learning Workshop, ECAI*, 2002.
16. C. Wroe, C. Goble, M. Greenwood, P. Lord, S. Miles, J. Papay, T. Payne, and L. Moreau. Automating Experiments Using Semantic Data on a Bioinformatics Grid. *IEEE Intelligent Systems*, 19(1):48–55, 2004.
17. C. Wroe, R. Stevens, C. Goble, A. Roberts, and M. Greenwood. A Suite of DAML+OIL Ontologies to Describe Bioinformatics Web Services and Data. *Journal of Cooperative Information Science*, 2003.

Applying KAoS Services to Ensure Policy Compliance for Semantic Web Services Workflow Composition and Enactment

Andrzej Uszok[1], Jeffrey M. Bradshaw[1], Renia Jeffers[1], Austin Tate[2], and Jeff Dalton[2]

[1] Institute for Human and Machine Cognition (IHMC),
40 S. Alcaniz, Pensacola, FL 32501, USA
{auszok, jbradshaw, rjeffers}@ihmc.us
[2] Artificial Intelligence Applications Institute, University of Edinburgh,
Edinburgh EH8 9LE, UK
{a.tate, j.dalton}@ed.ac.uk

Abstract. In this paper we describe our experience in applying KAoS services to ensure policy compliance for Semantic Web Services workflow composition and enactment. We are developing these capabilities within the context of two applications: Coalition Search and Rescue (CoSAR-TS) and Semantic Firewall (SFW). We describe how this work has uncovered requirements for increasing the expressivity of policy beyond what can be done with description logic (e.g., role-value-maps), and how we are extending our representation and reasoning mechanisms in a carefully controlled manner to that end. Since KAoS employs OWL for policy representation, it fits naturally with the use of OWL-S workflow descriptions generated by the AIAI I-X planning system in the CoSAR-TS application. The advanced reasoning mechanisms of KAoS are based on the JTP inference engine and enable the analysis of classes and instances of processes from a policy perspective. As the result of analysis, KAoS concludes whether a particular workflow step is allowed by policy and whether the performance of this step would incur additional policy-generated obligations. Issues in the representation of processes within OWL-S are described. Besides what is done during workflow composition, aspects of policy compliance can be checked at runtime when a workflow is enacted. We illustrate these capabilities through two application examples. Finally, we outline plans for future work.

1 Introduction

Despite rapid advances in Web Services, the demanding requirements of the user community continue to outstrip currently available technology solutions. To help close this gap, advocates of Semantic Web Services have begun to define and implement many new and significant capabilities (*http://www.swsi.org/*). These new capabilities are intended to more fully harness the power of Web Services through explicit representations of the semantics underlying Web resources and the development of intelligent Web infrastructure capable of fully exploiting them.

S.A. McIlraith et al. (Eds.): ISWC 2004, LNCS 3298, pp. 425–440, 2004.

Semantic Web Languages such as OWL extend RDF to allow users to specify ontologies composed of taxonomies of classes and inference rules.

Semantic Web Services can be effectively used not only by people but also by software agents [10]. Agents will increasingly use the combination of semantic markup languages and Semantic Web Services to understand and autonomously manipulate Web content in significant ways. Agents will discover, communicate, and cooperate with other agents and services and, as described in this paper, will rely on policy-based management and control mechanisms to ensure that human-imposed constraints on agent interaction are respected. Policy-based controls of Semantic Web Services can also be used to govern interaction with traditional (non-agent) clients.

2   Policies and Semantic Web Services

Policies, which constrain the behavior of system components, are becoming an increasingly popular approach to dynamic adjustability of applications in academia and industry (*http://www.policy-workshop.org/*). Elsewhere we have pointed out the many benefits of policy-based approaches, including reusability, efficiency, extensibility, context-sensitivity, verifiability, support for both simple and sophisticated components, protection from poorly-designed, buggy, or malicious components, and reasoning about their behavior [2]. Policies have important analogues in animal societies and human cultures [6].

Policy-based network and distributed system management has been the subject of extensive research over the last decade (*http://www-dse.doc.ic.ac.uk/Research/ policies/*) [18]. Policies are often applied to automate network administration tasks, such as configuration, security, recovery, or quality of service (QoS). In the network management field, policies are expressed as sets of rules governing choices in the behavior of the network. There are also ongoing standardization efforts toward common policy information models and frameworks. The Internet Engineering Task Force, for instance, has been investigating policies as a means for managing IP-multiservice networks by focusing on the specification of protocols and object-oriented models for representing policies (*http://www.ietf.org/html.charters/policy-charter.html*).

The scope of policy management is increasingly going beyond these traditional applications in significant ways. New challenges for policy management include:

- Sources and methods protection, digital rights management, information filtering and transformation, and capability-based access;
- Active networks, agile computing, pervasive and mobile systems;
- Organizational modeling, coalition formation, formalizing cross-organizational agreements;
- Trust models, trust management, information pedigrees;
- Effective human-machine interaction: interruption and notification management, presence management, adjustable autonomy, teamwork facilitation, safety; and
- Support for humans trying to retrieve, understand, and analyze all policies relevant to some situation.

Multiple approaches for policy specification have been proposed that range from formal policy languages that can be processed and interpreted easily and directly by a computer, to rule-based policy notation using an if-then-else format, to the representation of policies as entries in a table consisting of multiple attributes.

In the Web Services world, standards for SOAP-based message security[1] and XML-based languages for access control (e.g., XACML[2]) have begun to appear. However the immaturity of the current tools along with the limited scope and semantics of the new languages make them less-than-ideal candidates for the sorts of sophisticated Web-based applications its visionaries have imagined for the next decade [7; 12].

The use of XML as a standard for policy expression has both advantages and disadvantages. The major advantage of using XML is its straightforward extensibility (a feature shared with languages such as RDF and OWL, which are built using XML as a foundation). The problem with mere XML is that its semantics are mostly *implicit*. Meaning is conveyed based on a shared understanding derived from human consensus. The disadvantage of implicit semantics is that they are rife with ambiguity, promote fragmentation into incompatible representation variations, and require extra manual work that could be eliminated by a richer representation. However Semantic Web-based policy representations, such as those described in this paper, could be mapped to lower level representations if required by an implementation by applying contextual information.

In addition to our own work on KAoS (see below), some initial efforts in the use of Semantic Web representations for basic security applications (authentication, access control, data integrity, and encryption) of policy have begun to bear fruit. For example, Denker *et al.* have integrated a set of ontologies (credentials, security mechanisms) and security extensions for OWL-S Service profiles with the CMU Semantic Matchmaker [12] to enable security brokering between agents and services. Future work will allow security services to be composed with other services. Kagal *et al.* [8] are developing Rei, a Semantic Web language-based policy language that is being used as part of the described above OWL-S Service profiles extension and other applications.

In another promising direction, Li, Grosof, and Feigenbaum [9] have developed a logic-based approach to distributed authorization in large-scale, open, distributed systems.

3   KAoS Policy and Domain Management Services

KAoS is one of the first efforts to represent policy using a Semantic Web language—in this case OWL[3]. KAoS services and tools allow for the specification, management, conflict resolution, and enforcement of policies within the specific contexts established by complex organizational structures represented as *domains* [2; 3; 16; 17]. While initially oriented to the dynamic and complex requirements of software

---

[1] e.g., *http://www-106.ibm.com/developerworks/webservices/library/ws-secure/*

[2] *http://www.oasis-open.org/committees/tc_home.php?wg_abbrev=security*

[3] A comparison among two semantically-rich representations of policy (KAoS, Rei) and a more traditional policy language (Ponder[5]) can be found in [15].

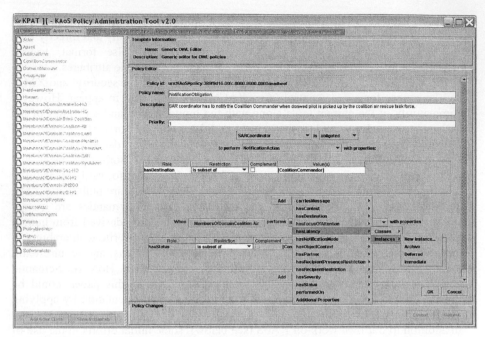

Fig. 1. Graphical interface of the OWL policy editor and administration tool: KPAT.

agent applications, KAoS services have been extended to work equally well with both agent and traditional clients on a variety of general distributed computing platforms (e.g., CORBA, Web Services, Grid Computing (Globus GT3)).

3.1 Ontological Representation of KAoS Policies

KAoS uses ontology concepts (encoded in OWL) to build policies. During its bootstrap, KAoS first loads a KAoS Policy Ontology (KPO) defining concepts used to describe a generic actors' environment and policies within this context (*http://ontology.ihmc.us/*). Then KAoS loads additional ontology, extending concepts from the generic ontology, with notions specific to the particular controlled environment.

The KAoS Policy Service distinguishes between *authorizations* (i.e., constraints that permit or forbid some action) and *obligations* (i.e., constraints that require some action to be performed when a state- or event-based trigger occurs, or else serve to waive such a requirement) [4]. Other policy constructs (e.g., delegation, role-based authorization) are built out of the basic primitives of domains plus these four policy types.

KAoS policy's OWL definition of (Fig. 1 shows the tool to define such policies) is an instance of one of four basic policy classes, that is: *PositiveAuthorization*, *NegativeAuthorization*, *PositiveObligation* or *NegativeObligation*. The property values determine management information for a particular policy (for example, its priority). The type of policy instance determines the kind of constraint KAoS should apply to the action, while a policy's action class is used to determine a policy's applicability in a given situation. The action class uses OWL restrictions to narrow scopes-of-action properties to a particular policy's needs. Every action contains a definition of the range of actors performing it. This range can be defined using any available OWL construct. For example, the range can be an enumeration of actor instances, a class of actors defining its type, or any description of the actor context (for instance, the class of actors executed on some host and possessing a given resource). The same is true for the action class's other properties but additionally XML Schema expressions can be used to restrict ranges of datatype properties. Consequently, policy can contain arbitrarily complex definitions of a situation. So, KAoS policies represent policies without conditional rules, relying instead on the context restrictions associated with the action class to determine policy applicability in a given situation

An action class helps classify action instances that actors intend to take or are currently undertaking. Components (such as KAoS Guards) that are interested in checking policy impact on these actions construct RDF descriptions of action instances. KAoS classifies these instances, relying on the inference capabilities of Stanford University's Java Theorem Prover (JTP, *www.ksl.stanford.edu/software/ JTP*). It then obtains a list of any policies whose action classes are relevant to the current situation. In the next step, KAoS determines the relative precedence of the obtained policies and sorts them accordingly in order to find the dominating authorization policy. If the dominating authorization is positive, KAoS then collects, in order of precedence, obligations from any triggered obligation policies. KAoS returns the result to the interested parties—in most cases, these parties are the enforcement mechanisms that are jointly responsible for blocking forbidden actions and assuring the performance of obligations.

Representing policies in OWL facilitates reasoning about the controlled environment, policy relations and disclosure, policy conflict detection, and harmonization. It also facilitates reasoning about domain structure and concepts exploiting the description logic subsumption and instance classification algorithms. KAoS can identify and, if desired, harmonize conflicting policies through algorithms that we have implemented in JTP.

3.2   Important KAoS Features

We highlight a few important features of KAoS below:

- *Homogeneous policy representation.* Because all aspects of KAoS policy representation are encoded purely in OWL, any third-party tool or environment supporting OWL can perform specialized analyses of the full knowledge base completely independently of KAoS itself, thus easing integration with an increasingly sophisticated range of new OWL tools and language enhancements in the future.
- *Maturity.* Over the past few years, KAoS has been used in a wide range of applications and operating environments.
- *Comprehensiveness.* Unlike many approaches that deal with only simple forms of access control or authorization, KAoS supports both authorization and

obligation policies. In addition, a complete infrastructure for policy management has been implemented including a full range of capabilities from sophisticated user interfaces for policy specification and analysis to a generic policy disclosure mechanism. Facilities for policy enforcement automation (i.e., automatic generation of code for enforcers) are under further development.

- *Pluggability.* Platform-specific and application-specific ontology is easily loaded on top of the core concepts. Moreover, the policy enforcement elements have been straightforwardly adapted to a wide range of computing environments, both traditional distributed computing platforms (e.g., Web Services, Grid Computing, CORBA) and various software and robotic agent platforms (e.g., Nomads, Brahms, SFX, CoABS Grid, Cougaar).

- *Scalability and performance.* We optimized the policy disclosure methods such that response to a query from an enforcer is provided on average in less than 1 ms. This performance is due in part to our reliance on efficient and logically decideable description logic subsumption and classification methods. Furthermore, queries can be executed concurrently by multiple enforcers, letting KAoS export multiprocessor machines. In rigorous evaluations in the DARPA UltraLog program, we've found that performance is acceptable even in large societies of more than a thousand agents, running on a dozen or more platforms, with hundreds of policies. Here, dynamic policy updates can be committed, deconflicted, and distributed in a matter of a few seconds. Further enhancements to underlying reasoners and advances in computer hardware will continue to improve this performance.

3.3   Beyond Description Logic for Policy Representation

Until recently, KAoS used only OWL-DL (initially DAML) to describe policy-governed entities and their actions. The semantic richness OWL enables in comparison to traditional policy languages allowed us much greater expressivity in specifying policies. However, we found ourselves limited in situations where we needed to define policies where one element of an action's context depended on the value of another part of the context. A simple example is an action of loop communication, where you must constrain the source and the destination of communication so that they're one and the same. A more complex example would be when we want to constrain the action to return the results of a calculation to only the parties that provided the data used to perform it (or to the specific entities the data's providers authorized). Such an action description might be needed to specify a policy controlling the distribution of calculation results. All such action descriptions go beyond what OWL-DL can express.

The required missing aspect of representational semantics has, however, been well studied under the name of role-value maps [10]. These maps should express equality or containment of values that has been reached through two chains of instance properties. The emerging standard for OWL rules, the Semantic Web Rule Language (SWRL, www.daml.org/2003/11/swrl), allows the use of role-value-map semantics. However, the required syntax is complex, and we've begun to think that an OWL-based representation expressing this same semantics might be valuable for a broad range of uses. For instance, the OWL-S developers found the need to express similar dataflow semantics and developed their own formulation (process:sameValues) that allowed the representation of such chains, albeit with the limitation that they could contain only single-chain elements [11].

We have equipped KAoS with mechanisms that will allow adding role-value-map semantics to defined policy action using the KAoS Policy Administration Tool. For the interim, we're basing our syntax for this semantics on the current version of the SWRL OWL ontology. However, the code that generates this syntax is encapsulated in a specialized Java class allowing later modification if the SWRL ontology changes or if an OWL-based syntax eventually emerges. Our classification algorithm can also use this information to classify action instances. This algorithm verifies if an instance satisfies the OWL-DL part of the action class and, if so, checks the appropriate role-value-map constraints. For example, if KAoS needs to determine whether an intercepted communication is a loop communication, it would determine whether the current communication source is also one of the values of the property describing the communication's destination.

To perform more complex policy analyses relying on role-value-map semantics, we've begun joint exploration with Stanford on extending JTP to allow subsumption reasoning on role-value-map semantics.

4   Example Application Contexts

In the remainder of the paper, we will discuss how KAoS is being extended to address two complementary requirements in a Semantic Web Services context:

- Verification for policy compliance for Semantic Web Services workflow composition (section 5),
- Enforcement of policies during the workflow enactment (section 6).

In this section, we briefly introduce the application contexts that motivate these investigations.

4.1   Coalition Search and Rescue Scenario

Within the CoSAR-TS[1] (Coalition Search and Rescue Task Support) project we are testing the integration of KAoS and AIAI's I-X technology with Semantic Web Services. Search and rescue operations, especially coalition based, by nature require the kind of rapid dynamic composition of available policy-constrained heterogeneous resources that make it a good use case to describe them using Semantic Web technologies. Additionally, military operations usually are conducted according to the well defined procedure, which however have to be concretized and grounded to the given situation. This presents a good planning under policy imposed constrained.

---

[1] *http://www.aiai.ed.ac.uk/project/cosar-ts/*

Other participants in this application include BBN Technologies, SPAWAR, AFRL, and Carnegie Mellon University.

The fictitious scenario, which is an extension of the well-know collation agent experiment CoAX[2], begins with an event that reports a downed airman between the coastlines of four fictional nations bordering the Red Sea: Agadez, Binni and Gao (to the West), and Arabello (to the East). In this initial scenario it is assumed that excellent location knowledge is available, and that there are no local threats to counter or avoid in the rescue. The airman reports his own injuries via his suit sensors. Next is an investigation of the facilities available to rescue the airman. There are different possibilities: a US ship-borne helicopter; a Gaoan helicopter from a land base in Binni; a patrol boat from off the Arabello coastline, etc. Finally, there is a process to establish available medical facilities for the specialized injury reported using the information provided about the countries in the region.

Selection of these resources is constrained by different policies originated from different partners of the coalition. If for instance a hospital in Arabello is best placed to provide the facilities, due to the fact that it has the necessary treatment facilities, choices of rescues resources are then restricted. There is a coalition policy that no Gaoan helicopters may be used by coalition members to transport injured airmen.

In addition to IHMC's KAoS, the CoSAR-TS application relies on a variety of I-X technologies from AIAI. I-X Process Panels (*http://i-x.info*; [13; 14]) provide task support by reasoning about and exchanging with other agents and services any combination of Issues, Activities, Constraints and Annotations (elements of the <I-N-C-A> ontology). I-X can therefore provide collaborative task support and exchange of structured messages related to plans, activity and the results of such activity. These types of information can be exchanged with other tools via OWL, RDF or other languages. The system includes a planner that can compose a suitable plan for the given tasks when provided with a library of standard operating procedures or processes, and knowledge of other agents or services that it may use.

Figure 2 shows an I-X Process Panel (I-P^2) and associated I-X Tools. The I-Space tool maintains agent relationships. The relationships can be obtained from agent services such as KAoS. I-X Process Panels can also link to semantic web information and web services, and can be integrated via "I-Q" adaptors [11] to appear in a natural way during planning and in plan execution support.

I-X work has concentrated on dynamically determined workflows at execution time, using knowledge of services, other agent availability, and so on. However, it also offers a process editor for creating process models (I-DE) to populate the domain model and an AI planner (I-Plan), which allows for hierarchical plan creation, precondition achievement, consistent binding of multiple variables, temporal constraint checking, and so forth.

4.2 Semantic Firewall

Another application area allowing us to validate our approach is the Semantic Firewall (SFW) project, developed in collaboration with University of Southampton,

---

2 *http://www.aiai.ed.ac.uk/project/coax/*

Domain Editor   **Process Panel**   **Map Tool**

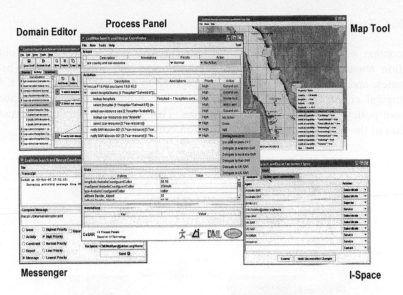

Messenger   I-Space

Fig. 2. I-X Process Panel for a Coalition Search and Rescue Task

IT Innovation, and SRI International [1][1]. In addition to performing standard policy management functions, the system will take as an input a desired client workflow of Grid Services invocations and verify whether the client is authorized to execute such a workflow in the domain controlled by a given instance of the SFW environment. Additionally the policy system may generate obligations in the form of grid service invocations. These obligations have to be executed during the original workflow; for instance in order to preserving provenance[2] of the calculation results. In effect, the initial workflow can be modified and amended with the policies. The resulting policies embedded within the contract governing the transaction will be then enforced by the system as the workflow is enacted.

5   Verification for Policy Compliance in Semantic Web Services Workflow Composition

As a research topic, automatic composition of feasible workflows from a dynamic set of available Semantic Web Services is drawing increasing attention [19]. We argue for applying existing technology and mapping of already developed planners input and output formats to the emerging Semantic Web Services Process Model standard (www.daml.org/services/owl-s/1.0). To this end, we are extending our implementations of I-X and KAoS.

---

[1]   See *http://ontology.ihmc.us/SemanticServices/S-F/Example/index.html* for an example scenario with policies encoded using the KAoS Policy syntax.

[2]   *http://www.pasoa.org/index.html*

5.1   I-K-C Tool

In the context of CoSAR-TS, we've integrated KAoS and I-X to let I-X obtain information about the role relationships among human and software actors (peers, subordinates, and superiors, for example) represented in domains and stored in KAoS as ontological concepts. I-X can also use the KAoS policy disclosure interface to learn about policy impact on its planned actions. This is the first step toward mutual integration of the planning and policy verification components.

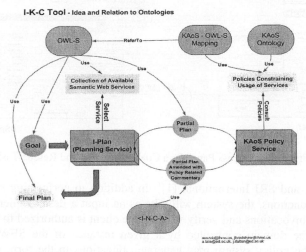

I-K-C Tool - Idea and Relation to Ontologies

Fig. 3. Cooperation between I-X and KAoS in the process of semantic workflow composition

The new I-K-C tool goes beyond the initial integration of I-X and KAoS to enable Semantic Web Services workflow composition consistent with policies that govern composition and enactment (see Figure 3). This approach lets I-X import services described in OWL-S into the planner, augmenting any predefined processes already in the process library. KAoS verifies constructed partial plans for policy compliance. We can export the final plan, represented in OWL-S ontology form, and use it in various enactment systems or to guide the dynamic reactive execution of those plans in I-P^2.

5.2   Mapping the OWL-S Representation of Process to the KAoS Concept of Action

The OWL-S concept of *Process* maps semantically to the KAoS concept of Action[1]. Unfortunately, OWL-S made a dramatic change in representing workflow processes in the transitioning from the earlier ontology called DAML-S. In DAML-S, processes were represented as classes whose instances were process executions and whose input and output parameters were defined as properties of those classes. Parameter restrictions were represented as range constraints on those parameter properties. In

---

[1]   *http://ontology.ihmc.us/Action.owl*

contrast, OWL-S represents processes as instances, and parameters are defined as instances of the class Parameter or its subclasses Input and Output, with their corresponding parameter restrictions defined by the value of the *process:parameterType* property for each parameter. This significant change does not allow for a straightforward mapping between OWL-S and KAoS concepts using *owl:equivalentClass* and *owl:equivalentProperty* as it had been previously possible in the case of DAML-S. OWL-S will define process executions as instances of a *ProcessInstance* class that refers to its process type. This approach is similar to that taken in the Process Specification Language (PSL) [20].

In order to use KAoS reasoning capabilities it is now necessary to create an OWL class based on the OWL-S process definition instance. This is done by changing the *process:parameterType* mentioned above to represent the appropriate restrictions. We are using OWL-S API[2] to load OWL-S process workflows, to find all processes within a workflow, and then to get detailed definitions in order to build, using Jena[1], the corresponding OWL class which is a subclass of the KAoS Action class.

The change in the representation of the process from DAML-S to OWL-S has other consequences:

- You can't build process hierarchies at different abstraction levels using *rdfs:subClassOf*, while you can in the KAoS ontology of actions.

- You can't represent an actual instance of a process—a very concrete realization of the process. Again, in KAoS we use the instance of an action to describe the currently enacted event and then to find whether policies exist that apply to this situation. The envisioned process control ontology, announced as part of OWL-S's future release, will clearly need methods to represent actual events and their relation to processes.

- The process instance doesn't represent the actual event anymore, so the fact that the process in OWL-S is a subclass of *time-entry:IntervalEvent* carried over from DAML-S is a self-contradiction. (OWL-S's developers have promised to resolve this issue in the near future.)

In short, the change of representation of processes between DAML-S and OWL-S was motivated by difficulties related to usage of classes of processes in collections and other issues. However, addressing this problem has created the challenges in the representation of policies in KAoS mentioned above. We hope that the promised improvements in future versions of OWL-S will help to address these issues.

5.3   KAoS Capabilities for Analyzing Action Classes

After KAoS extracts a particular action from the workflow and converts it to a corresponding action class, we examine the action to determine its compliance with the relevant policies in force. The process of workflow policy compliance checking differs from that of checking authorization and obligations of an action instance in policy enforcement that we described earlier. In workflow policy compliance checking, we're not dealing with an action instance but an action class. So, we must

---

[2] *http://www.mindswap.org/2004/owl-s/api/*
[1] *http://jena.sourceforge.net/*

use subsumption reasoning instead of classification reasoning - KAoS must find relations between the current action class and action classes associated with policies. Fortunately, we use this kind of reasoning to perform policy analyses such as policy deconfliction.8 These analyses also involve discovering relations (subsumption or disjointness, for example) between action classes associated with policies.

Such analyses will often lead to deterministic conclusions - for example, that a given process will be authorized or forbidden or that it will definitely generate an obligation. Results will always be deterministic if the given action class representing the investigated process is a subclass of either a single policy action class or a union of some policy action classes, respectively representing either authorization or obligation policies.

Sometimes, however, the analyses can be nondeterministic—that is, we might be able to conclude only that a given process instance could possibly be authorized or that it might generate obligations. This kind of result will occur if the given action class, representing the process in question, is neither fully subsumed nor fully disjoint, with a single policy action class or their unions respectively representing either authorization or obligation policies. In this case, KAoS can build a representation of the action class (either the class that corresponds to the portion of the action class in the authorization request or the one that generates a given obligation) by computing the difference between the current action class and the relevant policy action class. The algorithm is identical to the one we have previously described [3] for policy harmonization. However, we're still working out how to generically translate that new class to an OWL-S process instance representation.

We've developed a first cut of additional KAoS ontology components, enabling workflow annotation with the results of the policy analyses we described. The appropriate markup was added to the original OWL-S workflow using the OWL-S API and sent back from KAoS to the I-X planner.

5.4   Example: Planning Rescue Operation Under Coalition Policy Constraints

The CoSAR-TS scenario described in section 4 is being used to test the capabilities just described. Each time a new search and rescue situation is undertaken; the SAR coordinator gathers available information about the accident and constructs an appropriate goal for the planner. The goal could, for instance, contain information about the kind of injuries sustained and the approximate location of the victim. The planner begins with the selection of an initial plan template that is best for the given situation. It then builds OWL-S profiles for each of the necessary services and queries the Coalition Matchmaker to learn about OWL-S descriptions of registered search and rescue resources. This results in the first approximation of the plan expressed as the OWL-S Process Model. For instance, if the downed pilot has serious burn injuries, the planner will ask the Matchmaker about which services are offered by the burn injuries treatment unit in each medical care center. Subsequently it will ask for available rescue resources, which can pick-up pilot from the sea and deliver it to the chosen hospital (i.e., Arabello). The best result is selected and the OWL-S Process Model is submitted for verification. During workflow analysis, KAoS determines that there is an obligation policy requiring notification of the coalition commander when the downed pilot is successfully recovered. The appropriate process invoking the Notification Service available in the environment as the Web service is inserted into the model and returned to the planner.

6   Enforcement of Policies During Workflow Enactment

Not every aspect of policy compliance can be checked at planning time. Moreover, sometimes the possibility of buggy or malicious code requires runtime checking of compliance. Thus we have designed KAoS so that the policy service can independently enforce policies during workflow execution. The policies governing both authorization and obligation of clients and servers are stored in KAoS and checked by authorized parties. Whereas other approaches to securing Semantic Web Services are limited to either marking service advertisement with requirements for authentication and communication and enforcing compliance with these requirements [5] or by attaching conditions to inputs, outputs and effects of services, KAoS can automatically enforce any sort of policy through integration of Semantic Web Services with KAoS enforcers. These enforcers intercept requests to a service and consult KAoS about relevant authorizations and obligatiosn. KAoS is able to reason about the entire action performed by the services, not just about security credentials attached to the request. Additionally, KAoS is used to generate obligations created during use of the services, not just up front during initial service invocation.

6.1   Matchmaker Policy Enforcement – CoSAR-TS Scenario

While annotation of the Semantic Matchmaker service profiles allows registered service providers to describe required security profiles [5], it does not allow owners of infrastructure resources (e.g., computers, networks), client organizations (coalition organizations, national interest groups), or individuals to specify or enforce policy from their unique perspectives. For example, the policy that coalition members cannot use Gaoan transports is not something that can always be anticipated and specified within the Matchmaker service profile. Neither would Matchmaker service profile annotations be an adequate implementation for a US policy obligating encryption, prioritizing the allocation of network bandwidth, or requiring the logging of certain sorts of messages.

Moreover, the semantics of these policies cannot currently be expressed in terms of the current OWL-S specification of conditional constraints. Even if they were expressible, organizations and individuals may prefer to keep policy stores, reasoners, and enforcement capabilities within their private enclaves. This may be motivated by both the desire to maintain secure control over sensitive components as well as to keep other coalition members from becoming aware of private policies. For example, coalition members may not want Gao to be aware that the offer of their helicopters to rescue the downed airman will be automatically filtered out by policy.

6.2   Generic Semantic Web Service Enforcer

We have defined enforcers that intercept SOAP messages from the Matchmaker and filter results consistent with coalition policies. In our CoSAR-TS demonstration, these policies prevent the use of Gaoan resources.

Our implementation of a SOAP-enabled enforcer is capable of understanding arbitrary Semantic Web Service invocations so it can apply appropriate authorization policies to them. Additionally, it is equipped with a mechanism to perform obligation policies, which will be in the form of other Web Service invocations. For instance, an obligation policy may require the recording of certain kinds of service transactions through a logging service.

7   Conclusions

KAoS provides necessary capabilities to verify and enforce user-defined policy in the automatic process of planning and executing workflows of semantically described processes in the area of processes building such workflows. Future work will investigate how to take a context surrounding the process (i.e., processes and control constructs) in a given workflow into account.

Currently, KAoS is able to analyze OWL-S encoded workflows, however it can be extended to understand other form of descriptions (e.g., WSMO (Web Service Modeling Ontology)[1]) that share similar concepts of basic process and workflow composition abstractions.

Acknowledgements. This material is based on research sponsored by the Defense Advanced Research Projects Agency (DARPA) CoABS, DAML, and Ultra*Log programs the US Air Force Research Laboratory under agreement numbers F30602-00-2-0577 and F30602-03-2-0014, by NASA IS and X-Enterprise grants, by ONR, and the Army Research Labs. The U.S. Government, IHMC, and the University of Edinburgh are authorized to reproduce and distribute reprints and on-line copies for their purposes notwithstanding any copyright annotation hereon. Thanks to the other members of the KAoS project team: Maggie Breedy, Larry Bunch, Matthew Johnson, Hyuckchul Jung, Shri Kulkarni, James Lott, William Taysom, and Gianluca Tonti. We are also grateful for the contributions of Mark Burstein, Pat Hayes, Luc Moreau, Grit Denker, Darren Marvin, Mike Surridge, Ron Ashri, Terry Payne, Katia Sycara, Massimo Paolucci, Naveen Srinivasan, Niranjan Suri, Paul Feltovich, Richard Fikes, Jessica Jenkins, Bill Millar, Deborah McGuinness, Rich Feiertag, Timothy Redmond, Rebecca Montanari, Sue Rho, Ken Ford, Mark Greaves, Jack Hansen, James Allen, Lars Olson, and Robert Hoffman.

---

http://www.wsmo.org/

References

[1]   Ashri, R., Payne, T. R., & Surridge, M. (2004). Towards a Semantic Web Security Infrastructure. *AAAI Spring Symposium on Semantic Web Services*. Stanford University,

[2]   Bradshaw, J. M., Beautement, M. Breedy, L. Bunch, S. Drakunov, P. Feltovich, P., Raj, A., Johnson, M., Kulkarni, S., Suri, N. & A. Uszok (2004). Making agents acceptable to people. In N. Zhong & J. Liu (Ed.), *Intelligent Technologies for Information Analysis: Advances in Agents, Data Mining, and Statistical Learning*. (pp. 361-400). Berlin: Springer Verlag.

[3]   Bradshaw, J. M., Uszok, A., Jeffers, R., Suri, N., Hayes, P., Burstein, M. H., Acquisti, A., Benyo, B., Breedy, M. R., Carvalho, M., Diller, D., Johnson, M., Kulkarni, S., Lott, J., Sierhuis, M., & Van Hoof, R. (2003). Representation and reasoning for DAML-based policy and domain services in KAoS and Nomads. *Proceedings of the Autonomous Agents and Multi-Agent Systems Conference (AAMAS 2003)*. Melbourne, Australia, New York, NY: ACM Press,

[4]   Damianou, N., Dulay, N., Lupu, E. C., & Sloman, M. S. (2000). *Ponder: A Language for Specifying Security and Management Policies for Distributed Systems, Version 2.3*. Imperial College of Science, Technology and Medicine, Department of Computing, 20 October 2000.

[5]   Denker, G., Kagal, L., Finin, T., Paolucci, M., & Sycara, K. (2003). Security for DAML Web Services: Annotation and Matchmaking. In D. Fensel, K. Sycara, & J. Mylopoulos (Ed.), *The Semantic Web—ISWC 2003. Proceedings of the Second International Semantic Web Conference, Sanibel Island, Florida, USA, October 2003, LNCS 2870*. (pp. 335-350). Berlin: Springer.

[6]   Feltovich, P., Bradshaw, J. M., Jeffers, R., Suri, N., & Uszok, A. (2004). Social order and adaptability in animal and human cultures as an analogue for agent communities: Toward a policy-based approach. In *Engineering Societies in the Agents World IV*. (pp. 21-48). Berlin, Germany: Springer-Verlag.

[7]   Fensel, D., Hendler, J., Lieberman, H., & Wahlster, W. (Ed.). (2003). *Spinning the Semantic Web*. Cambridge, MA: The MIT Press.

[8]   Kagal, L., Finin, T., & Joshi, A. (2003). A policy-based approach to security for the Semantic Web. In D. Fensel, K. Sycara, & J. Mylopoulos (Ed.), *The Semantic Web— ISWC 2003. Proceedings of the Second International Semantic Web Conference, Sanibel Island, Florida, USA, October 2003, LNCS 2870*. (pp. 402-418).: Springer.

[9]   Li, N., Grosof, B. N., & Feigenbaum, J. (2003). Delegation logic: A logic-based approach to distributed authorization. *ACM Transactions on Information Systems Security (TISSEC)*, 1-42.

[10] McIlraith, S. A., Son, T. C., & Zeng, H. (2001). Semantic Web Services. *IEEE Intelligent Systems*, 46-53.

[11] Potter, S., Tate, A., & Dalton, J. (2003). I-X Task support on the Semantic Web. *Poster and Demonstration Proceedings for the Second International Semantic Web Conference (ISWC 2003)*. Sanibel Island, FL,

[12] Seamons, K. E., Winslett, M., Yu, T., Smith, B., Child, E., Jacobson, J., Mills, H., & Yu, L. (2002). Requirements for policy languages for trust negotiation. *Proceedings of the Third International Workshop on Policies for Distributed Systems and Networks (POLICY 2002)*. Monterey, CA,

[13] Tate, A. (2003). Coalition task support using I-X and <I-N-C-A>. In *Proceedings of the Third International Central and Eastern European Conference on Multi-Agent Systems (CEEMAS 2003), 16-18 June, Prague, Czech Republic, LNAI 2691*. (pp. 7-16). Berlin: Springer.

[14] Tate, A., Dalton, J., Siebra, C., Aitken, S., Bradshaw, J.M. and Uszok, A. (2004) Intelligent Agents for Coalition Search and Rescue Task Support, AAAI-2004 Intelligent Systems Demonstrator, in Proceedings of the Nineteenth National Conference of the American Association of Artificial Intelligence, (AAAI-2004), San Jose, California, USA, July 2004.,

[15] Tonti, G., Bradshaw, J. M., Jeffers, R., Montanari, R., Suri, N., & Uszok, A. (2003). Semantic Web languages for policy representation and reasoning: A comparison of KAoS, Rei, and Ponder. In D. Fensel, K. Sycara, & J. Mylopoulos (Ed.), *The Semantic Web—ISWC 2003. Proceedings of the Second International Semantic Web Conference, Sanibel Island, USA, 2003, LNCS 2870.* (pp. 419-437). Berlin: Springer.

[16] Uszok, A., Bradshaw, J. M., Hayes, P., Jeffers, R., Johnson, M., Kulkarni, S., Breedy, M. R., Lott, J., & Bunch, L. (2003). DAML reality check: A case study of KAoS domain and policy services. *Submitted to the International Semantic Web Conference (ISWC 03).* Sanibel Island, Florida,

[17] Uszok, A., Bradshaw, J. M., Jeffers, R., Suri, N., Hayes, P., Breedy, M. R., Bunch, L., Johnson, M., Kulkarni, S., & Lott, J. (2003). KAoS policy and domain services: Toward a description-logic approach to policy representation, deconfliction, and enforcement. *Proceedings of Policy 2003.* Como, Italy,

[18] Wright, S., Chadha, R., & Lapiotis, G. (2002). Special Issue on Policy-Based Networking. *IEEE Network*, 16(2), 8-56.

[19] Wu, D., Parsia, B., Sirin, E., Hendler, J., & Nau, D. (2003). Automating DAML-S Web Services composition using SHOP2. In D. Fensel, K. Sycara, & J. Mylopoulos (Ed.), *The Semantic Web—ISWC 2003. Proceedings of the Second International Semantic Web Conference, Sanibel Island, Florida, USA, October 2003, LNCS 2870.* (pp. 195-210). Berlin: Springer.

[20] Schlenoff, C., Gruninger M., Tissot, F., Valois, J., Lubell, J., Lee, J. (2000). The Process Specification Language (PSL): Overview and Version 1.0 Specification," NISTIR 6459, *National Institute of Standards and Technology*, Gaithersburg, MD.

Knowledge-Intensive Induction of Terminologies from Metadata

Floriana Esposito, Nicola Fanizzi, Luigi Iannone, Ignazio Palmisano, and
Giovanni Semeraro

Dipartimento di Informatica, Università degli Studi di Bari
Via Orabona 4, 70125 Bari, Italy
{esposito,fanizzi,iannone,palmisano,semeraro}@di.uniba.it

Abstract. We focus on the induction and revision of terminologies from
metadata. Following a Machine Learning approach, this setting can be
cast as a search problem to be solved employing operators that traverse the search space expressed in a structural representation, aiming
at correct concept definitions. The progressive refinement of such definitions in a terminology is driven by the available extensional knowledge
(metadata). A knowledge-intensive inductive approach to this task is
presented, that can deal with on the expressive Semantic Web representations based on Description Logics, which are endowed with well-
founded reasoning capabilities. The core inferential mechanism, based
on multilevel counterfactuals, can be used for either inducing new concept descriptions or refining existing (incorrect) ones. The soundness of
the approach and its applicability are also proved and discussed[1].

1 Introduction

The Semantic Web (SW) relies on ontological knowledge in order to gain a semantic interoperability for organizing and processing resources on the ground
of their meaning. Though SW actors adopt ontologies as a formal tool for semantic convergence, these are the outcome of a complex engineering process of
acquisition and harmonization that is still limitedly machine-aided. Automated
reasoning is typically exploited to assist knowledge engineers in the detection
of failures in the ontologies. However, harder problems involving (non standard)
inferences, such as the induction or revision of defective semantic knowledge is
typically delegated to knowledge engineers. The actors ought to be able not only
to detect inconsistent sections in the knowledge bases shared with their *peers*,
but also to adopt proper counter-measures to revise them accordingly and maintain a sound source of semantic information. A particular aspect of this kind of

[1] This research was partially funded by the European Commission under the IST Integrated Project VIKEF - Virtual Information and Knowledge Environment Framework (Contract no. 507173 - more information at http://www.vikef.net) and by
National Ministry of Instruction University and Research Project COFIN 2003 "Tec-
niche di intelligenza artificiale per il reperimento di informazione di qualita' sul Web".

problems is investigated. A domain ontology, supposed to be described by an ontology data model, proves itself incorrect (incomplete or inconsistent) with respect to processed assertional knowledge (metadata). Such a flawed information undermines the very foundations of semantic interoperability. Ideally, the required knowledge revision should be operated in a (semi)automatic fashion at a machine level so that the knowledge engineer's duties reduce to the mere checking of the outcomes. The induction and revision of structural knowledge is not new issue for *Machine Learning*, though it has been investigated for poorly expressive languages. Description Logics (henceforth DLs) and derived markup languages are a sort of *de facto* standard for representing ontologies owing to their well-founded semantics and available reasoning services [1]. DLs represent a peculiar fragment of First Order Logic that is comparable to graph representations. The induction of such a structural knowledge is known as a hard task [2]. Recently, in *Logic Programming* contexts, attempts have been made to extend relational learning techniques toward more expressive languages such as *prenex conjunctive normal forms* [3] or hybrid representations [4,5]. In order to cope with the complexity issues, former methods use heuristic search and generally implement bottom-up algorithms, such as the *least common subsumer* (*lcs*) [6]. Yet this induces overly specific concept definitions, which may have poor predictive capabilities (the phenomenon of *overfitting*). Moreover, for many DLs, it is well known that lcs's do not yield a compact representation of the generalizations [7]. Hence, other works propose heuristic generalizations [8].

Further approaches have shown that also a top-down search of concept definitions is feasible [9], yet the proposed methods are less operational. They can be considered as a theoretical study of the search space properties since the exploitation of the assertions in the refinement process is neglected, in favor of a generate and test strategy that can turn out to be in practice very inefficient.

A more knowledge-intensive refinement method is needed for concept definitions. Besides, when new assertions become available and turn out to be inconsistent w.r.t. the previously defined ontology, it is computationally expensive to re-build the the concept definitions accordingly. Thus the revision process should be possibly performed incrementally on the ground of the metadata.

In our investigation the learning problem is cast as a search problem in the space determined by an expressive DL representation. Imposing an order over the space of concept descriptions, we give the definition of theoretical operators that can traverse the space seeking a solution to the problem. Intending to give operational instruments for inference and refinement of conceptual descriptions, we introduce an algorithm based on multilevel counterfactuals [10] for operating with an $\mathcal{ALC}$ [11] representation (yet extensions to other DLs should be possible).

The method is based on mutually recursive cycles of specialization and generalization with respect to the (newly) available assertions (examples) regarding the concepts to be revised. The intuition is that specialization can be obtained learning exceptions, while generalizations stand as exceptions to exceptions, so on. We show how this method can be adapted to the DLs representation,

Table 1. The constructors for $\mathcal{ALC}$ descriptions and their interpretation.

NAME	SYNTAX	SEMANTICS
top concept	$\top$	$\Delta^{\mathcal{I}}$
bottom concept	$\bot$	$\emptyset$
concept negation	$\neg C$	$\Delta^{\mathcal{I}} \setminus C^{\mathcal{I}}$
concept conjunction	$C_1 \sqcap C_2$	$C_1^{\mathcal{I}} \cap C_2^{\mathcal{I}}$
concept disjunction	$C_1 \sqcup C_2$	$C_1^{\mathcal{I}} \cup C_2^{\mathcal{I}}$
existential restriction	$\exists R.C$	$\{x \in \Delta^{\mathcal{I}} \mid \exists y \; (x,y) \in R^{\mathcal{I}} \wedge y \in C^{\mathcal{I}}\}$
universal restriction	$\forall R.C$	$\{x \in \Delta^{\mathcal{I}} \mid \forall y \; (x,y) \in R^{\mathcal{I}} \rightarrow y \in C^{\mathcal{I}}\}$

converging to correct concept definitions (with respect to the intended model of the knowledge).

The paper is organized as follows. After the next preliminary section introducing the representation, in Sect. 3 the search space and its properties are presented. The method for learning and refining DL concept definitions is illustrated in Sect. 4, where its applicability is also briefly analyzed. Finally, possible extensions of the method are discussed in Sect. 5.

2   Syntax and Semantics

Most of the SW languages (RDF Schema, DAML+OIL, OWL) have their theoretical foundations in Description Logics. These formalisms are fragments of First Order Logic with different degrees of expressive powers. They rely on well-founded descriptive style semantics and offer efficient reasoning services (deductive inferences) such as subsumption, consistency and instance check. It is straightforward that the efficiency of reasoning is strongly dependent on the language expressiveness [1]. In this section we recall syntax and semantics for the reference representation $\mathcal{ALC}$ [11] adopted in the paper, although the method is also extensible to other DLs. Moreover, examples are shown where the DL constructs are mapped onto the descriptions in SW languages.

In a DL language, primitive *concepts* $N_C = \{C, D, \ldots\}$ are interpreted as subsets of a certain domain of objects (resources) and primitive *roles* $N_R = \{R, S, \ldots\}$ are interpreted as binary relations on such a domain (properties). More complex concept descriptions are built using atomic concepts and primitive roles by means of the constructors in Table 1. Their meaning is defined by an *interpretation* $\mathcal{I} = (\Delta^{\mathcal{I}}, \cdot^{\mathcal{I}})$, where $\Delta^{\mathcal{I}}$ is the *domain* of the interpretation and the functor $\cdot^{\mathcal{I}}$ stands for the *interpretation function*, mapping the intension of concepts and roles to their extension.

A *knowledge base* $\mathcal{K} = \langle \mathcal{T}, \mathcal{A} \rangle$ contains two components: a T-box $\mathcal{T}$ and an A-box $\mathcal{A}$. $\mathcal{T}$ is a set of concept definitions $C \equiv D$, meaning $C^{\mathcal{I}} = D^{\mathcal{I}}$, where C is the concept name and D is a description given in terms of the language constructors. $\mathcal{A}$ contains extensional assertions on concepts and roles, e.g. $C(a)$ and $R(a,b)$, meaning, respectively, that $a^{\mathcal{I}} \in C^{\mathcal{I}}$ and $(a^{\mathcal{I}}, b^{\mathcal{I}}) \in R^{\mathcal{I}}$.

The semantic notion of *subsumption* between concepts (or roles) can be given in terms of the interpretations:

Definition 2.1 (subsumption). *Given two concept descriptions C and D in $\mathcal{T}$, C subsumes D, denoted by $C \sqsupseteq D$, iff for every interpretation $\mathcal{I}$ of $\mathcal{T}$ it holds that $C^{\mathcal{I}} \supseteq D^{\mathcal{I}}$. Hence, $C \equiv D$ amounts to $C \sqsupseteq D$ and $D \sqsupseteq C$.*

Example 2.1. An instance of concept definition in the proposed language is:
$Father \equiv Human \sqcap Male \sqcap \exists hasChild.Human$
which translates the sentence: *"a father is a male human that has some humans as his children"*. A-box assertions look like:
$Father(Tom)$, $Father(Bill)$, $hasChild.Human(Bill, Joe)$ and so on.
Now, if we define two new concepts:
$FatherWithoutSons \equiv Human \sqcap Male \sqcap \exists hasChild.Human \sqcap \forall hasChild.(\neg Male)$
$Parent \equiv Human \sqcap (Male \sqcup Female) \sqcap \exists hasChild.Human$
then it is easy to see that $Father \sqsupseteq FatherWithoutSons$ and $Parent \sqsupseteq Father$, yet $Father \not\sqsupseteq Parent$ and $FatherWithoutSons \not\sqsupseteq Father$
The corresponding OWL/XML representation can be found in Figure 1.

Many semantically equivalent (yet syntactically different) descriptions can be given for the same concept. However they can be reduced to a canonical form by means of rewriting rules that preserve their equivalence, e.g. $\forall R.C_1 \sqcap \forall R.C_2 \equiv \forall R.(C_1 \sqcap C_2)$ (see [1] for normalization and simplification issues). Preliminarily, some notation is needed to name the different parts of an $\mathcal{ALC}$ description: $prim(C)$ is the set of all the concepts at the top-level conjunction of C; if there exists a universal restriction $\forall R.C'$ on the top-level of C then $val_R(C) = C'$ otherwise $val_R(C) = \top$ (a single one because of the equivalence mentioned above). Finally, $ex_R(C)$ is the set of the concept descriptions C' appearing in existential restrictions $\exists R.C'$ at the top-level conjunction of C.

Definition 2.2 (normal form). *A concept description D is in $\mathcal{ALC}$ normal form iff $D \equiv \bot$ or $D \equiv \top$ or if $D = D_1 \sqcup \cdots \sqcup D_n$ with*

$$D_i = \prod_{A \in prim(D_i)} A \sqcap \prod_{R \in N_R} \left[\prod_{V \in val_R(D_i)} \forall R.V \sqcap \prod_{E \in ex_R(D_i)} \exists R.E \right]$$

where, for all $i = 1, \ldots, n$, $D_i \not\equiv \bot$ and, for any R, every sub-description in $ex_R(D_i)$ and $val_R(D_i)$ is in normal form.

This form will be employed for defining an ordering over the concept descriptions and the refinement operators.

3 Induction as Search

The problem of induction in its simplest form can be now formally defined as a supervised learning task:

```
<!ENTITY ns1 "http://www.myontos/Friend#">
<rdf:RDF ... >
  <owl:Class rdf:about="&ns1;FatherWithoutSons">
    <rdfs:subClassOf>
      <owl:Restriction>
        <owl:onProperty><rdf:Property rdf:about="&ns1;hasChild"/>
        </owl:onProperty>
        <owl:minCardinality>1</owl:minCardinality>
      </owl:Restriction>
    </rdfs:subClassOf>
    <rdfs:subClassOf><owl:Class rdf:about="&ns1;Male"/>
    </rdfs:subClassOf>
    <rdfs:subClassOf>
      <owl:Restriction>
        <owl:onProperty><rdf:Property rdf:about="&ns1;hasFemaleChild"/>
        </owl:onProperty>
        <owl:maxCardinality>0</owl:maxCardinality>
      </owl:Restriction>
    </rdfs:subClassOf>
  </owl:Class>
  <owl:Class rdf:about="&ns1;Female">
    <rdfs:subClassOf><owl:Class rdf:about="&ns1;Human"/>
    </rdfs:subClassOf>
  </owl:Class>
  <owl:Class rdf:about="&ns1;MaleOrFemale">
    <owl:unionOf rdf:parseType="Collection">
      <owl:Class rdf:about="&ns1;Male"/>
      <owl:Class rdf:about="&ns1;Female"/>
    </owl:unionOf>
  </owl:Class>
  <owl:Class rdf:about="&ns1;Parent">
    <rdfs:subClassOf rdf:resource="&ns1;Human"/>
    <rdfs:subClassOf rdf:resource="&ns1;MaleOrFemale"/>
  </owl:Class>
  <owl:Class rdf:about="&ns1;Male">
    <rdfs:subClassOf rdf:resource="&ns1;Human"/>
  </owl:Class>
  <rdf:Property rdf:about="&ns1;hasFemaleChild">
    <rdfs:range rdf:resource="&ns1;Female"/>
    <rdfs:subPropertyOf rdf:resource="&ns1;hasChild"/>
  </rdf:Property>
</rdf:RDF>
```

Fig. 1. OWL/XML representation of Example 2.1

Definition 3.1 (learning problem). *In a search space* $(\mathcal{S}, \succeq)$
Given a knowledge base $\mathcal{K} = \langle \mathcal{T}, \mathcal{A} \rangle$ *and a set of positive and negative assertions* $\mathcal{A}_C = \mathcal{A}_C^+ \cup \mathcal{A}_C^-$ *regarding the membership (or non-membership) of some*

individuals to a concept C such that: $\mathcal{T} \not\models \mathcal{A} \cup \mathcal{A}_C$
Find *a new T-box* $\mathcal{T}' = (\mathcal{T} \setminus \{C \equiv D\}) \cup \{C \equiv D'\}$ *such that:* $\mathcal{T}' \models \mathcal{A} \cup \mathcal{A}_C$

Thus, if a concept C is not defined in the terminology $\mathcal{T}$ we have a case of an *induction problem* requiring to find definitions $C \equiv D$ entailing the (new) assertions in $\mathcal{A}_C$. Conversely, when an existing definition in $\mathcal{T}$ proves to be incorrect i.e. it is uncapable of entailing the positive assertions in $\mathcal{A}_C$ (*incomplete* definition) or it entails negative ones (*inconsistent* definition), this yields a *refinement problem* where a new correct definition $C \equiv D'$ is to be found on the ground of the previous one and the new examples.

The induction of the definitions can be modeled as a search in the space of candidate definitions. First, the search space of concept descriptions must be taken into account for the target language. This space is defined once a quasi-ordering on the descriptions is adopted (i.e. subsumption); then, definitions of refinement operators should be given for deciding the traversal of the search space. The (algebraic) properties of the *search space* obviously depend on the ordering imposed over its components (concept descriptions). This notion, in turn, induces a generalization model (a quasi-ordering) that gives a criterion for traversing the space of solutions by means of suitable operators.

In order to traverse the search space seeking for correct concept definitions solving the learning problem, we will employ the notion of particular operators:

Definition 3.2 (refinement operators). *In a quasi-ordered space* $(\mathcal{S}, \succeq)$, *a downward (respectively upward) refinement operator* ρ *(resp.* δ*) is a mapping from* $\mathcal{S}$ *to* $2^{\mathcal{S}}$, *such that* $D' \in \rho(D)$ *implies* $D \succeq D'$ *(resp.* $D' \in \delta(D)$ *implies* $D' \succeq D$*).* D' *is called a* specialization *(resp.* generalization*) of* D

Here the order should be based on the subsumption relationship. It is now possible to specify refinement operators for the reference search space. Preliminarily, the definition of a difference operator is needed for both conjunctive and disjunctive descriptions. In the former case, $C = C_1 \sqcap \cdots \sqcap C_n$, the difference is the generalized conjunct resulting from removing one conjunct: $C - C_i = \sqcap_{k \neq i} C_k$. In the latter case, $D = D_1 \sqcup \cdots \sqcup D_m$, the difference is the specialized disjunct $D - D_j = \bigsqcup_{k \neq j} D_k$. Taking into account the $\mathcal{ALC}$ normal form, each level of a concept description interleaves disjunctive or conjunctive descriptions. Thus, the operators should accommodate either case.

Definition 3.3 (downward operator). *In the search space* $(\mathcal{ALC}, \sqsupseteq)$, *the downward refinement operator* $\rho_{\sqcup}$ *for disjunctive concept descriptions (in $\mathcal{ALC}$ normal form)* $D = D_1 \sqcup \cdots \sqcup D_n$ *is defined as follows:*

- $D' \in \rho_{\sqcup}(D)$ *if* $D' = D - D_i$ *for some* $1 \leq i \leq n$
- $D' \in \rho_{\sqcup}(D)$ *if* $D' = (D - D_i) \sqcup D_i'$ *for some* $D_i' \in \rho_{\sqcap}(D_i)$, $1 \leq i \leq n$

where the downward refinement operator $\rho_{\sqcap}$, *given a conjunctive concept description* $C = C_1 \sqcap \cdots \sqcap C_m$, *is defined as follows:*

$C' \in \rho_{\sqcap}(C)$ *if* $C' = C \sqcap C_{j+1}$ *for some* $C_{j+1} \not\sqsupseteq C$

- $C' \in \rho_\sqcap(C)$ if $C' = (C - C_j) \sqcap C'_j$ for some $1 \le j \le m$, where:
  - $C'_j = \exists R.D'_j$, $C_j = \exists R.D_j$ and $D'_j \in \rho_\sqcup(D_j)$ or
  - $C'_j = \forall R.D'_j$, $C_j = \forall R.D_j$ and $D'_j \in \rho_\sqcup(D_j)$

It is straightforward to define the dual upward operator that seeks for more general hypotheses by dropping disjuncts or refining them.

Definition 3.4 (upward operator). *In the search space* $(\mathcal{ALC}, \sqsupseteq)$*, the upward refinement operator* $\delta_\sqcup$ *for disjunctive concept descriptions (in* $\mathcal{ALC}$ *normal form)* $D = D_1 \sqcup \cdots \sqcup D_n$ *is defined as follows:*

- $D' \in \delta_\sqcup(D)$ if $D' = D \sqcup D_{n+1}$ for some D_{n+1} such that $D_{n+1} \not\sqsubseteq D$
- $D' \in \delta_\sqcup(D)$ if $D' = (D - D_i) \sqcup D'_i$ for some $D'_i \in \delta_\sqcap(D_i)$, $1 \le i \le n$

where the upward refinement operator $\delta_\sqcap$, *given a conjunctive concept description* $C = C_1 \sqcap \cdots \sqcap C_m$, *is defined:*

- $C' \in \delta_\sqcap(C)$ if $C' = C - C_j$ for some $1 \le j \le m$
- $C' \in \delta_\sqcap(C)$ if $C' = (C - C_j) \sqcap C'_j$ for some $1 \le j \le m$, where:
  - $C'_j = \exists R.D'_j$, $C_j = \exists R.D_j$ and $D'_j \in \delta_\sqcup(D_j)$ or
  - $C'_j = \forall R.D'_j$, $C_j = \forall R.D_j$ and $D'_j \in \delta_\sqcup(D_j)$

Several properties of the refinement operators may be investigated such as *completeness, ideality, minimality* and *non-redundancy* [9]. Although theoretical results for these operators have been found (i.e. non ideality, completeness, local finiteness), these issues are beyond the intended scope of this paper. Defining both upward and downward operators allows for the specification of an inductive algorithm for T-box refinement that exploits the information provided by the examples and that is presented in the following section.

4   Induction of Concept Descriptions Based on Assertions

The main idea is to combine theoretic refinement operators with heuristics in order to converge toward a solution of the learning problem. The efficiency of this method derives from biasing inductive search with information coming from assertions. These, indeed, can indicate the search directions in order to avoid mere generate and test refinements and converge more rapidly to the solution. The methodology for the induction and refinement of T-boxes proposed in this work is based on the notion of counterfactuals built on the ground of residual learning problems [10]. We discuss its correctness, applicability and some issues related to its complexity.

4.1   The Method

It is assumed that the learning process can start exclusively from the examples and counterexamples in the A-box of the concept for which a new definition is required. This classification is assumed to be given by a trainer (the knowledge engineer). However, the methodology would apply also for a similar yet different setting where the starting hypothesis for the target concept is already available in a given T-box, which may have turned out to be incorrect (overly general) for entailing some (new) assertions that have been classified as being negative for the target concept.

Each assertion is not processed as such: it is supposed that a representative at the concept language level (*single representation trick*) is preliminarily derived in the form of *most specific concept* (*msc*). The msc required by the algorithm is a maximally specific DL concept description that entails the given assertion. Since, in some DL it does not exist, we consider their approximations up to a certain depth [12]. Hence, in the algorithm the positive and negative examples will be very specific conjunctive descriptions obtained by means of the *realization* [13] of the assertions concerning the target concept. For many DLs the msc cannot be easily computed or simply it is not unique. For our purposes it suffices to have good (upper) approximations. The algorithm relies on two interleaving routines (see Figure 2) performing, respectively, generalization and specialization, that call each other for converging at a correct concept definition.

The generalization algorithm is a greedy covering one: it tries to explain the positive examples by constructing a disjunctive definition. At each outer iteration, a very specialized definition (the msc of an example) is selected as a starting seed for a new partial generalization; then, iteratively, the hypothesis is generalized by means of the upward operator δ (with a heuristic that privileges the refinements that cover the most of the positives) until all positive concept representatives are covered or some negative representatives are explained. In such a case, the current concept definition *ParGen* has to be specialized by some counterfactuals. The co-routine, which receives the covered examples as its input, finds a sub-description K that is capable of ruling out the negative examples previously covered. In the routine for building counterfactuals, given a previously computed hypothesis *ParGen*, which is supposed to be complete (covering the positive assertions) yet inconsistent with respect to some negative assertions, the aim is finding those counterfactuals to be conjuncted to the initial hypothesis for restoring a correct definition, that can rule out the negative instances. The algorithm is based on the construction of residual learning problems based on the sub-descriptions that caused the subsumption of the negative examples, represented by their msc's. In this case, for each model a residual is derived by considering that part of the incorrect definition *ParGen* that did not play a role in the subsumption. The residual will be successively employed as a positive instance of that part of description that should be ruled out of the definition (through negation). Analogously the msc's derived from positive assertions will play the opposite role of negative instances for the residual learning problem under construction. Finally, this problem is solved by calling the co-routine which generalizes these example descriptions and then conjoining its negation of the returned result.

generalization(*Positives, Negatives, Generalization*)
input *Positives, Negatives*: positive and negative instances at concept level;
output *Generalization*: generalized concept definition
begin
ResPositives ← *Positives*
Generalization ← ⊥
while *ResPositives* ≠ ∅ **do**
   ParGen ← select_seed(*ResPositives*)
   CoveredPos ← {*Pos* ∈ *ResPositives* | *ParGen* ⊒ *Pos*}
   CoveredNeg ← {*Neg* ∈ *Negatives* | *ParGen* ⊒ *Neg*}
   while *CoveredPos* ≠ *ResPositives* **and** *CoveredNeg* = ∅ **do**
     ParGen ← select(δ(*ParGen*), *ResPositives*)
     CoveredPos ← {*Pos* ∈ *ResPositives* | *ParGen* ⊒ *Pos*}
     CoveredNeg ← {*Neg* ∈ *Negatives* | *ParGen* ⊒ *Neg*}
   if *CoveredNeg* ≠ ∅ **then**
     K ← **counterfactuals**(*ParGen, CoveredPos, CoveredNeg*)
     ParGen ← *ParGen* ⊓ ¬*K*
   Generalization ← *Generalization* ⊔ *ParGen*
   ResPositives ← *ResPositives* \ *CoveredPos*
return *Generalization*
end

counterfactuals(*ParGen, CoveredPos, CoveredNeg, K*)
input *ParGen*: inconsistent concept definition
   CoveredPos, CoveredNeg: covered positive and negative descriptions
output *K*: counterfactual
begin
NewPositives ← ∅
NewNegatives ← ∅
for each N_i ∈ *CoveredNeg* **do**
   $NewP_i$ ← residual(N_i, *ParGen*)
   NewPositives ← *NewPositives* ∪ {$NewP_i$}
for each P_j ∈ *CoveredPos* **do**
   $NewN_j$ ← residual(P_j, *ParGen*)
   NewNegatives ← *NewNegatives* ∪ {$NewN_j$}
K ← **generalization**(*NewPositives, NewNegatives*)
return *K*
end

Fig. 2. The co-routines used in the method.

Example 4.1. Suppose to have the RDF metadata fragment as in Figure 3, the resulting A-box[2] is:
$\mathcal{A}$ = {$IP(j), \neg IP(f), \neg IP(m), \neg IP(h), R(j), F(j, j_1), I(j_1), F(j, j_2), I(j_2),$
  $R(f), R(m), F(m, m_1), I(m_1), F(m, m_2), F(h, h_1), F(h, h_2), I(h_2)$}

---

[2] where *R* stands for *rich*, *I* stands for *influential* and *F* stands for the *hasFriend* relationship (an example taken from [9]).

The msc's of the examples in the A-Box are the following[3]:

$$msc(j) R \sqcap \exists F.I \sqcap \forall F.I \qquad mmsc(f) = R$$
$$msc(m) = R \sqcap \exists F.I \qquad mmsc(h) = \exists F.I \sqcap \forall F.I$$

The algorithm is presented with the incorrect definition $G_1 = \top$ for the target concept IP. This definition turns out to cover the example description $msc(j)$ and all the counterexample descriptions. Thus the routine *counterfactuals* is in charge for building a residual learning problem by computing the new examples.

Then, $Neg_j^1 = msc(j)$ is the only counterexample and $Pos_f^1 = msc(f)$, $Pos_m^1 = msc(m)$ and $Pos_h^1 = msc(h)$ are the examples for the new learning problem. Suppose Pos_f^1 is chosen as a seed description G_2. It turns out to be overly general since it would cover Pos_f^1, Pos_m^1 and Neg_j^1 but not Pos_h^1. In a new inner call, *counterfactuals* computes the following residuals (beside $Neg_m^2 = \top$):

$$Pos_j^2 = Neg_j^1 - G_2 = (R \sqcap \exists F.I \sqcap \forall F.I) \sqcup \neg R = \top \sqcap ((\exists F.I \sqcap \exists \forall F.I) \sqcup \neg R) = (\exists F.I \sqcap \forall F.I) \sqcup \neg R$$

$$Neg_m^2 = Pos_m^1 - G_2 = (R \sqcap \exists F.I) \sqcup \neg R = \top \sqcap (\neg R \sqcup \exists F.I) = \neg R \sqcup \exists F.I$$

Now, a trivial generalization G_3 amounts to the example description Pos_j^2 that does not cover the negative example description Neg_m^2. Then, returning from the inner call, we got a new specialized generalization $G_2 := G_2 \sqcap \neg G_3 = R \sqcap \neg ((\exists F.I \sqcap \forall F.I) \sqcup \neg R) = R \sqcap (\neg (\exists F.I \sqcap \forall F.I) \sqcap R) = R \sqcap \neg (\exists F.I \sqcap \forall F.I)$ which is consistent because it now rules out Neg_j^1. Yet it is not complete for it covers Pos_f^1 and Pos_m^1 but not Pos_h^1; then a new generalization problem is issued for producing a second disjunct.

The very Pos_h^1 is used as a seed for the new generalization G_2'. Since it covers the negative description Neg_j^1. Then the counterfactual found for this small problem is $K_2 := Neg_j^1 - Pos_h^1 = (R \sqcap \exists F.I \sqcap \forall F.I) \sqcup \neg (\exists F.I \sqcap \forall F.I) = (R \sqcup \neg (\exists F.I \sqcap \forall F.I)) \sqcap \top = R \sqcup \neg (\exists F.I \sqcap \forall F.I)$ and the corresponding generalization is $G_2' = Pos_h^1 \sqcap \neg K_2 = (\exists F.I \sqcap \forall F.I) \sqcap \neg (R \sqcup \neg (\exists F.I \sqcap \forall F.I)) = \neg R \sqcap (\exists F.I \sqcap \forall F.I)$ that covers Pos_h^1 but not Neg_j^1.

Recollecting the two disjuncts $G_2 = (R \sqcap \neg (\exists F.I \sqcap \forall F.I)) \sqcup (\neg R \sqcap (\exists F.I \sqcap \forall F.I))$. Finally, the complete and consistent generalization for the original problem is $G_1 := G_1 \sqcap \neg G_2 = \top \sqcap \neg ((R \sqcap \neg (\exists F.I \sqcap \forall F.I)) \sqcup (\neg R \sqcap (\exists F.I \sqcap \forall F.I))) = \neg (R \sqcap \neg (\exists F.I \sqcap \forall F.I)) \sqcap \neg (\neg R \sqcap (\exists F.I \sqcap \forall F.I)) = (\neg R \sqcup (\exists F.I \sqcap \forall F.I)) \sqcap (R \sqcup \neg (\exists F.I \sqcap \forall F.I)) = (R \sqcap (\exists F.I \sqcap \forall F.I)) \sqcup (\neg R \sqcap \neg (\exists F.I \sqcap \forall F.I))$. This generalization is complete and consistent. Its OWL/XML serialization is reported in Figure 4.

4.2   Discussion

For the sake of simplicity, the generalization routine described in the method is non-deterministic in the points where heuristic choices have to be made: among the possible upward refinements computed by the operator δ, those that maximize the number of covered positives should be preferred. The residual operator

---

Value restriction can be included by making a temporary domain closure assumption, ose extent is limited to the time the msc's computation is being performed. After we adopt the Open Domain Assumption, as usual in inductive reasoning.

```
<!ENTITY ns1 "http://www.myontos/Friend#">
...
<rdf:RDF xmlns:ns0='http://www.myontos/Friend#' ... >
 <owl:Ontology rdf:about=''/>
 <owl:ObjectProperty rdf:about='&ns1;F'/>
  <rdf:Description rdf:about='&ns1;f'>
   <rdf:type><owl:Class rdf:about='&ns1;R'/></rdf:type>
  </rdf:Description>
  <owl:Thing rdf:about='&ns1;h'>
    <ns0:F rdf:resource='&ns1;h1'/><ns0:F rdf:resource='&ns1;h2'/>
  </owl:Thing>
  <rdf:Description rdf:about='&ns1;j'>
   <rdf:type><owl:Class rdf:about='&ns1;R'/></rdf:type>
    <ns0:F rdf:resource='&ns1;j1'/><ns0:F rdf:resource='&ns1;j2'/>
  </rdf:Description>
  <rdf:Description rdf:about='&ns1;m'>
   <rdf:type><owl:Class rdf:about='&ns1;R'/></rdf:type>
    <ns0:F rdf:resource='&ns1;m1'/><ns0:F rdf:resource='&ns1;m2'/>
  </rdf:Description>
  <owl:Thing rdf:about='&ns1;h1'/>
  <rdf:Description rdf:about='&ns1;h2'>
   <rdf:type><owl:Class rdf:about='&ns1;I'/></rdf:type>
  </rdf:Description>
  <rdf:Description rdf:about='&ns1;j1'>
   <rdf:type><owl:Class rdf:about='&ns1;I'/></rdf:type>
  </rdf:Description>
  <rdf:Description rdf:about='&ns1;j2'>
   <rdf:type><owl:Class rdf:about='&ns1;I'/></rdf:type>
  </rdf:Description>
  <rdf:Description rdf:about='&ns1;m1'>
   <rdf:type><owl:Class rdf:about='&ns1;I'/></rdf:type>
  </rdf:Description>
  <owl:Thing rdf:about='&ns1;m2'/>
</rdf:RDF>
```

Fig. 3. OWL/RDF representation of Example 4.1

is essentially a difference function [14]. In general a possible definition of the operator could be $C - D = \max \{E \mid E \sqcap D \equiv C\}$, where the maximum depends on the ordering induced by subsumption. Depending on the representation language, other forms of difference are possible, as discussed in [12]. In the case $\mathcal{ALC}$, the difference can be simply defined as $C - D = C \sqcup \neg D$.

Now let us turn to prove that the method actually converges to a solution of the learning problem:

Theorem 4.1 (correctness). *The algorithm eventually terminates computing a correct concept definition.*

Proof. *The two routines are discussed separately.*

```
<!ENTITY ns1 "http://www.myontos/Friend#">
...
<owl:Class rdf:about="&ns1;Learned">
 <rdfs:subClassOf>
  <owl:Class><owl:unionOf rdf:parseType="Collection">
   <owl:Class><owl:intersectionOf rdf:parseType="Collection">
    <owl:Class rdf:about="&ns1;R"/>
    <owl:Class><owl:intersectionOf rdf:parseType="Collection">
     <owl:Restriction><owl:onProperty rdf:resource="&ns1;F"/>
      <owl:someValuesFrom><owl:Class rdf:about="&ns1;I"/>
      </owl:someValuesFrom></owl:Restriction>
     <owl:Restriction><owl:onProperty rdf:resource="&ns1;F"/>
      <owl:allValuesFrom><owl:Class rdf:about="&ns1;I"/>
      </owl:allValuesFrom></owl:Restriction>
    </owl:intersectionOf></owl:Class>
   </owl:intersectionOf></owl:Class>
   <owl:Class><owl:intersectionOf rdf:parseType="Collection">
    <owl:Class><owl:complementOf><owl:Class rdf:about="&ns1;R"/>
    </owl:complementOf></owl:Class>
    <owl:Class><owl:complementOf>
     <owl:Class><owl:intersectionOf rdf:parseType="Collection">
      <owl:Restriction><owl:onProperty rdf:resource="&ns1;F"/>
       <owl:someValuesFrom><owl:Class rdf:about="&ns1;I"/>
       </owl:someValuesFrom></owl:Restriction>
      <owl:Restriction><owl:onProperty rdf:resource="&ns1;F"/>
       <owl:allValuesFrom><owl:Class rdf:about="&ns1;I"/>
       </owl:allValuesFrom></owl:Restriction>
     </owl:intersectionOf></owl:Class>
    </owl:complementOf></owl:Class>
   </owl:intersectionOf></owl:Class>
  </owl:unionOf></owl:Class>
 </rdfs:subClassOf>
</owl:Class>
```

Fig. 4. Induced Concept Description in the Example 4.1

(generalization) *The routine is controlled by the outer cycle that produces one disjunct at each iteration, accommodating at least one positive example which is successively removed. Thus eventually the termination of the routine is guaranteed, provided that the inner loop terminates. The inner loop generalizes monotonically the starting seed-definition (a conjunct) by applying δ. Eventually, the loop terminates either because the generalization is correct or because it covers some negative example. This is the case when the counterfactuals co-routine is invoked.*

posing that the latter is correct, the former can terminate by conjoining the tion of the counterfactuals produced to the incorrect definition, thus covering h iteration new positives and no negative assertion.

(counterfactuals) *This routine contains two initial loops that are controlled by the sizes of the example sets in the input. Each iteration produces a residual concept definition to be used for the successive generalization. Provided that the other routine terminates with a correct generalization of the residual concept then also the counterfactual routine terminates. As regards the correctness, it is to be proven that, on return from the routine, the following relations hold:*

1. $\forall Pos \in CoveredPos: (ParGen \sqcap \neg K) \sqsupseteq Pos$
2. $\forall Neg \in Negatives: (ParGen \sqcap \neg K) \not\sqsupseteq Neg$. *If the call to* generalization *succeeds then for all* $NewN_j \in NewNegatives: K \not\sqsupseteq NewN_j$. *By definition of* $NewNegatives$, $P_j \in Positives$ *implies that the* residual$(P_j, ParGen) \in NewNegatives$. *Hence* $K \not\sqsupseteq$ residual$(P_j, ParGen)$. *Since* $\forall Pos \in Positives = CoveredPos: ParGen \sqsupseteq Pos$ *the first condition is proven. For the other condition, recall that* $(ParGen \sqcap \neg K) \not\sqsupseteq Neg$ *iff* $ParGen \not\sqsupseteq Neg$ *or* $ParGen \sqsupseteq Neg$ *and* $K \sqsupseteq$ residual$(Neg, ParGen)$. *Now, considering all* $Neg \in Negatives$, *if* $ParGen \not\sqsupseteq Neg$ *we have immediately the truth of the condition. Otherwise, if* $ParGen \sqsupseteq Neg$ *then the routine builds a residual element* residual$(Neg, ParGen)$ *for* $NewPositives$. *Thus, on return from the call to* generalization, K *is a generalization of every description in* $NewPositives$, *and hence* $K \sqsupseteq$ residual$(Neg, ParGen)$.

The algorithm may fail in two cases: a call to counterfactuals with null positive and negative descriptions indicates that it is impossible to discriminate between two identical descriptions. The second case is when generalization fails, which is unlikely to happen because trivially there exists the disjunction of all positive examples descriptions as basic generalization. Such cases should be eliminated beforehand by preprocessing the examples for obtaining the msc's. The counterfactuals algorithm is linear except for the dependency on the generalization algorithm. Then it suffices to discuss the complexity of such an algorithm. The generalization proposed here is a generic divide and conquer algorithm which performs a greedy search using the refinement operator δ. Introducing a better refinement operator based on examples, the heuristic information conveyed by the examples can be better exploited so to have a faster convergency. The cycles are linear on the number of instances. The subsumption tests, that are PSpace-complete in $\mathcal{ALC}$ [11], represent the real source of complexity. As mentioned in the introduction, an easy solution to the learning problem could be computing the minimal generalization: lcs(msc(Pos_1), ..., msc(Pos_m), msc$(\neg Neg_1)$, ..., msc$(\neg Neg_n)$). Yet, suffers from lacking of predictive power, fitting precisely only the known examples (while it may turn out to be inconsistent wrt new ones). Moreover, for many expressive DLs, such as $\mathcal{ALE}$, msc's are difficult to compute (provided they exist). In $\mathcal{ALC}$, although lcs is simply the disjunction of the inputs, there is no algorithm for computing msc's. Our algorithm processes approximations of the msc's, for it is endowed with the specialization mechanism of the counterfactuals, whereas the lcs can only generalize starting from very specialized definitions. The algorithm could be the skeleton for similar ones, based on different DL representations. In such cases, it suffices to change the operator for calculating residuals and proper methods to conjoin the counterfactual to the starting description should be devised.

5   Conclusions and Future Work

Structural knowledge is expected to play an important role in the Semantic Web. Yet, while techniques for deductive reasoning for such knowledge bases are now very well assessed, their construction is a hard task for knowledge engineers even for limited domains; they could be supported by (semi)automatic inductive tools that still require investigation. In this paper, we have investigated on the induction concept definitions in structural representations both theoretically casting the task as a search problem and operationally, presenting a method for inducing and/or refining concept definitions. The method illustrated in this paper (actually initially presented in [15]) has been implemented in a refinement system (YINGYANG, *Yet another INduction Yields A New Generalization*) that induces or refines $\mathcal{ALC}$ knowledge bases which can be maintained by means of OWL markup. This will allow to design a learning and refinement service for the Semantic Web. The proposed framework could be extended along three directions. First, an investigation on the properties of the refinement operators on DL languages is required. In order to increase the efficiency of learning, redundancy during the search for solutions is to be avoided. This can be done by defining minimal refinement operators [9]. Secondly, the method can be extended to other DLs by changing the residual operator and devising a proper representation for counterfactuals. Another promising direction is the study of *constructive induction* methods to overcome the mentioned problem of inadequate language bias to represent the concepts instantiated in the A-box, under the interactive supervision of the knowledge engineer as an oracle.

References

[1] Baader, F., Calvanese, D., McGuinness, D., Nardi, D., Patel-Schneider, P., eds.: The Description Logic Handbook. Cambridge University Press (2003)

[2] Haussler, D.: Learning conjunctive concepts in structural domains. Machine Learning 4 (1989) 7–40

[3] Nienhuys-Cheng, S., Laer, W.V., Ramon, J., Raedt, L.D.: Generalizing refinement operators to learn prenex conjunctive normal forms. In: Proceedings of the International Conference on Inductive Logic Programming. Volume 1631 of LNAI., Springer (1999) 245–256

[4] Rouveirol, C., Ventos, V.: Towards learning in CARIN-$\mathcal{ALN}$. In Cussens, J., Frisch, A., eds.: Proceedings of the 10th International Conference on Inductive Logic Programming. Volume 1866 of LNAI., Springer (2000) 191–208

Kietz, J.U.: Learnability of description logic programs. In Matwin, S., Sammut, C., eds.: Proceedings of the 12th International Conference on Inductive Logic Programming. Volume 2583 of LNAI., Sydney, Springer (2002) 117–132

[6] Cohen, W., Hirsh, H.: Learning the CLASSIC description logic. In Torasso, P., Doyle, J., Sandewall, E., eds.: Proceedings of the 4th International Conference on the Principles of Knowledge Representation and Reasoning, Morgan Kaufmann (1994) 121–133

[7] Baader, F., Turhan, A.Y.: TBoxes do not yield a compact representation of least common subsumers. In: Working Notes of the International Description Logics Workshop. Volume 49 of CEUR Workshop Proceedings., Stanford, USA (2001)

[8] Kietz, J.U., Morik, K.: A polynomial approach to the constructive induction of structural knowledge. Machine Learning **14** (1994) 193–218

[9] Badea, L., Nienhuys-Cheng, S.H.: A refinement operator for description logics. In Cussens, J., Frisch, A., eds.: Proceedings of the 10th International Conference on Inductive Logic Programming. Volume 1866 of LNAI., Springer (2000) 40–59

[10] Vere, S.: Multilevel counterfactuals for generalizations of relational concepts and productions. Artificial Intelligence **14** (1980) 139–164

[11] Schmidt-Schauß, M., Smolka, G.: Attributive concept descriptions with complements. Artificial Intelligence **48** (1991) 1–26

[12] Brandt, S., Küsters, R., Turhan, A.Y.: Approximation and difference in description logics. In Fensel, D., Giunchiglia, F., McGuinness, D., Williams, M.A., eds.: Proceedings of the International Conference on Knowledge Representation, Morgan Kaufmann (2002) 203–214

[13] Nebel, B.: Reasoning and Revision in Hybrid Representation Systems. Volume 422 of LNAI. Springer (1990)

[14] Teege, G.: A subtraction operation for description logics. In Torasso, P., Doyle, J., Sandewall, E., eds.: Proceedings of the 4th International Conference on Principles of Knowledge Representation and Reasoning, Morgan Kaufmann (1994) 540–550

[15] Esposito, F., Fanizzi, N., Iannone, L., Palmisano, I., Semeraro, G.: Induction and revision of terminologies. In de Mataras, R.L., Saitta, L., eds.: Proceedings of the 16th European Conference on Artificial Intelligence, IOS Press (2004) 1007–1008

Inferring Data Transformation Rules to Integrate Semantic Web Services

Bruce Spencer and Sandy Liu

National Research Council of Canada
46 Dineen Drive, Fredericton, New Brunswick, E3B 9W4
{Bruce.Spencer, Sandy.Liu}@nrc.ca, http://iit.nrc.gc.ca/il.html

Abstract. OWL-S allows selecting, composing and invoking Web Services at different levels of abstraction: selection uses high level abstract descriptions, invocation uses low level grounding ones, while composition needs to consider both high and low level descriptions. In our setting, two Web Services are to be composed so that output from the upstream one is used to create input for the downstream one. These Web Services may have different data models but are related to each other through high and low level descriptions. Correspondences must be found between components of the upstream data type and the downstream ones. Low level data transformation functions may be required (e.g. unit conversions, data type conversions). The components may be arranged in different XML tree structures. Thus, multiple data transformations are necessary: reshaping the message tree, matching leaves by corresponding types, translating through ontologies, and calling conversion functions. Our prototype compiles these transformations into a set of data transformation rules, using our tableau-based $\mathcal{ALC}$ Description Logic reasoner to reason over the given OWL-S and WSDL descriptions, as well as the related ontologies. A resolution-based inference mechanism for running these rules is embedded in an inference queue that conducts data from the upstream to the downstream service, running the rules to perform the data transformation in the process.

1   Introduction

Some envision that software components can be described sufficiently so that they can be autonomously found and incorporated, can pass data that will be automatically understood and processed, can recover from faults, and can prove and explain their actions and results. The OWL-S specification for Semantic Web Services [2] has recently been released in which these components are Web Services described using the Web Ontology Language, OWL [13].

The OWL-S release 1.0 proposes to describe Web Services in three layers: the service profile, service model, and service grounding, describing respectively what the service does, how it does it, and how to access it. The service profile gives the information necessary for discovering and for combining (composing) Web Services. By convention, it may describe the services only abstractly and not in

S.A. McIlraith et al. (Eds.): ISWC 2004, LNCS 3298, pp. 456–470, 2004.

complete detail; the inputs, outputs, preconditions, and effects of the service may be advertised at a high level for faster but imperfect matching. The grounding layer is where the complete details would be found for each of the components in these objects, expressed both in OWL-S grounding and Web Service Description Language (WSDL) [12], a low-level specification. By separating the abstract from the concrete specifications, the tasks for which the service profile are used, discovery and composition, are greatly simplified, making the whole architecture more viable.

In general several Web Services can be selected to work together, but in this paper we consider the case where only two Web Services have been selected: one as the producer and the other as the consumer of a stream of data messages. The producer, or *upstream* service will deliver one input message at a time to the *downstream* service, which will consume it. We imagine that one or both of these services were not previously designed to work together, and that they were selected to work together based on their service profiles; now the two service groundings must be coupled autonomously, using descriptions of both levels as well as ontologies available. The setting can be seen as a special case of data integration assisted by semantic markup.

We consider two use cases, a simple one for converting dates from year / month / day order as given by the upstream service, into month / day / year order as required by the downstream service. This simple case allows us to explain the various steps in the proposals. In the second use case we convert flight information from one format to another, reshaping the XML tree containing the data and invoking two different kinds of conversions.

In section 2 we discuss the integration problem in light of two use cases, and give the general technique for building the rules in Section 3. Section 4 gives a presentation of inference queues used to run the rules. In the last two sections, we give related and future work and conclusions.

2   Grounding Level Integration

We intend to automatically integrate Web Services. In our setting, the integration task is done at several levels. We assume that a high-level plan has determined which Web Services can be integrated, based on descriptions of the effects produced by upstream services, and the preconditions required by the downstream one. The abstract planning level will have determined that the data produced by the upstream services provide information needed by the downstream service. Matching upstream to downstream services should be done without knowledge of minor differences in the concrete types of data to be transferred, if reasoning at this level is to be kept unencumbered by overwhelming detail. Once compatibility is established at the upper level, the task of matching at the lower level can begin. Two similar or identical descriptions at the abstract level can refer to very different descriptions at the concrete level.

Therefore, our objective is to create a message of the downstream data type from one or more upstream messages. We assume there exist ontologies describ-

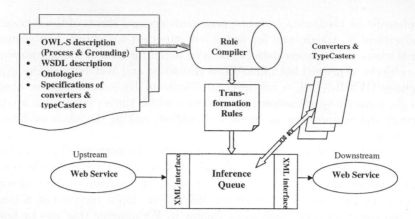

Fig. 1. System Architectural Overview

ing both the upstream messages and downstream messages, and in particular description logic, possibly OWL-S specifications containing the leaf-level parts of these messages. Figure 1 shows the overall system architecture to perform the grounding level integrations. The rule compiler takes the OWL-S descriptions, WSDL descriptions, auxiliary ontologies, and specifications of data converters as inputs, and creates data transformation rules. If the semantic integration is attempted but is not feasible, this will be indicated by a failure to create the rules.

At service invocation time, the set of transformation rules can be run to actually perform the data transformation from upstream to downstream. The intermediate carrier is called an inference queue [11], which accepts input data encoded as facts and rules in first-order logic, and can perform inferences on those facts so that both the input facts and inferred facts are transmitted as output. Such an inference queue loaded with data transformation rules at service composition time, and loaded with upstream data at runtime, will be able to convert that data to the appropriate form and deliver it to the downstream service.

Because the inference queue includes a theorem prover for definite clauses, it is capable of some of the other tasks we identified as necessary for robustness: it can detect when the upstream data is not convertible into data acceptable by the downstream service; it can also perform sanity test on the data. The OWL-S proposal allows us to express preconditions expected by the downstream service and effects expected from the upstream service. Since we may not have control over how these Web Services are written, we should attempt to verify that the expected effects were produced and expected preconditions were met. These checks would also be performed by the rule engine.

In the real world many data types that are not identical syntactically are still convertible, such as temperatures expressed in either Fahrenheit or Celsius, currency in either dollars or Yen, etc. We assume the existence of some mappings between data types, called *converters*, intended to be used for converting data from one type to another. We also assume that low-level type conversion such as converting between string and numeric can be performed through type casters. The functions of the converters and type casters can be specified, then they can be used by the rule compilers to generate the proper transformation rules. As a result, a number of these standard conversions can be expressed as relations in the bodies of rules, and at runtime the inference engine will perform the conversion.

2.1 Use Cases

Consider the following example: Suppose a Web Service produces a date in the conventional U.S. order month / day / year. In a typical usage scenario this date would be part of a larger message, but for simplicity we consider that this is the entire contents of the message. Suppose this Web Service has been selected as the upstream service so it will provide data to the downstream Web Service. The downstream message will also be composed of just a date, but in this case in the ISO order year / month / day. The decision to connect these two Web Services in this way would be done by a planning system, designed in accordance with the current OWL-S proposal [2]. While building the abstract plan, it determined that these messages are compatible, using only the information at the OWL-S profile and process levels. An ontology of dates states that ISO and U.S. dates are both subclasses of the class date and are composed of a year, a month and a day, as in Figure 2. The planner did not look into the lower level, where the types of the date are slightly different; these differences were considered to be

```
<owl:Class rdf:ID="Date">
</owl:Class>
<owl:ObjectProperty rdf:ID="hasYear">
    <rdfs:domain rdf:resource="#Date"/>
    <rdfs:range rdf:resource="#Year"/>
</owl:ObjectProperty>
<owl:ObjectProperty rdf:ID="hasMonth"/>
    <rdfs:domain rdf:resource="#Date"/>
    <rdfs:range rdf:resource="#Month"/>
</owl:ObjectProperty>
<owl:ObjectProperty rdf:ID="hasDay"/>
    <rdfs:domain rdf:resource="#Date"/>
    <rdfs:range rdf:resource="#Day"/>
</owl:ObjectProperty>
<owl:Class rdf:ID="ISODate">
    <rdfs:subClassOf rdf:resource="#Date"/>
</owl:Class>
<owl:Class rdf:ID="USDate">
    <rdfs:subClassOf rdf:resource="#Date"/>
</owl:Class>
```

Fig. 2. A Date Ontology in OWL

```
<grounding:WsdlAtomicProcessGrounding
    rdf:ID="WSDLGrounding_CalendarMgmt_setVisitDate">
  <grounding:wsdlInputMessageParts rdf:parseType="owl:collection">
    <grounding:WsdlMessageMap>
      <grounding:damlsParameter rdf:resource="&pm_file;#year"/>
      <grounding:wsdlMessagePart>
        <xsd:uriReference rdf:value="http://lclhst/calendar.wsdl#arg0"/>
      </grounding:wsdlMessagePart>
    </grounding:WsdlMessageMap>
    <grounding:WsdlMessageMap>
      <grounding:owlsParameter rdf:resource="&pm_file;#month"/>
      <grounding:wsdlMessagePart>
        <xsd:uriReference rdf:value="http://lclhst/calendar.wsdl#arg1"/>
      </grounding:wsdlMessagePart>
    </grounding:WsdlMessageMap>
    <grounding:WsdlMessageMap>
      <grounding:damlsParameter rdf:resource="&pm_file;#day"/>
      <grounding:wsdlMessagePart>
        <xsd:uriReference rdf:value="http://lclhst/calendar.wsdl#arg2"/>
      </grounding:wsdlMessagePart>
    </grounding:WsdlMessageMap>
  </grounding:wsdlInputMessageParts>
</grounding:WsdlAtomicProcessGrounding>
```

Fig. 3. Snippet from the Downstream Grounding in OWL

inessential at planning time. The specific types of date from the upstream and downstream services are described in WSDL as three integers, and these integers are given more meaning by the OWL-S grounding specification. Figure 3 shows a snippet of OWL-S grounding specification for the downstream Web Service.

We compile the data transformation into a rule to be invoked to do this transformation. The messages are passed from upstream to downstream via an inference queue. An inference queue is a conduit for data that contains an inference engine. Data are considered facts, and rules are "plugged in" to tell how to infer new facts, which become the output of the queue. We illustrate the data transformation rules using a Prolog notation, where variables are shown with an upper case letter. The current prototype directly uses the XML messages, but it is possible to use RuleML [1] or SWRL [3]. Any upstream message is assumed to be given to the inference queue as a fact using the unary predicate symbol up, where the argument is a Prolog term, in this case containing a date in month / day / year order. The inference queue produces a message meant for the downstream service, also as a fact with the unary predicate symbol down and the arguments in ISO order.

The rule for data transformation in this case is

```
down(isoDate(Year, Month, Day)) :- up(usDate(Month, Day, Year)).
```

When a fact, say, up(usDate(12, 31, 1999)) is entered to the inference queue, a resolution step is done, in which Month is bound to 12, Day to 31 and Year to

1999. The inference drawn is `down(isoDate(1999, 12, 31))`. This is expelled from the downstream end of the inference, to be delivered to the downstream Web Service.

For the second use case, suppose that a European-based Web Service producing flight information is selected to provide input to a Canadian-based Web Service accepting flight information. For the upstream (producing) Web Service the flight has three data items: a source city, a destination city and a cost quoted in Euros. The downstream service expects the flight to be described with two pieces of information: the cost in Canadian dollars and a flight manifest, which itself consists of two pieces of information, the code of the departure airport and arrival airport, respectively. In this case we make use of two converters: from Euros to dollars, and from cities to airport codes. We also need to have the translation mechanism create a message with an internal structure, the manifest object. The final rule generated for this case follows:

```
down(canadaFlight(DollarCurrency,
    manifest(DepartureAirportCode, ArrivalAirportCode))):-
  up(euroFlight(SourceCity, DestCity, EuroCurrency)),
  stringToDouble(EuroCurrency, EuroCurrencyDouble),
  euro2Dollar(EuroCurrencyDouble, DollarCurrency),
  city2AirportCode(SourceCity, DepartureAirportCode),
  city2AirportCode(DestCity, ArrivalAirportCode).
```

There are three tasks: creating the appropriate structure, converting the currency, and converting the two airport locators. Each needs to be reflected in the translation rules. The structure of the both up- and downstream messages must be reflected in the rule. In this case the downstream message, which is the argument of the down predicate, contains the term `canadaFlight` which itself contains two arguments, one for the dollar currency and other for the flight manifest, represented by the function symbol (or XML tag) `manifest` and containing two airport codes. So the rule constructor must be aware of and reflect all of the inner structure of both messages. These XML structures are inferred from the OWL-S grounding and WSDL information. Figure 4(a) and (b) shows these two trees representing the XML structure of the messages.

The second task is to place a call to a converter in the body of a rule. It is straightforward in the case of converting the currency amount in the upstream message to a dollar amount in the downstream message. There is a converter available, `euro2Dollar` whose specification shows that has the appropriate types; it maps Euros to dollars. In the conversion rule that is constructed, a call to this converter is included as a goal in the body of the clause. The first argument of this goal is a variable for the Euro amount that is shared within the up literal, as the first argument of the `canadaFlight` term. The second argument of the call to `euroToDollar` converter is a variable for the dollar amount that appears also in the down literal. All of these placements are straighforward because the types of the converter and the types of the message match. The arrow in Figure 4(c) from `EuroCurrency` to `DollarCurrency` was easy to place because of the type correspondences. It is not always so simple.

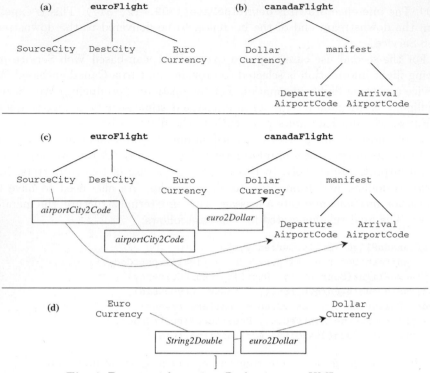

Fig. 4. Data transformation: Reshaping two XML trees

One complication arises because the output type of the converter may not match the required type. If the output type is a subtype of what is required, it must be promoted to the required type. But from a typing point of view, the converter can be used since it is guaranteed to produce a value of the required type. Alternately, if the output type is a supertype of what is required, it must be demoted to the required type. The converter may be still be useful, but a check must be done at runtime to ensure that the actual value is appropriate. On the input side of the converter, similar cases apply.

Yet the discussion so far does not fully account for the rule above. Two airport cities of different types, source and destination, need to be converted to airport codes. We want these two outputs to be of type departure and arrival airport codes, respectively. The converter, `city2AirportCode` will create data values of type airport code, but not specifically of type arrival airport code or departure airport code. Thus requires to promote the input of the converter and demote the output. But there is information lost in the promote step, which leads to confusion. (This will be illustrated in case (a) in Figure 6.) In our first attempt to write this rule, the rule compiler mixed up the types and created calls to the `airportCity2Code` converter in which the `SourceCity` was converted to the `ArrivalAirportCode`, instead of the `DestinationAirportCode`. Promoting the type from `SourceCity` to the more general type `City` causes information about the specialization to be lost.

$$\begin{aligned}
\text{SourceCity} &= \text{SourceLocation} \sqcap \text{City} \\
\text{DestCity} &= \text{DestLocation} \sqcap \text{City} \\
\text{DepartureAirportCode} &= \text{DepartureLocation} \sqcap \text{AirportCode} \\
\text{ArrivalAirportCode} &= \text{ArrivalLocation} \sqcap \text{AirportCode} \\
\text{SourceLocation} &= \text{DepartureLocation} \\
\text{DestLocation} &= \text{ArrivalLocation} \\
\text{EuroCurrency} &\sqsubseteq \text{Currency} \\
\text{DollarCurrency} &\sqsubseteq \text{Currency}
\end{aligned}$$

Fig. 5. Description Logic Axioms for Airport Example

One impractical way to solve this problem would be to provide one converter that takes a source city and creates an departure airport code, and another which converts a destination city to an arrival airport code. In this way the types of the converters would exactly match the types from the input and output messages. This is unreasonable because the programs for these two different converters would be identical, and each converter would be less useful than the original general converter. Moreover all of these converters would have to be written before the web services were encountered, defeating the goal of dealing with unforeseen Web Services.

Instead, our strategy is to create special converters dynamically from our library of general converters. The input and output types are specialized so they are closer to what is required. In this example, the concept of a SourceCity is actually defined as the intersection of a SourceLocation and a City, shown in Figure 5, while DepartureAirportCode is defined as the intersection of a DepartureLocation and AirportCode. Moreover, the set DepartureLocation is declared to be identical to the set SourceLocation. Thus the mapping from SourceCity to DepartureAirportCode can be seen as a specialization of the mapping from City to AirportCode. (This will be illustrated in case (a.1) in Figure 6.) Using this specialized mapping to convert the provided SourceCity gives us the right value for our DepartureAirportCode.

To create the correct specializations, we need to do some description logic reasoning. We have a tableau-based implementation of an $\mathcal{ALC}$ reasoner incorporated into our prototype. It is capable of searching among the ancestors (supersets) of a given concept. If two specific concepts are given and it is asked whether the first one can be converted to the second, a search is made among the superconcepts of each, to find some pair of ancestors that is most specific such that a converter is available from one to the other. In our example the ancestor types of the SourceCity are SourceLocation and City and the ancestors of DepartureAirportCode are DepartureLocation and AirportCode. We have a converter between two of these ancestors: SourceCity and AirportCode). The other two types, SourceLocation and DepartureLocation, are declared to be equivalent. From this information, the arrow in Figure 4(c) from SourceCity to DepartureAirportCode can be drawn.

Note that the rule also pays attention to the fact that the Euro currency was reported as an XML Schema string and needs to be converted to a decimal number (double) before being passed to the euro2Dollar converter. See Figure 4(d).

3   Creating Transformation Rules

The general procedure of creating the rule can now be described. A desired downstream Web Service message type is to be constructed, and we have a (set of) candidate upstream message type(s) that may provide values to be used. At higher level of abstraction, a reasoning system, such as a planner, has determined that these messages are compatible. A rule is required that at run-time creates the desired downstream message from the upstream message(s). The rule must contain a **down** conclusion in the head and this must match the structure of the downstream message, in that internal structures are reproduced within the Prolog term structure. An **up** goal with a reproduction of the upstream message is always added to the body of the rule. For each leaf-level data item in the downstream message, given its data type R_2, we need to identify a source R_1 among the data types available in the upstream message.

There are several possibilities. An upstream data type may exactly match or be a subconcept of the downstream data type: $R_1 \sqsubseteq R_2$. In that case we identify this upstream data as the source for the downstream data. For example, if R_1 is `EuroCurrency` and R_2 is `Currency` then we are assured that the value in R_1 is appropriate for R_2. Two occurrences of a shared variable are placed in the rule, one in the position of the target datum in the downstream message and one in the position in this upstream message of the selected matching datum.

An upstream data type may be a superconcept of the target downstream type: $R_1 \sqsupseteq R_2$. In that case the datum provided at runtime may or may not be of the appropriate type for the downstream message. In this case a check can be placed in the goal to verify that that datum a is of the downstream type, $a \in R_2$, if such a runtime check is possible. For example if R_1 is `Currency` and R_2 is `EuroCurrency` then at runtime we should check that value in R_1 is indeed a `EuroCurrency`.

The other possibilities come from the converters. A converter is defined as a mapping of data values from one type to another where both an element and its image represent the same individual. For example, a converter might map measurements in the imperial system to the metric system, but must map a quantity in one system to an equal quantity in the other. We assume that a converter C maps $S_1 \rightarrow S_2$.

Suppose there is a converter C available to generate data of the target downstream type R_2 from some available upstream type R_1; in other words by good fortune the types exactly match $R_1 = S_1$ and $R_2 = S_2$. Then add a goal to the body of the rule that calls that converter, where in loss at both endts input variable is shared with the position in the upstream message of the identified source datum, and the converter's output variable is shared with the target downstream datum.

Next suppose that the types do not match exactly. There are four cases to consider, shown as Figure 6(a-d), where the S's are either subsets or proper supersets of the R's.

Given a data value of type R_1 if it is guaranteed to be in S_1, as in cases (a) and (b), we can consider the data to have type S_1, promoting it so that we can use it as the input to the converter. If not, then $S_1 \sqsubset R_1$, and since the type is demoted, a check at runtime for being in S_1 is needed to be sure we can use this converter. This check is added as a condition of the rule. Similarly for cases (b) and (d) the output of the converter is guaranteed to be in R_2, while for cases (a) and (c), which are demotions, an additional check is needed.

However, for case (a) information is lost during promotion. It was this problem that mixed up our early prototype when it converted the SourceCity into the ArrivalAirportCode. It may be possible to retain this information, to preserve the mapping. Suppose that there exists a type T such that $R_1 = S_1 \sqcap T$ and $R_2 = S_2 \sqcap T$. Then we may assume that calling the converter with a datum of type R_1 will generate a datum of type R_2. See Figure 6(a.1). In our example from the previous section, we were able to restrict the domain and range of C by T, as follows: $S_1 = $ City, $S_2 = $ AirportCode, $R_1 = $ SourceCity, $R_2 = $ DepartureAirportCode, and $T = $ SourceLocation $= $ DepartureLocation.

If no such T exists, it may still be possible to specialize the converter. Suppose that there exist types T_1 and T_2 such that $R_1 = S_1 \sqcap T_1$ and $R_2 = S_2 \sqcap T_2$. If $T_1 \sqsubseteq T_2$ then the converted value is sure to be a member of R_2. See Figure 6(a.2). Otherwise if $T_1 \sqsupseteq T_2$ there is a chance that the output of the converter provided is not in R_2, and another goal should be placed into the rule checking that it is.

If there are two sources of upstream information available for the downstream type, this may mean that the data is not described in sufficient detail to make a unique determination. More semantic information may needed to disambiguate the situation. Ambiguity may also arise if there are different converters that could be applied. We can state that one converter is a better match than the other if it provides the exact types needed. However there seems to be no general technique to prefer using one converter over another. If ambiguities arise at rule generation time, several strategies could be employed: abort, ask a human, deliver a set of candidate rules, choose a probabilistically best one if a model of probability can be imposed, etc. We did not consider this problem further.

Note that in many ways the semantic integration of these Web Serices may fail and even if a rule is produced, it may not map data correctly. This could arise if the OWL-S descriptions are not sufficiently detailed, if no ontology is available to connect the data model of the upstream service to that of the downstream service, and many other reasons. We feel that more experience with marking up real life Web Services is needed before we can prescribe the sufficient conditions for producing valid data transformation rules, and the necessary conditions for succeeding to produce a rule.

In this discussion we have ignored the concrete (syntactic) data types, but at run time, when Web Service data is actually given, it is important to consider the XML Schema datatypes in which the data will delivered, either as xsd:string,

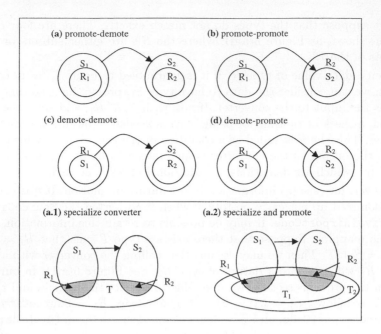

Fig. 6. Cases for specializing the converter

one of the numeric types, etc. The downstream Web Service and the converter will need to be called with the appropriate data type so a type casting (sometime called type conversion) may need to be done. Our compiler also considers this type casting and generates rules with these conversions inserted as necessary. See Figure 4(d).

The rule compiler is written in Prolog, and uses our Prolog implementation of a tableau-based $\mathcal{ALC}$ description logic engine.

4   Inference Queues

The inference queue plays a fundamental role in the delivery system from the upstream to the downstream Web Service. As a queue it provides two main functions: **insert** and **remove**, which are asynchronous calls (i.e. they can be called by separate threads in any order.) The insert operation accepts facts and rules and places them into the queue. It is non-blocking in that at any time a call to insert will succeed without any infinite delays. The remove operation produces facts that are logical consequences of the already inserted facts and rules. It is also non-blocking in the following sense; if there is some fact to be removed, there will be an at most finite delay. Usually any delay is extremely short.

In Section 3 we discuss how the inference queue is incorporated into an engine for composing Web Services. The inference queue takes on the role of transporting the messages from one Web Service to the next. The messages are

NewFacts is a priority queue of facts, ordered by $\preceq$, that have not yet been processed. *OldFacts* is a list of facts that have already been processed. *Rules* is a list of rules, and the first condition of each is designated the *selected goal*. *backgroundProcessingIsComplete* is a boolean variable which recalls whether processing has been done since the most recent **remove** and is initially true. *mostRecentlyRemovedFact* is a fact which has a valid value when *background-ProcessingIsComplete* is false.

synchronized **insert**(c)
    if not *backgroundProcessingIsComplete*
        performBackgroundProcessing(*mostRecentlyRemovedFact*)
    endif
    process(c)
    notify
end insert

synchronized Fact **remove**()
    if not *backgroundProcessingIsComplete*
        performBackgroundProcessing(*mostRecentlyRemovedFact*)
    endif
    repeat
        while *NewFacts* is empty
            wait
        end while
        select and remove a new fact f_{new} from *NewFacts*
    until f_{new} is not subsumed by any member of *OldFacts*
    set *backgroundProcessingIsComplete* to false
    set *mostRecentlyRemovedFact* to f_{new}
    return f_{new}
end remove

synchronized **performBackgroundProcessing**(f_{new})
    for each rule r whose first condition unifies with f_{new}
        resolve r against f_{new} producing r_1
        process(r_1)
    end for each
    set *backgroundProcessingIsComplete* to true
    add f_{new} to *OldFacts*
end performBackgroundProcessing

process(c)
    if c is a rule
        add c to *Rules*
        for each old fact f_{old} unifying with the selected goal of c
            resolve c with f_{old} to produce the new result n
            process(n)
        end for each
    else
        add c to *NewFacts*
    end if
end process

Fig. 7. Inference Queue Operations: insert and remove

in XML, but while they are in the inference queue, they are considered to be terms in logic.

The inference queue has six properties that make it suitable for our task. (See [11] for proofs.) (1) The engine computes only **sound** conclusions, which means they are correct according to the meaning of the given formulas. (2) It computes a **complete** set of conclusions, which means that if a conclusion logically follows from the facts and rules that have been inserted into the queue, then such a conclusion will be produced by the inference queue. (3) The output is **irredundant** in that a fact, once produced, will not be produced again. Moreover, suppose one fact is more specific than another, as $p(a)$ is more specific than $p(X)$ for all values X. Then the inference queue will not generate the more specific fact after it has already produced the more general one. (4) The conclusions are generated by **fairly**. This means for every implied conclusion, either it or a more general one will eventually be chosen as the output to a remove request; it will not be infinitely often deferred. Combining this property with completeness means we are guaranteed that every conclusion will eventually be produced, given a sufficient number of remove requests. To ensure this, the inference queue depends on a partial order, $\preceq$ between the facts, and produces them in accordance with this order. (5) The calls to insert and to remove are **thread safe** which means that these calls can occur simultaneously without the risk of the mechanism getting into an unsafe state. (6) Calls to insert and remove are **responsive** which means that there will not be an infinite delay between calls. This remains true even if the facts and rules have an infinite number of consequences.

Figure 7 shows the details of how the inference queue operations are defined. Note that it uses the convention that methods declared to be *synchronized* are mutually exclusive; there can not be threads active in two such methods at once. The insert and remove methods also communicate via *wait* and *notify*, which allows remove to block if the queue is currently empty, but to return a value when a fact becomes available.

Other features of the inference queue can contribute to other parts of a robust Web Services architecture, including the ability to detect, report and recover from errors during service invocation. The inference queue is based on the jDREW open-source libraries [10], which are found on SourceForge.

5   Related Work

The task we perform is similar to that proposed for a broker [4], in that messages from one Web Service are translated to an appropriate form for another, where these Web Services are not in direct communication, but pass through a third party. The abstraction algorithm in [4] is similar to our proposal, but it does not consider converters.

A recent proposal [5] to align OWL-S to DOLCE, is motivated in part by the difficulty to state in OWL-S that the output of one process is the input of another. We are interested in this work and look forward to seeing more details on how the proposal would handle the converters that we have employed.

A number of recent proposals for integration of Semantic Web Services have been presented. We are not aware of any other work chosing to compile the integration tasks into rules, yet the integration tasks are similar. For example, the merge-split of Xu and Embley [14] corresponds to our XML tree reshaping, and their superset/subset value matching corresponds to our matching of basic elements, as described in Section 3. They seem not to have incorporated converter rules. Likewise the work of Giunchglia and Shvaiko [8] and that of Silva and Rocha [9] consider mapping Web Services descriptions. Each of these papers offers insights for using semantic descriptions to assist with the integration problems. We are less focused on this task, and more on the rule compilation and execution tasks, so the approaches can be considered complementary. Indeed, the problem of dynamically specialing converters seems not to have been addressed in related field of database integration.

The inference queue appears related to rule-based systems, with a long history from OPS-5 [6] to modern implementations [7]. They include rules for reacting to an event E under conditions C to perform action A with postcondition P; hence are sometimes called ECAP rules. These systems do not usually have a model theoretic semantics and usually allow one to delete facts. Our system computes one model incrementally and does not allow deletion of facts; instead they are preserved. The RETE match algorithm [6] on which most rule-based systems are implemented bears a resemblance to the resolution-based system we propose in the inference queue, in that it activates the goals in a rule in left-to-right order and does high-speed matches from facts, or working memory elements, to the conditions in the rules. Rule-based systems have a notion of negation as the non-existence of a fact; we propose to allow negation in the inference queue in the future.

6   Conclusion and Future Work

To conclude, we introduce a rule-based approach for integrating semantic Web Services at the grounding level. Suppose a pair of Web Services is selected by an abstract reasoning system, such as a planner, such that the output of one, intended as the upstream service, semantically matches the input of the other, intended to be downstream. Our approach is capable of generating data transformation rules; data from the upstream Web Service is transformed into the data model of the downstream service such that the meaning is preserved. The core transformation steps include reshaping the XML structure (complex data types), followed by mapping the leaf level elements (the basic components). Special convertors can also be employed as built-in utilities for semantic type conversions or type casting between the basic components. The inference queue is proposed to generate messages in their desired formats. Given a set of transformation rules, the inference queue can produce sound, complete, and irredundant results. It is also fair, responsive, and thread safe. We illustrate with two use cases. Our approach compensates for the inflexibility of third-party code and completes the integration solution after Semantic Web Services discovery and composition.

We plan to add a form of negation to the inference queue. Given a stratification of the literals that is consistent with the partial order $\preceq$ employed by the inference queue, we could then guarantee that any consequence removed from the queue is consistent with the model of data so far inserted into the queue. If negative information is later inserted or derived, those previously removed consequences may not be consistent with the model including the new information. We will consider whether such a system could be useful in the realm of Web Services.

Our rules for performing the data transformation are definite clauses for which all of the reasoning in the descrption-logic level has already been done. We also consider to compile to SWRL [3] and defer some description logic reasoning until invocation time, as the data passes through the inference queue. In future work we propose to give the inference queue DL reasoning ability.

References

1. Harold Boley. The rule markup initiative. http://www.ruleml.org, 2003.
2. The OWL Service Coalition. OWL-S 1.0 Release. "http://www.daml.org/services/owl-s/1.0/", 2004.
3. Ian Horrocks et al. SWRL: A Semantic Web Rule Language Combing OWL and RuleML. http://www.daml.org/2003/11/swrl/, 2003.
4. Massimo Paolucci et al. A Broker for OWL-S Web Services. In *Semantic Web Services: Papers from the 2004 AAAI Spring Symposium*, pages 92–99. AAAI Press, 2004.
5. Peter Mika et al. Foundations for OWL-S: Aligning OWL-S to DOLCE. In *Semantic Web Services: Papers from the 2004 AAAI Spring Symposium*, pages 52–59. AAAI Press, 2004.
6. C. Forgy. Rete: A fast algorithm for the many patterns/many objects match problem. *Artificial Intelligence*, 19:17–37, 1982.
7. Ernest Friedman-Hill. Jess, the expert system shell for the java platform. Technical report, http://herzberg.ca.sandia.gov/jess/, 2002.
8. Fausto Giunchiglia and Pavel Shvaiko. Semantic matching. In AnHai Doan, Alon Halevy, Natasha Noy, editor, *Proceedings of the Semantic Integration Workshop*, volume Vol-82. CEUR-WS.org, 2003.
9. Nuno Silva and Joao Rocha. Service-oriented ontology mapping system. In AnHai Doan, Alon Halevy, Natasha Noy, editor, *Proceedings of the Semantic Integration Workshop*, volume Vol-82. CEUR-WS.org, 2003.
10. Bruce Spencer. A Java Deductive Reasoning Engine for the Web. www.jdrew.org, 2004. Accessed 2004 Jan 12.
11. Bruce Spencer and Sandy Liu. Inference Quenes for Communicating and Monitoring Declarative Information between Web Services. In *Proceedings of RuleML-2003*, number 2876 in Lecture Notes in Artificial Intelligence, 2003.
12. W3C. Web Services Description Language. "http://www.w3.org/tr/wsdl", 2001.
13. W3C. Web ontology language reference. "http://www.w3.org/TR/owl-ref/", 2004.
14. Li Xu and David W. Embley. Using domain ontology to discover direct and indirect matches for schema for schema elements. In AnHai Doan, Alon Halevy, Natasha Noy, editor, *Proceedings of the Semantic Integration Workshop*, volume Vol-82. CEUR-WS.org, 2004.

Using Vampire to Reason with OWL

Dmitry Tsarkov, Alexandre Riazanov, Sean Bechhofer, and Ian Horrocks

Department of Computer Science
The University of Manchester
Manchester, UK
{tsarkov|riazanov|seanb|horrocks}@cs.man.ac.uk

Abstract. OWL DL corresponds to a Description Logic (DL) that is a fragment of classical first-order predicate logic (FOL). Therefore, the standard methods of automated reasoning for full FOL can potentially be used instead of dedicated DL reasoners to solve OWL DL reasoning tasks. In this paper we report on some experiments designed to explore the feasibility of using existing general-purpose FOL provers to reason with OWL DL. We also extend our approach to SWRL, a proposed rule language extension to OWL.

1   Introduction

It is well known that OWL DL corresponds to the $\mathcal{SHOIN}D_n^-$ Description Logic (DL), and that, like most other DLs, $\mathcal{SHOIN}D_n^-$ is a fragment of classical first-order predicate logic (FOL) [8,17,1]. This suggests the idea of using standard methods of automated reasoning for full FOL as a mechanism for reasoning with OWL DL, not necessarily with a view to replacing dedicated DL reasoners, but perhaps as a supplementary mechanism that can be used in development, testing and to attempt problems that are outside the expressive range of existing DL reasoners.

This might be done by trying to create from scratch new architectures for reasoning in full FOL, which would be specialised for dealing efficiently with typical DL reasoning tasks. A much less expensive option is to use existing implementations of FOL provers, with the possibility of making adjustments that exploit the structure of DL reasoning tasks. In this paper we investigate, experimentally, the viability of the latter approach. It should be noted that our current implementation is very simplistic, and is only intended as a preliminary feasibility study.

Our main experiment is organised as follows. We use a DL reasoner, FaCT++, to classify three reasonably realistic OWL ontologies (DL knowledge bases): Galen, Tambis and Wine. A large number of nontrivial class (concept) subsumption subtasks are extracted, translated into FOL and submitted to Vampire, a state-of-the-art general-purpose resolution-based FOL prover. This allows us to compare the performance of the two systems on the same problem set.

Although by no means suggesting that dedicated DL reasoners are redundant, the results of our experiment are quite encouraging, and show that Vampire can cope with the vast majority of problems derived from the classification of these ontologies. Moreover, our experiments show that some fairly simple pre-processing optimisations can greatly improve Vampire's performance on ontology derived problems, and suggest that there

S.A. McIlraith et al. (Eds.): ISWC 2004, LNCS 3298, pp. 471–485, 2004.

may be scope for further significant improvements. At the same time, a significant number of tests were too hard for the FOL prover, which indicates that there may be a place for DL reasoning oriented optimisations in the Vampire architecture. Finally, a valuable byproduct of this experiment is a large set of realistic FOL problems which may be of interest to developers of other FOL systems.

In a second experiment, we use FOL translation and Vampire to solve problems from the OWL Test suite [25] designed to test reasoners for OWL DL. Although OWL DL corresponds to an expressive description logic for which the consistency problem is known to be decidable, there is as yet no effective decision procedure known for the complete language,[1] and consequently no implemented DL reasoners [18,17]. Since no tableaux procedure is known for this DL, it is interesting to check if a general-purpose FO system can at least cope with some of the tasks in the OWL Test suite [25]. In fact it turns out that Vampire can solve the vast majority of these problems.

Finally, we show how the simplicity and flexibility of our FOL translation approach allows it to be trivially extended to deal with the Semantic Web Rule Language (SWRL), a proposed rule language extension to OWL [13].

2   Preliminaries

There have been earlier investigations of the use of FOL provers to reason with description logics. Paramasivam and Plaisted, for example, have investigated the use of FOL reasoning for DL classification [26], while Ganzinger and de Nivelle have developed decision procedures for the guarded fragment, a fragment of FOL that includes many description logics [10]. The most widely known work in this area was by Hustadt and Schmidt [20], who used the SPASS FOL prover to reason with propositional modal logics, and, via well known correspondences [30], with description logics. Their technique involved the use of a relatively complex functional translation which produces a subset of FOL for which SPASS can be tuned so as to guarantee complete reasoning. The results of this experiment were quite encouraging, with performance of the SPASS based system being comparable, in many cases, with that of state of the art DL reasoners. The tests, however, mainly concentrated on checking the satisfiability of (large) single modal logic formulae (equivalently, OWL class descriptions/DL concepts), rather than the more interesting task (in an ontology reasoning context) of checking the satisfiability of formulae w.r.t. a large theory (equivalently, an OWL ontology/DL knowledge base).

In all of the above techniques, the DL is translated into (the guarded fragment of) FOL in such a way that the prover can be used as a decision procedure for the logic—i.e., reasoning is sound, complete and terminating. Such techniques have, however, yet to be extended to the more expressive DLs that underpin Web ontology languages such as DAML+OIL and OWL DL [16], and it is not even clear if such an extension would be possible.

An alternative approach, and the one we investigate here, is to use a simple "direct" translation based on the standard first order semantics of DLs (see, e.g., [1]). Using this approach, an ontology/knowledge base (a set of DL axioms), is translated into a FO

---

[1] Briefly, the interaction between inverse roles, nominals and number restrictions causes problems for existing algorithms.

theory (a set of FO axioms). A DL reasoning task w.r.t. the knowledge base (KB) is then transformed into a FO task that uses the theory. Unlike methods such as Hustadt and Schmidt's functional translation, this does not result in a decision procedure for the DL. The direct translation approach can, however, be used to provide reasoning services (albeit without any guarantee of completeness) for the expressive DLs underlying Web ontology languages, DLs for which no effective decision procedure is currently known. Moreover, the translation approach can easily deal with language extensions such as SWRL (see Section 5).

In recent years, a number of highly efficient FO provers have been implemented [23, 33,29]. These provers compete annually on a set of tasks, and the results are published [7]. One of the most successful general-purpose provers has been Vampire [29], and we have chosen this prover to use in our comparison.

2.1 Translation Issues

We will only discuss the translation from DL to FOL as the correspondence between OWL DL and $\mathcal{SHOIND}_n^-$ is well known [17]. The translation ϕ maps DL concept C and role name R into unary and binary predicates $\phi_C(x)$ and $\phi_R(x, y)$ respectively. Complex concepts and axioms are mapped into FO formulae and axioms in the standard way [6, 1]. For example, subsumption and equivalence axioms are translated into, respectively, FO implication and equivalence (with the free variables universally quantified).

As an example, let's see a translation of a couple of concept and role axioms:

DL	FOL
$R \sqsubseteq S$	$\forall x \forall y (\phi_R(x,y) \rightarrow \phi_S(x,y))$
$C \doteq D \sqcap \exists R.(E \sqcup$	$\forall x(\phi_C(x) \equiv \phi_D(x) \land \exists y(\phi_R(x,y) \land (\phi_E(y) \lor$
$\qquad \forall S^-.F)$	$\forall x(\phi_S(x,y) \land \phi_F(x)))))$
$A \sqsubseteq \geqslant 3\,R.B$	$\forall x(\phi_A(x) \rightarrow \exists y_1 \exists y_2 \exists y_3(\phi_R(x,y_1) \land \phi_B(y_1) \land$
	$\qquad \phi_R(x,y_2) \land \phi_B(y_2) \land \phi_R(x,y_3) \land \phi_B(y_3) \land$
	$\qquad (y_1 \neq y_2) \land (y_2 \neq y_3) \land (y_1 \neq y_3))$
Transitive(T)	$\forall x \forall y \forall z(\phi_T(x,y) \land \phi_T(y,z) \rightarrow \phi_T(x,z))$

Simple DLs (like $\mathcal{ALC}$) can be translated into the FOL class $\mathcal{L}^2$ (the FOL fragment with no function symbols and only 2 variables), which is known to be decidable [22]. The above translations of the role inclusion axiom and concept equality axiom are, for example, in $\mathcal{L}^2$. When number restrictions are added to these DLs, they can be translated into $\mathcal{C}^2$—equivalent to $\mathcal{L}^2$ with additional "counting quantifiers"—which is also known to be decidable [12].

The FOL translation of more expressive description logics, e.g., with transitive roles ($\mathcal{SHIQ}$, OWL Lite and OWL DL) and/or complex role axioms ($\mathcal{RIQ}$ [19]), may lead to the introduction of three or more variables.[2] The above transitivity axiom for role T is an example of this case. FOL with three variables is known to be undecidable [6].

OWL DL also provides for XML schema *datatypes* [5], equivalent to a very simple form of *concrete domains* [18]. The minimum requirement for OWL DL reasoners is that

---

[2] In some cases, the effects of transitive roles can be axiomatised in $\mathcal{C}^2$ [35].

they support xsd:integer and xsd:string datatypes, where support means providing a theory of (in)equality for integer and string values [27].

Our translation encodes the required datatype theory by mapping datatypes into predicates and data values into new constants. Lexically equivalent data values are mapped to the same constant, with integers first being canonicalised in the obvious way, and axioms are added that assert inequality between all the string and integer data constants introduced. If a data value DV and a datatype DT are mapped to DV and DT respectively, and DV is of type DT, then an axiom $DT(DV)$ is also added. As the xsd:integer and xsd:string interpretation domains are disjoint, we add an axiom to that effect. Finally, we add an axiom asserting the disjointness of the datatype domain (the set of data values) and the abstract domain (the set of individuals).

In accordance with the OWL DL semantics, other "unsupported" data types are treated opaquely, i.e., data values are mapped to the same constant if they are lexically identical, but no other assumptions are made (we do *not* assume inequality if the lexical forms are not identical) [27].

2.2   Key Reasoning Tasks

Given a DL *Knowledge Base* $\mathcal{K}$ (equivalently an OWL DL *ontology*) consisting of a set of axioms about concepts, roles, individuals and (possibly) datatypes, key reasoning tasks w.r.t. $\mathcal{K}$ include: Knowledge Base (KB) consistency (do the axioms in $\mathcal{K}$ lead to a contradiction); concept consistency (is it consistent for a concept to have at least one instance); concept subsumption (are the instances of one concept necessarily instances of another); instance checking (does a given class contain a given instance); instance retrieval (find all KB instances for a given class); classification (compute the subsumption partial ordering of concept names in $\mathcal{K}$); and entailment (does $\mathcal{K}$ entail all of the axioms in another KB). All of these tasks are reducible to KB consistency or, equivalently, concept consistency w.r.t. a KB [17] (in fact they are reducible to concept consistency w.r.t. an empty KB via internalisation [1]).

The tests presented here include several classification tasks, and a set of OWL DL consistency and entailment tasks. Each classification task transforms into a (usually quite large) set of concept subsumption/consistency tasks.

As a standard DL reasoner we will use FaCT++ version 0.85 beta. This system is a next generation of the well-known FaCT reasoner [15], being developed as part of the EU WonderWeb project (see http://wonderweb.semanticweb.org/). This implementation is based on the same tableaux algorithms as the original FaCT, but has a different architecture and is written in C++ instead of LISP. The goal of developing FaCT++ was to create a modern reasoner for complex DLs (like $\mathcal{SHIQ}$ and OWL DL) with good performance, improved extensibility and internal data structures that are better able to handle very large knowledge bases.

As an FOL prover we used Vampire v6 [29]. Vampire is a general-purpose FOL prover developed by Andrei Voronkov and Alexandre Riazanov. Given a set of first-order formulas in the full FOL syntax, Vampire transforms it into an equisatisfiable set of clauses, and then tries to demonstrate inconsistency of the clause set by saturating it with ordered resolution and superposition (see [3,24]). If the saturation process terminates without finding a refutation of the input clause set, it indicates that the clause set, and therefore the original formula set, is satisfiable, provided that the variant of the calculus used is refutationally complete and that a fair strategy[3] has been used for saturation. The main input format of Vampire is the TPTP syntax [31], although a parser for a subset of KIF [11] has been added recently.

Vampire is one of the most competitive general-purpose provers, which is demonstrated by its performance in the last five CASC competitions [7]. However, we would like to stress that Vampire uses no optimisations targeting specific needs of ontological reasoning. Moreover, most of the strong features of the implementation are not very useful in the experiments presented here. In particular, Vampire's implementation is highly optimised towards finding refutations, often at the cost of using incomplete procedures, whereas the majority of subsumption tests in our current experiment require the detection of satisfiability. Also, the needs of light-weight reasoning, when one needs to solve relatively easy problems very fast, have never been addressed. Most of the core implementation features, such as a number of complex term indexing techniques, introduce noticeable overhead during the first seconds of a run, which only pays off on reasonably hard problems.

3   Ontology Reasoning Comparison

3.1   Test Ontologies

We used three ontologies (KBs) in the test: the Tambis ontology[4] has a small size and very simple structure; the Wine ontology[5] has a similar size, but a much more complex structure and 150 general concept inclusion axioms (GCIs)[6] [1]; the Galen ontology[7] has a very large size with quite a simple concept language (only conjunction and existential restrictions), but with transitive roles and more than 400 GCIs. Table 1 gives the size of the ontologies along with the number of (positive and negative) subsumption tests performed by FaCT++ during classification.

Table 1. Ontologies used for the comparison

Ontology	Concepts	Roles	Total subs	Pos subs	Neg subs
Tambis	345	107	597	25	572
Wine	346	16	2221	465	1756
Galen	2749	207	25631	3561	22070

---

[3] i.e., all generated clauses are eventually processed

[4] A biochemistry ontology developed in the Tambis project [4].

[5] A wine and food ontology which forms part of the OWL test suite [25].

[6] A GCI is an axiom of the form $C \sqsubseteq D$, where C may be an arbitrarily complex class description. The presence of GCIs can significantly decreases the performance of a tableaux reasoner.

[7] A medical terminology ontology developed in the Galen project [28].

3.2   Experimental Methodology

We used the following comparison scheme. For a given ontology, the DL reasoner performed the classification process. In the case where a subsumption test is necessary, a task was also generated for the FO prover, and the result of the DL testing was noted for future comparison. After finishing the classification process, the set of problems that were solved had been generated. The FO prover was then run on this set of problems. The results were recorded and then compared with the DL ones.

In the experiments with Galen, Wine and Tambis we used the default settings of Vampire with the following two adjustments. Firstly, the default saturation procedure may apply an incomplete strategy, so we replaced it by a complete one (--main_alg otter). Secondly, the literal selection function, which is one of the most important resolution strategy parameters, was set to simulate positive hyperresolution (--selection 2), as this strategy showed the best results on a training set of tasks randomly selected from the given problems. All tests with Vampire and FaCT++ were made on Pentium III, 1000 Mhz running Linux. We ran Vampire with a time limit of 300 seconds and a memory limit of 350Mb per task.

Note that the actual number of comparisons performed in order to classify an ontology depends on the DL system's classification algorithm. If the algorithm is optimised (i.e., exploits concept structure, results of previous operations, etc.), then the number of (logical) subsumption tests may be much smaller than the number required by a naive (unoptimised) algorithm. In the FaCT++ classifier, for example, the number of actually performed subsumption tests is typically only 0.5-2% of those that would be required in a "brute force" implementation (see [2]). Moreover, relatively few of these tests give a positive result (i.e., one in which a subsumption is proved), because most subsumptions are "obvious", and do not need to be computed using a logical subsumption test.

The comparisons were generated by FaCT++ running in its standard (optimised) mode. This resulted in all of the general axioms in the test ontologies being *absorbed* [14], i.e., axioms of the form $C \sqsubseteq D$ (where C is a complex concept) were re-written as axioms of the form $CN \sqsubseteq D'$ (where CN is a primitive concept name). Absorbed axioms can be more efficiently dealt with by FaCT++'s tableaux algorithm.

3.3   Basic Translation Tests

Results using the basic translation (see Section 2.1 for details) are presented in Table 2. The number of (solved) tasks is given, along with the average time (in seconds) per solved task. The results are broken down into positive tasks (ones where subsumption is proved) and negative tasks (ones where non-subsumption is proved). Tasks that are not solved don't influence this parameter.

Vampire can solve every positive task for Tambis, 93% for Wine and 99% for Galen. It could not solve any negative subsumption task for Wine, but it solved 78% of negative tasks for Galen.

3.4   Relevant-Only Translation Tests

One problem with the results presented in the previous section is that Vampire receives *all* of the axioms that occur in the ontology when usually only a small fraction of them

Table 2. Results for basic translation

Ontology	Task type	Tasks	Solved tasks		Av. time (secs)	
			FaCT++	Vampire	FaCT++	Vampire
Tambis	pos	25	25	25	< 0.01	0.31
	neg	572	572	572	< 0.01	0.31
Wine	pos	465	465	433	< 0.01	41.94
	neg	1756	1756	0	0.037	—
Galen	pos	3561	3561	3536	< 0.01	23.75
	neg	22070	22070	17260	0.027	24.20

are actually relevant to a given subsumption problem. Unlike FaCT++, Vampire is not optimised to deal efficiently with large numbers of irrelevant axioms, and so is at a significant disadvantage.

An obvious way to correct this situation is to remove all irrelevant information from the FO task given to Vampire. We call an axiom *irrelevant* to a subsumption test $C \sqsubseteq D$ if we can easily show (i.e., via a syntactic analysis) that removing it from the ontology would not affect the interpretation of either C or D; other axioms are called *relevant*. Note that not every "relevant axiom" really *will* affect the computation of the test $C \sqsubseteq D$, but we cannot (easily) rule out the possibility that it *may* affect the computation. In the rest of paper, we will say that an FO-translation is *relevant-only* if it contains only FO-translations of axioms relevant (in the above sense) to the given subsumption test.

A concept or role expression *depends* on every concept or role that occurs in it, and a concept or role C depends on a concept or role D if D occurs in the definition of C. In addition, a concept C depends on every GCI in the ontology. *Relevance* is the transitive closure of depends. An algorithm for computing relevant information is quite straightforward and is described in detail in [36].

Table 3. Results for relevant-only translation

Ontology	Task type	Tasks	Solved tasks		Av. time (secs)	
			FaCT++	Vampire	FaCT++	Vampire
Tambis	pos	25	25	25	< 0.01	0.03
	neg	572	572	572	< 0.01	0.03
Wine	pos	465	465	461	< 0.01	3.44
	neg	1756	1756	1243	0.037	14.32
Galen	pos	3561	3561	3561	< 0.01	2.48
	neg	22070	22070	17271	0.027	1.73

Results using the relevant-only translation are presented in Table 3. Note that here only Vampire running times are changed (the additional overhead for creating relevant-only tasks is negligible, and we did not include it in the comparison).

The removal of irrelevant information results in a big improvement for Vampire. For the large but quite simple Galen ontology, the number of solved tests increased, and the average time was significantly reduced. In particular, Vampire solved all positive tests. For the complex Wine ontology, the majority of negative subsumption tests were solved, whereas none were solved before.

3.5 Non-absorbed Translation Tests

In our test ontologies, all GCIs were successfully absorbed. In general, however, not every GCI can be absorbed. It is well known that non-absorbed GCIs lead to a significant degradation in the performance of DL reasoners [15], so we decided to compare the effect of non-absorbed GCI's on Vampire and FaCT++ by switching off the absorption optimisation in FaCT++. The results of this test are presented in Table 4.

Table 4. Results for non-absorbed translation

Ontology	Task type	Tasks	Solved tasks		Av. time (secs)	
			FaCT++	Vampire	FaCT++	Vampire
Tambis	pos	25	25	25	< 0.01	0.30
	neg	572	572	572	< 0.01	0.31
Wine	pos	465	465	465	0.035	4.85
	neg	1756	1756	0	1.33	—
Galen	pos	3561	0	3550	—	18.38
	neg	22070	0	17263	—	17.95

In this test Vampire can solve all positive tasks with the smaller ontologies and 99% with the Galen one. It could not solve any negative subsumption tasks for Wine, but 78% of Galen's negative tasks were solved. FaCT++ could not solve any subsumption tests for the Galen ontology, and shows significantly (up to 2 orders) worse results for the Wine ontology. This test also demonstrates that a FO prover may be able to solve some subsumption tests that are very hard for a tableaux based DL reasoner.

It is interesting to note that the results for Vampire are similar to those for the basic translation given in Table 2, with the average solution time for the positive Wine problems actually being 9 times longer for the basic translation. This seems to be due to the increased number of complex clauses generated by the absorption optimisation (as we can see in Table 6, the fraction of non-horn clauses grows 4 times in the absorbed case for the Wine ontology), which makes the proving process harder for Vampire.

An example illustrating how absorption can increase the number of non-horn clauses is given in Table 5. Here C, D, E and F are concept names. The GCI $C \sqsubseteq F$ is absorbed into the axiom $D \sqsubseteq F \sqcup E$, and the corresponding formula becomes non-horn.

3.6 Translation Result Profiles

To give the reader an idea of the syntactic complexity of the first-order proof tasks which Vampire has to deal with in our experiments, we present in Table 6 the integral syntactic characteristics of the clause sets obtained by clausifying the input provided by FaCT++. In addition to some standard parameters (i.e. number of non-horn clauses and number of clauses with positive equalities), we count the number of so-called *chain clauses*,

Table 5. Explanation of non-horn clause introduction

Ontology	DL axiom	FO axiom	Clause type
Non absorbed	$C \equiv D \sqcap \neg E$	$\forall x(\phi_C(x) \equiv (\phi_D(x) \wedge \neg\phi_E(x)))$	
	$C \sqsubseteq F$	$\forall x(\phi_C(x) \to \phi_F(x))$	horn
Absorbed	$C \equiv D \sqcap \neg E$	$\forall x(\phi_C(x) \equiv (\phi_D(x) \wedge \neg\phi_E(x)))$	
	$D \sqsubseteq F \sqcup E$	$\forall x(\phi_D(x) \to (\phi_F(x) \vee \phi_E(x)))$	non-horn

i.e., clauses of the form $\pm p(x_1, \ldots, x_n) \vee \pm q(x_1, \ldots, x_n)$, where p and q are different predicates. This is not directly related to our current experiments, but the high proportion of chain clauses in our tests supports the thesis of applicability of *chain resolution* [34] to terminological reasoning, and may be a valuable observation for future work.

Table 6. Syntactic profiles of the test suites

	Tambis			Galen			Wine		
translation type	Bas.	Rel.	N.A.	Bas.	Rel.	N.A.	Bas.	Rel.	N.A.
num. of clauses	576	42	576	6111	1715	6146	3354	1223	3123
% nonhorn	0	0	0	0	0	0	12	32	3
% chain	24	29	24	60	72	61	64	71	61
% with pos. eq.	5	4	5	2	3	2	7	8	8
lit. per clause	2.05	2.03	2.05	2.71	3.88	2.59	2.58	3.65	2.12
symbols per lit.	2.4	2.35	2.4	2.52	2.57	2.51	2.54	2.68	2.42

4   OWL Tests Comparison

The W3C WebOnt working group[8] have been responsible for the definition of the OWL Web Ontology Language. A key facet of the WebOnt activity has been to define a suite of OWL Tests [25]. These consist of a number of tasks categorised according to their type (consistency, entailment, etc.) and the expected result (positive or negative). In the main, the problems are trivial in terms of reasoning, and are intended primarily to illustrate the features of the language. A number of tests have, however, been translated from other test collections (notable the DL98 tests [9]), and these provide more challenging problems for reasoners, testing both correctness (e.g., termination on problems with no finite interpretation) and efficiency (e.g., of searching large spaces of possible interpretations).

Because no existing DL reasoner can deal with the complete OWL language, we decided to use Vampire to try to prove (or disprove) the correctness of (some of) the OWL tests. Not all of the OWL tests were attempted as some are, e.g., designed to test parsers or OWL Full reasoners, and some use unsupported datatypes. The tests we attempted here are the consistency tests (both positive and negative) for OWL DL ontologies that use no datatypes other than xsd:string or xsd:integer.

---

[8] http://www.w3.org/2001/sw/WebOnt

In order to use Vampire with these tests, the OWL DL ontologies were translated into FO axioms as described in Section 2.1; we then tried to prove the inconsistency (consistency) of the resulting FO theory. In principle it would also be possible to use Vampire with the positive entailment tests by trying to prove the inconsistency of the premise theory augmented with the negated conclusion theory, but this would require a more sophisticated translation in order to deal correctly with anonymous individuals in the negated conclusion theory [17].

The current conversion strategy ignores OWL annotations, i.e., comments that are intended to have no formal semantics. This has no impact on the Consistency and Inconsistency tests. For entailment tests, however, further investigation would be needed as annotations do have an impact on entailment (in particular negative entailment) [27].

4.1 Test Results

We categorise the test results as follows. *Pass*—the prover returned a definitive result which is as expected. *Fail*—the prover returned a definitive result which is not as expected. *Unknown*—the prover failed as a result of technical problems with the translation or with Vampire. *Timeout*—the prover ran out of time (the prover is currently allowed up to 300 seconds to find a proof).

Strictly speaking, any result other than pass should be taken as a failure. A wrong answer is, however, clearly a much more serious failure than an inability to find a proof (timeout) or an inability to deal with the problem (unknown).

Table 7. OWL test results

Type	Attempted	Pass	Fail	Unknown	Timeout	Pass (%)
Inconsistent	66	64	0	1	1	97%
Consistent	46	43	0	1	2	93%
Total	112	107	0	2	3	96%

A summary of the current results is shown in Table 7. As can be seen, Vampire was able to pass over 95% of the tests. Moreover, of the 2 tests returning Unknown, one was due to the presence of large cardinality constraints (with values >500) in the original problem. The number of variables introduced in the translation results in a very large source file for the problem, causing technical difficulties in parsing and converting the test.

5   Extension to SWRL

An attractive feature of the use of a first order prover is its extensibility. The proposed "Semantic Web Stack" includes further layers that build on the Ontology or Logical layer provided by OWL (or similar languages). These layers are likely to add expressivity that moves us out of the fragments of FOL supported by Description Logic reasoners, so alternative techniques will be required to handle these extensions.

One such proposed extension to OWL is the Semantic Web Rule Language (SWRL) [13], which extends OWL with Horn-like rules. Note that SWRL is different from languages such as CARIN [21], where the combination of a relatively inexpressive DL ($\mathcal{ALCNR}$), and rather severe syntactic restrictions on rules, are used to ensure the decidability of the combined language. In contrast, SWRL's underlying logic is much more expressive, and the form of rules is much less restrictive, with the result that the combined language is no longer decidable. Using the translation approach, however, we can easily extend our first-order translation to incorporate these rules and provide a simple implementation of a SWRL reasoner.

5.1 Translating SWRL Rules

Rules in SWRL are of the form:

$$B_1, \ldots, B_m \rightarrow H_1, \ldots, H_n$$

where each of the B_i or H_j are rule *atoms*. Possible rule atoms are shown in Table 8. Here C is an OWL class description, R an OWL property and i and j are either OWL individual names or SWRL variables. We consider a simplification of the proposal in

Table 8. Rule Atoms

Atom	Type
C(i)	Class Atom
R(i,j)	Property Atom
i==j	Equality Atom
i!=j	Inequality Atom

[13], where C must be a class name (rather than arbitrary class descriptions), and R must be an object property. The first of these restrictions does not affect the expressivity of the language, as new class names can be introduced into the ontology to represent any complex descriptions required in rules. The restriction to object properties simplifies our implementation, but the translation we describe could easily be extended to handle data valued properties.

The translation of rules exactly follows the semantics of the rules as given in [13]. Each rule is translated as an implication, and any free variables in the rule are assumed to be universally quantified. Thus a rule:

$$B_1, \ldots, B_m \rightarrow H_1, \ldots, H_n$$

is translated to an axiom:

$$\forall x_1, x_2, \ldots, x_k . T(B_1) \wedge \ldots \wedge T(B_m) \rightarrow T(H_1) \wedge \ldots \wedge T(H_n)$$

where $x_1, x_2, \ldots, x_k$ are all the variables occurring in the B_i and H_j.

Table 9. Rule Atom Translation

Atom	Translation
C(i)	$C(i)$
R(i,j)	$R(i,j)$
i==j	$i=j$
i!=j	$i \neq j$

Translation of atoms is trivial and is shown in Table 9. Combining this translation with the translation from OWL to FOL described in Section 2 provides us with a prototype implementation of a SWRL reasoner. Given an ontology and a collection of rules relating to that ontology, we translate the ontology to FOL, and then add the FOL axioms generated by translating the rules. The resulting theory is passed to a FO prover, where it can be used for reasoning tasks such as satisfiability checking and instance checking. Of course the effectiveness of such a naive approach is open to question, but this does at least provide us with a reasoner *for the complete language* (rather than for some fragment that can be handled by a rule or DL reasoner) that can be used for illustrative and test purposes.

5.2   Examples

The proposed rule language extends the expressivity of OWL, in particular allowing us to provide extra information about properties. A standard example of this is the following definition of "uncle", which cannot be expressed in OWL alone:

```
hasParent(?x,?y), hasSibling(?y, ?z), Male(?z)
      ⇒ hasUncle(?x,?z)
```

If our ontology additionally includes the axiom and facts (expressed here using standard DL syntax):

```
Uncle ≡ ∃hasUncle⁻.⊤
⟨Robert, Paul⟩ : hasParent
⟨Paul, Ian⟩ : hasSibling
```

then the reasoner can infer not only hasUncle(Robert, Ian), but also that Ian is an instance of the Uncle class.

Another interesting aspect of the language is illustrated by the following rule:

```
Beer(?x)  ⇒  Happy(Sean)
```

This expresses the fact that for any instances of the class Beer, Sean must be an instance of Happy. This effectively allows us to express an existential quantification over the class Beer: if we can prove the existence of an instance of this class, then Sean will be Happy. Note that we do not actually have to provide a name for such an instance. For example, if our ontology includes the fact:

```
Sean : ∃drinks.Beer
```

then the reasoner can infer that Sean must be Happy as we now know that there exists *some* instance of Beer—even though this instance is unnamed.

6   Discussion

As can be seen from the results, the performance of Vampire is much worse than that of FaCT++ when tested with reasoning tasks derived from a naive translation of subsumption tests (w.r.t. an ontology). When a suitably optimised translation is used, however, the performance of Vampire improves dramatically: for the small ontology it is comparable with that of FaCT++, although for the more complex Galen and Wine ontologies it is still in the order of 100 times slower (and this does not take into consideration the tests which Vampire is unable to solve within the 300s time limit).

Vampire is able to solve the vast majority of tasks within the time limit, but for the complex ontologies it still fails on a significant number of negative tests (non-subsumption). Unfortunately, the vast majority of tests performed during ontology classification are negative tests. It should also be pointed out that performing each subsumption test in isolation puts Vampire at a considerable disadvantage, as fixed startup costs are incurred in every test, and information from previous tests cannot be reused.

The performance of Vampire is sufficiently encouraging to suggest that further investigations of FO theorem proving techniques for OWL ontology derived tasks would be worthwhile. The FO tasks generated in the tests are in the TPTP format [32], which is a de-facto standard for the theorem proving community, making it easy to use other FO provers in a similar comparison. Given that the performance of FO provers can vary greatly depending on the type of problem, it may be that another FO prover would give better performance on DL subsumption reasoning tasks. On the other hand, the performance gap with respect to FaCT++ is sufficiently large that the designers of FO provers might be encouraged to consider adding some DL reasoning oriented optimisations to their systems.

Although the results presented here do not suggest that FO provers might be used to replace dedicated DL reasoners, they do illustrate that a FO prover can be a useful tool for ontology reasoning. A FO prover might, for example, be used as part of the infrastructure for developing new algorithms and reasoners for various languages, in particular for debugging, prototyping, and for checking the status of newly developed test problems (such as those in the OWL test suite).

It might also be useful to use a FO prover in a hybrid tool for dealing with very expressive languages, e.g., for OWL DL, where reasoning with the complete language is beyond the scope of existing DL algorithms, or for SWRL, where the complete language no longer corresponds to a DL (or to any other decidable fragment of FOL). In these cases, it would be possible to use a FO prover to compute some or all of the relevant inferences. Although there would inevitably be problems with the speed of response, and with incompleteness, there would still be an improvement in performance given that existing DL reasoners currently can't deal with these situations *at all*.

References

1. Franz Baader, Diego Calvanese, Deborah McGuinness, Daniele Nardi, and Peter F. Patel-Schneider, editors. *The Description Logic Handbook: Theory, Implementation and Applications*. Cambridge University Press, 2002.

2. Franz Baader, Bernhard Hollunder, Bernhard Nebel, Hans-Jürgen Profitlich, and Enrico Franconi. An empirical analysis of optimization techniques for terminological representation systems. In *Proc. of the 3rd Int. Conf. on the Principles of Knowledge Representation and Reasoning (KR'92)*, pages 270–281. Morgan Kaufmann, Los Altos, 1992.

3. L. Bachmair and H. Ganzinger. Resolution Theorem Proving. In A. Robinson and A. Voronkov, editors, *Handbook of Automated Reasoning*, volume I, chapter 2, pages 19–99. Elsevier Science, 2001.

4. P. G. Baker, A. Brass, S. Bechhofer, C. Goble, N. Paton, and R. Stevens. Tambis: Transparent access to multiple bioinformatics information sources: an overview. In *Proceedings of the Sixth International Conference on Intelligent Systems for Molecular Biology, ISMB98*, pages 25–34. AAAI Press, 1998.

5. Paul V. Biron and Ashok Malhotra. XML schema part 2: Datatypes. W3C Recommendation, May 2001. http://www.w3.org/TR/xmlschema-2/.

6. Alexander Borgida. On the relative expressiveness of description logics and predicate logics. *Artificial Intelligence*, 82(1–2):353–367, 1996.

7. The CASC web page. http://www.cs.miami.edu/~tptp/CASC/.

8. Mike Dean, Dan Connolly, Frank van Harmelen, James Hendler, Ian Horrocks, Deborah L. McGuinness, Peter F. Patel-Schneider, and Lynn Andrea Stein. OWL Web Ontology Language Reference. W3C Recommendation, 10 February 2004.
http://www.w3.org/TR/owl-ref/.

9. DL'98 test suite. http://dl.kr.org/dl98/comparison/.

10. Harald Ganzinger and Hans de Nivelle. A superposition decision procedure for the guarded fragment with equality. In *Proc. IEEE Conference on Logic in Computer Science (LICS)*, pages 295–304, 1999.

11. M. R. Genesereth and R. E. Fikes. Knowledge Interchange Format Version 3.0 Reference Manual. Technical Report Logic Group Report Logic-92-1, Stanford University, 2001.
http://logic.stanford.edu/kif/Hypertext/kif-manual.html.

12. E. Gradel, M. Otto, and E. Rosen. Two-variable logic with counting is decidable. In *Proceedings of LICS 1997*, pages 306–317, 1997.

13. I. Horrocks, P. F. Patel-Schneider, H. Boley, S. Tabet, B. Grosof, and M. Dean. SWRL: A Semantic Web Rule Language Combining OWL and RuleML.
http://www.daml.org/2003/11/swrl/, 2003.

14. I. Horrocks and S. Tobies. Reasoning with axioms: Theory and practice. In *Proc. of the 7th Int. Conf. on the Principles of Knowledge Representation and Reasoning (KR'2000)*, pages 285–296, 2000.

15. Ian Horrocks. Using an expressive description logic: FaCT or fiction? In *Proc. of the 6th Int. Conf. on Principles of Knowledge Representation and Reasoning (KR'98)*, pages 636–647, 1998.

16. Ian Horrocks and Peter F. Patel-Schneider. The generation of DAML+OIL. In *Proc. of the 2001 Description Logic Workshop (DL 2001)*, pages 30–35. CEUR Electronic Workshop Proceedings, http://ceur-ws.org/Vol-49/, 2001.

17. Ian Horrocks and Peter F. Patel-Schneider. Reducing OWL entailment to description logic satisfiability. In Dieter Fensel, Katia Sycara, and John Mylopoulos, editors, *Proc. of the 2003 International Semantic Web Conference (ISWC 2003)*, number 2870 in Lecture Notes in Computer Science, pages 17–29. Springer, 2003.

18. Ian Horrocks and Ulrike Sattler. Ontology reasoning in the $\mathcal{SHOQ}(D)$ description logic. In *Proc. of the 17th Int. Joint Conf. on Artificial Intelligence (IJCAI 2001)*, pages 199–204, 2001.

19. Ian Horrocks and Ulrike Sattler. The effect of adding complex role inclusion axioms in description logics. In *Proc. of the 18th Int. Joint Conf. on Artificial Intelligence (IJCAI 2003)*, pages 343–348. Morgan Kaufmann, Los Altos, 2003.

20. U. Hustadt and R. A. Schmidt. MSPASS: Modal reasoning by translation and first-order resolution. In R. Dyckhoff, editor, *Automated Reasoning with Analytic Tableaux and Related Methods, International Conference (TABLEAUX 2000)*, volume 1847 of *Lecture Notes in Artificial Intelligence*, pages 67–71. Springer, 2000.

21. Alon Y. Levy and Marie-Christine Rousset. CARIN: A representation language combining horn rules and description logics. In *European Conference on Artificial Intelligence*, pages 323–327, 1996.

22. M. Mortimer. On languages with two variables. *Zeitschr. für math. Logik und Grundlagen der Math.*, 21:135–140, 1975.

23. Max Moser, Ortrun Ibens, Reinhold Letz, Joachim Steinbach, Christoph Goller, Johann Schumann, and Klaus Mayr. SETHEO and e-SETHEO - the CADE-13 systems. *Journal of Automated Reasoning*, 18(2):237–246, 1997.

24. R. Nieuwenhuis and A. Rubio. Paramodulation-Based Theorem Proving. In A. Robinson and A. Voronkov, editors, *Handbook of Automated Reasoning*, volume I, chapter 7, pages 371–443. Elsevier Science, 2001.

25. OWL test suite. http://www.w3.org/TR/owl-test/.

26. M. Paramasivam and David A. Plaisted. Automated deduction techniques for classification in description logic systems. *J. of Automated Reasoning*, 20(3):337–364, 1998.

27. Peter F. Patel-Schneider, Patrick Hayes, and Ian Horrocks. OWL web ontology language semantics and abstract syntax. W3C Recommendation, 10 February 2004. Available at http://www.w3.org/TR/owl-semantics/.

28. A. L. Rector, W. A. Nowlan, and A. Glowinski. Goals for concept representation in the GALEN project. In *Proc. of the 17th Annual Symposium on Computer Applications in Medical Care (SCAMC'93)*, pages 414–418, Washington DC, USA, 1993.

29. A. Riazanov and A. Voronkov. The Design and Implementation of Vampire. *AI Communications*, 15(2-3):91–110, 2002.

30. Klaus Schild. A correspondence theory for terminological logics: Preliminary report. In *Proc. of the 12th Int. Joint Conf. on Artificial Intelligence (IJCAI'91)*, pages 466–471, 1991.

31. G. Sutcliffe and C. Suttner. The TPTP Problem Library. TPTP v. 2.4.1. Technical report, University of Miami, 2001.

32. G. Sutcliffe and C. Suttner. The TPTP Problem Library. TPTP v. 2.4.1. Technical report, University of Miami, 2001.

33. T. Tammet. Gandalf. *Journal of Automated Reasoning*, 18(2):199–204, 1997.

34. Tanel Tammet. Extending Classical Theorem Proving for the Semantic Web. In R. Volz, S. Decker, and I. Cruz, editors, *Proceedings of the First International Workshop on Practical and Scalable Semantic Systems*, October 2003. http://km.aifb.uni-karlsruhe.de/ws/psss03/proceedings.

35. Stephan Tobies. *Complexity Results and Practical Algorithms for Logics in Knowledge Representation*. PhD thesis, LuFG Theoretical Computer Science, RWTH-Aachen, Germany, 2001.

36. Dmitry Tsarkov and Ian Horrocks. DL reasoner vs. first-order prover. In *Proc. of the 2003 Description Logic Workshop (DL 2003)*, volume 81 of *CEUR (http://ceur-ws.org/)*, pages 152–159, 2003.

Generating On the Fly Queries for the Semantic Web: The ICS-FORTH Graphical RQL Interface (GRQL)[1]

Nikos Athanasis[1,2], Vassilis Christophides[1,2], and Dimitris Kotzinos[2]

[1] Institute of Computer Science, Foundation for Research and Technology – Hellas,
P.O. Box 1385, 71110 Heraklio, Greece
{athanasi, christop}@ics.forth.gr
[2] Department of Computer Science, University of Crete,
P.O. Box 2208, 71110 Heraklio, Greece
kotzino@csd.uoc.gr

Abstract. Building user-friendly GUIs for browsing and filtering RDF/S description bases while exploiting in a transparent way the expressiveness of declarative query/view languages is vital for various Semantic Web applications (e.g., e-learning, e-science). In this paper we present a novel interface, called GRQL, which relies on the full power of the RDF/S data model for constructing on the fly queries expressed in RQL. More precisely, a user can navigate graphically through the individual RDF/S class and property definitions and generate transparently the RQL path expressions required to access the resources of interest. These expressions capture accurately the meaning of its navigation steps through the class (or property) subsumption and/or associations. Additionally, users can enrich the generated queries with filtering conditions on the attributes of the currently visited class while they can easily specify the resource's class(es) appearing in the query result. To the best of our knowledge, GRQL is the first application-independent GUI able to generate a unique RQL query which captures the cumulative effect of an entire user navigation session.

1 Introduction

Semantic Web (SW) technology and in particular the Resource Description Framework (RDF) [12] and its Schema definition language (RDFS) [3] are increasingly gaining acceptance by modern web applications (e.g., e-learning, e-science) striving to describe, retrieve and process large volumes of information resources spread worldwide. In this context, several declarative languages for querying and specifying views over RDF/S description bases have been proposed in the literature such as RQL [12], and RVL [15] (see [14] for an extensive comparison of SW QLs). However, these languages are mainly targeting experienced users, who need to understand not

---

[1] This work was partially supported by the EU Projects MesMuses (IST-2000-26074) and Selene (IST-2001-39045).

S.A. McIlraith et al. (Eds.): ISWC 2004, LNCS 3298, pp. 486–501, 2004.

only the RDF/S data model but also the syntax and the semantics of each language in order to formulate a query or a view in some textual form. Building user-friendly GUIs for browsing and filtering RDF/S description bases while exploiting in a transparent way the expressiveness of declarative languages like RQL/RVL is still an open issue for emerging SW technology.

The idea of using suitable visual abstractions in order to access data collections originates from the early days of the database systems. Commercial systems like the IBM QBE [21] and Microsoft Query Builder [16], as well as research prototypes like PESTO [8], IVORY [5], Lorel's DataGuide-driven GUI [10], BBQ [17], QURSED [18], and XQBE [2] are just few examples of graphical front-ends to relational, object or semistructured/XML databases assisting end-users in formulating queries to the underlying language (e.g., SQL, OQL, or XPath/XQuery) of the DBMS. These visual querying interfaces essentially rely on a graphical representation of the schema constructs (i.e., relations, object classes, XML elements/attributes) supported in each data model along with appropriate end-user interactions allowing to construct custom views and display their results in a default fashion. They are usually implemented as standalone applications targeting experienced users who need to understand not only the schema of the underlying database but also a great part of the functionality of the supported query language (i.e., joins, projections, etc.).

In the context of Semantic Web Portals, several browsing interfaces have been proposed (like RDF Distillery [9], OntoWeb [11], OntoPortal [4], ODESeW [7]) for accessing ontologies and their related information resources. These visual browsing interfaces offer a graphical view of the entire ontology as a tree or a graph of related classes and properties where users can either access directly the classified resources or formulate (attribute-value) filtering queries. They are usually implemented as Web applications for the "general public" using the programming APIs supported by the underlying ontology repository. As a result of their API limitations, the resources accessed each time correspond only to the most recently performed browsing action, regardless of the navigation paths traversed by a user. Thus, SW browsing interfaces ignore the class associations followed by users when visiting one class after the other.

The graphical interface presented in this paper aims to combine the simplicity of SW browsers with the expressiveness of DB query generators in order to navigate the Semantic Web by generating queries on the fly. The proposed interface, called GRQL, relies on the full power of the RDF/S data model for constructing, in a transparent to the end-user way, queries expressed in a declarative language such as RQL. More precisely, after choosing an entry point, users can discover the individual RDF/S class and property definitions and continue browsing by generating at each step the RQL path expressions required to access the resources of interest. These path expressions capture accurately the meaning of its navigation steps through the class (or property) subsumption and/or associations. Additionally, at each navigation step users can enrich the generated queries with filtering conditions on the attributes of the currently visited class while they can easily specify which class of resources should be finally included in the query result. To the best of our knowledge, GRQL is the first application-independent graphical interface able to generate a unique RQL query which captures the cumulative effect of an entire user navigation session. This functionality is vital for Semantic Web Portals striving to support conceptual bookmarks and personalized knowledge maps build on demand according to user's navigation history [19].

The rest of the paper is organized as follows. Section 2 presents the graphical generation of RQL queries using different navigation scenarios related to an example RDF/S schema. Section 3 details the implementation of our generic query generation algorithm including the internal representation model of RDF/S schemas and RQL queries, as well as the GUI demonstrating the intuitive use of GRQL by non-expert users. Finally, Section 4 summarizes our contributions and outlines our future work.

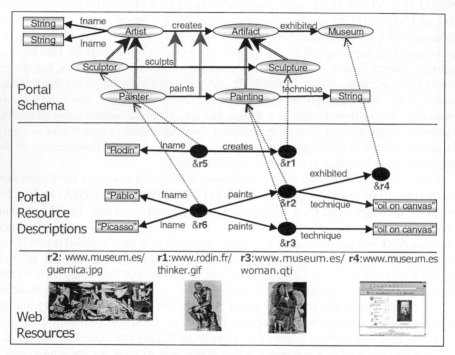

Fig. 1. RDF/S Descriptions of Web Resources in a Cultural Portal

2   From RDF/S Schema Browsing to RQL Queries

In this section we will present our graphical RQL interface (GRQL) and in particular the translation of the browsing actions performed by a user on the RDF/S class (or property) subsumption and/or associations to appropriate RQL path expressions and filters. To this end, we will use a fairly well known example schema originally employed in [12] to present the functionality of RQL.

Fig. 1 illustrates the RDF/S descriptions of four available resources: a sculpture image (resource identified as *r1*), two painting images (resources identified as *r2* and *r3*) and a museum web site (resource identified as *r4*). These descriptions have been created according to an RDF/S schema for cultural applications comprising three top-level classes, namely *Artist*, *Artifact* and *Museum*, which are associated thought the properties *creates* and *exhibited*. Given the flexibility of the RDF/S data model, both classes and properties can be specialized through subsumption relationships. In our example, the class *Artist* is specialized to *Sculptor* and *Painter* while class *Artifact* to *Sculpture* and *Painting*. In the same way the property *creates* (with domain the class *Artist* and range the class *Artifact*) is specialized to *sculpts* (with domain the class *Sculptor* and range the class *Sculpture*) and *paints* (with domain the class *Painter* and range the class *Painting*). Properties *fname, lname,* and *technique* play the role of attributes and range over the literal type *string* (or more generally an XML Schema data type [1, 20]). Then, resource *r2* can be described as an instance of the class *Painting* with an attribute *technique* having as value *"oil on canvas"* and it is associated with resource *r4* though the property *exhibited*.

It is fairly obvious that users of our cultural portal need to navigate through the schema in order to access the corresponding resource descriptions. Nevertheless this navigation should take place without having to learn an RDF query language and construct the necessary queries by themselves. Furthermore, they want to distinguish *Artifact* resources for which information about their creator is available (e.g., *r1, r2, r3*) from *Artifact* resources having additional information about their exhibiting museum (e.g., *r2*). In other words, as in the case of static hyperlinks between web pages, users should be able to browse the Semantic Web in order to access resources according to the navigation paths traversed in the conceptual space defined by an RDF/S schema. This is a non-trivial task given that users can arbitrary browse back and forth through both the subsumption relationships of classes (or properties) and the associations of classes captured by properties. In the rest of this section, we will detail how the translation algorithm of the GRQL interface supports the desired functionality.

2.1 Browsing Class Associations

GRQL provides a tree-shaped graphical representation of the class (or property) subsumption relationships defined in an RDF/S schema, as for instance, the cultural example of Fig. 1. Then, users can choose one of the available classes (or properties) to begin their navigation session, while the definition of the selected class (i.e., its subclasses, attributes and associations) is displayed in order to enable them to browse further the DAG of class associations[2]. This elementary browsing action is translated into an appropriate RQL query, which essentially specifies a dynamic view over the underlying resource descriptions according to the performed schema navigation. Table 1 depicts the choice of the class *Artist* as entry point, as well as the generated RQL query returning all resources classified under *Artist* and recursively its subclasses (i.e., resources *r5* and *r6*). At each browsing step, GRQL displays the path(s) of classes and properties visited insofar during a navigation session. In this way, GRQL not only informs users about their navigation history but also provides the ability to return to a previous browsing step. As we will see later on in this paper, this is useful for specifying which class of resources will be finally included in the con-

---

[2] Cyclic properties, having as domain and range the same class, are not considered in this paper.

structed view, as well as for navigating through multiple schema paths (see subsection 2.3).

Table 1. Choice of class *Artist* as entry point to the schema navigation

Navigation	RQL query	Path
Artist ❶	select X1 from Artist{X1}	Artist

After displaying the definition of the class *Artist* the user can access the resources of other associated classes, as for instance, the class *Artifact* (through the *creates* relationship). Now the user's view is extended with property *creates* relating instances of the class *Artist* with instances of the class *Artifact*. Table 2 shows the performed browsing action, the generated RQL query and the corresponding navigation path. Note that the path expression *creates* in the from clause of the RQL query considers resources associated by this property and any of its subproperties such as *paints* and *sculpts* (i.e., *Artifact* resources *r1, r2* and *r3*). By default, the resources included in the final result i.e., the select clause of the RQL query, correspond to the current class (or property) selection in the navigation path, as in this example the range class of the property *creates*.

Table 2. Navigation to associated class *Artifact* through property *creates*

Navigation	RQL query	Path
Artist ❶ →creates→ Artifact ❷	select X2 from {X1}creates{X2}	Artist→creates→Artifact

In the same manner, users can continue their navigation from class *Artifact* to *Museum* through the property *exhibited* and the available view is now specified by the following RQL query: select X3 from {X1}creates{X2}.exhibited{X3}. In this example, the constructed view comprises the *Museum* resource *r6*.

2.2 Browsing Subsumption Relationships

In addition, GRQL gives the ability to interleave at any step browsing on class associations with browsing on class (or property) subsumption relationships. For instance, after the navigation illustrated in Table 2 a user may choose to visit the subclass *Painting* of *Artifact*. As is shown in Table 3, this browsing action has the effect to narrow the user's view only to *Painting*(s) created by an *Artist*. Compared to the RQL query of Table 2, the path expression in the from clause has been now accordingly modified to {X1}creates{X2;Painting} where the range of the property instead of the default *Artifact* class (and thus initially omitted) is now restricted to *Painting*.

Table 3. Navigation to specialized classes

Navigation	RQL query	Path
	select X2 from {X1}creates{X2;Painting}	Artist→creates→Painting

Then, users can either continue browsing through more specialized subclasses, if available, or visit other associated classes of class *Painting*. Note that RDF/S subclasses may have additional associations and attributes, as for instance, *technique*. The user can alternatively return to a previous step in the navigation path by clicking on the name of an already visited class or property (or more generally by clicking the *back* button of a Web browser).

Table 4. Navigating back to an already visited class

Navigation	RQL query	Path
	select X2 from {X1}creates{X2;Painting}	Artist→creates→Painting
	select X1 from {X1}creates{X2;Painting}	Artist→creates→Painting

As shown in Table 4 (solid arrows represent the current position of the user in a navigation path), this browsing action affects only the target class of resources, which are going to be included in the user view i.e., the select clause of the generated RQL query. For example, while the first scenario considers in the view resources of the class *Painting* (represented by variable *X2*), the second scenario returning back to the initial navigation step, considers resources of the class *Artist* (represented by variable *X1*). It should be stressed that, although the user visits the same class *Artist* in both the initial and the final browsing step, the constructed views are different (see Tables 4, 1), since they capture the effect of a sequence of performed browsing actions.

Table 5. Navigating to sibling subclasses in a path

Navigation	RQL query	Path
Artist creates Artifact / Painting Sculpture	select X2 from {X1}creates{X2;Painting }, Sculpture{X2}	Artist→creates→Painting Sculpture

2.3 Browsing Multiple Navigation Paths

If a user revisits the class *Artifact* from the scenario of Table 4, the constructed view remains the same as illustrated in Table 3. This ensures that the GRQL interface does not generate redundant RQL queries in the case where a user loops in the navigation path. However, since the definition of class *Artifact* is made available once more, the user may choose to visit another subclass such as *Sculpture*. In this scenario, the view contains the *Artist*(s) and their *Painting*(s) computed previously, which are also *Sculpture*(s). As it can be seen in Table 5 this browsing action is translated into a conjunction of two RQL path expressions, given that the user was firstly interested to *Painting*(s) and then to *Sculpture*(s). Note that conjunctive path expressions in the from clause of an RQL query share common resource variables (e.g., variable X2). In this way GRQL interface captures the fact that the same URL may be classified under several unrelated through subsumption classes. The class of resources included in the final result of the view corresponds, as usual, to the current position of the user in the navigation path(s), but there is also the ability to obtain all the resources (e.g., represented by variables X1, X2 and X3) involved in its navigational view by selecting the special *"Include All"* GRQL button.

Users may in turn decide to revisit the class *Painting* displayed in the first navigation path and select the associated class *Museum* through the property *exhibited*. In this scenario, its view provides access to *Museum*(s) exhibiting *Painting*(s) that have been created by *Artist*(s), with the additional condition that these *Painting*(s) are also *Sculpture*(s). The generated RQL query by this browsing action is shown in Table 6.

Table 6. Navigating to associated classes that belong to different navigation paths

Navigation	RQL query	Path
Artist creates Artifact / Painting creates Museum Sculpture	select X3 from {X1}creates{X2;Pa inting}. {;Painting}exhibi ted{X3}, Sculpture{X2}	Sculpture Artist→creates→Painting→ →exhibited→Museum

Table 7. Navigating to specialized properties

Navigation	RQL query	Path
	Select X1, X2 from {X1}paints{X2}.{;Painting}exhibited{X3}, Sculpture{X2}	Sculpture Painter→paints→Painting→ →exhibited→Museum

As a different navigation scenario, we consider browsing through specialized properties, like *paints*, which can be reached in our example by clicking on the property *creates* already appearing in the first navigation path of Table 6. Compared to subclasses (see Table 3), browsing subproperties has as effect to alter both the domain and range classes of properties included in a navigation path. As shown in Table 7, this browsing action will construct a new view containing those *Painter*(s) that have *paint*ed *Painting*(s) *exhibited* in a *Museum* with the additional condition that these *Painting*(s) are also *Sculpture*(s). Since these classes are the default domain-range definitions of *paint*, the corresponding restrictions can be omitted in the from clause of the generated RQL query.

Finally, as a last navigation scenario, we consider browsing through different paths that converge to the same class. This class is the common range of properties (same or different) traversed by distinct branching paths. In Table 8, we assume that the user has navigated twice to the class *Museum* through the property *exhibited*: first from the class *Painting* and then from the class *Sculpture*. Given the semantics of the navigation to sibling classes (Table 5), our user is interested in *Painting(s)*, which are also *Sculpture(s)*, and the previous browsing action results to the addition only of the subpath Painting→exhibited→Museum. Note that the addition of the subpath Sculpture→exhibited→Museum is redundant, since the generated RQL query will always return the same results as previously: the corresponding view provides access to *Painters* that have created *Painting*, which are also *Sculptures*, exhibited in a *Museum*.

It becomes clear that GRQL enables users to browse towards all directions in an RDF/S schema (i.e., subsumption and association relationships of classes and properties), including backtracking and choice of branching navigation paths. The views

Table 8. Navigating to an associated class from multiple different paths

Navigation	RQL query	Path
	select X3 from {X1}paints{X2}.{;Painting}exhibited{X3}, Sculpture{X2}	Sculpture Painter→paints→Painting →exhibited→Museum

constructed at each step carry the information of the previous navigation and augment it with the additional resources that can be actually accessed by the current browsing action. In other words, GRQL creates dynamic views based on the incremental construction of adequate RQL queries capturing the effect of browsing actions performed by a user during its navigation session. To begin a new session, users have just to return back to the initial tree-shaped interface of class (or property) subsumption relationships and choose another entry point to the schema.

2.4   Enriching Path Expressions with Filtering Conditions

In addition to the ability to navigate through the RDF schema paths, users can formulate filtering conditions on the attributes of the class visited at each navigation step. The comparison operators which can be used in these conditions are related to the data types of the class attributes specified in XML Schema [1, 20], e.g. strings, datetime, numerical like integer and float, and enumerations. Thus, GRQL enables users to select graphically the desirable filtering condition that can be used with a particular attribute data type and fill the comparison values in a dedicated text area.

For example, if the RQL query of Table 4 should be restricted to obtain *Artists*, whose last name (attribute named *last_name*) contains a "P", the user has to insert the required information ("P") and select the "like" operator for filtering. The constructed conjunctive RQL query is given below:

select X1 from {X1}:creates{X2;Painting}, {X1}last_name{X4} where X4 like "*P*"

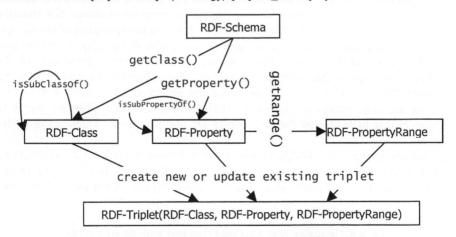

Fig. 2. The GRQL Java classes representation of RDF/S schemas

It becomes clear that filtering provides the ability to select resources that their attributes conform to user specified conditions in conjunction with their associations to other resources specified by the user schema navigation paths. As a result RQL queries can define custom views that present to users a snapshot of the underlying RDF/S description base by hiding unnecessary information.

3 Implementation of the GRQL Translation Algorithm and GUI

In this section we detail the translation algorithm of the user browsing actions on an RDF/S schema into appropriate RQL queries. To this end, we first introduce the GRQL interface internal representation of RDF/S schemas and RQL queries. Finally, we present the GRQL GUI, which allows browsing arbitrary RDF/S schemas and resource descriptions by generating RQL queries on the fly.

3.1 GRQL Internal Model of RDF/S Schemas and RQL Queries

An RDF/S schema is first loaded into the main memory during the GRQL system initialization by using appropriate Java classes. That way, schema navigation is efficiently implemented by accessing directly the required, at each step, class and property definitions instead of generating new RQL queries (e.g., to obtain subclasses or subproperties). Note that, GRQL is able to obtain during initialization the entire schema information stored in a RSSDB database [0] through a single RQL query.

As we can see in Fig. 2, the result of the initial schema query is processed by the java class RDF-Schema, while each RDF class is represented by the java class RDF-Class and each RDF property by the java class RDF-Property (java class RDF-PropertyRange captures either a literal type or a class serving as range of a property). Schema navigation performed by the user is represented as a list of objects of type RDF-Triplet containing references to objects of type RDF-Property, RDF-Class and RDF-PropertyRange. Then methods (like getDomain(), getRange(), isSubClassOf(), isSubPropertyOf()) are used to construct the appropriate RDF-Triplets according to the browsing actions performed by a user.

3.2 GRQL Translation Algorithm of Browsing Actions

The creation of dynamic views during the user's navigation relies on the generation of an appropriate RQL query. In order to create correctly this query we have implemented an algorithm translating the user navigation into schema triplets, which are used in the sequel to produce the corresponding RQL query, as well as visualize the traversed navigation paths. The algorithm relies on the RDF/S schema information represented by the Java classes of Fig. 2. A triplet consists of statements of the form <subject, predicate, object> where predicate captures the properties while subject and object capture the classes traversed during schema navigation.

Recall that GRQL interface allows users to navigate though classes and subclasses, as well as properties and subpropeties. Note also that properties are selected either explicitly by their name, or implicitly by their range given a specific domain class in the navigation path. At each browsing action performed by a user the GRQL translation algorithm will either create a new triplet or modify an existing one or leave everything unchanged in case of loops. The triplets belong either to the same path that the user is currently traversing (in which case the new triplet's domain is the range of the current triplet), thus creating a chain or to a new path (in which case the new triplet's domain is the same with the domain of the current triplet), thus creating tree-shaped paths. Thus, GRQL is able to construct and manipulate any kind of navigation path, including linear and branching paths with common origin and/or destination as depicted in Fig. 3. The pseudocode of the GRQL translation algorithm is given in Fig. 4 (the class and property selected by a user are denoted as selClass and selProp).

Going back to the first navigation scenario of the previous section, one can easily correlate the triplets created by our algorithm with the navigation paths traversed by a user and consequently with the generated RQL queries. So the initial selection of the *Artist* class as an entry point produces the first triplet: *<Artist, empty, empty>* (lines 2 – 5 of Fig. 4). Then, when the user navigates to an associated class, i.e. selects the *Artifact*(s) *create*(d) by the *Artist*(s), the triplet is modified to *<Artist, creates, Artifact>*. It should be stressed that we could obtain the same triplet in one step, if in the initial selection the property *creates* was chosen instead of the class *Artist* (lines 34 – 37). In any case, by selecting a subclass (*Painting*) the user chooses a more specific description about the available resources and thus the triplet is once more modified to *<Artist, creates, Painting>* (lines 15 – 18).

In the backtracking scenario when the user revisits a class, the triplets produced insofar remain the same. On the other hand, when the user selects a class not specializing the domain of the current triplet (i.e., sibling), the algorithm creates a new triplet corresponding to a branching path. For example, by selecting *Sculpture*(s) *create*(d) by *Artist*(s) instead of *Painting(s)*, the triplet *<empty, empty, Sculpture>* is added to the list of existing triplets (lines 20 – 25). Once again users could alternatively have chosen to view the *Sculpture*(s) *sculpt*(ed) by the *Sculptor*(s) by navigating through the subproperty *sculpts* of *creates*, which results to the modification of the triple *<Artist, creates, Painting>* to *<Sculptor, sculpts, Sculpture>* (lines 43 - 44) and the addition of the triplet *<empty, empty, Painting>* (lines 51 – 55). In both cases the user's navigation path has two branches and the RQL query is updated accordingly.

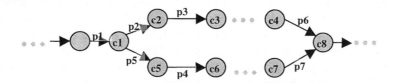

Fig. 3. Schema navigation paths constructed and manipulated by GRQL

Assuming now that the user wants to further expand his navigation along the initial path (*<Artist, creates, Artifact>*) in order to also obtain the *Museum*s that the *Artifact*s are exhibited at, the new triplet *<Artifact, exhibited, Museum>* will be added (lines 64 - 69) to the list of existing triples. If the user narrows the scope of its navigation by selecting the subclass *Painting,* this browsing action affects both triplets having *Artifact* as subject or object by modifying them to *<Artist, creates, Painting>*, *<Painting, exhibited, Museum>* (lines 15 – 18 and 10 – 13 respectively).

```
(00)  if (user navigates through subclasses)
(01)  {
(02)    if (the navigation path is empty)
(03)    {//create a new triplet where its domain is the selected class
(04)      create triplet (selClass, empty, empty);
(05)    }
(06)    else
(07)      //iterate through the already created triplets
(08)      for each triplet (c1,p,c2) in list of navigation paths
(09)      {//if the selected class is a subclass of triplet's domain
(10)        if (selClass.isSubClassOf(c1) )
(11)        {//modify the triplet's domain to the selected class
(12)          modify triplet (selClass, p, c2);
(13)        }
(14)        //if the selected class is a subclass of triplet's range
(15)        else if (selClass.isSubClassOf(c2))
(16)            {//modify the triplet's range to the selected class
(17)              modify triplet (c1, p, selClass);
(18)            }
(19)          //if the selected class is a sibling of triplet's domain/range
(20)          else if (selClass.isSubClassOf(p.getDomain()) or
(21)                  selClass.isSubClassOf(p.getRange()))
(22)              {//create a new branching triplet for path nodes
(23)                  if (candidate triplet is not in list of navigation paths
(24)                      and not exist other triplets in path specializing the
                          candidate triplet)
(25)                    create triplet (selClass, empty, empty); }
(26)      }
(27)  }
(28)  // user navigates through properties and subproperties
(29)  else
(30)  {//get the domain of the selected property
(31)    domain = selProp.getDomain();
(32)    //get the range of the selected property
(33)    range = selProp.getRange();
(34)    if (the list of navigation paths is empty)
(35)    {//create a triplet with the selected property, its domain and range
(36)      create triplet (domain, selprop, range);
(37)    }
(38)    else
(49)      //iterate through the already created triplets
(40)      for each triplet (c1,p,c2) in list of navigation paths
(41)      { //if the selected property selProp is a subproperty of the current
(42)        //triplet's property
(43)        if (selProp.isSubPropertyOf(p))
(44)          {//modify the property of the current triplet to selProp
(45)            modify triplet (domain, selProp, range);
(46)            //if triplet's domain is sibling of the selProp's domain
(47)            if !((domain==c1) or (domain.isSubClassOf(c1))
(48)              // create a new branching triplet for path nodes
(49)              if (candidate triplet is not in list of navigation paths)
(50)                  create triplet (c1, empty, empty);
(51)            //if triplet's range is sibling of the selProp's range
(52)            if !((range==c2) or (range.isSubClassOf(c2))
(53)              // create a new branching triplet for path nodes
(54)              if (candidate triplet is not in list of navigation paths)
(55)                  create triplet (empty, empty, c2);
(56)          }
(57)        //if the selected property differs from the triplet's property
(58)        else if (selProp != p)
(59)            {//adjust the domain of the immediate following triples in path
(60)              if (range.isSubClassOf(c1))
(61)              { //modify the triplet's domain to the selected property range
(62)                modify triplet (range, p, c2);
(63)              }
(64)              //if current triplet differs from the selected property
(65)              else if ((c1 != domain) and (c2 != range))
(66)              { //create a new branching triplet for path edges
(67)                  if (candidate triplet is not in list of navigation paths
(68)                      and not exist other triplets in path specializing the
                          candidate triplet)
(69)                    create triplet (domain, selProp, range);
(70)              }
(71)          }
(72)      }
(73)  }
```

Fig. 4. Pseudocode of the class navigation triplet construction

In the same manner, triplets are created when users add filtering conditions to their navigation paths. In this case though, triplets are constructed based on the attribute, its value and corresponding condition and the associated class. Referring to the example presented in 2.4 and for exactly the same RQL query the constructed triplets will be: *<Artist, creates, Painting>, <Artist, last_name, like "*P*">*.

It becomes clear that the GRQL translation algorithm captures successfully a sequence of complex browsing actions performed by a user at the schema level. Then, at each navigation step the generated triples are employed to construct dynamically the RQL query defining a user view. Last but not least, the GRQL translation algorithm ensures that the generated RQL queries are minimal, i.e., there do not exist other less complex RQL queries, which can produce the same result. As a matter of fact, our algorithm computes at each browsing step the minimal RQL query corresponding to the conjunction of the current and the previous navigation paths. For instance, assuming that a user selects initially the property *creates*, then refines its range to the subclass *Painter* and finally narrows its view to the subproperty *paints*, GRQL generates three RQL queries for which the following containment relationships are true:

Q3 select *   **Q2** select *   **Q1** select *
   from {X1}paints{X2} $\subseteq$ from {X1;Painter}creates{X2} $\subseteq$ from {X1}creates{X2}
Since the result of **Q2** is contained in the result of **Q1**, the conjunction of the queries (or more precisely of their path expressions) generated at the current (2) and previous steps (1) results to a redundant RQL query, which can be simplified as follows:
Q2 select *   **Q2'** select *
   from{X1;Painter}creates{X2} $\equiv$ from{X1;Painter}creates{X2},{X1}creates{X2}
In the same way, the minimal RQL query produced at the navigation step 3 is **Q3**. Readers are referred to [6] for formal foundations of RQL query containment.

3.3   The GRQL Graphical User Interface

The GRQL GUI consists of three basic interaction areas. The left area provides a tree-shaped display of the subsumption hierarchies[3] of both the classes and properties defined in an RDF/S schema. Selecting the name of a class or property, results to a new navigation session. This session considers the selected class or property as entry point for further schema browsing. In this respect, the right upper area of the GRQL GUI allows users to explore progressively the individual RDF/S class and property definitions and generate navigational and/or filtering RQL queries. Finally, the right lower area visualizes the constructed query/view results. A snapshot of the GRQL GUI is illustrated in Fig. 5.

The left area of the GUI displays the predefined views over the class and property hierarchies (e.g., corresponding to a particular RDF/S schema namespace). Each tree node is labeled with a class or a property name and users can access their subclasses

---

[3] In case of multiple subsumption, the same class or property appears as a child of all its parent nodes.

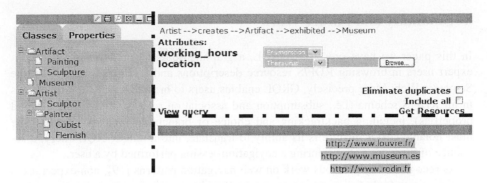

Fig. 5. A Snapshot of the GRQL GUI after navigating at the schema level

and subproperties by expanding the tree nodes. Each tree node is essentially a hyperlink that, after activation, fetches in the right area of the GUI the complete definition of the selected class or property. More precisely, for each selected class the following items are displayed: its subclasses, its associations with other classes and its attributes. For each selected property the domain and range classes are displayed, as well as its subproperties. As have presented in the previous section, selections on classes associations and/or subsumption result to the construction of appropriate schema navigation paths.

GRQL also supports navigation at the resource level. When the *"Get Resources"* hyperlink is activated, the lower area of the GUI will display the resources matching the generated RQL path expressions and filters, i.e., populating the constructed view. If the *"Include All"* button is also selected, the resources of all the classes taking part in the navigation path(s) will be displayed. In the opposite, (and this is the default behavior), only the resources of the last visited class will be displayed (or the resources in the domain and range of the last visited property). Additionally the user has the ability to *"Eliminate Duplicates"*, if such an action is desirable. For educational purposes, a user has the ability to inspect the generated RQL query by clicking on the *"View Query"* hyperlink. After computing the resources that correspond to a current position in the navigation path, users can select a specific resource URI to obtain its full semantic description (i.e., the classes under which are classified, their attribute values and associations to other resources) or they can continue their navigation at the schema level.

Finally, an appropriate navigation bar is employed to visualize the navigation history of a user and therefore the so-constructed RQL query. Hyperlinks of all constituent path parts enable users to revisit a class or property and follow an alternative navigation path. In a nutshell, GRQL GUI supports unconstrained browsing through both RDF/S resource descriptions and schemas.

4 Summary and Future Work

In this paper we have presented GRQL, a graphical query generator assisting non-expert users in browsing RDF/S resource descriptions and schemas available on the Semantic Web. More precisely, GRQL enables users to browse towards all directions in an RDF/S schema (i.e., subsumption and association relationships of classes and properties), including backtracking and choice of branching navigation paths. The most notable GRQL feature is its ability to translate, into a unique RQL query, a sequence of browsing actions during a navigation session performed by a user.

As recognized by previous work on web navigation patterns [19], non-expert users need intuitive tools for capturing resources they have visited in previous navigation steps. We believe that GRQL addresses successfully this need, by enabling SW applications to support conceptual bookmarks and personalized knowledge maps build on demand according to users' navigation history. We are currently implementing this functionality in the context of the ICS-FORTH Semantic Web Portal Generator[4].

Finally, we are planning to extend the GRQL graphical interface to also support disjunctive queries, as well as updates of RDF/S descriptions and schemas. In this way, users will be equipped with a uniform graphical interface for navigating, filtering and updating RDF/S description bases and schemas without needing to learn dedicated declarative languages or to program in application-specific APIs.

References

0.   Alexaki S., Christophides V., Karvounarakis G., Plexousakis D., Tolle K.: *The ICS-FORTH RDFSuite: Managing Voluminous RDF Description Bases*. In Proceedings of the 2nd International Workshop on the Semantic Web (SemWeb), in conjunction with the Tenth International World Wide Web Conference (WWW), Hongkong, May 1, 2001.
1.   Biron P. V., and Malhotra A.: *XML SchemaPart 2: Datatypes*. W3C Recommendation 02 May 2001.
     http://springerlink.metapress.com/openurl.asp?genre=article&issn=0302-9743&
     volume=2992&spage=848
2.   Braga D., Campi A., and Ceri S.: *XQBE: A Graphical Interface for XQuery Engines*. In Proceeding of the 9th International Conference on Extending Database Technology (EDBT), Heraklion, Crete, Greece, March 14-18, 2004.
3.   Brickley D., Guha R.V., and McBride B.: *RDF Vocabulary Description Language 1.0: RDF Schema*, W3C Recommendation 10 February 2004.
4.   Carr L., Kampa S., and Miles-Board T.: *OntoPortal: Building Ontological Hypermedia with the OntoPortal Framework*. MetaPortal Final Report 2001. The semantic portal is available at: http://www.ontoportal.org.uk
5.   Chang S., Lee D and Kim H. A.: *Visual Browse/Query Tool for Navigating and Retrieving Multimedia Data on Object Databases*. In Proceedings of the First International Conference on Advanced Multimedia Content Processing Osaka, Japan, November 1998.

---

[4] http://athena.ics.forth.gr:8999/RQLdemo/

6. Christophides V., Karvounarakis G., Koffina I., Kokkinidis G., Magkanaraki A., Plexousakis D., Serfiotis G., and Tannen V.: *The ICS-FORTH SWIM: A Powerful Semantic Web Integration Middleware*, First International Workshop on Semantic Web and Databases (SWDB), collocated with VLDB 2003, Humboldt-Universitat, Berlin, Germany, September 7-8, 2003.
7. Corcho, O., Gómez-Pérez, A., López-Cima, A., and del Carmen Suárez-Figueroa, M.: *ODESeW: Automatic Generation of Knowledge Portals for Intranets and Extranets*. The semantic portal is available at: http://www.esperonto.net/semanticportal/jsp/frames.jsp
8. Carey M., Haas L., Maganty V., and Williams J.: *PESTO: An Integrated Query/Browser for Object Databases*. In Proceedings of the 22nd International Conference on Very Large Data Bases (VLDB), September 3-6, 1996, Bombay, India.
9. Gibson, D.: *The RDF Distillery*. University of Queensland, 2002. Available at: http://www.kvocentral.com/reports/diongibsonthesis.pdf
10. Goldman R., and Widom J.: DataGuides: *Enabling Query Formulation and Optimization in Semi-structured Databases*. Stanford Technical Report 1997. Available at: http://www-db.stanford.edu/lore/pubs/dataguide.pdf
11. Jarrar M., Majer B., Meersman R., Spyns P., Studer R., Sure Y., and Volz R.: *OntoWeb Portal: Complete ontology and portal*. In Proceedings of the 17th National Conference on Artificial Intelligence, Austin/TX, USA, July 30-August 3, 2000, AAAI Press/MIT Press.
12. Karvounarakis G., Alexaki S., Christophides V., Plexousakis D., and Scholl M.: *RQL: A Declarative Query Language for RDF*, The Eleventh International World Wide Web Conference (WWW), Honolulu, Hawaii, USA, May 7-11, 2002.
13. Klyne G., Carroll J.J, and McBride B.: *Resource Description Framework (RDF): Concepts and Abstract Syntax*. W3C Recommendation. 10 February 2004.
14. Magkanaraki A., Karvounarakis G., Christophides V., Plexousakis D., and Anh T..: *Ontology Storage and Querying*. ICS-FORTH Technical Report No 308, April 2002.
15. Magkanaraki A., Tannen V., Christophides V., and Plexousakis D.: *Viewing the Semantic Web Through RVL Lenses*. In Proceedings of the Second International Semantic Web Conference (ISWC), Sanibel Island, Florida, USA, 20-23 October, 2003.
16. Microsoft Visual InterDev, Available at http://msdn.microsoft.com/vinterdev/
17. Munroe K., and Papakonstantinou Y.: *BBQ: A Visual Interface for Browsing and Querying XML*. In Proceedings of the 5th IFIP 2.6 Working Conference on Visual Database Systems Fukuoka – Japan, May 10-12, 2000.
18. Petropoulos M., Papakonstantinou Y. and Vassalos V.: *Graphical Query Interfaces for Semistructured Data: The QURSED System*. In ACM Transactions on Internet Technology (TOIT), vol 5/2, 2005.
19. Tauschcr L., and Greenberg S.: *How People Revisit Web Pages: Empirical Findings and Implications for the Design of History Systems*. In International Journal of Human Computer Studies, Special issue on World Wide Web Usability 1997. 47(1): p.97-137.
20. Thompson H.S., Beech D., Maloney M., and Mendelsohn N.: *XML Schema Part 1: Structures*. W3C Recommendation 2 May 2001.
21. Zloof, M.: *Query By Example*. In Proceedings of the National Compute Conference, AFIPS, Vol. 44, 1975, pp. 431-438.

A Comparison of RDF Query Languages

Peter Haase[1], Jeen Broekstra[2], Andreas Eberhart[1], and Raphael Volz[1]

[1] Institute AIFB, University of Karlsruhe, D-76128 Karlsruhe, Germany
{haase, eberhart, volz}@aifb.uni-karlsruhe.de
[2] Vrije Universiteit Amsterdam, The Netherlands
jbroeks@cs.vu.nl

Abstract. The purpose of this paper is to provide a rigorous comparison of six query languages for RDF. We outline and categorize features that any RDF query language should provide and compare the individual languages along these features. We describe several practical usage examples for RDF queries and conclude with a comparison of the expressiveness of the particular query languages. The use cases, sample data and queries for the respective languages are available on the web[6].

1 Introduction

The Resource Description Framework (RDF) is considered to be the most relevant standard for data representation and exchange on the Semantic Web. The recent recommendation of RDF has just completed a major clean up of the initial proposal [11] in terms of syntax [1], along with a clarification of the underlying data model [10], and its intended interpretation [7]. Several languages for querying RDF documents and have been proposed, some in the tradition of database query languages (i.e. SQL, OQL), others more closely inspired by rule languages. No standard for RDF query language has yet emerged, but the discussion is ongoing within both academic institutions, Semantic Web enthusiasts and the World Wide Web Consortium (W3C). The W3C recently chartered a working group[1] with a focus on accessing and querying RDF data. We present a comparison of six representative query languages for RDF, highlighting their common features and differences along general dimensions for query languages and particular requirements for RDF. Our comparison does not claim to be complete with respect to the coverage of all existing RDF query languages. However, we try to maintain an up-to-date version of our report with an extended set of languages on our website[6]. This extended set of languages also includes RxPath[2] and RDFQL[3].

Related Work. Two previous tool surveys [12,4] and diverse web sites[4] have collected and compared RDF query languages and their associated prototype

---

[1] http://www.w3.org/2001/sw/DataAccess/
[2] http://rx4rdf.liminalzone.org/RxPath
[3] http://www.intellidimension.com/
[4] http://www.w3.org/2001/11/13-RDF-Query-Rules/\#implementations

S.A. McIlraith et al. (Eds.): ISWC 2004, LNCS 3298, pp. 502–517, 2004.
© Springer-Verlag Berlin Heidelberg 2004

implementations. The web sites are usually focused on collecting syntactic example queries along several use cases. We follow this approach of illustrating a language but instantiate general categories of orthogonal language features to avoid the repetitiveness of use cases and capture a more extensive range of language features. Two tool surveys [12],[4] were published in 2002 and focused mainly only the individual prototype implementations comparing criteria like quality of documentation, robustness of implementation and to a minor extent the query language features[5] which changed tremendously in the past two years. We detail the feature set and illustrate supported features through example queries. [5] analyzes the foundational aspects of RDF data and query languages, including computational aspects of testing entailment and redundancy.

It should be stressed that our comparison does not involve performance figures, as the focus is on the RDF query languages, not the tools supporting these languages.

The paper is organized as follows. Section 2 elicits several dimensions that are important for designing and comparing RDF query languages. Section 3 introduces the six languages that are compared in this paper along with the implementations that we have used. Section 4 demonstrates RDF query use cases, which are grouped into several categories. These use cases are used to compare the individual languages and expose the set of features supported by each language. Section 5 presents a wish list for further important but yet unsupported query language features. We conclude in Section 6 with a summary of our results.

2   Language Dimensions

2.1   Support for RDF Data Model

The underlying data model directly influences the set of operations that should be provided by a query language. We therefore recapitulate the basic concepts of RDF and make note of their implications for the requirements on an RDF query language.

RDF abstract data model. The underlying structure of any RDF document is a collection of triples. This collection of triples is usually called the RDF graph. Each triple states a relationship (aka. edge, property) between two nodes (aka. resource) in the graph. This abstract data model is independent of a concrete serialization syntax. Therefore query languages usually do not provide features to query serialization-specific features, e.g. order of serialization.

Formal semantics and Inference. RDF has a formal semantics which provides a dependable basis for reasoning about the meaning of an RDF graph. This reasoning is usually called entailment. Entailment rules state which implicit information can be inferred from explicit information. Hence, RDF query languages can consider such entailment and might convey means to distinguish implicit from explicit data.

Support for XML schema data types. XML data types can be used to represent data values in RDF. XML Schema also provides an extensibility framework

---

[5] cf. [12][Table 2 on page 16] for the most extensive summary

suitable for defining new datatypes for use in RDF. Data types should therefore be supported in an RDF query language.

Free support for making statements about resources. In general, it is not assumed that complete information about any resource is available in the RDF query. A query language should be aware of this and should tolerate incomplete or contradicting information.

2.2   Query Language Properties

In addition to eliciting the support for the above RDF language features we will discuss the following properties for each language.

- *Expressiveness.* Expressiveness indicates how powerful queries can be formulated in a given language. Typically, a language should at least provide the means offered by relational algebra, i.e. be relationally complete. Usually, expressiveness is restricted to maintain other properties such as safety and to allow an efficient (and optimizable) execution of queries.
- *Closure.* The closure property requires that the results of an operation are again elements of the data model. This means that if a query language operates on the graph data model, the query results would again have to be graphs.
- *Adequacy.* A query language is called adequate if it uses all concepts of the underlying data model. This property therefore complements the closure property: For the closure, a query result must not be outside the data model, for adequacy the entire data model needs to be exploited.
- *Orthogonality.* The orthogonality of a query language requires that all operations may be used independently of the usage context.
- *Safety.* A query language is considered safe, if every query that is syntactically correct returns a finite set of results (on a finite data set). Typical concepts that cause query languages to be unsafe are recursion, negation and built-in functions.

3   Query Languages

This section briefly introduces the query languages and actual systems that were used in our comparison.

3.1   RQL

RQL [8] is a typed language following a functional approach, which supports generalized path expressions featuring variables on both nodes and edges of the RDF graph. RQL relies on a formal graph model that captures the RDF modeling primitives and permits the interpretation of superimposed resource descriptions by means of one or more schemas. The novelty of RQL lies in its ability to smoothly combine schema and data querying while exploiting the taxonomies of labels and multiple classification of resources. RQL follows an OQL-like syntax: `select Pub from {Pub} ns3:year {y} where y = "2004" using namespace ns3 = ...` RQL is orthogonal, but not closed, as queries return variable bindings instead of graphs. However, RQL's semantics is not completely compatible with the RDF Semantics: a number of additional restrictions are placed on RDF models to allow querying with RQL[6].

RQL is implemented in ICS-FORTH's RDF Suite[7], and an implementation of a subset of it is available in the Sesame system[8]. For our evaluation we used Sesame version 1.0, which was released on March 25, 2004.

3.2 SeRQL

SeRQL [3] stands for Sesame RDF Query Language and is a querying and tranformation language loosely based on several existing languages, most notably RQL, RDQL and N3. Its primary design goals are unification of best practices from query language and delivering a light-weight yet expressive query language for RDF that addresses practical concerns.

SeRQL syntax is similar to that of RQL though modifications have been made to make the language easier to parse. Like RQL, SeRQL is based on a formal interpretation of the RDF graph, but SeRQL's formal interpretation is based directly on the RDF Model Theory.

SeRQL supports generalized path expressions, boolean constraints and optional matching, as well two basic filters: select-from-where and construct-from-where. The first returns the familiar variable-binding/table result, the second returns a matching (optionally transformed) subgraph. As such, SeRQL construct-from-where-queries fulfill the closure and orthogonality property and thus allow composition of queries. SeRQL is not safe as it provides various recursive built-in functions.

SeRQL is implemented and available in the Sesame system, which we have used for our comparison in the version 1.0. A number of querying features are still missing from the current implementation. Most notable of these are functions for aggregation (minimum, maximum, average, count) and query nesting.

3.3 TRIPLE

The term Triple denotes both a query and rules language as well as the actual runtime system [16]. The language is derived from F-Logic [9]. RDF triples `(S,P,O)` are represented as F-Logic expressions `S[P->O]`, which can be nested. For example, the expression `S[P1->O1, P2->O2[P3->O3]]` corresponds to three RDF triples `(S,P1,O1)`, `(S,P2,O2)`, and `(O2,P3,O3)`.

---

[6] An example of such a restriction is that every property must have *exactly* one domain and range specified.

[7] `http://139.91.183.30:9090/RDF/`

[8] `http://www.openrdf.org/`

Triple does not distinguish between rules and queries, which are simply headless rules, where the results are bindings of free variables in the query. For example, `FORALL X <- ( X[rdfs:label->"foo"] )@default:ln`. returns all resources which have a label "foo". Since the output is a table of variables and possible bindings, Triple does not fulfill the closure property. Triple is not safe in the sense that it allows unsafe rules such as `FORALL X ( X[rdfs:label->"foo"] <- ( a[rdfs:label->"foo"] )@default:ln`.. While Triple is adequate and closed for its own data model, the mapping from RDF to Triple is not lossless. For example, anonymous RDF nodes are made explicit. Triple is able to deal with several RDF models simultaneously, which are identified via a suffix @model.

Triple does not encode a fixed RDF semantics. The desired semantics have to be specified as a set of rules along with the query. Datatypes are not supported by Triple. For the comparison, we used Triple in the latest version from March 14th, 2002 along with XSB 2.5 for Windows.

3.4 RDQL

RDQL currently has the status of a W3C submission [15].

The syntax of RDQL follows a SQL-like select pattern, where a from clause is omitted. For example, `select ?p where (?p, <rdfs:label>, "foo" )` collects all resources with label "foo" in the free variable p. The select clause at the beginning of the query allows projecting the variables. Namespace abbreviations can be defined in a query via a separate "using" clause. RDF Schema information is not interpreted. Since the output is a table of variables and possible bindings, RDQL does not fulfill the closure and orthogonality property. RDQL is safe and offers preliminary support for datatypes.

For the comparison, we worked with Jena 2.0 of August 2003.

3.5 N3

Notation3 (N3) provides a text-based syntax for RDF. Therefore the data model of N3 conforms to the RDF data model. Additionally, N3 allows to define rules, which are denoted using a special syntax, for example: `?y rdfs:label "foo" => ?y a :QueryResult` Such rules, whilst not a query language per se, can be used for the purpose of querying. For this purpose queries have to be stored as rules in a dedicated file, which is used in conjunction with the data. The CWM filter command allows to automatically select the data that is generated by rules. Even though N3 fulfills the orthogonality, closure and safety property, using N3 as a query language is cumbersome.

N3 is supported by two freely available systems, i.e. Euler [14] and CWM [2]. None of these systems do automatically adhere to the RDF semantics. The semantics has to be provided by custom rules. For our comparison, we worked with CWM in the version of March 21, 2004.

3.6   Versa

Versa takes an interesting approach in that the main building block of the language is a list of RDF resources. RDF triples play a role in the so-called traversal operations, which have the form `ListExpr - ListExpr -> BoolExpr`. These expressions return a list of all objects of matching triples. For instance, the traversal expression `all() - rdfs:label -> *` would return a list containing all labels. Within a traversal expression, we can alternatively select the subjects as well by placing a vertical bar at the beginning of the arrow symbol. Thus, `all() |- rdfs:label -> eq("foo")` would yield all resources having the label "foo". The fact that a traversal expression is again a list expression, allows us to nest expressions in order to create more complex queries.

The given data structures and expression tree make it hard to project several values at once. Versa uses the distribute operator to work around this limitation. It creates a list of lists, which allows selecting several properties of a given list of resources.

Versa offers some support for rules since it allows traversing predicates transitively. Custom built-ins, views, multiple models, and data manipulation are not implemented. However, Versa fulfills the orthogonality and safety criteria.

The Versa language is supported by 4Suite, which is a set of XML and RDF tools[9]. We used 4Suite version 1.0a3 for Windows from July 4, 2003 along with Python 2.3.

4   Use Cases

In this section we present use cases for the querying of RDF data and evaluate how the six query languages support them. In the following tables, "-" indicates no support, "•" full support and "o" partial support.

4.1   Sample Data

For our comparison, we have used a sample data set[10]. It describes a simple scenario of the computer science research domain, modelling persons, publications and a small topic hierarchy. The data set covers the main features of the RDF data model. It includes a class hierarchy with multiple inheritance, data types, resources with multiple instantiations, reification, collections of resources, etc. These variety of features are exploited in the following use cases.

4.2   Use Case Graph

Due to RDF's graph-based nature, a central feature of most query languages is the support for graph matching.

---

[9] http://www.4suite.org
[10] Available at
http://www.aifb.uni-karlsruhe.de/WBS/pha/rdf-query/sample.rdf

Table 1. Path expression query in all languages

N3	Triple
{ ?y s:author ?z. ?z ?p ?x. ?x a s:Person; s:name ?result. } => { ?result a :QueryResult.}.	FORALL C,X,A,N <- (s:Paper[s:author->C] AND C[X->A] AND A[s:name->N])@rdfschema(s:ln).
RDQL	**Versa**
SELECT ?n WHERE <s:Paper>, <s:author>, ?c), (?c, ?collection, ?a), (?a, <s:name>, ?n) USING s FOR ...	QUERY=((s:Paper - s:author -> *) - properties(.) -> *) - s:name -> *
SeRQL	**RQL**
select PersonName from {X} <s:author> {} <rdfs:member> {} <s:name> {PersonName} using namespace s = <!...>	select PersonName from {X} s:author {y}. rdfs:member {z}. s:name {PersonName} using namespace s = ... rdfs = ...

The namespace s is bound to that of the sample data.

Path Expressions. The central feature used to achieve this matching of graphs is a so-called path expression, which is typically used to traverse a graph. A path expression can be decomposed into several joins and is often implemented by joins. It comes at no surprise that path expressions are offered - in various syntactic forms (cf. Table 1) - by all RDF query languages.

Return the names of the authors of publication X

Query	RDQL	Triple	SeRQL	Versa	N3	RQL
Path	•	•	•	•	•	•

Optional Path Expressions. The RDF graph represents a semi-structured data model. Its weak structure allows to represent irregular and incomplete information. Therefore RDF query languages should provide means to deal with irregularities and incomplete information. A particular irregularity, which has to be accounted for in the following query, is that a given value may or may not be present.

What are the name and, if known, the e-mail of the authors of all available publications ?

Query	RDQL	Triple	SeRQL	Versa	N3	RQL
Optional Path	-	-	•	•	-	○

Unfortunately, only two languages - namely Versa and SeRQL - provide built-in means for dealing with incomplete information. For example, the SeRQL language provides so-called optional path expressions (denoted by square brackets) to match paths whose presence is irregular:

```
SELECT PersonName, Email FROM
{X} <ns3:author> {} <rdfs:member>
{p} <ns3:name> {PersonName};
[<ns3:email> {Email}]
USING NAMESPACE
    ns3 = <!...>
```

Usually, such optional path expressions can be simulated, if a language provides set union and negation. A correct answer is provided by unifying the results of two select-queries, where the first argument of the union retrieves all persons with an e-mail address, the second those without an e-mail address. Consequently, RQL gets partial credit since these operations are supported. Another workaround is possible in rule languages like N3 and Triple by defining a rule, which infers a dummy value in absence of other data. In our example, an optional path would carry the dummy email address. Since this workaround might create undesired results if the absence of values is checked in other parts of the query, we do not credit the respective languages. Versa's distribute operator allows formulating the query by converting the list of authors into a list of lists of (optional) attributes.

4.3   Use Case Relational

RDF is frequently used to model relational structures. In fact, n-ary tables such as found in the the relational data model can easily be encoded in RDF triple.

Basic algebraic operations. In the relational data model several basic algebraic operations are considered, i.e. (i) selection, (ii) projection, (iii) cartesian product, (iv) set difference and (v) set union. These operations can be combined to express other operations such as set intersection, several forms of joins, etc. The importance of these operations is accounted by the definition of relational completeness. In the relational world, a given query languages is known to be relationally complete, if it supports the full range of basic algebraic operations mentioned above.

The three basic algebraic operations selection, projection, product are supported by all languages and have been used in the path expression query of the previous use case *Graph*. We therefore concentrate on the other two basic operations mentioned above, i.e. union and difference, in this section.

Union. As we have seen in the previous section, union is provided by RQL. Versa contains an explicit union operator as well. N3 and Triple can simulate union with rules.

Return the labels of all topics that and (union) the titles of all publications

Query	RDQL	Triple	SeRQL	Versa	N3	RQL
Union	-	●	-	●	●	●

Difference. Difference is a special form of negation:

Return the labels of all topics that are not titles of publications

Query	RDQL	Triple	SeRQL	Versa	N3	RQL
Difference	-	-	-	∘	-	●

While difference is described in the Versa documentation (but not implemented) RQL also provides an implementation of this algebraic operator.
The following RQL query provides the correct answer:

```
( select title
  from s:Topic{T}. rdfs:label {title}
) minus (
  select title
  from s:Publication{P}. s:title {title} )
using namespace
  s = ... , rdfs = ...
```

Quantification. An existential predicate over a set of resources is satisfied if at least one of the values satisfies the predicate. Analogously, a universal predicate is satisfied if all the values satisfy the predicate. As any selection predicate implicitly has existential bindings, we here consider universal quantification.

Return the persons who are authors of all publications.

Query	RDQL	Triple	SeRQL	Versa	N3	RQL
Universal	-	-	-	-	-	●

RQL is the only language providing the universal quantification needed to answer this query:

```
SELECT person
FROM s:Person{person}
WHERE FORALL z IN
    (SELECT x FROM s:Publication{x} )
  SUCH THAT EXISTS p IN
    (SELECT Y FROM {z} s:author {}. rdfs:member {y})
  SUCH THAT person = p
USING NAMESPACE s = ..., rdfs = ...
```

4.4   Use Case Aggregation and Grouping

Aggregate functions compute a scalar value from a multi-set of values. These functions are regularly needed to count a number of values. For example, they are needed to identify the minimum or maximum of a set of values. Grouping additionally allows aggregates to be computed on groups of values.

Aggregation. A special case of aggregation tested in the following query is a simple count of the number of elements in a set:

Count the number of authors of a publication.

Query	RDQL	Triple	SeRQL	Versa	N3	RQL
Counting	-	-	-	●	●	●

Counting is supported by N3, Versa and RQL. The following N3 rule gives the appropriate answer:

```
{?y.sam:author math:memberCount ?result .} =>
{:Query :Result ?result}.
```

Grouping. None of the compared query languages allows to group values, such as provided with the SQL GROUP BY clause[11].

4.5   Use Case Recursion

Recursive queries often appear in information systems, typically if the underlying relationship is transitive in nature. Note that the RDF query engine must handle *schema* recursion, i.e. the transitivity of the subClassOf relation. The scope of this use case is *data* recursion introduced by the application domain. In the sample datasettopics are defined along with their subtopics, where the subtopic property is transitive. This must be expressed in the query.

Return all subtopics of topic "Information Systems", recursively.

Query	RDQL	Triple	SeRQL	Versa	N3	RQL
Recursion	-	●	-	●	●	-

Triple (and N3), being rule-based systems, naturally can support the required recursion through the definition of auxiliary rules:

```
FORALL O,P,V  O[acm:SubTopic->V] <-
   EXISTS W  (O[acm:SubTopic->W] AND W[acm:SubTopic->V])@default:ln.
FORALL Y <-
   ('...#ACMTopic/':Information_Systems[acm:SubTopic->Y])@default:ln.
```

Versa does not support general recursion, but provides a keyword "traverse", which effects a transitive interpretation of a specified property. This suffices to answer our recursive query:

```
traverse(@"...#ACMTopic/Information_Systems",
   acm:SubTopic, vtrav:forward, vtrav:transitive )
```

---

[11] The RQL query language allows the computation of global aggregate values such as required for a query such as selecting the publication with the maximum number of authors.

4.6   Use Case Reification

Reification is a unique feature of RDF. It adds a meta-layer to the graph and allows treating RDF statements as resources themselves, such that statements can be made about statements. In the sample data reification is used to state who entered publication data. Hence, the following query is of interest:

Return the person who has classified the publication X.

Query	RDQL	Triple	SeRQL	Versa	N3	RQL
Reification	○	○	●	○	-	○

SeRQL and Triple support reification with a special syntax. In SeRQL, a path expression representing a single statement can be written between the curly brackets of a node:

```
select Person
from {{X} <s:isAbout> {}} <dc:creator> {Person}
using namespace s = <!...>
```

In Triple statements can be reified by placing them in angle brackets and using this within another statement: FORALL V,W,X,Y,Z <- (V[W-><X[Y->Z]>]). However, we were only able to use this feature in the native F-Logic syntax, since the reified statements in the RDF sample data were not parsed correctly.

While N3 cannot syntactically represent RDF reification, RDQL, RQL and Versa treat reified statements as nodes in the graph, which can be addressed through normal path expressions by relying on the RDF normalization of reification. This allows treating the reification use case like any other query. We show the Versa example below:

```
QUERY=(all() |- rdf:predicate -> s:isAbout) - dc:creator -> *
```

4.7   Use Case Collections and Containers

RDF allows to define groups of entities using collections (a closed group of entities) and containers, namely *Bag*, *Sequence* and *Container*, which provide an intended meaning of the elements in the container. A query language should be able to retrieve the individual and all elements of these collections and containers, along with order information, if applicable, as in the following query:

Return the last author of Publication X

Query	RDQL	Triple	SeRQL	Versa	N3	RQL
Sequences	○	○	○	○	○	○

Although none of the query languages provide explicit support for the processing of containers (as known for example from the processing of sequences in XQuery), in all query languages it is possible to query for a particular element in a container with the help of the special predicate <rdf:_n>, which allows to address the nth element in a container. However, this approach only allows to retrieve the last element of a container if its size is known before.

None of the query languages provide explicit support for ordering or sorting of elements, except for Versa which features a special sort operator. RQL does have specific operators for retrieval of container elements according to its specification, but this feature is not implemented in the current engine.

4.8   Use Case Namespaces

Namespaces are an integral part of any query language for web-based data. The various examples presented so far showed how the languages allow introducing namespace abbreviations in order to keep the queries concise. This use case evaluates which operations are possible on the namespaces themselves. Given a set of resources, it might be interesting to query all values of properties from a certain namespace or a namespace with a certain pattern. The following query addresses this issue. Pattern matching on namespaces is particularly useful for versioned RDF data, as many versioning schemes rely on the namespace to encode version information.

Return all resources whose namespace starts with "http://www.aifb.uni-karlsruhe.de/".

Query	RDQL	Triple	SeRQL	Versa	N3	RQL
Namespace	○	–	●	–	●	●

SeRQL, RQL and N3 allow for pattern matching predicates on URIs in the same manner as for literals, which allows to realize the query as shown in the following for N3:

```
{?a ?b ?c. ?a log:rawUri ?d.
 ?d string:startsWith "http://www.aifb.uni-karlsruhe.de/" } =>
{:Query :Result ?d}.
```

For RDQL, the string match operator is defined in the grammar, however the implementation is incomplete. Versa has a contains operator, which apparently only works for string literals, not URIs.

4.9   Use Case Language

RDF allows to use XML-style language tagging. The XML tag enclosing an RDF literal can optionally carry an xml:lang attribute. The respective value identified the language used in the text of the literal. Possible values include en for english or de for german. This use case examines, whether the various languages support this RDF feature.

Return the German label of the topic whose English label is "Database Management"

Query	RDQL	Triple	SeRQL	Versa	N3	RQL
Language	-	-	•	-	-	-

Out of the compared languages, SeRQL is the only one that has explicit support to query language specific information. SeRQL provides a special function to retrieve the language information from a literal:

```
select deLabel
from {} <rdfs:label> {deLabel, enLabel}
where lang(deLabel) = "de" and lang(enLabel) = "en" and
     label(enLabel) = "Database Management"
```

4.10   Use Case Literals and Datatypes

Literals are used to identify values such as numbers and dates by means of a lexical representation. In addition to plain literals, RDF supports the type system of XML Schema to create typed literals. An RDF query language should support the XML Schema datatypes. A datatype consists of a lexical space, a value space and lexical to value mapping. This distinction should also be supported by an RDF query language. The sample data for example contains a typed integer literal to represent the page number of a publication, with the following two queries we will query both the lexical space and the value space:

Return all publications where the page number is the lexical value '08'

Query	RDQL	Triple	SeRQL	Versa	N3	RQL
Lexical Space	•	•	•	•	•	•

Return all publications where the page number is the integer value 8

Query	RDQL	Triple	SeRQL	Versa	N3	RQL
Value Space	○	-	•	-	-	•

All query languages are able to query the lexical space, but most query languages have no or only preliminary support for datatypes and do not support the distinction between lexical and value space. RDQL and SeRQL provide support for datatypes using a special syntax to indicate the datatype. However, the RDQL query did not work correctly in the implementation.

4.11   Use Case Entailment

RDF Schema vocabulary supports the entailment of implicit information. Two typical use cases in the context of RDF are:

– Subsumptions between classes and properties that are not explicitly stated in the RDF Schema,

– Classification of resources: For a resource having a property for which we know its domain – or analogously the range – is restricted to a certain class, we can infer the resource to be an instance of that class.

With the following query we evaluate the support of the query languages for RDF Schema entailment. The query is expected to return not only the resources for which the class membership is provided explicitly, but also those whose class membership can be inferred based on the entailment rules. Obviously, several other queries would be necessary to test the full RDF-S support. Due to space limitations, we restrict ourselves to the following query:

Return all instances of that are members of the class Publication

Query	RDQL	Triple	SeRQL	Versa	N3	RQL
Entailment	○	○	●	-	○	●

Discussion. Regarding the support for RDF-S entailment, the query languages take different approaches: RQL and SeRQL support entailment natively and even allow to distinguish between subclasses and direct subclasses. RDQL leaves entailment completely up to the implementation of the query engine, it is thus not part of the semantics of RDQL. Nevertheless, it gets partial credit, since Jena provides an optional mechanism for attaching an RDF-S reasoner such that the query processor takes advantage of it. N3 and Triple require an axiomatization of the RDF-S semantics, i.e. a set of rules. Versa provides no support.

The following sample shows how the query is realized in RQL:

```
select publications
from ns3:Publication{publications}
using namespace
  ns3 = <!http://www.aifb.uni-karlsruhe.de/WBS/pha/rdf-query/sample.rdf#>
```

5   Wish List

In the previous sections we have seen that the currently available query languages for RDF support a wide variety of operations. However, several important features - listed in the following text - are not well supported, or even not supported at all.

Grouping and Aggregation. Many of the existing proposals support very little functionality for grouping and aggregation. Functions such as min, max, average and count provide important tools for analysing data.

Sorting. Perhaps surprisingly, except for Versa, no language is capable to do sorting and ordering on the output. Related to this seems to be that many query languages do not support handling of ordered collections.

Optional matching. Due to the semi-structured nature of RDF, support for optional matches is crucial in any RDF query language and should be supported with a dedicated syntax.

Adequacy. Overall, the languages' support for RDF-specific features like containers, collections, XML Schema datatypes, language tags, and reification is quite poor. Since these are features of the data model, the degree of adequacy among the languages is low. For instance, it would be desirable for a query language to support operators on XML Schema datatypes, as defined in [13], as built-ins.

6   Conclusion

We believe that defining a suitable RDF query language should be a top priority in terms of standardization. Querying is a very fundamental functionality required in almost any Semantic Web application. Judging from the impact of SQL to the database community, standardization will definitely help the adoption of RDF query engines, make the development of applications a lot easier, and will thus help the Semantic Web in general.

We have evaluated six query language proposals with quite different approaches, goals, and philosophies. Consequently, it is very hard to compare the different proposals and come up with a ranking. From our analysis, we identify a small set of key criteria, which differ vastly between the languages.

A key distinction is the support for RDF Schema semantics. Languages like N3 and Triple do not make a strict distinction between queries and rules. Thus, a logic program representing the desired semantics, in this case RDF-S, can optionally supplement a query. SeRQL and RQL support RDF-S semantics internally. Versa takes a pragmatic approach by supporting the transitive closure as a special operator. While this is not very flexible, it solves most of the problems like traversing a concept hierarchy. RDQL's point of view is that entailment should be completely up to the RDF repository.

Orthogonality is a very desirable features, since it allows combining a set of simple operators into powerful constructs. Out of the six candidates, RQL, SeRQL, N3, and Versa support this property. Versa uses sets of resources as the basic data structure, whereas RQL, N3 and SeRQL operate on graphs. Triple can mimic orthogonality via rules, whereas RDQL does not support it.

Furthermore, we consider the extent to which the various use cases are supported. Obviously, one would have to distinguish between features like the support for recursive queries that fundamentally cannot be expressed in a language and a feature that simply has not been implemented in the respective system like a simple string match operator. However, since this distinction is often hard to make, we simply add up the queries that could be expressed. If the query could be formulated with a workaround, we count half a point. Using this metric, RQL and SeRQL appear to be the most complete languages, covering 10.5 and 8.5 out of 14 use case queries. Versa and N3 follow with 7.5 and 7. Triple and RDQL were able to answer the least queries and got 5.5 and 4.5 points.

Finally, we consider the readability and usability of a language. Obviously, this depends very much on personal taste. Syntactically, RQL, RDQL, and SeRQL are very similar due to their SQL / OQL heritage. Triple and N3 share the rules character. The Triple syntax allows for some nice syntactic variants. Versa's style is quite different, since a query directly exposes the operator tree.

Acknowledgments. Research reported in this paper has been partially financed by the EU in the project IST-2003-506826 SEKT.

References

1. D. Beckett. RDF/XML Syntax Specification (Revised). W3C Working Draft, 2003. Internet: http://www.w3.org/TR/rdf-syntax/.
2. T. Berners-Lee. CWM - closed world machine. Internet: http://www.w3.org/2000/10/swap/doc/cwm.html, 2000.
3. Jeen Broekstra and Arjohn Kampman. SeRQL: An RDF Query and Transformation Language. To be published, 2004. http://www.cs.vu.nl/~jbroeks/papers/SeRQL.pdf.
4. D. Fensel and A. Perez. A survey on ontology tools. Technical Report OntoWeb Deliverable 1.3, OntoWeb consortium, May 2002. http://www.ontoweb.org/download/deliverables/D13_v1-0.zip.
5. Claudio Gutiérrez, Carlos A. Hurtado, and Alberto O. Mendelzon. Foundations of semantic web databases. In *Proceedings of the Twenty-third Symposium on Principles of Database Systems (PODS), June 14-16, 2004, Paris, France*, pages 95–106, 2004.
6. Peter Haase, Jeen Broekstra, Andreas Eberhart, and Raphael Volz. A comparison of rdf query languages. Technical report, University of Karlsruhe, 2004. http://www.aifb.uni-karlsruhe.de/WBS/pha/rdf-query/.
7. Patrick Hayes. Rdf semantics. http://www.w3.org/TR/2004/REC-rdf-mt-20040210/\#rules.
8. G. Karvounarakis, S. Alexaki, V. Christophides, D. Plexousakis, and M. Schol. RQL: A Declarative Query Language for RDF. In *Proceedings of the Eleventh International World Wide Web Conference (WWW'02)*, Honolulu, Hawaii, USA, May7-11 2002.
9. M. Kifer, G. Lausen, and J. Wu. Logical foundations of object-oriented and frame-based languages. *Journal of the ACM*, 42, 1995.
10. G. Klyne and J. Carroll. Resource Description Framework (RDF): Concepts and Abstract Data Model. W3C Working Draft, 2003. Internet: http://www.w3.org/TR/rdf-concepts/.
11. O. Lassila and R. Swick. Resource Description Framework (RDF) Model and Syntax Specification. W3C Working Draft, 1999. Internet: http://www.w3.org/TR/REC-rdf-syntax/.
12. A. Maganaraki, G. Karvounarakis, V. Christophides, D. Plexousakis, and T. Anh. Ontology storage and querying. Technical Report 308, Foundation for Research and Technology Hellas, Institute of Computer Science, Information Systems Laboratory, April 2002.
13. Ashok Malhotra, Jim Melton, and Norman Walsh. Xquery 1.0 and xpath 2.0 functions and operators, w3c working draft 12 november 2003. http://www.w3.org/TR/xpath-functions/.
14. J. De Roo. Euler proof mechanism. Internet: http://www.agfa.com/w3c/euler/, 2002.
15. Andy Seaborne. Rdql - a query language for rdf, w3c member submission 9 january 2004, 2004. http://www.w3.org/Submission/2004/SUBM-RDQL-20040109/.
16. M. Sintek and S. Decker. TRIPLE - an RDF query, inference and transformation language. In *Deductive Databases and Knowledge Management (DDLP)*, 2001.

Information Retrieval Support for Ontology Construction and Use

Willem Robert van Hage*, Maarten de Rijke, and Maarten Marx

Informatics Institute, University of Amsterdam
Kruislaan 403, 1098 SJ Amsterdam
wrvhage,mdr,marx@science.uva.nl

Abstract. Information retrieval can contribute towards the construction of ontologies and the effective usage of ontologies. We use collocation-based keyword extraction to suggest new concepts, and study the generation of hyperlinks to automate the population of ontologies with instances. We evaluate our methods within the setting of digital library project, using information retrieval evaluation methodology. Within the same setting we study retrieval methods that complement the navigational support offered by the semantic relations in most ontologies to help users explore the ontology.

1   Introduction

Today's prevalent methods of searching, navigating, and organizing Internet information builds on several decades of research in information retrieval (IR) [2]. Based, ultimately, on general statistical laws governing human language use, these methods are being used not just in document retrieval but also in semantically richer tasks such as question answering [28]. One vision of the Semantic Web is that it will be much like the Web as we know it today, except that documents will be enriched with machine understandable markup [18]. These annotations will provide metadata about the documents and machine interpretable statements capturing some of the semantics of documents' content [7]. We discuss how the IR paradigm can contribute to this effort, by aiding the architects of non-trivial ontologies. IR techniques can aid in defining, populating, and checking the consistency of ontologies. Specifically, eight stages can be distinguished in the ontology building process [1]:

1. Determine the scope of the ontology.
2. Consider reusing (parts of) existing ontologies.
3. Enumerate all the concepts you want to include.
4. Define the taxonomy of these concepts.
5. Define properties of the concepts.
6. Define facets of the concepts such as cardinality, required values etc.
7. Define instances.
8. Check the consistency of the ontology.

---

* Current affiliation: TNO TPD and the Free University Amsterdam.

S.A. McIlraith et al. (Eds.): ISWC 2004, LNCS 3298, pp. 518–533, 2004.

Of these stages, we address 3 and 7 with IR-based techniques as we believe that these stages can be usefully tackled using retrieval technology available today. While equally suitable for automation, stage 4 is far from being a solved problem [21], and stage 8 is best left for purely symbolic reasoning methods as implemented in, e.g., the FACT and RACER provers.

In addition to being used to assist ontology builders, IR techniques can also assist users in searching, browsing, and providing serendipity. People will want to use the Semantic Web to search not just for documents, but also for information about specific semantic relationships, for instance in the setting of digital libraries [24]. Thus, we explore approaches to "retrieval within a concept hierarchy," where exact-match search as provided by most navigation tools and ontology editors may not be adequate [25].

By making today's document retrieval algorithms useful to building and exploiting the Semantic Web infrastructure, improvements in the former lead directly to improvements in the latter. But we have a more methodological reason for bringing IR and Semantic Web efforts closer together. The IR community has long emphasized the importance of evaluation. With the advent of the Text REtrieval Conferences (TREC, [26]), experimental evaluation of retrieval related tasks received a significant boost, which led to rapid progress in the tasks evaluated. Similar benefits occur with other retrieval-related evaluation exercises (CLEF [5], INEX [9], NTCIR [20]), and with efforts to evaluate semantically richer language processing tasks (e.g., CoNLL [6] and Senseval [23]). The Semantic Web community would benefit from a stronger emphasis on evaluation, and on tasks that can be evaluated, than it has so far had. Eating our own dog food, we conduct experimental evaluations for all tasks addressed in this paper.

Section 2 discusses the setting in which our work takes place: the Logic and Language Links (*LoLaLi*) project, aimed at providing ontology-based access to an electronic handbook on the interface of linguistics and logic. In Section 3 we discuss the automation of stage 3 and its evaluation. In Section 4 we discuss the automation of stage 7 and its evaluation. In Section 5 we discuss and evaluate search in the *LoLaLi* concept hierarchy. We conclude in Section 6.

2 LoLaLi: Logic and Language Links

Our work, and the experiments on which we report below, take place in the setting of a digital library project. Specifically, the *Logic and Language Links* (LoLaLi) project [4,15] explores methods to extend the traditional format of scientific handbooks with electronic tools. These tools help readers explore the content of the handbook and make it easier to locate relevant information.

As a case study the project focuses on the *Handbook of Logic and Language* [27], a 20 chapter, 1200 page publication; for our experiments we used the LaTeX sources (about 4.5MB of text). The *LoLaLi* project uses a WordNet-like concept hierarchy to provide access to (an electronic version of) the handbook. Concept hierarchies are often used for navigating through large collections of documents [29,16]. They are useful for the organization, display and exploration

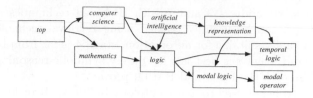

Fig. 1. An excerpt from the *LoLaLi* concept hierarchy.

of a large amount of information, and users carrying out a hypertext search task who have hierarchical browsing patterns perform better than users with sequential browsing paths [19]. Hence, architectures for electronic handbooks should allow for, or even enforce, hierarchical patterns: a concept hierarchy is a good way of doing this. The *LoLaLi* concept hierarchy is being built by hand, by domain experts, who have currently collected, organized, and related close to 600 concepts. At the back-end, a Sesame-based server stores the hierarchy information, which is edited and updated through a collection of purpose-built scripts and Protege. In Section 3 we discuss how basic IR techniques can help concept authors determine which concepts to consider for inclusion in the hierarchy.

Each concept in the *LoLaLi* hierarchy is annotated with a gloss, which briefly describes it. Moreover, concepts come with a longer description, also provided by the authors of the concept. The hierarchy consists of a TOP concept, with four main branches underneath it: *computer science, mathematics, linguistics*, and *philosophy*, organized by relations of subtopic-supertopic. The latter relations are *typed*, and the types include 'is-a' and 'part-of.' The *LoLaLi* hierarchy is a graph rather than a strict tree, as multiple parenthood is allowed; see Figure 1. Non-hierarchical relations are also allowed, and are used for navigational purposes; these include 'sibling,' 'other meanings,' and 'associated concepts.' Concepts in the *LoLaLi* hierarchy are also connected to external resources. Chief among these is the *Handbook of Logic and Language*; other examples include links to highly relevant online tools and demos. The (hypertext) links to the *Handbook* take a concept in the hierarchy as source and highly relevant segments in the *Handbook* as targets. In Section 4 we describe how IR techniques help address this task.

At present, users can access an early 'alpha' version of the hierarchy. Following the outcomes of an early user study, navigation along the semantic relations mentioned above has been complemented with search facilities that allow users to locate concepts in the hierarchy in an arbitrary manner. In Section 5 we describe and assess the underlying IR techniques.

3   Assisting Ontology Builders

When building an ontology for an established scientific domain, as in the *LoLaLi* project, there is a wealth of literature whose content should be "covered" by the ontology. We report on IR support for addressing the following question: Which concepts should be included in the ontology? Rather than manually mining the

Table 1. Precision at different ranks in the result lists.

rank	10	25	50	100	250	750
precision at rank (*Handbook*)	1.00	0.96	0.9	0.85	0.79	0.55
precision at rank (relative to the CLEF corpus)	1.00	1.00	0.98	0.99	0.94	0.80

literature, we describe methods to identify candidate concepts from domain specific text using term extraction. Concept names are usually noun phrases. Hence, recognizing noun phrases is likely to be a good first step for detecting candidate concepts. We distinguish between two cases, as they exploit different techniques: single word candidates and multi-word candidates.

3.1   Single Noun Concepts

To discover interesting nouns, we first POS-tag the *Handbook* text, and then select all nouns. We used two ways to rank them: by raw frequency, and by relative frequency, that is, by the number of occurrences divided by the number of occurrences in a general purpose document collection (we used the English CLEF collection [5]). The resulting lists were assessed by three assessors who were asked, for each noun in the result lists whether they would include it in a comprehensive list of important or useful notions in the domain, aimed at novices and experts. For our "gold standard", a noun was considered relevant if the majority of assessors deemed it relevant.

With this gold standard, we computed precision @ n scores (what fraction of the top n results is relevant?), for increasing values of n; see Table 1, where the second row concerns the result list ordered by raw frequency, and the third the result list ordered by relative frequency. Surprisingly, even the raw frequency result list, is of very high quality, with now non-relevant high-frequency nouns in the top. And by taking into account domain specificity (as in the list ordered by relative frequency), very high precision scores can be obtained. What about recall? It is hard, if not impossible, to compile an exhaustive list of important or useful nouns in the domain of the *Handbook*. Instead, we decided to approximate recall by using *concept recall* (CR): what fraction of the single noun concepts in the *LoLaLi* hierarchy did we identify, and what were their ranks in the result lists? Of the 522 concepts in the version of the concept hierarchy used, 158 are single nouns; hence, CR was measured against those 158. The noun extraction algorithm identified 77% (121) of the single noun concepts in the *LoLaLi* hierarchy; 70% of these are in the top 750. While this is not a perfect recall score, our ontology builders found the suggestions to be very helpful in further development of the hierarchy, telling us that the suggestions often inspired them to think of additional concepts, hence indirectly addressing the recall problem.

Table 2. Part-of-speech tag patterns for collocation filtering.

POS-tag pattern	example collocation
Adjective Noun	*logical study*
Noun Noun	*computer science*
Adjective Adjective Noun	*floating decimal point*
Adjective Noun Noun	*recursive enumerable set*
Noun Adjective Noun	*card programmed calculator*
Noun Noun Noun	*program storage unit*
Noun Preposition Noun	*theory of computation*

Table 3. The top 10 collocations extracted from the *Handbook* (left) and our web collection (right), with "usefulness" assessments by all three assessors, together with the "gold standard" (last column).

noun-collocation	useful?	noun-collocation	useful?
natural language	yes yes yes *yes*	computer science	yes yes yes *yes*
computer science	yes yes yes *yes*	other hand	no no no *no*
modal logic	yes yes yes *yes*	natural language	yes yes yes *yes*
lambda calculus	yes yes yes *yes*	university press	no no no *no*
situation theory	yes yes yes *yes*	modal logic	yes yes yes *yes*
discourse representation	no yes yes *yes*	induction hypothesis	yes yes yes *yes*
artificial intelligence	yes yes yes *yes*	first order	yes yes yes *yes*
phrase structure	yes yes yes *yes*	district page	no no no *no*
other hand	no no no *no*	description post	no no no *no*
proof theory	yes yes yes *yes*	post manual ref	no no no *no*

3.2   Multi-word Noun Phrases

Let us turn to the extraction of multi-word noun phrases now. We present a simple yet useful method that is based on collocations and that can be subdivided into three steps: (1) Shallow parse the text. (2) Filter out word sequences with interesting POS-tag patterns for closer examination. (3) Decide for each word sequence if it is a noun collocation. Step 1 is done with Schmid's *Tree-Tagger* POS-tagger [22]. Step 2 is accomplished by a method due to Justeson and Katz [11,17], which uses the POS-tag patterns shown in Table 2. We scan the tagged text and discard everything that does not match one of the listed POS-tag patterns. Step 3 is done by testing whether the words in the sequence occur together significantly more often than is to be expected if all the words in the text would be ordered randomly. Following Krenn and Evert [14], who addressed the related task of detecting PP-Verb collocations, we use the the t-test for addressing Step 3. Our null hypothesis will be that, in the text, the words that make up the sequence appear completely independently of each other.

When we apply our multi-word method to the *Handbook of Logic and Language*, we get promising results. As an example, the 10 noun collocations with the highest t-scores are shown in Table 3. Exactly how well did we do? As in the single noun case, we use concept recall (CR) and precision (P) to answer this question. Of the 522 concepts in the version of the concept hierarchy used, 364

Table 4. Precision at different ranks in the result list.

rank	10	25	50	100	250	750
precision at rank	0.90	0.76	0.74	0.65	0.67	0.63

are multi-word expressions; hence, CR was measured against those 364. Working on the *Handbook* our algorithm yielded 3896 collocations, 99 of which are concepts from the hierarchy. I.e., we found 28% of the multi-word concepts; 73% of these are in the top 750. Concerning P, we asked our three assessors to assess the candidate concepts returned (as in the earlier single noun case). Table 3 contains a sample of results produced, together with human assessments. Table 4 contains the resulting precision scores, at different ranks; the precision drops sharply as we move down the result list.

While precision, and especially early precision, is at an acceptable level, concept recall leaves something to be desired. There are several ways to improve recall: develop more extraction patterns, make the patterns less strict, or increase the amount of data they work on. The second option might hurt precision too much, and the first likely yields highly specific patterns, making little or no difference in terms of concept recall. We go for the third option: many interesting noun phrases only occur once in the *Handbook*, and since our detection method essentially works through redundancy we will not be able to find those words.

To create a larger corpus of relevant data, we proceeded as follows. Each of the 522 concepts in the *LoLaLi* hierarchy was fed to a web search engine (as a separate query), while restricting the output to PDF files (assuming that this restriction would increase the chance of retrieving scientific papers in our domain, rather than arbitrary documents). Per query, the top 20 results were kept; text was extracted using *pstotext*, producing 358MB of usable text. We extracted 206,475 collocations; a total of 197 (out of 364) concepts were found, and more importantly, 44% of those were found amongst the top 750 results. So, CR has certainly gone up, when compared against the results of running our algorithm against the *Handbook* text. The top 10 results (Table 3, right) reveal that early precision is seriously hurt by moving to our Web collection. The precision at various ranks in the result list for the Web collection does not drop as dramatically as for the *Handbook*; in fact, it goes up (Table 5, row 3). In Table 5 we also list the precision figures for the Web collection, relative to the CLEF corpus (bringing in domain specifity, as in the earlier single noun case). Domain specificity helps to get rid of expressions such as 'other hand', but it pushes expressions such as 'next section' to the top of the ranking, which explains the low p@10 score in row 3.

To examine the interplay between precision and recall, we looked at the *concept* precision (in addition to concept recall, both in terms of concepts from the *LoLaLi* hierarchy), and compiled plots for concept precision and concept recall. In Figure 3.2 we plotted concept recall (Left) and concept precision (Right) of collocations found, in the *Handbook*, in our Web collection, and in the latter, relative to the CLEF collection; the rank (plotted on the X-axis) is obtained by sorting by *t*-test score. As is to be expected, for the larger Web collection, con-

Table 5. Precision at different ranks in the result list, *Handbook* vs. Web collection.

rank	10	25	50	100	250	750
precision at rank (*Handbook*)	0.90	0.76	0.74	0.65	0.67	0.63
precision at rank (*Web collection*)	0.50	0.40	0.56	0.53	0.56	0.47
precision at rank (*Web collection, rel. to CLEF corpus*)	0.20	0.52	0.54	0.60	0.62	0.55

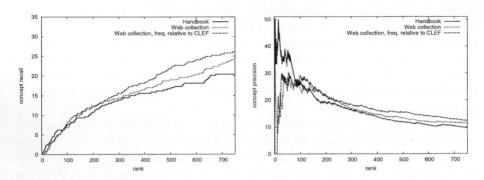

Fig. 2. (Left) The percentage of concepts present in the *LoLaLi* hierarchy identified at different points in the ranking. (Right) The fraction of concepts present in the *LoLaLi* hierarchy at different points in the ranking.

cept recall is highest, followed by the Web collection-relative-to-CLEF, followed by the *Handbook*. For concept precision, the relative order is reversed.

3.3   Conclusions and Further Steps

A simple single noun method and a simple collocation-based method can both yield valuable suggestions for concepts to be included in a concept hierarchy, thus addressing step 3 from Antoniou and Van Harmelen's list (see Section 1). For extracting multi-word expressions, more data proves useful to improve recall. Our results were further improved by filtering out the generic English expressions. Our scores are far from perfect, but as a source of suggestions, our ontology builders found the output of our methods extremely valuable. It may help to make our Web collection more focussed; if some concepts are available before collocation detection takes place, they could be used to constrain the text: new interesting concepts can be expected to occur in the proximity of the old ones.

4   Automatically Defining Instances

Ontologies rarely exist for their own sake, and their envisaged usage determines how ontologies should be populated. In settings where ontology-like structures are being used as navigational aids, an important group of instances are hypertext links to (fragments of) documents. In this section we describe and evaluate methods for automatically defining such instances, again within the setting of

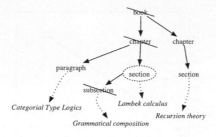

Fig. 3. Eliminating overlapping units of retrieval

the *LoLaLi* project. The task we are addressing is to link concepts in the *LoLaLi* hierarchy to highly relevant text fragments in the *Handbook*. We view this task as a high-precision information retrieval task by treating every concept as a topic and every text fragment as a document: to define the required instances, we need to identify highly relevant text fragments for every concept in the *LoLaLi* hierarchy. How much of the specific digital library and ontology aspects that we have access to, can usefully exploited to address the task at hand. Our strategy is an incremental one: starting from a simple baseline we determine the impact of exploiting document structure, text markup cues, and collocations.

4.1   Under the Hood

The document collection in which we have to identify link targets consists of LaTeX documents: semi-structured data with explicit markup of segments: \chapter, \section, \subsection, etc. These annotations provide a segmentation of the entire *Handbook* into (we assume) topically coherent text fragments. As hyperlink targets (that is, as units to be returned by the retrieval engine), we allow any segment at any level, from chapter down to paragraph. While it is sensible to allow this (as some topics are discussed in a single paragraph only, while others may exhaustively cover bigger units), it does raise a problem. If a subsection contains a relevant piece of text, then so does the section it belongs to and so does any larger surrounding annotation. How do you decide how small or large the unit of retrieval should be? Following our experience with XML retrieval [12], we decided not to allow returning overlapping pieces of text. In cases where we have to decide between two overlapping units of retrieval we choose the one ranked highest by the retrieval system. This is illustrated in Figure 3: if we choose to return the section then we are not allowed to return anything contained in that section or anything that contains the section [13].

To simplify the evaluation of the hyperlink generation task, we made use of the entries from the back-of-the-book index of the *Handbook*. Specifically, we used all entries in the back-of-the-book index that also occur in the *LoLaLi* hierarchy; there are 141 such entries. Each entry is explicitly marked up in the LaTeX source of the *Handbook* (with the \index{<entry>} command); on average, an entry comes with three occurrences of the corresponding \index{..} tag. Our "gold

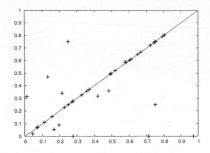

Fig. 4. An example quantile plot of the baseline compared to a run that exploits emphasis annotations.

standard" used for assessment consists of the 141 concepts mentioned as our "topics" (in IR parlance). A text segment is considered relevant for a topic if it is marked up with the corresponding \index{..} command. Clearly, the quality of our results depends on the quality of the back-of-the-book index.

We use *Incremental R-Precision* as our metric; it returns 0 when none of the relevant documents have been found for a given topic, and 1 when all have been found. It has a higher value when a returned document appears high in the ranking than when it appears further down in the ranking. Given a topic, $p@n$ (precision at n) is $|\{d \in Relevant \mid \text{rank}(d) \leq n\}|/n$, and

$$Incremental\ R\text{-}Precision = \sum_{n=1}^{|Relevant|} \frac{p@n}{|Relevant|},$$

where *Relevant* is the set of relevant documents for the given topic. The score for a run or experiment is obtained by averaging over all topics.

If the distribution of the performance differences is not skewed and if there are few outliers then it is safe to use the paired t-test for the evaluation of information retrieval [8]. These two conditions can be tested with quantile plots. The points in such a plot are supposed to be balanced around the identity line. We checked that this is the case for all our data; an example is shown in Figure 4. Hence, we test how significant the differences between two methods are by comparing the results per query with the paired t-test. Significant differences (95% confidence, $t \geq 1.645$) are marked with $\triangle, \triangledown$ and material differences (99% confidence, $t \geq 2.346$) with $\blacktriangle, \blacktriangledown$. Insignificant differences are not marked.

4.2   Experiments

Our baseline uses a standard *tf.idf* weighting scheme [2], and we reduce all words to their stem using the *TreeTagger* lemmatizer [22]. On top of that we experimented with additional layout cues, and with collocations. First, words that appear inside the titles of units (such as sections) are likely to be good indicators of the main topic covered by those units. Word sequences that are emphasized (the *Handbook* convention is to use \emph{..} and {\em ..}) seem

Table 6. Link generation experiments. (Top) Runs that exploit layout cues. (Bottom) Runs that exploit collocations.

Experiment	Inc. R-Precision
baseline	.35
title bonuses	.41 ▲
emphasis bonuses	.33
title and emphasis bonuses	.39 △
collocation bonus	.35
title and collocation bonus	.46 ▲ (relative to .41)
emphasis and collocation bonus	.33

more important than others. We implement the preference for terms with a certain annotation, or occurring in a certain context, fairly naively, by increasing the score of the text segment at hand. If a segment starts with a title and that title contains the query words we double the segment's score. If the segment's title contains nothing else, i.e., it coincides with the query, we double the segment's score again. If a document contains \em or \emph environments that literally contain the query we double the score; and if the emphasis is on nothing but the query we double it again. The experimental outcomes are shown in Table 6 (Top). There is a material difference for runs that prefer titles, but no significant difference between runs that prefer emphasized text and those that do not: even though emphasis is frequently used to stress key phrases, there appear to be more cases where it is used to stress unimportant words.

With the resources developed in the previous section, we tried to boost the performance of our link generation method. Using the collocations obtained from our Web collection, we increased a segment's score for a topic whenever it contained a collocation from the topic. Using a similar naive scoring mechanism as before, whenever a segment contains one or more collocations its score is doubled. (A segment's score can only be doubled once.) The idea is to bring some word order to the topic-segment matching process, which should increase precision whenever we know that word order may matter (as is the case for our collocations: e.g., *proof theory* is likely to be more informative than *theory proof*). Table 6 (Bottom) shows the results of the experiments with collocation bonuses. There is no significant difference between the baseline and runs that only exploit collocations, but when we combine title and collocation preference there is a material difference with the baseline and even with the title preference only run: the literal occurrence of the query in a segment's body or emphasized text does not say more about a segment's probability of being relevant to the query than its *tf.idf* score. However, the (literal) occurrence of query terms in both a segment's title and body is overwhelming evidence of relevancy.

4.3   Conclusions and Further Steps

We showed that exploiting title fields and collocations can improve the performance of automatic hyperlinking. The methods we used are quite crude and it is very likely that further improvements can be realized by optimization. A more careful method to combine the evidence provided by *tf.idf*, title markup and collocations could be beneficial to the results, thus leading us to consider more sophisticated weighting schemes that standard ones used here.

5   Searching in Ontologies

After Sections 3 and 4, which were aimed at IR support for ontology construction, we change tack and address support for end users that access ontologies for navigational purposes. The process of browsing through the ontology to find a concept can give the user a good impression about how the ontology (and the underlying domain) is organized and how the concepts are related, but it can also be a difficult and laborious process. Examples where browsing frustrates the information access process are well-known, and include such things as not knowing were in the hierarchy a concept might be located, using a different vocabulary, or simply getting lost because of the sheer size of the ontology. In such cases IR techniques can help address these information needs. Instead of following the semantic relations hard-wired in an ontology, IR offers random access to an ontology and a flexible interpretation of a user's information need.

The task we want to address in the remainder of this section is the following: given a query, find relevant concepts in a concept hierarchy. In other words, users' information needs are formulated using arbitrary keywords, while the "documents" to be returned are concepts, in the *LoLaLi* hierarchy.

5.1   Under the Hood

When trying to retrieve relevant concepts from an ontology, we have to deal with a number of issues. (1) The queries tend to be very short. The number of keywords per topic can be expected to be roughly equal to that of web search engine queries, on average two keywords per topic [10,3]. (2) The documents are very short too. Even if we have an extended description of the concepts (as many of the concepts in the *LoLaLi* hierarchy do), the documents to be retrieved are short compared to standard test collections. (On average, the descriptions are 23.3 words long, and the concept names 1.8 words; so the average document is about 26 words long.) (3) The document collection is small. This means that recall may be an issue. Summing up, retrieval against the *LoLaLi* hierarchy is a high precision task, but, potentially, with high recall requirements.

Our topics, of which there are 26, have been made by four different authors and are based on what first-year artificial intelligence students of the University of Amsterdam typed into a prototype search engine in a user test of the *LoLaLi* user interface. A "gold standard" was established using three assessors, in the same manner as for the link generation task addressed in Section 4. The metric used is also the same as in Section 4: incremental R-precision.

All documents and topics are stripped of all non-word characters except hyphens and, as with the hyperlinking task described in Section 4, lemmatized

Table 7. (Top) Results of collocation and exact match bonuses. (Bottom) Results of concept relation based reranking.

	Inc. R-Precision
baseline	.53
only collocations	.55
only exact match	.56
coll. and exact match	.58
grouping	.65 ▲
grouping adding context	.68 ▲
grouping with coll. and exact match	.67 ▲
grouping adding context with coll. and exact match	.74 ▲

using *TreeTagger* [22]. Each topic is then compared to documents in the inverted index, producing a ranked list of documents, which is presented to the user.

5.2   Experiments

As a baseline we choose a simple *tf.idf* based retrieval model. As in the previous section, we are interested in finding out to which extent the structure of the concepts and concept hierarchy can help improve retrieval effectiveness. Specifically, we tried the following ideas on top of the baseline, all aimed at high precision without hurting recall: (1) Give concepts of which the name exactly matches the topic a bonus over other concepts. e.g. If the user types in 'logic' then the concept 'logic' would be preferred over 'modal logic'. (2) Give concepts that share a collocation with the topic a bonus over concepts that share the constituents in some other order. (3) Group concepts that are related to each other together, allowing concepts that are related to concepts in the top of the ranking to benefit.

The first thing we try to improve over the baseline is to exploit characteristics of the syntax of the documents. The results from our automatic hyperlinking experiments suggests that we should prefer words in titles to words in the body of a section. Similarly, we will prefer occurrences of query terms in a concept's name to cases where it appears only in its description; in the former case the scores are simply doubled. Since the concept hierarchy is filled with very specific terms, the influence of word order can be expected to be even greater in this experiment than with the automatic hyperlinking. So we will try applying the same method as with that experiment too. When a concept contains a collocation that also appears in the query, we double its score. When a concept's name is exactly equal to the topic it is unlikely that the user desires another concept. So we apply the same technique as before: we double the concept's score.

The results of these techniques are shown in Table 7 (Top). Given the small number of topics we can not conclude that the improvement is significant. We can only say with about 90% confidence that there is a difference.

We now turn to further improvements over the baseline, ones that try to exploit the semantics that are encoded by the relations in the concept hierar-

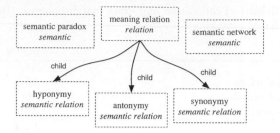

Fig. 5. Sometimes related concepts are better than concepts that match the query well.

chy. For brevity we only report on the use of the subsumption relations is-a and subclass-of for this purpose. Concepts inherit information from their parents and specify them in some way; the converse holds for parent concepts in relation to their children. Queries have to be answered as precisely as possible: not too general, and not too specific. Often, the concept that gets the highest score from a weighting scheme is the right concept, but sometimes things are more complicated, as in Figure 5. Here, the query is 'semantic relation' and the desired concept is 'meaning relation,' but the only concepts that contain 'semantic relation' literally are the children of 'meaning relation.' To address this problem we propose to rerank the list of concepts produced by the weighting scheme in such a way that related concepts appear close to each other. This allows concepts that are related to a concept that gets a high score to benefit from this relation and move up the ranking. The rules we use to group related concepts together are listed below:

1. Every matching concept should be clustered under its parent; this parent concept shows the context of the concept.
2. Matching concepts with the same parent should be put together under that common parent, ordered by their own score.
3. Every chain of parent-child related matching concepts should end in a non-matching concept that shows the context of the chain.
4. Unrelated clusters are joined together as a forest, ordered by the maximum score of the cluster.
5. When parents have the same children they are joined together and get the highest of the two scores.

These rules let parents benefit from their children and vice versa, and they let siblings benefit from higher scoring siblings.

To constrain the size of the groups, and, hence, to allow more than one group to fill the top of the ranking, we discard everything after a certain discrete cut-off point and apply grouping on the concepts that are left. After some experimentation, we chose 10 as the cut-off point, based on the average number of relevant documents per topic. An overview of the retrieval-plus-reranking process is shown in Figure 6. The results of the grouping rules are shown in Table 7 (Bottom). Even with the small number of queries we can conclude that there is a

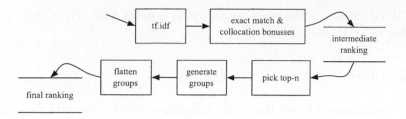

Fig. 6. Overview of the concept grouping process.

material improvement of the scores when we exploit concept relations, and that the combination of all techniques discussed so far improves most, suggesting that distinct techniques have distinct effects.

5.3   Conclusion and Further Steps

While search in a concept hierarchy has special features that may require special IR approaches, we have seen that standard retrieval techniques offer acceptable levels of performance, but that material improvements can be achieved by exploiting the structure of the concept hierarchy. This, we believe, is a very interesting combination of IR and Semantic Web techniques. Obvious further steps worth exploring to improve ontology search include using additional relations from the hierarchy, as well as using different retrieval models.

6   Conclusion

We used collocation-based keyword extraction to suggest new concepts, and we studied the automatic generation of hyperlinks to automate the population of ontologies with instances. We evaluated our methods within the setting of an ontology-based digital library project. Within the same setting we explored retrieval methods aimed at helping users search an ontology, and found that a mixture of IR techniques and result reranking based on the underlying concept hierarchy was the most effective method.

We should point out that, except for the grouping methods deployed in the previous section, the IR methods that we used are mostly standard ones; however, their applications in the Semantic Web setting are novel. The methods and results on which we reported in this paper should be interpreted as providing baselines for their respective tasks. There is a wealth of IR methods that, we believe, can make further contributions to ontology construction, and to the effective usage of ontologies.

Acknowledgments. Maarten de Rijke was supported by the Netherlands Organization for Scientific Research (NWO), under project numbers 612-13-001, 365-20-005, 612.069.006, 612.000.106, 220-80-001, 612.000.207, 612.066.302, and

264-70-050. Maarten Marx was supported by a grant from NWO under project number 612.000.106.

References

1. G. Antoniou and F. van Harmelen. *A Semantic Web Primer*. MIT Press, 2004.
2. R. Baeza-Yates and N. Ribeiro-Neto. *Modern Information Retrieval*. ACM Press, 1999.
3. N.J. Belkin, C. Cool, D. Kelly, G. Kim, J.-Y. Kim, H.-J. Lee, G. Muresan, M.-C Tang, and X.-J Yuan. Query length in interactive information retrieval. In *Proc. of SIGIR*, 2003.
4. C. Caracciolo. Towards modular access to electronic handbooks. *Journal of Digital Information*, 3(4), 2003. Article No. 157, 2003-02-19.
5. CLEF. Cross-Language Evaluation Forum, 2003. URL: `http://www.clef-campaign.org/`.
6. CoNLL. Conference on Natural Language Learning, 2003. URL: `http://cnts.uia.ac.be/signll/conll.html`.
7. J. Heflin, J. Hendler, and S. Luke. Shoe: A prototype language for the semantic web. *Linköping Electronic Articles in Computer and Information Science*, 6, 2001. URL: `http://www.ep.liu.se/ea/cis/2001/003/`.
8. D. Hull. Evaluating evaluation measure stability. In *Proc. of SIGIR 2000*, 2000.
9. INEX. INitiative for the Evaluation of XML Retrieval, 2004. URL: `http://inex.is.informatik.uni-duisburg.de:2004/`.
10. B.J. Jansen. An investigation into the use of simple queries on web ir systems. *Information Research: An Electronic Journal*, 6(1), 2000.
11. J.S. Justeson and S.M. Katz. Technical terminology: some linguistic properties and an algorithm for identification in text., 1995.
12. J. Kamps, M. Marx, M. de Rijke, and B. Sigurbjörnsson. XML retrieval: What to retrieve? In *Proc. of SIGIR*, 2003.
13. G. Kazai, M. Lalmas, and A. de Vries. The overlap problem in content-oriented XML retrieval evaluation. In *Proc. of SIGIR*, 2004.
14. B. Krenn and S. Evert. Can we do better than frequency? A case study on extracting PP-verb collocations. In *Proc. ACL Workshop on Collocations*, 2001.
15. LoLaLi. Logic and Language Links, 2003. URL: `http://lolali.net/`.
16. M. Dewey. Dewey Decimal Classification, 1870. URL: `http://www.oclc.org/dewey`.
17. C.D. Manning and H. Schütze. *Foundations of statistical language processing*. The MIT Press, 1999.
18. J. Mayfield and T. Finin. Information retrieval on the Semantic Web: Integrating inference and retrieval. In *Proc. SIGIR 2003 Semantic Web Workshop*, 2003.
19. J.E. McEneaney. Visualizing and assessing navigation in hypertext. In *Proc. ACM Conference on Hypertext and Hypermedia*, pages 61–70, 1999.
20. NTCIR. NII-NACSIS Test Collection for IR Systems, 2003. URL: `http://research.nii.ac.jp/ntcir/`.
21. M. Sanderson and B. Croft. Deriving concept hierarchies from text. In *Pro. SIGIR 1999*, pages 206–213, 1999.
22. H. Schmid. Probabilistic part-of-speech tagging using decision trees. In *Proc. of International Conference on New Methods in Language Processing*, 1994.

23. Senseval. Evaluation of Systems for the Semantic Analysis of Text, 2003. URL: http://www.senseval.org/.
24. U. Shah, T. Finin, A. Joshi, R.S. Cost, and J. Mayfield. Information retrieval on the semantic web. In *Proc. CIKM 2002*, 2002.
25. H. Stuckenschmidt and F. van Harmelen. Approximating terminological queries. In *Proc. FQAS'02*, 2002.
26. TREC. Text REtrieval Conference, 2003. URL: http://trec.nist.gov/.
27. J. van Benthem and A. Ter Meulen, editors. *Handbook of Logic and Language*. Elsevier, 1997.
28. E.M. Voorhees. Overview of the TREC 2003 Question Answering Track. In *NIST Special Publication 500-255: TREC 2003*, 2004.
29. Yahoo! Yahoo!, 1995. URL: http://www.yahoo.com/.

Rules-By-Example – A Novel Approach to Semantic Indexing and Querying of Images

Suzanne Little[1,2] and Jane Hunter[1]

[1] DSTC Pty Ltd, The University of Queensland,
St Lucia, Queensland, Australia
{slittle, jane}@dstc.edu.au
[2] ITEE Dept., The University of Queensland,
St Lucia, Queensland, Australia

Abstract. Images represent a key source of information in many domains and the ability to exploit them through their discovery, analysis and integration by services and agents on the Semantic Web is a challenging and significant problem. To date the semantic indexing of images has concentrated on applying machine-learning techniques to a set of manually-annotated images in order to automatically label images with keywords. In this paper we propose a new hybrid, user-assisted approach, Rules-By-Example (RBE), which is based on a combination of RuleML and Query-By-Example. Our RBE user interface enables domain-experts to graphically define domain-specific rules that can infer high-level semantic descriptions of images from combinations of low-level visual features (e.g., color, texture, shape, size of regions) which have been specified through examples. Using these rules, the system is able to analyze the visual features of any given image from this domain and generate semantically meaningful labels, using terms defined in the domain-specific ontology. We believe that this approach, in combination with traditional solutions, will enable faster, more flexible, cost-effective and accurate semantic indexing of images and hence maximize their potential for discovery, re-use, integration and processing by Semantic Web services, tools and agents.

1 Introduction

Images constitute a significant and under-utilized proportion of information in many domains and semantic indexing of images is essential if they are to be discovered and fully exploited by Web search engines, services, agents and applications. Because of the complexity and multidimensional nature of image data, manual annotation is slow, expensive and predisposed to high subjectivity. Significant progress has been made in recent years on the automatic recognition of low-level features within images. However, comparatively little progress has been made on the machine-generation of high-level semantic descriptions of images.

In this paper we describe a unique, user-assisted approach to generating ontology-based semantic descriptions of images from low-level automatically extracted features. Our approach enables domain-experts to define rules specific to their domain which map particular combinations of low-level visual features (colour, texture, shape, size) to high-level semantic terms defined in their domain ontology. Such

S.A. McIlraith et al. (Eds.): ISWC 2004, LNCS 3298, pp. 534–548, 2004.

descriptions enable more sophisticated semantic querying of the images in terms familiar to the user's domain whilst still ensuring that the information and knowledge within the images has a much greater chance of being discovered and exploited by services, agents and applications on the Web. The use of ontologies reduces the potential subjectivity of the semantic descriptions and the documentation of the inference rules provides a mechanism for capturing and sharing human domain knowledge, in the form of the analysis methods employed by the domain experts.

Query-By-Example (QBE) is a well-recognized approach to image retrieval. In QBE, the user provides the system with an example image or examples of the visual features that they are seeking and the system attempts to retrieve similar images by matching the visual features. In order to define semantic inferencing rules for images, users need to be able to specify values for low-level visual features. Consider, for example, an oncologist labelling CAT scans of brains, in order to enable the search and retrieval of particular types of brain tumours:

IF [(color is like this) AND (texture is like this) AND (shape is like this)]
THEN (the object is an astrocytoma)

The simplest and most intuitive way to specify such rules is to provide a QBE-type interface by which users can specify colour, texture, shape and size through visual examples, drawing from images within their collection of interest. Hence we decided to develop a Graphical User Interface (GUI) which provides users with color palettes, texture palettes, pre-defined shapes or drawing tools, by which they can define their own semantic inferencing rules. The GUI is generated from and dependent on the pre-selected back-end (OWL) ontology (specified at time of system configuration) which defines and constrains the semantic descriptions that can be generated. The system can be migrated to a different domain by supplying a different back-end ontology. Graphically-defined rules are saved as RuleML which can be applied to image metadata from that particular domain to generate semantic descriptions.

In order to test and evaluate our proposed approach we wanted a domain in which image analysis played a key role and in which a certain amount of knowledge was already available in the form of existing but informal models, vocabularies and image analysis methods which could be represented within ontologies and inference rules. Discussions with the Centre for Microscopy and Microanalysis at The University of Queensland led us to the fuel cell community and their problem of optimization of fuel cells. This application is typical of many eScience applications in that it requires the analysis of large numbers of microstructural images and their assimilation with related information such as performance data and manufacturing parameters. Because the efficiency of fuel cells is dependent on the internal structure of the fuel cell layers and the interfaces between them, an analysis of electron microscopy images of cross-sectional samples through fuel cells can reveal valuable new information. Simple macro-level information such as the thickness of the cell layers, surface area, roughness and densities can be used to determine gas permeation of the electrode materials. Nano-level information about the electrode's internal interface structure provides data on the efficiency of exchange reactions. Figure 1 illustrates a sample of the image data obtainable at different magnifications which needs to be analyzed and semantically indexed in order to fully mine the potential knowledge held within the images.

Fig. 1. Microscopic images of a fuel cell at 3 different magnifications

The remainder of this paper describes in more detail the semantic indexing system which we built and its application and evaluation within the context of the fuel cell domain. Although we have chosen one particular community in which to test our approach, the design is such that it applies to any image-analysis domain e.g., remote-sensing, satellite or medical images. The paper is structured as follows:

- Section 2 describes previous research on the generation of semantic image descriptions from low-level features;
- Section 3 describes the overall architecture of our system and its main components:
    - The ontologies which we developed;
    - The automatic image analysis programs which we invoked to extract low-level features and to generate MPEG-7 descriptions;
    - How we applied semantic inferencing rules to image data and the challenges this involved;
- Section 4 describes the Rules-By-Example graphical user interface which we developed;
- Section 5 contains empirical results obtained by testing our approach on real fuel cell images;
- Section 6 contains our conclusions and describes future plans for this research.

2   Previous Work

Most recent research in image or video indexing and retrieval has focused on query-by-example (QBE) [1-3]. However semantic querying or query-by-keyword (QBK) has recently motivated research into semantic indexing of images and video content. A number of research efforts have investigated the use of automatic recognition techniques to extract different low-level visual or audio features which together can be used to generate improved semantic descriptions of multimedia content. Recent attempts include work by Naphade et. al. [4] which proposes a statistical factor graph framework to bridge the gap between low-level features and semantic concepts. Chang et. al. [5] use a library of examples approach, which they call semantic visual templates. Adams et. al. [6] manually annotate atomic audio and video features in a set of training videos and from these develop explicit statistical models to automatically label the video with high-level semantic concepts. Zhao and Grosky [7] employ a latent semantic indexing technique which integrates a variety of automatically extracted visual features (global and sub-image colour histograms and anglograms for shape-based and colour-based representations) to enable semantic indexing and retrieval of images.

Overall the use of machine learning techniques to bridge the semantic gap between image features and high-level semantic annotations provides a relatively powerful method for discovering complex and hidden relationships or mappings. However the 'black-box' method often employed can be difficult to develop and maintain as its effectiveness relies upon the design and configuration of multiple variables and options. In addition, extensive and detailed training corpuses are required to ensure optimum performance from the system. The main disadvantage of machine learning-based systems is that they are built specifically for one particular domain and document type (e.g., images or speech) and cannot easily accommodate other domains or information sources.

In their recent paper, Marques and Barman [8] used machine-learning techniques to semantically annotate images with semantic descriptions defined within ontologies. Our approach is to replace or augment the machine-learning component with domain-specific inferencing rules defined by domain-experts through an intuitive user-friendly interface. Hatala and Richards [9] applied a similar approach to generating semantic descriptions for learning objects - relevant values for a particular metadata field are suggested by applying ontologies and rules – but they have not applied this approach to image content.

We believe that our approach enables some of the limitations in existing image annotation approaches (such as difficulty determining the distinguishing features and adapting to different domains) to be overcome. We do this through the complementary use of semantic web technologies and an interface which allows domain experts to intuitively and interactively develop and define semantic inferencing rules in an interoperable, machine-understandable and shareable format.

3 System Architecture

Figure 2 illustrates the overall system components and architecture for the knowledge management system that we developed to manage the manufacturing, performance, microscopy and image data captured from the fuel cell components.

The MPEG-7 (Multimedia Content Description) [10] standard is used to describe the low-level image features. The OME (Open Microscopy Environment) [11] standard is used to capture associated microscope details and settings – essential provenance information within any scientific context. An additional metadata schema (FUSION [12]) was developed specifically to satisfy the descriptive requirements of fuel cell analysts. We developed both XML Schemas [13] to define and validate the metadata descriptions, and OWL [14] ontologies, to define the semantics and semantic relationships between the terms used in each of these schemas. User-specified RuleML rules define the relationships between low-level automatically-extracted MPEG-7 features and high-level FUSION concepts or terms and are applied by an inferencing engine. All of the generated and validated metadata is stored in a central knowledge repository. A query engine, visualization engine and knowledge capture (annotation) tools sit on top of the knowledge repository. Together these enable users to access, interpret, assimilate and mine the stored data.

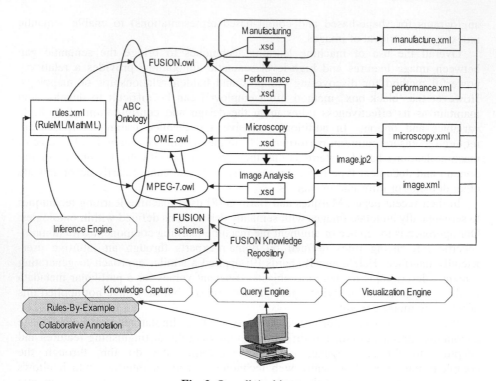

Fig. 2. Overall Architecture

A key aspect of our approach is the separation (as far as possible) of rules from facts. The rules are contained within explicit definitions in the RuleML files (rules.xml) and within implicit class/property relationships of the ontologies. Together these produce rules which are more flexible and able to be easily abstracted e.g., if a given rule applies to mpeg7:Color then it will also apply to mpeg7:DominantColor. The facts are built from the knowledge repository elements which are defined by both XML Schema (syntactic) definitions and ontological (semantic) definitions. Applying the rules through a reasoning engine, produces more "facts" which are inserted into the knowledge repository and defined within the related XML Schema and OWL ontology.

In order to enable semantic interoperability between the MPEG-7, OME and FUSION metadata vocabularies, and to define the semantic and inferencing relationships between the terms in these different schemas, we needed to develop ontologies for each of these vocabularies and harmonize or relate them. We used the top-level or core ABC ontology [15] developed within the Harmony project to do this. The ABC ontology provides a global and extensible model that expresses the basic concepts that are common across a variety of domains and provides the basis for specialization into domain-specific concepts and vocabularies. Brief descriptions of the MPEG-7, OME and FUSION ontologies together with figures illustrating a subset of these ontologies are provided below.

3.1 The MPEG-7 Ontology

Figure 3 illustrates graphically a subset of the MPEG-7 OWL ontology [16] which we developed to define the semantics of terms used within the MPEG-7 standard for describing multimedia/image content – and in particular low level visual features. Figure 3 shows only those classes for which "color" is a visual descriptor and the five sub-properties of color. A complete description of the MPEG-7 ontology is available at [17].

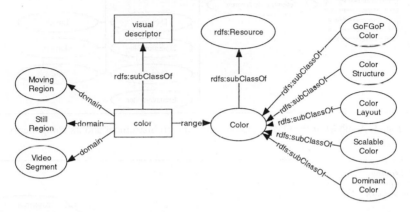

Fig. 3. The MPEG-7 Visual Descriptor "Color".

3.2 The OME Ontology

The OME (Open Microscopy Environment) [18] is an open source collaborative software project which aims to develop a common environment for the analysis, management and exchange of biological microscopic images. A key component of the OME is an XML-encoded file standard for the storage, analysis and exchange of image data output from microscopy procedures. A common standard for recording microscope-related metadata is essential for capturing the provenance or source of microscopy images and it includes such information as: the microscope manufacturer, serial and model, instrument settings, detectors, filters and light sources. An OME ontology was developed from the OME CoreSemanticTypes [19]. It defines the semantics associated with microscope output data and settings and enables them to be related to the image descriptors defined by MPEG-7 and FUSION ontologies. Figure 4 illustrates a subset of the OME OWL ontology that we developed.

3.3 The FUSION Ontology

Figure 5 illustrates the key classes or concepts and their relationships, as defined in the FUSION ontology that we developed for the fuel cell community. This was developed in collaboration with domain experts using the approach recommended in [20] and was used to generate the high-level semantic descriptions or terms which the fuel-cell experts use when searching and retrieving images.

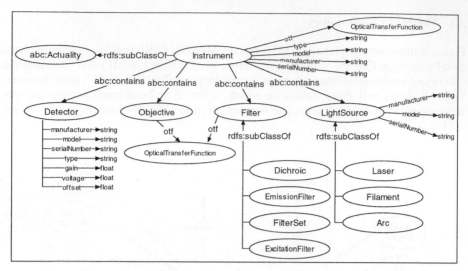

Fig. 4. A subset of the OME ontology showing an instrument and its components

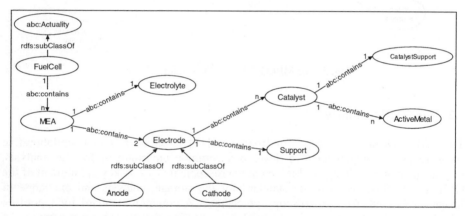

Fig. 5. A subset of the Fuel Cell ontology showing components of a fuel cell.

3.4 Automatic Feature Extraction

Automatic feature extraction for images [21] is a significant research area and a wide variety of tools and mechanisms exist for analyzing scientific and other types of images (e.g. [22]). Within the scope of this project, we are not particularly interested in the underlying method by which these programs process images but we are interested in the outputs or features that such programs produce and whether they can be used to generate MPEG-7 descriptions from which higher-level semantic concepts can be inferred. For our system we have chosen to use MATLAB [23] because it is a popular and powerful tool which is currently being widely used by microscopists and scientists for analyzing scientific images. MATLAB is capable of producing a large amount of low-level data about the features and objects within an image e.g., area, location, pixel colour, centroid, eccentricity, orientation etc. Currently we are calling MATLAB analysis methods directly but plan to employ SOAP [24], WSDL [25] and OWL-S [26] to make the automatic feature extraction modules of MATLAB available as web services. This would allow greater flexibility and adaptability by enabling the optimum extraction and analysis tools or services to be plugged in at runtime. The data produced by MATLAB analysis methods is transformed to MPEG-7 descriptions using Python scripts.

3.5 Defining and Invoking Semantic Inferencing Rules

Many challenges need to be overcome, when implementing inferencing rules within a Semantic Web application. [27] provides a useful discussion of the current approaches to rules within the Semantic Web and examines some of the motivations and difficulties. The three main issues faced by our project were: what recording syntax to choose; how to build or generate the rules; and how to apply the rules.

The recording syntax had to be flexible, machine-processable and interoperable with existing tools and standards (e.g., XML Schema, OWL). By using an XML-based rule definition language such as RuleML, the rules, ontologies and metadata schemas can be linked through the use of URIs, namespaces and semantic attributes defined in the XML Schema documents (see [28] for further details on this approach). In addition, as noted by Boley et. al. [29], XML-based rules provide a sharable, application-independent form of knowledge which can easily be processed for each application using transformation methods such as XSLT or others of the growing variety of generic tools for the creation, modification and management of XML data. Several possible XML formats exist for representing inference rules. The most popular markup language for rules and the current most likely candidate for adoption by the Semantic Web community is RuleML [30], the Rule Markup Language. Although still under active development, RuleML has a wide user base, a reasonable level of available tool support in the form of reasoning engines and transformation options and provides an XML description of inference rules. Alternative markup languages which were examined included the eXtensible Rule Markup Language (XRML) [31] and the Description Logic Markup Language (DLML) [32] both of which lacked the breadth of users and tool support available for RuleML. A promising emerging approach, the Semantic Web Rule Language (SWRL) [33, 34] which combines OWL and RuleML, is also under-development and may be considered for use within this project as its stability and support base expands. In addition MathML [35], the W3C's Mathematical Markup Language, was also investigated in order to support the description of more complex mathematical relationships and models relating to the fuel cell domain.

While XML-based rules have many advantages, they can be very difficult and time consuming to create and in the case of image data, rely on the specification of low-level features which can be highly complex (e.g., colour histograms). The size of the resulting XML file is also a serious issue. For example, the simple rule provided in the introduction to this paper would convert to approximately 40 lines of RuleML. The translation from rules specified in a natural language format to RuleML is not necessarily a one-to-one mapping. For example, *color is 'one of' set* can have multiple possible RuleML representations. In order to assist domain experts in the creation, refinement and application of the semantic inferencing rules, we developed the Rules-By-Example GUI – an intuitive user interface generated from the configured backend ontologies that allows users to build complex RuleML rules quickly and easily. This is described in detail in the next section.

Once the rules have been defined and recorded they need to be processed and applied to the specified data using an inferencing engine. Possible candidates for the inferencing engine include: JESS (Java Expert System Shell) [36]; and Mandarax [37], a Java RuleML engine. Problems that often arise when invoking the semantic inferencing rules include: slow processing speed; the need to convert data to in-memory RuleML facts and the lack of native RuleML support for applying standard string and mathematical relations (e.g., greater than, equal to, etc.). Mandarax provides some internal representation and processing options (ZKB) which can be used to overcome these issues. Alternatively using wrapper scripts and relational or XML databases can also be used to improve performance and flexibility.

4   Rules-By-Example Implementation and Interface

Figure 6 illustrates the dataflow within the Rules-By-Example (RBE) system. The RBE GUI enables the user to specify values for visual features from palettes of sample colors and textures, drawing tools or by specifying example images selected from the knowledge repository. For example, using the graphical tools, users can easily specify that 'color' should be 'like this region in this image'. By generating the GUI's pull-down menus from MPEG-7 descriptions generated by the image analysis services and the ontologies specified at configuration time, the GUI enables domain experts to easily define complex rules and store them in RuleML format without understanding the complexities of image analysis or RuleML.

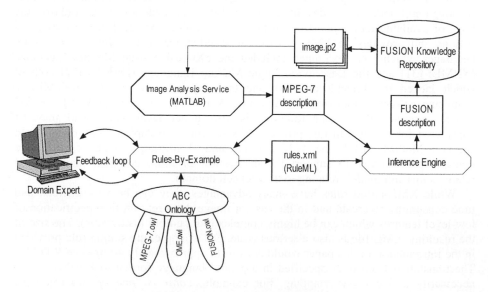

Fig. 6. Rules-By-Example Dataflow

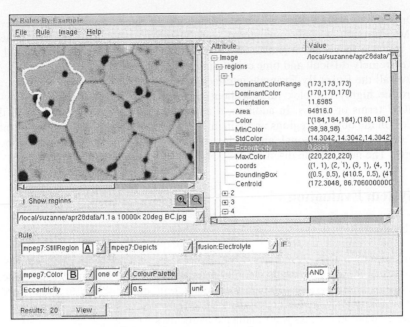

Fig. 7. Screenshot of user interface prototype

Figure 7 illustrates a screenshot of the prototype RBE interface developed. The menu options within the interface are populated dynamically from the back-end ontologies specified during system configuration. For example, the initial menu (marked A) identifies the MPEG-7 Media element to which the rule applies. Consequently the drop-down menu displays subclasses of the Region class of the MPEG-7 ontology. In this case the user has selected the StillRegion sub-class. Further use of relationships derived from ontologies can be seen in the menu marked B. Depending on the media element selection made in menu A, menu B displays all possible properties (or attributes) which have that element or its superclass as the domain. The possible operators and values for a property, are also generated from its range definition e.g., if the type is *string* then relationships such as *less than* are irrelevant. This type of dynamic population of the user interface provides both user support and domain independence – both strengths of this system. Standard logical operators (AND/OR) enable the specification of more advanced, composite, logic-based rules. The window in the upper right-hand section of Figure 7 shows the metadata which has been automatically extracted for the highlighted region.

In order to specify the values of atoms within a rule's body, the user is able to select an existing image (or set of images) and choose regions or segments of the image to use as examples. For instance, in the screenshot above, the color specification within this rule states that for the rule to be true (that is for the *StillRegion* to depict *Electrolyte*) then color must be one or more of the set shown on the palette. The palette displays all of the colors in the selected segment and the user is able select one or more. An additional complexity when searching for visual features is the fuzzy matching problem. Similarity rather than exact matches are usually required. To support this, the interface provides the ability to set a threshold value for individual image attributes or features.

Once the user is satisfied with a rule definition, it can be transformed and saved in RuleML format (possibly augmented with MathML). The RuleML file generated from the rule in Figure 7 is available[1]. Manual creation of such a rule would have been extremely difficult and time consuming.

Overall the Rules-By-Example interface allows the user to quickly develop, apply and refine highly complex rules without needing to understand complex low-level MPEG-7 terms or values. In addition, it enables users to direct the system so that it focuses on the objects, regions or distinguishing features of highest priority or interest – in contrast to traditional approaches which require pre-selection of important features. The next section discusses the results of initial system evaluation.

5   System Evaluation

5.1   Evaluation Process

Initial evaluation tests were carried out using a set of sample fuel cell images. The objectives of these experiments were: to determine how the semantic labels generated by our rules-based system compare with manual annotations; and to gather feedback on the usability and expediency of the RBE interface.

The evaluation process was conducted as follows:

1.   Twelve microscopy images, of equivalent magnification (10000x) and from the same fuel cell component (electrolyte of a ceramic fuel cell) were manually segmented by defining region boundaries. The images were all grayscale and either high quality JPEG or TIFF images of average size 2560x1920 pixels. Two main region types were present: large pale gray 10% yttria-stabilized zirconia (10YSZ) grains and smaller, darker alumina grains.

2.   The images were analyzed using the MATLAB image processing toolbox and low level data (including: Boundary Coordinates, Area, BoundingBox, Eccentricity, Color (lightest, darkest, mean, standard deviation, dominant color, dominant range of colors)) were extracted and saved to a MySQL database.

3.   The RBE interface was used by the system designers to manually assign labels to all of the regions in the images (total of 274 regions).

4.   The RBE interface was then used by the fuel cell experts to build six sample RuleML rules (three describing the 10YSZ grains and three describing the alumina grains) based on a region's Area, Eccentricity, DominantColor and DominantColorRange. Feedback on the usability of the interface was recorded during this phase.

5.   A Python script converted the data in the database into RuleML facts describing the features of each region. Some filtering and preprocessing of the facts was necessary to remove tiny (<100 pixel) areas that were detected by the segmenting software but which do not represent relevant regions. These regions can greatly reduce the speed of the inferencing engine. Secondly, as discussed in section 3.5, mathematical relationships defined within the rules (e.g., *greater than*) are not processed by Mandarax. So in order for the inferencing engine to apply rules such as, "DominantColor must be greater than (165,165,165)", a Python pre-

---

[1]   http://metadata.net/sunago/fusion/sample.ruleml

processing script was required to generate additional facts e.g., declaring those regions with attribute values greater than the nominated threshold.

6. A sample RuleML query was defined and the rule, query and facts were combined into a rulebase and processed using the Mandarax inferencing engine. The list of regions which matched the query were saved and compared with the labels of the manually annotated regions to calculate the precision and recall of the RBE system.

5.2 Evaluation Results

Table 1 shows the results of initial evaluation tests generated by applying the six rules specified below the table. Initial results demonstrate exceptional precision but only mediocre recall. The high precision is a direct result of the RBE interface which enables users to interactively adapt and refine their rules and filter out erroneous rules, based on system feedback. However this also encourages users to mould rules to fit the test set, potentially at the expense of performance or accuracy when applied to a larger size or range of images. The improvement in recall shown when two rules were combined (Rules 3 and 6) demonstrates how this tendency can be overcome and leveraged to improve the results.

Table 1. Summary of initial evaluation results

	1	2	3	4	5	6
Total regions which match the rule (I)	66	52	102	24	24	33
Regions which match the rule and have the equivalent label in the database (H)	66	52	102	23	24	32
Total regions labeled as *component* in the database (C)	167	167	167	53	53	53
Precision (C/I)	100	100	100	95.83	100	95.83
Recall (C/H)	39.52	31.14	61.08	43.4	45.28	60.38

1. mpeg7:Region mpeg7:Depicts 10YSZ IF mpeg7:DominantColor is '(1,1,1)' AND DominantColorRange is '(6,6,6)'
2. mpeg7:Region mpeg7:Depicts 10YSZ IF Area < 5000 and Eccentricity < 0.5
3. mpeg7:Region mpeg7:Depicts 10YSZ IF Rule1 OR Rule2
4. mpeg7:Region mpeg7:Depicts alumina IF mpeg7:DominantColor is > '(165,165,165)' and mpeg7:DominantColor < '(200,200,200)'
5. mpeg7:Region mpeg7:Depicts alumina IF Area > 100000 and Eccentricity > 0.5
6. mpeg7:Region mpeg7:Depicts alumina IF Rule4 OR Rule5

The homogeneous nature of the images also contributed to the high precision of the results. The images were highly consistent because they originated from the same fuel cell component (albeit at different cross-sections) and were created under exactly the same microscopy conditions. This consistency, together with the presence of only two distinct region types, made the creation of precise rules relatively simple.

However, the slow performance of the system was a serious problem. The size of the images, the number of regions and the size of the associated data (100MB text files generated by MATLAB) significantly affected the performance and responsiveness of the RBE interface. Processing even a simple query and rule over a large set of facts took up to 10 minutes. A number of solutions (e.g., closer integration of database functionality, use of MATLAB APIs and faster image processing techniques) are currently being investigated.

User's feedback on the interface produced several useful requests including: the ability to compare and contrast selected sample regions; a 'sketch' interface integrated with feature measurements such as *eccentricity*, to assist in describing shape; and enabling the definitions of the ontology terms used to populate the dropdown menus to be displayed. These interface issues are currently being addressed.

6 Future Work and Conclusions

The initial test results were very encouraging. A comparison of the semantic labels generated automatically (by applying user-defined rules) with the semantic labels manually attached to the same images, has demonstrated very high correlation. Given the semantic descriptions generated by applying the rules defined within the RBE GUI, domain-experts are able to perform much more complex and sophisticated queries over the image data, in terms which are useful and familiar to their domain e.g., "give me all of the images depicting Catalysts with high ActiveMetal density".

However further testing is required – using larger image sets and images from other domains. Future tests will also involve more formal interface evaluation (user interviews, observation, task analysis) and more comprehensive investigation of methods for improving performance and scalability. We also plan to compare the performance of the system with machine learning based methods for image analysis.

Additional future plans include: supporting user suggestions gathered from the initial trials; including confidence ratings with rule specifications; extending the approach described here to the semantic indexing of video content (exploiting automatically-extracted audio and moving object features); adding an annotation component to allow shared evaluation of experimental data.

To conclude, we have described in this paper a new approach to the semi-automatic semantic indexing of images. Rules-By-Example (RBE) combines RuleML with a Query-By-Example type interface to enable domain-experts to graphically define domain-specific rules that can infer high-level semantic descriptions of images from combinations of low-level visual features (e.g., color, texture, shape, size of regions). By applying these rules, the system is able to analyze the visual features of any given image from this domain and generate semantically meaningful descriptions, using terms defined in the domain-specific ontology. We believe that the advantages of this approach include:

- Faster, more accurate cost-effective semantic indexing of images;
- A graphical user interface which provides an intuitive, user-friendly means by which domain-experts can interactively develop, apply and refine semantic inferencing rules for images;
- A flexible architecture which enables any ontology to be easily linked to the system at configuration time, dynamically customizing the system for a particular domain;

- The ability to plug in the optimum or most appropriate automatic image analysis tools/services at runtime;
- The use of machine-understandable XML-based image metadata standards, schemas, ontologies and rule languages which ensure maximum interoperability of the system and data;
- A knowledge capture system which accurately and easily captures the knowledge of domain experts and maximizes the potential of their image content to be discovered, re-used and assimilated by communities, services, tools and agents on the Web.

Acknowledgements. The work reported in this paper has been funded in part by the Co-operative Research Centre for Enterprise Distributed Systems Technology (DSTC) through the Australian Federal Government's CRC Programme (Department of Education, Science and Training). Thanks also to staff from the Centre for Microscopy and Microanalysis at the University of Queensland for their feedback and the images used in this project.

References

1. Deng, Y. and Manjunath, B. S. "Content-based search of video using color, texture and motion." in International Conference on Image Processing (ICIP '97). Washington, DC, USA, October 26-29, 1997.
2. Marchand-Maillet, S., "Content-Based Video Retrieval: An Overview." University of Geneva, Geneva, Switzerland. 2000. Technical Report No. 00.06, CUI.
3. Zhang, H., Wang, A., and Altunbasak, Y. "Content-based video retrieval and compression: a unified solution." in IEEE International Conference on Image Processing. Santa Barbara, CA, Oct 1997.
4. Naphade, M. R., et al. "A Factor Graph Framework for Semantic Indexing and Retrieval in Video", in IEEE Workshop on Content-based Access of Image and Video Libraries (CBAIVL'00). Hilton Head, South Carolina, June 16 2000.
5. Chang, S. F., Chen, W., and Sundaram, H. "Semantic Visual Templates: linking visual features to semantics", in IEEE International Conference on Image Processing (ICIP '98). Chicago, Illinois, 1998.
6. Adams, B., et al., Semantic Indexing of Multimedia Content Using Visual, Audio and Text Cues. EURASIP Journal on Applied Signal Processing. 2003.
7. Zhao, R. and Grosky, W. I., Negotiating The Semantic Gap: From Feature Maps to Semantic Landscapes. Pattern Recognition. 35(3): p. 51-58, 2002.
8. Marques, O. and Barman, N. "Semi-automatic Semantic Annotation of Images Using Machine Learning Techniques", in International Semantic Web Conference. Florida, October 2003.
9. Hatala, M. and Richards, G. "Value-added Metatagging: Ontology and Rule based Methods for Smarter Metadata", in Rules and Rule Markup Languages for the Semantic Web (RuleML2003), 2003.
10. ISO/IEC 15938-5 FDIS Information Technology, "Multimedia Content Description Interface - Part 5: Multimedia Description Schemes". MPEG7, Sydney. July 2001.
11. Open Microscopy Environment, OME, (http://www.openmicroscopy.org/).
12. FUSION Project, (http://metadata.net/sunago/fusion.htm).
13. W3C, XML Schema Specifications (Part 0: Primer, Part 1: Structures, and Part 2: Datatypes), W3C Recommendation, May 2001, (http://www.w3.org/XML/Schema#dev).

14. W3C, OWL Web Ontology Language Overview, W3C Recommendation, 10 Feb 2004, Edited by Deborah L. McGuinness and Frank van Harmelen, (http://www.w3.org/TR/owl-features/).
15. Lagoze, C. and Hunter, J., The ABC Ontology and Model (v3.0). Journal of Digital Information. 2(2), 2001.
16. Hunter, J. "Adding Multimedia to the Semantic Web - Building an MPEG-7 Ontology", in International Semantic Web Working Symposium (SWWS). Stanford, July 30 - August 1, 2001.
17. MPEG-7 Ontology, (http://metadata.net/harmony/MPEG7/mpeg7.owl).
18. Swedlow, J. R., et al., Informatics and Quantitative Analysis in Biological Imaging. SCIENCE. 300: p. 100-102, 2003.
19. Open Microscopy Environment, OMECoreSemanticTypes.ome, 4 Sep 2003, (http://openmicroscopy.org/XMLschemas/STD/RC2/OMECoreTypes.ome).
20. Noy, N. and McGuinness, D., "Ontology development 101: A Guide to Creating Your First Ontology". Stanford University, 2001. Technical Report SMI-2001-0880.
21. Nixon, M. and Aguado, A., Feature Extraction and Image Processing. 2002: Newnes.
22. Internet Analysis Tools Registry, (http://www.cma.mgh.harvard.edu/iatr/display.php?search_type=all).
23. MathWorks, MATLAB, (http://www.mathworks.com/products/imageprocessing/).
24. W3C, SOAP Version 1.2 Part 0: Primer, W3C Recommendation, 24 June 2003, Edited by Nilo Mitra, (http://www.w3.org/TR/2003/REC-soap12-part0-20030624/).
25. Christensen, E., et al., Web Services Description Language (WSDL) 1.1, W3C Note, 15 March 2001, (http://www.w3.org/TR/wsdl).
26. The DAML Services Coalition, OWL-S: Semantic Markup for Web Services, May 2003, (http://www.daml.org/services/owl-s/1.0/).
27. Staab, S., et al., Trends & controversies - Where are the rules? Intelligent Systems, IEEE. 18(5): p. 76, 2003.
28. Hunter, J. and Lagoze, C. "Combining RDF and XML Schemas to Enhance Interoperability Between Metadata Application Profiles", in WWW10. HongKong, May 2001.
29. Boley, H., Tabet, S., and Wagner, G. "Design Rationale of RuleML: A Markup Language for Semantic Web Rules", in Semantic Web Working Symposium (SWWS), 2001.
30. The Rule Markup Initiative, RuleML, (http://www.dfki.uni-kl.de/ruleml).
31. eXtensible Rule Markup Language, XRML, (http://xrml.kaist.ac.kr/).
32. Description Logic Markup Language, DLML, (http://co4.inrialpes.fr/xml/dlml/).
33. Horrocks, I., et al., "SWRL: A Semantic Web Rule Language Combining OWL and RuleML". 19 November 2003. proposal
34. Grosof, B. N., et al. "Description Logic Programs: Combining Logic Programs with Description Logic", in 12th Intl. Conf. on the World Wide Web (WWW-2003). Budapest, Hungary, May 20-23, 2003.
35. W3C, Mathematical Markup Language (MathML), W3C Proposed Edited Recommendation, 04 August 2003, Patrick Ion Edited by David Carlisle, Robert Miner and Nico Poppelier, (http://www.w3.org/TR/2003/PER-MathML2-2003080).
36. Friedman-Hill, E., Jess, The Expert Shell for the Java Platform, (http://herzberg.ca.sandia.gov/jess/).
37. Dietrich, J., The Mandarax Project, (http://www.mandarax.org/).

Query Answering for OWL-DL with Rules

Boris Motik[1], Ulrike Sattler[2], and Rudi Studer[1]

[1] FZI Research Center for Information Technologies, Univ. of Karlsruhe, Germany
{motik,studer}@fzi.de
[2] Department of Computer Science, Univ. of Manchester, UK
sattler@cs.man.ac.uk

Abstract. Both OWL-DL and function-free Horn rules[1] are decidable logics with interesting, yet orthogonal expressive power: from the rules perspective, OWL-DL is restricted to tree-like rules, but provides both existentially and universally quantified variables and full, monotonic negation. From the description logic perspective, rules are restricted to universal quantification, but allow for the interaction of variables in arbitrary ways. Clearly, a combination of OWL-DL and rules is desirable for building Semantic Web ontologies, and several such combinations have already been discussed. However, such a combination might easily lead to the undecidability of interesting reasoning problems. Here, we present a *decidable* such combination which is, to the best of our knowledge, more general than similar decidable combinations proposed so far. Decidability is obtained by restricting rules to so-called *DL-safe* ones, requiring each variable in a rule to occur in a non-DL-atom in the rule body. We show that query answering in such a combined logic is decidable, and we discuss its expressive power by means of a non-trivial example. Finally, we present an algorithm for query answering in $\mathcal{SHIQ}(\mathbf{D})$ extended with DL-safe rules based on the reduction to disjunctive datalog.

1 Introduction

OWL-DL [20] is a W3C recommendation language for ontology representation in the Semantic Web. It is a syntactic variant of the $\mathcal{SHOIN}(\mathbf{D})$ description logic (DL), offering a high level of expressivity while still being decidable. For example, $\mathcal{SHOIN}(\mathbf{D})$ provides full negation, disjunction, and (a restricted form of) universal and existential quantification of variables. A related logic, $\mathcal{SHIQ}(\mathbf{D})$ [13,12], distinguished from $\mathcal{SHOIN}(\mathbf{D})$ mainly by not supporting nominals (or named objects), has been successfully implemented in practical reasoning systems, such as Racer [9] and FaCT [10]. Description logics have been found useful in numerous applications such as information integration [1, ch. 16], software engineering [1, ch. 11], and conceptual modeling [1, ch. 10].

Although OWL-DL is very expressive, it is a *decidable* fragment of first-order logic, and thus cannot express arbitrary axioms: the only axioms it can express are of a certain tree-structure [8]. In contrast, decidable rule-based formalism such as function-free Horn rules do not share this restriction, but lack

---

[1] Throughout this paper, we use "rules" and "clauses" synonymously, following [11].

S.A. McIlraith et al. (Eds.): ISWC 2004, LNCS 3298, pp. 549–563, 2004.

some of the expressive power of OWL-DL: they are restricted to universal quantification and lack negation in their basic form. To overcome the limitations of both approaches, OWL-DL was extended with rules in [11], but this extension is undecidable [11]. Intuitively, the undecidability is due to the fact that adding rules to OWL-DL causes the loss of any form of *tree model property*. In a logic with such a property, every satisfiable knowledge base has a model of a certain tree-shaped form. As a consequence, to decide satisfiability (i.e. the existence of a model of a knowledge base), we can search only for such tree-shaped models. For most DLs, it is possible to ensure termination of such a search. To see how rules can destroy this property, consider e.g. the rule $hasAunt(x, y) \leftarrow hasParent(x, z), hasSibling(z, y), Female(y)$, which obviously has only non-tree models.

It is natural to ask what kind of (non-tree) rules can be added to OWL-DL while preserving decidability. This follows a classic line of research in knowledge representation, investigating the trade-off between expressivity and complexity, and providing formalisms with varying expressive power and complexity. It not only provides insight into the causes for the undecidability of the full combination, but also enables a more detailed complexity analysis and, ultimately, the design of "specialized" decision procedures. Applications that do not require the expressive power of the full combination can use such procedures, relying upon known upper time and space bounds required to return a correct answer. Finally, in the last decade, it turned out that many specialized decision procedures are amenable to optimizations, thus achieving surprisingly good performance in practice even for logics with high worst-case complexity [1, ch. 9].

In this paper, we propose a decidable combination of OWL-DL with rules, where decidability is obtained by restricting the rules to so-called *DL-safe* ones. Importantly, we do not restrict the component languages, but only reduce the interface between them. Generalizing the approaches of other decidable combinations of rules and description logics [16,5], in DL-safe rules, concepts and roles are allowed to occur in both rule bodies and heads as unary, respectively binary predicates in atoms, but each variable of a rule is required to occur in some body literal whose predicate is neither a concept nor a role. We discuss the expressive power and limitations of our approach by means of an example, and show that query answering for it is decidable.

Moreover, we present an algorithm for query answering in the extension of $\mathcal{SHIQ}(\mathbf{D})$ with DL-safe rules which is based on a novel technique for reducing $\mathcal{SHIQ}(\mathbf{D})$ knowledge bases to disjunctive datalog programs [15,14]. This yields a query answering algorithm which follows the principle of "graceful degradation": the user "pays" only for the features she actually uses. Although a full evaluation is not yet finished, our partial evaluation from [18] is very promising, and we believe that this algorithm can be efficiently realized in practice.

Please note that we are primarily concerned with the semantic and decidability aspects of hybrid reasoning, and not with the infrastructure aspects, such as the syntax or the exchange of rules on the Web. For these issues, we refer the reader to [11] since our approach is fully compatible with the one proposed there.

2 Preliminaries

OWL-DL is a syntactic variant of the $\mathcal{SHOIN}(\mathbf{D})$ description logic [11]. Hence, although several XML and RDF syntaxes for OWL-DL exist, in this paper we use the traditional description logic notation since it is more compact. For the correspondence between this notation and various OWL-DL syntaxes, see [11].

$\mathcal{SHOIN}(\mathbf{D})$ supports reasoning with concrete datatypes, such as strings or integers. For example, it is possible to define a minor as a person whose age is less than or equal to 18 in the following way: $Minor \equiv Person \sqcap \exists age. \leq_{18}$. Instead of axiomatizing concrete datatypes in logic, $\mathcal{SHOIN}(\mathbf{D})$ employs an approach similar to [2], where the properties of concrete datatypes are encapsulated in so-called *concrete domains*. A *concrete domain* is a pair $(\triangle_{\mathbf{D}}, \Phi_{\mathbf{D}})$, where $\triangle_{\mathbf{D}}$ is an interpretation domain and $\Phi_{\mathbf{D}}$ is a set of concrete domain predicates with a predefined arity n and an interpretation $d^{\mathbf{D}} \subseteq \triangle_{\mathbf{D}}^{n}$. An *admissible* concrete domain $\mathbf{D}$ is equipped with a decision procedure for checking satisfiability of finite conjunctions over concrete predicates. Satisfiability checking of admissible concrete domains can successfully be combined with logical reasoning for many description logics [17].

We use a set of concept names N_C, sets of abstract and concrete individuals N_{I_a} and N_{I_c}, respectively, and sets of abstract and concrete role names N_{R_a} and N_{R_c}, respectively. An *abstract role* is an abstract role name or the inverse S^- of an abstract role name S (concrete roles do not have inverses). In the following, we assume that $\mathbf{D}$ is an admissible concrete domain.

An *RBox* $\mathcal{R}$ consists of a finite set of transitivity axioms $\mathsf{Trans}(R)$, and role inclusion axioms of the form $R \sqsubseteq S$ and $T \sqsubseteq U$, where R and S are abstract roles, and T and U are concrete roles. The reflexive-transitive closure of the role inclusion relationship is denoted with $\sqsubseteq^*$. A role not having transitive subroles (w.r.t. $\sqsubseteq^*$, for a full definition see [13]) is called a *simple* role.

The set of $\mathcal{SHOIN}(\mathbf{D})$ *concepts* is defined by the following syntactic rules, where A is an atomic concept, R is an abstract role, S is an abstract simple role, $T_{(i)}$ are concrete roles, d is a concrete domain predicate, a_i and c_i are abstract and concrete individuals, respectively, and n is a non-negative integer:

$$C \rightarrow A \mid \neg C \mid C_1 \sqcap C_2 \mid C_1 \sqcup C_2 \mid \exists R.C \mid \forall R.C \mid \geq n\, S \mid \leq n\, S \mid \{a_1, \ldots, a_n\} \mid$$
$$\mid \geq n\, T \mid \leq n\, T \mid \exists T_1, \ldots, T_n.D \mid \forall T_1, \ldots, T_n.D$$
$$D \rightarrow d \mid \{c_1, \ldots, c_n\}$$

A *TBox* $\mathcal{T}$ consists of a finite set of concept inclusion axioms $C \sqsubseteq D$, where C and D are concepts; an *ABox* $\mathcal{A}$ consists of a finite set of concept and role assertions and individual (in)equalities $C(a)$, $R(a,b)$, $a \approx b$, and $a \not\approx b$, respectively. A $\mathcal{SHOIN}(\mathbf{D})$ *knowledge base* $(\mathcal{T}, \mathcal{R}, \mathcal{A})$ consists of a TBox $\mathcal{T}$, an RBox $\mathcal{R}$, and an ABox $\mathcal{A}$.

The $\mathcal{SHIQ}(\mathbf{D})$ description logic is obtained from $\mathcal{SHOIN}(\mathbf{D})$ by disallowing nominal concepts of the form $\{a_1, \ldots, a_n\}$ and $\{c_1, \ldots, c_n\}$, and by allowing qualified number restrictions of the form $\geq n\, S.C$ and $\leq n\, S.C$, for C a $\mathcal{SHIQ}(\mathbf{D})$ concept and S a simple role.

Table 1. Translation of $\mathcal{SHOIN}(\mathbf{D})$ into FOL

Mapping Concepts to FOL	
$\pi_y(\top, X){=}\top$	$\pi_y(\bot, X){=}\bot$
$\pi_y(A, X){=}A(X)$	$\pi_y(\neg C, X){=}\neg\pi_y(C, X)$
$\pi_y(C \sqcap D, X){=}\pi_y(C, X) \wedge \pi_y(D, X)$	$\pi_y(C \sqcup D, X){=}\pi_y(C, X) \vee \pi_y(D, X)$
$\pi_y(\forall R.C, X){=}\forall y : R(X, y) \rightarrow \pi_x(C, y)$	$\pi_y(\exists R.C, X){=}\exists y : R(X, y) \wedge \pi_x(C, y)$

$$\pi_y(\{a_1 \ldots, a_n\}, X){=}X \approx a_1 \vee \ldots \vee X \approx a_n$$
$$\pi_y(\leq n\,R.C, X){=}\forall y_1, \ldots, y_{n+1} : \bigwedge R(X, y_i) \wedge \bigwedge \pi_x(C, y_i) \rightarrow \bigvee y_i \approx y_j$$
$$\pi_y(\geq n\,R.C, X){=}\exists y_1, \ldots, y_n : \bigwedge R(X, y_i) \wedge \bigwedge \pi_x(C, y_i) \wedge \bigwedge y_i \not\approx y_j$$
$$\pi_y(\forall T_1, \ldots, T_m.d, X){=}\forall y_1^{\mathsf{c}}, \ldots, y_m^{\mathsf{c}} : \bigwedge T_i(X, y_i^{\mathsf{c}}) \rightarrow d(y_1^{\mathsf{c}}, \ldots, y_m^{\mathsf{c}})$$
$$\pi_y(\exists T_1, \ldots, T_m.d, X){=}\exists y_1^{\mathsf{c}}, \ldots, y_m^{\mathsf{c}} : \bigwedge T_i(X, y_i^{\mathsf{c}}) \wedge d(y_1^{\mathsf{c}}, \ldots, y_m^{\mathsf{c}})$$
$$\pi_y(\leq n\,T, X){=}\forall y_1^{\mathsf{c}}, \ldots, y_{n+1}^{\mathsf{c}} : \bigwedge T(X, y_i^{\mathsf{c}}) \rightarrow \bigvee y_i^{\mathsf{c}} \approx y_j^{\mathsf{c}}$$
$$\pi_y(\geq n\,T, X){=}\exists y_1^{\mathsf{c}}, \ldots, y_n^{\mathsf{c}} : \bigwedge T(X, y_i^{\mathsf{c}}) \wedge \bigwedge y_i^{\mathsf{c}} \not\approx y_j^{\mathsf{c}}$$

Mapping Axioms to FOL	
$\pi(C(a)){=}\pi_y(C, a)$	$\pi(R(a, b)){=}R(a, b)$
$\pi(a \approx b)){=}a \approx b$	$\pi(a \not\approx b)){=}a \not\approx b$
$\pi(C \sqsubseteq D){=}\forall x : \pi_y(C, x) \rightarrow \pi_y(D, x)$	
$\pi(R \sqsubseteq S){=}\forall x, y : R(x, y) \rightarrow S(x, y)$	
$\pi(\mathsf{Trans}(R)){=}\forall x, y, z : R(x, y) \wedge R(y, z) \rightarrow R(x, z)$	

Mapping KB to FOL
$\pi(KB){=}\bigwedge_{R \in N_R} \forall x, y : R(x, y) \leftrightarrow R^-(y, x) \wedge \bigwedge_{\alpha \in KB_\mathcal{R} \cup KB_\mathcal{T} \cup KB_\mathcal{A}} \pi(\alpha)$

where X is a meta variable and is substituted by the actual variable
and π_x is defined as π_y by substituting x and x_i for all y and y_i, respectively.

Since the algorithms we present in Section 5 are based on resolution, instead of using a direct model-theoretic semantics to $\mathcal{SHOIN}(\mathbf{D})$ [13], we present an equivalent semantics by translation into multi-sorted first-order logic. To separate the interpretations of the abstract and the concrete domain, we introduce the sorts a and c, and use the notation x^{c} and f^{c} to denote that x and f are of sort c. We translate each atomic concept into a unary predicate of sort a, each n-ary concrete domain predicate into a predicate with arguments of sort c, and each abstract (concrete) role into a binary predicate of sort $\mathsf{a} \times \mathsf{a}$ ($\mathsf{a} \times \mathsf{c}$). The translation operator π is presented in Table 1.

For rules, we use the standard definitions. Let N_P be a set of predicate symbols such that $N_C \cup N_{R_a} \cup N_{R_c} \subseteq N_P$. A *term* is either a constant (denoted by a, b, c) or a variable (denoted by x, y, z). An *atom* has the form $P(s_1, \ldots, s_n)$, where P is a predicate symbol and s_i are terms. A *rule* has the form

$$H \leftarrow B_1, \ldots, B_n$$

where H and B_i are atoms; H is called the *rule head*, and the set of all B_i is called the *rule body*. A *program* P is a finite set of rules. For the semantics, we define a rule $H \leftarrow B_1, \ldots, B_n$ to be equivalent to the clause $H \vee \neg B_1 \vee \ldots \vee \neg B_n$. This yields a monotonic formalism compatible with the one from [11].

Table 2. Example Knowledge Base

$Person(Peter)$	Peter is a person.
$Person \sqsubseteq \exists father.Person$	Each person has a father who is a person.
$\exists father.(\exists father.Person) \sqsubseteq Grandchild$	Things having a father of a father who is a person are grandchildren.

3   Reasons for the Undecidability of OWL-DL with Rules

In [11], the following problem was shown to be undecidable: given an OWL-DL knowledge base KB and a program P, is there a common model of $\pi(KB)$ and P, i.e. is KB consistent with P? As a consequence, subsumption and query answering w.r.t. knowledge bases and programs is also undecidable. Investigating this proof and the ones in [16] more closely, we note that the undecidability is caused by the interaction between some very basic features of description logics and rules. In this section, we try to give an intuitive explanation of this result and its consequences.

Consider the simple knowledge base KB from Table 2. It is not too difficult to see that this knowledge base implies the existence of an infinite chain of fathers: since *Peter* must have a father, there is some x_1 who is a *Person*. In turn, x_1 must have some father x_2, which must be a *Person*, and so on. An infinite model with such a chain is shown in Figure 1, upper part a). Observe that *Peter* is a grandchild, since he has a father of a father.

Let us now check whether $KB \models Grandchild(Jane)$; this is the case if and only if $KB \cup \{\neg Grandchild(Jane)\}$ is unsatisfiable, i.e. if it does not have a model. We can check this by trying to build such a model; if we fail, then we conclude that $KB \cup \{\neg Grandchild(Jane)\}$ is unsatisfiable. However, we have a problem: starting from *Peter*, a naïve approach to building a model will expand the chain of Peter's fathers indefinitely, and will therefore not terminate.

This very simple example intuitively shows that we have to be careful if we want to ensure termination of a satisfiability checking algorithm. For many DLs, termination can be ensured without losing correctness because we can restrict our attention to certain "nice" models. For numerous DLs, we can restrict our attention to *tree models*, i.e. to models where the underlying relational structure forms a tree [22]. This is so because every satisfiable knowledge base has such

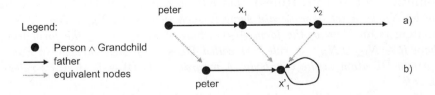

Fig. 1. Two Similar Models

a tree model (to be precise, for some DLs we consider tree-like abstractions of non-tree-like models). Even if such a tree model is infinite, we can *wind* this infinite tree model into a finite one. In our example, since *KB* does not require each father in the chain to be distinct, the model in Figure 1, lower part b) is the result of this "winding" of a tree into a "nice" model. Due to their regular structure, these "windings" of tree models can be easily constructed in an automated way. To understand why every satisfiable $\mathcal{SHIQ}(\mathbf{D})$ knowledge base has a tree model [13], consider the mapping π in Table 1 more closely (we abstract some technicalities caused by the transitive roles): in all formulae obtained by transforming the result of π into prenex normal form, variables are connected by roles only in a tree-like manner, as shown in the following example:

$$\exists S.(\exists R.C \sqcap \exists R.D) \sqsubseteq Q \qquad \Rightarrow$$
$$\forall x : \{[\exists y : S(x,y) \wedge (\exists x : R(y,x) \wedge C(x)) \wedge (\exists x : R(y,x) \wedge D(x))] \rightarrow Q(x)\} \ \Rightarrow$$
$$\forall x, x_1, x_2, x_3 : \{S(x,x_1) \wedge R(x_1,x_2) \wedge C(x_2) \wedge R(x_1,x_3) \wedge D(x_3) \rightarrow Q(x)\}$$

Let us contrast these observations with the kind of reasoning required for function-free Horn rules. In such rules, all variables are universally quantified, i.e. there are no existentially quantified variables in rule consequents. Hence, we never have to infer the existence of "new" objects. Thus, reasoning algorithms must consider only individuals explicitly introduced in the knowledge base and will never run into the termination problems outlined above. Hence, the rules, such as the one defining $hasAunt(x,y)$ from the introduction, are allowed to enforce arbitrary but finite, non-tree relational models, and not only "nice" models.

Now let us see what happens if we extend, eg. $\mathcal{SHIQ}$, with function-free Horn rules. Then, we combine a logic whose decidability is due to the fact that we can restrict our attention to "nice" models (but with individuals whose existence may be implied by a knowledge base) with the one whose decidability is due to the fact that we can restrict our attention to "known" individuals (but with arbitrary relations between them). Unsurprisingly, this and similar combinations are undecidable [16,11].

4   DL-Safe Rules

As a reaction to the observations in Section 3, in this section we define the formalism of *DL-safe* rules, discuss its benefits and drawbacks, and prove that query answering in $\mathcal{SHOIN}$ with DL-safe rules is decidable.

Definition 1 (DL-safe Rules). *Let KB be a $\mathcal{SHOIN}(\mathbf{D})$ knowledge base, and let N_P be a set of predicate symbols such that $N_C \cup N_{R_a} \cup N_{R_c} \subseteq N_P$. A DL-atom is an atom of the form $A(s)$, where $A \in N_C$, or of the form $R(s,t)$, where $R \in N_{R_a} \cup N_{R_c}$. A rule r is called DL-safe if each variable in r occurs in a non-DL-atom in the rule body. A program P is DL-safe if all its rules are DL-safe.*

The semantics of the combined knowledge base (KB, P) *is given by translation into first-order logic as $\pi(KB) \cup P$. The main inference in (KB, P) is* query answering, *i.e. deciding whether $\pi(KB) \cup P \models \alpha$ for a ground atom α.*

Some remarks are in order. Firstly, DL-safety is similar to the safety in datalog. In a safe rule, each variable occurs in a positive atom in the body, and may therefore be bound only to constants explicitly present in the database. Similarly, DL-safety makes sure that each variable is bound only to individuals explicitly introduced in the ABox. For example, if *Person*, *livesAt*, and *worksAt* are concepts and roles from *KB*, the following rule is not DL-safe:

$$Homeworker(x) \leftarrow Person(x), livesAt(x,y), worksAt(x,y)$$

The reason for this is that both variables x and y occur in DL-atoms, but do not occur in a body atom with a predicate outside of *KB*. This rule can be made DL-safe by adding special non-DL-literals $\mathcal{O}(x)$ and $\mathcal{O}(y)$ to the rule body, and by adding a fact $\mathcal{O}(a)$ for each individual a. In Subsection 4.1 we discuss the consequences that this transformation has on the semantics.

Secondly, DL-safety only allows atomic concepts to occur in a rule. This is not really a restriction: for a complex concept C, one may introduce an atomic concept A_C, add the axiom $C \sqsubseteq A_C$ to the TBox, and use A_C in the rule.

4.1   Expressivity of DL-Safe Rules

In our approach, to achieve decidability, we do not restrict the component languages. Rather, we combine full $\mathcal{SHOIN}(\mathbf{D})$ with function-free Horn rules, and thus extend both formalisms. DL-safety only restricts the interchange of consequences between the component languages to those consequences involving individuals explicitly introduced in the ABox.

To illustrate the expressive power of DL-safe rules, we extend the example from Table 2 with the TBox axioms and rules from Table 3. We use a rule to define the only non-DL-predicate *BadChild* as a grandchild which hates some of its siblings (or itself). Notice that this rule involves relations forming a triangle between two siblings and a parent and thus cannot be expressed in a description logic such as $\mathcal{SHOIN}(\mathbf{D})$. Moreover, it is not DL-safe because each variable in the rule does not occur in a non-DL-atom in the rule body.

Now consider the first group of ABox facts. Since *Cain* is a *Person*, as in Section 3 one may infer that *Cain* is a *Grandchild*. Since *Cain* and *Abel* are children of *Adam*, and *Cain* hates *Abel*, *Cain* is a *BadChild*.

Similarly, *Romulus* has a father who is a father of *Remus*, and *Romulus* hates *Remus*, so *Romulus* is a *BadChild* as well. We are able to derive this without knowing exactly who the father of *Romulus* is[2].

Consider now the DL-safe rule defining *BadChild'* (assuming that the ABox contains $\mathcal{O}(a)$ for each individual a): since the father of *Cain* and *Abel* is known by name (i.e. *Adam* is in the ABox), the literal $\mathcal{O}(y)$ from the rule for *BadChild'* can be matched to $\mathcal{O}(Adam)$, and we may conclude that *Cain* is a *BadChild'*. In contrast, the father of *Romulus* and *Remus* is not known in the ABox. Hence,

---

[2] Historically, the father of Romulus and Remus is Mars, but for illustration purposes we assume that the modeler does not know that.

Table 3. Example with DL-safe Rules

$father \sqsubseteq parent$	Fatherhood is a kind of parenthood.
$BadChild(x) \leftarrow Grandchild(x),$ $\quad parent(x,y), parent(z,y), hates(x,z)$	A bad child is a grandchild who hates one of his siblings.
$BadChild'(x) \leftarrow Grandchild(x),$ $\quad parent(x,y), parent(z,y), hates(x,z),$ $\quad \mathcal{O}(x), \mathcal{O}(y), \mathcal{O}(z)$	DL-safe version of a bad child.
$Person(Cain)$	Cain is a person.
$father(Cain, Adam)$	Cain's father is Adam.
$father(Abel, Adam)$	Abel's father is Adam.
$hates(Cain, Abel)$	Cain hates Abel.
$Person(Romulus)$	Romulus is a person.
$\exists father.\exists father^{-}.\{Remus\}(Romulus)$	Romulus' father is a father of Remus.
$hates(Romulus, Remus)$	Romulus hates Remus.
$Child(x) \leftarrow GoodChild(x), \mathcal{O}(x)$	Good children are children.
$Child(x) \leftarrow BadChild'(x), \mathcal{O}(x)$	Bad children are children.
$(GoodChild \sqcup BadChild')(Oedipus)$	Oedipus is a good or a bad child.
$\mathcal{O}(\alpha)$ for each explicitly named individual α	Enumeration of all ABox individuals.

the literal $\mathcal{O}(y)$ from the DL-safe rule cannot be matched to the father's name, so the rule does not derive that *Romulus* is a *BadChild'*.

This may seem confusing. However, DL-safe rules do have a "natural" reading: just append the phrase "where the identity of all objects is known" to the meaning of the rule. For example, the rule defining *BadChild'* can be read as "A *BadChild'* is a *known* grandchild for which we *know* a parent, and who hates one of his *known* siblings".

Combining description logics with DL-safe rules increases the expressivity of both languages. Namely, a $\mathcal{SHOIN}(\mathbf{D})$ knowledge base cannot imply that *Cain* is a *BadChild'* because the "triangle" rule cannot be expressed using $\mathcal{SHOIN}(\mathbf{D})$ constructs. Similarly, a set of function-free Horn rules cannot imply this either: we know that Cain has a grandfather because Cain is a person, but we do not know who he is. Hence, we need the existential quantifier to *infer* the existence of ancestors, and then to infer that *Cain* is a *Grandchild*.

Finally, we would like to point out that it is incorrect to compute all consequences of the description logic component first, and then to apply the rules to the consequences. Consider the *KB* part about *Oedipus*: he is a *GoodChild* or a *BadChild'*, but we do not know exactly which. Either way, one of the rules derives that *Oedipus* is a *Child*, so $(KB, P) \models Child(Oedipus)$. This would not be derived by applying the rules to the consequences of *KB*, since $KB \not\models GoodChild(Oedipus)$ and $KB \not\models BadChild'(Oedipus)$.

4.2 Decidability of Query Answering

We now sketch a proof for the decidability of query answering for $\mathcal{SHOIN}$ extended with DL-safe rules, which is by a non-deterministic reduction of the query answering problem to the satisfiability problem for $\mathcal{SHOIN}$ without rules.

Theorem 1. *For a $\mathcal{SHOIN}$ knowledge base KB and a DL-safe program P, query answering in (KB, P) is decidable.*

Proof. Clearly $(KB, P) \models \alpha$ iff $\pi(KB) \cup P'$ is unsatisfiable, where $P' = P \cup \{\neg\alpha\}$. Let P^g be the set of ground instances of P', i.e. P^g contains all possible ground instantiations of rules in P' with individuals from KB and P.

We now show that $\pi(KB) \cup P'$ is satisfiable iff $\pi(KB) \cup P^g$ is satisfiable. The ($\Rightarrow$) direction is trivial. For the ($\Leftarrow$) direction, let I be a model of $\pi(KB) \cup P^g$. Since $\pi(KB) \cup P^g$ does not contain non-DL-atoms with variables, we may safely assume that the interpretation of each non-DL-predicate contains only tuples of the form $(\alpha_1, \ldots, \alpha_n)$, such that, for each α_i, there is a constant a_i with $a_i^I = \alpha_i$. Let r be a rule from P. Since r is DL-safe, each variable in r occurs in a body non-DL-atom. Hence, for each valuation replacing a variable in r with an individual α, for which there is no such constant a with $a^I = \alpha$, there will be a body atom of r which is false in I, making r true in I. Thus, I is a model of $\pi(KB) \cup P'$.

Satisfiability of $\pi(KB) \cup P^g$ can be decided by case analysis as follows: each model of P^g satisfies at least one literal per rule. Hence, we don't-know non-deterministically choose one literal per clause in P^g and, for L^c the resulting set of literals, we test the satisfiability of $\pi(KB) \cup L^c$. Clearly, $\pi(KB) \cup P^g$ is satisfiable iff there exists a "choice" of L^c such that $\pi(KB) \cup L^c$ is satisfiable.

Next, let $L_{DL}^c \subseteq L^c$ be the set of (ground) literals in L^c involving DL predicates. Clearly, $\pi(KB) \cup L^c$ is unsatisfiable iff either L^c contains a complementary pair of ground literals or $\pi(KB) \cup L_{DL}^c$ is unsatisfiable. The first case can be checked easily, and the second case can be reduced to standard $\mathcal{SHOIN}$ reasoning as follows: L_{DL}^c can be viewed as an ABox, apart from literals of the form $\neg R(a, b)$. However, each such literal can be transformed into an equivalent $\mathcal{SHOIN}$ ABox assertion $(\forall R.\neg\{b\})(a)$. Thus we have reduced query answering to deciding satisfiability of a $\mathcal{SHOIN}$ knowledge base. This problem is decidable because (*i*) transitivity axioms can be eliminated from $\mathcal{SHOIN}$ knowledge bases in the same way as this is done for $\mathcal{SHIQ}$ in [14] and (*ii*) the resulting logic is a syntactic variant of the two variable fragment of first-order logic with counting quantifiers, which is known to be decidable [7]. □

We strongly believe that Theorem 1 also holds for $\mathcal{SHOIN}(\mathbf{D})$: (*i*) the decidability proof of $\mathcal{SHOIN}$ should be easily adaptable to $\mathcal{SHOIN}(\mathbf{D})$, and (*ii*) the same non-deterministic reduction of ground DL-safe rules to sets of ground literals as for $\mathcal{SHOIN}$ is applicable to $\mathcal{SHOIN}(\mathbf{D})$. To work out the details of this proof is part of our future work.

5   Query Answering with DL-Safe Rules

In the proof of the Theorem 1, we have presented a decision procedure for query answering in the full combination from Section 4. However, this procedure is likely to be hopelessly inefficient in practice, mainly due to the huge amount of don't-known non-determinism. Hence, in this section, we describe a practical reasoning algorithm for the following fragment: (i) the description logic is $\mathcal{SHIQ}(\mathbf{D})$, and (ii) in rules, DL-atoms are restricted to concepts and simple roles. Our algorithm is based on reducing the description logic knowledge base to a positive disjunctive datalog program which entails the same set of ground facts as the original knowledge base. DL-safe rules (with the above restriction to concepts and simple roles) can simply be appended to such a program. For unary coding of numbers and assuming a bound on the arity of predicates in rules, our algorithm runs in deterministic exponential time, which makes it optimal since $\mathcal{SHIQ}$ is ExpTime-complete [21].

The full presentation of the algorithm and a proof of its correctness are technically involved and lengthy. Here, we just provide an overview of the procedure, without going into details. For a complete presentation of the procedure and for the proofs of its correctness, we direct the interested reader to [14,15].

Our algorithm does not support all of $\mathcal{SHOIN}(\mathbf{D})$ since it does not support nominals: to the best of our knowledge, no decision procedure has yet been implemented for $\mathcal{SHOIN}(\mathbf{D})$. The development of such a decision procedure is part of our ongoing work. Namely, the combination of nominals, inverse roles, and number restriction is known to be difficult to handle, which is confirmed by the increase in complexity from ExpTime to NExpTime [21].

5.1   Reducing $\mathcal{SHIQ}(\mathbf{D})$ to Disjunctive Datalog

Let KB be a $\mathcal{SHIQ}(\mathbf{D})$ knowledge base. The reduction of KB to a disjunctive datalog program $\mathrm{DD}(KB)$ can be computed by an algorithm schematically presented in Figure 2. We next explain each step of the algorithm.

Elimination of Transitivity Axioms. Our core algorithms cannot handle transitivity axioms, basically because in their first-order logic formulation they involve three variables. However, we can eliminate transitivity axioms by encoding KB into an equisatisfiable knowledge base $\Omega(KB)$. Roughly speaking, for each transitive role S, each role $S \sqsubseteq^* R$, and each concept $\forall R.C$ occurring in KB, it is sufficient to add an axiom $\forall R.C \sqsubseteq \forall S.(\forall S.C)$. Intuitively, this axiom propagates all relevant concept constraints through transitive roles. Whereas KB and $\Omega(KB)$ entail the same set of ground facts concerning simple roles, they do not entail the same set of ground facts concerning complex roles. This is the reason for the restriction (ii) which allows only simple roles to occur in DL-safe rules.

Translation into Clauses. The next step is to translate $\Omega(KB)$ into clausal first-order logic. We first use π as defined in Table 1 and then transform the result

Fig. 2. Algorithm for Reducing $\mathcal{SHIQ}(\mathbf{D})$ to Datalog Programs

$\pi(\Omega(KB))$ into clausal form using *structural transformation* to avoid exponential blow-up [19]. We call the result $\Xi(KB)$.

Saturation by Basic Superposition. We next saturate the RBox and TBox clauses of $\Xi(KB)$ by basic superposition [4] — a clausal calculus optimized for theorem proving with equality. In this key step of the reduction, we compute all non-ground consequences of KB. We can prove that saturation terminates because application of each rule of basic superposition produces a clause with at most one variable and with functional terms of depth at most two. This yields an exponential bound on the number of clauses we can compute, and thus an exponential time complexity bound for our algorithm so far.

Elimination of Function Symbols. Saturation of RBox and TBox of $\Xi(KB)$ computes all non-ground consequences of KB. If we add ABox assertions to this saturated clause set, all "further" inferences by basic superposition will produce only ground clauses. Moreover, the resulting ground clauses contain only ground functional terms of depth one. Hence, it is possible to simulate each functional term $f(a)$ with a new constant a_f. For each function symbol f, we introduce a binary predicate S_f, and for each individual a, we add an assertion $S_f(a, a_f)$. Finally, if a clause contains the term $f(x)$, we replace it with a new variable x_f and add the literal $\neg S_f(x, x_f)$, as in the following example:

$$\neg C(x) \lor D(f(x)) \Rightarrow \neg S_f(x, x_f) \lor \neg C(x) \lor D(x_f)$$

We denote the resulting function-free set of clauses with $\mathsf{FF}(KB)$. In [14], we show that each inference step of basic superposition in $\Xi(KB)$ can be simulated by an inference step in $\mathsf{FF}(KB)$, and vice versa. Hence, KB and $\mathsf{FF}(KB)$ are equisatisfiable.

Conversion to Disjunctive Datalog. Since $\mathsf{FF}(KB)$ does not contain functional terms and all its clauses are safe, we can rewrite each clause into a positive disjunctive rule. We use $\mathsf{DD}(KB)$ for the result of this rewriting.

The following theorem summarizes the properties of our algorithm (we use $\models_c$ for cautions entailment in disjunctive datalog, which coincides on ground facts with first-order entailment for positive datalog programs [6]):

Theorem 2 ([14]). *Let KB be an $\mathcal{SHIQ}(\mathbf{D})$ knowledge base, defined over an admissible concrete domain $\mathbf{D}$, such that satisfiability of finite conjunctions over $\Phi_{\mathbf{D}}$ can be decided in deterministic exponential time. Then the following claims hold:*

1. *KB is unsatisfiable if and only if $\mathsf{DD}(KB)$ is unsatisfiable.*
2. *$KB \models \alpha$ if and only if $\mathsf{DD}(KB) \models_c \alpha$, for α of the form $A(a)$ or $S(a, b)$, A an atomic concept, and S a simple role.*
3. *$KB \models C(a)$ if and only if $\mathsf{DD}(KB \cup \{C \sqsubseteq Q\}) \models_c Q(a)$, for C a non-atomic concept, and Q a new atomic concept.*
4. *Let $|KB|$ be the length of KB with numbers in number restrictions coded in unary. The number of rules in $\mathsf{DD}(KB)$ is at most exponential in $|KB|$, the number of literals in each rule is at most polynomial in $|KB|$, and $\mathsf{DD}(KB)$ can be computed in time exponential in $|KB|$.*

Adding DL-safe Rules. The disjunctive program $DD(KB)$ can be combined with DL-safe rules by simply appending the rules to the program. The following theorem shows that (KB, P) and $DD(KB) \cup P$ entail the same sets of ground facts:

Theorem 3 ([14]). *Let* KB *be a* $\mathcal{SHIQ}(\mathbf{D})$ *knowledge base and* P *a DL-safe disjunctive datalog program. Then* $(KB, P) \models \alpha$ *if and only if* $DD(KB) \cup P \models_c \alpha$, *where* α *is a DL-atom* $A(a)$ *or* $S(a, b)$ *for* S *a simple role, or* α *is a ground non-DL-atom.*

5.2   Evaluating Queries in Datalog Program

Answering queries in disjunctive datalog programs is computationally more expensive than in non-disjunctive programs [6]. Furthermore, if disjunction is not used in a knowledge base, our algorithm should not introduce a performance penalty. To address that, we have devised an algorithm for evaluating queries in disjunctive programs, which we outline next. For details, please see [14].

Let P be a positive datalog program and let Q be a query predicate not occurring in the body of a rule of P. This is not a limitation since one can always introduce a new predicate A_Q and add the rule $A_Q(\mathbf{x}) \leftarrow Q(\mathbf{x})$. To compute all answers of $\mathbf{a}$ to Q w.r.t. P, i.e. all $\mathbf{a}$ such that $P \models_c Q(\mathbf{a})$, we saturate P by hyperresolution and perform paramodulation inferences between ground clauses to deal with equality. It is well-known that this calculus remains complete if ground literals are totally ordered under an arbitrary ordering $\succ$, and inferences are performed on maximal literals only [3]. This ordering has the useful property that, in each ground disjunction, exactly one literal is maximal. Hence, instead of performing an inference on each literal of a ground fact, it is sufficient to do so on the maximal literal only, which dramatically improves performance.

In [14] we have shown that, if all literals involving the predicate Q are minimal w.r.t. $\succ$, then all ground consequences of P will be derived as *unit* ground clauses in the saturation. To compute all answers to a query, it is sufficient to saturate P only once using an appropriate ordering $\succ$. Thus, our algorithm computes all consequences by a single saturation.

An example of a hyperresolution inference is presented in Figure 3. The maximal literals in the premises are underlined, and only these literals can participate in an inference. When performing hyperresolution, premises are matched to a disjunctive rule exactly as in the non-disjunctive case, the variables in the rule

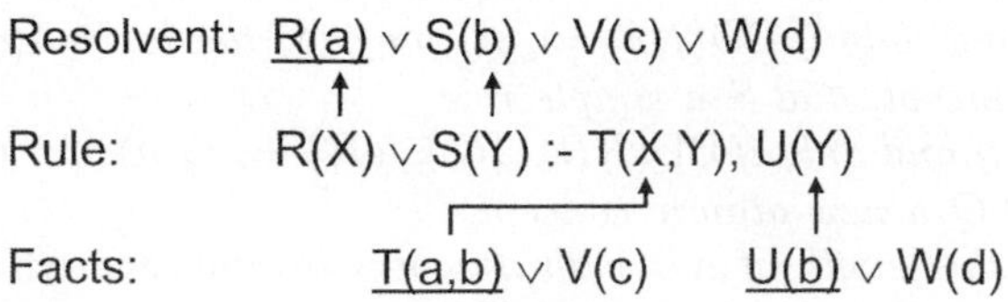

Resolvent: $\underline{R(a)} \vee S(b) \vee V(c) \vee W(d)$

Rule: $R(X) \vee S(Y) :\text{-} T(X,Y), U(Y)$

Facts: $\underline{T(a,b)} \vee V(c) \quad\quad \underline{U(b)} \vee W(d)$

Fig. 3. Hyperresolution Example

head are instantiated, and the remaining literals from the rule body are transferred to the rule head. Observe that, if premises and the rule are not disjunctive, then hyperresolution becomes exactly the least fixpoint operator used to evaluate non-disjunctive datalog programs. The consequences of the least fixpoint operator can be computed in polynomial time, so we get tractable behavior. In this way our algorithm supports the principle of "graceful degradation": the user pays a performance penalty only for features actually used.

6   Related Work

$\mathcal{AL}$-log [5] is a logic which combines a TBox and ABox expressed in the basic description logic $\mathcal{ALC}$ with datalog rules, which may be constrained with unary atoms having $\mathcal{ALC}$ concepts as predicates in the body. Query answering in $\mathcal{AL}$-log is decided by a variant of constrained resolution, combined with a tableaux algorithm for $\mathcal{ALC}$. The combined algorithm is shown to run in single non-deterministic exponential time. The fact that atoms with concept predicates can occur only as constraints in the body makes rules applicable only to explicitly named objects. Our restriction to DL-safe rules has the same effect. However, our approach is more general in the following ways: (i) it supports a more expressive description logic, (ii) it allows using both concepts and roles in DL-atoms and (iii) DL-atoms can be used in rule heads as well. Furthermore, (iv) we present a query answering algorithm as an extension of deductive database techniques which runs in deterministic exponential time. A comprehensive study of the effects of combining datalog rules with description logics is presented in [16]. The logic considered is $\mathcal{ALCNR}$, which, although less expressive than $\mathcal{SHOIN}(\mathbf{D})$ or $\mathcal{SHIQ}(\mathbf{D})$, contains constructors that are characteristic of most DL languages. The results of the study can be summarized as follows: (i) answering conjunctive queries over $\mathcal{ALCNR}$ TBoxes is decidable, (ii) query answering in a logic obtained by extending $\mathcal{ALCNR}$ with non-recursive datalog rules, where both concepts and roles can occur in rule bodies, is also decidable, as it can be reduced to computing a union of conjunctive query answers, (iii) if rules are recursive, query answering becomes undecidable, (iv) decidability can be regained by disallowing certain combinations of constructors in the logic, and (v) decidability can be regained by requiring rules to be *role-safe*, where at least one variable from each role literal must occur in some non-DL-atom. As in $\mathcal{AL}$-log, query answering is decided using constrained resolution and a modified version of the tableaux calculus. Besides the fact that we treat a more expressive logic, in our approach all variables in a rule must occur in at least one non-DL-atom, but concepts and roles are allowed to occur in rule heads. Hence, when compared to the variant (v), our approach is slightly less general in some, and slightly more general in other aspects.

   The OWL Rule Language (ORL) [11] combines OWL-DL with rules in which concept and role predicates are allowed to occur in the head and in the body, without any restrictions. As mentioned before, this combination is undecidable but, as pointed out by the authors, (incomplete) reasoning in such a logic can be performed using general first-order theorem provers. Our approach trades some expressivity for decidability. Furthermore, we provide an optimal query answering algorithm covering a significant portion of OWL-DL.

Finally, [8] describes a natural, decidable intersection of description logic and logic programming. This provides a useful insight into the relationship between these two formalisms, but yields a combination which is less expressive than our approach, since it does not support existential quantifiers, negation, or disjunction in the axiom consequent.

7   Summary and Outlook

We have presented an approach for extending OWL-DL with DL-safe rules. Instead of reducing the component formalisms, we reduce the interface between them. As a consequence, rules apply only to individuals explicitly introduced in the ABox. We have discussed the effects of such a definition on a non-trivial example, which also shows that our approach increases the expressivity of its two components.

Besides a decidability result for $\mathcal{SHOIN}$ with DL-safe rules, we have presented an algorithm for answering queries over $\mathcal{SHIQ}(\mathbf{D})$ extended with DL-safe rules which we believe to be useful in practice. This algorithm transforms a $\mathcal{SHIQ}(\mathbf{D})$ knowledge base into a disjunctive datalog program. To attenuate the increased computational complexity introduced by using disjunctive datalog, we developed a query answering algorithm which supports the principle of "graceful degradation": the user only pays a performance penalty for the features actually used in a knowledge base.

In our future work, we shall try to extend the reduction algorithm to support all of OWL-DL. Furthermore, we are currently implementing the algorithms presented here in KAON2, a new hybrid reasoner, for which we shall conduct a thorough performance evaluation.

Acknowledgements. We thank Stefan Decker for his very valuable comments. This work was partially funded by the EU IST project DIP 507483.

References

1. F. Baader, D. Calvanese, D. McGuinness, D. Nardi, and P. Patel-Schneider, editors. *The Description Logic Handbook*. Cambridge University Press, January 2003.
2. F. Baader and P. Hanschke. A Scheme for Integrating Concrete Domains into Concept Languages. In *Proc. of the 12th Int'l Joint Conf. on Artificial Intelligence (IJCAI-91)*, pages 452–457, Sydney, Australia, 1991.
3. L. Bachmair and H. Ganzinger. Resolution Theorem Proving. In A. Robinson and A. Voronkov, editors, *Handbook of Automated Reasoning*, volume I, chapter 2, pages 19–99. Elsevier Science, 2001.
4. L. Bachmair, H. Ganzinger, C. Lynch, and W. Snyder. Basic Paramodulation. *Information and Computation*, 121(2):172–192, 1995.

5. F. M. Donini, M. Lenzerini, D. Nardi, and A. Schaerf. AL-log: Integrating Datalog and Description Logics. *J. of Intelligent Information Systems*, 10(3):227–252, 1998.

6. T. Eiter, G. Gottlob, and H. Mannila. Disjunctive Datalog. *ACM Transactions on Database Systems*, 22(3):364–418, 1997.

7. E. Grädel, M. Otto, and E. Rosen. Two-Variable Logic with Counting is Decidable. In *Proc. of 12th IEEE Symposium on Logic in Computer Science LICS '97*, Warsaw, Poland, 1997.

8. B. N. Grosof, I. Horrocks, R. Volz, and S. Decker. Description Logic Programs: Combining Logic Programs with Description Logic. In *Proc. of the Twelfth Int'l World Wide Web Conf. (WWW 2003)*, pages 48–57. ACM, 2003.

9. V. Haarslev and R. Möller. RACER System Description. In *1st Int'l Joint Conf. on Automated Reasoning (IJCAR-01)*, pages 701–706. Springer-Verlag, 2001.

10. I. Horrocks. Using an Expressive Description Logic: FaCT or Fiction? In *Proc. 6th Int'l. Conf. on Principles of Knowledge Representation and Reasoning (KR'98)*, pages 636–647. Morgan Kaufmann Publishers, 1998.

11. I. Horrocks and P. F. Patel-Schneider. A Proposal for an OWL Rules Language. In *Proc. of the Thirteenth Int'l World Wide Web Conf.(WWW 2004)*. ACM, 2004.

12. I. Horrocks and U. Sattler. Ontology Reasoning in the $\mathcal{SHOQ}(D)$ Description Logic. In B. Nebel, editor, *Proc. of the 17th Int'l Joint Conf. on Artificial Intelligence (IJCAI 2001)*, pages 199–204. Morgan Kaufmann, 2001.

13. I. Horrocks, U. Sattler, and S. Tobies. Practical Reasoning for Very Expressive Description Logics. *Logic Journal of the IGPL*, 8(3):239–263, 2000.

14. U. Hustadt, B. Motik, and U. Sattler. Reasoning for Description Logics around $\mathcal{SHIQ}$ in a Resolution Framework. Technical Report 3-8-04/04, FZI, Karlsruhe, Germany, April 2004. http://www.fzi.de/wim/publikationen.php?id=1172.

15. U. Hustadt, B. Motik, and U. Sattler. Reducing $\mathcal{SHIQ}^-$ Description Logic to Disjunctive Datalog Programs. In *Proc. of the 9th Conference on Knowledge Representation and Reasoning (KR2004)*. AAAI Press, June 2004.

16. A. Y. Levy and M.-C. Rousset. Combining Horn rules and description logics in CARIN. *Artificial Intelligence*, 104(1-2):165–209, 1998.

17. C. Lutz. Description Logics with Concrete Domains—A Survey. In *Advances in Modal Logics*, volume 4. King's College Publications, 2003.

18. B. Motik, A. Maedche, and R. Volz. Optimizing Query Answering in Description Logics using Disjunctive Deductive Databases. In *10th Int'l Workshop on Knowledge Representation meets Databases (KRDB-2003)*, Hamburg, Germany, September 15-16 2003.

19. A. Nonnengart and C. Weidenbach. Computing Small Clause Normal Forms. In A. Robinson and A. Voronkov, editors, *Handbook of Automated Reasoning*, volume I, chapter 6, pages 335–367. Elsevier Science, 2001.

20. P. F. Patel-Schneider, P. Hayes, I. Horrocks, and F. van Harmelen. OWL Web Ontology Language; Semantics and Abstract Syntax, W3C Candidate Recommendation. http://www.w3.org/TR/owl-semantics/, November 2002.

21. S. Tobies. *Complexity Results and Practical Algorithms for Logics in Knowledge Representation*. PhD thesis, RWTH Aachen, Germany, 2001.

22. M. Vardi. Why is modal logic so robustly decidable? In N. Immerman and P. Kolaitis, editors, *Descriptive Complexity and Finite Models*, volume 31 of *DIMACS Series in Discrete Mathematics and Theoretical Computer Science*, pages 149–184. AMS, 1997.

A Semantic Web Resource Protocol: XPointer and HTTP

Kendall Clark[1], Bijan Parsia[2], Bryan Thompson[3], and Bradley Bebee[4]

[1] University of Maryland, MIND Lab
8400 Baltimore Ave,
College Park MD 20742, USA
kendall@monkeyfist.com

[2] University of Maryland, MIND Lab
8400 Baltimore Ave,
College Park MD 20742, USA
bparsia@isr.umd.edu

[3] SAIC, Advanced Systems and Concepts
3811 N. Fairfax Dr., Suite 850
Arlington VA 22203, USA
BRYAN.B.THOMPSON@saic.com

[4] SAIC, Advanced Systems and Concepts
3811 N. Fairfax Dr., Suite 850
Arlington VA 22203, USA
bebeeb@saic.com

Abstract. Semantic Web resources — that is, knowledge representation formalisms existing in a distributed hypermedia system — require different addressing and processing models and capacities than the typical kinds of World Wide Web resources. We describe an approach to building a Semantic Web resource protocol — a scalable, extensible logical addressing scheme and transport protocol — by using and extending existing specifications and technologies. We introduce XPointer and some infrequently used, but useful features of HTTP/1.1, in order to support addressing and server side processing of resource and subresource operations. We consider applications of the XPointer Framework for use in the Semantic Web, particularly for RDF and OWL resources and subresources. We describe two initial implementations: filtering of RSS resources by date and item range; RDF subresource selection using RDQL. Finally, we describe possible application to the problem of OWL imports.

1 RDF, RDFS, and OWL

RDF, RDFS, and OWL form the middle layers of the so-called Semantic Web layer cake. They are also its transitional layers; the parts beneath RDF-RDFS-OWL are part of the existing Web and are not distinctively *semantic*. These lower layers — URIs, Unicode, XML, and W3C XML Schema (WXS) — are not KR formalisms, though they do contribute, especially XML and WXS, to the syntax and the semantics of RDF, RDFS, and OWL. RDF, RDFS, and OWL

S.A. McIlraith et al. (Eds.): ISWC 2004, LNCS 3298, pp. 564–575, 2004.

are minimalist formalisms, defined primarily as logics independent of particular theories of the world or of the Web. At best they have a thin upper ontology for representing aspects of their own abstract syntax and semantics. For example, the hierarchy of builtin classes of OWL Full, which is the richest of the OWL variants in terms of expressiveness and predefined ontology, contains a universal class (`rdfs:Resource`), several classes of classes and of properties (`rdfs:Class`, `owl:Class`, `rdf:Property`, `rdf:AnnotationProperty`, etc.), along with a few individuals (`rdf:nil`).[1]

Further, certain kinds of inference are licensed in RDF, RDFS, and OWL. If, for example, an RDF graph contains a triple (`s p o`), then there is at least one other triple (`p rdf:type rdf:Property`) that is RDF-entailed by that graph. This is unusual from a first order logic point of view; it is not merely a syntactically sensitive inference. Rather, it derives a claim *about* that syntax, which highlights the strong reflective modeling capabilities deemed essential to the Semantic Web. But putting aside, first, the desirability of such reflective modeling capabilities or, second, the specific capabilities of OWL Full, there are two ways in which the thin upper ontology formed by RDFS and OWL Full, together with the associated inference mechanisms, fails to cover existing, critical aspects of the Web and the Semantic Web:

1. There are no classes or properties to represent RDF graphs or documents themselves. RDF graphs are a fundamental kind of Semantic Web resource.
2. There is no connection between the defined semantics of URIs and the assertions, especially type assertions, using them. For example, it is not unreasonable, and it has sometimes been proposed, that `mailto:`' URIs only denote things that are mailboxes or mail address endpoints.

Since there appears to be no consensus for specific sets of URI as to their proper associated type, standardization of such inferences would be premature. However, it is important to be able easily to coin sensible URIs for mailboxes, Web pages, people, and RDF graphs. Taking just the case of RDF graphs, it is simple enough to offer some sensible principles to resource publishers and URI owners.[2] For example, treat RDF graphs as normal Web accessible information resources. The simplest application of this principle is to publish RDF graphs as RDF/XML documents on the Web, allowing others to interact with those graphs using HTTP.[3] This deployment practice will suffice if two conditions are

---

[1] Of course, in OWL Full all classes and properties are `rdfs:Resource` and, thus, individuals in the domain as well.

[2] The canonical discussion of URI ownership is [10], especially section 2.2.1.1.

[3] Or, as [10] puts it,

A URI owner may, upon request, provide representations of the resource identified by the URI. For example, when a URI owner uses the HTTP protocol to provide those representations, the HTTP origin server...is the software agent acting on behalf of the URI owner to provide the authoritative representations for the resource identified by that URI. The owner is also responsible for accepting or rejecting requests to modify the resource identified by that URI...

met: first, that the graphs we want to manipulate directly are relatively small; and, second, that we can anticipate the subgraphs users will need and provide the appropriate document interface to them.

When RDF graphs or OWL ontologies are very large[4], retrieving the entire graph as a document to be processed locally by the client is often impractical, especially if the graph is dynamic or if the client is resource-constrained. Further, it is not at all clear that standard techniques for mapping resource representations to documents fits Semantic Web resource representations very well. While for many applications RDF data has an obvious document chunking — for example, individual Web resource metadata can be embedded or associated with the corresponding resource — it can be difficult to anticipate the range of kinds of queries a client may need to execute. And many common queries may cut across the obvious or common case RDF chunking. While it is natural to associate creator information with created resources, it is perfectly sensible to want to know all the creators for a site, all the resources created by the current page's creators, and so on. In such cases, having to aggregate the chunking RDF is worse than simply downloading a very large RDF/XML document.

These problems and constraints point to the need for a logical, extensible means of identifying and addressing Semantic Web resources, preferably in a way that is as consonant as possible with existing standards and deployed systems.

2   Web Addressing and Fragment Identifiers

According to [2], in order to authoritatively interpret a URI fragment identifier,[5] a user-agent must dereference the URI containing the fragment identifier, using the Internet Media Type (IMT) [7] of the retrieved representation to apply an authoritative interpretation function[6] to the fragment identifier.

When dereferencing URIs that return HTML representations, the user-agent is usually acting on behalf of a human person who is navigating web hypermedia resources. In this case the semantics of the fragment identifier are interpreted by a web browser such that the subresource identified by the fragment identifier

---

[4] For example, the National Cancer Institute's Cancer Ontology, an OWL version of the NCI Thesaurus, is made up of more than 500,000 RDF triples, 17,000 concepts, and is roughly 35 megabytes. Or consider the RDF/XML serialization of UniProt (Universal Protein Resource) KB which is about 134,000,000 triples and 8 gigabytes.

[5] A fragment identifier, according to [10],

allows indirect identification of a secondary resource by reference to a primary resource and additional identifying information. The secondary resource may be some portion or subset of the primary resource, some view on representations of the primary resource, or some other resource defined or described by those representations.

[6] See [10], section 3.3.1.

is made visible in the browser window. Fragment identifiers do not allow user-agents to manipulate subresources directly; they are, rather, processed by the user-agent only after the resource representation has been retrieved. In fact, HTTP does not even transmit the fragment identifier as part of the `Request-URI`. Origin servers never see the fragment identifier component of the URI.

HTTP does, however, provide an extensible mechanism for user-agents to interact with a range of the resource representation, using the `Range` header. The only range-unit that is explicitly described by the HTTP/1.1 RFC is "bytes". User-agents may address one or more byte ranges in the retrieved resource representation. The bytes range-unit is useful for some IMTs; for example, retrieving a byte-range of a URI that returns a binary image as its representation. The HTTP specification breaks transparency and encourages caches to combine byte ranges under certain validity conditions. The bytes range-unit is obviously much less useful for Semantic Web resources because it isn't appropriate for directly addressing and manipulating *logical* or *semantic* subresources.

3   XPointer and HTTP

The XPointer Framework [9] provides an extensible mechanism for addressing XML subresources. The XPointer Working Group defined a core set of XPointer addressing schemes — [4], [8], and [5] — in addition to the fundamental XPointer Framework. Since XPointer is an extensible scheme, we can define new XPointer schemes and adopt existing XPointer schemes for addressing subresources of specific XML vocabularies. For example, SVG [6] defines a scheme for interpreting fragment identifiers as logical views into a rendered SVG document.

Of the existing W3C-standardized XPointer schemes, the `element()` scheme is too weak and the `xpointer()` scheme is so complex that it is rarely implemented. But it is simple enough to declare and implement new schemes. Such schemes can be crafted specifically for the specific nature of particular resource types. Consider an XPointer addressing scheme, `xpath()`, that would facilitate addressing subresources using the widely adopted XPath Recommendation [3]. Or consider a scheme, `isbn()`, that would facilitate addressing metadata resources about books by ISBN identifier.

We want to shape our XPointer schemes such that they will serve dual use: not only will they provide a data access mechanism for subresources, but they will also make it possible for authorized user-agents to directly manipulate those subresources. A card catalog resource, for example, could be maintained by interchanging XML fragments that represent metadata about books in a library's collection.

3.1   Server-Side XPointer

How can we use the XPointer Framework and HTTP to address and manipulate resources and subresources *directly*? The key pieces include an XPointer scheme and three HTTP headers: `Accept-Range`, `Range`, and `Content-Type`.

First, the origin server uses the `Accept-Range:` xpointer header-key/value pair to signal its support for the XPointer Framework. Second, the client sends a subresource request via the `Range:` `[xpointer-scheme]` `=` `[pointer-parts]` header-key/value pair. Third, the server provides a partial content response using the `Content-Type:` `multipart/mixed` header-key/value pair.

Our main proposal is very simple: the user agent creates an HTTP `Range` request header using the fragment identifier, which makes the fragment identifier a visible part of the request sent to the origin server. That way XPointer schemes may be processed by the origin server, and so user agents do not have to retrieve an entire representation just in order to apply an XPointer scheme, the intention of which may very well be to work with only a subresource. In sum, the only new requirement imposed by our scheme on a user agent is that, when it prepares an HTTP request, it must create a `Range` header, the value of which is the fragment identifier.[7] xpointer in the `Range` header specifies the range-unit. The range-unit signals the server as to the appropriate interpretation of the range-specifier, which in this case is `element`.

Consider the following example. The user agent's request:

```
GET /resource HTTP/1.1
Host: example.org
Accept: text/xml
Range: xpointer=element(a12)
```

The origin server's response:

```
HTTP/1.1 206 Partial Content
Content-Type: multipart/mixed; boundary="simple boundary"

--simple boundary

Content-type: text/xml; charset=ISO-8859-1

<bar>Hello</bar>

--simple boundary--
```

When the server uses an XPointer processor to evaluate the XPointer expression — the `element(a12)` range-specification from the `Range` header — against the negotiated representation[8] of the current state of the resource, the result is a node set consisting of the single XML element whose ID type attribute has

---

[7] User agents must also be able to process the response by recognizing the HTTP status code 206 Partial Content and must be able to handle the `multipart/mixed` IMTs.

[8] Recall that the semantics of any particular fragment identifier are defined in terms of a particular IMT and are applied to the negotiated, retrieved representation of the resource. When a user agent is smart about the use of fragment identifiers, it can correctly choose the right fragment identifier for the desired content type, which

the value "a12". The response, then, contains a single XML fragment, which is the serialization of that XML element. However, since there could have been multiple matched XML subresources in the general case, the individual XML subresources are returned as the body parts of a multipart/mime response entity. The HTTP status code is a 2xx series, indicating success; but the 206 status code is used to indicate that partial content is being returned by the server in response to the Range header included by the client.

3.2   Addressing Multiple Subresources

Consider an XPointer scheme named xpath(). Since it's not an official XPointer scheme, it *must* be placed into an explicit namespace using the XPointer xmlns() scheme. This provision for explicit namespaces on XPointer schemes is partially responsible for XPointer's extensibility.

The user agent's request:

```
GET /mydoc HTTP/1.1
Host: example.org
Accept: text/xml
Range: xpointer=xmlns(xp=http://example.org/xptr/xpath)xpath(//bar)
```

The origin server's response:

```
HTTP/1.1 206 Partial Content
Content-Type: multipart/mixed; boundary="simple boundary"

--simple boundary

Content-type: text/xml; charset=ISO-8859-1

<bar id="a12">Hello</bar>

--simple boundary

Content-type: text/xml; charset=ISO-8859-1

<bar id="a13">World</bar>

--simple boundary--
```

---

is done using the HTTP Accept request header. However, if the user agent attempts to apply a fragment identifier that has no semantics for the retrieved IMT-typed representation, then the evaluation of the fragment identifier will fail. So, given a link to an SVG resource using the svgView() fragment identifier, a user agent that does not support SVG may negotiate for a JPEG representation of the resource. The svgView() scheme is not defined against the JPEG IMT, and thus the user agent, for example, a browser, will not be able to establish the correct viewport onto the retrieved image.

The response entity now contains one body part for each matched node in the addressed XML resource. Further, the MIME body parts are presented to the client in document order, just as they would be identified if you applied that XPath expression directly to the negotiated text/xml representation of that resource.

4   RDF Query Language and XPointer

There is a large and growing number of query languages for RDF. The W3C has chartered the Data Access Working Group to create a recommendation for both an RDF query language and a data access protocol. Since XPointer is an extensible framework, we can choose any RDF query language — including, but not limited to one standardized by the Data Access Working Group — and develop a notation for that query language that is consistent with the XPointer Framework. Once that is done, we can encode a query in a URI and use the techniques described above to address subresources — for example, subgraphs of an RDF graph, all the classes in an OWL ontology, the creator of an RDF snippet — identified by that query language.

Consider an XPointer scheme, rdql(), for RDQL [11]. Since rdql() isn't an officially specified W3C XPointer scheme, we use the xmlns() scheme to setup the namespace context so that rdql() is correctly recognized by the XPointer processor. Once the namespace context has been established, we set the resulting XPointer expression as the value of the Range header. When the request is received by the server it will use an XPointer processor to evaluate that expression on behalf of the client and ship back the results.

The user agent's request:

```
GET /myStore HTTP/1.1
Accept: application/rdf+xml
Range: xmlns(q=http://www.myorg.org/xpointer-scheme/rdql)
      rdql(
         SELECT (?x foaf:mbox ?mbox)
          WHERE (?x foaf:name "John Smith")
                (?x foaf:mbox ?mbox)
          USING foaf FOR <http://xmlns.com/foaf/0.1/>
      )
```

The origin server's response:

```
HTTP/1.1 206 Partial Content
Content-Type: application/rdf+xml

<rdf:RDF xmlns:rdf="...">...</rdf:RDF>
```

Notice that in this case multiple subresources are being returned using an atomic, as opposed to a multipart, IMT. We can do this for three reasons: First, we are using a logical as opposed to syntactic addressing scheme. Second, we are assuming that any subresources of an RDF graph are also RDF graphs, which is to say that you can't address anything more simple than an RDF triple. Third, any RDF graph can be interchanged as a single `application/rdf+xml` document.

5 RDF, OWL, and XPointer

Our proposal enables user agents to delegate the evaluation of the fragment identifier to the origin server. The client is essentially declaring that it only needs those subresource(s) that are actually addressed by the fragment identifier. `rdf()` and `owl()` XPointer schemes would allow for appropriate kinds of server (and, subsequently, client-side) processing of Semantic Web resources. But what about the reflective modeling questions raised above?

5.1 Reflective RDF Modeling and Management

Consider a Semantic Web application which allows RDF graphs to be collected and aggregated. One approach to managing such an application is to include provenance information about each bit of RDF in the snippet itself. That is, for each RDF graph, it would contain explicit triples asserting, for example, the creator of the snippet, as well as the date the snippet was submitted and the date it was updated. Thus, a query for the metadata about a particular RDF snippet might retrieve every assertion with the snippet's URI as the subject; but that approach has some obvious problems.

A more tractable solution is to store the metadata about each snippet separately from the RDF graph about which that metadata makes assertions. Storing the metadata about an RDF graph outside the graph has some obvious advantages; suppose, for example, that we want to assert that the content of some snippet is untrustworthy or outdated. Presumably that characterization of the assertions in the graph is not intended to apply to the characterization itself. That is, we might very well want to say things about the whole graph which were not meant to be said of the graph's metadata.

This point exposes a modeling problem for RDF data and the Semantic Web generally. We want to treat RDF documents as web resources, one of the general uses of which is to make assertions about other resources. But we also want to be able to make assertions about RDF graphs, *qua* Web resources, themselves. We want, therefore, some measure of reflective or second-order expressiveness about all web resources, including the ones that are RDF and OWL. One approach to achieving this kind of reflective expressivity is to establish a URI convention for the metadata of a graph — by, say, appending a "/rdf" URI path segment to any URI. Setting aside the widespread breakage that might impose, it's not a very elegant solution. It is far more reasonable to create an XPointer scheme, say `metadata()` that, in conjunction with our server-side XPointer proposal, would be taken by Semantic Web origin servers to be a query or retrieval of information *about* a resource rather than *of* the resource.

This approach is similar to the URIQA [13] proposal in that both approaches avoid the needless proliferation of URIs. We, however, want to have a URIRef for the metadata about a resource as well. The URIQA approach — to create new HTTP methods, most notably MGET — effectively hides the switch from resource to metadata about the resource in the request.[9] Which says nothing, of course, about the non-technical intractability of standardizing a new set of core HTTP methods.

5.2   OWL Partial Imports

OWL ontologies are usually encoded, published, and exchanged as RDF/XML documents. One way in which the needs of the Semantic Web, *quo* a KR-like system, are not fully served by the typical implementation of HTTP/1.1 is the importation of third party OWL ontologies. We think the proposed Semantic Web resource protocol described herein can address some of the problems associated with OWL partial imports.

In order to understand the utility of our proposal for OWL imports, it's important to review its semantics. Using owl:imports in ontology A to import ontology B has the effect of merging the set of RDF triples which constitute the two ontologies. One of the problems with multi-ontology Semantic Web applications is selective use of a term or terms from another ontology. For example, consider an OWL ontology about biological research, which may need to use a few terms from a very large ontology about proteins, but which, for practical reasons, does not want to simply owl:imports the very large ontology. Since the only semantics of owl:imports is something like "graph concatenation", the choices seem to be either import the entire large ontology, do not import any of it, or shadow some of its terms by declaring equivalent classes in the host ontology. Each of these options has real disadvantages.

But using the techniques described herein, we can specify *partial imports* of resources which are, in fact, subresources addressed and retrieved by means of RDF or OWL or even arbitrary XQuery or XPath queries. By providing a URI that contains an XPointer scheme — for example, the rdql scheme described above — as the value of an owl:imports, we can specify a complex query to filter a published OWL ontology to a subresource that only contains the triples we need.

Such filtered, partial imports may well be semantically problematic in light of the original ontology creator's intention; but whatever semantic perturbations

---

[9] URIQA not only proposes three new HTTP methods, MGET, MPUT, and MDELETE, but it also requires clients and origins servers to support a new HTTP header, URIQA-uri: "it is recommended that when submitting a URIQA request where the request URI contains a fragment identifier, the full URI should be redundantly specified using the special HTTP message header URIQA-uri." The proposal herein has the relative advantage of using only extant headers and URI serialization forms.

are created by a partial import are no different in principle than the perturbations that may be created by an ordinary import. The publisher of an OWL ontology has no control over what happens to it once it is imported into an arbitrary ontology.

A partial import has the advantage of neither touching the original creator's URI space nor requiring some kind of shadow resource or document. It does require coordination of XPointer schemes between the user agent and origin server, however; though, as we point out in the next section, this does not impose a very high burden of implementation. Furthermore, we can imagine future XPointer schemes that would allow us to address subresources of OWL ontologies that are OWL specific; for example, addressing and retrieving the subresource of an ontology that is a particular class and all its subclasses.

6   Implementation Experience

As a test of our claims herein we have developed software to support two XPointer schemes for server-side processing.

6.1   Partial OWL Imports in Pellet

The Pellet OWL Reasoner [12] is a Java DL reasoner implemented, using the tableaux algorithm, by members of the UMD Mindlab, including one of the authors of this paper. The developers of Pellet support a subset of RDQL queries as a kind of conjunctive ABox query. As a proof of the concepts described in this paper, we deployed Pellet in a simple HTTP application environment wherein it used the `Accept-Range: xpointer` HTTP header to advertise its ability to process XPointer URIs.

We were then able to address and retrieve representations of subresources of the very large NCI cancer ontology using RDQL and Pellet. We were able to do this with very simple HTTP user agents; for example, we used the Unix command line tool `wget`, which allows the insertion of an arbitrary HTTP header into every request. With this environment we are able to create complex RDQL queries, use those queries to address and retrieve subresources of the NCI cancer ontology, and we're able to do this with very little implementation burden. The user agent implementation is very minimal, and the origin server burden is equally minimal.

6.2   RSS Querying

RSS 1.0 [1] is an RDF vocabulary for representing and exchanging typed web site event streams. These event streams, known colloquially as "channels", are published on the Web and referred to by URI. Because it is an RDF vocabulary, the kinds of events that it can serialize are limited only by RDF itself. As further proof of the concepts described herein, we implemented an XPointer scheme, `rss`, that allowed querying of an RSS channel in two ways.

First, the rss scheme supports queries by list slice semantics; that is, taking the channel to be a list of events, you can address a subresource of the channel by indexing into the list in the same way as you index a list in a high-level programming language. Because we used Python as our implementation language, we simply exposed a subset of the Python list slice semantics to the rss scheme. For example, rss(-1) addresses the last entry of the channel; and rss(0:5) addresses the first five channel entries.

Second, we implemented support for arbitrary date range queries. One of the standard properties of the entries of an RSS channel is a date property. For example, rss(2004-05-05:2004-05-07) addresses the subresource constituted by all the RSS events occurring on or between 2004-0505 and 2004-05-07.

7   Conclusion and Future Work

The nature of most Semantic Web resources, represented by RDF and OWL documents, is significantly different from World Wide Web resources, represented by HTML and XML documents. The latter are intended for human consumption and syntactic interoperability. The former are KR formalisms and are amenable to logical query languages and KR-sensitive addressing schemes. But the Semantic Web is still supposed to be the Web, which suggests that extensions of existing addressing and protocol technologies are appropriate.

We have described herein one such extension, which has as its goal the creation of a Semantic Web resource protocol using the extensible XPointer addressing scheme and some features of HTTP/1.1. The benefits of this proposal include *scalability*, derived from XPointer processing at the origin server rather than by the client, as well as *extensibility*, which allows for addressing and interaction models that are sensitive to RDF and OWL. In particular our proposal offers a way of handling the resource/resource-metadata distinction without the needless propagation of URIs, as well as offering some traction for the problems of OWL imports.

We conclude that the proposal described herein is practically realizable on a large scale, such realization being primarily a matter of multiparty agreement as to the semantics of particular XPointer schemes. We anticipate more detailed analyses of the semantics of RDF and OWL-specific XPointer schemes in conjunction with HTTP methods like DELETE, PUT, POST, LINK and UNLINK.

References

1. G. Beged-Dov, D. Brickley, R. Dornfest, I. Davis, L. Dodds, and et. al. RDF Site Summary (RSS) 1.0. http://web.resource.org/rss/1.0/spec.
2. T. Berners-Lee, R. Fielding, and L. Masinter. Uniform Resource Identifier (URI): Generic Syntax. IETF Network Working Group Internet Draft, http://gbiv.com/protocols/uri/rev-2002/rfc2396bis.html.
3. J. Clark and S. DeRose. XML Path Language (XPath) Version 1.0. W3C Recommendation 16 November 1999 http://www.w3.org/TR/xpath/.

4. S. DeRose, E. Maler, and R. Daniel Jr. XPointer xpointer() Scheme. W3C Working Draft 19 December 2002 http://www.w3.org/TR/xptr-xpointer/.
5. S. J. DeRose, R. Daniel Jr., E. Maler, and J. Marsh. XPointer xmlns() Scheme. W3C Recommendation 25 March 2003 http://www.w3.org/TR/xpointer-xmlns/.
6. J. Ferraiolo, F. Jun, and D. Jackson. Scalable Vector Graphics (SVG) 1.1 Specification. W3C Recommendation 14 January 2003 http://www.w3.org/TR/SVG11/.
7. N. Freed and N. Borenstein. Multipurpose Internet Mime Extensions (MIME) Part Two: Media Types. IETF Network Working Group RFC 2046, http://www.ietf.org/rfc/rfc2046.txt.
8. P. Grosso, E. Maler, J. Marsh, and N. Walsh. XPointer elemnet() Scheme. W3C Recommendation 25 March 2003 http://www.w3.org/TR/xptr-element/.
9. P. Grosso, E. Maler, J. Marsh, and N. Walsh. XPointer Framework. W3C Recommendation 25 March 2003 http://www.w3.org/TR/xptr-framework/.
10. I. Jacobs. Architecture of the World Wide Web. W3C Working Draft 9 December 2003 http://www.w3.org/TR/webarch/.
11. A. Seaborne. RDQL - A Query Language for RDF. W3C Member Submission 9 January 2004, http://www.w3.org/Submission/RDQL/.
12. E. Sirin and B. Parsia. Pellet OWL Reasoner. http://www.mindswap.org/2003/pellet/.
13. P. Stickler. The Nokia URI Query Agent Model. http://sw.nokia.com/uriqa/URIQA.html.

On the Emergent Semantic Web and Overlooked Issues

Yannis Kalfoglou[1], Harith Alani[1], Marco Schorlemmer[2], and Chris Walton[3]

[1] Advanced Knowledge Technologies (AKT), School of Electronics and Computer Science,
University of Southampton, UK
{y.kalfoglou,ha}@ecs.soton.ac.uk

[2] Escola de Tecnologies d'Informació i Comunicació,
Universitat Internacional de Catalunya, Spain
marco@cir.unica.edu

[3] Advanced Knowledge Technologies (AKT), CISA, School of Informatics,
University of Edinburgh, UK
cwd@inf.ed.ac.uk

Abstract. The emergent Semantic Web, despite being in its infancy, has already received a lot of attention from academia and industry. This resulted in an abundance of prototype systems and discussion most of which are centred around the underlying infrastructure. However, when we critically review the work done to date we realise that there is little discussion with respect to the vision of the Semantic Web. In particular, there is an observed dearth of discussion on how to deliver knowledge sharing in an environment such as the Semantic Web in effective and efficient manners. There are a lot of overlooked issues, associated with agents and trust to hidden assumptions made with respect to knowledge representation and robust reasoning in a distributed environment. These issues could potentially hinder further development if not considered at the early stages of designing Semantic Web systems. In this perspectives' paper, we aim to help engineers and practitioners of the Semantic Web by raising awareness of these issues.

1 Introduction

The *Semantic Web* (SW) is on its early stages of research and development – not more than five years in life loosely counting from appearances of early publications in the literature and W3C blueprints and design notes – and there has been considerable progress in both academic and industrial fronts. The emergent SW, however, still falls short of expectations and hasn't realised the vision outlined in [5]. This statement is bound to be subjective as many would interpret the "SW expectations" differently depending on their experiences with SW technologies and their successes or failures. In this paper we aim to put in perspective these views and critically review the SW vision and work done to date. We reflect on the expectations created by the SW literature, but our aim is not to conclusively discount the idea of the SW. Rather, we aim to raise awareness of overlooked issues with respect to: (a) provision of robust reasoning on the SW, (b) usage of mechanised forms of trust, (c) enabling software agents on the SW, and (d) cultural legacy from a Web user's point of view. We base our critique on personal experiences with involvement in the design, development, and deployment of SW-enabled applications, thus our discussion is targeted to practitioners and engineers and the focus is on technical issues and limitations of current technology.

S.A. McIlraith et al. (Eds.): ISWC 2004, LNCS 3298, pp. 576–590, 2004.

From an ethnographical point of view, this sort of critique and analyses of a new technology is sparse in the SW literature. For example, in the past three SW events – starting with the SWWS'01 symposium and followed by two ISWC conferences – there have been 135 papers published but, to our judgment, we only found 3 critiquing papers highlighting problems, experiences and issues emerged. Similar dearth of critiquing is found in SW related events organised by adjacent communities like the WWW or major Artificial Intelligence (AI) conferences. Based on this evidence and seeing all this excitement and work done so far, an average Web user would wonder: *the SW should be already out there and I could use it as I use the Web?*. However, this is not true yet, as current users of the emergent SW are mostly its engineers and practitioners rather than the general public.

These two are the main anchor points upon which we unravel our argumentation: review work done to date and highlight issues that could hinder future development by focusing on the expectations of the SW from a Web user's point of view. We start with a brief overview of the emergent SW in section 2 before elaborating on emerging issues in the following sections. In particular, in section 3 we argue for the role of agency and mechanised trust as the means to realise the benefits of a SW. These are closely related with our ability to operationalise robust reasoners on the SW, an issue related with Knowledge Representation (KR). We elaborate on known limitations of KR for the SW in section 4, and we put together all these issues under a pragmatics' lens in section 5 where we speculate on the impact of these issues and pinpoint to directions that could help us come closer to realise the SW vision before concluding our perspectives' paper in section 6.

2   The Emergent Semantic Web

The SW endeavour is well underway with the majority of work concentrating on infrastructure issues. As semantics are seen as the differentiating factor from the Web, one of the first deliverables of the SW, namely RDF [29], was aiming to assist content providers with annotation of their data with semantic information. The adoption and use of RDF though has not been unproblematic, as reported in [24]. In [42] the authors elaborate further on the problems associated with RDF syntax and notation , in particular when it is used with the W3C's recommended Web Ontology Language (OWL) [36]. OWL emerged in the last few years as an ontology language that, hopefully, will become a *de facto* language in which to represent SW ontologies. The design of this carefully crafted language was influenced by AI products, such as Frame Logic and Description Logic (DL). These formalisms have their own peculiarities which are inherited in the language itself but we will elaborate on them in the next section.

As RDF preceded OWL, early adopters of this technology used sophisticated, but ad-hoc ways of providing AI-style inferencing in early systems (for example, the *OntoBroker* system [10]). As OWL became widely available and backed by the W3C we are beginning to see content annotated with OWL syntax not only for ontology encoding but for describing instances too (ABoxes in DL). A number of tools are already available, including robust APIs like HP's Jena[1] and the OWL-API[2].

---

[1] http://jena.sourceforge.net

[2] http://sourceforge.net/projects/owlapi

But despite the sophisticated machinery for annotating content and reasoning over it, the main driver of the SW seems to be simplicity and ease of use. This is evident since the early days of designing the SW [4], when the widespread belief was to keep things simple and to compromise on KR principles that shaped most of the KR practice in AI for years, as we will discuss in the next section. To quote Berners-Lee [4]: "The Semantic Web is what we will get if we perform the same globalisation process to Knowledge Representation that the Web initially did to Hypertext. We remove the centralised concepts of absolute truth, total knowledge, and total provability, and see what we can do with limited knowledge." Similar statements are found in the SW literature almost 5 years after these design notes were written, as for example in McBride's report [34]:

> [...] the perception that the Semantic Web is concerned with AI is not helpful to its widespread adoption in the IT industry [...] this perception is understandable. The Semantic Web is often presented as the technology that will achieve marvelous things [...] much of the excitement and motivational power of such scenarios come from the handling of speech, NLP, general problem solving, scheduling, common sense reasoning and other features commonly associated with intelligence. These are not what the Semantic Web is about. The Semantic Web is about creating an infrastructure in which information from a variety of sources can be integrated on demand to achieve some task. The Semantic Web provides mechanisms that enable access to and integration of data.

There is a hidden antithesis in these two, chronologically distant, but similar calls for compromised KR and infrastructure. McBride's call for infrastructure reflects much of the work done to date, but the infrastructure call presupposes a non-compromised KR, as the tasks envisaged for this infrastructure require the full strength of today's best KR practices. You can't have a compromised KR to support an infrastructure that aims to provide the means for accessing and integrating disparate data in semantically rich manners. At least not with the current state-of-the-art in KR and SW infrastructure. So, there is a comprise on both ends, KR and infrastructure, as it is evident on early, successful, SW systems and demonstrators.

For example, the 2003 SW challenge award-winner CS AKTive space[3] strikes a balance between aggregation of vast amounts of semantically annotated data from a variety of disparate sources and provision of robust reasoning services. For instance, as the focus is on infrastructure, more attention has been paid on performance and scaling issues[4] rather than robust reasoning, as for example resolving the ever so re-occurring problem of referential integrity [1]. On the other hand, systems like KAON [51], provide more robust reasoning services but compromise on scale and, arguably, on the principle of decentralization and distributiveness of the SW as KAON is a stand-alone application server with its processing centralised. The list of early prototypes who compromise on either scale and distributiveness or KR capabilities is long to mention in this paper but to the best of our knowledge none of those developed so far, have managed both.

An issue closely related with the ability to provide robust reasoning over distributed resources is not so much the capabilities of the reasoner but the usefulness of the external

---

[3] http://www-agki.tzi.de/swc/csaktivespace.html

[4] One of the biggest RDF triplestores available today with more than 25 million RDF triples in store.

resources. In an environment the size of the SW these could be assessed by some form of mechanised trust and accessed with software agents, as it is envisaged in the literature. There are open issues, however, when we call upon agency and trust which we review in the next section.

3   The Role of Agency and Trust

The SW is predicated on the notion of *agents* as the key consumers of SW information. This is expressed in [5]: "The real power of the Semantic Web will be realised when people create many programs that collect Web content from diverse sources, process the information and exchange the results with other programs. The effectiveness of such software agents will increase exponentially as more machine-readable Web content and automated services (including other agents) become available.". The underlying assumption in this description is that agents will be able to *automatically* utilise the information on the Web once semantic annotation has been provided. Nonetheless, there are many challenges associated with the use of agency in this manner, and a solution to many of the issues is far from clear. We outline a number of these challenges in this section, with reference to state-of-the-art techniques for addressing the associated issues.

What is an agent? The first issue concerns the definition of the term "software agent" itself. There is a surprising lack of consensus in the agency community over how this term should be defined. Indeed, the term is applied to a wide range of systems, ranging from simple distributed objects, to complex autonomous entities [41]. The reason for this lack of consensus is primarily because the term is used generically to refer to a heterogeneous body of AI research, rather than a specific implementation. From the perspective of the SW, it is unclear what kind of agency is required. The increasing use of Web services[5] to express computation on the SW points to a purely procedural notion of agency, while the kinds of reasoning which are envisaged in the description of the SW appear to require something more complex, e.g. proactive behaviour. Thus, to address this issue, a number of systems that combine autonomous agents with Web services have been proposed (e.g., [52]).

Agent Coordination. It can be argued that a precise definition of agency on the SW is unimportant, provided that the agents can cooperate in meaningful ways. This is further expressed in [5]: "[...] even agents that were not expressly designed to work together can transfer data among themselves when the data come with semantics.". From this description it appears that the semantic markup itself is intended to solve the problem of coordination among heterogeneous agents. However, it is far from clear how this can be achieved. The problem of coordinating agents with semantic markup introduces the issues associated with semantic interoperability (see section 4). For example, if two agents wish to cooperate, and they have different internal representations of the domain in question, then they must perform a mapping between (or a subset of) their knowledge. This must be done automatically if the agents are to cooperate autonomously in the SW. There are a number of proposed solutions, e.g., the adoption of a standard upper ontology

---

[5] http://www.w3.org/TR/ws-arch/

such as OWL-S[6], or the use of partial mappings [23]. However, it is likely that this will be an open issue for some time to come.

A popular basis for coordination among agents is the use of *performative* languages. These languages have their roots in the theory of *speech acts*. This theory identifies a class of performative verbs (e.g. inform, promise, request) that have the characteristics of physical actions, in that they change the state of the world. The use of performatives to express interactions between agents has been enthusiastically adopted by the agency community and this is most visible in the development of Agent Communication Languages (ACLs), such as the Foundation for Intelligent Physical Agents ACL (FIPA-ACL[7]). In these languages, the model of interaction between agents is based on the exchange of messages. FIPA-ACL defines a set of performatives (message types) that express the intended meaning of these messages.

Sincerity. There is a significant issue in the use of performative languages in an open environment. There is an underlying *sincerity assumption* in these languages which demands that agents always act in accordance with their intentions. It will always be possible for an insincere agent to simulate any required internal state, and we cannot verify the sincerity of an agent as we have no access to its internal mental states. This problem is termed the *semantic verification* problem and is detailed in [54]. In order to address the sincerity issues, a number of alternatives have been proposed which we now discuss. The proposals all address sincerity by restricting the kinds of behaviours that the agents can exhibit and exposing the internal state of the agents. Thus, agents who are not acting in accordance with the intended dialogue can be readily identified.

Dialogue protocols. The first of these imposes a layer of control above the performative language, through the use of *dialogue protocols* (e.g., [49]). In this approach, the performative language defines only *how* agents can communicate, while the dialogue protocol defines *if and when* agents should communicate. The underlying concept in the Electronic Institutions (EI) approach is that human interactions are never completely unconstrained, rather they are always guided by formal and informal conventions such as customs, etiquette, and laws. EI are a means of representing and controlling these conventions within multi-agent systems (MAS). Dialogue protocols greatly assist in the design of MAS as they impose structure on the agents, co-ordinate tasks between agents, and define commitments which agents must satisfy. Nonetheless, there are a number of pertinent issues which need to be addressed in the EI framework. The most serious of these is that there is no straightforward means to disseminate the institutions, and thus the agents must be explicitly designed (in advance) for a specific institution.

Social policy. Another alternative is the use of social policy to control agent interaction. The key concept of the social commitment model is the establishment of shared commitments between agents. A social commitment between agents is a binding agreement from one agent to another. The commitment distinguishes between the creditor who commits to a course of action, and the debtor on whose behalf the action is done. Establishing a commitment constrains the subsequent actions of the agent until the commitment is discharged. Commitments are stored as part of the social state of the MAS and are verifiable. A theory which combines speech acts with social commitments is outlined in

---

[6] http://www.daml.org/services/
[7] http://www.fipa.org

[17], though there remain considerable implementation issues in maintaining a suitable store of shared commitments.

Dialogue games. A further approach involves the use of dialogue games, which trace their origins to the philosophical tradition of Aristotle. Dialogue games have been used to study fallacious reasoning, for natural language processing and generation, and to develop a game-theoretic semantics for various logics. These games can also be utilised as the basis for interaction between autonomous agents. A group of agents participate in a dialogue game in which their utterances correspond to moves in this game. Different rules can be applied to the game, which correspond to different dialogue types, e.g. persuasion, negotiation, enquiry [53]. For example, a persuasion dialogue begins with an assertion and ends when the proponent withdraws the claim or the opponent concedes the claim. A framework which permits different kinds of dialogue games, and also meta-dialogues is outlined in [35]. However, this framework is only defined at a formal level, and an implementation has yet to be realised.

Dynamic scripting. The final approach which we describe here relaxes the requirement that the agent coordination must be statically defined before evaluation can take place. Rather, we can take a script-based approach to coordination, where the script is built dynamically during evaluation, as the agents communicate. In general, a great deal of conversation is an expression of protocol. For example, the question *"Can you tell me the time?"* implies that the next step in the protocol is for the other party to respond with the time. We express the coordination as an executable protocol, which is passed between agents as the communication happens. This approach is detailed in [47], where the scripting language is derived from the Calculus of Communication Systems [39].

Trust

One of the needs for software agents' cooperation on the SW is the ability to use automated methods for measuring trust. This is exemplified in [5]: "Lucy's agent, having complete trust in Pete's agent in the context of the present task, automatically assisted by supplying access certificates..." *Trust* is placed at the top of the proposed SW "layer cake"[8]. The trustworthiness of knowledge-base statements have generally been accepted without any proof [50]. Van Harmelen argues that some measurement of trust will be needed when dealing with distributed knowledge sources. In [32] the authors highlight some of the issues that need to be incorporated into the SW service architecture to enable exchanging trust and reputation and to control policies and negotiations. There are several issues to consider with respect to trust and the SW. For example, *how can trust be modelled and exchanged between agents and SW services*? *Where should trust annotations be stored and made available*? *What kind of knowledge is required to measure trust and where will this knowledge come from*? *What trust features need to be considered (e.g. subjectivity, propagations, transitivity)*? and *how do they effect trust in general*?

Modelling & representation. For trust to be used by SW agents it must first be formalised and modelled in an agreed fashion. The first computational model of trust was introduced in [31], which inspired much work in this domain. Modelling trust helps to untangle its

---

[8] http://www.w3c.org/2000/Talks/1206-xml2k-tbl/slide10-0.html

complexity and understand its main components and evolution. However, the accuracy and completeness of such models is one thing, and their suitability and integration into MAS communication is a totally different thing. In [19] the authors are calling for security and trust to be added to the systems design process, rather than trying to attach them to already existing systems which might not be compatible. They argue that modelling trust and security should be closely related to where they will be applied and used, which raises questions about the actual applicability of generic trust models.

There is a clear need for semantic language support for representing trust. In [16] the authors suggested to use a semantic policy language to enable annotating security and belief. Representing trust explicitly can significantly improve knowledge exchange and outsourcing performance between agents [13]. There are some emerging standards such as SOAP security extension and PICS which was originally designed for rating Web pages. However, none of these languages are sophisticated enough to represent trust efficiently.

Sourcing. There is still no agreement about whether trust information is best gathered and broadcasted in centralised units, or left in a distributed format for agents to collect and reach their own conclusions. In [18] the authors developed a centralised system to help users annotate sources to highlight alternative, probably contradictory, sources. Users feedback can then be used to assess information sources. Another example is proposed in [33] for a centralised agent to measure the reputation of Web services by monitoring and collecting outcomes and client feedback, and making this information available to other agents. Such centralised systems raise the question of how trustworthy are the users or agents who provided the feedback in the first place, and why such trust warehouses should be trusted [13]. For example, in [16] the authors argue against centralised units for measuring trust because of their scalability limitations and the implicit trust measurement mechanisms they adopt.

Measuring trust. To reduce the risk of online trading on the SW, there must be a way to infer trust and reputation electronically [40]. However, there is no consensus about how this can be done. In [55] the authors state the need for agents to combine their own experience with the experience of other agents when measuring the trustworthiness of a specific agent. This raises the issue of availability and accessibility of such experience outcome over the SW, and whether trust can still be measured in their absence.

Several approaches have been introduced in an attempt to extract trust values from decentralised, interconnected semantic networks. In [22] the authors argue that trust can be propagated through relatively short paths connecting entities in small world networks. They believe that modern information networks will be decentralised and highly dynamic, where traditional trust control methods will no longer apply. They used an algorithm based on the *small world theory* [38] to measure trust between entities that are not directly connected. Similarly, in [20] the authors applied techniques to measure trust over a FOAF network, extended with trust relations while in [46] the authors applied path algebra and probabilistic algorithms to measure the trustworthiness of users along a network of trust connections explicitly specified by users. All these approaches seem to rely to some extent on trust values given explicitly by users. One observation made in [45] with respect to *eBay* is that users feedback is almost always positive. The authors note that most people do not like giving negative feedback, unless revenge is a motivation.

Furthermore, scalability becomes a serious issue when relying solely on users trust feedback.

Context. One major problem with many approaches proposed for measuring trust is the lack of context, which is a basic feature of trust [13]. You may trust your colleague to write a good project proposal, but you might not trust him to fix your car. Associating trust measurement with specific contexts will inevitably increase its calculation and representation complexity, but nevertheless is crucial for the resulting trust values to be on any use. Transitivity of trust is a complex issue that also needs to be investigated to determine how trust should propagate along the SW. Some argue that trust is not strictly transitive, and that the transitivity of trust is subjective and context dependent [12].

It should now be clear that the capitalisation of agency and trust in the SW will require a significant number of challenges to be addressed. The focus of our attention has been on the provision of a coordination framework for agents, and mechanised ways for measuring trust. However, even with such a framework in place and a well-connected network upon which network analysis algorithms will measure trust, we are still dependent on robust reasoners that will operate in such an environment.

4   Knowledge Representation and Reasoning on the Semantic Web

Robust reasoning. Intimately connected with the ability to operationalise our reasoners on the SW is how we handle *soundness* and *completeness*. These are precise technical terms that describe properties of formal systems or sets of sentences, and they get their meaning from the field of mathematical logic. A formal system is *sound* when every sentence produced by the system's inference rules operating on the system's initial set of axioms logically follows from that set; it is *complete* when every sentence that logically follows from the system's initial set of axioms can be formally derived using the inference rules. In addition a set of sentences is said to be *complete* if for every sentence of the logical language, either it or its negation can be proven from the set, using the rules of the formal system.

These notions are tightly connected to the story of first-order logic (FOL), which, among all logics, has a special status due to its expressive power, its natural deductive systems, and its intuitive model theory based on sets. It is because of FOL's success in providing rigorous definitions of mathematical truth and proof, that, from the early days of the field of AI, knowledge representation and reasoning (KRR) has been developed primarily around FOL and its model-theoretic semantics.

From a practical point of view, to render the SW operational, it is understandable that current standardisation efforts for SW technology have primarily focused around traditional views of KRR, using FOL's model theory as its semantic underpinning. FOL is well understood, both mathematically and computationally, and is also well established via many customised representation languages and highly optimised inference engines that have been developed for a plethora of different subsets and variants of FOL. Hence, it comes at no surprise that OWL is based on well-studied DL theory and technology, very well following FOL's traditional model-theoretic semantics [36].

But, despite of FOL's prominent status in mathematical logic, and besides the practical reasons for adopting FOL's model theory as semantic underpinning to get the SW up and running, it would be a mistake to base the current emergent SW technology solely, or primarily, around the traditional KRR paradigm. In [15] the author has nicely summarised the strengths and limitations of the model-theoretic approach to the SW, which situates many of the envisioned applications of the SW clearly beyond the capacity of FOL-based, and consequently DL-based SW technology.

Soundness and completeness, for instance, have a different dimension when it comes to the SW. As it is reported in [50]: "[...] some of the assumptions underlying current KR technology [that] will have to be revised when applied to the Semantic Web." While scale and change rate are regarded as big obstacles that test current KR technology to its limits, the crux of the problem with preserving and mechanizing *soundness* and *completeness* on the SW is lack of referential integrity and inconsistent knowledge produced by multiple knowledge sources, as they will exist in the SW. There is call for more robust inferencing [50]:

> In an environment the of size of the web we must abandon the classical idea of sound and complete reasoners, our reasoners will almost certainly have to be incomplete (no longer guaranteeing to return all logically valid results), but most likely also unsound: sometimes jumping to a logically unwarranted conclusion. Furthermore, the degrees of such incompleteness or unsoundness must be a function of the available resources. Answers will have to be approximate.

Open and closed worlds. We visit a key notion that has been used in the past to tackle incompleteness, and it is revised in the context of agents' research to become more operational when applied at a large scale. *Closed World Assumption* (CWA) states that everything that is not known or cannot proved to be true, must be false. CWA originates from AI and database research in the late 70s (for example, Reiter's work on CWA [44] as an implementation of McCarthy's investigations on the *Frame Problem*) and the same fundamental assumption still holds for most of databases' design today. Despite its similarities, it has a different interpretation when studied in DL, as it is stated in [2]: "a database instance represents exactly one interpretation, namely the one where classes and relations in the schema are interpreted by the objects and tuples in the instance [...] an ABox represents many different interpretations, namely all its models." So, absence of information in a database instance is interpreted as *negative information*, while absence of information in an ABox only indicates *lack of knowledge*. Thus, while the information in a database is always understood to be complete, the information in an ABox is in general viewed as incomplete, and that leads to the perception of ABoxes semantics as "open world", while the traditional semantics of databases is characterised as "closed world".

This view that ABoxes (set of instances or facts that comprise a knowledge base) have an "open world" semantics is clearly reflected in the current SW technologies which originate from DL (for instance, in OWL). For this reason, CWA has received a rather controversial perception. In the W3C OWL requirements recommendation [25], the ability to state closed worlds is seen as an objective, rather than a requirement[9] and its value is praised by the author: "[...] the language must be able to state that a given ontology

---

[9] The difference being, that a W3C requirement is a feature that the OWL language must have as opposed to an objective which is not mandatory but nice to have.

can be regarded as complete. This would sanction additional inferences to be drawn from that ontology. The precise semantics of such statement (and the corresponding set of inferences) remains to be defined, but examples might include assuming complete property information about individuals, assuming completeness of class-membership, and assuming exhaustiveness of subclasses.". These features are indeed what a SW reasoner would expect to find in a knowledge source on the SW in order to draw complete, and possibly sound inferences.

But, providing the right machinery to automate the task of asserting information about the completeness of a knowledge source is not an easy job and solutions vary across disciplines. For example, in the logic programming realm, the use of extra-logical operators, embedded in the syntax of the language, are common, like the use of *not* operator in some implementations of Prolog. Similar attempts are reported in the software engineering domain [30], whereas in [6] the authors use techniques from Answer Set Programming (ASP), which allow to draw conclusions based on the lack of evidence of the contrary. Their approach augments the semantics of SW languages' constructs, in particular that of the DAML daml:subClassOf, with ASP programs to be fed into an ASP solver in order to allow drawn, default inferences to be dropped if opposite knowledge is found in the knowledge source. A promising approach emerged in the agents' community as an extension of the classical CWA, namely *Local World Assumption* - hereafter, LCW. It was first applied in the XII planner [21] to reduce the planning time when dealing with external information. LCW allows closed-world information to be obtained on subsets of information that are known to be complete, while still allowing other information to be treated as unknown. A problem acknowledged with early LCW approaches though, was the assumption that there must exist a priory knowledge of the local completeness of the information sources. And that assumption cannot be operational in an environment the size and scale of the Web. In [26] a proposed solution to this is to provide the means for facilitating the assertion of local completeness information in SW languages themselves, thus enabling SW content providers to annotate their resources with LCW statements. However, the issue of how to acquire knowledge of local completeness in the first place still remains unsolved. The plausible assumption made here, is that the content providers should possess that knowledge and they only need to annotate their content with it. Still, this leave some open issues with respect to the consistency of their content, as LCW could easily introduce contradictions if not handled properly when applied at huge resources.

Semantic interoperability. Spurred by the need to be able to reuse knowledge-based systems and to make them interoperable, the effort in achieving knowledge sharing has carried this tradition in KR over to the research on information system ontologies. In such a highly distributed and decentralised environment as that envisioned for the SW, ontologies were quickly adopted as its semantic backbone: The proposed layer diagram[10] reflecting the SW architecture includes a layer for "ontological vocabulary". But the proliferation of ontologies and ontology representation languages has highlighted the need of standardisation, similarly to that achieved at lower levels of the proposed architecture diagram, which encapsulate already *de facto* standards of current Web technology, such as URI's and XML syntax. As already mentioned in section 2, in the past years RDF and

---

[10] http://www.w3c.org/2000/Talks/1206-xml2k-tbl/slide10-0.html

RDF Schema, with their model-theoretic semantics, have emerged as recommendations for formalisms for defining the semantic content of the Web [29].

Within ontologies' field, many proposals for standard ontologies have arisen in various domains, and the difficulty of consensus has not hindered the continuing work on even the old dream of philosophy of building representations of common-sense knowledge in so called "upper" or "top-level" ontologies such as Cyc[11] and IEEE's Standard Upper Ontology.[12] These efforts attempt to provide generic "objective" representations of knowledge about our world on which ideally particular domain-specific knowledge would define their primitive terminology.

Without questioning the value and necessity of standardisation efforts of this kind, such centralised ontologies may basically make sense for small communities. But large standard ontologies bring back the rigidity of centralised agencies organised under classical codification-based management philosophies [9]. The very distributed and decentralised nature of the web makes the proliferation of ontologies and of formalisms to represent these an unavoidable reality. This has put forward the need to support the interoperability and integration of communities on the semantic level, for instance by means of technology that supports the mapping and merging of ontologies [28].

Corrêa da Silva et al. have shown situations in which even a shared conceptualisation as explicitly specified by means of an ontology is not enough for achieving flawless knowledge sharing [8]: A knowledge base whose inference engine is based on linear logic that poses a query to a knowledge base with the same ontology, but whose inference engine is based on relevance logic should not accept answers as valid if the inference carried out in order to answer the query was using the contraction inference rule, which is not allowed in linear logic. Here, we have clearly an issue of *trust* on the other knowledge base's inference engine, which results from each knowledge base being based on different logical systems.

In [15] Farrugia suggests that, before any meaning negotiation between two agents can start, first the "logical setup" needs to be established, for which he points to Meseguer's notion of *logical system* [37]. This contrasts with the mainstream effort within the SW community where semantic interoperability is sought within the context of standardised representation languages based on Tarskian model-theoretic semantics.

Alternative approaches for a logic based on precise mathematical models of information as a necessary requirement for designing and operating information-processing systems have been advocated e.g., [11,3]. We have recently explored how mathematical theories of information may provide a different angle from which to approach the distributive nature of semantics on the Semantic Web. As it seems, an information-theoretic approach such as that of Barwise and Seligman's channel theory [3] may be suitable to accommodate various understandings of semantics like those occurring in the Web, and also allows for the establishing of ontology mappings that accommodate the particular way different communities use their terminology in their respective contexts, as defined by the use and classification of particular instances with respect to local concepts [27].

---

[11] http://www.cyc.com
[12] http://suo.ieee.org

5 Pragmatics

In sections 3 and 4 we reviewed and analysed a number of challenges that SW faces today. In this section we focus on their impact and put them in perspective when we consider short to medium term deliverables. As the challenges we reviewed cover a broad area of scientific research, it is not realistic to expect them to be fully resolved before the SW will be available and commercially exploitable. It will take time to come up with sound scientific and practical solutions to the problems of robust reasoning, agency coordination, and semantic interoperability, to name a few. In the meantime, the SW will continue to grow and attract attention based on short to medium term solutions. This model of evolution follows the Web legacy, when the SW's predecessor grew on the basis of a network effect. Early Web adopters volunteered to link up their content which resulted in the biggest distributed network ever build in modern computer science. This fundamental assumption is passed onto SW adopters as linked content is still the main deliverable. The difference which should be catered for, though, is that a broken semantic link in a futuristic SW will take more than an explanatory Web-style "404" error message to resolve. As mechanised reasoners will be the main crawlers of content, and not humans as it is often the case with the Web, there have to be automated ways of getting around broken semantic links. Safeguarding your inferences against such an event will be crucial for the quality of service a SW provider will aim to deliver.

Another consideration with respect to the network effect principle of building the SW, is that content management is no longer a carefully manifested process controlled by few but rather an ad-hoc procedure engaged by many. The side-effect of this, is that trust and interoperability will take centre stage as the means to ensure that only useful content will be fed into our reasoners. We also see from evidence from analysing the behaviour of users of the Internet as whole, that erosion of trust is something that we should become to expect in the future, as Blumenthal and Clark point out: "Of all the changes that are transforming the Internet, the loss of trust may be the most fundamental. The simple model of the early Internet - a group of mutually trusting users attached to a transparent network - is gone for ever. A motto for tomorrow may well be 'global communication with local trust'." [7]. Providing the means for local trust would relax the "tension between the demand for trustworthy overall operation and the inability to trust the behaviour of individual users"[7]. As we reported in section 3, laying out the technological foundations for operationalising this 'local trust' that Blumenthal and Clark call for is a whole new challenge in its own right.

The community's favourable route to provide reliable reasoning, is to build as robust as possible reasoning machines for the SW. This is clearly reflected in the latest OWL family of tools (e.g., OWL languages, OWL rules, OWL-S) but would probably not be enough to tackle flawed content. As we reported in section 4 the current state-of-the-art in KRR prevents us from providing guaranteed (i.e., complete) and trustworthy (i.e., sound) automated reasoning over incomplete and/or inconsistent content.

Furthermore, in [48] it is reported that the focus on the KR formalisms RDF and OWL does not include current computer technology, such as the query and modelling languages SQL and UML, into the SW in a satisfactory way. Such languages are widely used in database and software engineering circles, and they are more expressive than OWL. Any pragrmatic approach to the SW would also have to aim at a seamless integration of this technology into the SW architecture.

Lastly, but not least, we have to consider cultural issues related to users' expectations and *modus operandi*. As the SW is seen by many as the natural evolution of the Web, users' will become to expect the same, and probably, more advanced usability and functionality. For example, inspired by the unprecedented success of the Web browser, some have engaged in exploratory activities to build "semantic web browsers" (e.g., [14,43]). However, these are far from being fully operational or at least comparable with current Web browser technology. And we believe that this is a crucial point when it comes to promoting the SW idea to Web users as they have accumulated a 10 year experiences with the Web and only a truly superior product will win them over.

6 Conclusions

Despite using a pessimistic tone in pragmatics' section we are optimistic of the SW idea. We do, however, speculate on the process of building such an ambitious network and argue for a change of course. It seems more practical, and arguably easier to build and deliver in short time, to change the process of building *a* SW, to that of building a series of *Semantic Webs*, all of which will be smaller in size than the envisaged SW, but at least deliver – to the maximum degree possible – the vision outlined in Berners-Lee et al.'s Scientific American article. It could be argued that early SW prototypes are such small *Semantic Webs*. Once we master the art of managing these *Semantic Webs* and they reach a critical mass with satisfied users, the next natural step will be to link them, thus creating a *Web of Semantic Webs*, which eventually could evolve to the envisaged SW. This course is contrary to the current trend of hastingly annotating with dubious semantics masses of content in the hope that advanced, but yet-to-be-built, reasoners and intelligent services will exploit this content and deliver the output to eager users, thus creating the SW. Which approach is the best, time can only tell but it's worth exploring both.

Acknowledgments. This work is supported under the Advanced Knowledge Technologies (AKT) Interdisciplinary Research Collaboration (IRC), which is sponsored by the UK Engineering and Physical Sciences Research Council under grant number GR/N15764/01. The AKT IRC comprises the Universities of Aberdeen, Edinburgh, Sheffield, Southampton and the Open University. The views and conclusions contained herein are those of the authors and should not be interpreted as necessarily representing official policies or endorsements, either express or implied, of the EPSRC or any other member of the AKT IRC. M. Schorlemmer is supported by a *Ramón y Cajal* Fellowship from the Spanish Ministry of Science and Technology.

References

1. H. Alani, S. Dasmahapatra, N. Gibbins, H. Glasser, S. Harris, Y. Kalfoglou, K. O'Hara, and N. Shadbolt. Managing reference: Ensuring Referential Integrity of Ontologies for the Semantic Web. In *Proc. of 13th Int. Conf. on Knowledge Engineering and Knowledge Management (EKAW'02)*, pages 317–334, 2002.
2. F. Baader, D. Calvanese, D. McGuinness, D. Nardi, and P. Pater-Schneider. *The Description Logic Handbook*. Cambridge University Press, 2003.

3. J. Barwise and J. Seligman. *Information Flow*. Cambridge University Press, 1997.
4. T. Berners Lee. What the Semantic Web can represent. Web design Issues, 1998.
5. T. Berners-Lee, J. Hendler, and O. Lassila. The Semantic Web. *Scientific American*, May 2001.
6. E. Bertino, A. Provetti, and F. Salvetti. Local Closed-World assumptions for reasoning about Semantic Web data. In *Proc. of APPIA-GULP-PRODE Joint Conference on Declarative Programming, AGP'03*, 2003.
7. M. Blumenthal and D. Clark. Rethinking the Design of the Internet: The end-to-end arguments vs. the brave new world. *ACM Transactions on Internet Technology (TOIT)*, 1(1):70–109, 2001.
8. F. Corrêa da Silva, W. Vasconcelos, D. Robertson, V. Brilhante, A. de Melo, M. Finger, and J. Agustí. On the insufficiency of ontologies: Problems in knowledge sharing and alternative solutions. *Knowledge Based Systems*, 15(3):147–167, 2002.
9. F. da Silva and J. Agustí. *Knowledge Coordination*. John Wiley and Sons Ltd., 2003.
10. S. Decker, M. Erdmann, D. Fensel, and R. Studer. Ontobroker: Ontology Based Access to Distributed and Semi-Structured Information. In *Proc. of DS-8, Semantic Issues in Multimedia Systems*, pages 351–369, 1999.
11. K. Devlin. *Logic and Information*. Cambridge University Press, 1991.
12. T. Dimitrakos and J. Bicarregui. Towards a Framework for Managing Trust in e-services. In *Proc. of 4th Int. Conf. on Electronic Commerce Research*, pages 360–381, 2001.
13. L. Ding, L. Zhou, and T. Finin. Trust based Knowledge Outsourcing for Semantic Web agents. In *Proc. of 2nd International Conference on Web Intelligence (WI-2003)*, 2003.
14. M. Dzbor, J. Domingue, and E. Motta. Magpie— Towards a Semantic Web browser. In *Proc. of 2nd International Conference on the Semantic Web (ISWC'03)*, pages 690–705, 2003.
15. J. Farrugia. Logical Systems: Towards protocols for Web-based meaning negotiation. In *Proc. of AAAI 2002 Workshop on Meaning Negotiation*, pages 56–59, 2002.
16. T. Finin and A. Joshi. Agents, Trust, and Information access on the Semantic Web. Technical report, Dec. 2002. SIGMOD Record, Volume 31, Number 4.
17. R. A. Flores and R. C. Kremer. Bringing Coherence to Agent Conversations. In *Proc. of Agent-Oriented Software Engineering (AOSE 2001)*, LNCS 2222, pages 50–67, 2002.
18. Y. Gil and V. Ratnakar. Trusting Information sources: One citizen at a time. In *Proc. of 1st Int. Conf. on the Semantic Web (ISWC'02)*, pages 162–177, 2002.
19. P. Giorgini, F. Massaci, J. Mylopoulos, and N. Zannone. Requirements engineering meets trust management: model, methodology, and reasoning. In *Proc. of 2nd Int. Conf. on Trust Management (iTrust'04)*, 2004.
20. J. Golbeck, B. Parsia, and J. Hendler. Trust networks on the Semantic Web. In *Proc. of 7th Int. Workshop on Cooperative Information Agents (CIA-2003)*, 2003.
21. K. Golden, O. Etzioni, and D. Weld. Omnipresence without omnipresence. In *Proc. of 12th Nat. Conf. on Artificial Intelligence(AAAI'94)*, 1994.
22. E. Gray, J. Seigneur, Y. Chen, and C. Jensen. Trust propagation in small world. In *Proc. of 1st Int. Conf. on Trust Management (iTrust'03)*, 2003.
23. M. Burstein. Ontology Mapping for Dynamic Service Invocation on the Semantic Web. In *Proc.of AAAI Spring Symposium on Semantic Web Services*, 2004.
24. S. Haustein and J. Pleumann. Is participation in the Semantic Web too difficult? In *Proc. of 1st Int. Conf. on the Semantic Web (ISWC'02)*, pages 448–454, 2002.
25. J. Heflin. OWL Web Ontology Language use cases and requirements. Technical report, W3C, 2004. W3C Recommendation—10 Feb 2004.
26. J. Heflin and H. Munoz-Avila. LCW-based agent planning for the Semantic Web. In *Proc. of AAAI'02 Workshop on Ontologies and the Semantic Web (WS-02-11)*, 2002.
27. Y. Kalfoglou and M. Schorlemmer. IF-MAP: an ontology mapping method based on Information Flow theory. *Journal on Data Semantics*, 1:98–127, LNCS 2800, 2003.
28. Y. Kalfoglou and M. Schorlemmer. Ontology mapping: the state of the art. *The Knowledge Engineering Review*, 18(1):1–31, 2003.
29. O. Lassila and R. Swick. Resource Description Framework(RDF) Model and Syntax Specification. W3C recommendation, W3C, Feb 1999.

30. Luqi and D. Cooke. How to combine nonmonotonic logic and rapid prototyping to help maintain software. *Int. J. of Software Engineering and Knowledge Engineering*, 5(1):89–118, 1995.

31. S. Marsh. Formalising trust as a computational concept. PhD thesis, University of Stirling, 1994.

32. B. Matthews and T. Dimitrakos. Deploying trust policies on the Semantic Web. In *Proc. of 2nd Int. Conf. on Trust Management (iTrust'04)*, 2004.

33. M. Maximilien and P. Singh. An ontology for Web service ratings and reputations. In *Proc. of AAMAS 2003 Workshop on Ontologies in Agent Systems (OAS'03)*, 2003.

34. B. McBride. Four steps towards the widespread adoption of the Semantic Web. In *Proc. of the 1st Int. Conf. on the Semantic Web (ISWC'02)*, pages 419–423, 2002.

35. P. McBurney and S. Parsons. Games that agents play: A formal framework for dialogues between autonomous agents. *Journal of Logic, Language and Information*, 11(3):315–334, 2002.

36. D. McGuinness and F. van Harmelen. OWL Web Ontology Language. Technical report, W3C, 2004.

37. J. Meseguer. Formal Interoperability. In *Proc. of 5th Int. Symp. on Artificial Intelligence and Mathematics*, 1998.

38. S. Milgram. The small world problem. *Psychology Today*, pages 60–67, 1967.

39. R. Milner. *Communication and Concurrency*. Prentice Hall International, 1989. ISBN: 0131150073.

40. L. Mui, M. Mohtashemi, and A. Halberstadt. A computational model for trust and reputation. In *Proc. of 35th Hawaii Int. Conf. on System Sciences (HICSS-35)*, 2002.

41. H. S. Nwana. Software Agents: An Overview. *The Knowledge Engineering Review*, 11(3):1–40, 1996.

42. P. Patel-Schneider and D. Fensel. Layering the Semantic Web: Problems and directions. In *Proc. of 1st Int. Conf. on the Semantic Web (ISWC'02)*, pages 16–30, 2002.

43. D. Quan and D. Karger. How to make a Semantic Web browser. In *Proc. of 13th Int. World Wide Web Conf. (WWW'04)*, 2004.

44. R. Reiter. On Closed World databases. In *Proc. of 1978 ACM SIGMOD Int. Conf. on Management of Data*, 1978.

45. P. Resnick and R. Zeckhauser. Trust among strangers in Internet transactions: Empirical analysis of eBay's reputation system. *Advances in Applied Mircroelectronics*, 11, 2002.

46. M. Richardson, R. Agrawal, and P. Domingos. Trust management for the Semantic Web. In *Proc. of 2nd Int. Conf. on the Semantic Web (ISWC'03)*, pages 351–368, 2003.

47. D. Robertson. A Lightweight Method for Coordination of Agent Oriented Web Services. In *Proc. of the AAAI Spring Symposium on Semantic Web Services*, 2004.

48. J. Sowa. Architectures for Intelligent Systems. IBM Systems Journal, 41(3), pages 331-349, 2002.

49. J. A. Rodríguez, F. J. Martín, P. Noriega, P. Garcia, and C. Sierra. Towards a Formal Specification of Complex Social Structures in Multi-Agent Systems. In *Proc. of Collaboration between Human and Artificial Societies conference*, pages 284–300, 2000.

50. F. van Harmelen. How the Semantic Web will change KR: challenges and opportunities for a new research agenda. *The Knowledge Engineering Review*, 17(1):93–96, 2002.

51. R. Volz, D. Oberle, S. Staab, and B. Motik. KAON server: A Semantic Web management system. In *Proc. of the 12th Int. World Wide Web Conf. (WWW'03)*, 2003.

52. C. Walton. Model Checking Multi-Agent Web Services. In *Proc. of the AAAI Spring Symposium on Semantic Web Services*, 2004.

53. D. N. Walton and E. C. W. Krabbe. *Commitment in Dialogue: Basic Concepts of Interpersonal Reasoning*. SUNY Press, 1995.

54. M. Wooldridge. Semantic issues in the verification of agent communication languages. *Autonomous Agents and Multi-Agent Systems*, 3(1):9–31, 2000.

55. B. Yu and M. Singh. An evidential model of distributed reputation management. In *Proc. of the 1st Int. Joint Conf. On Autonomous Agents and Multi-Agent Systems (AAMAS'02)*, pages 294–301, 2002.

Metadata-Driven Personal Knowledge Publishing

Ikki Ohmukai[1], Hideaki Takeda[2], Masahiro Hamasaki[1], Kosuke Numa[1], and
Shin Adachi[3]

[1] Graduate University for Advanced Studies,
2-1-2 Hitotsubashi, Chiyoda-ku, Tokyo, Japan,
i2k@grad.nii.ac.jp,
http://www-kasm.nii.ac.jp/~i2k/
[2] National Institute of Informatics,
2-1-2 Hitotsubashi, Chiyoda-ku, Tokyo, Japan
[3] Waseda University,
3-4-1 Okubo, Shinjuku-ku, Tokyo, Japan

Abstract. We propose a personal knowledge publishing system called
Semblog is realized with integration of Semantic Web techniques and Weblog tools. Semblog suite provides an integrated environment for gathering, authoring, publishing, and making human relationship seamlessly
to enable people to exchange information and knowledge with easy and
casual fashion. We use a lightweight metadata format like RSS to activate the information flow and its activities. We define three level of
interest of information gathering and publishing i.e., "check", "clip" and
"post" and provide suitable ways to distribute information depending
on the interest level. Our system called Semblog platform consists of two
types of extended content aggregator and information retrieval / recommendation applications. We also design a new metadata module to
define personal ontology that realizes semantic relations among people
and Weblog sites.

1   Introduction

We propose a personal knowledge publishing system called *Semblog* is realized
with integration of Semantic Web techniques and Weblog tools. Semblog suite
provides an integrated environment for gathering, authoring, publishing, and
making human relationship seamlessly to enable people to exchange information
and knowledge with easy and casual fashion.

   We are aiming to build systems that support not only human information
but also human communication activities. We show the scheme of human information and communication activities in Fig.1. It is an extension of "Activities
and Relationships Table" proposed by Shneiderman[1]. The first layer has three
elements that concern information handling, i.e., collect, create and donate information. Three activities form a cycle, i.e., they are invoked repeatedly. The
second layer has also three elements that concerns communication handling, i.e.,

S.A. McIlraith et al. (Eds.): ISWC 2004, LNCS 3298, pp. 591–604, 2004.

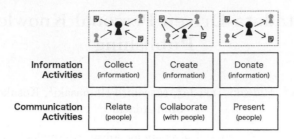

Information **Activities**	Collect (information)	Create (information)	Donate (information)
Communication **Activities**	Relate (people)	Collaborate (with people)	Present (people)

Fig. 1. Information and Communication Activities

relate, collaborate and present people. They also form a cycle. The two layers are not isolated rather closely related. Organization of information in the first layer is performed by the communication process of multiple people in the second layer. It implies that support for information activities requires support for communication activities, and vice versa.

We set Weblog as a platform for systems to support human information and communalization activities, because Weblog supports more these activities than Web. Web only supports publishing of information, and other information activities are left to other services like HTML editors and search engines. Weblog directly supports authoring and publishing in an integrated way, and furthermore it commits communication activities. Weblog users tend to refer to each other and form so-called "Weblog communities", and Weblog tools support such communication like TrackBack and ping. But the support is partially, indirectly, and not integrated.

Semblog suites extend Weblogs by adding flexible but uniform operations for Weblog sites and entries like aggregation and clipping, and facilities for searching and contacting to other Weblog sites. It means that Semblog suite supports communication activities as well as information activities.

The organization of the paper is as follows; in the following section, we discuss relationship between Weblog and Semantic Web. Then we identify architecture of Semblog in Section 4. We describe details of Semblog suites, first platforms of Semblog and then applications of Semblog in Section 5 and 6 respectively. We furthermore introduce ontology in Semblog platform in Section 6. Finally we conclude the paper in Section 7.

2   Semantic Web and Weblog

In this section, we overview the current situation of information distribution on Web, Semantic Web and Weblog. Web lacks functionality of information distribution and Semantic Web aims to fulfill the functionality by metadata. We support Semantic Web approach but it has difficulty of metadata annotation. So we focus on Weblog that also use metadata for information distribution.

2.1   Information Processing with Semantic Web Techniques

We propose a content distribution support system for individuals with Semantic Web techniques. Information distribution process does not mean just publishing but an integrated process containing information gathering and authoring. In the current web, however, there is no framework to support the whole process of information distribution despite the fact that Berners-Lee specified the first world wide web to support both authoring and publishing process equally[2]. Protrusion of information publishing just accelerates so-called information overload.

There is a great hope that the Semantic Web technologies will resolve information overload. According to the manifesto[3], Semantic Web is an environment, which consists of the contents with machine-readable (semantic) tags and the software agents, to realize autonomous information distribution and syndication. Resource Description Framework (RDF)[4] and other ontology definition languages[5] are recommended by W3C as elemental technologies of the Semantic Web and these are now in practical use.

However it is difficult to produce contents with semantic tags because of their complicated syntax and vocabulary. Ordinary people hardly find a merit of semantic annotation although it is a time-consuming task. It is also impossible to annotate the semantic tags to existing enormous information on the Internet. There are some researches about automatic annotation with AI techniques and natural language processing[6] however their effects are still unclear.

In our approach, we use lightweight metadata formats, i.e., RSS 1.0 (RDF Site Summary[7]), to activate the information flow and its activities. RSS is one of the metadata to describe a summary of a web site. It contains general attributes of the site i.e. title and publisher's name of the web site, and excerpt and updated date of its contents. A number of web sites already publish RSS metadata, and several applications and services called RSS aggregator are provided based on this trend.

An aggregator collects these RSS from various web sites and reform them to organize this large amount of contents to show at a glance. There are two types of aggregator; one is a standalone application that is executed on client PCs. The other is an aggregation service that runs on the internet server and the user access via her/his web browser. The former applications provide rapid browsing of RSS by their flexible user interface and the latter enables the user to access their information wherever she/he is.

Use of RSS and the aggregator decreases information gathering, but it is just a part of information distribution process as we mentioned. Gathering should be related to information authoring and publishing otherwise it will be another search engines without any selection or extraction.

2.2   Information Creation with Weblog

Weblog is one of the most advanced systems that use metadata in gathering, creating and publishing.

Recently Weblog has come into the spotlight in the Web[8]. There is no strict definition about Weblog but it is recognized as a web site that consists of miscellaneous notes updated daily[9]. In such sites the authors do not make efforts to knit up these contents because Weblog tools align them in chronological order with a well-designed HTML format. We call these frequently posted contents as small contents in this paper. Small contents include various subjects including journal, expertise and critique. One of most popular topics is the introductions and comments of the web sites ranging from news sites to the other small contents. Some Weblog sites attract the attention with their own editorial policy. The authors of Weblog sites reedit the existing web contents by quoting them. Moreover there are new types of Weblogs that criticize the other Weblogs so that these Weblogs are regarded to organize the "Weblog community". Now there are millions of weblog sites in the World. It is a surprising number because these people are now active information creators and distributors as well as information receivers thanks to weblog.

Most of Weblog sites use so-called Weblog tools that are a kind of content management systems (CMS). Weblog tools enable the author to describe and edit the small contents via a web browser and transform the contents form text format to HTML files. These tools are implemented based on MVC (Model / View / Controller) model which is the fundamental concept of web applications. The author defines a view template once then do not have to decorate the contents with various HTML tags. This model decreases the cost of publication remarkably in comparison with traditional style that requires local text editor and FTP. This feature contributes abundant production of the small contents.

Weblog tools usually generate RSS automatically. General attributes such as publisher's name are set as a profile by the user. Excerpt and updated date of each content are generated by the tools. Most of distributed RSS are generated by these Weblog tools. Main purpose of RSS aggregator is also to browse the Weblog site. Currently the number of news site feeding RSS is expanding.

3   Semblog Architecture

We propose a personal publishing system using Semantic Web techniques and Weblog tools. The system supports the whole process of information distribution which includes gathering, authoring and publishing. Furthermore it connects information distribution process of different people seamlessly, i.e., it also supports finding collaborating and advertising people for information distribution.

We divide system architecture into the following four levels, i.e., metadata format, metadata management, metadata aggregator, and metadata application. In Weblog, they correspond to RSS, Weblog tools, RSS aggregator, and various applications on Weblog respectively. In Semblog, Metadata on person and interpersonal relations is added in order to include activities on the communication levels. We adopt FOAF (Friend-Of-A-Friend) as person metadata. Content (RSS) and person metadata should be processed seamlessly in every level.

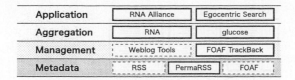

Fig. 2. Semblog Architecture

We build our systems by integrating new technologies and existing technologies shown in Fig.2. A box with solid line indicates our proposal and a box with dashed line an existing one.

In the following two sections, we explain platforms and application of Semblog. The former corresponds the first three levels and the latter the last level.

4   Semblog Platform

Fig.3 shows the system architecture of Semblog platform. Semblog system consists of the two types of extended RSS aggregator, semblog applications and conventional Weblog tools. Each module exchanges data in RSS format and communicates with XML-RPC protocol[10] for dynamic invocation. We use Movable Type system as Weblog tool[11], which supports RSS and XML-RPC call. In this section, we explain extended RSS aggregators that support authoring and publishing with different levels of interest.

4.1   Different Levels of Interest

We define the level of interest of information gathering and publishing i.e., "check", "clip" and "post". Our system provides different ways to distribute information depend on the interest level.

"Check" means that the user routinely browses particular web sites and information sources. The user does not know "what" is described at those sites exactly but she/he knows "what kind" of contents are included in these sites. We assume that these "what kind" knowledge are important for information distribution so that our system supports the user to present her/his interest by publishing the list of URIs she/he always accesses.

"Clip" makes shortcut to a content to which the user has strong interest among various contents of "Checked" sites. Our system automatically publishes the list of "clipped" contents. We suppose that "clip" link presents stronger interest of the user than "check" link because it points individual content directly. In addition, contents of "checked" links are changing momentary but those of "clipped" links are persistent (called "Permalink").

Online bookmark systems were developed for the same objective. These systems make a backup of "bookmark" or "favorite" of the user's web browser and she/he can obtain the list from anywhere. The user can also make the list to be public or not so the list will be a web content. However that bookmark is only

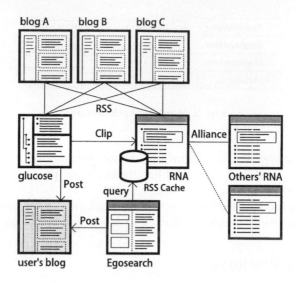

Fig. 3. System Architecture

a static list of URIs and is lacking functions for change in time. Therefore these online bookmark systems are not useful for everyone except the user.

Conventional bookmark systems do not distinguish the URIs between to a site and content. It is necessary to switch the way to distribute these links because they have different level of interest as described above.

"Post" means that the user quotes content, adds some comment, and publishes it as new information. In that case the user presents not only strong interest but also her/his personal opinion. In our system, "post" type of information publication is made by the Weblog tools.

Providing different levels for publishing reduces the psychological burden of publishing. In standard BBSs, it is said that lurkers show feeling of belonging to communities in sprite of their reluctant behavior[12]. This is important to involve ordinary people into the cycle of information gathering and publishing.

The all process is realized by metadata handling therefore it is open to other systems and applications. It enables seamless connection of information distribution of different people.

4.2 RNA: RSS Aggregation Service

RNA is an extended RSS aggregator described with Perl CGI. Fig.4(left) shows a snapshot of RNA. The user puts this script to her/his own web server and operates it. Basic function and interface of RNA are shown below.

- RSS registration and loading
  The user should register RSS in a configuration interface. Once she/he enters the URIs of RSS, RNA obtains these RSS files via HTTP. The user is able to

Fig. 4. Snapshot of RNA (left) and Glucose (right)

classify each RSS using categories. The list of registered sites is transformed into RSS and it can be used by the other applications. RNA can also import or export an OPML file which is standard format for the bookmarks.

– Building RSS tree

RNA parses multiple RSSs from various sites and builds a "global" RSS tree from each RSS tree. The global tree stores all information obtained by RNA. Next RNA recomposes the global tree into several sub trees according to rule templates. In default setting, RNA reproduces three types of sub trees i.e., list of contents sorted by chronological order and updated contents in each site. The user can describe own template script to generate a new sub tree.

– RSS redistribution

Generated sub trees are distributed as new RSS and are visualized by server / client side XSLT engine using XSL stylesheet. RNA can also transform these RSS into HTML with its own template system. With these templates, the user is easily able to customize an output style rather than XSLT since the syntax of template is similar to HTML.

– Content clipping

The user can register content to a clip list in one click. Clipped contents are stored in "clipped" RSS tree and it is published like the other RSS. Each element of RSS tree is changing momentary but those of "clipped" tree are persistent.

– Updating

It is necessary to get RSS and build trees occasionally since its contents are changeable with update of its distributor. RNA can update periodically by a Cron interface of the server. Update interface can be called both manually and remotely by XML-RPC message the Weblog tools automatically generated. The latter feature enables the author of a Weblog to notify her/his new content to RNA.

– TrackBack tracing

RNA also queries to registered Weblog tools whether its content has Track-Back links (reverse link provided by Weblog tools) or not. If exist, RNA extracts these links and adds them to RSS tree.

– Sanitizing and caching RSS

RNA checks syntax of acquired RSS and corrects them if they are not valid. Currently three versions of RSS are proposed i.e., 0.91, 1.0 and 2.0. RNA converts all versions into 1.0, which is based on RDF model. Every RSS is cached and decomposed to attach to each content as a fine-grained metadata.

"Antenna" services are already provided to check update of registered sites. Conventional antenna obtains HTTP LastModified header of each URI and sorts the site list by chronological order. Using RNA the user can get richer information than the antenna since RSS contains not only updated time but its excerpt and so on. RNA also enables the user to edit information in the contents level such as clip and TrackBack tracing.

4.3   Glucose: Standalone RSS Aggregator

Glucose is also an extended RSS aggregator but a standalone program for Windows. Fig.4(right) shows a snapshot of Glucose. Unlike orthodox aggregators, Glucose is developed to support information distribution process by coordination with RNA. Main functions and interfaces of Glucose are shown below.

- RSS registration
  Like in RNA, the user registers URIs of RSS or OPML site list. Glucose can access several news sites without RSS by "sensor" script which extracts articles and converts them to RSS.
- Three-pane interface
  Glucose has three panes interface. The left pane shows "RSS Channels" which is subscribed by the user. The upper right pane indicates the headline list of contents including title, updated time, source and category. The lower right pane shows original contents.
- TrackBack tracing
  Glucose can extract TrackBack links from each content. Obtained links are shown below the corresponding entry in headline pane with "Re:" just like a mailer.
- Posting to Weblog
  With a Weblog editor interface in Glucose, the user can post an entry to her/his Weblog if she/he has strong interest for content. This interface uses XML-RPC protocol.
- RNA clipping
  The user can post content to the clip list of own RNA using XML-RPC.
- P2P content recommendation
  Glucose runs as a P2P servant and the users automatically construct P2P network. In this network, several contents read by someone are distributed randomly and the other user may receive these contents as a recommendation. The user can clip or post it to her/his own system and can also register URI of its RSS to the site list.

We distribute RNA and Glucose in our web site (http://www.semblog.org/wiki/?en). About 2000 users downloaded RNA and over 20000 users downloaded Glucose from September 2003.

5   Application on Semblog Platform

Using functions on Semblog platform, we develop a new type of recommendation and retrieval systems.

5.1   RNA Alliance

Each RNA has XML-RPC interface that can send and receive its data dynamically. RNA alliance is a content recommendation system based on cooperation of multiple RNA.

We use FOAF metadata to identify each RNA. FOAF is RDF-based metadata format for describing human relationship. Besides the basic elements such as name, email and URI of the user, FOAF provides a statement that user X knows user Y.

The current version of RNA can generate FOAF data. RNA also has an interface for FOAF management to extend social network easily. We call this method as "FOAF TrackBack".

First the user X enters an RNA URI of the user Y in her/his own FOAF manager. The manager X asks the manager Y to acquire the FOAF data of Y, and writes "X knows Y" link in its FOAF. The manager Y records "Y isKnown X" link in its FOAF and notifies to the user Y. If the user Y agrees, her/his manager registers "Y knows X" link. Repeating this process, a personal network of the user is constructed. Following recommendation methods are performed in the network.

Collaborative Recommendation. Collaborative recommendation is based on difference of registered sites or clips among multiple RNAs. At first it calculates similarities: S_i between the user's RNA: R_0 and a RNA on the personal network: R_i $(1 < i < n)$. Each RNA has a list of URIs: $R_i = \{u_0, \dots, u_k\}$.

$$S_i = \frac{|R_0 \cap R_i|}{|R_0| + |R_i|}$$

The system gives recommendation score: $V(u)$ to each URI by the following formula:

$$V_i(u) = \begin{cases} S_i & \text{if } u \in R_i \\ 0 & \text{if } u \notin R_i \ (i = 1, \dots, n) \end{cases}$$

$$V(u) = \frac{\sum_{i=i}^{n} V_i(u)}{n}$$

This score is used for recommendation to R_0's user if URI u is not included in R_0.

The system shows the list of recommended URIs sorted by the score. The user can add these URI to her/his own "check" list.

Categorical Similarity and Recommendation. The user of RNA can categorize the sites and clips she/he registered. Using this category, relationship of *interest* among users can be identified and recommended. We apply a recommendation method based on a categorical similarity to this objective[13].

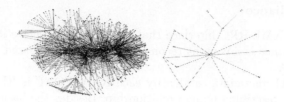

Fig. 5. Document-based (left) and Person-based (right) Network

Relational Filtering. Relational filtering method realizes access control of information using the categorized social network. By merging the personal network of every user, a large human network like a small world is constructed. This method extracts multiple communities from this network and enables information sharing in single community[14]. The user can manage her/his contents which have various level of disclosure through an unified interface.

5.2 Egocentric Search

Egocentric search provides subjective search which collects and evaluates information for each user[15]. We think that it is suitable for handling of the small contents like Weblog entries because connection is usually more subjective than other Web pages.

The users daily write and post contents to their Weblog sites with the editor interface. Egocentric search interface scans a content that the user is posting. If this content contains a hyperlink, the editor acquires the whole content and RSS of the link, and constructs an entry network around the user's content (Fig.5(left)). This network indicates not only relations of contents but also human relationships because all entries on Weblog are owned by some authors. Our method organizes a document network into person-based network (Fig.5(right)). Each path of the personal network is weighted relatively to the frequency of citation. Once the user cites some site as a topic in the new content (entry), the editor interface performs egocentric search and shows the result.

– Relative Chain Search
  Relative chain search returns the contents which is directly linked with the entry cited by the authoring content. This model is based on a simple model but consequently it seems most trustful. (Fig.6(a))
– Co-citation Search
  Co-citation search discovers the entries that link the same contents as the authoring entry links to. Co-citation entries are retrieved from the RSS cache and the search result contains the weight of authors. (Fig.6(b))
– Keyword Search
  Keyword search method picks up the entries by keyword matching from the RSS cache. Unlike the conventional search engines, our method targets only related sites around the user's Weblog. (Fig.6(c))

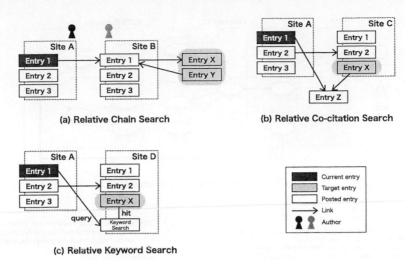

(a) Relative Chain Search

(b) Relative Co-citation Search

(c) Relative Keyword Search

Fig. 6. Egocentric Search Methods

The user can read search results by these methods with the right-hand side window while authoring, and can append the link of some helpful contents to the currently authoring content. This process expects to enrich the user's content and change the search result of the system in turn.

6 Personal Ontology

We propose a bottom-up personal ontology framework using RSS and FOAF metadata. To process small contents in various forms, we have to annotate a semantic markup with an ontology language to those contents. It is difficult to organize practical ontology hierarchy with top-down approach because building and maintaining such well-organized large ontology takes a lot of efforts. We aim to develop loose and bottom-up ontology system by combining personal classification, because we consider that personal knowledge will be represented with a routine work such as categorization and arrangement of information. Fig.9 indicates a conceptual architecture of the personal ontology system.

At first we define a personal ontology as a hierarchical system of categories. Everyone has those categories, and they routinely classify described and collected contents to the category. A label of a category can be named arbitrarily by user.

Unlike the conventional ontology, the personal ontology has to be related to the person who produces it. Therefore we apply FOAF metadata to link between the ontology and the person.

Personal ontology metadata consists of FOAF, RDFS Ontology and Contents RSS. The FOAF describes personal information, and the RDFS ontology shows a structure of the categories, and the contents RSS shows written and collected contents by the user.

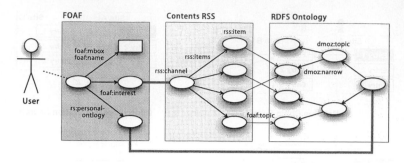

Fig. 7. Personal Ontology Framework

```
<rdf:RDF
 xmlns:rdf="http://www.w3.org/1999/02/22-rdf-syntax-ns#"
 xmlns:foaf="http://xmlns.com/foaf/0.1/"
 xmlns:rdfs="http://www.w3.org/2000/01/rdf-schema#"
 xmlns:rs="http://www.roughsemantics.org/rs/0.1/"
>

<foaf:Person>
<foaf:name>Ikki Ohmukai</foaf:name>
<foaf:nick>i2k</foaf:nick>
<foaf:mbox rdf:resource="mailto:i2k@grad.nii.ac.jp" />
<foaf:weblog rdf:resource="http://www.semblog.org/i2k/" />
<rdfs:seeAlso rdf:resource="http://www-kasm.nii.ac.jp/~i2k/foaf.rdf" />
<foaf:interest rdf:resource="http://www-kasm.nii.ac.jp/~i2k/index.rdf" />
<rs:personalontology
        rdf:resource="http://www-kasm.nii.ac.jp/~i2k/ontology.rdf" />
....

</foaf:Person>
</rdf:RDF>
```

(a) Extended FOAF

```
<RDF xmlns:rdf="http://www.w3.org/TR/RDF/"
     xmlns:dc="http://purl.org/dc/elements/1.0/"
     xmlns="http://directory.mozilla.org/rdf">

<Topic rdf:id="Top">
  <tag catid="1"/>
  <dc:Title>Top</dc:Title>
  <narrow rdf:resource="Top/Arts"/>
  <narrow rdf:resource="Top/Business"/>
  <narrow rdf:resource="Top/Economy"/>
  <narrow rdf:resource="Top/Tech"/>
  ....
</Topic>

<Topic rdf:id="Top/Arts">
  <tag catid="2"/>
  <dc:Title>Top/Arts</dc:Title>
  <narrow rdf:resource="Top/Arts/Fine"/>
  ....
</Topic>
```

(b) RDFS Ontology

```
<item rdf:about="http://www.semblog.org/i2k/archives/000304.html">
<title>Blog Hacks</title>
<link>http://www.semblog.org/i2k/archives/000304.html</link>
<description>
Monday's child is fair of face, Tuesday's child is full of grace,
Wednesday's child is full of woe, Thursday's child has far to go,
Friday's child is loving and giving, Saturday's child works hard for his living,
And the child that is born on the Sabbath day is bonny and blithe, and good and gay. ...
</description>
<dc:subject>trivia</dc:subject>
<foaf:topic rdf:resource="http://www-kasm.nii.ac.jp/~i2k/ontology.rdf#Top/Arts">
<dc:creator>i2k</dc:creator>
<dc:date>2004-04-09T01:24:16+09:00</dc:date>
</item>
```

(c) Contents RSS

Fig. 8. Personal Ontology Metadata

We add two elements to basic FOAF model shown in Fig.8 (a). One is <foaf:interest> which is to point the contents RSS, and the other is <rs:personalontology> that is originally defined by our Rough Semantics project (http://www.roughsemantics.org/) to indicate the RDFS ontology.

The RDFS ontology is described with the form of Open Directory RDFS format shown in Fig.8 (b). Each node has a fragment ID.

The contents RSS is similar to a conventional RSS. Our RSS uses <foaf:topic> to point a category on the RDFS ontology, while the conven-

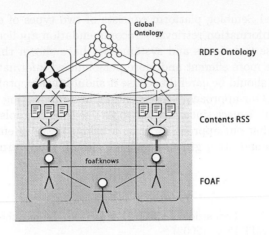

Fig. 9. Bottom-up Ontology

tional model applies `<dc:subject>` to express a thesis of a content. This makes our RSS to have backward compatibility. Example of this RSS is shown in Fig.8 (c). It should be noted that topics pointed by this tag are not restricted to those in their own ontology, rather any topics in others' and some global ontology. Separating ontology and instances enables such flexible management.

FOAF, RDFS ontology, and RSS are described in separate files so that we can keep compatibility with existing applications on these formats. This is a great benefit that our system can cope with such existing applications via these files.

Our framework enables applications and services to produce new types of search or recommendation. For example, mapping methods between two directories or bookmarks are applicable to the personal ontology. Egocentric search is also able to realize easily by building a social network with `<foaf:knows>` in the users' FOAF.

Unlike these peer-to-peer model, we can calculate a similarity among a personal ontology and the global ontologies such like WordNet and ODP in advance. Multiple personal ontology can be matched each other via the global ontology and this method needs less computation cost as shown in Fig.9. In addition, it is not necessary to modify that algorithm in P2P model and personal-global model because both ontology has the same structure.

7   Conclusion

In this paper we propose a personal publishing system with Semantic Web techniques and Weblog tools. We use a lightweight metadata format like RSS to activate the information flow and its activities. We define three level of interest of information gathering and publishing i.e., "check", "clip" and "post" and provide suitable ways to distribute information depending on the interest level.

Our system called Semblog platform consists of two types of extended content aggregator and information retrieval / recommendation applications.

Through these techniques and systems, we have shown that metadata can be used to realize more efferent and more personalized information distribution. Metadata design should be careful because it should be acceptable by many people and systems. Our approach, i.e., extending and integrating RSS and FOAF, is successful in this aspect since existing tools like Weblog tools are ready to use them. We hope that our approach will be a bridge between emerging Semantic Web technologies and other growing technologies on the Internet.

References

1. Shneiderman, B.: Leonardo's Laptop: Human Needs and the New Computing Technologies. MIT Press (2002)
2. Berners-Lee, T.: Weaving the Web. HarperCollins (1999)
3. Berners-Lee, T.: A roadmap to the Semantic Web. http://www.w3.org/DesignIssues/Semantic.html (1998)
4. World Wide Web Consortium (W3C): Resource Description Framework (RDF) Model and Syntax Specification. http://www.w3.org/TR/REC-rdf-syntax (1999)
5. World Wide Web Consortium (W3C): OWL Web Ontology Language Overview. http://www.w3.org/TR/owl-features/ (2003)
6. Dill, S., Eiron, N., Gibson, D., et al.: SemTag and Seeker: Bootstrapping the Semantic Web via Automated Semantic Annotation. Proceedings of the Twelfth International World Wide Web Conference (WWW2003) (2003)
7. RDF Site Summary 1.0 Specification Working Group: RDF Site Summary (RSS) 1.0. http://web.resource.org/rss/1.0/spec (2001)
8. Blood, R.: We've Got Blog: How Weblogs are Changing Our Culture. Perseus Publishing (2002)
9. Aimeur, E., Brassard, G., Paquet, S.: Using Personal Knowledge Publishing to Facilitate Sharing Across Communities. Workshop on (Virtual) Community Informatics, Held in conjunction with the Twelfth International World Wide Web Conference (WWW2003) (2003)
10. UserLand Software: XML-RPC Specification. http://www.xmlrpc.com/spec (1999)
11. Six Apart: Movable Type. http://www.movabletype.org/ (2003)
12. B.Nonnecke, J.Preece: Shedding light on Lurkers in Online Communities. Ethnographic Studies in Real and Virtual Environments: Inhabited Information Spaces and Connected Communities (1999) 123–128
13. M.Hamasaki, H.Takeda: Find better friends? – re-configuration of personal networks by the neighborhood matchmaker method –. In: The International Workshop on Semantic Web Foundations and Application Technologies (SWFAT). (2003) 73–76
14. I.Ohmukai, H.Takeda: Social Scheduler: A Proposal of Collaborative Personal Task Management. Proceedings of Web Intelligence (WI2003) (2003)
15. I.Ohmukai, K.Numa, H.Takeda: Egocentric Search Method for Authoring Support in Semantic Weblog. Workshop on Knowledge Markup and Semantic Annotation (Semannot2003), the Second International Conference on Knowledge Capture (K-CAP2003) (2003)

An Extensible Directory Enabling Efficient Semantic Web Service Integration

Ion Constantinescu, Walter Binder, and Boi Faltings

Artificial Intelligence Laboratory
Swiss Federal Institute of Technology,
IN (Ecublens), CH–1015 Lausanne, Switzerland.
{ion.constantinescu,walter.binder,boi.faltings}@epfl.ch

Abstract. In an open environment populated by large numbers of heterogeneous information services, integration is a major challenge. In such a setting, the efficient coupling between directory-based service discovery and service composition engines is crucial. In this paper we present a directory service that offers specific functionality in order to enable efficient service integration. The directory implementation relies on a compact numerical encoding of service parameters and on a multidimensional index structure. It supports isolated service integration sessions providing a consistent view of the directory data. During a session a client may issue multiple queries to the directory and retrieve the results incrementally. In order to optimize the interaction of the directory with different service composition algorithms, the directory supports custom ranking functions that are dynamically installed with the aid of mobile code. The ranking functions are written in Java, but the directory service imposes severe restrictions on the programming model in order to protect itself against malicious or erroneous code (e.g., denial-of-service attacks). With the aid of user-defined ranking functions, application-specific ordering heuristics can be deployed directly. Experiments on randomly generated problems show that they significantly reduce the number of query results that have to be transmitted to the client by up to **5 times**.[1]

Keywords: Incremental service integration, service directories, service discovery, service ranking.

1 Introduction

Service composition is an exciting area which has received a significant amount of interest in the last period. Initial approaches to web service composition [28] used a simple forward chaining technique which can result in the discovery of large numbers of services. There is a good body of work which tries to address the service composition problem by applying planning techniques based either on theorem proving (e.g., Golog [21,22], SWORD [24]) or on hierarchical task planning (e.g., SHOP-2 [32]).

[1] Work presented in this paper was partly carried out in the framework of the EPFL Center for Global Computing and supported by the Swiss National Science Foundation as part of the project MAGIC (FNRS-68155), as well as by the Swiss National Funding Agency OFES as part of the European projects KnowledgeWeb (FP6-507482) and DIP (FP6-507483).

S.A. McIlraith et al. (Eds.): ISWC 2004, LNCS 3298, pp. 605–619, 2004.

The advantage of this kind of approach is that complex constructs like loops (Golog) or processes (SHOP-2) can be handled. All these approaches assume that the relevant service descriptions are initially loaded into the reasoning engine and that no discovery is performed during composition.

Still the current and future state of affairs regarding web services will be quite different since due to the large number of services and to the loose coupling between service providers and consumers we expect that services will be indexed in directories. Consequently, planning algorithms will have to be adapted to a situation where operators are not known a priori, but have to be retrieved through queries to these directories. Recently, Lassila and Dixit [19] have addressed the problem of interleaving discovery and integration in more detail, but they have considered only simple workflows where services have one input and one output.

Our approach to automated service composition is based on matching input and output parameters of services using type information in order to constrain the ways how services may be composed [12]. Our composition algorithm allows for *partially matching* types and handles them by computing and introducing *switches* in the integration plan. Experimental results carried out in various domains show that using partial matches decreases the failure rate by up to *7 times* compared with an integration algorithm that supports only complete matches [12].

We have developed a directory service with specific features to ease and make more efficient service composition but without fully solving it. Queries may not only search for complete matches, but may also retrieve *partially matching* directory entries [10]. As the number of (partially) matching entries may be large, the directory supports *incremental retrieval* of the results of a query. This is achieved through *sessions*, during which a client issues queries and retrieves the results in chunks of limited size. Sessions are well isolated from each other, also concurrent modifications of the directory (i.e., new service registrations, updates, and removal of services from the directory) do not affect the sequence of results after a query has been issued. We have implemented a simple but very efficient concurrency control scheme which may delay the visibility of directory updates but does not require any synchronization activities within sessions. Hence, our concurrency control mechanism has no negative impacts on the scalability with respect to the number of concurrent sessions [9].

As in a large-scale directory the number of (partially) matching results for a query may be very high, it is crucial to order the result set within the directory according to heuristics and transfer first the better matches to the client. If the ranking heuristics work well, only a small part of the possibly large result set has to be transferred, thus saving network bandwidth and boosting the performance of a directory client that executes a service composition algorithm (the results are returned incrementally, once a result fulfills the client's requirements, no further results need to be transmitted). However, the ranking heuristics depend on the concrete composition algorithm. For each service composition algorithm (e.g., forward chaining, backward chaining, etc.), a different ranking heuristic may be better adapted. Because research on service composition is still in the beginning and the directory cannot anticipate the needs of all possible service integration algorithms, our directory supports *user-defined ranking functions*.

Custom ranking-functions allow the execution of user-defined application-specific heuristics directly within the directory, close to the data, in order to transfer the best results for a query first. They dramatically increase the flexibility of our directory, as the client is able to tailor the processing of directory queries according to its needs. The ranking functions are written in Java and dynamically installed during service composition sessions by means of *mobile code*. Because the support of mobile code increases the vulnerability of systems and custom ranking functions may be abused for various kinds of attacks, such as denial-of-service attacks consuming a vast amount of memory and processing resources within the directory, our directory imposes severe restrictions on the code of these functions.

As the main contributions of this paper, we show how our directory supports service integration sessions and user-defined ranking functions. We present some parts of the session API and explain the restricted programming model for ranking functions. Moreover, we explain how our directory protects itself against malicious code. Performance evaluations point up the necessity to support heuristic ranking functions that are tailored to specific service composition algorithms.

This paper is structured as follows: In Section 2 we explain how service descriptions can be numerically encoded as sets of intervals and we give an overview of the index structure for multidimensional data on which our directory implementation is based. In Section 3 we discuss extensions of the directory specific to service composition that enable consistent views of the directory data during the service integration process. In Section 4 we show how the directory can be dynamically extended by user-defined ranking functions. We discuss some implementation details, in particular showing how the directory protects itself against malicious code. In Section 5 we present some experimental results that illustrate the need for dynamically installing application-specific heuristic ranking functions. Finally, Section 6 concludes this paper.

2   Service Composition with Directories

Since we assume a large-scale open environment with a high number of available services, the integration process has to be able to discover relevant services incrementally through queries to the service directory. Interleaving the integration process with service discovery in a large-scale directory is a novelty of our approach.

Our composition algorithm builds on forward chaining, a technique well known for planning [6] and more recently for service integration [28]. Most previous work on service composition has required an explicit specification of the control flow between basic services in order to provide value-added services.

For instance, in the eFlow system [8], a composite service is modeled as a graph that defines the order of execution of different processes. The Self-Serv framework [2] uses a subset of statecharts to describe the control flow within a composite service. The Business Process Execution Language for Web Services (BPEL4WS) [7] addresses compositions where the control flow of the process and the bindings between services are known in advance. In service composition using Golog [22], logical inferencing techniques are applied to pre-defined plan templates.

More recently, planning techniques have been applied to the service integration problem [25,33,34]. Such an approach does not require a pre-defined process model of the composite service, but returns a possible control flow as a result. Other approaches to planning, such as planning as model checking [15], are being considered for web service composition and would allow more complex constructions such as loops.

Informally, the idea of composition with forward chaining is to iteratively apply a possible service S to a set of input parameters provided by a query Q (i.e., all inputs required by S have to be available). If applying S does not solve the problem (i.e., still not all the outputs required by the query Q are available) then a new query Q' can be computed from Q and S and the whole process is iterated. This part of our framework corresponds to the planning techniques currently used for service composition [28]. Details on our service composition algorithm, which also supports partial matches, can be found in [12].

2.1   Directories of Web Services

Currently, UDDI is the state of the art for directories of web services (see [9] for an overview of other service directory systems). The standard is clear in terms of data models and query API, but suffers from the fact that it considers service descriptions to be completely opaque.

A more complex method for discovering relevant services from a directory of advertisements is matchmaking. In this case the directory query (requested capabilities) is formulated in the form of a service description template that presents all the features of interest. This template is then compared with all the entries in the directory and the results that have features compatible with the features of interest are returned. A good amount of work exists in the area of matchmaking including LARKS [27], and the newer efforts geared towards OWL-S [23]. Other approaches include the Ariadne mediator [17].

Regarding service descriptions, in this paper we partially build on existing developments, such as [31], [1], and [13], by considering a simple table-based formalism where each service is described through a set of tuples mapping service parameters (unique names of inputs or outputs) to parameter types (the spaces of possible values for a given parameter). For efficiency reasons, we represent the DG numerically. Details concerning the encoding can be found in [10].

2.2   Match Types

We consider four match relations between a query Q and a service S (see example for input parameters in Fig. 1):

- **Exact** - S is an exact match of Q.
- **PlugIn** - S is a plug-in match for Q, if S could be always used instead of Q.
- **Subsumes** - Q contains S. In this case S could be used under the condition that Q satisfies some additional runtime constraints such that it is specific enough for S.
- **Overlap** - Q and S have a given intersection. In this case, runtime constraints both over Q and S have to be taken into account.

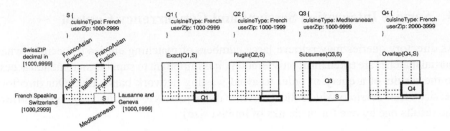

Fig. 1. Match types of inputs of query Q and service S by "precision": **Exact, PlugIn, Subsumes, Overlap**.

In the example we show how the match relation is determined between the inputs available from the queries Q1, Q2, Q3, Q4 and the inputs required by service S.

Given that a **Subsumes** match requires the specification of supplementary constraints we can order the types of match by "precision" as following: **Exact, PlugIn, Subsumes, Overlap**. We consider **Subsumes** and **Overlap** as "partial" matches. The first three relations have been previously identified by Paolucci in [23] and the forth, **Overlap**, was identified by Li [20] and Constantinescu [10].

Determining one match relation between a query description and a service description requires that subsequent relations are determined between all the inputs of the query Q and service S and between the outputs of the service S and query Q (note the reversed order of query and services in the match for outputs). Our approach is more complex than the one of Paolluci in that we take also into account the relations between the properties that introduce different inputs or outputs (equivalent to parameter names). This is important for disambiguating services with equivalent signatures (e.g., we can disambiguate two services that have two string outputs by knowing the names of the respective parameters).

2.3   Multidimensional Access Methods – GiST

The need for efficient discovery and matchmaking leads to a need for search structures and indexes for directories. We consider numerically encoded service descriptions as multidimensional data and use techniques related to the indexing of such kind of information in the directory. This approach leads to local response times in the order of milliseconds for directories containing tens of thousands (10^4) of service descriptions.

The indexing technique that we use is based on the Generalized Search Tree (GiST), proposed as a unifying framework by Hellerstein [16]. The design principle of GiST arises from the observation that search trees used in databases are balanced trees with a high fanout in which the internal nodes are used as a directory and the leaf nodes point to the actual data. Each internal node holds a key in the form of a predicate P and a number of pointers to other nodes (depending on system and hardware constraints, e.g., filesystem page size). To search for records that satisfy a query predicate Q, the paths of the tree that have keys P satisfying Q are followed.

3   Service Integration Sessions and Concurrency Control

As directory queries may retrieve large numbers of matching entries (especially when partial matches are taken into consideration), it is important to support incremental access to the results of a query in order to avoid wasting network bandwidth. Our directory service offers *sessions* which allow a user to issue queries to the directory and to retrieve the results one by one (or in chunks of limited size).

3.1   Session API

Fig. 2 presents the UML diagram of our directory service API. Sessions have a limited time-span after which session methods cannot be invoked anymore (timeout). The directory has per-session resource usage limits regarding the number of created ranking functions and the size of the result set of a query. The directory also checks for non-conforming ranking functions (see Section 4) and invalid service IDs.

The `Directory` interface is used to create a service integration session. Within a session several queries may be issued. The `Query` interface allows the sequential retrieval of query results, i.e., the directory entries that match the requirements of the query (see above Section 2.2 or [23]).

There is no particular order in which the results are returned (the order depends on the internal organization of the directory tree), unless a user-defined ranking function has been provided by the client (see Section 4). A session may define multiple ranking functions and associate a different ranking function with each query. Identifiers for declared ranking functions remain valid throughout a session, unless they are destroyed explicitly. Explicit destruction of ranking function IDs may be needed if the directory enforces a strict limit on the number of ranking functions active within a session. The ranking function is provided as bytecode of a compiled Java class.

The `getNextResult()` and `getNextResults()` methods do not return full service descriptions, but IDs that can be used later to retrieve the associated service description using the `getService()` method. The IDs remain valid and unique during the whole session. This approach allows the service integration client to cache retrieved service descriptions (the same service description may be returned in several queries) and thus helps to reduce the network traffic with the directory. The complete service description may be much larger than its ID of 64 bits.

Within a session several queries may be started in parallel. For each query the directory has to maintain some internal state. If there are too many concurrent queries in a session or a query requires too much processing or memory allocation within the

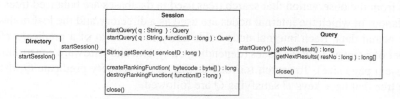

Fig. 2. The session API.

directory, an appropriate exception is thrown. When a session is closed, all its queries are closed automatically, too, and returned IDs of service descriptions may become invalid.

3.2   Session Implementation

The session guarantees a consistent view of the directory, i.e., the directory structure and contents as seen by a session does not change. Concurrent updates (service registration, update, and removal) do not affect the sequence of query results returned within a session; sessions are isolated from concurrent modifications.

Previous research work has addressed concurrency control in generalized search trees [18]. However, these concurrency control mechanisms only synchronize individual operations in the tree, whereas our directory supports long-lasting sessions during which certain parts of the tree structure must not be altered. This implies that insertion and deletion operations may not be performed concurrently with query sessions, as these operations may significantly change the structure of the tree (splitting or joining of nodes, balancing the tree, etc.).

The following assumptions underly the design of our concurrency control mechanism:

1. Read accesses (i.e., queries within sessions and the incremental retrieval of the results) will be much more frequent than updates.
2. High concurrency for read accesses (high number of concurrent query sessions).
3. Read accesses shall not be delayed.
4. Updates may become visible with a significant delay, but feedback concerning the update (success/failure) shall be returned immediately.
5. The duration of a session may be limited (timeout).

A simple solution would be to create a private copy of the result set of each query. However, as we want to support a high number of concurrent sessions, such an approach is inefficient, because it wastes memory and processing resources to copy the relevant data. Hence, such a solution may not scale well and is not in accord with our first two assumptions. Another solution would be to support transactions. However, this seems to be too heavy weight. The directory shall be optimized for the common case, i.e., for read accesses (first assumption). This distinguishes directory services from general-purpose databases. Concurrency protocols based on locking techniques are not in accord with these assumptions either. Because of assumption 3, sessions shall not have to wait for concurrent updates.

In order to meet the assumptions above, we have designed a mechanism which guarantees that sessions operate on read-only data structures that are not subject to changes. In our approach the in-memory structure of the directory tree (i.e., the directory index) is replicated up to 3 times, while the actual service descriptions are shared between the replicated trees.

When the directory service is started, the persistent representation of the directory tree is loaded into memory. This master copy of the directory tree is always kept up to date, i.e., updates are immediately applied to that master copy and are made persistent, too. Upon start of the directory service, a read-only copy of the in-memory master copy is allocated. Sessions operate only on this read-only copy. Hence, session management is trivial, there are no synchronization needs. Periodically, the master copy is duplicated to create a new read-only copy. Afterwards, new sessions are redirected to the new read-only copy. The old read-only copy is freed when the last session operating on it completes (either by an explicit session termination by the client or by a timeout).

We require the session timeout to be smaller than the update frequency of the read-only copy (the duplication frequency of the master copy). This condition ensures that there will be at most 3 copies of the in-memory representation of the directory at the same time: The master where updates are immediately applied (but which is not yet visible to sessions), as well as the previous 2 read-only copies used for sessions. When a new read-only copy is created, the old copy will remain active until the last session operating on it terminates; this time span is bounded by the session timeout.

In our approach only updates to the master copy are synchronized. Updates are immediately applied to the master copy (yielding immediate feedback to the client requesting an update). Only during copying the directory is blocked for further updates. In accord with the third assumption, the creation of sessions requires no synchronization.

4   Custom Ranking Functions

Sessions allow a service integration engine to incrementally retrieve service descriptions from the directory that (partially) match some of the requirements of the query. The order in which matching service descriptions are returned depends on the actual structure of the directory search tree. However, depending on the service integration algorithm, ordering the results of a query according to certain heuristics may significantly improve the performance of service composition. In order to avoid the transfer of a large number of service descriptions, the ranking and sorting according to application-dependent heuristics should occur directly within the directory. As for each service integration algorithm a different order may be advantageous, our directory allows its clients to define custom ranking functions which are used to sort the results of a query. This approach can be seen as a form of remote evaluation [14].

4.1   API for Ranking Functions

The ranking function receives as arguments information concerning the matching of a service description in the directory with the current query. It returns a value which represents the quality of the match. The bigger the return value, the better the service description matches the requirements of the query. The sequence of results as returned by the directory is sorted in descending order of the values calculated by the ranking function (a higher value means a better match). Results for which the ranking function evaluates to zero come at the end, a negative value for the ranking function indicates that the match is too poor to be returned, i.e., the result is discarded and not passed to the client.

As arguments the client-defined ranking function takes four ParamSet objects corresponding to the input and output parameter sets of the query, and respectively of the service. The `ParamSet` object provides methods like size, membership, union, intersection, and difference (see below Fig. 3). The size and membership methods have as single argument the current `ParamSet` object while the union, intersection and difference methods use two arguments - the current object and a second `ParamSet` object passed as parameter.

It is very important to note that some of the above methods address two different issues in the same time:

1. basic **set operations**, where a set member is defined through a parameter name and it's type ; for deciding the equality of parameters with same name and different types a user-specified expression is used.
2. **computation of new types** for some parameters in the resulting sets ; when a parameter is common to the two argument sets it's type in the resulting set is computed using a user-specified expression.

The explicit behavior of the `ParamSet` methods is the following:

– `size` - returns the number of parameters in the current set.
– `containsParam` - this method returns true when the current set contains a parameter with the same name as that passed as parameter regardless of it's type.
– `union` - this method returns all parameters in the two argument sets. For any parameter that is common to the two argument sets the type in the resulting set is computed accordingly to the user-specified expression `newTypeExpr`.
– `intersection` - this method returns the parameters that are common to the two sets **AND** for which the respective types conform to the equality test specified by the `eqTestExpr`. Those parameters are added to the resulting set, with a type computed accordingly to the user-specified expression `newTypeExpr`.
– `minus` - this method returns the parameters that are either present only in the `ParamSet` object on which the method is called or in the case of common parameters only those that **DO NOT** conform to the equality test specified by the `eqTestExpr`. For the latter kind of parameters the type in the resulting set is computed accordingly to the user-specified expression `newTypeExpr`.

The expressions used in the `eqTestExpr` and `newTypeExpr` parameters have the same format and they are applied to parameters that are common to the two arguments of a `union`, `intersection` or `minus` method. For such kind of parameter we note it's type in the two argument sets as A and B. The expressions are created from these two types possibly by using some extra constructors based on the Description Logic language OWL [30] like $\top$, $\bot$, $\neg$, $\sqcap$, $\sqcup$, $\sqsubseteq$, $\equiv$. The expressions are build by specifying a constructor type and which of the argument types A and B should be considered negated. For the single type constructors $\top$ and $\bot$ negation cannot be specified and for the constructors A and B the negation is allowed only for the respective type (e.g., for constructor type A only $\neg A$ can be set).

We represent an expression as a bit vector having a value corresponding to it's respective constructor type. For encoding the negation of any of the types that are arguments to the constructor two masks can be applied to the constructor types: NEG_A and

Table 1. Possible expressions for constructors of parameter sets.

Constructor type	$\neg A$?	$\neg B$?	Possible expressions
THING	-	-	$\top$
NOTHING	-	-	$\bot$
A	Y/N	-	$A, \neg A$
B	-	Y/N	$B, \neg B$
UNION	Y/N	Y/N	$A \sqcup B, A \sqcup \neg B, \neg A \sqcup B, \neg A \sqcup \neg B$
INTERSECTION	Y/N	Y/N	$A \sqcap B, A \sqcap \neg B, \neg A \sqcap B, \neg A \sqcap \neg B$
SUBCLASS	Y/N	Y/N	$A \sqsupseteq B, A \sqsupseteq \neg B, \neg A \sqsupseteq B, \neg A \sqsupseteq \neg B$
SUPERCLASS	Y/N	Y/N	$A \sqsubseteq B, A \sqsubseteq \neg B, \neg A \sqsubseteq B, \neg A \sqsubseteq \neg B$
SAMECLASS	Y/N	Y/N	$A \equiv B, A \equiv \neg B, \neg A \equiv B, \neg A \equiv \neg B$

```
public interface Ranking {
  double rank( ParamSet qin, ParamSet qout, ParamSet sin, ParamSet sout );
}

public interface ParamSet {
  static final int THING=1, NOTHING=2, A=3, B=4, UNION=5, INTERSECTION=6,
  SUBCLASS=7, SUPERCLASS=8, SAMECLASS=9, NEG_A=16, NEG_B=32;

  int size();
  boolean containsParam( String paramName );
  ParamSet union( ParamSet p, int newTypeExpr );
  ParamSet minus( ParamSet p, int eqTestExpr, int newTypeExpr );
  ParamSet intersection( ParamSet p, int eqTestExpr, int newTypeExpr );
}
```

Fig. 3. The API for ranking functions.

NEG_B. For the actual encoding see Table 1. For example, $A \sqcap \neg B$ will be expressed as `ParamSet.INTERSECTION | ParamSet.NEG_B`.

As an example of API usage, assume we need to select the parameters that are common to two sets X and Y, which have in X a type that is more specific than the one in Y. We would like to preserve in the result set the type values in X. The following statement can be used for this purpose: `X.intersection(Y, ParamSet.SUPERCLASS, ParamSet.A)`.

The directory supports ranking functions written in a subset of the Java programming language. The code of the functions is provided as a compiled Java class. The class has to implement the `Ranking` interface shown in Fig. 3.

On one hand, this API allows to write rather generic ranking functions that take into account only the number of parameters in a certain matching relationship between the description of the query and the description of the service. On the other hand, the ranking function may be customized for a query for which the existance of particular parameters is important by using the set membership test (e.g., if a required output is known to be very hard to be found, a service description that provides exactly this output may receive a higher ranking).

4.2   Exemplary Ranking Functions

In the example in Fig. 4 two basic ranking functions are shown, the first one more appropriate for a service composition algorithms using forward chaining, the second for algorithms using backward chaining with complete type matches.

```
public final class ForwardRanking implements Ranking {
 public double rank( ParamSet qin, ParamSet qout,
                     ParamSet sin, ParamSet sout ) {
  // services that provide more required parameters are better;
  // the provided output has to be more specific than the required one
  return (double)sout.intersection(qout, ParamSet.SUPERCLASS, ParamSet.A).size();
 }
}

public final class BackwardCompleteRanking implements Ranking {
 public double rank( ParamSet qin, ParamSet qout,
                     ParamSet sin, ParamSet sout ) {
  // services that reduce most the number of required outputs are better
  ParamSet remaining = qout.minus(sout, ParamSet.SUBCLASS, ParamSet.A);
  ParamSet newRequired = sin.minus(qin, ParamSet.SUBCLASS, ParamSet.A);
  ParamSet required = remaining.union(newRequired, ParamSet.INTERSECTION);
  return 1 / (double)(1+required.size());
 }
}
```

Fig. 4. Exemplary ranking functions.

4.3   Safe and Efficient Execution of Ranking Functions

Using a subset of Java as programming language for ranking functions has several advantages: Java is well known to many programmers, there are lots of programming tools for Java, and, above all, it integrates very well with our directory service, which is completely written in Java.

Compiling and integrating user-defined ranking functions into the directory leverages state-of-the-art optimizations in recent JVM implementations. For instance, the HotSpot VM [26] first interprets JVM bytecode and gathers execution statistics. If code is executed frequently enough, it is compiled to optimized native code for fast execution. In this way, frequently used ranking functions are executed as efficiently as algorithms directly built into the directory.

The class containing the ranking function is analyzed by our special bytecode verifier which ensures that the user-defined ranking function always terminates within a well-defined time span and does not interfere with the directory implementation. Efficient, extended bytecode verification to enforce restrictions on JVM bytecode for the safe execution of untrusted mobile code has been studied in the JavaSeal [29] and in the J-SEAL2 [3,4] mobile object kernels. Our bytecode verifier ensures the following conditions:

- The Ranking interface is implemented.
- Only a single method is provided.
- The control-flow graph of the rank() method is acyclic. The control-flow graph

is created by an efficient algorithm with execution time linear with the number of JVM instructions in the method.

- No exception handlers (using malformed exception handlers, certain infinite loops can be constructed that are not detected by the standard Java verifier, as shown in [5]). If the ranking function throws an exception (e.g., due to a division by zero), its result is to be considered zero by the directory.

- No JVM subroutines (they result from the compilation of finally{} clauses).

- No explicit object allocation. As there is some implicit object allocation in the set operations in ParamSet, the number of set operations and the maximum size of the resulting sets are limited.

- Only the interface methods of ParamSet may be invoked, as well as a well-defined set of methods from the standard mathematics package.

- Only the static fields defined in the interface ParamSet may be accessed.

- No fields are defined.

- No synchronization instructions.

These restrictions ensure that the execution time of the custom ranking function is bounded by the size of its code. Hence, an attacker cannot crash the directory by providing, for example, a ranking function that contains an endless loop. Moreover, ranking functions cannot allocate memory. Our extended bytecode verification algorithm is highly efficient, its performance is linear with the size of the ranking method. As a prevention against denial-of-service attacks, our directory service allows to set a limit for the size of ranking functions.

Ranking functions are loaded by separate classloaders, in order to support multiple versions of classes with the same name (avoiding name clashes between multiple clients) and to enable garbage collection of the class structures. The loaded class is instantiated and casted to the Ranking interface that is loaded by the system classloader. The directory implementation (which is loaded by the system classloader) accesses the user-defined functions only through the Ranking interface.

As service integration clients may use the same ranking functions in multiple sessions, our directory keeps a cache of ranking functions. This cache maps a hashcode of the function class to a structure containing the function bytecode as well as the loaded class. In case of a cache hit the user-defined function code is compared with the cache entry, and if it matches, the function in the cache is reused, skipping verification and avoiding to reload it with a separate classloader. Due to the restrictions mentioned before, multiple invocations of the same ranking function cannot influence each other. The cache employs a least-recently-used replacement strategy. If a function is removed from the cache, it becomes eligible for garbage collection as soon as it is not in use by any service integration session.

Service composition sessions that do not define custom ranking functions require only a small amount of memory within the directory in order to keep track of the traversal of the directory tree. However, when custom ranking functions are used, the directory has to allocate a temporary data structure in order to sort the matching entries according to the ranking function. In order to protect the directory from attacks, queries issued in sessions that employ custom ranking functions are rejected if the size of the result set exceeds a certain threshold defined by the directory service provider. In such a case, the

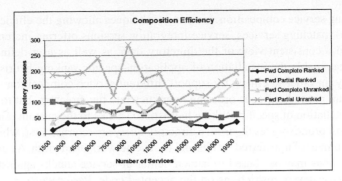

Fig. 5. Impact of ranking functions on composition algorithms.

client has either to do without the custom ranking function, or the query has to be made more specific in order to reduce the number of results.

5   Evaluation

We have evaluated our approach by carrying out tests on random service descriptions and service composition problems that were generated as described in [11]. As we consider directory accesses to be a computationally expensive operation we use them as a measure of efficiency.

The problems have been solved using two forward chaining composition algorithms: one that handles only complete type matches and another that can compose partially matching services, too [12]. When running the algorithms we have used two different directory configuration: The first configuration was using the extensible directory described in this paper which supports custom ranking functions, in particular using the forward chaining ranking function described in Fig. 4. In the second configuration we used a directory which is not aware of the service composition algorithm (e.g., forward complete, backward, etc.) and cannot be extended by client ranking functions. This directory implements a generic ordering heuristic by considering the number of overlapping inputs in the query and in the service, plus the number of overlapping outputs in the query and in the service.

For both directories we have used exactly the same set of service descriptions and at each iteration we have run the algorithms on exactly the same random problems. As it can be seen in Fig. 5 using custom ranking functions consistently improves the performance of our algorithms. In the case of complete matches the improvement is up to a factor of 5 (for a directory of 10500 services) and in the case of partial matches the improvement is of a factor of 3 (for a directory of 9000 of services).

6   Conclusion

Efficient service integration in an open environment populated by a large number of services requires a highly optimized interaction between large-scale directories and service integration engines. Our directory service addresses this need with special features for supporting service composition: indexing techniques allowing the efficient retrieval of (partially) matching services, service integration sessions offering incremental data retrieval and a consistent view of the directory data, as well as user-defined ranking functions that enable the installation of application-specific ranking heuristics within the directory. In order to efficiently support different service composition algorithms, it is important not to hard-code ordering heuristics into the directory, but to enable the dynamic installation of specific ranking heuristics. Thanks to the custom ranking functions, the most promising results from a directory query are returned first, which helps to reduce the number of transferred results and to save network bandwidth. As user-defined ranking functions may be abused to launch denial-of-service attacks against the directory, we impose severe restrictions on the accepted code. Performance measurements underline the need for applying application specific heuristics to order the results that are returned by a directory query.

References

1. D.-S. C. A. Ankolekar, M. Burstein, J. R. Hobbs, O. Lassila, D. Martin, D. McDermott, S. A. McIlraith, S. Narayanan, M. Paolucci, T. Payne, and K. Sycara. DAML-S: Web service description for the Semantic Web. *Lecture Notes in Computer Science*, 2342, 2002.
2. B. Benatallah, Q. Z. Sheng, and M. Dumas. The self-serv environment for web services composition. *IEEE Internet Computing*, 7(1):40–48, 2003.
3. W. Binder. Design and implementation of the J-SEAL2 mobile agent kernel. In *The 2001 Symposium on Applications and the Internet (SAINT-2001)*, San Diego, CA, USA, Jan. 2001.
4. W. Binder, J. Hulaas, A. Villazón, and R. Vidal. Portable resource control in Java: The J-SEAL2 approach. In *ACM Conference on Object-Oriented Programming, Systems, Languages, and Applications (OOPSLA-2001)*, Tampa Bay, Florida, USA, Oct. 2001.
5. W. Binder and V. Roth. Secure mobile agent systems using Java: Where are we heading? In *Seventeenth ACM Symposium on Applied Computing (SAC-2002)*, Madrid, Spain, Mar. 2002.
6. A. L. Blum and M. L. Furst. Fast planning through planning graph analysis. *Artificial Intelligence*, 90(1–2):281–300, 1997.
7. BPEL4WS. Business process execution language for web services version 1.1, http://www.ibm.com/developerworks/library/ws-bpel/.
8. F. Casati, S. Ilnicki, L. Jin, V. Krishnamoorthy, and M.-C. Shan. Adaptive and dynamic service composition in eflow. Technical Report HPL-2000-39, Hewlett Packard Laboratories, 2000.
9. I. Constantinescu, W. Binder, and B. Faltings. Directory services for incremental service integration. In *First European Semantic Web Symposium (ESWS-2004)*, Heraklion, Greece, May 2004.
10. I. Constantinescu and B. Faltings. Efficient matchmaking and directory services. In *The 2003 IEEE/WIC International Conference on Web Intelligence*, 2003.
11. I. Constantinescu, B. Faltings, and W. Binder. Large scale testbed for type compatible service composition. In *ICAPS 04 workshop on planning and scheduling for web and grid services*, 2004.
12. I. Constantinescu, B. Faltings, and W. Binder. Large scale, type-compatible service composition. In *IEEE International Conference on Web Services (ICWS-2004)*, San Diego, CA, USA, July 2004.
13. DAML-S. DAML Services, http://www.daml.org/services.
14. A. Fuggetta, G. P. Picco, and G. Vigna. Understanding Code Mobility. *IEEE Transactions on Software Engineering*, 24(5):342–361, May 1998.

15. F. Giunchiglia and P. Traverso. Planning as model checking. In *European Conference on Planning*, pages 1–20, 1999.
16. J. M. Hellerstein, J. F. Naughton, and A. Pfeffer. Generalized search trees for database systems. In U. Dayal, P. M. D. Gray, and S. Nishio, editors, *Proc. 21st Int. Conf. Very Large Data Bases, VLDB*, pages 562–573. Morgan Kaufmann, 11–15 1995.
17. C. A. Knoblock, S. Minton, J. L. Ambite, N. Ashish, I. Muslea, A. Philpot, and S. Tejada. The Ariadne Approach to Web-Based Information Integration. *International Journal of Cooperative Information Systems*, 10(1-2):145–169, 2001.
18. M. Kornacker, C. Mohan, and J. M. Hellerstein. Concurrency and recovery in generalized search trees. In J. M. Peckman, editor, *Proceedings, ACM SIGMOD International Conference on Management of Data: SIGMOD 1997: May 13–15, 1997, Tucson, Arizona, USA*, 1997.
19. O. Lassila and S. Dixit. Interleaving discovery and composition for simpleworkflows. In *Semantic Web Services, 2004 AAAI Spring Symposium Series*, 2004.
20. L. Li and I. Horrocks. A software framework for matchmaking based on semantic web technology. In *Proceedings of the 12th International Conference on the World Wide Web*, 2003.
21. S. McIlraith, T. Son, and H. Zeng. Mobilizing the semantic web with daml-enabled web services. In *Proc. Second International Workshop on the Semantic Web (SemWeb-2001)*, Hongkong, 2001.
22. S. A. McIlraith and T. C. Son. Adapting golog for composition of semantic web services. In D. Fensel, F. Giunchiglia, D. McGuinness, and M.-A. Williams, editors, *Proceedings of the 8th International Conference on Principles and Knowledge Representation and Reasoning (KR-02)*, pages 482–496, San Francisco, CA, Apr. 22–25 2002. Morgan Kaufmann Publishers.
23. M. Paolucci, T. Kawamura, T. R. Payne, and K. Sycara. Semantic matching of web services capabilities. In *Proceedings of the 1st International Semantic Web Conference (ISWC)*, 2002.
24. S. R. Ponnekanti and A. Fox. Sword: A developer toolkit for web service composition. In *In 11th World Wide Web Conference (Web Engineering Track)*, 2002.
25. B. Srivastav. Automatic web services composition using planning. In *International Conference on Knowledge Based Computer Systems (KBCS-2002)*, 2002.
26. Sun Microsystems, Inc. Java HotSpot Technology. Web pages at http://java.sun.com/products/hotspot/.
27. K. Sycara, J. Lu, M. Klusch, and S. Widoff. Matchmaking among heterogeneous agents on the internet. In *Proceedings of the 1999 AAAI Spring Symposium on Intelligent Agents in Cyberspace*, Stanford University, USA, March 1999.
28. S. Thakkar, C. A. Knoblock, J. L. Ambite, and C. Shahabi. Dynamically composing web services from on-line sources. In *Proceeding of the AAAI-2002 Workshop on Intelligent Service Integration*, pages 1–7, Edmonton, Alberta, Canada, July 2002.
29. J. Vitek, C. Bryce, and W. Binder. Designing JavaSeal or how to make Java safe for agents. Technical report, University of Geneva, July 1998.
30. W3C. OWL web ontology language 1.0 reference, http://www.w3.org/tr/owl-ref/.
31. W3C. Web services description language (wsdl) version 1.2, http://www.w3.org/tr/wsdl12.
32. D. Wu, B. Parsia, E. Sirin, J. Hendler, and D. Nau. Automating DAML-S web services composition using SHOP2. In *Proceedings of 2nd International Semantic Web Conference (ISWC2003)*, 2003.
33. Wu, Dan and Parsia, Bijan and Sirin, Evren and Hendler, James and Nau, Dana. Automating DAML-S Web Services Composition Using SHOP2. In *Proceedings of 2nd International Semantic Web Conference (ISWC2003)*, 2003.
34. J. Yang and M. P. Papazoglou. Web component: A substrate for Web service reuse and composition. *Lecture Notes in Computer Science*, 2348, 2002.

Working with Multiple Ontologies on the Semantic Web

Bernardo Cuenca Grau[1,2], Bijan Parsia[1], and Evren Sirin[1]

[1] Maryland Information and Network Dynamics Laboratory, USA
[2] Department of Computer Science, University of Valencia, Spain

Abstract. The standardization of the second generation Web Ontology Language, OWL, leaves a crucial issue for Web-based ontologies unsatisfactorily resolved: how to represent and reason with multiple distinct, but linked, ontologies. OWL provides the owl:imports construct which, roughly, allows Web ontologies to include other Web ontologies, but only by merging all the linked ontologies into a single logical "space." Recent work on multidimensional logics, fusions and other combinations of modal logics, distributed and contextual logics, and the like have tried to find formalisms wherein knowledge bases (and their logic) are kept more distinct but yet affect each other. These formalisms have various degrees of robustness in their computational complexity, their modularity, their expressivity, and their intuitiveness to modelers. In this paper, we explore a family of such formalisms, grounded in $\mathcal{E}$-connections as extensions to OWL, with emphasis on a novel sub-formalism that seems very straightforward to implement on existing tableau OWL reasoners, as witnessed by our implementation of this formalism in the OWL reasoner Pellet. We discuss how to integrate those formalisms into OWL, as well as some of the issues that modelers have to face when using such formalisms in the context of a large number of heterogeneous, independently developed, richly interconnected ontologies that we expect to be the norm on the Semantic Web.

1 Introduction

Combining ontologies in a controlled and scalable way is crucial for the success of the Semantic Web. However, at the current stage, the means provided by the Web Ontology Language (OWL) for such a purpose are clearly insufficient. OWL provides a construct, 'owl:imports'[1], that allows to include by reference in a knowledge base the axioms contained in another ontology, presumably retrievable from the Web and identified by a URI. However, the functionality provided by owl:imports is unsatisfactory for a number of reasons.

First, it does not support information hiding or filtering, which means that everything in (the transitive closure of the imports of) the imported ontologies gets into the original ontology. Thus, it relies on developer discipline to avoid

---

[1] Throughout, we abbreviate the URI, http://www.w3.org/TR/2004/REC-owl-semantics-20040210/#*owl_imports*, with the pseudo-qname 'owl:imports'.

S.A. McIlraith et al. (Eds.): ISWC 2004, LNCS 3298, pp. 620–634, 2004.

unmanageable blow up of ontology size. Indeed, as ontology reuse via owl:imports increases, so does the chance than an innocuous owl:imports will bring into the local ontology a large chunk of the Semantic Web. Second, none of the imported axioms or facts retain their context. While it is possible to track down the originator(s) of some assertions by inspection of the imported ontology, OWL reasoning does not take such context into account. Finally, the use of a "foreign" URI reference without a corresponding owl:imports brings *nothing* from any of the foreign owner's ontologies

Hence, with owl:imports, OWL can let in either all the axioms of a foreign ontology, or none. The primary distinction, in practical terms, between using owl:imports and directly adding all the assertions in the imported ontology is that with owl:imports, the modeler can break an ontology into different documents. This is a very important distinction, but it is not quite the distinction many hope for.

2   Logical Formalisms for Combining Knowledge Bases

Fortunately, there is a growing body of work about combining multiple ontologies in ways that strike a middle ground between importing all and nothing. In this paper, we consider two formalisms, which are natural extensions of OWL-DL: Distributed Description Logics (DDLs) [2], and $\mathcal{E}$-connections [4].

2.1   Distributed Description Logics

Distributed Description Logics (DDL) [2] is a formalism for combining different DL knowledge bases in a loosely coupled information system. The idea of the combination is to preserve the "identity" and independence of each local ontology. The coupling is established by allowing a new set of inter-ontology axioms, called bridge rules. A bridge rule is an expression of one of the following forms[2]

$$C_i \overset{\sqsubseteq}{\Rightarrow} C_j; \qquad ; C_i \overset{\sqsupseteq}{\Rightarrow} C_j ; \qquad a_i \rightarrow b_j$$

Where, C_i, C_j are classes and a_i, b_j individuals in the ontologies O_i, O_j respectively.

From the modeling point of view, bridge rules have been conceived for establishing directional ("view dependent") subsumption relationships between classes and correspondences between individuals in different ontologies. The motivation for bridge rules, hence, covers a wide variety of intuitive modeling scenarios on the Semantic Web. For example, suppose that in ontology O_1 we have a class "Beer" defined as a subclass of "GermanProduct" and which doesn't exist in ontology O_2. However, in ontology O_2 there is a class "Drink", but there is no class modeling the concept of "Beer". Both ontologies could be linked by

---

[2] We will consider bridge rules without complete individual correspondences along the paper

using a bridge rule stating that "Beer" in ontology O_1 is a subclass of "Drink" in O_2 .

These kind of modeling scenarios are appealing, because they nicely fit in the vision of the Semantic Web in which the notion of a universal upper ontology is abandoned by the notion of a web of distributed, linked and independently developed ontologies. Researchers in the Semantic Web community are starting to realize the importance of extending OWL with a suitable formalism that provides inter-ontology mappings with a precise logical semantics. A first attempt in this direction resulted in C-OWL [3], a syntax and semantic extension of OWL that adds the DDL formalism to the language.

However, C-OWL, as presented in [3] has some difficulties. First, no reasoning support is provided for the language. Extending the existing tableau reasoners to deal with such an extension is certainly a crucial issue. Second, some expressive features that are beyond DDLs (and also beyond $\mathcal{E}$-connections), like the inclusion of inter-ontology role subsumption statements, are included in the language without the required discussion. This kind of expressive power could even make the reasoning undecidable. Finally, from the modeling perspective, no distinction is made between the idea of partially importing concepts from a foreign KB and the idea of linking ontologies through the use of inter-ontology subsumption relationships. It is unclear whether the semantics of DDLs capture that idea of linking, as we will discuss in section 5.

2.2 $\mathcal{E}$-Connections

The $\mathcal{E}$-connections technique [4] is a method for combining logical formalisms that are expressible in the Abstract Description System (ADS) framework. ADSs are a generalization of description, modal and epistemic logics and many logics of time and space (see [1] for a detailed discussion).

The advantages of this technique are twofold: On one hand, $\mathcal{E}$-connections provide a quite expressive way for combining knowledge bases written in a wide variety of logical languages, while, on the other hand, the coupling between the combined logical formalisms is loose enough for ensuring the decidability of the combined formalism. Hence, $\mathcal{E}$-connections provide a trade-off between the tightness of the coupling between the component logical languages and the computational robustness of the combination.

The $\mathcal{E}$-connection method can be applied, for example, to the following setting. Assume that we have n disjoint domains $D_1, ..., D_n$ and two languages l_1 and l_2 for talking about them, and suppose that l_1 and l_2 are two propositionally closed description logics (two extensions of ALC) with decidable satisfiability (and hence subsumption) problem and such that they can be expressed as an Abstract Description System. Assume we want to define a combined formalism $C(l_1, l_2)$ which talks about the domains and also about the relationships among them. First, we define countable and disjoint sets ϵ_{ij} with $i, j = 1, ..., n; i \neq j$ of link names. A link $E \in \epsilon_{ij}$ can be seen as a property that relates elements from the domain D_i to elements of the domain D_j, as opposed to object properties, which relate elements of the same interpretation domain.

For example, let K_1 and K_2 be two knowledge bases written in l_1 and l_2 respectively. The knowledge base K_1 deals with people, while K_2 describes the domain of Pets; then we can define the links $Owns \in \epsilon_{12}$, and $LovesToPlayWith \in \epsilon_{21}$. Intuitively, the link $Owns$ represent the relationships of a person to own a pet, while the link $lovesToPlayWith$ would represent the relation of pets liking to play with people. In its basic form, the syntax of the combination is specified by extending the syntax of l_1 and l_2 with two new constructors: existential and value restrictions on links. For example, in our ontologies K_1, K_2 it is possible to define in K_1 a "DogOwner" as a person who owns at least one dog and in K_2 an "unfriendly pet" as a pet that doesn't like to play with people:

$$DogOwner \equiv Person \sqcap \exists Owns.Dog$$
$$UnfriendlyPet \equiv Pet \sqcap \forall LovesToPlayWith.(\neg Person)$$

Finally, we can also use inverses on the links and define an "Unhappy Cat" in K_2 as a cat that is *owned by* a "Dog Owner":

$$UnhappyCat \equiv Cat \sqcap \exists Owns^{-}(DogOwner)$$

Given n ontologies, the semantics of the combined KB, written in $C(l_1, l_2)$, is given by a combined interpretation $I = (\{I_i\}_{i=1}^{n}\epsilon_{ij}^{I})$, where $I_i = (W_i, \cdot^{I_i})$ is an interpretation and $W_i \cap W_j = \emptyset, \forall i \neq j$. A link $E \in \epsilon_{ij}$ is interpreted as a cross-domain relation $E^{I} \subseteq W_i \times W_j$, and its inverse E^{-} as the relation $(E^{-})^{I} = \{(a,b) \in W_j \times W_i | (b,a) \in E^{I}\}$. Finally, the expressions $\exists E.C$, and $\forall E.C$, where $E \subset \epsilon_{ij}$ and C a concept in the jth KB, are interpreted as subsets of W_i, as follows:

$$(\exists E.C)^{I} = \{x \in W_i | \exists y \in W_j, (x,y) \in E^{I}, y \in C^{I}\}$$
$$(\forall E.C)^{I} = \{x \in W_i | \forall y \in W_j, if\ (x,y) \in E^{I}, \rightarrow y \in C^{I}\}$$

$\mathcal{E}$-connections are strictly more expressive than DDLs (without individual correspondences), and in [4] it is shown how DDLs can be translated into axioms in an $\mathcal{E}$-connection.

3   Integrating $\mathcal{E}$-Connections into OWL

In this section, we define a syntax and semantic extension of OWL that integrates the $\mathcal{E}$-connections formalism into the language in a compact and natural way. The extension is based on the definition of a new set of properties, called links, that stand for the inter-ontology relations in the $\mathcal{E}$-connections framework. The OWL-DL[3] language is then enriched with a new set of constructors that basically allow to define new classes by placing restrictions on the link properties.

---

[3] We are considering OWL-DL/OWL-Lite along the paper because OWL-Full is beyond the ADS framework, and hence $\mathcal{E}$-connections cannot be used to combine OWL-Full with OWL-DL KBs

3.1   Abstract Syntax

The syntax presented in this section is an extension of the normative OWL abstract syntax, as described in the OWL abstract syntax and semantics recommendation [5]. We use the same Extended BNF syntax as in the normative document. A new set of properties, called link properties, are named using a URI, and hence a *linkID* is defined to be a *URIreference*

In order to ensure the separation of vocabularies, a URI-reference cannot be both a linkID, an individual-valued property ID, a datatype property ID, an annotation property ID or an ontology property ID. Intuitively, while individual-valued properties relate individuals to other individuals in the same ontology, while link properties relate individuals corresponding to different interpretation domains. Thus, link properties act as a bridge between different ontologies, which remain separate, and keep their own identity.

Our proposal extends OWL-DL with a new kind of property axiom, by adding the following production rule:

> **axiom**::= 'Link('**linkID**['Deprecated'] { **annotation** }
>   ['inverseOf(' linkID ')']
>   { ' domain (' **Description**')' }
>   { ' range ('**Description**')' }
>   'ForeignOntology (' **OntologyID**')

Informally, link properties are used to bring or import class descriptions from a foreign OWL ontology to the local context, without having to import the whole external knowledge base. The addition of inverses in link properties is a distinguishing feature of $\mathcal{E}$-connections, which has important consequences, both conceptually and in practice.

Link properties can be used to define new classes by means of restrictions on them. Intuitively, a restriction on a link property is applied to a concept in a foreign ontology, and returns a concept defined over the local interpretation domain.

> **restriction**::= 'Restriction('**linkID**
>   **linkRestrictionComponent**
>   { **linkRestrictionComponent** } ')'

> **linkRestrictionComponent**::= 'allValuesFrom('**Description**)'
> | 'someValuesFrom('**Description**)'

The intuition is that the classes specified in link restriction properties are evaluated according to the semantics of the foreign ontology specified in the definition of the link property. Finally, the set of facts is defined by extending the set of facts in OWL in order to provide the means for instantiating link properties. This is achieved by simply adding to the OWL abstract syntax a new alternative to the non-terminal "value"

value ::= 'value(' linkID individualID ')'

Essentially, link properties are similar to Datatype properties. In OWL DL, datatypes constitute a domain disjoint from the domain of classes. Similarly, classes defined in foreign ontologies belong to a domain separate from the domain of classes defined in the importing ontology. The reasoning about datatypes is done by a so-called "Datatype Oracle" and this process is a black-box operation for the rest of the reasoning procedure. Analogously, reasoning about link properties are done with respect to the foreign ontology in an isolated process.

3.2   Direct Model-Theoretic Semantics

The semantics starts with the notion of vocabulary.

Definition 1. *(Combined OWL Vocabulary)*
   A combined OWL vocabulary V consists of a tuple $V = \{V_1, ..., V_n, V_{link}\}$, where $V_1, ..., V_n$ is a set of OWL vocabularies, as defined in [5], and V_{link} is a set whose elements are triples of the form:

$$(O_i, O_j, L_k), \; i, j = 1, ..., n, i \neq j$$

Where O_j, O_i are ontologyIDs with $i \neq j$, L_k a linkID (a URI), and where none of the linkIDs are contained in any of the $V_i, i = 1..., n$

Definition 2. *(Combined OWL interpretation)*
   A combined OWL interpretation with vocabulary $V = \{V_1, ..., V_n, V_{link}\}$ is a tuple of the form:

$$I = (\{I_i\}_{i=1}^n, \epsilon_{ij} = (O_i, O_j, L_k)^I), i, j = 1, ..., n; i \neq j;$$

Where $I_i, i = 1, ..., n$ is an abstract OWL interpretation with vocabulary V_i, and with respect to a datatype map D_i, and domain W_i, and $(O_i, O_j, L_k)^I = W_i \times W_j$, for $(O_i, O_j, L_k) \in V_{link}$.
   Class and property axioms are interpreted as in OWL-DL, with the remark that now the concepts built using the new constructors can appear in class axioms and the semantics applied to them must be the semantics of table 1.

Definition 3. *($\mathcal{E}$−Connection of OWL ontologies)*
   A combined OWL ontology is a combined KB $\Sigma = \{O_1, ..., O_n\}$ written in the extended abstract syntax, such that it is closed under 'owl:imports' and for every ontology in Σ, all the link properties it contains refer to a foreign ontology which is also contained in Σ.

Finally, we say that a combined interpretation I satisfies Σ, iff it satisfies all the axioms of all the ontologies in it.

Table 1. Semantics

Abstract Syntax	EC Syntax	Semantics
$Link(L_k)$ defined in O_i $ForeignOntology(O_j)$	L_k^{ij}	$(L_k^{ij})^I \subseteq W_i \times W_j$
inverseOf$((E_m))$	$L_k^{ij} \equiv (E_m^{ji})^-$	$((L_k)ij)^I = ((E_m^{ji})^I)^-$
domain(C)		$(L_k^{ij})^I \subseteq C^I \times W_j$
range(D)		$(L_k^{ij})^I \subseteq W_i \times D^I$
restriction$(L_k$ $someValuesFrom(C))$	$\exists L_k^{ij}(C)$	$(\exists L_k^{ij}(C))^I = \{x \in W_i \mid \exists y \in W_j, [x,y] \in (L_k^{ij})^I \text{ and } y \in C^I\}$
restriction$(L_k$ $allValuesFrom(C))$	$\forall L_k^{ij}(C)$	$(\forall L_k^{ij}(C))^I = \{x \in W_i \mid \forall y \in W_j, \text{ if } [x,y] \in (L_k^{ij})^I \rightarrow y \in C^I\}$
value ($t\ L_k\ o$)	$(t,o) : L_k^{ij}$	$(t^I, o^I) : (L_k^{ij})^I$

4 Reasoning with $\mathcal{E}$-Connections on the Semantic Web

Finding efficient and easy to implement algorithms for reasoning on $\mathcal{E}$-connections is a challenging task. Two possible ways of simplifying the problem are, on one hand, defining subformalisms of $\mathcal{E}$-connections which still preserve most of the expressive power of $\mathcal{E}$-connections, and, on the other hand, restricting to particular ADS of special practical relevance.

In this paper we do both. We define Perspectival $\mathcal{E}$-connections (PECs), an expressive sublanguage of $\mathcal{E}$-connections, and we restrict ourselves to combinations of OWL-Lite (SHIF(D)) ontologies without ABoxes. We will use the notation $C^\epsilon(SHIF(D))$, for the PEC language that enables the combination of OWL-Lite ontologies.

The main motivation for introducing PECs is that they can be implemented in a quite straightforward way by extending the existing tableaux-based DL reasoners, at least for logics that do not include nominals (hence the restriction to SHIF(D)/OWL-Lite).

4.1 Perspectival $\mathcal{E}$-Connections

Perspectival $\mathcal{E}$-connections (PECs) are obtained from $\mathcal{E}$-connections by disallowing the use of inverses on link properties. This implies that links cannot be "navigated" in both directions anymore. In the abstract syntax, PECs would be obviously defined by suppressing the inverse clause in the definition of link properties. In our example of persons and pets, we would still be able to define the concept of a "dog owner" and "unhappy pet owner" in K_1, but not the concept of "unhappy cat" in K_2.

As a consequence of the restrictions imposed to the formalism, PECs are strictly less expressive than $\mathcal{E}$-connections, but remain strictly more expressive than DDLs.

The syntax and semantics of the combined language $C^\epsilon(SHIF(D))$ is defined as follows:

Definition 4. *Let $C_i, R_i, \delta_i, \epsilon_{ij}$ be disjoint sets, for $i, j = 1...n; i \neq j$, where the $C_i, R_i, \delta_i, \epsilon_{ij}$ are respectively sets of concept, role, datatype properties, and link*

Table 2. Semantics of i-concepts

Syntax	Semantics
R^-	$(R^-)^I = \{(a,b)\|(b,a) \in R^I\}$
$\neg C$	$(\neg C)^I = W_i - C^I$
$C \sqcap D$	$(C \sqcap D)^I = C^I \cap D^I$
$C \sqcup D$	$(C \sqcup D)^I = C^I \cup D^I$
$\exists R.C$	$(\exists R.C)^I = \{x \in W_i \| \exists y \in W_i, (x,y) \in R^I, y \in C^I\}$
$\forall R.C$	$(\forall R.C)^I = \{x \in W_i \| \forall y \in W_i, (x,y) \in R^I \to y \in C^I\}$
$\leq 1S$	$(\leq 1S)^I = \{x \in W_i \| \forall y, z, if\ (x,y) \in S^I \wedge (x,z) \in S^I \to y = z\}$
$\geq 2S$	$(\geq 2S)^I = \{x \in W_i \| \exists y, z : (x,y) \in S^I, (x,z) \in S^I, \wedge y \neq z\}$
$\exists U.d$	$(\exists U.d)^I = \{x \in W_i \| \exists y \in \Delta_D, (x,y) \in U^I, y \in d^D\}$
$\forall U.d$	$(\forall U.d)^I = \{x \in W_i \| \forall y \in \Delta_D, (x,y) \in U^I \to y \in d^D\}$
$\exists G.Z$	$(\exists G.Z)^I = \{x \in W_i \| \exists y \in W_j, (x,y) \in G^I, y \in Z^I\}$
$(\forall G.Z)$	$(\forall G.Z)^I = \{x \in W_i \| \forall y \in W_j, if\ (x,y) \in G^I, \to y \in Z^I\}$

names. The set of i-roles is the set $R_i \cup \{R^- \| R \in R_i\}$. We will use the notation $Inv(R) = S$ if $R = S^-$.

For R, S i-roles, a role inclusion axiom is an assertion of the form $R \sqsubseteq S$. An i-role axiom is either a role inclusion axiom, an assertion of the form $Inv(R) = S$ or a transitivity axiom $Trans(R)$, with $R \in R_i$. An i-role box $\Re_i$ is a finite set of i-role axioms. The combined role box is given by the tuple $\Re = (\Re_1, ..., \Re_n)$. An i-role R is called simple if for $\sqsubseteq^*$ the transitive reflexive closure of $\sqsubseteq$ on $\Re_i$, and for each i-role S, $S \sqsubseteq^* R$ implies $Trans(R) \notin \Re_i$. The set of ij-links is the set of atomic links ϵ_{ij}, and the set of i-datatype properties is the set δ_i.

Finally, the set of i-concepts in $C^\epsilon(SHIF(D))$ is recursively defined, for $i = 1, ..., n$ as the smallest set such that each concept name $A \in C_i$, is an i-concept and, for R an i-role, U an i-datatype property, S a simple i-role, $G \in \epsilon_{ij}$ C, D i-concepts, and Z a j-concept, the following constructions are also valid i-concepts:

- $C \sqcap D$, $C \sqcup D$, $\neg C$, $\forall R.C$, $\exists R.C$, $(\leq 1S)$, $(\geq 2S)$, $\forall U.d$, $\exists U.d$
- $\exists G.Z$, $\forall G.Z$

A combined TBox is defined as $K = (K_1, ..., K_n)$, where K_i is a set of assertions of the form $C \sqsubseteq D$, with both C, D i-concepts. The semantics is given by means of an interpretation $I = (\{I_i\}\epsilon_{ij}^I)$, $i, j = 1, ..., n; i \neq j$ where $I_i = (W_i, \cdot^{I_i})$, with $W_i \cap W_j = \emptyset$. The interpretation function maps every atomic concept $A \in N_{C_i}$ to $A^I \subseteq W_i$, every role $R \in N_{R_i}$ to $R^I \subseteq W_i \times W_i$, every link $G \in \epsilon_{ij}$ to $G^I \subseteq W_i \times W_j$, every i-datatype property U to $U^I \subseteq W_i \times \Delta_D$, and every datatype d to $d^D \subseteq \Delta_D$. Table 1 shows the extension of the interpretation function to complex descriptions. In the table, C, D are i-concepts, R is an i-role, S is an simple i-role, U is an i-datatype property, Z is a j-concept, $G \in \epsilon_{ij}$, and d is a datatype.

An interpretation satisfies an i-role inclusion axiom $R \sqsubseteq S$, if $R^{I_i} \subseteq S^{I_i}$, where R, S are both i-roles and the axiom is in $\Re_i$, and satisfies a transitivity axiom $Trans(R)$, iff $R^{I_i} = (R^{I_i})^+$. An interpretation satisfies the combined role box $\Re$ iff it satisfies all the axioms in each $\Re_i$. If C, D are i-concepts, an interpretation satisfies the axiom $C \sqsubseteq D$ if $C^I \subseteq D^I$, and satisfies the combined TBox K iff it satisfies all the axioms in each K_i. A combined knowledge base is defined as $\Sigma = (T, \Re)$, where K is a combined TBox and $\Re$ a combined role box. An interpretation satisfies Σ if it satisfies both K and $\Re$. An i-concept C is satisfiable wrt Σ iff there is an interpretation I such that it satisfies Σ, and $C^I \neq \emptyset$. Such an interpretation is called a model of C w.r.t. Σ. An i-concept C is subsumed by another i-concept D wrt Σ iff $C^I \subseteq D^I$, for each interpretation satisfying Σ.

We can transform each component K_i of a combined TBox K into a single equivalent concept equation $\top_i \equiv C_{K_i}$, where:

$$C_{K_i} = \sqcap_{C_j^i \sqsubseteq D_j^i \in K_i} (\neg C_j^i \sqcup D_j^i)$$

An interpretation I will satisfy the TBox K iff $\top_i = C_{K_i}^I$, for $i = 1, ..., n$.

5   A Combined Tableau for $C^\epsilon(SHIF(D))$

We will assume concepts written in NNF. To transform an i-concept into NNF, we can push negation inwards using De Morgan's laws and the following equivalences:

For R an i-role, U an i-datatype role S an i-simple role, $E \in \epsilon_{ij}, i, j = 1, ..., n; i \neq j$, C an i-concept, Z a j-concept and d a datatype:

$$\neg \exists R.C \equiv \forall R.\neg C \qquad \neg \forall R.C \equiv \exists R.\neg C \qquad \neg \geq 2S \equiv \leq 1S \qquad \neg \leq 1S \equiv \geq 2S$$
$$\neg \exists U.d \equiv \forall U.\neg d \qquad \neg \forall U.d \equiv \exists U.\neg d \qquad \neg \exists E.Z \equiv \forall E.\neg Z \qquad \neg \forall E.Z \equiv \exists D.\neg Z$$

We will use the notation $\sim C$ for the NNF of $\neg C$.

Let X be an i-concept, then the set $sub_i(X, \Re)$ of i-subconcepts of X w.r.t. the combined role box $\Re$ is defined as follows, for all $i, j = 1, ..., n; i \neq j$:

- If X is an atomic primitive i-concept or its negation, then $sub_i(X, \Re) = \{X\}$, $sub_j(X, \Re) = \emptyset$
- If X is of the form $\exists R.C$ where $\exists R.C$ is an i-concept, then $sub_i(X, \Re) = \{X\} \cup sub_i(C, \Re)$, $sub_j(X, \Re) = sub_j(C, \Re)$
- If X is of the form $\forall R.C$, where $\forall R.C$ is an i-concept then $sub_i(X, \Re) = \{X\} \cup sub_i(C, \Re) \bigcup_k \{\forall S_k.C\}$ for every $S_k \sqsubseteq^* R$, with $Trans(S_k)$ in $\Re_i$. Again, $sub_j(X, \Re) = sub_j(C, \Re)$
- If X is of the form $C_1 \sqcap C_2$, or $C_1 \sqcup C_2$ where C_1 and C_2 are i-concepts, then $sub_i(X) = \{X, \Re\} \cup sub_i(C_1, \Re) \cup sub_i(C_2, \Re)$, $sub_j(X, \Re) = sub_j(C_1, \Re) \cup sub_j(C_2, \Re)$
- If X is of the form $\leq nS$ or $\geq nS$, where S is a simple role, then $sub_i(X, \Re) = \{X\}$ and $sub_j(X, \Re) = \emptyset$
- If X is a concept of the form $\exists U.d$, or $\forall U.d$, where U is a datatype property and d a datatype, then $sub_i(X, \Re) = \{X\} \cup \{d\}$ and $sub_j(X, \Re) = \emptyset$

- If X is an i-concept of the form $\exists G.D$ or $\forall G.D$, where $G \in \epsilon_{ij}$, D a j-concept, then $sub_i(X, \Re) = \{X\} \cup sub_i(D, \Re)$, $sub_j(X, \Re) = sub_j(D, \Re)$

For X and a combined knowledge base Σ, we define $sub_i(X, \Sigma)$ as the union of $sub_i(X, \Re)$ and all the $sub_i(C_{T_k}, \Re)$, $k = 1, ..., n$. From now on, we will call ρ_i and δ_i to the set of i-roles and i-datatype properties respectively occurring in X, Σ, and ϵ_{ij} will be the set of ij-links appearing in X, Σ

Definition 5. *(Combined Tableau)*
*Let X be a valid i-concept (written in NNF), and Σ a combined KB. A **combined tableau** T for X wrt Σ is defined as a tuple $T = (\{T_i\}, \epsilon_X)$, $i = 1, ..., n$ where:*

- $T_i = (O_i, L_i, \alpha_i, \mu_i)$, *with O_i a set of individuals, and:*
  - $L_i : O_i \to 2^{sub_i(X, \Sigma)}$
  - $\alpha_i : \rho_i \to 2^{O_i \times O_i}$
  - $\mu_i : \delta_i \to 2^{O_i \times \Delta_D}$
- $\epsilon_X : \epsilon_{ij} \to 2^{O_i \times O_j}$

In a combined tableau for an i-concept X, there must exist n individuals $o_j \in O_j$ such that $\{X, C_{K_j}\} \subseteq L_j(o_j)$ if $j = i$ and $\{C_{K_j}\} \subseteq L_j(o_j)$ otherwise, for all $j = 1, ..., n$.

Moreover, for all $i, j = 1, ..., n; i \neq j$, $s_i, t_i \in O_i, C, D \in sub_i(X, \Sigma)$, $Z \in sub_j(X, \Sigma)$, $R, S \in \rho_i$, $E \in \epsilon_{ij}$ $U \in \delta_i$, and d a datatype, the following conditions must hold:

1. *If $C \in L_i(s_i)$, then $\neg C \notin L_i(s_i)$*
2. *If $(C \sqcap D) \in L_i(s_i)$, then $C \in L_i(s_i)$, and $D \subset L_i(s_i)$*
3. *If $(C \sqcup D) \in L_i(s_i)$, then $C \in L_i(s_i)$, or $D \in L_i(s_i)$*
4. *If $\forall R.C \in L_i(s_i)$, and $(s_i, t_i) \in \alpha_i(R)$, then $C \in L_i(t_i)$*
5. *If $\exists R.C \in L_i(s_i)$, then there is some $t_i \in O_i$ such that $(s_i, t_i) \in \alpha_i(R)$, and $C \in L_i(t_i)$*
6. *If $\forall R.C \in L_i(s_i)$, and $(s_i, t_i) \in \alpha_i(S)$, for some $S \sqsubseteq^* R$ with $Trans(S)$, then $\forall S.C \in L_i(t_i)$*
7. *If $(\leq 1R) \in L_i(s_i)$, and $(s_i, t_i) \in \alpha_i(R)$, and $(s_i, t_i') \in \alpha_i(R)$, then $t_i = t_i'$*
8. *If $(\geq 2R) \in L_i(s_i)$, then there are some $t_i, t_i' \in O_i$, such that $(s_i, t_i) \in \alpha_i(R)$, $(s_i, t_i') \in \alpha_i(R)$, and $t_i \neq t_i'$*
9. *If $(s_i, t_i) \in \alpha_i(R)$ and $R \sqsubseteq^* S$, then $(s_i, t_i) \in \alpha_i(S)$*
10. *$(s, t) \in \alpha_i(R)$ iff $(t, s) \in \alpha_i(Inv(R))$*
11. *If $\forall U.d \in L_i(s_i)$, and $(s_i, t_i) \in \mu_i(U)$, then $t_i \in d^D$*
12. *If $\exists U.d \in L_i(s_i)$, then there is some $t_i \in \Delta_D$ such that $(s_i, t_i) \in \mu_i(U)$, and $t_i \in d^D$*
13. *If $\forall E.Z \in L_i(s)$ where $s \in O_i$, and $(s, t) \in \epsilon_X(E)$, then $Z \in L_j(t)$, $t \in O_j$*
14. *If $\exists E.Z \in L_i(s)$, where $s \in O_i$, then there exists some $t \in O_j$ such that $(s, t) \in \epsilon_X(E)$, and $Z \in L_j(t)$*

Lemma 1. *An i-concept X in $C^\epsilon(SHIF(D))$ is satisfiable wrt a combined knowledge base Σ iff X has a combined tableau wrt Σ.*

5.1   Description of the Algorithm

We suggest a tableaux-based reasoning algorithm for determining the satisfiability of i-concepts (i=1,2) wrt a combined knowledge base Σ in the language $C^\epsilon(SHIF(D))$.

From the structure of a combined TBox it is easy to see that the combined TBox K cannot be internalized into a single concept. This means that we cannot directly use a concept satisfiability algorithm with empty TBox as a decision procedure for the reasoning problems in the combined TBox. We add a rule $\rightarrow CE$ that ensures that every i-node contains the concept C_{K_i}.

The algorithm works on a *finite combined completion*, which is a forest of $SHIF(D)$ completion trees. The labels of the i-nodes in the model are restricted to subsets of $sub_i(X, \Sigma)$.

The algorithm tries to build a combined tableau for the input concept. If it succeeds, it returns "satisfiable", while if it fails to build the tableau, it returns "unsatisfiable".

The algorithm generates n kinds of nodes, called i-nodes, and can generate n different types of trees, called i-trees. An i-tree is expanded using the $SHIF(D)$ rules, plus the additional rules and can contain i-nodes and j-nodes, $i \neq j$. The root node of an i-tree is always an i-node and the j-nodes of the i-trees are always leaves. The algorithm will keep track of all the generated i-trees, together with the dependencies between them. If the algorithm is building an i-tree T and during the process generates a new j-tree, the algorithm will continue expanding T, potentially generating new j-trees on the way, which are all processed after T is finished. A j-node g in an i-tree contains a clash iff the corresponding j-tree contains a clash when expanded. Otherwise, it is satisfiable and g is marked with the label "visited".

The algorithm adds three new expansion rules:

- $\rightarrow \exists_{link}$ **Rule:** If $\exists E.C$ is in $L_i(x)$ ($E \in \epsilon_{ij}$), x is not blocked and has no E-successor y with $L(x,y) = \{E\}$, and $\{C\} \in L_j(y)$, then create a new E-successor (a j-node) y of x with $L_j(y) = \{C\}$. A new j-tree is created with root y labeled with $L_j(y)$. The j-tree won't be expanded until no more rules apply in the i-tree.
- $\rightarrow \forall_{link}$ **Rule:** If $\forall E.C$ is in $L_i(x)$ ($E \in \epsilon_{ij}$), x is not blocked and there exists an E-successor y of x, such that $C \notin L_j(y)$, then $L_j(y) = L_j(y) \cup \{C\}$.
- $\rightarrow CE$ **Rule:** If $C_{K_i} \notin L_i(x)$, then $L_i(x) \leftarrow L_i(x) \cup \{C_{K_i}\}$

However, the algorithm as we have described it so far may not terminate. In order to ensure termination an extra blocking condition is required. Each time the algorithm starts expanding a new i-tree T with root g, created as a successor of a certain j-node, the algorithm checks if there exists a node x in a not yet completed i-tree such that $L_i(g) \subseteq L_i(x)$. In that case the algorithm blocks the root of the new tree, which returns "satisfiable". Given as an input an i-concept X and a combined KB Σ the algorithm creates an i-tree with a single i-node x_i, labeled $L_i(x_i) = \{X\}$, and a j-tree for each $j = 1, ..., n; j \neq i$, each with a single j-node labelled with the emptyset.

A tree is **complete** when some node in it contains a (SHIF(D)) clash, or when none of the rules is applicable in the i-nodes and all the j-nodes it contains are marked as "visited".

If for the input i-concept X, the expansion rules can be applied to all the trees in such a way that each initial tree yields to a complete, clash-free completion tree, then the algorithm returns "X is satisfiable", and "X is unsatisfiable" otherwise.

The algorithm presented in this section is a decision procedure for satisfiability and subsumption of i-concepts w.r.t. a combined knowledge base Σ, as a direct consequence of the following lemma:

Lemma 2. *Let* $\Sigma = (K, \Re)$ *a combined knowledge base in the PEC* $C^\epsilon(SHIF(D))$ *and let X be an i-concept. Then:*

1. *The algorithm terminates when applied to Σ and X*
2. *The rules can be applied such that they generate a clash-free and complete combined completion iff X is satisfiable w.r.t. Σ*

This technique shows that the generated i-trees in a combined completion are independent, in the sense that they do not affect each other, and hence the decision procedure we have presented has a "black box" property. A a slight modification of existing DL reasoners suffices for implementing the algorithm. However, this technique cannot be straightforwardly extended to basic $\mathcal{E}$-connections. If the algorithm is naively applied to the basic $\mathcal{E}$-connections case, then it happens to be unsound.

As an example, consider the concept in the pet ontology:

$$Man \sqcap \exists Owns(\forall Owns^-(\neg Man))$$

The concept is clearly unsatisfiable; however, the algorithm will return the wrong answer. The unsoundness is caused by the presence of inverses on the links, which breaks the black box property of the algorithm.

Nominals (presence of the oneOf constructor) also cause unsoundness if the algorithm is naively extend to PECs whose component logics contain nominals. For example, a concept of the form:

$$\exists E.(\{o\} \sqcap A) \sqcap \exists F.(\{o\} \sqcap \neg A)$$

Would be unsatisfiable. However, a straightforward extension of the algorithm would return the wrong answer[4]. Similar considerations do apply to the $C^\epsilon(SHIF(D))$ combination when ABoxes are included.

---

[4] We would like to thank the anonymous reviewer of the DL-2004 workshop that pointed out this example to us in an earlier presentation of some of this work

5.2   Implementation

We have implemented the algorithm in the OWL reasoner Pellet, a tableau based DL reasoner specifically developed to work with OWL ontologies. The reasoner also supports XML Schema datatypes and includes a datatype oracle for this purpose.

In Pellet, an OWL ontology is normally parsed into one KB that has the associated TBox/ABox components. The effect of importing an OWL ontology results in the merging of these two KBs. For PECs, the component ontologies should be kept separate. Hence, each ontology is loaded into a disjoint KB during the parsing process. A global ontology manager stores this set of ontologies along with the cached results of satisfiability results for the different KBs. Please note that we are considering combinations of an arbitrary number of ontologies.

The modification to the existing tableau algorithm implies marking each node with the ontology it belongs to. When a successor node is being created due to a link property, the new node is marked as belonging to the ontology which defined that link. The clash detection for the nodes that belong to foreign ontologies is performed by the ontology manager.

This ensures termination and also provides some caching of the satisfiability results. For each ontology two different caches are stored: one for satisfiable concepts and the other for unsatisfiable concepts. After a satisfiability test succeeds, the labels of all the nodes in the resulting completion tree are added to the satisfiability cache of that ontology. In the case of an unsatisfiable concept, only the label of the root node is stored in the unsatisfiability cache. When a new satisfiability test is asked, these caches are first searched for the previous answers.

6   Difficulties When Modeling with C-OWL and DDLs

Consider the ontology Figure 1a. The ontology O defines two disjoint concepts *Flying* and *NonFlying*, the concept *Bird* and the concept *Penguin*. The axioms in O state that all birds fly and also that a penguin is a bird, but it doesn't fly. In this case, in which all the axioms are gathered in a single logical space, the concept *Penguin* would be clearly unsatisfiable.

Now, imagine that we split the knowledge about the domain in two coupled ontologies, shown in Figure 1b. The ontology A states that the concepts *Flying* and *NonFlying* are disjoint and states that all birds fly. On the other hand, the ontology B defines the concept *Penguin* and states, using DDL subsumption links, that a penguin doesn't fly and that a penguin is a bird. However, it is easy to see by direct application of the semantics that in this case the obvious (and relevant) contradiction is not detected, and *Penguin* is satisfiable in the coupled system.

The reason for this is that what bridge rules actually do is to place restrictions on a link property, which is nothing but an "ordinary" $\mathcal{E}$-connection link. Intuitively, there's nothing contradictory in these bridge rules in the same way that

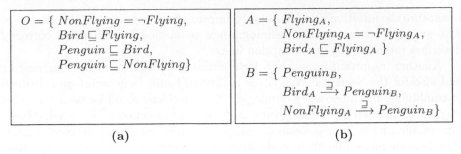

$$O = \{\ NonFlying = \neg Flying,$$
$$Bird \sqsubseteq Flying,$$
$$Penguin \sqsubseteq Bird,$$
$$Penguin \sqsubseteq NonFlying\}$$

$$A = \{\ Flying_A,$$
$$NonFlying_A = \neg Flying_A,$$
$$Bird_A \sqsubseteq Flying_A\ \}$$

$$B = \{\ Penguin_B,$$
$$Bird_A \xrightarrow{\sqsupseteq} Penguin_B,$$
$$NonFlying_A \xrightarrow{\sqsupseteq} Penguin_B\}$$

$$(a) \qquad\qquad (b)$$

Fig. 1. Figure (a) shows a single ontology where concept *Penguin* is unsatisfiable. Figure (b) shows the same definition with bridge rules where contradiction cannot be detected anymore

there is no inconsistency between two axioms like $Father \sqsubseteq \exists hasChild.Male$ and $Father \sqsubseteq \exists hasChild.\neg Male$ in an ordinary ontology.

This result, together with the fact that inter-ontology subsumption links do not propagate transitively, shows that DDLs can be misleading and counterintuitive, and do not seem to capture the notion of subsumption links across a "Web of ontologies". The example suggests that a formalism for dealing with inter-ontology subsumption relationships is still lacking. $\mathcal{E}$-connections, though suitable for covering a wide variety of relevant modeling scenarios in the Semantic Web context, do not capture the idea of linking ontologies with subsumption relationships, but, as opposed to DDLs, were not conceived for such a purpose.

7   Conclusion and Future Work

One of the most important challenges for the Semantic Web is to understand how to represent and reason with multiple, distinct, independently developed, but linked ontologies in a distributed environment. In this paper, we have explored the $\mathcal{E}$-connections framework as a powerful formalism for combining OWL ontologies.

We argue that $\mathcal{E}$-connections capture the intuition behind many relevant modeling scenarios in which ontology developers "partially import" concepts from other ontologies and use them for the definition of new concepts without having to bring to the local logical space all the axioms in the foreign ontology. We have shown how to integrate the formalism into OWL in a natural and compact way. The resulting syntax and semantic extension of OWL is strictly more expressive than earlier proposals, like C-OWL.

We have defined an expressive subformalism of $\mathcal{E}$-connections, strictly more expressive than DDLs, which can be implemented in a quite straightforward way for the combination of OWL-Lite ontologies by extending existing tableaux-based reasoners. The resulting algorithm has been satisfactorily implemented in the OWL reasoner Pellet. Finally, we have shown how DDLs seem unsatisfactory, because on one hand they are too inexpressive for the modeling scenarios for which $\mathcal{E}$-connections are suitable, and on the other hand because they seem not to capture the intuitive idea behind subsumption links across multiple ontologies. This suggests further work in defining a new semantics for DDLs that correctly describes inter-ontology subsumption links.

Another important application for $\mathcal{E}$-connections for knowledge engineering and also for the Semantic Web is the ability to factor large ontologies. Instead of combining and integrating ontologies, $\mathcal{E}$-connections could be used the other way round, namely for decomposing large and heterogeneous[5] knowledge bases into smaller, more homogeneous $\mathcal{E}$-connected ontologies. When ontologies grow, they become more difficult to understand for modelers and also harder to reuse. Hence, the ability to "break" large ontologies into smaller, connected pieces may yield to the development of more effective and modular knowledge modeling techniques. Factoring ontologies in this way may also result in a computational efficiency gain when performing reasoning, since the number of non-absorbable general concept inclusion axioms in the original knowledge base is partitioned into different sets, corresponding to the different ontologies in the combination, which may result in a remarkable performance gain.

Future work includes the development of reasoning techniques for handling nominals in the combination (and hence OWL-DL ontologies), and also to explore the transition from PECs to full $\mathcal{E}$-connections. We also plan to extend the algorithm presented here to reason with Aboxes. When reasoning with individuals using this technique, we expect a major performance gain, since the number of individuals in the original ontology is divided among the different ontologies in the combination. Finally, we are also looking into integrating support for multiple ontologies in the SWOOPed ontology editor in order to make these formalisms as usable and intuitive as possible for modelers, which is crucial for successfully bringing them to the Semantic Web.

References

1. F. Baader, C. Lutz, H.Sturm, and F.Wolter. Fusions of description logics and abstract description systems. *Journal of Artificial Intelligence Research (JAIR), 16:1-58*, 2003.
2. A. Borgida and L. Serafini. Distributed description logics: Assimilating information from peer sources. *Journal of Data Semantics, 1:153-184*, 2003.
3. Paolo Bouquet, Fausto Giunchiglia, Frank van Harmelen, Luciano Serafini, and Heiner Stuckenschmidt. C-owl: Contextualizing ontologies. In *Proc. of the 2003 International Semantic Web Conference (ISWC 2003)*, 2003.
4. O. Kutz, C. Lutz, F. Wolter, and M. Zakharyaschev. E-connections of abstract description systems. *Artificial Intelligence 156(1):1-73*, 2004.
5. P.F. Patel-Schneider, P. Hayes, and I.Horrocks. Web ontology language (owl) abstract syntax and semantics. *W3C Recommendation*, 2004.

---

[5] The word heterogeneous is used here to state that a certain ontology covers different topics or domains

Opening Up Magpie via Semantic Services

Martin Dzbor, Enrico Motta, and John Domingue

Knowledge Media Institute, The Open University, Milton Keynes, UK
{M.Dzbor, E.Motta, J.B.Domingue}@open.ac.uk

Abstract. Magpie is a suite of tools supporting a 'zero-cost' approach to semantic web browsing: it avoids the need for manual annotation by automatically associating an ontology-based semantic layer to web resources. An
important aspect of Magpie, which differentiates it from superficially similar
hypermedia systems, is that the association between items on a web page and
semantic concepts is not merely a mechanism for dynamic linking, but it is the
enabling condition for locating services and making them available to a user.
These services can be manually activated by a user (pull services), or opportunistically triggered when the appropriate web entities are encountered during a
browsing session (push services). In this paper we analyze Magpie from the
perspective of building semantic web applications and we note that earlier implementations did not fulfill the criterion of "open as to services", which is a
key aspect of the emerging semantic web. For this reason, in the past twelve
months we have carried out a radical redesign of Magpie, resulting in a novel
architecture, which is open both with respect to ontologies and semantic web
services. This new architecture goes beyond the idea of merely providing support for semantic web browsing and can be seen as a software framework for
designing and implementing semantic web applications.

1 Introduction

Magpie [5-7] is a suite of tools supporting a 'zero-cost' approach to semantic web
browsing. It avoids the need for manual annotation by automatically associating an
ontology-based semantic layer to web resources. There are many ways to characterize
Magpie. One view, emphasized in earlier papers, is to consider Magpie as a tool supporting the *interpretation of web pages*. Specifically, one can see the automatic recognition of entities in web pages and the linking of these entities to semantic concepts
as a way to bring an interpretative context to bear, which can help users in making
sense of the information presented in a web page. For instance, we are using Magpie
in a learning context to help students of a course in climate science in understanding
the vast mass of information about climate change that can be found on the web. In
such a context, using Magpie can be seen as adopting the viewpoint of an expert in
the field, and use this as an aid for navigating the web.

Another way to look at Magpie is as a *semantic web browser*. If we take this view,
then Magpie can be seen as providing an efficient way to integrate semantic and
'standard' (i.e., non-semantic) web browsing, through the automatic association of
semantics to web pages and the provision of user-interface support. This allows the

S.A. McIlraith et al. (Eds.): ISWC 2004, LNCS 3298, pp. 635–649, 2004.
© Springer-Verlag Berlin Heidelberg 2004

user to navigate the web using both semantic and hypertext links, and helps him/her to invoke the services appropriate for a given class of ontological entities.

A third viewpoint we can use to characterize Magpie is as a *framework for developing semantic web applications*. According to this view, the Magpie suite of tools can be seen as a 'shell' for building semantic web applications, which provides generic mechanisms for bringing together ontologies, web resources and (semantic) web services. For instance, the climate science example mentioned above can be viewed as a semantic web application, characterized by a number of ontology-based services, which are made available to students opportunistically, when the 'right web page' is encountered. The key feature of Magpie here is that it allows developers to focus on the semantic functionalities, i.e., specifying and populating the ontology and defining the services, with no need to identify, let alone annotate web resources.

Although the idea of Magpie as a framework for building semantic web applications has informed our research since the very beginning, the implementations described in earlier papers fall somewhat short of realizing this vision. In particular, the original Magpie architecture was open with regard to ontologies, but not with respect to services, which had to be statically coupled with the ontology. In other words, they had to be designed by a Magpie developer, much like in a 'closed system' scenario. This approach goes against the vision of the web as an open architecture and more importantly goes against the vision of the semantic web as an open web of interoperable applications [1], which can be opportunistically located and composed, either manually (web services) or automatically (semantic web services).

For these reasons, in the past twelve months we have carried out a radical redesign of Magpie, resulting in a novel architecture, which is open both with respect to ontologies and with respect to functionalities, the latter delivered through semantic web services. This new architecture goes beyond the idea of providing support for semantic web browsing and can be seen as software framework for designing and implementing semantic web applications. Among other things, the new Magpie opens up new communication modalities allowing bi-directional exchange of information among services and users. This is crucial for going beyond the traditional 'click&go' modality of existing hypermedia systems, such as COHSE, and realizing the 'semantic web of applications' vision described above.

In this paper we describe this new architecture for Magpie and we illustrate its functionalities using the example of the Open University's course on climate science, which we mentioned earlier. The paper is structured as follows. In section 2 we illustrate the Magpie functionalities from an end user's perspective. Section 3 describes the new architecture in detail. In section 4 we elaborate the concept of "open publishing", further stressing its importance in the context of the semantic web. Finally, we conclude the paper by reviewing related work in section 5, and by reiterating its key contributions in section 6.

2   Magpie as a Resource Aggregator in Education

At The Open University, students enrolling in a level-one climatology course receive printed and multimedia educational material. In addition, they are expected to use web resources that are often complex scientific analyses and technical reports of climate scientists, as well as technical news stories related to the subject. Magpie facili-

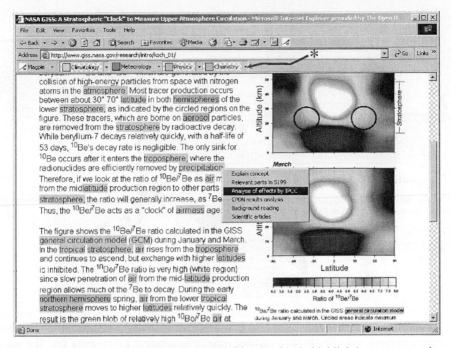

Fig. 1. A climate science related web page with Magpie plug-in highlighting concepts relevant from the perspective of climatology course for a particular student. Menu shown in the center is associated with the concept of '*precipitation*'.

tates a course-specific perspective on such texts. It enables students to relate the content of third-party documents to the relevant course concepts, materials, activities, and knowledge they are expected to gain from studying the course.

Fig. 1 shows a student's web browser with a web page describing stratospheric circulation. This is a relevant but complex text, so the student interacts with it using the Magpie plug-in. The web page[1] is first annotated with several course-specific ontological concepts by selecting some of the ontology-specific toolbar buttons. In this course the student can annotate concepts in four scientific areas: *Climatology*, *Meteorology*, *Physics*, and *Chemistry*. Annotated and highlighted concepts become 'hotspots' to allow the user to request a menu with relevant functionalities for a relevant item. In Fig. 1, the contextual right-click on the '*precipitation*' reveals a menu of semantic services. The choices depend on the ontological classification of a particular concept in the selected ontology.

Our new, services-oriented framework supports composition of such semantic menus from the services available for a particular ontology. These services can be in principle implemented by different knowledge providers. For instance, service '*Relevant parts in S199*' is an internal index to the course material. On the contrary, the '*Background reading*' service is provided by a different university that uses its own, proprietary encyclopedia to provide contextually related reading on a particular concept/topic. Yet another type of service is '*Explain concept*'. This is an aggregating

---

[1] The original text is a property of NASA Goddard Institute for Space Studies, and the page can be accessed at http://www.giss.nasa.gov/research/intro/koch_01/.

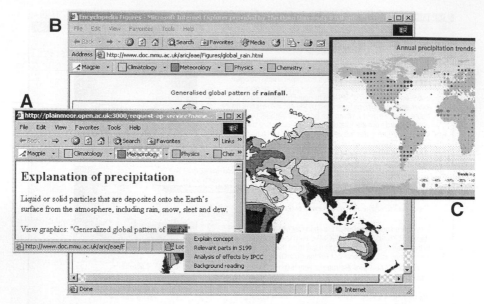

Fig. 2. Results of the '*Explain concept*' semantic query invoked for the '*precipitation*' concept by the semantic menu action depicted in Fig. 1. Window A shows a brief explanation drawing on course glossary and a link to the associated image originating at a third-party site. The actual image related to the concept based on its semantic proximity is in window B. Window C shows a sample analysis relevant to the same concept by Intergovernmental Panel on Climate Change.

service using sophisticated ontology-based reasoning to combine chunks of textual and visual knowledge explaining a particular concept. The combination is based on having access to simpler services retrieving semantically annotated knowledge chunks from several sources and appreciating their semantic 'closeness'. Obviously, the degree of sophistication of the services is independent of the Magpie architecture, which considers all services as black boxes.

Thus, the '*Explain concept*' service in Fig. 1 generates a textual explanation from the course glossary, and attempts to attach a related image or scheme if this exists in its repository of annotated materials (e.g. Fig. 2B). The answer as shown in Fig. 2A does not explicitly exist in the course books, and indeed it is an interpretative viewpoint of the selected ontology. It facilitates an expert's view – as if a tutor was associating different materials together. Because the answer to a semantic query may be a web resource in its own right, it can be further browsed or annotated semantically. Here Magpie merges the independent mechanisms for recognizing semantic relevance and browsing the resulting web resources.

Entirely different strategy is employed by the '*Analysis of effects by IPCC*' service. Unlike the services mentioned earlier, this focuses more on computing the answer rather than linking to any relevant document. A sample response to invoking this semantic service for concept '*precipitation*' may look as shown in Fig. 2C.

The support Magpie provides for trigger services, is based on the 'subscribe&acquire' rather than 'click&go' user-system interaction modality. Our dedicated interfaces, called *collectors*, visualize the results of such services. For example, the collector in Fig. 3 aggregates those concepts appearing in the web page that can be

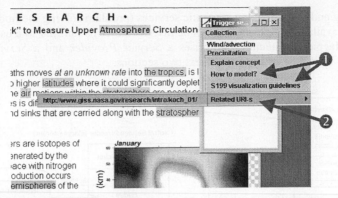

Fig. 3. A simple trigger service aggregating all those concepts from a page, which could be further investigated by the users. This 'further investigation' usually comprises a hands-on modeling exercise with their customized climate model (courtesy of the climate*prediction*.net project) – see pointer ❶. In addition to providing dedicated guidance, the trigger service also serves as a semantic bookmarking tool remembering where particular concepts appeared (see pointer ❷).

modeled or visualized using the state-of-the-art climate model each student runs on his/her computer. As shown in the figure, the list of collected items differs from the highlighted concepts because the model is constrained to run a sub-set of possible analyses. This alternative way of delivering information to the students might implement a tutor's pedagogical goal of providing additional information to those students who are interested in a deeper understanding of the topic. Magpie collectors also offer a range of other functionalities, such as semantic bookmarking or browsing history management. These are discussed in detail e.g. in [5].

This example presents Magpie as an application development framework for building semantic web applications. In this case, a course-specific ontology supports students in making sense of information about climate science, independently of where this information resides on the web. The application is built by selecting or constructing the appropriate ontology and by defining the appropriate services. This example highlights the desirability of an architecture open with respect to services, so that more functionalities can be made available to students, using standard mechanisms for interoperability on the web. This openness facilitates more focused approach to using scarce resources, and enables better personalization. In the next section we look at the backend infrastructure required to support openness with respect to services.

3   An Open Semantic Services Architecture

We now describe the architecture, which allows Magpie users to define, publish and use their own semantic services (shown in Fig. 4). It uses an infrastructure we have developed – IRS-II [13], which supports the publishing and invocation of semantic services. IRS-II is based on the UPML framework [8], and therefore differentiates between *tasks*, *problem solving methods* (generic reasoners) and *domain models*. By distinguishing between tasks and problem solving methods we separate the activity of specifying and implementing semantic services (problem solving methods) from making them available in a form that can be invoked in terms familiar to a user (tasks).

The Magpie architecture comprises a *Service Provider* and a *Service Recipient*. These are briefly described in the next two sections.

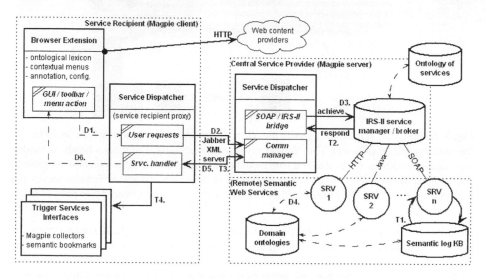

Fig. 4. Schematic architecture of "open services" Magpie framework

3.1   Service Recipient Components

On the service recipient side the framework features: the *Magpie Browser Extension* (of Internet Explorer), the *Magpie Client-Side Service Dispatcher*, and *Trigger Service Interfaces*. The Magpie Browser Extension has already been described in detail in earlier papers [5, 7], and therefore does not need to be discussed again. In a nutshell it provides the basic Magpie functionality, by automatically matching items in a web page to items in the selected ontology and by allowing users to bring up a menu of services contextualized for ontological concepts.

The Magpie Client-Side Service Dispatcher acts as a dedicated service proxy for the user. It manages the communication between the Browser Extension and the service dispatcher embedded in the Magpie server. The Dispatcher delivers both user requests and the responses from providers, using customized XML messages, e.g. to be used by collectors. These are a form of Magpie Trigger Service Interfaces, which are able to visualize the data pushed by the specific trigger services a user subscribes to.

Trigger services are an important innovation in the Magpie infrastructure. Unlike contextual, menu-based services, trigger services are activated based on patterns and relations among concepts recognized in the page and automatically asserted in a semantic log. The subscription system allows the user to filter only 'useful' items to be collected. Since a lot of spam is due to 'pushing' unsolicited content to the users, the principle of trigger services is different. They are not designed for 'blanket coverage' of all users browsing a particular page. They are selected and activated by the user and only push information to him/her when a specific pattern emerges on the page.

The Client-Side Service Dispatcher handles the interactions between the user, the Magpie-enabled browser and the Magpie service providers. In principle, it is an alternative to the GET/POST requests available for standard hypermedia. Although Magpie supports such requests, a growing number of services are available in formats not suitable for integration with a standard web browser, and for this reason the Magpie architecture supports a more generic approach to service mediation.

In particular, the Magpie dispatcher acts on behalf of the user and can be identified as such. Hence, it is possible to communicate service requests/responses *asynchronously*. This is an important extension of standard hypermedia protocol, which assumes synchronous interactions. This capability is also critical for supporting trigger services or generally, semantically-filtered 'pushed content'. Such a *two-way communication* is not possible in standard HTTP-based hypermedia systems.

The support for asynchronous interaction between the client and the server makes the Magpie architecture extremely flexible. For instance, trigger messages may be redirected to a more appropriate user interface than a standard web browser (e.g. a graphic visualization widget). The possibility of bi-directional information exchange is also useful to support negotiation. For instance, different degrees of response granularity may be available, or ontologies may be stored in different formats. Our dispatchers may make it possible for the user to customize the ontology used for interpreting the web pages; e.g. by selecting "a relevant sub-set" of an extensive domain model.

3.2   Service Provider Components

A number of components on the service provider side manage value-added functionalities such as semantic logging, the association of semantic services with ontological classes, and reasoning for trigger services. Two criteria important for designing this "back-office support" for semantic enrichment of web browsing in Magpie are:

- Open as to the definition of new semantic services, which may use an existing ontology and a require access to the semantic log, and
- Allowing users to customize how the output of a service is rendered.

The rationale for these criteria is similar to that of the envisaged Semantic Web [1]. Rather than authors hard-wiring the relationships into the content of web resources, the users are allowed to (re-)use data and services, and adapt them to different contexts. Our Magpie service manager caters for authors publishing new services, and for users selecting or subscribing to a particular set of services. Since Magpie relies on ontologies for associating services with web content, the authors have to publish semantic descriptions of their services. In other words, given the ontology-centric nature of Magpie, a key requirement here is to integrate Magpie with an architecture for *semantic* web services, rather with standard (i.e., non-semantic) web services.

As already mentioned, we have fulfilled this requirement by integrating Magpie with the IRS-II architecture [13], and the Magpie service manager uses the IRS-II framework to handle the subscriptions of individual users to individual services. The service manager also communicates with the IRS broker, whose job is to locate the appropriate web service when a request is made to achieve a task.

Conceptually, the integration between Magpie and the IRS is achieved by defining a top-level *Magpie task,* which takes as input an ontological identifier of a concept, various related arguments and a choice of a visual renderer specifying the desirable output format (typically HTML). Specific semantic services inherit from this generic task, and extend it with specific input or output roles (e.g., the semantic service 'Explain concept' described in section 2 takes a concept from a specific category as input and a textual definition or a pair of textual/graphical definitions as its output).

In IRS-II a task can be handled by one or more *problem-solving methods* (PSMs). PSMs are the knowledge-level descriptions of code for reasoning with particular input roles as specified by the task definition. PSMs tackle a particular task, and introduce a system of *pre-conditions* (e.g. an argument supplied mustn't be a 'Physics' or 'Chemistry' concept), and *post-conditions* (e.g. show graphics if available). While PSMs are crucial for reasoning, the end-user only interacts at the task level – thus specifying what needs to be achieved rather than how to achieve it. The IRS-II framework supports different modes of service publishing and invocation, as well as other emerging standards such as WSDL [13]. Regardless of the publication, IRS-II generates a unique "access URI" where the web service can be invoked. These URIs are then used in Magpie to achieve a particular task when a user right-clicks a particular 'hotspot' item in a web page.

4   Defining Magpie Semantic Services

The process of manual definition of semantic services for different ontologies by the knowledge engineer is not feasible on a larger scale. We argued in section 3.2 that the publication procedure has to be open. Before describing the technical details of defining semantic services using the web services framework, we re-consider the educational example from section 2 to highlight key benefits for the end-user.

4.1   Benefits of Open Services Architecture

Magpie shows the *on-demand services menu* whenever the mouse hovers over a recognized entity. This menu is context-dependent, but so-far, we have used a one-size-fits-all semantic context defined by the membership of a particular entity to a particular ontological class. The class membership is defined in the ontology, and is essentially the same for all users subscribing to a particular ontology. This acknowledges a certain degree of commonality of purpose among the subscribers, but it is a rather superficial commonality. For example, if a tutor decides to divide the students into 'standard' and 'advanced' learners, Magpie should reflect this pedagogic strategy by offering suitable services to the sub-groups of students based on the tutor's choice.

Another issue concerns the development of such educational resources. Institutions accelerate their course production and update procedures, but with printed materials this may still take some time. In Magpie framework, new semantic services for students could be developed and updated continuously. Because of the nature of the framework, new services are accessible to the end users (students) with 'near-zero' delay since their development.

4.2   Defining Magpie Tasks

The generic Magpie framework comes with core ontologies that define a) a basic domain ontology of items such as 'Thing' and 'HTML', b) a task ontology defining the top-level Magpie task, and c) a basic PSM ontology of default Magpie services (e.g. rendering HTML and XML-based output). The magpie-generic-request-task is a top-level, generic description taking three inputs: user's identity (UID), ontological concept identifier (OID), and rendering. Its output has to be a result that complies with the rendering provided as an input argument, and it can be in form of RDF, HTML or a generic list. Specific Magpie tasks inherit from this generic request task.

magpie-explain thing-task (magpie-generic-request-task)

input roles: has_oid   // task is invoked for a given item
 has_user   // task is invoked by a given user
 has_rendering   // result rendered as ...

output role: has_result   // the result of the service

constraints: type-of (has_oid) = (or Climatology Meteorology Physics Chemistry)   ❶
 cardinality (has_oid) = 1
 value (has-pretty-name) = "Explain concept"   ❷

has-goal-expression: value = (kappa (?task ?sol)
 (= ?sol (magpie-render-function (role-value ?task has-rendering)
 (request-explain-thing-function (role-value ?task has-oid)))))   ❷

Fig. 5. Schematic task description for Magpie service 'Explain concept' in IRS-II

A task description for the service *'Explain concept'* containing optional graphics (from section 2) is shown in Fig. 5. Marker '❶' highlights parts that re-define the generic task; e.g. restricting the concept OID to be an instance of Climatology or Meteorology classes. These classes come from a specific, climate course reference ontology. Hence, the *'Explain concept'* task is defined in an ontology that inherits from both a generic ontology of Magpie tasks and from the course ontology.

The definition of the magpie-explain-thing-task contains two extra slots (see markers '❷'): has-pretty-name labels the task in the displayed semantic menu, and has-goal-expression plays two roles. Firstly, it specifies what the task does for a human reader. Secondly, the expression enables knowledge-level reasoning about the task for the purposes of automatic service location or composition.

4.3   Defining Magpie PSMs

Having described what a particular task can do for a particular ontology, the semantic web application developer describes the actual methods tackling it. Fig. 6 shows a PSM description, which looks similar to that of a task. The main difference is that the developer defines different PSMs to implement a particular task for different types of input. For instance, let's assume that we have already defined a generic (empty) PSM for the *'Explain concept'* service, and now want to narrow it for the class *'Climatology'*. Constraining a PSM for a particular class means introducing an additional applicability condition (the input has to be a Climatology concept) that must be satisfied before invoking this method. This condition semantically annotates the code that implements it and makes it applicable only to this class. In practice this may mean that different providers can handle different categories of data using mutually incompatible approaches or techniques. Our PSMs take this fully into account.

```
magpie-explain-climatology-provider    (magpie-explain-thing-provider)
  tackles-task:                         magpie-explain-thing-task
  has-applicability-condition:    (kappa (?p)
                                    (climatology-category (role-value ?p has-oid)))
```

Fig. 6. PSM description for Magpie service tackling the task '*Explain concept*' (see Fig. 5) for the '*Climatology*' class (category)

Applicability conditions enable the broker to select from several PSMs tackling the same task. There may be several distinct descriptions (e.g. with or without graphical explanation), but the user needs to refer to a single task ('Explain concept'). The service manager can invoke a specific PSM and its implementation depending on the type of the submitted argument or user preference. This also explains why semantic menus for different categories may use the same label to identify a service (task) that delivers different functionality in a different context (through different PSMs).

4.4   Publishing and Invoking Magpie Services

The final step is to write a snippet of code in Java (for example), and to make it available by publishing it via IRS-II. Publishing is explained in [13]; here it suffices to say that it essentially means creating wrappers turning a piece of proprietary code into a web service and associating that service with an appropriate PSM. The associations are stored in a registry, which is referred to whenever a user makes a request to achieve a particular task with a particular set of arguments. The IRS-II takes care of invoking the appropriate service provider code, passing the necessary arguments, and processing the results.

All the activities described so-far were done by service or semantic web application developers – outside of the Magpie end user scope of attention. The implications of such a standard means of publishing services for the end user are in the simplification of the entire interaction. Once the user decides which classes in the selected ontology he/she is interested in, the Magpie plug-in uses the Dispatcher to request the semantic services applicable to each chosen class. The generator of semantic menus is itself a service that takes a (top-level) class name as an input, and sends back a list of URIs to invoke applicable tasks. The generator takes all tasks published for a particular ontology, where at least one argument matches a given class; i.e. the input type is either the given class or is a subclass of the given class. Each service is rendered as a pair ⟨pretty-name, URI⟩; for example (the 'XXXN' replaces the actual values):

Explain concept
http://irsserver:3000/achieve-task?ontology=climateprediction-kb& task=request-explain-thing-task&has_oid=XXX1& has_user=XXX2 & has_rendering=XXX3

The actual execution of a particular service from a semantic services menu in a Magpie-enabled web browser invokes the task behind the 'pretty label' (through URI). The benefit to the user is the task-based reference to semantic services. Instead of knowing (and labeling) the individual methods, the user refers to a particular functionality using a single label, regardless of the context. This reduces the maintenance overhead. New variations of a service for different contexts can be added without changing the structure of the displayed menus; the implementation or location of an individual service can be changed transparently.

4.5   Specifics of Trigger Services

Magpie trigger services can be defined following the same procedure as for the on-demand services (described in previous sections). However, there is one major difference; a generic 'trigger task' has no particular concept (OID) as its input. It does not make sense for a trigger service to invoke it for a single specific item (e.g., 'airmass'). An access to regularly updated semantic log, which resides on one of the central Magpie servers, is required instead. Since services (including trigger ones) can be defined by anyone, and may be distributed, there is a problem in accessing the central semantic log. This cannot be replicated because of security issues, and for this reason, each trigger service needs to monitor it for a particular (approved) pattern.

As a result, both the task and PSM definitions of trigger services use a simple extension to the standard service specification mechanism. First, the author declares that a particular trigger name is associated with a particular pattern. The pattern is then typically defined in terms of applicable antecedents for an 'IF...THEN...' rule. For example, a trigger may generate experiment guidelines to investigate concepts found in a web page (for which some guideline exists). The pattern would look like this:

(and (climatology-category ?X) (has-link-to ?X ?Y) (experiment-guide ?Y))

The author then associates a task invocation with the pattern. The actual implementation of the trigger task calls a central, shared service monitoring the semantic log with this specific pattern as one of the arguments. In other words, once a user registers with a particular trigger task, the respective pattern is forwarded to the semantic log monitor, where it is applied whenever the log is updated. Otherwise, the trigger task behaves as a standard service; it takes the asserted data as an input and distributes an alert to all those users who subscribed to the trigger. An example of how this trigger functionality has been used to facilitate team collaboration is discussed in [6].

5   Related Work

A tool that functionally resembles Magpie is the KIM plug-in for Internet Explorer [14]. Knowledge and Information Management (KIM) is a platform for automatic semantic annotation, web page indexing and retrieval. As Magpie, it uses named entities as a foundation for document semantics, and assigns ontological definitions to the entities in the text. The platform uses a massive populated ontology of common 'upper-level' concepts (e.g. locations, dates, organizations or money) and their instances.

Unlike Magpie, KIM is based on the GATE platform [4] but it extends its flat NER rules with ontological hierarchies. The entities are recognized by the KIM proxy, and in parallel they are associated with respective instances in the ontology. GATE supports the recognition of acronyms, incomplete names and co-references thus enabling KIM to work with both already-known and new named entities.

Magpie differs from KIM in a number of respects. While KIM is coupled with a specific, large knowledge base, Magpie is open with respect to ontologies, allowing users to select a particular semantic viewpoint and use this to enrich the browsing experience. Another important difference is that while KIM is very much steeped in the classic 'click&go' hypermedia paradigm, Magpie is open with respect to services, as discussed in this paper. Hence, as already pointed out Magpie goes beyond KIM in the direction of providing a framework for building semantic web applications, rather than simply supporting semantic annotation and semantic web browsing.

Magpie also differs from 'free-text' document annotation tools [9, 10] by intertwining entity recognition, annotation and ontological reasoning. Annotation using ontological lexicons outperforms 'free-text' annotations in terms of >90-95% recall rate and similar precision for in-domain resources. Yet, free-hand annotations are useful for ad-hoc, personal, customized interpretation of the web resources. Magpie does not currently support manual semantic annotation, which is a limitation. To address this issue we will shortly begin work on integrating Magpie with MnM, a semantic annotation framework developed at the Knowledge Media Institute [16].

From user interface adaptability perspective Magpie is relevant to projects such as Letizia [11] with its reconnaissance agents. This type of agent "looks ahead of the user on the links on the current web page". Such pre-filtering may use semantic knowledge to improve the relevance and usefulness of browsing. Magpie implements functionality similar to that of Letizia ("logged entities reconnaissance") through semantic logging and trigger services, and thus provides a more general and flexible framework for implementing push services, than the one provided by Letizia.

Another system superficially similar to Magpie is COHSE, which implements an open hypermedia approach [2]. The similarity between the two systems is due to the fact that (at a basic level of analysis) both work with web resources and use similar user interaction paradigms ('click&go'). However, beyond the superficial similarity there are very major differences between these two systems. The main goal of COHSE is to provide dynamic linking between documents – i.e., the basic unit of information for COHSE is a document. Dynamic linking is achieved by using the ontology as a mediator between terms appearing in two different documents. COHSE uses a hypertext paradigm to cross-link documents through static and dynamic anchors. In contrast with COHSE, Magpie is not about linking documents.

As emphasized in the introduction, there are three ways we can look at Magpie: as a way to support semantic web browsing, as a tool to support interpretation of web resources through 'ontological lenses' and as a framework for building semantic web applications. In particular, if we take the latter perspective, Magpie goes beyond the notion of hypermedia systems, by providing a platform for integrating semantic services into the browsing experience, both in pull and push modalities. In a nutshell, Magpie uses a different paradigm. It views web as a knowledge-based servicing of various user needs. Using Magpie's "web as computation" paradigm, we not only provide information about one concept, but can easily offer knowledge dependent on *N-ary relationships* among concepts. This is impossible in any hypermedia system –

one can't use one click to follow multiple anchors simultaneously, and reach a single target document or a piece of knowledge.

Moreover, Magpie supports the publishing of new services without altering the servers or the plug-in. Service publishing leaves the users in control by allowing them to subscribe to selected services. It also makes the development of a semantically rich application more modular; thus cheaper and easier for domain experts rather than knowledge engineers. This is more powerful than the mechanisms used by open hypermedia systems, which are largely based on the "editorial choice of links". Magpie explores the actual knowledge space as contrasted with navigating through hypertext as one of its explicit manifestations. Mere link following (in open or closed hypermedia) is not sufficient to facilitate document interpretation. We complement the familiar 'click&go' model by two new models: (i) 'publish&subscribe' (for services) and (ii) 'subscribe&acquire' (for data and knowledge).

To conclude we want to note a growing recognition by the research community of the need to make the semantic web accessible to "ordinary" users. Two approaches follow similar, lightweight and near-zero overhead principles as Magpie; albeit for different purposes. The authors of Haystack [15] and Mangrove [12] argue that the major issue with Semantic Web is the gap between the power of authoring languages such as RDF(S) or OWL and sheer simplicity of HTML. In response to this concern, Magpie separates the presentation of semantic knowledge, service authoring, and publishing from the underlying knowledge-level reasoning mechanisms.

6   Concluding Remarks

In this paper we described the Magpie framework focusing on how semantic services can be deployed and used in an open fashion. Magpie is an *open architecture* in respect to the technological infrastructure; it is not bound to a single 'services standard'. The separation of the user interface from a 'thin communication client', the Client-Side Service Dispatcher, offers several benefits, and enables us to implement dynamically defined/updated on-demand and trigger services. By combining semantic web, browsing technologies and semantic web services we created an open framework that maximizes flexibility. A Magpie user is free to select both the overall viewpoint, captured within an ontology, and the associated services. Semantic web application developers are free to customize and extend the available services including a number of core Magpie services such as the NER and lexicon generation.

As we showed in our example, Magpie enables lay members of the public to explore rich scientific resources (such as climatology and climate prediction, for example). Thus, the semantic browsing capabilities of Magpie may serve as an *enabling technology* for the increased public understanding of science. In the past papers, we presented Magpie as a tool for browsing the Semantic Web. However, as Tim Berners-Lee argues: "Semantic Web is about integration of resources rather than browsing."[2]. Leaving aside the philosophical issue of what constitutes "*the semantic web browser*", the extended Magpie framework can be seen as a display *integrating* knowledge resources *distributed throughout* the Semantic Web. Web services offer

---

[2]   Quote from Tim Berners-Lee's keynote speech delivered at the 2nd International Semantic Web Conference, Sanibel Island, Florida, US, October 2003.

small, easier to maintain modules of a larger semantic web application, could be authored independently, and stored as a distributed system.

Whether the Semantic Web is about browsing, computation or integration, the main contribution of our research is in allowing users to browse the standard Web whilst utilizing the concepts and relationships captured within a selected ontology. The semantic services (whether on-demand or triggered) that are offered through the Magpie framework enhance web interoperability and user interaction with knowledge. Magpie plug-in acts more as an end-user interface for accessing and interacting with the distributed semantic web services rather than a mere "web browser".

For the future, a number of issues remain open. As mentioned earlier, we want to integrate Magpie with a framework for semantic annotation [16], to allow seamless integration of browsing, service invocation and annotation. This would enable the users to extend and/or customize the existing ontological commitments. We are also working on more powerful named entity recognition mechanisms, both ontology-based and general-purpose (such as GATE [4]). Finally, we are working on a set of support tools that would enable web developers to publish their applications for the Magpie users quickly and simply. This is critical in order to reduce the development time for any subsequent applications of our framework.

Once this publishing facility is in place, a comprehensive usability study needs to be performed to back our assumptions and design principles. Nonetheless, our initial experiments with tools supporting the application developers seem to support our experience-driven requirement for reducing the complexity of interacting with semantic web services. Magpie is clearly geared towards high recall/precision annotation *within a specific domain*. Early evidence suggests there is a benefit for naïve users and novices in interacting with the domain knowledge in such a constrained way. However, to measure the value-added of Magpie more objective usability study is planned.

Acknowledgments. The Magpie effort is supported by the climate*prediction*.net and the Advanced Knowledge Technologies (AKT) projects. Climate*prediction*.net is sponsored by the UK Natural Environment Research Council and UK Department of Trade e-Science Initiative, and involves Oxford University, CLRC Rutherford Appleton Labs and The Open University. AKT is an Interdisciplinary Research Collaboration (IRC) sponsored by the UK Engineering and Physical Sciences Research Council by grant no. GR/N15764/01. The AKT IRC comprises the Universities of Aberdeen, Edinburgh, Sheffield, Southampton and The Open University.

References

[1]   Berners-Lee, T., Hendler, J., and Lassila, O., *The Semantic Web*. Scientific American, 2001. **279**(5): p.34-43.
[2]   Carr, L., Bechhofer, S., Goble, C., *et al. Conceptual Linking: Ontology-based Open Hypermedia*. In *Proc. of the 10th Intl. WWW Conf.* 2001. Hong-Kong.
[3]   Ciravegna, F., Chapman, S., Dingli, A., *et al. Learning to Harvest Information for the Semantic Web*. In *1st European Semantic Web Symposium*. 2004. Greece.

[4]   Cunningham, H., Maynard, D., Bontcheva, K., *et al. GATE: A Framework and Graphical Development Environment for Robust NLP Tools and Applications.* In *Proc. of the 40th Anniversary Meeting of the Association for Computational Linguistics (ACL).* 2002. Pennsylvania, US.

[5]   Domingue, J., Dzbor, M., and Motta, E. *Magpie: Supporting Browsing and Navigation on the Semantic Web.* In *Proc. of the Intelligent User Interfaces Conf. (IUI).* 2004. Portugal.

[6]   Domingue, J., Dzbor, M., and Motta, E. *Collaborative Semantic Web Browsing with Magpie.* In *1st European Semantic Web Symposium.* 2004. Greece.

[7]   Dzbor, M., Domingue, J., and Motta, E. *Magpie: Towards a Semantic Web Browser.* In *Proc. of the 2nd Intl. Semantic Web Conf.* 2003. Florida, USA.

[8]   Fensel, D. and Motta, E., *Structured Development of Problem Solving Methods.* IEEE Transactions on Knowledge and Data Engineering, 2001. **13**(6): p.913-932

[9]   Handschuh, S., Staab, S., and Maedche, A. *CREAM - Creating relational metadata with a component-based, ontology driven annotation framework.* In *Intl. Semantic Web Working Symposium (SWWS).* 2001. California, USA.

[10] Kahan, J., Koivunen, M.-R., Prud'Hommeaux, E., *et al. Annotea: An Open RDF Infrastructure for Shared Web Annotations.* In *Proc. of the 10th Intl. WWW Conf.* 2001. Hong-Kong.

[11] Lieberman, H., Fry, C., and Weitzman, L., *Exploring the web with reconnaissance Agents.* Comm. of the ACM, 2001. **44**(8): p.69-75.

[12] McDowell, L., Etzioni, O., Gribble, S.D., *et al. Mangrove: Enticing Ordinary People onto the Semantic Web via Instant Gratification.* In *Proc. of the 2nd Intl. Semantic Web Conf.* 2003. Florida, USA.

[13] Motta, E., Domingue, J., Cabral, L., *et al. IRS-II: A Framework and Infrastructure for Semantic Web Services.* In *Proc. of the 2nd Intl. Semantic Web Conf.* 2003. Florida, USA.

[14] Popov, B., Kiryakov, A., Kirilov, A., *et al. KIM - Semantic Annotation Platform.* In *Proc. of the 2nd Intl. Semantic Web Conf.* 2003. Florida, USA.

[15] Quan, D., Huynh, D., and Karger, D.R. *Haystack: A Platform for Authoring End User Semantic Web Applications.* In *Proc. of the 2nd Intl. Semantic Web Conf.* 2003. Florida, USA.

[16] Vargas-Vera, M., Motta, E., Domingue, J., *et al. MnM: Ontology Driven Semi-automatic and Automatic Support for Semantic Markup.* In *Proc. of the 13th European Knowledge Acquisition Workshop (EKAW).* 2002. Spain.

Towards a Symptom Ontology for Semantic Web Applications

Kenneth Baclawski[1], Christopher J. Matheus[2], Mieczyslaw M. Kokar[1],
Jerzy Letkowski[3], and Paul A. Kogut[4]

[1] Northeastern University
[2] Versatile Information Systems, Inc.
[3] Western New England College
[4] Lockheed Martin

Abstract. As the use of Semantic Web ontologies continues to expand there is a growing need for tools that can validate ontological consistency and provide guidance in the correction of detected defects and errors. A number of tools already exist as evidenced by the ten systems participating in the W3C's evaluation of the OWL Test Cases. For the most part, these first generation tools focus on experimental approaches to consistency checking, while minimal attention is paid to how the results will be used or how the systems might interoperate. For this reason very few of these systems produce results in a machine-readable format (for example as OWL annotations) and there is no shared notion across the tools of how to identify and describe what it is that makes a specific ontology or annotation inconsistent. In this paper we propose the development of a Symptom Ontology for the Semantic Web that would serve as a common language for identifying and describing semantic errors and warnings that may be indicative of inconsistencies in ontologies and annotations; we refer to such errors and warnings as *symptoms*. We offer the symptom ontology currently used by the ConsVISor consistency-checking tool, as the starting point for a discussion on the desirable characteristics of such an ontology. Included among these characteristics are 1) a hierarchy of common symptoms, 2) clear associations between specific symptoms and the axioms of the languages they violate and 3) a means for relating individual symptoms back to the specific constructs in the input file(s) through which they were implicated. We conclude with aa number of suggestions for future directions of this work including its extension to syntactic symptoms.

1 Introduction

As the Semantic Web initiative and the use of the Web Ontology Language (OWL) [1] continue to develop and grow in popularity, there will be an increasing need for ways to validate ontological consistency and provide guidance in the correction of defects and errors in OWL documents. Even with relatively simple OWL documents, identifying inconsistencies within their XML markup can be a major challenge beyond the capabilities of most writers of ontologies and annotations. Fortunately, formal and heuristic techniques exist for automatically detecting certain types of inconsistencies, and several tools, called "validators" or "consistency checkers", already provide some limited capabilities. The W3C's OWL Test Results page [2] shows nine systems capable of detecting at least some forms of inconsistencies within

S.A. McIlraith et al. (Eds.): ISWC 2004, LNCS 3298, pp. 650–667, 2004.

OWL documents; additional tools with consistency-checking capabilities can be found in [3] and at [4]. As automated consistency-checking techniques continue to mature they will eventually become an integral part of most if not all OWL tools and application development suites. Given the formative stage of these tools, now is the time to consider how they might evolve and explore ways of fostering their ultimate effectiveness and interoperability with other tools.

In this paper we focus on the nature of the output of consistency-checking tools, both in terms of what they are like now and what they might be in the future. In particular we are concerned with the format and content of the output reports these tools generate, which currently vary widely in the inconsistencies they identify, the identification and description of the detected symptoms of the inconsistencies and the format in which the results are delivered. We begin by reviewing the content and format of the results returned by several existing tools and argue that the lack of a consistent and well-grounded (semantically speaking) approach to the representation of results makes these tools difficult to use, especially by automated programs intended to leverage the results of one or more of them. The situation as it currently exists seems to be begging for the development of a common, shared ontology for describing the symptoms of the inconsistencies discovered in OWL documents. As an example of how such an ontology might work, we present the symptom ontology used by **ConsVISor** [5], the authors' consistency-checking tool, and offer it as an initial step towards the establishment of a symptom ontology for Semantic Web applications. In closing we discuss the strengths and limitations of this nascent ontology along with making a number of suggestions for future improvements and extensions.

2   Review of Existing Consistency Reports

We have analyzed the output from several freely available consistency-checking tools but for this paper we limit attention to the following five: **ConsVISor** [6], **Euler** [7], **FOWL** [8], **Pellet** [9] and **vOWLidator** [10]. The first four of these systems participated in the W3C OWL Test Cases demonstration [2] and either provided links to their full output reports for each test or they were available as Web services from which their results could be easily obtained. The fifth system was included due to its early popularity as a DAML+OIL [11] (the predecessor to OWL) validation tool and because it exhibits some desirable characteristics worth noting. For the sake of comparing the various outputs, we used just one of the W3C's DL inconsistency test cases (DL 109) to produce the sample output reports that appear in Figures 1-5.

Many consistency-checking tools also perform syntax checking. As defined in the OWL standard, a syntax checker makes a determination of the language level of the OWL document being examined. A consistency checker makes no such determination: the OWL language level must be explicitly asserted by the user. Because many tools perform both functions, the distinction between these two types of tools is often blurred. In this paper we consider only consistency checkers.

In our analysis, we were not as concerned with the correctness of the results as we were with the general nature of the content and format of the reports. On the chosen test case all of the first four systems correctly identified the document as being inconsistent; the fifth system was unable to perform a consistency test due to an error

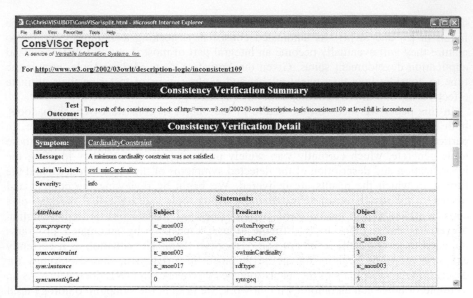

Fig. 1. ConsVISor Sample Output Report (condensed HTML version)

produced by the parser it happens to use. Of greater interest to us were the answers to three simple questions.

1. What language does the tool use to format its output? In other words, is the output report written in plain text, structured HTML, RDF, OWL or some non-standard language? The answer to this question conveys a lot about how easy it is to automatically process the results with other programs. It also identifies whether there is a well-defined semantics for interpreting the results. While natural language output can be very useful when humans are reading the output of a tool, it is of little use for automated processing. In this paper we focus on the extent to which these tools produce output that can processed automatically, and we do not comment on how readable the output might be to a human reader. We also do not speculate on whether one might be able to interact with a tool on the source code level (such as via some API).

2. Did the tool identify specific symptoms of the inconsistencies within the document? This question is not about whether the tool correctly identified the presence of one or more inconsistencies (i.e., that it responded "Inconsistent" or "Consistent") but rather whether the specific nature of the inconsistencies was identified; just knowing that a document is inconsistent is not as helpful as knowing why. In the ideal case a tool would associate each symptom of an inconsistency with the specific axiom or axioms of the ontology language (i.e., OWL Lite, OWL DL, OWL Full) that were violated.

3. How useful to the document's author is the output report in identifying and helping to correct the cause(s) of the inconsistency(s)? Being told that a complex document violates a specific OWL axiom will not necessarily provide sufficient information for the author to locate and correct the error, even if she is a highly skilled ontologist. Ideally a tool will, when possible, indicate the line number and character position of the symptom(s) indicative of the underlying inconsistencies.

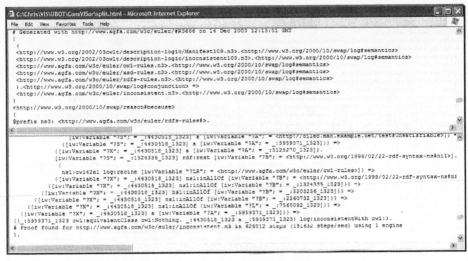

Fig. 2. Euler Sample Output Report (condensed)

Table 1 provides a summary of the answers to the three questions for the five analyzed systems. The intent of this table is not to pass judgment on particular systems but to indicate the disparate nature of the output of current systems. In the following subsections we discuss each of our three questions and their answers in more detail. In the fourth subsection we describe the differences between statements made by some of the systems pertaining to *errors*, *warnings*, *information* and *fatal failures*, some of which go beyond the mere identification of symptoms of inconsistencies.

Table 1. Summary of Answers to Three Questions

System	Output Language	Axiom Violations Ided	Location
ConsVISor	HTML or OWL	Yes	yes, if possible
Euler	non-standard	difficult to determine	no
FOWL	non-standard	difficult to determine	no
Pellet	text (html markup)	No	no
vOWLidator	structured HTML	Sometimes	no

2.1   Question 1: Output Language

The W3C OWL test results show that in the case of the set of all inconsistency tests no single participating system is currently capable of detecting every inconsistency across all language species (i.e., Full, DL, Lite). This is not very surprising given that the tools employ different techniques for detecting inconsistencies and many of them are still in the early stages of development. Moreover, because OWL Full is undecidable, it is impossible for a single tool to detect every possible inconsistency. These observations, however, suggest that one should run an OWL document through more than one of these systems. It is fair to say that writing a program to automatically

Fig. 3. FOWL Sample Output Report

run all five systems (or even some reasonable subset) on a given OWL document and then combine the results into a meaningful summary would be challenging. Even if one succeeded in creating such a program it would require tweaking whenever any of the tool authors changed the output representation of their systems or when new, more powerful systems come along, each having its own unique output format. Of the 5 consistency checkers surveyed, only one (ConsVISor) can produce ontologically-based output, and only one other tool (vOWLidator) can produce well structured output.

If the intent is to be able to have consistency-checking tools that can interoperate with other tools or amongst themselves, then it is paramount that these systems at least provide the option for outputting their results in an ontology language such as OWL. Once this conclusion is accepted it becomes necessary to consider what should belong in the ontology created for this purpose. Before addressing this issue, however, there are two additional factors we would like to consider regarding the nature of the output of consistency-checking tool.

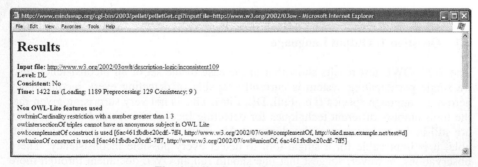

Fig. 4. Pellet Sample Output Report

2.2   Question 2: Axiom Violation

The guidelines provided with the W3C OWL Test Cases specify that a consistency-checking tool "takes a document as input and returns one word being Consistent, Inconsistent, or Unknown" [12]. This approach is fine if all you wish to know is whether an ontology is consistent or not. A Semantic Web browser, for example, may only need this level of feedback from a consistency checker in order to determine whether or not it should attempt to render a document; if the checker returns Inconsistent the browser can simply refuse to process it further. If, on the other hand, you are an author needing to produce a consistent document, having a tool that simply tells you your document is Inconsistent is not very helpful; rather, you would like to receive some indication of what it is about your document that makes it inconsistent.

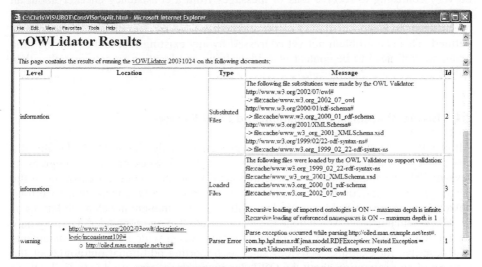

Fig. 5. vOWLidator Sample Output Report

So what makes an OWL document inconsistent? An OWL document is inconsistent if there is no interpretation for the RDF graph defined by the document's triples [13]. An interpretation exists if and only if there are no contradictions in the set of triples consisting of the document triples plus all of the derived triples entailed by the axioms of the OWL language. In theory, if a consistency checker discovers a contradiction in this set of triples it should be possible to trace the contradiction to a specific violation or violations of the OWL language semantics specified in [13]. Ideally, a consistency-checking tool should describe the detected symptoms of inconsistencies in terms of the specific language axioms that are violated. By doing so it provides a means for verifying that the tool "understands" what it is talking about. In other words, if a tool can state why it believes there is an inconsistency we have a means for determining whether it is correct. We currently have no systematic way of knowing if the reasoning behind the Consistent and Inconsistent responses we get from the tools is sound. What we need is an agreed upon approach for how tools indicate the axiom violations they detect – yet another reason for the creation of a common symptom ontology.

2.3   Question 3: Symptom Location

In addition to identifying the nature of a violation, an ideal consistency checker would indicate the precise location and nature of the "bug" or "bugs" discovered in an OWL document. For example, the tool might tell you that "in the Ontology element you forgot to include an import for the XYZ ontology" or "you mistyped the name of the resource at line 10 character position 5". Unfortunately the precise identification of the underlying cause or causes of an inconsistency, let alone its location, is often not possible. This situation can result from limitations in the methods these tools use to detect inconsistencies, but it can also be due to the fact that it is frequently impossible to determine the original intentions of the author. In either case what these first generation tools usually detect are "symptoms" of problems rather than the problems themselves, and in many cases a single problem can lead to multiple symptoms. It can be very confusing to receive tens of messages from a consistency checker about an undefined resource and yet receive no mention of the construct causing the error itself, such as a typo in the id of the element where the resource was supposedly defined. This is a problem not yet addressed by any existing tool and so for the time being we will need to be content with identifying and locating symptoms rather than bugs.[1]

2.4   Errors, Warnings, Information, and Fatal Failures

All problems are not created equal. In the process of analyzing an OWL document a consistency-checking tool may encounter a variety of issues of various degrees of severity. The most egregious are those that clearly violate one or more axioms of the language semantics; these are clearly identifiable as *errors*. In addition to errors, however, there are several types of identifiable "issues" that are not clear violations of the OWL semantics but which none the less indicate that an unintended meaning may be implicit in the document. Consequently, many tools provide *informative* statements that describe, for example, activities such as importing additional ontologies or the making of an assumption about the OWL language class being used (e.g. Full, DL or Lite). *Warnings* represent the identification of constructs (or often, lack there of) that indicate the author may have constructed something other than what was intended, even though it is perfectly valid. For example, it is perfectly permissible in OWL full to use a resource as a property without defining it as such, but it is often the case that doing so represents an oversight in the definition of the property or perhaps a misspelling of the resource name. Informative statements and warnings are not actually indicators of inconsistencies but they are often helpful in providing information that the author can use to ensure the ultimate document conveys the intended meaning. There is finally another type of "issue" not quite captured by any of the other three and that is what we call a *fatal failure*. A fatal failure occurs when the system failed to complete the consistency check because it either crashed or ran out of resources. In such cases the tool (if it can) should return "Unknown" as its

---

[1]   The authors are working on a second generation tool, called BugVISor, that attempts to reason from observed symptoms back to the root problems, i.e., the "bugs", that caused them; unfortunately this topic is beyond the scope of the current paper.

result and ideally include as much information as may be useful in determining the cause of the failure.

As with the case of symptom location, there is the question of "where" and "how" to report information about these various types of issues. Once again, having a common ontology would provide the vehicle for representing such information in a consistent and meaningful manner usable by humans and machines alike.

3 Proposed Solution

For the purpose of giving an account of the symptoms of inconsistencies detected in an OWL document by a consistency-checking tool, various approaches are possible. A natural approach, and one chosen by several existing tools, is the use of a plain textual description describing the problem(s) in human readable terms. An obvious extension to this is to beautify the output with HTML markup or to add some structure to the results using, for example, HTML tables. While the latter approach makes it possible to write programs to "screen scrape" the content of the results from the HTML, none of these approaches is well suited to the automated processing and interpretation of the results by machines. As discussed above, there are several advantages to making consistency-checking results machine processible, and, given the intended audience of this paper, we do not believe it is necessary to belabor the argument. Given that the use of a formal language is desirable the question then becomes one of choosing which one based on the requirements of the information that needs to be conveyed. Clearly we will need to define at least a class to represent instances of symptoms and this class will need properties to associate individual symptoms with the specific resources involved, axioms violated, and location information, at the least. These requirements represent a clear case for use of an ontology language and in the context of the Semantic Web the natural choice is of course OWL itself.

If we agree it is worthwhile to develop a common ontology in OWL for use in annotating the results of consistency-checking tools, we can then turn our attention to the question of what it needs to contain. As we have argued, symptoms are about as much as one can expect to receive from the current generation of tools, and even with the advent of more sophisticated systems capable of identifying actual bugs there will always be situations where the best one can do is cite the symptom(s) indicative of a possible bug (this is so because there will always be situations where a system cannot unequivocally determine the intent of the author). For this reason we believe the symptom class should be the focus of the ontology, and have placed it at the center of our proposed high-level design shown in Fig. 6. So what makes up a symptom? First, a symptom is always attributable to a specific OWL document, i.e., the one in which it was detected. In fact, since the output of the tool may actually include multiple symptoms it would be convenient to define a high-level class to describe the OWL document and associate with it the (possibly empty) set of symptoms that were detected. One could also associate it with other meta-data about the document, such as the high-level conclusion reached by the tool (i.e., `Consistent`, `Inconsistent` or `Unknown`).

Another characteristic of a symptom is that there should always be (in theory at least) an axiom of the ontology language that was violated and which serves as the justification for claiming the symptom represents an inconsistency. This allows a client to examine the original language references that define the OWL language. This can be represented using a property on the symptom class that connects it with a class representing axioms. In addition, a symptom is always manifested by the characteristics of one or more RDF statements (i.e., triples) found in or inferred from the OWL document. It is possible to identify various types of symptom sub-classes based on the statement characteristics they share; when we consider the ontology used by **ConsVISor** in the next section we present an example of a set of symptom subclasses defined in this manner. This idea of creating symptom subclasses based on shared characteristics is appealing because we can then define the relationships between the statements comprising a subclass of symptoms through the definition of appropriate property constraints on the subclass. The examples in the next section will make this more clear, but for now the point is that the ontology needs to be able to associate symptoms with specific statements specified in or inferred from the OWL document, and one convenient way to do this is by defining various symptom subclasses based on shared statement characteristics.

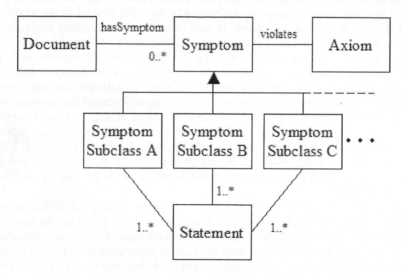

Fig. 6. Proposed High-Level Design for a Shared Symptom Ontology

The UML diagram in Fig. 6 shows a high-level view of the proposed design for a common symptom ontology, as described in the preceding paragraphs. This design is intended to capture the general concepts that we hope can be agreed upon by the Semantic Web user community and thereby serve as a starting point for discussion; consequently, many of the details of a complete solution – including what fully defines the Axiom and Document classes – are left unspecified. In the next section we describe the design decisions made during the creation of **ConsVISor**'s symptom ontology and offer the implementation as a case study from which to draw ideas for a community-defined solution.

4   ConsVISor's Symptom Ontology

ConsVISor is a rule-based tool for checking the consistency of OWL Full, OWL DL and OWL Lite documents. At the time of this writing it is freely available for use as a Web service at http://www.vistology.com/**ConsVISor**. **ConsVISor**'s development was initiated as a DARPA funded project in 2002, at which time the target languages were DAML+OIL and RDF and the implementation was done in Prolog and Java. During the conversion from DAML+OIL to OWL in 2003 the system underwent a number of changes including a re-implementation in Jess and Java and the introduction of a symptom ontology for use in producing OWL-annotated results. The success of this ontology-based approach to generating consistency reports led to the conceptualization of this paper. In the rest of this section we describe the design of the **ConsVISor** symptom ontology and offer it as an initial step towards the ultimate realization of a common symptom ontology for Semantic Web applications.

As stated earlier, a symptom is an indication of a possible problem in an ontology. As with human disease symptoms, such an indication can be benign or it can be severe. The actual diagnosis is not addressed by this ontology. It is only concerned with those conditions that may be of some use in a determination that the ontology has a problem that should be addressed.

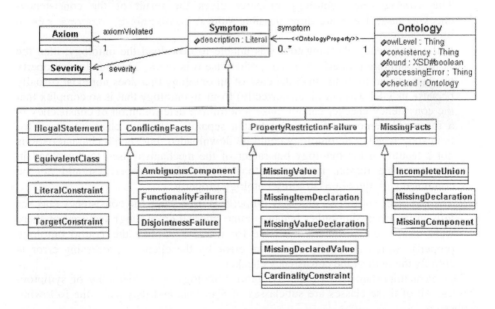

Fig. 7. ConsVISor's Symptom Ontology (simplified for display purposes)

As discussed in the previous section, a particular symptom individual is always characteristic of some particular ontology. Since symptoms are properties of an ontology, they must somehow be linked with the ontology being checked. However, it would be inappropriate to link the symptom directly with the ontology being checked because the symptom is not an intrinsic property of the ontology. It is only a property of the particular invocation of the consistency checker on that ontology. If one regards the symptoms as being in a *report* generated by a tool, then the symptoms should properly reside in that report, and the report (along with many others) can refer to the ontology being checked. Since such a report consists of OWL statements, it is itself an OWL ontology. The instances of the Ontology class in Fig. 7 are these reports, and symptoms in this report are explicitly linked with the report to which they belong by the symptom ontology property. By defining the collection of symptoms generated by a consistency checker to be an OWL ontology, it can itself be checked for consistency, as well as processed by any OWL-aware tool. Consistency checking reports have a number of other ontology properties that are used to specify the context within which the consistency checker produced them, such as:

- The consistency-checking tool that produced the collection of symptoms is specified by the checked ontology property.
- There are three language levels for OWL ontologies. This level is not intrinsic to the ontology, and a single ontology can be regarded as belonging to any one of the three. The owlLevel ontology property specifies the level that was used for the consistency checking operation. Some tools require that the user specify the level for consistency checking, while others report the level of the ontology as part of their output. The former can be regarded as performing three consistency-checking tasks: one for each level.
- The consistency ontology property gives the result of the consistency-checking task. There are three possible values: Consistent, Inconsistent and Unknown.
- If the consistency-checking tool was unable to download the ontology, then the found ontology property is false, otherwise it is true. This ontology property was introduced to distinguish the case of an ontology that does not exist (usually because its URI was not given correctly) from an ontology that is so complex that the consistency checker cannot make a definitive determination of consistency in a reasonable amount of time. At first a separate symptom class was used for indicating whether an ontology could be downloaded, but such a characteristic is not a feature of the ontology but rather of the mechanism used to download it. For the same reason, it was felt that this ontology property should not be combined with the consistency ontology property.
- The processingError ontology property is used when the consistency checker fails in its processing either because some internal error (bug) occurred or there were insufficient resources available for the task. Unlike the found ontology property, which is usually due to an error by the client, a processing error is entirely the fault of the consistency checker.

The most important part of the Symptom Ontology is its hierarchy of symptom classes. All of these classes are subclasses of Symptom, and they share the following properties:

- The description of a symptom is an explanation, using ordinary natural language, of the symptom that occurred.
- There are four severity levels for symptoms:
  1. Symptoms having no effect on consistency are at the info level. These symptoms are simply reporting on entailments that might possibly be indicators of a problem. For example, a resource that was used as the predicate of a statement but was not declared to be a property would generate such a symptom. It is considered to be only informational because the fact

that the resource is a property is entailed by its use as a predicate. However, not all entailments result in symptoms. Subsumptions, for example, are too common and routine to merit explicit mention. Currently there is no clear boundary between those entailments that should produce a symptom and those that should not.

2. A warning is a symptom that is not just the result of an entailment, but that also is not a clear indicator of an inconsistency. Ideally, there should not be any of these as they represent a situation in which the consistency checking tool has been unable to decide between consistency and inconsistency. However, every tool has its limitations because consistency checking is computationally very hard in the worst case (and even undecidable for OWL Full).

3. An error symptom is a clear indication of an inconsistency. Such a symptom is definitely a problem.

4. A fatal error means that processing of the ontology did not complete normally. If a fatal error occurs then there will normally also be a processingError ontology property. A fatal error gives more detailed information about the error, such as its location.

- The OWL language reference does not have a single listing of all of the axioms of the language. The specification of the three language levels is stated in several ways, some of which do not specify the axioms of all the language constructs. To deal with this complexity, each symptom specifies one or more references to items in the OWL language reference documents that are responsible for the symptom. Each symptom is linked with at most one member of the Axiom class via the axiomViolated property. Each such axiom, in turn, is linked to specific places in the OWL language reference documents via the reference property. This allows a client to examine the original sources that define the OWL language. Unfortunately, these sources are not formally specified, so these links are only meaningful to a person.

The subclasses of Symptom differ from one another with respect to the properties that apply; these differences are depicted in Fig. 8. All of these other properties are alike in linking a symptom to one or more resources of type Statement. The Statement class is one of the built-in classes of RDF (and therefore also OWL). A resource of type Statement is a reified statement. The reified statements linked with a symptom indicate the statements that were responsible for the symptom. There are several reasons for using reified statements.

- Reified statements are not asserted so they do not represent statements in the consistency checker report. One would certainly expect that the report generated by a consistency checker should itself be consistent so that it can be processed by the same tools that process any other ontology or annotation. If the statements were asserted they would, in general, reproduce the same inconsistencies in the report that exist in the ontology being checked.

- Reified statements are resources, so one can make statements about them. The statements in this case are explanations of the reasons for a symptom being generated.

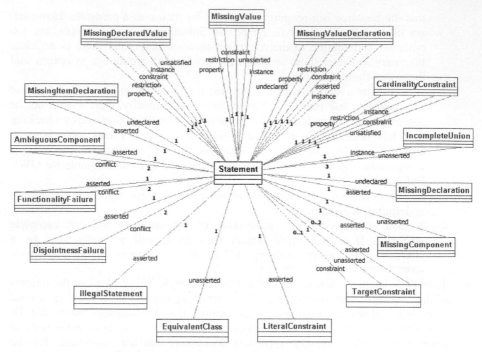

Fig. 8. Property Associations for each Symptom Class

- One could certainly have explained each symptom by referring to various resources. This was the case in an early version of the Symptom Ontology. However, this design was complex because it required one to introduce a number of auxiliary classes to express all of the concepts. We found that by using reified statements one could eliminate the auxiliary classes. For a while the design used both reified statements and direct references to literals and resources. Eventually the design evolved until all such direct references were eliminated and all explanations were specified using reified statements. The resulting design achieved significant simplifications.

Another design alternative that was considered for some time was for the symptom explanations to be proofs. Some of the symptom classes have sufficient information (including references to axioms in the OWL languages reference documents) to construct a proof. However, we chose not to give complete proof traces because it would make processing of the resulting report much more difficult (both by humans and by software agents). In addition, it would make comparing the reports of different consistency checkers much more difficult if not impossible.

4.1   The Symptom Classes

In this section we define the fifteen symptom classes and identify their properties. The association between the symptom classes and properties are visually depicted in Fig. 8. Every symptom class can occur at any language level, but not necessarily at every severity. If the possible severity levels are not mentioned, then a symptom class can occur at every severity level.

AmbiguousComponent. An inverse functional property maps two resources to the same resource. If the two resources are different, then this symptom signals an inconsistency. **Properties**: The `conflict` property gives the conflicting facts, and the `asserted` property gives the inverse functionality constraint assertion.

CardinalityConstraint. A cardinality constraint was not satisfied. This includes max, min and equal cardinality constraints. For a max cardinality constraint to result in an error, the set of resources must be distinct as well as have too large a cardinality, otherwise the symptom will only be informational. Similarly, for a min cardinality constraint to result in an error, the set of possible resources must be limited in some way (such as by using an enumeration). **Properties**: The cardinality constraint that was asserted is given by the `constraint` property. The property that is being constrained is given by `property`. The resource that is mapped to the wrong number of other resources is given by the `instance` property. The numerical relation (equality or inequality) that failed to hold is given by the `unsatisfied` property. Cardinality constraints are usually specified by asserting a subclass constraint between a class and a relation. This fact is given by the `restriction` property.

ConflictingFacts. Two facts conflict with one another. In other words, they cannot both hold and still be consistent. This is the superclass of several other symptom classes that specify more specific kinds of conflict. A symptom of this kind is either informational or an error. **Properties**: The `conflict` property gives the conflicting facts. When there is an explicitly asserted statement that acts as a constraint (such as a functionality constraint on a property) then the assertion is given by the `asserted` property. The difference between the asserted fact and the conflicting facts is that the two conflicting facts are at the same "level" and are similar (such as two resources mapped to the same resource), while the asserted fact is on a different "level" (such as a functionality constraint). If the constraint is built-in then the `asserted` property will not have a value.

DisjointnessFailure. Two disjoint classes have an instance in common. A symptom of this kind can be either informational or an error. **Properties:** The `conflict` property gives the conflicting facts. When an explicit assertion of disjointness was made, then the `asserted` property gives this statement. Built-in disjointness constraints will not have a value for the `asserted` property.

FunctionalityFailure. A functional property maps a resource to two resources. If the two resources are different, then this symptom signals an inconsistency. A symptom of this kind can be either informational or an error. **Properties**: the `conflict` property gives the conflicting facts, and the `asserted` property gives the functionality constraint assertion.

IllegalStatement. A statement was asserted that is not allowed at the specified language level. A symptom of this kind is either informational or an error. **Properties:** The `asserted` property gives the asserted illegal statement. Sometimes there will also be an `element` item. This occurs when a list of a particular kind (given by the asserted property) contains an illegal element.

IncompleteUnion. A union or enumeration class has an instance that does not occur in the component classes (for a union) or is not one of the enumerators. **Properties:** When there is an explicitly stated union or enumeration constraint, then it is given by the `constraint` property. Built-in constraints are not given. The instance of the union or enumeration is given by the `instance` property. For a union class, the instance should be an instance of one (or more) component classes. These facts may be given using the `unasserted` property. Similarly for enumeration classes.

LiteralConstraint. A literal was asserted to have a datatype with which its value is incompatible. A symptom of this kind is always an error. **Properties:** The `asserted` property gives the statement that the literal has the datatype.

MissingComponent. A required resource is missing. For example, `rdf:first` must always have exactly one value. This is a special case of a minimum cardinality constraint, but this symptom class is not a subclass of `CardinalityConstraint`. This symptom is informational only because the necessary statements are entailed. **Properties:** The `asserted` property gives the statement that uses the resource in question. The `unasserted` property gives the statement that should have been asserted. The object of this statement does not exist, so shown as `sym:unspecifiedEntity`. However, this is just a placeholder. If two symptoms of this kind occur, the unspecified entities need not be the same.

MissingDeclaration. A resource was used in a manner that requires that it be an instance of particular class, but the resource was never explicitly declared to be such an instance. These symptoms are informational only, since the `unasserted` statement is immediately entailed. However, these symptoms are some of the most useful for catching errors. Spelling errors, for example, will result in a `MissingDeclaration` symptom. **Properties:** The `asserted` property gives the statement that uses the resource in question. The `undeclared` property gives the statement that should have been asserted.

MissingDeclaredValue. This is a combination of `MissingComponent` and `MissingDeclaration`. The value is not only missing, it also must be declared to be an instance of a particular class. This symptom arises from an `owl:someValuesFrom` constraint. This symptom is informational only because the necessary statements are entailed. **Properties:** The `owl:someValuesFrom` constraint is specified using property, restriction and constraint as in the `CardinalityConstraint` symptom. The instance is given by the `instance` property. The missing value is given by `unasserted` as in `MissingComponent`, and the missing declaration is given by `undeclared`.

MissingItemDeclaration. An item in a collection is required to be an instance of a particular class, but it was not declared to be in this class. This is an informational symptom only because the declarations are entailed. **Properties:** The `asserted` property gives the collection-valued statement that constrains the elements of the collection. The particular item that was not declared is given by the `item` property. The declaration that was not asserted is given by the `undeclared` property.

MissingValue. A particular case of an `owl:hasValue` constraint was not satisfied. This is informational only as the statement is entailed. **Properties:** The `owl:hasValue` constraint is specified using property, restriction and constraint as in the `CardinalityConstraint` symptom. The instance is given by the `instance` property. The missing fact is given by `unasserted` property.

MissingValueDeclaration: A particular case of an `owl:allValuesFrom` constraint was not satisfied. This is informational only as the declaration is entailed. **Properties:** The `owl:allValuesFrom` constraint is specified using property, restriction and constraint as in the `CardinalityConstraint` symptom. The instance is given by the `instance` property. The statement mapping the instance by the property to an undeclared value is given by the `asserted` property. The missing declaration is given by `undeclared` property.

TargetConstraint: Any of several constraints such as domain and range constraints that have exactly one asserted and exactly one unasserted statement. These are usually informational symptoms, but in some cases the symptom is an error when asserting the unasserted statement is not allowed. **Properties:** The constraint (such as a domain constraint) is given by the `constraint` property. The statement (such as a mapping of a resource that does not satisfy the constraint) that gave rise to the constraint failure is given by the `asserted` property. The statement that should have been asserted is given by the `unasserted` property.

The symptom classes given above cover all possible violations of the axioms of OWL at any of the language levels. They were designed to have a level of detail that includes the RDF statements that participate in the axiom being violated. While there may be some redundancy among the classes (i.e., there may be overlap among classes other than the overlap due to the subclass relationship), an attempt was made to minimize such occurrences.

5   Possible Extensions and Enhancements

If a Symptom Ontology for OWL is accepted, then it could be the beginning of a trend toward formalizing the output of many other tools. OWL is most commonly represented using RDF and XML Schema, so that the first step in consistency checking is parsing RDF and XML Schema files (which, in turn, requires parsing XML documents). Both RDF and XML Schema have complex semantics that require their own forms of consistency checking. In fact, RDF has a suite of test cases that is as extensive as the OWL test case suite. [14] The same kind of Symptom Ontology can be developed for RDF as we have done for OWL. Although most of the symptoms would be syntactic, RDF has nontrivial semantics, which, as in the case of OWL ontologies, should be checked for consistency. Both RDF and OWL use XML Schema for the representation of literals, and one can also develop a Symptom ontology for validating XML Schema data types and literals.

More generally, one could formalize the output of compilers for languages other than OWL, RDF and XML Schema. This would allow one to automate the validation of compilers. It would also make it possible to build tools (such as integrated development environments) that process and present the output of whichever compiler one chooses to use.

While developing the Symptom Ontology, we found that there were many constraints that were not expressible in OWL. For example, a FunctionalityFailure symptom has two reified statements that conflict with one another. The subjects of these two reified statements must be the same. One cannot express such a constraint using OWL alone. However, it is possible to do so using rules. When an OWL rule language is available, it will be possible to give a more complete theory of symptoms.

6   Conclusion

In their Scientific American article, Tim Berners-Lee, James Hendler and Ora Lassila envisioned the Semantic Web to be "an extension of the current web in which information is given well-defined meaning, better enabling computers and people to work in cooperation" [15]. The success of the Semantic Web depends on tools to ensure that meaning is really "well-defined", i.e., that information is consistent and reflects the intentions of the authors. Many first generation tools have now established that consistency checking of Semantic Web ontologies is feasible. However, for the most part these tools have not themselves adhered to the Semantic Web vision of well-defined meaning and interoperability. Few of them produce results that can be processed by machine, and there is no shared notion of how to describe the flaws that they detect in Semantic Web ontologies and annotations.

To remedy this situation, we have proposed a common language for identifying and describing semantic errors and warnings that may be indicative of inconsistencies in ontologies and annotations. This language is expressed as an OWL ontology called the Symptom Ontology. This language is currently used by our **ConsVISor** consistency-checking tool. Some of the characteristics that we have proposed as being important for such an ontology include those that should be supported by any tool (such as a compiler or interpreter) that requires semantic consistency; namely, a hierarchy of common symptoms and a means of relating the symptoms to the constructs in the source document that gave rise to them. We have also proposed that symptoms should be associated with the axioms of the language that are violated. The latter proposal goes beyond what compilers and other consistency checkers currently do but is essential for achieving the goal of the Semantic Web in which all information is well defined.

We see the Symptom Ontology as an example of how many tools that currently produce informal, idiosyncratic output can be Semantic Web enabled. Virtually every software tool generates errors and warnings when anomalous situations arise. By formalizing these errors and warnings, their meanings will be formally defined and grounded in the standard for the language, thereby contributing to the Semantic Web vision of meaning and interoperability.

References

1. W3C Recommendation, OWL Web Ontology Language Overview, February 2004. http://www.w3.org/TR/owl-features/
2. W3C, OWL Test Results Page, March 2004. http://www.w3.org/2003/08/owl-systems/test-results-out

3. European OntoWeb Consortium, A Survey of Ontology Tools, May 2002. http://ontoweb.aifb.uni-karlsruhe.de/About/Deliverables/D13_v1-0.zip
4. InfoEther & BBN Technologies, SemWebCentral Validation Tools Assessment. http://semwebcentral.org/assessment/report?type=category&category=Validation
5 K. Baclawski, M. Kokar, R. Waldinger and P. Kogut, Consistency Checking of Semantic Web Ontologies. 1st International Semantic Web Conference (ISWC)}, Lecture Notes in Computer Science, LNCS 2342, Springer, pp. 454--459, 2002.
6. Versatile Information Systems, Inc., ConsVISor. http://www.vistology.com/consvisor/
7. AGFA, Euler. http://www.agfa.com/w3c/euler/
8. UMBC, FOWL. http://fowl.sourceforge.net
9. University of Maryland Institute for Advanced Computer Studies, Pellet. http://www.mindswap.org/2003/pellet/
10. BBN, vOWLidator. http://owl.bbn.com/validator/
11. DAML, DARPA Agent Markup Language. http://www.daml.org/
12. W3C, OWL Test Cases, February 2004. http://www.w3.org/TR/owl-test/
13. W3C Recommendation, OWL Web Ontology Language Semantics and Abstract Syntax, February 2004. http://www.w3.org/TR/owl-semantics/
14. W3C Recommendation, RDF Test Cases, February 2004. http://www.w3.org/TR/rdf-testcases/
15. T. Berners-Lee, J. Hendler and O. Lassila, The Semantic Web: A new form of Web content that is meaningful to computers will unleash a revolution of new possibilities. Scientific American, May 2001.

Patching Syntax in OWL Ontologies

Sean Bechhofer[1] and Raphael Volz[2]

[1] University of Manchester, UK
http://www.cs.man.ac.uk
seanb@cs.man.ac.uk
[2] Institute AIFB, University of Karlsruhe, Germany
http://www.aifb.uni-karlsruhe.de
rvo@aifb.uni-karlsruhe.de

Abstract. An analysis of OWL ontologies represented in RDF/XML on the Web shows that a majority are OWL Full. In many cases this may not be through a desire to use the expressivity provided by OWL Full, but is rather due to syntactic errors or accidental misuse of the vocabulary. We present a "rogues gallery" of common errors encountered, and describe how robust parsers that attempt to cope with such errors can be produced.

1 Introduction

In Feb 2004, the World Wide Web Consortium (W3C) announced the release of the OWL Web Ontology Language Standard[1]. OWL is intended to provide the "Ontology Layer" of the oft-cited Semantic Web stack and in order to fulfill this, has an RDF carrier syntax [8] that will allow RDF-aware applications to make use of data marked up in OWL.

The publication of the OWL Recommendation does not, of course, mean that our work is done in terms of Ontology Languages. We must now support users and application builders in the development of ontologies and applications that use them. This is the rationale behind activities such as the Semantic Web Best Practices Working Group[2].

A key aspect of the OWL design is the layering of different language sub-species. All OWL documents can be represented using the same RDF/XML carrier concrete syntax, and OWL has three language variants with increasing expressivity: Lite, DL and Full. All Lite documents are DL, and all DL documents are Full, but the converse is not true. The constraints on the expressivity of OWL DL have been made in such a manner as to produce a language for which there exists sound and complete decision procedures. The task of species recognition – determining which particular species an ontology is in – thus becomes important, as an OWL DL application needs to know whether it can apply the appropriate semantics and inference procedures to an ontology. See [2] for a detailed discussion of the issues concerning parsing and recognition.

---

[1] http://www.w3.org/News/2004##item14

[2] http://www.w3.org/2001/sw/BestPractices/

S.A. McIlraith et al. (Eds.): ISWC 2004, LNCS 3298, pp. 668–682, 2004.

The designers of OWL expect that a significant number of ontologies will use the Lite and DL subspecies. However, in a simple analysis reported here, we discover that the proportion of OWL Lite and DL ontologies currently on the web is small. It appears, however, that the reasons for this are often due to accidental syntactic errors or vocabulary misuse rather than modelling intention. For example, the rules about OWL DL are strict in their requirements for explicit typing of all classes used in the ontology. Such problems can be tackled through provision of tools supporting the production of ontologies, which ensure that correct and appropriate syntax is used.

As a parallel approach, we propose the use of robust parsers that can cope with syntactic errors and apply "fixups" or patches (as initially discussed in [2]) wherever necessary[3] in order to produce OWL DL ontologies. This approach is predicated on the assumption that we *are* interested in working with OWL DL ontologies – a hypothesis that we feel is valid (the number of implementors building OWL DL and Lite reasoners[4] bears witness to this).

The paper is structured as follows. Section 2 describes an experiment in analysing a number of Web ontologies in order to determine which particular species they fell into. Section 3 provides an analysis of the detailed reasons for membership (or non-membership) of a particular species – these reasons can be classified into a number of more general reasons (such as missing type triples) providing us with a rogues gallery of the "usual suspects" or kinds of syntactic malforms we may encounter that contribute towards non-membership of DL or Lite. Section 4 describes possible patches that can be applied to these classes of error in order to obtain OWL DL or Lite ontologies. Section 5 describes extensions to an OWL parser that provides a more robust tool that will attempt to cope with a number of different "error" conditions. We conclude with remarks on related work and a summary of our contribution.

2   Ontology Sources

Our initial motivation was to answer the question "how much OWL is there on the Web?" Of course, any RDF graph is, in fact, an OWL (Full) graph, but such documents can not necessarily be used with tools targeted at OWL DL or Lite. Thus, an alternative, and perhaps more interesting, question is "how much *OWL DL* is there on the Web?"

2.1   Ontology Library

Our first port of call was the largest library of ontologies in the Web - the DAML ontology library[5] - which contained 282 ontologies of various formats at the time of our experiment. Of these 282 we selected those which we considered

---

[3] Of course, as discussed in the paper, we must be careful when applying patches in such situations as the semantics may be impacted.

[4] http://www.w3.org/2001/sw/WebOnt/impls

[5] http://daml.org/ontologies/

Table 1. Species Breakdown

Collection	Total	Full	DL	Lite
DAML Library	76	63 (83%)	3 (4%)	10 (13%)
Google	201	174 (86%)	19 (10%)	8 (4%)

to be *candidates* for OWL DL ontologies. Our heuristic to judge whether an ontology is a candidate was based on usage of the OWL namespace. If an RDF graph fails to mention the OWL namespace, we can be sure that it will not be an OWL DL graph, as there can be no explicit typing as required by the OWL DL rules[6].

Unfortunately most of the ontologies in this library (193 ontologies) were definitely not candidates as they were no longer available, had XML errors, or used previous Web ontology languages such as OIL or DAML-ONT. Seventy-six ontologies, however, were available, were valid XML, and used elements from the OWL vocabulary.

2.2   Google

This small set of 76 ontologies was not considered satisfactory, so we chose to expand our collection by searching for OWL ontologies using Google. A simple search for `OWL` is of course too broad and leads to more than 4 million web pages, most of which are not ontologies. Two refined searches for `filetype:.owl owl` and `filetype:.rdf owl` provided 264[7] more appropriate documents, of which 56 documents were suitable, e.g. they were HTML pages, and 15 documents were no longer available online. In conclusion we actually found 201 candidate ontologies. Obviously, these ontologies do not necessarily constitute all available ontologies, since we missed those that departed from the syntactic search pattern used or were not made publicly available[8].

3   Analysis

A breakdown of the species distribution of the candidate ontologies from the DAML Library and Google search is shown in Table 1. This initial analysis reveals that a majority of the ontologies found are not directly usable by OWL DL or OWL Lite-aware systems. Our hypothesis, however, is that most of these ontologies are not intentionally OWL Full, but become OWL Full through various errors made by the designer of the ontologies. We therefore had a closer

---

[6] An exception to this, of course, is the trivially empty graph, relatively uninteresting in this context.

[7] The reader may note that the Google estimate displayed with the search results is not correct.

[8] For example ontologies held in repositories such as Sesame [4] will not necessarily be apparent to Google unless the owners of the repository have taken steps to publish information about them.

look at the 174 OWL Full ontologies found by Google and the 63 OWL Full ontologies found in the DAML library[9]. We could identify 20 different reasons why those ontologies were OWL Full (cf. Table 2). As discussed before, these reasons are seen as errors for OWL DL and OWL Lite processors. The errors can be aggregated into five more general categories of fault, which are described below.

Note that here we are making an assumption that our desired intention *is* that ontologies should be in the OWL DL or Lite subspecies. Thus we use the term "error" to describe a situation where an ontology does not belong to DL or Lite.

Missing typing: This category occurred most frequently and in almost all of the OWL Full ontologies. A good example for missing typing is when a property was not specified to be a datatype or object property. Missing type information often occurred together for various types of elements, for example in 154 (89%) of the OWL Full ontologies found by Google;

Namespace problems: Namespace problems occurred in about half of all full ontologies, but more frequently in the ontologies from the DAML library. Namespace problems are (i) a violation of the namespace separation mandated in OWL, (ii) usage of the OWL namespace itself (one may not declare classes, properties or instances in the OWL namespace) and a (iii) redefinition of elements of OWL itself, e.g. OWL class.

Wrong vocabulary: 32 (18%) of the OWL Full ontologies found by Google were using the wrong vocabulary. But this was the second most frequent (78%) error category for the DAML ontologies. Usage of the wrong vocabulary, for example `rdf:Class` instead of `owl:Class`, `rdf:Property` instead of `owl:Property` or usage of `owl:sameAs` on classes, can be accounted to mistakes in legacy migration. With no exceptions all of the ontologies in this category also had missing type information and namespace problems, which are both direct results of using wrong vocabulary;

OWL Full: Around 20% of the ontologies in both data sets were definitely OWL Full, since either (i) complex object properties were declared to be transitive[10] or (ii) illegal subproperty statements were made. The latter refers to making a datatype property a subproperty of an object property or vice versa[11].

OWL/RDF Irregularities: 20 (11%) of the Google ontologies and 15 (24%) of the DAML ontologies contained various OWL/RDF irregularities. This refers to (i) Unused RDF Triples, (ii) Malformed Lists, (iii) Anonymous

---

[9] More detailed results concerning the analysis can be found at:
http://owl.man.ac.uk/patching.

[10] In order to ensure that OWL DL is decidable, there are extra side conditions on the use of transitive properties. *Complex properties* are those that are functional, are involved in cardinality restrictions, or have a complex inverse or superproperty. Such properties cannot be declared to be transitive. See [8] for details.

[11] With a single exception, the definitely Full ontologies found by Google also had also namespace problems and were missing type information.

Table 2. Frequent Error Types

Error Type	DAML Library		Google	
	Absolute	Relative	Absolute	Relative
OWL Full (Total)	63	100%	174	100%
Missing Typing	**63**	**100%**	**167**	**96%**
Untyped Ontology	5	7%	24	13%
Untyped Object Property	34	53%	131	75%
Untyped Individual	37	58%	137	78%
Untyped Datatype	18	28%	10	5%
Untyped Data Property	18	28%	134	77%
Untyped Class	58	92%	148	85%
Untyped Functional Property	1	1%	4	2%
Namespace Problems	**41**	**65%**	**76**	**43%**
Redefinition of built in vocabulary	23	36%	50	28%
OWL Namespace Used	14	22%	35	20%
Namespace Separation Violated	33	52%	68	39%
Wrong Vocabulary	**49**	**77%**	**32**	**18%**
SameAs with Class	0	0%	2	1%
RDF Property Used	9	14%	27	15%
RDF Class Used	48	76%	23	13%
OWL Full	**13**	**20%**	**31**	**17%**
Illegal Sub Property	14	22%	28	16%
Complex role declared Transitive	1	1%	3	1%
OWL/RDF Irregularities	**15**	**23%**	**20**	**11%**
Unused Triples	12	19%	10	5%
Structure Sharing	0	0%	4	2%
Malformed Restriction	9	14%	2	1%
Malformed List	2	3%	8	4%
Anonymous Class Creation	3	4%	8	4%

Class Creation, (iv) Structure Sharing and (v) Malformed Restrictions. With no exceptions all of the ontologies in this category also had missing type information and namespace problems, which comes at no surprise since these errors are directly effected by the OWL/RDF irregularities.

Note that the categories are not disjoint – an ontology could have both missing type information and illegal sub property axioms. Note also that the summary figures (e.g. Missing Typing) summarise *any* of the subcategories referred to, e.g. untyped class, untyped individual etc.

We can identify several other problems that could theoretically occur, but were not found in the data set. These include particular RDF malforms such as malformed descriptions or `owl:AllDifferent` axioms, the use of Inverse Functional Data Properties [8], cycles in bnodes or `owl:sameAs` applied to Object or Datatype Property.

4   Patching

Adopting the terminology as introduced in [2], errors can be classified into *external* and *internal* errors. *Internal* errors are those where the triples correspond to an OWL ontology, but the ontology makes use of expressivity outside of the required species. *External* errors are those where the RDF graph is in some way incorrectly formed. We can also identify a third class of *syntactic* errors to cover those situations where there are problems with the underlying concrete presentation of the ontology – for example the XML concrete syntax is malformed. Such situations are likely to be best dealt with by the underlying XML parsers – we do not devote much attention to these here, and concentrate mainly on addressing *external* errors such as missing type information. In addition, we would expect that as more and more ontologies are produced by tools, malformed XML will become a thing of the past. Similarly, if ontologies are held in RDF repositories (such as Sesame [4]) we would hope to see less malformed XML as the repository takes responsibility for the production of the concrete representation. Some *internal* errors, in general those arising from imports, can be tackled, and we discuss these here.

4.1   Missing Type Information

Fortunately the most frequent error of missing type information is also the most easy to deal with. OWL DL requires that URI references used in particular contexts (e.g. as a class) must be explicitly typed as such. This requirement for complete information about the typing of resources is effectively a restriction on the *syntax*. Contrast this with the *semantics* [8] of OWL, which applies an open world assumption, allowing incomplete information.

As we have seen in the previous section almost all of the OWL Full ontologies tested failed to belong to OWL DL primarily because of such missing information.

There are a number of situations that we can identify as *Class Contexts* – those where a URI is expected to be an `owl:Class`. Such situations include:

- The subject or object of an `rdfs:subClassOf` triple.
- The object of an `rdf:type` triple.
- The object of an `owl:someValuesFrom` or `owl:allValuesFrom` triple where the subject of the triple is also the subject of an `owl:onProperty` triple with an `owl:ObjectProperty` as the object.
- The object of an `rdf:domain` triple.
- The object of an `rdf:range` triple where the subject is an `owl:ObjectProperty`.

In these cases, we can be fairly sure that the intention *is* that the URI is intended to be an `owl:Class` and can add an appropriate `rdf:type` triple.

Similarly, we can identify *Object Property Contexts*, those where an `owl:ObjectProperty` is expected. These include:

- The object of an `owl:onProperty` triple where the subject of the triple is also the subject of an `owl:someValuesFrom` or `owl:allValuesFrom` triple with an `owl:Class` as the object.
- The subject of an `rdf:range` triple where the object is an `owl:Class`.

Data Property Contexts encapsulate those situations where an `owl:DatatypeProperty` is expected. These include:

- The object of an `owl:onProperty` triple where the subject of the triple is also the subject of an `owl:someValuesFrom` or `owl:allValuesFrom` triple with a Datatype[12] as the object.
- The subject of an `rdf:range` triple where the object is a Datatype.

Note that the identification of `owl:ObjectProperty` and `owl:DatatypeProperty` usage requires some analysis of the surrounding context.

These possible contexts may interact and it may be the case that it is **not** possible to disambiguate. For example, consider the following fragment:

```
<rdf:Property rdf:about='#p'>
  <rdf:range rdf:resource='#D'/>
</rdf:Property>
```

One possible patch here would be to consider p as an `owl:ObjectProperty` and D as an `owl:Class`. An alternative would be to consider p as a `owl:DatatypeProperty` and D as an `rdfs:Datatype`. Either would provide a valid OWL DL ontology.

Patching is, of course, not always possible (as the ontology may use expressiveness that results in an OWL Full ontology). In the following fragment:

```
<rdf:Description rdf:about="#a">
  <rdf:type rdf:resource="#A"/>
</rdf:Description>
<rdf:Description rdf:about="#A">
  <rdf:type rdf:resource="#B"/>
</rdf:Description>
```

There is no combination of type triples that we can add here to produce an OWL DL ontology as there is an implicit use of classes as instances (and thus a violation of the requirement for a *separated vocabulary* [8]) as A is both given a type and used as a type. This example serves to illustrate that there may not always be an appropriate patch that can be applied.

The order in which the contexts are addressed has an impact. For example, if `rdf:Property` (rather than `owl:ObjectProperty`) has been used in an ontology, analysing the use of the property in `owl:someValuesFrom` or `owl:allValuesFrom` triples is likely to yield more information than, for example `owl:cardinality` triples (which do not tell us anything about the characteristics of the property). Thus the entire context of the ontology can prove useful in disambiguating such situations.

---

[12] When we refer to Datatypes we mean either an `rdfs:Datatype` or a known XML Schema Datatype.

Another "hard" case is where the intention is that a property is used for annotation. Take the following ontology:

```
<?xml version="1.0" encoding="ISO-8859-1"?>
<rdf:RDF xmlns:owl="http://www.w3.org/2002/07/owl#"
    xmlns:rdf="http://www.w3.org/1999/02/22-rdf-syntax-ns#"
    xmlns:rdfs="http://www.w3.org/2000/01/rdf-schema#"
    xml:base="http://owl.man.ac.uk/ontologies/whatever"
    xmlns="http://owl.man.ac.uk/ontologies/whatever#">
<owl:Ontology rdf:about=""/>
<owl:Class rdf:about="#A"/>
<rdf:Description rdf:about="#A">
  <author rdf:resource="http://www.cs.man.ac.uk/~seanb"/>
</rdf:Description>
</rdf:RDF>
```

In this example, A is explicitly declared to be an owl:Class. However, we have no type for the property author. In this particular case, by choosing to type author as an owl:AnnotationProperty we can produce an OWL DL ontology. Choosing to type author as an owl:ObjectProperty would also require us to treat http://www.cs.man.ac.uk/~seanb as an individual (and thus provide a type), but would then push us into OWL Full due to the treatment of A as class and instance. Thus in this case, to obtain an OWL DL ontology, we need to treat author as an owl:AnnotationProperty.

In situations like this, it is unlikely that an automated approach will be appropriate – we are in a situation where *user input* is needed in order to make the ultimate decision as to how to resolve the problem. Tools can, however, provide a degree of support in determining what needs to be done and suggest appropriate course of action.

4.2   Import of OWL or RDF Schemas

A common occurrence in OWL ontologies is the import of OWL or RDF schemas. This is not necessary in order to produce OWL ontologies, and in fact will *always* result in an OWL-Full (and not OWL-DL) ontology as the import of the schema results in triples using terms from the *disallowed vocabulary* (see Section 4 of [8] for details) as subjects in triples. Although it may be the case that importing the OWL schema *is* sometimes required or intended – for example if we wish to extend the OWL Schema itself – in the majority of cases this is unnecessary.

Resources in RDF namespace. OWL does not completely forbid the use of URIs from the RDF and RDF(S) namespaces. For example, rdf:Bag can be used as a Class in an OWL DL ontology. Addition of type triples is, however, necessary in certain situations in order to ensure that such RDF schemas are OWL DL. For example, we need to say that rdf:Bag is being treated as an owl:Class. Similarly, the RDF container properties rdf:_1, rdf:_2, etc. can be used as properties, but must be typed appropriately.

4.3 Use of Vocabularies Without Appropriate Import

This also belongs to the category of missing type information, but is worth special attention. A number of standard vocabularies are often used in ontologies without the necessary definitions. For example, in the ontologies analysed, we encounter Dublin Core properties such as `dc:author` or `dc:title` used without import of the Dublin Core schema or explicit definition of the property. Even if the schema at `http://purl.org/dc/elements/1.1` *is* included, however, this does not necessarily alleviate the position, as that particular schema is itself an OWL Full document due to the use of `rdf:Property` rather than a more specific OWL property. In general, we might expect a property from the Dublin Core to be treated as an `owl:AnnotationProperty`.

4.4 Misuse of `owl:sameAs`

According to the OWL semantics [8], the `owl:sameAs` property should be used to represent the fact that two *individuals* are the same. Using `owl:sameAs` to relate two Classes is thus **not** the same thing as relating them using `owl:equivalentClass` (the latter states that the classes are extensionally equivalent, e.g. have the same members while the former asserts that the two classes are to be interpreted as the same object). Using `owl:sameAs` to relate two Classes results in an OWL Full ontology. The situation is similar with properties, although here we would expect to see `owl:equivalentProperty` rather than `owl:sameAs`. It is likely that in such situations, the modeller may have intended to use `owl:equivalentClass` or `owl:equivalentProperty` rather than `owl:sameAs`.

4.5 `xml:base` and `xmlns` Confusion

The use of `xml:base` and the default namespace `xmlns` often causes confusion and can be the source of missing type information. The confusion arises due to the fact that in an RDF/XML file, elements are resolved with respect to the default namespace, whereas attribute values are resolved with respect to the XML base [7]. If no `xml:base` attribute is explicitly set, then this is the URI where the file is retrieved from. If `xml:base` is not set and the document is moved, this can then cause problems as the URIs of the classes and properties declared in the ontology may not match those used in the ontology. For example, assume the following ontology is available at `http://owl.man.ac.uk/ontologies/base`:

```
<?xml version="1.0" encoding="ISO-8859-1"?>
<rdf:RDF xmlns:rdf="http://www.w3.org/1999/02/22-rdf-syntax-ns#"
    xmlns:rdfs="http://www.w3.org/2000/01/rdf-schema#"
    xmlns:owl="http://www.w3.org/2002/07/owl#"
    xmlns:xsd="http://www.w3.org/2001/XMLSchema#"
    xmlns="http://owl.man.ac.uk/ontologies/base#">
<owl:Class rdf:about="#A"/>
<A rdf:about="#a"/>
</rdf:RDF>
```

```
<?xml version="1.0" encoding="ISO-8859-1"?>
<rdf:RDF xmlns:owl="http://www.w3.org/2002/07/owl#"
    xmlns:rdf="http://www.w3.org/1999/02/22-rdf-syntax-ns#"
    xmlns:rdfs="http://www.w3.org/2000/01/rdf-schema#"
    xml:base="http://owl.man.ac.uk/ontologies/broken"
    xmlns="http://owl.man.ac.uk/ontologies/broken#">
<owl:Ontology rdf:about=""/>
<!-- B should be a class -->
<owl:Class rdf:about="#A">
  <rdfs:subClassOf rdf:resource="#B"/>
</owl:Class>
</rdf:RDF>
```

Fig. 1. Not OWL DL

This particular ontology will validate as OWL DL. If, however, we move the file to http://owl.man.ac.uk/ontologies/base2 and then attempt to validate, validation will fail as the owl:Class typing triple will now apply to the URL http://owl.man.ac.uk/ontologies/base2#A. Use of an xml:base declaration would alleviate this problem.

Unfortunately there is not much we can do in terms of applying patches here. The resolution of URIs is, in general, dealt with by the XML parser and the information regarding the base and default namespaces may not actually be available to the RDF processing phase. However, it is worth mentioning here as this *is* an issue that those publishing ontologies need to be aware of and sensitive to.

5   Implementation

The OWL Validator [2] provided with the WonderWeb OWL API [3] checks the species of OWL ontologies represented using RDF/XML. It does this through a combination of syntactic checks on the structure of the triple graph, and further checks on the expressiveness used in the ontology[13].

The Validator reports any violations of the OWL DL/Lite rules encountered during the parse – this information can then be used to try and provide patches for such violations. The implementation of the Validator has been extended to provide such a Patcher, applying the heuristics described in the paper in order to try and obtain OWL DL ontologies.

5.1   Additions

A number of different approaches can be taken to producing "patches". In the case of errors of omission, such as missing type information, we can try and provide a collection of triples that need to be added to the ontology in order to provide OWL DL. We cannot always assume, however, that we have

---

[13] The Validation and Patching services described in this paper are available at:
http://owl.man.ac.uk/services.shtml

```
<?xml version="1.0" encoding="ISO-8859-1"?>
<rdf:RDF xmlns:owl="http://www.w3.org/2002/07/owl#"
    xmlns:rdf="http://www.w3.org/1999/02/22-rdf-syntax-ns#"
    xmlns:rdfs="http://www.w3.org/2000/01/rdf-schema#">
<owl:Ontology rdf:about="">
  <owl:imports>
    <owl:Ontology rdf:about="http://owl.man.ac.uk/ontologies/broken"/>
  </owl:imports>
</owl:Ontology>
<owl:Class rdf:about="http://owl.man.ac.uk/ontologies/broken#B"/>
</rdf:RDF>
```

Fig. 2. OWL DL

access to the source of the ontology – indeed in most cases we will not as the ontologies are referred to via URLs. In order to cope with this, we can produce a new ontology which uses `owl:imports` to import the checked ontology and then adds the necessary type triples. For example, say that at `http://owl.man.ac.uk/ontologies/broken` we find the RDF shown in Figure 1. The results of the patcher will be a new OWL ontology as shown in Figure 2.

Addition of extra triples can be considered to be a "safe" manipulation of the graph. In this case, any entailments (in the RDF sense) that held will continue to hold, due to the *monotonicity* of RDF entailment [6].

5.2   Deletions

For situations such those described in Sections 4.2 (the import of the OWL schema), the change required to the ontology is effectively a *deletion*, e.g. removing the offending `owl:import` triple. Again, if the ontology source is not within our control, removing such a triple is impossible. We can, however, instruct the parser to ignore particular import statements when parsing. In contrast to the addition of triples, after deletions, RDF entailments from the original graph may no longer hold. We must be sure that this is not done silently – the ontology obtained when we ignore an `owl:import` triple is *not* the same ontology as that obtained when the triple is processed. Note, however, that in terms of entailments that can be drawn using OWL DL semantics, the question is moot, as the original graph is not OWL DL, and thus cannot have the OWL DL semantics applied to it.

Similarly, for vocabulary misuse such as the `owl:sameAs` problem described in Section 4.4 we can tell the parser to treat `owl:sameAs` triples as if they were `owl:equivalentClass` or `owl:equivalentProperty` as appropriate (depending on context).

Once the processor has identified all the possible patches it can apply, it attempts to revalidate the ontology in the light of those patches and reports its findings.

```
<?xml version="1.0" encoding="UTF-8"?>
<rdf:RDF xmlns:rdf="http://www.w3.org/1999/02/22-rdf-syntax-ns#"
         xmlns="http://www.daml.org/tools/tools-ont#">
  <Project rdf:ID="DAML">
    <name>DAML</name>
  </Project>
  <Tool rdf:ID="SiRPAC">
    <name>Simple RDF Parser And Compiler (SiRPAC)</name>
    <description>RDF parser, from W3C</description>
    <site>http://www.w3.org/RDF/Implementations/SiRPAC/</site>
    <category>RDF Parser</category>
  </Tool>
  <Tool rdf:ID="SiLRI">
    <name>Simple Logic-based RDF Interpreter (SiLRI)</name>
    <description>a main-memory logic-based inference engine</description>
    <site>http://www.ontoprise.de/download/</site>
    <uses rdf:resource="#SiRPAC"/>
    <category>Inference Engine</category>
  </Tool>
  ...
</rdf:RDF>
```

Fig. 3. DAML Tools Ontology (fragment)

Table 3. Results of Patching Non-DL Ontologies

Collection	Attempted	Patched by Type Triples	Patched by Schema Handling
DAML Library	50	16 (32%)	1 (2%)
Google Search	140	78 (56%)	2 (1%)

The outcome of the process is thus a combination of things:

- A report on the errors encountered during the parse/validation.
- A collection of type triples that need to be added to the ontology.
- Identification of imports that cause problems (such as the OWL Schema).

As an example of this process, the DAML pages provide an ontology of tools at http://www.daml.org/tools/tools.owl. This is a vanilla RDF (and thus OWL Full) file that does not validate as OWL DL due to the presence of a number of untyped properties and classes. A fragment of the source is shown in Figure 3. In this case, an analysis of the RDF suggests that Tool is intended to be an owl:Class, properties such as name and site are instances of DatatypeProperty, and uses is an owl:ObjectProperty. After adding these triples to the ontology (using the owl:imports mechanism as described above), we find that the resulting graph does indeed validate as OWL DL.

5.3 Results

The ontologies analysed in the initial experiment were run through the Patcher in order to see whether OWL DL ontologies could be produced. Results are summarised in Table 3. Of the 63 candidates from the DAML Library, 13 were definitely OWL Full due to the expressiveness used (for example subproperty axioms were asserted between Object and Datatype Properties), leaving 50 potentially available for patching. Of the ontologies gathered using Google, 31 were definitely OWL Full, leaving 140 potentially available for patching.

6 Related Work

Approaches to parsing OWL in RDF are described in [2,1]. The application described here extends the approach of trying to construct an abstract syntax tree representing the OWL ontology. In contrast, the Jena recognizer attempts to classify nodes according to their occurrence within the RDF graph. The graph validates as a particular species if the classification of the nodes meets certain conditions. This approach may well also be amenable to patching as described here as the node categories provide pointers to the expected types of the nodes.

BBN's OWL Validator[14] is a tool to "...check OWL markup for problems beyond simple syntax errors...". It is able to spot some missing type errors, but does not (as yet) supply detailed information on how these errors could or should be addressed.

7 Conclusion

The widespread use of ontology languages like OWL is at a rather early stage, and a number of the "rough edges" still need to be smoothed out. Providing tools that support the production of ontologies that conform to the rules and conditions relating to OWL sublanguages is, we feel, a useful step in the right direction. This paper can be seen as complementary to Appendix E of the OWL Reference [5] and the Working Group Note on Parsing [1]. The former provides "Rules of Thumb" to ensure that ontologies are in OWL Lite or DL, while the latter describes how to parse OWL ontologies in RDF/XML. This work describes how, in some sense, one might *retrospectively* apply the Rules of Thumb to existing ontologies.

Our results are encouraging. As we see in Section 5, over half of the searched ontologies that were originally found to be OWL Full can in fact be "retrofitted" to the OWL DL requirements through the addition of the missing type triples or judicious handling of imports. For those in the DAML Library, we were able to handle around a third. The solutions we describe here are admittedly rather simple – the latter example in Section 4.1 gives a glimpse of the complex dependencies that may arise from missing types and we do not (as yet) offer automated

---

[14] http://owl.bbn.com/validator/

solutions to such problems. However the results reported show that even with simple approaches, we are able to handle a significant number of ontologies.

A key message here is that care should be taken when applying such heuristics – the underlying semantics of the ontology *are* being changed (see Sections 5.1 and 5.2), and tools must ensure that users are aware of the fact that this is happening. We are not advocating that applications should feel free to arbitrarily rewrite ontologies they find on the web – this is likely to compromise interoperability. Rather, the procedures we describe here can form a first cut in a process of "cleaning up" information on the Web.

An analogy can be made with HTML processors. A significant proportion of HTML pages which are available on the web do not, in fact, conform to schema such as the XHTML standard. It is often the case that, for example, closing tags are missing. HTML parsers such as those found in browsers have been carefully honed to try and deal with these situations. Indeed, it is unlikely that the web would have met with the success it has if browsers were not able to handle poorly structured documents. We should be careful not to stretch this analogy too far, however. In general, HTML pages are targeted at a human interpreter – humans are fairly robust in terms of their ability to deal with incomplete or dirty information. Software agents are a different matter, and care must be taken when applying patching heuristics to ensure that the end user is aware that such an approach is being taken. In addition, even with what seems to be "broken" or dirty information, it may be the case that the original syntactic presentation *is* exactly what was intended.

Support for the migration from vanilla RDF to OWL is also of interest here. As discussed in the introduction, the number of OWL DL/Lite ontologies currently on the web is small. Indeed the number of ontologies that even use the OWL vocabulary is small – many more schemas are currently represented using RDF. It would be useful if such schemas could be made accessible to OWL processors whenever possible. Again, we surmise that in a large proportion of the RDF schemas available on the web, the schemas are not inherently OWL Full due to the expressivity used, but are rather OWL Full because they do not meet the *syntactic* restrictions imposed by OWL DL. Translating these to valid OWL DL ontologies is not, as we have seen, simply a case of replacing vocabulary. However, with the application of appropriate heuristics, we can move towards the support of automatic migration of RDF vocabularies to OWL DL and Lite.

Another issue that we touch on here, but do not examine in much depth is that of the provision of ontology libraries. The success of the Semantic Web relies, in part, on the provision of ontologies and the *sharing* of those ontologies. Not only must we author the ontologies, but they must also be published and made available to applications. The initial analysis reported here used a somewhat crude mechanism (searching Google) in order to find OWL ontologies. There are a small number of ontology libraries on the web (for example the DAML ontology library[15] which is probably the largest) but these are not partic-

---

[15] http://www.daml.org/ontologies

ularly comprehensive, and in the main are rather *lightweight*[16]. For example, our experience of encountering Dublin Core properties in OWL ontologies suggests that an available OWL DL or Lite schema for the Dublin Core properties[17] is likely to be a useful resource.

In conclusion, although the initial answer to the question "how much OWL DL is there on the Web?" is "not much", with the provision of some quite simple tool support, we believe we can increase this to at least "a little bit".

Acknowledgments. This work was supported by the WonderWeb project (EU grant IST-2001-33052). Sean Bechhofer would like to thank Peter Patel-Schneider and Jeremy Carroll for their invaluable assistance in deciphering the minutiae of OWL syntax.

References

1. Sean Bechhofer. OWL Web Ontology Language Parsing OWL in RDF/XML. W3C Working Group Note, World Wide Web Consortium, January 2004. http://www.w3.org/TR/owl-parsing.
2. Sean Bechhofer and Jeremy J. Carroll. Parsing OWL DL: Trees or Triples? In *Proceedings of World Wide Web Conference, WWW2004*. ACM Press, May 2004.
3. Sean Bechhofer, Raphael Volz, and Phillip Lord. Cooking the Semantic Web with the OWL API. In *2nd International Semantic Web Conference, ISWC*, volume 2870 of *Lecture Notes in Computer Science*, Sanibel Island, Florida, October 2003. Springer.
4. Jeen Broekstra, Arjohn Kampman, and F. van Harmelen. Sesame: A Generic Architecture for Storing and Querying RDF. In Ian Horrocks and James Hendler, editors, *Proceedings of the International Semantic Web Conference, ISWC2002*, volume 2342 of *Lecture Notes in Computer Science*, pages 54–68. Springer-Verlag, June 2002.
5. Mike Dean and Guus Schreiber. OWL Web Ontology Language Reference. W3C Recommendation, World Wide Web Consortium, 2004. http://www.w3.org/TR/owl-ref/.
6. P. Hayes. RDF Semantics. W3C Recommendation, World Wide Web Consortium, 2004. http://www.w3.org/TR/rdf-mt/.
7. Jonathan Marsh. XML Base. W3C Recommendation, World Wide Web Consortium, 2004. http://www.w3.org/TR/xmlbase/.
8. P. Patel-Schneider, P. Hayes, and I. Horrocks. OWL Web Ontology Language Abstract Syntax and Semantics. W3C Recommendation, World Wide Web Consortium, 2004. http://www.w3.org/TR/owl-semantics/.

---

[16] By lightweight here we mean ontologies that do not extend much beyond the expressivity supported by RDF Schema.

[17] http://www.aifb.uni-karlsruhe.de/WBS/rvo/ontologies/dublincore.owl

QOM – Quick Ontology Mapping

Marc Ehrig and Steffen Staab

Institute AIFB, University of Karlsruhe

Abstract. (Semi-)automatic mapping — also called (semi-)automatic alignment — of ontologies is a core task to achieve interoperability when two agents or services use different ontologies. In the existing literature, the focus has so far been on improving the quality of mapping results. We here consider QOM, Quick Ontology Mapping, as a way to trade off between effectiveness (i.e. quality) and efficiency of the mapping generation algorithms. We show that QOM has lower run-time complexity than existing prominent approaches. Then, we show in experiments that this theoretical investigation translates into practical benefits. While QOM gives up some of the possibilities for producing high-quality results in favor of efficiency, our experiments show that this loss of quality is marginal.

1 Introduction

Semantic mapping[1] between ontologies is a necessary precondition to establish interoperation between agents or services using different ontologies. In recent years we have seen a range of research work on methods proposing such mappings [1,2,3]. The focus of the previous work, however, has been laid exclusively on improving the *effectiveness* of the approach (i.e. the quality of proposed mappings such as evaluated against some human judgement given either a posteriori or a priori). When we tried to apply these methods to some of the real-world scenarios we address in other research contributions [4], we found that existing mapping methods were not suitable for the ontology integration task at hand, as they all neglected *efficiency*. To illustrate our requirements: We have been working in realms where light-weight ontologies are applied such as the ACM Topic hierarchy with its 10^4 concepts or folder structures of individual computers, which corresponded to 10^4 to 10^5 concepts. Finally, we are working with Wordnet exploiting its 10^6 concepts (cf. [5]). When mapping between such light-weight ontologies, the trade-off that one has to face is between effectiveness and efficiency. For instance, consider the knowledge management platform built on a Semantic Web And Peer-to-peer basis in SWAP [4]. It is not sufficient to provide its user with the best possible mapping, it is also necessary to answer his queries within a few seconds — even if two peers use two different ontologies and have never encountered each other before.

In this paper we present an approach that considers both the quality of mapping results as well as the run-time complexity. Our hypothesis is that mapping algorithms may be streamlined such that the loss of quality (compared to a standard baseline) is marginal, but the improvement of efficiency is so tremendous that it allows for the ad-hoc mapping of large-size, light-weight ontologies. To substantiate the hypothesis, we outline

---

[1] Frequently also called alignment.

S.A. McIlraith et al. (Eds.): ISWC 2004, LNCS 3298, pp. 683–697, 2004.
© Springer-Verlag Berlin Heidelberg 2004

a comparison of the worst-case run-time behavior (given in full detail in [6]) and we report on a number of practical experiments. The approaches used for our (unavoidably preliminary) comparison represent different classes of algorithms for ontology mapping. Comparing to these approaches we can observe that our new efficient approach QOM achieves good quality. The complexity of QOM is of $O(n \cdot log(n))$ (measuring with n being the number of the entities in the ontologies) against $O(n^2)$ for approaches that have similar effective outcomes.

The remainder of the paper starts with a clarification of terminology (Section 2). To compare the worst-case run-time behavior of different approaches, we then describe a canonical process for ontology mapping that subsumes the different approaches compared in this paper (Section 3). The process is a core building block for later deriving the run-time complexity of the different mapping algorithms. Section 4 presents our toolbox to analyze these algorithms. In Section 5, different approaches for proposing mappings are described and aligned to the canonical process, one of them being our approach QOM. The way to derive their run-time complexity is outlined in Section 6. Experimental results (Section 7) complement the comparison of run-time complexities. We close this paper with a short section on related work and a conclusion.

2   Terminology

2.1   Ontology

As we currently focus on light-weight ontologies, we build on RDF/S[2] to represent ontologies. To facilitate the further description, we briefly summarize its major primitives and introduce some shorthand notations. An RDF model is described by a set of statements, each consisting of a subject, a predicate and an object. An ontology O is defined by its set of Concepts C (instances of "rdfs:Class") with a corresponding subsumption hierarchy H_C (a binary relation corresponding to "rdfs:subClassOf"). Relations R (instances of "rdf:Property") exist between single concepts. Relations are arranged alike in a hierarchy H_R ("rdfs:subPropertyOf"). An entity $i \in I$ may be an instance of a class $c \in C$ ("rdf:type"). An instance $i \in I$ may have one j or many role fillers from I for a relation r from R. We also call this type of triple (i, r, j) a property instance.

2.2   Mapping

We here define our use of the term "mapping". Given two ontologies O_1 and O_2, mapping one ontology onto another means that for each entity (concept C, relation R, or instance I) in ontology O_1, we try to find a corresponding entity, which has the same intended meaning, in ontology O_2.

Definition 1. *We define an ontology mapping function,* map, *based on the vocabulary,* $\mathcal{E}$, *of all terms* $e \in \mathcal{E}$ *and based on the set of possible ontologies,* $\mathcal{O}$, *as a partial function:*

$$\text{map} : \mathcal{E} \times \mathcal{O} \times \mathcal{O} \rightharpoonup \mathcal{E},$$

with $\forall e \in O_1 (\exists f \in O_2 : \text{map}(e, O_1, O_2) = f \vee \text{map}(e, O_1, O_2) = \bot).$

---

[2] http://www.w3.org/RDFS/

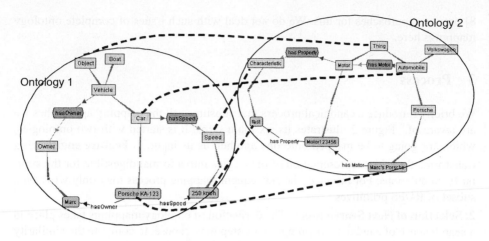

Fig. 1. Example Ontologies and their Mappings

Table 1. Mapping Table for Relation $\text{map}_{O_1,O_2}(e, f)$

Ontology O_1	Ontology O_2
Object	Thing
Car	Automobile
Porsche KA-123	Marc's Porsche
Speed	Characteristic
250 km/h	fast

A term c interpreted in an ontology O is either a concept, a relation or an instance, i.e. $e_{|O} \in \mathcal{C} \cup \mathcal{R} \cup \mathcal{I}$. We usually write e instead of $e_{|O}$ when the ontology O is clear from the context of the writing. We write $\text{map}_{O_1,O_2}(e)$ for $\text{map}(e, O_1, O_2)$. We derive a relation map_{O_1,O_2} by defining $\text{map}_{O_1,O_2}(e, f) \Leftrightarrow \text{map}_{O_1,O_2}(e) = f$. We leave out O_1, O_2 when they are evident from the context and write $\text{map}(e) = f$ and $\text{map}(e, f)$, respectively. Once a (partial) mapping, map, between two ontologies O_1 and O_2 is established, we also say *"entity c is mapped onto entity f"* iff $\text{map}(e, f)$. An entity can either be mapped to at most one other entity. A pair of entities (e, f) that is not yet in map and for which appropriate mapping criteria still need to be tested is called a *candidate mapping*.

2.3   Example

The following example illustrates a mapping. Two ontologies O_1 and O_2 describing the domain of car retailing are given (Figure 1). A reasonable mapping between the two ontologies is given in Table 1 as well as by the dashed lines in the figure.

Apart from one-to-one mappings as investigated in this paper one entity often has to be mapped to a complex composite such as a concatenation of terms (first and last name) or an entity with restrictions (a sports-car is a car going faster than 250 km/h). [7,

8] propose approaches for this. We do not deal with such issues of complete ontology mappings here.

3   Process

We briefly introduce a canonical process that subsumes all the mapping approaches we are aware of.[3] Figure 2 illustrates its six main steps. It is started with two ontologies, which are going to be mapped onto one another, as its input: **1. Feature engineering** transforms the initial representation of ontologies into a format digestible for the similarity calculations. For instance, the subsequent mapping process may only work on a subset of RDFS primitives.

2. Selection of Next Search Steps. The derivation of ontology mappings takes place in a search space of candidate mappings. This step may choose, to compute the similarity of a restricted subset of candidate concepts pairs $\{(e, f)|e \in O_1, f \in O_2\}$ and to ignore others.

3. Similarity Computation determines similarity values of candidate mappings.

4. Similarity Aggregation. In general, there may be several similarity values for a candidate pair of entities e, f from two ontologies O_1, O_2, e.g. one for the similarity of their labels and one for the similarity of their relationship to other terms. These different similarity values for one candidate pair must be aggregated into a single aggregated similarity value.

5. Interpretation uses the individual or aggregated similarity values to derive mappings between entities from O_1 and O_2. Some mechanisms here are, to use thresholds for similarity mappings [2], to perform relaxation labelling [3], or to combine structural and similarity criteria.

6. Iteration. Several algorithms perform an iteration over the whole process in order to bootstrap the amount of structural knowledge. Iteration may stop when no new mappings are proposed. Note that in a subsequent iteration one or several of steps 1 through 5 may be skipped, because all features might already be available in the appropriate format or because some similarity computation might only be required in the first round.

Eventually, the output returned is a mapping table representing the relation map_{O_1, O_2}.

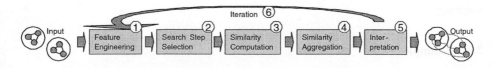

Fig. 2. Mapping Process

---

[3] The process is inspired by CRISP-DM, http://www.crisp-dm.org/, the CRoss Industry Standard Process for Data Mining.

4 A Toolbox of Data Structures and Methods

The principal idea of this section is to provide a toolbox of data structures and methods common to many approaches that determine mappings. This gives us a least common denominator based on which concrete approaches instantiating the process depicted in Figure 2 can be compared more easily.

4.1 Features of Ontological Entities

To compare two entities from two different ontologies, one considers their characteristics, i.e. their features. The features may be specific for a mapping generation algorithm, in any case the features of ontological entities (of concepts, relations, instances) need to be extracted from extensional and intensional ontology definitions. See also [9] and [10] for an overview of possible features and a classification of them. Possible characteristics include:

- *Identifiers*: i.e. strings with dedicated formats, such as unified resource identifiers (URIs) or RDF labels.
- *RDF/S Primitives*: such as properties or subclass relations
- *Derived Features*: which constrain or extend simple RDFS primitives (e.g. most-specific-class-of-instance)
- *Aggregated Features*: i.e. aggregating more than one simple RDFS primitive, e.g. a sibling is every instance-of the parent-concept of an instance
- *OWL Primitives*: such as an entity being the sameAs another entity
- *Domain Specific Features* are features which only apply to a certain domain with a predefined shared ontology. For instance, in an application where files are represented as instances and the relation hashcode-of-file is defined, we use this feature to compare representations of concrete files.

Example. We again refer to the example in Figure 1. The actual feature consists of a juxtaposition of relation name and entity name. The Car concept of ontology 1 is characterized through its (label, Car), the concept which it is linked to through (subclassOf, Vehicle), its (concept sibling, boat), and the (direct property, hasSpeed). Car is also described by its instances through (instance, Porsche KA-123). The relation hasSpeed on the other hand is described through the (domain, Car) and the (range, Speed). An instance would be Porsche KA-123, which is characterized through the instantiated (property instance, (hasOwner, Marc)) and (property instance, (hasSpeed, 250 km/h)).

4.2 Similarity Computation

Definition 2. *We define a similarity measure for comparison of ontology entities as a function as follows (cf. [11]):*

$$\text{sim} : \mathcal{E} \times \mathcal{E} \times \mathcal{O} \times \mathcal{O} \to [0, 1]$$

Different similarity measures $\text{sim}_k(e, f, O_1, O_2)$ are indexed through a label k. Further, we leave out O_1, O_2 when they are evident from the context and write $\text{sim}_k(e, f)$. The following similarity measures are needed to compare the features of ontological entities at iteration t.

- *Object Equality* is based on existing logical assertions — especially assertions from previous iterations: $\text{sim}_{obj}(a, b) := \{1$ iff $\text{map}_{t-1}(a) = b, 0$ otherwise$\}$
- *Explicit Equality* checks whether a logical assertion already forces two entities to be equal: $\text{sim}_{exp}(a, b) := \{1$ iff $statement(a, \text{"}sameAs\text{''}, b), 0$ otherwise$\}$
- *String Similarity* measures the similarity of two strings on a scale from 0 to 1 (cf. [12]) based on Levenshtein's edit distance, ed [13].
  $\text{sim}_{str}(c, d) := max(0, \frac{min(|c|,|d|)-ed(c,d)}{min(|c|,|d|)})$
- *SimSet*: For many features we have to determine to what extent two sets of entities are similar. To remedy the problem, multidimensional scaling [14] measures how far two entities are from all other entities and assumes that if they have very similar distances to all other entities, they must be very similar:
  $\text{sim}_{set}(E, F) = \frac{\sum_{e \in E} e}{|E|} \cdot \frac{\sum_{f \in F} f}{|F|}$
  with $e = (\text{sim}(e, e_1), \text{sim}(e, e_2), \dots, \text{sim}(e, f_1), \text{sim}(e, f_2), \dots)$, f analogously.

These measures are all input to the similarity aggregation.

4.3   Similarity Aggregation

Similarities are aggregated by:
$\text{sim}_{agg}(e, f) = \frac{\sum_{k=1\dots n} w_k \cdot adj(\text{sim}_k(e,f))}{\sum_{k=1\dots n} w_k}$
with w_k being the weight for each individual similarity measure, and adj being a function to transform the original similarity value ($adj : [0, 1] \rightarrow [0, 1]$), which yields better results.

4.4   Interpretation

From the similarity values we derive the actual mappings. The basic idea is that each entity may only participate in one mapping and that we assign mappings based on a threshold t and a greedy strategy that starts with the largest similarity values first. Ties are broken arbitrarily by $arg\tilde{m}ax_{(g,h)}$, but with a deterministic strategy.
$P(\bot, \bot, E \cup \{\bot\}, E \cup \{\bot\})$.
$P(g, h, U \backslash \{e\}, V \backslash \{f\}) \leftarrow P(e, f, U, V) \wedge \text{sim}(g, h) > t$
$\wedge (g, h) = arg\tilde{m}ax_{(g,h) \in U \backslash \{e\} \times V \backslash \{f\}} \text{sim}_{agg}(g, h)$.
$\text{map}(e, f) \leftarrow \exists X_1, X_2 P(e, f, X_1, X_2) \wedge (e, f) \neq (\bot, \bot)$.

5   Approaches to Determine Mappings

In the following we now use the toolbox, and extend it, too, in order to define a range of different mapping generation approaches. In the course of this section we present our novel Quick Ontology Mapping approach — QOM.

5.1   Standard Mapping Approaches

Our Naive Ontology Mapping (NOM)[9] constitutes a straight forward baseline for later comparisons. It is defined by the steps of the process model as follows. Where appropriate we point to related mapping approaches and briefly describe the difference in comparison to NOM.

1. Feature Engineering. Firstly, the ontologies have to be represented in RDFS. We use features as shown in Section 4.1.

For PROMPT and Anchor-PROMPT [2] any ontology format is suitable as long as it can be used in the Protege environment. GLUE [3] learns in advance, based on a sample mapping set, a similarity estimator to identify equal instances and concepts.

2. Search Step Selection. All entities of the first ontology are compared with all entities of the second ontology. Any pair is treated as a candidate mapping.

This is generally the same for other mapping approaches, though the PROMPT algorithm can be implemented more efficiently by sorting the labels first, thus only requiring the comparison of two neighboring elements in the list.

3. Similarity Computation. The similarity computation between an entity of O_1 and an entity of O_2 is done by using a wide range of similarity functions. Each similarity function is based on a feature (Section 4.1) of both ontologies and a respective similarity measure (Section 4.2). For NOM they are shown in Table 2.

The PROMPT system determines the similarity based on the exact equality (not only similarity) of labels. Anchor-PROMPT adds structural components. In GLUE the similarity is gained using the previously learned Similarity Estimator. It further adds other features using Relaxation Labelling based on the intuition that mappings of a node are typically influenced by the node's neighborhood.

4. Similarity Aggregation. NOM emphasizes high individual similarities and de-emphasizes low individual similarities by weighting individual similarity results with a sigmoid function first and summing the modified values then. To produce an aggregated similarity (cf. Section 4.2) NOM applies $adj(x) = \frac{1}{1+e^{-5(x-0.5)}}$. Weights w_k are assigned by manually maximizing the f-measure on overall training data from different test ontologies.

In systems with one similarity value such as PROMPT or GLUE this step does not apply.

5. Interpretation. NOM interprets similarity results by two means. First, it applies a threshold to discard spurious evidence of similarity. Second, NOM enforces bijectivity of the mapping by ignoring candidate mappings that would violate this constraint and by favoring candidate mappings with highest aggregated similarity scores.

As PROMPT is semi-automatic this step is less crucial. It presents all pairs with a similarity value above a relatively low threshold value and the users can decide to carry out the merging step or not. The relaxation labelling process of GLUE can also be seen as a kind of interpretation.

6. Iteration. The first round uses only the basic comparison method based on labels and string similarity to compute the similarity between entities. By doing the computation in several rounds one can access the already computed pairs and use more sophisticated structural similarity measures. Therefore, in the second round and thereafter NOM relies on all the similarity functions listed in Table 2.

Table 2. Features and Similarity Measures for Different Entity Types Contributing to Aggregated Similarity in NOM. The corresponding ontology is indicated through an index.

Comparing	No.	Feature	Similarity Measure
Concepts	1	(label,X_1)	string similarity(X_1, X_2)
	2	(URI_1)	string equality(URI_1, URI_2)
	3	(X_1,sameAs,X_2) relation	explicit equality(X_1, X_2)
	4	(direct properties,Y_1)	SimSet(Y_1, Y_2)
	5	all (inherited properties,Y_1)	SimSet(Y_1, Y_2)
	6	all (super-concepts,Y_1)	SimSet(Y_1, Y_2)
	7	all (sub-concepts,Y_1)	SimSet(Y_1, Y_2)
	8	(concept siblings,Y_1)	SimSet(Y_1, Y_2)
	9	(direct instances,Y_1)	SimSet(Y_1, Y_2)
	10	(instances,Y_1)	SimSet(Y_1, Y_2)
Relations	1	(label,X_1)	string similarity(X_1, X_2)
	2	(URI_1)	string equality(URI_1, URI_2)
	3	(X_1,sameAs,X_2) relation	explicit equality(X_1, X_2)
	4	(domain,X_d1) and (range,X_r1)	object equality(X_{d1}, X_{d2}), (X_{r1}, X_{r2})
	5	all (super-properties,Y_1)	SimSet(Y_1, Y_2)
	6	all (sub-properties,Y_1)	SimSet(Y_1, Y_2)
	7	(property siblings,Y_1)	SimSet(Y_1, Y_2)
	8	(property instances,Y_1)	SimSet(Y_1, Y_2)
Instances	1	(label,X_1)	string similarity(X_1, X_2)
	2	(URI_1)	string equality(URI_1, URI_2)
	3	(X_1,sameAs,X_2) relation	explicit equality(X_1, X_2)
	4	all (parent-concepts,Y_1)	SimSet(Y_1, Y_2)
	5	(property instances,Y_1)	SimSet(Y_1, Y_2)
Property-Instances	1	(domain,X_d1) and (range,X_r1)	object equality(X_{d1}, X_{d2}), (X_{r1}, X_{r2})
	2	(parent property,Y_1)	SimSet(Y_1, Y_2)

PROMPT also requires these iterations after feedback has been given by the user. The GLUE system heavily relies on iterations for the relaxation labelling process. Both do not change the strategies during the iterations.

5.2   QOM — Quick Ontology Mapping

The goal of this paper is to present an efficient mapping algorithm. For this purpose, we optimize the effective, but inefficient NOM approach towards our goal. The outcome is QOM — Quick Ontology Mapping. We would also like to point out that the efficiency gaining steps can be applied to other mapping approaches as well.

1. Feature Engineering. Like NOM, QOM exploits RDF triples.

2. Search Step Selection. A major ingredient of run-time complexity is the number of candidate mapping pairs which have to be compared to actually find the best mappings. Therefore, we use heuristics to lower the number of candidate mappings. Fortunately we can make use of ontological structures to classify the candidate mappings into promising and less promising pairs.

In particular we use a dynamic programming approach [15]. In this approach we have two main data structures. First, we have candidate mappings which ought to be investigated. Second, an agenda orders the candidate mappings, discarding some of them entirely to gain efficiency. After the completion of the similarity analysis and their interpretation new decisions have to be taken. The system has to determine which candidate mappings to add to the agenda for the next iteration. The behavior of initiative and ordering constitutes a search strategy.

We suggest the subsequent strategies to propose new candidate mappings for inspection:

Random. A simple approach is to limit the number of candidate mappings by selecting either a fixed number or percentage from all possible mappings.

Label. This restricts candidate mappings to entity pairs whose labels are near to each other in a sorted list. Every entity is compared to its "label"-neighbors.

Change Propagation. QOM further compares only entities for which adjacent entities were assigned new mappings in a previous iteration. This is motivated by the fact that every time a new mapping has been found, we can expect to also find similar entities adjacent to these found mappings. Further, to prevent very large numbers of comparisons, the number of pairs is restricted.

Hierarchy. We start comparisons at a high level of the concept and property taxonomy. Only the top level entities are compared in the beginning. We then subsequently descend the taxonomy.

Combination. The combined approach used in QOM follows different optimization strategies: it uses a label subagenda, a randomness subagenda, and a mapping change propagation subagenda. In the first iteration the label subagenda is pursued. Afterwards we focus on mapping change propagation. Finally we shift to the randomness subagenda, if the other strategies do not identify sufficiently many correct mapping candidates.

With these multiple agenda strategies we only have to check a fixed and restricted number of mapping candidates for each original entity.[4] Please note that the creation of the presented agendas does require processing resources itself.

3. Similarity Computation. QOM, just like NOM, is based on a wide range of ontology feature and heuristic combinations. In order to optimize QOM, we have restricted the range of costly features as specified in Table 3. In particular, QOM avoids the complete pair-wise comparison of trees in favor of a(n incomplete) top-down strategy. The marked comparisons in the table were changed from features which point to complete inferred sets to features only retrieving limited size direct sets.

4. Similarity Aggregation. The aggregation of single methods is only performed once per candidate mapping and is therefore not critical for the overall efficiency. Therefore, QOM works like NOM in this step.

5. Interpretation. Also the interpretation step of QOM is the same as in NOM.

6. Iteration. QOM iterates to find mappings based on lexical knowledge first and based on knowledge structures later.

---

[4] We have also explored a number of other strategies or combinations of strategies with simple data sets but they did not outperform results of QOM presented here.

Table 3. Features and Similarity Measures for Different Entity Types Contributing to Aggregated Similarity in QOM. The lower case "a" indicates that the feature has been modified for efficiency considerations.

Comparing	Change	Feature	Similarity Measure
Concepts	5	all (inherited properties, Y_1)	SimSet(Y_1, Y_2)
	$\longrightarrow$ 5a	(properties of direct super-concepts, Y_1)	SimSet(Y_1, Y_2)
	6	all (inherited super-concepts, Y_1)	SimSet(Y_1, Y_2)
	$\longrightarrow$ 6a	(direct super-concepts, Y_1)	SimSet(Y_1, Y_2)
	7	all (inherited sub-concepts, Y_1)	SimSet(Y_1, Y_2)
	$\longrightarrow$ 7a	(direct sub-concepts, Y_1)	SimSet(Y_1, Y_2)
	10	all (inherited instances, Y_1)	SimSet(Y_1, Y_2)
	$\longrightarrow$ 10a	(instances of direct sub-concepts, Y_1)	SimSet(Y_1, Y_2)
Relations	5	all (inherited super-properties, Y_1)	SimSet(Y_1, Y_2)
	$\longrightarrow$ 5a	(direct super-properties, Y_1)	SimSet(Y_1, Y_2)
	6	all (inherited sub-properties, Y_1)	SimSet(Y_1, Y_2)
	$\longrightarrow$ 6a	(direct sub-properties, Y_1)	SimSet(Y_1, Y_2)
Instances	4	all (inherited parent-concepts, Y_1)	SimSet(Y_1, Y_2)
	$\longrightarrow$ 4a	(direct parent-concepts, Y_1)	SimSet(Y_1, Y_2)

In all our tests we have found that after ten rounds hardly any further changes occur in the mapping table. This is independent from the actual size of the involved ontologies. QOM therefore restricts the number of runs.

Assuming that ontologies have a fixed percentage of entities with similar lexical labels, we will easily find their correct mappings in the first iteration. These are further evenly distributed over the two ontologies, i.e. the distance to the furthest not directly found mapping is constant. Through the change propagation agenda we pass on to the next adjacent mapping candidates with every iteration step. The number of required iterations remains constant; it is independent from the size of the ontologies.

6   Comparing Run-Time Complexity

We determine the worst-case run-time complexity of the algorithms to propose mappings as a function of the size of the two given ontologies. Thereby, we wanted to base our analysis on realistic ontologies and not on artifacts. We wanted to avoid the consideration of large ontologies with n leaf concepts but a depth of the concept hierarchy H_C of $n - 1$. [16] have examined the structure of a large number of ontologies and found, that concept hierarchies on average have a branching factor of around 2 and that the concept hierarchies are neither extremely shallow nor extremely deep. The actual branching factor can be described by a power law distribution. Hence, in the following we base our results on their findings.

Theorem 1. *The worst case run-time behaviors of NOM, PROMPT, Anchor-PROMPT, GLUE and QOM are given by the following table:*

NOM	$O(n^2 \cdot log^2(n))$
PROMPT[5]	$O(n \cdot log(n))$
Anchor-PROMPT	$O(n^2 \cdot log^2(n))$
GLUE[6]	$O(n^2)$
QOM	$O(n \cdot log(n))$

Proof Sketch 1. *The different algorithmic steps contributing to complexity[7] are aligned to the canonical process of Section 3.*

For each of the algorithms, one may then determine the costs of each step. First, one determines the cost for feature engineering (feat). The second step is the search step i.e. candidate mappings selection (sele). For each of the selected candidate mappings (comp) we need to compute k different similarity functions sim_k and aggregate them (agg). The number of entities involved and the complexity of the respective similarity measure affect the run-time performance. Subsequently the interpretation of the similarity values with respect to mapping requires a run-time complexity of inter. Finally we have to iterate over the previous steps multiple times (iter).

Then, the worst case run-time complexity is defined for all approaches by:

$$c = (feat + sele + comp \cdot (\textstyle\sum_k sim_k + agg) + inter) \cdot iter$$

Depending on the concrete values that show up in the individual process steps the different run-time complexities are derived in detail in [6].

7   Empirical Evaluation and Results

In this section we show that the worst case considerations carry over to practical experiments and that the quality of QOM is only negligibly lower than the one of other approaches. The implementation itself was coded in Java using the KAON-framework[8] for ontology operations.

7.1   Test Scenario

Metrics. We use standard information retrieval metrics to assess the different approaches (cf. [17]):

Precision $p = \frac{\#correct\_found\_mapping}{\#found\_mappings}$

Recall $r = \frac{\#correct\_found\_mappings}{\#existing\_mappings}$

F-Measure $f_1 = \frac{2pr}{p+r}$

---

[5] This complexity assumes an ideal implementation of PROMPT using a sorted list. The tool itself requires $O(n^2)$.

[6] This result is based on optimistic assumptions about the learner.

[7] In this paper we assume that the retrieval of a statement of an ontology entity from a database can be done in constant access time, independent of the ontology size, e.g. based on sufficient memory and a hash function.

[8] http://kaon.semanticweb.org/

Data Sets. Three separate data sets were used for evaluation purposes. As real world ontologies and especially their mappings are scarce, students were asked to independently create and map ontologies.[9]

Russia 1. In this first set we have two ontologies describing Russia. The students created the ontologies with the objectives to represent the content of two independent travel websites about Russia. These ontologies have approximately 400 entities each, including concepts, relations, and instances. The total number of possible mappings is 160, which the students have assigned manually.

Russia 2. The second set again covers Russia, but the two ontologies are more difficult to map. After their creation they have been altered by deleting entities and changing the labels at random. They differ substantially in both labels and structure. Each ontology has 300 entities with 215 possible mappings, which were captured during generation.

Tourism. Finally, the participants of a seminar created two ontologies which separately describe the tourism domain of Mecklenburg-Vorpommern. Both ontologies have an extent of about 500 entities. No instances were modelled with this ontology though, they only consist of concepts and relations. The 300 mappings were created manually.

Strategies. We evaluated the mapping strategies described in the previous sections:

- PROMPT — As the PROMPT algorithm is rather simple and fast we use it as a baseline to evaluate the speed. The empirical evaluation is based on the actual implementation of PROMPT rather than its theoretic potential, as described in the previous section.
- NOM / Anchor-PROMPT — Naive Ontology Mapping is an approach making use of a wide range of features and measures. Therefore it reaches high levels of effectiveness and represents our quality baseline. In terms of structural information used and complexity incurred it is similar to Anchor-PROMPT.
- QOM — Quick Ontology Mapping is our novel approach focusing on efficiency.

To circumvent the problem of having semi-automatic merging tools (PROMPT and Anchor-PROMPT) in our fully automatic mapping tests, we assumed that every proposition of the system is meaningful and correct. Further, as we had difficulties in running Anchor-PROMPT with the size of the given data sets, we refer to the results of the somewhat similar NOM. For GLUE we face another general problem. The algorithm has a strong focus on example instance mappings. As we can not provide this, we refrained from running the tests on a poorly trained estimator which would immediately result in poor quality results.

7.2   Results and Discussion

We present the results of the strategies on each of the data sets in Figures 3 and 4. The tourism dataset shows similar characteristics as Russia 1 and is therefore not plotted. The x-axis shows the elapsed time on a logarithmic scale, the y-axis corresponds to the f-measure. The symbols represent the result after each iteration step.

---

[9] The datasets are available from http://www.aifb.uni-karlsruhe.de/WBS/meh/mapping/.

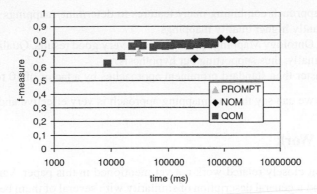

Fig. 3. Mapping quality reached over time with Russia 1 ontologies.

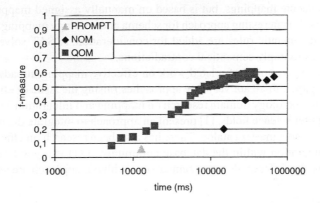

Fig. 4. Mapping quality reached over time with Russia 2 ontologies.

Depending on the scenario PROMPT reaches good results within a short period of time. Please notice that for ontologies with a small number of similar labels (Figure 4) this strategy is not satisfactory (f-measure 0.06). In contrast, the f-measure value of the NOM strategy rises slowly but reaches high absolute values of up to 0.8. Unfortunately it requires a lot of time. Finally the QOM Strategy is plotted. It reaches high quality levels very quickly. In terms of absolute values it also seems to reach the best quality results of all strategies. This appears to be an effect of QOM achieving an about 20 times higher number of iterations than NOM within the given time frame.

Lessons Learned. We had the hypothesis that faster mapping results can be obtained with only a negligible loss of quality. We here briefly present the bottom line of our considerations in this paper:

1. Optimizing the mapping approach for efficiency — like QOM does — decreases the overall mapping quality. If ontologies are not too large one might prefer to rather avoid this.
2. Labels are very important for mapping, if not the most important feature of all, and alone already return very satisfying results.

3. Using an approach combining many features to determine mappings clearly leads to significantly higher quality mappings.
4. The Quick Ontology Mapping approach shows very good results. Quality is lowered only marginally, thus supporting our hypothesis.
5. QOM is faster than standard prominent approaches by a factor of 10 to 100 times.

Recapitulating we can say that our mapping approach is very effective and efficient.

8   Related Work

We only present closely related work not yet mentioned in this paper. Various authors have tried to find a general description of similarity with several of them being based on knowledge networks. [18] give a general overview of similarity.

Original work on mapping is presented by [19] in their tool ONION, which uses inferencing to execute mappings, but is based on manually assigned mappings or very simple heuristics. An interesting approach for schema and ontology mapping is presented by [20]. Explicit semantic rules are added for consideration. A SAT solver is used to prevent mappings to imply semantical contradictions.

Despite the large number of related work on effective mapping already mentioned throughout this paper, there are very few approaches raising the issue of efficiency.

Apart from the ontology domain research on mapping and integration has been done in various computer science fields. [1] present an approach to integrate documents from different sources into a master catalog. There has also been research on efficient schema and instance integration within the database community. [21] is a good source for an overview. Due to the different domain comparisons with our approach are very difficult.

9   Conclusion

The problem of mapping two ontologies effectively and efficiently arises in many application scenarios [4,5]. We have devised a generic process model to investigate and compare different approaches that generate ontology mappings. In particular, we have developed an original method, QOM, for identifying mappings between two ontologies. We have shown that it is on a par with other good state-of-the-art algorithms concerning the quality of proposed mappings, while outperforming them with respect to efficiency — in terms of run-time complexity ($O(n \cdot log(n))$ instead of $O(n^2)$) and in terms of the experiments we have performed (by a factor of 10 to 100).

Acknowledgements. Research reported in this paper has been partially financed by the EU in the IST projects WonderWeb (IST-2001-33052), SWAP (IST-2001-34103) and SEKT (IST-2003-506826).

References

1. Agrawal, R., Srikant, R.: On integrating catalogs. In: Proceedings of the tenth international conference on World Wide Web, ACM Press (2001) 603–612

2. Noy, N.F., Musen, M.A.: The PROMPT suite: interactive tools for ontology merging and mapping. International Journal of Human-Computer Studies **59** (2003) 983–1024

3. Doan, A., Domingos, P., Halevy, A.: Learning to match the schemas of data sources: A multistrategy approach. VLDB Journal **50** (2003) 279–301

4. Ehrig, M., Haase, P., van Harmelen, F., Siebes, R., Staab, S., Stuckenschmidt, H., Studer, R., Tempich, C.: The SWAP data and metadata model for semantics-based peer-to-peer systems. In: Proceedings of MATES-2003. First German Conference on Multiagent Technologies. LNAI, Erfurt, Germany, Springer (2003)

5. Hotho, A., Staab, S., Stumme, G.: Ontologies improve text document clustering. In: Proceedings of the International Conference on Data Mining — ICDM-2003, IEEE Press (2003)

6. Ehrig, M., Staab, S.: Quick ontology mapping with QOM. Technical report, University of Karlsruhe, Institute AIFB (2004)
   http://www.aifb.uni-karlsruhe.de/WBS/meh/mapping/.

7. Do, H., Rahm, E.: COMA - a system for flexible combination of schema matching approaches. In: Proceedings of the 28th VLDB Conference, Hong Kong, China (2002)

8. Dhamankar, R., Lee, Y., Doan, A., Halevy, A., Domingos, P.: imap: discovering complex semantic matches between database schemas. In: Proceedings of the 2004 ACM SIGMOD international conference on Management of data. (2004) 383–394

9. Ehrig, M., Sure, Y.: Ontology mapping - an integrated approach. In Bussler, C., Davis, J., Fensel, D., Studer, R., eds.: Proceedings of the 1st ESWS. Volume 3053 of Lecture Notes in Computer Science., Heraklion, Greece, Springer Verlag (2004) 76–91

10. Euzenat, J., Valtchev, P.: An integrative proximity measure for ontology alignment. In Doan, A., Halevy, A., Noy, N., eds.: Proceedings of the Semantic Integration Workshop at ISWC-03. (2003)

11. Bisson, G.: Why and how to define a similarity measure for object based representation systems. Towards Very Large Knowledge Bases (1995) 236–246

12. Maedche, A., Staab, S.: Measuring similarity between ontologies. In: Proceedings of the European Conference on Knowledge Acquisition and Management (EKAW), Springer (2002)

13. Levenshtein, I.V.: Binary codes capable of correcting deletions, insertions, and reversals. Cybernetics and Control Theory (1966)

14. Cox, T., Cox, M.: Multidimensional Scaling. Chapman and Hall (1994)

15. Boddy, M.: Anytime problem solving using dynamic programming. In: Proceedings of the Ninth National Conference on Artificial Intelligence, Anaheim, California, Shaker Verlag (1991) 738–743

16. Tempich, C., Volz, R.: Towards a benchmark for semantic web reasoners - an analysis of the DAML ontology library. In Sure, Y., ed.: Evaluation of Ontology-based Tools (EON2003) at Second International Semantic Web Conference (ISWC 2003). (2003)

17. Do, H., Melnik, S., Rahm, E.: Comparison of schema matching evaluations. In: Proceedings of the second int. workshop on Web Databases (German Informatics Society). (2002)

18. Rodríguez, M.A., Egenhofer, M.J.: Determining semantic similarity among entity classes from different ontologies. IEEE Transactions on Knowledge and Data Engineering (2000)

19. Mitra, P., Wiederhold, G., Kersten, M.: A graph-oriented model for articulation of ontology interdependencies. Lecture Notes in Computer Science **1777** (2000) 86+

20. Bouquet, P., Magnini, B., Serafini, L., Zanobini, S.: A SAT-based algorithm for context matching. In: IV International and Interdisciplinary Conference on Modeling and Using Context (CONTEXT'2003), Stanford University (CA, USA) (2003)

21. McCallum, A., Nigam, K., Ungar, L.H.: Efficient clustering of high-dimensional data sets with application to reference matching. In: Knowledge Discovery and Data Mining. (2000) 169–178

An API for Ontology Alignment

Jérôme Euzenat

INRIA Rhône-Alpes, Montbonnot, France,
Jerome.Euzenat@inrialpes.fr

Abstract. Ontologies are seen as the solution to data heterogeneity on the web. However, the available ontologies are themselves source of heterogeneity. This can be overcome by aligning ontologies, or finding the correspondence between their components. These alignments deserve to be treated as objects: they can be referenced on the web as such, be completed by an algorithm that improves a particular alignment, be compared with other alignments and be transformed into a set of axioms or a translation program. We present here a format for expressing alignments in RDF, so that they can be published on the web. Then we propose an implementation of this format as an Alignment API, which can be seen as an extension of the OWL API and shares some design goals with it. We show how this API can be used for effectively aligning ontologies and completing partial alignments, thresholding alignments or generating axioms and transformations.

1 Introduction

Like the web, the semantic web will have to be distributed and heterogeneous. Its main problem will be the integration of the resources that compose it. For contributing solving this problem, data will be expressed in the framework of ontologies. However, ontologies themselves can be heterogeneous and some work will have to be done to achieve interoperability.

Semantic interoperability can be grounded on ontology reconciliation: finding relationships between concepts belonging to different ontologies. We call this process "ontology alignment". The ontology alignment problem can be described in one sentence: given two ontologies each describing a set of discrete entities (which can be classes, properties, rules, predicates, etc.), find the relationships (e.g., equivalence or subsumption) holding between these entities.

Imagine that one agent wants to query another for bibliographic data but they do not use the same ontology (see Table 1). The receiver of the query can produce some alignment for merging both ontologies and understanding the message or for translating the query in terms of its favorite ontology. Additionally, it could store the alignment for future use or choose to communicate it to its partner for it to translate messages. The ability to align ontologies can be seen as a service provided to the agents. As such it will benefit for some explicit representation of the alignment.

"Reifying" alignment results in a standardized format can be very useful in various contexts:

- for collecting, hand-made or automatically created, alignments in libraries that can be used for linking two particular ontologies;

S.A. McIlraith et al. (Eds.): ISWC 2004, LNCS 3298, pp. 698–712, 2004.
© Springer-Verlag Berlin Heidelberg 2004

- for modularizing alignments algorithms, e.g., by first using terminological alignment methods for labels, having this alignment agreed or amended by a user and using it as input for a structural alignment method;
- for comparing the results with each others or with possible "standard" results;
- for generating from the output of different algorithms, various forms of interoperability enablers. For instance, one might generate transformations from one source to another, bridge axioms for merging two ontologies, query wrappers (or mediators) which rewrite queries for reaching a particular source, inference rules for transferring knowledge from one context to another.

The problem is thus to design an alignment format which is general enough for covering most of the needs (in terms of languages and alignment output) and developed enough for offering the above functions. We propose an alignment format and an application programming interface (API) for manipulating alignments, illustrated through a first implementation. Providing an alignment format is not solely tied to triggering alignment algorithms but can help achieving other goals such as:

- allowing a user to select parts of alignments to be used,
- transforming the alignment into some translation programme or articulation axioms,
- thresholding correspondence in an alignment on some criterion,
- improving a partial alignment with a new algorithm,
- comparing alignment results,
- publishing ontology alignments on the web.

The design of this API follows that of the OWL API [1] in separating the various concerns that are involved in the manipulation and implementation of the API.

In the remainder, we shall define the current alignment format (§2), present it as an alignment API (§3) and its implementation on top of the OWL-API (§4). Then we will demonstrate the extension of the system by adding new algorithms (§5), composing alignments (§6), generating various output formats (§7) and comparing the alignments (§8).

2 Alignment Format

As briefly sketched above and before ([4]), in first approximation, an alignment is a set of pairs of elements from each ontology. However, as already pointed out in [9], this first definition does not cover all needs and all alignments generated. So the alignment format is provided on several levels, which depend on more elaborate alignment definitions.

2.1 Alignment

The alignment description can be stated as follows:

a level used for characterizing the type of correspondence (see below);

a set of correspondences which express the relation holding between entities of the first ontology and entities of the second ontology. This is considered in the following subsections;

an arity (default 1:1): Usual notations are 1:1, 1:m, n:1 or n:m. We prefer to note if the mapping is injective, surjective and total or partial on both side. We then end up with more alignment arities (noted with, 1 for injective and total, ? for injective, + for total and * for none and each sign concerning one mapping and its converse): ?:?, ?:1, 1:?, 1:1, ?:+, +:?, 1:+, +:1, +:+, ?:*, *:?, 1:*, *:1, +:*, *:+, *:*. These assertions could be provided as input (or constraint) for the alignment algorithm or as a result by the same algorithm.

This format is simpler than the alignment representation of [7], but is supposed producible by most alignment tools.

2.2   Level 0

The very basic definition of a correspondence is the one of a pair of discrete entities in the language. This first level of alignment has the advantage not to depend on a particular language. Its definition is roughly the following:

entity1: the first aligned entity. It is identified by an URI and corresponds to some discrete entity of the representation language.
entity2: the second aligned entity with the same constraint as entity1.
relation: (default "=") the relation holding between the two entities. It is not restricted to the equivalence relation, but can be more sophisticated operators (e.g., subsumption, incompatibility [5], or even some fuzzy relation).
strength: (default 1.) denotes the confidence held in this correspondence. Since many alignment methods compute a strength of the relation between entities, this strength can be provided as a normalized measure. This measure is by no mean characterizing the relationship (e.g., as a fuzzy relation which should be expressed in the relation attribute), but reflects the confidence of the alignment provider in the relation holding between the entities. Currently, we restrict this value to be a float value between 0. and 1.. If found useful, this could be generalised into any lattice domain.
id: an identifier for the correspondence.

A simple pair can be characterised by the default relation "=" and the default strength "1.". These default values lead to consider the alignment as a simple set of pairs.

On this level, the aligned entities may be classes, properties or individuals. But they also can be any kind of complex term that is used by the target language. For instance, it can use the concatenation of firstname and lastname considered in [11] if this is an entity, or it can use a path algebra like in:

```
hasSoftCopy.softCopyURI = hasURL
```

However, in the format described above and for the purpose of storing it in some RDF format, it is required that these entities (here, the paths) are discrete and identifiable by a URI.

Level 0 alignments are basic but found everywhere: there are no algorithm that cannot account for such alignments. It is, however, somewhat limited: there are other aspects of alignments that can be added to this first approximation.

2.3   Level 1

Level 1 replaces pairs of entities by pairs of sets (or lists) of entities. A level 1 correspondence is thus a slight refinement of level 0, which fills the gap between level 0 and level 2. However, it can be easily parsed and is still language independent.

2.4   Level 2 (L)

Level 2 considers sets of expressions of a particular language (L) with variables in these expressions. Correspondences are thus directional and correspond to a clause:

$$\forall \overline{x_f}(f \implies \exists \overline{x_g} g)$$

in which the variables of the left hand side are universally quantified over the whole formula and those of the right hand side (which do not occur in the left hand side) are existentially quantified. This level can express correspondences like:

$$\forall x, z\ grandparent(x, z) \implies \exists y; parent(x, y) \land parent(y, z)$$

This kind of rules (or restrictions) is commonly used in logic-based languages or in the database world for defining the views in "global-as-view" of "local-as-view" approaches [2]. It also resembles the SWRL rule language [6] when used with OWL (see §7.3 for a simple example of such rules). These rules can also be generalised to any relation and drop the orientation constraint.

Level 2 can be applied to other languages than OWL (SQL, regular expressions, F-Logic, etc.). For instance, the expression can apply to character strings and the alignment can denote concatenation like in

```
name = firstname+" "+lastname
```

This alignment format has been given an OWL ontology and a DTD for validating it in RDF/XML. Given such a format, we will briefly describe how is an API designed around it (§3) before explaining its implementation (§4) and functions (§5-§8).

3   Alignment API

A JAVA API can be used for implementing this format and linking to alignment algorithms and evaluation procedures. It is briefly sketched here.

3.1   Classes

The OWL API is extended with the (org.semanticweb.owl.align) package which describes the Alignment API. This package name is used for historical reasons. In fact, the API itself is fully independent from OWL or the OWL API.

It is essentially made of three interfaces. We present here, under the term "features", the information that the API implementation must provide. For each feature, there are the usual reader and writer accessors:

Alignment: The Alignment interface describes a particular alignment. It contains a specification of the alignment and a list of cells. Its features are the following:

    level: (values "0", "1", "2*") indicates the level of alignment format used;

    type: (values: "11", "1?", "1+", "1*", "?1", "??", "?+", "?*", "+1", "+?", "++", "+*", "*1", "*?", "?+", "**") the type of alignment;

    onto1: (value: URL) the first ontology to be aligned;

    onto2: (value: URL) the second ontology to be aligned;

    map: (value: Cell*) the set of correspondences between entities of the ontologies.

Cell: The Cell interface describes a particular correspondence between entities. It provides the following features:

    rdf:resource: (value: URI) the URI identifying the current correspondence;

    entity1: (value: URI) the URI of some entity of the first ontology;

    entity2: (value: URI) the URI of some entity of the second ontology;

    measure: (value: float between 0. and 1.) the confidence in the assertion that the relation holds between the first and the second entity (the higher the value, the higher the confidence);

    relation: (value: Relation) the relation holding between the first and second entity.

Relation: The Relation interface does not mandate any particular feature.

To these interfaces, implementing the format, are added a couple of other interfaces:

AlignmentProcess: The AlignmentProcess interface extends the Alignment interface by providing an align method. This interface must be implemented for each alignment algorithm.

Evaluator: The Evaluator interface describes the comparison of two alignments (the first one could serve as a reference). Its features are the following:

    align1: (value: URI) a first alignment, sometimes the reference alignment;

    align2: (value: URI) a second alignment which will be compared with the first one;

3.2   Functions

Of course, this API does provide support for manipulating alignments. It offers a number of services for manipulating the API. As in [1], these functions are separated in their implementation. The following primitives are available:

parsing/serializing an alignment from a file in RDF/XML (AlignmentParser.read(), Alignment.write());

computing the alignment, with input alignment (Alignment.align(Alignment, Parameters));

thresholding alignment with threshold as argument (Alignment.cut(double));

hardening an alignment by considering that all correspondences are absolute (Alignment.harden(double));

comparing one alignment with another (Evaluator.eval(Parameters)) and serialising them (Evaluator.write());

outputting alignment in a particular format (rule, axioms, transformations)
  (Alignment.render(stream,visitor));

These functions are more precisely described below.

In addition, alignment and evaluation algorithms accept parameters. These are put in a structure that allows storing and retrieving them. The parameter name is a string and its value is any Java object. The parameters can be the various weights used by some algorithms, some intermediate thresholds or the tolerance of some iterative algorithms.

4   Implementation and Example

For validating the API, we carried out a first implementation, on top of the OWL API [1], which is presented here and illustrated in the following sections.

4.1   Default Implementation

A (default) implementation of this API can be found in the fr.inrialpes.exmo.-align.impl package. It implements the API by providing the simple basic classes: BasicAlignment, BasicCell, BasicRelation, BasicParameters and Basic-Evaluator. These classes provide all the necessary implementation for the API but the algorithm specific methods (Alignment.align() and Evaluator.eval()). It also provides an RDF/XML parser that can parse the format into an Alignment object.

Along with these basic classes the default implementation provides a library of other classes, mentioned below.

4.2   Command-Line Interface

There is a stand-alone program (fr.inrialpes.exmo.align.util.Procalign) which:

- Reads two OWL/RDF ontologies;
- Creates an alignment object;
- Computes the alignment between these ontologies;
- Displays the result.

This programme implements the standard structure for using the API.
  Additionally, a number of options are available:

- displaying debug information (-d);
- controlling the way of rendering the output (-r);
- deciding the implementation of the alignment method (-i);
- providing an input alignment (-a).

4.3   Processing an Example

Using this alignment processor works in the following way (assuming that $CWD corresponds to the current directory):

```
$ java -jar lib/procalign.jar -i fr.inrialpes.exmo.align.impl.SubsDistNameAlignment
    file://localhost$CWD/rdf/onto1.owl file://localhost$CWD/rdf/onto2.owl
    -o aligns/sample.owl
```

This asks for aligning the ontology onto1.rdf and onto2.rdf with the SubsDist NameAlignment class which implements a substring based distance on the labels of classes and properties, and output the result to the sample.owl file. Since the results are not very satisfying, the program can be called again by asking to threshold under .6:

```
$ java -jar lib/procalign.jar -i fr.inrialpes.exmo.align.impl.SubsDistNameAlignment
    file://localhost$CWD/rdf/onto1.owl file://localhost$CWD/rdf/onto2.owl  -t .6
```

which returns:

```
<?xml version='1.0' encoding='utf-8' standalone='no'?>
<!DOCTYPE rdf:RDF SYSTEM "align.dtd">

<rdf:RDF xmlns='http://knowledgeweb.semanticweb.org/heterogeneity/alignment'
         xmlns:rdf='http://www.w3.org/1999/02/22-rdf-syntax-ns#'
         xmlns:xsd='http://www.w3.org/2001/XMLSchema#'>
<Alignment>
  <xml>yes</xml>
  <level>0</level>
  <type>**</type>
  <onto1>http://www.example.org/ontology1</onto1>
  <onto2>http://www.example.org/ontology2</onto2>
  <map>
    <Cell>
      <entity1 rdf:resource='http://www.example.org/ontology1#reviewedarticle'/>
      <entity2 rdf:resource='http://www.example.org/ontology2#article'/>
      <measure rdf:datatype='&xsd;float'>0.6363636363636364</measure>
      <relation>=</relation>
    </Cell>
    <Cell>
      <entity1 rdf:resource='http://www.example.org/ontology1#journalarticle'/>
      <entity2 rdf:resource='http://www.example.org/ontology2#journalarticle'/>
      <measure rdf:datatype='&xsd;float'>1.0</measure>
      <relation>=</relation>
    </Cell>
  </map>
</Alignment>
</rdf:RDF>
```

4.4   Example Data

In order to provide a simple example, we picked up, on the web, two bibliographic ontologies described in OWL:

- eBiquity Publication Ontology Resource[1],
- BibTeX Definition in Web Ontology Language[2].

These ontologies are obviously based on BibTeX (see Table 1). This explains the relative ease of alignment with very simple algorithms. The only purpose of this example is to

---

[1] http://ebiquity.umbc.edu/v2.1/ontology/publication.owl
[2] http://visus.mit.edu/bibtex/0.1/

Table 1. Classes and properties in the three ontologies (From BibTeX, this table avoids technical terms like key and crossref). Standard BibTeX classes have been separated from non-standard ones (some of the non-standard-but-common are mentioned in parenthesis).

BibTeX	UMBC	MIT	BibTeX	UMBC	MIT
	Resource			SoftCopy	
	Publication	Entry			
		Unpublished			Conference
article	Article	Article	book	Book	Book
inbook	InBook	Inbook	incollection	InCollection	Incollection
inproceedings	InProceedings	Inproceedings	mastersthesis	MastersThesis	Mastersthesis
misc	Misc	Misc	phdthesis	PhdThesis	Phdthesis
proceedings	Proceedings	Proceedings	techreport	TechReport	Techreport
			booklet		Booklet
title	title	hasTitle	author	author	hasAuthor
editor	editor	hasEditor	publisher	publisher	hasPublisher
edition	edition	hasEdition	chapter	chapter	hasChapter
series	series	hasSeries	pages	pages	hasPages
volume	volume	hasVolume	number	number	hasNumber
note	note	hasNote	address	address	hasAddress
organization	organization	hasOrganization	journal	journal	hasJournal
booktitle	booktitle	hasBooktitle	shool	school	hasSchool
howpublished		howPublished	institution	institution	hasInstitution
type	type	hasType	year	year	hasYear
annotation		hasAnnotation			
(affiliation)		hasAffiliation	(abstract)	abstract	hasAbstract
(copyright)		hasCopyright	(content)	hasContent	
(keywords)	keywords	hasKeywords			
(URL)	softCopyURI	hasURL	(ISBN)		hasISBN
(size)	softCopySize	hasSize	(ISSN)		hasISSN
(location)		hasLocation	(LCCN)		hasLCCN
(language)		hasLanguage	(price)		hasPrice
	softCopy			relatedProject	
	softCopyFormat			counter	
	version			description	
	publishedOn				pageChapterData
	firstAuthor				humanCreator

demonstrate the use of the API and its implementation. However, both ontologies display a number of differences, especially in the name of properties.

The expected alignments of both ontologies is the one given in Table 1. It as been described in the alignment format for the purpose of evaluating the results of the various algorithms (see §8).

5   Adding an Algorithm

There are many different methods for computing alignments. However, they always need at least two ontologies as input and provide an alignment as output (or as an intermediate step because some algorithms are more focussed on merging the ontologies for instance). Sometimes they can take an alignment or various other parameters as input.

5.1   Extending the Implemented Algorithms

The API enables the integration of the algorithms based on that minimal interface. It is used by creating an alignment object, providing the two ontologies, calling the `align` method which takes parameters and initial alignment as arguments. The alignment object then bears the result of the alignment procedure.

Adding new alignments methods amounts to create a new `AlignmentProcess` class implementing the interface. Generally, this class can extend the proposed `Basic-Alignment` class. The `BasicAlignment` class defines the storage structures for ontologies and alignment specification as well as the methods for dealing with alignment display. All methods can be refined (no one is final). The only method it does not implement is `align` itself.

5.2   Collection of Predefined Algorithms

Several algorithms have been run to provide the alignments between these two ontologies:

NameEqAlignment: Simply compares the equality of class and property names (once downcased) and align those objects with the same name;

EditDistNameAlignment: Uses an editing (or Levenstein) distance between (downcased) entity names. It thus has to build a distance matrix and to choose the alignment from the distance;

SubsDistNameAlignment: Computes a substring distance on the (downcased) entity name;

StrucSubsDistNameAlignment: Computes a substring distance on the (downcased) entity names and uses and aggregates this distance with the symmetric difference of properties in classes.

These simple algorithms should increase the accuracy of the alignment results. We will see what happens in §8.

6   Composing Alignments

One of the claimed advantages of providing a format for alignments is the ability to improve alignments by composing alignment algorithms. This would allow iterative alignment: starting with a first alignment, followed by user feedback, subsequent alignment rectification, and so on. A previous alignment can, indeed, be passed to the `align` method as an argument. The correspondences of this alignment can be incorporated in those of the alignment to be processed.

For instance, it is possible to implement the `StrucSubsDistNameAlignment`, by first providing a simple substring distance on the property names and then applying a structural distance on classes. The new modular implementation of the algorithm yields the same results.

Moreover, modularizing these alignment algorithms offers the opportunity to manipulate the alignment in the middle, for instance, by thresholding. As an example, the algorithm used above can be obtained by:

- aligning the properties;
- thresholding those under `threshold`;
- aligning the classes with regard to this partial alignment;
- generating axioms (see below);

Selecting by other criterion (only retaining the alignments on classes or in some specific area of the ontology) is also possible this way.

7 Generating Output

The obtained alignment can, of course, be generated in some RDF serialisation form like demonstrated by the example of §4.3. However, there are other formats available.

The API provides the notion of a visitor of the alignment cells. These visitors are used in the implementation for rendering the alignments. So far, the implementation is provided with four such visitors:

RDFRendererVisitor displays the alignment in the RDF format described in §2.
OWLAxiomsRendererVisitor generates an ontology merging both aligned ontologies and comprising OWL axioms for expressing the subsumption, equivalence and exclusivity relations.
XSLTRendererVisitor generates an XSLT stylesheet for transforming data expressed in the first ontology in data expressed in the second ontology;
SWRLRendererVisitor generates a set of SWRL [6] rules for inferring from data expressed in the first ontology the corresponding data with regard of the second ontology.

Some of these methods, like XSLT or SWRL, take the first ontology in the alignment as the source ontology and the second one as the target ontology.

7.1 Generating Axioms

OWL itself provides tools for expressing axioms corresponding to some relations that we are able to generate such as subsumption (`subClassOf`) or equivalence (`equivalentClass`). From an alignment, the `OWLAxiomsRendererVisitor` visitor generates an ontology that merges the previous ontologies and adds the bridging axioms corresponding to the cells of the alignment.

They can be generated from the following command-line invocation:

```
$ java -jar lib/procalign.jar -i fr.inrialpes.exmo.align.impl.SubsDistNameAlignment
    file://localhost$CWD/rdf/onto1.owl file://localhost$CWD/rdf/onto2.owl -t .6
    -r fr.inrialpes.exmo.align.impl.OWLAxiomsRendererVisitor
```

which returns:

```
<rdf:RDF
    xmlns:owl="http://www.w3.org/2002/07/owl#"
    xmlns:rdf="http://www.w3.org/1999/02/22-rdf-syntax-ns#"
    xmlns:rdfs="http://www.w3.org/2000/01/rdf-schema#">

  <owl:Ontology rdf:about="">
    <rdfs:comment>Aligned ontollogies</rdfs:comment>
    <owl:imports rdf:resource="http://www.example.org/ontology1"/>
    <owl:imports rdf:resource="http://www.example.org/ontology2"/>
  </owl:Ontology>

  <owl:Class rdf:about="http://www.example.org/ontology1#reviewedarticle">
    <owl:equivalentClass rdf:resource="http://www.example.org/ontology2#article"/>
  </owl:Class>

  <owl:Class rdf:about="http://www.example.org/ontology1#journalarticle">
    <owl:equivalentClass rdf:resource="http://www.example.org/ontology2#journalarticle"/>
  </owl:Class>

</rdf:RDF>
```

7.2   Generating Translations

Alignments can be used for translation as well as for merging. Such a transformation can be made on a very syntactic level. The most neutral solution seems to generate translators in XSLT. However, because it lacks deductive capabilities, this solution is only suited for transforming data (i.e., individual descriptions) appearing in a regular form.

We have implemented an XSLTRendererVisitor, which generates transformations that recursively replace the names of classes and properties in individuals. The renderer produces stylesheets like:

```
<xsl:stylesheet xmlns:xsl="http://www.w3.org/1999/XSL/Transform" version="1.0"
    xmlns:owl="http://www.w3.org/2002/07/owl#"
    xmlns:rdf="http://www.w3.org/1999/02/22-rdf-syntax-ns#"
    xmlns:rdfs="http://www.w3.org/2000/01/rdf-schema#"
    xmlns:xsd="http://www.w3.org/2001/XMLSchema#">

  <xsl:template match="http://www.example.org/ontology1#reviewedarticle">
    <xsl:element name="http://www.example.org/ontology2#article">
      <xsl:apply-templates select="*|@*|text()"/>
    </xsl:element>
  </xsl:template>

  <xsl:template match="http://www.example.org/ontology1#journalarticle">
    <xsl:element name="http://www.example.org/ontology2#journalarticle">
      <xsl:apply-templates select="*|@*|text()"/>
    </xsl:element>
  </xsl:template>

  <!-- Copying the root -->
  <xsl:template match="/">
    <xsl:apply-templates/>
  </xsl:template>

  <!-- Copying all elements and attributes -->
  <xsl:template match="*|@*|text()">
    <xsl:copy>
      <xsl:apply-templates select="*|@*|text()"/>
    </xsl:copy>
  </xsl:template>

</xsl:stylesheet>
```

7.3   Generating SWRL Rules

Finally, this transformation can be implemented as a set of rules which will "interpret" the correspondence. This is more adapted than XSLT stylesheets because, we can assume that a rule engine will work semantically (i.e., it achieves some degree of completeness with regard to the semantics) rather than purely syntactically.

The SWRLRendererVisitor transforms the alignment into a set of SWRL rules which have been defined in [6]. The result on the same example will be the following:

```
<?xml version="1.0" encoding="UTF-8"?>

<swrlx:Ontology swrlx:name="generatedAl"
                xmlns:swrlx="http://www.w3.org/2003/11/swrlx#"
                xmlns:owlx="http://www.w3.org/2003/05/owl-xml"
                xmlns:ruleml="http://www.w3.org/2003/11/ruleml#">
  <owlx:Imports rdf:resource="http://www.example.org/ontology1"/>

  <ruleml:imp>
    <ruleml:_body>
      <swrlx:classAtom>
        <owlx:Class owlx:name="http://www.example.org/ontology1#reviewedarticle"/>
        <ruleml:var>x</ruleml:var>
      </swrlx:classAtom>
    </ruleml:_body>
    <ruleml:_head>
      <swrlx:classAtom>
        <owlx:Class owlx:name="http://www.example.org/ontology2#journalarticle"/>
        <ruleml:var>x</ruleml:var>
      </swrlx:classAtom>
    </ruleml:_head>
  </ruleml:imp>

...
</swrlx:Ontology>
```

Of course, level 2 alignments would require specific renderers targeted at their particular languages.

8   Comparing Alignments

Last, but not least, one of the reasons for having a separate alignment format is to be able to compare the alignments provided by various alignment algorithms. They can be compared with each other or against a "correct" alignment. For that purpose, the API proposes the Evaluator interface.

8.1   Implementing Comparison

The implementation of the API provides a BasicEvaluator which implements a container for the evaluation (it has no eval method).

Implementing a particular comparator thus consists in creating a new subclass of BasicEvaluator and implementing its eval method that will compare two alignments (the first one can be considered as the reference alignment). Currently available subclasses are:

PRecEvaluator, which implements a classical precision/recall/fallout evaluation as well as the derived measures introduced in [3]. Precision is the ratio between true positive and all aligned objects; Recall is the ratio between the true positive and all the correspondences that should have been found.

SymMeanEvaluator, which implements a weighted symmetric difference between the entities that are in one alignment and those common to both alignments (missing alignments count for 0., others weight 1. complemented by the difference between their strengths). This is thus a measure for the similarity of two alignments. The result is here split between the kinds of entity considered (Class/Property/Individual).

8.2   Examples

We provided, by hand, an alignment file that corresponds to the alignment of the classes and properties in Table 1. Each cell, is ranked with strength 1. and relation "=". The result of applying a particular evaluator (here PRecEvaluator) is obtained by calling a simple command-line evaluation on the files representing the standard alignment (bibref.owl) and the result of the application of a particular alignment method (here EditDistName.owl):

```
$ java -cp lib/procalign.jar fr.inrialpes.exmo.align.util.EvalAlign
  -i fr.inrialpes.exmo.align.impl.PRecEvaluator
  file://localhost$CWD/aligns/bibref.owl file://localhost$CWD/aligns/EditDistName.owl
```

The result is:

```
<?xml version='1.0' encoding='utf-8' standalone='yes'?>
<rdf:RDF xmlns:rdf='http://www.w3.org/1999/02/22-rdf-syntax-ns#'
  xmlns:map='http://www.atl.external.lmco.com/projects/ontology/ResultsOntology.n3#'>
  <map:output rdf:about=''>
    <map:precision>0.6976744186046512</map:precision>
    <map:recall>0.9375</map:recall>
   <fallout>0.3023255813953488</fallout>
    <map:fMeasure>0.8000000000000002</map:fMeasure>
    <map:oMeasure>0.53125</map:oMeasure>
    <result>1.34375</result>
  </map:output>
</rdf:RDF>
```

As can be noted, we use the format developed at Lockheed[3] extended with a few attributes, but any other format could have been generated. We have used these comparisons for providing the figures of Table 2.

Table 2. Performance measure for the algorithms presented in §5 with the ontologies presented in §4 (the reference alignment has 32 correspondences).

	eqstring	editdist	substring	substring property	substring property threshold=.4	substring property threshold=.7
Precision	1.	.70	.72	.72	.82	.97
Recall	.31	.94	.97	.97	.97	.94
Weighted	.48	.63	.71	.70	.75	.82

---

[3] http://www.atl.external.lmco.com/projects/ontology/

9   Conclusion

In order to exchange and evaluate results of alignment algorithms, we have provided an alignment format. A Java API has been proposed for this format and a default implementation described. We have shown how to integrate new alignment algorithms, compose algorithms, generate transformations and axioms and compare alignments.

This API and its implementation could fairly easily be adapted to other representation languages than OWL. In particular, if there were some ontology API, that would constitute a better basis for the implementation than the OWL API. It is unlikely that this format and API will satisfy all needs, but there is no reason why it could not be improved.

To our knowledge, there is no similar API. There are some attempts at defining ontology alignment or ontology mapping either very close to a particular use [5,11] or instead a very abstract definition which is neither immediately implementable nor sharable [7]. This was the analysis of [9], which led to the conclusion that alignment algorithms are not comparable and that their results are different. So, there would be no alignment format. On the contrary, our position is that it is better to define an alignment challenge as general as possible and that we use it, not for identifying the best tool, but for characterising strengths and weaknesses of these algorithms. Moreover, the advantage of having an alignment format that can generate – nearly for free – transformations, axioms and merged ontologies, should be an incentive for algorithm developers to generate that format.

The closest works we know are the RDFT and MAFRA systems. The main goal of RDFT is to represent mappings that can be executed and imported in a transformation process [10]. These mappings correspond to sets of pairs between simple entities (RDFS classes and properties) with a qualification of the relation holding. The ontology is expressed in DAML+OIL. Surprisingly, if the correspondences are generated by Bayes techniques no strength is retained. This format is aimed at using the mapping but no hints are given for adding alignment algorithms or extending the format. MAFRA provides an explicit notion of semantic bridges modelled in a DAML+OIL ontology [8]. The MAFRA Semantic bridges share a lot with the mapping format presented here: they can be produced, serialised, manipulated and communicated through the web. Moreover, the semantic bridges are relatively independent from the mapped languages (though they can map only classes, attributes and relations). They have, however, been built for being used with the MAFRA system, not to be open to external uses, so the classes of the ontology are rather fixed and cannot easily be extended towards new relations or new kinds of mappings. This format is also tailored to the processing architecture used (with non declarative primitives in the transformations).

All the software and the examples presented here are available to everyone [4]. The sources of the API and its implementation are available through an anonymous CVS server. Readers are invited to use it and report any need that is not covered in the current state of the API.

---

[4] http://co4.inrialpes.fr/align

Acknowledgements. This work has been partly supported by the European Knowledge Web network of excellence (IST-2004-507482). It had benefited from discussions with Petko Valtchev, Paolo Bouquet and Sergio Tessaris. The author thanks the OWL API developers for their great work.

References

1. Sean Bechhofer, Rapahel Voltz, and Phillip Lord. Cooking the semantic web with the OWL API. In *Proc. 2nd International Semantic Web Conference (ISWC), Sanibel Island (FL US)*, 2003.
2. Diego Calvanese, Giuseppe De Giacomo, and Maurizio Lenzerini. A framework for ontology integration. In Isabel Cruz, Stefan Decker, Jérôme Euzenat, and Deborah McGuinness, editors, *The emerging semantic web*, pages 201–214. IOS Press, Amsterdam (NL), 2002.
3. Hong-Hai Do, Sergey Melnik, and Erhard Rahm. Comparison of schema matching evaluations. In *Proc. GI-Workshop "Web and Databases", Erfurt (DE)*, 2002. http://dol.uni-leipzig.de/pub/2002-28.
4. Jérôme Euzenat. Towards composing and benchmarking ontology alignments. In *Proc. ISWC-2003 workshop on semantic information integration, Sanibel Island (FL US)*, pages 165–166, 2003.
5. Fausto Giunchiglia and Pavel Shvaiko. Semantic matching. In *Proc. IJCAI 2003 Workshop on ontologies and distributed systems, Acapulco (MX)*, pages 139–146, 2003.
6. Ian Horrocks, Peter Patel-Schneider, Harold Boley, Said Tabet, Benjamin Grosof, and Mike Dean. SWRL: a semantic web rule language combining OWL and RuleML, 2003. www.daml.org/2003/11/swrl/.
7. Jayant Madhavan, Philip Bernstein, Pedro Domingos, and Alon Halevy. Representing and reasoning about mappings between domain models. In *Proc. 18th National Conference on Artificial Intelligence (AAAI 2002), Edmonton (CA)*, pages 122–133, 1998. http://citeseer.nj.nec.com/milo98using.html.
8. Alexander Mädche, Boris Motik, Nuno Silva, and Raphael Volz. MAFRA – a mapping framework for distributed ontologies. In *Proc. ECAI workshop on Knowledge Transformation for the Semantic web, Lyon (FR)*, pages 60–68, 2002.
9. Natasha Noy and Mark Musen. Evaluating ontology-mapping tools: requirements and experience. In *Proc. 1st workshop on Evaluation of Ontology Tools (EON2002), EKAW'02*, 2002.
10. Borys Omelayenko. Integrating vocabularies: discovering and representing vocabulary maps. In *Proc. 1st International Semantic Web Conference (ISWC-2002), Chia Laguna (IT)*, pages 206–220, 2002.
11. Erhard Rahm and Philip Bernstein. A survey of approaches to automatic schema matching. *VLDB Journal*, 10(4):334–350, 2001.

Specifying Ontology Views by Traversal

Natalya F. Noy and Mark A. Musen

Stanford Medical Informatics, Stanford University,
251 Campus Drive, x-215, Stanford, CA 94305, USA
{noy, musen}@smi.stanford.edu

Abstract. One of the original motivations behind ontology research was
the belief that ontologies can help with reuse in knowledge representation. However, many of the ontologies that are developed with reuse in
mind, such as standard reference ontologies and controlled terminologies,
are extremely large, while the users often need to reuse only a small part
of these resources in their work. Specifying various views of an ontology
enables users to limit the set of concepts that they see. In this paper, we
develop the concept of a *Traversal View*, a view where a user specifies the
central concept or concepts of interest, the relationships to traverse to
find other concepts to include in the view, and the depth of the traversal.
For example, given a large ontology of anatomy, a user may use a Traversal View to extract a concept of *Heart* and organs and organ parts that
surround the heart or are contained in the heart. We define the notion of
Traversal Views formally, discuss their properties, present a strategy for
maintaining the view through ontology evolution and describe our tool
for defining and extracting Traversal Views.

1 Ontology Views

Ontologies constitute an integral and important part of the Semantic Web. For
the Semantic Web to succeed, developers must create and integrate numerous
ontologies, from general top-level ontologies, to domain-specific and task-specific
ontologies. One of the original motivations behind ontology research was the
belief that ontologies can help with reuse in knowledge representation [5]. By
virtue of being formal and explicit representations of a domain, ontologies could
represent shared domain descriptions that different applications and agents use.
When a person developing a new application chooses to reuse a published shared
ontology of the domain rather than to create his own model, he gains a number
of advantages: not having to reinvent the wheel, using an ontology that has
already been tested in other applications, and, perhaps, most important of all,
tremendously facilitating the path to information integration among different
applications that use the same ontology.

Currently, there are several efforts to develop standard reusable ontologies
in various domains and to make them available on the Semantic Web: from
the generic upper-level ontology of SUO[1] and lexical corpus of WordNet [3] to

---

[1] http://suo.ieee.org/

S.A. McIlraith et al. (Eds.): ISWC 2004, LNCS 3298, pp. 713–725, 2004.

domain-specific ontologies such as UMLS [9]. Consider for example the Foundational Model of Anatomy (FMA)—a declarative representation of anatomy developed at the University of Washington [15]. The ontology represents the result of manual and disciplined modeling of the structural organization of the human body. While the FMA ontology is a relatively recent development, many in medical informatics already consider it to be a tremendous resource that will facilitate sharing of information among applications that use anatomy knowledge. However, the size and complexity of the ontology is immense: approximately 70,000 concepts at the time of this writing. As a result, the project authors often get requests for self-contained portions of the ontology that describe only specific organs and organ parts.

In general, while providing a shared, tested, and well-accepted vocabulary, many of the large standard resources pose a formidable challenge to Semantic Web users: these resources are huge, often containing tens of thousands of concepts. However, many Semantic Web users need only a small fraction of the resource for their application. Currently such a user still needs to make sense of the complete resource, importing it as a whole, and dragging along this extra "baggage" of concepts, most of which he is never going to use. In addition to the cognitive challenge of understanding the large resource (or at least figuring out which swaths of it are not relevant and can be safely ignored), there can be a computational penalty as well if the user needs to perform reasoning with the whole ontology.

Therefore, users need the ability to extract self-contained portions of ontologies and to use these portions in their applications. For example, we can imagine the user of the FMA specifying that he needs everything that is directly related to the *heart* as well as definitions of all organs and organ parts that surround the heart. The user may also ask to include organs and organ parts that are "twice removed" from the heart. Or, the user may ask for everything related to the heart concept—a transitive closure of all relations in which the concept participates.

The notion of creating a self-contained portion of a resource has long been an area of research in databases. A database *view* provides exactly that: users specify a query that extracts a portion of database instances satisfying the query, creating a specific *view* on the data in the database. Similarly, we call a portion of an ontology an **ontology view**.

In databases, a view is specified as a query: all instances satisfying the query constitute the view. Current research on ontology views (see Section 6) takes a similar approach: an ontology view is specified as a query in some ontology-query language. However, this query-based approach does not allow users to specify a portion of an ontology that results from a particular traversal of ontology links, as in the *heart* example above. Therefore, we suggest a complementary way of defining ontology views: by **traversal specification**. In such a specification, we define a starter concept or concepts, the "central" or "focus" concepts in the result, and the details of the relationship to traverse, starting at these concepts. We call such a view a **Traversal View**.

We believe that various types of view definitions—query-based and traversal-based, and perhaps several others—are necessary to provide full flexibility to Semantic Web users in extracting specific parts of an ontology. We are developing a suite of tools that provides a convenient interface to allow users to specify views in different ways, to examine the resulting views, and to use them in their applications. In this paper, we focus on Traversal Views, defining their properties, describing an algorithm for computing them, and presenting our user-centered tools for specifying and using them.

More specifically, this paper makes the following contributions:

- defines the approach of specifying ontology views through traversal of concepts
- presents an algorithm for finding the results of traversal-view definitions
- identifies properties of Traversal Views
- presents a strategy for maintaining Traversal Views through ontology evolution
- describes a user-oriented tool for specifying Traversal Views

2 Specification of Traversal Views

In this work, we mainly consider ontologies expressed in RDF Schema and therefore consisting of classes, their properties, and instances [18]. Although, as we discuss in Section 3, our approach can be easily adapted to ontologies expressed in OWL (in fact, our implementation, which we describe in Section 5, works both with RDFS and OWL ontologies).

We combine all the properties related to a class or an instance in a **concept definition**:

Definition 1 (Concept definition). *Given an RDF class or individual C, the definition of C, $Def(C)$, is a set of RDF triples such that:*

- *any RDF triple with C as a subject is in $Def(C)$*
- *for any property P such that C is in the domain of P (as defined by $rdfs : domain$), any triple with P as a subect is in $Def(C)$*

No other triples are in $Def(C)$.

This definition implies for example, that a definition for a class C includes all the property domain statements for all the properties that contain C in their domain. Similarly, they include all the triples specifying property values for C.

We can now define the notion of Traversal Views. Traversal Views help users exploring a new ontology to find its subset that covers a particular "topic." For instance, one may not be interested in the entire human anatomy, but just in the heart and the organs that are physically close to it (say, separated from it by at most one other anatomical structure). Traversal Views enable users to extract a manageable and self-contained portion of the ontology relevant to their needs, allowing them to use and extend it for their own purposes.

Intuitively, we specify a Traversal View by specifying a starter concept (e.g., *Heart*), a list of relationships (property names) that should be traversed and the maximum distance to traverse along each of the relationships.

Example 1. We can specify a traversal view that starts at the class *Heart* and traverses the *partOf* relationship for 2 steps and the *containedIn* relationship for 1 step. We then compute the view in the following way:

1. *Heart* is included in the view
2. If *Heart* is in the domain of the property *partOf* or the property *containedIn*, then all classes in the range of these properties are also included in the view
3. If *Heart* was also an instance (RDF Schema does not prevent classes from being instances as well) and had a value for properties *partOf* and *containedIn*, those values are also included in the view

The view resulting from this process contains the traversal along the *partOf* and *containedIn* properties of length 1. We then apply the same procedure to all classes in the resulting view but consider only the *partOf* property to compute the traversal along the *partOf* property of length 2 (Recall that we requested a traversal of length 1 along the *containedIn* property.)

We now present a formal definition of a traversal view. The definition consists of two parts: the view specification (Definitions 2 and 3) and the view computation (Definitions 4 and 5).

Definition 2 (Traversal Directive). *A **traversal directive** D for ontology O is a pair $\langle C_{st}, \mathcal{PT} \rangle$ where*

- *C_{st} is a class or an instance in O (the starter concept of the traversal);*
- *$\mathcal{PT}$ is a set of **property directives**. Each property directive is a pair $\langle P, n \rangle$, where P is a property in O and n is a nonnegative integer or infinity (∞), which specifies the depth of the traversal along the property P. If $n = \infty$, then the traversal includes a transitive closure for P starting with C_{st}.*

In Example 1 we defined a single traversal directive, with *Heart* playing the role of the starter concept C_{st} and two property directives in $\mathcal{PT}$: $\langle partOf, 2 \rangle$ and $\langle containedIn, 1 \rangle$.

Definition 3 (Traversal View Specification). *A **Traversal View specification** T is a set of traversal directives $\mathcal{TD}$*

The view specification in Example 1 contained only one traversal directive.

Example 2. Suppose in addition to the concept *Heart* and its related concepts from the view in Example 1, we also want to include all parts of the lung in the view (without limiting the depth of the traversal). We will then include the following directive into the view specification (in addition to the directives in Example 1):

- $C_{st} = Lung$

$- \mathcal{PT} = \{\langle has\ part, \infty \rangle\}$

We define the procedure for computing Traversal Views recursively as follows.

Definition 4 (Traversal Directive Result).
*Given a traversal directive $D = \langle C_{st}, \mathcal{PT} \rangle$ for an ontology O, a **traversal directive result** $D(O)$ (the result of applying directive D to O) is a set of instance and class definitions (in the sense of Definition 1) from O such that*

1. *C_{st} is in $D(O)$ (the starter concept is in the result)*
2. *For each property directive $D_s \in \mathcal{PT}$, where $D_s = \langle P, n \rangle$, $n > 0$,*
   - *if C_{st} is a class in the domain of the property P, and a class $C \in O$ is in the range definition for P at C_{st}, then C in $D(O)$*
   - *if C_{st} is an instance and it has a value for the property P, and this value is another class or instance $F \in O$, then F is in $D(O)$*
3. *$\mathcal{PT}_{next}$ is a set of property directives such that for each property directive $D_s = \langle P, n \rangle$ in $\mathcal{PT}$, the directive $\langle P, n - 1 \rangle$ is in $\mathcal{PT}_{next}$. If $n = \infty$, then $n - 1 = \infty$. For each class or instance F that was added to $D(O)$ in step 2, the traversal directive result for a traversal directive $D_F = \langle F, \mathcal{PT}_{next} \rangle$ is in $D(O)$.*

No other concepts are in $D(O)$.

This definition describes the procedure that we followed in finding the view in Example 1. Note that along with the concept itself, we include its definition in the view, which includes the property values for the concept, as well as range, cardinality, and other constraint statements for the properties for which the concept serves as a domain.

Finally, we define the concept of a traversal view.

Definition 5 (Traversal View). *Given an ontology O and a Traversal View specification T, consisting of a set of traversal directives $\mathcal{TD}$, a **traversal view** $TV(O, T)$ is the union of traversal directive results for each traversal directive $D \in \mathcal{TD}$*

In other words, a Traversal View is a subset of an ontology that consists of classes and instances on the path of the traversal specified in the view.

Note that if the user wants to specify a view that contains the starter concept and everything that is related to it—the transitive closure of all relations emanating from the starter concept—he needs to specify all the properties in the ontology and set the infinite depth of traversal on all of them (The user interface that we describe later makes this operation easy by having a single **"everything"** button.)

Standard properties. In addition to the properties defined in the ontology, traversal directives can include standard relations such as *rdf:subclassOf*, *rdf:type*, and so on. In fact, a useful directive could include a starter concept, and some specific number of levels of its subclasses (or superclasses). To include these standard ontology relations in the traversal directives, internally, we treat them as properties: Each class has a property *direct-subclasses*; the values of this property are all subclasses of the class. Similarly, there are properties *direct-superclasses*, *direct-instances, type-of*.[2] Therefore, these properties can be used in traversal directives just as all the regular properties.

View Boundary. When we extract a portion of an ontology for the view, we inevitably leave some of the definitions in the ontology incomplete. For instance, a view may include a class C_1 but not a class C_2 which is a range for a property P for C_1. Therefore, the definition of C_1 in the view is incomplete. At the same time, we may not be able to include C_2 in the view since it will violate the specific directives in the view definition.

In this case, we say that the concept C_2 in this example is in the **boundary** of the view definition: it is referenced by one of the concepts in the view but it is not itself included in the view. Maintaining the list of concepts in the view boundary is extremely useful for interactive specification of a view: the user can see which concepts are missing from the definition of the view and add them to the specification.

Traversal Views for Description Logics formalisms. While we used RDF Schema to define Traversal Views, we can also specify views for description-logic ontologies, such as ontologies in OWL [2]. Classes and properties in OWL are similar to classes and properties in RDF Schema. Definitions 2, 3, 5 are trivially adapted by adjusting terminology.

In the Step 2 of Definition 4 we consider all properties that have the starter concept as part of their *domain*. There are a number of ways to restrict a property value in OWL, by using *allValuesFrom, someValuesFrom*, or *hasValue* restrictions. These restrictions have classes or individuals as their values. More specifically, we add the following concepts to $D(O)$ in Step 2 of the Definition:

- *If an object property P (a property that specifies relations between instances of classes) has a restriction for C_{st}, the classes specified in the restriction (whether for* allValuesFrom, someValuesFrom, hasValue*) are in $D(O)$*
- *If an object property P has C_{st} in its domain, the classes in the range of P are in $D(O)$*
- *If an object property P has a value for C_{st} as an individual, that value is in $D(O)$*

The view designed in such a way has all the same properties that we discuss for general Traversal Views in the next section.

3   Properties of Traversal Views

We now discuss the properties of Traversal Views that follow from Definitions 2 through 5. We consider compositional properties of single traversal directives

---

[2] The Protégé ontology-editing environment, which was the platform for our implementation discussed later, takes exactly this approach.

and complete views. We then discuss completeness of our definition and computational cost of computing the view. Finally we discuss the issue of using Traversal Views to answer queries.

3.1 Composition of Directives and Views

Composition of traversal directives. It is easy to show, based on Definitions 2 and 4, that traversal directives are *commutative* with respect to composition: the set of concepts in the traversal view does not depend on the order of traversal directives in the view. Each directive is applied to the complete source ontology, thus traversal directive results are not affected by other directives. The result of the view is the union of the results of applying each directive.

Traversal directives are also *distributive*. Recall that a traversal directive D consists of a starter concept C_{st} and a set of property directives. Consider two traversal directives D_1 and D_2 with the same starter concept C_{st}. It follows from Definition 4 that composition of traversal directives is distributive:

$$\langle C_{st}, \mathcal{PT}_1 \rangle \oplus \langle C_{st}, \mathcal{PT}_2 \rangle = \langle C_{st}, \mathcal{PT}_1 \circ \mathcal{PT}_2 \rangle \tag{1}$$

Here the composition of the sets of property directives $\mathcal{PT}_1$ and $\mathcal{PT}_2$ is the union of the directives in each set.

Composition and chaining of Traversal Views. Given an ontology O and two Traversal View specifications T_1 and T_2, we define **composition** of T_1 and T_2 as applying both T_1 and T_2 to O and then taking the union of the result:

$$T_1 \oplus T_2 = TV(O, T_1) \cup TV(O, T_2) \tag{2}$$

Composition defined in this way is *commutative*: the results of applying directives in one of the traversal views does not depend on the other view, since both are applied to the complete ontology O.

Chaining of Traversal Views T_1 and T_2 is the result of applying T_2 to *the result of* applying T_1 to O:

$$T_1 \circ T_2 = TV(TV(O, T_2), T_1) \tag{3}$$

Chaining of Traversal Views is *not commutative*: When the view T_2 applied to T_1, the set of concepts in T_2 is limited by the concepts that were included in T_1. These concepts may not include some of the concepts that would have been in T_2 if it was applied to all of the ontology O. In fact, the specification of the view T_2 may not even be a valid view specification since some of the starter concepts in traversal directives in T_2 may not even be in T_1. Thus, Traversal Views are not commutative with respect to chaining.

3.2 Completeness and Complexity

Completeness. Traversal Views are complete in the sense that for any subset of concepts in an ontology there is a (not necessarily unique) Traversal View that defines it. Let $\{c_1, ..., c_n\}$ be a subset of concepts. A Traversal View consisting of a set traversal directives $\{td_1, ...td_n\}$ such that $td_k = (c_k, \emptyset)$ defines exactly of the set $\{c_1, ..., c_n\}$. In other words, for each concept in the subset, we create a traversal directive containing that concept as a starter concept and no property directives.

Computational Properties. Let t be the number of traversal directives in a view definition and n be the number of concepts in the ontology. Then the running time of computing the Traversal View is $O(t * n)$. In other words, if the number of traversal directives in a view is limited by some constant c, computation of a Traversal View is linear in the size of the ontology. Indeed, computation of each traversal directive, which simply follows Definition 4, needs to examine each concept in the ontology exactly once. Suppose a concept C was examined during iteration i. If C is visited at any subsequent iterations in computing the same traversal directive, we do not need to compute the traversal directive $\langle C, \mathcal{PT}_{next} \rangle$: the depths for all the property directives will be necessarily less than at iteration i and therefore computing this directive will not add any new concepts to the view.

3.3   Using Traversal Views in Inference

Consider an ontology O and a Traversal View specification T. If the ontology O is consistent (for example, based on the interpretation of RDF Schema Semantics [4]), then the Traversal View $TV(O, T)$ also represents a consistent ontology based on this semantic interpretation: According to Definition 4, we do not add any new triples to $TV(O, T)$ that did not already exist in O. Further, given the fact that the constructs available in RDF Schema are monotonic, if a set of triples is consistent according to the RDF Semantics interpretation, then its subset is also consistent. Therefore, any relation between concepts in the view $TV(O, T)$ that is entailed by the view definition, is also entailed by the definitions in the full ontology O.

Note that this property of views is not true in general for Traversal Views for OWL ontologies. Consider for example the notion of disjointness in OWL. If the disjointness axiom is not included in the view, we may conclude that two entities are equivalent that should not be equivalent if disjointness is considered. We are currently working on identifying a set of syntactic constraints for an OWL ontology that would allow us to assert that any relation between two entities that is entailed by $TV(O, T)$ is also entailed by O.

4   Traversal Views and Ontology Evolution

It is inevitable that ontologies change and users need to work with different versions of the same ontology. After using Traversal Views to extract a portion of an ontology, and then getting a new version of this ontology, the user should be able to determine (1) whether the view definition is still valid for the new version (that is, all the starter concepts and all the properties explicitly mentioned in the view definition are present in the new version of the ontology); and (2) whether the subset of the ontology specified by the view is unchanged.

Noy and Musen [11] have developed the PROMPTDIFF algorithm to compare different versions of the same ontology. We integrated PROMPTDIFF with Traversal Views to answer the questions above.

Given two versions of an ontology V_{old} and V_{new}, for each concept in V_{old}, PROMPTDIFF determines a corresponding concept in V_{new} if there is one. (It uses a set of heuristics to find correspondences for classes and properties that changed their names or definitions). Using this information we determine whether a view T, which was defined for V_{old}, is still valid for V_{new}. If for each concept from V_{old} that is explicitly used in T as a starter concept or a property name, there is a corresponding concept in V_{new}, then the view is valid. Furthermore, if any of the concepts explicitly used in T have changed, the user has the option of updating the view T to refer to the corresponding new concepts.

If the view has been materialized, we can use a similar technique to determine if the materialized view needs to be updated by examining the view to determine whether each concept in the view has a corresponding concept in the new version.

5   Implementation

We have implemented Traversal Views as a plugin to the Protégé ontology-development environment.[3] Protégé provides an intuitive graphical user interface for ontology development, a rich knowledge model, and an extensible architecture that provides API access both to the Protégé knowledge bases and to its user-interface components.

Figure 1 presents the user interface for Traversal View specification. First, the user selects a starter concept by browsing the ontology (Figure 1A). Then the user specifies property directives. Specification may simply include checking some of the built-in relationships, such as subclasses or superclasses (Figure 1B). If the user wants to specify a more detailed directive, he does this through an additional dialog (Figure 1C), specifying the depth of traversal for each property. In addition, the user can select the "everything" option and set the same depth of traversal for all the properties in the ontology.

After the user specifies and issues a traversal directive, we materialize the directive by copying the concepts in the view to the user's local space. In addition, we save the traversal directives as instances in an *ontology of traversal directives*.

When the user saves the results of his work, both the materialized view (the extracted portion of the source ontology) and the ontology representing the traversal directive (the view definition) are saved. The user then has the option of automatically "replaying" these directives on the source ontology. Another possibility would be to "mark" concepts from the ontology that belong to the view rather than to materialize the view.

---

[3] http://protege.stanford.edu

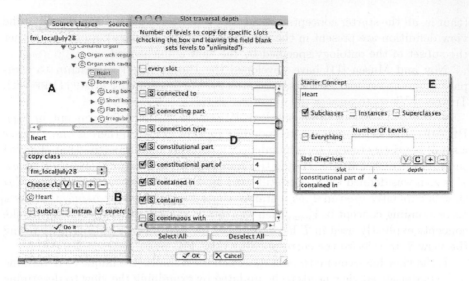

Fig. 1. Specifying and examining Traversal Views. The user chooses the starter concept by browsing the hierarchy (A), specifies the traversal along the built-in properties (B), brings up a separate window (C), which lists all the properties in the ontology and built-in properties (D). The user can examine and edit the defined views through a simple form-based interface of Protégé (E).

Using an ontology to store the directive is likely to lower the level of expertise required from the user to update the directive: In Protégé users browse and edit ontology instances (which is exactly what traversal directives are) through a simple form interface. To many, editing traversal directives through this interface (Figure 1E) is easier than writing an SQL query. Furthermore, a user can open the ontology with saved traversal directives in an ontology editor, such as Protégé, and use this simple interface to change the directives before applying them again.

6   Related Work

Our work is complementary to the work of using queries to define ontology views. Volz and colleagues [16,17], for instance, define a view language based on the RQL query language [7]. In this framework, a view represents a new class or property in the ontology. The authors restrict the RQL queries that can be used in the view to ensure that the view returns only unary or binary relations (classes or properties respectively).

In theory, query-based approaches to defining ontology views are equivalent to our traversal-based approach in terms of their completeness: Just as we showed that any subset of an ontology can be produced by a combination of trivial traversal directives, we can show that any subset of an ontology can be produced by a combination of trivial queries. However, depending on what the user needs in the view and what information he can specify about the view result, a query-based or a traversal-based approach may be more appropriate.

Magkanaraki and colleagues [10] take the approach of defining query-based views further. In their RVL language, which also uses RQL for querying ontologies, the authors propose mechanisms for restructuring the original class and property hierarchies, allowing the creation of new resources, property values, classes, or properties. Therefore, a view definition includes not only the query itself, but also a set of statements that define these new structures, linking them to the query results. We can take a similar approach with Traversal Views, allowing the users to rename or reorganize the concepts in the view.

XML query languages, such as XQuery [1] are also based on traversing structures. There are, however, important differences between languages such as XQuery and Traversal Views: In XQuery, the traversal is aimed at collecting the *data* themselves rather than the schema and at presenting the data in the result according to a particular structure specified in the query. Traversal Views are aimed at traversing and collecting the schema elements themselves in the result.

Researchers in the Process Interchange Format (PIF) Project have introduced the notion of Partially Shared Views as a way of allowing different groups to extend a shared standard [8]. A Partially Specified View includes of the type hierarchy and templates, which are similar to concept definition. In this sense, Partially Specified Views are reminiscent of Traversal Views: they include definitions of concepts themselves rather that their instantiations.

A combination of views as a mechanism for extracting ontology subsets and mechanisms that allow for renaming or slight reorganization of concepts in the view is crucial to encouraging ontology reuse. This reuse, in turn, can facilitate the problem of integrating ontologies. Orbst [13] suggests creating application views of ontologies as a means of enabling applications to use standard well-developed ontologies. This approach combines views or "perspectives" with mappings between concepts in the view and in the application. The task of creating the mappings becomes much easier if the ontology to map to is smaller and contains only the concepts that are relevant to the application. Ontology views as means for extracting self-contained subsets of standard ontologies can help in this task.

7   Summary and Open Issues

We have presented *Traversal Views* as a way of defining an ontology view. In a Traversal View, a user specifies a subset of an ontology to include in the view by specifying of starter concepts to include, the links to follow from those concepts, and how deep. This mechanism enables users to extract self-contained portions of an ontology related to a particular concept or a set of concepts (such as all parts and components of the Heart).

Database researchers have done a lot of work on using views directly to *answer queries* [6]. Since database views are themselves queries, this area of research centers on reformulating the user's query to express it in terms of existing views. While Traversal Views do not map to queries directly, whether we can use their definitions directly in answering (perhaps a restricted set of) queries is an open research issue.

Interfaces that enable users to browse the views while "popping out" to the original ontology when hitting the boundary of the view are also necessary. Developers may omit or forget something when defining a view and enabling users to see more of the original context for concepts in the view may be helpful.

Traversal Views enable users to extract classes and instances to include in the view, thus simplifying the original ontology for them. However, these classes and instances can have definitions that are themselves very complex. The next step would be to allow *pruning the definitions*, hiding some of the parts or presenting some the parts differently, based on the user's perspective.

We limited a *concept definition* for a concept C to RDF triples where C is the subject and to ranges of properties where C is a domain. This definition can be generalized to include a wider "neighborhood" of the concept C in an RDF graph. For example, it can include an *anonymous closure* of an RDF graph [14], which is computed by following graph edges, from subject to object of statements, until an anonymous RDF resource or RDF Literal is found. This extension will include, for example, all members of an RDF collection of values for a property of C in the concept definition of C. This, and similar, extensions to a concept definition, effect what a Traversal View ultimately includes.

A similar issue is the treatment of *transitive properties* for languages such as OWL. Suppose a Traversal View includes a traversal directive with a starter concept C_{st} and a property directive $\langle P, 1 \rangle$, where P is a transitive property. If we issue a query for all concepts X such that $P(C_{st}, X)$, looking for all the concepts directly related to C_{st} through property P, we will get all concepts in the transitive closure of C_{st} with respect to P, rendering the depth of traversal meaningless. One possibility to handle limited traversal of transitive properties is to distinguish between explicit and inferred triples in the ontology definition.

As part of future work, we plan to perform user studies to evaluate different approaches to these issues to determine which ones provide Traversal Views that correspond most closely to users' intuition.

Finally, we would like to link query-based view, Traversal Views and other types of view-definition techniques in a unified framework to enable users to combine the different means of defining ontology views. Furthermore, we consider definition and manipulation of ontology views to be part of the general framework for ontology management. We have developed a suite of tools—PROMPT [12]—that supports various tasks in ontology management, such as comparing ontologies, merging them together, maintaining and comparing different versions, and so on. For example, the users can compare or merge views of different ontologies, find diffs between different versions of a view, integrate two views into a single ontology.

Acknowledgments. This work was supported by a grant from the DARPA, executed by the U.S. Army Medical Research and Materiel Command/TATRC

Cooperative Agreement, Contract # W81XWH-04-2-0012. This work was conducted using the Protégé resource, which is supported by grant LM007885 from the United States National Library of Medicine. The Prompt suite is available as a plugin to the Protégé ontology-development environment at http://protege.stanford.edu/plugins/prompt/prompt.html

References

1. S. Boag, D. Chamberlin, M. F. Fernṭndez, D. Florescu, J. Robie, and J. SimŽon. XQuery 1.0: An XML query language. Technical report, W3C, 2003.
2. M. Dean, D. Connolly, F. v. Harmelen, J. Hendler, I. Horrocks, D. L. McGuinness, P. F. Patel-Schneider, and L. A. Stein. Web ontology language (OWL) reference version 1.0, http://www.w3.org/tr/owl-guide/, 2002.
3. C. Fellbaum, editor. *WordNet: An Electronic Lexical Database.* MIT Press, Cambridge, 1998.
4. R. Fikes and D. L. McGuinness. An axiomatic semantics for RDF, RDF-S, and DAML+OIL. Technical report, World Wide Web Committee (W3C) Note, 2001.
5. T. R. Gruber. A translation approach to portable ontology specification. *Knowledge Acquisition*, 5:199–220, 1993.
6. A. Halevy. Answering queries using views: a survey. *VLDB Journal*, 2001.
7. G. Karvounarakis, S. Alexaki, V. Christophides, D. Plexousakis, and M. Scholl. RQL: A declarative query language for RDF. In *Eleventh International World Wide Web Conference*, page 592–603, Honolulu, Hawaii, USA, 2002.
8. J. Lee and T. W. Malone. Partially shared views: a scheme for communicating among groups that use different type hierarchies. *ACM Transactions on Information Systems (TOIS)*, 8(1):1–26, 1990.
9. D. Lindberg, B. Humphreys, and A. McCray. The Unified Medical Language System. *Methods of Information in Medicine*, 32(4):281, 1993.
10. A. Magkanaraki, V. Tannen, V. Christophides, and D. Plexousakis. Viewing the semantic web through RVL lenses. In *Second International Semantic Web Conference*, volume 2870, pages 96–112, Sanibel Island, FL, 2003. Springer-Verlag.
11. N. F. Noy and M. A. Musen. PromptDiff: A fixed-point algorithm for comparing ontology versions. In *18th Conf. on Artificial Intelligence (AAAI-2002)*, Edmonton.
12. N. F. Noy and M. A. Musen. The PROMPT suite: Interactive tools for ontology merging and mapping. *International Journal of Human-Computer Studies*, 59(6):983–1024, 2003.
13. L. Obrst, H. Liu, and R. Wray. Ontologies for corporate web applications. *AI Magazine*, 24(3):49–62, 2003.
14. M. Palmer, A. Naeve, and F. Paulsson. The SCAM framework: helping semantic web applications to store and access metadata. In *1st European Semantic Web Symposium (ESWS 2004)*, Heraklion, Greece, 2004.
15. C. Rosse and J. L. V. Mejino. A reference ontology for bioinformatics: The foundational model of anatomy. *Journal of Biomedical Informatics.*, 2004.
16. R. Volz, D. Oberle, and R. Studer. On views in the semantic web. In *2nd Int. Workshop on Databases, Documents and Information Fusion (DBFUSION02)*, 2002.
17. R. Volz, D. Oberle, and R. Studer. Implementing views for light-weight web ontologies. In *IEEE Database Engineering and Application Symposium (IDEAS)*, Hong Kong, China, 2003.
18. W3C. Resource description framework (RDF), 2000.

Automatic Generation of Ontology for Scholarly Semantic Web

Thanh Tho Quan[1], Siu Cheung Hui[1], A.C.M. Fong[1], and Tru Hoang Cao[2]

[1] School of Computer Engineering, Nanyang Technological University
Singapore
{PA0218164B, asschui, ascmfong}@ntu.edu.sg
[2] Faculty of Information Technology, Hochiminh City University of Technology
Vietnam
tru@dit.hcmut.edu.vn

Abstract. Semantic Web provides a knowledge-based environment that enables information to be shared and retrieved effectively. In this research, we propose the Scholarly Semantic Web for the sharing, reuse and management of scholarly information. To support the Scholarly Semantic Web, we need to construct ontology from data which is a tedious and difficult task. To generate ontology automatically, Formal Concept Analysis (FCA) is an effective technique that can formally abstract data as conceptual structures. To enable FCA to deal with uncertainty in data and interpret the concept hierarchy reasonably, we propose to incorporate fuzzy logic into FCA for automatic generation of ontology. The proposed new framework is known as Fuzzy Formal Concept Analysis (FFCA). In this paper, we will discuss the Scholarly Semantic Web, and the ontology generation process from the FFCA framework. In addition, the performance of the FFCA framework for ontology generation will also be evaluated and presented.

1 Introduction

Semantic Web was introduced as a common framework that allows data to be shared and reused across application, enterprise and community boundaries[1]. And ontology is used to represent knowledge on the Semantic Web. Ontology is a conceptualization of a domain into a human understandable, but machine-readable format consisting of entities, attributes, relationships and axioms[2]. Thus, the knowledge metadata designed in the Semantic Web using ontologies should be sufficiently expressive to represent and model the domain it applies to. As such, programs can then access the knowledge carried by the Semantic Web and use the knowledge for processing information in a semantic manner.

Recently, much research has investigated the use of ontology to represent data. As the source data is usually stored in unstructured, semi-structured or fully structured format (e.g. textual documents or database schemata), it needs to be processed in order to generate the ontology in an appropriate format for representation. Some tools such as Protégé 2000[3] and OLIEd[4] have been

S.A. McIlraith et al. (Eds.): ISWC 2004, LNCS 3298, pp. 726–740, 2004.

developed to help users to edit ontology. However, it is a very difficult and cumbersome task to manually derive ontology from data. Some recent researches have been carried out to tackle this problem through the learning of ontology from free text[5], semi-structured data (e.g., HTML or XML) or structured data from a database[6].

To represent conceptual organization of the corresponding context of data, concepts are usually organized into multiple levels as a hierarchy, in which concepts at lower levels are more specific in terms of meaning than those at higher levels. Generally, to generate ontology from a database automatically, we need to perform the following two steps: (1) to abstract data items as ontology concepts and (2) to construct relations between concepts. Ontology concepts can be extracted quite efficiently from free text documents. However, it remains a hard problem to generate ontology relations automatically due to the complexity of Natural Language Processing (NLP). Relations represented in semi-structured and structured data can be extracted as ontology relations. This can be done using data mining techniques such as association rules mining and clustering[5,7].

Conceptual clustering techniques such as COBWEB[7] were proposed to discover knowledge that is more meaningful and comprehensible. COBWEB can cluster data into conceptual clusters, which are clusters associated with conceptual descriptions. The generated clusters can then be organized as a concept hierarchy. However, as COBWEB uses statistical models to describe clusters conceptually, it is unable to give the "real" conceptual organization, in terms of descriptions and relations. Moreover, since COBWEB is based on the hierarchical clustering technique to generate clusters of hierarchical relations, the concept hierarchy generated has a tree-like form. It means that a subconcept is only inherited from one superconcept. This way of conceptual representation cannot really reflect real-life concept organization. For instance, "fuzzy clustering technique" can be considered as a concept inherited from two superconcepts, "clustering technique" and "fuzzy theory".

Formal Concept Analysis (FCA)[8], which is a data analysis technique based on ordered lattice theory, has been used for conceptual knowledge discovery[9]. FCA offers better conceptual representations compared with traditional conceptual clustering techniques such as COBWEB as it provides formal definitions of concepts and its hierarchical relationships of concepts are organized as a lattice rather than a simple hierarchical tree. However, this technique still suffers from the drawback on its in capabilities on representing vague information and extracting "real" concepts. In this paper, we propose a new formal framework known as Fuzzy Formal Concept Analysis (FFCA) for constructing ontology for Scholarly Semantic Web that supports citation-based retrieval of scientific publications for the Semantic Web. The FFCA framework extends Formal Concept Analysis with fuzzy logic[10] which can represent vague and uncertain information. In addition, we also propose a conceptual clustering technique based on the FFCA framework to construct ontology of "real" concepts.

The rest of this paper is organized as follows. Section 2 discusses the Scholarly Semantic Web. Section 3 discusses the Fuzzy Formal Concept Analysis framework. Section 4 discusses conceptual clustering based on FFCA. Ontology generation is given in Section 5. The ontology generation process using an experimental citation database is discussed in Section 6. The performance results are given in Section 7. Finally, Section 8 concludes the paper.

2   Scholarly Semantic Web

Scholars are defined as individuals working in scientific areas. They could be researchers, scientists or academics. Obviously, scholars always need to acquire new information related to their academic activities in order to support their work and research. Such information will help researchers to obtain useful knowledge in their research areas, and enable them to make contributions in their scholarly activities, such as publishing papers or attending conferences.

The enormous growth of the Internet in recent years has urged scholars to use the Web for conducting scientific research. Digital libraries[11] and in particular, citation-based retrieval systems such as ISI (Institute for Scientific Information)[12] and CiteSeer (or Research Index)[13] are some of the tools that have been developed to help researchers to search related scientific information over the Web. In scientific documents, other papers or books that are useful for the understanding of its contents are usually cited as references. Citation indices contain references that the documents cite. They provide linking between source documents to the cited documents or papers. Thus, citation indices provide useful information to help researchers when conducting scientific research, such as identifying researchers working on their research areas, finding publications from a certain research area, and analyzing research trends. This helps researchers avoid doing research that had already been done by others. Citation indices are stored in a citation database.

Due to the lack of semantic information in the traditional Web, researchers can only rely on traditional search or retrieval systems to retrieve scientific publications. To provide more advanced and semantic-based search, research has recently been carried out based on Semantic Web for scholarly activities. The E-scholar Knowledge Inference Model (ESKIMO)[14] investigates the use of hypertext links on the traditional Web to develop a scholarly system for the Semantic Web. Using the Semantic Web, ESKIMO can retrieve scholarly information, such as finding researchers and institutions that are related to a particular document, or finding similar journals. However, in ESKIMO, the ontology building approach is still largely based on manual methods.

In this research, we aim to develop a Scholarly Semantic Web to support scholarly activities based on citation databases. Figure 1 gives the architecture of the Scholarly Semantic Web. As shown in Figure 1, scientific publications stored in the citation database are used as the source for automatic construction of ontology. The proposed FFCA technique is then applied to the citation database to construct the Scholarly Ontology. Web Services can be provided to enable the knowledge stored in the Scholarly Ontology be accessible by other programs. Semantic Search Engine can also be developed to support seman-

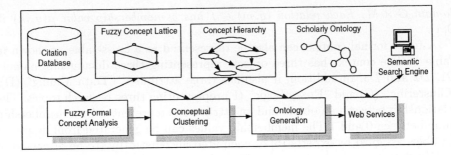

Fig. 1. The proposed approach for automatic generation of concept hierarchy

tic search functions to locate information on the Scholarly Ontology. As such, knowledge stored in the Scholarly Ontology can be shared and retrieved. The major components of the Scholarly Semantic Web are briefly discussed below:

- Fuzzy Formal Concept Analysis: It generates *fuzzy formal context* from the citation database. Citation information extracted from scientific documents is used to generate the necessary fuzzy information in order to construct the fuzzy formal context. In addition, it also generates *fuzzy formal concepts* from the *fuzzy formal context* and organizes the generated concepts as a *fuzzy concept lattice*.
- Conceptual Clustering: It clusters concepts on the *fuzzy concept lattice* and generates a *concept hierarchy.*
- Ontology Generation: It generates the Scholarly Ontology from the *concept hierarchy.*
- Web Services: It enables other programs to access the knowledge stored in the Scholarly Ontology. In addition, advanced search features can also be provided.
- Semantic Search Engine: It enables users to query the ontology stored in the Scholarly Ontology.

This paper focuses only on the ontology generation process that involves components including Fuzzy Formal Concept Analysis, Conceptual Clustering and Ontology Generation. Web Services and Semantic Search Engine will not be discussed in this paper.

3   Fuzzy Formal Concept Analysis

In this section, we propose the Fuzzy Formal Concept Analysis, which incorporates fuzzy logic into Formal Concept Analysis, to represent vague information.

Definition 1. *A fuzzy formal context is a triple $K = (G, M, I = \varphi(G \times M))$ where G is a set of objects, M is a set of attributes, and I is a fuzzy set on* domain $G \times M$. Each relation $(g,m) \in I$ has a membership value $\mu(g,m)$ in $[0,1]$.

A fuzzy formal context can also be represented as a cross-table as shown in Table 1. The context has three objects representing three documents, namely $D1$, $D2$ and $D3$. In addition, it also has three attributes, "Data Mining" (D), "Clustering" (C) and "Fuzzy Logic" (F) representing three research topics. The relationship between an object and an attribute is represented by a membership value between 0 and 1.The membership values can be generated from linguistic variables assigned by experts[15] or computed automatically (to be discussed in Section 6).

Table 1. A cross-table of a fuzzy formal context.

	D	C	F
D1	0.8	0.12	0.61
D2	0.9	0.85	0.13
D3	0.1	0.14	0.87

Table 2. Fuzzy formal context in Table 1 with $T = 0.5$.

	D	C	F
D1	0.8	-	0.61
D2	0.9	0.85	-
D3	-	-	0.87

A *confidence threshold* T can be set to eliminate relations that have low membership values. Table 2 shows the cross-table of the fuzzy formal context given in Table 1 with $T = 0.5$.

Generally, we can consider the attributes of a formal concept as the description of the concept. Thus, the relationships between the object and the concept should be the intersection of the relationships between the objects and the attributes of the concept. Since each relationship between the object and an attribute is represented as a membership value in fuzzy formal context, then the intersection of these membership values should be the minimum of these membership values, according to fuzzy theory[16].

Definition 2. *Given a fuzzy formal context $K=(G, M, I)$ and a confidence threshold T, we define $A^* = \{m \in M | \forall g \in A: \mu(g,m) \geq T\}$ for $A \subseteq G$ and $B^* = \{g \in G | \forall m \in B: \mu(g,m) \geq T\}$ for $B \subseteq M$. A fuzzy formal concept (or fuzzy concept) of a fuzzy formal context (G, M, I) with a confidence threshold T is a pair $(A_f = \varphi(A), B)$ where $A \subseteq G$, $B \subseteq M$, $A^* = B$ and $B^* = A$. Each object $g \in \varphi(A)$ has a membership μ_g defined as*

$$\mu_g = \min_{m \in B} \mu(g,m)$$

where $\mu(g,m)$ is the membership value between object g and attribute m, which is defined in I. Note that if $B = \{\}$ then $\mu_g = 1$ for every g.

Definition 3. *Let (A_1, B_1) and (A_2, B_2) be two fuzzy concepts of a fuzzy formal context (G, M, I). $(\varphi(A_1), B_1)$ is the subconcept of $(\varphi(A_2), B_2)$, denoted as $(\varphi(A_1), B_1) \leq (\varphi(A_2), B_2)$, if and only if $\varphi(A_1) \subseteq \varphi(A_2)(\Leftrightarrow B_2 \subseteq B_1)$. Equivalently, (A_2, B_2) is the superconcept of (A_1, B_1).*

Definition 4. *A fuzzy concept lattice of a fuzzy formal context K with a confidence threshold T is a set F (K) of all fuzzy concepts of K with the partial order $\leq$ with the confidence threshold T.*

Definition 5. *The similarity of a fuzzy formal concept $K_1 = (\varphi(A_1), B_1)$ and its subconcept $K_2 = (\varphi(A_2), B_2)$ is defined as $E(K_1, K_2) = \frac{|\varphi(A_1) \cap \varphi(A_2)|}{|\varphi(A_1) \cup \varphi(A_2)|}$.*

Figure 2 gives the traditional concept lattice generated from Table 1. Figure 3 gives the fuzzy concept lattice generated from the fuzzy formal context given in Table 2. As shown from the figures, the fuzzy concept lattice can provide additional information, such as membership values of objects in each fuzzy formal concept and similarities of fuzzy formal concepts, that are important for the construction of concept hierarchy.

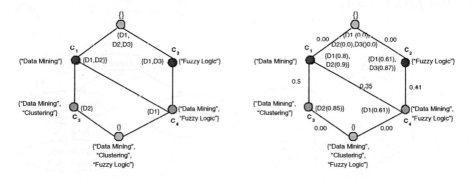

Fig. 2. A concept lattice generated from traditional FCA.   **Fig. 3.** A fuzzy concept lattice generated from FFCA.

4   Conceptual Clustering

As in traditional concept lattice, the formal concepts are generated mathematically, objects that have small differences in terms of attribute values are classified into distinct formal concepts. At a higher level, such objects should belong to the same concept when they are interpreted by human. Based on this observation, we propose to cluster formal concepts into conceptual clusters using fuzzy conceptual clustering. The conceptual clusters generated have the following properties:

- Conceptual clusters have hierarchical relationships that can be derived from fuzzy formal concepts on the fuzzy concept lattice. That is, a concept represented by a conceptual cluster can be a subconcept or superconcept of other concepts represented by other conceptual clusters.
- A formal concept must belong to at least one conceptual cluster, but it can also belong to more than one conceptual cluster. This property is derived from the characteristic of concepts that an object can belong to more than

one concept. For example, a scientific document can belong to more than one research area.

Conceptual clusters are generated based on the premise that if a formal concept A belongs to a conceptual cluster R, then its subconcept B also belongs to R if B is similar to A. We can use a *similarity confidence threshold* T_S to determine whether two concepts are similar or not.

Definition 6. *A conceptual cluster of a concept lattice K with a similarity confidence threshold T_S is a sublattice S_K of K which has the following properties:*

1. *S_K has a supremum concept C_S that is not similar to any of its superconcepts.*
2. *Any concept $C \neq C_S$ in S_K must have at least one superconcept $C' \in S_K$ such that $E(C, C') > T_S$.*

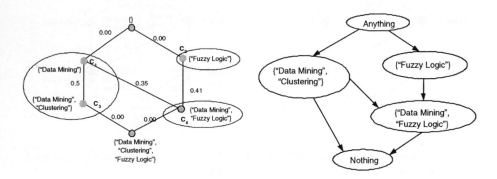

Fig. 4. Conceptual clusters.   **Fig. 5.** Concept hierarchy.

Figure 4 shows the conceptual clusters that are generated from the concept lattice given in Figure 3 with the similarity confidence threshold $T_S = 0.5$. Figure 5 shows the corresponding concept hierarchy, in which each concept is represented by a set of attributes of objects from the corresponding conceptual cluster.

Figure 6 gives the algorithm that generates conceptual clusters from a concept C_S which is called the *starting concept* on a fuzzy concept lattice $F(K)$. To generate all conceptual clusters of $F(K)$, we choose C_S as the supremum of $F(K)$, or $C_S = \sup(F(K))$.

5   Ontology Generation

After the construction of the concept hierarchy, we need to convert it into ontology for the Semantic Web. Since ontology strongly supports hierarchical representation, the conversion is done as follows:

```
Algorithm: Conceptual_Cluster_Generation
Input: Starting concept C_S of concept lattice F(K) and a similarity threshold T_S
Output: A set of generated conceptual clusters S_C
Process:
1:  S_C ← {}
2:  F'(K) ← An empty concept lattice
3:  Add C_S to F'(K)
4:  for each subconcept C' of C_S in F(K) do
5:      F'(C') ← Conceptual_Cluster_Generation(C', F(K), T_S)
6:      if E(C_S, C') = |C_S ∩ C'| / |C_S ∪ C'| < T_S then
7:          S_C ← S_C ∪ { F'(C') }
8:      else
9:          Insert F'(C') to F'(K) with sup(F'(K)) as a subconcept of C_S
10:     endif
11: endfor
12: S_C ← S_C ∪ {F'(K)}
```

Fig. 6. The fuzzy conceptual clustering algorithm.

- Each concept in the hierarchy is represented as an ontology class.
- The concepts' relations are preserved for the corresponding generated ontology classes. That is, if S_1 is the superconcept of S_2, then C_1 is the superclass of C_2 where C_1 and C_2 are the corresponding classes for S_1 and S_2 respectively.
- Each attribute of a concept is represented as a property of the corresponding class.
- Each object in a concept is represented as an instance of the corresponding class.
- The value of an instance's property is the membership value of the corresponding object's attribute. In future research, we will apply fuzzy logic to convert the membership value into linguistic terms, so that the generated ontology will be more informative and comprehensible.

We use DMAL+OIL[17] to annotate the generated ontology. DMAL+OIL is an RDF-based ontology description language that can represent ontology class properties and relations effectively. For illustration, Figure 7 gives the ontology for the concept hierarchy given in Figure 5.

6 Scholarly Ontology for Scholarly Semantic Web

In order for evaluating the proposed Fuzzy Formal Concept Analysis framework for ontology generation for the Scholarly Semantic Web, we have collected a set of 1400 scientific documents on the research area "Information Retrieval" published in 1987-1997 from the Institute for Scientific Information's (ISI) web-site

```
<rdf:RDF>
xmlns:rdf ="http://www.w3.org/1999/02/22-rdf-syntax-ns#"
xmlns:rdfs="http://www.w3.org/2000/01/rdf-schema#"
xmlns:xsd ="http://www.w3.org/2000/10/XMLSchema#"
xmlns:daml="http://www.w3.org/2001/10/daml+oil#"
<daml:Ontology rdf:about="Scholarly Information">
<daml:versionInfo>
$Id: daml+oil-ex.daml,v 1.8 2001/03/27 21:24:04 horrocks Exp $
< /daml:versionInfo>
<rdfs:comment>
An ontology of Scholarly Information
< /rdfs:comment>
<daml:imports rdf:resource="http://www.w3.org/2001/10/daml+oil"/>
<daml:Class rdf:ID="Concept1">
<dmal:label> "Data Mining"</daml:label>
< /daml:Class>
<daml:Class rdf:ID="Concept2">
<dmal:label> Fuzzy Logic</daml:label>
< /daml:Class>
<daml:Class rdf:ID="Concept3">
<dmal:label> "Data Mining, Fuzzy Logic"</daml:label>
<rdfs:subClassOf rdf:resource="#Concept1"/>
<rdfs:subClassOf rdf:resource="#Concept2"/>
< /daml:Class>
<document rdf:ID = "Document3">
<instanceOf>
<resourceRef xlink:href="#Concept2"/>
< /instanceOf>
<FuzzyLogic>
<FuzzyLogicValue>0.87</FuzzyLogicValue>
< /FuzzyLogic>
< /document>
< /daml:Ontology>
< /rdf:RDF>
```

Fig. 7. The ontology for the concept hierarchy given in Figure 5.

[11]. The downloaded documents are preprocessed to extract related information such as the title, authors, citation keywords, and other citation information. The extracted information is then stored as a citation database. We then apply FFCA, conceptual clustering and ontology generation to the citation database as follows.

For each document, we have extracted the 10 most frequent citation keywords. We then construct a fuzzy formal context $K_f = \{G, M, I\}$, with G as the set of documents and M as the set of keywords. The membership value of a document D on a citation keyword C_K in K_f is computed as

$$\mu(D, C_K) = \frac{n_1}{n_2}$$

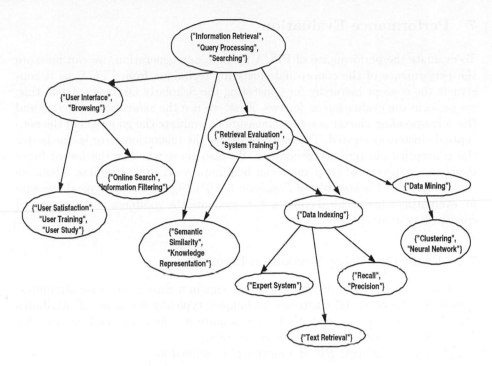

Fig. 8. An example concept hierarchy generated

where n_1 is the number of documents that cited D and contained C_K and n_2 is the number of documents that cited D. This formula is based on the premise that the more frequent a keyword occurs in the citing paper, the more important the keyword is in the cited paper.

Then, conceptual clustering is performed from the fuzzy formal context. As each conceptual cluster represents a real concept, the concepts to be discovered are the research areas. They form a hierarchy of research areas from the main research area on "Information Retrieval".

Figure 8 shows a part of the generated research hierarchy when $T_S = 0.7$. As shown in Figure 8, each research area is represented by a set of most frequent keywords occurring in the documents that belong to that research area. Research areas given by the hierarchy are considered as sub-areas of the research area "Information Retrieval". Hierarchical relationships between research areas including sub-areas and super-areas, which correspond to the definitions of subconcept and superconcept in FFCA, are also given. According to FFCA, sub-areas inherit keywords from their super-areas. Note that the inherited keywords are not shown in Figure 8 when labeling the concepts. Only keywords specific to the concepts are used for labeling.

Then, the generated concept hierarchy is converted into the Scholarly Ontology as discussed in Section 5.

7   Performance Evaluation

To evaluate the performance of FFCA for ontology generation, we can measure the performance of the conceptual clustering technique from FFCA, as it constructs the concept hierarchy for generating the Scholarly Ontology. To do this, we perform the evaluation as follows. First, we use the *relaxation error*[18] and the corresponding cluster goodness measure to evaluate the goodness of the conceptual clusters generated. Typically, the lower the relaxation error is, the better the conceptual clusters are generated. We also show whether the use of fuzzy membership instead of crisp value can help improve cluster goodness. Then, we use the *Average Uninterpolated Precision* (AUP)[19], which is a typical measure for evaluating a hierarchical construct, to evaluate the goodness of the generated concept hierarchy.

7.1   Evaluation Using Relaxation Error

Relaxation error implies dissimilarities of items in a cluster based on attributes' values. Since conceptual clustering techniques typically use a set of attributes for concept generation, relaxation error is quite a commonly used measure for evaluating the goodness of conceptual clusters.

The relaxation error RE of a cluster C is defined as

$$RE(C) = \sum_{a \in A} \sum_{i=1}^{n} \sum_{j=1}^{n} P(x_i)P(x_j)d^a(x_i, x_j)$$

where A is the set of attributes of items in C, $P(x_i)$ is the probability of item x_i occurring in C and $d^a(x_i, x_j)$ is the distance of x_i and x_j on attribute a. In this experiment, $d^a(x_i, x_j) = |m(i,a) - m(j,a)|$ where $m(i,a)$ and $m(j,a)$ are the membership values of objects x_i and x_j on attribute a respectively. The cluster goodness G of cluster C is defined as

$$G(C) = 1 - RE(C)$$

Obviously, the smaller the cluster relaxation error is, the better the cluster goodness is.

The relaxation error and the cluster goodness measure reflect respectively the dissimilarities and similarities of items in clusters. If we use a crisp number (that is, only values of 0 and 1 are used) for items' attributes as in typical FCA methods, we are unable to represent the similarities between items. Instead, the fuzzy membership value can be used to represent such similarities, thereby improving the cluster goodness.

In the experiment, we first measure the *fuzzy cluster goodness* (*FCG*) of clusters generated using the objects' fuzzy memberships. Then, we replace the objects' fuzzy memberships by crisp values. This is done as follows. If the membership value is greater than 0.5, it is replaced by 1, otherwise it is replaced by 0. Then, we measure the *crisp cluster goodness* (*CCG*) using the replaced crisp

Table 3. Performance results for fuzzy cluster goodness and crisp cluster goodness.

		T_s=0.2	T_s=0.3	T_s=0.4	T_s=0.5	T_s=0.6	T_s=0.7	T_s=0.8	T_s=0.9
N=2	FCG	0.85	0.77	0.79	0.85	0.86	0.86	0.84	0.85
	CCG	0.7	0.7	0.7	0.7	0.67	0.77	0.76	0.76
N=3	FCG	0.84	0.91	0.81	0.81	0.72	0.88	0.75	0.85
	CCG	0.72	0.72	0.72	0.71	0.65	0.71	0.69	0.69
N=4	FCG	0.9	0.74	0.82	0.76	0.75	0.81	0.73	0.75
	CCG	0.73	0.65	0.63	0.62	0.62	0.65	0.64	0.65
N=5	FCG	0.86	0.78	.075	0.8	0.76	0.75	0.72	0.77
	CCG	0.71	0.63	0.61	0.61	0.61	0.63	0.61	0.61
N=6	FCG	0.91	0.76	0.79	0.76	0.7	0.74	0.8	0.8
	CCG	0.73	0.65	0.61	0.61	0.6	0.62	0.63	0.63
N=7	FCG	0.91	0.79	0.73	0.73	0.73	0.84	0.78	0.74
	CCG	0.76	0.66	0.64	0.63	0.62	0.63	0.65	0.65
N=8	FCG	0.95	0.81	0.73	0.84	0.77	0.82	0.84	0.77
	CCG	0.8	0.71	0.64	0.63	0.62	0.63	0.65	0.65
N=9	FCG	0.91	0.88	0.76	0.84	0.71	0.75	0.77	0.85
	CCG	0.84	0.75	0.66	0.63	0.63	0.65	0.65	0.65
N=10	FCG	0.94	0.85	0.83	0.73	0.74	0.84	0.84	0.73
	CCG	0.85	0.77	0.65	0.64	0.63	0.64	0.66	0.66

values. We vary the number of keywords N extracted from documents from 2 to 10 and the similarity threshold T_S from 0.2 to 0.9 for conceptual clustering. The results are given in Table 3.

As can be seen from Table 3, the FCG obtained is generally better than the CCG. It has shown the advantage of using fuzzy membership values for representing object attributes. Since the relaxation error is an important factor for approximate query answering[20], the experimental results have shown that the use of fuzzy logic in FFCA can potentially improve retrieval performance on conceptual clustering.

In addition, the experimental results have also shown that better cluster goodness is obtained when the number of extracted keywords is small. It is expected because smaller number of keywords will cause smaller differences in objects in terms of keywords' membership values. Therefore, the relaxation error will be smaller. However, as we will see later in Section 7.2, smaller number of extracted keywords will cause poor performance in retrieval.

7.2 Evaluation Using Average Uninterpolated Precision

The Average Uninterpolated Precision (AUP) is defined as the sum of the precision value at each point (or node) in a hierarchical structure where a relevant item appears, divided by the total number of relevant items. Typically, AUP implies the goodness of a hierarchical structure.

We have manually classified the downloaded documents into classes based on their research themes. For each class, we extract 5 most frequent keywords

Table 4. Performance results for AUP^H and AUP^U.

		T_s=0.2	T_s=0.3	T_s=0.4	T_s=0.5	T_s=0.6	T_s=0.7	T_s=0.8	T_s=0.9
N=2	AUP^H	0.0503	0.0503	0.0503	0.05	0.042	0.043	0.0467	0.0464
	AUP^U	0.0325	0.0325	0.0325	0.0325	0.0251	0.0175	0.0175	0.0175
N=3	AUP^H	0.1088	0.1088	0.1083	0.1076	0.0849	0.0763	0.0818	0.0831
	AUP^U	0.0721	0.0721	0.0721	0.0721	0.0492	0.0305	0.0292	0.0292
N=4	AUP^H	0.1609	0.1552	0.1452	0.1418	0.1373	0.1338	0.1404	0.1461
	AUP^U	0.1458	0.1166	0.1029	0.0985	0.0855	0.0655	0.0636	0.0636
N=5	AUP^H	0.2066	0.1871	0.179	0.1779	0.1761	0.1772	0.1876	0.1965
	AUP^U	0.1924	0.1555	0.1448	0.1429	0.1300	0.1076	0.1065	0.1065
N=6	AUP^H	0.2983	0.2688	0.2625	0.2696	0.2733	0.2737	0.2833	0.2938
	AUP^U	0.2846	0.2424	0.2263	0.2237	0.2077	0.1819	0.1792	0.1797
N=7	AUP^H	0.3534	0.328	0.3149	0.3159	0.3295	0.2737	0.2833	0.2938
	AUP^U	0.352	0.2985	0.2677	0.2651	0.2556	0.2431	0.2316	0.2309
N=8	AUP^H	0.3619	0.3368	0.3215	0.3212	0.3306	0.3366	0.3417	0.3605
	AUP^U	0.36	0.3	0.2687	0.2659	0.2556	0.2422	0.2303	0.2297
N=9	AUP^H	0.3723	0.3459	0.3296	0.3267	0.3353	0.341	0.346	0.3657
	AUP^U	0.3704	0.3114	0.2771	0.2741	0.2635	0.2498	0.2377	0.237
N=10	AUP^H	0.3768	0.351	0.3345	0.3294	0.3381	0.3439	0.3485	0.3686
	AUP^U	0.3747	0.317	0.2824	0.2793	0.2685	0.2548	0.2426	0.242

from the documents in the class. Then, we use these keywords as inputs to form retrieval queries and evaluate the retrieval performance using AUP. This is carried out as follows. For each document, we will generate a set of *document keywords*. There are two different ways to generate document keywords. The first way is to use the set of keywords, known as *attribute keywords*, from each conceptual cluster as the document keywords. The second way is to use the keywords from each document as the document keywords. Then, we vectorize the document keywords and the input query, and calculate the vectors' distance for measuring the retrieval performance.

We refer the AUP measured using the first way to as *Hierarchical Average Uninterpolated Precision* (AUP^H), as each concept inherits attribute keywords from its superconcepts. Whereas the AUP measured using the second way is referred to as *Unconnected Average Uninterpolated Precision* (AUP^U). Table 4 gives the performance results for AUP^H and AUP^U using different numbers of extracted keywords N and similarity thresholds T_S for conceptual clustering. Generally, when N gets larger, the performance on both AUP^H and AUP^U gets better. It has shown that the number of keywords extracted for conceptual clustering has affected the retrieval accuracy. In addition, the performance on AUP^H is generally better than that of AUP^U. It means that the attribute keywords generated for conceptual clusters are quite appropriate concepts to be represented in the hierarchical structure.

8   Conclusions

In this paper, we have proposed a new framework called Fuzzy Formal Concept Analysis that extends Formal Concept Analysis for ontology generation for the Scholarly Semantic Web. As compared to traditional FCA, FFCA can deal with uncertainty in data. Moreover, we have also proposed a conceptual clustering technique that can cluster the fuzzy concept lattice to generate a concept hierarchy, which can then be converted into Scholarly Ontology. The proposed framework is used to construct Semantic Scholarly Web from a citation database. The FFCA framework has been evaluated and good performance has been achieved. As for future research, we intend to restructure the generated ontology for supporting multiple-level concepts corresponding to multiple levels of abstractions. Moreover, we will also use fuzzy logic to convert fuzzy property values of the generated ontology into linguistic terms to make the generated ontology more informative and comprehensible.

References

1. T. Berners-Lee, J. Hendler and O. Lassila, "The Semantic Web", *Scientific American,* Available at: <http://www.sciam.com/2001/0501issue/0501berners-lee.html>, 2001.
2. N. Guarino and P. Giaretta, *Ontologies and Knowledge Bases: Towards a Terminological Clarification. Toward Very Large Knowledge Bases: Knowledge Building and Knowledge Sharing,* IOS Press, Amsterdam, 1995.
3. N. Noy and D. L. McGuinness, "Ontology Development 101: A Guide to Creating Your First Ontology", *Report SMI-2001-0880,* Department of Mechanical and Industrial Engineering, University of Toronto, 2001.
4. S. Bechhofer, I. Horrocks, P. Patel-Schneider and S. Tessaris, "A Proposal for a Description Logic Interface", In *Proceedings of the International Workshop on Description Logics,* 1999, pp. 33-36.
5. A. Maedche and S. Staab, "Mining Ontologies from Text", In *EKAW-2000 - 12th International Conference on Knowledge Engineering and Knowledge Management,* Juan-les-Pins, France. LNAI, Springer, 2000.
6. A. Doan, J. Madhavan, P. Domingos and A.Y. Halevy, "Learning to Map Between Ontologies on the Semantic Web", In *Proceedings of the Eleventh International World Wide Web Conference, WWW2002,* Honolulu, Hawaii, USA, 2002, pp. 662-673.
7. A.K Jain and R.C Dubes, *Algorithms for Clustering Data,* Prentice-Hall, 1988.
8. B. Ganter and R. Wille, *Formal Concept Analysis,* Springer, Berlin – Heidelberg, 1999.
9. A. Hotho, S. Staab and G. Stumme, "Explaining Text Clustering Results using Semantic Structures", In *Proceedings of Principles of Data Mining and Knowledge Discovery, 7th European Conference, PKDD 2003,* Croatia, 2003, pp. 217-228.
10. L.A. Zadeh, "Fuzzy Logic and Approximate Reasoning", *Synthese,* Vol. 30, 1975, pp. 407-428.
11. G. Wiederhold, *Digital Libraries, Value, and Productivity,* Communications of the ACM, Vol. 38, No. 4, 1995, pp. 85-96.

12. ISI, *Institute for Scientific Information*, Available at: <http://www.isinet.com>, 2000.
13. K. Bollacker, S. Lawrence and C. Giles, "Discovering Relevant Scientific Literature on the Web", *IEEE Intelligent Systems*, Vol. 15, No. 2, 2000, pp. 42-47.
14. S. Kampa, T. Miles-Board and L. Carr, "Hypertext in the Semantic Web", In *Proceedings ACM Conference on Hypertext and Hypermedia*, Aarhus, Denmark, 2001, pp. 237-238.
15. L.A. Zadeh, "The concept of a linguistic variable and its application to approximate reasoning". Part I: *Inf. Science 8*,199-249; Part II: *Inf. Science 8,* 301-357; Part III: *Inf. Science 9,* 43-80, 1975.
16. L.A. Zadeh, "Fuzzy Sets", *Journal of Information and Control*, Vol. 8, 1965, pp. 338-353.
17. DARPA, *DAML-ONT Initial Release,* Available at: <http://www.daml.org/2000/10/daml-ont.html>, 2000.
18. W. Chu and K. Chiang, "Abstraction of High Level Concepts from Numerical Values in Databases", In *Proceedings of AAAI Workshop on Knowledge Discovery in Databases*, 1994, pp. 133-144.
19. N. Nanas, V. Uren and A. de Roeck, "Building and Applying a Concept Hierarchy Representation of a User Profile", In *Proceedings of the 26th annual international ACM SIGIR Conference on Research and Development in Information Retrieval*, ACM Press, 2003.
20. W. Chu and Q. Chen, "Neighborhood and associative query answering", *Journal of Intelligent Information Systems*, Vol. 1, No. 3, 1992.

Querying Real World Services Through the Semantic Web*

Kaoru Hiramatsu, Jun-ichi Akahani, and Tetsuji Satoh

NTT Communication Science Laboratories
Nippon Telegraph and Telephone Corporation
2-4, Hikaridai, Seika-cho, Soraku-gun, Kyoto 619-0237 Japan
{hiramatu,akahani}@cslab.kecl.ntt.co.jp, satoh.tetsuji@lab.ntt.co.jp

Abstract. We propose a framework for querying real world services using meta data of Web pages and ontologies and implement a prototype system using standardized technologies developed by the Semantic Web community. The meta data and the ontologies enable systems to infer related classes while modifying the queries and retrieving approximate result and help them smooth obstacles in interaction while querying. The standardized technologies help us to describe the meta data and the ontologies in RDF (Resource Description Framework) and OWL (Web Ontology Language) formally and enable us to share them on the network. In this paper, we illustrate details of the framework and the prototype system, demonstrate how it works using practical data in Kyoto, Japan, and discuss requirements for actualizing this framework on the network.

1 Introduction

Some of the most popular and frequently used content on the Internet is information on real world services, such as that containing location information (e.g. store locations and hours of business) and services (e.g. timetables and route maps of public transportation systems). Much of this information is accessible as Web pages, and users can search for them with keywords using major search engines as they can with other kinds of contents by trial and error. In searching for real world services, locality is one of the most important factors; therefore it is necessary for users to specify a region geographically in order to find the real world services efficiently. However, because of the ambiguity of location names, users have to enter an exact address or use some heuristics (e.g. use a zip code as a keyword instead of an exact address) that are often noted on help pages for local searches.

Such inflexibility and heuristics on the current Internet are mainly caused by the ambiguity of terms extracted from Web pages by the search engines and queries submitted by users. To handle this ambiguity, much research has been done on meta data of the Web pages with respect to information retrieval [1], natural language processing [2][3], and databases [4][5]. Although these academic approaches show steady improvement and some of them mention sharing and reusing the meta data, no standardized frameworks and languages have yet come into wide use.

---

* Previous version of this paper was presented at the demonstration session of the 2nd International Semantic Web Conference

S.A. McIlraith et al. (Eds.): ISWC 2004, LNCS 3298, pp. 741–751, 2004.
© Springer-Verlag Berlin Heidelberg 2004

The Semantic Web [6] is expected to play an important role in improving the situation on the Internet. Thanks to Semantic Web activity at the World Wide Web Consortium (W3C), Resource Description Framework (RDF)[1] and Web Ontology Language (OWL)[2] have been standardized as frameworks of the Semantic Web. They enable us to describe meta data of the Web pages and the ontologies formally. The formalized meta data and the ontologies are regarded as being machine-readable semi-structured knowledge and as sharable on the Internet without ambiguity. Such knowledge will not only enable the search engines to handle terms extracted from the Web pages and the queries more accurately, but also help the systems provide users with various related information using the taxonomic knowledge in the ontologies.

In this paper, we propose a framework for querying information on real world services and implement a prototype system based on the framework utilizing standardized technologies developed by the Semantic Web community. Taxonomic knowledge and database schemata of the real world services are integrated into the ontologies that are described in OWL. Based on these ontologies, the meta data of the Web pages concerning real world services such as location, hours of business, and service types, is extracted from the Web pages by a scraping program, converted into RDF data, and stored in service provider agents separately according to their area of responsibility and service categories. The meta data and the ontologies help systems avoid ambiguity of terms extracted from Web pages and queries, and enable them to infer related classes for modifying the queries and searching for approximate results.

The prototype system accepts queries in natural language sentences and displays search results in several styles (e.g. map view and tree-structure view) according to meta data of the search results. As in the upper example of Fig. 1, the prototype system accepts a query "Find traditional Japanese restaurants near a bus stop that will be open around 2 p.m. tomorrow[3]," then returns three search result sets that include a restaurant and a bus stop, respectively. The prototype system utilizes the meta data and the ontologies to smooth interactive querying. For example, if no result satisfies the initial query, the prototype system will extend its search range using the meta data and the ontologies (e.g. find a category "Restaurant" that is a superordinate category of "Japanese Restaurant.")

The accepted queries are translated into queries in extended SQL [7] and submitted to a mediator agent, which coordinates the optimal combination of service provider agents according to advertisements for the service provider agents in DAML-S [8]. Then, the mediator agent submits the query to the coordinated service provider agents and a service integrator agent integrates the search results returned from them. As the lower example in Fig. 1 shows, when a user submits the query "find a route to Kyoto station and a bank on the way to Kyoto station," the prototype system forwards the query to two service provider agents, a route finding service and a location information service, and outputs integrated results on a result viewer (lower right of Fig. 1.) Moreover, to enable the users to digress from the search results, the prototype system extracts meta data of selected search results as default values of future queries.

---

[1] RDF: http://www.w3c.org/RDF/

[2] OWL: http://www.w3c.org/2001/sw/WebOnt/

[3] As in the screenshot (Fig. 1), this version of the prototype system only accepts queries in Japanese.

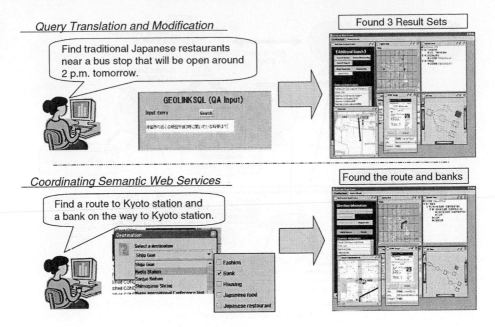

Fig. 1. Example of the prototype system

In the remainder of this paper, we illustrate details of the framework and the prototype system, and demonstrate how it works using practical data in Kyoto, Japan. We also discuss requirements for actualizing this framework on the network through comparing it with related work.

2   Framework and Prototype System

2.1   Overview

Information on real world services is provided by many directory services (e.g. Yahoo![4] and Zagat survey[5].) and rendered in various styles. Almost all of entries in them include names, addresses, hours of business, and telephone numbers. These fields are regarded as basic and common data. The other fields such as ratings, reputations, and atmospheres of places are also familiar and useful for users to make their choice. All these data are important and meaningful for sharing as meta data of information on real world services. However, in contrast to the former fields that are objective, the latter fields are filled in by reporters subjectively; consequently, it is necessary for inference engines to take account of mutual trust between reporters and users. To simplify the prototype system, we mainly utilize the former fields as the meta data of the information on real world services.

In order to collect meta data of information on real world services, we implemented a scraping program based on Web robots. It accesses Web pages according to a URL

---

[4] Yahoo!: http://www.yahoo.com/
[5] Zagat survey: http://www.zagat.com/

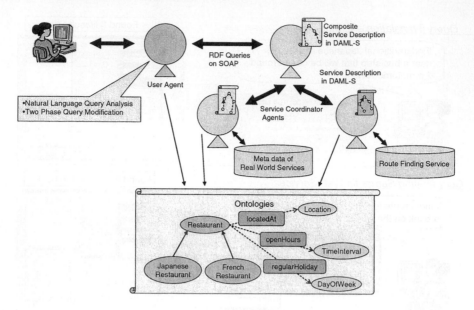

Fig. 2. System overview

list and downloads them recursively. It then analyzes the downloaded Web pages using morphological analysis and pattern matching and extracts fields of names, addresses, and business hours of the real world services. In this analysis, we utilize digital map data as dictionaries for extracting the names and the addresses and assigning geographic coordinates to the downloaded Web pages belonging to the real world services. The extracted fields are converted to RDF data and stored in service provider agents separately according to their area of responsibility and service category. However, it is difficult and unreasonable for the scraping program to extract meta data of all the information residing in route planners and dynamic databases in the same manner. Therefore, we utilize a service description in DAML-S instead of employing their meta data.

Ontologies of the meta data are described in OWL. The ontologies are utilized to determine field extraction by the scraping program and to infer related and superordinate categories by user agents. As shown in Fig. 2, the ontologies include data schemata of the extracted fields and related knowledge such as hierarchies of service categories and addresses.

The prototype system based on this framework consists of a user agent and service coordinator agents (Fig. 2). In this prototype system, one service coordinator agent performs one or more roles of a service provider agent, a mediator agent, a service wrapper agent, and a service integrator agent. We will describe the details of these agents in Section 2.3. These modules are implemented using Java[6], Jena[7] for manipulating

---

[6] http://java.sun.com/

[7] a Java API for manipulating RDF models, http://www.hp.hp.com/semweb/

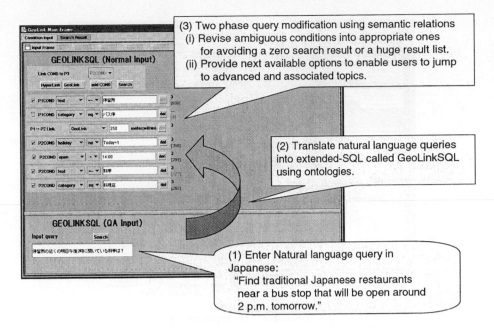

Fig. 3. Query translation

RDF models, PostgresSQL[8] for storing RDF data, and Jun for Java[9] for displaying tree structures of search results in the result viewer. These modules utilize SOAP (Simple Object Access Protocol) for message passing.

The user agent behaves as a front-end of the prototype system. As Fig. 3 shows, the user agent can accept queries either in natural language style or in form style, which is equivalent to queries in extended SQL. The query entered as the natural sentence is classified as a query type using SAIQA[10] and translated into a query in extended SQL using a template that is derived from the query type.

The query in extended SQL is submitted to the mediator agent. According to advertisements of the service provider agents in DAML-S, the mediator agent coordinates optimal combination of the service provider agents, divides the query according to the combination, and submits the divided query to the organized service provider agents. The service provider agents accept the query and returns search results that satisfy the queries based on the meta data of the real world services that the service provider agents store according to their area of responsibility and service category. The service integrator agent then integrates search results which are returned from the service provider agents into result sets based on relations that are specified in the query in extended SQL.

While processing a query, the prototype system applies two-phase query modification [9] to it. We will explain the details of this modification in Section 2.2.

---

[8] an open source Object-Relational DBMS, http://www.postgresql.org/
[9] a 3D graphics class library, http://www.sra.co.jp/people/nisinaka/Jun4Java/
[10] a question answering system developed by NTT Communication Science Laboratories

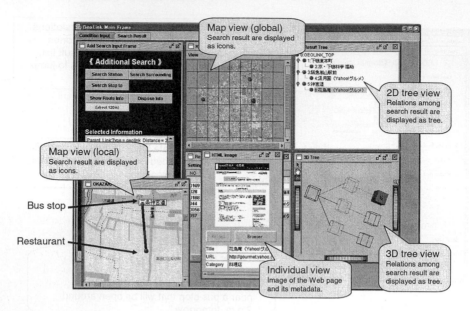

Fig. 4. Screenshot of the result viewer

After the query processing, the user agent displays search results using a result viewing frame. As shown in Fig. 4, the result viewing frame includes a map view, a 2D tree view, a 3D tree view, an individual view, and an add-search-input frame. The map view displays search results as icons on a digital map, while the 2D and 3D tree views show the search results (e.g. three sets of a restaurant and a bus stop) using the tree style. In both tree views, a node in the tree view expresses a Web page that includes information on a real world service, where an edge stands for a relation between real world services (e.g. hyperlinks between Web pages and geographical relationships.) The individual view enables the user to browse images of the Web page and its meta data by clicking the icons on the map view or the nodes in the 2D and 3D views. The add-search-input frame prompts the user to conduct the next search by showing available search options that are coordinated from meta data of one or all of the initial search results and preset user profiles. To conform with popular design guidelines for user interfaces, the available search options are displayed as enabled buttons, while the others are displayed as disabled buttons.

This query processing of the prototype system is based on an augmented Web space [7] that enables the system to search for a set of Web pages with relations by specifying conditions of the Web page attributes, hyperlinks, and implicit geographic relations between the Web pages. In the augmented Web space, the implicit geographic relations are calculated as geographical generic links, which are created dynamically according to implicit geographic relations, such as distance and directions, between objects that are described in the Web pages. Owing to this function, the prototype system can find sets of search results that satisfy the queries. Although the original augmented Web space is designed to utilize only geographic relations, we extended it to handle the meta data for creating semantic links.

2.2 Two-Phase Query Modification

We employ two-phase query modification [9] to the prototype system for driving users to evolve interactive queries. This query modification is divided into two phases:

1. Revising ambiguous conditions into appropriate ones to obtain an adequate number of search results.
2. Providing next available options that enable users to jump to advanced and associated topics.

Both phases are processed tightly coupled with query processing in accordance with the meta data and the ontologies.

In the first phase, the user agent prefetches a number of search results of each term condition in the query and identifies ambiguous term conditions in accordance with the number of search results. It then revises them into appropriate ones automatically using the ontologies. For example, if a term extracted from the query is too ambiguous and an enormous amount of search results are matched, the term will be replaced with a more specific term along with word relations in the taxonomic knowledge. On the other hand, if a keyword results in a zero search result, then the keyword will be replaced with a hypernym or a superordinate category name. After that, while joining the retrieved Web pages, if a geographic condition between Web pages is too narrow, in that an adequate result cannot be produced, the condition will be expanded into a wider area in accordance with the characteristics of distribution of the meta data. In contrast, if a geographic condition is too wide, the condition will be shortened. The user agent applies this query modification repeatedly until an adequate search result is obtained.

In the second phase, the prototype system provides the users with the next available options, which are advanced queries from the initial one and associated topics with the original target. Since the search result has a tree structure, the next available options are developed from root and leaf nodes of the search result and from characteristics of links between Web pages, according to the meta data and the ontologies. After the initial search result is returned to the user, he/she is prompted to choose one of the next available options, which are explicitly displayed in the add-search-input frame of the result viewer. In the second phase, all the next options are displayed on the result viewer so that the user can select and browse them repeatedly through trial and error. We suppose this helps users deepen and broaden their interests, even if they do not have a clear search intention when they start querying.

2.3 Coordinating Real-World Services

Various pieces of information on real world services is available on networks and each of them is responsible for a type of information such as restaurant directories or route guides. It is thus necessary to find adequate services to coordinate search results. We therefore need to introduce service coordinator agents into our framework. In our framework, one service coordinator agent performs one or both of the following roles.

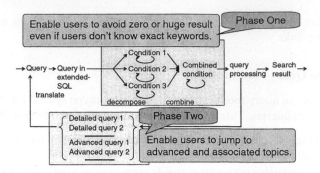

Fig. 5. Two-phase query modification

1. Service provider agents that provide services. Each service provider agent advertises its service description in DAML-S.
2. Mediator agents that forward queries to suitable service provider agents based on the service descriptions of the service provider agents.

Moreover, the service provider agents are categorized into the following two types.

1. Service wrapper agent that wraps Web services.
2. Service integrator agent that integrates services provided by other service provider agents. Each service integrator agent advertises a composite service description.

In the prototype system, we utilize two types of Web services: service provider agents and a route finding service. These Web services are wrapped by the service wrapper agents and are accessible in accordance with service descriptions in DAML-S. We have also implemented a service integrator agent that can integrate these two services.

3   Typical Example

For this prototype system, we prepared a test data set by extending the data originally created for the Digital City Kyoto prototype [10]. We constructed a URL list that includes about 5,000 Web pages of real world services in Kyoto, Japan, and extracted meta data from them using the scraping program. The meta data, such as names, hours of business, and addresses, are stored in service provider agents separately according to service area for which they were responsible, and service category. We collected service descriptions of the service provider agents and the real world services that coordinate search results dynamically.

To illustrate how the prototype system works, we employ the two example queries shown in Figure 1. The first is "find traditional Japanese restaurants near a bus stop that will be open around 2 p.m. tomorrow," and the second is "find a route to Kyoto station and a bank on the way to Kyoto station."

In the first example, a user inputs the example query into the field for a natural sentence. Then, the user agent analyzes the query and translates it into a query in extended

```
SELECT p2.url
FROM p1,link,p2
    p1.keyword =~ 'traditional'
    p1.keyword =~ 'Japanese restaurant'
    is_open(p1,'14:00')
    link AS diatance(p1,p2) < 250m
    p2.keyword =~ 'bus stop'
```

Fig. 6. Translated query in extended SQL

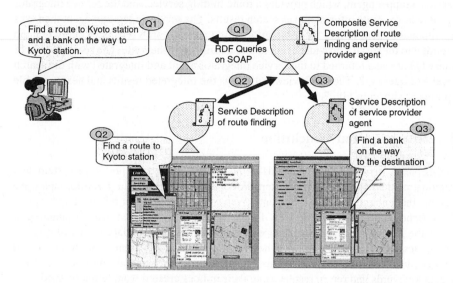

Fig. 7. Coordinating the agents of the real world services

SQL (Fig. 6). After translation, the user agent divides the query into term conditions and relational conditions, optimizes a processing order for them based on statistics of the test data set, and transmits them to a service coordinator agent. The service coordinator agent distributes the term conditions and the relational conditions to service provider agents based in a service area and service category for which they are responsible, and ask them to process each condition in the optimized order. While this processing occurs, the first phase of the query modification process is applied. The number of matching results for each term condition in the translated query is estimated by the query processing modules of the service provider agents. In this example, there is no term condition where the estimated result is zero or beyond the preset thresholds; if there is such a condition, then it will be replaced with more adequate term conditions using semantic relations in the ontologies.

Next, matching results are retrieved from the service provider agents and integrated into the search result in accordance with the link conditions in the query. As shown in the upper right of Fig. 1, the example query succeeded in retrieving three sets of a restaurant and a bus stop as the search result; however, if a link condition based on geographic distance is inadequate, the system extends or shortens the distance in order to obtain an adequate result. Also, if the combined result becomes invalid even though each condition is successfully processed, the system backtracks to the term replacement process and recombines the results until an adequate result is obtained.

The second example is conjunctive, meaning that the prototype system divides and processes it as in Fig. 7. The user agent translates a query and submits it to a mediator agent. In this phase, the mediator agent divides query Q1 into two: one is "find a route to Kyoto station" (Q2), and the other is "find a bank on the way to the destination" (Q3) according to the service descriptions. The mediator agent first submits query Q2 to a service wrapper agent, which provides a route finding service, and the service integrator agent receives route information as search results. The service integrator agent then asks the mediator agent to add the route information in the search results to query Q3 and submit it to the service provider agent to find a bank along the route. The search results of query Q3 are also returned to the service integrator agent and integrated with the search results of query Q2. The result viewer displays the integrated results and next available options as shown in Fig. 7.

4   Discussion and Conclusion

In this paper, we illustrated the details of the framework and the prototype system, and demonstrated how the prototype system works using practical data in Kyoto, Japan. We assume that enlargement of the Semantic Web will lead to a closer relationship between the Internet and real world services. To accelerate such evolution, we are planning to refine the framework and the prototype system along with meta data and ontologies.

As described in Section 1, many heuristics are diffused for searching for real world services using current search engines on the Internet. In general, the search engines accept keywords and return results using their indices created from terms scraped from the Web pages. This simple framework contributes to scalability and performance of the search engines, but it restricts users to conducting related information and cascading the result flexibly. In contrast to these search engines, users can utilize meta data of search results (e.g. names and locations of real world services) as default values of future searches using other information sources in our framework. However, extracting such meta data while processing queries causes a reduction in system performance. To avoid this tradeoff would be difficult; therefore it is necessary to estimate the quantity and quality of meta data.

As described in Section 2.1, we utilized common and objective meta data of information on real world services in the prototype system. Other meta data such as atmosphere, reputations, and ratings of real world services, are also meaningful for comparison, though such subjective meta data requires systems and users to confirm author information and date of creation and update. Such confirmation, which is regarded as a component of mutual trust is a difficult but worthwhile challenge in the Semantic Web.

The scraping program extracts meta data of the real world services based on the ontologies automatically using morphological processing and pattern matching. However, due to incomprehensive descriptions in Web pages and imperfect performance of natural language processing, the scraping program cannot always work correctly. To minimize the effect of errors, we need to investigate robust query processing and error checking by inferring engines that use ontologies.

Acknowledgment. Thanks are due to content holders for the permission to use their Web pages concerned with Kyoto, and to Yuji Nagato and Yoshikazu Furukawa of NTT Comware Corporation for their great contributions to demonstrating the system.

References

1. Jones, C.B., Purves, R., Ruas, A., Sanderson, M., Sester, M., van Kreveld, M., Weibel, R.: Spatial Information Retrieval and Geographic Ontologies An Overview of the SPRIT Project. In: Proceedings of the 25th Annual International ACM SIGIR Conference on Research and Development in Information Retrieval (SIGIR02). (2002) 387–388
2. Smith, D.A., Crane, G.: Disambiguating Geographic Names in a Historical Digital Library. In: Proceedings of the 5th European Conference on Research and Advanced Technology for Digital Libraries. (2001)
3. Krovetz, R., Croft, W.B.: Lexical ambiguity and information retrieval. ACM Transactions on Information Systems (TOIS) **10** (1992) 115–141
4. Knoblock, C.: Agents for Gathering, Integrating, and Monitoring Information for Travel Planning. IEEE Intelligent Systems **17** (2002) 63–66
5. Chen, C.C., Thakkar, S., Knoblock, C.A., Shahabi, C.: Automatically Annotating and Integrating Spatial Datasets. In: Proceedings of the Eighth International Symposium on Spatial and Temporal Databases (SSTD 2003). (2003)
6. Berners-Lee, T., Hendler, J., Lassila, O.: The Semantic Web. Scientific America (2001)
7. Hiramatsu, K., Ishida, T.: An Augmented Web Space for Digital Cities. In: The 2001 Symposium on Application and the Internet (SAINT2001). (2001) 105–112
8. Coaliation, T.D.S.: DAML-S: Web Service Description for the Semantic Web. In: The First International Semantic Web Conference (ISWC). (2002)
9. Hiramatsu, K., Akahani, J., Satoh, T.: Two-phase Query Modification using Semantic Relations based on Ontologies. In: Proceedings of IJCAI-03 Workshop on Information Integration on the Web (IIWeb-03). (2003) 155–158
10. Ishida, T., Akahani, J., Hiramatsu, K., Isbister, K., Lisowski, S., Nakanishi, H., Okamoto, M., Miyazaki, Y., Tsutsuguchi, K.: Digital City Kyoto: Towards A Social Information Infrastructure. In: Cooperative Information Agents III. Volume 1652 of Lecture Notes in Computer Science. (1999) 34–46

Public Deployment of
Semantic Service Matchmaker
with UDDI Business Registry

Takahiro Kawamura[1], Jacques-Albert De Blasio[1], Tetsuo Hasegawa[1],
Massimo Paolucci[2], and Katia Sycara[2]

[1] Research and Development Center, Toshiba Corp.
[2] The Robotics Institute, Carnegie Mellon University

Abstract. Public deployment of the semantic service matchmaker to a
UDDI registry for half a year is shown in this paper. UDDI is a standard registry for Web Services, but if we consider it a search engine,
its functionality is limited to a keyword search. Therefore, the Matchmaker was developed to enhance UDDI by service capability matching.
Then, we have deployed the Matchmaker to one of four official UDDI
registries operated by NTT-Communications since September 2003. In
this paper, we first introduce the Matchmaker with UDDI, and illustrate client tools which lower the threshold of use of semantics. Then,
we evaluate this deployment by benchmarks in terms of performance
and functionality. Finally, we discuss user requirements obtained by two
ways: questionnaire and observation of search behaviour.

1   Introduction

The recent spread of web services reveals the needs of sophisticated discovery
mechanism. Although UDDI[1] is emerging as a de-facto standard registry for
web services, the search functionality provided by UDDI is the keyword search
only on names, comments and keys of businesses and services descriptions. Unfortunately, the keyword search fails to recognize the similarities and differences
between the capabilities provided by web services. To address this problem, we
developed the Matchmaker in collaboration with Carnegie Mellon University[2],
which enhances the search functionality of UDDI by making use of semantic
information. Then, we initiated an experiment on a publicly available UDDI
maintained by NTT-Communications, one of four official UDDI operators[3].
Since started from September 2003, we have evaluated the scalability and feasibility of our approach with performance and functional comparison and collected
user requirements through half a year.

In this paper, we first introduce the Matchmaker in section 2, and the one
deployed with UDDI in section 3. After illustrating supporting tools that provide
user interfaces to the Matchmaker in section 4, we will present the evaluation in
section 5.

S.A. McIlraith et al. (Eds.): ISWC 2004, LNCS 3298, pp. 752–766, 2004.

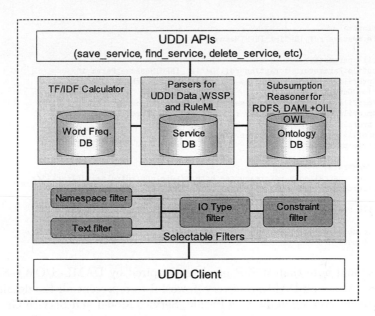

Fig. 1. Matchmaker

2   Semantic Service Matchmaker

Figure 1 shows the architecture of the Matchmaker.

2.1   Service Description

First of all, we mention Web Service Semantic Profile (WSSP), a way to encode semantic information with WSDL. WSDL specifies the programming interface of a service to be used at invocation time. To this account it specifies the name of the function to invoke and the types of data that the service expects as inputs and outputs. The data types describe how the information is formatted, but because there are arbitrarily many ways of encoding the same information in data types, they fail to express the semantics of the information, which is needed to express the capability of the service.

The aim of WSSP is to enrich WSDL with the basic semantic information to represent the services capabilities. As in WSDL we can define input and output parameters, the ontologies of those parameters are defined in WSSP. Further, WSSP offers the possibility to add constraints to those parameters to represent conditions for the service invocation more accurately. Since automatic service composition is out of our experiment for now, preconditions and effect (postcondition) will be our next priorities. An example of the WSSP is given below, in which the ontology for the parameter in RDFS[4], DAML+OIL[5] or OWL[6], facts and rules in RDF-RuleML[7] as the constraints, and the original WSDL parameter are encoded.

```
<profile:input>
  <profile:message rdf:ID="1st_INPUTMessage">

    <profile:parameter>
      <profile:ParameterDescription rdf:ID="1st_INPUTMessage_Param_1">
        <profile:parameterName>Param_1</profile:parameterName>
        <!-- Ontology -->
        <profile:restrictedTo rdf:resource="http://ont.com/Onto.owl#class1"/>
        <profile:wsdlParam>xPointer to wsdl parameter</profile:wsdlParam>
        <profile:datatype>XMLSchema.xsd#String</profile:datatype>
      </profile:ParameterDescription>
    </profile:parameter>

    <!-- Constraint -->
    <profile:constrainedBy rdf:resource="http://rule.com/rdfrules.rdf#fact1"/>
    <profile:constrainedBy rdf:resource="http://rule.com/rdfrules.rdf#rule1"/>

    <profile:wsdlMessage>xPointer to wsdl message</profile:wsdlMessage>

  </profile:message>
</profile:input>
```

We should note that WSSP has been inspired by DAML-S/OWL-S Service Profile[8]. Although DAML-S is very powerful to represent all the details about the service by combining Service Profile, Service Model and Service Grounding, it is difficult to use only the Service Profile without adopting the Process Model and the Grounding because of relationship among those three modules. Further, we would have redundancy if we use both the Service Profile and WSDL. Thus, we adopted the basic ideas of the Service Profile, and imported them into WSSP. Due to the highest priority on the standards, if any standard language will allow to express the same information as WSSP near future, we will be pleased to adopt it.

2.2   Matchmaking Mechanism

In brief we describe how the matching of capabilities is performed. Ideally, when the requester looks for a service, the matchmaker will retrieve a service that matches exactly the service that the requester expects. But, in practice it is very unlikely that such a service is available, instead the matchmaker will retrieve a service whose capabilities are *similar* to the capabilities expected by the requester. To address this problem, the matchmaker identifies the three levels of matching.

Exact match is the highest degree of matching, it results when the two descriptions are equivalent.

Plug-in match results when the service provided is more general than the service requested, but in practice it can be used in place of the ideal system that the requester would like to use. To this extent the result can be "plugged in" place of the correct match.

Relaxed match. The relaxed match has a weakest semantic interpretation. It is used to indicate the degree of similarity between the advertisement and the request.

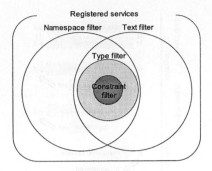

Fig. 2. Four filters

The second aspect of our matchmaker is to provide a series of four filters (Fig. 2), which are independent from each other, and narrow the set of registered services with respect to a given criterion. User may select any combination of these filters at the search time, considering the trade-off between accuracy and speed of the search. We briefly illustrate each filter as follows. Further details are provided in Sycara et al.[9]. The degree of the match are calculated as the sum of scores at the passed filters.

1. Namespace Filter

Pre-checking process which determines whether or not the requested service and the registered ones have at least one shared namespace (a url of an ontology file). The intersection of namespaces can be considered shared knowledge between the request and the advertisement. Therefore, only the registered services which have at least one shared namespace go into the next filter. Namespaces of default like rdf, rdfs, xsd, etc. are not considered the intersection. Of course, there is a case that the relation between two nodes of different ontology files does exist, although the distance would be relatively long. This filter and the next filter are meant for the reduction of the computation time of the last two filters.

2. Text Filter

Pre-checking process for human-readable service explanation parts such as comment and text descriptions. It utilizes the well-known information retrieval (IR) technique called Term Frequency Inverse Document Frequency (TF/IDF) method. This filter help to minimize the risk to miss the services which have any relation to the requested one.

3. I/O Type Filter

Type Filter checks to see if the ontologies of the input and output match. A set of subtype inferencing rules mainly based on structural algorithm are used to determine in this filter. Such a match is determined if: (Fig. 3)

- the types and number of input/output parameters exactly matches, OR
- outputs of the registered service can be subsumed by outputs of the requested service, and the number of outputs of the registered service is greater than the number of outputs of the requested service, AND/OR

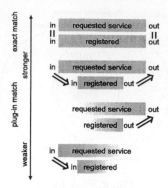

Fig. 3. Levels of plug-in match

- inputs of the requested service can be subsumed by inputs of the registered service, and the number of inputs of the requested service is greater than the number of inputs of the registered service.

If there is a mismatch in the number of parameters, then the filter attempts to pair up parameters in the registered one with those in the request, by seeking the registered one's parameters that are sub-types of the requested one's parameters.

Further, the request may not have a model of what inputs may be required, and may need to obtain this information from the returned service. To support this, inputs and inputs' constraints in the next section also match when those of the request are empty.

4. Constraint Filter

The responsibility of this filter is to verify whether the subsumption relationship for each of the constraints are logically valid. The constraints filter compares the constraints to determine if the registered service is less constrained than the request. The Matchmaker computes the logical implication among constraints by using polynomial θ-subsumption checking for Horn clauses. Matching is achieved by performing conjunctive pair-wise comparisons for the constraints.

The constraints for inputs and outputs are defined for the request (R_I and R_O) and for each registered service (A_I and A_O). The constraints for inputs R_I is compared with A_I, and a match is determined if A_I subsumes R_I, i.e.

$$match(R_I, A_I) \Leftarrow (\forall j, \exists i : (i \in R_I) \wedge (j \in A_I) \wedge subs(j, i)) \vee R_I = \emptyset$$

where $subs(j, i)$ is true when j subsumes i. The constraints for outputs match when all the elements in R_O subsumes elements in A_O, i.e.

$$match(R_O, A_O) \Leftarrow \forall i, \exists j : (i \in R_O) \wedge (j \in A_O) \wedge subs(i, j)$$

3   Matchmaker Deployed with UDDI

At the design phase of this development, we have collected VOCs (Voice Of the Customer) from system integrators and user companies of web services. The

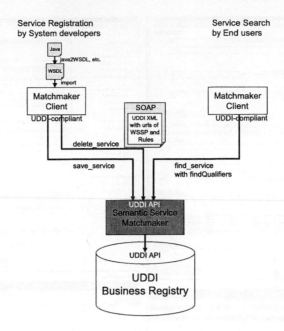

Fig. 4. UDDI and Matchmaker

first request from both of the integrators and the users was the reduction of the cost of development and administration. Then, the second requirement was interoperability with the current systems running or selling in their companies. The third ones were a track record and security in general. As a consequence, we have decided to obey the standards as much as possible. This means not only the improvement of the interoperability, but also the reduction of the cost because it will give users and developers freedom of choice at the selection of the private UDDI registry product and the client tools. Besides, we hope this public deployment contributes to the track record.

The architecture of the Matchmaker with UDDI is shown in Fig. 4. It strives to be compliant with the current standards of web services such as SOAP and WSDL. Also, the Matchmaker API is equivalent to UDDI API to facilitate the users seamless connection. Furthermore, the format of the results returned adopts the same format of the results returned by UDDI. So that we hope the Matchmaker can be added as a part of the common e-Business platform.

4   Supporting Tools

The above VOCs also showed the most important thing in a service search engine was ease of use and search speed. Although using the semantics surely has higher value on the service capability matching than the keyword search, it needs much expense in time and effort. Therefore, we introduce our client tools, which support to lower the threshold of use of semantics.

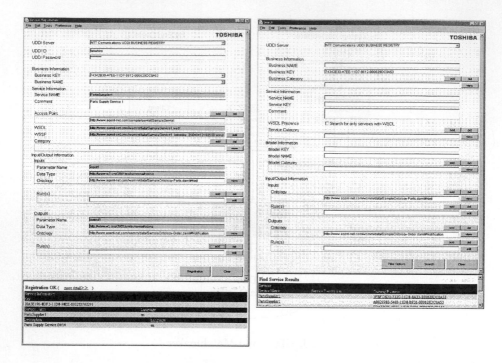

Fig. 5. Matchmaker Client

4.1   Registration of Business Service

Registration of *Business Service* (UDDI terminology) are shown in the left side of
Fig. 5 (field names are corresponding to UDDI Data Structure). Firstly, the user
can import a WSDL file, which may have been generated automatically from
Java source code to *Matchmaker Client*. The Client will automatically complete
some of the fields (gray ones in the figure) from the information in the WSDL.

Then, the user can annotate the input and output with the ontology using *Ontology Viewer*(Fig. 6), which parses ontology files written by RDFS,
DAML+OIL, or OWL, then show them as graphical trees. The only necessary
to annotate each parameter is to click a node in the trees. Also, the user can
add constraints on each parameter using *Rule Editor* described later.

Next, the user can register the service to the Matchmaker and the UDDI as a
consequence. The semantic service description, WSSP is automatically generated
by the Client, and uploaded to the Matchmaker. Upon receiving the registration,
the Matchmaker extracts the semantic annotation, and stores it after loading all
the ontologies it refers to. Then, the Matchmaker registers the service to the
UDDI.

The user may decide not to annotate any parameter with the ontology or
constraints. If this is the case, the Client registers the service just to the UDDI.
Note that the Matchmaker has the same API as the UDDI, so the Client can be
used as a UDDI client for any UDDI registry.

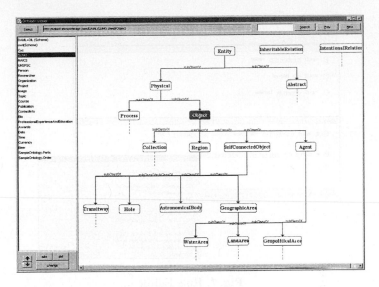

Fig. 6. Ontology Viewer

4.2 Search of Business Service

Search of *Business Service* are shown in the right side of Fig. 5. In addition
to the ordinary UDDI search conditions like keywords for service names, the
Client allow to specify the capability of the desired service, such as the number
of inputs and outputs, the meaning of each parameter, that is, the ontology,
and the constraints if necessary. Then, the Client sends a search request to the
Matchmaker.

Upon receiving the request, the Matchmaker searches for services that is
similar enough to the requested from the registered services. After making the
matching results, the Matchmaker retrieves the detailed information of those
results from the UDDI, and return them to the Client.

The user may also decide to restrict his search to the UDDI keyword search.
If so, the Client searches just in the UDDI.

4.3 Rule Editor

Writing rules precisely is a difficult and wordy task even for logic experts. To
address this problem, we developed Rule Editor (Fig. 7) which allows anyone
to easily write facts and rules, as if they were writing natural sentences. The
user can just select any predicate for fact or rule as constraint on a parameter.
The parameter corresponds to variable in the fact or rule. After creating the
constraints, they appear in "Rule" field the Client, and RDF-RuleML files will
be automatically generated.

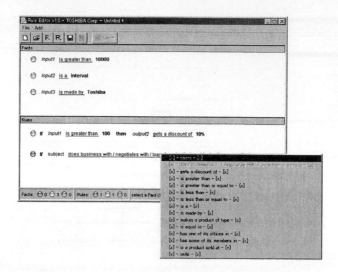

Fig. 7. Rule Editor

5   Evaluation

We have publicly deployed our Matchmaker to the official NTT UDDI registry for half a year since September 2003. In this section, we evaluate the Matchmaker in terms of performance with UDDI and functionality with other matchmakers.

5.1   Performance Comparison

In order to compare the performance of UDDI with UDDI with the Matchmaker, firstly we made a number of datasets and measure the average search time of each filter for a query, which always returns 10% of each dataset as matched. The dataset has a certain number of registered services, each of which has 3 input parameters and 2 outputs parameters, and each parameter has 1 constraint rule. Further, we used one of the largest ontology Cyc[10], and randomly put a node in the Cyc to each input and output parameter. The result is shown in Fig. 8

Although some items are difficult to see in the figure, all the search time are almost linearly increasing along with the size of the dataset even in UDDI. However, the rate of increase for Type and Constraint filter is relatively higher than UDDI. This was caused by the fact that UDDI is running at the very high-performance server machine, although the Matchmaker is sitting at just a common PC server with RedHat 7.3 on Intel Xeon 2.7GHz, and the keyword search costs much lower than our logical computation. But we can say at least that our Matchmaker succeeded to avoid the exponential increase of the logical computation time.

Secondarily, we constructed a search model for the users and measured the total search time for a query. In this model four filters are sequentially connected,

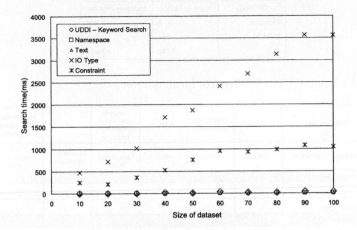

Fig. 8. Search time at each filter

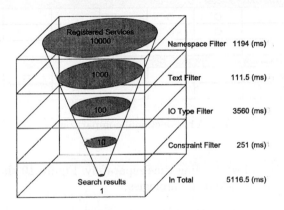

Fig. 9. A search model

and every filter outputs 10% of the services inputted from the previous one. Figure 9 illustrates this model, and the search time for each and in total.

UDDI currently stores at most 10,000 services in its database, so that it's enough realistic to have 10,000 services as the initial dataset. Further, we annotated each input and output parameter by the Cyc. We believe this setting is one of the largest cases in scale which can be taken at the present. Therefore, the search time, 5 seconds in total proves that our Matchmaker can be deployed in the practical business use.

We also note that the above search does not include the loading time of any new ontology, because as a way of performance improvement all the ontology that the Matchmaker encounters at the service registration will be immediately loaded and parsed in a fast-accessible internal form. Thus we assumed that in most cases the ontologies are already loaded before the service search. Therefore,

Ontology	Num. of Nodes	Loading time (s)
WordNet	6	0.690
SUMO	631	4.246
Cyc	1740	49.461

Fig. 10. Loading time

System Name	UDDI	Web Serivce Matchmaker	InfoSleuth	Semantic Web based matchmaking prototype	n/a	WebSphere Matchmaking Environment
Developer / Organizaion	OASIS	Toshiba	MCC	HP Laboratories Bristol	University of Manchester	IBM Zurich Research Laboratory
Syntactical matching						
Keyword Search	O					O
IR / Text mining		O				O
Semantic matching						
Ontological Subsumption		O	O	O	◎	
Constraints / Rules		O	◎	O	O	O
Compliance with Web Services Standards						
UDDI	O	O				
SOAP	O	O				O
WSDL	O	O				O
Compliance with Semantic Web						
DAML+OIL / OWL		O		O	O	
DAML-S / OWL-S				O	O	

Fig. 11. Functional comparison

we measured the ontology loading time separately. Figure 10 shows the loading time for some of the well-known ontologies.

5.2 Functional Comparison

We picked up the following matchmakers from academic and industrial activities, and summarised the comparison in Fig. 11 and the following list, in which criteria were syntactical matching like keyword search, semantic matching like ontology, and compliance with the standards for web services and semantic web.

- UDDI, OASIS
  - A standard of Web Services registry, linked to WSDL and SOAP.
  - Search functionality is limited to the keyword search.
- InfoSleuth, MCC[11]
  - Based on constraint-based reasoning, a broker of information gathering agents.
  - The original service capability and constraint description, LDL++.
  - No explicit relationship to Web Services standards.
- Semantic Web based matchmaking prototype, HP Lab.[12]

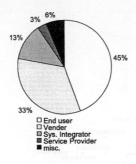

Fig. 12. Target users

- Based on ontological subsumption and rules similar to ours.
- The original service description and rule language.
- No integration to UDDI.
- WebSphere Matchmaking Environment, IBM Zurich Research Lab.[13]
  - A add-on for IBM Web application server WebSphere.
  - Search conditions can be written in a script, which is sent to the matchmaker.
  - Semantics seems to be not considered.
- Ian Horrocks et al., University of Manchester[14]
  - Based on highly functional DL (Description Logics) reasoner Racer with DAML-S.
  - Semantic matchmaker without any IR techniques like TF/IDF and prefiltering for the reduction of computation time.
  - No compliance to Web Service standards.

6   Discussion

This section shows user requirements for the Matchmaker explicitly obtained by questionnaires at the download of the Matchmaker Client, and implicitly recognised by our observation of users' search behaviour.

6.1   Explicit Requirements

The targets of this questionnaire are users who intentionally accessed our Matchmaker web page (www.agent-net.com) and downloaded the Client. That is, the targets are people keeping their eyes on the trend of web services. Figure 12 shows the breakdown of the targets, which are selected as valid votes. We got future improvements by adapting DFACE (Define–Focus–Analyze–Create–Evaluate) methodology, which is a version of "Design for Six Sigma"[15] developed by Stanford University, to user requirements described in the questionnaire. Figure 13 shows Cost–Worth analysis for the conceivable improvements, in which

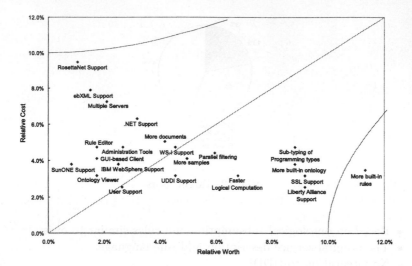

Fig. 13. Cost-Worth analysis

you will see for example, compliance to web services standards is so much important, and automatic service invocation should be discussed after the service search. We couldn't describe the process to get this analysis in detail due to the page limitation, but basically it was calculated by proportional distribution from user requirements considering CSM (Customer Satisfaction Measurement) and workload.

6.2   Implicit Requirements

The following lists are part of users' indirect suggestions gotten from the log files which record every action in the Matchmaker.

– IO Type filter: we found that some amount of users specify the ontology only to an output. This means that search conditions for the human users are somewhat vague, and they are willing to manually choose the most desirable one from the results. This behaviour inevitably reduces the accuracy of logical matching due to the lack of semantic information for the request. Therefore, matchmakers relying only on the ontology and rules would need to incorporate other aspects like conventional IR techniques to be practically deployable. However, for automatic service search and composition by machines in future ambiguous requests are not allowed, so logical matching has more importance.

– IO Type filter: some users tend to give just a keyword as the ontology. It seems that they are thinking the ontology can be automatically specified from an arbitrary word such that a specific category is determined by any keyword in Yahoo!. Therefore, pre-process to reason about a specific ontology node from a keyword would be useful for them.

- Constraint filter: it seems that the most familiar predicates for the users are numerical ones like equals, greaterThan, lessThan, etc. This is because the meanings and effects of those rules are easily imaginable for the users. On the other hand, putting facts and rules with generic predicate seems to be difficult enough for the users. This means that our Rule Editor which now automatically generates the rules from the user's simple selection of predicates need to be improved to make the user understand what happens when you choose it. The same things would be said to precondition and effect in future.
- Text filter: most of registered services do not have a certain length of comments. Therefore, adopting IR techniques only to comment parts has some limitation. So we are trying to take other parts of service description like parameter names and related web pages of the service provider referring to syntactic approaches of service search like Wang et al.[16].
- Namespace filter: since this filter is the first one, it compares a request to all the registered services. To reduce the burden of this filter, and to increase the accuracy even in the above-mentioned case that the user specifies the ontology only to an output, we are planning to take Category field for Business and Services in UDDI Data Structure specified by NAICS, UNSPSC, etc. into account before this filter. In case that the number of results is less than the user wants, the services in other categories can be checked by the filters. This also means more tightly integration to UDDI.
- In general: as you see Link Popularity has one of the biggest roles in Google, we will have to consider the heuristics even for the logical service matching. We are now examining some of the ideas on the analogy of web search engines. We hope to show their effectiveness and efficiency in near future.

7   Conclusion

In this paper, we evaluated the deployment of the semantic service matchmaker to the UDDI in public, and discussed scalability in performance, feasibility in functionality, and future works from users' explicit and implicit requirements. According to the future works, we will make improvement on the Matchmaker and client tools, and keep our deployment to get further feedbacks near future.

References

1. Universal Description, Discovery and Integration, http://www.uddi.org/.
2. M. Paolucci, T. Kawamura, T. R. Payne, K. Sycara, "Semantic Matching of Web Services Capabilities", Proceedings of First International Semantic Web Conference (ISWC 2002), IEEE, pp. 333-347, 2002.
3. T. Kawamura, J. D. Blasio, T. Hasegawa, M. Paolucci, K. Sycara, "Preliminary Report of Public Experiment of Semantic Service Matchmaker with UDDI Business Registry", Proceedings of First International Conference on Service Oriented Computing (ICSOC 2003), pp. 208-224, 2003.

4. Resource Description Framework, http://www.w3.org/RDF/.
5. DAML Language, http://www.daml.org/language/.
6. Web-Ontology Working Group, http://www.w3.org/2001/sw/WebOnt/.
7. The Rule Markup Initiative, http://www.dfki.uni-kl.de/ruleml/.
8. DAML Services, http://www.daml.org/services/.
9. K. Sycara, S. Widoff, M. Klusch, J. Lu, "LARKS: Dynamic Matchmaking Among Heterogeneous Software Agents in Cyberspace". In Autonomous Agents and Multi-Agent Systems, Vol.5, pp.173-203, 2002.
10. Cyc, http://www.cyc.com/2002/04/08/cyc.daml.
11. M. H. Nodine, J. Fowler, T. Ksiezyk, B. Perry, M. Taylor, and A. Unruh, "Active information gathering in infosleuth", International Journal of Cooperative Information Systems, pp. 3-28, 2000.
12. J. G. Castillo, D. Trastour, and C. Bartolini, "Description Logics for Matchmaking of Services", Proceedings of Workshop on Application of Description Logics, 2001.
13. WebSphere Matchmaking Environment, http://www.zurich.ibm.com/wme/.
14. L. Li, I. Horrocks, "A software framework for matchmaking based on semantic web technology", Proceedings of the Twelfth International World Wide Web Conference (WWW 2003), pp. 331-339, 2003.
15. Six Sigma Academy, http://www.6-sigma.com/.
16. Y. Wang, E. Stroulia, "Semantic Structure Matching for Assessing Web-Service Similarity", Proceedings of First International Conference on Service Oriented Computing (ICSOC 2003), pp. 194-207, 2003.

SemanticOrganizer: A Customizable Semantic Repository for Distributed NASA Project Teams

Richard M. Keller[1], Daniel C. Berrios[2], Robert E. Carvalho[1], David R. Hall[3],
Stephen J. Rich[4], Ian B. Sturken[3], Keith J. Swanson[1], and Shawn R. Wolfe[1]

[1] Computational Sciences Division, NASA Ames Research Center, Moffett Field, CA
{rkeller, rcarvalho, kswanson, swolfe}@arc.nasa.gov
[2] University of California, Santa Cruz, NASA Ames Research Center, Moffett Field, CA
dberrios@arc.nasa.gov
[3] QSS Group, Inc. NASA Ames Research Center, Moffett Field, CA
{dhall, isturken}@arc.nasa.gov
[4] SAIC, NASA Ames Research Center, Moffett Field, CA
srich@arc.nasa.gov

Abstract. SemanticOrganizer is a collaborative knowledge management system designed to support distributed NASA projects, including multidisciplinary teams of scientists, engineers, and accident investigators. The system provides a customizable, semantically structured information repository that stores work products relevant to multiple projects of differing types. SemanticOrganizer is one of the earliest and largest semantic web applications deployed at NASA to date, and has been used in varying contexts ranging from the investigation of Space Shuttle Columbia's accident to the search for life on other planets. Although the underlying repository employs a single unified ontology, access control and ontology customization mechanisms make the repository contents appear different for each project team. This paper describes SemanticOrganizer, its customization facilities, and a sampling of its applications. The paper also summarizes some key lessons learned from building and fielding a successful semantic web application across a wide-ranging set of domains with disparate users.

1 Introduction

Over the past five years, the semantic web community has been busily designing languages, developing theories, and defining standards in the spirit of the vision set forth by Berners-Lee [1]. There is no lack of publications documenting progress in this new area of research. However, practical semantic web applications in routine daily use are still uncommon. We have developed and deployed a semantic web application at NASA with over 500 users accessing a web of 45,000 information nodes connected by over 150,000 links. The SemanticOrganizer system [2] has been used in diverse contexts within NASA ranging from support for the Shuttle Columbia accident investigation to the search for life on other planets; from the execution of Mars mission simulations to the analysis of aviation safety and study of malarial disease in Kenya. This paper describes our system and some of the practical challenges of building and fielding a successful semantic web application across a

S.A. McIlraith et al. (Eds.): ISWC 2004, LNCS 3298, pp. 767–781, 2004.

wide-ranging set of domains. One of the key lessons we learned in building a successful application for NASA is to understand the limits of shared ontologies and the importance of tuning terminology and semantics for specific groups of users performing specific tasks. We describe the methods, compromises, and workarounds we developed to enable maximal sharing of our ontology structure across diverse teams of users.

SemanticOrganizer is a collaborative knowledge management application designed to support distributed project teams of NASA scientists and engineers. Knowledge management systems can play an important role by enabling project teams to communicate and share information more effectively. Toward this goal, SemanticOrganizer provides a semantically-structured information repository that serves as a common access point for all work products related to an ongoing project. With a web interface, users can upload repository documents, data, images, and other relevant information stored in a wide variety of file formats (image, video, audio, document, spreadsheet, project management, binary, etc.). The repository stores not only files, but also metadata describing domain concepts that provide context for the work products. Hardware or software systems that generate these project data products can access the repository via an XML-based API.

Although there are many document management tools on the market to support basic information-sharing needs, NASA science and engineering teams have some specialized requirements that justify more specialized solutions. Examples of such teams include scientific research teams, accident investigation teams, space exploration teams, engineering design teams, and safety investigation teams, among others. Some of their distinctive requirements include:

- *sharing of heterogeneous technical information*: teams must exchange various types of specialized scientific and technical information in differing formats;
- *detailed descriptive metadata*: teams must use a precise technical terminology to document aspects of information provenance, quality, and collection methodology;
- *multi-dimensional correlation and dependency tracking*: teams need to interrelate and explore technical information along a variety of axes simultaneously and to make connections to new information rapidly;
- *evidential reasoning*: teams must be able to store hypotheses along with supporting and refuting facts, and methodically analyze causal relationships;
- *experimentation*: teams must test hypotheses by collecting systematic measurements generated by specialized scientific instruments and sensors;
- *security and access control*: information being collected and analyzed may be highly proprietary, competitively sensitive, and/or legally restricted; and
- *historical record:* project teams must document their work process and products – including both successes and failures – for subsequent scrutiny (e.g., to allow follow-on teams to validate, replicate, or extend the work; to capture lessons learned; or to satisfy legal requirements).

Aside from satisfying the above requirements, we faced several other major technical challenges in building the SemanticOrganizer repository system. One of the most difficult challenges was to make the information easily and intuitively accessible to members of different collaborating teams, because each team employs different terms, relationships, and models to mentally organize their work products. Rather than organizing information using generic indexing schemes and organizational models, we felt it was important to employ terms, concepts, and natural distinctions that make sense in users' own work contexts. A second and related challenge was to develop a single application that could be rapidly customized to meet the needs of many different types of teams simultaneously. Many of the candidate user teams consisted of just two or three people, so they could not afford the overhead of running their own server installation or handling system administration. Thus, the system had to be centrally deployed while still being customized for each teams' distinctive work context. A third key challenge involved knowledge acquisition and the automatic ingestion of information. With the large volume of information generated during NASA science and engineering projects and the complexity of the semantic interrelationships among information, users cannot be expected to maintain the repository without some machine assistance. A final challenge is providing rapid, precise access to repository information despite the large volume.

We found that a semantic web framework provided a sound basis for our system. Storing information in a networked node and link structure, rather than a conventional hierarchical structure, addressed the need to connect information along multiple dimensions to facilitate rapid access. Using formal ontologies provided a customizable vocabulary and a structured mechanism for defining heterogeneous types of information along with their associated metadata and permissible relationships to other information. We employed an inference system to assist with acquiring and maintaining repository knowledge automatically. However, we also found it necessary to add a host of practical capabilities on top of the basic semantic web framework: access control mechanisms, authentication and security, ontology renaming and aliasing schemes, effective interfaces for accessing semantically-structured information, and APIs to enable ingestion of agent-delivered information.

The balance of the paper is organized as follows. Section 2 describes the basic SemanticOrganizer system in more detail. Section 3 describes the mechanisms we have developed to differentially customize the system for multiple groups of simultaneous users. Section 4 highlights some NASA applications developed using SemanticOrganizer and describes extra functionality implemented to support these applications. Section 5 summarizes lessons learned from our experience building a practical semantic web application. Section 6 discusses related work, and Section 7 presents future directions.

2   The SemanticOrganizer System

SemanticOrganizer consists of a network-structured semantic hypermedia repository [3] of typed *information items*. Each repository item represents something relevant to a project team (e.g., a specific person, place, hypothesis, document, physical sample, subsystem, meeting, event, etc.). An item includes a set of descriptive metadata properties and optionally, an attached file containing an image, dataset, document, or other relevant electronic product. The items are extensively cross-linked via semantically labeled relations to permit easy access to interrelated pieces of information. For example, Figure 1 illustrates a small portion of a semantic repository that was developed for a NASA accident investigation team. The item in the center of the diagram represents a faulty rotor assembly system that caused an accident in a wind tunnel test. The links between items indicate that the rotor assembly was operated by a person, John Smith, who is being investigated as part of the CRW

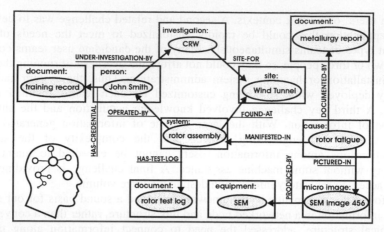

Fig. 1. Portion of semantic repository network for CRW accident investigation

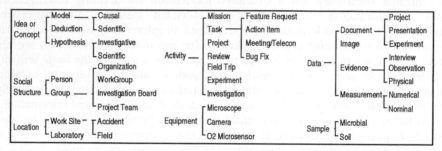

Fig. 2. Representative classes from SemanticOrganizer's master ontology. The entire ontology has over 350 classes and reaches a maximum depth of six.

investigation. Rotor fatigue is hypothesized as a possible accident cause, manifesting itself in the failed rotor assembly. The fatigue is documented by evidence consisting of a metallurgy report and a scanning electron microscope (SEM) image. These types of items and relationships are natural for this domain, whereas others would be required to support a different application area.

A master ontology (Figure 2) describes all the different types (i.e., classes) of items for SemanticOrganizer applications, and defines properties of those items, as well as links that can be used to express relationships between the items. A link (i.e., a relation) is defined by specifying its name and its domain and range classes, along with the name of its reverse link. (All links are bidirectional.) Property and link inheritance is supported. We began development of SemanticOrganizer in 1999, prior to the standardization of semantic web languages; as a result, the system was built using a custom-developed language. This language has the representational power of RDFS [4], except that it does not permit the subclassing of relationships.

SemanticOrganizer was built using Java and its ontology and associated instances are stored in a MySQL database. The system includes an inference component that is built on top of Jess [5]. Explicit rules can be defined that create or modify items/links in the repository or establish item property values. The rules can chain together to perform inference, utilizing subsumption relationships defined in the ontology.

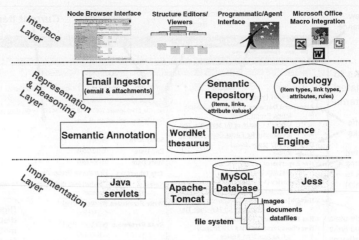

Fig. 3. SemanticOrganizer's architectural components

SemanticOrganizer includes an email distribution and archiving facility that allows teams to create ad-hoc email lists. Email sent to a SemanticOrganizer distribution list is forwarded to recipients and archived as an email message item within the team's repository. Attachments are preserved along with the message body, and instances representing the sender and recipients are automatically linked to the message. A more experimental system component under development is the Semantic Annotator, which parses text documents, such as email messages, and links them to relevant items in the repository. The Semantic Annotator employs WordNet [6], as well as other sources of information, to select relevant items for linking.

SemanticOrganizer's various components are depicted in Figure 3. For conceptual clarity, in the diagram we distinguish between the ontology, which stores the class and link types, and the semantic repository, which stores the interlinked item instances. In practice, these components are implemented using a single representational mechanism that stores both classes and instances. Although the repository is stored on a single server, access control and ontology customization mechanisms make the repository format and content appear different for each group of users. In essence, SemanticOrganizer is a set of *virtual repositories*, each built upon the same representational framework and storage mechanisms, yet each custom-designed to suit the needs of its specific users. This is described further in Section 3.

SemanticOrganizer users create and interlink items using a servlet-driven Web interface that enables them to navigate through the semantic network repository, upload and view files, enter metadata, and search for specific items (see Figure 4). The interface restricts the types of links that users can create between items based on their item types and the domain/range specifications defined in the ontology. The core interface uses only HTML and basic JavaScript to maximize compatibility with standard browsers. Aside from the HTML-based Web interface, the system also includes some specialized applets for visualizing and editing specific interlinked structures of items. (A more general graphical network visualization component is currently under development.) SemanticOrganizer features an XML-based API that enables external agents to access the repository and manipulate its contents. In addition, we have developed a set of Visual Basic macros that provide an interface

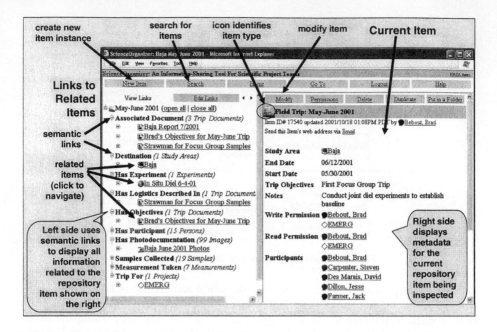

Fig. 4. SemanticOrganizer's Web interface displaying a scientific 'field trip' item at right. Note individual and group permissions for the item. Links to related items are displayed at left.

between Microsoft® Office documents and SemanticOrganizer using the Office application's menu bar.

Security and authentication are handled by HTTPS encryption and individual user logins. No access is permitted to users without an assigned login as part of one or more established project teams. Once inside the repository, user access to items is controlled by a permission management system. This system limits users' access to a defined subnet within the overall information space that contains information relevant to their team. As part of this access control system, each instance in the repository has a set of read and write permissions recording the individual users or groups (i.e., sets of users) that can view and modify the instance.

A set of successively more sophisticated search techniques is available to SemanticOrganizer users. A basic search allows users to locate items by entering a text string and searching for matching items. The user can specify where the match must occur: in an item name, in a property value for an item, or in the text of a document attached to an item. In addition, the user can limit the search to one or more item types. An intermediate search option allows the user to specify property value matching requirements involving a conjunction of constraints on numeric fields, enumerated fields, and text fields. Finally, a sophisticated semantic search is available to match patterns of multiply interlinked items with property value constraints [7].

3 Application Customization Mechanisms

SemanticOrganizer is specifically designed to support multiple deployments across different types of distributed project teams. Knowledge modelers work with each new group of users to understand their unique requirements. The modelers add or reuse ontology classes to form a custom application suitable for the team. To encourage reuse of class, property, and link definitions, the system contains a single unified ontology that addresses the needs of users involved in more than 25 different project teams. Each of these teams uses only a subset of the classes defined in the ontology. Ontology classes are assigned to users through a process illustrated in Figure 5.

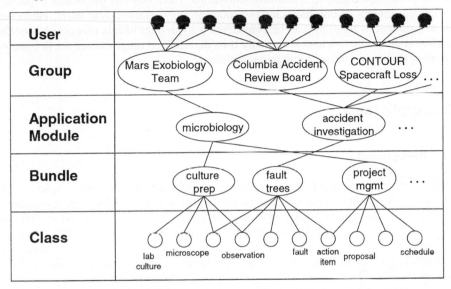

Fig. 5. Mapping ontology classes to users via bundles, application modules, and groups

At the lowest levels, classes are grouped into *bundles*, where each bundle defines a set of classes relevant to a specific task function. For example, all of the classes relevant to growing microbial cultures (e.g., physical samples, microscopes, lab cultures, culturing media) might constitute one bundle; all classes relevant to project management (e.g., project plans, project documents, funding sources, proposals, meetings) might be another bundle. Aside from grouping related classes, bundles provide a mechanism for aliasing classes to control their interface presentation to users. For example, the ontology includes a class called 'field site'. A field site is simply a location away from the normal place of business where investigation activities are conducted. Although there may be a general consensus about this definition across different application teams, the terminology used to describe the concept may differ. For example, whereas geologists may be perfectly comfortable with the term 'field site', accident investigators may prefer the term 'accident site'. Although this distinction may seem trivial, employing appropriate terminology is essential to user acceptance. The bundling mechanism allows domain modelers to alias classes with a new name. (Note that renaming of properties is not supported, at present, but would also prove useful.)

At the next level up in Figure 5, sets of bundles are grouped together as *application modules*. These modules contain all the bundles that correspond to relevant tasks for a given application. For example, there might be a microbiology investigation team growing microbial cultures as part of a scientific research project. In this case, the application builder would simply define a module that includes the microbial culture bundle and the project management bundle. At the top levels of Figure 5, modules are assigned to groups of users, and finally through these groups, individual users gain access to the appropriate classes for their application. A user can be assigned more than one module if he or she is involved in more than one group. For example, a microbiologist involved in the Mars Exobiology team may also be on the Columbia Accident Review Board as a scientific consultant. Note that this discussion explicitly covers assignment of ontology classes – not ontology relations – to users. However, the assignment of relations can be considered a byproduct of this process. A specific relation is available to a user if and only if its domain and range classes are in bundles assigned to the user via an application module.

4   Applications

4.1   Background

With over 500 registered users and over a half-million RDF-style triples in its repository, SemanticOrganizer is one of the largest semantic technology applications that has been fielded at NASA to date. The system was first deployed in 2001 to support a small group of collaborating research scientists. As of April 2004, over 25 different collaborating groups – ranging in size from 2 people to over 100 – have used SemanticOrganizer in conjunction with their projects. System users are drawn from more than 50 different organizations throughout NASA, industry, and academia. The overall ontology contains over 350 classes and over 1000 relationships. Over 14,000 files have been uploaded into the system and more than 12,000 email messages have been distributed and archived.

SemanticOrganizer has found application within two primary user communities: the NASA scientific community (where the system is known as *ScienceOrganizer*), and the NASA safety and accident investigation community (where the system is known as *InvestigationOrganizer* or *IO*). In the following sections, we describe prototypical applications within these distinct SemanticOrganizer user communities.

4.2   ScienceOrganizer

ScienceOrganizer was originally developed to address the information management needs of distributed NASA science teams. These teams need to organize and maintain a body of information accumulated through scientific fieldwork, laboratory experimentation, and data analysis. The types of information stored by scientific teams are diverse, and include scientific measurements, publication manuscripts, datasets, field site descriptions and photos, field sample records, electron microscope images, genetic sequences, equipment rosters, research proposals, etc. Various relationships among these types of information are represented within ScienceOrganizer, and they are used to link the information together within the repository. For example, a field sample can be: *collected-at* a field site; *collected-by* a person; *analyzed-by* an instrument; *imaged-under* a microscope; etc. We have selected two ScienceOrganizer applications to highlight in this section: EMERG and Mobile Agents.

The Early Microbial Ecosystems Research Group (EMERG) was an early adopter of ScienceOrganizer, and provided many of the requirements that drove its development. EMERG is an interdisciplinary team of over 35 biologists, chemists, and geologists, including both U.S. and international participants across eight institutions. Their goal is to understand extreme environments that sustain life on earth and help characterize environments suitable to life beyond the planet. EMERG focuses on understanding the evolution of microbial communities functioning in algae mats located in high salinity or thermally extreme environments. As part of their research, they conduct field trips and collect mat samples in various remote locations, perform field analysis of the samples, and ship the results back to laboratories at their home institutions. There, they perform experiments on the samples, grow cultures of the organisms in the mats, analyze data, and publish the results.

ScienceOrganizer was used across EMERG to store and interlink information products created at each stage of their research. This enabled the distributed team to work together and share information remotely. As a side benefit, the repository served as an organizational memory [8], retaining a record of previous work that could be useful when planning subsequent scientific activities. As part of the collaboration with EMERG, we developed a capability within ScienceOrganizer that allows scientists to set up and initiate automated laboratory experiments on microbial mat samples. The scientist defines an experiment within ScienceOrganizer by specifying its starting time and providing details of the experimental parameters to be used. A software agent is responsible for controlling internet-accessible laboratory hardware and initiating the experiment at the specified time. When the experiment is complete, the agent deposits experimental results back within ScienceOrganizer so they can be viewed by the scientist. This capability allows remote users to initiate experiments and view results from any location using ScienceOrganizer.

The second project, Mobile Agents [9], is a space mission simulation that uses mobile software agents to develop an understanding of how humans and robots will collaborate to accomplish tasks on the surface of other planets or moons. As part of the mission simulation, humans (acting as astronauts) and robots are deployed to a remote desert location, where they conduct a mock surface mission. In this context, ScienceOrganizer is used as a repository for information products generated during the mission, including photos, measurements, and voice notes, which are uploaded by autonomous software agents using the system's XML-based API. ScienceOrganizer also serves as a two-way communication medium between the mission team and a second team that simulates a set of earth-bound scientists. The science team views the contents of ScienceOrganizer to analyze the field data uploaded by the mission team. In response, the science team can suggest activities to the mission team by uploading recommended plans into ScienceOrganizer for execution by the mission team.

4.3   InvestigationOrganizer

When an accident involving NASA personnel or equipment occurs, NASA policy requires the creation of an accident investigation board to determine the cause(s) of the mishap and formulate recommendations to prevent future accidents. Information management, correlation, and analysis are integral activities performed by an accident investigation board. Their primary tasks include the following: collecting and managing evidence; performing different types of analyses (e.g., chemical, structural, forensic) that generate derivative evidence; connecting the evidence together to support or refute accident hypotheses; resolving accident causal factors; and making recommendations. The heterogeneous nature of the evidence in NASA accidents coupled with the complex nature of the relationships among evidence and hypotheses make the use of a system like SemanticOrganizer quite natural in this setting. NASA accident investigation teams typically are composed of engineers, scientists, and safety personnel from NASA's ten field centers geographically distributed across the country. Each team is composed of specialists with expertise pertinent to the accident. Distributed information sharing is an essential capability for accident investigation teams. Although the team may start out colocated, evidence gathering and analysis often take team members to different sites. With lengthy investigations, the logistics of centralizing personnel and information at one location are unworkable. Teams have relied on standard information-sharing technology in past investigations: email, phone, fax, and mail courier. From many perspectives – security, timeliness, and persistence – these approaches are largely inadequate.

InvestigationOrganizer was developed in partnership with NASA engineers and mission assurance personnel to support the work of distributed NASA mishap investigation teams. The types of data stored by these teams include a wide variety of information: descriptions and photos of physical evidence; schematics and descriptions of the failed system; witness interviews; design and operational readiness documents; engineering telemetry; operator logs; meeting notes; training records; hypothesized contributory accident factors; supporting and refuting evidence for those factors; etc. Various relationships among these types of information are represented within InvestigationOrganizer and serve to link information (e.g., as in Figure 1). For instance, a design document can: *describe* a physical system; be *authored-by* a contractor employee; *refute* a hypothesized accident factor; be *requested-from* a contracting organization; etc.

To date, InvestigationOrganizer has been used with four NASA mishap investigations ranging in scope from minor localized investigations to major distributed investigations. The major investigations included the loss of the Space Shuttle Columbia and the loss of the CONTOUR unmanned spacecraft, which broke apart while escaping earth orbit.

Within the Columbia and CONTOUR investigations, InvestigationOrganizer was used to track information pertaining to almost every aspect of the investigation. The system also supported analysis of the data in terms of fault models and temporal event models that were built to understand the progression and causes of the accidents. Mishap investigators in these cases went beyond the system's basic capabilities to support evidence collection and correlation; they used InvestigationOrganizer to explicitly record and share investigators' reasoning processes as the investigations proceeded. For Columbia, an added benefit to recording these processes was a preservation of the chain of evidence from hypotheses and theories to findings and recommendations. This chain of evidence is currently being used in NASA's efforts to return the Space Shuttles to flight, allowing engineers to trace the reasoning behind the conclusions reached by the investigation board.

5   Lessons Learned

Our experience deploying SemanticOrganizer across numerous domains, and working with a very diverse set of users, has given us a glimpse into the promise and the perils associated with semantic repository applications. In this section we discuss some of our key lessons learned.

5.1   Network-Structured Storage Models Present Challenges to Users

Despite the ubiquity of the Web, we found that people are not initially comfortable using network structures for storing and retrieving information. Most information repositories use the familiar hierarchical structure of folders and subfolders to organize files. While network structures have advantages, the notion of connecting information using multiple, non-hierarchical relationships was very disorienting to some users. Even with training, they would either fail to comprehend the network model or reject it as overly complex and unnecessary for their needs. In response to users' desire to organize information hierarchically, we introduced nested folder structures into our repository with limited success. Folders were typed and linked to their contents via a 'contains' relation. Users could create folders of people, photos, biological samples, etc. However, this model was unfamiliar to users expecting to place a set of mixed items in a folder without constraint. Our attempt to graft hierarchical structures onto networks left much room for improvement and we continue to seek better, more intuitive methods of combining these two models.

5.2   Need for Both 'Loose' and 'Tight' Semantics

People have widely differing styles regarding the manner in which they wish to organize information. At one end of the spectrum are the meticulous organizers who strove to understand and use the full power of the semantic representations in our system. They would carefully weave the semantic network around their repository content and suggest precise revisions and extensions to the global ontology. They appreciated the increased descriptive power of a "tight" (i.e., more precise) semantics and didn't mind taking the additional time required to annotate and link the new material appropriately. At the other end of the spectrum are the casual organizers – users who simply wanted to add their document to the repository as quickly as possible. If their new material didn't align easily with the existing semantics, they became frustrated. They wanted "loose" semantics that would minimally cover their situation so they could quickly add and link their material, yet feel comfortable it was at least reasonably correct. SemanticOrganizer was designed with the meticulous organizers in mind and we had to relax our notion of what was semantically correct to accommodate the casual organizers. However, we found that in our attempt to craft compromises and simultaneously accommodate both styles of use, we sometimes failed to serve either group properly.

5.3 Principled Ontology Evolution Is Difficult to Sustain

Because we often had a half dozen projects in active development, ontology sharing and evolution became much harder than expected. Our knowledge modelers understood the importance of reuse and initially, there was sufficient momentum to evolve common ontology components to meet the changing needs of different projects. However, as workload and schedule pressures increased, it became increasingly difficult to coordinate discussions and create consensus on how to evolve the global ontology. In an effort to meet individual project needs, modelers would simply start cloning portions of the ontology and then evolve them independently. Cloning serves immediate local project needs and offers the freedom to quickly make decisions and updates without seeking global consensus. Because our tools for merging classes or morphing instances into new classes were not well developed, modelers were also reluctant to expend the effort required to recreate a more globally coherent ontology. We expect this will continue to be a difficult problem to address.

5.4 Navigating a Large Semantic Network Is Problematic

Typical projects in SemanticOrganizer contain more than 5000 informational nodes with 30,000 to 50,000 semantic interconnections. A common user complaint with SemanticOrganizer is the difficulty of orienting themselves in the information space. The standard system interface (Figure 4) presents the details of a single node along side a hyperlinked listing of its direct neighbors, organized by the semantic type of the link. This interface is convenient for editing the informational content of a node and linking it to new neighbors, but it does not help with non-local navigation. The degree of the node connectivity is bimodal with a small, but significant, percentage of the nodes being connected to many tens of nodes, while 30 to 40 percent of the nodes have 3 or fewer links. Imagine trying to explore a city having several massive central intersections where hundreds of streets meet. Most of these streets are narrow paths leading thru smaller intersections and ending in a cul-de-sac. Visual approaches that allow users to understand the overall topology of the information space and that permit a smooth transition from a local to a global perspective are critical to providing an effective means of navigating through semantic repositories [10].

5.5 Automated Knowledge Acquisition Is Critical

The original design concept for SemanticOrganizer was that teams would primarily manage their repository space manually, using the web interface to add links, enter new information, and upload artifacts such as documents or scientific measurements. But we quickly found that the task of adding information to the repository and linking to existing content is time consuming and error prone when the volume of information is large or when many people are involved. To address this need, SemanticOrganizer evolved to incorporate various forms of automated knowledge acquisition: an inference engine that uses rules to create links between items and maintain the semantic consistency of the repository; an API that allows software agents to add artifacts, modify meta-knowledge, and create links; a Microsoft® Office macro that give users the ability to upload information directly from an Office application; and an email processing system that incorporates user email directly into SemanticOrganizer. We now understand the importance of developing knowledge acquisition methods that allow users to seamlessly add new repository content as a by-product of their normal work practices, without imposing the burden of new tools or procedures.

6   Related Work

We have identified four categories of Web-based systems that share important characteristics with SemanticOrganizer: conventional Web portals, content/document management systems, semantic portals, and semantic repositories. Conventional Web portals, as exemplified by sites such as MyYahoo, typically allow users to selectively subscribe to various published content and customize its presentation. Content or document management systems (e.g., BSCW, Documentum, FileNet, Vignette, and DocuShare) are more focused on supporting daily work processes than on publishing. They allow users to upload, store, and share content (including intermediary work products). To summarize the difference, portals are intended to publish finished content, whereas document management systems manage transient and unfinished work products that are not necessarily appropriate for external or even internal publication. Neither type of system is semantically based.

Semantic portals [11-14] and semantic repositories [15] can be viewed as analogous to "regular" portals and content management systems, respectively, except that they use an underlying ontology to enhance their content with semantics. As a generalization, the primary difference between them is that semantic portals are intended to publish finalized information, whereas semantic repositories are intended to manage work products in process. SemanticOrganizer is a prime example of a semantic repository; it is intended to provide semantics-enhanced content management support across various phases of a project lifecycle. ODESeW [16] has characteristics of both a semantic repository and a semantic portal because it allows management of internal, preliminary documents, yet also supports external publishing and presentation of finalized documents.

7   Conclusions and Future Directions

Developing the SemanticOrganizer system has left us with a solid foundation of experience in developing practical semantic web applications. The application domains and users we've directly supported are extremely diverse and have ranged from a few highly specialized research scientists exploring microscopic evidence for signs of life on Mars, to high-ranking generals and executives of major aerospace companies, leading the investigation into the tragic loss of Columbia.

SemanticOrganizer represents a microcosm of the benefits and challenges that will emerge as part of the broadly distributed semantic web vision of the future.

The jury is still deliberating over the ultimate utility of semantically structured repositories. Some of our users have become enthusiastic evangelists for SemanticOrganizer and have engaged its use across multiple projects. They find the organization, access, and search capabilities provided by the system to be highly intuitive and functional. In contrast, other users consider the complex, cross-linked information space to be confusing and disorienting, and prefer familiar folder hierarchies. Some of the usability problems experienced by these users can be traced to poor interface design; others are due to the use of large and overly complex ontologies. But there are deeper concerns about whether we are taxing the limits of human cognitive and perceptual abilities to understand complex information structures. Clearly human-computer interaction considerations are extremely important in developing an effective system. NASA, in collaboration with Xerox Corporation's DocuShare Business Unit, is currently working with HCI experts to address some of these issues and develop an improved interface and user experience as part of a commercial reimplementation of InvestigationOrganizer.

Most of our system components were designed prior to recent semantic web standardization efforts, so we are currently re-architecting our system to improve interoperability with emerging technologies. For example, we now have the ability to export and import our ontology and instances in RDF and OWL. Heeding our own lessons learned, we are developing new visualization techniques to provide users with an enhanced ability to understand and navigate our repository. We are also building acquisition tools that will automatically analyze text from documents and produce semantic annotations that link documents to related items in SemanticOrganizer.

Acknowledgments. We gratefully acknowledge funding support by the NASA Intelligent Systems Project and by NASA Engineering for Complex Systems Program. This work would not have been successful without dedicated application partners in various scientific and engineering disciplines. Tina Panontin and James Williams provided invaluable guidance and direction on the application of SemanticOrganizer to accident investigation. They also took a leading role in the deployment of SemanticOrganizer for the Shuttle Columbia accident investigation, as well as other investigations. Brad Bebout provided essential long-term guidance and support for the application of SemanticOrganizer to astrobiology and life science domains. Maarten Sierhuis provided support for application to space mission simulation testbeds. Our sincere appreciation goes to our colleagues Sergey Yentus, Ling-Jen Chiang, Deepak Kulkarni, and David Nishikawa for their contributions to system development.

References

1.   T. Berners-Lee, "A Roadmap to the Semantic Web," 1998, http://www.w3.org/Design Issues/Semantic.html.
2.   R. M. Keller, "SemanticOrganizer Web Site," 2004, http://sciencedesk.arc.nasa.gov.

3.   B. R. Gaines and D. Madigan, "Special Issue on Knowledge-based Hypermedia," International Journal of Human-Computer Studies, vol. 43, pp. 281-497, 1995.
4.   D. Brickley and R. V. Guha, "RDF Vocabulary Description Language 1.0: RDF Schema," W3C, 2004, http://www.w3.org/TR/rdf-schema/.
5.   E. Friedman-Hill, "Jess: The rule engine for the Java platform," 2004, http://herzberg.ca.sandia.gov/jess/index.shtml.
6.   G. A. Miller, "WordNet: A Lexical Database for English," Communications of the ACM, vol. 38, pp. 39-41, 1995.
7.   D. C. Berrios and R. M. Keller, "Developing a Web-based User Interface for Semantic Information Retrieval," Proc. ISWC 2003 Workshop on Semantic Web Technologies for Searching and Retrieving Scientific Data, C. Goble, Ed. Sanibel Island, FL, pp. 65-70.
8.   R. Dieng-Kuntz and N. Matta, "Knowledge Management and Organizational Memories", Boston: Kluwer Academic Publishers, 2002,
9.   M. Sierhuis, W. J. Clancey, C. Seah, J. P. Trimble, and M. H. Sims, "Modeling and Simulation for Mission Operations Work Systems Design," Journal of Management Information Systems, vol. 19, pp. 85-128, 2003.
10.   V. Geroimenko and C. Chen, "Visualizing the Semantic Web: XML-based Internet and Information Visualization", London: Springer-Verlag, 2003,
11.   Y. Jin, S. Xu, S. Decker, and G. Wiederhold, "OntoWebber: a novel approach for managing data on the Web", International Conference on Data Engineering, 2002.
12.   N. Stojanovic, A. Maedche, S. Staab, R. Studer, and Y. Sure, "SEAL - a framework for developing semantic portals", Proceedings of the International Conference on Knowledge capture, pp. 155-162, 2001.
13.   P. Spyns, D. Oberle, R. Volz, J. Zheng, M. Jarrar, Y. Sure, R. Studer, and R. Meersman, "OntoWeb - a semantic Web community portal", Fourth International Conference on Practical Aspects of Knowledge Management, 2002.
14.   E. Bozsak, M. Ehrig, S. Handschuh, A. Hotho, A. Maedche, B. Motik, D. Oberle, C. Schmitz, S. Staab, L. Stojanovic, N. Stojanovic, R. Studer, G. Stumme, Y. Sure, J. Tane, R. Volz, and V. Zacharias, "KAON-towards a large scale Semantic Web," Proceedings of EC-Web, 2002.
15.   BrainEKP Software Application, Santa Monica, CA: TheBrain Technologies Corporation, 2004, http://www.thebrain.com.
16.   O. Corcho, A. Gomez-Perez, A. Lopez-Cima, V. Lopez-Garcia, and M. Suarez-Figueroa, "ODESeW. Automatic generation of knowledge portals for Intranets and Extranets," The Semantic Web - ISWC 2003, vol. LNCS 2870, pp. 802-817, 2003.

SWS for Financial Overdrawn Alerting

José Manuel López-Cobo, Silvestre Losada, Oscar Corcho, Richard Benjamins,
Marcos Niño, and Jesús Contreras

Intelligent Software Components, S.A. (iSOCO)
C/ Pedro de Valdivia, 10. 28006 Madrid, Spain
{ozelin,slosada,ocorcho,rbenjamins,
marcosn,jcontreras}@isoco.com

Abstract. In this paper, we present a Notification Agent designed and implemented using Semantic Web Services. The Notification Agent manages alerts
when critical financial situations arise discovering and selecting notification
services. This agent applies open research results on the Semantic Web Services technologies including on-the-fly composition based on a finite state machine and automatic discovery of semantic services. Financial Domain ontologies, based on IFX financial standard, have been constructed and extended for
building agent systems using OWL and OWL-S standard (as well as other approaches like DL or f-Logic). This agent is going to be offered through integrated Online Aggregation systems in commercial financial organizations.

Keywords: Semantic Web Services, Ontologies, Composition, Intelligent
Agent.

1 Introduction

The objective of the distributed system described in this paper (the Customer Notification Agent) is to provide added value to customers of financial services. This added
value consists in a fully customizable and configurable set of aggregations and estimation functionalities on account balance evolution, as well as SMS and email alerts
(among others), which will allow customers to have more efficient information about
his financial position.

This system reuses existing technology for aggregation available at our company
(iSOCO GETsee ®), and migrates it to Semantic Web Services technology. The integrated use of Semantic Web technologies and Web Services allows us to describe and
reason with pieces of code understandable for machines, discharging the sometimes
tedious task of checking the online accounts to a software system. This system is able
to engage with other commercial solutions for aggregation and to detect at run-time
and raise alerts if some conditions are detected (for example, a possible overdrawn of
a customer saving account, due to the future payment of an invoice).

We have developed different ontologies to express the needed knowledge for this
application. These ontologies are divided into three groups: general ontologies, which

S.A. McIlraith et al. (Eds.): ISWC 2004, LNCS 3298, pp. 782–796, 2004.

represent common sense knowledge reusable across domains; domain ontologies, which represent reusable knowledge in a specific domain; and application-dependent ontologies, which represent the application-dependent knowledge needed.

We have defined three high-level services for performing the task of the Customer Notification Agent. The *GETseeSWS Service* accesses the online accounts of the customer and the invoices associated with them, and calculates the balance for these accounts. The *NotificationService* notifies customers with different types of messages (discharging in 3rd party providers the execution of the actual notification) and finally, the *EstimationService* estimates, using different kinds of arithmetical functions, the expectable amount of an invoice for preventing an overdrawn situation.

One of the main innovations of our systems is the proposal of a finite state diagram to represent the composition of atomic processes into composite ones using conditions as a way to choose between different choices. Such an approach allows at run-time the discovery and invocation of services which comply with the conditions defined for the transition from one state to another. This allows describing a composite process at design-time by defining its behaviour and leaving the selection of the specific service to the execution time. This is an innovation with respect to other approaches where the selection of the specific services is done also during the design time.

The paper is organized as follows. Section 2 describes a sample scenario where the Notification Agent can be used, showing the main actors and agents involved in the overall process and the steps usually followed by them. Section 3 describes the ontologies that we have developed, either from scratch or by reusing other ontologies or vocabularies already available elsewhere. Section 4 describes the Semantic Web services created for the system, which have been implemented using OWL-S, DL and f-Logic. Section 5 describes one of the main contributions of this paper, namely the proposal for service composition using finite state diagrams. Finally, section 6 provides some conclusions of our work and future lines of research.

2 Scenario Description

Let us suppose that we are working on the scenario presented in figure 1. In this scenario we have a customer with several banking accounts where he/she has different amounts of money. This customer has also contracts with some consumer goods companies such as a telephone company, and gas and electricity providers, among others.

Everyday, the Customer Notification Agent will detect whether any of the customer accounts is going to be in an overdrawn situation. Bank accounts may have different invoices associated from different consumer good companies. If the amount of the invoice is bigger than the amount of money of the account, there could be an overdrawn situation. To help the customer, the system calculates an estimation of the amount of every invoice expected for that account before its value date and notifies the customer if the balance of the saving account is less than the expected invoice amount. The system will choose any of the notification channels available for the customer and will notify him/her about the overdraw possibility.

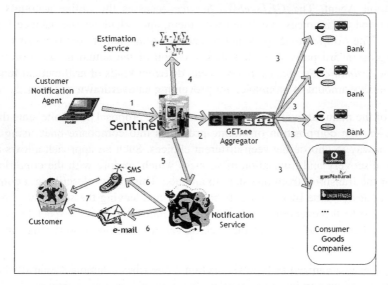

Fig. 1. Sample scenario diagram for the Notification Agent.

In this scenario, the following actors are involved: the customer, the banks, and the consumer goods companies. And the following agents are involved: customer notification agent (CNA), Sentinel and some estimation services. Finally, the iSOCO GETsee® application is at the core of this scenario, in charge of the aggregation of data from bank accounts and consumer goods companies.

The following steps will be normally done:

Step 1: Everyday, the Customer Notification Agent dynamically configures and invokes the Sentinel Service. This agent has the entire customer's information needed for invoking the composed service (online username, password and other data). The update frequency of this agent can be customized.

Step 2: The Sentinel Service uses iSOCO GETsee® for collecting information from the customer's accounts.

Step 3: iSOCO GETsee® collects the amount balance of all the customer's accounts (of banks B1, B2, …, Bn). In one (or more) of this accounts some consumer goods companies (E1, E2, …, En) can charge invoices. The invoices have their notification and value dates. The frequency of those invoices is always the same (weekly, monthly, bimonthly, annually).

Step 4: For each invoice of consumer goods companies (E1, E2, ..., En) associated with the account, the Estimation Service estimates the probable amount at the end of the period, Ae (estimated amount) in terms of heuristics or mathematical models. Ae has a relationship with a consumer good company (Ee) and an account of a bank (ABe). If the Ae is less than the established threshold for the account, then an alert has to be raised.

Step 5: The Notification Service looks in a (de)centralized registry different ways to communicate with the user. It can find different services involving many different devices (phone calls using VoIP, SMS, electronic mail, telegram) and personal data (phone number, cell phone number, e-mail, postal address). The services discovered must have the ability to perform the action defined in the Notification Service.

Step 6: The invocation engine sorts in terms of cost, time to deliver, etc., the different possibilities and chooses the first service in this particular ranking. Some data mediation could be needed if terms of the ontology used differ from the one used by the Notification Service. If the service chosen has an irrecoverable mismatching of process or data, or some communication error occurs in the invocation, the service has to be able to choose another service and invoke it.

Step 7: The service chosen is invoked and the user is notified.

In summary, the objective of the Notification Agent is to provide added value to the user including a fully customizable and configurable set of aggregations and estimation functionalities on balance evolution as well as SMS and email alerts, allowing the customer to have more efficient information about his financial position in the incoming time period.

Several estimation functionalities allow calculating balance evolution on different accounts according to expected invoices and payments. The foreseen value of account balances will allow firing alert rules defined by the user and managed by the Notification Agent application. Those alerts could let him anticipate any trouble that could occur in his accounts or avoid missing any business opportunity.

3   Ontology Structure for the CNA

In this section we describe briefly the ontologies that model the domain presented in our scenario, and which will be used by the Semantic Web services developed for it and described in section 4. These ontologies have been implemented in OWL [3] using the Protégé-2000 ontology tool [5], with the OWL-plug-in [6]. A graphical outline of the main relationships between these ontologies is presented in figure 2.

According to the classifications of Van Heijst and colleagues [1] and of Mizoguchi and colleagues [2], we can distinguish the following types of ontologies:

- *General ontologies*, which represent common sense knowledge reusable across domains. In this group we can include our ontologies about users and notifications, which include basic concepts related to persons and their contact information, and our ontology about estimation parameters, which is based on statistical concepts.

- *Domain ontologies*, which represent reusable knowledge in a specific domain. In this group we can include our ontologies about financial products and financial services.

- *Application ontologies*, which represent the application-dependent knowledge needed. In this group we can include our ontologies about saving accounts and invoice payments, and our ontology about overdrawn situations. The reason why we classify them under this group does not mean that they might not be reusable in other ontology-based applications; instead it means that we have not designed them taking into account such objective.

We will first describe the general ontologies. The ontologies about users and notifications include basic concepts related to persons (users of information systems), such as name, surname, birth date, etc, and related to their contact information , such as email addresses, postal addresses, phone and fax numbers, etc. The same message can be sent in many different types of notifications, using the same or different physical devices. For instance, if you want to communicate with someone sending him a fax and an e- mail, the receiver will have two different communications, one in the facsimile device and the other in his e-mail inbox.

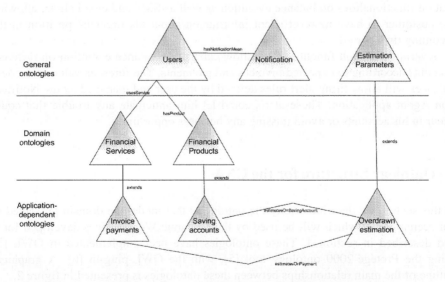

Fig. 2. Ontologies developed for the Customer Notification Agent for Financial Overdrawn.

With regard to the ontology about estimation parameter, it describes the basic arithmetical functions that can be used, among others, to estimate the amount of the spending of an invoice (or whatever other numerical concept which has an historical evolution). This ontology considers parameters related to linear estimation factors, statistical information, heuristics, etc.

Regarding the domain ontologies defined, we have two different ones, as shown in figure 2: financial services and financial products. These ontologies are based on the IFX financial standard [12], so that they will be easier to reuse by other ontology-based applications.

The ontology about financial products contains the different types of products provided by a bank (loans, investment accounts, saving accounts, investment funds, etc.). In all of them the bank and the customer sign a contract where the bank stores or lend money from or to the customer. Each financial product has their own specific attributes, and is related to the corresponding user(s) of the ontology about users. Each product can be owned by many holders and vice versa.

The ontology about financial services represents those services that banks can provide to their customers and which arc not financial products. These financial services provide added value to the relationship between a bank and their customers. They include loyalty cards, paying invoices by direct debit, Internet connection advantages, information provision about stock markets, etc.

The application-dependent ontologies describe more specific concepts and relationships related to our system. One of these ontologies is the one related to invoice payment, which represents the service that the bank offers to their customers, allowing to charge directly to a saving account of the customer the payment of many different things (taxes, shopping, subscriptions, consumer goods companies consumes like gas, water or phone). The ontology related to saving accounts includes concepts related to the types of saving accounts that can be contracted with the banks with which we are working.

Finally, the last application-dependent ontology extends the general ontology about estimation parameters, focusing on the specific case of overdrawn situations like the ones presented in the previous section.

4 Discovery of Notification Semantic Web Services

The following top-level services are available, as shown in figure 3: GETsee Service, Notification Service and Estimation Service.

Besides, the figure shows how the GETsee Service is decomposed into five atomic services (openSession, getAccounts, getInvoices, getBalance, closeSession). These five services are annotated using the same ontology as the GETsee service (although this is not mandatory in our approach). Those atomic services invoke other services, which are annotated according to other ontologies. In these cases, data mediation is needed for the exchange of messages, although this is out of the scope of this paper.

At last, the Notification Service looks for a service able to notify something to a person and finds at least two services (notification by SMS and notification by e-mail), which might be annotated according to other two more ontologies.

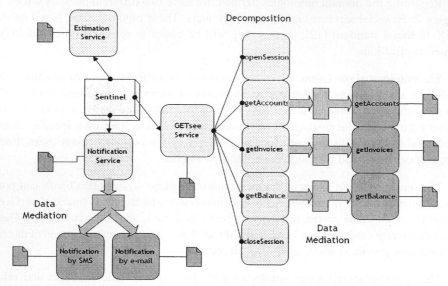

Fig. 3. A diagram of the Semantic Web services used for our notification scenario.

As commented in the previous section, the Semantic Web services used in our scenario have been annotated with OWL-S, DL and f-Logic [4, 10]. OWL-S uses the class Service as a complete description of the content and behaviour of a service. It has three differentiated parts. First of all, the Service Profile explains "what the service does". The Process Model describes "how the service works" and finally the Service Grounding maps the content and format of the messages needed to interact with the service. It provides a mapping from the semantic form of the messages exchanged as defined in the Process Model, to the syntactic form as defined in the WSDL input and output specifications.

For a further understanding about how is supposed to work the Discovery of Notification Services [17], we put the description (using DL) of two services (defined by their capabilities) and a Request from a User and depict how they will be matched.

Some domain-level facts:

```
Notification ⊑ Action
EmailNotification ⊑ Notification
⊤    ⊑  =1 from
```

Capability and a Request:
```
Cap_A ≡
EmailNotification   ⊓ ∃ from.User ⊓ ∃ to.User ⊓ ∀to.User ⊓
∃usedProvider.{Provider_A} ⊓ ∃sendingTime.Timestamp ⊓ ∃content.String ⊓
∀acknowledgement.=_F ⊓ ∃cost. =_5
```

Req ≡
ElectronicNotification ⊓ ∃ from.{User$_x$} ⊓ ∃ to.{User$_Y$} ⊓ ∃ to.{User$_z$} ⊓
=2to ⊓ ∀ usedProvider.Provider ⊓ ∃ sendTime ≤ $_{200406250900}$ ⊓ ∃ con-
tent.String ⊓ ∀ acknowledgment =$_T$ ⊓ ∀ cost ≤$_5$

With respect to the ontology schema introduced above the DL-based discovery component will match requests and capabilities using DL inferences. The basic idea of the DL-based discovery matching is to check whether the conjunction of a request and a capability is satisfiable, i.e. there can at least be one instance which they have in common. If Request ⊓ Capability$_X$ ⊑ ⊥ holds true there is no such common instance and the request cannot be fulfilled by this capability.

Other useful approach would be use f-Logic and a reasoner for describe capabilities and goals [8] and make queries for matchmake capabilities and goals. For the goal we model the postcondition (the state of the information space that is desired). We express this by a fact in f-logic (here we use the flora2 syntax [16]).

```
myGoal:goal[
   postCondition->myNotification].
myNotification:notification[
   ntf_userToBeNotified -> johndoe,
   ntf_date-> d040606:date[dayOfMonth->5, monthOfYear->5,
                           year->2004],
   paymentMethod -> creditCard, cost -> 0.2,
   ntf_body -> "Your Account Z will be in minus in 2 weeks",
   ntf_from -> sentinel].
johndoe:user[
   nif ->123, name -> "John Doe", password -> "p", login -> "l",
   firstPreference -> jdMobile,
   contacts ->>
   {jdEmaill:eml_account[eml_account->"jon@doe.com"],
    jdMobile:phone[phn_number->"0123456", phn_type->mobile],
    jdHome:phone[phn_number->"6543210", phn_type->home]}].
sentinel:user[
   name -> "Sentinel System",
   contacts ->> {jdEmaill:eml_account[
      eml_account->"sentinel@isoco.com"]}].
```

The capability postcondition describes the state of the information space the service has after its execution. Here we use some prolog build in predicate e.g. '//' which is an integer division, but that might also be replaced by more declarative predicate names like "integerDivision(X,Y,Z)".

```
smsProvider[postcondition] :-
_AnyNotification:notificationSMS[
   phn_number -> _X:phone[phn_type->mobile],
   ntf_receiptAcknowledgement -> false,
   ntf_time -> Time:dateAndTime,
   content -> AnyMessage:message,
   payment -> Payment],
is_charlist(
AnyMessage.msg_body, AnyMessageLength)@prolog(),
AnyMessageLength < 800,
Tokens is '//'(AnyMessageLength,160)@prolog()+1,
Cost is Tokens * 0.05,
```

```
Payment.cost >= Cost,
(Payment.paymentMode=creditCard; Payment.paymentMode=account),
secondsBetween(currentDate,Time,X),    X < 5*60.
```

In the F-Logic approach for discovery we are checking if the capability entails the goal (capability ≤ goal). Current limitations with respect to available reasoners led to the current modelling, where we have the goal-postcondition as a fact (which may not be fully specified) and the capability-postcondition as a rule.

We would like to extend this approach on the one hand to overcome the limitations due to the modelling of the goal as fact (i.e. that makes it hard to express ranges and constraints) and on the other hand to extend it to other matching semantics (e.g. if the intersection is satisfiable like in the DL approach).

5 Composition Using Finite State Diagram

The functionality of the non-atomic processes could be decomposed in a structured (or not) set of atomic processes for performing the same task. This composition (or decomposition, viewed from the opposite side) can be specified by using control constructs such as *Sequence* and *If-then-else*. Such decomposition normally shows, among other things, how the various inputs of the process are accepted by particular subprocesses, and how its various outputs are returned by particular subprocesses.

A CompositeProcess must have a *composedOf* property by which is indicated the control structure of the composite, using a *ControlConstruct*

```
<rdf:Property rdf:ID="composedOf">
  <rdfs:domain rdf:resource="#CompositeProcess"/>
  <rdfs:range rdf:resource="#ControlConstruct"/>
</rdf:Property>
<owl:Class rdf:ID="ControlConstruct"/>
```

Each control construct, in turn, is associated with an additional property called *components* to indicate the ordering and conditional execution of the sub processes (or control constructs) from which it is composed. For instance, the control construct, *Sequence*, has a *components* property that ranges over a *ProcessComponentList* (a list whose items are restricted to be *ProcessComponents*, which are either processes or control constructs).

This property allows managing the control flow of the execution of a Composite-Process but, in counterpart, binds the ontologies to contain information about the data and control flow, what is not always desirable [13,14].

For that reason, in our system we have developed a mechanism to describe finite state machines (finite state diagrams). The situation calculus introduces first-order terms called *situations*, [15]. The intuition behind the situation calculus is that the world persists in one state until an *action* is performed that changes it to a new state. Time is discrete, one action occurs at a time, time durations do not matter, and actions are irreducible entities. Actions are conceptualized as objects in the universe of discourse, as are states of the world. Hence, states and actions are reified. All changes to the world are the result of *actions,* which correspond to our atomic processes. The situation that holds on entry to an action is different to that which holds on exit. The exit situation is said to be the *successor* of the entry situation. Sequences of actions combine to form histories that describe composite situations – in essence the state that holds at the end of the sequence. Given this interpretation we can clarify the meaning of preconditions. A precondition is a condition that must be true of the situation on entry to an atomic process. However, sometimes these preconditions cannot be computed in terms of the input that is in terms of the domain ontology. That kind of preconditions are also called *assumptions.*

So, speaking in terms of Semantic Web Services, each *state* can be seen as a situation, stable, after or before any *action.* The set of preconditions that must be true in this state are part of the preconditions of the atomic processes that make change that state. Following in this interpretation, transitions in the state diagram represent each atomic process needed for fulfil part of the goal, as is presented in figure 4.

At this very moment there are several efforts to describe preconditions, postconditions, effects and assumptions in the research area, but few consensus has been reached to determine a final good candidate (SWRL, F-Logic, OWL, DRS). In order to describe our current needs we define a naïve solution to model conditions. Of course, making use of the reuse, we can import references to other conditions expressed in other ontologies.

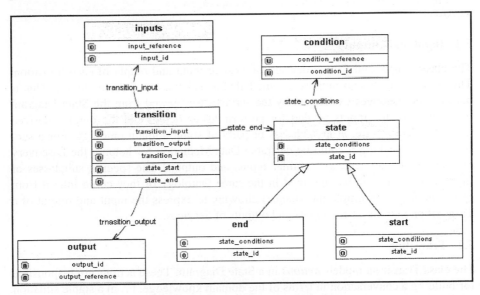

Fig. 4. Finite state diagram ontology.

The class *Condition* represents conditions, that is, statements which can be true or false in a particular state of the world (depicted in the state diagram). These conditions could be expressed in the same way (in fact, they are exactly the same) that we use to describe conditions in Semantic Web Services. Conditions of a State are modelled as instances of this class (or subclasses defined by an Ontology designer). This class is defined as subclass of [...] Process.owl#Condition and [...] Process.owl#Effect defined in the OWL-S Process Ontology for model conditions and effects. Using this technique, expressing conditions in the state diagram in the same way as in the Services will favor any attempt to matchmake Services with Transitions.

```
<owl:Class rdf:ID="condition">
  <rdfs:subClassOf rdf:resource="Process.owl#Condition"/>
  <rdfs:subClassOf rdf:resource="Process.owl#Effect"/>
</owl:Class>
```

5.1 State

The class State models a state inside a state diagram. A state is represented as a node of the Graph which models a state machine. Each node is labelled with conditions, using the relationship *state_conditions*. Besides, each node is identified with a unique id, the slot *state_id*. A state in a Service Composition represents an intermediary step in the execution of two services.

The states (when we are talking of a concrete State Diagram) are represented as instances:
```
<state rdf:ID="estimated">
  <state_conditions rdf:resource="#logged_in"/>
</state>
```

5.2 Input and Output

The classes Input and Output defines the desired input and output of each transition. The specific inputs and outputs are modelled as subclasses of these classes. This is because the messages exchanged by the services (or viewed from the State Diagram point of view, the inputs needed for performing an action and the outputs derived from this actions) are, at last, classes or parts of some domain ontology. For a successful matchmaking it could be desirable Data Mediation for helping the Discovery Service to find services with similar inputs and outputs. The specific subclasses of Input and Output can be described in the same Ontology or they could inherit from other Ontologies (multiple inheritance) allowing to express the input and output of a Transaction in terms of the inputs and outputs of Services.

5.3 Transition

The class Transition models *actions* in a State Diagram. These actions are responsible for building a conversation in terms of the domain knowledge. From a stable situation (a state) and in presence of some conditions (which are true), some action is performed and some transition from the previous state to his successor is made. In a state diagram this transition is represented using an arrow from the starting state to the ending state. In a Composite Service framework, a Transition models the execution of an operation (in terms of Semantic Web Services this could be done by an Atomic Process or by another Composite Process).

The class Transition has the following attributes and relationships:

- State_start, State_end: They are the starting and ending state of the transition. They are instances of the class State. Each state is labeled with conditions which serve to refer to the preconditions and effect of the transition.

- Transition_input, Transition_output: Defines, in the domain ontology, the desired input and output for the transition. They references to subclasses of the class Input or Output (described before) or they could be a simple data type. This restriction makes mandatory the description of this ontology in OWL-full because OWL-DL doesn't allow this kind of description.

There are two special states labelled in a special way to denote what is the starting state and the ending state. Doing this, we always know what the first subgoal which can be achieved is and what is the final subgoal. With this information, some reasoning could be done forward or backward. To be able to transit from one state to another, The Discovery Service has to be able to find some Semantic Web Service with the same set of preconditions, effects, inputs and outputs which has the instance of Transition representing the transition between the states in the following terms:

- Preconditions: These conditions label the starting state.

- Effects: They are the conditions present on the ending state but missing in the starting state.

- Inputs: Define which part of the domain ontology need the service to be executed. Some data mediation could be needed if there are 3rd party services using other ontology.

- Outputs: Define which part of the domain ontology is the result of the execution of the service. Some data mediation could be needed if there are 3rd party services using other ontology.

For obtaining a more precise understanding of the relationship between the State Diagram and the Services (for the sake of matchmaking), see the figure 5.

This is the state diagram which models the functionality of Sentinel. It could be easily translated to the State Diagram Ontology, previously described. With this ontology and the description of the Service, an agent could accomplish the task described with the state machine. The agent will need to make some decision about what transition to take (i.e. what service has to execute) and some reasoner (with storage functionalities) will be needed to perform the control flow. Two instances of transitions can be seen below.

```
<transition rdf:ID="KB_044630_Individual_84">
    <state_end rdf:resource="#Logged"/>
    <state_start>
        <stateStart rdf:ID="initState"/>
    </state_start>
    <transition_id>GETseeSWSlogin</transition_id>
    <transition_input rdf:resource="#input_user"/>
    <transition_output rdf:resource="XMLSchema#boolean"/>
</transition>
```

```
<transition rdf:ID="KB_044630_Individual_92">
  <transition_input rdf:resource="#input_output_savingAccounts"/>
  <transition_input rdf:resource="#input_user"/>
  <transition_id>GETseeSWSgetinvoices</transition_id>
  <transition_output rdf:resource="#output_InvoicesPayments"/>
  <state_start rdf:resource="#AccountsLoaded"/>
  <state_end rdf:resource="#InvoicesLoaded"/>
</transition>
```

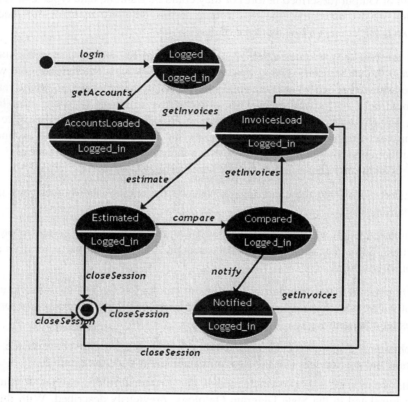

Fig. 5. Relationships between the state diagram and the Sentinel service.

6   Conclusions

We have described the Customer Notification Agent which makes use of an aggregation system, developed by iSOCO, called GETsee. ISOCO GETsee® application is able to aggregate information coming from different sources. It can be financial information (saving accounts, credit cards, investment funds, etc.), different invoices from consumer goods companies, loyalty cards, insurance companies or e-mail accounts from different Web Portals.

The Customer Notification Agent focuses on the dynamic configuration of a system that generates notifications and suggestions for transactions to the customer related to conciliation between financial accounts and pending invoices.

Integration of applications is one of the most ambitious goals of the Semantic Web Services. The existence of different agents or legacy applications must not interfere in the shared use of information. Exploiting the advantages of semantic interoperability and loose-coupled services will allow us to interconnect different applications and integrate data and information through messages. So, the system to be built leans upon an existing iSOCO's commercial application and others agents or services built *ad hoc*.

For adding semantics to the system, we have defined, or reused, different ontologies to express the needed knowledge. Besides, we have defined three services for perform the task of the Customer Notification Agent. The GETseeSWS Service access the online accounts of the customer, the invoices associated with them and calculates the balance for these accounts. The Notification Service notifies the user any message and finally, the Estimation Service estimates, using some arithmetical functions, the expectable amount of an invoice for preventing an overdrawn situation.

A Finite state diagram has been used for representing the composition of Atomic Processes, allowing in run-time the discovering and invocation of services which comply with the conditions defined for transition from a state to another. This allows us describe a Composite Process in design-time, defining its behaviour and leaving the selection of the particular service to the execution time.

Some open research issues have been explored in this work as the composition on-the-fly and the discovery of Services using different approaches. These approaches will contribute to the testing of the contents of WSMO [8] and the SWWS-CA [18]. The projects SWWS and DIP, supporting this work, are devoted to the contribution and dissemination of WSMO.

Acknowledgements. This work is supported by the IST project SWWS (IST-2001-37134) and the IST project DIP(FP6 – 507483). We would like to thank Pablo Gómez, Andrés Cirugeda and Ignacio González for their contributions.

References

1. van HeijstG, Schreiber ATh, Wielinga BJ (1997). *Using explicit ontologies in KBS development* .International Journal of Human-Computer Studies 45:183-192
2. Mizoguchi R, Vanwelkenhuysen J, Ikeda M (1995). *Task Ontology for reuse of problem solving knowledge*. In: Mars N (ed) Towards Very Large Knowledge Bases: Knowledge Building and Knowledge Sharing (KBKS'95). University of Twente, Schede, The Netherlands. IOS Press, Amsterdam, The Netherlands.

3.   OWL. Web Ontology Language.
     http://www.w3.org/TR/2004/REC-owl- features- 20040210/
4.   OWL-S. OWL for Services. http://www.daml.org/services/owl-s/1.0/
5.   Protégé 2000. Stanford Medical Informatics. http://protege.stanford.edu/
6.   OWL Plugin: A Semantic Web Ontology Editor for Protégé.
     http://protege.stanford.edu/plugins/owl/
7.   ezOWL Plugin for Protégé 2000. http://iweb.etri.re.kr/ezowl/plugin.html
8.   WSMO. Web Service Modeling Framework.
     http://www.nextwebgeneration.org/projects/wsmo/
9.   SWRL: A Semantic Web Rule Language Combining OWL and RuleML.
     http://www.daml.org/2003/11/swrl/
10. Michael Kifer, Georg Lausen, James Wu , Logical Foundations of Object Oriented and
     Frame Based Languages. Journal of ACM 1995, vol. 42, p. 741-843
11. DRS: A Set of Conventions for Representing Logical Languages in RDF. Drew McDer-
     mott, January 2004. http://www.daml.org/services/owl-s/1.0/DRSguide.pdf
12. IFX. Interactive Financial eXchange. http://www.ifxforum.org
13. D. Berardi, F. De Rosa, L. De Santis, and M. Mecella. Finite state automata as conceptual
     model for e-services. In Proc. of the IDPT 2003 Conference, 2003. To appear.
14. S. Narayanan and S. McIlraith. Simulation, Verification and Automated Composition of
     Web Services. In *Proc. of WWW 2002*.
15. H. Levesque, F. Pirri, R. Reiter. Foundations of the Situation Calculus. Linköping Elec-
     tronic Articles in Computer and Information Science, Vol 3, nr 18.
     http://www.ep.liu.se/ea/cis/1998/018. December 1998
16. *FLORA*-2: An Object-Oriented Knowledge Base Language. http://flora.sourceforge.net
17. S. Grimm, H. Lausen. Discussion document SWWS Service Description / Discovery. May
     2004
18. C. Priest. SWWS-CA A Conceptual Architecture for Semantic Web Services. May 2004

ONTOVIEWS
– A Tool for Creating Semantic Web Portals

Eetu Mäkelä, Eero Hyvönen, Samppa Saarela, and Kim Viljanen

Helsinki Institute for Information Technology (HIIT), University of Helsinki
P.O. Box 26, 00014 UNIV. OF HELSINKI, FINLAND
{Firstname.Lastname}@cs.Helsinki.FI
http://www.cs.helsinki.fi/group/seco/

Abstract. This paper presents a semantic web portal tool ONTOVIEWS for publishing RDF content on the web. ONTOVIEWS provides the portal designer with a content-based search engine server, Ontogator, and a link recommendation system server, Ontodella. The user interface is created by combining these servers with the Apache Cocoon framework. From the end-user's viewpoint, the key idea of ONTOVIEWS is to combine the multi-facet search paradigm, developed within the information retrieval research community, with semantic web RDFS ontologies, and extend the search service with a semantic browsing facility based on ontological reasoning. ONTOVIEWS is presented from the viewpoints of the end-user, architecture, and implementation. The implementation described is modular, easily modified and extended, and provides a good practical basis for creating semantic portals on the web. As a proof of concept, application of ONTOVIEWS to a deployed semantic web portal is discussed.

Keywords: Semantic web, information retrieval, multi-facet search, view-based search, recommendation system.

1 Introduction

Much of the semantic web content will be published using semantic portals[1] [1]. Such portals typically provide the end-user with two basic services: 1) a search engine based on the semantics of the content [2] and 2) dynamic linking between pages based on the semantic relations in the underlying knowledge base [3].

This paper presents ONTOVIEWS — a tool for creating semantic portals — that facilitates these two services combined with user interface and Web Services functionality inside the Apache Cocoon framework[2]. The search service of ONTOVIEWS is based on the idea of combining multi-facet search [4,5] with RDFS ontologies. The dynamic linking service is based on logical rules that define associations of interest between RDF(S) resources. Such associations are rendered on the user interface as links with labels that explain the nature the semantic linkage to the end-user.

These ideas were initially developed and tested as a stand-alone Java application [6] and as a Prolog-based HTML generator [7]. ONTOVIEWS combines and extends these

---

[1] See, e.g., http://www.ontoweb.org/.
[2] http://cocoon.apache.org/

S.A. McIlraith et al. (Eds.): ISWC 2004, LNCS 3298, pp. 797–811, 2004.
© Springer-Verlag Berlin Heidelberg 2004

two systems by separating the search and link recommendation services into independent servers (Ontogator and Ontodella) to be used on the Semantic Web, and by providing a clear logic-based interface by which ontology and annotation schema specific RDF(S) structures can be hidden from the servers.

In the following, ONTOVIEWS is first presented from the viewpoint of the end-user. We present an application developed using the tool: MUSEUMFINLAND[3] [8]. This system is a deployed semantic portal for publishing heterogeneous museum collections on the Semantic Web. After this the architecture and the implementation of the framework are discussed mostly from the portal designer's viewpoint. In conclusion, benefits and limitations of the system are summarized, related work is discussed, and directions for further research are outlined.

2   ONTOVIEWS from the End-User's Perspective

ONTOVIEWS provides the end-user with a semantic view-based search engine and a recommendation system. In MUSEUMFINLAND, these services are provided to the end-user via two different user interfaces: one for desktop computers and one for mobile devices. In below the desktop computer web interface is first presented.

2.1   A Multi-facet Search Engine

The search engine of ONTOVIEWS is based on the multi-facet search paradigm [4,5]. Here the concepts used for indexing are called *categories* and are organized systematically into a set of hierarchical, orthogonal taxonomies. The taxonomies are called subject *facets* or *views*. In multi-facet search the views are exposed to the end-user in order to provide her/him with the right query vocabulary and for presenting the repository contents and search results along different views.

In MUSEUMFINLAND, the content consists of collections of cultural artifacts and historical sites in RDF format consolidated from several heterogeneous Finnish museum databases [9]. The RDF content is annotated using a set of seven ontologies. From the seven ontologies, nine view-facets are created. The ontologies underlying the application consist of some 10,000 RDF(S) classes and individuals, half of which are in use in the current version on the web. There are some 7,600 categories in the views and 4,500 metadata records of collection artifacts and old cultural sites in Finland.

Figure 1 shows the search interface of MUSEUMFINLAND. The nine facet hierarchies, such as Artifact ("Esinetyyppi") and Material ("Materiaali"), are shown (in Finnish) on the left column. For each facet hierarchy, the next level of sub-categories is shown as links. A query is formulated by selecting a category by clicking on its name. When the user selects a category c in a facet f, the system constrains the search by leaving in the result set only such objects that are annotated in facet f with some sub-category of c or c itself. The result set is shown on the right grouped by the sub-categories of the last selection. In this case the user has selected "Tools", whose sub-categories include Textile making tools ("tekstiilityövälineet") and Tools of folk medicine ("kansanlääkinnän työvälineet").

---

[3] http://museosuomi.cs.helsinki.fi/

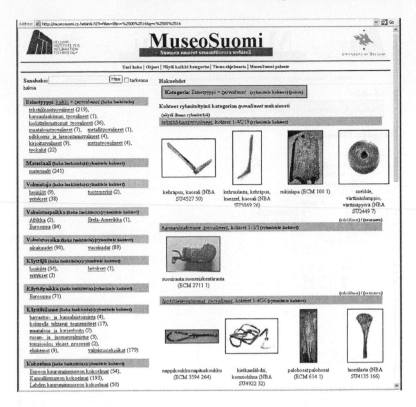

Fig. 1. MUSEUMFINLAND search interface after selecting the category link Tools ("työvälineet").

Hits in different categories are separated by horizontal bars and can be paged through independently in each category.

When answering the query, the result sets resulting from the selection of each category seen on the screen are recomputed, and a number (n) is shown to the user after the category name. It tells that if the category is selected next, then there will be n hits in the result set. For example, in figure 1, the number 193 in the Collection facet ("Kokoelma") on the bottom tells that there are 193 tools in the collections of the National Museum ("Kansallismuseon kokoelmat"). A selection leading to an empty result set ($n = 0$) is removed from its facet (or alternatively disabled and shown grayed out, depending on the user's preference). In this way, the user is hindered from making a selection leading to an empty result set, and is guided toward selections that are likely to constrain the search appropriately. The query can be relaxed by making a new selection on a higher level in the facet or by dismissing the facet totally from the query.

Above, the category selection was made among the direct sub-categories listed in the facets. An alternative way is to click on the link Whole facet ("koko luokittelu") on a facet. The system then shows all possible selections in the whole facet hierarchy with hit counts. For example, in figure 2 the user selected in the situation of figure 1 the link Whole facet of the facet Time of Creation ("Valmistusaika"). The system shows how the

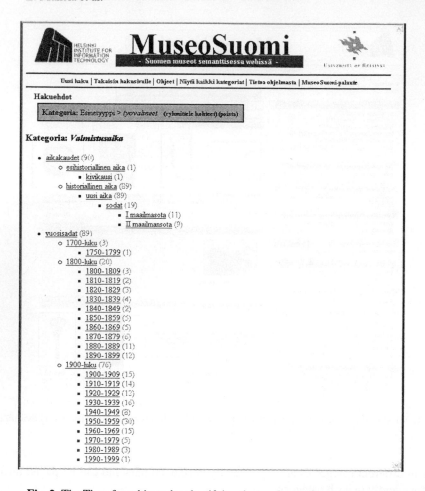

Fig. 2. The Time facet hierarchy classifying the result set of tools in figure 1.

tools in the current result set are classified according to the selected facet. This gives the user a good overview of the distribution of items over a desired dimension. With the option of graying out categories with no hits, it is also immediately obvious where the collections are lacking artifacts.

When the user is capable of expressing her information need straightforward in terms of keywords, then a Google-like keyword search interface is usually preferred. ONTO-VIEWS seamlessly integrates this functionality in the following way: First, the search keywords from the search form are matched against category names in the facets. A new dynamic facet is created in the user interface, containing all facet categories matching the keyword shown with the corresponding facet name. Second, a result set of object hits is shown. This result set contains all objects contained in any of the categories matched in addition to all objects whose metadata directly contains the keyword, grouped by the categories found. This way, the keyword search also solves the search problem of finding relevant categories in facets that may contain thousands of categories.

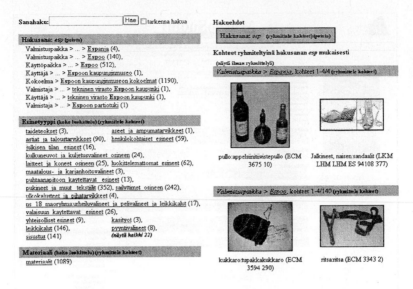

Fig. 3. Using the keyword search for finding categories.

A sample keyword search is shown in figure 3. Here, a search for "esp" has matched, for example, the categories Spain ("Espanja" in Finnish) and Espoo in the facet Location of Creation and the category Espoo City Museum ("Espoon kaupunginmuseo") in the facet User ("Käyttäjä"). The categories found can be used to constrain the multi-facet search as normal, with the distinction that selections from the dynamic facet replace selections in their corresponding facets and dismiss the dynamic facet.

2.2   The Item View with Semantic Links

At any point during multi-facet search the user can select any hit found by clicking on its image. The corresponding data object is then shown as a web page, such as the one in figure 4. The example depicts a special part, distaff ("rukinlapa" in Finnish) used in a spinning wheel. The page contains the following information and links:

1. On top, there are links to directly navigate in the groups and results of the current query.
2. The image(s) of the object is (are) depicted on the left.
3. The metadata of the object is shown in the middle on top.
4. All facet categories that the object is annotated with are listed in the middle bottom as hierarchical link paths. A new search can be started by selecting any category there.
5. A set of semantic links on the right provided by a semantic recommendation system.

The semantic links on the right reveal to the end-user a most interesting aspect of the collection items: the implicit semantic relations that relate collection data with their context and each other. The links provide a *semantic browsing* facility to the end-user.

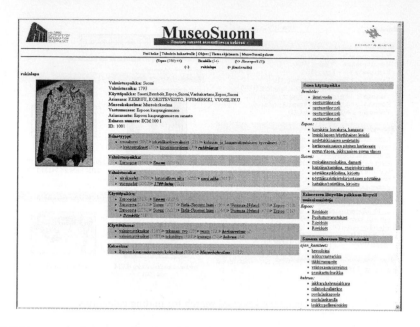

Fig. 4. Web page depicting a collection object, its metadata, facet categories, and semantic recommendation links to other collection object pages.

For example, in figure 4 there are links to objects used at the same location (categorized according to the name of the common location), to objects related to similar events (e.g., objects used in spinning, and objects related to concepts of time, because the distaff in question has a year carved onto it), to objects manufactured at the same time, and so on. Since a decoratively carved distaff used to be a typical wedding gift in Finland, it is also possible to recommend links to other objects related to the wedding event, such as wedding rings. In ONTOVIEWS, such associations can be exposed to the end-user as link groups whose titles and link names explain to the user the reason for the recommendation.

2.3   The Mobile User Interface

Using ONTOVIEWS the same content and services can easily be rendered to the end-users in different ways. To demonstrate this, we created another user interface for MUSEUM-FINLAND to be used by WAP 2.0 (XHTML/MP) compatible devices. ONTOVIEWS is a particularly promising tool for designing a mobile user interface due to the following reasons. Firstly, empty results can be eliminated, which is a nice feature in an environment where data transfer latencies and costs are still often high. Secondly, the elimination of infeasible choices makes it possible to use the small screen size more efficiently for displaying relevant information. Thirdly, the semantic browsing functionality is a simple and effective navigation method in a mobile environment.

The mobile interface repeats all functionality of the PC interface, but in a layout more suitable to the limited screen space of mobile devices. In addition, to better facilitate finding interesting starting points for browsing, some mobile-specific search shortcuts were created. The search results are shown first up front noting the current search parameters for easy reference and dismissal, as seen in figure 5. Below this, the actual search facets are shown. In the mobile user interface selectable sub-categories are not shown as explicit links as in the PC interface, but as drop-down lists that replace the whole view when selected. This minimizes screen space usage while browsing the facets, but maximizes usability when selecting sub-categories from them. In-page links are provided for quick navigation between search results and the search form.

Fig. 5. Results of a mobile geolocation search initiated somewhere near Ruuhijärvi, Finland.

The item page (corresponding to figure 4) is organized in a similar fashion, showing first the item name, images, metadata, annotations, semantic recommendations, and finally navigation in the search result. There are also in-page links for jumping quickly between the different parts of the page.

The mobile user interface also provides two distinct services aimed specifically for mobile use. Firstly, the interface supports search by the geolocation of the mobile device in the same manner as in the concept-based ONTOVIEWS keyword search. Any entries in the Location ontology near the current location of the mobile user are shown in a dynamic facet as well as all data objects made *or* used in any of these locations. In addition, any objects directly annotated with geo-coordinates near the mobile user are shown grouped as normal. This feature gives the user a one-click path to items of likely immediate interest. Secondly, because navigation and search with mobile devices is tedious, any search state can be "bookmarked", sent by email to a desired address, and inspected later in more detail by using the more convenient PC interface.

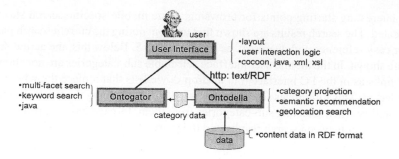

Fig. 6. The components of ONTOVIEWS.

3   Architecture and Implementation

ONTOVIEWS consists of the three major components shown in figure 6. The logic server of ONTOVIEWS, Ontodella, provides the system with reasoning services, such as category generation and semantic recommendations. It is based on the HTTP server version of SWI-Prolog[4]. It has also been extended to provide simple point-of-interest search based on geo-coordinates. It is queried via a HTTP connection.

The multi-facet search engine of ONTOVIEWS, Ontogator, is a generic view-based RDF search engine. It defines and implements an RDF-based query interface that is used to separate view-based search logic from the user interface. The interface is defined as an OWL ontology[5]. It can be used to query for category hierarchies and items grouped by and/or constrained by these. Both categories and items can also be queried using keywords. Given a set of category and/or keyword-based constraints, Ontogator filters categories that would lead to an empty result set. Alternatively, filtering the categories, for example by graying out, can be left for the user interface. This is possible since Ontogator (optionally) tags every category with a number of hits. There are also a number of other general options (e.g. accepted language) and restrictions (e.g. max items/categories returned) that can be used, for example, to page the results by categories and/or items. Ontogator replies to queries in RDF/XML that has a fixed structure. Since the search results are used in building the user interface, every resource is tagged with an rdfs:label.

The third component in figure 6, User Interface, binds the services of Ontogator and Ontodella together, and is responsible for the user interfaces and interaction. This component is built on top of the Apache Cocoon framework[6]. Cocoon is a framework based wholly on XML and the concept of pipelines constructed from different types of components, as illustrated in figure 7. A pipeline always begins with a generator, that generates an XML-document. Then follow zero or more transformers that take an XML-document as input and output a document of their own. The pipeline always ends

---

[4] http://swi-prolog.org/

[5] http://www.cs.helsinki.fi/group/seco/ns/2004/03/ontogator#

[6] http://cocoon.apache.org/

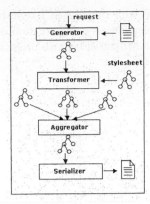

Fig. 7. The components of a Cocoon pipeline.

in a serializer that serializes its input into the final result, such as an HTML-page, a PDF-file, or an image. It is also possible for the output of partial pipelines to be combined via aggregation into a single XML-document for further processing. Execution of these pipelines can be tied to different criteria, e.g, to a combination of the request URI and requesting user-agent.

In ONTOVIEWS, all of the intermediate components produce not only XML, but valid RDF/XML. Figure 8 depicts two pipelines of the ONTOVIEWS system. The pipe lines look alike, but result in quite different pages, namely in the search result page seen in figure 1 (and another similar page used for depicting results of the keyword search), and in the item page seen in figure 4. This is due to the modular nature of the pipelines, which makes it possible to split a problem into small units and reuse components.

Every pipeline that is tied to user interaction web requests begins with a user state generator that generates an RDF/XML representation of the user's current state. While browsing, the state is encoded wholly in the request URL, which allows for easy book-marking and also furthers the possibilities of using multiple servers. This user state is then combined with system state information in the form of facet identifiers and query hit counts, and possible user geolocation based information. This information is then transformed into appropriate queries for the Ontogator and Ontodella servers depending on the pipeline.

In the Search Page pipeline on the left, an Ontogator query returning grouped hits and categories is created. In the Item Page pipeline on the right, Ontogator is queried for the properties and annotations of a specific item and its place in the result set, while On-todella is queried for the semantic links relating to that item. The Ontogator search engine is encapsulated in a Cocoon transformer, while the Ontodella transformer is actually a generic Web Services transformer that creates a HTTP-query from its input, executes it, and creates SAX events from the HTTP-response. The RDF/XML responses from the search engines are then given to user interface transformers depending on the pipeline and the device that originated the request. These transform the results into appropriate XHTML or to any other format, which is then run through an internationalization trans-former for language support and serialized. Most of the transformations into queries and XHTML are implemented with simple XSLT-stylesheets. In this way, changes to layout are very simple to implement, as is the creation of new interfaces for different media. The mobile interface to MUSEUMFINLAND discussed earlier was created in this way quite quickly.

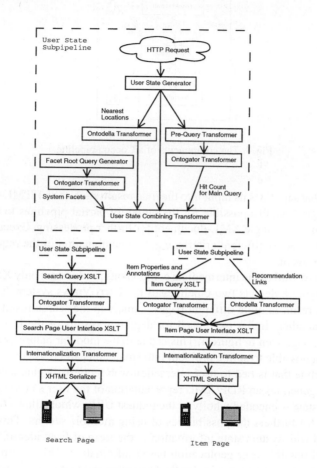

Fig. 8. Two Cocoon pipelines used in ONTOVIEWS.

All of the transformer components can also be made available for use in other web applications as Web Services, by creating a pipeline that generates XML from an HTTP-query and returns its output as XML. In this way, other web applications could make use of the actual RDF-data contained in the system, querying the Ontogator and On-todella servers directly for content data in RDF/XML-format. It also provides a way of distributing the processing in the system to multiple servers. For example, ONTO-VIEWS instances running Ontogator could be installed on multiple servers, and a main ONTOVIEWS handling user interaction could distribute queries among these servers in a round-robin fashion to balance load.

4   Adapting OntoViews to New Data

OntoViews is capable of supporting any RDF-based input data (e.g., OWL). To adapt the system to new data, the following steps must be taken: First, create rules describing how categories are generated and items connected to them for the view based search. Second, create rules describing how links are generated for the recommendations. Third, possibly change the layout templates.

In the following, we describe how the logic rules needed are defined in our system using Prolog. The layout templates are straightforward XSLT and will not be discussed.

4.1   Category View Generation

A view is a hierarchical index-like decomposition of category resources where each category is associated with a set of subcategories and data items. A view is defined in Ontodella, the logic server of OntoViews, by specifying a view predicate called `ontodella_view` with the following information: 1) the root resource URI, 2) a binary subcategory relation predicate, and 3) a binary relation predicate that maps the hierarchy categories with the items used as leaves in the view. In addition, each view must have a label.

An example[7] of a view predicate is given below:

```
ontodella_view(
    'http://www.cs.helsinki.fi/seco/ns/2004/03/places#earth',
    place_sub_category,
    place_of_use_leaf_item,
    [fi:'K\"{a}ytt\"{o}paikka', en:'Place of Use'] % the labels
).
```

Here the URI on the second line is the root resource, `place_sub_category` is the name of the subcategory relation predicate and `place_of_use_leaf_item` is the leaf predicate. The label list contains the labels for each supported language. In our case, we support both Finnish (fi) and English (en).

The binary subcategory predicate can be based, e.g., on a containment property in the following way:

```
place_sub_category( ParentCategory, SubCategory ) :-
    SubCategoryProperty =
        'http://www.cs.helsinki.fi/seco/ns/2004/03/places#isContainedBy',
    rdf( SubCategory, SubCategoryProperty, ParentCategory ).
```

The leaf predicate describes when a given resource item is a member of the given category. For example, `place_of_use_leaf_item` in our example above can be described as follows:

```
place_of_use_leaf_item( ResourceURI, CategoryURI ) :-
    Relation = 'http://www.cs.helsinki.fi/seco/ns/2004/03/artifacts#usedIn',
    rdf( ResourceURI, Relation, CategoryURI ).
```

---

[7] The syntax is slightly simplified due to presentation reasons. We use SWI-Prolog (http://www.swi-prolog.org) as the inference engine and SWI-Prolog syntax in the examples.

Based on these rules, the categories can be generated by iterating through the predicate ontodella_view, and by recursively creating the category hierarchies using the subcategory rules starting from the given root category. At every category, all relevant leaf resources are attached to the category based on the leaf rules. When the categories have been generated, they can be navigated using the Ontogator module presented earlier.

4.2   Recommendation Link Generation

Link generation is based on rules that describe when two resources should be linked. Each link rule can be arbitrary complex and is defined by a domain specialist. A linking rule is described by a predicate of the form $p(SubjectURI, TargetURI, Explanation)$ that should succeed with the two resources $SubjectURI$ and $TargetURI$ are to be linked. The variable $Explanation$ is then bound to an explanatory label (string) for the link. In the following, one of the more complex rules — linking items related to a common event — is presented as an example:

```
related_by_event( Subject, Target, Explanation ) :-

ItemTypeProperty =
   'http://www.cs.helsinki.fi/seco/ns/2004/03/artifacts#item_type',
ItemTypeToEventRelatingProperty =
   'http://www.cs.helsinki.fi/seco/ns/2004/03/mapping#related_to_event',

% check that both URIs correspond in fact to artifacts
isArtifact(Subject),
isArtifact(Target),
% and are not the same
Subject \= Target,

% find all the item types the subject item belongs to
rdf(Subject, ItemTypeProperty, SubjectItemType),
rdfs_transitive_subClassOf(SubjectItemType,SubClassOfSubjectItemType),

% find all the events any of those item types are related to
rdf(SubClassOfSubjectItemType, ItemTypeToEventRelatingProperty, Event),
% and events they include or are part of
(
   rdfs_transitive_subClassOf(Even, SubOrSuperClassOfEvent),
   DescResource=TransitiveSubOrSuperClassOfEvent;
   % or
   rdfs_transitive_subClassOf(SubOrSuperClassOfEvent, Event),
   DescResource=Event;
),

% find all item types related to those events
rdf(TargetItemType, ItemTypeToEventRelatingProperty, SubOrSuperClassOfEvent),
% and all their superclasses
rdfs_transitive_subClassOf(SuperClassOfTargetItemType, TargetItemType),

% don't make uninteresting links between items of the same type
SuperClassOfTargetItemType \= SubjectItemType,
not(rdfs_transitive_subClassOf(SuperClassOfTargetItemType, SubjectItemType)),
not(rdfs_transitive_subClassOf(SubjectItemType, SuperClassOfTargetItemType)),

% finally, find all items related to the linked item types
rdf(Target, ItemTypeProperty, SuperClassOfTargetItemType),

list_labels([DescResource], RelLabel),
Explanation=[commonResources(DescResource), label(fi:RelLabel)].
```

The rule goes over several ontologies, first discovering the object types of the objects, then traversing the object type ontology, relating the object types to events, and finally traversing the event ontology looking for common resources. Additional checks are made to ensure that the found target is an artifact and that the subject and target are not the same resources. Finally, information about the relation is collected, such as the URI and the label of the common resource, and the result is returned as the link label.

The links for a specific subject are generated when the ONTOVIEWS main module makes an HTTP query to the Ontodella. As a result, the Ontodella returns an RDF/XML message containing the link information (the target URI and the relation description). These links are then shown to the user using the User Interface (cf. figure 6).

5   Discussion

5.1   Benefits and Limitations

The example application MUSEUMFINLAND shows that the multi-facet search paradigm combined with ontologies is feasible as a basis for search on the Semantic Web. The paradigm is especially useful when the user is not just searching for a particular piece of information, but is interested in getting a broader view of the contents of the repository, and in browsing of the contents in the large. The addition of keyword-based searching complements multi-facet searching nicely, better addressing the search needs of people with a clear idea of what they want and with means of expressing it. Such a search can be integrated seamlessly into the user interaction logic and visualization of the user interface. It can be used to also solve the search problem of finding appropriate concepts in the ontologies to be used as a basis in multi-facet search. The semantic recommendation system provides further browsing possibilities by linking the items semantically with each other by relations that cannot be expressed with the hierarchical categorizations used in the multi-facet search.

The Cocoon-based implementation of the ONTOVIEWS is eminently portable, extendable, modifiable, and modular when compared to our previous test implementations. This flexibility is a direct result of designing the application around the Cocoon concepts of transformers and pipelines, in contrast to servlets and layout XSLT. The generality and flexibility of ONTOVIEWS has been verified in creating the mobile device interface for MUSEUMFINLAND. Furthermore, we have used ONTOVIEWS in the creation of a semantic yellow page portal [10], and (using a later version of the tool) a test portal based on the material of the Open Directory Project (ODP)[8]. These demonstrations are based on ontologies and content different from MUSEUMFINLAND. With the ODP material, the system was tested to scale up to 2.3 million data items and 275,000 view categories with search times of less then 5 seconds on an ordinary PC server.

The use of XSLT in most of the user interface and query transformations makes it easy to modify the interface appearance and to add new functionality. However, it has also led to some quite complicated XSLT templates in the more involved areas of user interaction logic, e.g., when (sub-)paging and navigating in the search result pages. In using XSLT with RDF/XML there is also the problem that the same RDF triple can

---

[8] http://www.dmoz.org/

be represented in XML in different ways but an XSLT template can be only tied to a specific representation. In our current system, this problem can be avoided because the RDF/XML serialization formats used by each of the subcomponents of the system are known, but in a general web service environment, this could cause complications. However, the core search engine components of OntoViews would be unaffected even in this case because they handle their input with true RDF semantics.

When applying OntoViews, the category and linking rules are described by a domain specialist. She selects what should be shown in the views and what relations between data items should be presented to the user as semantical links. With the help of the rules, any RDF data can be used as input for OntoViews. The prize of the flexibility is that somebody must create the rules, which can be a difficult task if the input data is not directly suitable for generating the wanted projections and links.

5.2   Related Work

Much of the web user interface and user interaction logic in OntoViews and Museum-Finland pertaining to multi-facet search is based on Flamenco [5]. In OntoViews, however, several extensions to this baseline have been added, such as the tree view of categories (figure 2), the seamless integration of concept-based keyword and geolocation search, extended navigation in the result set, and semantic browsing. The easy addition of these capabilities was made possible by basing the system on RDF. We feel it would have been much more difficult to implement the system by using the traditional relational database model. Our approach also permits OntoViews to load and publish any existing RDF data, once the rules defining the facet projections and semantic links are defined.

5.3   Future Work

OntoViews is a research prototype. The test with the material of the Open Directory Project has proved it quite scalable with regards to the amount of data, but the response-time of the system currently scales linearly with respect to the number of simultaneous queries. Further optimization work would be needed to make the system truly able to handle large amounts of concurrent users. The benefits observed applying the XML-based Cocoon pipeline concept to RDF handling has lead us to the question, whether it would be possible to create a true "Semantic Cocoon" based on RDF semantics and an RDF-transformation language.

References

1. A. Maedche, S. Staab, N. Stojanovic, R. Struder, and Y. Sure, "Semantic portal — the SEAL approach," Institute AIFB, University of Karlsruhe, Germany, Tech. Rep., 2001.
2. S. Decker, M. Erdmann, D. Fensel, and R. Studer, "Ontobroker: Ontology based access to distributed and semi-structured unformation," in *DS-8*, 1999, pp. 351–369, citeseer.nj.nec.com/article/decker98ontobroker.html.
3. C. Goble, S. Bechhofer, L. Carr, D. D. Roure, and W. Hall, "Conceptual open hypermedia = the semantic web?" in *Proceedings of the WWW2001, Semantic Web Workshop, Hongkong*, 2001.

4. A. S. Pollitt, "The key role of classification and indexing in view-based searching," University of Huddersfield, UK, Tech. Rep., 1998, http://www.ifla.org/IV/ifla63/63polst.pdf.
5. M. Hearst, A. Elliott, J. English, R. Sinha, K. Swearingen, and K.-P. Lee, "Finding the flow in web site search," *CACM*, vol. 45, no. 9, pp. 42–49, 2002.
6. E. Hyvönen, S. Saarela, and K. Viljanen, "Application of ontology-based techniques to view-based semantic search and browsing," in *Proceedings of the First European Semantic Web Symposium, May 10-12, Heraklion, Greece.* Springer–Verlag, Berlin, 2004.
7. E. Hyvönen, M. Holi, and K. Viljanen, "Designing and creating a web site based on RDF content," in *Proceedings of WWW2004 Workshop on Application Design, Development, and Implementation Issues in the Semantic Web, New York, USA.* CEUR Workshop Proceedings, Vol-105, 2004, http://ceur-ws.org.
8. E. Hyvönen, M. Junnila, S. Kettula, E. Mäkelä, S. Saarela, M. Salminen, A. Syreeni, A. Valo, and K. Viljanen, "Finnish Museums on the Semantic Web. User's perspective on MuseumFinland," in *Proceedings of Museums and the Web 2004 (MW2004), Seleted Papers, Arlington, Virginia, USA,* 2004, http://www.archimuse.com/mw2004/papers/hyvonen/hyvonen.html.
9. E. Hyvönen, M. Salminen, S. Kettula, and M. Junnila, "A content creation process for the Semantic Web," in *Proceeding of OntoLex 2004: Ontologies and Lexical Resources in Distributed Environments, May 29, Lisbon, Portugal,* 2004.
10. M. Laukkanen, K. Viljanen, M. Apiola, P. Lindgren, and E. Hyvönen, "Towards ontology-based yellow page services," in *Proceedings of WWW2004 Workshop on Application Design, Development, and Implementation Issues in the Semantic Web, New York, USA.* CEUR Workshop Proceedings, Vol-105, 2004, http://ceur-ws.org.

Applying Semantic Web Technology to the Life Cycle Support of Complex Engineering Assets

David Price and Rob Bodington

Eurostep Limited, Cwttir Lane, St. Asaph, Denbighshire, LL17 0LQ, UK
david.price@eurostep.com

Abstract. Complex engineering assets, such as ships and aircraft, are designed to be in-service for many years. Over its life, the support of such an asset costs an organization many times more than the original cost of the asset itself. An industry/government initiative has resulted in an International Standard information model aimed at satisfying three significant business requirements for owners of these assets: 1) reducing the cost of total ownership of such assets, 2) protecting the investment in produce data through life, and 3) increasing the use of the asset to deliver enhanced business performance. This standard, called Product Life Cycle Support (PLCS), defines a domain-specific, but flexible, information model designed to be tailored by using organizations through the use of Reference Data. This paper describes the approach used to take advantage of the Web Ontology Language (OWL) in the definition of Reference Data and how it is being applied in pilot projects. The use of Semantic Web technology for Reference Data is a first step towards the application of that technology in the Life Cycle Support domain. The relationship between the information model, and its modelling language called EXPRESS, and OWL is also explored.

1   What Is Product Life Cycle Support?

Product Life Cycle Support (PLCS) is an ISO standard for the support of complex engineering assets, such as ships and aircraft, through life. PLCS defines a comprehensive information model for describing a set of products needing support and the work required to sustain such products in an operational condition. Because of its broad scope and variety of using organizations, the PLCS information model is designed to be used in conjunction with Reference Data (RD). Reference Data is used to extend the semantics of the information model using a classification capability designed into the information model itself. PLCS data instances may be classified using a, potentially external, library of Reference Data.

Formally, PLCS is ISO 10303-239 Product Life Cycle Support [1] and is one of a suite of standards called STEP – the Standard for the Exchange of Product Model Data. Other standards that are part of STEP have been successfully deployed on major industrial projects such as the Eurofighter Typhoon aircraft program where the prime partners used STEP to exchange product data. Organizations have "reduced design development times by 10 to 40 percent, and realized cost savings of 5 to 30 percent in

S.A. McIlraith et al. (Eds.): ISWC 2004, LNCS 3298, pp. 812–822, 2004.
© Springer-Verlag Berlin Heidelberg 2004

the management of technical data" [2] through the use of STEP. The STEP standards are defined in ISO Technical Committee 184, Subcommittee 4 Industrial Data [3].

Figure 1 shows the relationship between the PLCS information model and the Reference Data. The full semantics required by implementations include those defined in the information model and those defined in the Reference Data.

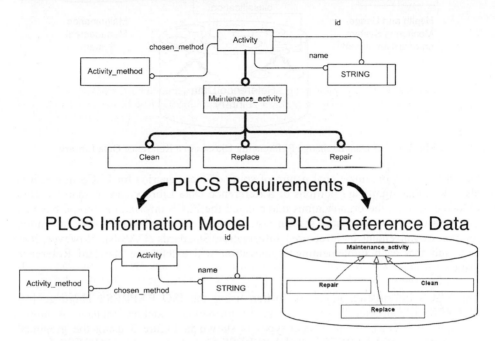

Fig. 1. The Relationship between the PLCS Information Model and Reference Data

As an example, the PLCS information model includes the representation of an activity and that the activity is performed using a chosen method. However, it does not standardize the different kinds of activities, such as the maintenance activities repair or replace. Instead, those concepts are defined in the Reference Data.

2 More on Reference Data

In the PLCS context, a Reference Data Library (RDL) is a set of Reference Data made available to a PLCS implementation. For example, an aircraft Health and Usage Monitoring System (HUMS) may use PLCS to provide information about the state of the aircraft to a Maintenance Management System (MMS). Rather than including all the details about particular equipment fitted to the aircraft, both the HUMS and the MMS applications have access to the RDL and references to the categories of equipment in the RDL are provided to the MMS. The properties of the types of equipment are then available to the MMS from the RDL. Figure 2 illustrates that scenario.

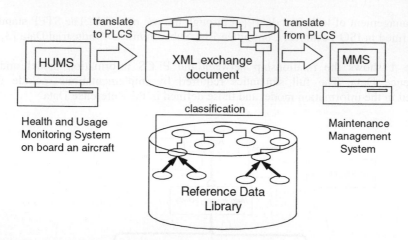

Fig. 2. PLCS Data Exchange Referencing Classes in a Reference Data Library

Given the cross-organizational nature of some of the scenarios for PLCS usage, it is also clear that significant portions of a Reference Data Library can be shared across industry. In fact, the organizations that created the PLCS information model have an initiative underway to create a standard set of core Reference Data in the Organization for the Advancement of Structured Information Standards (OASIS). However, it is expected that each implementing organization will extend the standard Reference Data.

The PLCS information model is written using the ISO EXPRESS language [4]. EXPRESS is a structurally object-oriented information modeling language. A simple example of EXPRESS entity data types is shown in Figure 3 using the graphical representation of EXPRESS called EXPRESS-G and using the EXPRESS lexical form. One issue arising from the PLCS use of Reference Data is defining the specific relationship between the EXPRESS constructs and the RDL. In order to ensure the appropriate use of Reference Data with respect to the information model, the links to the elements in that model from the Reference Data are being defined in that standard core RDL. In order to maintain the integrity of the information model-RDL links, organization-specific extensions to the RDL are only allowed to be related to the standard RDL, rather than the information model itself.

PLCS is, therefore, actually the combination of an ISO standardized EXPRESS information model, a related implementation method (e.g. XML exchange document) and industry-standardized Reference Data that together define a framework for organization-specific extension and use in Life Cycle Support applications.

3   Implementing PLCS

The broad scope of the PLCS information model supports an extensive business process model [5]. It is unlikely that any individual application will support the

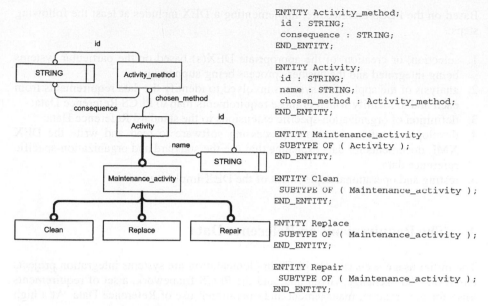

```
ENTITY Activity_method;
   id : STRING;
   consequence : STRING;
END_ENTITY;

ENTITY Activity;
   id : STRING;
   name : STRING;
   chosen_method : Activity_method;
END_ENTITY;

ENTITY Maintenance_activity
   SUBTYPE OF ( Activity );
END_ENTITY;

ENTITY Clean
   SUBTYPE OF ( Maintenance_activity );
END_ENTITY;

ENTITY Replace
   SUBTYPE OF ( Maintenance_activity );
END_ENTITY;

ENTITY Repair
   SUBTYPE OF ( Maintenance_activity );
END_ENTITY;
```

Fig. 3. A Simple Example of EXPRESS Entity Data Types

complete PLCS information model, or that the complete scope of the PLCS business processes will be deployed immediately. Therefore, a number of business critical process flows have been identified along with the subsets of the information model required to support these process. These subsets of the information model are referred to as Data Exchange Sets (DEXs). In order to support implementations of DEXs, usage guidance is developed and will be published through the OASIS Product Life Cycle Support Technical Committee.

The DEXs are defined using an XML-based document publication facility called DEXLib. As the DEX is where guidance related to implementation is defined, DEXLib is also the place where the standard Reference Data is defined. As was mentioned previously, how the Reference Data relates to the PLCS EXPRESS information model is also defined as part of the Reference Data Library.

For each DEX, a related XML Schema is generated for use as the data exchange implementation method and is standardized in OASIS as well. An in-process ISO mapping from EXPRESS to XML Schema [6] is implemented in DEXLib.

For many planned applications of PLCS, the Reference Data Libraries are expected to be very large hierarchies of classes and properties. For example, a library of equipment types could contain tens of thousands of types with numerous properties associated with each type. It is expected that they will be made available via the Internet in many cases so that these large libraries need not be duplicated within every implementing organization.

Based on the PLCS architecture, implementing a DEX includes at least the following steps:

1. selection, or creation, of the appropriate DEX(s) based on the particular systems being integrated and the business process being supported;
2. analysis of the application systems involved to identify the data requirements from each and to identify which of those requirements map to PLCS Reference Data;
3. definition of organization-specific extensions to the standard Reference Data;
4. development of pre- and post-processing software to read and write the DEX XML documents for data exchange that use the standard and organization-specific reference data;
5. testing and operational deployment of the DEX implementation.

4   The Requirements on Reference Data

The initial usage scenarios for PLCS implementation are systems integration projects based on data exchange. Given that, and the PLCS framework, a set of requirements arise for the creation, management and operational use of Reference Data. At a high level, these requirements are:

1. a method for representing the PLCS EXPRESS model concepts in order to be able to define the relationship of the standard Reference Data to that model;
2. a method for defining classes, a class hierarchy, properties of the classes and the necessary associated documentation;
3. a method for publishing the standard Reference Data easily allowing browsing and operational use both on the Internet and in applications internal to the implementing organization;
4. a method by which organization-specific extensions to the standard Reference Data can be defined, including formally relating those extensions to the standard Reference Data;
5. a method by which the organization-specific extensions may be integrated into the standard Reference Data over time and as appropriate;
6. enabling Web-centric implementation;
7. support for very large Reference Data Libraries;
8. use of technology supporting XML-based exchange mechanisms;
9. use of technology allowing Reference Data to be embedded, exchanged or referenced;
10. support for the addition of business rules and constraints where required by the usage scenario.

Non-functional requirements for PLCS implementation are also important. Use of information technology that is broad-based and for which experience already exists in implementing organizations is seen as critical given the broad scope and long life of PLCS applications.

5   Our Conclusion: Use OWL for Reference Data

Several approaches for PLCS Reference data were considered. Initially, a project specific XML DTD was defined and integrated into DEXLib. Two other ISO standards, ISO 15926 Process Plants including Oil and Gas facilities life-cycle data [7] and ISO 13584 PLIB - Parts Library [8], were then considered. The publication of the OWL Candidate Recommendation raised its profile in the PLCS community and it was included in the analysis. After comparing the requirements against the capabilities of each approach, considering the non-functional requirements and after early successes based on the use of the Stanford University Protégé tool and its OWL Plug-in, it was clear that OWL was the best choice for the PLCS Reference Data Library. We demonstrated and recommended OWL and Protégé to the OASIS PLCS Technical Committee and the approach was accepted.

The rationale for the choice of OWL for the PLCS RDL included the following:

- OWL satisfies the RDL modelling requirements with its support for classes, multiple inheritance, properties, datatypes, instances, and reuse of ontologies;
- the Object Management Group has support for OWL under development [9] resulting in a graphical Reference Data Language standard;
- OWL satisfies RDL IT requirements having an XML syntax and being Web-enabled;
- OWL aligns well with the ISO standards involving reference data we considered, particularly ISO 15926, and so reuse of Reference Data may be possible;
- industry and academic interest and support including open-source tools;
- proven support for very large libraries; and
- it was easy to envision how Semantic Web technologies might be used in life cycle support applications in the future, and choosing OWL sets the stage for evolution in that direction.

6   Pilot Projects

PLCS pilot projects implementing the approach described in this paper are currently underway. These pilot projects are coordinated with the OASIS PLCS Technical Committee. At present, the pilot projects are being driven by the Ministries of Defence in the United Kingdom, Sweden and Norway. Figure 4 shows the systems, XML data exchange document, standard Reference Data, and organization-specific Reference Data.. The systems involved are Maintenance Feedback systems, As-Operated Configuration Management systems and Maintenance Planning systems.

The approach taken with OWL and the Reference Data in support of these pilot projects has four major aspects:

1. the translation of the subset of the PLCS EXPRESS model to which the PLCS classification capability can be applied into OWL;

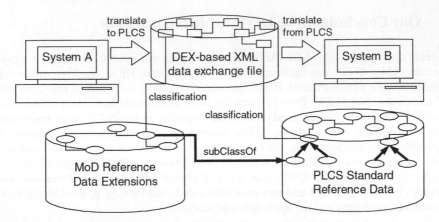

Fig. 4. Scenario used in the MoD PLCS Pilot Projects

2. the definition of the standard RDL OWL classes and their relationship to the OWL representation of the EXPRESS model;
3. the organization-extensions to the standard RDL OWL classes;
4. supporting the documentation of the RDL OWL classes and properties.

For documentation, the decision was made to use an OWL representation of the Dublin Core [10] as annotation properties. This approach also avoided the need to define class-of-class relationships in the OWL ontology so that the RDL is OWL DL.

An XSLT stylesheet was developed to translate from the XML representation of the PLCS EXPRESS into OWL. Only a subset of the EXPRESS was mapped. The EXPRESS entity types that can be classified according to PLCS are mapped into OWL classes. The EXPRESS supertype/subtype graph is mapped into the OWL class hierarchy as well.

The Reference Data itself is defined as OWL classes, including the class hierarchy, and OWL properties. After considering the semantics of what the combination of the EXPRESS schema as OWL and the Reference Data as OWL meant, it was determined that the OWL classes representing Reference Data are actually subclasses of those representing the EXPRESS entity types which they can classify. As was shown in Figure 1, completing the semantics of the model is left to the Reference Data.

Finally, the organization-specific Reference Data is defined by the pilot projects as OWL classes and properties. The organization-specific ontologies use the OWL import capability to include the entire standard PLCS ontology and can then extend it as required. However, extension is limited to defining subclasses of the standard Reference Data classes to ensure that their semantics are properly defined with respect to the PLCS information model.

7   Related Sources of Reference Data for the Pilot Projects

For the MoD pilot projects, much of the required Reference Data for PLCS already exists. The MoDs, NATO, ISO and other organizations publish standards, catalogues and classification schemes that can be reused for PLCS.

One such source is a standard aimed and large scale, data warehouse-based applications in the Oil and Gas industry, ISO 15926 [7]. ISO 15926 is also known as the EPISTLE Framework. The basis of ISO 15926 is a very generic, 4-dimensional upper ontology written using EXPRESS, standardized as ISO 15926-2 and also known as the EPISTLE Core Model [11]. ISO 15926-2 is aimed at supporting a universal scope and therefore any domain semantics are represented using reference data in a manner similar to that used for PLCS. An initial set of Oil and Gas reference data is undergoing standardization as ISO 15926-4. Efforts are underway to reuse ISO 15926-4 reference data as part of the PLCS pilot implementations.

8   Making Use of the Full Semantic Web Capabilities

The proper relationship between the STEP suite of standards and the Semantic Web is not obvious. STEP was essentially designed to be a data exchange standard and the EXPRESS language is based on a type-instance paradigm without any expectation for use with inference engines or reasoners.

A straightforward mapping from the STEP EXPRESS models to OWL can be defined that covers many of the EXPRESS constructs used in those standards. For example, the EXPRESS entity type hierarchy can map to an OWL class hierarchy. The EXPRESS select types can map to OWL classes defined as unions of classes and become part of the OWL class hierarchy as well. However, some of the EXPRESS models include the capability to exchange the definitions of categories and classes. Therefore, some entity instances based on STEP models represent what would properly be defined as OWL classes in an ontology while others would properly map to OWL individuals. As the determination about which entity types model the concept of a class and which are themselves classes is model-specific, a generic mapping from EXPRESS to OWL supporting reasoning is not possible. STEP schema-specific mappings are required. A prototype EXPRESS to OWL translator is under development as an open-source project called Express for Free [12]. Once that is complete, the translation of the PLCS Reference Data and associated DEX XML data exchange documents into an OWL ontology can begin to be investigated properly.

The benefits of the use of Semantic Web technology in support of the long-life assets that are the domain of PLCS are clear. Rather than integrating various support applications, a knowledge base of the entire history of the asset can be built and used to more efficiently maintain that asset. Because of the distributed nature of the Semantic Web technology, that history does not have to be maintained in a single repository in order to support reasoners and other applications. Each creator of engineering data about the asset can simply publish that data into the organization

Intranet. While the other standards in the STEP suite do not all have the same long-life context, it is expected that a similar approach can be applied. Those standards include the following domains: Configuration Controlled 3D Design, Electronic assembly, interconnect, and packaging design, Ship structures, and Systems engineering data representation.

Figure 5 illustrates the example of a United Kingdom Ministry of Defence (MoD) Maintenance Management System exporting or publishing data about tasks performed as part of an OWL repository. The individuals related to those tasks can be aggregated with the existing information related to a specific MoD ship, in this case HMS Illustrious. The PLCS RDL and the MoD-specific extensions that are currently being developed to support the DEX-based exchange scenarios can be the basis for this future scenario. That scenario enables automation, through reasoning and other technologies, that will become more prevalent in the day-to-day operations of the MoD over the coming years.

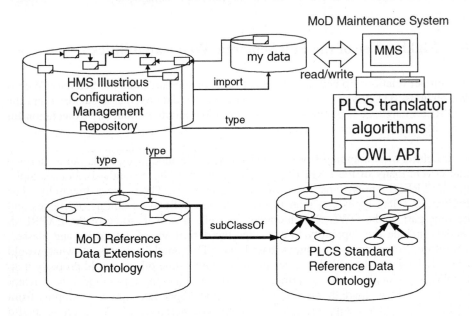

Fig. 5. Publish Maintenance Data In a Semantic Web Environment

While Figure 5 shows a Maintenance Management System publishing information about maintenance performed on a particular ship, a more interesting use of the Semantic Web capabilities might be based on the periodic publications of information about the ship such as distance traveled, oceans in which the travel occurred, weather conditions under which the travel occurred, and current location. Then, based on that information and other information from naval shipyards including their location, availability of spare parts and skilled workers, a future maintenance activity can be planned using an intelligent agent. This scenario is shown in Figure 6.

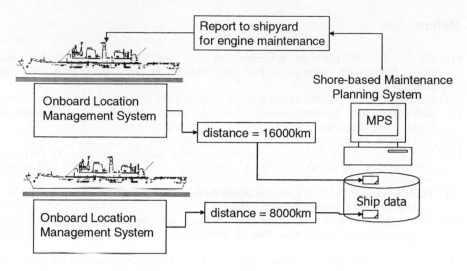

Fig. 6. Automated planning of ship maintenance

9   Conclusions

This paper describes an approach for the use of OWL in the context of supporting a complex asset over its long life. The initial data exchange scenario does not take full advantage of the Semantic Web capabilities typically enabled through the use of OWL. However, the approach is a significant first step in that direction by an active group within the STEP community – a community with more than 15 years of models, and modelling expertise, that can be applied across many engineering domains.

The next steps in the evolution of STEP towards full use of the Semantic Web are being investigated. The relationship between the EXPRESS language and OWL will be formally defined, likely in an ISO standard mapping between the languages. In the longer term, the adoption of Semantic Web languages such as OWL by the STEP community modellers in domains where an ontological approach is required will certainly be proposed.

The relationship of OWL and other standards within the same ISO subcommittee producing STEP is also being investigated. The OMPEK (Ontologies for Modeling Process Engineering Knowledge) [13] project is exploring the use of ISO 15926 as an upper level ontology by mapping it into OWL. ISO 15926 is also the basis for some of the PLCS Reference Data described in this paper. Synergy between these two activities is just beginning to be explored but may also provide another means for the application of Semantic Web technology to the ISO STEP-standardized engineering disciplines.

References

[1] ISO 10303-239, Industrial automation systems and integration — Product data representation and exchange — Part 239: Application protocols: Product life cycle support.
[2] Introducing STEP — The Foundation for Product Data Exchange in the Aerospace and Defence Sectors, National Research Council Canada. Available on the Internet at http://strategis.ic.gc.ca/epic/internet/inad-ad.nsf/en/ad03581e.html.
[3] SC4 Online. Available on the Internet at http://www.tc184-sc4.org.
[4] ISO 10303-11:2004, Industrial automation systems and integration — Product data representation and exchange — Part 11: Description methods: The EXPRESS language reference manual.
[5] PLCS Process Model, PLCS, Inc. Available on the Internet at http://www.plcsinc.org/process/index.htm.
[6] ISO 10303-28, Industrial automation systems and integration — Product data representation and exchange — Part 28: Implementation methods: EXPRESS to XML Schema bindings.
[7] ISO 15926, Industrial automation systems and integration — Integration of life-cycle data for process plants including oil and gas production facilities.
[8] ISO 13584, Industrial automation systems and integration — Parts library.
[9] Object Management Group Ontology Definition Metamodel Request For Proposal. Available on the Internet at http://www.omg.org/docs/ad/03-03-40.pdf
[10] Dublin Core Metadata Initiative Metadata Terms. Available on the Internet at http://www.dublincore.org/documents/dcmi-terms/.
[11] Standard Upper Ontology Working Group – 4D Ontology. Available on the Internet at http://suo.ieee.org/SUO/SUO-4D/index.html.
[12] exff is exPRESS for free . Available on the Internet at http://www.exff.org.
[13] The OMPEK (Ontologies for Modeling Process Engineering Knowledge) Project. Available on the Internet at http://www.ompek.org.

ORIENT: Integrate Ontology Engineering into Industry Tooling Environment[*]

Lei Zhang[1], Yong Yu[1], Jing Lu[1], ChenXi Lin[1],
KeWei Tu[1], MingChuan Guo[1], Zhuo Zhang[1],
GuoTong Xie[2], Zhong Su[2], and Yue Pan[2]

[1] APEX Data and Knowledge Management Lab,
Department of Computer Science and Engineering,
Shanghai JiaoTong University, Shanghai, 200030, China.
{zhanglei,yyu,robertlu,linchenxi,tkw,gmc,zhuoz}@apex.sjtu.edu.cn
[2] IBM China Research Lab
NO.7, 5th Ave., ShangDi, Beijing, 100085, China.
{xieguot,suzhong,panyue}@cn.ibm.com

Abstract. ORIENT is a project to develop an ontology engineering tool that integrates into existing industry tooling environments – the Eclipse platform and the WebSphere Studio developing tools family. This paper describes how two important issues are addressed during the project, namely tool integration and scalability. We show how ORIENT morphs into the Eclipse platform and achieves UI and data level integration with the Eclipse platform and other modelling tools. We also describe how we implemented a scalable RDF(S) storage, query, manipulation and inference mechanism on top of a relational database. In particular, we report the empirical performance of our RDF(S) closure inference algorithm on a DB2 database.

1 Introduction

Ontology is the backbone that provids semantics to the Semantic Web. The development of the Semantic Web thus depends heavily on the engineering of high quality ontologies. Numerous tools supporting this task have been developed in the past such as Protégé [1], OilEd [2] and WebODE [3]. Based on the R&D experiences and results of these tools, we initiated the ORIENT (Ontology engineeRIng ENvrionmenT) project[1] that develops an ontology engineering tool that integrates into existing industry tooling environments – the open-source Eclipse platform [4] and the WebSphere Studio™ developing tools family.

In this paper, we describe how two important issues are addressed during the project, namely tool integration and scalability. The importance of tool integration comes from three requirements on the tool and can not be underestimated.

---

[*] Opinions expressed and claims made in this paper are of the authors. They do not represent the opinions and claims of the International Business Machine Corporation.
[1] http://apex.sjtu.edu.cn/projects/orient/, also available from IBM Semantics Toolkit at http://www.alphaworks.ibm.com/tech/semanticstk

S.A. McIlraith et al. (Eds.): ISWC 2004, LNCS 3298, pp. 823–837, 2004.
© Springer-Verlag Berlin Heidelberg 2004

First, to be a complete ontology engineering tool, it must integrate different tools for different sub-tasks of ontology engineering such as building, mapping, merging and evaluation. Second, because applying ontologies in real applications requires the tool be used together with other tools to accomplish a certain task, tool integration is thus required to reduce the cost of switching between different tools. Finally, if the tool can be integrated with exisiting tooling environment e.g. the Eclipse platform and the WebSphere Developing tools family, it will be much more developer-friendly and easier to use. The success story of the Protégé tool on the integration of numerous plugins also remind us on the advantages of tool integration. In the ORIENT project, instead of designing the tool as a stand-alone application, we decided to build it as a set of Eclipse plugins that make it morph into the Eclipse platform. This strategy proves to be effective in satisfying the above requirements and achieves both data and UI level integration with other tools. In section 5, an example showing how ORIENT can be integrated with an UML editing tool is presented. Futhermore, because WebSphere Studio developing tools are also built on the Eclipse platform, this strategy paves a direct way to the product family.

In addition to tool integration, scalability is another important issue in ORIENT. Since ontologies[2] in real applications tend to have a large size, managing large volume ontology in industry applications is thus not a feature but a necessity. In this paper, we describe how we implemented a scalable RDF(S) storage, query, manipulation and inference mechanizm on top of a relational database and report the empirical performance of this implementation. In particular, we describe how an algorithm is carefully designed to calculate RDF(S) closure on a relational database and give the experiment result of its performance test. To our best knowledge, we do not know any previous report on RDF(S) closure inference performance on databases yet, although there are reports on RDF(S) storage and query performance on databases e.g. RQL[5] and Jena2[6].

The rest of the paper is organized as follows. Section 2 introduces the Eclipse platform and section 3 describes the Eclipse-based ORIENT architecture. We then describe the integration with Eclipse UI in section 4 and the integration with other modelling tools in section 5. The RDF(S) storage, query, manipulation and inference implementation and empirical performance analysis is presented in section 6. We conclude this paper in section 7.

2   Eclipse Tools Integration Platform

As stated in its technical overview [4], Eclipse is an open extensible IDE for anything and nothing in particular. It provides a unified mechanism to expose extension points and develop plugins that leads to seamlessly-integrated tools. The Eclipse architecture is designed around the concepts of plugins, extension points and extensions. New tools and functionalities can be integrated into the

---

[2] In this paper, the term *ontology* refers to a knowledge base that includes concepts, relations, instances and instance relations that together model a domain

platform as plugins. Through this plugin architecture, Eclipse platform thus provides a solid foundation for tools integration.

Besides its well-designed plugin architecture, the Eclipse platform also offers an extensible user interface paradigm for various plugins to share and extend. The UI paradigm is based on editors, views and perspectives. A perspective groups and arranges a set of editors and views on the screen. New types of editors, views and perspectives can be added to the platform UI through its plugin mechanism. Actually, ORIENT adds its own perspective with 8 views and editors to the Eclipse platform.

The above gives a very brief description of the Eclipse platform. We refer interested readers to the technical overview [4] and various articles on the Eclipse.org web site for more in-depth information about the Eclipse platform. The WebSphere Studio developing tools are also built on the Eclipse platform.

3   ORIENT Architecture

In the design of the ORIENT architecture, the most influential factor is tool integration at both the data and UI level . The demanding need for tool integration actually arises from three aspects. Firstly, ontology engineering has a complex life cycle [7,8] that needs different tools for different sub-tasks (e.g. building, mapping, merging and evaluation, etc.). Although the sub-task tools may be developed by different people at different time, they must be integrated to form a complete ontology engineering environment. For example, it will be preferable if the ontology evaluation tool can be tightly integrated with the ontology building tool to provide real-time feedback on the quality of the ontology.

Secondly, applying ontology in real applications requires that the ontology engineering tool be used together with other tools to accomplish a certain task. For example, annotating Web pages with semantic tags needs both an ontology browsing tool and an annotation tool. Building and testing a Semantic Portal [9] may involve ontology building, portal customization, and portal generation tools (e.g. in OntoWeaver [10]). Users of these tools have to switch back and forth between them to get their work done. If the tools can be seamlessly integrated at both the data and UI level in a single development environment, the cost associated with switching between them will be greatly reduced. In addition, if other modelling tools (e.g. ER and UML tools) can be integrated, it will enable users not familiar with ontology engineering to use our tool through another familiar tool. It can also leverage existing knowledge on data and application modelling to help them learn and get familiar with ontology engineering. This actually is in accordance with many researchers' opinion that the Semantic Web should come as an evolution rather than a revolution.

Finally, it will be much more developer-friendly and easier to use, if the tool can be integrated with the Eclipse platform or the WebSphere Developing tools product family and appear not as a brand new tool for users to learn but as a new integrated set of functionalities. In addition, the user base of the industry tooling environments will also help the ontology engineering tool reach a wider

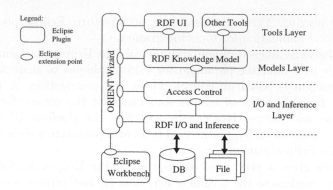

Fig. 1. The ORIENT architecture using RDF plugins as an example

developer community. We demonstrate how ORIENT morphs into the Eclipse platform in section 4.

Based on the above considerations, we decided not to design the tool as a new stand-alone application but as a set of loosely-coupled cooperative Eclipse plugins. The plugins are organized into a three layer architecture as shown in Fig.1. RDF related plugins are used in Fig.1 as concrete examples. The architecture layers are defined and separated by Eclipse extension points. Plugins in each layer are only required to correctly extend (implement) the extension points. This enables flexible mix-and-match of different plugins (possibly from different vendors) to compose an ontology engineering tool. For example, one may choose to use an RDF DB plugin to provide storage function for an OWL knowledge model plugin. Actually, the ORIENT Wizard plugin (at the left side of Fig.1) does exactly the job of helping users compose and manage plugins from different layers.

In the architecture, the models layer provides an in-memory model and access API for the ontology and it enables the sharing of the same model among different tools in the tools layer. For tools using different models, a translation between models is needed to integrate them at the data level. An example of this is shown in section 5.

Note that the lowest layer in the architecture is I/O and inference layer that manages the storage and inference of ontologies. Because it is usually hard to load a very large ontology entirely into the main memory, better inference algorithm can be designed if we know how the ontology is stored on the permanent storage. At the same time, the design of the inference algorithm may also impose certain requirements on the storage schema. Therefore, we purposely put the inference function down in this layer for better scalability.

Finally, this Eclipse plugin-centered architecture makes ORIENT seamlessly morph into the Eclipse platform. This greatly improves the tool's usability and lays a foundation for tool integration.

4   Integration with the Eclipse Platform

In this section, we show several examples of the UI level integration of the
ORIENT tool with the Eclipse platform.

First, ORIENT uses an ontology file to represent an ontology in the Eclipse
platform. The file stores information such as which plugins should be activated
to access the ontology, where the ontology is stored, etc. Once the file is opened,
an ORIENT perspective with editors and views will be opened for editing the
ontology. In this way, ontologies can be put as files into any existing Eclipse
project and sit side-by-side with other resources in the project. This makes incorporating, using and managing ontologies in a project very easy. Furthermore,
switching between ORIENT and other tools can be done by simply double-clicking
on different resources in an Eclipse project. This is where tool integration helps
user quickly switch between different tools to accomplish a task in a project.
In addition to ontology files, ORIENT also supports creating ontology projects
that contain one or more ontologies. Fig.2 shows the ORIENT New Ontology
File/Project Wizard in the WebSphere Studio Application Developer V5.1.

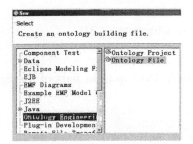
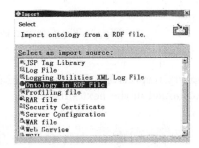

Fig. 2. New Ontology File/Project wizard   **Fig. 3.** RDF Import/Export Wizard

Second, ORIENT provides an ontology import/export function for users
to import/export ontologyes stored in ORIENT from/to external files. This
import/export functionality is also integrated with the general Eclipse im-
port/export UI and can be accessed very easily. Fig.3 shows a screenshot of
the ORIENT RDF import function entry in the WebSphere Studio Application
Developer V5.1 import UI.

Finally, ORIENT offers a dedicated Eclipse perspective that groups its ontology related views and editors. Fig.4 is a screen shot of the ORIENT perspective.
Currently, the ORIENT perspective contains one editor and eight views for users
to view and edit an RDF ontology. The eight views are grouped into list views,
hierarchy views and information views. The three list views (i.e. *Resource List,
Class List* and *Property List*) show all the existing resources, classes and properties respectively. The two hierarchy views (i.e. *Class Hierarchy* and *Property
Hierarchy*) display the hierarchy trees of classes and properties. The three information views are used to display detailed information of a resource, a class or a

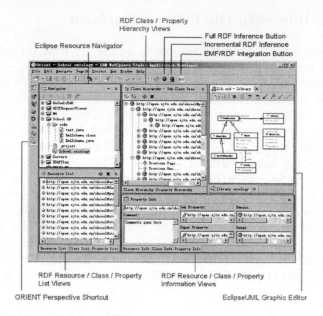

Fig. 4. The ORIENT Perspective with EclipseUML

property respectively. The EclipseUML editor in the top right part of the figure is explained in the next subsection.

5   Integration with Other Tools

The above section has demonstrated the UI level integration of ORIENT with the Eclipse platform. What may be more important is how ORIENT is integrated at the data level with other tools. In this section, we show how ORIENT can be integrated at the data level with Eclipse tools that are based on the Ecore model.

Ecore model is a central part of the Eclipse Modeling Framework (EMF)[3]. Currently, it provides the class digram modeling capabilities of UML. For example, Ecore provides modeling elements such as EClass, EAttribute and EReference etc. Several tools have been developed (or are under development) based on the Ecore model. Eclipse EMF plugin is a tool that provides a Java framework and code generation facility for building tools and other applications based on the Ecore model. EclipseUML[4] is a simple graphical UML editing tool that bases its model on Ecore. UML2 is an Eclipse tool project[5] that develops an Ecore and EMF-based tool for the UML 2.0 meta-model.

---

[3] Ecore and EMF can be found at http://www.eclipse.org/emf

[4] EclipseUML can be found at http://www.omondo.com

[5] UML2 can be found at http://www.eclipse.org/uml2

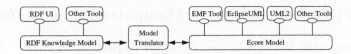

Fig. 5. The Integration of ORIENT and Ecore Tools

As we have mentioned in section 3, if modeling tools such as UML can be integrated with ORIENT, it will enable users not familiar with ontology engineering to use ORIENT through another familiar tool (e.g. UML tool) and it can also leverage existing industry knowledge on data and application modeling to help users learn and get familiar with ontology engineering. This is the main motivation to integrate ORIENT and the Ecore model based tools. The actual data level integration is done through a model translator. The model translator works between the ORIENT model layer and the Ecore model. It captures the two sides' model changes, translates the changes and applies them to the models accordingly so as to keep them synchronized.

Fig.5 shows this idea visually. This integration enables users to utilize different tools to work on the same model even if the model is expressed in different formalisms. Users can, for example, first edit the model in a graphical UML tool (e.g. EclipseUML) and then switch to ORIENT to view it through the RDF perspective and finally export it in RDF. On the contrary, users may also be able to visualize an RDF model through a graphical UML tool and save it as a UML model. This demonstrates the power of tool integration and how it benefits the users.

However, the difficulties come from maximally preserving the model seman tics in the model translator. Currently, we are doing a translation between RDF and Ecore in ORIENT. Detailed explaination of this translation is beyond the scope of this paper. The following lists some important translation rules in the current implementation:

- `EClass` elements of Ecore are converted as `rdfs:Class` resources and their hierarchical relationships are preserved using `rdfs:subClassOf`.
- `EAttribute` elements in Ecore are converted as `rdf:Property` resources.
- EMF elements of types other than `EClass` and `EAttribute`, when converted as RDF resources, take on their Ecore types(such as `EReferences`) as the value of their `rdf:type` properties.

The current translation is by no means perfectly sound and complete. It is a further research issue in ontology transformation and mapping and in ontology development using UML [11].

Aided by the UI level tool integration, the results of the data level tool integration are immediately visible to the end users. In Fig.4, ORIENT is actually used together with EclipseUML. Both the ORIENT views and the EclipseUML graphical editor are shown to the user (note the EclipseUML graphical editor at the top right corner). Changes in each tool's view will be instantly reflected in the other tool's view once the they are saved.

6   RDF(S) Storage, Query, Manipulation, and Inference

6.1   Query and Manipulation Through RQML

In the current ORIENT I/O and Inference Layer, a Default ORIENT RDF DB plugin is implemented to provide RDF(S) storage, query, manipulation and inference capabilities to the upper layers. For both users and programs to query and manipulate RDF data in an uniform manner, a declarative RDF Query and Manipulation Language (RQML) is defined in the plugin. Based on RQML, RDF models on top of the I/O and inference layer can provide higher level object-oriented APIs for easier program access. RQML is designed based on previous RDF query languages such as RQL[5], RDQL[6] and SeRQL[12].

RQML tries to be maximally syntax-compatible with RDQL while at the same time borrows features like path expression from SeRQL. In addition, it also introduces some new commands not available in previous languages like INSERT, DELETE and UPDATE. For example,

```
UPDATE (?p, <!http://employee/level>, ''Senior Engineer'')
WHERE  (?p, <!http://employee/level>, ''Engineer''),
       (?p, <!http://employee/hasCert>, ''Linux'').
```

6.2   Inference Capabilities

Reasoning on existing knowledge to discover implicit information is an important process on the Semantic Web. It is also very useful in an ontology engineering tool. Common queries such as what are the (direct and indirect) sub-classes and instances of an exiting class, what instances has an interested relationship with a given instance may all involve inference. According to the RDF Semantics document [13], RDF(S) closure contains all the triples that can be inferred from an RDF(S) ontology. In ORIENT, an algorithm for calculating the RDF(S) closure is implemented to provide RDF(S) inference support. As we have metioned in section 3, the inference algorithm is purposely embedded in the Default ORIENT RDF DB plugin. This improves the performance of the inference algorithm on a relational database. In section 6.5, we report the algorithm's empirical performance on a DB2 database. To our best knowledge, we do not know any previous report on RDF(S) closure inference performance on databases yet, although there are reports on RDF(S) storage and query performance on databases e.g. RQL[5] and Jena2[6].

The RDF(S) closure calculation is based on a core subset of the RDF(S) entailment rules defined in the RDF Semantics document [13] and can be used in either full mode or incremental mode. In the full mode, RDF(S) closure is not calculated until the plugin is told to do so and a full re-calculation is performed. In the incremental mode, every modification to the RDF(S) ontology will trigger a calculation on the change to the RDF(S) closure. The full mode is suitable for batch update to the ontology and may take a long time to complete while the incremental mode is suitable for fast response to small update. Once the RDF(S) closure is calculated, it can be transparently queried and manipulated through

RQML. At the same time, users of RQML can also distinguish between inferred and non-inferred data in the closure and process them differently.

6.3   Storage Schema

In order to support efficient RQML processing and RDF(S) closure calculation, we carefully designed a relational database schema to store RDF(S) ontology. We followed the following principles in the design of the storage schema:

- For high performance RQML processing and RDF(S) closure calculation, we trade storage space for speed.
- Although the storage schema should be able to handle arbitrary RDF(S) data, it must optimize for normal data distribution and typical queries in ontology engineering scenarios.

Table.1 lists the major database tables in the current storage schema design. Since the RDFStatement table already holds all RDF triples, all other tables can be seen as redundant. In addition, we store inferred data with non-inferred data together in the tables. This can also be seen as a redundancy. However, this redundancy design greatly facilitates and speeds up query processing and RDF(S) closure calculation. For example, because inferred data are directly stored, answering queries involving inference is almost as fast as queries without inference. The drawback of this design is that much care must be taken to maintain consistency among the tables.

To quickly answer typical queries about class hierarchies, property hierarchies/domains/ranges and instance types, the tables RDFSubClass, RDFSubProp, RDFDomain, RDFRange and RDFType are created. They can quickly provide answers to these typical queries. In order to support RQML literal comparison and calculation, the RDFLiteralInteger, RDFLiteralFloat, RDFLiteralBoolean, and RDFLiteralString talbes are created (not listed in Table.1) to hold common data type literals and leverage native SQL data type comparison and calcu-

Table 1. Major database tables

Table Name	Table Description
RDFSubPropSubProp	This table holds all triples (x, rdfs:subPropertyOf, rdfs:subPropertyOf).
RDFSubProp	This table holds all triples (x, rdfs:subPropertyOf, y).
RDFDomain	This table holds all triples (x, rdfs:domain, y).
RDFRange	This tables holds all triples (x, rdfs:range, y).
RDFSubClass	This table holds all triples (x, rdfs:subClassOf, y).
RDFType	This table holds all triples (x, rdf:type, y).
RDFStatement	This table holds all triples (x, y, z).
RDFResource	This table holds all RDF resources.
RDFUserProp	This table holds the names of user specified properties.
RDFProp*	These tables hold user specified property groups.

lation. We also borrowed Jena2's Property Tables design [6] in the `RDFUserProp` and `RDFProp*` tables to speed up property lookup.

In addition to the above considerations, the design of the tables are also influenced by and closely related to the RDF(S) closure calculation algorithm which is detailed in the next subsection.

6.4   RDF(S) Closure Calculation Algorithm

The closure calculation algorithm works in either full mode or incremental mode. For brevity, we only describe the full mode here. The algorithm supports a core subset of the RDF(S) entailment rules including `rdf1,rdfs2 -- rdfs11` (as defined in the RDF Semantics document [13]). We call these eleven rules *the rule set* and the involved five RDFS vocabularies `rdfs:domain`, `rdfs:range`, `rdfs:type`, `rdfs:subPropertyOf`, and `rdfs:subClassOf` *the reserved vocabularies*. The rules are selected based on their importance and wide usage in common RDF ontology engineering scenarios. Further development of ORIENT may support more RDF(S) entailment rules.

A well known fast forward-chaining rule algorithm is Rete [14]. It minimizes the impact to the rule system caused by the adding or removing of facts. However, it still falls into repetitive loops if the rules contain cycles. Because the RDF(S) rule set contains cycles, we try to manually remove them as much as possible to obtain an almost one-pass algorithm. By analyzing the rule set, we found that the cycles stem from the following two problems:

P1:   The two transitive predicates `rdfs:subPropertyOf` and `rdfs:subClassOf` give rise to cyclic repetitive calculation.

P2:   The rules in the rule set and the `rdfs:subPropertyOf` predicate create interdependent derivation relationships among the predicates.

However, scrutinizing the second problem P2 reveals that under certain circumstances the cyclic repetitive calculation can be reduced to just one pass. Fig.6 shows a simplified graph of the predicates' derivation relationships caused by the rule set. Edge lables are names of the rules that cause the derivation relation. Two set of derivation relations are omitted from the graph:

R1:   Rules `rdf1`, `rdfs2`, `rdfs3`, `rdfs4a` and `rdfs4b` may derive `rdf:type` from any predicate.

R2:   Rule `rdfs7` may derive any predicate from any predicate due to possible `rdfs:subPropertyOf` relations.

The self loops caused by `rdfs5`, `rdfs11`, and `rdfs9` in the figure actually represent the problem P1. Without considering P1, it is now clear from Fig.6 that `rdfs6`, `rdfs8`, `rdfs10` and R2 create big and complex loops in the derivation graph. We now introduce the Original Semantics Assumption that removes these loops.

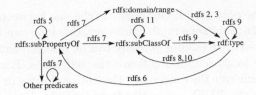

Fig. 6. Derivation Relationships among Predicates in The Rule Set

Original Semantics Assumption. Let $\mathcal{A}$ be the set of RDFS axiomatic triples defined in the RDF Semantics document [13]. Let $\mathcal{T}$ be the closure of $\mathcal{A}$ under the rule set. Let Ω be the closure of the current RDF knowledge base under the rule set and $\mathcal{R} \subseteq \Omega$ be the set of all the triples whose subject is in the set {rdfs:domain, rdfs:range, rdfs:type, rdfs:subPropertyOf, rdfs:subClassOf}. The original semantics assumption supposes that $\mathcal{R} \subseteq \mathcal{T}$.

This assumption actually assumes that the RDF knowledge base does not strengthen the semantics of the five reserved RDF(S) vocabularies. They still keep their original meaning defined by the axiomatic facts. In most RDF(S) ontology engineering scenarios, this assumption is natural and can be satisfied because most applications does not require the change of the original RDF(S) semantics.

Under this assumption[6], the rdfs6 and rdfs10 rules

  rdfs6: (uuu rdf:type rdf:Property) $\rightarrow$ (uuu rdfs:subPropertyOf uuu)
  rdfs10: (uuu rdf:type rdfs:Class) $\rightarrow$ (uuu rdfs:subClassOf uuu)

become trivial. If the rdf:type closure is obtained, the two rules can be applied only once on the rdf:type triples and we can be sure that no more triples can be obtained from them. That is, they can not create loops in the derivation graph. Now let's look at the rdfs8 rule:

  rdfs8: (uuu rdf:type rdfs:Class) $\rightarrow$ (uuu rdfs:subClassOf rdfs:Resource)

Under the original semantics assumption, rdfs:subClassOf can not be other property's sub-property and rdfs:Resource can not be other resource's subclass. Therefore if the rdf:type closure is obtained, this rule can be applied only once on the rdf:type triples and we can be sure that no more triples can be derived from it. Hence this rule can not create loops in the derivation graph either. We can now safely remove the back lines caused by rdfs6, rdfs8, and rdfs10 from Fig.6.

Finally, let's review R2. Because of the original semantics assumption, the rdfs:subPropertyOf relation can only hold from other predicates to the five reserved vocabularies. Hence the rdfs7 rule can only create derivation relation from "other predicates" to the five reserved vocabularies in Fig.6. If R2 is now

---

[6] The Original Semantics Assumption is actually stronger than what we really needed. However, it is easier to explain and understand.

drawn on Fig.6, the only loop it can create is the one between the "other predicates" and the `rdfs:subPropertyOf`. However, this loop can be broken because the `rdfs:subPropertyOf` closure actually can be independently calculated[7].

Now, the only loops left in Fig.6 are the self loops. Except for these self loops, our algorithm can thus calculate the entire closure in one pass. The algorithm first adds the RDFS axiomatic facts into the database. It then calculates the `rdfs:subPropertyOf` and `rdfs:subClassOf` closure using a variant of the Floyd algorithm. After that, the closures of `rdfs:domain`, `rdfs:range` and `rdf:type` are obtained in this order without repetitive calculation because all the closures they depend on are already obtained. Finally, we can calculate the `rdfs7` rule closure of the "other predicates". Note that this closure can also be gained without repetitive calculation if we follow the topology order created by the `rdfs:subPropertyOf` relation among the "other predicates". This one-pass algorithm's performance is confirmed by real data experiments shown in the next subsection. The correctness is also verified using W3C RDF test cases.

6.5   Query and Inference Performance

In this section we report the results of the experiments performed to empirically evaluate the performance of query and inference of the current ORIENT RDF DB plugin. The inference performance test is first presented followed by the query performance test.

Two data sets are used in the experiments. One is an artificial data set called "T57" that consists of only `rdfs:subClassOf` and `rdfs:subPropertyOf` relation triples that construct a class hierarchy tree and a property hierarchy tree. Both the two trees have a maximum height of 7 and a constant fan-out of 5. Another data set is "WN", which is the RDF representation of WordNet[8]. All experiments are performed on a PC with one Pentium-4 2.4GHz CPU and 1GB memory running Windows XP Pro, using J2SDK 1.4.1 and Eclipse-SDK-2.1.1 connecting to a local machine DB2 UDB V8.1 Workgroup Server. All data are stored in the database. The inference time is measured as the time cost to transform a database state of containing only original triples to one that also containing all inferred triples. The query time is measured from the time when the query is sent to the time when all results are fetched one by one from the database.

In our one-pass RDF(S) closure inference algorithm, the major component that determines the order of magnitude of time complexity is the calculation of the transitive closure of `rdfs:subPropertyOf` and `rdfs:subClassOf` using Floyd algorithm on databases. The T57 data set is specifically designed to measure the empirical time complexity of it. By growing the two trees in T57 via adding one level of height each time (with constant fan-out of 5) until the height of 7 is reached, a series of growing data set for inference is got. The result is shown in Fig.7. The T57-1 line shows the relation between the inference time

---

[7] For brevity, the detailed method is not shown here
[8] Available at http://www.semanticweb.org/library/

and the number of original triples. The T57-2 line shows the relation between the inference time and the number of triples after inference.

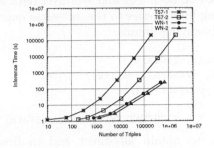

Fig. 7. RDF(S) Inference Performance   **Fig. 8.** RQML Query Performance

Different from T57, the WordNet data set has a very small RDF Schema with a very large set of instances and instance relations. The instance data in the four WordNet RDF files are sampled at the same speed. The number of sampled triples are multiplied by 5 each time and the triples from the four files are put together to get a series of growing data set for inference. The result is also shown in Fig.7. The WN-1 line shows the relation between the inference time and the original number of triples and the WN-2 line shows the relation between the inference time and the number of triples after inference.

Both the X-axis and Y-axis of Fig.7 are in log10 scale. The two T57 lines show a linear trend when the number of triples are large (> 1000). Linear regression analysis of the last four points at the end of each T57 line shows that the slopes are 1.87 and 1.75 for T57-1 and T57-2 respectively. This indicates approximately $O(n^{1.87})$ and $O(n^{1.75})$ time complexity. In theory, calculating transitive closure using Floyd algorithm has worst-case time complexity $O(n^3)$. When the algorithm is performed on a database, many factors of the RDBMS may further affect the performance. Combining the experiment result, we tend to empirically predicate that, when performed on a largely tree hierarchy ontology like T57 on a relational database, the time complexity of our inference algorithm is around $O(n^2)$.

Because the WordNet RDF data consists mostly of instance data, its number of inferred triples and inference time are much lower than T57. It, however, shows the same trend of linear relation in Fig.7. Linear regression analysis of the last four data points at the end of each WN line indicates approximately $O(n^{0.92})$ and $O(n^{0.93})$ time complexity. Similarly, we empirically expect that, when performed on a largely instance data ontology like WordNet on a relational database, the time complexity of our inference algorithm is around $O(n)$.

We can see in Fig.7 that, in the experiments, the number of the triples after inference is in linear proportion to that of the original triples.If a normal RDF(S) ontology satisfies this property and the Original Semantics Assumption in section 6.4, with characteristics between T57 and WordNet, we empirically estimate that its inference time complexity on a relational database is likely between $O(n)$ and $O(n^2)$. The n here can represent either the number of the original triples or the number of the triples after inference.

The RQML query performance is tested on both T57 and WordNet data set with inferred triples. We used the following four queries to test sub-class query, simple query, query with join and query involving literals:

```
Q1: SELECT ?X WHERE (?X, <rdfs:subClassOf>, [aClass])
Q2: SELECT ?X WHERE (?X, <wn:similarTo>, [randomAdjective])
Q3: SELECT ?Y WHERE ([randomNoun] <wn:hyponymOf>, ?X),
                    (?X, <wn:wordForm>, ?Y)
Q4: SELECT ?X WHERE (?X, <wn:wordForm>, ?Y) SUCHTHAT ?Y=[randomWordForm]
```

Q1 is performed on the T57 data set to obtain all direct and in-direct subclasses of a given class. For each T57 data sample, and for each height of the tree hierarchy in that sample, Q1 is executed once using a class in that height. The query time of Q1 is then obtained as the average of the execution times. Q2, Q3 and Q4 are performed on the WordNet inferred data sets. The query time is averaged over 1000 query executions by randomly selecting a WordNet constant to replace the random constant in the above queries. The whole result is shown in Fig.8.

Both axis of Fig.8 is in log10 scale. Lines in Fig.8 are in linear trend, especially Q1. Linear regression analysis of the four lines shows approximately $O(n^{0.84})$, $O(n^{0.89})$, $O(n^{1.06})$, and $O(n^{1.05})$ time complexity for them. In theory, the worst-case time complexity of querying on a database table with index is $O(n \log n)$. The actual query time also depends on the size of the result set. This test shows that the query time has a strong tendency of linear time $O(n)$ complexity and the query is executed quite speedy.

Although the above experiments shows an encouraging query and inference performance result, they are not very thorough and conclusive and the result is still empirical. In the future, more experiments will be performed to further verify the results obtained here.

7   Conclusion and Future Work

ORIENT is a project to develop an ontology engineering tool that integrates into existing industry tooling environments. In this paper, we have described how we addressed the tool integration and scalability issues in the project. By designing ORIENT as a set of Eclipse plugins, we make ORIENT morph into the Eclipse platform and achieve both data and UI level integration with other tools. We have showed how we implemented a scalable RDF(S) storage, query, manipulation and inference mechanism on top of relational databases. In particular, we have reported the empirical performance of our RDF(S) closure inference algorithm on a DB2 database. Future work of the ORIENT project includes adding OWL support and better visualization methods, improving the integration with Ecore and potentially XMI, and further optimizing and tuning the performance.

References

1. H.Gennari, J., A.Musen, M., W.Fergerson, R., E.Grosso, W., Crubézy, M., Eriksson, H., F.Noy, N., W.Tu, S.: The evolution of Protégé: An environment for knowledge-based systems development. Technical Report SMI-2002-0943, Stanford Medical Informatics (2002)
2. Bechhofer, S., Horrocks, I., Goble, C., Stevens, R.: OilEd: a reason-able ontology editor for the semantic web. In: Proceedings of the Joint German/Austrian Conference on AI. LNCS 2174 (2001) 396–408
3. Corcho, O., López, M.F., Pérez, A.G., Vicente, O.: WebODE: An integrated workbench for ontology representation, reasoning, and exchange. In: Proceedings of EKAW 2002. LNCS 2473 (2002) 138–153
4. Eclipse.org: Eclipse platform technical overview. Technical report, http://www.eclipse.org/whitepapers/eclipse-overview.pdf (2003)
5. G.Karvounarakis, S.Alexaki, V.Christophides, D.Plexousakis, Scholl, M.: RQL: A declarative query language for RDF. In: Proceedings of the Eleventh International World Wide Web Conference (WWW02). (2002)
6. Wilkinson, K., Sayers, C., Kuno, H., Reynolds, D.: Efficient RDF storage and retrieval in Jena2. In: Proceedings of the first International Workshop on Semantic Web and Databases (SWDB), Berlin,Germany (2003) 131–150
7. López, M.F., Pérez, A.G., Amaya, M.D.R.: Ontology's crossed life cycles. In: Proceedings of the EKAW 2000. LNCS 1937 (2000) 65–79
8. Sure, Y., Studer, R.: On-To-Knowledge methodology - final version. Technical report, Institute AIFB, University of Karlsruhe (2002) On-To-Knowledge Deliverable 18, available at http://www.ontoknowledge.org/downl/del18.pdf.
9. Maedche, A., Staab, S., Stojanovic, N., Studer, R., Sure, Y.: SEAL – a framework for developing semantic web portals. In: Proceedings of the 18th British National Conference on Databases. Volume 2097 of LNCS. (2001) 1–22
10. Lei, Y., Motta, E., Domingue, J.: Design of customized web applications with OntoWeaver. In: Proceedings of the 2nd International Conference on Knowledge Capture (KCAP 2003), FL, USA (2003) 54–61
11. Kogut, P., Cranefield, S., Hart, L., Dutra, M., Baclawski, K., Kokar, M., Smith, J.: UML for ontology development. Knowledge Engineering Review 17 (2002)
12. Broekstra, J., Kampman, A., van Harmelen, F.: Sesame: A generic architecture for storing and querying RDF and RDF Schema. In: Proceedings of the 1st International Semantic Web Conference (ISWC02). LNCS 2342 (2002) 54–68
13. Hayes, P., McBride, B.: RDF Semantics. W3C Recommendation, W3C (2004) http://www.w3.org/TR/2004/REC-rdf-mt-20040210/.
14. Forgy, C.: Rete: A fast algorithm for the many pattern/many object pattern match problem. Artificial Intelligence 19 (1982) 17–37

Author Index

Lecture Notes in Computer Science

For information about Vols. 1–3206

please contact your bookseller or Springer

Vol. 3255: A. Benczúr, J. Demetrovics, G. Gottlob (Eds.), Advances in Databases and Information Systems. XI, 423 pages. 2004.

Vol. 3254: E. Macii, V. Paliouras, O. Koufopavlou (Eds.), Integrated Circuit and System Design. XVI, 910 pages. 2004.

Vol. 3253: Y. Lakhnech, S. Yovine (Eds.), Formal Techniques, Modelling and Analysis of Timed and Fault-Tolerant Systems. X, 397 pages. 2004.

Vol. 3252: H. Jin, Y. Pan, N. Xiao, J. Sun (Eds.), Grid and Cooperative Computing - GCC 2004 Workshops. XVIII, 785 pages. 2004.

Vol. 3251: H. Jin, Y. Pan, N. Xiao, J. Sun (Eds.), Grid and Cooperative Computing - GCC 2004. XXII, 1025 pages. 2004.

Vol. 3250: L.-J. (LJ) Zhang, M. Jeckle (Eds.), Web Services. X, 301 pages. 2004.

Vol. 3249: B. Buchberger, J.A. Campbell (Eds.), Artificial Intelligence and Symbolic Computation. X, 285 pages. 2004. (Subseries LNAI).

Vol. 3246: A. Apostolico, M. Melucci (Eds.), String Processing and Information Retrieval. XIV, 332 pages. 2004.

Vol. 3245: E. Suzuki, S. Arikawa (Eds.), Discovery Science. XIV, 430 pages. 2004. (Subseries LNAI).

Vol. 3244: S. Ben-David, J. Case, A. Maruoka (Eds.), Algorithmic Learning Theory. XIV, 505 pages. 2004. (Subseries LNAI).

Vol. 3243: S. Leonardi (Ed.), Algorithms and Models for the Web-Graph. VIII, 189 pages. 2004.

Vol. 3242: X. Yao, E. Burke, J.A. Lozano, J. Smith, J.J. Merelo-Guervós, J.A. Bullinaria, J. Rowe, P. Tiňo, A. Kabán, H.-P. Schwefel (Eds.), Parallel Problem Solving from Nature - PPSN VIII. XX, 1185 pages. 2004.

Vol. 3241: D. Kranzlmüller, P. Kacsuk, J.J. Dongarra (Eds.), Recent Advances in Parallel Virtual Machine and Message Passing Interface. XIII, 452 pages. 2004.

Vol. 3240: I. Jonassen, J. Kim (Eds.), Algorithms in Bioinformatics. IX, 476 pages. 2004. (Subseries LNBI).

Vol. 3239: G. Nicosia, V. Cutello, P.J. Bentley, J. Timmis (Eds.), Artificial Immune Systems. XII, 444 pages. 2004.

Vol. 3238: S. Biundo, T. Frühwirth, G. Palm (Eds.), KI 2004: Advances in Artificial Intelligence. XI, 467 pages. 2004. (Subseries LNAI).

Vol. 3236: M. Núñez, Z. Maamar, F.L. Pelayo, K. Pousttchi, F. Rubio (Eds.), Applying Formal Methods: Testing, Performance, and M/E-Commerce. XI, 381 pages. 2004.

Vol. 3235: D. de Frutos-Escrig, M. Nunez (Eds.), Formal Techniques for Networked and Distributed Systems - FORTE 2004. X, 377 pages. 2004.

Vol. 3234: M.J. Egenhofer, C. Freksa, H.J. Miller (Eds.), Geographic Information Science. VIII, 345 pages. 2004.

Vol. 3233: K. Futatsugi, F. Mizoguchi, N. Yonezaki (Eds.), Software Security - Theories and Systems. X, 345 pages. 2004.

Vol. 3232: R. Heery, L. Lyon (Eds.), Research and Advanced Technology for Digital Libraries. XV, 528 pages. 2004.

Vol. 3231: H.-A. Jacobsen (Ed.), Middleware 2004. XV, 514 pages. 2004.

Vol. 3230: J.L. Vicedo, P. Martínez-Barco, R. Muñoz, M. Saiz Noeda (Eds.), Advances in Natural Language Processing. XII, 488 pages. 2004. (Subseries LNAI).

Vol. 3229: J.J. Alferes, J. Leite (Eds.), Logics in Artificial Intelligence. XIV, 744 pages. 2004. (Subseries LNAI).

Vol. 3226: M. Bouzeghoub, C. Goble, V. Kashyap, S. Spaccapietra (Eds.), Semantics of a Networked World. XIII, 326 pages. 2004.

Vol. 3225: K. Zhang, Y. Zheng (Eds.), Information Security. XII, 442 pages. 2004.

Vol. 3224: E. Jonsson, A. Valdes, M. Almgren (Eds.), Recent Advances in Intrusion Detection. XII, 315 pages. 2004.

Vol. 3223: K. Slind, A. Bunker, G. Gopalakrishnan (Eds.), Theorem Proving in Higher Order Logics. VIII, 337 pages. 2004.

Vol. 3222: H. Jin, G.R. Gao, Z. Xu, H. Chen (Eds.), Network and Parallel Computing. XX, 694 pages. 2004.

Vol. 3221: S. Albers, T. Radzik (Eds.), Algorithms – ESA 2004. XVIII, 836 pages. 2004.

Vol. 3220: J.C. Lester, R.M. Vicari, F. Paraguaçu (Eds.), Intelligent Tutoring Systems. XXI, 920 pages. 2004.

Vol. 3219: M. Heisel, P. Liggesmeyer, S. Wittmann (Eds.), Computer Safety, Reliability, and Security. XI, 339 pages. 2004.

Vol. 3217: C. Barillot, D.R. Haynor, P. Hellier (Eds.), Medical Image Computing and Computer-Assisted Intervention – MICCAI 2004. XXXVIII, 1114 pages. 2004.

Vol. 3216: C. Barillot, D.R. Haynor, P. Hellier (Eds.), Medical Image Computing and Computer-Assisted Intervention – MICCAI 2004. XXXVIII, 930 pages. 2004.

Vol. 3215: M.G.. Negoita, R.J. Howlett, L.C. Jain (Eds.), Knowledge-Based Intelligent Information and Engineering Systems. LVII, 906 pages. 2004. (Subseries LNAI).

Vol. 3214: M.G.. Negoita, R.J. Howlett, L.C. Jain (Eds.), Knowledge-Based Intelligent Information and Engineering Systems. LVIII, 1302 pages. 2004. (Subseries LNAI).

Vol. 3213: M.G.. Negoita, R.J. Howlett, L.C. Jain (Eds.), Knowledge-Based Intelligent Information and Engineering Systems. LVIII, 1280 pages. 2004. (Subseries LNAI).

Vol. 3212: A. Campilho, M. Kamel (Eds.), Image Analysis and Recognition. XXIX, 862 pages. 2004.

Vol. 3211: A. Campilho, M. Kamel (Eds.), Image Analysis and Recognition. XXIX, 880 pages. 2004.

Vol. 3210: J. Marcinkowski, A. Tarlecki (Eds.), Computer Science Logic. XI, 520 pages. 2004.

Vol. 3209: B. Berendt, A. Hotho, D. Mladenic, M. van Someren, M. Spiliopoulou, G. Stumme (Eds.), Web Mining: From Web to Semantic Web. IX, 201 pages. 2004. (Subseries LNAI).

Vol. 3208: H.J. Ohlbach, S. Schaffert (Eds.), Principles and Practice of Semantic Web Reasoning. VII, 165 pages. 2004.

Vol. 3207: L.T. Yang, M. Guo, G.R. Gao, N.K. Jha (Eds.), Embedded and Ubiquitous Computing. XX, 1116 pages. 2004.